Twenty-first Edition

Economics

AP EDITION

PRINCIPLES, PROBLEMS, AND POLICIES

Campbell R. McConnell
University of Nebraska

Stanley L. Brue
Pacific Lutheran University

Sean M. Flynn
Scripps College

Mc Graw Hill Education

ECONOMICS: PRINCIPLES, PROBLEMS, AND POLICIES, AP® EDITION, TWENTY-FIRST EDITION

Published by McGraw-Hill Education, 2 Penn Plaza, New York, NY 10121.

This book is printed on acid-free paper.

2 3 4 5 6 7 8 9 LWI 21 20 19 18 17

ISBN 978-0-07-900157-3 (student edition)
MHID 0-07-900157-2 (student edition)

Chief Product Officer, SVP Products & Markets: *G. Scott Virkler*
Vice President, General Manager, Products & Markets: *Marty Lange*
Vice President, Content Design & Delivery: *Betsy Whalen*
Managing Director: *Susan Gouijnstook*
Senior Brand Manager: *Katie Hoenicke*
Director, Product Development: *Rose Koos*
Product Developer: *Adam Huenecke*
Senior Director, Digital Content Development: *Douglas Ruby*
Marketing Manager: *Virgil Lloyd*
Director, Content Design & Delivery: *Linda Avenarius*
Program Manager: *Mark Christianson*
Content Project Managers: *Harvey Yep (Core); Bruce Gin (Assessment)*
Buyer: *Laura Fuller*
Design: *Tara McDermott*
Cover Image: © *Getty Images/Kativ*
Content Licensing Specialists: *Shawntel Schmitt (Image); Beth Thole (Text)*
Typeface: *Stix Mathjax MAIN 10/12*
Compositor: *Aptara®, Inc.*
Printer: *LSC Communications*

Library of Congress Cataloging-in-Publication Data

Names: McConnell, Campbell R., author. | Brue, Stanley L., 1945- author. | Flynn, Sean Masaki, author.
Title: Economics : principles, problems, and policies / Campbell R. McConnell, University of Nebraska, Stanley L. Brue, Pacific Lutheran University, Sean M. Flynn, Scripps College.
Description: 21 Edition. | Dubuque : McGraw-Hill Education, [2018] | Revised edition of the authors' Economics, 2015.
Identifiers: LCCN 2016043780 | ISBN 9780079001573 (alk. paper) | ISBN 0079001572 (alk. paper)
Subjects: LCSH: Economics.
Classification: LCC HB171.5 .M47 2018 | DDC 330—dc23 LC record available at https://lccn.loc.gov/2016043780

2013038889

mheonline.com/ap

BRIEF CONTENTS

ABOUT THE AUTHORS

CAMPBELL R. MCCONNELL earned his Ph.D. from the University of Iowa after receiving degrees from Cornell College and the University of Illinois. He taught at the University of Nebraska–Lincoln from 1953 until his retirement in 1990. He is also coauthor of *Contemporary Labor Economics,* eleventh edition, and *Essentials of Economics,* third edition, and has edited readers for the principles and labor economics courses. He is a recipient of both the University of Nebraska Distinguished Teaching Award and the James A. Lake Academic Freedom Award and is past president of the Midwest Economics Association. Professor McConnell was awarded an honorary Doctor of Laws degree from Cornell College in 1973 and received its Distinguished Achievement Award in 1994. His primary areas of interest are labor economics and economic education. He has an extensive collection of jazz recordings and enjoys reading jazz history.

STANLEY L. BRUE did his undergraduate work at Augustana College (South Dakota) and received its Distinguished Achievement Award in 1991. He received his Ph.D. from the University of Nebraska–Lincoln. He is retired from a long career at Pacific Lutheran University, where he was honored as a recipient of the Burlington Northern Faculty Achievement Award. Professor Brue has also received the national Leavey Award for excellence in economic education. He has served as national president and chair of the Board of Trustees of Omicron Delta Epsilon International Economics Honorary. He is coauthor of *Economic Scenes,* fifth edition (Prentice-Hall); *Contemporary Labor Economics,* eleventh edition; *Essentials of Economics,* third edition; and *The Evolution of Economic Thought,* eighth edition (Cengage Learning). For relaxation, he enjoys international travel, attending sporting events, and going on fishing trips.

SEAN M. FLYNN did his undergraduate work at the University of Southern California before completing his Ph.D. at U.C. Berkeley, where he served as the Head Graduate Student Instructor for the Department of Economics after receiving the Outstanding Graduate Student Instructor Award. He teaches at Scripps College (of the Claremont Colleges) and is the author of *Economics for Dummies,* second edition (Wiley) and coauthor of *Essentials of Economics,* third edition. His research interests include finance, behavioral economics, and health economics. An accomplished martial artist, he has represented the United States in international aikido tournaments and is the author of *Understanding Shodokan Aikido* (Shodokan Press). Other hobbies include running, traveling, and enjoying ethnic food.

To Mem and to Terri and Craig, and to past instructors

AP CONTENTS

For ease-of-use we have color coded our AP edition.

Microeconomics Parts and Chapters are indicated with green

Macroeconomics Parts and Chapters are indicated with purple

Parts and Chapters that **cover both content** are indicated with combined green and purple

AP KEY GRAPHS

I. GENERAL CONCEPTS:

II. MICROECONOMICS:

PREFACE AP

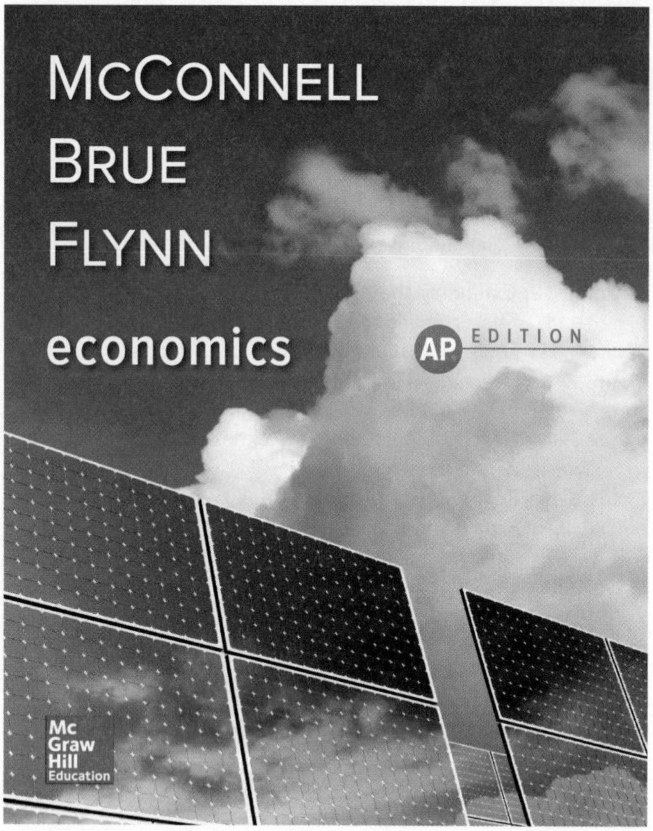

Welcome to the 21st edition of *Economics,* the best-selling economics textbook in the world. We are pleased that *Economics* continues to meet the market test: nearly one out of five U.S. college students in principles courses used the 20th edition. The AP® Edition continues to be a market leader, preparing thousands of students each year for the AP Microeconomics and AP Macroeconomics Exams.

Fundamental Objectives

We have three main goals for *Economics AP® Edition:*

- Help the beginning student master the principles essential for understanding the economizing problem, specific economic issues, and policy alternatives.
- Help the student understand and apply the economic perspective and reason accurately and objectively about economic matters.
- Promote a lasting student interest in economics and the economy.

What's New and Improved?

One of the benefits of writing a successful text is the opportunity to revise—to delete the outdated and install the new, to rewrite misleading or ambiguous statements, to introduce more relevant illustrations, to improve the organizational structure, and to enhance the learning aids.

We trust that you will agree that we have used this opportunity wisely and fully. Some of the more significant changes include the following.

AP Edition Streamlined and Reorganized

In order to tighten the focus of the AP® Edition to include only the most important content for AP Microeconomics and AP Macroeconomics, we have placed the enrichment content online. Teachers now have the freedom to use extension topics such as health care, immigration, technology and R&D, or the economics of developing countries to enrich the core AP content that appears in the print and digital student editions.

Color-coded sidebars help students and teachers easily identify foundational content that is important for both micro- and macroeconomics students as well as focused content for each of the disciplines. This is illustrated in the walkthrough on page xxvii and in the Table of Contents.

Separate Presentations of Monopolistic Competition and Oligopoly

In response to feedback, we have split the material on monopolistic competition and oligopoly that had together comprised a single chapter in previous editions into two separate chapters. The separated chapters have been made modular so that skipping either or covering both will be equally viable options for teachers. This should be particularly helpful to teachers who want to spend more time on oligopoly.

Modernized Presentation of Fixed Exchange Rates and Currency Interventions

For this new edition, we have reorganized and rewritten large parts of Chapter 35 (The Balance of Payments, Exchange Rates, and Trade Deficits). The key revision has to do with our presentation of fixed exchange rates. We now show with greater clarity that under a fixed exchange rate regime, changes in the balance of payments generate automatic changes in both foreign exchange reserves and the domestic money supply that then have to be dealt with by a nation's central bank. Our new presentation uses China as an example of these forces and how they often lead to "sterilization" actions on the part of the central banks that are engaged in currency pegs. Our new presentation also clarifies the relationship between trade deficits and foreign exchange reserves under a currency peg.

We have also inserted additional examples into our presentation of flexible exchange rates and have introduced a new Last Word on optimal currency areas to give students insight into some of the European Monetary Union's current problems and how they relate to the fact that a monetary union is equivalent to simultaneous multilateral currency pegs. For instructors who wish to give a larger historical perspective, we have created a brief appendix that covers the gold standard era as well as the Bretton Woods period.

New "Consider This" and "Last Word" Pieces

Our "Consider This" boxes are used to provide analogies, examples, or stories that help drive home central economic ideas in a student-oriented, real-world manner. For instance, a "Consider This" box titled "McHits and McMisses" illustrates consumer sovereignty through a listing of successful and unsuccessful products. How businesses exploit price discrimination is driven home in a "Consider This" box that explains why ballparks charge different admission prices for adults and children but only one set of prices at their concession stands. These brief vignettes, each accompanied by a photo, illustrate key points in a lively, colorful, and easy-to-remember way.

Our "Last Word" pieces are lengthier applications or case studies that are placed near the end of each chapter. For example, the "Last Word" section for Chapter 1 (Limits, Alternatives, and Choices) examines pitfalls to sound economic reasoning, while the "Last Word" section for Chapter 4 (Market Failures: Public Goods and Externalities) examines cap-and-trade versus carbon taxes as policy responses to excessive carbon dioxide emissions.

If you are unfamiliar with *Economics,* we encourage you to thumb through the chapters to take a quick look at these highly visible features.

CONSIDER THIS . . .

A Bright Idea

Source: © Federico Rostagno/Shutterstock.com

In sunny areas, a solar panel can make up for the cost of its installation in just a few years by greatly reducing or even eliminating a household's electricity bill. After those years of payback are finished, there will be almost nothing but benefits because the solar panel will continue to provide free electricity at only modest maintenance costs. Consequently, nearly every household in sunny areas could rationally profit from installing solar panels.

Unfortunately, myopia discourages most people from wanting to reap the net benefits. Because people are myopic, they focus too strongly on the upfront costs of installing solar panels while at the same time discounting the long-run benefits from being able to generate their own electricity. The result is major inefficiency as most homeowners end up foregoing solar panels.

A company called Solar City has figured out a way to work with rather than against people's myopia. It does so by offering leasing and financing options that eliminate the need for consumers to pay for the upfront costs of installing a solar system. Instead, Solar City pays for the upfront costs and then makes its money by splitting the resulting savings on monthly electricity bills with consumers.

This arrangement actually benefits from myopia because consumers get to focus on instant savings rather than initial costs. The same strategy can also be used to promote other investments that would normally be discouraged by myopia, such as installing energy-efficient furnaces, air conditioners, and appliances.

LAST WORD

Antitrust Online

The Internet Has Presented Antitrust Authorities with Both Old and New Causes for Concern.

© grzegorz knec/Alamy Stock Photo

The Airline Tariff Publishing case was the first important example of how digital communication platforms could be used by businesses to engage in price-fixing. In the late 1980s, U.S. airlines began to post both current and future prices for airline tickets on a centralized computer system known as the Airline Tariff Publishing Company. The system was set up so that travel agents could comparison shop for their clients. But the airlines used the system's ability to list start dates and end dates for ticket purchases as a way of colluding.

As an example, suppose that American Airlines and Delta Airlines had both been charging $200 for a one-way ticket between New York and Chicago. American could then post a higher price of $250 for the route with the stipulation that nobody could start buying tickets at that price until the next month. Delta could then respond by also saying that it would start selling tickets at the higher price next month. In that way, the two airlines could tacitly coordinate their price setting ahead of time so as to collude on a major price increase.

The antitrust authorities at the U.S. Department of Justice stopped this practice in 1994 by getting the airlines to agree to the behavioral

The most recent threat to competition spawned by the Internet is the rise of collusion via pieces of software that use pricing algorithms (automatically applied rules for setting prices) to constantly adjust a company's the online prices in response to seeing what rival firms are charging for similar products. The problem for regulators

New AP Quick Reviews

AP Quick Review boxes help students keep up with most important AP economic content. Concepts are reexamined in a clear and concise manner. AP Quick Reviews are ideal study tools for chapter quizzes and tests as well as the AP Exams.

AP QUICK REVIEW 3.1

- ✓ Demand is a schedule or curve showing the quantity of a product that buyers are willing and able to buy, in a particular time period, at each per unit price.
- ✓ The law of demand states that, other things equal, the quantity of a good purchased varies inversely with its price. At lower prices more is purchased; at higher prices less is purchased.
- ✓ The demand curve shifts, because of changes in (a) consumer tastes, (b) the number of buyers in the market, (c) consumer income, (d) the prices of substitute or complementary goods, (e) consumer expectations, and (f) tastes.
- ✓ A change in demand is a shift of the entire demand curve. A change in quantity demanded is a movement from one point to another point along the demand curve.

Enhanced Coverage of Game Theory and Strategic Behavior

The online economy and the tech sector present students with many high-profile examples of oligopolistic firms and industries. A grasp of strategic behavior is consequently more important than ever for principles students. To that end, the 21st edition features extended coverage of game theory and strategic behavior. The new material covers topics related to sequential games, including backward induction, the game-tree (extensive form) representation of strategic games, and subgame perfect Nash equilibrium.

In previous editions, a substantial portion of our game theory coverage appeared in an appendix to a chapter that covered both monopolistic competition and oligopoly. With the material on monopolistic competition now located in a separate chapter, we have been able to eliminate the appendix and fully integrate the game theory material that had appeared there with the treatment of oligopoly that had appeared in the main body of text. The result is our new Chapter 13, which is titled, "Oligopoly and Strategic Behavior."

This integrated presentation facilitates student comprehension of both game theory and oligopoly because strategic interactions are always presented in an accessible, intuitive context. Students already understand that Google's actions affect those of rivals like Facebook, and vice versa. So integrating oligopoly with game theory illuminates both sets of material.

New Discussions of Unconventional Monetary Policy and Interest-Rate Normalization

Our macroeconomics chapters on monetary policy have been rewritten in many places to reflect the historically unprecedented monetary policy regimes that have been instituted by central banks since the Financial Crisis. Thus, for instance, we have included material that will allow students to comprehend the negative interest rates that are now common in Europe. Also necessary was a revised treatment of the federal funds rate to reflect the fact that monetary policy has been implemented in recent years in the United States by means of open-market interventions aimed at quantitative easing rather than open-market interventions aimed at lowering the federal funds rate, which has been stuck near the zero lower bound since the Great Recession.

We have also been sure to include intuitive coverage of the monetary policy tools that the Federal Reserve says it will be using in coming years to "normalize" monetary policy and raise short-term interest rates in the context of massive excess bank reserves. To that end, we have truncated our coverage of the federal funds market because the Fed has stated that it intends to normalize via the repo market and the interest rate that it pays banks on excess reserves (IOER). We cover those mechanisms in detail and explain how the Fed intends to use them in coming years.

New AP Appendices on Real and Nominal Interest Rates and Loanable Funds

Additional information specific for AP students has been added to Chapters 27 (Fiscal Policy, Deficits, and Debt) and 30 (Interest Rates and Monetary Policy). In Chapter 27, the appendix includes extended coverage of the loanable funds market. This discussion is vital because it shows the process by which the savers of funds (businesses, households, and the foreign sector) interact with the demanders of funds (business investors, households purchasing homes or expensive items with payments over time, and governments funding deficits). An equilibrium real interest rate results from this interaction. Thus, when governments fund deficits, they must enter the loanable funds market to borrow funds, raising the real interest rate, and reducing private sector investment (referred to as crowding out), a critique of deficit spending offered by fiscal conservatives.

The appendix for Chapter 30 discusses the Federal Reserve's control over nominal and real interest rates and introduces the Fisher equation. AP students need this information because investment and savings decisions tend to be motivated by the real interest rate that incorporates price level changes or inflation. The observed interest rate or the nominal interest rate does not explicitly show price level changes. The Fisher equation which shows the real interest rate as the nominal interest rate minus the rate of expected price change links these concepts.

Full Support for Flipped Classroom Teaching Strategies

We have also designed our new materials to facilitate flipped-classroom teaching strategies, wherein students learn basic material at home, before class, before being challenged in class to reach higher levels of understanding. In K–12 math programs, for example, students study short videos on new content at home before coming to class to work problems. That sequence of learning activities assures that a teacher is present at the stage where students encounter the most difficulties, namely, when they attempt to apply the material. By contrast, the traditional (non-flipped) method for teaching elementary math presents new content in class before sending students home to work problems by themselves. That sequence leaves students without expert help when they are most vulnerable to misunderstandings and errors.

We have designed our materials to facilitate the flipped-classroom method by leveraging the adaptive learning materials that are already available in our Connect online learning platform. In particular, students can be assigned new material before class via SmartBook, which is an adaptive-learning technology that tutors students through the basic concepts and skills presented in each section of the book. We also recommend that students work before class on end-of-chapter problems and LearnSmart (which also come with adaptive feedback thanks to Connect).

Those pre-class activities will allow students to master the lower levels of Bloom's Taxonomy of learning objectives—things like remembering and understanding—*before* they come to class. They will then be ready to attack the higher levels of Bloom's Taxonomy—things like applying, analyzing, and evaluating.

We are consequently happy to be offering students and teachers yet another first, namely, the first high-quality, proven, flipped-classroom package available for principles of economics classes. Not every teacher will choose to use this format, but we are confident that those who do will wish that it had arrived much sooner.

Current Discussions and Examples

The 21st edition of *Economics* refers to and discusses many current topics. Examples include surpluses and shortages of tickets at the Olympics; applications of game theory; the most rapidly expanding and disappearing U.S. jobs; oil and gasoline prices; occupational licensing; state lotteries; consumption versus income inequality; conditional and unconditional cash transfers; the difficulty of targeting fiscal stimulus; the rapid rise in college tuition; the slow recovery from the Great Recession; ballooning federal budget deficits and public debt; the long-run funding shortfalls in Social Security and Medicare; the effect of rising dependency ratios on economic growth; innovative Federal Reserve policies, including quantitative easing, the zero interest rate policy, and explicit inflation targets; the massive excess reserves in the banking system; the jump in the size of the Fed's balance sheet; the effect of the zero interest rate policy on savers; regulation of "too big to fail" banks; trade adjustment assistance; changes in exchange rates; and many other current topics.

Chapter-by-Chapter Changes

Each chapter of *Economics,* AP® edition, contains updated data reflecting the current economy, revised Learning Objectives, and reorganized and expanded end-of-chapter content. Every chapter also contains one or more AP Quick Review boxes to help students review and solidify content as they are reading along.

Chapter-specific updates include:

Chapter 1: Limits, Alternatives, and Choices features two refreshed Consider This pieces as well as revised new examples and working improvements to clarify the main concepts.

Chapter 2: The Market System and the Circular Flow contains updated examples and a brief new introduction to the concept of residual claimant.

Chapter 3: Demand, Supply, and Market Equilibrium includes a new Last Word on how student lending raises college tuition as well as data updates and updated examples.

Chapter 4: Market Failures: Public Goods and Externalities features updated examples and a new Key Word on Pigovian taxes.

Chapter 5: Government's Role and Government Failure has a new Consider This on government agencies violating government laws, several new examples, and wording revisions for increased clarity.

Chapter 6: Elasticity contains several updated examples.

Chapter 7: Utility Maximization incorporates updated examples and a new Consider This vignette on consumers applying maximizing behavior to the calorie data that are now printed on restaurant menus.

Chapter 8: Behavioral Economics contains a new Consider This piece on the myopia-busting business model employed by Solar City as well as a new Last Word describing the activities of the Behavioral Insights Team.

Chapter 8: Businesses and the Costs of Production incorporates a few wording updates to facilitate rapid comprehension.

Chapter 9: Pure Competition in the Short Run features several wording changes to improve student understanding of the end-of-chapter questions and problems.

Chapter 10: Pure Competition in the Long Run contains several updated examples to keep the content relevant for today's students.

Chapter 11: Pure Monopoly has a new Last Word about individualized online price discrimination as well as updated examples.

Chapter 12: Monopolistic Competition was previously part of a chapter that covered both monopolistic competition and oligopoly. We have split that chapter into two parts for the 21st edition so that instructors who wish to skip either set of material may easily do so.

Chapter 13: Oligopoly and Strategic Behavior was previously part of a chapter that covered both monopolistic competition and oligopoly. The material on oligopoly constitutes the basis for this stand-alone chapter, which also extends the game theory material found in the previous edition. Our extended coverage of game theory and strategic behavior includes extensive-form (game-tree) representations of sequential games and the concept of subgame-perfect Nash equilibrium. As with prior editions, all game theory material is kept concrete by presenting it in the context of strategic behavior among oligopoly firms.

Chapter 14: The Demand for Resources incorporates light data updates as well as an entirely new Last Word on capital-labor substitution. This discussion uses ATM machines as its main example, just as the Last Word in the previous edition did. But an update was required because recent research indicates that the main premise of the old Last Word no longer holds true: ATMs did not in fact replace human tellers in the aggregate, at least not after managers adjusted to the new technology. The new Last Word updates the story.

Chapter 15: Wage Determination features extensive data updates, improved wording for clarity, and a new Last Word on how unnecessary occupational licensing requirements are reducing employment opportunities.

Chapter 16: Rent, Interest, and Profit incorporates wording improvements, data updates, and a new Consider This on the subject of profits.

Chapter 17: Public Finance: Expenditures and Taxes contains extensive data updates and several new examples.

Chapter 18: Antitrust Policy and Regulation has a new Last Word that covers both antitrust prosecutions against human managers who intentionally engage in anticompetitive practices as well as the newly evolving area of price-fixing by artificial intelligence algorithms that unintentionally collude to fix prices when they interact with each other.

Chapter 19: Income Inequality, Poverty, and Discrimination contains a new Consider This about welfare cliffs as well as extensive data updates and several new examples.

Chapter 20: An Introduction to Macroeconomics incorporates data updates, wording improvements, and several new examples.

Chapter 21: Measuring Domestic Output and National Income features extensive data updates and a short new section discussing the importance of paying attention to intermediate economic activity as measured by gross output.

Chapter 22: Economic Growth contains data updates, new examples, and a new discussion of the slowdown in productivity growth that has occurred since the Great Recession.

Chapter 23: Business Cycles, Unemployment, and Inflation features both a new Consider This on deflationary spirals as well as an extended discussion of negative interest rates.

Chapter 24: Basic Macroeconomic Relationships features data updates and a new Last Word that humorously illustrates the multiplier concept in the same parody style that was used in the Last Word piece that this all-new story replaces.

Chapter 25: The Aggregate Expenditures Model contains data updates and minor wording improvements.

Chapter 26: Aggregate Demand and Aggregate Supply incorporates updates to both data and examples.

Chapter 27: Fiscal Policy, Deficits, and Debt uses extensive data updates to reflect the current U.S. fiscal situation and place it in an international context.

Chapter 28: Money, Banking, and Financial Institutions features a new Last Word on central bank bailouts for insolvent as well as illiquid financial institutions, a policy derided by some as "extend and pretend."

Chapter 29: Money Creation incorporates a few data updates as well as a new section explaining the demise of the federal funds market after the Financial Crisis of 2007–2008.

Chapter 30: Interest Rates and Monetary Policy features new material on the unorthodox monetary policy of the last 10 years. Coverage of the federal funds market has been slashed, reflecting the fact that the massive excess reserves in the banking system mean that the Fed now uses open-market operations for quantitative easing rather than adjustments to the federal funds rate (which is constantly forced toward zero by those massive excess bank reserves). We also give an in-depth explanation of the Federal Reserve's plan to normalize monetary policy by using reverse repos and the rate of interest on excess reserves (IOER) to raise short-term interest rates in the coming years. To aid comprehension of how repos and reverse repos work, we have also added a new Consider This piece.

Chapter 31: Financial Economics has extensive data updates and a new Consider This on how increased institutional stock ownership may have exacerbated the principal-agent problem and thereby engendered a greater amount of self-serving behavior on the part of corporate managers.

Chapter 32: Extending the Analysis of Aggregate Supply incorporates data updates and new material that updates our discussion of the empirical validity of the Phillips Curve by including the most recent data on inflation and unemployment.

Chapter 33: Current Issues in Macro Theory and Policy contains a new section explaining the Federal Reserve's 2-percent inflation target as well as a new Last Word describing Market Monetarism.

Chapter 34: International Trade contains new examples and data updates.

Chapter 35: The Balance of Payments, Exchange Rates, and Trade Deficits is heavily revised for this edition. There is an entirely new presentation of fixed exchange rates and how the balance of payments under a fixed exchange rate determines the direction of change of both foreign exchange reserves as well as the domestic money supply. This presentation is illustrated with a new Consider This on China's currency peg as well as a new Last Word on whether common currencies (which are implicit pegs) are a good idea. This chapter also has a new appendix that includes the material on previous (pre-Bretton Woods) exchange rate systems.

Details about the updates to the extension chapters can be found in the Instructor's Resource section, accessible through the Library tab in Connect

Distinguishing Features

Comprehensive Explanations at an Appropriate Level

Economics is comprehensive, analytical, and challenging yet fully accessible to a wide range of students. The thoroughness and accessibility enable teachers to select topics for special classroom emphasis with confidence that students can read and comprehend other independently assigned material in the book. Where needed, an extra sentence of explanation is provided. Brevity at the expense of clarity is false economy.

Fundamentals of the Market System Many economies throughout the world are still making difficult transitions from planning to markets while a handful of other countries such as Venezuela seem to be trying to reestablish government-controlled, centrally planned economies. Our detailed description of the institutions and operation of the market system in Chapter 2 (The Market System and the Circular Flow) is therefore even more relevant than before. We pay particular attention to property rights, entrepreneurship, freedom of enterprise and choice, competition, and the role of profits because these concepts are often misunderstood by beginning students worldwide.

Extensive Treatment of International Economics We give the principles and institutions of the global economy extensive treatment. The appendix to Chapter 3 (Demand, Supply, and Market Equilibrium) has an application on exchange rates. Chapter 34 (International Trade) examines key facts of international trade, specialization and comparative advantage, arguments for protectionism, impacts of tariffs and subsidies, and various trade agreements. Chapter 35 (The Balance of Payments, Exchange Rates, and Trade Deficits) discusses the balance of payments, fixed and floating exchange rates, and U.S. trade deficits.

Chapter 34 (International Trade) is constructed such that teachers who want to cover international trade early in the course can assign it immediately after Chapter 3. Chapter 34 requires only a good understanding of production possibilities analysis and supply and demand analysis to comprehend.

International competition, trade flows, and financial flows are integrated throughout the micro and macro sections. "Global Perspective" boxes add to the international flavor of the book.

Early and Extensive Treatment of Government The public sector is an integral component of modern capitalism. This book introduces the role of government early. Chapter 4 (Market Failures: Public Goods and Externalities) systematically discusses public goods and government policies toward externalities. Chapter 5 (Government's Role and Government Failure) details the factors that cause government failure. And Chapter 17 (Public Finance: Expenditures and Taxes) examines taxation and government expenditures in detail. Both the micro and the macro sections of the text include issue- and policy-oriented chapters.

Stress on the Theory of the Firm We have given much attention to microeconomics in general and to the theory of the firm in particular, for two reasons. First, the concepts of microeconomics are difficult for most beginning students; abbreviated expositions usually compound these difficulties by raising more questions than they answer. Second, we wanted to couple analysis of the various market structures with a discussion of the impact of each market arrangement on price, output levels, resource allocation, and the rate of technological advance.

Step-by-Step, Two-Path Macro As in the previous edition, our macro continues to be distinguished by a systematic step-by-step approach to developing ideas and building models. Explicit assumptions about price and wage stickiness are posited and then systematically peeled away, yielding new models and extensions, all in the broader context of growth, expectations, shocks, and degrees of price and wage stickiness over time.

In crafting this step-by-step macro approach, we took care to preserve the "two-path macro" that many instructors appreciated. Instructors who want to bypass the immediate short-run model (Chapter 25: The Aggregate Expenditures Model) can proceed without loss of continuity directly to the short-run AD-AS model (Chapter 26: Aggregate Demand and Aggregate Supply), fiscal policy, money and banking, monetary policy, and the long-run AD-AS analysis.

Emphasis on Technological Change and Economic Growth This edition continues to emphasize economic growth. Chapter 1 (Limits, Alternatives, and Choices) uses the production possibilities curve to show the basic ingredients of growth. Chapter 22 (Economic Growth) explains how growth is measured and presents the facts of growth. It also discusses the causes of growth, looks at productivity growth, and addresses some controversies surrounding economic growth. Chapter 22's "Last Word" examines whether economic growth can survive demographic decline.

Organizational Alternatives

Although instructors generally agree on the content of principles of economics courses, they sometimes differ on how to arrange the material. *Economics* includes 11 parts, and thus provides considerable organizational flexibility. We place microeconomics before macroeconomics because this ordering is consistent with how contemporary economists view the direction of linkage between the two components. The introductory material of Parts 1 and 2, however, can be followed immediately by the macro analysis of Parts 7 and 8. Similarly, the two-path macro enables covering the full aggregate expenditures model or advancing directly from the basic macro relationships chapter to the AD-AS model.

Some instructors will prefer to intersperse the microeconomics of Parts 4 and 5 with the issues chapters of Part 6. Chapter 34 on international trade can easily be moved up to immediately after Chapter 3 on supply and demand for instructors who want an early discussion of international trade.

Pedagogical Aids for AP

Economics is highly student-oriented. The AP edition is also accompanied by a variety of high-quality supplements that help students master the subject and help teachers implement customized courses.

Digital Tools

Adaptive Reading Experience SmartBook contains the same content as the print book, but actively tailors that content to the needs of the individual through adaptive probing. Instructors can assign SmartBook reading assignments for points to create incentives for students to come to class prepared.

Extensive Algorithmic and Graphing Assessment Robust, auto-gradable question banks for each chapter now include even more questions that make use of the Connect graphing tool. More questions featuring algorithmic variations have also been added.

Interactive Graphs This new assignable resource within Connect helps students see the relevance of subject matter by providing visual displays of real data for students to manipulate. All graphs are accompanied by assignable assessment questions and feedback to guide students through the experience of learning to read and interpret graphs and data.

Videos New to this edition are videos that provide support for key economics topics. These short, engaging explanations are presented at the moment students may be struggling to help them connect the dots and grasp challenging concepts.

Math Preparedness Tutorials Our math preparedness assignments have been reworked to help students refresh on important prerequisite topics necessary to be successful in economics.

Digital Image Library Every graph and table in the text is available in the Instructor's Resource section in Connect.

Content Review Test Banks Each question in the content review test banks for Economics maps to a specific learning objective. All Test Bank questions are organized by learning objective, topic, and Bloom's Taxonomy guidelines.

Test Bank III contains more than 600 pages of short-answer questions and problems created in the style of the book's end-of-chapter questions. Test Bank III can be used to construct student assignments or design essay and problem exams. Suggested answers to the essay and problem questions are included.

Supplements for AP Students and Teachers

The NEW *Focus Review Guide to accompany McConnell Economics AP® Edition*

The *Focus Review Guide* was designed to support students' complete understanding and application of the most important AP economics concepts. Written by experienced AP teacher and Exam Reader Lisa Ellison, the *Focus Review Guide* highlights AP concepts and offers additional explanation and practice along with insightful guidance.

Key features include:

- **AP Key Concept** review is a perfect study tool
- **A Closer Look** explains the concepts in different ways to ensure complete understanding
- **Practice** questions, often using graphs, allow students to apply the concepts
- **Graphing Guidance** provides instruction and tips for graphing in class and on the Exam
- **Caution** features help students avoid common pitfalls or mistakes common to AP students
- **Keep in Mind** offers tips and advice for earning the highest score on the AP Exam
- **Economically Speaking** reviews key vocabulary and economic terms

AP Teacher's Manual Designed specifically with the AP Economics teacher and course in mind, this resource has been written and reviewed by expert, experienced AP Teachers and Exam Readers.

The AP Teacher Manual provides:

- Chapter overviews
- Instructional objectives
- Answers to end-of-chapter Discussion Questions, AP Review Questions, and Problems
- Comments and teaching suggestions to help promote understanding and stimulate discussion
- A pacing guide
- Lecture notes

A **Student Stumbling Blocks** section identifies typical areas of difficulty for the high school student in the study of economics, and provides ideas for helping students move past these sources of frustration.

AP-Style Test Banks These chapter banks, specific to *Economics* AP Edition, give students additional practice answering **AP-style multiple-choice questions and free response questions**. Teachers can easily edit and deliver these tests online for chapter quizzes, unit tests, or AP Exam practice. Automatic grading is available for each multiple choice question, while scoring rubrics and detailed explanations are provided for each free-response question.

TestGen Test Banks TestGen is a complete, state-of-the-art test generator and editing application software that allows instructors to quickly and easily select test items from McGraw-Hill's AP and content review test banks. The teachers can then organize, edit, and customize questions and answers to rapidly generate tests for paper or online administration. TestGen's random generator provides the option to display different text or calculated number values each time questions are used. With both quick-and-simple test creation and flexible and robust editing tools, TestGen is a complete test generator system for today's educators.

You can use our test bank software, TestGen, or *Connect Economics* to easily query for learning outcomes and objectives that directly relate to the learning objectives for your course. You can then use the reporting features to aggregate student results in a similar fashion, making the collection and presentation of assurance-of-learning data simple and easy.

AP Macroeconomics Correlation This chart correlates book content to specific AP Macroeconomics topics and learning objectives to help teachers target critical content and prepare students for the AP exam.

AP Microeconomics Correlation This chart correlates book content to specific AP Microeconomics topics and learning objectives to help teachers target critical content and prepare students for the AP exam.

Instructor's Manual The revised *Instructor's Manual* includes, chapter summaries, teaching tips and suggestions, learning objectives, chapter outlines, extra questions and problems, and answers to the end-of-chapter questions and problems, plus correlation guides mapping content to learning objectives. All of these resources are available in the Instructor's Resource section, accessible through the Library tab in Connect.

PowerPoint Presentations Each chapter is accompanied by a concise yet thorough tour of the key concepts. Teachers can use these presentations in the classroom, and students can use them on their computers.

Digital Solutions

ONboard™ for AP Economics

ONboard™ is a series of self-paced, online, interactive modules that help students master the skills and content necessary to be successful in AP coursework and on the AP Exams. Research-based and developed with teaching experts, *ONboard*™ features high-interest videos and interactive activities. Students self-check to ensure comprehension while the pre-test and comprehensive final assessment helps teachers identify skill and knowledge gaps.

McGraw-Hill *Connect® Economics*

Less Managing. More Teaching. Greater Learning. *Connect Economics* is an online assignment and assessment solution that offers a number of powerful tools and features that make managing assignments easier so faculty can spend more time teaching. With *Connect Economics*, students can engage with their coursework anytime and anywhere, making the learning process more accessible and efficient.

SCOREboard™ AP Economics

SCOREboard™ is the first Advanced Placement Exam Preparation solution that truly adapts to each student's learning needs, delivering personalized learning to ensure student comprehension as they prepare in the weeks and months leading up to the AP Exam. **This is especially valuable for students who take AP Economics in the fall, but will not take the exam until the spring.** *SCOREboard*™ features adaptive content review, targeted instruction, and two complete AP Practice Exams each for Macroeconomics and Microeconomics.

Tegrity Campus: Lectures 24/7

Tegrity Campus is a service that makes class time available 24/7 by automatically capturing every lecture in a searchable format for students to review when they study and complete assignments. With a simple one-click start-and-stop process, you capture all computer screens and corresponding audio. Students can replay any part of any class with easy-to-use browser-based viewing on a PC or Mac.

To learn more about Tegrity, you can watch a two-minute Flash demo at **tegritycampus.mhhe.com.**

We have made it simple for you to find the course content you are looking for!

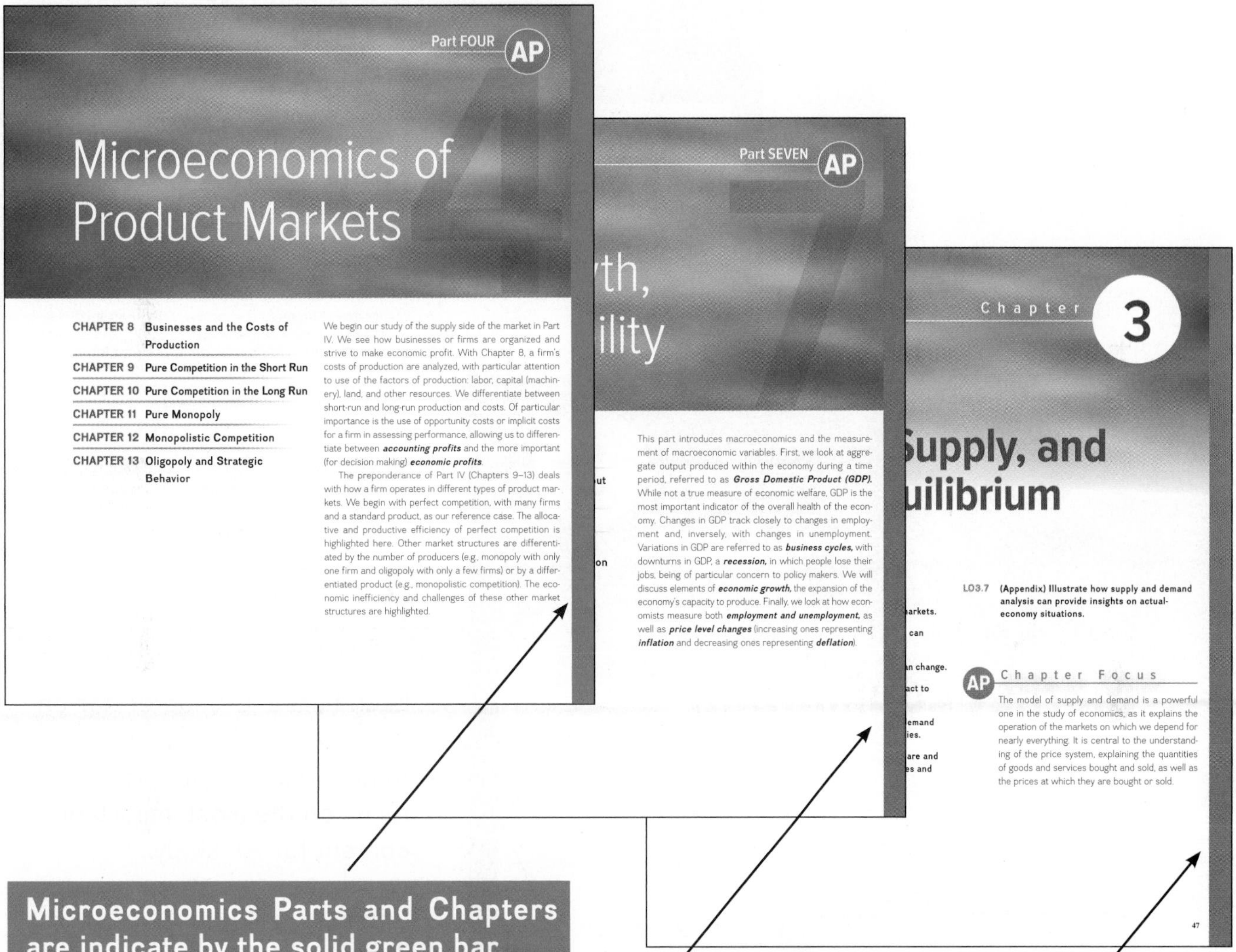

Microeconomics Parts and Chapters are indicate by the solid green bar.

Macroeconomics Parts and Chapters are indicate by the solid purple bar.

Parts and Chapters that cover both are indicate by the gradient bar.

AP Part TWO

2 Price, Quantity, and Efficiency

In Chapter 3, this critical part of the study of economics introduces you to the functioning of a competitive product market. The ***law of demand*** which leads to consumers having an inverse relationship between product price and the quantity demanded of a product is explained. The ***law of supply*** which leads to producers having a positive or direct relationship between product price and the quantity supplied of a product is explained. Then the fundamental concept of ***equilibrium*** price and quantity in the product market is shown, as well as the beneficial result, called ***allocative efficiency*** by economists, when quantity demanded is equal to quantity supplied.

Chapter 4 then introduces the concept of ***market failure***, or situations where the competitive equilibrium does not prevail. In this chapter important to microeconomics, we will see how consumers can be harmed with a loss of consumer surplus and/or how producers can be harmed with a loss of ***producer surplus***. Public goods and externalities, possible causes of market failures, are discussed here.

Finally, in Chapter 5 we introduce you to the challenges facing government in a market economy. Even when the preponderance of economic decisions are made by the market, there is still a role for government to help direct the economy and to provide some goods and services, like public education, roads, and national defense.

Chapter 3

Demand, Supply, and Market Equilibrium

Learning Objectives

LO3.1 Characterize and give examples of markets.

LO3.2 Describe *demand* and explain how it can change.

LO3.3 Describe *supply* and explain how it can change.

LO3.4 Relate how supply and demand interact to determine market equilibrium.

LO3.5 Explain how changes in supply and demand affect equilibrium prices and quantities.

LO3.6 Identify what government-set prices are and how they can cause product surpluses and shortages.

LO3.7 (Appendix) Illustrate how supply and demand analysis can provide insights on actual-economy situations.

AP Chapter Focus

The model of supply and demand is a powerful one in the study of economics, as it explains the operation of the markets on which we depend for nearly everything. It is central to the understanding of the price system, explaining the quantities of goods and services bought and sold, as well as the prices at which they are bought or sold.

47

Each Part and Chapter has an **AP-specific introduction** to help teachers and students focus on the most important content for AP study.

The most important **Figures and Tables** for AP students are clearly marked.

CHAPTER 3 Demand, Supply, and Market Equilibrium | 51

AP **FIGURE 3.3 Changes in the demand for corn.** A change in one or more of the determinants of demand causes a change in demand. An increase in demand is shown as a shift of the demand curve to the right, as from D_1 to D_2. A decrease in demand is shown as a shift of the demand curve to the left, as from D_1 to D_3. These changes in demand are to be distinguished from a change in quantity demanded, which is caused by a change in the price of the product, as shown by a movement from, say, point *a* to point *b* on fixed demand curve D_1.

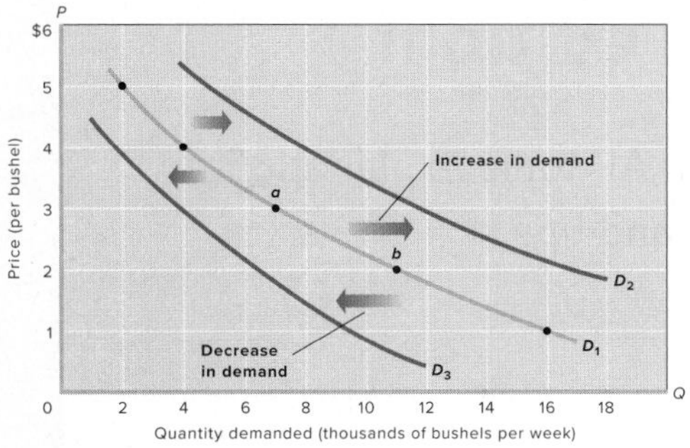

Market Demand for Corn, 200 Buyers, (D_1)	
(1) Price per Bushel	(2) Total Quantity Demanded per Week
$5	2,000
4	4,000
3	7,000
2	11,000
1	16,000

AP QUICK REVIEW 3.1

- ✓ Demand is a schedule or curve showing the quantity of a product that buyers are willing and able to buy, in a particular time period, at each per unit price.
- ✓ The law of demand states that, other things equal, the quantity of a good purchased varies inversely with its price. At lower prices more is purchased; at higher prices less is purchased.
- ✓ The demand curve shifts, because of changes in (a) consumer tastes, (b) the number of buyers in the market, (c) consumer income, (d) the prices of substitute or complementary goods, (e) consumer expectations, and (f) tastes.
- ✓ A change in demand is a shift of the entire demand curve. A change in quantity demanded is a movement from one point to another point along the demand curve.

AP Quick Review boxes help students keep up with most important AP economic content. Concepts are reexamined in a clear and concise manner.

AP-style Multiple Choice and Free-Response Questions at the end of each chapter and complete **AP Microeconomics and Macroeconomics Practice Exams** at the end of the book provide additional practice answering AP-style questions.

AP REVIEW QUESTIONS

1. What effect will each of the following have on the demand for small, fuel efficient automobiles such as the Mini-Cooper and Fiat 500? LO3.2
   - **a.** Small automobiles become more fashionable.
   - **b.** The price of large automobiles rises (with the price of small autos remaining the same).
   - **c.** Income declines and small autos are an inferior good.
   - **d.** Consumers anticipate that the price of small autos will greatly come down in the near future.
   - **e.** The price of gasoline substantially drops.
2. True or False: A "change in quantity demanded" is a shift of the entire demand curve to the right or to the left. LO3.2
3. What effect will each of the following have on the supply of auto tires? LO3.3
   - **a.** A technological advance in the methods of producing tires.
   - **b.** A decline in the number of firms in the tire industry.
   - **c.** An increase in the prices of rubber used in the production of tires.
   - **d.** The expectation that the equilibrium price of auto tires will be lower in the future than currently.
   - **e.** A decline in the price of the large tires used for semi trucks and earth-hauling rigs (with no change in the price of auto tires).
   - **f.** The levying of a per-unit tax on each auto tire sold.
   - **g.** The granting of a 50-cent-per-unit subsidy for each auto tire produced.
4. Peanut butter and jelly sandwiches continue to be a mainstay of packed lunches across America. If the price of peanut butter declines, the demand curve for the jelly will: LO3.4
   - **a.** Shift to the left, since jelly is a substitute.
   - **b.** Shift to the right, since peanut butter and jelly are complements.
   - **c.** Decrease, since jelly is a substitute.
   - **d.** Remain unchanged.
   - **e.** Shift to the left, since peanut butter and jelly are complements.
5. Suppose that in the market for computer memory chips, the equilibrium price is $50 per chip. If the current price is $55 per chip, then there will be ____________ of memory chips. LO3.4
   - **a.** A shortage.
   - **b.** A surplus.
   - **c.** An equilibrium.
   - **d.** A future increase in the production.
   - **e.** None of the above.
6. If price is above the equilibrium level, competition among sellers to reduce the resulting: LO3.5
   - **a.** Surplus will increase quantity demanded and decrease quantity supplied.
   - **b.** Shortage will decrease quantity demanded and increase quantity supplied.
   - **c.** Surplus will decrease quantity demanded and increase quantity supplied.
   - **d.** Shortage will increase quantity demanded and decrease quantity supplied.
   - **e.** Equilibrium will take no action to change.
7. Label each of the following scenarios with the set of symbols that best indicates the price change and quantity change that occur in the scenario. In some scenarios, it may not be possible from the information given to determine the direction of a particular price change or a particular quantity change. We will symbolize those cases as, respectively, "P?" and "Q?". The four possible combinations of price and quantity changes are: LO3.5

   P↓ Q?   P? Q↓

   P↑ Q?   P? Q↑

NEW *Focus Review Guide* to work hand in hand with the student edition!

Featuring additional AP topic explanations, practice, guidance, and tips.

While providing a summary overview of the most important AP concepts covered in the *Student Edition*, the *Focus Review Guide* also provides reinforcement and extra practice for select key topics (marked with the AP icon AP) essential for students to master.

AP Demand

LO3.2 Describe *demand* and explain how it can change.

Demand is a schedule or a curve that shows the various amounts of a product that consumers are willing and able to purchase at each of a series of possible prices during a specified period of time.[1] Demand shows the quantities of a product that will be purchased at various possible prices, *other things equal*. Demand can easily be shown in table form. The table in Figure 3.1 is a hypothetical **demand schedule** for a *single consumer* purchasing bushels of corn.

The table reveals the relationship between the various prices of corn and the quantity of corn a particular consumer would be willing and able to purchase at each of these prices. We say "willing and able" because willingness alone is not effective in the market. You may be willing to buy a plasma television set, but if that willingness is not backed by the necessary dollars, it will not be effective and, therefore, will not be reflected in the market. In the table in Figure 3.1, if the price of corn were $5 per bushel, our consumer would be willing and able to buy 10 bushels per week; if it were $4, the consumer would be willing and able to buy 20 bushels per week; and so forth.

Demand

Refer to pages 48–53 of your textbook.

A CLOSER LOOK The Demand Curve

The **demand** curve shows the quantity of products consumers are willing and able to buy at various prices. It is a downward-sloping curve, showing the inverse relationship between the price and the quantity demanded. According to the **Law of Demand,** when the price falls, the quantity demanded increases; when the price rises, the quantity demanded falls. You know this to be true from purchases you have made. If you had a choice of paying $100 or $75 for the very same pair of shoes, which price would you be more willing and able to pay?

So what makes the Law of Demand operate as it does? Three factors create this effect. The first is **diminishing marginal utility.** As a consumer gets more and more of a product, the satisfaction he gets from each additional product falls; therefore, he is not willing to pay as much for additional products. A pencil is very useful for school work, and if you really need one, you might be willing to pay $1 for it. A second pencil is still useful, but not as much as that first one was, so you might only be willing to pay 50¢ for it. In order to entice you to buy more, the producer must lower the price for additional products.

The second factor is the **income effect.** At a lower price, a consumer can afford to buy more of the product. Say you go to the store, expecting to pay $2 for a box of pencils. But you find that the store is having a sale, with a price of only $1 for the box of pencils. You now have a dollar left over, which you might use to buy a second box of pencils. When the price falls, people are able to buy more.

The third factor is the **substitution effect.** At a lower price, a customer may choose to substitute one product for another. If you went to the store planning to pay $2 for a box of pens, but saw the box of pencils on sale for $1, you might be willing to buy the pencils instead of the pens. When the price falls, people are willing to buy more.

To draw a demand curve, you must first create a demand schedule, showing how many products the consumer is willing and able to buy at each price. Then you can plot the points into the graph and connect those points to draw the curve.

A Closer Look provides additional information and explanation to ensure complete understanding.

PRACTICE **The Demand Curve**

Use the demand schedule to draw a demand curve for pizzas per night at Cameron's Pizza Shop.

Price	Quantity
$ 4	50
$ 6	40
$ 8	20
$10	10

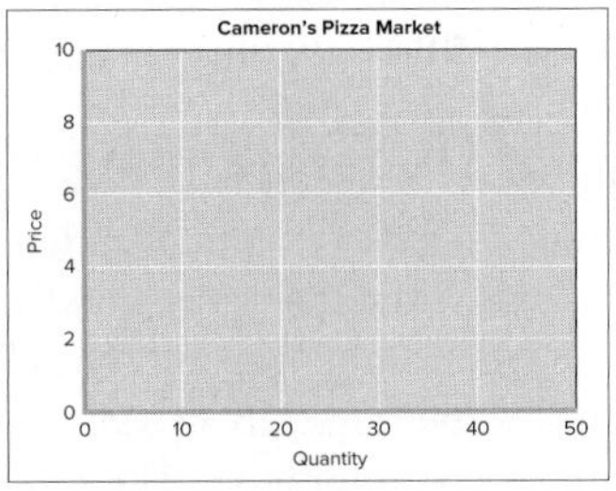

1. _______ How many pizzas will be sold at $6?
2. _______ How many pizzas will be sold at $7?
3. _______ What price should be set to sell 20 pizzas?
4. _______ What price should be set to sell 15 pizzas?
5. _______ If the shop wants to sell 25 pizzas and it now charges $8, should it raise or lower the price?

Practice sections include questions and graphing exercises that allow students additional practice in applying AP concepts.

Valuable features, such as **Caution, Graphing Guidance, Keep in Mind,** and **Economically Speaking** give students tips, advice, and study tools to help them avoid common mistakes and earn high scores on the AP Exams.

Economically Speaking

- **Allocative Efficiency** the mark
- **Ceteris Paribus** the assumptio changes
- **Change in Demand/Supply** a shift of the entire demand/supply curve
- **Change in Quantity Demanded** response to a price change
- **Complements** products that are
- **Demand** the willingness and ab
- **Diminishing Marginal Utility** as satisfaction s/he gets from each
- **Equilibrium Price** the price wh
- **Equilibrium Quantity** the quant
- **Income Effect** at a lower price,
- **Inferior Goods** when income d
- **Law of Demand** when the price quantity demanded falls
- **Law of Supply** when the price quantity supplied falls
- **Market Demand** total demand from all consumers in the market
- **Market Supply** total supply fro
- **Normal Goods** when income i
- **Price Ceiling** the maximum pri
- **Price Floor** the minimum price
- **Productive Efficiency** a produ
- **Shortage** the quantity demand
- **Subsidy** a government paymen
- **Substitutes** products that can
- **Substitution Effect** at a lower product for a higher-priced one
- **Supply** the willingness and abil
- **Surplus** the quantity supplied i

Graphing Guidance

It is very important to shift demand curves *directly* to the right or left, *not* up and down or at angles. An increase in demand shows that *at this same price*, consumers are demanding more products. So the quantity would increase, but the price would not.

Caution

It is important to distinguish between the *substitution effect* (which changes the quantity demanded) and a *change in the price of substitutes* (which shifts the demand curve). The substitution effect focuses on the consumer's reaction to the change in price of a product. If you intended to buy chips and found the chips on sale for a lower price, you might buy more chips. Your demand curve for chips didn't shift; you simply responded to the lower price by buying more, which is a movement from one point to another point on your demand curve. However, if the price of a *different* product like pretzels fell, you might buy the pretzels instead of the chips, and your entire demand curve for chips would shift. The key is to look at whether the price of the specific *product* changed (so your quantity demanded changed) or the price of a *different* product changed, causing you to buy less of the original product (so your demand for the product at all prices changed).

Keep in Mind

The proper labeling of graphs is *essential* to earn full scores on the free-response portion of an AP Economics exam.

1. Label each axis (price on the vertical; quantity on the horizontal)
2. Label each curve (supply and demand)
3. Draw equilibrium lines and label equilibrium price and quantity (such as P and Q)
4. Distinguish each curve that shows movement (such as D_1 and D_2)
5. Draw arrows between the original and new curves to show the direction of movement
6. Draw new equilibrium lines and label your new equilibrium price and quantity to distinguish them from the originals (such as P_1 and P_2, and Q_1 and Q_2)

Because scoring rubrics allocate points specifically for correctly labeled graphs, you can earn points just for getting that far—or easily lose points on an otherwise excellent response simply due to sloppy labeling. So maximize your potential score and label carefully!

About the AP Micro and Macro Economics Courses

Course Themes and Structure

The Advanced Placement (AP) program was created by the College Board, which also developed the SAT exam. Each of the AP Microeconomics and AP Macroeconomics courses has an exam. The exams are written by AP Economics Micro- or Macro- Course Development Committees, which consists of college Economics professors and high school teachers with experience teaching the AP Economics course. In developing the exams, these committees review the course descriptions and course contents from hundreds of university Economics professors to determine which concepts to include in the AP Economics course descriptions and in the AP Economics Exams. The College Board requires audits of high school courses with the AP designation to ensure that the high school curriculum meets standards equivalent to the college Economics courses. Test development committees are constantly reviewing university course descriptions and discussing AP course revisions.

Microeconomics and Macroeconomics are generally two one-semester courses that explore different aspects of our economy. Microeconomics focuses on the small picture of economic decisions made by households, as consumers and as suppliers of inputs like labor and of firms and suppliers of output and demanders of inputs. Macroeconomics considers the behavior of the aggregate economy and its performance. Particular attention is paid to macroeconomic challenges with unemployment, inflation, and economic growth. International finance is considered in the Macroeconomics course, while international trade is included both in both the Microeconomics and in the Macroeconomics courses.

About the Exam

The AP Microeconomics Exam and AP Macroeconomics Exam are entirely separate exams. Students may opt to take either exam or both. Each exam is scheduled for two hours and ten minutes, with one test in the morning and the other in the afternoon of the same day. Students are given 70 minutes to answer 60 multiple-choice questions. Then, after a ten-minute reading period, students have 50 minutes to write answers to three free- response questions.

Understanding the Format

As we explained earlier, each of the AP Economics Exams—Microeconomics and Macroeconomics—is a two-hour and ten-minute exam. The College Board schedules these exams on the same day in May, with one exam in the morning and one in the afternoon. The multiple-choice section accounts for two-thirds of the score, and a free-response section provides the other one-third of the score.

Multiple-Choice Questions

The first portion of the exam consists of sixty multiple-choice questions, which are to be answered within seventy minutes. The multiple-choice questions can include a wide range of information, including definitions and applications

Table 1A: Breakdown of the AP Microeconomics Exam

Percentage of Questions	Topics	Chapters in this book related to the Exam
8-14%	Basic Economic Concepts	1, 2, 3, 4
55-70%	The Nature and Functions of Product Markets	3, 6, 7, 8, 9, 10, 11, 12, 13
10-18%	Factor Markets	14, 15, 16,
12-18%	Market Failure and the Role of Government	4, 17, 18, 19

Table 1B: Breakdown of the AP Macroeconomics Exam

Percentage of Questions	Topics	Chapters in this book related to the Exam
8-12%	Basic Economic Concepts	1, 2, 3, 5
12-16%	Measurement of Economic Performance	20, 21, 22, 23,
10-15%	National Income and Price Determination	24, 25, 26
15-20%	Financial Sector	28, 29, 30,
20-30%	Stabilization Policies	24, 27, 31, 32
5-10%	Economic Growth	22
10-15%	Open Economy: International Trade and Finance	33, 34, 35

of principles, calculations, interpretations of graphs, explanations of the causes or results of an economic action, and choosing an appropriate economic policy to deal with an economic event.

Free-Response Questions

The second portion of the exam consists of three free-response questions, with approximately half of the score given for the first written response and the rest divided between the other two written responses. The sixty minutes of free-response time begins with a mandatory ten-minute reading period, during which you may begin outlining your answers. The College Board suggests that you spend approximately twenty-five minutes writing the long response and divide the other twenty-five minutes between the shorter responses. The long response generally involves interconnections among several different concepts central to the course, while the shorter responses generally focus on one specific concept or a pair of related concepts.

Table 2: Breakdown of the AP Economics Exam Format

Summary of Exam Format		
Section I:	Multiple Choice 60 questions Time: 70 minutes	No calculators are allowed. Use a #2 pencil with a very good eraser for this section.
	[10-minute break]	
Section II:	Free Response Three free-response questions Time: 50 minutes One long question (25 minutes) and two short questions (25 minutes together)	There is a 10 minute required reading period before writing the answers to the three free-response questions. This time can also be used to begin outlining answers. No calculators are allowed. Use blue or black ink for this section.

Table 3: Overall Grade Distribution

Grade Distribution	
Multiple Choice:	67%
Free Response:	33% The long (first) free-response question represents 50% of the free-response score, while each of the other two free-response questions represents 25% of the free-response score.

Practice Questions

AP Central has an exam page for each course. Here is the link to the AP Macro- and Micro- questions and rubrics. http://apcentral.collegeboard.com/apc/members/exam/exam_information/2083.html

Look at the screen shot of the AP Central Homepage. Look down the left side. There is a section called Exam Information. That link takes you to the list of exam homepages from which you can get past history of the annual AP free response questions, their answers, and their grading. There are also released exams of multiple-choice questions, typically every five years.

A great way to testing your knowledge of Micro- and Macroeconomics is by working these past test questions. They are excellent preparation for taking the exam.

Grading of the AP Exam

The multiple-choice section of the exam is scored electronically, while readers grade the free-response sections. The College Board then applies a weighted formula and combines the raw multiple-choice and free-response scores to create a composite score. Finally, a conversion factor is used to award the student one of five final scores with a 5 being extremely well qualified and a 1 being no recommendation.

Because the AP Microeconomics and Macroeconomics courses are intended to represent the two one-semester college courses, the two AP Exams are scored independently. You may opt to take either exam or to take both exams. A passing score on either exam can provide college credit for institutions that accept AP credit, but colleges and universities differ markedly in requirements and credits offered. Some schools accept a score of 3 for credit, while other schools may require a 4 or a 5 in order to receive credit.

Multiple-Choice Questions

Each question has five potential answers labeled A-E. Each correct answer is worth one point, while questions left blank earn no points.

To guess or not to guess?

The College Board will assess no penalty for wrong answers. While you will earn no credit for a wrong answer, you will not face any additional penalty for guessing. So it is in your best interest to answer every question on the exam.

Free-Response Questions

AP Economics responses are quite different from the formal essays written for some other AP subjects, which require thesis statements and five-paragraph development structure. AP Economics free-response questions generally consist of a series of questions and sub-questions which can be answered in several sentences. Responses should directly answer the questions asked.

Keep in mind the economic concept of efficiency and apply that to your free-response writing. Be complete, but be efficient about it. Directly answer the question asked and explain why that answer is correct. The best answers use the appropriate terms and the clearest language to explain the situation, causes and effects, and reasoning. The readers want to see a clear analysis and your understanding.

Many of the free-response questions also require you to draw one or more graphs. As the exam directions indicate, it is very important that you correctly label your graphs. Your axis labels should be clear (for example, Price and Quantity, or Price Level and Real Output). Every curve should be appropriately labeled. If you want to indicate the shift of a curve, be sure to draw arrows between the curves to show the direction of movement, and label the second curve differently (for example, D1 and D2). Draw equilibrium points where appropriate and indicate those equilibrium prices or quantities on the axes of your graph. Remember that the readers want to award you points for every correct portion of your response, so make their job as easy as possible.

Hints and Strategies

Multiple-Choice Questions

Because the College Board no longer places an additional penalty on wrong answers, you should answer every question in the multiple-choice section of the exam. It is best to answer questions in the order they appear, rather than skipping questions throughout the test, out of concern that you might skip a line and mismark subsequent answers. Make a note of answers you want to go back to review once you've finished, but don't skip a question entirely. Carefully erase corrections completely.

Be careful not to overanalyze questions. In many cases, the answer may seem to be too obvious when it is correct. Don't second-guess yourself. The AP Exam questions are designed to test information you should have learned in the course, not reach for the most obscure concepts. While some questions will test your ability to discern concepts (for example, the difference between a change in demand and a change in quantity demanded), they are not designed to trick you if you understand those concepts.

With that in mind, also remember that several of the test questions will be written at a high level in order to identify students deserving scores of 4 and 5. You may face test questions about concepts you have not studied or do not remember, but it is still important to answer every question. If you can eliminate a couple of obviously wrong answers, you are that much closer to a correct answer.

Watch carefully for key terms in a question that can help you rule out incorrect answers. For example, "long run" and "short run" result in different graphs for firms entering and exiting the industry in Micro, and a different slope for aggregate supply and Phillips Curves in Macro. The terms "nominal" and "real" can help you differentiate the effects of inflation. If you pay careful attention to the terms, you may be able to rule out two or more of the potential answers.

For questions regarding graphical analysis, quickly draw yourself a graph to visualize the answer. Don't just rely on your memory; seeing the graph can help you to remember the relative locations of the average total cost and average variable cost curves, or how a change in aggregate demand affects real output and price levels. It is important to use these visual aids to avoid simple mistakes that cost you points.

Calculators cannot be used during the AP Economics exam. Generally, the math involved in multiple-choice questions is simple enough that if you understand the formulas, the answer will be clear. For example, reserve requirement ratios will tend to be 5%, 10%, 20%, or 25% to make it easy for you to calculate money multipliers. The opportunity costs involved in calculating comparative advantage will reduce to numbers that are easy to compare.

It is important to watch your pace as you move through the exam questions. You have just over one minute to answer each question. Some questions, such as definitions, can be answered very quickly, while others may require deeper analysis or time to draw a graph to find the answer. The key is to keep moving and keep an eye on the time. If you finish early, double check that you have answered every question on your answer sheet, and review the questions you had made a note to review one last time.

Free-Response Questions

At the beginning of the free-response portion of the exam, you will have a mandatory ten-minute reading period. Use that time to very carefully review each question. Start to sketch graphs and write notes right on the question page, so you can outline your answers.

One key to writing a good free response is to focus on the verbs in the free- response questions. "Identify" calls for a brief, direct answer to the question, while "explain" calls for an actual explanation of the reasoning for your answer. "Define" means to do exactly that—define what the term means. It is not enough to give an example of the concept in action. Some students have found that circling all of the verbs on the question sheet helps them to identify what they should do for each part of the question.

Organization is essential for a good free-response answer. Be sure to answer the questions in the order they were asked. Directly answer the question that was asked. For example, if the question asks you what will happen to employment, don't answer by explaining what you think will happen to the unemployment rate; answer about employment.

In writing your answers, it is critical to make linkages between concepts. This is one issue readers have consistently identified as a weakness in the responses they read. In Micro, why does an increase in the price of strawberries lead to an increase in the demand for grapes? In Macro, why does an increase in the money supply cause an increase in new home sales? Be sure to explain how a change in one factor affects other factors, and the mechanisms that cause that change to happen.

Remember that in the free-response portion of the exam, readers give you points for correct answers, rather than subtracting points for incorrect answers. However, if the question asks about a specific policy solution such as an open market operation, and you answer by discussing changes in the discount rate, even if your answer pertaining to the discount rate is correct, you will not earn the point because you did not answer the question that was asked.

It is important to look for details in the question that will help you to correctly draw your graphs. Look for terms like "short run" and "long run". A Micro question may ask you to draw a graph showing a firm making an initial short-run profit. Drawing a graph in long-run equilibrium will cost you easy points. In the same way, a Macro question may ask you to draw a graph illustrating an economy in short-run equilibrium at less than full-employment output. In order to illustrate that lower output, you will have to draw a vertical long-run aggregate supply curve to the right of current equilibrium. Be careful to label every axis and curve and show any curve shifts and equilibrium.

When you have finished, it is very important to reread each question and sub-question to be sure you have answered every single part of the question. Because readers give points for correct answers, rather than subtracting for incorrect answers, it is in your best interest to guess. What will happen to the price? What will happen to exports? What will happen to the number of workers hired? The only possible answers are "increase", "decrease", or "no change", so make your best effort even if you are not entirely sure of your answer.

One last consideration: handwriting. You must write your answer in blue or black ink. Use your best handwriting to make it easy for your reader to find and read your answers, so you can earn all of the points you deserve.

We are grateful for the contributions of the following AP experts in the preparation of this AP Edition and the *Focus Review Guide to accompany McConnell Economics AP® Edition.*

Dr. Clark Ross
Frontis W. Johnston Professor of Economics at Davidson College, Davidson, North Carolina

Dr. Ross has been active in Advanced Placement Economics since the inception of the program in 1988. From 1998 to 2005, he served as chief faculty consultant for AP Economics. He currently serves as the co-chair of the AP Macroeconomics Test Development Committee and offers frequent workshops for AP economics teachers.

Lisa Ellison
AP Economics Teacher, Kokomo High School, Kokomo, IN (retired)

Lisa Ellison taught AP Microeconomics and Macroeconomics since 1988 and is a Reader for AP Economics exams. She was a writer and advisor for McGraw-Hill Education's ONboard for AP® Economics and published nearly three dozen articles and lessons on economic education. She serves as a reviewer for EconEdLink and is the teacher representative to the Indiana Council for Economic Education Executive Committee.

Sally Meek
AP Macroeconomics Teacher, Plano West Senior High School, Plano, Texas

Sally Meek has been teaching AP Macroeconomics for 17 years. She has been working with the College Board since 1998 and has been presenting AP Workshops since 2000. She has served in many roles with the College Board: as a member of the AP Test Development Committee, an Advisor to the AP Macroeconomics Development Committee, a Reader, a Table Leader, and a Question Leader.

Part ONE AP

Introduction to Economics and the Economy

CHAPTER 1 Limits, Alternatives, and Choices

CHAPTER 2 The Market System and the Circular Flow

This introduction to economics is vitally important. In the first chapter we learn about ***scarcity,*** and how society's aggregate wants for goods and services have always exceeded the society's ability to produce goods and services. Society's production is limited by the availability of resources, or inputs (labor, capital or machinery, land, and natural resources), and the state of technology. With scarce resources and a resulting scarcity of output, choices must be made relating to production. Analyzing such choices is the fundamental objective of the discipline of economics, a relatively new discipline (from the 18th century) that addresses problems that predate recorded history. As we look at such choices, we shall learn an important concept: ***opportunity cost.*** As we pursue one course of action or production, what have we given up? For example, as you study economics, what are you not doing? Would you be studying another subject or exercising, perhaps?

Scarcity introduces four economic problems. First, ***what goods should be produced?*** Contemporary choices range from computers to food to clothing, among so many others. Opportunity cost will be quite evident when we look at a ***production possibilities curve*** that elaborates the choices of what a society can feasibly produce. Second, ***how to produce the goods?*** Should much land and little labor be used to produce wheat? Or the converse? Third, ***how much of current output or resources should be used to enhance growth in the future?*** Consider the classic case of seed corn. If we eat all our corn today, we shall have no seed corn for future production. Finally and fourth, ***who should get the goods and services that are produced?*** If we do not have enough to satisfy everyone, how do we divide these goods and services within the population?

These questions are addressed by the economic system that characterizes the society. From ***tradition*** to ***market capitalism*** to the ***command economy*** of the former Soviet Union, there are differing systems to address economic questions.

In Chapter 2 we look at how the capitalist market system addresses the four problems associated with scarcity as outlined above. With a market system, the forces of consumer demand and producer supply will determine output levels in the markets for goods and services. We will see that equilibrium prices in competitive markets can balance the demand and the supply for a good. The vast majority of the contemporary world's population live in societies where markets, both competitive and less competitive, play an important, if not vital, role in deciding economic outcomes.

1 Chapter

Limits, Alternatives, and Choices

Learning Objectives

LO1.1 **Define economics and the features of the economic perspective.**

LO1.2 **Describe the role of economic theory in economics.**

LO1.3 **Distinguish microeconomics from macroeconomics and positive economics from normative economics.**

LO1.4 **Explain the individual's economizing problem and how trade-offs, opportunity costs, and attainable combinations can be illustrated with budget lines.**

LO1.5 **List the categories of scarce resources and delineate the nature of society's economizing problem.**

LO1.6 **Apply production possibilities analysis, increasing opportunity costs, and economic growth.**

LO1.7 **Explain how economic growth and international trade increase consumption possibilities.**

LO1.8 **(Appendix) Understand graphs, curves, and slopes as they relate to economics.**

AP Chapter Focus

(Review understanding graphs in this chapter's appendix.) People's wants are numerous and varied. At a basic level, people need air, water, food, clothing, and shelter. In modern society, however, people want goods and services that help provide a more comfortable standard of living.

The study of economics, then, uses the scientific method and mathematical modeling as decision-making tools to help in developing economic policies towards the goal of providing all people with goods and services to their satisfaction.

Fortunately, we possess resources like labor, tools, and land to help us produce the goods and services that people want. The blunt reality, however, is that our economic wants far exceed the productive capacity of our resources. As a result, we are forced to make choices.

This unyielding reality underlies the fundamentals in economics. The essential question is how do and should individuals, institutions, and society make optimal (best) choices under conditions of scarcity.

AP The Economic Perspective

LO1.1 Define economics and the features of the economic perspective.

Economists view things from a unique perspective. This **economic perspective,** or economic way of thinking, has several critical and closely interrelated features.

Scarcity and Choice

The economic resources needed to make goods and services are in limited supply. This **scarcity** restricts options and demands choices. Because we "can't have it all," we must decide what we will have and what we must forgo.

At the core of economics is the idea that "there is no free lunch." You may be treated to lunch, making it "free" from your perspective, but someone bears a cost. Because all resources are either privately or collectively owned by members of society, ultimately society bears the cost. Scarce inputs of land, equipment, farm labor, the labor of cooks and waiters, and managerial talent are required. Because society could have used these resources to produce other things, it sacrifices those other goods and services in making the lunch available. Economists call such sacrifices **opportunity costs:** To obtain more of one thing, society forgoes the opportunity of getting the next best thing that could have been created with those resources. That sacrifice is the opportunity cost of the choice.

Purposeful Behavior

Economics assumes that human behavior reflects "rational self-interest." Individuals look for and pursue opportunities to increase their **utility**—the pleasure, happiness, or satisfaction obtained from consuming a good or service. They allocate their time, energy, and money to maximize their satisfaction. Because they weigh costs and benefits, their economic decisions are "purposeful" or "rational," not "random" or "chaotic."

Consumers are purposeful in deciding what goods and services to buy. Business firms are purposeful in deciding what products to produce and how to produce them. Government entities are purposeful in deciding what public services to provide and how to finance them.

"Purposeful behavior" does not assume that people and institutions are immune from faulty logic and therefore are perfect decision makers. They sometimes make mistakes. Nor does it mean that people's decisions are unaffected by emotion or the decisions of those around them. Indeed, economists acknowledge that people are sometimes impulsive or emulative. "Purposeful behavior" simply means that people make decisions with some desired outcome in mind.

Rational self-interest is not the same as selfishness. In the economy, increasing one's own wage, rent, interest, or profit normally requires identifying and satisfying *somebody else's* wants! Also, people make personal sacrifices for others. They contribute time and money to charities because they derive pleasure from doing so. Parents help pay for their children's education for the same reason. These self-interested, but unselfish, acts help maximize the givers' satisfaction as much as any personal purchase of goods or services. Self-interested behavior is simply behavior designed to increase personal satisfaction, however it may be derived.

CONSIDER THIS . . .

Source: © Mar Photographics/Alamy Stock Photo

Free for All?

Free products are seemingly everywhere. Sellers offer free apps, free cell phones, and free checking accounts. Dentists give out free toothbrushes. At state visitor centers, there are free brochures and maps.

Does the presence of so many free products contradict the economist's assertion that "There is no free lunch"? No! Resources are used to produce each of these products, and because those resources have alternative uses, society gives up something else to get the "free" good. Because alternatives must be forsaken, there is no such thing as a free lunch.

So why are these goods offered for free? In a word: marketing! Firms sometimes offer free products to entice people to try them, hoping they will then purchase those goods later. Getting to try out the free version of an app may eventually entice you to buy the pay version that has more features. In other cases, a product is free only in conjunction with a larger purchase. To get the free bottle of soda, you must buy the large pizza. To get the free cell phone, you need to sign up for a year's worth of cell phone service.

But while "free" products may come at no cost to the individuals receiving them, they are never free to society because their manufacture requires the use of resources that could have been put to alternative uses.

Marginal Analysis: Comparing Benefits and Costs

The economic perspective focuses largely on **marginal analysis**—comparisons of marginal benefits and marginal costs, usually for decision making. To economists, "marginal" means "extra," "additional," or "a change in." Most choices or decisions involve changes in the status quo, meaning the existing state of affairs.

Should you attend school for another year? Should you study an extra hour for an exam? Should you supersize your fries? Similarly, should a business expand or reduce its output? Should government increase or decrease its funding for a missile defense system?

Each option involves marginal benefits and, because of scarce resources, marginal costs. In making choices rationally, the decision maker must compare those two amounts. Example: You and your fiancée are shopping for an engagement ring. Should you buy a $\frac{1}{2}$-carat diamond, a $\frac{3}{4}$-carat diamond, a 1-carat diamond, or something even larger? The marginal cost of a larger-size diamond is the added expense beyond the cost of the smaller-size diamond. The marginal benefit is the perceived lifetime pleasure (utility) from the larger-size stone. If the marginal benefit of the larger diamond exceeds its marginal cost (and you can afford it), buy the larger stone. But if the marginal cost is more than the marginal benefit, you should buy the smaller diamond instead—even if you can afford the larger stone!

In a world of scarcity, the decision to obtain the marginal benefit associated with some specific option always includes the marginal cost of forgoing something else. The money spent on the larger-size diamond means forgoing some other product. An opportunity cost—the value of the next best thing forgone—is always present whenever a choice is made.

CONSIDER THIS . . .

Source: © Syracuse Newspapers/The Image Works

Fast-Food Lines

The economic perspective is useful in analyzing all sorts of behaviors. Consider an everyday example: the behavior of fast-food customers. When customers enter the restaurant, they go to the shortest line, believing that line will minimize their time cost of obtaining food. They are acting purposefully; time is limited, and people prefer using it in some way other than standing in line.

If one fast-food line is temporarily shorter than other lines, some people will move to that line. These movers apparently view the time saving from the shorter line (marginal benefit) as exceeding the cost of moving from their present line (marginal cost). The line switching tends to equalize line lengths. No further movement of customers between lines occurs once all lines are about equal.

Fast-food customers face another cost-benefit decision when a clerk opens a new station at the counter. Should they move to the new station or stay put? Those who shift to the new line decide that the time saving from the move exceeds the extra cost of physically moving. In so deciding, customers must also consider just how quickly they can get to the new station compared with others who may be contemplating the same move. (Those who hesitate are lost!)

Customers at the fast-food establishment do not have perfect information when they select lines. Thus, not all decisions turn out as expected. For example, you might enter a short line only to find that someone in front of you is ordering hamburgers and fries for 40 people in the Greyhound bus parked out back (and also that the guy taking orders in your new line is a trainee)! Nevertheless, at the time you made your decision, you thought it was optimal.

Finally, customers must decide what food to order when they arrive at the counter. In making their choices, they again compare marginal costs and marginal benefits in attempting to obtain the greatest personal satisfaction for their expenditure.

Economists believe that what is true for the behavior of customers at fast-food restaurants is true for economic behavior in general. Faced with an array of choices, consumers, workers, and businesses rationally compare marginal costs and marginal benefits when making decisions.

Theories, Principles, and Models

LO1.2 Describe the role of economic theory in economics.

Like the physical and life sciences, as well as other social sciences, economics relies on the **scientific method.** That procedure consists of several elements:

- Observing real-world behavior and outcomes.
- Based on those observations, formulating a possible explanation of cause and effect (hypothesis).
- Testing this explanation by comparing the outcomes of specific events to the outcome predicted by the hypothesis.
- Accepting, rejecting, and modifying the hypothesis, based on these comparisons.
- Continuing to test the hypothesis against the facts. If favorable results accumulate, the hypothesis evolves into a theory. A very well-tested and widely accepted theory is referred to as an economic law or an **economic principle**—a statement about economic behavior or the economy that enables prediction of the probable effects of certain actions. Combinations of such laws or principles are incorporated into models, which are simplified representations of how something works, such as a market or segment of the economy.

Economists develop theories of the behavior of individuals (consumers, workers) and institutions (businesses, governments) engaged in the production, exchange, and consumption of goods and services. Theories, principles, and models are "purposeful simplifications." The full scope of economic reality itself is too complex and bewildering to be understood as a whole. In developing theories, principles, and models economists remove the clutter and simplify.

Economic principles and models are highly useful in analyzing economic behavior and understanding how the economy operates. They are the tools for ascertaining cause and effect (or action and outcome) within the economic system. Good theories do a good job of explaining and predicting. They are supported by facts concerning how individuals and institutions actually behave in producing, exchanging, and consuming goods and services.

There are some other things you should know about economic principles.

- ***Generalizations*** Economic principles are generalizations relating to economic behavior or to the economy itself. Economic principles are expressed as the tendencies of typical or average consumers, workers, or business firms. For example, economists say that consumers buy more of a particular product when its price falls. Economists recognize that some consumers may increase their purchases by a large amount, others by a small amount, and a few not at all. This "price-quantity" principle, however, holds for the typical consumer and for consumers as a group.
- ***Other-things-equal assumption*** In constructing their theories, economists use the *ceteris paribus* or **other-things-equal assumption**—the assumption that factors other than those being considered do not change. They assume that all variables except those under immediate consideration are held constant for a particular analysis. For example, consider the relationship between the price of Pepsi and the amount of Pepsi that is purchased. Assume that of all the factors that might influence the amount of Pepsi purchased (for example, the price of Pepsi, the price of Coca-Cola, and consumer incomes and preferences), only the price of Pepsi varies. This is helpful because the economist can then focus on the relationship between the price of Pepsi and purchases of Pepsi in isolation without being confused by changes in other variables.
- ***Graphical expression*** Many economic models are expressed graphically. Be sure to read the special appendix at the end of this chapter as a review of graphs.

AP Microeconomics and Macroeconomics

LO1.3 Distinguish microeconomics from macroeconomics and positive economics from normative economics.

Economists develop economic principles and models at two levels.

Microeconomics

Microeconomics is the part of economics concerned with decision making by individual customers, workers, households, and business firms. At this level of analysis, we observe the details of their behavior under a figurative microscope. We measure the price of a specific product, the number of workers employed by a single firm, the revenue or income of a particular firm or household, or the expenditures of a specific firm, government entity, or family. In microeconomics, we examine the sand, rocks, and shells, not the beach.

Macroeconomics

Macroeconomics examines the performance and behavior of the economy as a whole. It focuses its attention on economic growth, the business cycle, interest rates, inflation, and the behavior of major economic aggregates such as the government, household, and business sectors. An **aggregate** is a collection of specific economic units treated as if they were one unit. Therefore, we might lump together the millions of consumers in the U.S. economy and treat them as if they were one huge unit called "consumers."

In using aggregates, macroeconomics seeks to obtain an overview, or general outline, of the structure of the economy and the relationships of its major aggregates. Macroeconomics speaks of such economic measures as total output, total employment, total income, aggregate expenditures, and the general level of prices in analyzing various economic problems. Very little attention is given to the specific units making up the various aggregates.

Figuratively, macroeconomics looks at the beach, not the pieces of sand, the rocks, and the shells.

The micro–macro distinction does not mean that economics is so highly compartmentalized that every topic can be readily labeled as either micro or macro; many topics and subdivisions of economics are rooted in both. Example: While the problem of unemployment is usually treated as a macroeconomic topic (because unemployment relates to aggregate production), economists recognize that the decisions made by *individual* workers on how long to search for jobs and the way *specific* labor markets encourage or impede hiring are also critical in determining the unemployment rate.

Positive and Normative Economics

Both microeconomics and macroeconomics contain elements of positive economics and normative economics. **Positive economics** focuses on facts and cause-and-effect relationships. It includes description, theory development, and theory testing. Positive economics avoids value judgments. It tries to establish scientific statements about economic behavior and deals with what the economy is actually like. Such scientific-based analysis is critical to good policy analysis.

Economic policy, on the other hand, involves **normative economics,** which incorporates value judgments about what the economy should be like or what particular policy actions should be recommended to achieve a desirable goal. Normative economics looks at the desirability of certain aspects of the economy. It underlies expressions of support for particular economic policies.

Positive economics concerns *what is,* whereas normative economics embodies subjective feelings about *what ought to be*. Examples: Positive statement: "The unemployment rate in France is higher than that in the United States." Normative statement: "France ought to undertake policies to make its labor market more flexible to reduce unemployment rates." Whenever words such as "ought" or "should" appear in a sentence, you are very likely encountering a normative statement.

Most of the disagreement among economists involves normative, value-based policy questions. Of course, economists sometime disagree about which theories or models best represent the economy and its parts, but they agree on a full range of economic principles. Most economic controversy thus reflects differing opinions or value judgments about what society should be like.

AP QUICK REVIEW 1.1

- ✓ Economics examines how individuals, institutions, and society behave under conditions of scarcity.
- ✓ The economic perspective stresses (a) resource scarcity and the necessity of making choices, (b) the assumption of purposeful (or rational) behavior, and (c) comparisons of marginal benefit to marginal cost.
- ✓ In making choices, people incur an opportunity cost—the value of the next-best option.
- ✓ Economists establish scientific economic theories—cause-effect generalizations about the economic behavior of individuals and institutions.
- ✓ Microeconomics focuses on specific decision-making units within the economy, such as the consumer or a firm (business). Macroeconomics examines the economy as a whole.
- ✓ Positive economics deals with factual statements that can be derived from theory or inferred from actual data ("what is" statements); normative economics involves value judgments ("what ought to be" statements).

Individual's Economizing Problem

LO1.4 Explain the individual's economizing problem and how trade-offs, opportunity costs, and attainable combinations can be illustrated with budget lines.

A close examination of the **economizing problem**—the need to make choices because economic wants exceed economic means—will enhance your understanding of economic models and the difference between microeconomic and macroeconomic analysis. Let's first build a microeconomic model of the economizing problem faced by an individual.

Limited Income

We all have a finite amount of income, even the wealthiest among us. Even Bill Gates must decide how to spend his money! And the majority of us have much more limited means. Our income comes to us in the form of wages, interest, rent, and profit, although we may also receive money from government programs or family members. As Global Perspective 1.1 shows, the average income of Americans in 2014 was $55,200. In the poorest nations, it was less than $500.

GLOBAL PERSPECTIVE 1.1

Average Income, Selected Nations

Average income (total income/population) and therefore typical individual budget constraints vary greatly among nations.

Country	Country Per Capita Income, 2014 (U.S. dollars, based on exchange rates)
Norway	$103,630
Sweden	61,610
United States	55,200
Singapore	55,150
France	42,960
South Korea	27,090
Mexico	9,870
China	7,400
Iraq	6,500
India	1,570
Madagascar	440
Malawi	250

Source: The World Bank, **www.worldbank.org.**

Unlimited Wants

For better or worse, most people have virtually unlimited wants. We desire various goods and services that provide utility. Our wants extend over a wide range of products, from *necessities* (for example, food, shelter, and clothing) to *luxuries* (for example, perfumes, yachts, and sports cars). Some wants such as basic food, clothing, and shelter have biological roots. Other wants, for example, specific kinds of food, clothing, and shelter, arise from the conventions and customs of society.

Over time, as new and improved products are introduced, economic wants tend to change and multiply. Only recently have people wanted wi-fi connections, tablet computers, or flying drones because those products did not exist a few decades ago. Also, the satisfaction of certain wants may trigger others: the acquisition of a Ford Focus or a Honda Civic has been known to whet the appetite for a Lexus or a Mercedes.

Services, as well as goods, satisfy our wants. Car repair work, the removal of an inflamed appendix, legal and accounting advice, and haircuts all satisfy human wants. Actually, we buy many goods, such as automobiles and washing machines, for the services they render. The differences between goods and services are often smaller than they appear to be.

For most people, the desires for goods and services cannot be fully satisfied. Bill Gates may have all that he wants for himself, but his massive charitable giving suggests that he keenly wants better health care for the world's poor. Our desires for a particular good or service can be satisfied; over a short period of time we can surely get enough toothpaste or pasta. And one appendectomy is plenty. But our broader desire for more goods and services and higher-quality goods and services seems to be another story.

Because we have only limited income (usually through our work) but seemingly insatiable wants, it is in our self-interest to economize: to pick and choose goods and services that maximize our satisfaction given the limitations we face.

A Budget Line

We can clarify the economizing problem facing consumers by visualizing a **budget line** (or, more technically, a *budget constraint*). It is a schedule or curve that shows various combinations of two products a consumer can purchase with a specific money income. Although we assume two products, the analysis generalizes to the full range of products available to consumers.

To understand the idea of a budget line, suppose that you received an Amazon gift card as a birthday present. The $120 card is soon to expire. You go online to Amazon.com and confine your purchase decisions to two alternatives: movies and paperback books. Movies are $20 each and paperback books are $10 each. Your purchase options are shown in the table in Figure 1.1.

At one extreme, you might spend all of your $120 "income" on 6 movies at $20 each and have nothing left to spend on books. Or, by giving up 2 movies and thereby gaining $40, you can have 4 movies at $20 each and 4 books at $10 each. And so on to the other extreme, at which you could buy 12 books at $10 each, spending your entire gift card on books with nothing left to spend on movies.

The graph in Figure 1.1 shows the budget line. Note that the graph is not restricted to whole units of movies and books as is the table. Every point on the graph represents a possible combination of movies and books, including fractional quantities. The slope of the graphed budget line measures the ratio of the price of books (P_b) to the price of movies (P_m); more

FIGURE 1.1 A consumer's budget line. The budget line (or budget constraint) shows all the combinations of any two products that can be purchased, given the prices of the products and the consumer's money income.

The Budget Line: Whole-Unit Combinations of Movies and Paperback Books Attainable with an Income of $120

Units of Movies (Price = $20)	Units of Books (Price = $10)	Total Expenditure
6	0	$120 (= $120 + $0)
5	2	$120 (= $100 + $20)
4	4	$120 (= $80 + $40)
3	6	$120 (= $60 + $60)
2	8	$120 (= $40 + $80)
1	10	$120 (= $20 + $100)
0	12	$120 (= $0 + $120)

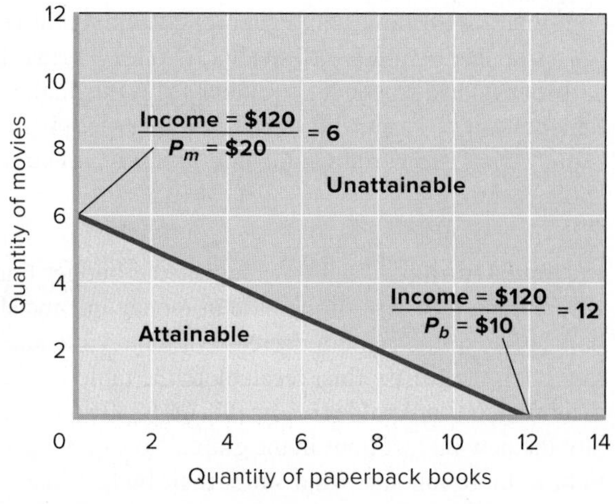

precisely, the slope is $P_b/P_m = \$-10/\$+20 = -\frac{1}{2}$. So you must forgo 1 movie (measured on the vertical axis) to buy 2 books (measured on the horizontal axis). This yields a slope of $-\frac{1}{2}$ or $-.5$.

The budget line illustrates several ideas.

Attainable and Unattainable Combinations All the combinations of movies and books on or inside the budget line are *attainable* from the $120 of money income. You can afford to buy, for example, 3 movies at $20 each and 6 books at $10 each. You also can obviously afford to buy 2 movies and 5 books, thereby using up only $90 of the $120 available on your gift card. But to achieve maximum utility you will want to spend the full $120. The budget line shows all combinations that cost exactly the full $120.

In contrast, all combinations beyond the budget line are *unattainable*. The $120 limit simply does not allow you to purchase, for example, 5 movies at $20 each and 5 books at $10 each. That $150 expenditure would clearly exceed the $120 limit. In Figure 1.1 the attainable combinations are on and within the budget line; the unattainable combinations are beyond the budget line.

Trade-Offs and Opportunity Costs The budget line in Figure 1.1 illustrates the idea of trade-offs arising from limited income. To obtain more movies, you have to give up some books. For example, to obtain the first movie, you trade off 2 books. So the opportunity cost of the first movie is 2 books. To obtain the second movie the opportunity cost is also 2 books. The straight-line budget constraint, with its constant slope, indicates constant opportunity cost. That is, the opportunity cost of 1 extra movie remains the same (= 2 books) as more movies are purchased. And, in reverse, the opportunity cost of 1 extra book does not change (= $\frac{1}{2}$ movie) as more books are bought.

Choice Limited income forces people to choose what to buy and what to forgo to fulfill wants. You will select the combination of movies and paperback books that you think is "best." That is, you will evaluate your marginal benefits and marginal costs (here, product price) to make choices that maximize your satisfaction. Other people, with the same $120 gift card, would undoubtedly make different choices.

Income Changes The location of the budget line varies with money income. An increase in money income shifts the budget line to the right; a decrease in money income shifts it to the left. To verify this, recalculate the table in Figure 1.1, assuming the card value (income) is (a) $240 and (b) $60, and plot the new budget lines in the graph. No wonder people like to have more income: That shifts their budget lines outward and enables them to buy more goods and services. But even with more income, people will still face spending trade-offs, choices, and opportunity costs.

CONSIDER THIS . . .

Source: © Helga Esteb/Shutterstock.com

Did Zuckerberg, Seacrest, and Swift Make Bad Choices?

Opportunity costs come into play in decisions well beyond simple buying decisions. Consider the different choices people make with respect to college. The average salaries earned by college graduates are nearly twice as high as those earned by persons with just high school diplomas. For most capable students, "Go to college, stay in college, and earn a degree" is very sound advice.

Yet Facebook founder Mark Zuckerberg and media personality Ryan Seacrest both dropped out of college, while pop singer Taylor Swift never even bothered to start classes. What were they thinking? Unlike most students, Zuckerberg faced enormous opportunity costs for staying in college. He had a vision for his company, and dropping out helped to ensure Facebook's success. Similarly, Seacrest landed a professional DJ job at his local radio station when he was in high school before moving to Hollywood and eventually becoming America's top radio and TV personality. Finishing his college degree might have interrupted the string of successes that made his career possible. And Swift knew that staying on top in the world of pop takes unceasing work. So after her first album became a massive hit for her at age 16, it made sense for her to skip college in order to relentlessly pursue continuing success.

So Zuckerberg, Seacrest, and Swift understood opportunity costs and made their choices accordingly. The size of opportunity costs matters greatly in making individual decisions.

AP QUICK REVIEW 1.2

- ✓ Because their wants exceed their incomes, individuals face an economizing problem; they must decide what to buy and what to forgo.
- ✓ A budget line (budget constraint) shows the various combinations of two goods that a consumer can purchase with a specific money income.
- ✓ Straight-line budget constraints imply constant opportunity costs for both goods or constancy of price for each good.

Society's Economizing Problem

LO1.5 List the categories of scarce resources and delineate the nature of society's economizing problem.

Society must also make choices under conditions of scarcity. It, too, faces an economizing problem. Should it devote more of its limited resources to the criminal justice system (police, courts, and prisons) or to education (teachers, books, and schools)? If it decides to devote more resources to both, what other goods and services does it forgo? Health care? Energy development?

Scarce Resources

Society has limited or scarce **economic resources,** meaning all natural, human, and manufactured resources that go into the production of goods and services. This includes the entire set of factory and farm buildings and all the equipment, tools, and machinery used to produce manufactured goods and agricultural products; all transportation and communication facilities; all types of labor; and land and mineral resources.

Resource Categories

Economists classify economic resources into four general categories.

Land Land means much more to the economist than it does to most people. To the economist **land** includes all natural resources ("gifts of nature") used in the production process. These include forests, mineral and oil deposits, water resources, wind power, sunlight, and arable land.

Labor The resource **labor** consists of the physical actions and mental activities that people contribute to the production of goods and services. The work-related activities of a logger, retail clerk, machinist, teacher, professional football player, and nuclear physicist all fall under the general heading "labor."

Capital For economists, **capital** (or capital goods) includes all manufactured aids used in producing consumer goods and services. Included are all factory, storage, transportation, and distribution facilities, as well as tools and machinery. Economists use the term **investment** to describe spending that pays for the production and accumulation of capital goods.

Capital goods differ from consumer goods because consumer goods satisfy wants directly, whereas capital goods do so indirectly by aiding the production of consumer goods. For example, large commercial baking ovens (capital goods) help make loaves of bread (consumer goods). Note that the term "capital" as used by economists refers not to money but to tools, machinery, and other productive equipment. Because money produces nothing, economists do not include it as an economic resource. Money (or money capital or financial capital) is simply a means for purchasing goods and services, including capital goods.

Entrepreneurial Ability Finally, there is the special human resource, distinct from labor, called **entrepreneurial ability.** It is supplied by **entrepreneurs,** who perform several critically important economic functions:

- The entrepreneur takes the initiative in combining the resources of land, labor, and capital to produce a good or a service. Both a sparkplug and a catalyst, the entrepreneur is the driving force behind production and the agent who combines the other resources in what is hoped will be a successful business venture.
- The entrepreneur makes the strategic business decisions that set the course of an enterprise.
- The entrepreneur innovates. He or she commercializes new products, new production techniques, or even new forms of business organization.
- The entrepreneur bears risk. Innovation is risky, as nearly all new products and ideas are subject to the possibility of failure as well as success. Progress would cease without entrepreneurs who are willing to take on risk by devoting their time, effort, and ability—as well as their own money and the money of others—to commercializing new products and ideas that may enhance society's standard of living.

Because land, labor, capital, and entrepreneurial ability are combined to produce goods and services, they are called the **factors of production,** or simply "inputs."

AP Production Possibilities Model

LO1.6 Apply production possibilities analysis, increasing opportunity costs, and economic growth.

Society uses its scarce resources to produce goods and services. The alternatives and choices it faces can best be understood through a macroeconomic model of production possibilities. To keep things simple, let's initially assume:

- ***Full employment*** The economy is employing all of its available resources.
- ***Fixed resources*** The quantity and quality of the factors of production are fixed.
- ***Fixed technology*** The state of technology (the methods used to produce output) is constant.
- ***Two goods*** The economy is producing only two goods: pizzas and industrial robots. Pizzas symbolize **consumer goods,** products that satisfy our wants directly; industrial robots (for example, the kind used to weld automobile frames) symbolize **capital goods,** products that satisfy our wants indirectly by making possible more efficient production of consumer goods.

TABLE 1.1 Production Possibilities of Pizzas and Industrial Robots

	Production Alternatives				
Type of Product	A	B	C	D	E
Pizzas (in hundred thousands)	0	1	2	3	4
Robots (in thousands)	10	9	7	4	0

Production Possibilities Table

A production possibilities table lists the different combinations of two products that can be produced with a specific set of resources, assuming full employment. Table 1.1 presents a simple, hypothetical economy that is producing pizzas and industrial robots; the data are, of course, hypothetical, too. At alternative A, this economy would be devoting all its available resources to the production of industrial robots (capital goods); at alternative E, all resources would go to pizza production (consumer goods). Those alternatives are unrealistic extremes; an economy typically produces both capital goods and consumer goods, as in B, C, and D. As we move from alternative A to E, we increase the production of pizzas at the expense of the production of industrial robots.

Because consumer goods satisfy our wants directly, any movement toward E looks tempting. In producing more pizzas, society increases the satisfaction of its current wants. But there is a cost: More pizzas mean fewer industrial robots. This shift of resources to consumer goods catches up with society over time because the stock of capital goods expands more slowly, thereby reducing potential future production. By moving toward alternative E, society chooses "more now" at the expense of "much more later."

By moving toward A, society chooses to forgo current consumption, thereby freeing up resources that can be used to increase the production of capital goods. By building up its stock of capital this way, society will have greater future production and, therefore, greater future consumption. By moving toward A, society is choosing "more later" at the cost of "less now."

Generalization: At any point in time, a fully employed economy must sacrifice some of one good to obtain more of another good. Scarce resources prohibit a fully employed economy from having more of both goods. Society must choose among alternatives. There is no such thing as a free pizza, or a free industrial robot. Having more of one thing means having less of something else.

Production Possibilities Curve

The data presented in a production possibilities table are shown graphically as a **production possibilities curve.** Such a curve displays the different combinations of goods and services that society can produce in a fully employed economy, assuming a fixed availability of supplies of resources and fixed technology. We arbitrarily represent the economy's output of capital goods (here, industrial robots) on the vertical axis and the output of consumer goods (here, pizzas) on the horizontal axis, as shown in **Figure 1.2 (Key Graph).**

Each point on the production possibilities curve represents some maximum output of the two products. The curve is a "constraint" because it shows the limit of attainable outputs. Points on the curve are attainable as long as the economy uses all its available resources. Points lying inside the curve are also attainable, but they reflect less total output and therefore are not as desirable as points on the curve. Points inside the curve imply that the economy could have more of both industrial robots and pizzas if it achieved full employment of its resources. Points lying beyond the production possibilities curve, like *W*, would represent a greater output than the output at any point on the curve. Such points, however, are unattainable with the current availability of resources and technology.

Law of Increasing Opportunity Costs

Figure 1.2 clearly shows that more pizzas mean fewer industrial robots. The number of units of industrial robots that must be given up to obtain another unit of pizzas, of course, is the opportunity cost of that unit of pizzas.

In moving from alternative *A* to alternative *B* in Table 1.1, the cost of 1 additional unit of pizzas is 1 fewer unit of industrial robots. But when additional units are considered—*B* to *C*, *C* to *D*, and *D* to *E*—an important economic principle is revealed: For society, the opportunity cost of each additional unit of pizzas is greater than the opportunity cost of the preceding one. When we move from *A* to *B*, just 1 unit of industrial robots is sacrificed for 1 more unit of pizzas; but in going from *B* to *C* we sacrifice 2 additional units of industrial robots for 1 more unit of pizzas; then 3 more of industrial robots for 1 more of pizzas; and finally 4 for 1. Conversely, confirm that as we move from *E* to *A*, the cost of an additional unit of industrial robots (on average) is $\frac{1}{4}$, $\frac{1}{3}$, $\frac{1}{2}$, and 1 unit of pizzas, respectively, for the four successive moves.

Our example illustrates the **law of increasing opportunity costs.** As the production of a particular good increases, the opportunity cost of producing an additional unit rises.

Shape of the Curve The law of increasing opportunity costs is reflected in the shape of the production possibilities curve: The curve is bowed out from the origin of the graph. Figure 1.2 shows that when the economy moves from *A* to *E*, it must give up successively larger amounts of industrial robots (1, 2, 3, and 4) to acquire equal increments of pizzas (1, 1, 1, and 1). This is shown in the slope of the production possibilities curve, which becomes steeper as we move from *A* to *E*.

Economic Rationale The law of increasing opportunity costs is driven by the fact that economic resources are not

AP KEY GRAPH

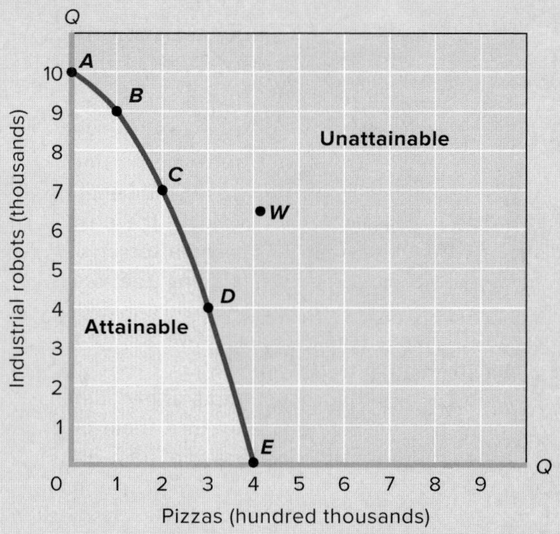

FIGURE 1.2 The production possibilities curve. Each point on the production possibilities curve represents some maximum combination of two products that can be produced if resources are fully employed. When an economy is operating on the curve, more industrial robots means fewer pizzas, and vice versa. Limited resources and a fixed technology make any combination of industrial robots and pizzas lying outside the curve (such as at *W*) unattainable. Points inside the curve are attainable, but they indicate that full employment is not being realized.

QUICK QUIZ FOR FIGURE 1.2

1. Production possibilities curve *ABCDE* is bowed out from the origin because:
- **a.** the marginal benefit of pizzas declines as more pizzas are consumed.
- **b.** the curve gets steeper as we move from *E* to *A*.
- **c.** it reflects the law of increasing opportunity costs.
- **d.** resources are scarce.

2. The marginal opportunity cost of the second unit of pizza is:
- **a.** 2 units of robots.
- **b.** 3 units of robots.
- **c.** 7 units of robots.
- **d.** 9 units of robots.

3. The total opportunity cost of 7 units of robots is:
- **a.** 1 unit of pizza.
- **b.** 2 units of pizza.
- **c.** 3 units of pizza.
- **d.** 4 units of pizza.

4. All points on this production possibilities curve necessarily represent:
- **a.** society's optimal choice.
- **b.** less than full use of resources.
- **c.** unattainable levels of output.
- **d.** full employment.

Answers: 1. c; 2. a; 3. b; 4. d

completely adaptable to alternative uses. Many resources are better at producing one type of good than at producing others. Consider land. Some land is highly suited to growing the ingredients necessary for pizza production. But as pizza production expands, society has to start using land that is less bountiful for farming. Other land is rich in mineral deposits and therefore well-suited to producing the materials needed to make industrial robots. That land will be the first land devoted to the production of industrial robots. But as society steps up the production of robots, it must use land that is less and less suited to making their components.

If we start at *A* and move to *B* in Figure 1.2, we can shift resources whose productivity is relatively high in pizza production and low in industrial robots. But as we move from *B* to *C*, *C* to *D*, and so on, resources highly productive in pizzas become increasingly scarce. To get more pizzas, resources whose productivity in industrial robots is relatively great will be needed. Increasingly more of such resources, and hence greater sacrifices of industrial robots, will be needed to achieve each 1-unit increase in pizzas. This lack of perfect flexibility, or interchangeability, on the part of resources is the cause of increasing opportunity costs for society.

Optimal Allocation

Of all the attainable combinations of pizzas and industrial robots on the curve in Figure 1.2, which is optimal (best)? That is, what specific quantities of resources should be allocated to pizzas and what specific quantities should be allocated to industrial robots in order to maximize satisfaction?

Recall that economic decisions center on comparisons of marginal benefit (MB) and marginal cost (MC). Any economic activity should be expanded as long as marginal

AP **FIGURE 1.3 Optimal output: MB = MC.** Achieving the optimal output requires the expansion of a good's output until its marginal benefit (MB) and marginal cost (MC) are equal. No resources beyond that point should be allocated to the product. Here, optimal output occurs at point *e*, where 200,000 units of pizzas are produced.

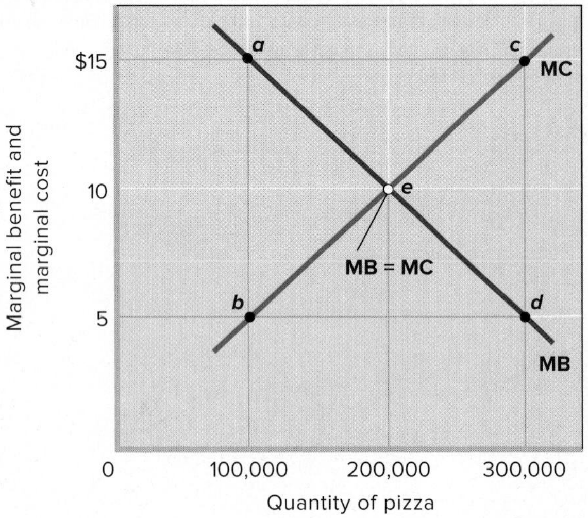

benefit exceeds marginal cost and should be reduced if marginal cost exceeds marginal benefit. The optimal amount of the activity occurs where MB = MC. Society needs to make a similar assessment about its production decision.

Consider pizzas. We already know from the law of increasing opportunity costs that the marginal cost of additional units of pizza will rise as more units are produced. At the same time, we need to recognize that the extra or marginal benefits that come from producing and consuming pizza decline with each successive unit of pizza. Consequently, each successive unit of pizza brings with it both increasing marginal costs and decreasing marginal benefits.

The optimal quantity of pizza production is indicated in Figure 1.3 by point *e* at the intersection of the MB and MC curves: 200,000 units. Why is this amount the optimal quantity? If only 100,000 units of pizzas were produced, the marginal benefit of an extra unit of pizza (point *a*) would exceed its marginal cost (point *b*). In money terms, MB is $15, while MC is only $5. When society gains something worth $15 at a marginal cost of only $5, it is better off. In Figure 1.3, net gains can continue to be realized until pizza-product production has been increased to 200,000.

In contrast, the production of 300,000 units of pizzas is excessive. There the MC of an added unit is $15 (point *c*) and its MB is only $5 (point *d*). This means that 1 unit of pizza is worth only $5 to society but costs it $15 to obtain. This is a losing proposition for society!

So resources are being efficiently allocated to any product when the marginal benefit and marginal cost of its output are equal (MB = MC). Suppose that by applying the same analysis to industrial robots, we find that the optimal (MB = MC) quantity of robots is 7,000. This would mean that alternative *C* (200,000 units of pizzas and 7,000 units of industrial robots) on the production possibilities curve in Figure 1.2 would be optimal for this economy.

CONSIDER THIS . . .

Source: © Royalty-Free/Corbis RF

The Economics of War

Production possibilities analysis is helpful in assessing the costs and benefits of waging the post-9/11 war on terrorism, including the wars in Afghanistan and Iraq. At the end of 2015, the estimated cumulative cost of these efforts exceeded $1.7 trillion.

If we categorize all U.S. production as either "defense goods" or "civilian goods," we can measure them on the axes of a production possibilities diagram such as that shown in Figure 1.2. The opportunity cost of using more resources for defense goods is the civilian goods sacrificed. In a fully employed economy, more defense goods are achieved at the opportunity cost of fewer civilian goods—health care, education, pollution control, personal computers, houses, and so on. The cost of war and defense is the other goods forgone. The benefits of these activities are numerous and diverse but clearly include the gains from protecting against future loss of American lives, assets, income, and well-being.

Society must assess the marginal benefit (MB) and marginal cost (MC) of additional defense goods to determine their optimal amounts—where to locate on the defense goods–civilian goods production possibilities curve. Although estimating marginal benefits and marginal costs is an imprecise art, the MB-MC framework is a useful way of approaching choices. An optimal allocation of resources requires that society expand production of defense goods until MB = MC.

The events of September 11, 2001, and the future threats they foreshadowed increased the marginal benefits of defense goods, as perceived by Americans. If we label the horizontal axis in Figure 1.3 "defense goods" and draw in a rightward shift of the MB curve, you will see that the optimal quantity of defense goods rises. In view of the concerns relating to September 11, the United States allocated more of its resources to defense. But the MB-MC analysis also reminds us we can spend too much on defense, as well as too little. The United States should not expand defense goods beyond the point where MB = MC. If it does, it will be sacrificing civilian goods of greater value than the defense goods obtained.

AP QUICK REVIEW 1.3

- ✓ Economists categorize economic resources as land, labor, capital, and entrepreneurial ability. They are referred to as factors of production, or inputs.
- ✓ The production possibilities curve illustrates several ideas: (a) scarcity of resources is implied by the area outside the curve; (b) choice among outputs is reflected by the points along the curve; (c) the downward slope of the curve shows the opportunity cost; (d) the law of increasing opportunity costs is reflected in the bowed-outward shape of the curve.
- ✓ A comparison of marginal benefits (MB) and marginal costs (MC) can be used to determine the best or optimal output mix for society, as modeled on a production possibilities curve. The optimal amount of the activity occurs when MB = MC.

AP Unemployment, Growth, and the Future

LO1.7 Explain how economic growth and international trade increase consumption possibilities.

In the depths of the Great Depression of the 1930s, one-quarter of U.S. workers were unemployed and one-third of U.S. production capacity was idle. Subsequent downturns have been much less severe. During the deep 2007–2009 recession, for instance, production fell by a comparably smaller 3.7 percent and 1-in-10 workers was without a job.

Almost all nations have experienced widespread unemployment and unused production capacity from business downturns at one time or another. Since 2010, for example, many nations—including Argentina, Italy, Russia, Japan, and France—have had economic downturns and elevated unemployment.

How do these realities relate to the production possibilities model? Our analysis and conclusions change if we relax the assumption that all available resources are fully employed. The five alternatives in Table 1.1 represent maximum outputs; they illustrate the combinations of pizzas and industrial robots that can be produced when the economy is operating at full employment. With unemployment, this economy would produce less than each alternative shown in the table.

Graphically, we represent situations of unemployment by points inside the original production possibilities curve (reproduced here in Figure 1.4). Point *U* is one such point. Here the economy is falling short of the various maximum combinations of pizzas and industrial robots represented by the points on the production possibilities curve. The arrows in Figure 1.4 indicate three possible paths back to full employment. A move toward full employment would yield a greater output of one or both products.

AP FIGURE 1.4 Unemployment and the production possibilities curve. Any point inside the production possibilities curve, such as *U*, represents unemployment or a failure to achieve full employment. The arrows indicate that by realizing full employment, the economy could operate on the curve. This means it could produce more of one or both products than it is producing at point *U*.

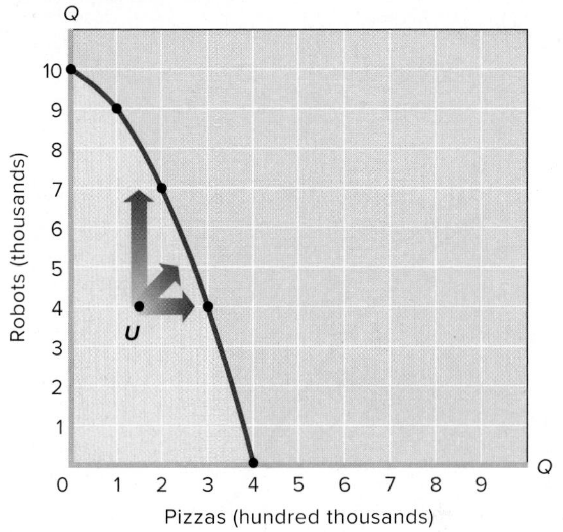

A Growing Economy

When we drop the assumptions that the quantity and quality of resources and technology are fixed, the production possibilities curve shifts positions and the potential maximum output of the economy changes.

Increases in Resource Supplies Although resource supplies are fixed at any specific moment, they change over time. For example, a nation's growing population brings about increases in the supplies of labor and entrepreneurial ability. Also, labor quality usually improves over time via more education and training. Historically, the economy's stock of capital has increased at a significant, though unsteady, rate. And although some of our energy and mineral resources are being depleted, new sources are also being discovered. The development of irrigation systems, for example, adds to the supply of arable land.

The net result of these increased supplies of the factors of production is the ability to produce more of both consumer goods and capital goods. Thus, 20 years from now, the production possibilities may supersede those shown in Table 1.1. The new production possibilities might look like those in the table in Figure 1.5. The greater abundance of resources will result in a greater potential output of one or both products at each alternative. The economy will have achieved economic growth in the form of expanded potential output. Thus, when an increase in the quantity or quality of resources occurs, the production possibilities curve shifts outward and to the right,

AP **FIGURE 1.5 Economic growth and the production possibilities curve.** The increase in supplies of resources, improvements in resource quality, and technological advances that occur in a dynamic economy move the production possibilities curve outward and to the right, allowing the economy to have larger quantities of both types of goods.

	Production Alternatives				
Type of Product	**A′**	**B′**	**C′**	**D′**	**E′**
Pizzas (in hundred thousands)	0	2	4	6	8
Robots (in thousands)	14	12	9	5	0

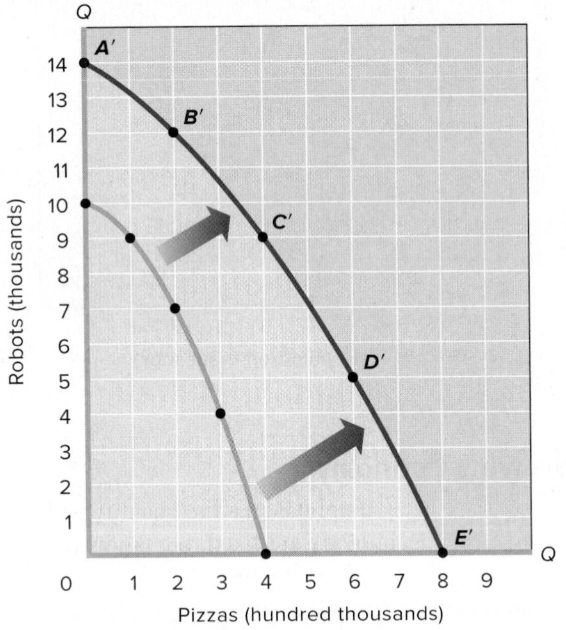

as illustrated by the move from the inner curve to curve $A'B'C'D'E'$ in Figure 1.5. This sort of shift represents growth of economic capacity, which, when used, means **economic growth:** a larger total output.

Advances in Technology An advancing technology brings both new and better goods and improved ways of producing them. For now, let's think of technological advance as being only improvements in the methods of production, for example, the introduction of computerized systems to manage inventories and schedule production. These advances alter our previous discussion of the economizing problem by allowing society to produce more goods with available resources. As with increases in resource supplies, technological advances make possible the production of more industrial robots *and* more pizzas.

A real-world example of improved technology is the recent surge of new technologies relating to computers, communications, and biotechnology. Technological advances have dropped the prices of computers and greatly increased their speed. Improved software has greatly increased the everyday usefulness of computers. Cellular phones and the Internet have increased communications capacity, enhancing production and improving the efficiency of markets. Advances in biotechnology have resulted in important agricultural and medical discoveries. These and other new and improved technologies have contributed to U.S. economic growth (outward shifts of the nation's production possibilities curve).

Conclusion: Economic growth is the result of (1) increases in supplies of resources, (2) improvements in resource quality, and (3) technological advances. The consequence of growth is that a full-employment economy can enjoy a greater output of both consumption goods and capital goods. Whereas static, no-growth economies must sacrifice some of one good to obtain more of another, dynamic, growing economies can have larger quantities of both goods.

Present Choices and Future Possibilities

An economy's current choice of positions on its production possibilities curve helps determine the future location of that curve. Let's designate the two axes of the production possibilities curve as "goods for the future" and "goods for the present," as in Figure 1.6. Goods for the future are such things as capital goods, research and education, and preventive medicine. They increase the quantity and quality of property resources, enlarge the stock of technological information, and improve the quality of human resources. As we have already seen, goods for the future such as capital goods are the ingredients of economic growth. Goods for the present are consumer goods such as food, clothing, and entertainment.

Now suppose there are two hypothetical economies, Presentville and Futureville, that are initially identical in every respect except one: Presentville's current choice of positions on its production possibilities curve strongly favors present goods over future goods. Point *P* in Figure 1.6a indicates that choice. It is located quite far down the curve to the right, indicating a high priority for goods for the present, at the expense of less goods for the future. Futureville, in contrast, makes a current choice that stresses larger amounts of future goods and smaller amounts of present goods, as shown by point *F* in Figure 1.6b.

Now, other things equal, we can expect Futureville's future production possibilities curve to be farther to the right than Presentville's future production possibilities curve. By currently choosing an output more favorable to technological advances and to increases in the quantity and quality of resources, Futureville will achieve greater economic growth than Presentville. In terms of capital goods, Futureville is choosing to make larger current additions to its "national factory" by devoting more of its current output to capital than

FIGURE 1.6 Present choices and future locations of production possibilities curves. (a) Presentville's current choice to produce more "present goods" and fewer "future goods," as represented by point *P*, will result in a modest outward shift of the production possibilities curve in the future. (b) Futureville's current choice of producing fewer "present goods" and more "future goods," as depicted by point *F*, will lead to a greater outward shift of the production possibilities curve in the future.

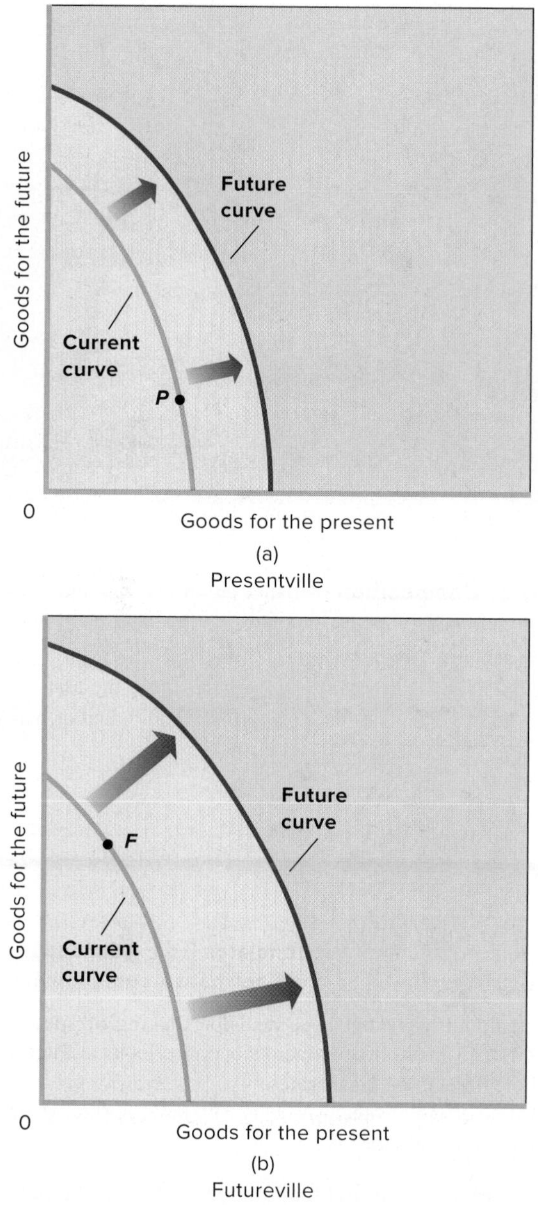

does Presentville. The payoff from this choice for Futureville is greater future production capacity and economic growth. The opportunity cost is fewer consumer goods in the present for Futureville to enjoy.

Is Futureville's choice thus necessarily "better" than Presentville's? That, we cannot say. The different outcomes simply reflect different preferences and priorities in the two countries. But each country will have to live with the economic consequences of its choice.

A Qualification: International Trade

Production possibilities analysis implies that an individual nation is limited to the combinations of output indicated by its production possibilities curve. But we must modify this principle when international specialization and trade exist.

You will see in later chapters that an economy can circumvent, through international specialization and trade, the output limits imposed by its domestic production possibilities curve. Under international specialization and trade, each nation first specializes in the production of those items for which it has the lowest opportunity costs (due to an abundance of the necessary resources). Countries then engage in international trade, with each country exchanging the items that it can produce at the lowest opportunity costs for the items that other countries can produce at the lowest opportunity costs.

International specialization and trade allow a nation to get more of a desired good at less sacrifice of some other good. Rather than sacrifice three units of domestically produced robots to get a third unit of domestically produced pizza, as in Table 1.1, a nation that engages in international specialization and trade might be able to do much better. If it specializes in robots while another country specializes in pizza, then it may be able to obtain the third unit of pizza by trading only two units of domestically produced robots for one unit of foreign-produced pizza. Specialization and trade have the same effect as having more and better resources or discovering improved production techniques; both increase the quantities of capital and consumer goods available to society. Expansion of domestic production possibilities and international trade are two separate routes for obtaining greater output.

AP QUICK REVIEW 1.4

- ✓ Unemployment causes an economy to operate at a point inside its production possibilities curve.
- ✓ Increases in resource supplies, improvements in resource quality, and technological advance cause economic growth, which is depicted as an outward shift of the production possibilities curve.
- ✓ An economy's present choice of capital and consumer goods helps determine the future location of its production possibilities curve. Producing more capital goods today will result in fewer consumer goods today, but with enhanced future opportunities, i.e., economic growth with an outward shift of the PPC.
- ✓ International specialization and trade enable a nation to consume beyond its production possibilities curve.

LAST WORD

Pitfalls to Sound Economic Reasoning

Because They Affect Us So Personally, We Often Have Difficulty Thinking Accurately and Objectively about Economic Issues.

Here are some common pitfalls to avoid in successfully applying the economic perspective.

Biases Most people bring a bundle of biases and preconceptions to the field of economics. For example, some may think that corporate profits are excessive or that lending money is always superior to borrowing money. Others may believe that government is necessarily less efficient than businesses or that more government regulation is always better than less. Biases cloud thinking and interfere with objective analysis. All of us must be willing to shed biases and preconceptions that are not supported by facts.

Loaded Terminology The economic terminology used in newspapers and broadcast media is sometimes emotionally biased, or loaded. The writer or spokesperson may have a cause to promote or an ax to grind and may slant comments accordingly. High profits may be labeled "obscene," low wages may be called "exploitative," or self-interested behavior may be "greed." Government workers may be referred to as "mindless bureaucrats" and those favoring stronger government regulations may be called "socialists." To objectively analyze economic issues, you must be prepared to reject or discount such terminology.

Source: © James Leynse/Corbis RF

Fallacy of Composition Another pitfall in economic thinking is the assumption that what is true for one individual or part of a whole is necessarily true for a group of individuals or the whole. This is a logical fallacy called the *fallacy of composition;* the assumption is not correct. A statement that is valid for an individual or part is not

SUMMARY

LO1.1 Define economics and the features of the economic perspective.

Economics is the social science that examines how individuals, institutions, and society make optimal choices under conditions of scarcity. Central to economics is the idea of opportunity cost: the value of the next-best good or service forgone to obtain something.

The economic perspective includes three elements: scarcity and choice, purposeful behavior, and marginal analysis. It sees individuals and institutions as making rational decisions based on comparisons of marginal costs and marginal benefits.

LO1.2 Describe the role of economic theory in economics.

Economists employ the scientific method, in which they form and test hypotheses of cause-and-effect relationships to generate theories, laws, and principles. Economists often combine theories into representations called models.

LO1.3 Distinguish microeconomics from macroeconomics and positive economics from normative economics.

Microeconomics examines the decision making of specific economic units or institutions. Macroeconomics looks at the economy as a whole or its major aggregates.

Positive economic analysis deals with facts; normative economics reflects value judgments.

LO1.4 Explain the individual's economizing problem and how trade-offs, opportunity costs, and attainable combinations can be illustrated with budget lines.

Individuals face an economizing problem. Because their wants exceed their incomes, they must decide what to purchase and what to forgo. Society also faces an economizing problem. Societal wants exceed the available resources necessary to fulfill them. Society therefore must decide what to produce and what to forgo.

Graphically, a budget line (or budget constraint) illustrates the economizing problem for individuals. The line shows the various necessarily valid for the larger group or whole. Noneconomic example: You may see the action better if you leap to your feet to see an outstanding play at a football game. But if all the spectators leap to their feet at the same time, nobody—including you—will have a better view than when all remained seated.

Here are two economic examples: An individual stockholder can sell shares of, say, Google stock without affecting the price of the stock. The individual's sale will not noticeably reduce the share price because the sale is a negligible fraction of the total shares of Google being bought and sold. But if all the Google shareholders decide to sell their shares the same day, the market will be flooded with shares and the stock price will fall precipitously. Similarly, a single cattle ranch can increase its revenue by expanding the size of its livestock herd. The extra cattle will not affect the price of cattle when they are brought to market. But if all ranchers as a group expand their herds, the total output of cattle will increase so much that the price of cattle will decline when the cattle are sold. If the price reduction is relatively large, ranchers as a group might find that their income has fallen despite their having sold a greater number of cattle because the fall in price overwhelms the increase in quantity.

Post Hoc Fallacy You must think very carefully before concluding that because event A precedes event B, A is the cause of B. This kind of faulty reasoning is known as the *post hoc, ergo propter hoc,* or "after this, therefore because of this," fallacy. Noneconomic example: A professional football team hires a new coach and the team's record improves. Is the new coach the cause? Maybe. Perhaps the presence of more experienced and talented players or an easier schedule is the true cause. The rooster crows before dawn but does not cause the sunrise.

Economic example: Many people blamed the Great Depression of the 1930s on the stock market crash of 1929. But the crash did not cause the Great Depression. The same severe weaknesses in the economy that caused the crash caused the Great Depression. The depression would have occurred even without the preceding stock market crash.

Correlation but Not Causation Do not confuse correlation, or connection, with causation. Correlation between two events or two sets of data indicates only that they are associated in some systematic and dependable way. For example, we may find that when variable *X* increases, *Y* also increases. But this correlation does not necessarily mean that there is causation—that increases in *X* cause increases in *Y*. The relationship could be purely coincidental or dependent on some other factor, *Z,* not included in the analysis.

Here is an example: Economists have found a positive correlation between education and income. In general, people with more education earn higher incomes than those with less education. Common sense suggests education is the cause and higher incomes are the effect; more education implies a more knowledgeable and productive worker, and such workers receive larger salaries.

But might the relationship be explainable in other ways? Are education and income correlated because the characteristics required for succeeding in education—ability and motivation—are the same ones required to be a productive and highly paid worker? If so, then people with those traits will probably both obtain more education and earn higher incomes. Greater education will not be the sole cause of the higher income.

combinations of two products that a consumer can purchase with a specific money income, given the prices of the two products.

LO1.5 List the categories of scarce resources and delineate the nature of society's economizing problem.

Economic resources are inputs into the production process and can be classified as land, labor, capital, or entrepreneurial ability. Economic resources are also known as factors of production or inputs.

Economists illustrate society's economizing problem through production possibilities analysis. Production possibilities tables and curves show the different combinations of goods and services that can be produced in a fully employed economy, assuming that resource quantity, resource quality, and technology are fixed.

LO1.6 Apply production possibilities analysis, increasing opportunity costs, and economic growth.

An economy that is fully employed and thus operating on its production possibilities curve must sacrifice the output of some types of goods and services to increase the production of others. The gain of one type of good or service is always accompanied by an opportunity cost in the form of the loss of some of the other type of good or service.

Because resources are not equally productive in all possible uses, shifting resources from one use to another creates increasing opportunity costs. The production of additional units of one product requires the sacrifice of increasing amounts of the other product.

The optimal (best) point on the production possibilities curve represents the most desirable mix of goods and is determined by expanding the production of each good until its marginal benefit (MB) equals its marginal cost (MC).

LO1.7 Explain how economic growth and international trade increase consumption possibilities.

Over time, technological advances and increases in the quantity and quality of resources enable the economy to produce more of all goods and services, that is, to experience economic growth. Society's choice as to the mix of consumer goods and capital goods in current output is a major determinant of the future location of the production possibilities curve and thus of the extent of economic growth.

International trade enables a nation to obtain more goods from its limited resources than its production possibilities curve indicates.

TERMS AND CONCEPTS

economics
economic perspective
scarcity
opportunity cost
utility
marginal analysis
scientific method
economic principle
other-things-equal assumption
microeconomics
macroeconomics
aggregate
positive economics
normative economics
economizing problem
budget line
economic resources
land
labor
capital
investment
entrepreneurial ability
entrepreneurs
factors of production
consumer goods
capital goods
production possibilities curve
law of increasing opportunity costs
economic growth

The following and additional problems can be found in connect

DISCUSSION QUESTIONS

1. What is an opportunity cost? How does the idea relate to the definition of economics? Which of the following decisions would entail the greater opportunity cost: allocating a square block in the heart of New York City for a surface parking lot or allocating a square block at the edge of a typical suburb for such a lot? Explain. LO1.1
2. Cite three examples of recent decisions that you made in which you, at least implicitly, weighed marginal cost and marginal benefit. LO1.1
3. What is meant by the term "utility" and how does the idea relate to purposeful behavior? LO1.1
4. What are the key elements of the scientific method and how does this method relate to economic principles and laws? LO1.2
5. State (a) a positive economic statement of your choice, and then (b) a normative economic statement relating to your first statement. LO1.3
6. How does the slope of a budget line illustrate opportunity costs and trade-offs? How does a budget line illustrate scarcity and the effect of limited incomes? LO1.4
7. What are economic resources? What categories do economists use to classify them? Why are resources also called factors of production? Why are they called inputs? LO1.5
8. Why is money not considered to be a capital resource in economics? Why is entrepreneurial ability considered a category of economic resource, distinct from labor? What are the major functions of the entrepreneur? LO1.5
9. Specify and explain the typical shapes of marginal-benefit and marginal-cost curves. How are these curves used to determine the optimal allocation of resources to a particular product? If current output is such that marginal cost exceeds marginal benefit, should more or fewer resources be allocated to this product? Explain. LO1.6
10. Suppose that, on the basis of a nation's production possibilities curve, an economy must sacrifice 10,000 pizzas domestically to get the 1 additional industrial robot it desires but that it can get the robot from another country in exchange for 9,000 pizzas. Relate this information to the following statement: "Through international specialization and trade, a nation can reduce its opportunity cost of obtaining goods and thus 'move outside its production possibilities curve.'" LO1.7
11. **LAST WORD** Studies indicate that married men on average earn more income than unmarried men of the same age and education level. Why must we be cautious in concluding that marriage is the cause and higher income is the effect?

AP REVIEW QUESTIONS

1. Match each term with the correct definition. LO1.1
   economics
   opportunity cost
   marginal analysis
   utility
   a. The next-best thing that must be forgone in order to produce one more unit of a given product.
   b. The pleasure, happiness, or satisfaction obtained from consuming a good or service.
   c. The social science concerned with how individuals, institutions, and society make optimal (best) choices under conditions of scarcity.
   d. Making choices based on comparing marginal benefits with marginal costs.
2. Indicate whether each of the following statements applies to microeconomics or macroeconomics: LO1.3
   a. The unemployment rate in the United States was 5.1 percent in September 2015.

b. A U.S. software firm discharged 15 workers last month and transferred the work to India.
c. An unexpected freeze in central Florida reduced the citrus crop and caused the price of oranges to rise.
d. U.S. output, adjusted for inflation, increased by 2.4 percent in 2014.
e. Last week Wells Fargo Bank lowered its interest rate on business loans by one-half of 1 percentage point.
f. The consumer price index rose by 0.2 percent from August 2014 to August 2015.

3. Suppose that you initially have $100 to spend on books or movie tickets. The books start off costing $25 each and the movie tickets start off costing $10 each. For each of the following situations, would the attainable set of combinations that you can afford increase or decrease? **LO1.4**
   a. Your budget increases from $100 to $150 while the prices stay the same.
   b. Your budget remains $100, the price of books remains $25, but the price of movie tickets rises to $20.
   c. Your budget remains $100, the price of movie tickets remains $10, but the price of a book falls to $15.
4. Suppose that you are given a $100 budget at work that can be spent only on two items: staplers and pens. If staplers cost $10 each and pens cost $2.50 each, then the opportunity cost of purchasing one stapler is: **LO1.4**
   a. 10 pens.
   b. 5 pens.
   c. zero pens.
   d. 4 pens.
   e. 2 pens.
5. For each of the following situations involving marginal cost (MC) and marginal benefit (MB), indicate whether it would be best to produce more, fewer, or the current number of units. **LO1.4**
   a. 3,000 units at which MC = $10 and MB = $13.
   b. 11 units at which MC = $4 and MB = $3.
   c. 43,277 units at which MC = $99 and MB = $99.
6. Explain how (if at all) each of the following events affects the location of a country's production possibilities curve: **LO1.6**
   a. The quality of education increases.
   b. The number of unemployed workers increases.
   c. A new technique improves the efficiency of extracting copper from ore.
   d. A devastating earthquake destroys numerous production facilities.
   e. The flow of oil, an essential resource, is decreased due to bad weather in the Gulf of Mexico.
7. Which of the following shows two major ways in which an economy can grow and push out its production possibilities curve? **LO1.7**
   a. Better weather and nicer cars.
   b. Higher taxes and lower spending.
   c. Increases in resource supplies and advances in technology.
   d. Increases in trade and lower investment spending.
   e. Lower taxes and government subsidies.
8. Begin each question with a new production possibilities curve (PPC) for country Nicola. Assume two goods (X measured on the horizontal axis and Y on the vertical axis) and increasing opportunity costs. Show the following:
   a. Use point F to show a possible situation in which country Nicola has significant unemployment of resources.
   b. Show both the original PPC and a new PPC if there is an increase in Nicola's labor force.
   c. Show both the original PPC and a new PPC if there is technological change in the production of good X.

PROBLEMS

1. Potatoes cost Janice $1 per pound, and she has $5.00 that she could possibly spend on potatoes or other items. If she feels that the first pound of potatoes is worth $1.50, the second pound is worth $1.14, the third pound is worth $1.05, and all subsequent pounds are worth $0.30, how many pounds of potatoes will she purchase? What if she only had $2 to spend? **LO1.1**
2. Pham can work as many or as few hours as she wants at the college bookstore for $9 per hour. But due to her hectic schedule, she has just 15 hours per week that she can spend working at either the bookstore or other potential jobs. One potential job, at a café, will pay her $12 per hour for up to 6 hours per week. She has another job offer at a garage that will pay her $10 an hour for up to 5 hours per week. And she has a potential job at a daycare center that will pay her $8.50 per hour for as many hours as she can work. If her goal is to maximize the amount of money she can make each week, how many hours will she work at the bookstore? **LO1.1**
3. Suppose you won $15 on a lotto ticket at the local 7-Eleven and decided to spend all the winnings on candy bars and bags of peanuts. Candy bars cost $0.75 each while bags of peanuts cost $1.50 each. **LO1.5**
   a. Construct a table showing the alternative combinations of the two products that are available.
   b. Plot the data in your table as a budget line in a graph. What is the slope of the budget line? What is the opportunity cost of one more candy bar? Of one more bag of peanuts? Do these opportunity costs rise, fall, or remain constant as additional units are purchased?
   c. Does the budget line tell you which of the available combinations of candy bars and bags of peanuts to buy?
   d. Suppose that you had won $30 on your ticket, not $15. Show the $30 budget line in your diagram. Has the number of available combinations increased or decreased?
4. Suppose that you are on a desert island and possess exactly 20 coconuts. Your neighbor, Friday, is a fisherman, and he is willing to trade 2 fish for every 1 coconut that you are willing to give him. Another neighbor, Kwame, is also a fisherman, and he is willing to trade 3 fish for every 1 coconut. **LO1.5**
   a. On a single figure, draw budget lines for trading with Friday and for trading with Kwame. (Put coconuts on the vertical axis.)
   b. What is the slope of the budget line from trading with Friday?
   c. What is the slope of the budget line from trading with Kwame?
   d. Which budget line features a larger set of attainable combinations of coconuts and fish?
   e. If you are going to trade coconuts for fish, would you rather trade with Friday or Kwame?

5. Refer to the following production possibilities table for consumer goods (automobiles) and capital goods (forklifts): LO1.6
   a. Show these data graphically. Upon what specific assumptions is this production possibilities curve based?
   b. If the economy is at point C, what is the cost of one more automobile? Of one more forklift? Which characteristic of the production possibilities curve reflects the law of increasing opportunity costs: its shape or its length?
   c. If the economy characterized by this production possibilities table and curve were producing 3 automobiles and 20 forklifts, what could you conclude about its use of its available resources?
   d. Is production at a point outside the production possibilities curve currently possible? Could a future advance in technology allow production beyond the current production possibilities curve? Could international trade allow a country to consume beyond its current production possibilities curve?

	Production Alternatives				
Type of Production	**A**	**B**	**C**	**D**	**E**
Automobiles	0	2	4	6	8
Forklifts	30	27	21	12	0

6. Look at Figure 1.3. Suppose that the cost of cheese falls, so that the marginal cost of producing pizza decreases. Will the MC curve shift up or down? Will the optimal amount of pizza increase or decrease? LO1.6
7. Referring to the table in problem 5, suppose improvement occurs in the technology of producing forklifts but not in the technology of producing automobiles. Draw the new production possibilities curve. Now assume that a technological advance occurs in producing automobiles but not in producing forklifts. Draw the new production possibilities curve. Now draw a production possibilities curve that reflects technological improvement in the production of both goods. LO1.7
8. Because investment and capital goods are paid for with savings, higher savings rates reflect a decision to consume fewer goods for the present in order to be able to invest in more goods for the future. Households in China save 40 percent of their annual incomes each year, whereas U.S. households save less than 5 percent. At the same time, production possibilities are growing at roughly 9 percent per year in China but only about 3.5 percent per year in the United States. Use graphical analysis of "present goods" versus "future goods" to explain the difference between China's growth rate and the U.S. growth rate. LO1.7

Graphs and Their Meaning

LO1.8 Understand graphs, curves, and slopes as they relate to economics.

If you glance quickly through this text, you will find many graphs. Some seem simple, while others seem more formidable. All are included to help you visualize and understand economic relationships. Physicists and chemists sometimes illustrate their theories by building arrangements of multicolored wooden balls, representing protons, neutrons, and electrons, that are held in proper relation to one another by wires or sticks. Economists most often use graphs to illustrate their models. By understanding these "pictures," you can more readily comprehend economic relationships.

Construction of a Graph

A *graph* is a visual representation of the relationship between two economic quantities, or variables. The table in Figure 1 is a hypothetical illustration showing the relationship between income and consumption for the economy as a whole. Without even studying economics, we would logically expect that people would buy more goods and services when their incomes go up. Thus, it is not surprising to find in the table that total consumption in the economy increases as total income increases.

The information in the table is expressed graphically in Figure 1. Here is how it is done: We want to show visually how consumption changes as income changes. We therefore represent income on the **horizontal axis** of the graph and consumption on the **vertical axis.**

Now we arrange the vertical and horizontal scales of the graph to reflect the ranges of values of consumption and income and mark the scales in convenient increments. As you can see, the values marked on the scales cover all the values in the table. The increments on both scales are $100.

Because the graph has two dimensions, each point within it represents an income value and its associated consumption value. To find a point that represents one of the five income-consumption combinations in the table in Figure 1, we draw straight lines from the appropriate values on the vertical and horizontal axes. For example, to plot point *c* (the $200 income–$150 consumption point), we draw straight lines up from the horizontal (income) axis at $200 and across from the vertical (consumption) axis at $150. These lines intersect at point *c*, which represents this particular income-consumption combination. You should verify that the other income-consumption combinations shown in the table are properly located in the graph in Figure 1. Finally, by assuming that the same general relationship between income and consumption prevails for all other incomes, we draw a line or smooth curve to connect these points. That line or curve represents the income-consumption relationship.

If the curve is a straight line, as in Figure 1, we say the relationship is *linear.* (It is permissible, and even customary, to refer to straight lines in graphs as "curves.")

Direct and Inverse Relationships

The line in Figure 1 slopes upward to the right, so it depicts a direct relationship between income and consumption. By a **direct relationship** (or positive relationship) we mean that two variables—in this case, consumption and income—change in the *same* direction. An increase in consumption is

FIGURE 1 Graphing the direct relationship between consumption and income. Two sets of data that are positively or directly related, such as consumption and income, graph as an upsloping line.

Income per Week	Consumption per Week	Point
$ 0	$ 50	*a*
100	100	*b*
200	150	*c*
300	200	*d*
400	250	*e*

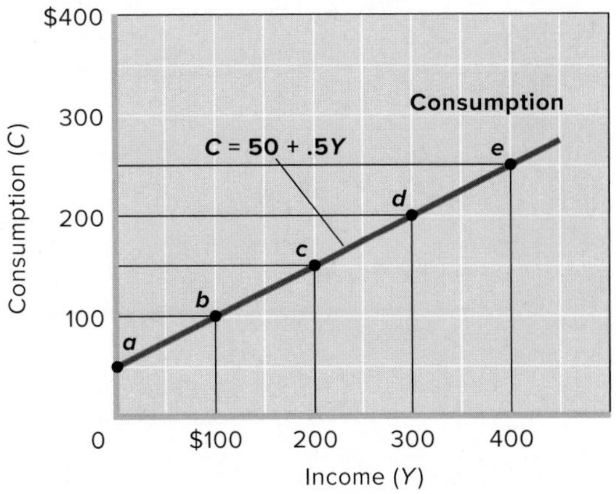

associated with an increase in income; a decrease in consumption accompanies a decrease in income. When two sets of data are positively or directly related, they always graph as an *upsloping* line, as in Figure 1.

In contrast, two sets of data may be inversely related. Consider the table in Figure 2, which shows the relationship between the price of basketball tickets and game attendance at Gigantic State University (GSU). Here we have an **inverse relationship** (or negative relationship) because the two variables change in *opposite* directions. When ticket prices decrease, attendance increases. When ticket prices increase, attendance decreases. The six data points in the table in Figure 2 are plotted in the graph. Observe that an inverse relationship always graphs as a *downsloping* line.

Dependent and Independent Variables

Although it is not always easy, economists seek to determine which variable is the "cause" and which is the "effect." Or, more formally, they seek the independent variable and the dependent variable. The **independent variable** is the cause or source; it is the variable that changes first. The **dependent variable** is the effect or outcome; it is the variable that changes because of the change in the independent variable. As in our income-consumption example, income generally is the independent variable and consumption the dependent variable. Income causes consumption to be what it is rather than the other way around. Similarly, ticket prices (set in advance of the season and printed on the ticket) determine attendance at GSU basketball games; attendance at games does not determine the printed ticket prices for those games. Ticket price is the independent variable and the quantity of tickets purchased is the dependent variable.

You may recall from your high school courses that mathematicians put the independent variable (cause) on the horizontal axis and the dependent variable (effect) on the vertical axis. Economists are less tidy; their graphing of independent and dependent variables is more arbitrary. Their conventional graphing of the income-consumption relationship is consistent with mathematical convention, but economists put price and cost data on the vertical axis. Hence, economists' graphing of GSU's ticket price–attendance data differs from normal mathematical procedure. This does not present a problem, but we want you to be aware of this fact to avoid any possible confusion.

Other Things Equal

Our simple two-variable graphs purposely ignore many other factors that might affect the amount of consumption occurring at each income level or the number of people who attend GSU basketball games at each possible ticket price. When economists plot the relationship between any two variables, they employ the *ceteris paribus* (other-things-equal) assumption. Thus, in Figure 1 all factors other than income that might affect the amount of consumption are presumed to be constant or unchanged. Similarly, in Figure 2 all factors other than ticket price that might influence attendance at GSU basketball games are assumed constant. In reality, "other things" are not equal; they often change, and when they do, the relationship represented in our two tables and graphs will change. Specifically, the lines we have plotted would *shift* to new locations.

Consider a stock market "crash." The dramatic drop in the value of stocks might cause people to feel less wealthy and therefore less willing to consume at each level of income. The result might be a downward shift of the consumption line. To see this,

FIGURE 2 Graphing the inverse relationship between ticket prices and game attendance. Two sets of data that are negatively or inversely related, such as ticket price and the attendance at basketball games, graph as a downsloping line.

Ticket Price	Attendance, Thousands	Point
$50	0	*a*
40	4	*b*
30	8	*c*
20	12	*d*
10	16	*e*
0	20	*f*

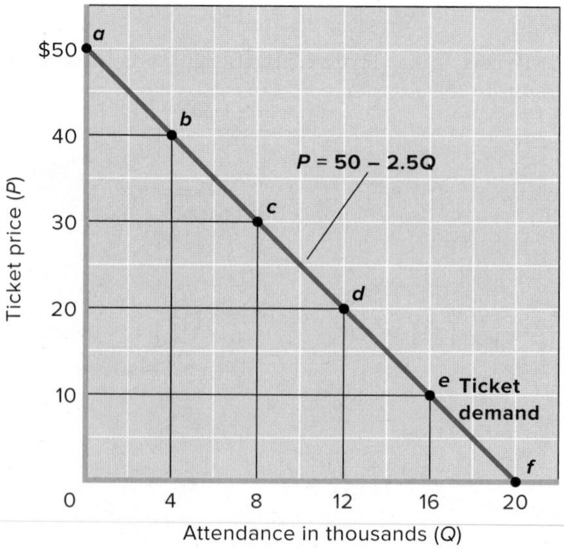

you should plot a new consumption line in Figure 1, assuming that consumption is, say, \$20 less at each income level. Note that the relationship remains direct; the line merely shifts downward to reflect less consumption spending at each income level.

Similarly, factors other than ticket prices might affect GSU game attendance. If GSU loses most of its games, attendance at GSU games might be less at each ticket price. To see this, redraw Figure 2 assuming that 2,000 fewer fans attend GSU games at each ticket price.

Slope of a Line

Lines can be described in terms of their slopes. The **slope of a straight line** is the ratio of the vertical change (the rise or drop) to the horizontal change (the run) between any two points of the line.

Positive Slope Between point *b* and point *c* in Figure 1, the rise or vertical change (the change in consumption) is +\$50 and the run or horizontal change (the change in income) is +\$100. Therefore:

$$\text{slope} = \frac{\text{vertical change}}{\text{horizontal change}} = \frac{+50}{+100} = \frac{1}{2} = .5$$

Note that our slope of or .5 is positive because consumption and income change in the same direction; that is, consumption and income are directly or positively related.

The slope of .5 tells us there will be a \$0.50 increase in consumption for every \$1 increase in income. Similarly, there will be a \$0.50 decrease in consumption for every \$1 decrease in income.

Negative Slope Between any two of the identified points in Figure 2, say, point *c* and point *d*, the vertical change is −10 (the drop) and the horizontal change is +4 (the run). Therefore:

$$\text{Slope} = \frac{\text{vertical change}}{\text{horizontal change}} = \frac{-10}{+4}$$

$$= -2\frac{1}{2} = -2.5$$

This slope is negative because ticket price and attendance have an inverse relationship.

Note that on the horizontal axis attendance is stated in thousands of people. So the slope of −10/+4 or −2.5 means that lowering the price by \$10 will increase attendance by 4,000 people. That ratio also implies that a \$2.50 price reduction will increase attendance by 1,000 persons.

Slopes and Measurement Units The slope of a line will be affected by the choice of units for either variable. If, in our ticket price illustration, we had chosen to measure attendance in individual people, our horizontal change would have been 4,000 and the slope would have been

$$\text{slope} = \frac{-10}{+4{,}000} = \frac{-1}{+400} = -.0025$$

The slope depends on the way the relevant variables are measured.

Slopes and Marginal Analysis Recall that economics is largely concerned with changes from the status quo. The concept of slope is important in economics because it reflects marginal changes—those involving 1 more (or 1 fewer) unit. For example, in Figure 1 the .5 slope shows that \$0.50 of extra or marginal consumption is associated with each \$1 change in income. In this example, people collectively will consume \$0.50 of any \$1 increase in their incomes and reduce their consumption by \$0.50 for each \$1 decline in income.

Infinite and Zero Slopes Many variables are unrelated or independent of one another. For example, the quantity of wristwatches purchased is not related to the price of bananas. In Figure 3a we represent the price of bananas on the vertical axis and the quantity of watches demanded on the horizontal axis. The graph of their relationship is the line parallel to the vertical axis. The line's vertical slope indicates that the same quantity of watches is purchased no matter what the price of bananas. The slope of vertical lines is *infinite*.

Similarly, aggregate consumption is completely unrelated to the nation's divorce rate. In Figure 3b we put consumption

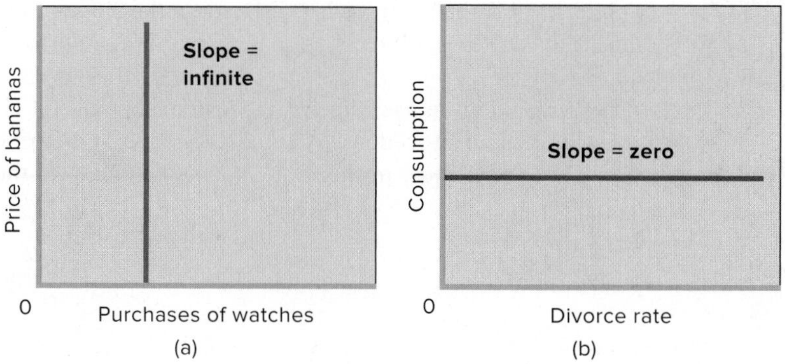

FIGURE 3 Infinite and zero slopes. (a) A line parallel to the vertical axis has an infinite slope. Here, purchases of watches remain the same no matter what happens to the price of bananas. (b) A line parallel to the horizontal axis has a slope of zero. In this case, consumption remains the same no matter what happens to the divorce rate. In both (a) and (b), the two variables are totally unrelated to one another.

on the vertical axis and the divorce rate on the horizontal axis. The line parallel to the horizontal axis represents this lack of relatedness because the amount of consumption remains the same no matter what happens to the divorce rate. The slope of horizontal lines is *zero*.

Vertical Intercept

A line can be positioned on a graph (without plotting points) if we know just two things: its slope and its vertical intercept. We have already discussed slope. The **vertical intercept** of a line is the point where the line meets the vertical axis. In Figure 1 the intercept is \$50. This intercept means that if current income were zero, consumers would still spend \$50. They might do this through borrowing or by selling some of their assets. Similarly, the \$50 vertical intercept in Figure 2 shows that at a \$50 ticket price, GSU's basketball team would be playing in an empty arena.

Equation of a Linear Relationship

If we know the vertical intercept and slope, we can describe a line succinctly in equation form. In its general form, the equation of a straight line is

$$y = a + bx$$

where y = dependent variable
a = vertical intercept
b = slope of line
x = independent variable

For our income-consumption example, if C represents consumption (the dependent variable) and Y represents income (the independent variable), we can write $C = a + bY$. By substituting the known values of the intercept and the slope, we get

$$C = 50 + .5Y$$

This equation also allows us to determine the amount of consumption C at any specific level of income. You should use it to confirm that at the \$250 income level, consumption is \$175.

When economists reverse mathematical convention by putting the independent variable on the vertical axis and the dependent variable on the horizontal axis, then y stands for the independent variable, rather than the dependent variable in the general form. We noted previously that this case is relevant for our GSU ticket price–attendance data. If P represents the ticket price (independent variable) and Q represents attendance (dependent variable), their relationship is given by

$$P = 50 - 2.5Q$$

FIGURE 4 Determining the slopes of curves. The slope of a nonlinear curve changes from point to point on the curve. The slope at any point (say, *B*) can be determined by drawing a straight line that is tangent to that point (line *bb*) and calculating the slope of that line.

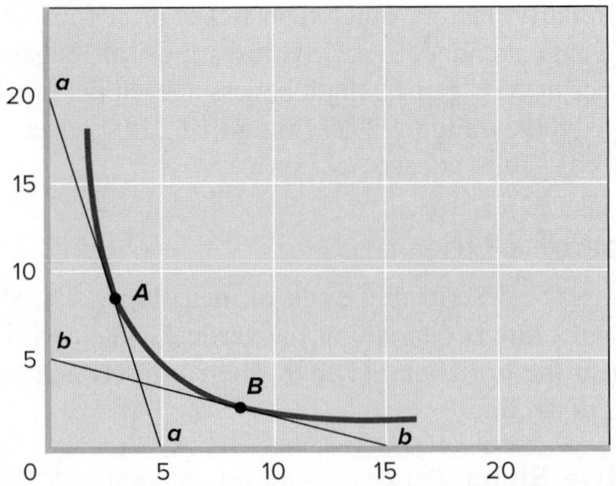

where the vertical intercept is 50 and the negative slope is $-2\frac{1}{2}$, or -2.5. Knowing the value of P lets us solve for Q, our dependent variable. You should use this equation to predict GSU ticket sales when the ticket price is \$15.

Slope of a Nonlinear Curve

We now move from the simple world of linear relationships (straight lines) to the more complex world of nonlinear relationships (curvy lines). The slope of a straight line is the same at all its points. The slope of a line representing a nonlinear relationship changes from one point to another. Such lines are always referred to as *curves*.

Consider the downsloping curve in Figure 4. Its slope is negative throughout, but the curve flattens as we move down along it. Thus, its slope constantly changes; the curve has a different slope at each point.

To measure the slope at a specific point, we draw a straight line tangent to the curve at that point. A straight line is *tangent* at a point if it touches, but does not intersect, the curve at that point. Thus line *aa* is tangent to the curve in Figure 4 at point *A*. The slope of the curve at that point is equal to the slope of the tangent line. Specifically, the total vertical change (drop) in the tangent line *aa* is -20 and the total horizontal change (run) is $+5$. Because the slope of the tangent line *aa* is $-20/+5$, or -4, the slope of the curve at point *A* is also -4.

Line *bb* in Figure 4 is tangent to the curve at point *B*. Following the same procedure, we find the slope at *B* to be $-5/+15$, or $-\frac{1}{3}$. Thus, in this flatter part of the curve, the slope is less negative.

APPENDIX SUMMARY

LO1.8 Understand graphs, curves, and slopes as they relate to economics.

Graphs are a convenient and revealing way to represent economic relationships.

Two variables are positively or directly related when their values change in the same direction. The line (curve) representing two directly related variables slopes upward.

Two variables are negatively or inversely related when their values change in opposite directions. The line (curve) representing two inversely related variables slopes downward.

The value of the dependent variable (the "effect") is determined by the value of the independent variable (the "cause").

When the "other factors" that might affect a two-variable relationship are allowed to change, the graph of the relationship will likely shift to a new location.

The slope of a straight line is the ratio of the vertical change to the horizontal change between any two points. The slope of an upsloping line is positive; the slope of a downsloping line is negative.

The slope of a line or curve depends on the units used in measuring the variables. The slope is especially relevant for economics because it measures marginal changes.

The slope of a horizontal line is zero; the slope of a vertical line is infinite.

Together, the vertical intercept and slope of a line determine its location; they are used in expressing the line—and the relationship between the two variables—as an equation.

The slope of a curve at any point is determined by calculating the slope of a straight line tangent to the curve at that point.

APPENDIX TERMS AND CONCEPTS

horizontal axis	inverse relationship	slope of a straight line
vertical axis	independent variable	vertical intercept
direct relationship	dependent variable	

The following and additional problems can be found in connect

APPENDIX DISCUSSION QUESTIONS

1. Briefly explain the use of graphs as a way to represent economic relationships. What is an inverse relationship? How does it graph? What is a direct relationship? How does it graph? **LO1.8**
2. Describe the graphical relationship between ticket prices and the number of people choosing to visit amusement parks. Is that relationship consistent with the fact that, historically, park attendance and ticket prices have both risen? Explain. **LO1.8**
3. Look back at Figure 2, which shows the inverse relationship between ticket prices and game attendance at Gigantic State University. (a) Interpret the meaning of both the slope and the intercept. (b) If the slope of the line were steeper, what would that say about the amount by which ticket sales respond to increases in ticket prices? (c) If the slope of the line stayed the same but the intercept increased, what can you say about the amount by which ticket sales respond to increases in ticket prices? **LO1.8**

APPENDIX REVIEW QUESTIONS

1. Indicate whether each of the following relationships is usually a direct relationship or an inverse relationship. **LO1.8**
   - **a.** A sports team's winning percentage and attendance at its home games.
   - **b.** Higher temperatures and sweater sales.
   - **c.** A person's income and how often he or she shops at discount stores.
   - **d.** Higher gasoline prices and miles driven in automobiles.
2. Erin grows pecans. The number of bushels (B) that she can produce depends on the number of inches of rainfall (R) that her orchards get. The relationship is given algebraically as follows: $B = 3{,}000 + 800R$. Match each part of this equation with the correct term. **LO1.8**

B	slope
3,000	dependent variable
800	vertical intercept
R	independent variable

APPENDIX PROBLEMS

1. Graph and label as either direct or indirect the relationships you would expect to find between (a) the number of inches of rainfall per month and the sale of umbrellas, (b) the amount of tuition and the level of enrollment at a university, and (c) the popularity of an entertainer and the price of her concert tickets. **LO1.8**
2. Indicate how each of the following might affect the data shown in the table and graph in Figure 2 of this appendix: **LO1.8**
   - **a.** GSU's athletic director schedules higher-quality opponents.
   - **b.** An NBA team locates in the city where GSU plays.
   - **c.** GSU contracts to have all its home games televised.

3. The following table contains data on the relationship between saving and income. Rearrange these data into a meaningful order and graph them on the accompanying grid. What is the slope of the line? The vertical intercept? Write the equation that represents this line. What would you predict saving to be at the $12,500 level of income? **LO1.8**

Income per Year	Saving per Year
$15,000	$1,000
0	−500
10,000	500
5,000	0
20,000	1,500

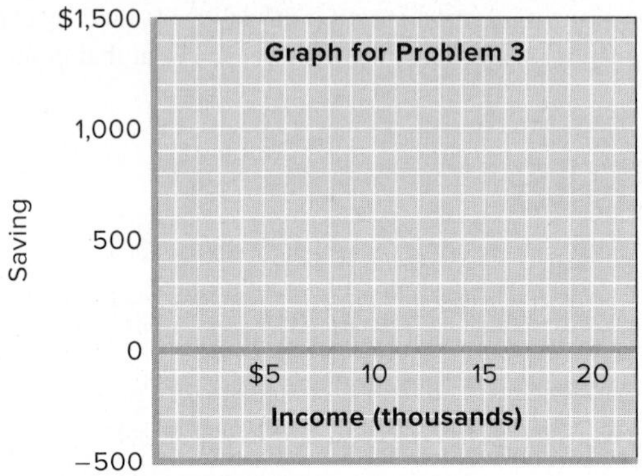

4. Construct a table from the data shown in the accompanying graph. Which is the dependent variable and which is the independent variable? Summarize the data in equation form. **LO1.8**

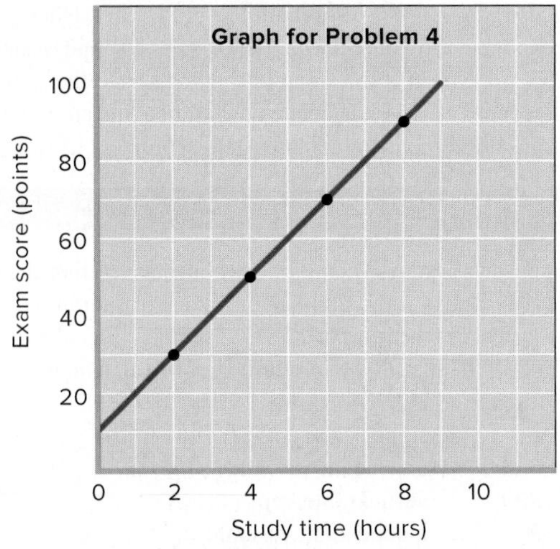

5. Suppose that when the interest rate on loans is 16 percent, businesses find it unprofitable to invest in machinery and equipment. However, when the interest rate is 14 percent, $5 billion worth of investment is profitable. At 12 percent interest, a total of $10 billion of investment is profitable. Similarly, total investment increases by $5 billion for each successive 2-percentage-point decline in the interest rate. Describe the relevant relationship between the interest rate and investment in a table, on a graph, and as an equation. Put the interest rate on the vertical axis and investment on the horizontal axis. In your equation use the form $i = a + bI$, where i is the interest rate, a is the vertical intercept, b is the slope of the line (which is negative), and I is the level of investment. **LO1.8**

6. Suppose that $C = a + bY$, where C = consumption, a = consumption at zero income, b = slope, and Y = income. **LO1.8**
   a. Are C and Y positively related or are they negatively related?
   b. If graphed, would the curve for this equation slope upward or slope downward?
   c. Are the variables C and Y inversely related or directly related?
   d. What is the value of C if $a = 10$, $b = 0.50$, and $Y = 200$?
   e. What is the value of Y if $C = 100$, $a = 10$, and $b = 0.25$?

7. The accompanying graph shows curve XX' and tangents at points A, B, and C. Calculate the slope of the curve at these three points. **LO1.8**

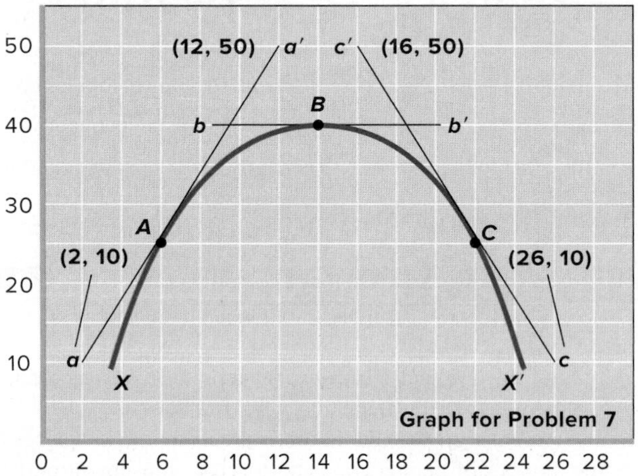

8. In the accompanying graph, is the slope of curve AA' positive or negative? Does the slope increase or decrease as we move along the curve from A to A'? Answer the same two questions for curve BB'. **LO1.8**

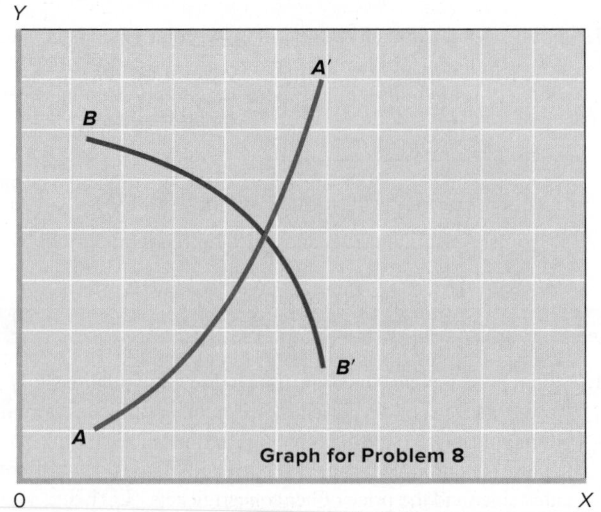

Chapter 2

The Market System and the Circular Flow

Learning Objectives

LO2.1 **Differentiate between laissez-faire capitalism, the command system, and the market system.**

LO2.2 **List the main characteristics of the market system.**

LO2.3 **Explain how the market system answers the five fundamental questions of what to produce, how to produce, who obtains the output, how to adjust to change, and how to promote progress.**

LO2.4 **Explain the operation of the "invisible hand" and why market economies usually do a better job than command economies at efficiently transforming economic resources into desirable output.**

LO2.5 **Describe the mechanics of the circular flow model.**

LO2.6 **Explain how the market system deals with risk.**

AP Chapter Focus

Ever wonder how decisions are made about which goods and services will be available for consumption in an economy? How do producers of goods and services decide which technology and types of resources to use, and what accounts for new or improved products and services? Who obtains these products and services? The answers to these questions depend on the type of economic system that is in place. Chapter 2 examines these systems, focusing on the market system.

The next essential economic model to learn—the circular flow model—is introduced in this chapter. Study this model carefully. It will be expanded over the course of study to include more "players" that interact in the marketplace.

AP Economic Systems

LO2.1 Differentiate between laissez-faire capitalism, the command system, and the market system.

Every society needs to develop an **economic system**—a particular set of institutional arrangements and a coordinating mechanism—to respond to the economizing problem. The economic system has to determine what goods are produced, how they are produced, who gets them, how to accommodate change, and how to promote technological progress.

Economic systems differ as to (1) who owns the factors of production and (2) the method used to motivate, coordinate, and direct economic activity.

Economics systems can be classified by the degree to which they rely upon decentralized decision making based upon markets and prices or centralized government control based upon orders and mandates. At one extreme lies *laissez-faire capitalism,* in which government intervention is at a very minimum and markets and prices are allowed to direct nearly all economic activity. At the other extreme lie *command systems,* in which governments have total control over all economic activity. The vast majority of national economies lie somewhere in the middle, utilizing some mixture of centralized government regulation and decentralized markets and prices. These economies are said to have *market systems* or *mixed economies.*

Laissez-Faire Capitalism

In **laissez-faire capitalism**—or "pure capitalism"—the government's role would be limited to protecting private property from theft and aggression and establishing a legal environment in which contracts would be enforced and people could interact in markets to buy and sell goods, services, and resources.

The term "laissez-faire" is the French for "let it be," that is, keep the government from interfering with the economy. Proponents of laissez-faire believe that such interference reduces human welfare. They maintain that any government that intervenes widely in the economy will end up being corrupted by special interests that will use the government's economic influence to benefit themselves rather than society at large.

To prevent that from happening, the proponents of laissez-faire argue that government should restrict itself to preventing individuals and firms from coercing each other. By doing so, it will ensure that only mutually beneficial economic transactions get negotiated and completed. That should lead to the highest possible level of human satisfaction because, after all, who knows better what people want than the people themselves?

It is important to note, however, that no society has ever employed a laissez-faire system. In fact, no government has *ever* limited its economic actions to the short list of functions that would be allowed under laissez-faire. Instead, every government known to history has undertaken a wider range of economic activities, many of which are widely popular and which include industrial safety regulations, various taxes and subsidies, occupational licensing requirements, and income redistribution.

Thus, you should think of laissez-faire capitalism as a hypothetical system that is viewed by proponents as the ideal to which all economic systems should strive—but which is opposed by those who welcome greater government intervention in the economy.

The Command System

The polar opposite of laissez-faire capitalism is the **command system,** in which government owns most property resources and economic decision making is set by a central economic plan created and enforced by the government. The command system is also known as *socialism* or *communism.*

Under the command system, a central planning board appointed by the government makes all the major decisions concerning the use of resources, the composition and distribution of output, and the organization of production. The government owns most of the business firms, which produce according to government directives. The central planning board determines production goals for each enterprise and specifies the amount of resources to be allocated to each enterprise so that it can reach its production goals. The division of output between capital and consumer goods is centrally decided, and capital goods are allocated among industries on the basis of the central planning board's long-term priorities.

A pure command economy would rely exclusively on a central plan to allocate the government-owned property resources. But, in reality, even the preeminent command economy—the Soviet Union—tolerated some private ownership and incorporated some markets before its collapse in 1992. Subsequent reforms in Russia and most of the eastern European nations have, to one degree or another, transformed their command economies to capitalistic, market-oriented systems. China's reforms have not gone as far, but they have greatly reduced China's reliance on central planning. Although government ownership of resources and capital in China is still extensive, the nation has increasingly relied on free markets to organize and coordinate its economy. North Korea and Cuba are the last prominent remaining examples of largely centrally planned economies. Other countries using mainly the command system include Turkmenistan, Laos, Belarus, Myanmar, Venezuela, and Iran. Later in this chapter, we will explore the main reasons for the general demise of command systems.

The Market System

The vast majority of the world's economies utilize the **market system,** which is also known as *capitalism* or the *mixed economy.*

The market system is characterized by a mixture of centralized government economic initiatives and decentralized actions taken by individuals and firms. The precise mixture varies from country to country, but in each case the system features the private ownership of resources and the use of markets and prices to coordinate and direct economic activity.

In the market system, individuals and businesses seek to achieve their economic goals through their own decisions regarding work, consumption, or production. The system allows for the private ownership of capital, communicates through prices, and coordinates economic activity through markets—places where buyers and sellers come together to buy and sell goods, services, and resources.

Participants act in their own self-interest, and goods and services are produced and resources are supplied by whoever is willing and able to do so. The result is competition among independently acting buyers and sellers of each product and resource and an economic system in which decision making is widely dispersed.

The market system also offers high potential monetary rewards that create powerful incentives for existing firms to innovate and for entrepreneurs to pioneer new products and processes despite the financial risks involved and despite most innovations failing to catch on with consumers.

It is the case, however, that in the capitalism practiced in the United States and most other countries, the government plays a substantial role in the economy. It not only provides the rules for economic activity but also promotes economic stability and growth, provides certain goods and services that would otherwise be underproduced or not produced at all, and modifies the distribution of income. The government, however, is not the dominant economic force in deciding what to produce, how to produce it, and who will get it. That force is the market.

AP Characteristics of the Market System

LO2.2 List the main characteristics of the market system.

An examination of some of the key features of the market system in detail will be very instructive.

Private Property

In a market system, private individuals and firms, not the government, own most of the property resources (land and capital). It is this extensive private ownership of capital that gives capitalism its name. This right of **private property,** coupled with the freedom to negotiate binding legal contracts, enables individuals and businesses to obtain, use, and dispose of property resources as they see fit. The right of property owners to designate who will receive their property when they die helps sustain the institution of private property.

The most important consequence of property rights is that they encourage people to cooperate by helping to ensure that only *mutually agreeable* economic transactions take place. To consider why this is true, imagine a world without legally enforceable property rights. In such a world, the strong could simply take whatever they wanted from the weak without giving them any compensation. But in a world of legally enforceable property rights, any person wanting something from you has to get you to agree to give it to them. And you can say no. The result is that if they really want what you have, they must offer you something that you value more highly in return. That is, they must offer you a mutually agreeable economic transaction—one that benefits you as well as them.

Property rights also encourage investment, innovation, exchange, maintenance of property, and economic growth. Nobody would stock a store, build a factory, or clear land for farming if someone else, or the government itself, could take that property for his or her own benefit.

Property rights also extend to intellectual property through patents, copyrights, and trademarks. Such long-term protection encourages people to write books, music, and computer programs and to invent new products and production processes without fear that others will steal them and the rewards they may bring.

Moreover, property rights facilitate exchange. The title to an automobile or the deed to a cattle ranch assures the buyer that the seller is the legitimate owner. Also, property rights encourage owners to maintain or improve their property so as to preserve or increase its value. Finally, property rights enable people to use their time and resources to produce more goods and services, rather than using them to protect and retain the property they have already produced or acquired.

Freedom of Enterprise and Choice

Closely related to private ownership of property is freedom of enterprise and choice. The market system requires that various economic units make certain choices, which are expressed and implemented in the economy's markets:

- **Freedom of enterprise** ensures that entrepreneurs and private businesses are free to obtain and use economic resources to produce their choice of goods and services and to sell them in their chosen markets.
- **Freedom of choice** enables owners to employ or dispose of their property and money as they see fit. It also allows workers to try to enter any line of work for which they are qualified. Finally, it ensures that consumers are free to buy the goods and services that best satisfy their wants and that their budgets allow.

These choices are free only within broad legal limitations, of course. Illegal choices such as selling human organs or buying illicit drugs are punished through fines and imprisonment. (Global Perspective 2.1 reveals that the degree of economic freedom varies greatly from economy to economy.)

Self-Interest

In the market system, **self-interest** is the motivating force of the various economic units as they express their free choices. Self-interest simply means that each economic unit tries to achieve its own particular goal, which usually requires delivering something of value to others. Entrepreneurs try to maximize profit or minimize loss. Property owners try to get the highest price for the sale or rent of their resources. Workers try to maximize their utility (satisfaction) by finding jobs that offer the best combination of wages, hours, fringe benefits, and working conditions. Consumers try to obtain the products they want at the lowest possible price and apportion their

GLOBAL PERSPECTIVE 2.1

Index of Economic Freedom, Selected Economies

The Index of Economic Freedom measures economic freedom using 10 major groupings such as trade policy, property rights, and government intervention, with each category containing more than 50 specific criteria. The index then ranks 179 economies according to their degree of economic freedom. A few selected rankings for 2015 are listed below.

FREE

1 Hong Kong

3 New Zeland

5 Switzerland

MOSTLY FREE

12 United States

20 Japan

28 Colombia

MOSTLY UNFREE

117 Brazil

128 India

143 Russia

REPRESSED

169 Argentina

171 Iran

178 North Korea

Source: The Heritage Foundation, **www.heritage.org**.

expenditures to maximize their utility. The motive of self-interest gives direction and consistency to what might otherwise be a chaotic economy.

Competition

The market system depends on **competition** among economic units. The basis of this competition is freedom of choice exercised in pursuit of a monetary return. Very broadly defined, competition requires

- Two or more buyers and two or more sellers acting independently in a particular product or resource market. (Usually there are many more than two buyers and two sellers.)
- Freedom of sellers and buyers to enter or leave markets, on the basis of their economic self-interest.

Competition among buyers and sellers diffuses economic power within the businesses and households that make up the economy. When there are many buyers and sellers acting independently in a market, no single buyer or seller can dictate the price of the product or resource because others can undercut that price.

Competition also implies that producers can enter or leave an industry; no insurmountable barriers prevent an industry's expanding or contracting. This freedom of an industry to expand or contract provides the economy with the flexibility needed to remain efficient over time. Freedom of entry and exit enables the economy to adjust to changes in consumer tastes, technology, and resource availability.

The diffusion of economic power inherent in competition limits the potential abuse of that power. A producer that charges more than the competitive market price will lose sales to other producers. An employer who pays less than the competitive market wage rate will lose workers to other employers. A firm that fails to exploit new technology will lose profits to firms that do. A firm that produces shoddy products will be punished as customers switch to higher-quality items made by rival firms. Competition is the basic regulatory force in the market system.

Markets and Prices

We may wonder why an economy based on self-interest does not collapse in chaos. If consumers want breakfast cereal, but businesses choose to produce running shoes and resource suppliers decide to make computer software, production would seem to be deadlocked by the apparent inconsistencies of free choices.

In reality, the millions of decisions made by households and businesses are highly coordinated with one another by markets and prices, which are key components of the market system. They give the system its ability to coordinate millions of daily economic decisions. A **market** is an institution or mechanism that brings buyers ("demanders") and sellers ("suppliers") into contact. A market system conveys the decisions made by buyers and sellers of products and resources. The decisions made on each side of the market determine a set of product and resource prices that guide resource owners, entrepreneurs, and consumers as they make and revise their choices and pursue their self-interest.

Just as competition is the regulatory mechanism of the market system, the market system itself is the organizing and coordinating mechanism. It is an elaborate communication network through which innumerable individual free choices are recorded, summarized, and balanced. Those who respond to market signals and heed market dictates are rewarded with greater profit and income; those who do not respond to those signals and choose to ignore market dictates are penalized. Through this mechanism society decides what the economy should produce, how production can be organized efficiently, and how the fruits of production are to be distributed among the various units that make up the economy.

AP QUICK REVIEW 2.1

- ✓ The market system rests on the concepts of private ownership of property and on freedom of enterprise and freedom of choice.
- ✓ Property rights encourage people to cooperate and make mutually agreeable economic transactions.
- ✓ The market system permits consumers, resource suppliers, and businesses to pursue and further their self-interest. It brings together buyers and sellers.
- ✓ Competition diffuses economic power and limits the actions of any single seller or buyer.
- ✓ The coordinating mechanism of capitalism is a system of markets with flexible prices that respond to demand for and supply of a product.

Technology and Capital Goods

In the market system, competition, freedom of choice, self-interest, and personal reward provide the opportunity and motivation for technological advance. The monetary rewards for new products or production techniques accrue directly to the innovator. The market system therefore encourages extensive use and rapid development of complex capital goods: tools, machinery, large-scale factories, and facilities for storage, communication, transportation, and marketing.

Advanced technology and capital goods are important because the most direct methods of production are often the least efficient. The only way to avoid that inefficiency is to rely on capital goods. It would be ridiculous for a farmer to go at production with bare hands. There are huge benefits to be derived from creating and using such capital equipment as plows, tractors, and storage bins. More efficient production means much more abundant output.

Specialization

The extent to which market economies rely on **specialization** is extraordinary. Specialization means using the resources of an individual, firm, region, or nation to produce one or a few goods or services rather than the entire range of goods and services. Those goods and services are then exchanged for a full range of desired products. The majority of consumers produce virtually none of the goods and services they consume, and they consume little or nothing of the items they produce. The person working nine to five installing windows in commercial aircraft may rarely fly. Many farmers sell their milk to the local dairy and then buy margarine at the local grocery store. Society learned long ago that self-sufficiency breeds inefficiency. The jack-of-all-trades may be a very colorful individual but is certainly not an efficient producer.

Division of Labor Human specialization—called the **division of labor**—contributes to a society's output in several ways:

- ***Specialization makes use of differences in ability.*** Specialization enables individuals to take advantage of existing differences in their abilities and skills. If LeBron is strong, athletic, and good at shooting a basketball and Beyoncé is beautiful, agile, and can sing, their distribution of talents can be most efficiently used if LeBron plays professional basketball while Beyoncé records songs and gives concerts.
- ***Specialization fosters learning by doing.*** Even if the abilities of two people are identical, specialization may still be advantageous. By devoting time to a single task, a person is more likely to develop the skills required and to improve techniques than by working at a number of different tasks. You learn to be a good lawyer by studying and practicing law.
- ***Specialization saves time.*** By devoting time to a single task, a person avoids the loss of time incurred in shifting from one job to another. Also, time is saved by not "fumbling around" with tasks that one is not trained to do.

For all these reasons, specialization increases the total output society derives from limited resources.

Geographic Specialization Specialization also works on a regional and international basis. It is conceivable that oranges could be grown in Nebraska, but because of the unsuitability of the land, rainfall, and temperature, the costs would be very high. And it is conceivable that wheat could be grown in Florida, but such production would be costly for similar geographical reasons. So Nebraskans produce products—wheat in particular—for which their resources are best suited, and Floridians do the same, producing oranges and other citrus fruits. By specializing, both economies produce more than is needed locally. Then, very sensibly, Nebraskans and Floridians swap some of their surpluses—wheat for oranges, oranges for wheat.

Similarly, on an international scale, the United States specializes in producing such items as commercial aircraft and software, which it sells abroad in exchange for mobile phones from China, bananas from Honduras, and woven baskets from Thailand. Both human specialization and geographic specialization are needed to achieve efficiency in the use of limited resources.

Use of Money

A rather obvious characteristic of any economic system is the extensive use of money. Money performs several functions, but first and foremost it is a **medium of exchange.** It makes trade easier.

Specialization requires exchange. Exchange can, and sometimes does, occur through **barter**—swapping goods for

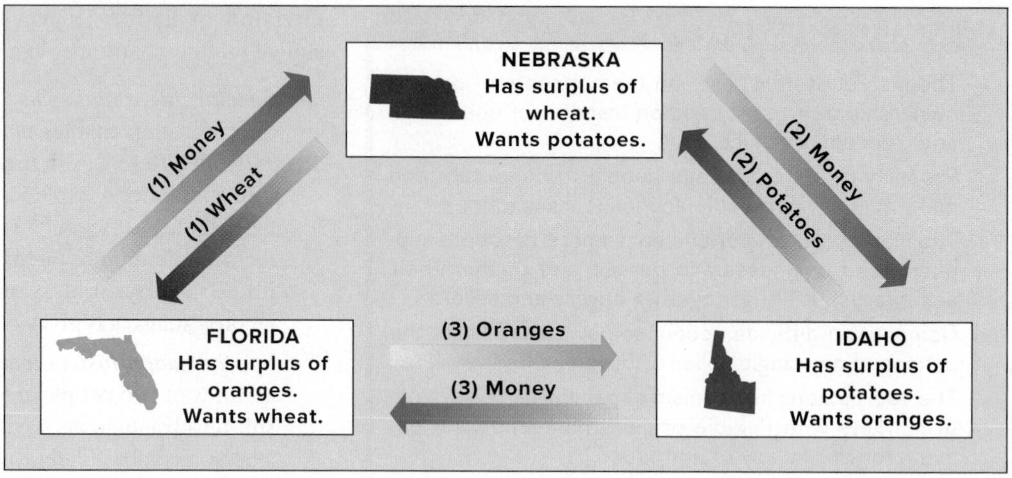

FIGURE 2.1 Money facilitates trade when wants do not coincide. The use of money as a medium of exchange permits trade to be accomplished despite a noncoincidence of wants. (1) Nebraska trades the wheat that Florida wants for money from Floridians; (2) Nebraska trades the money it receives from Florida for the potatoes it wants from Idaho; (3) Idaho trades the money it receives from Nebraska for the oranges it wants from Florida.

goods, say, wheat for oranges. But barter poses serious problems because it requires a *coincidence of wants* between the buyer and the seller. In our example, we assumed that Nebraskans had excess wheat to trade and wanted oranges. And we assumed that Floridians had excess oranges to trade and wanted wheat. So an exchange occurred. But if such a coincidence of wants is missing, trade is stymied.

Suppose that Nebraska has no interest in Florida's oranges but wants potatoes from Idaho. And suppose that Idaho wants Florida's oranges but not Nebraska's wheat. And, to complicate matters, suppose that Florida wants some of Nebraska's wheat but none of Idaho's potatoes. We summarize the situation in Figure 2.1.

In none of the cases shown in the figure is there a coincidence of wants. Trade by barter clearly would be difficult. Instead, people in each state use **money,** which is simply a convenient social invention to facilitate exchanges of goods and services. Historically, people have used cattle, cigarettes, shells, stones, pieces of metal, and many other commodities, with varying degrees of success, as money. To serve as money, an item needs to pass only one test: It must be generally acceptable to sellers in exchange for their goods and services. Money is socially defined; whatever society accepts as a medium of exchange *is* money.

Today, most economies use pieces of paper as money. The use of paper dollars (currency) as a medium of exchange is what enables Nebraska, Florida, and Idaho to overcome their trade stalemate, as demonstrated in Figure 2.1.

On a global basis, specialization and exchange are complicated by the fact that different nations have different currencies. But markets in which currencies are bought and sold make it possible for people living in different countries to exchange goods and services without resorting to barter.

Active, but Limited, Government

An active, but limited, government is the final characteristic of market systems in modern advanced industrial economies. Although a market system promotes a high degree of efficiency in the use of its resources, it has certain inherent shortcomings, called "market failures." We will discover in subsequent chapters that governments can often increase the overall effectiveness of a market system in several ways. That being said, governments have their own set of shortcomings that can themselves cause substantial misallocations of resources. Consequently, we will also investigate several types of "government failure."

AP QUICK REVIEW 2.2

- ✓ Modern market systems are characterized by extensive use of technologically advanced capital goods, fostering competition, freedom of choice, self-interest, and personal reward. Greater production efficiency is achieved.
- ✓ Specialization is extensive in market systems; it enhances efficiency and output by enabling individuals, regions, and nations to produce the goods and services for which their resources are best suited.
- ✓ Money is a social invention to facilitate the exchange of goods and services, and to serve as a store of value.

AP Five Fundamental Questions

LO2.3 Explain how the market system answers the five fundamental questions of what to produce, how to produce, who obtains the output, how to adjust to change, and how to promote progress.

The key features of the market system help explain how market economies respond to five fundamental questions:

- What goods and services will be produced?
- How will the goods and services be produced?
- Who will get the goods and services?
- How will the system accommodate change?
- How will the system promote progress?

CONSIDER THIS . . .

McHits and McMisses

Source: © The McGraw-Hill Education/John Flournoy, photographer

McDonald's has introduced several new menu items over the decades. Some have been profitable "hits," while others have been "misses." In a market system, consumers ultimately decide whether a menu item is profitable and therefore whether it stays on the McDonald's menu.

- Hulaburger (1962)—McMiss
- Filet-O-Fish (1963)—McHit
- Strawberry shortcake (1966)—McMiss
- Big Mac (1968)—McHit
- Hot apple pie (1968)—McHit
- Egg McMuffin (1975)—McHit
- Drive-thru (1975)—McHit
- Chicken McNuggets (1983)—McHit
- Arch Deluxe (1996)—McMiss
- McSalad Shaker (2000)—McMiss
- McGriddle (2003)—McHit
- Snack Wrap (2006)—McHit
- Fish McBites (2012)—McMiss

Sources: Passikoff, Robert, "McDonald's Fish McBites Flounders," *Forbes,* March 12, 2013, forbes.com; Machan, Dyan, "Polishing the Golden Arches," *Forbes,* June 15, 1998, pp. 42–43, updated.

These five questions highlight the economic choices underlying the production possibilities curve discussed in Chapter 1. They reflect the reality of scarce resources in a world of unlimited wants. All economies, whether market or command, must address these five questions.

What Will Be Produced?

How will a market system decide on the specific types and quantities of goods to be produced? The simple answer is this: The goods and services that can be produced at a continuing profit will be produced, while those whose production generates a continuing loss will be discontinued. Profits and losses are the difference between the total revenue (TR) a firm receives from the sale of its products and the total cost (TC) of producing those products. (For economists, total costs include not only wage and salary payments to labor, and interest and rental payments for capital and land, but also payments to the entrepreneur for organizing and combining the other resources to produce a product.)

Continuing economic profit (TR > TC) in an industry results in expanded production and the movement of resources toward that industry. Existing firms grow and new firms enter. The industry expands. Continuing losses (TC > TR) in an industry lead to reduced production and the exit of resources from that industry. Some existing firms shrink in size; others go out of business. The industry contracts. In the market system, consumers are sovereign (in command). **Consumer sovereignty** is crucial in determining the types and quantities of goods produced. Consumers spend their income on the goods they are most willing and able to buy. Through these **"dollar votes"** they register their wants in the market. If the dollar votes for a certain product are great enough to create a profit, businesses will produce that product and offer it for sale. In contrast, if the dollar votes do not create sufficient revenues to cover costs, businesses will not produce the product. So the consumers are sovereign. They collectively direct resources to industries that are meeting consumer wants and away from industries that are not meeting consumer wants.

The dollar votes of consumers determine not only which industries will continue to exist but also which products will survive or fail. Only profitable industries, firms, and products survive. So firms are not as free to produce whatever products they wish as one might otherwise think. Consumers' buying decisions make the production of some products profitable and the production of other products unprofitable, thus restricting the choice of businesses in deciding what to produce. Businesses must match their production choices with consumer choices or else face losses and eventual bankruptcy.

The same holds true for resource suppliers. The employment of resources derives from the sale of the goods and services that the resources help produce. Autoworkers are employed because automobiles are sold. There are few remaining professors of early Latin because there are few people desiring to learn the Latin language. Resource suppliers, desiring to earn income, are not truly free to allocate their resources to the production of goods that consumers do not value highly. Consumers register their preferences in the market; producers and resource suppliers, prompted by their own self-interest, respond appropriately.

How Will the Goods and Services Be Produced?

What combinations of resources and technologies will be used to produce goods and services? How will the production be organized? The answer: In combinations and ways that minimize the cost per unit of output. This is true because inefficiency drives up costs and lowers profits. As a result, any firm wishing to maximize its profits will make great efforts to minimize production costs. These efforts will include using the right mix of labor and capital, given the prices and productivity of those resources. They also mean locating production facilities optimally to hold down production and transportation expenses.

Those efforts will be intensified if the firm faces competition, as consumers strongly prefer low prices and will shift their purchases over to the firms that can produce a quality product at the lowest possible price. Any firm foolish enough to use higher-cost production methods will go bankrupt as it is undersold by its more efficient competitors who can still make a profit when selling at a lower price. Simply stated: Competition eliminates high-cost producers.

Least-cost production means that firms must employ the most economically efficient technique of production in producing their output. The most efficient production technique depends on

- The available technology, that is, the available body of knowledge and techniques that can be used to combine economic resources to produce the desired results.
- The prices of the needed resources.

A technique that requires just a few inputs of resources to produce a specific output may be highly inefficient economically if those resources are valued very highly in the market. Economic efficiency requires obtaining a particular output of product with the least input of scarce resources, when both output and resource inputs are measured in dollars and cents. The combination of resources that will produce, say, $15 worth of bathroom soap at the lowest possible cost is the most efficient.

Suppose there are three possible techniques for producing the desired $15 worth of bars of soap. Suppose also that the quantity of each resource required by each production technique and the prices of the required resources are as shown in Table 2.1. By multiplying the required quantities of each resource by its price in each of the three techniques, we can determine the total cost of producing $15 worth of soap by means of each technique.

Technique 2 is economically the most efficient because it is the least costly. It enables society to obtain $15 worth of output by using a smaller amount of resources—$13 worth—than the $15 worth required by the two other techniques. Competition will dictate that producers use technique 2. Thus, the question of how goods will be produced is answered. They will be produced in a least-cost way.

A change in either technology or resource prices, however, may cause a firm to shift from the technology it is using. If the price of labor falls to $0.50, technique 1 becomes more desirable than technique 2. Firms will find they can lower their costs by shifting to a technology that uses more of the resource whose price has fallen. Exercise: Would a new technique involving 1 unit of labor, 4 of land, 1 of capital, and 1 of entrepreneurial ability be preferable to the techniques listed in Table 2.1, assuming the resource prices shown there?

Who Will Get the Output?

The market system enters the picture in two ways when determining the distribution of total output. Generally, any product will be distributed to consumers on the basis of their ability and willingness to pay its existing market price. If the price of some product, say, a small sailboat, is $3,000, then buyers who are willing and able to pay that price will "sail, sail away." Consumers who are unwilling or unable to pay the price will be "sitting on the dock of the bay."

The ability to pay the prices for sailboats and other products depends on the amount of income that consumers have, along with the prices of, and preferences for, various goods. If consumers have sufficient income and want to spend their money on a particular good, they can have it. The amount of income they have depends on (1) the quantities of the property and human resources they supply and (2) the prices those resources command in the resource market. Resource prices (wages, interest, rent, profit) are crucial in determining the size of each person's income and therefore each person's ability to buy part of the economy's output. If a lawyer earning $130 an hour and a janitor earning $13 an hour both work the same number of hours each year, then each year the lawyer will be able to purchase 10 times more of society's output than the janitor.

How Will the System Accommodate Change?

Market systems are dynamic: Consumer preferences, technologies, and resource supplies all change. This means that the particular allocation of resources that is now the most efficient for a specific pattern of consumer tastes, range of

TABLE 2.1 Three Techniques for Producing $15 Worth of Bar Soap

		Units of Resource					
		Technique 1		Technique 2		Technique 3	
Resource	Price per Unit of Resource	Units	Cost	Units	Cost	Units	Cost
Labor	$2	4	$ 8	2	$ 4	1	$ 2
Land	1	1	1	3	3	4	4
Capital	3	1	3	1	3	2	6
Entrepreneurial ability	3	1	3	1	3	1	3
Total cost of $15 worth of bar soap			$15		$13		$15

technological alternatives, and amount of available resources will become obsolete and inefficient as consumer preferences change, new techniques of production are discovered, and resource supplies change over time. Can the market economy adjust to such changes?

Suppose consumer tastes change. For instance, assume that consumers decide they want more fruit juice and less milk than the economy currently provides. Those changes in consumer tastes will be communicated to producers through an increase in spending on fruit and a decline in spending on milk. Other things equal, prices and profits in the fruit juice industry will rise and those in the milk industry will fall. Self-interest will induce existing competitors to expand output and entice new competitors to enter the prosperous fruit industry and will in time force firms to scale down—or even exit—the depressed milk industry.

The higher prices and greater economic profit in the fruit-juice industry will not only induce that industry to expand but also give it the revenue needed to obtain the resources essential to its growth. Higher prices and profits will permit fruit producers to attract more resources from less urgent alternative uses. The reverse occurs in the milk industry, where fewer workers and other resources are employed. These adjustments in the economy are appropriate responses to the changes in consumer tastes. This is consumer sovereignty at work.

The market system is a gigantic communications system. Through changes in prices and profits, it communicates changes in such basic matters as consumer tastes and elicits appropriate responses from businesses and resource suppliers. By affecting price and profits, changes in consumer tastes direct the expansion of some industries and the contraction of others. Those adjustments are conveyed to the resource market. As expanding industries employ more resources and contracting industries employ fewer, the resulting changes in resource prices (wages and salaries, for example) and income flows guide resources from the contracting industries to the expanding industries.

This directing or guiding function of prices and profits is a core element of the market system. Without such a system, a government planning board or some other administrative agency would have to direct businesses and resources into the appropriate industries. A similar analysis shows that the system can and does adjust to other fundamental changes—for example, to changes in technology and in the prices of various resources.

How Will the System Promote Progress?

Society desires economic growth (greater output) and higher standards of living (greater output *per person*). How does the market system promote technological improvements and capital accumulation, both of which contribute to a higher standard of living for society?

Technological Advance The market system provides a strong incentive for technological advance and enables better products and processes to supplant inferior ones. An entrepreneur or firm that introduces a popular new product will gain revenue and economic profit at the expense of rivals. Firms that are highly profitable one year may find they are in financial trouble just a few years later. Technological advance also includes new and improved methods that reduce production or distribution costs. By passing part of its cost reduction on to the consumer through a lower product price, a firm can increase sales and obtain economic profit at the expense of rival firms.

Moreover, the market system promotes the *rapid spread* of technological advance throughout an industry. Rival firms must follow the lead of the most innovative firm or else suffer immediate losses and eventual failure. In some cases, the result is **creative destruction:** The creation of new products and production methods completely destroys the market positions of firms that are wedded to existing products and older ways of doing business. Example: Compact discs largely demolished vinyl records before MP3 players and then online streaming subsequently supplanted compact discs.

Capital Accumulation Most technological advances require additional capital goods. The market system provides the resources necessary to produce additional capital goods through increased dollar votes for those goods. That is, the market system acknowledges dollar voting for capital goods as well as for consumer goods.

But who counts the dollar votes for capital goods? Answer: Entrepreneurs and business owners. As receivers of profit income, they often use part of that income to purchase capital goods. Doing so yields even greater profit income in the future if the technological innovation that required the additional capital goods is successful. Also, by paying interest or selling ownership shares, the entrepreneur and firm can attract some of the income of households as saving to increase their dollar votes for the production of more capital goods.

AP QUICK REVIEW 2.3

- ✓ The output mix of the market system is determined by business producing to seek economic profits, which, in turn, depend heavily on consumer preferences. Consumer sovereignty means that "dollar votes" signal consumer wants in the marketplace. Note that dollar votes reflect relative income levels.
- ✓ Competition forces industries to use the least costly production methods.
- ✓ In a market economy, consumer income and product prices determine which output will be produced and how it is distributed within the society.
- ✓ The directing or guiding function of prices and profits helps individuals and businesses see the changes in the market and react appropriately.
- ✓ Competitive markets create incentives for technological advance and capital accumulation, both of which contribute to increases in standards of living.

The "Invisible Hand"

LO2.4 Explain the operation of the "invisible hand" and why market economies usually do a better job than command economies at efficiently transforming economic resources into desirable output.

In his 1776 book *The Wealth of Nations,* Adam Smith first noted that the operation of a market system creates a curious unity between private interests and social interests. Firms and resource suppliers, seeking to further their own self-interest and operating within the framework of a highly competitive market system, will simultaneously, as though guided by an **"invisible hand,"** promote the public or social interest. For example, we have seen that in a competitive environment, businesses seek to build new and improved products to increase profits. Those enhanced products increase society's well-being. Businesses also use the least costly combination of resources to produce a specific output because doing so is in their self-interest. To act otherwise would be to forgo profit or even to risk business failure. But, at the same time, to use scarce resources in the least costly way is clearly in the social interest as well. It "frees up" resources to produce other things that society desires.

Self-interest, awakened and guided by the competitive market system, is what induces responses appropriate to the changes in society's wants. Businesses seeking to make higher profits and to avoid losses, and resource suppliers pursuing greater monetary rewards, negotiate changes in the allocation of resources and end up with the output that society wants. Competition controls or guides self-interest such that self-interest automatically and quite unintentionally furthers the best interest of society. The invisible hand ensures that when firms maximize their profits and resource suppliers maximize their incomes, these groups also help maximize society's output and income.

Of the various virtues of the market system, three merit reemphasis:

- ***Efficiency*** The market system promotes the efficient use of resources by guiding them into the production of the goods and services most wanted by society. It forces the use of the most efficient techniques in organizing resources for production, and it encourages the development and adoption of new and more efficient production techniques.
- ***Incentives*** The market system encourages skill acquisition, hard work, and innovation. Greater work skills and effort mean greater production and higher incomes, which usually translate into a higher standard of living. Similarly, the assuming of risks by entrepreneurs can result in substantial profit incomes. Successful innovations generate economic rewards.
- ***Freedom*** The major noneconomic argument for the market system is its emphasis on personal freedom. In contrast to central planning, the market system coordinates economic activity without coercion. The market system permits—indeed, it thrives on—freedom of enterprise and choice. Entrepreneurs and workers are free to further their own self-interest, subject to the rewards and penalties imposed by the market system itself.

Of course, no economic system, including the market system, is flawless. In Chapter 4 we will explain two well-known shortcomings of the market system and examine the government policies that try to remedy them.

The Demise of the Command Systems

Our discussion of how a market system answers the five fundamental questions provides insights on why the command systems of the Soviet Union, eastern Europe, and China (prior to its market reforms) failed. Those systems encountered two insurmountable problems.

The Coordination Problem The first difficulty was the coordination problem. The central planners had to coordinate the millions of individual decisions by consumers, resource suppliers, and businesses. Consider the setting up of a factory to produce tractors. The central planners had to establish a realistic annual production target, for example, 1,000 tractors. They then had to make available all the necessary inputs—labor, machinery, electric power, steel, tires, glass, paint, transportation—for the production and delivery of those 1,000 tractors.

Because the outputs of many industries serve as inputs to other industries, the failure of any single industry to achieve its output target caused a chain reaction of repercussions. For example, if iron mines, for want of machinery or labor or transportation, did not supply the steel industry with the required inputs of iron ore, the steel mills were unable to fulfill the input needs of the many industries that depended on steel. Those steel-using industries (such as tractor, automobile, and transportation) were unable to fulfill their planned production goals. Eventually the chain reaction spread to all firms that used steel as an input and from there to other input buyers or final consumers.

The coordination problem became more difficult as the economies expanded. Products and production processes grew more sophisticated and the number of industries requiring planning increased. Planning techniques that worked for the simpler economy proved highly inadequate and inefficient for the larger economy. Bottlenecks and production stoppages became the norm, not the exception. In trying to cope, planners further suppressed product variety, focusing on one or two products in each product category.

A lack of a reliable success indicator added to the coordination problem in the Soviet Union and China prior to its market reforms. We have seen that market economies rely on profit as a success indicator. Profit depends on consumer demand, production efficiency, and product quality. In contrast, the major success indicator for the command economies usually was a quantitative production target that the central planners assigned. Production costs, product quality, and product mix were secondary considerations. Managers and workers often sacrificed product quality and variety because they were being awarded bonuses for meeting quantitative, not qualitative, targets. If meeting production goals meant sloppy assembly work and little product variety, so be it.

It was difficult at best for planners to assign quantitative production targets without unintentionally producing distortions in output. If the plan specified a production target for producing nails in terms of *weight* (tons of nails), the enterprise made only large nails. But if it specified the target as a *quantity* (thousands of nails), the firm made all small nails, and lots of them! That is precisely what happened in the centrally planned economies.

The Incentive Problem

The command economies also faced an incentive problem. Central planners determined the output mix. When they misjudged how many automobiles, shoes, shirts, and chickens were wanted at the government-determined prices, persistent shortages and surpluses of those products arose. But as long as the managers who oversaw the production of those goods were rewarded for meeting their assigned production goals, they had no incentive to adjust production in response to the shortages and surpluses. And there were no fluctuations in prices and profitability to signal that more or less of certain products was desired. Thus, many products were unavailable or in short supply, while other products were overproduced and sat for months or years in warehouses.

The command systems of the former Soviet Union and China before its market reforms also lacked entrepreneurship. Central planning did not trigger the profit motive, nor did it reward innovation and enterprise. The route for getting ahead was through participation in the political hierarchy of the Communist Party. Moving up the hierarchy meant better housing, better access to health care, and the right to shop in special stores. Meeting production targets and maneuvering through the minefields of party politics were measures of success in "business." But a definition of business success based solely on political savvy was not conducive to technological advance, which is often disruptive to existing products, production methods, and organizational structures.

CONSIDER THIS . . .

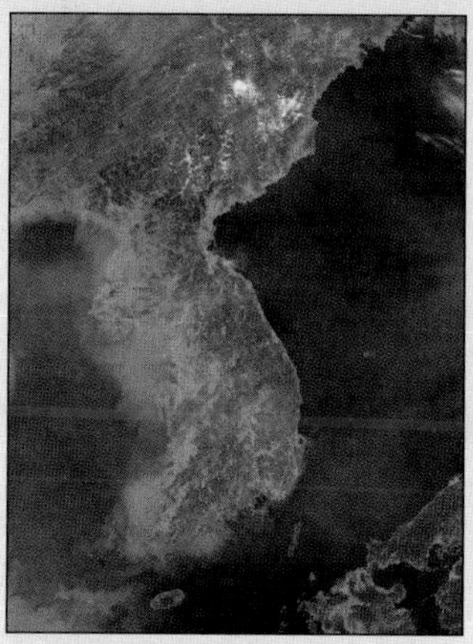

Source: © Stocktrek Images/Getty Images RF

The Two Koreas

North Korea is one of the few command economies still standing. After the Second World War, the Korean peninsula was divided into North Korea and South Korea. North Korea, under the influence of the Soviet Union, established a command economy that emphasized government ownership and central government planning. South Korea, protected by the United States, established a market economy based upon private ownership and the profit motive. Today, the differences in the economic outcomes of the two systems are striking:

	North Korea	South Korea
GDP	\$40 billion*	\$1.8 trillion*
GDP per capita	\$1,800*	\$34,200*
Exports	\$2.2 billion	\$911 billion
Imports	\$4.4 billion	\$815 billion
Agriculture as % of GDP	23 percent	2.3 percent

*Based on purchasing power equivalencies to the U.S. dollar.

Source: CIA World Fact Book, 2014, **www.cia.gov**.

AP The Circular Flow Model

LO2.5 Describe the mechanics of the circular flow model.

The dynamic market economy creates continuous, repetitive flows of goods and services, resources, and money. The **circular flow diagram,** shown in **Figure 2.2 (Key Graph),** illustrates those flows for a simplified economy in which there is no government. Observe that in the diagram we group this economy's decision makers into *businesses* and *households*. Additionally, we divide this economy's markets into the *resource market* and the *product market*.

Households

The blue rectangle on the right side of the circular flow diagram in Figure 2.2 represents **households,** which are defined as one or more persons occupying a housing unit. There are currently about 118 million households in the U.S. economy. Households buy the goods and services that businesses make available in the product market. Households obtain the income needed to buy those products by selling resources in the resource market.

All the resources in our no-government economy are ultimately owned or provided by households. For instance, the members of one household or another directly provide all of the labor and entrepreneurial ability in the economy. Households also own all of the land and all of the capital in the economy either directly, as personal property, or indirectly, as a consequence of owning all of the businesses in the economy

AP KEY GRAPH

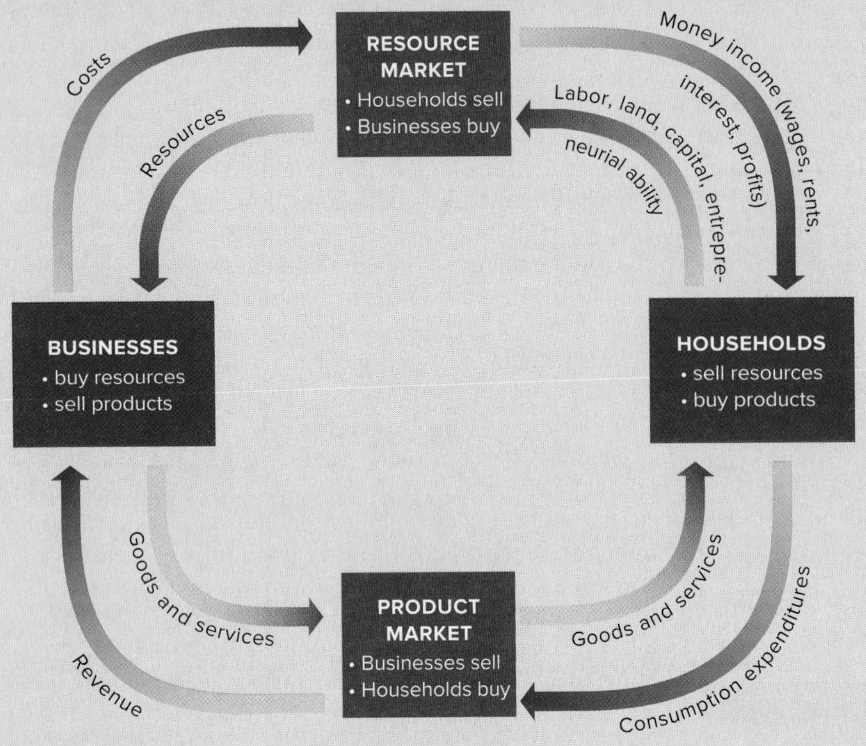

FIGURE 2.2 The circular flow diagram. Resources flow from households to businesses through the resource market, and products flow from businesses to households through the product market. Opposite these real flows are monetary flows. Households receive income from businesses (their costs) through the resource market, and businesses receive revenue from households (their expenditures) through the product market.

QUICK QUIZ FOR FIGURE 2.2

1. The resource market is the place where:
- **a.** households sell products and businesses buy products.
- **b.** businesses sell resources and households sell products.
- **c.** households sell resources and businesses buy resources (or the services of resources).
- **d.** businesses sell resources and households buy resources (or the services of resources).

2. Which of the following would be determined in the product market?
- **a.** a manager's salary.
- **b.** the price of equipment used in a bottling plant.
- **c.** the price of 80 acres of farmland.
- **d.** the price of a new pair of athletic shoes.

3. In this circular flow diagram:
- **a.** money flows counterclockwise.
- **b.** resources flow counterclockwise.
- **c.** goods and services flow clockwise.
- **d.** households are on the selling side of the product market.

4. In this circular flow diagram:
- **a.** households spend income in the product market.
- **b.** firms sell resources to households.
- **c.** households receive income through the product market.
- **d.** households produce goods.

Answers: 1. c; 2. d; 3. b; 4. a

(and thereby controlling all of the land and capital owned by businesses). Thus, all of the income in the economy—all wages, rents, interest, and profits—flows to households because they provide the economy's labor, land, capital, and entrepreneurial ability.

Businesses

The blue rectangle on the left side of the circular flow diagram represents **businesses,** which are commercial establishments that attempt to earn profits for their owners by offering goods and services for sale. Businesses fall into three main categories.

- A **sole proprietorship** is a business owned and managed by a single person. The proprietor (the owner) may work alone or have employees. Examples include a woman who runs her own tree-cutting business and an independent accountant who, with two assistants, helps his clients with their taxes.
- The **partnership** form of business organization is a natural outgrowth of the sole proprietorship. In a

partnership, two or more individuals (the partners) agree to own and operate a business together. They pool their financial resources and business skills to operate the business, and they share any profits or losses that the business may generate. Many law firms and dental practices are organized as partnerships, as are a wide variety of firms in many other industries.

- A **corporation** is an independent legal entity that can—on its own behalf—acquire resources, own assets, produce and sell products, incur debts, extend credit, sue and be sued, and otherwise engage in any legal business activity.

The fact that a corporation is an independent legal entity means that its owners bear no personal financial responsibility for the fulfillment of the corporation's debts and obligations. For instance, if a corporation has failed to repay a loan to a bank, the bank can sue the corporation but not its owners. Professional managers run most corporations. They are hired and supervised by a board of directors that is elected annually by the corporation's owners. Google, Ford, and American Airlines are examples of large corporations, but corporations come in all sizes and operate in every type of industry.

There currently are about 30 million businesses in the United States, ranging from enormous corporations like Walmart, with 2012 sales of $444 billion and 2.2 million employees, to single-person sole proprietorships with sales of less than $100 per day.

Businesses sell goods and services in the product market in order to obtain revenue, and they incur costs in the resource market when they purchase the labor, land, capital, and entrepreneurial ability that they need to produce their respective goods and services.

Product Market

The red rectangle at the bottom of the diagram represents the **product market,** the place where the goods and services produced by businesses are bought and sold. Households use the income they receive from the sale of resources to buy goods and services. The money that they spend on goods and services flows to businesses as revenue.

Resource Market

Finally, the red rectangle at the top of the circular flow diagram represents the **resource market** in which households sell resources to businesses. The households sell resources to generate income, and the businesses buy resources to produce goods and services. Productive resources flow from households to businesses, while money flows from businesses to households in the form of wages, rents, interest, and profits.

To summarize, the circular flow model depicts a complex web of economic activity in which businesses and households are both buyers and sellers. Businesses buy resources and sell products. Households buy products and sell resources. The counterclockwise flow of economic resources and finished products that is illustrated by the red arrows in Figure 2.2 is paid for by the clockwise flow of money income and consumption expenditures illustrated by the blue arrows.

AP QUICK REVIEW 2.4

✓ Competition directs individuals and firms to unwittingly promote the social interest (the "invisible hand"), as measured by economic surplus to consumers, producers, and owners of factors of production.

✓ The circular flow model illustrates how resources flow from households to businesses and how payments for those resources flow from businesses to households. The product market is where goods and services produced by business are bought and sold. The resource market is where households sell their resources to businesses.

How the Market System Deals with Risk

LO2.6 Explain how the market system deals with risk.

Producing goods and services is risky. Input shortages can suddenly arise. Consumer preferences can quickly change. Natural disasters can destroy factories and cripple supply chains.

For an economic system to maximize its potential, it must develop methods for assessing and managing risk. The market system does so by confronting business owners with the financial consequences of their decisions. If they manage risks well, they may prosper. If they manage risks poorly, they may lose everything.

The Profit System

As explained in Chapter 1, entrepreneurial ability is the economic resource that organizes and directs the other three resources of land, labor, and capital toward productive uses. The owners of a firm may attempt to supply the entrepreneurial ability themselves. Or they can hire professional managers to supply the necessary leadership and decision making. Either way, it falls to those acting as the firm's entrepreneurs to deal with risk.

They are guided toward sensible decisions by the so-called *profit system.* This system is actually a *profit and loss* system because the entrepreneurs who must deal with risk and uncertainty gain profits if they choose wisely but suffer losses if they choose poorly. That provides them with a large financial incentive to avoid unnecessary risks and make prudent decisions.

By contrast, risk management tends to be done very poorly in command economies because the central planners who must allocate resources and deal with risk do not themselves face the possibility of losing money if they make bad decisions. As government employees, they tend to receive the same salaries whether things go well or poorly.

Shielding Employees and Suppliers from Business Risk

Under the market system, only a firm's owners are subject to business risk and the possibility of losing money. By contrast, the firm's employees and suppliers are shielded from business risk because they are legally entitled to receive their contracted wages and payments on time and in full regardless of whether the firm is earning a profit or generating a loss.

To see how this works, consider a pizza parlor that is being started in a small town. Its investors put up $50,000 to get it going. They rent a storefront, lease ovens, purchase computers, and leave some money set aside as a reserve.

The firm then has to attract employees. To do so, it will offer wage contracts that promise to pay employees every two weeks without regard to whether the firm is making a profit or generating a loss. This guarantee shields the firm's employees from the risks of owning and operating the business. They will get paid even if the pizza parlor is losing money.

In the same way, the contracts that the firm signs with its suppliers and with anyone who loans the firm money (for instance, the local bank) will also specify that they will be paid on time and in full no matter how the firm is doing in terms of profitability.

Because everyone else is legally entitled to get paid before the firm's owners, the firm's owners are referred to as **residual claimants** in business law. The owners are obligated to receive (claim) whatever profit or loss remains (is residual) after all other parties have been paid.

Dealing with Losses So what happens if the firm starts losing money? In that case, the owners will take the financial hit. To be concrete, suppose that the pizza parlor loses $1,500 during the month of October because it runs up $11,500 in costs but generates only $10,000 in revenue. In that situation, the investors' wealth will shrink by $1,500 as the firm is forced to dip into its reserve to cover the loss. If the firm continues to lose money in subsequent months and exhausts the reserve, the owners will then have to decide whether they want to close the shop or put in additional money in the hope that things will turn around.

But throughout all those months of losses, the suppliers and employees are safeguarded. Because they are paid on time and in full, they are shielded from the firm's business risks and whether it is generating a profit or a loss.

CONSIDER THIS . . .

Source: © Robert J. Bennett/AGE Fotostock RF

Insurance

Insurance promotes economic growth and investment by transferring risk from those who have a low tolerance for risk to those who have a high tolerance for risk.

Consider fire insurance. Homeowners pay a monthly premium in exchange for which their insurance company guarantees to reimburse them if their house burns down. That guarantee transfers the risk of fire damage from the homeowners (who do not want to bear the risk) to the insurance company's owners (who are happy to bear the risk as a business proposition).

The insurance company will save the premiums that it receives from homeowners to help cover the rebuilding costs of any homes that do end up burning down. But it is quite possible that there will be so many fires that the insurance company will spend more money repairing fire damage than it received in premiums.

If that happens, the insurance company will suffer a loss that will fall upon the insurance company's owners. Their personal wealth will decline in order to make up for the unexpectedly high number of fires. Thus, the insurance company's owners ultimately bear the fire risk; it is to them that the insurance contract transfers risk.

But if the number of fires is unexpectedly small, the insurance company will turn a nice profit and the insurance company's owners will benefit from having been willing to bear the fire risk that the homeowners did not wish to bear.

More importantly, the economy's overall level of investment rises because the availability of insurance means that those who dislike risk are much more willing to invest their savings into the construction and purchase of capital goods like houses, cars, and factories.

As a result, however, they are not legally entitled to share in the profits if the firm does end up being profitable. That privilege is reserved under the market system for the firm's owners as their reward for bearing business risk. In exchange for making sure that everyone else is shielded if things go badly, the owners are legally entitled to take all of the profits if things go well.

Benefits of Restricting Business Risk to Owners

There are two major benefits that arise from the market system's restriction of business risk to owners and investors.

LAST WORD

Shuffling the Deck

Economist Donald Boudreaux Marvels at the Way the Market System Systematically and Purposefully Arranges the World's Tens of Billions of Individual Resources.

In *The Future and Its Enemies,* Virginia Postrel notes the astonishing fact that if you thoroughly shuffle an ordinary deck of 52 playing cards, chances are practically 100 percent that the resulting arrangement of cards has never before existed. *Never.* Every time you shuffle a deck, you produce an arrangement of cards that exists for the first time in history.

The arithmetic works out that way. For a very small number of items, the number of possible arrangements is small. Three items, for example, can be arranged only six different ways. But the number of possible arrangements grows very large very quickly. The number of different ways to arrange five items is 120 . . . for ten items it's 3,628,800 . . . for fifteen items it's 1,307,674,368,000.

The number of different ways to arrange 52 items is 8.066×10^{67}. This is a *big* number. No human can comprehend its enormousness. By way of comparison, the number of possible ways to arrange a mere 20 items is 2,432,902,008,176,640,000—a number larger than the total number of seconds that have elapsed since the beginning of time ten billion years ago—and this number is Lilliputian compared to 8.066×10^{67}.

What's the significance of these facts about numbers? Consider the number of different resources available in the world—my labor, your labor, your land, oil, tungsten, cedar, coffee beans, chickens, rivers, the Empire State Building, [Microsoft] Windows, the wharves at Houston, the classrooms at Oxford, the airport at Miami, and on and on and on. No one can possibly count all of the different productive resources available for our use. But we can be sure that this number is at least in the tens of billions.

When you reflect on how incomprehensibly large is the number of ways to arrange a deck containing a mere 52 cards, the mind boggles at the number of different ways to arrange all the world's resources.

If our world were random—if resources combined together haphazardly, as if a giant took them all into his hands and tossed them down like so many [cards]—it's a virtual certainty that the resulting combination of resources would be useless. Unless this chance arrangement were quickly rearranged according to some productive logic, nothing worthwhile would be produced. We would all starve to death. Because only a tiny fraction of possible arrangements serves human ends, any arrangement will be useless if it is chosen randomly or with inadequate knowledge of how each and every resource might be productively combined with each other.

Source: © Royalty-Free/Corbis RF

And yet, we witness all around us an arrangement of resources that's productive and serves human goals. Today's arrangement of resources might not be perfect, but it is vastly superior to most of the trillions upon trillions of other possible arrangements.

How have we managed to get one of the minuscule number of arrangements that works? The answer is private property—a social institution that encourages mutual accommodation.

Private property eliminates the possibility that resource arrangements will be random, for each resource owner chooses a course of action only if it promises rewards to the owner that exceed the rewards promised by all other available courses.

[The result] is a breathtakingly complex and productive arrangement of countless resources. This arrangement emerged over time (and is still emerging) as the result of billions upon billions of individual, daily, small decisions made by people seeking to better employ their resources and labor in ways that other people find helpful.

Source: Abridged from Donald J. Boudreaux, "Mutual Accommodation," *Ideas on Liberty,* May 2000, pp. 4–5. Used by permission of *The Freeman.*

Attracting Inputs Many people deeply dislike risk and would not be willing to participate in a business venture if they were exposed to the possibility of losing money. That is the case with many workers, who just want to do their jobs and get paid twice a month without having to worry about whether their employer is doing well or not. The same is true for most suppliers, who just want to get paid on time and in full for the inputs they supply to the firm.

For both groups, the concentration of business risk on owners and investors is very welcome because they can supply their resources to a firm without having to worry about the firm's profitability. That sense of security makes it much easier for firms to attract labor and other inputs, which in turn helps the economy innovate and grow.

Focusing Attention The profit system helps to achieve prudent risk management by focusing both the responsibility and the rewards for successfully managing risk onto a firm's owners. They can provide the risk-managing input of entrepreneurial ability themselves or hire it by paying a skilled manager. But either way, some individual's full-time job includes the specialized task of managing risk and making prudent decisions about the allocation of resources. By contrast, in a command system, the responsibility for managing risk tends to be spread out over several layers of government and many different committees so that nobody is personally responsible for bad outcomes.

AP QUICK REVIEW 2.5

- ✓ The market system incentivizes the prudent management of business risk by concentrating any profit or loss upon a firm's owners and investors.
- ✓ The market system generally shields employees, suppliers, and lenders from business risks, but in exchange for that protection, they are excluded from any profit that may be earned.
- ✓ By focusing risk on owners and investors, the market system (a) creates an incentive for owners and investors to hire managerial and entrepreneurial specialists to prudently manage business risks and (b) encourages the participation of workers, suppliers, and lenders who dislike risk.

SUMMARY

LO2.1 Differentiate between laissez-faire capitalism, the command system, and the market system.

Laissez-faire capitalism is a hypothetical economic system in which government's role would be restricted to protecting private property and enforcing contracts. All real-world economic systems have featured a more extensive role for government. Governments in command systems own nearly all property and resources and make nearly all decisions about what to produce, how to produce it, and who gets the output. Most countries today, including the United States, have market systems in which the government does play a large role, but in which most property and resources are privately owned and markets are the major force in determining what to produce, how to produce it, and who gets it.

LO2.2 List the main characteristics of the market system.

The market system is characterized by the private ownership of resources, including capital, and the freedom of individuals to engage in economic activities of their choice to advance their material well-being. Self-interest is the driving force of such an economy and competition functions as a regulatory or control mechanism.

In the market system, markets, prices, and profits organize and make effective the many millions of individual economic decisions that occur daily.

Specialization, use of advanced technology, and the extensive use of capital goods are common features of market systems. Functioning as a medium of exchange, money eliminates the problems of bartering and permits easy trade and greater specialization, both domestically and internationally.

LO2.3 Explain how the market system answers the five fundamental questions of what to produce, how to produce, who obtains the output, how to adjust to change, and how to promote progress.

Every economy faces five fundamental questions: (a) What goods and services will be produced? (b) How will the goods and services be produced? (c) Who will get the goods and services? (d) How will the system accommodate change? (e) How will the system promote progress?

The market system produces products whose production and sale yield total revenue sufficient to cover total cost. It does not produce products for which total revenue continuously falls short of total cost. Competition forces firms to use the lowest-cost production techniques.

Economic profit (total revenue minus total cost) indicates that an industry is prosperous and promotes its expansion. Losses signify that an industry is not prosperous and hasten its contraction.

Consumer sovereignty means that both businesses and resource suppliers are subject to the wants of consumers. Through their dollar votes, consumers decide on the composition of output.

The prices that a household receives for the resources it supplies to the economy determine that household's income. This income determines the household's claim on the economy's output. Those who have income to spend get the products produced in the market system.

By communicating changes in consumer tastes to entrepreneurs and resource suppliers, the market system prompts appropriate adjustments in the allocation of the economy's resources. The market system also encourages technological advance and capital accumulation, both of which raise a nation's standard of living.

LO2.4 Explain the operation of the "invisible hand" and why market economies usually do a better job than command economies at efficiently transforming economic resources into desirable output.

Competition, the primary mechanism of control in the market economy, promotes a unity of self-interest and social interests. As if directed by an invisible hand, competition harnesses the self-interested motives of businesses and resource suppliers to further the social interest.

The command systems of the Soviet Union and pre-reform China met their demise because of coordination difficulties caused by central planning and the lack of a profit incentive. The coordination problem resulted in bottlenecks, inefficiencies, and a focus on a limited number of products. The incentive problem discouraged product improvement, new product development, and entrepreneurship.

LO2.5 Describe the mechanics of the circular flow model.

The circular flow model illustrates the flows of resources and products from households to businesses and from businesses to households, along with the corresponding monetary flows. Businesses are on the buying side of the resource market and the selling side of the product market. Households are on the selling side of the resource market and the buying side of the product market.

LO2.6 Explain how the market system deals with risk.

By focusing business risks onto owners, the market system encourages the participation of workers and suppliers who dislike risk while at the same time creating a strong incentive for owners to manage business risks prudently.

TERMS AND CONCEPTS

economic system	specialization	households
laissez-faire capitalism	division of labor	businesses
command system	medium of exchange	sole proprietorship
market system	barter	partnership
private property	money	corporation
freedom of enterprise	consumer sovereignty	product market
freedom of choice	dollar votes	resource market
self-interest	creative destruction	residual claimant
competition	invisible hand	
market	circular flow diagram	

The following and additional problems can be found in connect

DISCUSSION QUESTIONS

1. Contrast how a market system and a command economy try to cope with economic scarcity. LO2.1
2. How does self-interest help achieve society's economic goals? Why is there such a wide variety of desired goods and services in a market system? In what way are entrepreneurs and businesses at the helm of the economy but commanded by consumers? LO2.2
3. Why is private property, and the protection of property rights, so critical to the success of the market system? How do property rights encourage cooperation? LO2.2
4. What are the advantages of using capital in the production process? What is meant by the term "division of labor"? What are the advantages of specialization in the use of human and material resources? Explain why exchange is the necessary consequence of specialization. LO2.2
5. What problem does barter entail? Indicate the economic significance of money as a medium of exchange. What is meant by the statement "We want money only to part with it"? LO2.2
6. Evaluate and explain the following statements: LO2.2
   a. The market system is a profit-and-loss system.
   b. Competition is the disciplinarian of the market economy.
7. Some large hardware stores, such as Home Depot, boast of carrying as many as 20,000 different products in each store. What motivated the producers of those individual products to make them and offer them for sale? How did the producers decide on the best combinations of resources to use? Who made those resources available, and why? Who decides whether these particular hardware products should continue to be produced and offered for sale? LO2.3

8. What is meant by the term "creative destruction"? How does the emergence of MP3 (or iPod) technology relate to this idea? LO2.3
9. In a sentence, describe the meaning of the phrase "invisible hand." LO2.4
10. In market economies, firms rarely worry about the availability of inputs to produce their products, whereas in command economies input availability is a constant concern. Why the difference? LO2.4
11. Distinguish between the resource market and the product market in the circular flow model. In what way are businesses and households both sellers and buyers in this model? What are the flows in the circular flow model? LO2.5
12. How does shielding employees and suppliers from business risk help to improve economic outcomes? Who is responsible for managing business risks in the market system? LO2.6
13. **LAST WORD** What explains why millions of economic resources tend to get arranged logically and productively rather than haphazardly and unproductively?

AP REVIEW QUESTIONS

1. Decide whether each of the following descriptions most closely corresponds to being part of a command system, a mixed economic system, or a pure market system. LO2.1
   a. A woman who wants to start a flower shop finds she cannot do so unless the central government has already decided to allow a flower shop in her area.
   b. Shops stock and sell the goods their customers want.
   c. The only taxes levied by the government are to pay for national defense, law enforcement, and a legal system designed to enforce contracts between private citizens.
2. Match each term with the correct definition. LO2.2
   private property
   freedom of enterprise
   mutually agreeable
   freedom of choice
   self-interest
   competition
   market
   a. An institution that brings buyers and sellers together.
   b. The right of private persons and firms to obtain, control, employ, dispose of, and bequeath land, capital, and other property.
   c. The presence in a market of independent buyers and sellers who compete with one another and who are free to enter and exit the market as they each see fit.
   d. The freedom of firms to obtain economic resources, decide what products to produce with those resources, and sell those products in markets of their choice.
   e. What each individual or firm believes is best for itself and seeks to obtain.
   f. Economic transactions willingly undertaken by both the buyer and the seller because each feels that the transaction will make him or her better off.
   g. The freedom of resource owners to dispose of their resources as they think best; of workers to enter any line of work for which they are qualified; and of consumers to spend their incomes in whatever way they feel is most appropriate.
3. True or False: Money must be issued by a government for people to accept it. LO2.2
4. The product market is the place where: LO2.3
   a. Households sell products and businesses buy products.
   b. Businesses sell resources and households sell products.
   c. Households sell resources and businesses buy resources.
   d. Businesses sell resources and households buy resources.
   e. Businesses sell products and households buy products
5. Households and businesses: LO2.3
   a. Are both buyers in the resource market.
   b. Are both sellers in the product market.
   c. Are sellers in the resource and product markets, respectively.
   d. Are sellers in the product and resource markets, respectively.
   e. Do not interact in the resource maket
6. The invisible-hand concept suggests that: LO2.4
   a. Government action is necessary to correct for market failures.
   b. Changes in product demands are only randomly reflected in changes in the demands for resources.
   c. Profit maximization is inconsistent with an efficient allocation of resources.
   d. The profit motive of firms drives all other firms from the marketplace
   e. When competitive firms maximize their profits, the correct allocation of outputs will be produced
7. Consider the market for apple pickers. Respectively, who sells labor services (to pick apples) in the resource market, and who buys labor services (needing apples to be picked) in the resource market? LO2.5

	Sells	Buys
a.	households	firms
b.	households	households
c.	firms	firms
d.	firms	households
e.	firms	individuals

8. Franklin, John, Henry, and Harry have decided to pool their financial resources and business skills in order to open up and run a coffee shop. They will share any profits or losses that the business generates and will be personally responsible for making good on any debt that their business undertakes. Their business should be classified as a: LO2.6
   a. corporation.
   b. sole proprietorship.
   c. partnership.
   d. none of the above.
9. Ted and Fred are the owners of a gas station. They invested $150,000 each and pay an employee named Lawrence $35,000 per year. This year revenues are $900,000, while costs are $940,000. Who is legally responsible for bearing the $40,000 loss? LO2.6
   a. Lawrence.
   b. Ted.
   c. Fred.
   d. Ted and Fred.
   e. Lawrence, Ted, and Fred.

PROBLEMS

1. Table 2.1 contains information on three techniques for producing $15 worth of bar soap. Assume that we said "$15 worth of bar soap" because soap costs $3 per bar and all three techniques produce 5 bars of soap ($15 = $3 per bar × 5 bars). So you know each technique produces 5 bars of soap. **LO2.3**
   a. What technique will you want to use if the price of a bar of soap falls to $2.75? What if the price of a bar of soap rises to $4? To $5?
   b. How many bars of soap will you want to produce if the price of a bar of soap falls to $2.00?
   c. Suppose that the price of soap is again $3 per bar but that the prices of all four resources are now $1 per unit. Which is now the least-profitable technique?
   d. If the resource prices return to their original levels (the ones shown in the table), but a new technique is invented that can produce 3 bars of soap (yes, 3 bars, not 5 bars!), using 1 unit of each of the four resources, will firms prefer the new technique?
2. Suppose Natasha currently makes $50,000 per year working as a manager at a cable TV company. She then develops two possible entrepreneurial business opportunities. In one, she will quit her job to start an organic soap company. In the other, she will try to develop an Internet-based competitor to the local cable company. For the soap-making opportunity, she anticipates annual revenue of $465,000 and costs for the necessary land, labor, and capital of $395,000 per year. For the Internet opportunity, she anticipates costs for land, labor, and capital of $3,250,000 per year as compared to revenues of $3,275,000 per year. (a) Should she quit her current job to become an entrepreneur? (b) If she does quit her current job, which opportunity would she pursue? **LO2.3**
3. With current technology, suppose a firm is producing 400 loaves of banana bread daily. Also assume that the least-cost combination of resources in producing those loaves is 5 units of labor, 7 units of land, 2 units of capital, and 1 unit of entrepreneurial ability, selling at prices of $40, $60, $60, and $20, respectively. If the firm can sell these 400 loaves at $2 per unit, what is its total revenue? Its total cost? Its profit or loss? Will it continue to produce banana bread? If this firm's situation is typical for the other makers of banana bread, will resources flow toward or away from this bakery good? **LO2.3**
4. Let's put dollar amounts on the flows in the circular flow diagram of Figure 2.2. **LO2.5**
   a. Suppose that businesses buy a total of $100 billion of the four resources (labor, land, capital, and entrepreneurial ability) from households. If households receive $60 billion in wages, $10 billion in rent, and $20 billion in interest, how much are households paid for providing entrepreneurial ability?
   b. If households spend $55 billion on goods and $45 billion on services, how much in revenues do businesses receive in the product market?

AP Part TWO

2 Price, Quantity, and Efficiency

In Chapter 3, this critical part of the study of economics introduces you to the functioning of a competitive product market. The ***law of demand*** which leads to consumers having an inverse relationship between product price and the quantity demanded of a product is explained. The ***law of supply*** which leads to producers having a positive or direct relationship between product price and the quantity supplied of a product is explained. Then the fundamental concept of ***equilibrium*** price and quantity in the product market is shown, as well as the beneficial result, called ***allocative efficiency*** by economists, when quantity demanded is equal to quantity supplied.

Chapter 4 then introduces the concept of ***market failure***, or situations where the competitive equilibrium does not prevail. In this chapter important to microeconomics, we will see how consumers can be harmed with a loss of consumer surplus and/or how producers can be harmed with a loss of ***producer surplus***. Public goods and externalities, possible causes of market failures, are discussed here.

Finally, in Chapter 5 we introduce you to the challenges facing government in a market economy. Even when the preponderance of economic decisions are made by the market, there is still a role for government to help direct the economy and to provide some goods and services, like public education, roads, and national defense.

Chapter 3

Demand, Supply, and Market Equilibrium

Learning Objectives

LO3.1 Characterize and give examples of markets.

LO3.2 Describe *demand* and explain how it can change.

LO3.3 Describe *supply* and explain how it can change.

LO3.4 Relate how supply and demand interact to determine market equilibrium.

LO3.5 Explain how changes in supply and demand affect equilibrium prices and quantities.

LO3.6 Identify what government-set prices are and how they can cause product surpluses and shortages.

LO3.7 (Appendix) Illustrate how supply and demand analysis can provide insights on actual-economy situations.

AP Chapter Focus

The model of supply and demand is a powerful one in the study of economics, as it explains the operation of the markets on which we depend for nearly everything. It is central to the understanding of the price system, explaining the quantities of goods and services bought and sold, as well as the prices at which they are bought or sold.

Markets

LO3.1 Characterize and give examples of markets.

Markets bring together buyers ("demanders") and sellers ("suppliers"). The corner gas station, an e-commerce site, the local bakery shop, a farmer's roadside stand—all are familiar markets. The New York Stock Exchange and the Chicago Board of Trade are markets in which buyers and sellers from all over the world communicate with one another to buy and sell bonds, stocks, and commodities. Auctioneers bring together potential buyers and sellers of art, livestock, used farm equipment, and, sometimes, real estate. In labor markets, new college graduates "sell" and employers "buy" specific labor services.

Some markets are local; others are national or international. Some are highly personal, involving face-to-face contact between demander and supplier; others are faceless, with buyer and seller never seeing or knowing each other.

To keep things simple, we will focus in this chapter on markets in which large numbers of independently acting buyers and sellers come together to buy and sell standardized products. Markets with these characteristics are the economy's most highly competitive. They include the wheat market, the stock market, and the market for foreign currencies. All such markets involve demand, supply, price, and quantity. As you will soon see, the price is "discovered" through the interacting decisions of buyers and sellers.

AP Demand

LO3.2 Describe *demand* and explain how it can change.

Demand is a schedule or a curve that shows the various amounts of a product that consumers are willing and able to purchase at each of a series of possible prices during a specified period of time.[1] Demand shows the quantities of a product that will be purchased at various possible prices, *other things equal*. Demand can easily be shown in table form. The table in Figure 3.1 is a hypothetical **demand schedule** for a *single consumer* purchasing bushels of corn.

The table reveals the relationship between the various prices of corn and the quantity of corn a particular consumer would be willing and able to purchase at each of these prices. We say "willing and able" because willingness alone is not effective in the market. You may be willing to buy a plasma television set, but if that willingness is not backed by the necessary dollars, it will not be effective and, therefore, will not be reflected in the market. In the table in Figure 3.1, if the price of corn were \$5 per bushel, our consumer would be willing and able to buy 10 bushels per week; if it were \$4, the consumer would be willing and able to buy 20 bushels per week; and so forth.

[1]This definition obviously is worded to apply to product markets. To adjust it to apply to resource markets, substitute the word "resource" for "product" and the word "businesses" for "consumers."

AP **FIGURE 3.1 An individual buyer's demand for corn.** Because price and quantity demanded are inversely related, an individual's demand schedule graphs as a downsloping curve such as *D*. Other things equal, consumers will buy more of a product as its price declines and less of the product as its price rises. (Here and in later figures, *P* stands for price and *Q* stands for quantity demanded or supplied.)

Demand for Corn	
Price per Bushel	Quantity Demanded per Week
\$5	10
4	20
3	35
2	55
1	80

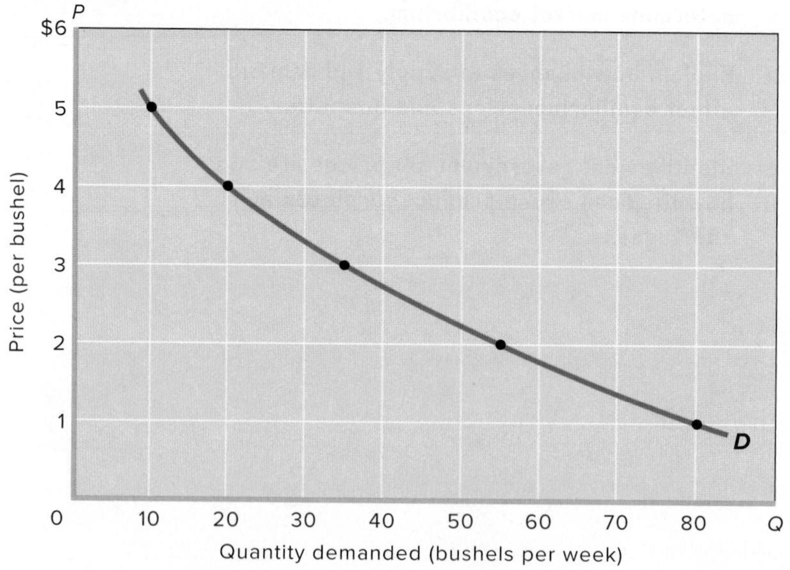

The table does not tell us which of the five possible prices will actually exist in the corn market. That depends on the interaction between demand and supply. Demand is simply a statement of a buyer's plans, or intentions, with respect to the purchase of a product.

To be meaningful, the quantities demanded at each price must relate to a specific period—a day, a week, a month. Saying "A consumer will buy 10 bushels of corn at $5 per bushel" is meaningless. Saying "A consumer will buy 10 bushels of corn *per week* at $5 per bushel" is meaningful. Unless a specific time period is stated, we do not know whether the demand for a product is large or small.

Law of Demand

A fundamental characteristic of demand is this: Other things equal, as price falls, the quantity demanded rises, and as price rises, the quantity demanded falls. In short, there is a negative or *inverse* relationship between price and quantity demanded. Economists call this inverse relationship the **law of demand.**

The other-things-equal assumption is critical here. Many factors other than the price of the product being considered affect the amount purchased. For example, the quantity of Nikes purchased will depend not only on the price of Nikes but also on the prices of such substitutes as Reeboks, Adidas, and New Balances. The law of demand in this case says that fewer Nikes will be purchased if the price of Nikes rises and if the prices of Reeboks, Adidas, and New Balances all remain constant. In short, if the *relative price* of Nikes rises, fewer Nikes will be bought. However, if the price of Nikes and the prices of all other competing shoes increase by some amount—say, $5—consumers might buy more, fewer, or the same number of Nikes.

Why the inverse relationship between price and quantity demanded? Let's look at three explanations, beginning with the simplest one:

- The law of demand is consistent with common sense. People ordinarily *do* buy more of a product at a low price than at a high price. Price is an obstacle that deters consumers from buying. The higher that obstacle, the less of a product they will buy; the lower the price obstacle, the more they will buy. The fact that businesses have "sales" to clear out unsold items is evidence of their belief in the law of demand.
- In any specific time period, each buyer of a product will derive less satisfaction (or benefit, or utility) from each successive unit of the product consumed. The second Big Mac will yield less satisfaction to the consumer than the first, and the third still less than the second. That is, consumption is subject to **diminishing marginal utility.** And because successive units of a particular product yield less and less marginal utility, consumers will buy additional units only if the price of those units is progressively reduced.
- We can also explain the law of demand in terms of income and substitution effects. The **income effect** indicates that a lower price increases the purchasing power of a buyer's money income, enabling the buyer to purchase more of the product than before. A higher price has the opposite effect. The **substitution effect** suggests that at a lower price buyers have the incentive to substitute what is now a less expensive product for other products that are now *relatively* more expensive. The product whose price has fallen is now "a better deal" relative to the other products.

For example, a decline in the price of chicken will increase the purchasing power of consumer incomes, enabling people to buy more chicken (the income effect). At a lower price, chicken is relatively more attractive and consumers tend to substitute it for pork, lamb, beef, and fish (the substitution effect). The income and substitution effects combine to make consumers able and willing to buy more of a product at a low price than at a high price.

The Demand Curve

The inverse relationship between price and quantity demanded for any product can be represented on a simple graph, in which, by convention, we measure *quantity demanded* on the horizontal axis and *price* on the vertical axis. In the graph in Figure 3.1 we have plotted the five price-quantity data points listed in the accompanying table and connected the points with a smooth curve, labeled *D*. Such a curve is called a **demand curve.** Its downward slope reflects the law of demand—people buy more of a product, service, or resource as its price falls. The relationship between price and quantity demanded is inverse (or negative).

The table and graph in Figure 3.1 contain exactly the same data and reflect the same relationship between price and quantity demanded. But the graph shows that relationship much more simply and clearly than a table or a description in words.

Market Demand

So far, we have concentrated on just one consumer. But competition requires that more than one buyer be present in each market. By adding the quantities demanded by all consumers at each of the various possible prices, we can get from *individual* demand to *market* demand. If there are just three buyers in the market, as represented in the table in Figure 3.2, it is relatively easy to determine the total quantity demanded at each price. Figure 3.2 shows the graphical summing procedure: At each price we sum horizontally the quantities demanded by Joe, Jen,

AP **FIGURE 3.2 Market demand for corn, three buyers.** The market demand curve *D* is the horizontal summation of the individual demand curves (D_1, D_2, and D_3) of all the consumers in the market. At the price of $3, for example, the three individual curves yield a total quantity demanded of 100 bushels (= 35 + 39 + 26).

Market Demand for Corn, Three Buyers

Price per Bushel	Quantity Demanded: Joe		Jen		Jay		Total Quantity Demanded per Week
$5	10	+	12	+	8	=	30
4	20	+	23	+	17	=	60
3	35	+	39	+	26	=	100
2	55	+	60	+	39	=	154
1	80	+	87	+	54	=	221

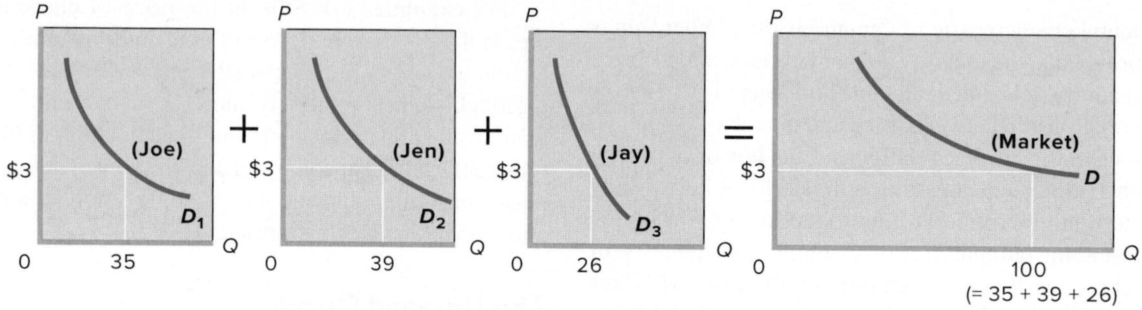

and Jay to obtain the total quantity demanded at that price; we then plot the price and the total quantity demanded as one point on the market demand curve. At the price of $3, for example, the three individual curves yield a total quantity demanded of 100 bushels (= 35 + 39 + 26).

Competition, of course, ordinarily entails many more than three buyers of a product. To avoid hundreds or thousands or millions of additions, we suppose that all the buyers in a market are willing and able to buy the same amounts at each of the possible prices. Then we just multiply those amounts by the number of buyers to obtain the market demand. That is how we arrived at the demand schedule and demand curve D_1 in Figure 3.3 for a market of 200 corn buyers, each with a demand as shown in the table in Figure 3.1.

In constructing a demand curve such as D_1 in Figure 3.3, economists assume that price is the most important influence on the amount of any product purchased. But economists know that other factors can and do affect purchases. These factors, called **determinants of demand,** are assumed to be constant when a demand curve like D_1 is drawn. They are the "other things equal" in the relationship between price and quantity demanded. When any of these determinants changes, the demand curve will shift to the right or left. For this reason, determinants of demand are sometimes referred to as *demand shifters.*

The basic determinants of demand are (1) consumers' tastes (preferences), (2) the number of buyers in the market, (3) consumers' incomes, (4) the prices of related goods, and (5) consumer expectations.

Changes in Demand

A change in one or more of the determinants of demand will change the demand data (the demand schedule) in the table accompanying Figure 3.3 and therefore the location of the demand curve there. A change in the demand schedule or, graphically, a shift in the demand curve is called a *change in demand.*

If consumers desire to buy more corn at each possible price than is reflected in column 2 in the table in Figure 3.3, that *increase in demand* is shown as a shift of the demand curve to the right, say, from D_1 to D_2. Conversely, a *decrease in demand* occurs when consumers buy less corn at each possible price than is indicated in column 2. The leftward shift of the demand curve from D_1 to D_3 in Figure 3.3 shows that situation.

Now let's see how changes in each determinant affect demand.

Tastes A favorable change in consumer tastes (preferences) for a product—a change that makes the product more desirable—means that more of it will be demanded at each price. Demand will increase; the demand curve will shift rightward. An unfavorable change in consumer preferences will decrease demand, shifting the demand curve to the left.

New products may affect consumer tastes; for example, the introduction of digital cameras greatly decreased the demand for film cameras. Consumers' concern over the health hazards of cholesterol and obesity have increased the demand

AP **FIGURE 3.3 Changes in the demand for corn.** A change in one or more of the determinants of demand causes a change in demand. An increase in demand is shown as a shift of the demand curve to the right, as from D_1 to D_2. A decrease in demand is shown as a shift of the demand curve to the left, as from D_1 to D_3. These changes in demand are to be distinguished from a change in quantity demanded, which is caused by a change in the price of the product, as shown by a movement from, say, point *a* to point *b* on fixed demand curve D_1.

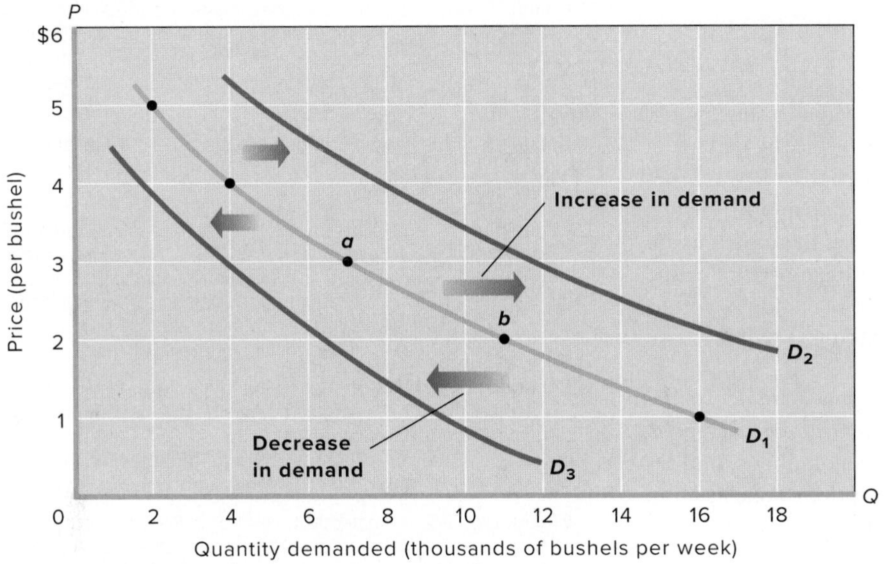

Market Demand for Corn, 200 Buyers, (D_1)	
(1) Price per Bushel	(2) Total Quantity Demanded per Week
$5	2,000
4	4,000
3	7,000
2	11,000
1	16,000

for broccoli, low-calorie beverages, and fresh fruit while decreasing the demand for beef, veal, eggs, and whole milk. Over the past twenty years, the demand for coffee drinks and table wine has greatly increased, driven by a change in tastes. So, too, has the demand for touch-screen mobile phones and fuel-efficient hybrid vehicles.

Number of Buyers An increase in the number of buyers in a market is likely to increase demand; a decrease in the number of buyers will probably decrease demand. For example, the rising number of older persons in the United States in recent years has increased the demand for motor homes, medical care, and retirement communities. Large-scale immigration from Mexico has greatly increased the demand for a range of goods and services in the Southwest, including Mexican food products in local grocery stores. Improvements in communications have given financial markets international range and have thus increased the demand for stocks and bonds. International trade agreements have reduced foreign trade barriers to American farm commodities, increasing the number of buyers and therefore the demand for those products.

In contrast, emigration (out-migration) from many small rural communities has reduced the population and thus the demand for housing, home appliances, and auto repair in those towns.

Income How changes in income affect demand is a more complex matter. For most products, a rise in income causes an increase in demand. Consumers typically buy more steaks, furniture, and electronic equipment as their incomes increase. Conversely, the demand for such products declines as their incomes fall. Products whose demand varies *directly* with money income are called *superior goods,* or **normal goods.**

Although most products are normal goods, there are some exceptions. As incomes increase beyond some point, the demand for used clothing, retread tires, and third-hand automobiles may decrease because the higher incomes enable consumers to buy new versions of those products. Rising incomes may also decrease the demand for soy-enhanced hamburger. Similarly, rising incomes may cause the demand for charcoal grills to decline as wealthier consumers switch to gas grills. Goods whose demand varies *inversely* with money income are called **inferior goods.**

Prices of Related Goods A change in the price of a related good may either increase or decrease the demand for a product, depending on whether the related good is a substitute or a complement:

- A **substitute good** is one that can be used in place of another good.
- A **complementary good** is one that is used together with another good.

Substitutes Häagen-Dazs ice cream and Ben & Jerry's ice cream are substitute goods or, simply, *substitutes.* When two products are substitutes, an increase in the price of one will increase the demand for the other. Conversely, a decrease in the price of one will decrease the demand for the other. For example, when the price of Häagen-Dazs ice cream rises, consumers will buy less of it and increase their demand for Ben & Jerry's ice cream. When the price of Colgate toothpaste declines, the demand for Crest decreases. So it is with other product pairs such as Nikes and Reeboks, Budweiser and Miller beer, or Chevrolets and Fords. They are *substitutes in consumption*.

Complements Because complementary goods (or, simply, *complements*) are used together, they are typically demanded jointly. Examples include computers and software, cell phones and cellular service, and snowboards and lift tickets. If the price of a complement (for example, lettuce) goes up, the demand for the related good (salad dressing) will decline. Conversely, if the price of a complement (for example, tuition) falls, the demand for a related good (textbooks) will increase.

Unrelated Goods The vast majority of goods are not related to one another and are called *independent goods*. Examples are butter and golf balls, potatoes and automobiles, and bananas and wristwatches. A change in the price of one has little or no effect on the demand for the other.

Consumer Expectations Changes in consumer expectations may shift demand. A newly formed expectation of higher future prices may cause consumers to buy now in order to "beat" the anticipated price rises, thus increasing current demand. That is often what happens in so-called hot real estate markets. Buyers rush in because they think the price of new homes will continue to escalate rapidly. Some buyers fear being "priced out of the market" and therefore not obtaining the home they desire. Other buyers—speculators—believe they will be able to sell the houses later at a higher price. Whichever their motivation, these buyers increase the current demand for houses.

Similarly, a change in expectations concerning future income may prompt consumers to change their current spending. For example, first-round NFL draft choices may splurge on new luxury cars in anticipation of lucrative professional football contracts. Or workers who become fearful of losing their jobs may reduce their demand for, say, vacation travel.

In summary, an *increase* in demand—the decision by consumers to buy larger quantities of a product at each possible price—may be caused by:

- A favorable change in consumer tastes.
- An increase in the number of buyers.
- Rising incomes if the product is a normal good.
- Falling incomes if the product is an inferior good.
- An increase in the price of a substitute good.
- A decrease in the price of a complementary good.
- A new consumer expectation that either prices or income will be higher in the future.

TABLE 3.1 Determinants of Demand: Factors That Shift the Demand Curve

Determinant	Examples
Change in buyer tastes	Physical fitness rises in popularity, increasing the demand for jogging shoes and bicycles; cell phone popularity rises, reducing the demand for landline phones.
Change in number of buyers	A decline in the birthrate reduces the demand for children's toys.
Change in income	A rise in incomes increases the demand for normal goods such as restaurant meals, sports tickets, and necklaces while reducing the demand for inferior goods such as cabbage, turnips, and inexpensive wine.
Change in the prices of related goods	A reduction in airfares reduces the demand for bus transportation (substitute goods); a decline in the price of DVD players increases the demand for DVD movies (complementary goods).
Change in consumer expectations	Inclement weather in South America creates an expectation of higher future coffee bean prices, thereby increasing today's demand for coffee beans.

You should "reverse" these generalizations to explain a *decrease* in demand. Table 3.1 provides additional illustrations of the determinants of demand.

Changes in Quantity Demanded

A *change in demand* must not be confused with a *change in quantity demanded.* A **change in demand** is a shift of the demand curve to the right (an increase in demand) or to the left (a decrease in demand). It occurs because the consumer's state of mind about purchasing the product has been altered in response to a change in one or more of the determinants of demand. Recall that "demand" is a schedule or a curve; therefore, a "change in demand" means a change in the schedule and a shift of the curve.

In contrast, a **change in quantity demanded** is a movement from one point to another point—from one price-quantity combination to another—on a fixed demand curve. The cause of such a change is an increase or decrease in the price of the product under consideration. In the table in Figure 3.3, for example, a decline in the price of corn from $5 to $4 will increase the quantity demanded of corn from 2,000 to 4,000 bushels.

In Figure 3.3 the shift of the demand curve D_1 to either D_2 or D_3 is a change in demand. But the movement from point *a* to point *b* on curve D_1 represents a change in quantity demanded: Demand has not changed; it is the entire curve, and it remains fixed in place.

AP QUICK REVIEW 3.1

- ✓ Demand is a schedule or curve showing the quantity of a product that buyers are willing and able to buy, in a particular time period, at each per unit price.
- ✓ The law of demand states that, other things equal, the quantity of a good purchased varies inversely with its price. At lower prices more is purchased; at higher prices less is purchased.
- ✓ The demand curve shifts, because of changes in (a) consumer tastes, (b) the number of buyers in the market, (c) consumer income, (d) the prices of substitute or complementary goods, (e) consumer expectations, and (f) tastes.
- ✓ A change in demand is a shift of the entire demand curve. A change in quantity demanded is a movement from one point to another point along the demand curve.

AP Supply

LO3.3 Describe *supply* and explain how it can change.

Supply is a schedule or curve showing the various amounts of a product that producers are willing and able to make available for sale at each of a series of possible prices during a specific period.[2] The table in Figure 3.4 is a hypothetical **supply schedule** for a single producer of corn. It shows the quantities of corn that will be supplied at various prices, other things equal.

[2]This definition is worded to apply to product markets. To adjust it to apply to resource markets, substitute "resource" for "product" and "owners" for "producers.

Law of Supply

The table in Figure 3.4 shows that a positive or direct relationship prevails between price and quantity supplied. As price rises, the quantity supplied rises; as price falls, the quantity supplied falls. This relationship is called the **law of supply.** A supply schedule tells us that, other things equal, firms will produce and offer for sale more of their product at a high price than at a low price. This, again, is basically common sense.

Price is an obstacle from the standpoint of the consumer, who is on the paying end. The higher the price, the less the consumer will buy. But the supplier is on the receiving end of the product's price. To a supplier, price represents *revenue,* which serves as an incentive to produce and sell a product. The higher the price, the greater this incentive and the greater the quantity supplied.

Consider a farmer who is deciding on how much corn to plant. As corn prices rise, as shown in the table in Figure 3.4, the farmer finds it profitable to plant more corn. And the higher corn prices enable the farmer to cover the increased costs associated with more intensive cultivation and the use of more seed, fertilizer, and pesticides. The overall result is more corn.

Now consider a manufacturer. Beyond some quantity of production, manufacturers usually encounter increases in *marginal cost*—the added cost of producing one more unit of output. Certain productive resources—in particular, the firm's plant and machinery—cannot be expanded quickly, so the firm uses more of other resources such as labor to produce more output. But as labor becomes more abundant relative to the fixed plant and equipment, the additional workers have relatively less space and access to equipment. For example, the added workers may have to wait to gain access to machines. As a result, each added worker produces less added output, and the marginal cost

AP **FIGURE 3.4 An individual producer's supply of corn.** Because price and quantity supplied are directly related, the supply curve for an individual producer graphs as an upsloping curve. Other things equal, producers will offer more of a product for sale as its price rises and less of the product for sale as its price falls.

Supply of Corn	
Price per Bushel	Quantity Supplied per Week
$5	60
4	50
3	35
2	20
1	5

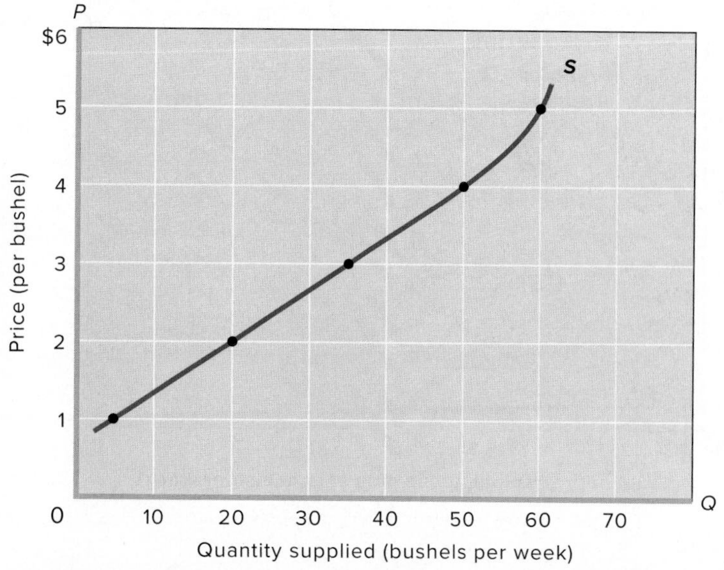

of successive units of output rises accordingly. The firm will not produce the more costly units unless it receives a higher price for them. Again, price and quantity supplied are directly related.

The Supply Curve

As with demand, it is convenient to represent individual supply graphically. In Figure 3.4, curve *S* is the **supply curve** that corresponds with the price–quantity supplied data in the accompanying table. The upward slope of the curve reflects the law of supply—producers offer more of a good, service, or resource for sale as its price rises. The relationship between price and quantity supplied is positive, or direct.

Market Supply

Market supply is derived from individual supply in exactly the same way that market demand is derived from individual demand. We sum the quantities supplied by each producer at each price. That is, we obtain the market supply curve by "horizontally adding" the supply curves of the individual producers. The price–quantity supplied data in the table accompanying Figure 3.5 are for an assumed 200 identical producers in the market, each willing to supply corn according to the supply schedule shown in Figure 3.4. Curve S_1 in Figure 3.5 is a graph of the market supply data. Note that the values of the axes in Figure 3.5 are the same as those used in our graph of market demand (Figure 3.3). The only difference is that we change the label on the horizontal axis from "quantity demanded" to "quantity supplied."

Determinants of Supply

In constructing a supply curve, we assume that price is the most significant influence on the quantity supplied of any product. But other factors (the "other things equal") can and do affect supply. The supply curve is drawn on the assumption that these other things are fixed and do not change. If one of them does change, a *change in supply* will occur, meaning that the entire supply curve will shift.

The basic **determinants of supply** are (1) resource prices, (2) technology, (3) taxes and subsidies, (4) prices of other goods, (5) producer expectations, and (6) the number of sellers in the market. A change in any one or more of these determinants of supply, or *supply shifters,* will move the supply curve for a product either right or left. A shift to the *right,* as from S_1 to S_2 in Figure 3.5, signifies an *increase* in supply: Producers supply larger quantities of the product at each possible price. A shift to the *left,* as from S_1 to S_3, indicates a *decrease* in supply: Producers offer less output at each price.

Changes in Supply

Let's consider how changes in each of the determinants affect supply. The key idea is that costs are a major factor underlying supply curves; anything that affects costs (other than changes in output itself) usually shifts the supply curve.

Resource Prices The prices of the resources used in the production process help determine the costs of production incurred by firms. Higher *resource* prices raise production costs and, assuming a particular *product* price, squeeze profits. That reduction in profits reduces the incentive for firms to supply output at each product price. For example, an increase in the price of sand, crushed rock, or Portland cement will increase the cost of producing concrete and reduce its supply.

In contrast, lower *resource* prices reduce production costs and increase profits. So when resource prices fall, firms

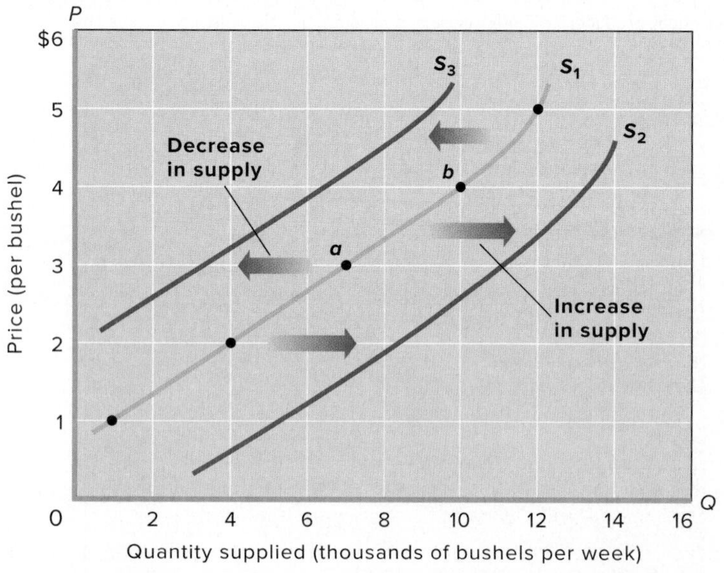

AP FIGURE 3.5 **Changes in the supply of corn.** A change in one or more of the determinants of supply causes a change in supply. An increase in supply is shown as a rightward shift of the supply curve, as from S_1 to S_2. A decrease in supply is depicted as a leftward shift of the curve, as from S_1 to S_3. In contrast, a change in the *quantity supplied* is caused by a change in the product's price and is shown by a movement from one point to another, as from *b* to *a* on fixed supply curve S_1.

Market Supply of Corn, 200 Producers, (S_1)

(1) Price per Bushel	(2) Total Quantity Supplied per Week
$5	12,000
4	10,000
3	7,000
2	4,000
1	1,000

supply greater output at each product price. For example, a decrease in the price of iron ore will decrease the price of steel.

Technology Improvements in technology (techniques of production) enable firms to produce units of output with fewer resources. Because resources are costly, using fewer of them lowers production costs and increases supply. Example: Technological advances in producing flat-panel computer monitors have greatly reduced their cost. Thus, manufacturers will now offer more such monitors than previously at the various prices; the supply of flat-panel monitors has increased.

Taxes and Subsidies Businesses treat most taxes as costs. An increase in sales or property taxes will increase production costs and reduce supply. In contrast, subsidies are "taxes in reverse." If the government subsidizes the production of a good, it in effect lowers the producers' costs and increases supply.

Prices of Other Goods Firms that produce a particular product, say, soccer balls, can sometimes use their plant and equipment to produce alternative goods, say, basketballs and volleyballs. The higher prices of these "other goods" may entice soccer ball producers to switch production to those other goods in order to increase profits. This *substitution in production* results in a decline in the supply of soccer balls. Alternatively, when the prices of basketballs and volleyballs decline relative to the price of soccer balls, producers of those goods may decide to produce more soccer balls instead, increasing their supply.

Producer Expectations Changes in expectations about the future price of a product may affect the producer's current willingness to supply that product. It is difficult, however, to generalize about how a new expectation of higher prices affects the present supply of a product. Farmers anticipating a higher wheat price in the future might withhold some of their current wheat harvest from the market, thereby causing a decrease in the current supply of wheat. In contrast, in many types of manufacturing industries, newly formed expectations that price will increase may induce firms to add another shift of workers or to expand their production facilities, causing current supply to increase.

Number of Sellers Other things equal, the larger the number of suppliers, the greater the market supply. As more firms enter an industry, the supply curve shifts to the right. Conversely, the smaller the number of firms in the industry, the less the market supply. This means that as firms leave an industry, the supply curve shifts to the left. Example: The United States and Canada have imposed restrictions on haddock fishing to replenish dwindling stocks. As part of that policy, the federal government has bought the boats of some of the haddock fishers as a way of putting them out of business and decreasing the catch. The result has been a decline in the market supply of haddock.

Table 3.2 is a checklist of the determinants of supply, along with further illustrations.

TABLE 3.2 Determinants of Supply: Factors That Shift the Supply Curve

Determinant	Examples
Change in resource prices	A decrease in the price of microchips increases the supply of computers; an increase in the price of crude oil reduces the supply of gasoline.
Change in technology	The development of more effective wireless technology increases the supply of cell phones.
Changes in taxes and subsidies	An increase in the excise tax on cigarettes reduces the supply of cigarettes; a decline in subsidies to state universities reduces the supply of higher education.
Change in prices of other goods	An increase in the price of cucumbers decreases the supply of watermelons.
Change in producer expectations	An expectation of a substantial rise in future log prices decreases the supply of logs today.
Change in number of suppliers	An increase in the number of tattoo parlors increases the supply of tattoos; the formation of women's professional basketball leagues increases the supply of women's professional basketball games.

Changes in Quantity Supplied

The distinction between a *change in supply* and a *change in quantity supplied* parallels the distinction between a change in demand and a change in quantity demanded. Because supply is a schedule or curve, a **change in supply** means a change in the schedule and a shift of the curve. An increase in supply shifts the curve to the right; a decrease in supply shifts it to the left. The cause of a change in supply is a change in one or more of the determinants of supply.

In contrast, a **change in quantity supplied** is a movement from one point to another on a fixed supply curve. The cause of such a movement is a change in the price of the specific product being considered.

Consider supply curve S_1 in Figure 3.5. A decline in the price of corn from $4 to $3 decreases the quantity of corn supplied per week from 10,000 to 7,000 bushels. This movement from point *b* to point *a* along S_1 is a change in quantity supplied, not a change in supply. Supply is the full schedule of prices and quantities shown, and this schedule does not change when the price of corn changes.

AP QUICK REVIEW 3.2

- ✓ Supply curves show the amount of a product that suppliers will offer for sale at each per unit price.
- ✓ Other things being equal, the quantity of a good supplied varies directly with its price. More will be supplied at higher prices; less, at lower prices.
- ✓ Supply curves shift due to changes in (a) resource prices, (b) technology, (c) taxes or subsidies, (d) future price expectations, and (e) number of suppliers. A change in supply is a shift of the entire supply curve. A change in quantity supplied is a movement from one point to another along the supply curve.

AP Market Equilibrium

LO3.4 Relate how supply and demand interact to determine market equilibrium.

With our understanding of demand and supply, we can now show how the decisions of buyers of corn and sellers of corn interact to determine the equilibrium price and quantity of corn. In the table in Figure 3.6, columns 1 and 2 repeat the market supply of corn (from the table in Figure 3.5), and columns 2 and 3 repeat the market demand for corn (from the table in Figure 3.3). We assume this is a competitive market so that neither buyers nor sellers can set the price.

Equilibrium Price and Quantity

We are looking for the equilibrium price and equilibrium quantity. The **equilibrium price** (or *market-clearing price*) is the price where the intentions of buyers and sellers match. It is the price where quantity demanded equals quantity supplied. The table in Figure 3.6 reveals that at $3, *and only at that price,* the number of bushels of corn that sellers wish to sell (7,000) is identical to the number consumers want to buy (also 7,000). At $3 and 7,000 bushels of corn, there is neither a shortage nor a surplus of corn. So 7,000 bushels of corn is the **equilibrium quantity:** the quantity at which the intentions of buyers and sellers match, so that the quantity demanded and the quantity supplied are equal.

Graphically, the equilibrium price is indicated by the intersection of the supply curve and the demand curve in **Figure 3.6 (Key Graph).** (The horizontal axis now measures both quantity demanded and quantity supplied.) With neither a shortage nor a surplus at $3, the market is *in equilibrium,* meaning "in balance" or "at rest."

Competition among buyers and among sellers drives the price to the equilibrium price; once there, it will remain there unless it is subsequently disturbed by changes in demand or supply (shifts of the curves). To better understand the uniqueness of the equilibrium price, let's consider other prices. At any above-equilibrium price, quantity supplied exceeds quantity demanded. For example, at the $4 price, sellers will offer 10,000 bushels of corn, but buyers will purchase only 4,000. The $4 price encourages sellers to offer lots of corn but discourages many consumers from buying it. The result is a **surplus** (or *excess supply*) of 6,000 bushels. If corn sellers produced them all, they would find themselves with 6,000 unsold bushels of corn.

Surpluses drive prices down. Even if the $4 price existed temporarily, it could not persist. The large surplus would prompt competing sellers to lower the price to encourage buyers to take the surplus off their hands. As the price fell, the incentive to produce corn would decline and the incentive for consumers to buy corn would increase. As shown in Figure 3.6, the market would move to its equilibrium at $3.

Any price below the $3 equilibrium price would create a shortage; quantity demanded would exceed quantity supplied. Consider a $2 price, for example. We see both from column 2 of the table and from the demand curve in Figure 3.6 that quantity demanded exceeds quantity supplied at that price. The result is a **shortage** (or *excess demand*) of 7,000 bushels of corn. The $2 price discourages sellers from devoting resources to corn and encourages consumers to desire more bushels than are available. The $2 price cannot persist as the equilibrium price. Many consumers who want to buy corn at this price will not obtain it. They will express a willingness to pay more than $2 to get corn. Competition among these buyers will drive up the price, eventually to the $3 equilibrium level. Unless disrupted by changes of supply or demand, this $3 price of corn will continue to prevail.

Rationing Function of Prices

The ability of the competitive forces of supply and demand to establish a price at which selling and buying decisions are consistent is called the rationing function of prices. In our case, the equilibrium price of $3 clears the market, leaving no burdensome surplus for sellers and no inconvenient shortage for potential buyers. And it is the combination of freely made individual decisions that sets this market-clearing price. In effect, the market outcome says that all buyers who are willing and able to pay $3 for a bushel of corn will obtain it; all buyers who cannot or will not pay $3 will go without corn. Similarly, all producers who are willing and able to offer corn for sale at $3 a bushel will sell it; all producers who cannot or will not sell for $3 per bushel will not sell their product.

Efficient Allocation

A competitive market such as that we have described not only rations goods to consumers but also allocates society's

AP KEY GRAPH

FIGURE 3.6 Equilibrium price and quantity. The intersection of the downsloping demand curve *D* and the upsloping supply curve *S* indicates the equilibrium price and quantity, here \$3 and 7,000 bushels of corn. The shortages of corn at below-equilibrium prices (for example, 7,000 bushels at \$2) drive up price. The higher prices increase the quantity supplied and reduce the quantity demanded until equilibrium is achieved. The surpluses caused by above-equilibrium prices (for example, 6,000 bushels at \$4) push price down. As price drops, the quantity demanded rises and the quantity supplied falls until equilibrium is established. At the equilibrium price and quantity, there are neither shortages nor surpluses of corn.

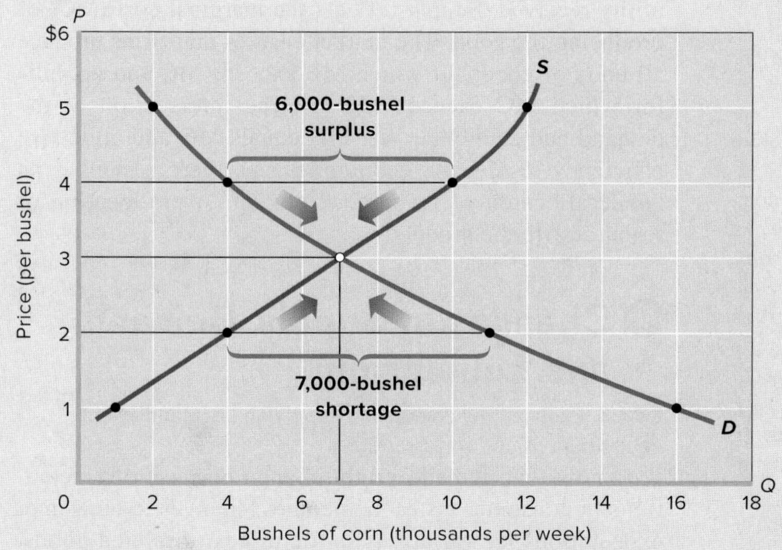

Market Supply of and Demand for Corn

(1) Total Quantity Supplied per Week	(2) Price per Bushel	(3) Total Quantity Demanded per Week	(4) Surplus (+) or Shortage (−)*
12,000	\$5	2,000	+10,000 ↓
10,000	4	4,000	+6,000 ↓
7,000	**3**	**7,000**	**0**
4,000	2	11,000	−7,000 ↑
1,000	1	16,000	−15,000 ↑

*Arrows indicate the effect on price.

QUICK QUIZ FOR FIGURE 3.6

1. Demand curve *D* is downsloping because:
   a. producers offer less of a product for sale as the price of the product falls.
   b. lower prices of a product create income and substitution effects that lead consumers to purchase more of it.
   c. the larger the number of buyers in a market, the lower the product price.
   d. price and quantity demanded are directly (positively) related.
2. Supply curve *S*:
   a. reflects an inverse (negative) relationship between price and quantity supplied.
   b. reflects a direct (positive) relationship between price and quantity supplied.
   c. depicts the collective behavior of buyers in this market.
   d. shows that producers will offer more of a product for sale at a low product price than at a high product price.
3. At the \$3 price:
   a. quantity supplied exceeds quantity demanded.
   b. quantity demanded exceeds quantity supplied.
   c. the product is abundant and a surplus exists.
   d. there is no pressure on price to rise or fall.
4. At price \$5 in this market:
   a. there will be a shortage of 10,000 units.
   b. there will be a surplus of 10,000 units.
   c. quantity demanded will be 12,000 units.
   d. quantity demanded will equal quantity supplied.

Answers: 1. b; 2. b; 3. d; 4. b

resources efficiently to the particular product. Competition among corn producers forces them to use the best technology and right mix of productive resources. If they didn't, their costs would be too high relative to the market price, and they would be unprofitable. The result is **productive efficiency:** the production of any particular good in the least costly way. When society produces corn at the lowest achievable per-unit cost, it is expending the least-valued combination of resources to produce that product and therefore is making available more-valued resources to produce other desired goods. Suppose society has only \$100 worth of resources available. If it can produce a bushel of corn using \$3 of those resources, then it will have available \$97 of resources remaining to produce other goods. This is clearly better than producing the corn for \$5 and having only \$95 of resources available for the alternative uses.

Competitive markets also produce **allocative efficiency:** the *particular mix* of goods and services most

CONSIDER THIS . . .

Source: Uber Manila Tips, **http://ubermanilatips.com/wp-content/uploads/2015/02/surge-price-icon.jpg**

Uber and Dynamic Pricing

The ride-sharing service known as Uber rose to prominence in 2013 by offering consumers an alternative to government-regulated taxi companies. Uber works via the Internet, matching people who need a ride with people who are willing to use their own vehicles to provide rides. Both parties can find each other easily and instantly via a mobile phone app and Uber makes its money by taking a percentage of the fare.

Uber is innovative in many ways, including empowering anybody to become a paid driver, breaking up local taxi monopolies, and making it effortless to arrange a quick pickup. But Uber's most interesting feature is dynamic pricing, under which Uber sets equilibrium prices in real time, constantly adjusting fares so as to equalize quantity demanded and quality supplied. The result is extremely short waiting times for both riders and drivers as Uber will, for instance, set a substantially higher "surge price" in a given location if demand suddenly increases due to, say, a bunch of people leaving a concert all at once and wanting rides. The higher fare encourages more Uber drivers to converge on the area, thereby minimizing wait times for both drivers and passengers.

The short wait times created by Uber's use of dynamic pricing stand in sharp contrast to taxi fares, which are fixed by law and therefore unable to adjust to ongoing changes in supply and demand. On days when demand is high relative to supply, taxi shortages arise. On days when demand is low relative to supply, drivers sit idle for long stretches of time. All of that inefficiency and inconvenience is eliminated by Uber's use of market equilibrium prices to equalize the demand and supply of rides.

highly valued by society (minimum-cost production assumed). For example, society wants land suitable for growing corn used for that purpose, not to grow dandelions. It wants diamonds to be used for jewelry, not crushed up and used as an additive to give concrete more sparkle. It wants streaming online music, not cassette players and tapes. Moreover, society does not want to devote all its resources to corn, diamonds, and streaming music. It wants to assign some resources to wheat, gasoline, and cell phones. Competitive markets make those allocatively efficient assignments.

The equilibrium price and quantity in competitive markets usually produce an assignment of resources that is "right" from an economic perspective. Demand essentially reflects the marginal benefit (MB) of the good, based on the utility received. Supply reflects the marginal cost (MC) of producing the good. The market ensures that firms produce all units of goods for which MB exceeds MC and no units for which MC exceeds MB. At the intersection of the demand and supply curves, MB equals MC and allocative efficiency results. As economists say, there is neither an "underallocaton of resources" nor an "overallocation of resources" to the product.

AP Changes in Supply, Demand, and Equilibrium

LO3.5 Explain how changes in supply and demand affect equilibrium prices and quantities.

We know that demand might change because of fluctuations in consumer tastes or incomes, changes in consumer expectations, or variations in the prices of related goods. Supply might change in response to changes in resource prices, technology, or taxes. What effects will such changes in supply and demand have on equilibrium price and quantity?

Changes in Demand

Suppose that the supply of some good (for example, health care) is constant and demand increases, as shown in Figure 3.7a. As a result, the new intersection of the supply and demand curves is at higher values on both the price and the quantity axes. Clearly, an increase in demand raises both equilibrium price and equilibrium quantity. Conversely, a decrease in demand such as that shown in Figure 3.7b reduces both equilibrium price and equilibrium quantity. (The value of graphical analysis is now apparent: We need not fumble with columns of figures to determine the outcomes; we need only compare the new and the old points of intersection on the graph.)

Changes in Supply

What happens if the demand for some good (for example, automobiles) is constant but supply increases, as in Figure 3.7c? The new intersection of supply and demand is located at a lower equilibrium price but at a higher equilibrium quantity. An increase in supply reduces equilibrium price but increases equilibrium quantity. In contrast, if supply decreases, as in Figure 3.7d, equilibrium price rises while equilibrium quantity declines.

AP FIGURE 3.7 Changes in demand and supply and the effects on price and quantity. The increase in demand from D_1 to D_2 in (a) increases both equilibrium price and equilibrium quantity. The decrease in demand from D_3 to D_4 in (b) decreases both equilibrium price and equilibrium quantity. The increase in supply from S_1 to S_2 in (c) decreases equilibrium price and increases equilibrium quantity. The decline in supply from S_3 to S_4 in (d) increases equilibrium price and decreases equilibrium quantity. The boxes in the top right corners summarize the respective changes and outcomes. The upward arrows in the boxes signify increases in equilibrium price (*P*) and equilibrium quantity (*Q*); the downward arrows signify decreases in these items.

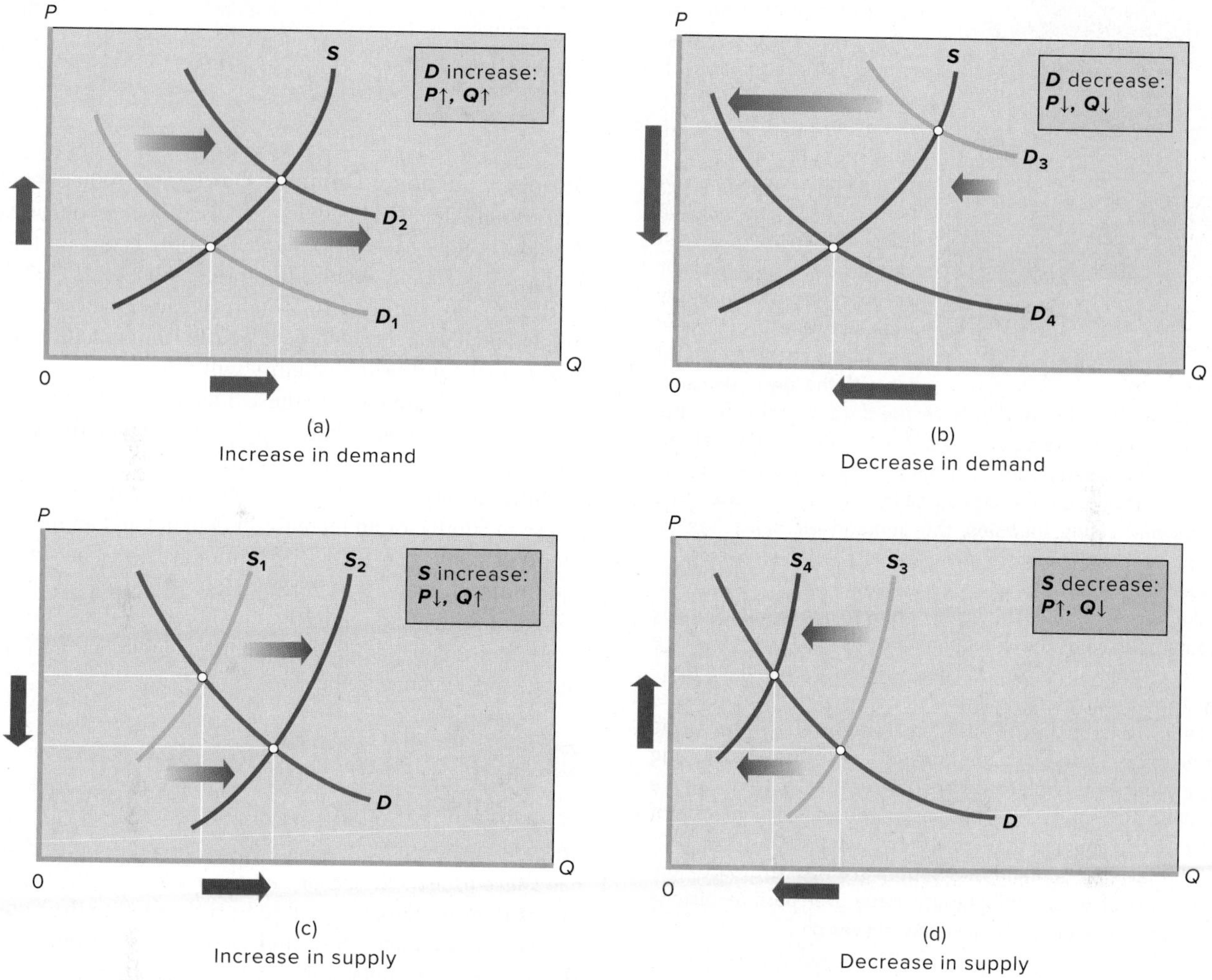

Complex Cases

When both supply and demand change, the effect is a combination of the individual effects.

Supply Increase; Demand Decrease What effect will a supply increase and a demand decrease for some good (for example, apples) have on equilibrium price? Both changes decrease price, so the net result is a price drop greater than that resulting from either change alone.

What about equilibrium quantity? Here the effects of the changes in supply and demand are opposed: the increase in supply increases equilibrium quantity, but the decrease in demand reduces it. The direction of the change in equilibrium quantity depends on the relative sizes of the changes in supply and demand. If the increase in supply is larger than the decrease in demand, the equilibrium quantity will increase. But if the decrease in demand is greater than the increase in supply, the equilibrium quantity will decrease.

Supply Decrease; Demand Increase A decrease in supply and an increase in demand for some good (for example, gasoline) both increase price. Their combined effect is an increase in equilibrium price greater than that caused by either change separately. But their effect on the equilibrium quantity is again indeterminate, depending on the relative sizes of the changes in supply and demand. If the decrease in

CONSIDER THIS . . .

© Nancy R. Cohen/Getty Images RF

Salsa and Coffee Beans

If you forget the other-things-equal assumption, you can encounter situations that *seem* to be in conflict with the laws of demand and supply. For example, suppose salsa manufacturers sell 1 million bottles of salsa at $4 a bottle in one year; 2 million bottles at $5 in the next year; and 3 million at $6 in the year thereafter. Price and quantity purchased vary directly, and these data seem to be at odds with the law of demand.

But there is no conflict here; the data do not refute the law of demand. The catch is that the law of demand's other-things-equal assumption has been violated over the three years in the example. Specifically, because of changing tastes and rising incomes, the demand for salsa has increased sharply, as in Figure 3.7a. The result is higher prices *and* larger quantities purchased.

Another example: The price of coffee beans occasionally shoots upward at the same time that the quantity of coffee beans harvested declines. These events seemingly contradict the direct relationship between price and quantity denoted by supply. The catch again is that the other-things-equal assumption underlying the upsloping supply curve is violated. Poor coffee harvests decrease supply, as in Figure 3.7d, increasing the equilibrium price of coffee and reducing the equilibrium quantity.

The laws of demand and supply are not refuted by observations of price and quantity made over periods of time in which either demand or supply curves shift.

supply is larger than the increase in demand, the equilibrium quantity will decrease. In contrast, if the increase in demand is greater than the decrease in supply, the equilibrium quantity will increase.

Supply Increase; Demand Increase What if supply and demand both increase for some good (for example, cell phones)? A supply increase drops equilibrium price, while a demand increase boosts it. If the increase in supply is greater than the increase in demand, the equilibrium price will fall. If the opposite holds, the equilibrium price will rise.

The effect on equilibrium quantity is certain: The increases in supply and demand both raise the equilibrium quantity. Therefore, the equilibrium quantity will increase by an amount greater than that caused by either change alone.

TABLE 3.3 Effects of Changes in Both Supply and Demand

Change in Supply	Change in Demand	Effect on Equilibrium Price	Effect on Equilibrium Quantity
1. Increase	Decrease	Decrease	Indeterminate
2. Decrease	Increase	Increase	Indeterminate
3. Increase	Increase	Indeterminate	Increase
4. Decrease	Decrease	Indeterminate	Decrease

Supply Decrease; Demand Decrease What about decreases in both supply and demand for some good (for example, new homes)? If the decrease in supply is greater than the decrease in demand, equilibrium price will rise. If the reverse is true, equilibrium price will fall. Because the decreases in supply and demand each reduce equilibrium quantity, we can be sure that equilibrium quantity will fall.

Table 3.3 summarizes these four cases. To understand them fully, you should draw supply and demand diagrams for each case to confirm the effects listed in this table.

Special cases arise when a decrease in demand and a decrease in supply, or an increase in demand and an increase in supply, exactly cancel out. In both cases, the net effect on equilibrium price will be zero; price will not change.

The optional appendix accompanying this chapter provides additional examples of situations in which both supply and demand change at the same time.

AP Application: Government-Set Prices

LO3.6 Identify what government-set prices are and how they can cause product surpluses and shortages.

Prices in most markets are free to rise or fall to their equilibrium levels, no matter how high or low those levels might be. However, government sometimes concludes that supply and demand will produce prices that are unfairly high for buyers or unfairly low for sellers. So government may place legal limits on how high or low a price or prices may go. Is that a good idea?

Price Ceilings on Gasoline

A **price ceiling** sets the maximum legal price a seller may charge for a product or service. A price at or below the ceiling is legal; a price above it is not. The rationale for establishing price ceilings (or ceiling prices) on specific products is that they purportedly enable consumers to obtain some "essential" good or service that they could not afford at the equilibrium price. Examples are rent controls and usury laws, which specify maximum "prices" in the forms of rent and interest that can be charged to borrowers.

AP **FIGURE 3.8 A price ceiling.** A price ceiling is a maximum legal price such as P_c. When the ceiling price is below the equilibrium price, a persistent product shortage results. Here that shortage is shown by the horizontal distance between Q_d and Q_s.

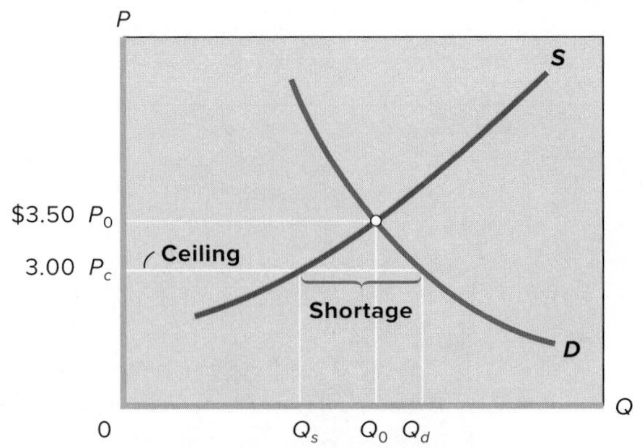

Graphical Analysis We can easily show the effects of price ceilings graphically. Suppose that rapidly rising world income boosts the purchase of automobiles and shifts the demand for gasoline to the right so that the market equilibrium price reaches $3.50 per gallon, shown as P_0 in Figure 3.8. The rapidly rising price of gasoline greatly burdens low- and moderate-income households, which pressure government to "do something." To keep gasoline prices down, the government imposes a ceiling price P_c of $3 per gallon. To impact the market, a price ceiling must be below the equilibrium price. A ceiling price of $4, for example, would have had no effect on the price of gasoline in the current situation.

What are the effects of this $3 ceiling price? The rationing ability of the free market is rendered ineffective. Because the ceiling price P_c is below the market-clearing price P_0, there is a lasting shortage of gasoline. The quantity of gasoline demanded at P_c is Q_d and the quantity supplied is only Q_s; a persistent excess demand or shortage of amount $Q_d - Q_s$ occurs.

The price ceiling P_c prevents the usual market adjustment in which competition among buyers bids up price, inducing more production and rationing some buyers out of the market. That process would normally continue until the shortage disappeared at the equilibrium price and quantity, P_0 and Q_0.

By preventing these market adjustments from occurring, the price ceiling poses two related problems.

Rationing Problem How will the available supply Q_s be apportioned among buyers who want the greater amount Q_d? Should gasoline be distributed on a first-come, first-served basis, that is, to those willing and able to get in line the soonest or stay in line the longest? Or should gas stations distribute it on the basis of favoritism? Since an unregulated shortage does not lead to an equitable distribution of gasoline, the government must establish some formal system for rationing it to consumers. One option is to issue ration coupons, which authorize bearers to purchase a fixed amount of gasoline per month. The rationing system might entail first the printing of coupons for Q_s gallons of gasoline and then the equal distribution of the coupons among consumers so that the wealthy family of four and the poor family of four both receive the same number of coupons.

Black Markets But ration coupons would not prevent a second problem from arising. The demand curve in Figure 3.8 reveals that many buyers are willing to pay more than the ceiling price P_c. And, of course, it is more profitable for gasoline stations to sell at prices above the ceiling. Thus, despite a sizable enforcement bureaucracy that would have to accompany the price controls, *black markets* in which gasoline is illegally bought and sold at prices above the legal limits will flourish. Counterfeiting of ration coupons will also be a problem. And since the price of gasoline is now "set by government," government might face political pressure to set the price even lower.

Rent Controls

About 200 cities in the United States, including New York City, Boston, and San Francisco, have at one time or another enacted rent controls: maximum rents established by law (or, more recently, maximum rent increases for existing tenants). Such laws are well intended. Their goals are to protect low-income families from escalating rents caused by perceived housing shortages and to make housing more affordable to the poor.

What have been the actual economic effects? On the demand side, the below-equilibrium rents attract a larger number of renters. Some are locals seeking to move into their own places after sharing housing with friends or family. Others are outsiders attracted into the area by the artificially lower rents. But a large problem occurs on the supply side. Price controls make it less attractive for landlords to offer housing on the rental market. In the short run, owners may sell their rental units or convert them to condominiums. In the long run, low rents make it unprofitable for owners to repair or renovate their rental units. (Rent controls are one cause of the many abandoned apartment buildings found in larger cities.) Also, insurance companies, pension funds, and other potential new investors in housing will find it more profitable to invest in office buildings, shopping malls, or motels, where rents are not controlled.

In brief, rent controls distort market signals and thus resources are misallocated: Too few resources are allocated to rental housing and too many to alternative uses. Ironically, although rent controls are often legislated to lessen the effects

LAST WORD

Student Loans and Tuition Costs

By Increasing Demand, Student Loans Increase the Price of Higher Education.

Since 1958, the federal government has attempted to make college more affordable by subsidizing student loans. The subsidies come in the form of lower interest rates and fewer credit checks than if students tried to borrow privately.

At first glance, that assistance appears to be entirely helpful. After all, college tuition costs are now very high after having risen steadily for decades. Between 1971-1972 school year and the 2014-2015 school year, the average cost of tuition, fees, room, and board increased from $2,929 to $42,419 at private four-year colleges and universities. Over the same period, they increased from $1,405 to $18,943 at public institutions.

It may seem obvious that student loans have helped students keep up with rising college costs. Under this commonly held hypothesis, college costs have risen over time due to outside factors like having to pay higher salaries to faculty and administrators, having to install the equipment necessary for digital classrooms and Internet connectivity, and having to hire larger staffs as colleges and universities added a wider variety of student services, including career centers and tutoring programs. From this point of view, outside factors increased costs and one of the only ways for students to keep up was by taking out loans.

But as far back as 1987, William Bennett, who was then the U.S. Secretary of Education, proposed that the commonly held hypothesis had things backward. Instead of loans helping students to keep up with rising tuition costs, loans were a major *cause* of rising tuition costs. As he wrote in the *New York Times,* ". . . increases in financial aid in recent years have enabled colleges and universities to blithely raise their tuitions, confident that Federal loan subsidies would help cushion the increase."

© baona/Getty Images RF

of perceived housing shortages, controls in fact are a primary cause of such shortages. For that reason, most American cities either have abandoned or are in the process of dismantling rent controls.

Price Floors on Wheat

A **price floor** is a minimum price fixed by the government. A price at or above the price floor is legal; a price below it is not. Price floors above equilibrium prices are usually invoked when society feels that the free functioning of the market system has not provided a sufficient income for certain groups of resource suppliers or producers. Supported prices for agricultural products and current minimum wages are two examples of price (or wage) floors. Let's look at the former.

Suppose that many farmers have extremely low incomes when the price of wheat is at its equilibrium value of $2 per bushel. The government decides to help out by establishing a legal price floor or price support of $3 per bushel.

What will be the effects? At any price above the equilibrium price, quantity supplied will exceed quantity demanded—that is, there will be a persistent excess supply or surplus of the product. Farmers will be willing to produce and offer for sale more than private buyers are willing to purchase at the price floor. As we saw with a price ceiling, an imposed legal price disrupts the rationing ability of the free market.

Graphical Analysis Figure 3.9 illustrates the effect of a price floor graphically. Suppose that *S* and *D* are the supply and demand curves for wheat. Equilibrium price and quantity are P_0 and Q_0, respectively. If the government imposes a price floor of P_f, farmers will produce Q_s but private buyers will purchase only Q_d. The surplus is the excess of Q_s over Q_d.

The government may cope with the surplus resulting from a price floor in two ways:

- It can restrict supply (for example, by instituting acreage allotments by which farmers agree to take a

Recent research by the New York Federal Reserve Bank confirms Bennett's view.[1] Each $1 increase in the average amount of student loans received per full-time student increases tuition costs by an average of 70 cents. In addition, researchers were able to demonstrate the order of causation because the federal government increased the borrowing limits on student loans in the mid-2000s. When the limits were raised, students borrowed more. And when they did, tuition increased. So the order of causation was clear: more loans lead to higher tuition (rather than higher tuition causing students to take out more loans).

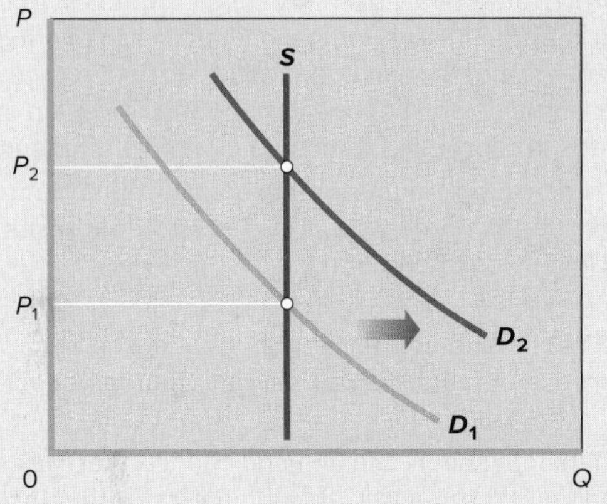

[1]David O. Lucca, Taylor Nauld, and Karen Shen, "Credit Supply and the Rise in College Tuition: Evidence from the Expansion in Federal Student Aid Programs," Staff Report No. 733, Federal Reserve Bank of New York, July 2015.

The model of demand and supply can explain why taking out more loans raises tuition. Take a look at the accompanying figure. At any given time, the quantity supplied of higher education is essentially fixed because it is not easy for colleges and universities to expand enrollments without constructing new classrooms. But the demand curve for higher education is not fixed. It shifts rightward whenever any factor increases either the willingness or ability of students to pay for higher education.

That is important because student loans increase the ability to pay. Student loans consequently shift the demand curve for higher education to the right from D_1 to D_2. That rightward shift in demand coupled with the fixed supply results in the equilibrium price of higher education rising from P_1 to P_2. More loans mean higher tuition costs.

This suggests that student loans are the wrong approach for the government to be taking in its attempt to increase access to higher education. With each $1 increase in the average amount of student loans received per full-time student causing a 70 cent increase in tuition, the student lending program is largely self-defeating as it ends up dramatically raising the price of the thing that it is striving to make more affordable.

One alternative would be for the government to redirect its efforts toward subsidizing supply rather than demand. If the government set up programs to increase the supply of higher education, the equilibrium price of higher education would naturally fall as the supply curve for higher education S shifted rightward. This was the approach taken after World War II, when the heavily subsidized state university systems expanded rapidly.

certain amount of land out of production) or increase demand (for example, by researching new uses for the product involved). These actions may reduce the difference between the equilibrium price and the price floor and that way reduce the size of the resulting surplus.

- If these efforts are not wholly successful, then the government must purchase the surplus output at the $3 price (thereby subsidizing farmers) and store or otherwise dispose of it.

Additional Consequences Price floors such as P_f in Figure 3.9 not only disrupt the rationing ability of prices but distort resource allocation. Without the price floor, the $2 equilibrium price of wheat would cause financial losses and force high-cost wheat producers to plant other crops or abandon farming altogether. But the $3 price floor allows them to continue to grow wheat and remain farmers. So society devotes too many of its scarce resources to wheat production and too few to

AP **FIGURE 3.9 A price floor.** A price floor is a minimum legal price such as P_f. When the price floor is above the equilibrium price, a persistent product surplus results. Here that surplus is shown by the horizontal distance between Q_s and Q_d.

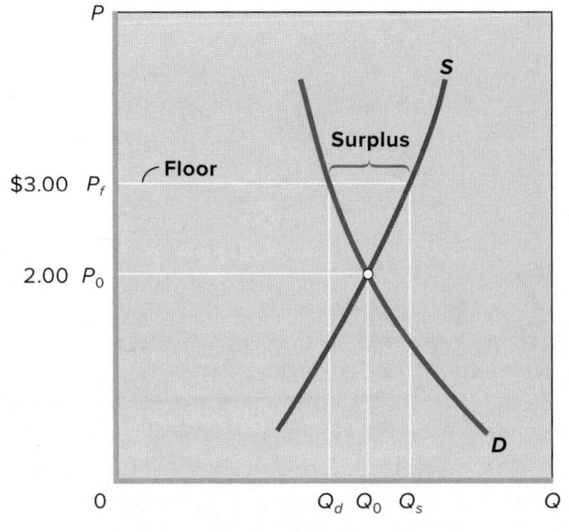

producing other, more valuable, goods and services. It fails to achieve allocative efficiency.

That's not all. Consumers of wheat-based products pay higher prices because of the price floor. Taxpayers pay higher taxes to finance the government's purchase of the surplus. Also, the price floor causes potential environmental damage by encouraging wheat farmers to bring hilly, erosion-prone "marginal land" into production. The higher price also prompts imports of wheat. But, since such imports would increase the quantity of wheat supplied and thus undermine the price floor, the government needs to erect tariffs (taxes on imports) to keep the foreign wheat out. Such tariffs usually prompt other countries to retaliate with their own tariffs against U.S. agricultural or manufacturing exports.

So it is easy to see why economists "sound the alarm" when politicians advocate imposing price ceilings or price floors such as price controls, rent controls, interest-rate lids, or agricultural price supports. In all these cases, good intentions lead to bad economic outcomes. Government-controlled prices cause shortages or surpluses, distort resource allocation, and produce negative side effects.

AP QUICK REVIEW 3.3

- ✓ In competitive markets, prices adjust to the equilibrium level, at which quantity demanded equals quantity supplied. In a competitive market, the equilibrium price performs a rationing function, insuring that the quantity produced equals the quantity demanded at the equilibrium price.
- ✓ The equilibrium price and quantity are indicated by the intersection of the supply and demand curves for any product or resource. Price is read from the vertical axis, and quantity is read from the horizontal axis.
- ✓ Both productive and allocative efficiency occur at market equilibrium, where products are produced in the least costly way (productive efficiency) and the mix of goods and services are optimal given consumer tastes and production costs (allocative efficiency).
- ✓ An increase in demand increases equilibrium price and quantity; a decrease in demand decreases equilibrium price and quantity.
- ✓ An increase in supply reduces equilibrium price, but increases equilibrium quantity; a decrease in supply increases equilibrium price, but reduces equilibrium quantity.
- ✓ When both supply and demand change, there is greater ambiguity. Frequently, the impact on **either** price or quantity will be known, while the impact on the other will be indeterminate. For instance, if the number of consumers increase and the number of producers increase, both demand and supply will increase. There will be an increase in the equilibrium quantity, but an indeterminate change in the equilibrium price.
- ✓ Government-controlled prices in the form of ceilings and floors, attempting to correct for perceived unfairness to buyers or sellers, disrupt the rationing function of prices, distort resource allocations, can produce negative side effects, and generate deadweight economic loss.

SUMMARY

LO3.1 Characterize and give examples of markets.

Markets bring buyers and sellers together. Some markets are local, others international. Some have physical locations while others are online. For simplicity, this chapter focuses on highly competitive markets in which large numbers of buyers and sellers come together to buy and sell standardized products. All such markets involve demand, supply, price, and quantity, with price being "discovered" through the interacting decisions of buyers and sellers.

LO3.2 Describe *demand* and explain how it can change.

Demand is a schedule or curve representing the willingness of buyers in a specific period to purchase a particular product at each of various prices. The law of demand implies that consumers will buy more of a product at a low price than at a high price. So, other things equal, the relationship between price and quantity demanded is negative or inverse and is graphed as a downsloping curve.

Market demand curves are found by adding horizontally the demand curves of the many individual consumers in the market.

Changes in one or more of the determinants of demand (consumer tastes, the number of buyers in the market, the money incomes of consumers, the prices of related goods, and consumer expectations) shift the market demand curve. A shift to the right is an increase in demand; a shift to the left is a decrease in demand. A change in demand is different from a change in the quantity demanded, the latter being a movement from one point to another point on a fixed demand curve because of a change in the product's price.

LO3.3 Describe *supply* and explain how it can change.

Supply is a schedule or curve showing the amounts of a product that producers are willing to offer in the market at each possible price during a specific period. The law of supply states that, other things equal, producers will offer more of a product at a high price than at a low price. Thus, the relationship between price and quantity supplied is positive or direct, and supply is graphed as an upsloping curve.

The market supply curve is the horizontal summation of the supply curves of the individual producers of the product.

Changes in one or more of the determinants of supply (resource prices, production techniques, taxes or subsidies, the prices of other goods, producer expectations, or the number of sellers in the market) shift the supply curve of a product. A shift to the right is an increase in supply; a shift to the left is a decrease in supply. In contrast, a change in the price of the product being considered causes a change in the quantity supplied, which is shown as a movement from one point to another point on a fixed supply curve.

LO3.4 Relate how supply and demand interact to determine market equilibrium.

The equilibrium price and quantity are established at the intersection of the supply and demand curves. The interaction of market demand and market supply adjusts the price to the point at which the quantities demanded and supplied are equal. This is the equilibrium price. The corresponding quantity is the equilibrium quantity.

The ability of market forces to synchronize selling and buying decisions to eliminate potential surpluses and shortages is known as the rationing function of prices. The equilibrium quantity in competitive markets reflects both productive efficiency (least-cost production) and allocative efficiency (producing the right amount of the product relative to other products).

LO3.5 Explain how changes in supply and demand affect equilibrium prices and quantities.

A change in either demand or supply changes the equilibrium price and quantity. Increases in demand raise both equilibrium price and equilibrium quantity; decreases in demand lower both equilibrium price and equilibrium quantity. Increases in supply lower equilibrium price and raise equilibrium quantity; decreases in supply raise equilibrium price and lower equilibrium quantity.

Simultaneous changes in demand and supply affect equilibrium price and quantity in various ways, depending on their direction and relative magnitudes (see Table 3.3).

LO3.6 Identify what government-set prices are and how they can cause product surpluses and shortages.

A price ceiling is a maximum price set by government and is designed to help consumers. Effective price ceilings produce persistent product shortages, and if an equitable distribution of the product is sought, government must ration the product to consumers.

A price floor is a minimum price set by government and is designed to aid producers. Effective price floors lead to persistent product surpluses; the government must either purchase the product or eliminate the surplus by imposing restrictions on production or increasing private demand.

Legally fixed prices stifle the rationing function of prices and distort the allocation of resources.

TERMS AND CONCEPTS

demand
demand schedule
law of demand
diminishing marginal utility
income effect
substitution effect
demand curve
determinants of demand
normal goods
inferior goods
substitute good
complementary good
change in demand
change in quantity demanded
supply
supply schedule
law of supply
supply curve
determinants of supply
change in supply
change in quantity supplied
equilibrium price
equilibrium quantity
surplus
shortage
productive efficiency
allocative efficiency
price ceiling
price floor

The following and additional problems can be found in connect

DISCUSSION QUESTIONS

1. Explain the law of demand. Why does a demand curve slope downward? How is a market demand curve derived from individual demand curves? LO3.2
2. What are the determinants of demand? What happens to the demand curve when any of these determinants change? Distinguish between a change in demand and a movement along a fixed demand curve, noting the cause(s) of each. LO3.2
3. Explain the law of supply. Why does the supply curve slope upward? How is the market supply curve derived from the supply curves of individual producers? LO3.3
4. What are the determinants of supply? What happens to the supply curve when any of these determinants change? Distinguish between a change in supply and a change in the quantity supplied, noting the cause(s) of each. LO3.3
5. In 2001 an outbreak of hoof-and-mouth disease in Europe led to the burning of millions of cattle carcasses. What impact do you think this had on the supply of cattle hides, hide prices, the supply of leather goods, and the price of leather goods? LO3.5
6. For each stock in the stock market, the number of shares sold daily equals the number of shares purchased. That is, the quantity of each firm's shares demanded equals the quantity supplied. So, if this equality always occurs, why do the prices of stock shares ever change? LO3.5
7. What do economists mean when they say "price floors and ceilings stifle the rationing function of prices and distort resource allocation"? LO3.6
8. **LAST WORD** Real (inflation-adjusted) tuition costs were nearly constant during the 1960s despite a huge increase in the number of college students as the very large Baby Boom generation came of age. What does this suggest about the supply of higher education during that period? When the much smaller Baby Bust generation followed in the 1970s, real tuition costs fell. What does that suggest about demand relative to supply during the 1970s?

AP REVIEW QUESTIONS

1. What effect will each of the following have on the demand for small, fuel efficient automobiles such as the Mini-Cooper and Fiat 500? LO3.2
   a. Small automobiles become more fashionable.
   b. The price of large automobiles rises (with the price of small autos remaining the same).
   c. Income declines and small autos are an inferior good.
   d. Consumers anticipate that the price of small autos will greatly come down in the near future.
   e. The price of gasoline substantially drops.
2. True or False: A "change in quantity demanded" is a shift of the entire demand curve to the right or to the left. LO3.2
3. What effect will each of the following have on the supply of auto tires? LO3.3
   a. A technological advance in the methods of producing tires.
   b. A decline in the number of firms in the tire industry.
   c. An increase in the prices of rubber used in the production of tires.
   d. The expectation that the equilibrium price of auto tires will be lower in the future than currently.
   e. A decline in the price of the large tires used for semi trucks and earth-hauling rigs (with no change in the price of auto tires).
   f. The levying of a per-unit tax on each auto tire sold.
   g. The granting of a 50-cent-per-unit subsidy for each auto tire produced.
4. Peanut butter and jelly sandwiches continue to be a mainstay of packed lunches across America. If the price of peanut butter declines, the demand curve for the jelly will: LO3.4
   a. Shift to the left, since jelly is a substitute.
   b. Shift to the right, since peanut butter and jelly are complements.
   c. Decrease, since jelly is a substitute.
   d. Remain unchanged.
   e. Shift to the left, since peanut butter and jelly are complements.
5. Suppose that in the market for computer memory chips, the equilibrium price is \$50 per chip. If the current price is \$55 per chip, then there will be ____________ of memory chips. LO3.4
   a. A shortage.
   b. A surplus.
   c. An equilibrium.
   d. A future increase in the production.
   e. None of the above.
6. If price is above the equilibrium level, competition among sellers to reduce the resulting: LO3.5
   a. Surplus will increase quantity demanded and decrease quantity supplied.
   b. Shortage will decrease quantity demanded and increase quantity supplied.
   c. Surplus will decrease quantity demanded and increase quantity supplied.
   d. Shortage will increase quantity demanded and decrease quantity supplied.
   e. Equilibrium will take no action to change.
7. Label each of the following scenarios with the set of symbols that best indicates the price change and quantity change that occur in the scenario. In some scenarios, it may not be possible from the information given to determine the direction of a particular price change or a particular quantity change. We will symbolize those cases as, respectively, "P?" and "Q?". The four possible combinations of price and quantity changes are: LO3.5

P ↓ Q?	P? Q ↓
P ↑ Q?	P? Q ↑

a. On a hot day, both the demand for lemonade and the supply of lemonade increase.

b. On a cold day, both the demand for ice cream and the supply of ice cream decrease.

c. When Hawaii's Mt. Kilauea erupts violently, the demand on the part of tourists for sightseeing flights increases but the supply of pilots willing to provide these dangerous flights decreases.

d. In a hot area of Arizona where they generate a lot of their electricity with wind turbines, the demand for electricity falls on windy days as people switch off their air conditioners and enjoy the breeze. But at the same time, the amount of electricity supplied increases as the wind turbines spin faster.

8. Suppose the total demand for wheat and the total supply of wheat per month in the Kansas City grain market are as shown in the following table. Suppose that the government establishes a price ceiling of $3.70 for wheat. Explain carefully the main effects. Demonstrate your answer graphically. Next, suppose that the government establishes a price floor of $4.60 for wheat. What will be the main effects of this price floor? Demonstrate your answer graphically. **LO3.6**

Thousands of Bushels Demanded	Price per Bushel	Thousands of Bushels Supplied
85	$3.40	72
80	3.70	73
75	4.00	75
70	4.30	77
65	4.60	79
60	4.90	81

9. A price ceiling will result in a shortage only if the ceiling price is __________ the equilibrium price. **LO3.6**

a. Less than.
b. Equal to.
c. Greater than.
d. Equal to and less than
e. Equal to and greater than

PROBLEMS

1. Suppose there are three buyers of candy in a market: Tex, Dex, and Rex. The market demand and the individual demands of Tex, Dex, and Rex are shown in the following table. **LO3.2**

a. Fill in the table for the missing values.

b. Which buyer demands the least at a price of $5? The most at a price of $7?

c. Which buyer's quantity demanded increases the most when the price is lowered from $7 to $6?

d. Which direction would the market demand curve shift if Tex withdrew from the market? What if Dex doubled his purchases at each possible price?

e. Suppose that at a price of $6, the total quantity demanded increases from 19 to 38. Is this a "change in the quantity demanded" or a "change in demand"?

Price per Candy	Individual Quantities Demanded: Tex		Dex		Rex		Total Quantity Demanded
$8	3	+	1	+	0	=	___
7	8	+	2	+	___	=	12
6	___	+	3	+	4	=	19
5	17	+	___	+	6	=	27
4	23	+	5	+	8	=	___

2. The figure below shows the supply curve for tennis balls, S_1, for Drop Volley Tennis, a producer of tennis equipment. Use the figure and the table below to give your answers to the following questions. **LO3.3**

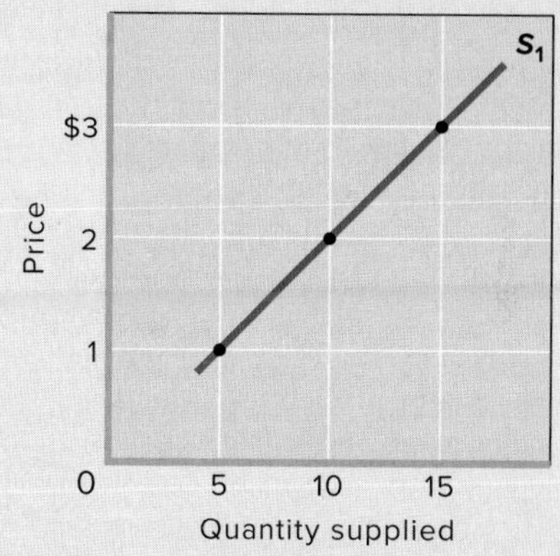

a. Use the figure to fill in the quantity supplied on supply curve S_1 for each price in the following table.

Price	S_1 Quantity Supplied	S_2 Quantity Supplied	Change in Quantity Supplied
$3	______	4	______
2	______	2	______
1	______	0	______

b. If production costs were to increase, the quantities supplied at each price would be as shown by the third column of the table ("S_2 Quantity Supplied"). Use those data to draw supply curve S_2 on the same graph as supply curve S_1.

c. In the fourth column of the table, enter the amount by which the quantity supplied at each price changes due to the increase in product costs. (Use positive numbers for increases and negative numbers for decreases.)

d. Did the increase in production costs cause a "decrease in supply" or a "decrease in quantity supplied"?

3. Refer to the following expanded table from review question 8. **LO3.4**

a. What is the equilibrium price? At what price is there neither a shortage nor a surplus? Fill in the surplus-shortage column and use it to confirm your answers.

b. Graph the demand for wheat and the supply of wheat. Be sure to label the axes of your graph correctly. Label equilibrium price *P* and equilibrium quantity *Q*.

c. How big is the surplus or shortage at \$3.40? At \$4.90? How big a surplus or shortage results if the price is 60 cents higher than the equilibrium price? 30 cents lower than the equilibrium price?

Thousands of Bushels Demanded	Price per Bushel	Thousands of Bushels Supplied	Surplus (+) or Shortage (−)
85	\$3.40	72	_____
80	3.70	73	_____
75	4.00	75	_____
70	4.30	77	_____
65	4.60	79	_____
60	4.90	81	_____

4. How will each of the following changes in demand and/or supply affect equilibrium price and equilibrium quantity in a competitive market; that is, do price and quantity rise, fall, or remain unchanged, or are the answers indeterminate because they depend on the magnitudes of the shifts? Use supply and demand to verify your answers. **LO3.5**

a. Supply decreases and demand is constant.

b. Demand decreases and supply is constant.

c. Supply increases and demand is constant.

d. Demand increases and supply increases.

e. Demand increases and supply is constant.

f. Supply increases and demand decreases.

g. Demand increases and supply decreases.

h. Demand decreases and supply decreases.

5. Use two market diagrams to explain how an increase in state subsidies to public colleges might affect tuition and enrollments in both public and private colleges. **LO3.5**

6. **ADVANCED ANALYSIS** Assume that demand for a commodity is represented by the equation $P = 10 - .2Q_d$ and supply by the equation $P = 2 + .2Q_s$, where Q_d and Q_s are quantity demanded and quantity supplied, respectively, and *P* is price. Using the equilibrium condition $Q_s = Q_d$, solve the equations to determine equilibrium price. Now determine equilibrium quantity. **LO3.5**

7. Suppose that the demand and supply schedules for rental apartments in the city of Gotham are as given in the following table. **LO3.6**

Monthly Rent	Apartments Demanded	Apartments Supplied
\$2,500	10,000	15,000
2,000	12,500	12,500
1,500	15,000	10,000
1,000	17,500	7,500
500	20,000	5,000

a. What is the market equilibrium rental price per month and the market equilibrium number of apartments demanded and supplied?

b. If the local government can enforce a rent-control law that sets the maximum monthly rent at \$1,500, will there be a surplus or a shortage? Of how many units? And how many units will actually be rented each month?

c. Suppose that a new government is elected that wants to keep out the poor. It declares that the minimum rent that can be charged is \$2,500 per month. If the government can enforce that price floor, will there be a surplus or a shortage? Of how many units? And how many units will actually be rented each month?

d. Suppose that the government wishes to decrease the market equilibrium monthly rent by increasing the supply of housing. Assuming that demand remains unchanged, by how many units of housing would the government have to increase the supply of housing in order to get the market equilibrium rental price to fall to \$1,500 per month? To \$1,000 per month? To \$500 per month?

connect

Additional Examples of Supply and Demand

LO3.7 Illustrate how supply and demand analysis can provide insights on actual-economy situations.

Our discussion has clearly demonstrated that supply and demand analysis is a powerful tool for understanding equilibrium prices and quantities. The information provided in the main body of this chapter is fully sufficient for moving forward in the book, but you may find that additional examples of supply and demand are helpful. The examples found in this appendix can provide strong reinforcement and provide a preview for further uses of the demand and supply model.

AP Changes in Supply and Demand

As Figure 3.7 of this chapter demonstrates, changes in supply and demand cause changes in price, quantity, or both. The following applications illustrate this fact in several real-world markets. The simplest situations are those in which either supply changes while demand remains constant or demand changes while supply remains constant. Let's consider two such simple cases first, before looking at more complex applications.

Lettuce

Every now and then we hear on the news that extreme weather has severely reduced the size of some crop. Suppose, for example, that a severe freeze destroys a sizable portion of the lettuce crop. This unfortunate situation implies a significant decline in supply, which we represent as a leftward shift of the supply curve from S_1 to S_2 in Figure 1. At each price, consumers desire as much lettuce as before, so the freeze does not affect the demand for lettuce. That is, demand curve D_1 does not shift.

What are the consequences of the reduced supply of lettuce for equilibrium price and quantity? As shown in Figure 1, the leftward shift of the supply curve disrupts the previous equilibrium in the market for lettuce and drives the equilibrium price upward from P_1 to P_2. Consumers respond to that price hike by reducing the quantity of lettuce demanded from Q_1 to Q_2. Equilibrium is restored at P_2 and Q_2.

Consumers who are willing and able to pay price P_2 obtain lettuce; consumers unwilling or unable to pay that price do not. Some consumers continue to buy as much lettuce as before, even at the higher price. Others buy some lettuce but not as much as before, and still others opt out of the market completely. The latter two groups use the money they would have spent on lettuce to obtain other products, say, carrots. (Because of our other-things-equal assumption, the prices of other products have not changed.)

FIGURE 1 The market for lettuce. The decrease in the supply of lettuce, shown here by the shift from S_1 to S_2, increases the equilibrium price of lettuce from P_1 to P_2 and reduces the equilibrium quantity from Q_1 to Q_2.

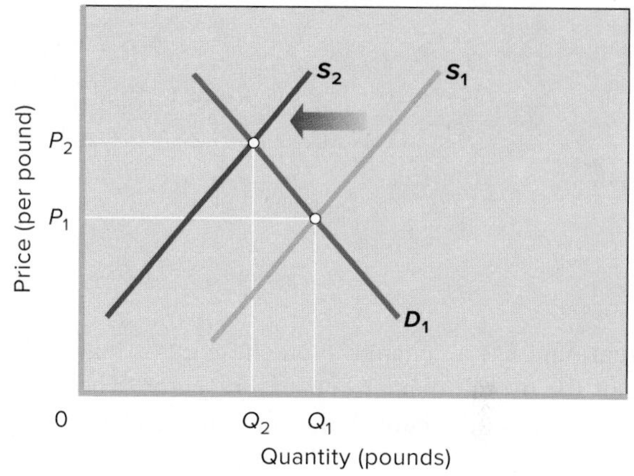

Exchange Rates

Exchange rates are the prices at which one currency can be traded (exchanged) for another. Exchange rates are normally determined in foreign exchange markets. One of the largest foreign exchange markets is the euro-dollar market in which the currency used in most of Europe, the *euro*, is exchanged for U.S. dollars. In the United States, this market is set up so that euros are priced in dollars—that is, the "product" being traded is euros and the "price" to buy that product is quoted in dollars. Thus, the market equilibrium price one day might be \$1.25 to buy 1 euro, while on another day it might be \$1.50 to buy 1 euro.

Foreign exchange markets are used by individuals and companies that need to make purchases or payments in a different currency. U.S. companies exporting goods to Germany, for instance, wish to be paid in U.S. dollars. Thus, their German customers will need to convert euros into dollars. The euros that they bring to the euro-dollar market will become part of the overall market supply of euros. Conversely, an American mutual fund may wish to purchase some French real estate outside of Paris. But to purchase that real estate, it will need to pay in euros because the current French owners will only accept payment in euros. Thus, the American

FIGURE 2 The market for euros. The increase in the demand for euros, shown here by the shift from D_1 to D_2, increases the equilibrium price of one euro from $1.25 to $1.50 and increases the equilibrium quantity of euros that are exchanged from Q_1 to Q_2. The dollar has depreciated.

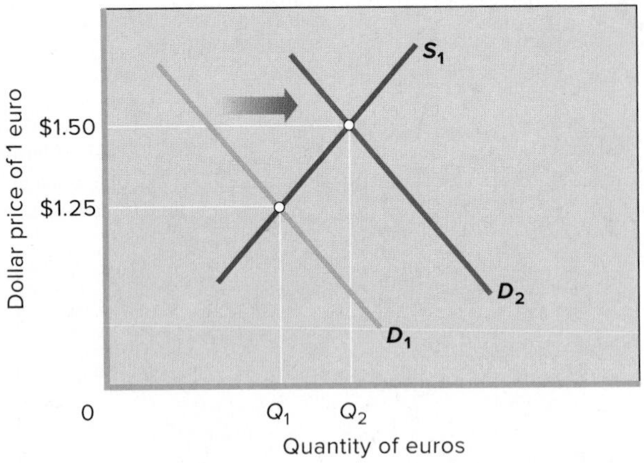

FIGURE 3 The market for pink salmon. In the last several decades, the supply of pink salmon has increased and the demand for pink salmon has decreased. As a result, the price of pink salmon has declined, as from P_1 to P_2. Because supply has increased by more than demand has decreased, the equilibrium quantity of pink salmon has increased, as from Q_1 to Q_2.

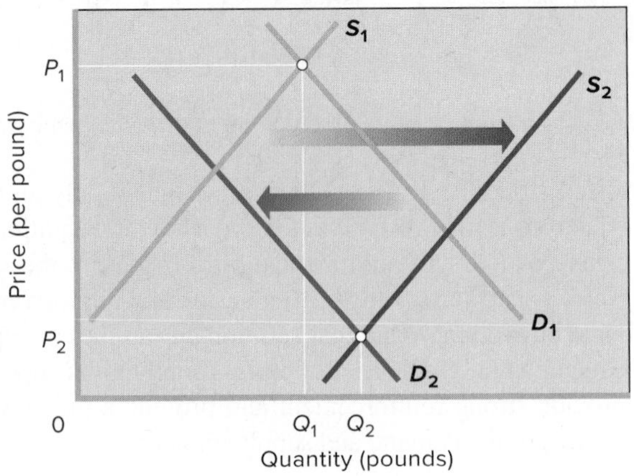

mutual fund has a demand to purchase euros that will form part of the overall market demand for euros. The fund will bring dollars to the euro-dollar foreign exchange market in order to purchase the euros it desires.

Sometimes, the demand for euros increases. This might be because a European product surges in popularity in foreign countries. For example, if a new German-made automobile is a big hit in the United States, American car dealers will demand more euros with which to pay for more units of that new model. This will shift the demand curve for euros to the right, as from D_1 to D_2 in Figure 2. Given the fixed euro supply curve S_1, the increase in demand raises the equilibrium exchange rate (the equilibrium number of dollars needed to purchase 1 euro) from $1.25 to $1.50. The equilibrium quantity of euros purchased increases from Q_1 to Q_2. Because a higher dollar amount is now needed to purchase one euro, economists say that the dollar has *depreciated*—gone down in value—relative to the euro. Alternatively, the euro has *appreciated*—gone up in value—relative to the dollar, because one euro now buys $1.50 rather than $1.25.

Pink Salmon

Now let's see what happens when both supply and demand change at the same time. Several decades ago, people who caught salmon earned as much as $1 for each pound of pink salmon—the type of salmon most commonly used for canning. In Figure 3 that price is represented as P_1, at the intersection of supply curve S_1 and demand curve D_1. The corresponding quantity of pink salmon is shown as Q_1 pounds.

As time passed, supply and demand changed in the market for pink salmon. On the supply side, improved technology in the form of larger, more efficient fishing boats greatly increased the catch and lowered the cost of obtaining it. Also, high profits at price P_1 encouraged many new fishers to enter the industry. As a result of these changes, the supply of pink salmon greatly increased and the supply curve shifted to the right, as from S_1 to S_2 in Figure 3.

Over the same years, the demand for pink salmon declined, as represented by the leftward shift from D_1 to D_2 in Figure 3. That decrease was caused by increases in consumer income and reductions of the price of substitute products. As buyers' incomes rose, consumers shifted demand away from canned fish and toward higher-quality fresh or frozen fish, including more-valued Atlantic, chinook, sockeye, and coho salmon. Moreover, the emergence of fish farming, in which salmon are raised in ocean net pens, lowered the prices of these substitute species. That, too, reduced the demand for pink salmon.

The altered supply and demand reduced the price of pink salmon to as low as $0.10 per pound, as represented by the drop in price from P_1 to P_2 in Figure 3. Both the supply increase and the demand decrease helped reduce the equilibrium price. However, in this particular case the equilibrium quantity of pink salmon increased, as represented by the move from Q_1 to Q_2. Both shifts reduced the equilibrium price, but equilibrium quantity increased because the increase in supply exceeded the decrease in demand.

Gasoline

The price of gasoline in the United States has increased rapidly several times during the past several years. For example, the average price of a gallon of gasoline rose from around $2.60 in October 2010 to about $3.90 in May 2011. What caused this 50 percent rise in the price of gasoline? How would we diagram this increase?

We begin in Figure 4 with the price of a gallon of gasoline at P_1, representing the $2.60 price. Simultaneous

FIGURE 4 The market for gasoline. An increase in the demand for gasoline, as shown by the shift from D_1 to D_2, coupled with a decrease in supply, as shown by the shift from S_1 to S_2, boosts equilibrium price (here from P_1 to P_2). In this case, equilibrium quantity increases from Q_1 to Q_2 because the increase in demand outweighs the decrease in supply.

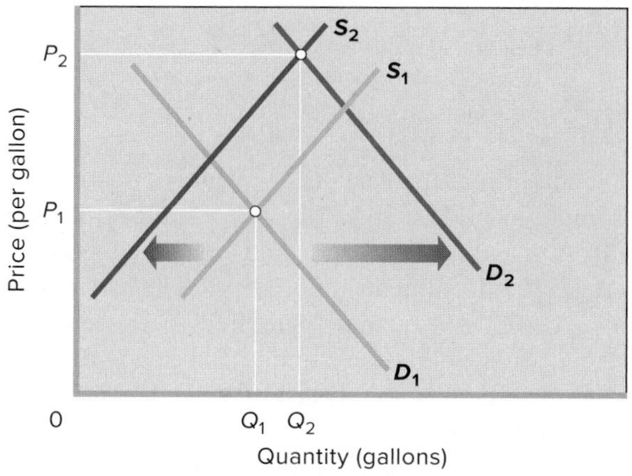

FIGURE 5 The market for sushi. Equal increases in the demand for sushi, as from D_1 to D_2, and in the supply of sushi, as from S_1 to S_2, expand the equilibrium quantity of sushi (here from Q_1 to Q_2) while leaving the price of sushi unchanged at P_1.

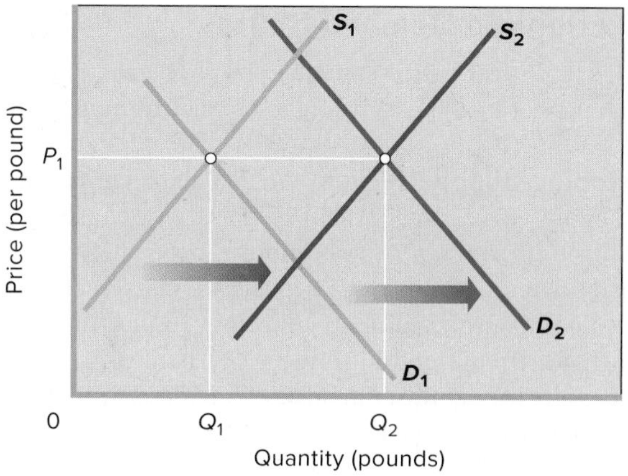

supply and demand factors disturbed this equilibrium. Supply uncertainties relating to Middle East politics and warfare and expanded demand for oil by fast-growing countries such as China pushed up the price of a barrel of oil from under \$80 per barrel in October 2010 to well over \$100 per barrel in May 2011. Oil is the main input for producing gasoline, so any sustained rise in its price boosts the per-unit cost of producing gasoline. Such cost rises decrease the supply of gasoline, as represented by the leftward shift of the supply curve from S_1 to S_2 in Figure 4. At times refinery breakdowns in the United States also contributed to this reduced supply.

While the supply of gasoline declined between October 2010 and May 2011, the demand for gasoline increased, as depicted by the rightward shift of the demand curve from D_1 to D_2. Incomes in general were rising over this period because the U.S. economy was expanding. Rising incomes raise demand for all normal goods, including gasoline. An increased number of low-gas-mileage SUVs and light trucks on the road also contributed to growing gas demand.

The combined decline in gasoline supply and increase in gasoline demand boosted the price of gasoline from \$2.60 to \$3.90, as represented by the rise from P_1 to P_2 in Figure 4. Because the demand increase outweighed the supply decrease, the equilibrium quantity expanded, here from Q_1 to Q_2.

In other periods the price of gasoline has *declined* as the demand for gasoline has increased. Test your understanding of the analysis by explaining how such a price decrease could occur.

Sushi

Sushi bars are springing up like Starbucks in American cities (well, maybe not that fast!). Consumption of sushi, the raw-fish delicacy from Japan, has soared in the United States in recent years. Nevertheless, the price of sushi has remained relatively constant.

Supply and demand analysis helps explain this circumstance of increased quantity and constant price. A change in tastes has increased the U.S. demand for sushi. Many consumers of sushi find it highly tasty when they try it. And, as implied by the growing number of sushi bars in the United States, the supply of sushi has also expanded.

We represent these supply and demand changes in Figure 5 as the rightward shift of the demand curve from D_1 to D_2 and the rightward shift of the supply curve from S_1 to S_2. Observe that the equilibrium quantity of sushi increases from Q_1 to Q_2 and equilibrium price remains constant at P_1. The increase in supply, which taken alone would reduce price, has perfectly offset the increase in demand, which taken alone would raise price. The price of sushi does not change, but the equilibrium quantity greatly increases because both the increase in demand and the increase in supply expand purchases and sales.

Simultaneous increases in demand and supply can cause price to either rise, fall, or remain constant, depending on the relative magnitudes of the supply and demand increases. In this case, price remained constant.

AP Upsloping versus Vertical Supply Curves

As you already know, the typical good or service possesses an upsloping supply curve because a higher market price will cause producers to increase the quantity supplied. There are, however, some goods and services whose quantities supplied are fixed and totally unresponsive to changes in price. Examples include the amount of land in a given area, the number of seats in a stadium, and the limited part of the electromagnetic spectrum that is reserved for cellular telephone transmissions. These sorts of goods and services have vertical supply curves because the same fixed amount is available no matter what price is offered to suppliers.

Reactions to Demand Shifts

Markets react very differently to a shift in demand depending upon whether they have upsloping or vertical supply curves.

Upsloping Supply Curves When a market has an upsloping supply curve, any shift in demand will cause both the equilibrium price *and* the equilibrium quantity to adjust. Consider Figure 2. When the demand for euros increases, the movement from the initial equilibrium to the final equilibrium involves the equilibrium price rising from \$1.25 to \$1.50 while the equilibrium quantity increases from Q_1 to Q_2. Price and quantity *both* change.

Vertical Supply Curves When a market has a vertical supply curve, any shift in demand will cause only the equilibrium price to change; the equilibrium quantity remains the same because the quantity supplied is fixed and cannot adjust.

Consider Figure 6, in which the supply of land in San Francisco is fixed at quantity Q_0. If demand increases from D_1 to D_2, the movement from the initial equilibrium at point *a* to the final equilibrium at point *b* is accomplished solely by a rise in the equilibrium price from P_1 to P_2. Because the quantity of land is fixed, the increase in demand cannot cause any change in the equilibrium quantity supplied. The entire adjustment from the initial equilibrium to the final equilibrium has to come in the form of a higher equilibrium price.

FIGURE 6 The market for land in San Francisco. Because the quantity of land in San Francisco is fixed at Q_0, the supply curve is vertical above Q_0 in order to indicate that the same quantity of land will be supplied no matter what the price is. As demand increases from D_1 to D_2, the equilibrium price rises from P_1 to P_2. Because the quantity of land is fixed at Q_0, the movement from equilibrium *a* to equilibrium *b* involves only a change in the equilibrium price; the equilibrium quantity remains at Q_0 due to land being in fixed supply.

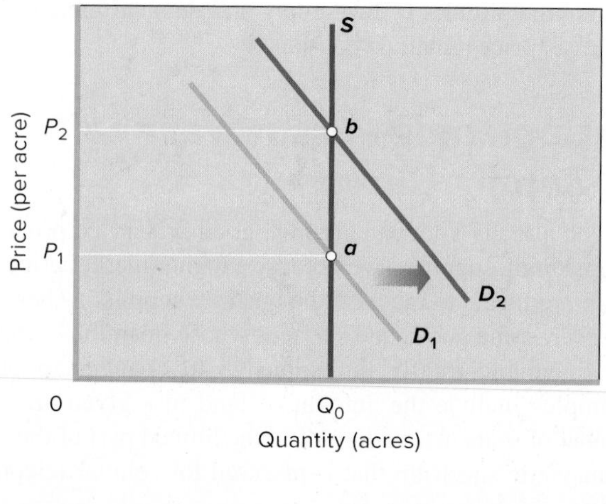

This fact explains why real estate prices are so high in San Francisco and other major cities. Any increase in demand cannot be met by a combination of increases in price and increases in quantity. With the quantity of land in fixed supply, any increase in demand results solely in higher equilibrium land prices.

Preset Prices

In the body of this chapter, we saw that an effective government-imposed price ceiling (legal maximum price) causes quantity demanded to exceed quantity supplied—a shortage. An effective government-imposed price floor (legal minimum price) causes quantity supplied to exceed quantity demanded—a surplus. Put simply: Shortages result when prices are set below, and surpluses result when prices are set above, equilibrium prices.

We now want to establish that shortages and surpluses can occur in markets other than those in which government imposes price floors and ceilings. Such market imbalances happen when the seller or sellers set prices in advance of sales and the prices selected turn out to be below or above equilibrium prices. Consider the following two examples.

Olympic Figure Skating Finals

Tickets for the women's figure skating championship at the Olympics are among the world's "hottest tickets." The popularity of this event and the high incomes of buyers translate into tremendous ticket demand. The Olympic officials set the price for the tickets in advance. Invariably, the price, although high, is considerably below the equilibrium price that would equate quantity demanded and quantity supplied. A severe shortage of tickets therefore occurs in this *primary market*—the market involving the official ticket office.

The shortage, in turn, creates a *secondary market* in which buyers bid for tickets held by initial purchasers rather than the original seller. Scalping tickets—selling them above the original ticket price—may be legal or illegal, depending on local laws.

Figure 7 shows how the shortage in the primary ticket market looks in terms of supply and demand analysis. Demand curve *D* represents the strong demand for tickets and supply curve *S* represents the supply of tickets. The supply curve is vertical because a fixed number of tickets are printed to match the capacity of the arena. At the printed ticket price of P_1, the quantity of tickets demanded, Q_2, exceeds the quantity supplied, Q_1. The result is a shortage of *ab*—the horizontal distance between Q_2 and Q_1 in the primary market.

If the printed ticket price had been the higher equilibrium price P_2, no shortage of tickets would have occurred. But at the lower price P_1, a shortage and secondary ticket market will emerge among those buyers willing to pay more than the printed ticket price and those sellers willing to sell their

FIGURE 7 The market for tickets to the Olympic women's figure skating finals. The demand curve *D* and supply curve *S* for the Olympic women's figure skating finals produce an equilibrium price that is above the P_1 price printed on the ticket. At price P_1 the quantity of tickets demanded, Q_2, greatly exceeds the quantity of tickets available, Q_1. The resulting shortage of *ab* (= $Q_2 - Q_1$) gives rise to a legal or illegal secondary market.

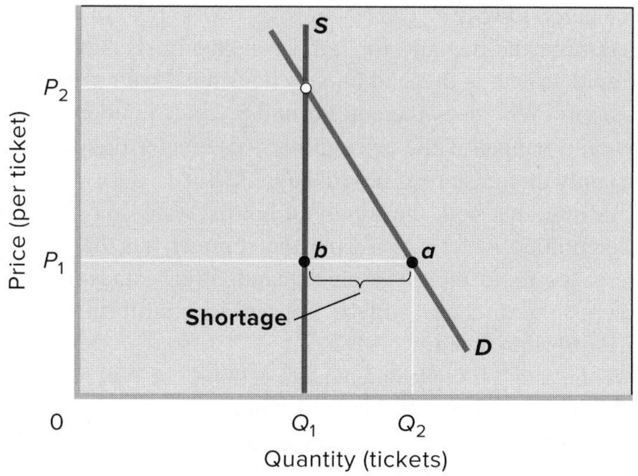

FIGURE 8 The market for tickets to the Olympic curling preliminaries. The demand curve *D* and supply curve *S* for the Olympic curling preliminaries produce an equilibrium price below the P_1 price printed on the ticket. At price P_1 the quantity of tickets demanded is less than the quantity of tickets available. The resulting surplus of *ba* (= $Q_1 - Q_2$) means the event is not sold out.

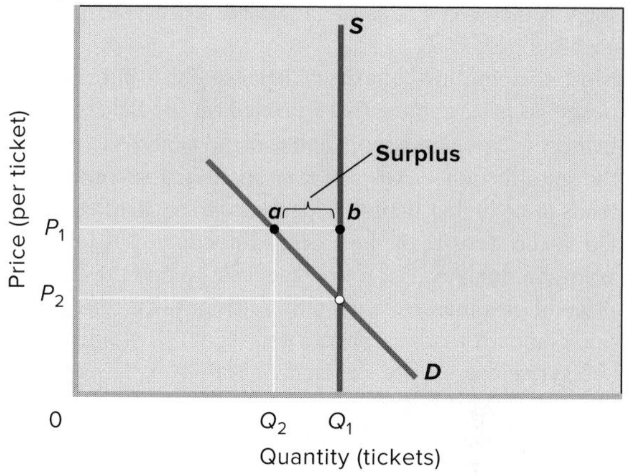

purchased tickets for more than the original price. Wherever there are shortages and secondary markets, it is safe to assume the original price was set below the equilibrium price.

Olympic Curling Preliminaries

Contrast the shortage of tickets for the women's figure skating finals at the Olympics to the surplus of tickets for one of the preliminary curling matches. For the uninitiated, curling is a sport in which participants slide a heavy round object called a "stone" down the ice toward a target while teammates called "sweepers" use brooms to alter the course of the stone when desired.

Curling is a popular spectator sport in a few nations such as Canada, but it does not draw many fans in most countries. So the demand for tickets to most of the preliminary curling events is not very strong. We demonstrate this weak demand as *D* in Figure 8. As in our previous example, the supply of tickets is fixed by the size of the arena and is shown as vertical line *S*.

We represent the printed ticket price as P_1 in Figure 8. In this case the printed price is much higher than the equilibrium price of P_2. At the printed ticket price, quantity supplied is Q_1 and quantity demanded is Q_2. So a surplus of tickets of *ba* (= $Q_1 - Q_2$) occurs. No ticket scalping occurs and there are numerous empty seats. Only if the Olympic officials had priced the tickets at the lower price P_2 would the event have been a sellout. (Actually, the Olympic officials try to adjust to demand realities for curling contests by holding them in smaller arenas and by charging less for tickets. Nevertheless, the stands are rarely full for the preliminary contests, which compete against final events in other winter Olympic sports.)

APPENDIX SUMMARY

LO3.7 Illustrate how supply and demand analysis can provide insights on actual-economy situations.

A decrease in the supply of a product increases its equilibrium price and reduces its equilibrium quantity. In contrast, an increase in the demand for a product boosts both its equilibrium price and its equilibrium quantity.

Simultaneous changes in supply and demand affect equilibrium price and quantity in various ways, depending on the relative magnitudes of the changes in supply and demand. Equal increases in supply and demand, for example, leave equilibrium price unchanged.

Products (such as land) whose quantities supplied do not vary with price have vertical supply curves. For these products, any shift in demand will lead to a change in the equilibrium price but no change in the equilibrium quantity.

Sellers set prices of some items such as tickets in advance of the event. These items are sold in the primary market that involves the original sellers and buyers. If preset prices turn out to be below the equilibrium prices, shortages occur and scalping in legal or illegal secondary markets arises. The prices in the secondary market then rise above the preset prices. In contrast, surpluses occur when the preset prices happen to exceed the equilibrium prices.

The following and additional problems can be found in connect

APPENDIX DISCUSSION QUESTIONS

1. Why are shortages or surpluses more likely with preset prices, such as those on tickets, than flexible prices, such as those on gasoline? LO3.7
2. Most scalping laws make it illegal to sell—but not to buy—tickets at prices above those printed on the tickets. Assuming that is the case, use supply and demand analysis to explain why the equilibrium ticket price in an illegal secondary market tends to be higher than in a legal secondary market. LO3.7
3. Go to the website of the Energy Information Administration, **www.eia.doe.gov,** and follow the links to find the current retail price of gasoline. How does the current price of regular gasoline compare with the price a year ago? What must have happened to either supply, demand, or both to explain the observed price change? LO3.7
4. Suppose the supply of apples sharply increases because of perfect weather conditions throughout the growing season. Assuming no change in demand, explain the effect on the equilibrium price and quantity of apples. Explain why quantity demanded increases even though demand does not change. LO3.7
5. Assume the demand for lumber suddenly rises because of a rapid growth of demand for new housing. Assume no change in supply. Why does the equilibrium price of lumber rise? What would happen if the price did not rise under the demand and supply circumstances described? LO3.7
6. Assume that both the supply of bottled water and the demand for bottled water rise during the summer but that supply increases more rapidly than demand. What can you conclude about the directions of the impacts on equilibrium price and equilibrium quantity? LO3.7
7. When asked for investment advice, humorist Will Rogers joked that people should "[b]uy land. They ain't making any more of the stuff." Explain his advice in terms of the supply and demand model. LO3.7

AP APPENDIX REVIEW QUESTIONS

1. Will the equilibrium price of orange juice increase or decrease in each of the following situations? LO3.7
   a. A medical study reporting that orange juice reduces cancer is released at the same time that a freak storm destroys half of the orange crop in Florida.
   b. The prices of all beverages except orange juice fall by half while unexpectedly perfect weather in Florida results in an orange crop that is 20 percent larger than normal.
2. Consider the market for coffee beans. Suppose that the prices of all other caffeinated beverages go up 30 percent while at the same time a new fertilizer boosts production at coffee plantations dramatically. Which of the following best describes what is likely to happen to the equilibrium price and quantity of coffee beans? LO3.7
   a. Both the equilibrium price and the quantity will rise.
   b. The equilibrium price will rise but the equilibrium quantity will fall.
   c. The equilibrium price may rise or fall but the equilibrium quantity will rise for certain.
   d. Neither the price change nor the quantity change can be determined for certain.
   e. None of the above.
3. Suppose that the demand for euros increases as more Americans travel to Europe for vacation. What is the effect on the market for euros? LO3.7
   a. The dollar will appreciate.
   b. The equilibrium price of one euro for one dollar would be higher.
   c. The equilibrium price of one euro for one dollar would be lower.
   d. The euro will stay the same equilibrium price for the dollar.
   e. The dollar will appreciate, and the euro will depreciate.
4. Suppose that you are the economic advisor to a local government that has to deal with a politically embarrassing surplus that was caused by a price floor that the government recently imposed. Your first suggestion is to get rid of the price floor, but the politicians don't want to do that. Instead, they present you with the following list of options that they hope will get rid of the surplus while keeping the price floor. Identify each one as either *could work* or *can't work*. LO3.7
   a. Restricting supply.
   b. Decreasing demand.
   c. Purchasing the surplus at the floor price.
5. Suppose both the demand for olives and the supply of olives decline by equal amounts over some time period. Use graphical analysis to show the effect on equilibrium price and quantity. LO3.7
6. When the supply curve is vertical, which statement is true? LO3.7
   a. Any shift in the demand curve will cause both equilibrium price and quantity to adjust.
   b. Any shift in the demand curve will cause only the equilibrium price to adjust.
   c. Any shift in the demand curve will cause only the equilibrium quantity to adjust.
   d. Any shift in the vertical supply curve will cause both the equilibrium price and quantity to adjust.
   e. There can be no equilibrium position between demand and supply.

APPENDIX PROBLEMS

1. Demand and supply often shift in the retail market for gasoline. Below are two demand curves and two supply curves for gallons of gasoline in the month of May in a small town in Maine. Some of the data are missing. LO3.7

	Quantities Demanded		Quantities Supplied	
Price	D_1	D_2	S_1	S_2
$4.00	5,000	7,500	9,000	9,500
____	6,000	8,000	8,000	9,000
2.00	____	8,500	____	8,500
____	____	9,000	5,000	____

   a. Use the following facts to fill in the missing data in the table. If demand is D_1 and supply is S_1, the equilibrium quantity is 7,000 gallons per month. When demand is D_2 and supply is S_1, the equilibrium price is $3.00 per gallon. When demand is D_2 and supply is S_1, there is an excess demand of 4,000 gallons per month at a price of $1.00 per gallon. If demand is D_1 and supply is S_2, the equilibrium quantity is 8,000 gallons per month.

   b. Compare two equilibriums. In the first, demand is D_1 and supply is S_1. In the second, demand is D_1 and supply is S_2. By how much does the equilibrium quantity change? By how much does the equilibrium price change?

   c. If supply falls from S_2 to S_1 while demand declines from D_2 to D_1, does the equilibrium price rise, fall, or stay the same? What if only supply falls? What if only demand falls?

   d. Suppose that supply is fixed at S_1 and that demand starts at D_1. By how many gallons per month would demand have to increase at each price level such that the equilibrium price per gallon would be $3.00? $4.00?

2. The following table shows two demand schedules for a given style of men's shoe—that is, how many pairs per month will be demanded at various prices at a men's clothing store in Seattle called Stromnord.

Price	D_1 Quantity Demanded	D_2 Quantity Demanded
$75	53	13
70	60	15
65	68	18
60	77	22
55	87	27

Suppose that Stromnord has exactly 65 pairs of this style of shoe in inventory at the start of the month of July and will not receive any more pairs of this style until at least August 1. LO3.7

   a. If demand is D_1, what is the lowest price that Stromnord can charge so that it will not run out of this model of shoe in the month of July? What if demand is D_2?

   b. If the price of shoes is set at $75 for both July and August and demand will be D_2 in July and D_1 in August, how many pairs of shoes should Stromnord order if it wants to end the month of August with exactly zero pairs of shoes in its inventory? What if the price is set at $55 for both months?

3. Use the following table to answer the questions that follow: LO3.7

   a. If this table reflects the supply of and demand for tickets to a particular World Cup soccer game, what is the stadium capacity?

   b. If the preset ticket price is $45, would we expect to see a secondary market for tickets? Would the price of a ticket in the secondary market be higher than, the same as, or lower than the price in the primary (original) market?

   c. Suppose for some other World Cup game the quantity of tickets demanded is 20,000 lower at each ticket price than shown in the table. If the ticket price remains $45, would the event be a sellout?

Quantity Demanded, Thousands	Price	Quantity Supplied, Thousands
80	$25	60
75	35	60
70	45	60
65	55	60
60	65	60
55	75	60
50	85	60

Chapter 4

Market Failures: Public Goods and Externalities

Learning Objectives

LO4.1 **Differentiate between demand-side market failures and supply-side market failures.**

LO4.2 **Explain the origin of both consumer surplus and producer surplus and explain how properly functioning markets maximize their sum, total surplus, while optimally allocating resources.**

LO4.3 **Describe free riding and public goods and illustrate why private firms cannot normally produce public goods.**

LO4.4 **Explain how positive and negative externalities cause under- and overallocations of resources.**

LO4.5 **Show why we normally won't want to pay what it would cost to eliminate every last bit of a negative externality such as air pollution.**

LO4.6 **(Appendix) Describe how information failures may justify government intervention in some markets.**

AP Chapter Focus

Competitive markets usually do a remarkable job of allocating a society's resources to their most highly valued uses. In this chapter we demonstrate how properly functioning markets efficiently allocate resources. We then explore what happens when markets don't function properly (referred to as **market failures**). In some circumstances, economically desirable goods are not produced at all, overproduced, or underproduced.

In such situations, an economic role for government may arise. We will examine that role as it relates to public goods and so-called externalities—situations where market failures lead to suboptimal outcomes that the government may be able to improve upon by using its powers to tax, spend, and regulate. The government may, for instance, pay for the production of goods that the private sector fails to produce. It may also act to reduce the production of those goods and services that the private sector overproduces. Implementing such policies can, however, be both costly and complicated. We conclude the chapter by noting the government inefficiencies that can hinder government efforts to improve economic outcomes.

Market Failures in Competitive Markets[1]

LO4.1 Differentiate between demand-side market failures and supply-side market failures.

In Chapter 3 we asserted that "competitive markets usually produce an assignment of resources that is 'right' from an economic perspective." We now want to focus on the word "usually" and discuss exceptions. We must do this because it is unfortunately the case that the presence of robust competition involving many buyers and many sellers may not, by itself, be enough to guarantee that a market will allocate resources correctly. Market failures sometimes happen in competitive markets. The focus of this chapter is to explain how and why such market failures can arise.

Fortunately, the broad picture is simple. Market failures in competitive markets fall into just two categories:

- **Demand-side market failures** happen when demand curves do not reflect consumers' full willingness to pay for a good or service.
- **Supply-side market failures** occur when supply curves do not reflect the full cost of producing a good or service.

Demand-Side Market Failures

Demand-side market failures arise because it is impossible in certain cases to charge consumers what they are willing to pay for a product. Consider outdoor fireworks displays. People enjoy fireworks and would therefore be *willing* to pay to see a fireworks display if the only way to see it was to have to pay for the right to do so. But because such displays are outdoors and in public, people don't actually *have* to pay to see the display because there is no way to exclude those who haven't paid from also enjoying the show. Private firms will therefore be unwilling to produce outdoor fireworks displays, as it will be nearly impossible for them to raise enough revenue to cover production costs.

Supply-Side Market Failures

Supply-side market failures arise in situations in which a firm does not have to pay the full cost of producing its output. Consider a coal-burning power plant. The firm running the plant will have to pay for all of the land, labor, capital, and entrepreneurship that it uses to generate electricity by burning coal. But if the firm is not charged for the smoke that it releases into the atmosphere, it will fail to pay another set of costs—the costs that its pollution imposes on other people. These include future harm from global warming, toxins that affect wildlife, and possible damage to agricultural crops downwind.

A market failure arises because it is not possible for the market to correctly weigh costs and benefits in a situation in which some of the costs are completely unaccounted for. The coal-burning power plant produces more electricity and generates more pollution than it would if it had to pay for each ton of smoke that it released into the atmosphere. The extra units that are produced are units of output for which the costs are *greater than* the benefits. Obviously, these units should not be produced.

AP Efficiently Functioning Markets

LO4.2 Explain the origin of both consumer surplus and producer surplus and explain how properly functioning markets maximize their sum, total surplus, while optimally allocating resources.

The best way to understand market failure is to first understand how properly functioning competitive markets achieve economic efficiency. We touched on this subject in Chapter 3, but we now want to expand and deepen that analysis, both for its own sake and to set up our discussion of public goods and externalities. Two conditions must hold if a competitive market is to produce efficient outcomes: The demand curve in the market must reflect consumers' full willingness to pay, and the supply curve in the market must reflect all the costs of production. If these conditions hold, then the market will produce only units for which benefits are at least equal to costs. It will also maximize the amount of "benefit surpluses" that are shared between consumers and producers.

Consumer Surplus

The benefit surplus received by a consumer or consumers in a market is called **consumer surplus.** It is defined as the difference between the maximum price a consumer is (or consumers are) willing to pay for a product and the actual price that they do pay.

The maximum price that a person is willing to pay for a unit of a product depends on the opportunity cost of that person's consumption alternatives. Suppose that Ted is offered the chance to purchase an apple. He would of course like to have it for free, but the maximum amount he would be willing to pay depends on the alternative uses to which he can put his money. If his maximum willingness to pay for that particular apple is $1.25, then we know that he is willing to forgo up to—but not more than—$1.25 of other goods and services. Paying even one cent more would entail having to give up too much of other goods and services.

It also means that if Ted is charged any market price less than $1.25, he will receive a consumer surplus equal to the

[1]Other market failures arise when there are not enough buyers or sellers to ensure competition. In those situations, the lack of competition allows either buyers or sellers to restrict purchases or sales below optimal levels for their own benefit. As an example, a monopoly—a firm that is the only producer in its industry—can restrict the amount of output that it supplies in order to drive up the market price and thereby increase its own profit.

TABLE 4.1 Consumer Surplus

(1) Person	(2) Maximum Price Willing to Pay	(3) Actual Price (Equilibrium Price)	(4) Consumer Surplus
Bob	$13	$8	$5 (= $13 – $8)
Barb	12	8	4 (= $12 – $8)
Bill	11	8	3 (= $11 – $8)
Bart	10	8	2 (= $10 – $8)
Brent	9	8	1 (= $ 9 – $8)
Betty	8	8	0 (= $ 8 – $8)

difference between the $1.25 maximum price that he would have been willing to pay and the lower market price. For instance, if the market price is $0.50 per apple, Ted will receive a consumer surplus of $0.75 per apple (= $1.25 – $0.50). In nearly all markets, consumers individually and collectively gain greater total utility or satisfaction in dollar terms from their purchases than the amount of their expenditures (= product price × quantity). This utility surplus arises because each consumer who buys the product only has to pay the market equilibrium price even though many of them would have been willing to pay more than the equilibrium price to obtain the product.

The concept of maximum willingness to pay also gives us another way to understand demand curves. Consider Table 4.1, where the first two columns show the maximum amounts that six consumers would each be willing to pay for a bag of oranges. Bob, for instance, would be willing to pay a maximum of $13 for a bag of oranges. Betty, by contrast, would only be willing to pay a maximum of $8 for a bag of oranges.

Notice that the maximum prices that these individuals are willing to pay represent points on a demand curve because the lower the market price, the more bags of oranges will be demanded. At a price of $12.50, for instance, Bob will be the only person listed in the table who will purchase a bag. But at a price of $11.50, both Bob and Barb will want to purchase a bag. And at a price of $10.50, Bob, Barb, and Bill will each want to purchase a bag. The lower the price, the greater the total quantity demanded as the market price falls below the maximum prices of more and more consumers.

Lower prices also imply larger consumer surpluses. When the price is $12.50, Bob only gets $0.50 in consumer surplus because his maximum willingness to pay of $13 is only $0.50 higher than the market price of $12.50. But if the market price were to fall to $8, then his consumer surplus would be $5 (= $13 – $8). The third and fourth columns of Table 4.1 show how much consumer surplus each of our six consumers will receive if the market price of a bag of oranges is $8. Only Betty receives no consumer surplus because her maximum willingness to pay exactly matches the $8 equilibrium price.

AP **FIGURE 4.1 Consumer surplus.** Consumer surplus—shown as the green triangle—is the difference between the maximum prices consumers are willing to pay for a product and the lower equilibrium price, here assumed to be $8. For quantity Q_1, consumers are willing to pay the sum of the amounts represented by the green triangle and the yellow rectangle. Because they need to pay only the amount shown as the yellow rectangle, the green triangle shows consumer surplus.

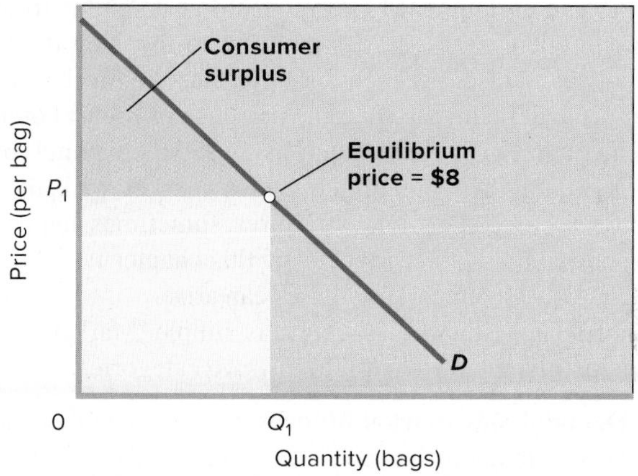

It is easy to show on a graph both the individual consumer surplus received by each particular buyer in a market as well as the collective consumer surplus received by all buyers. Consider Figure 4.1, which shows the market equilibrium price P_1 = $8 as well as the downsloping demand curve *D* for bags of oranges. Demand curve *D* includes not only the six consumers named in Table 4.1 but also every other consumer of oranges in the market. The individual consumer surplus of each particular person who is willing to buy at the $8 market price is simply the vertical distance from the horizontal line that marks the $8 market price up to that particular buyer's maximum willingness to pay. The collective consumer surplus obtained by all of our named and unnamed buyers is found by adding together each of their individual consumer surpluses. To obtain the Q_1 bags of oranges represented, consumers collectively are willing to pay the total amount shown by the sum of the green triangle and yellow rectangle under the demand curve and to the left of Q_1. But consumers need pay only the amount represented by the yellow rectangle (= $P_1 \times Q_1$). So the green triangle is the consumer surplus in this market. It is the sum of the vertical distances between the demand curve and the $8 equilibrium price at each quantity up to Q_1. Alternatively, it is the sum of the gaps between maximum willingness to pay and actual price, such as those we calculated in Table 4.1. Thus, consumer surplus can also be defined as the area that lies below the demand curve and above the price line that extends horizontally from P_1.

Consumer surplus and price are inversely (negatively) related. Given the demand curve, higher prices reduce consumer surplus; lower prices increase it. To test this generalization, draw in an equilibrium price above $8 in Figure 4.1

and observe the reduced size of the triangle representing consumer surplus. When price goes up, the gap narrows between the maximum willingness to pay and the actual price. Next, draw in an equilibrium price below $8 and see that consumer surplus increases. When price declines, the gap widens between maximum willingness to pay and actual price.

Producer Surplus

Like consumers, producers also receive a benefit surplus in markets. This **producer surplus** is the difference between the actual price a producer receives (or producers receive) and the minimum acceptable price that a consumer would have to pay the producer to make a particular unit of output available.

A producer's minimum acceptable price for a particular unit will equal the producer's marginal cost of producing that particular unit. That marginal cost will be the sum of the rent, wages, interest, and profit that the producer will need to pay in order to obtain the land, labor, capital, and entrepreneurship required to produce that particular unit. In this section, we are assuming that the marginal cost of producing a unit will include *all* of the costs of production. Unlike the coal-burning power plant mentioned previously, the producer must pay for all of its costs, including the cost of pollution. In later sections, we will explore the market failures that arise in situations where firms do not have to pay all their costs.

In addition to equaling marginal cost, a producer's minimum acceptable price can also be interpreted as the opportunity cost of bidding resources away from the production of other products. To see why this is true, suppose that Leah is an apple grower. The resources necessary for her to produce one apple could be used to produce other things. To get them directed toward producing an apple, it is necessary to pay Leah what it will cost her to bid the necessary resources away from other entrepreneurs who would like to use them to produce other products. Leah would, naturally, like to get paid as much as possible to produce the apple for you. But her minimum acceptable price is the lowest price you could pay her such that she can just break even after bidding away from other uses the land, labor, capital, and entrepreneurship necessary to produce the apple.

The size of the producer surplus earned on any particular unit will be the difference between the market price that the producer actually receives and the producer's minimum acceptable price. Consider Table 4.2, which shows the minimum acceptable prices of six different orange growers. With a market price of $8, Carlos, for instance, has a producer surplus of $5, which is equal to the market price of $8 minus his minimum acceptable price of $3. Chad, by contrast, receives no producer surplus because his minimum acceptable price of $8 just equals the market equilibrium price of $8.

Carlos's minimum acceptable price is lower than Chad's minimum acceptable price because Carlos is a more efficient producer than Chad, by which we mean that Carlos produces oranges using a less-costly combination of resources than Chad uses. The differences in efficiency between Carlos and Chad are likely due to differences in the type and quality of resources available to them. Carlos, for instance, may own land perfectly suited to growing oranges, while Chad has land in the desert that requires costly irrigation if it is to be used to grow oranges. Thus, Chad has a higher marginal cost of producing oranges.

TABLE 4.2 Producer Surplus

(1) Person	(2) Minimum Acceptable Price	(3) Actual Price (Equilibrium Price)	(4) Consumer Surplus
Carlos	$3	$8	$5 (= $8 – $3)
Courtney	4	8	4 (= $8 – $4)
Chuck	5	8	3 (= $8 – $5)
Cindy	6	8	2 (= $8 – $6)
Craig	7	8	1 (= $8 – $7)
Chad	8	8	0 (= $8 – $8)

The minimum acceptable prices that producers are willing to accept form points on a supply curve because the higher the price, the more bags of oranges will be supplied. At a price of $3.50, for instance, only Carlos would be willing to supply a bag of oranges. But at a price of $5.50, Carlos, Courtney, and Chuck would all be willing to supply a bag of oranges. The higher the market price, the more oranges will be supplied, as the market price surpasses the marginal costs and minimum acceptable prices of more and more producers. Thus, supply curves shown in this competitive market are both marginal-cost curves and minimum-acceptable-price curves.

The supply curve in Figure 4.2 includes not only the six producers named in Table 4.2 but also every other producer of oranges in the market. At the market price of $8 per bag, Q_1 bags are produced because only those producers whose minimum acceptable prices are less than $8 per bag will choose to produce oranges with their resources. Those lower acceptable prices for each of the units up to Q_1 are shown by the portion of the supply curve lying to the left of and below the assumed $8 market price.

The individual producer surplus of each of these sellers is thus the vertical distance from each seller's respective minimum acceptable price on the supply curve up to the $8 market price. Their collective producer surplus is shown by the blue triangle in Figure 4.2. In that figure, producers collect revenues of $P_1 \times Q_1$, which is the sum of the blue triangle and the yellow area. As shown by the supply curve, however, revenues of only those illustrated by the yellow area would be required to entice producers to offer Q_1 bags of oranges for sale. The sellers therefore receive a producer surplus shown by the blue triangle. That surplus is the sum of the vertical

AP **FIGURE 4.2 Producer surplus.** Producer surplus—shown as the blue triangle—is the difference between the actual price producers receive for a product (here $8) and the lower minimum payments they are willing to accept. For quantity Q_1, producers receive the sum of the amounts represented by the blue triangle plus the yellow area. Because they need to receive only the amount shown by the yellow area to produce Q_1, the blue triangle represents producer surplus.

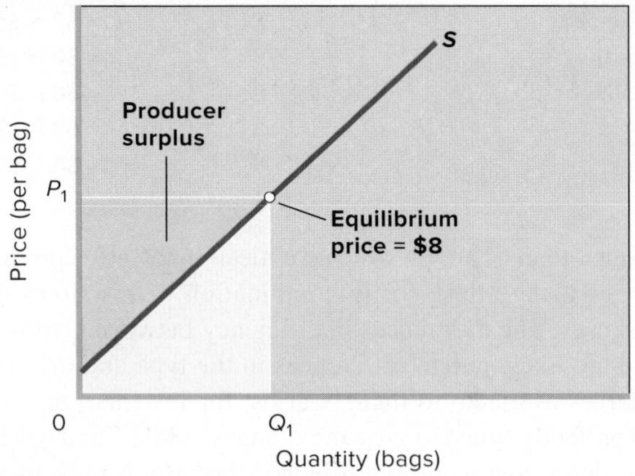

AP **FIGURE 4.3 Efficiency: maximum combined consumer and producer surplus.** At quantity Q_1 the combined amount of consumer surplus, shown as the green triangle, and producer surplus, shown as the blue triangle, is maximized. Efficiency occurs because, at Q_1, maximum willingness to pay, indicated by the points on the demand curve, equals minimum acceptable price, shown by the points on the supply curve.

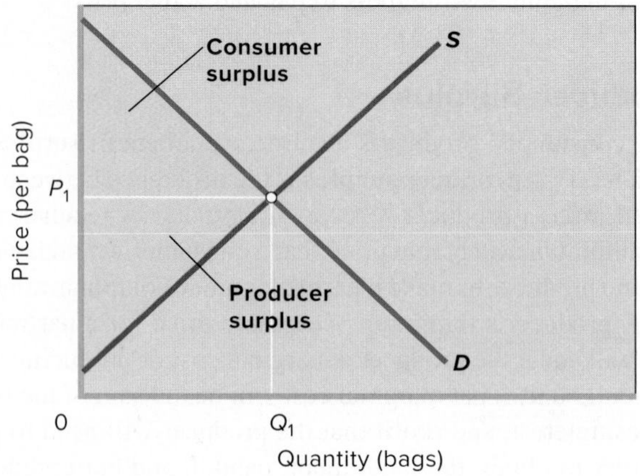

distances between the supply curve and the $8 equilibrium price at each of the quantities to the left of Q_1.

There is a direct (positive) relationship between equilibrium price and the amount of producer surplus. Given the supply curve, lower prices reduce producer surplus; higher prices increase it. If you pencil in a lower equilibrium price than $8, you will see that the producer surplus triangle gets smaller. The gaps between the minimum acceptable payments and the actual prices narrow when the price falls. If you pencil in an equilibrium price above $8, the size of the producer surplus triangle increases. The gaps between minimum acceptable payments and actual prices widen when the price increases.

Efficiency Revisited

In Figure 4.3 we bring together the demand and supply curves of Figures 4.1 and 4.2 to show the equilibrium price and quantity and the previously described regions of consumer and producer surplus. All markets that have downsloping demand curves and upsloping supply curves yield consumer and producer surplus.

Because we are assuming in Figure 4.3 that the demand curve reflects buyers' full willingness to pay and the supply curve reflects all of the costs facing sellers, the equilibrium quantity in Figure 4.3 reflects economic efficiency, which consists of productive efficiency and allocative efficiency.

- ***Productive efficiency*** is achieved because competition forces orange growers to use the best technologies and combinations of resources available. Doing so minimizes the per-unit cost of the output produced.
- ***Allocative efficiency*** is achieved because the correct quantity of oranges—Q_1—is produced relative to other goods and services.

There are two ways to understand why Q_1 is the correct quantity of oranges. Both involve realizing that any resources directed toward the production of oranges are resources that could have been used to produce other products. Thus, the only way to justify taking any amount of any resource (land, labor, capital, entrepreneurship) away from the production of other products is if it brings more utility or satisfaction when devoted to the production of oranges than it would if it were used to produce other products.

The first way to see why Q_1 is the allocatively efficient quantity of oranges is to note that demand and supply curves can be interpreted as measuring marginal benefit (MB) and marginal cost (MC). Recall from the discussion relating to Figure 1.3 that optimal allocation is achieved at the output level where MB = MC. We have already seen that supply curves are marginal cost curves. As it turns out, demand curves are marginal benefit curves. This is true because the maximum price that a consumer would be willing to pay for any particular unit is equal to the benefit that she would get if she were to consume that unit. Thus, each point on a demand curve represents both some consumer's maximum willingness to pay as well as the marginal benefit that he or she would get from consuming the particular unit in question.

Combining the fact that supply curves are MC curves with the fact that demand curves are MB curves, we see that points on the demand curve in Figure 4.3 measure the marginal benefit of oranges at each level of output, while points on the supply curve measure the marginal cost of oranges at each level of output. As a result, MB = MC where the demand and supply curves intersect—which means that the equilibrium quantity Q_1 must be allocatively efficient.

To gain a deeper understanding of why Q_1 is allocatively efficient, notice that for every unit up to Q_1 marginal benefit exceeds marginal cost (MB > MC). And because marginal cost includes the opportunity cost of not making other things with the resources needed to make these units, we know that people are made better off when the resources necessary to make these units are allocated to producing oranges rather than to producing anything else.

The second way to see why Q_1 is the correct quantity of oranges is based on our analysis of consumer and producer surplus and the fact that we can interpret demand and supply curves in terms of maximum willingness to pay and minimum acceptable price. In Figure 4.3, the maximum willingness to pay on the demand curve for each bag of oranges up to Q_1 exceeds the corresponding minimum acceptable price on the supply curve. Thus, each of these bags adds a positive amount (= maximum willingness to pay *minus* minimum acceptable price) to the *total* of consumer and producer surplus.

The fact that maximum willingness to pay exceeds minimum acceptable price for every unit up to Q_1 means that people gain more utility from producing and consuming those units than they would if they produced and consumed anything else that could be made with the resources that went into making those units. This is true because both the maximum willingness to pay and the minimum acceptable price take opportunity costs into account. As long as the maximum willingness to pay exceeds the minimum acceptable price, people are willing to pay more to consume a unit of the good in question (here, bags of oranges) than they would pay to consume anything else that could be made with the same resources. Only at the equilibrium quantity Q_1—where the maximum willingness to pay exactly equals the minimum acceptable price—does society exhaust all opportunities to produce units for which benefits exceed costs (including opportunity costs). Producing Q_1 units therefore achieves allocative efficiency because the market is producing and distributing only those units that make people happier with bags of oranges than they would be with anything else that could be produced with the same resources.

Geometrically, producing Q_1 units maximizes the combined area of consumer and producer surplus in Figure 4.3. In this context, the combined area is referred to as *total surplus*. Thus, when Q_1 units are produced, total surplus is equal to the large triangle formed by the green consumer-surplus triangle and the blue producer-surplus triangle.

When demand curves reflect buyers' full willingness to pay and when supply curves reflect all the costs facing sellers, competitive markets produce equilibrium quantities that maximize the sum of consumer and producer surplus. Allocative efficiency occurs at the market equilibrium quantity where three conditions exist simultaneously:

- MB = MC (Figure 1.3).
- Maximum willingness to pay = minimum acceptable price.
- Total surplus (= sum of consumer and producer surplus) is at a maximum.

Economists are enamored of markets because properly functioning markets automatically achieve allocative efficiency. Other methods of allocating resources—such as government central planning—do exist. But because other methods cannot do any better than properly functioning markets—and may, in many cases, do much worse—economists usually prefer that resources be allocated through markets whenever properly functioning markets are available.

Efficiency Losses (or Deadweight Losses)

Figures 4.4a and 4.4b demonstrate that **efficiency losses**—reductions of combined consumer and producer surplus—result from both underproduction and overproduction. First, consider Figure 4.4a, which analyzes the case of underproduction by considering what happens if output falls from the efficient level Q_1 to the smaller amount Q_2. When that happens, the sum of consumer and producer surplus, previously *abc,* falls to *adec*. So the combined consumer and producer surplus declines by the amount of the gray triangle to the left

AP **FIGURE 4.4 Efficiency losses (or deadweight losses).** Quantity levels either less than or greater than the efficient quantity Q_1 create efficiency losses. (a) Triangle *dbe* shows the efficiency loss associated with underproduction at output Q_2. (b) Triangle *bfg* illustrates the efficiency loss associated with overproduction at output level Q_3.

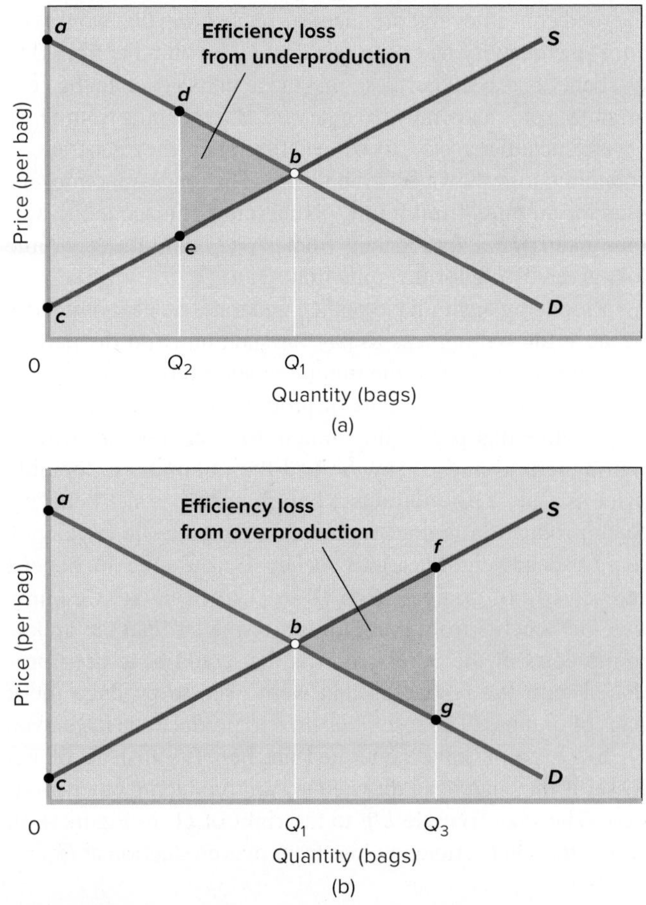

of Q_1. That triangle represents an efficiency loss to buyers and sellers. And because buyers and sellers are members of society, it represents an efficiency loss (or a so-called **deadweight loss**) to society.

For output levels from Q_2 to Q_1, consumers' maximum willingness to pay (as reflected by points on the demand curve) exceeds producers' minimum acceptable price (as reflected by points on the supply curve). By failing to produce units of this product for which a consumer is willing to pay more than a producer is willing to accept, society suffers a loss of net benefits. As a concrete example, consider a particular unit for which a consumer is willing to pay \$10 and a producer is willing to accept \$6. The \$4 difference between those values is a net benefit that will not be realized if this unit is not produced. In addition, the resources that should have gone to producing this unit will go instead to producing other products that will not generate as much utility as if those resources had been used here to produce this unit of this product. The triangle *dbe* in Figure 4.4a shows the total loss of net benefits that results from failing to produce the units from Q_2 to Q_1.

In contrast, consider the case of overproduction shown in Figure 4.4b, in which the number of oranges produced is Q_3 rather than the efficient level Q_1. In Figure 4.4b the combined consumer and producer surplus therefore declines by *bfg*—the gray triangle to the right of Q_1. This triangle subtracts from the total consumer and producer surplus of *abc* that would occur if the quantity had been Q_1. That is, for all units from 0 to Q_1, benefits exceed costs, so that those units generate the economic surplus shown by triangle *abc*. But the units from Q_1 to Q_3 are such that costs exceed benefits. Thus, they generate an economic loss shown by triangle *bfg*. The total economic surplus for all units from 0 to Q_3 is therefore the economic surplus given by *abc* for the units from 0 to Q_1 *minus* the economic loss given by *bfg* for the units from Q_1 to Q_3.

Producing any unit beyond Q_1 generates an economic loss because the willingness to pay for such units on the part of consumers is less than the minimum acceptable price to produce such units on the part of producers. As a concrete example, note that producing an item for which the maximum willingness to pay is, say, \$7 and the minimum acceptable price is, say, \$10 subtracts \$3 from society's net benefits. Such production is uneconomical and creates an efficiency loss (or deadweight loss) for society. Because the net benefit of each bag of oranges from Q_1 to Q_3 is negative, we know that the benefits from these units are smaller than the opportunity costs of the other products that could have been produced with the resources that were used to produce these bags of oranges. The resources used to produce the bags from Q_1 to Q_3 could have generated net benefits instead of net losses if they had been directed toward producing other products. The gray triangle *bfg* to the right of Q_1 in Figure 4.4b shows the total efficiency loss from overproduction at Q_3.

AP QUICK REVIEW 4.1

- ✓ Market failures in competitive markets occur when demand curves do not reflect the full benefits to society or supply curves do not reflect the full cost of production.
- ✓ Consumer surplus is the difference between the maximum price that a consumer is willing to pay for a product and the price actually paid.
- ✓ Producer surplus is the difference between the minimum price that a producer is willing to accept for a product and the price actually received.
- ✓ At the equilibrium price and quantity in competitive markets, marginal benefit equals marginal cost, and the sum (or total) of consumer surplus and producer surplus is maximized. The combination of consumer and producer surplus, called economic surplus, is maximized. Each of these conditions defines allocative efficiency.
- ✓ Quantities associated with underproduction and overproduction create efficiency losses, represented by lost economic surplus, called deadweight losses.

The magic of markets is that when demand reflects consumers' full willingness to pay and when supply reflects all costs, the market equilibrium quantity will automatically equal the allocatively efficient output level. Under these conditions, the market equilibrium quantity will ensure that there are neither efficiency losses from underproduction nor efficiency losses from overproduction. As we are about to see, however, such losses do happen when either demand does not reflect consumers' full willingness to pay or supply does not reflect all costs.

AP Public Goods

LO4.3 Describe free riding and public goods and illustrate why private firms cannot normally produce public goods.

Demand-side market failures arise in competitive markets when demand curves fail to reflect consumers' full willingness to pay for a good or service. In such situations, markets fail to produce all of the units for which there are net benefits because demand curves underreport how much consumers are willing and able to pay. This underreporting problem reaches its most extreme form in the case of a public good: Markets may fail to produce *any* of the public good because its demand curve may reflect *none* of its consumers' willingness to pay.

To understand public goods, we first need to understand the characteristics that define private goods.

Private Goods Characteristics

We have seen that the market system produces a wide range of **private goods**. These are the goods offered for sale in stores, in shops, and on the Internet. Examples include automobiles, clothing, personal computers, household appliances, and sporting goods. Private goods are distinguished by rivalry and excludability.

- **Rivalry** (in consumption) means that when one person buys and consumes a product, it is not available for another person to buy and consume. When Adams purchases and drinks a bottle of mineral water, it is not available for Benson to purchase and consume.
- **Excludability** means that sellers can keep people who do not pay for a product from obtaining its benefits. Only people who are willing and able to pay the market price for bottles of water can obtain these drinks and the benefits they confer.

Consumers fully express their personal demands for private goods in the market. If Adams likes bottled mineral water, that fact will be known by her desire to purchase the product. Other things equal, the higher the price of bottled water, the fewer bottles she will buy. So Adams's demand for bottled water will reflect an inverse relationship between the price of bottled water and the quantity of it demanded. This is simply *individual* demand, as described in Chapter 3.

The *market* demand for a private good is the horizontal summation of the individual demand schedules (review Figure 3.2). Suppose just two consumers comprise the market for bottled water and the price is $1 per bottle. If Adams will purchase 3 bottles and Benson will buy 2, the market demand will reflect consumers' demand for 5 bottles at the $1 price. Similar summations of quantities demanded at other prices will generate the market demand schedule and curve.

Suppose the equilibrium price of bottled water is $1. Adams and Benson will buy a total of 5 bottles, and the sellers will obtain total revenue of $5 (= $1 × 5). If the sellers' cost per bottle is $0.80, their total cost will be $4 (= $0.80 × 5). So sellers charging $1 per bottle will obtain $5 of total revenue, incur $4 of total cost, and earn $1 of profit on the 5 bottles sold.

Because firms can profitably "tap market demand" for private goods, they will produce and offer them for sale. Consumers demand private goods, and profit-seeking suppliers produce goods that satisfy the demand. Consumers willing to pay the market price obtain the goods; nonpayers go without. A competitive market not only makes private goods available to consumers but also allocates society's resources efficiently to the particular product. There is neither underproduction nor overproduction of the product.

Public Goods Characteristics

Public goods have the opposite characteristics of private goods. Public goods are distinguished by nonrivalry and nonexcludability.

- **Nonrivalry** (in consumption) means that one person's consumption of a good does not preclude consumption of the good by others. Everyone can simultaneously obtain the benefit from a public good such as national defense, street lighting, a global positioning system, or environmental protection.
- **Nonexcludability** means there is no effective way of excluding individuals from the benefit of the good once it comes into existence. Once in place, you cannot exclude someone from benefiting from national defense, street lighting, a global positioning system, or environmental protection.

These two characteristics create a **free-rider problem.** Once a producer has provided a public good, everyone, including nonpayers, can obtain the benefit.

Because most people do not voluntarily pay for something that they can obtain for free, most people become free riders. These free riders like the public good and would be willing to pay for it if producers could somehow force them to pay—but nonexcludability means that there is no way for producers to withhold the good from the free riders without also denying it to the few who do pay. As a result, free riding means that the willingness to pay of the free riders is not expressed in the market. From the viewpoint of producers, free riding reduces demand. The more free riding, the less demand. And if all consumers free ride, demand will collapse all the way to zero.

The low or even zero demand caused by free riding makes it virtually impossible for private firms to profitably provide public goods. With little or no demand, firms cannot effectively "tap market demand" for revenues and profits. As a result, they will not produce public goods. Society will therefore suffer efficiency losses because goods for which marginal benefits exceed marginal costs are not produced. Thus, if society wants a public good to be produced, it will have to direct government to provide it. Because the public good will still feature nonexcludability, the government won't have any better luck preventing free riding or charging people for it. But because the government can finance the provision of the public good through the taxation of other things, the government does not have to worry about profitability. It can therefore provide the public good even when private firms can't.

Examples of public goods include national defense, outdoor fireworks displays, the light beams thrown out by lighthouses, public art displays, public music concerts, MP3 music files posted to file-sharing websites, and ideas and inventions that are not protected by patents or copyrights. Each of these goods or services shows both nonrivalry and nonexcludability.

In a few special cases, private firms can provide public goods because the production costs of these public goods can be covered by the profits generated by closely related private

CONSIDER THIS . . .

Source: © Colin Young-Wolff/PhotoEdit

Street Entertainers

Street entertainers are often found in tourist areas of major cities. These entertainers illuminate the concepts of free riders and public goods.

Most street entertainers have a hard time earning a living from their activities (unless event organizers pay them) because they have no way of excluding nonpayers from the benefits of their entertainment. They essentially are providing public, not private, goods and must rely on voluntary payments.

The result is a significant free-rider problem. Only a few in the audience put money in the container or instrument case, and many who do so contribute only token amounts. The rest are free riders who obtain the benefits of the street entertainment and retain their money for purchases that they initiate.

Street entertainers are acutely aware of the free-rider problem, and some have found creative ways to lessen it. For example, some entertainers involve the audience directly in the act. This usually creates a greater sense of audience willingness (or obligation) to contribute money at the end of the performance.

"Pay for performance" is another creative approach to lessening the free-rider problem. A good example is the street entertainer painted up to look like a statue. When people drop coins into the container, the "statue" makes a slight movement. The greater the contributions, the greater the movement. But these human "statues" still face a free-rider problem: Nonpayers also get to enjoy the acts.

goods. For instance, private companies can make a profit providing broadcast TV—which is a nonrival, nonexcludable public good—because they control who gets to air TV commercials, which are rival and excludable private goods. The money that broadcasters make from selling airtime for ads allows them to turn a profit despite having to give their main product, broadcast TV, away for free.

Unfortunately, only a few public goods can be subsidized in this way by closely related private goods. For the large majority of public goods, private provision is unprofitable. As a result, there are only two remaining ways for a public good to be provided: private philanthropy or government provision. For many less expensive or less important public goods like fireworks displays or public art, society may feel comfortable relying on private philanthropy. But when it comes to public goods like national defense, people normally look to the government.

This leads to an important question: Once a government decides to produce a particular public good, how can it determine the optimal amount that it should produce? How can it avoid either underallocating or overallocating society's scarce resources to the production of the public good?

Optimal Quantity of a Public Good

If consumers need not reveal their true demand for a public good in the marketplace, how can society determine the optimal amount of that good? The answer is that the government has to try to estimate the demand for a public good through surveys or public votes. It can then compare the marginal benefit (MB) of an added unit of the good against the government's marginal cost (MC) of providing it. Adhering to the MB = MC rule, government can provide the "right," meaning "efficient," amount of the public good.

Demand for Public Goods

The demand for a public good is somewhat unusual. Suppose Adams and Benson are the only two people in the society, and their marginal willingness to pay for a public good, national defense, is as shown in columns 1 and 2 and columns 1 and 3 in Table 4.3. Economists might have discovered these schedules through a survey asking hypothetical questions about how much each citizen was willing to pay for various types and amounts of public goods rather than go without them.

Notice that the schedules in Table 4.3 are price-quantity schedules, implying that they are demand schedules. Rather than depicting demand in the usual way—the quantity of a product someone is willing to buy at each possible price—these schedules show the price someone is willing to pay for an extra unit at each possible quantity. That is, Adams is willing to pay $4 for the first unit of the public good, $3 for the second, $2 for the third, and so on.

Suppose the government produces 1 unit of this public good. Because of nonrivalry, Adams's consumption of the good does not preclude Benson from also consuming it, and vice versa. So both consume the good, and neither volunteers to pay for it. But from Table 4.3 we can find the amount these

TABLE 4.3 Demand for a Public Good, Two Individuals

(1) Quantity of Public Good	(2) Adams's Willingness to Pay (Price)		(3) Benson's Willingness to Pay (Price)		(4) Collective Willingness to Pay (Price)
1	$4	+	$5	=	$9
2	3	+	4	=	7
3	2	+	3	=	5
4	1	+	2	=	3
5	0	+	1	=	1

CONSIDER THIS . . .

Source: © Robert Kohlhuber/Getty Images RF

Responding to Digital Free Riding

Four teenage friends start a rock band. They practice hard, master their instruments, write their own songs, and do gig after gig for nearly nothing at local bars to gain experience and perfect their music.

After nearly five years of effort, they get signed to a major record label. But the year is 2005 and record sales are collapsing due to digital piracy. The rise of Internet file sharing has turned music into a public good and sales of recorded music have collapsed as hundreds of millions of music lovers have become digital free riders.

At first, the band struggles with the new reality. If they can't make a living selling music, they might have to quit music and get regular jobs. But then they realize that while recorded music is now free for anyone who wants it to be free, live music isn't. And neither are T-shirts or memorabilia.

So the band promotes itself online and allows free downloads to help propel its popularity. But then it charges steep prices at live concerts and makes sure that its T-shirts and memorabilia also generate substantial revenues. By doing so, the band adjusts to the new reality in which music has become a public good, but live concerts and T-shirts have not. They charge for the items that are still private goods.

two people would be willing to pay, together, rather than do without this 1 unit of the good. Columns 1 and 2 show that Adams would be willing to pay \$4 for the first unit of the public good; columns 1 and 3 show that Benson would be willing to pay \$5 for it. So the two people are jointly willing to pay \$9 (= \$4 + \$5) for this first unit.

For the second unit of the public good, the collective price they are willing to pay is \$7 (= \$3 from Adams + \$4 from Benson); for the third unit they would pay \$5 (= \$2 + \$3); and so on. By finding the collective willingness to pay for each additional unit (column 4), we can construct a collective demand schedule (a willingness-to-pay schedule) for the public good. Here we are *not* adding the quantities demanded at each possible price, as we do when we determine the market demand for a private good. Instead, we are adding the prices that people are willing to pay for the last unit of the public good at each possible quantity demanded.

Figure 4.5 shows the same adding procedure graphically, using the data from Table 4.3. Note that we sum Adams's and Benson's willingness-to-pay curves *vertically* to derive the collective willingness-to-pay curve (demand curve). The summing procedure is downward from the top graph to the middle graph to the bottom (total) graph. For example, the height of the collective demand curve D_c at 2 units of

AP FIGURE 4.5 The optimal amount of a public good. Two people—Adams and Benson—are the only members of a hypothetical economy. (a) D_1 shows Adams's willingness to pay for various quantities of a particular public good. (b) D_2 shows Benson's willingness to pay pay for these same quantities of this public good. (c) The collective demand for this public good is shown by D_c and is found by summing vertically Adams's and Benson's individual willingness-to-pay curves. The supply (S) of the public good is upsloping, reflecting rising marginal costs. The optimal amount of the public good is 3 units, determined by the intersection of D_c and S. At that output, marginal benefit (reflected in the collective demand curve D_c) equals marginal cost (reflected in the supply curve S).

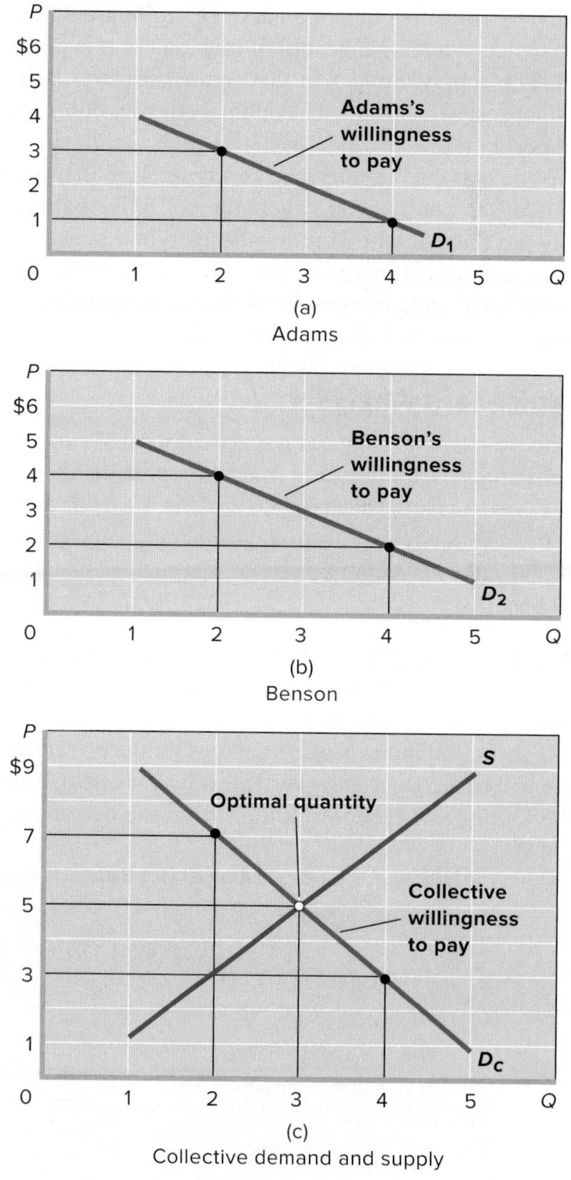

output in the bottom graph is $7, the sum of the amounts that Adams and Benson are each willing to pay for the second unit (= $3 + $4). Likewise, the height of the collective demand curve at 4 units of the public good is $3 (= $1 + $2).

What does it mean in Figure 4.5a that, for example, Adams is willing to pay $3 for the second unit of the public good? It means that Adams expects to receive $3 of extra benefit or utility from that unit. And we know from our discussion of diminishing marginal utility in Chapter 3 that successive units of any good yield less and less added benefit. This is also true for public goods, explaining the downward slope of the willingness-to-pay curves of Adams, Benson, and society. These curves, in essence, are marginal-benefit (MB) curves.

Comparing MB and MC

We can now determine the optimal quantity of the public good. The collective demand curve D_c in Figure 4.5c measures society's marginal benefit of each unit of this particular good. The supply curve *S* in that figure measures society's marginal cost of each unit. The optimal quantity of this public good occurs where marginal benefit equals marginal cost, or where the two curves intersect. In Figure 4.5c that point is 3 units of the public good, where the collective willingness to pay for the last (third) unit—the marginal benefit—just matches that unit's marginal cost ($5 = $5). As we saw in Chapter 1, equating marginal benefit and marginal cost efficiently allocates society's scarce resources.

Cost-Benefit Analysis

The above example suggests a practical means, called **cost-benefit analysis,** for deciding whether to provide a particular public good and how much of it to provide. Like our example, cost-benefit analysis (or marginal-benefit–marginal-cost analysis) involves a comparison of marginal costs and marginal benefits.

Concept Suppose the federal government is contemplating a highway construction plan. Because the economy's resources are limited, any decision to use more resources in the public sector will mean fewer resources for the private sector. There will be an opportunity cost, as well as a benefit. The cost is the loss of satisfaction resulting from the accompanying decline in the production of private goods; the benefit is the extra satisfaction resulting from the output of more public goods. Should the needed resources be shifted from the private to the public sector? The answer is yes if the benefit from the extra public goods exceeds the cost that results from having fewer private goods. The answer is no if the cost of the forgone private goods is greater than the benefit associated with the extra public goods.

Cost-benefit analysis, however, can indicate more than whether a public program is worth doing. It can also help the government decide on the *extent* to which a project should be pursued. Real economic questions cannot usually be answered simply by "yes" or "no" but, rather, involve questions such as "how much" or "how little."

Illustration Roads and highways can be run privately, as excludability is possible with toll gates. However, the federal highway system is almost entirely nonexclusive because anyone with a car can get on and off most federal highways without restriction any time they want. Federal highways therefore satisfy one characteristic of a public good, nonexcludability. The other characteristic, nonrivalry, is also satisfied by the fact that unless a highway is already extremely crowded, one person's driving on the highway does not preclude another person's driving on the highway. Thus, the federal highway system is effectively a public good. This leads us to ask: Should the federal government expand the federal highway system? If so, what is the proper size or scope for the overall project?

Table 4.4 lists a series of increasingly ambitious and increasingly costly highway projects: widening existing two-lane highways; building new two-lane highways; building new four-lane highways; building new six-lane highways. The extent to which government should undertake highway construction depends on the costs and benefits. The costs are largely the costs of constructing and maintaining the highways; the benefits are improved flows of people and goods throughout the country.[2]

[2] Because the costs of public goods typically are immediate while the benefits often accrue over longer time periods, economists convert both costs and benefits to present values for comparison. Doing so properly accounts for the time-value of money, discussed at length in later chapters.

TABLE 4.4 Cost-Benefit Analysis for a National Highway Construction Project (in Billions)

(1) Plan	(2) Total Cost of Project	(3) Marginal Cost	(4) Total Benefit	(5) Marginal Benefit	(6) Net Benefit (4) – (2)
No new construction	$ 0		$ 0		$ 0
A: Widen existing highways	4	$ 4	5	$ 5	1
B: New 2-lane highways	10	6	13	8	3
C: New 4-lane highways	18	8	23	10	5
D: New 6-lane highways	28	10	26	3	−2

The table shows that total annual benefit (column 4) exceeds total annual cost (column 2) for plans A, B, and C, indicating that some highway construction is economically justifiable. We see this directly in column 6, where total costs (column 2) are subtracted from total annual benefits (column 4). Net benefits are positive for plans A, B, and C. Plan D is not economically justifiable because net benefits are negative.

But the question of optimal size or scope for this project remains. Comparing the marginal cost (the change in total cost) and the marginal benefit (the change in total benefit) relating to each plan determines the answer. The guideline is well known to you from previous discussions: Increase an activity, project, or output as long as the marginal benefit (column 5) exceeds the marginal cost (column 3). Stop the activity at, or as close as possible to, the point at which the marginal benefit equals the marginal cost. Do not undertake a project for which marginal cost exceeds marginal benefit.

In this case plan C (building new four-lane highways) is the best plan. Plans A and B are too modest; the marginal benefits exceed the marginal costs, and there is a better option. Plan D's marginal cost ($10 billion) exceeds the marginal benefit ($3 billion) and therefore cannot be justified; it overallocates resources to the project. Plan C is closest to the theoretical optimum because its marginal benefit ($10 billion) still exceeds marginal cost ($8 billion) but approaches the MB = MC (or MC = MB) ideal.

This **marginal-cost–marginal-benefit rule** actually tells us which plan provides the maximum excess of total benefits over total costs or, in other words, the plan that provides society with the maximum net benefit. You can confirm directly in column 6 that the maximum net benefit (= $5 billion) is associated with plan C.

Cost-benefit analysis shatters the myth that "economy in government" and "reduced government spending" are synonymous. "Economy" is concerned with using scarce resources efficiently. If the marginal cost of a proposed government program exceeds its marginal benefit, then the proposed public program should not be undertaken. But if the marginal benefit exceeds the marginal cost, then it would be uneconomical or "wasteful" not to spend on that government program. Economy in government does not mean minimization of public spending. It means allocating resources between the private and public sectors and among public goods to achieve maximum net benefit.

Quasi-Public Goods

Government provides many goods that fit the economist's definition of a public good. However, it also provides other goods and services that could be produced and delivered in such a way that exclusion would be possible. Such goods, called **quasi-public goods**, include education, streets and highways, police and fire protection, libraries and museums, preventive medicine, and sewage disposal. They could all be priced and provided by private firms through the market system. But, because the benefits of these goods flow well beyond the benefit to individual buyers, these goods would be underproduced by the market system. Therefore, government often provides them to avoid the underallocation of resources that would otherwise occur.

The Reallocation Process

How are resources reallocated from the production of private goods to the production of public and quasi-public goods? If the resources of the economy are fully employed, government must free up resources from the production of private goods and make them available for producing public and quasi-public goods. It does so by reducing private demand for them. And it does that by levying taxes on households and businesses, taking some of their income out of the circular flow. With lower incomes and hence less purchasing power, households and businesses must curtail their consumption and investment spending. As a result, the private demand for goods and services declines, as does the private demand for resources. So by diverting purchasing power from private spenders to government, taxes remove resources from private use.

Government then spends the tax proceeds to provide public and quasi-public goods and services. Taxation releases resources from the production of private consumer goods (food, clothing, television sets) and private investment goods (wi-fi networks, boxcars, warehouses). Government shifts those resources to the production of public and quasi-public goods (post offices, submarines, parks), changing the composition of the economy's total output.

AP QUICK REVIEW 4.2

- ✓ Public goods are characterized by nonrivalry and nonexcludability. These characteristics create the free-rider problem, non-payers who obtain the benefits. For that reason, the demand curve may not reflect the full willingness of consumers to pay for a public good, like public radio broadcasts or national defense.
- ✓ The demand (marginal-benefit) curve for a public good is found by vertically adding the prices that all the members of society are willing to pay for the last unit of output at various output levels.
- ✓ The socially optimal amount of a public good is the amount at which the marginal cost and marginal benefit of the good are equal.
- ✓ Cost-benefit analysis is the method of evaluating alternative projects or sizes of projects by comparing the marginal cost and marginal benefit and applying the MC = MB rule.
- ✓ The government uses taxes to reallocate resources from the production of private goods to the production of public and quasi-public goods.

AP Externalities

LO4.4 Explain how positive and negative externalities cause under- and overallocations of resources.

In addition to providing public goods, governments can also improve the allocation of resources in the economy by correcting for market failures caused by externalities. An **externality** occurs when some of the costs or the benefits of a good or service are passed onto or "spill over to" someone other than the immediate buyer or seller. Such spillovers are called externalities because they are benefits or costs that accrue to some third party that is external to the market transaction.

There are both positive and negative externalities. An example of a negative externality is the cost of breathing polluted air; an example of a positive externality is the benefit of having everyone else inoculated against some disease. When there are negative externalities, an overproduction of the related product occurs and there is an overallocation of resources to this product. Conversely, underproduction and underallocation of resources result when positive externalities are present.

Negative Externalities

Negative externalities cause supply-side market failures. These failures happen because producers do not take into account the costs that their negative externalities impose on others. This failure to account for all production costs causes firms' supply curves to shift to the right of (or below) where they would be if firms properly accounted for all costs. Consider the costs of breathing polluted air that are imposed on third parties living downwind of smoke-spewing factories. Because polluting firms do not take account of such costs, they oversupply the products they make, producing units for which total costs (including those that fall on third parties) exceed total benefits. The same is true when airlines fail to account for the costs that noisy jet engines impose on people living near airports and when biodiesel factories that convert dead animal parts into fuel release foul smelling gases that disgust those living nearby.

Figure 4.6a illustrates how negative externalities affect the allocation of resources. When producers shift some of their costs onto the community as external costs, producers' marginal costs are lower than they would be if they had to pay for those costs. So their supply curves do not include or "capture" all the costs legitimately associated with the production of their goods. A polluting producer's supply curve such as *S* in Figure 4.6a therefore understates the total cost of production. The firm's supply curve lies to the right of (or below) the total-cost supply curve S_t, which would include the spillover cost. Through polluting and thus transferring costs to society, the firm enjoys lower production costs and has the supply curve *S*.

The outcome is shown in Figure 4.6a, where equilibrium output Q_e is larger than the optimal output Q_o. This means that resources are overallocated to the production of this commodity; too many units of it are produced. In fact, there is a net loss to society for every unit from Q_o to Q_e because, for those units, the supply curve that accounts for all costs, S_t, lies above the demand curve. Therefore, MC exceeds MB for those units. The resources that went into producing those units should have been used elsewhere in the economy to produce other things.

In terms of our previous analysis, the negative externality results in an efficiency loss represented by triangle *abc*.

Positive Externalities

Positive externalities cause demand-side market failures. These failures happen because market demand curves in such cases fail to include the willingness to pay of the third parties who receive the external benefits caused by the positive externality. This failure to account for all benefits shifts market demand curves to the left of (or below) where they would be if they included all benefits and the willingness to pay of both the third parties as well as the primary beneficiaries. Because demand curves fail to take into account all benefits when there are positive externalities, markets in such cases fail to produce all units for which benefits (including those that are received by third parties) exceed costs. As a result, products featuring positive externalities are underproduced.

Vaccinations are a good example of how positive externalities reduce demand and shift demand curves down and to the left. When John gets vaccinated against a disease, he benefits not only himself (because he can no longer contract the

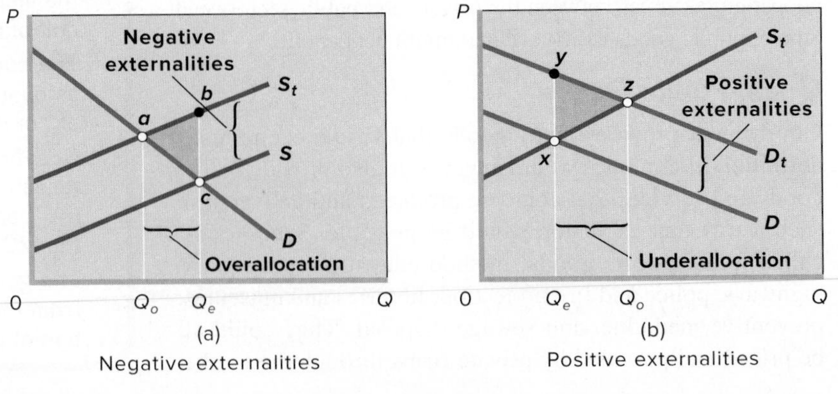

AP **FIGURE 4.6 Negative externalities and positive externalities.** (a) With negative externalities borne by society, the producers' supply curve *S* is to the right of (below) the total-cost supply curve S_t. Consequently, the equilibrium output Q_e is greater than the optimal output Q_o, and the efficiency loss is *abc*. (b) When positive externalities accrue to society, the market demand curve *D* is to the left of (below) the total-benefit demand curve D_t. As a result, the equilibrium output Q_e is less than the optimal output Q_o, and the efficiency loss is *xyz*.

disease) but also everyone else around him (because they know that in the future he will never be able to infect them). These other people would presumably be willing to pay some positive amount of money for the benefits they receive when John is vaccinated. But because his vaccination is a public good, there is no way to make them pay.

To see why his vaccination is a public good, note that the vaccination benefits that John provides to others feature nonrivalry and nonexcludability. There is nonrivalry because the protection his vaccination provides to one person does not lessen the protection that it provides to other people. There is nonexcludability because once he is vaccinated, there is no way to exclude anyone in particular from benefiting from his vaccination. Thus, the market demand for vaccinations will only include John's personal willingness to pay for the benefits that he personally receives from the vaccination. The market demand will fail to include the benefits that others receive. As a result, demand will be too low and vaccinations will be underproduced.

Figure 4.6b shows the impact of positive externalities on resource allocation. When external benefits occur, the market demand curve D lies to the left of (or below) the total-benefits demand curve, D_t. That is, D does not include the external benefits of the product, whereas D_t does.

The outcome is that the equilibrium output Q_e is less than the optimal output Q_o. The market fails to produce enough vaccinations, and resources are underallocated to this product. The underproduction implies that society is missing out on a significant amount of potential net benefits. For every unit from Q_e to Q_o, the demand curve that accounts for all benefits, D_t, lies above the supply curve that accounts for all costs—including the opportunity cost of producing other items with the resources that would be needed to produce these units. Therefore, MB exceeds MC for each of these units, and we know that society should redeploy some of its resources away from the production of other things in order to produce these units that generate net benefits.

In terms of our previous analysis, the positive externality results in an efficiency loss represented by triangle *xyz*.

Government Intervention

Government intervention may be called upon to achieve economic efficiency when externalities affect large numbers of people or when community interests are at stake. Government can use direct controls and taxes to counter negative externalities; it may provide subsidies or public goods to deal with positive externalities.

Direct Controls The direct way to reduce negative externalities from a certain activity is to pass legislation limiting that activity. Such direct controls force the offending firms to incur the actual costs of the offending activity. Historically, direct controls in the form of uniform emission standards—limits on allowable pollution—have dominated American air pollution policy. For example, the Clean Air Act of 1990 (1) forced factories and businesses to install "maximum achievable control technology" to reduce emissions of 189 toxic chemicals by 90 percent between 1990 and 2000; (2) required a 30 to 60 percent reduction in tailpipe emissions from automobiles by 2000; (3) mandated a 50 percent reduction in the use of chlorofluorocarbons (CFCs), which deplete the ozone layer (CFCs were used widely as a coolant in refrigeration, a blowing agent for foam, and a solvent in the electronics industry); and (4) forced coal-burning utilities to cut their emissions of sulfur dioxide by about 50 percent to reduce the acid-rain destruction of lakes and forests. Clean-water legislation limits the amount of heavy metals, detergents, and other pollutants firms can discharge into rivers and bays. Toxic-waste laws dictate special procedures and dump sites for disposing of contaminated soil and solvents. Violating these laws means fines and, in some cases, imprisonment.

Direct controls raise the marginal cost of production because the firms must operate and maintain pollution-control equipment. The supply curve S in Figure 4.7b, which does not

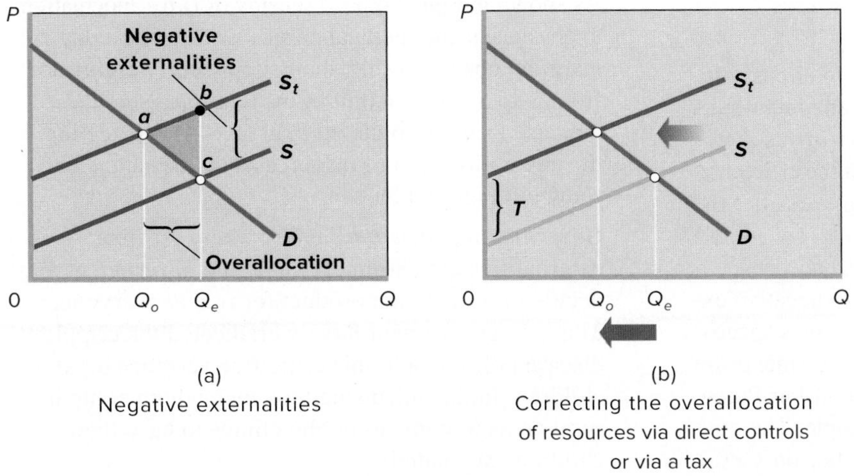

AP **FIGURE 4.7 Correcting for negative externalities.** (a) Negative externalities result in an overallocation of resources. (b) Government can correct this overallocation in two ways: (1) using direct controls, which would shift the supply curve from S to S_t and reduce output from Q_e to Q_o, or (2) imposing a specific tax T, which would also shift the supply curve from S to S_t, eliminating the overallocation of resources and thus the efficiency loss.

CONSIDER THIS . . .

Source: © Digital Vision/Getty Images RF

The Fable of the Bees

Economist Ronald Coase received the Nobel Prize for his so-called **Coase theorem**, which pointed out that under the right conditions, private individuals could often negotiate their own mutually agreeable solutions to externality problems through *private bargaining* without the need for government interventions like pollution taxes.

This is a very important insight because it means that we shouldn't automatically call for government intervention every time we see a potential externality problem. Consider the positive externalities that bees provide by pollinating farmers' crops. Should we assume that beekeeping will be underprovided unless the government intervenes with, for instance, subsidies to encourage more hives and hence more pollination?

As it turns out, no. Research has shown that farmers and beekeepers long ago used private bargaining to develop customs and payment systems that avoid free riding by farmers and encourage beekeepers to keep the optimal number of hives. Free riding is avoided by the custom that all farmers in an area simultaneously hire beekeepers to provide bees to pollinate their crops. And farmers always pay the beekeepers for their pollination services because if they didn't, then no beekeeper would ever work with them in the future—a situation that would lead to massively reduced crop yields due to a lack of pollination.

The "Fable of the Bees" is a good reminder that it is a fallacy to assume that the government must always get involved to remedy externalities. In many cases, the private sector can solve both positive and negative externality problems on its own.

reflect the external costs, shifts leftward to the total-cost supply curve, S_t. Product price increases, equilibrium output falls from Q_e to Q_o, and the initial overallocation of resources shown in Figure 4.7a is corrected. Observe that the efficiency loss shown by triangle *abc* in Figure 4.7a disappears after the overallocation is corrected in Figure 4.7b.

Pigovian Taxes A second policy approach to negative externalities is for government to levy taxes or charges specifically on the related good. These targeted tax assessments are often referred to as **Pigovian taxes** in honor of Arthur Pigou, the first economist to study externalities. Example: The government has placed a manufacturing excise tax on CFCs, which deplete the stratospheric ozone layer protecting the earth from excessive solar ultraviolet radiation. Facing such an excise tax, manufacturers must decide whether to pay the tax or expend additional funds to purchase or develop substitute products. In either case, the tax raises the marginal cost of producing CFCs, shifting the private supply curve for this product leftward (or upward).

In Figure 4.7b, a tax equal to T per unit increases the firm's marginal cost, shifting the supply curve from S to S_t. The equilibrium price rises, and the equilibrium output declines from Q_e to the economically efficient level Q_o. The tax thus eliminates the initial overallocation of resources and therefore the efficiency loss.

Subsidies and Government Provision Where spillover benefits are large and diffuse, as in our earlier example of inoculations, government has three options for correcting the underallocation of resources:

- ***Subsidies to buyers*** Figure 4.8a again shows the supply-demand situation for positive externalities. Government could correct the underallocation of resources, for example, to inoculations, by subsidizing consumers of the product. It could give each new mother in the United States a discount coupon to be used to obtain a series of inoculations for her child. The coupon would reduce the "price" to the mother by, say, 50 percent. As shown in Figure 4.8b, this program would shift the demand curve for inoculations from too-low D to the appropriate D_t. The number of inoculations would rise from Q_e to the economically optimal Q_o, eliminating the underallocation of resources and efficiency loss shown in Figure 4.8a.
- ***Subsidies to producers*** A subsidy to producers is a tax in reverse. Taxes are payments *to* the government that increase producers' costs. Subsidies are payments *from* the government that decrease producers' costs. As shown in Figure 4.8c, a subsidy of U per inoculation to physicians and medical clinics would reduce their marginal costs and shift their supply curve rightward from S_t to S_t'. The output of inoculations would increase from Q_e to the optimal level Q_o, correcting the underallocation of resources and efficiency loss shown in Figure 4.8a.
- ***Government provision*** Finally, where positive externalities are extremely large, the government may decide to provide the product for free to everyone. The U.S. government largely eradicated the crippling disease polio by administering free vaccines to all children. India ended smallpox by paying people in rural areas to come to public clinics to have their children vaccinated.

AP **FIGURE 4.8 Correcting for positive externalities.** (a) Positive externalities result in an underallocation of resources. (b) This underallocation can be corrected through a subsidy to consumers, which shifts market demand from D to D_t and increases output from Q_e to Q_o. (c) Alternatively, the underallocation can be eliminated by providing producers with a subsidy of U, which shifts their supply curve from S_t to S'_t, increasing output from Q_e to Q_o and eliminating the underallocation, and thus the efficiency loss, shown in graph a.

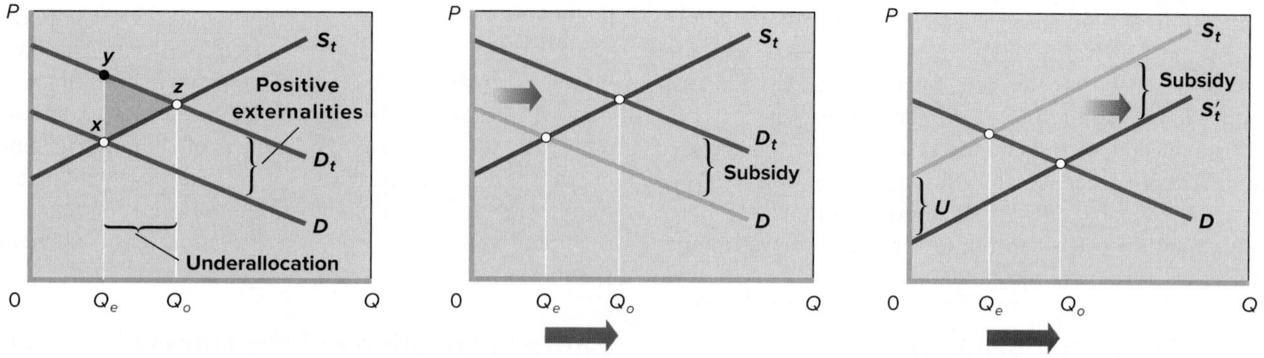

(a) Positive externalities

(b) Correcting the underallocation of resources via a subsidy to consumers

(c) Correcting the underallocation of resources via a subsidy to producers

TABLE 4.5 Methods for Dealing with Externalities

Problem	Resource Allocation Outcome	Ways to Correct
Negative externalities (spillover costs)	Overproduction of output and therefore overallocation of resources	1. Private bargaining 2. Liability rules and lawsuits 3. Tax on producers 4. Direct controls 5. Market for externality rights
Positive externalities (spillover benefits)	Underproduction of output and therefore underallocation of resources	1. Private bargaining 2. Subsidy to consumers 3. Subsidy to producers 4. Government provision

Table 4.5 lists several methods for correcting externalities, including those we have discussed thus far.

Society's Optimal Amount of Externality Reduction

LO4.5 Show why we normally won't want to pay what it would cost to eliminate every last bit of a negative externality such as air pollution.

Negative externalities such as pollution reduce the utility of those affected, rather than increase it. These spillovers are not economic goods but economic "bads." If something is bad, shouldn't society eliminate it? Why should society allow firms or municipalities to discharge *any* impure waste into public waterways or to emit *any* pollution into the air?

Economists answer these questions by pointing out that reducing pollution and negative externalities is not free. There are costs as well as benefits to reducing pollution. As a result, the correct question to ask when it comes to cleaning up negative externalities is not, "Do we pollute a lot or pollute zero?" That is an all-or-nothing question that ignores marginal costs and marginal benefits. Instead, the correct question is, "What is the optimal amount to clean up—the amount that equalizes the marginal cost of cleaning up with the marginal benefit of a cleaner environment?"

If we ask that question, we see that reducing a negative externality has a "price." Society must decide how much of a reduction it wants to "buy." High costs may mean that totally eliminating pollution might not be desirable, even if it is technologically feasible. Because of the law of diminishing returns, cleaning up the second 10 percent of pollutants from an industrial smokestack normally is more costly than cleaning up the first 10 percent. Eliminating the third 10 percent is more costly than cleaning up the second 10 percent, and so on. Therefore, cleaning up the last 10 percent of pollutants is the most costly reduction of all.

The marginal cost (MC) to the firm and hence to society—the opportunity cost of the extra resources used—rises as pollution is reduced more and more. At some point MC may rise so high that it exceeds society's marginal benefit (MB) of further pollution abatement (reduction). Additional actions to reduce pollution will therefore lower society's well-being; total cost will rise more than total benefit.

MC, MB, and Equilibrium Quantity

Figure 4.9 shows both the rising marginal-cost curve, MC, for pollution reduction and the downsloping marginal-benefit curve, MB, for pollution reduction. MB slopes downward because of the law of diminishing marginal utility: The more pollution reduction society accomplishes, the lower the utility (and benefit) of the next unit of pollution reduction.

The **optimal reduction of an externality** occurs when society's marginal cost and marginal benefit of reducing that externality are equal (MC = MB). In Figure 4.9 this optimal amount of pollution abatement is Q_1 units. When MB exceeds MC, additional abatement moves society toward economic efficiency; the added benefit of cleaner air or water exceeds the benefit of any alternative use of the required resources. When MC exceeds MB, additional abatement reduces economic efficiency; there would be greater benefits from using resources in some other way than to further reduce pollution.

FIGURE 4.9 Society's optimal amount of pollution abatement. The optimal amount of externality reduction—in this case, pollution abatement—occurs at Q_1, where society's marginal cost MC and marginal benefit MB of reducing the spillover are equal.

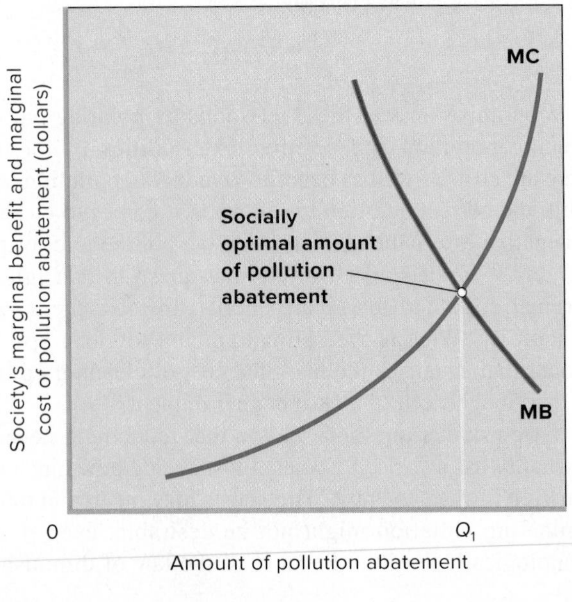

In reality, it is difficult to measure the marginal costs and benefits of pollution control. Nevertheless, Figure 4.9 demonstrates that some pollution may be economically efficient. This is so not because pollution is desirable but because beyond some level of control, further abatement may reduce society's net well-being. As an example, it would cost the government billions of dollars to clean up every last piece of litter in America. Thus, it would be better to tolerate some trash blowing around if the money saved by picking up less trash would yield larger net benefits when spent on other things.

Shifts in Locations of the Curves

The locations of the marginal-cost and marginal-benefit curves in Figure 4.9 are not forever fixed. They can, and probably do, shift over time. For example, suppose that the technology of pollution-control equipment improved noticeably. We would expect the cost of pollution abatement to fall, society's MC curve to shift rightward, and the optimal level of abatement to rise. Or suppose that society were to decide that it wanted cleaner air and water because of new information about the adverse health effects of pollution. The MB curve in Figure 4.9 would shift rightward, and the optimal level of pollution control would increase beyond Q_1. Test your understanding of these statements by drawing the new MC and MB curves in Figure 4.9.

Government's Role in the Economy

Market failures can be used to justify government interventions in the economy. The inability of private-sector firms to break even when attempting to provide public goods and the over- and underproduction problems caused by positive and negative externalities mean that government can have an important role to play if society's resources are to be efficiently allocated to the goods and services that people most highly desire.

Correcting for market failures is not, however, an easy task. To begin with, government officials must correctly identify the existence and the cause of any given market failure. That by itself may be difficult, time-consuming, and costly. But even if a market failure is correctly identified and diagnosed, government may still fail to take appropriate corrective action due to the fact that government undertakes its economic role in the context of politics.

To serve the public, politicians need to get elected. To stay elected, officials (presidents, senators, representatives, mayors, council members, school board members) need to satisfy their particular constituencies. At best, the political realities complicate government's role in the economy; at worst, they produce undesirable economic outcomes.

LAST WORD

Carbon Dioxide Emissions, Cap and Trade, and Carbon Taxes

Cap-and-Trade Systems and Carbon Taxes Are Two Approaches to Reducing Carbon Dioxide (CO_2) Emissions.

Externality problems are property rights problems. Consider a landfill. Because the owner of the landfill has full rights to his land, people wishing to dump their trash into the landfill have to pay him. This payment implies that there is no externality: He happily accepts their trash in exchange for a dumping fee. By contrast, because nobody owns the atmosphere, all air pollution is an externality, since there is no way for those doing the polluting to work out a payment to compensate those affected by the pollution or for those threatened with pollution to simply refuse to be polluted on.

Conventional property rights therefore cannot fix the externalities associated with air pollution. But that does not mean property rights can't help fight pollution. The trick to making them work is to assign property rights not to the atmosphere itself, but to *polluting* the atmosphere. This is done in "cap-and-trade" systems, under which the government sets an annual limit, or cap, to the number of tons of a pollutant that firms can emit into the atmosphere.

Consider carbon dioxide, or CO_2. It is a colorless, odorless gas that many scientists consider to be a contributing cause of climate change, specifically global warming. To reduce CO_2 emissions, the U.S. government might set a cap of 5 billion tons of CO_2 emissions per year in the United States (which would be about 25 percent below 2010 emissions levels for that molecule). The government then prints out emissions permits that sum to the limit set in the cap and distributes them to polluting firms. Once they are distributed, the only way a firm can legally emit a ton of CO_2 is if it owns a permit to do so.

Under this policy, the government can obviously adjust the total amount of air pollution by adjusting the cap. This by itself improves efficiency because the cap imposes scarcity. Because each firm has only a limited number of permits, each firm has a strong incentive to maximize the net benefit that it produces from every ton of pollution that it emits. But the *cap-and-trade* scheme leads to even greater improvements in efficiency because firms are free to trade (sell) them to each other in what are referred to as *markets for externality rights.*

For instance, suppose Smokestack Toys owns permits for 100 tons of CO_2 emissions and that it could use them to produce toy cars that would generate profits of $100,000. There is a power plant, however, that could make up to $1 million of profits by using those 100 tons of emissions permits to generate electricity. Because firms can trade their permits, Smokestack Toys will sell its permits to the power plant for more than the $100,000 in profits that it could make if it kept them and produced toy cars. And the power plant will gladly pay more than $100,000 for those permits because it can turn around and use them to make up to $1 million of profits by using them to generate electricity.

Society will benefit hugely from this transaction because while 100 tons of CO_2 will be emitted no matter which firm uses the permits, society will receive much greater net benefits when they are used by the power plant, as indicated by the fact that the power plant can produce much larger profits than the toy company when using the same amount of this scarce resource.

Source: © Larry Lee Photography/Corbis RF

Several words of caution, however! Cap-and-trade systems have proven very difficult to implement in cases where it is difficult for regulators to effectively check whether firms are obeying the system. This has been a major problem with the European Union's cap-and-trade system for CO_2 emissions. Because nearly every type of industrial activity releases CO_2 into the atmosphere, enforcement involves monitoring many thousands of factories of all sizes. That is very difficult and cheating has resulted. In addition, politically connected industries got politicians to give them exemptions or free permits.

By contrast, a cap-and-trade system on sulfur dioxide emissions from coal-burning public utilities has worked well in the United States since the 1980s. But in that case, there were only a few hundred polluting utilities, and they were already being monitored for emissions. So there was little ability to cheat. In addition, all of the firms were treated equally, with no firms allowed exemptions or free permits.

Due to the mixed results, many economists have concluded that a cap-and-trade system would not be the best way to curb CO_2 emissions in the United States. They believe that there are simply too many sources of pollution to make monitoring either possible or cost-effective. And it seems likely that politically connected industries will be granted exemptions. So, instead, many economists favor a carbon tax, which would involve taxing each ton of coal, each gallon of gasoline, and each barrel of oil on the basis of how much carbon it contains (and thus how much CO_2 will eventually be released into the atmosphere when it is used). By raising the cost of polluting, the tax would reduce consumption and lessen the externalities associated with CO_2 emissions. It would also be nearly impossible to evade, so that we would not have to worry about cheating.

In the political context, overregulation can occur in some cases; underregulation, in others. Some public goods and quasi-public goods can be produced not because their benefits exceed their costs but because their benefits accrue to firms located in states served by powerful elected officials. Inefficiency can easily creep into government activities because of the lack of a profit incentive to hold down costs. Policies to correct negative externalities can be politically blocked by the very parties that are producing the spillovers. In short, the economic role of government, although critical to a well-functioning economy, is not always perfectly carried out.

Economists use the term "government failure" to describe economically inefficient outcomes caused by shortcomings in the public sector.

AP QUICK REVIEW 4.3

- ✓ Negative externalities cause supply-side market failures involving overproduction, because producers do not take into account the costs that their negative externalities impose on others. Pollution that imposes costs on those living near the producer is an example of a negative externality.
- ✓ Positive externalities cause demand-side market failures involving underproduction, because market demand curves fail to include the willingness of the third parties who receive the external benefits caused by the positive externality to pay. Inoculations against infectious disease have a positive externality, as they protect both those who receive the inoculation, as well as those who have contact with the person.
- ✓ Policies for coping with the overallocation of resources, and therefore efficiency losses, caused by negative externalities are (a) private bargaining, (b) liability rules and lawsuits, (c) direct controls, (d) specific taxes, and (e) markets for externality rights (Last Word).
- ✓ Policies for correcting the underallocation of resources, and therefore efficiency losses, associated with positive externalities are (a) private bargaining, (b) subsidies to producers, (c) subsidies to consumers, and (d) government provision.
- ✓ The optimal amount of negative-externality reduction occurs where society's marginal cost and marginal benefit of reducing the externality are equal.

SUMMARY

LO4.1 Differentiate between demand-side market failures and supply-side market failures.

A market failure happens in a particular market when the market produces an equilibrium level of output that either overallocates or underallocates resources to the product being traded in the market. In competitive markets that feature many buyers and many sellers, market failures can be divided into two types: Demand-side market failures occur when demand curves do not reflect consumers' full willingness to pay; supply-side market failures occur when supply curves do not reflect all production costs, including those that may be borne by third parties.

LO4.2 Explain the origin of both consumer surplus and producer surplus and explain how properly functioning markets maximize their sum, total surplus, while optimally allocating resources.

Consumer surplus is the difference between the maximum price that a consumer is willing to pay for a product and the lower price actually paid; producer surplus is the difference between the minimum price that a producer is willing to accept for a product and the higher price actually received. Collectively, consumer surplus is represented by the triangle under the demand curve and above the actual price, whereas producer surplus is shown by the triangle above the supply curve and below the actual price.

Graphically, the combined amount of producer and consumer surplus is represented by the triangle to the left of the intersection of the supply and demand curves that is below the demand curve and above the supply curve. At the equilibrium price and quantity in competitive markets, marginal benefit equals marginal cost, maximum willingness to pay equals minimum acceptable price, and the combined amount of consumer surplus and producer surplus is maximized.

Output levels that are either less than or greater than the equilibrium output create efficiency losses, also called deadweight losses. These losses are reductions in the combined amount of consumer surplus and producer surplus. Underproduction creates efficiency losses because output is not being produced for which maximum willingness to pay exceeds minimum acceptable price. Overproduction creates efficiency losses because output is being produced for which minimum acceptable price exceeds maximum willingness to pay.

LO4.3 Describe free riding and public goods and illustrate why private firms cannot normally produce public goods.

Public goods are distinguished from private goods. Private goods are characterized by rivalry (in consumption) and excludability. One person's purchase and consumption of a private good precludes others from also buying and consuming it. Producers can exclude nonpayers (free riders) from receiving the benefits. In contrast, public goods are characterized by nonrivalry (in consumption) and nonexcludability. Public goods are not profitable to private firms because nonpayers (free riders) can obtain and consume those goods without paying. Government can, however, provide desirable public goods, financing them through taxation.

The collective demand schedule for a particular public good is found by summing the prices that each individual is willing to pay for an additional unit. Graphically, that demand curve is found by summing vertically the individual demand curves for that good. The resulting total demand curve indicates the collective willingness to pay for (or marginal benefit of) any given amount of the public good.

The optimal quantity of a public good occurs where the society's willingness to pay for the last unit—the marginal benefit of the good—equals the marginal cost of the good.

LO4.4 Explain how positive and negative externalities cause under- and overallocations of resources.

Externalities, or spillovers, are costs or benefits that accrue to someone other than the immediate buyer or seller. Such costs or benefits are not captured in market demand or supply curves and therefore cause the output of certain goods to vary from society's optimal output. Negative externalities (or spillover costs or external costs) result in an overallocation of resources to a particular product. Positive externalities (or spillover benefits or external benefits) are accompanied by an underallocaton of resources to a particular product.

Direct controls and specifically targeted Pigovian taxes can improve resource allocation in situations where negative externalities affect many people and community resources. Both direct controls (for example, smokestack emission standards) and Pigovian taxes (for example, taxes on firms producing toxic chemicals) increase production costs and hence product price. As product price rises, the externality, overallocation of resources, and efficiency loss are reduced since less of the output is produced.

Government can correct the underallocation of resources and therefore the efficiency losses that result from positive externalities in a particular market either by subsidizing consumers (which increases market demand) or by subsidizing producers (which increases market supply). Such subsidies increase the equilibrium output, reducing or eliminating the positive externality and consequent underallocation of resources and efficiency loss.

The Coase theorem suggests that under the right circumstances private bargaining can solve externality problems. Thus, government intervention is not always needed to deal with externality problems.

LO4.5 Show why we normally won't want to pay what it would cost to eliminate every last bit of a negative externality such as air pollution.

The socially optimal amount of externality abatement occurs where society's marginal cost and marginal benefit of reducing the externality are equal. With pollution, for example, this optimal amount of pollution abatement is likely to be less than a 100 percent reduction. Changes in technology or changes in society's attitudes toward pollution can affect the optimal amount of pollution abatement.

Market failures present government with opportunities to improve the allocation of society's resources and thereby enhance society's total well-being. But even when government correctly identifies the existence and cause of a market failure, political pressures may make it difficult or impossible for government officials to implement a proper solution.

TERMS AND CONCEPTS

market failures
demand-side market failures
supply-side market failures
consumer surplus
producer surplus
efficiency losses (or deadweight losses)
private goods
rivalry
excludability
public goods
nonrivalry
nonexcludability
free-rider problem
cost-benefit analysis
marginal-cost–marginal-benefit rule
quasi-public goods
externality
Coase theorem
Pigovian tax
optimal reduction of an externality

The following and additional problems can be found in connect

DISCUSSION QUESTIONS

1. Explain the two causes of market failures. Given their definitions, could a market be affected by both types of market failures simultaneously? LO4.1
2. Use the ideas of consumer surplus and producer surplus to explain why economists say competitive markets are efficient. Why are below- or above-equilibrium levels of output inefficient, according to these two sets of ideas? LO4.2
3. What are the two characteristics of public goods? Explain the significance of each for public provision as opposed to private provision. What is the free-rider problem as it relates to public

goods? Is U.S. border patrol a public good or a private good? Why? How about satellite TV? Explain. LO4.3

4. What divergences arise between equilibrium output and efficient output when (a) negative externalities and (b) positive externalities are present? How might government correct these divergences? Cite an example (other than the text examples) of an external cost and an external benefit. LO4.4
5. Why are spillover costs and spillover benefits also called negative and positive externalities? Show graphically how a tax can correct for a negative externality and how a subsidy to producers can correct for a positive externality. How does a subsidy to consumers differ from a subsidy to producers in correcting for a positive externality? LO4.4
6. An apple grower's orchard provides nectar to a neighbor's bees, while the beekeeper's bees help the apple grower by pollinating his apple blossoms. Use Figure 4.6b to explain why this situation of dual positive externalities might lead to an underallocation of resources to both apple growing and beekeeping. How might this underallocation get resolved via the means suggested by the Coase theorem? LO4.4
7. The LoJack car recovery system allows the police to track stolen cars. As a result, they not only recover 90 percent of LoJack-equipped cars that are stolen but also arrest many auto thieves and shut down many "chop shops" that take apart stolen vehicles to get at their used parts. Thus, LoJack provides both private benefits and positive externalities. Should the government consider subsidizing LoJack purchases? LO4.4
8. Explain why zoning laws, which allow certain land uses only in specific locations, might be justified in dealing with a problem of negative externalities. Explain why in areas where buildings sit close together tax breaks to property owners for installing extra fire prevention equipment might be justified in view of positive externalities. Explain why excise taxes on beer might be justified in dealing with a problem of external costs. LO4.5
9. **LAST WORD** Distinguish between a carbon-tax and a cap-and-trade strategy for reducing carbon dioxide and other so-called greenhouse gases (that are believed by many scientists to be causing global warming). Which of the two strategies do you think would have the most political support in an election in your home state? Explain your thinking.

AP REVIEW QUESTIONS

1. Draw a supply and demand graph and identify the areas of consumer surplus and producer surplus. Given the demand curve, what impact will an increase in supply have on the amount of consumer surplus shown in your diagram? Explain why. LO4.2
2. Assume that candle wax is traded in a perfectly competitive market in which the demand curve captures buyers' full willingness to pay while the supply curve reflects all production costs. For each of the following situations, indicate whether the total output should be increased, decreased, or kept the same in order to achieve allocative and productive efficiency. LO4.2
   a. Maximum willingness to pay exceeds minimum acceptable price.
   b. MC > MB.
   c. Total economic surplus is at a maximum.
   d. The current quantity produced exceeds the market equilibrium quantity.
3. Allocative efficiency occurs when LO4.2
   a. Marginal social benefit exceeds marginal social cost.
   b. Consumer surplus is maximized.
   c. When producer surplus is maximized.
   d. When economic surplus is maximized.
   e. Total revenue is maximized.
4. "Pollution should be completely eliminated." Evaluate this statement, supporting your answer using MB and MC analysis. LO4.3
5. Match each of the following characteristics or scenarios with either the term *negative externality* or the term *positive externality*. LO4.4
   a. Overallocation of resources.
   b. Tammy installs a very nice front garden, raising the property values of all the other houses on her block.
   c. Free flu vaccine reduces the incidence of flu by 35 percent compared to the prior year.
   d. Underallocation of resources.
   e. Water pollution from a factory forces neighbors to buy water purifiers.
6. Assume that tea is sold in a competitive market. LO4.2, 4.3, 4.4, 4.5
   a. Show the equilibrium price and quantity of tea.
   b. Shade the consumer surplus and the producer surplus at this market equilibrium.
   c. Assume that it is shown that tea consumption has modestly positive health benefits for consumers. Does that represent a positive or negative externality? How do you know?
   d. Given your answer to **part c,** is the output level identified in **part a,** allocatively efficient? Explain.
   e. What policy initiative could be implemented to achieve the allocatively efficient output level, given your answer to **part c**?
7. Use marginal cost/marginal benefit analysis to determine if the following statement is true or false: "The optimal amount of pollution abatement for some substances, say, dirty water from storm drains, is very low; the optimal amount of abatement for other substances, say, cyanide poison, is close to 100 percent." LO4.5

PROBLEMS

1. Refer to Table 4.1. If the six people listed in the table are the only consumers in the market and the equilibrium price is \$11 (not the \$8 shown), how much consumer surplus will the market generate? LO4.2
2. Refer to Table 4.2. If the six people listed in the table are the only producers in the market and the equilibrium price is \$6 (not the \$8 shown), how much producer surplus will the market generate? LO4.2

3. Look at Tables 4.1 and 4.2 together. What is the total surplus if Bob buys a unit from Carlos? If Barb buys a unit from Courtney? If Bob buys a unit from Chad? If you match up pairs of buyers and sellers so as to maximize the total surplus of all transactions, what is the largest total surplus that can be achieved? **LO4.2**

4. **ADVANCED ANALYSIS** Assume the following values for Figures 4.4a and 4.4b: $Q_1 = 20$ bags. $Q_2 = 15$ bags. $Q_3 = 27$ bags. The market equilibrium price is \$45 per bag. The price at *a* is \$85 per bag. The price at *c* is \$5 per bag. The price at *f* is \$59 per bag. The price at *g* is \$31 per bag. Apply the formula for the area of a triangle (Area = ½ × Base × Height) to answer the following questions. **LO4.2**
   a. What is the dollar value of the total surplus (producer surplus plus consumer surplus) when the allocatively efficient output level is being produced? How large is the dollar value of the consumer surplus at that output level?
   b. What is the dollar value of the deadweight loss when output level Q_2 is being produced? What is the total surplus when output level Q_2 is being produced?
   c. What is the dollar value of the deadweight loss when output level Q_3 is produced? What is the dollar value of the total surplus when output level Q_3 is produced?

5. On the basis of the three individual demand schedules in the following table, and assuming these three people are the only ones in the society, determine (a) the market demand schedule on the assumption that the good is a private good and (b) the collective demand schedule on the assumption that the good is a public good. **LO4.3**

P	$Q_d(D_1)$	$Q_d(D_2)$	$Q_d(D_3)$
\$8	0	1	0
7	0	2	0
6	0	3	1
5	1	4	2
4	2	5	3
3	3	6	4
2	4	7	5
1	5	8	6

6. Use your demand schedule for a public good, determined in problem 5, and the following supply schedule to ascertain the optimal quantity of this public good. **LO4.3**

P	Q_s
\$19	10
16	8
13	6
10	4
7	2
4	1

7. Look at Tables 4.1 and 4.2, which show, respectively, the willingness to pay and willingness to accept of buyers and sellers of bags of oranges. For the following questions, assume that the equilibrium price and quantity will depend on the indicated changes in supply and demand. Assume that the only market participants are those listed by name in the two tables. **LO4.4**
   a. What are the equilibrium price and quantity for the data displayed in the two tables?
   b. What if, instead of bags of oranges, the data in the two tables dealt with a public good like fireworks displays? If all the buyers free ride, what will be the quantity supplied by private sellers?
   c. Assume that we are back to talking about bags of oranges (a private good), but that the government has decided that tossed orange peels impose a negative externality on the public that must be rectified by imposing a \$2-per-bag tax on sellers. What is the new equilibrium price and quantity? If the new equilibrium quantity is the optimal quantity, by how many bags were oranges being overproduced before?

connect

Information Failures

LO4.6 Describe how information failures may justify government intervention in some markets.

This chapter discussed the two most common types of market failure, public goods and externalities. But there is also another, subtler, type of market failure. This one results when either buyers or sellers have incomplete or inaccurate information and their cost of obtaining better information is prohibitive. Technically stated, this market failure occurs because of **asymmetric information**—unequal knowledge possessed by the parties to a market transaction. Buyers and sellers do not have identical information about price, quality, or some other aspect of the good or service.

Sufficient market information is normally available to ensure that goods and services are produced and purchased efficiently. But in some cases inadequate information makes it difficult to distinguish trustworthy from untrustworthy sellers or trustworthy from untrustworthy buyers. In these markets, society's scarce resources may not be used efficiently, thus implying that the government should intervene by increasing the information available to the market participants. Under rare circumstances the government may itself supply a good for which information problems have prohibited efficient production.

Inadequate Buyer Information about Sellers

Inadequate information among buyers about sellers and their products can cause market failure in the form of underallocation of resources. Two examples will help you understand this point.

Example: Gasoline Market

Assume an absurd situation: Suppose there is no system of weights and measures established by law, no government inspection of gasoline pumps, and no law against false advertising. Each gas station can use whatever measure it chooses; it can define a gallon of gas as it pleases. A station can advertise that its gas is 87 octane when in fact it is only 75. It can rig its pumps to indicate that it is providing more gas than the amount being delivered.

Obviously, the consumer's cost of obtaining reliable information under such chaotic conditions is exceptionally high, if not prohibitive. Customers or their representatives would have to buy samples of gas from various gas stations, have them tested for octane level, and test the accuracy of calibrations at the pump. And these activities would have to be repeated regularly, since a station owner could alter the product quality and the accuracy of the pump at will.

Because of the high cost of obtaining information about the seller, many consumers would opt out of this chaotic market. One tankful of a 50 percent mixture of gasoline and water would be enough to discourage most motorists from further driving. More realistically, the conditions in this market would encourage consumers to vote for political candidates who promise to provide a government solution. The oil companies and honest gasoline stations would most likely welcome government intervention. They would realize that accurate information, by enabling this market to work, would expand their total sales and profits.

The government has in fact intervened in the market for gasoline and other markets with similar potential information difficulties. It has established a system of weights and measures, employed inspectors to check the accuracy of gasoline pumps, and passed laws against fraudulent claims and misleading advertising. Clearly, these government activities have produced net benefits for society.

Example: Licensing of Surgeons

Suppose now that anyone could hang out a shingle and claim to be a surgeon, much as anyone can become a house painter. The market would eventually sort out the true surgeons from those who are "learning by doing" or are fly-by-night operators who move into and out of an area. As people died from unsuccessful surgeries, lawsuits for malpractice eventually would identify and eliminate most of the medical impostors. People needing surgery for themselves or their loved ones could obtain information from newspaper reports, Internet sites, or people who have undergone similar operations.

But this process of obtaining information for those needing surgery would take considerable time and would impose unacceptably high human and economic costs. There is a fundamental difference between getting an amateurish paint job on one's house and being on the receiving end of heart surgery by a bogus physician. The marginal cost of obtaining information about sellers in the surgery market would be excessively high. The risk of proceeding without good information would result in much less surgery than desirable—an underallocation of resources to surgery.

The government has remedied this market failure through a system of qualifying tests and licensing. The licensing provides consumers with inexpensive information about a service they only infrequently buy. The government has taken a similar role in several other areas of the economy. For example, it approves new medicines, regulates the securities industry, and requires warnings on containers of potentially hazardous substances.

It also requires warning labels on cigarette packages and disseminates information about communicable diseases. And it issues warnings about unsafe toys and inspects restaurants for health-related violations.

Inadequate Seller Information about Buyers

Just as inadequate information about sellers can keep markets from achieving economic efficiency, so can inadequate information about buyers. The buyers may be consumers who buy products or firms that buy resources.

Moral Hazard Problem

Private markets may underallocate resources to a particular good or service for which there is a severe **moral hazard problem.** The moral hazard problem is the tendency of one party to a contract or agreement to alter her or his behavior, after the contract is signed, in ways that could be costly to the other party.

Suppose a firm offers an insurance policy that pays a set amount of money per month to people who suffer divorces. The attractiveness of such insurance is that it would pool the economic risk of divorce among thousands of people and, in particular, would protect spouses and children from the economic hardship that divorce often brings. Unfortunately, the moral hazard problem reduces the likelihood that insurance companies can profitably provide this type of insurance.

After taking out such insurance, some people would alter their behavior in ways that impose heavy costs on the insurer. For example, married couples would have less of an incentive to get along and to iron out marital difficulties. At the extreme, some people might be motivated to obtain a divorce, collect the insurance, and then continue to live together. Such insurance could even promote divorce, the very outcome that it is intended to protect against. The moral hazard problem would force the insurer to charge such high premiums for this insurance that few policies would be bought. If the insurer could identify in advance those people most prone to alter their behavior, the firm could exclude them from buying the insurance. But the firm's marginal cost of getting such information is too high compared with the marginal benefit. Thus, this market would fail.

Although divorce insurance is not available in the marketplace, society recognizes the benefits of insuring against the hardships of divorce. It has corrected for this underallocation of "hardship insurance" through child-support laws that dictate payments to the spouse who retains the children, when the economic circumstances warrant them. Alimony laws also play a role.

The government also supplies "divorce insurance" of a sort through the Temporary Assistance for Needy Families (TANF) program. Though aimed at helping poor children in general rather than children of divorce specifically, parents with children can receive TANF payments if they are left destitute by divorce. Because government does not have to earn a profit when supplying services, it can offer this type of "divorce insurance" despite the fact that it, too, may be susceptible to the moral hazard problem.

The moral hazard problem is also illustrated in the following statements:

- Drivers may be less cautious because they have car insurance.
- Medical malpractice insurance may increase the amount of malpractice.
- Guaranteed contracts for professional athletes may reduce the quality of their performance.
- Unemployment compensation insurance may lead some workers to shirk.
- Government insurance on bank deposits may encourage banks to make risky loans.

Adverse Selection Problem

Another information problem resulting from inadequate information about buyers is the **adverse selection problem.** This problem arises when information known by the first party to a contract or agreement is not known by the second and, as a result, the second party incurs major costs. Unlike the moral hazard problem, which arises after a person signs a contract, the adverse selection problem arises at the time a person signs a contract.

In insurance, the adverse selection problem is that people who are most likely to need insurance payouts are those who buy insurance. For example, those in poorest health will seek to buy the most generous health insurance policies. Or, at the extreme, a person planning to hire an arsonist to "torch" his failing business has an incentive to buy fire insurance.

Our hypothetical divorce insurance sheds further light on the adverse selection problem. If the insurance firm sets the premiums on the basis of the average divorce rate, many married couples who are about to obtain a divorce will buy insurance. An insurance premium based on average probabilities will make a great buy for those about to get divorced. Meanwhile, those in highly stable marriages will not buy it.

The adverse selection problem thus tends to eliminate the pooling of low and high risks, which is the basis of profitable insurance. Insurance rates then must be so high that few people would want to (or be able to) buy such insurance.

Where private firms underprovide insurance because of information problems, the government often establishes some type of social insurance. It can require that everyone in a particular group take the insurance and thereby can overcome the adverse selection problem. Example: Although the Social

Security system in the United States is partly insurance and partly an income transfer program, in its broadest sense it is insurance against poverty during old age. The Social Security program requires nearly universal participation: People who are most likely to need the minimum benefits that Social Security provides are automatically participants in the program. So, too, are those not likely to need the benefits. Consequently, no adverse selection problem emerges.

Qualification

Households and businesses have found many ingenious ways to overcome information difficulties without government intervention. For example, many firms offer product warranties to overcome the lack of information about themselves and their products. Franchising also helps overcome this problem. When you visit a Wendy's or a Marriott, you know what you are going to get, as opposed to stopping at Slim's Hamburger Shop or the Triple Six Motel.

Also, some private firms and organizations specialize in providing information to buyers and sellers. *Consumer Reports, Mobil Travel Guide,* and numerous Internet sites provide product information; labor unions collect and disseminate information about job safety; and credit bureaus provide information about credit histories and past bankruptcies to lending institutions and insurance companies. Brokers, bonding agencies, and intermediaries also provide information to clients.

Economists agree, however, that the private sector cannot remedy all information problems. In some situations, government intervention is desirable to promote an efficient allocation of society's scarce resources.

APPENDIX SUMMARY

LO4.6 Describe how information failures may justify government intervention in some markets.

Asymmetric information occurs when buyers and sellers do not have the same information about a product. It is a source of potential market failure, causing society's scarce resources to be allocated inefficiently.

Asymmetric information can cause a market to fail if the party that has less information decides to withdraw from the market because it fears that its lack of knowledge may be exploited by the party that has more information.

If the party that has less information reduces its participation in a market, the reduction in the size of the market may cause an underallocation of resources to the product produced for the market.

The moral hazard problem is the tendency of one party to a contract or agreement to alter its behavior in ways that are costly to the other party; for example, a person who buys insurance may willingly incur added risk.

The adverse selection problem arises when one party to a contract or agreement has less information than the other party and incurs a cost because of that asymmetrical information. For example, an insurance company offering "no medical-exam-required" life insurance policies may attract customers who have life-threatening diseases.

APPENDIX TERMS AND CONCEPTS

asymmetric information

moral hazard problem

adverse selection problem

The following and additional problems can be found in connect

APPENDIX DISCUSSION QUESTIONS

1. Because medical records are private, an individual applying for health insurance will know more about his own health conditions than will the insurance companies to which he is applying for coverage. Is this likely to increase or decrease the insurance premium that he will be offered? Why? **LO4.6**
2. Why is it in the interest of new homebuyers and builders of new homes to have government building codes and building inspectors? **LO4.6**
3. Place an "M" beside the items in the following list that describe a moral hazard problem and an "A" beside those that describe an adverse selection problem. **LO4.6**
   - **a.** A person with a terminal illness buys several life insurance policies through the mail.
   - **b.** A person drives carelessly because she has automobile insurance.
   - **c.** A person who intends to torch his warehouse takes out a large fire insurance policy.
   - **d.** A professional athlete who has a guaranteed contract fails to stay in shape during the off season.
   - **e.** A woman who anticipates having a large family takes a job with a firm that offers exceptional child care benefits.

APPENDIX REVIEW QUESTIONS

1. People drive faster when they have auto insurance. This is an example of: LO4.6
   a. Adverse selection.
   b. Asymmetric information.
   c. Moral hazard.
2. Government inspectors who check on the quality of services provided by retailers as well as government requirements for licensing in various professions are both attempts to resolve: LO4.6
   a. The moral hazard problem.
   b. The asymmetric information problem.
3. True or False: A market may collapse and have relatively few transactions between buyers and sellers if buyers have more information than sellers. LO4.6

APPENDIX PROBLEMS

1. Consider a used car market with asymmetric information. The owners of used cars know what their vehicles are worth but have no way of credibly demonstrating those values to potential buyers. Thus, potential buyers must always worry that the used car they are being offered may be a low quality "lemon." LO4.6
   a. Suppose that there are equal numbers of good and bad used cars in the market and that good used cars are worth $13,000 while bad used cars are worth $5,000. What is the average value of a used car?
   b. By how much does the average value exceed the value of a bad used car? By how much does the value of a good used car exceed the average value?
   c. Would a potential seller of a good used car be willing to accept the average value as payment for her vehicle?
   d. If a buyer negotiates with a seller to purchase the seller's used car for a price equal to the average value, is the car more likely to be good or bad?
   e. Will the used-car market come to feature mostly—if not exclusively—lemons? How much will used cars end up costing if all the good cars are withdrawn?

5 Chapter

Government's Role and Government Failure

Learning Objectives

LO5.1 Describe how government's power to coerce can be economically beneficial and list some of the difficulties associated with managing and directing the government.

LO5.2 Discuss "government failure" and explain why it happens.

LO5.3 (Appendix) Explain the difficulties of conveying economic preferences through majority voting.

AP Chapter Focus

Governments perform a variety of economic tasks in market economies. As discussed in various places in the book, these include promoting production and trade by defining property rights, enforcing contracts, and settling disputes; enforcing laws designed to maintain competition; redistributing income via taxes and transfers; reallocating resources by producing public goods and intervening to correct negative and positive externalities; and promoting economic growth and full employment.

In this chapter, we deepen our understanding of government's role in the market economy by examining some of the difficulties that democratic governments face when making specific laws related to the economy.

Government's Economic Role

LO5.1 Describe how government's power to coerce can be economically beneficial and list some of the difficulties associated with managing and directing the government.

As discussed in Chapter 2, the U.S. economy is a *market system* that uses mostly markets and prices to coordinate and direct economic activity. But the government also has a prominent role in how the economy functions. Among other things, the government sets the laws governing economic activity, provides goods and services that would otherwise be underproduced by private firms, and modifies the distribution of income. The government also promotes both economic stability and economic growth.

Government's Right to Coerce

One key difference between the economic activities of government and those of private firms and individuals is that government possesses the legal right to force people to do things. Whereas private-sector economic activities consist primarily of voluntary transactions, government has the legal right to enforce involuntary transactions. Among other things, the government can put you in jail if you do not pay your taxes, fine you if you violate pollution laws, jail you if you commit fraud, and remove your business license if you violate health and safety regulations.

Force and Economic Efficiency From an economic perspective, the government's ability to force people to do things can be quite beneficial because it can be used to increase economic efficiency.

Correcting for Market Failures Consider public goods and externalities. As discussed in Chapter 4, these market failures cause resource misallocations. When it comes to both public goods and products offering positive externalities, private producers fail to produce enough output because it is impossible to charge many of the beneficiaries for the benefits that they receive from the producers' products. In such cases, the government can improve economic efficiency by using involuntarily collected tax money to subsidize production.

By contrast, products that generate negative externalities are overproduced by the private sector because many of their costs are borne by third parties rather than by their producers. The government can reduce that overproduction and improve economic efficiency by using involuntary policies such as direct controls, pollution taxes, and cap-and-trade schemes to force producers to bear higher costs.

Reducing Private-Sector Economic Risks Government's ability to force people to do things is also crucial in reducing private-sector economic risks. To begin with, the government helps to ensure that only mutually agreeable transactions take place by making blackmail, extortion, and other forms of private coercion illegal. The government also uses its legal powers to outlaw various forms of theft, deception, and discrimination as well as restraints on trade, price-fixing, and refusal to honor a contract.

These limitations encourage economic activity by giving greater security to both individuals and firms. Because they know that the government will use its massive resources to arrest and punish those who break the law, they know that other individuals and firms are less likely to try to take advantage of them. That reduction in risk encourages higher levels of investment, the formation of more new businesses, and the introduction of more new goods and services. In economic terminology, both allocative and productive efficiency increase.

The Problem of Directing and Managing Government

As just discussed, the government can substantially improve allocative and productive efficiency if it directs its awesome coercive powers toward rectifying market failures and providing a low-risk economic environment for the private sector. However, it has only been in recent centuries that democratic political institutions have been able to tame government and direct it toward those goals. Until that happened, most governments were tyrannical, with their powers almost always directed toward enriching the small minority that controlled each government.

Because modern democratic governments serve much broader constituencies, they are much more likely to pursue economic policies with widespread social benefits. Their ability to deliver economically optimal outcomes is hindered, however, by the wide variety of government failures that this chapter will discuss in detail.

But before discussing them, it will be useful to first point out that governing a nation is not easy. In particular, governments face the daunting challenge of organizing millions of employees to carry out thousands of tasks—everything from cleaning sewers to researching cures for cancer to delivering the mail. An understanding of those challenges and complexities will give you a better sense of how well most governments manage to do *despite* all of the problems associated with government failure.

CONSIDER THIS . . .

Source: © Antenna/Getty Images RF

Does Big Government Equal Bad Government?

You will sometimes hear politicians (and maybe your grumpy uncle) complaining about Big Government. Their implication is that large government initiatives are inherently inefficient or incompetent.

Since economics is focused on efficiency, you might wonder where economists stand on the subject.

The answer is that economists focus not on bigness or smallness *per se*, but on marginal benefit (MB) and marginal cost (MC). Spending should be increased up to the point where MB = MC. For some programs, that will be a small dollar amount. For other programs, that will be a large dollar amount.

Thus, economists don't see much point in having an abstract debate over "big government" versus "small government." What matters is allocative and productive efficiency and directing government's limited resources toward the programs that generate the largest net benefits for society.

From that vantage point, we should not condemn large government programs just for being large. We must first compare MB with MC. Only if MB < MC should large programs be reduced or eliminated.

No Invisible Hand Government economic polices are not self-correcting. Unlike the private sector—where competitive forces and Adam Smith's "invisible hand" help to automatically direct resources to their best uses—poorly designed government policies can misallocate resources indefinitely unless active steps are taken by legislators or administrators.

Massive Size and Scope Identifying and correcting inefficient government policies is hampered by government's massive size and scope. Consider the U.S. federal government. In 2014, it had 4.2 million employees spread over 500 agencies that were collectively charged with enforcing hundreds of thousands of pages of laws and regulations while attempting to wisely spend $3.5 trillion.

The Need for Bureaucracy By law, those 4.2 million federal employees are ultimately supervised and directed by just 536 elected officials: one president, 435 representatives, and 100 senators. Because 536 elected officials could never hope to directly supervise 4.2 million people, governments rely on many layers of supervisors and supervisors-of-supervisors to manage the government's affairs. They collectively form a massive, hierarchical, many-layered bureaucracy.

The Need for Paperwork and Inflexibility To make sure that laws are uniformly enforced and do not vary at the whim of individual bureaucrats, the bureaucracy is regulated by detailed rules and regulations governing nearly every possible action that any individual bureaucrat might be called upon to make. These rules and regulations ensure that laws and regulations are uniformly applied. But they do so at the cost of massive amounts of paperwork and an inability to expeditiously process nonroutine situations and requests.

The Information Aggregation Problem Because of their massive size and scope, bureaucracies have difficulty with effectively aggregating and conveying information from their bottom layers to their top layers. As a result, top officials will tend to make many inefficient choices because they do not have enough information to sensibly compare the marginal benefits and marginal costs of individual programs and because they are unable to comprehensively assess opportunity costs and where to best spend funds across the wide variety of programs run by the government.

Lack of Accountability Governments also struggle with accountability. Democratic elections do take place for the elected officials at the top, but because the government undertakes so many activities simultaneously, it is difficult for the electorate to know the details of even a small fraction of what the government is up to at any particular time. As a result, hundreds or even thousands of individual programs may be poorly run without affecting the reelection chances of the incumbent politicians who are supposed to be supervising everything.

Within the bureaucracy itself, individual accountability is also hard to enforce because most bureaucrats have civil service protections that effectively guarantee them a job for life. Those protections reduce corruption by shielding bureaucrats from political pressures. But they also severely constrain the ability of elected officials to hold individual bureaucrats personally responsible for bad decisions.

AP QUICK REVIEW 5.1

- ✓ Government's ability to enforce nonvoluntary transactions can improve economic outcomes by compensating for resource misallocations and by providing a low-risk economic environment for individuals and firms.
- ✓ Government economic actions are not automatically self-correcting (as with the "invisible hand" in competitive markets).
- ✓ Democratic governments face several challenges in directing and supervising government's actions, including inflexibility, information aggregation, comparing marginal costs with marginal benefits, assessment of opportunity costs, and accountability.

AP Government Failure

LO5.2 Discuss "government failure" and explain why it happens.

The term **government failure** refers to economically inefficient outcomes caused by shortcomings in the public sector. One cause of government failure is the voting problems that we discuss at length in this chapter's appendix. But government failures caused by voting problems are somewhat unique in that they are driven by a lack of information about voter preferences. By contrast, most instances of government failure happen *despite* government officials knowing what voters prefer.

In these situations, government failures occur because the incentive structures facing government officials lead them to either put their own interests ahead of voter interests or to put the interests of a minority of voters ahead of those of the majority of voters. Let's examine what economic theory has to say about these situations.

Representative Democracy and the Principal-Agent Problem

Our system of representative democracy has the advantage of allowing us to elect full-time representatives who can specialize in understanding the pros and cons of different potential laws and who have more time to digest their details than the average citizen. But the system also suffers from principal-agent problems.

Principal-agent problems are conflicts that arise when tasks are delegated by one group of people (principals) to another group of people (agents). The conflicts arise because the interests of the agents may not be the same as the interests of the principals, so that the agents may end up taking actions that are opposed by the principals whom they are supposed to be representing.

In the business world, principal-agent problems often arise when the company's managers (the agents) take actions that are not in the best interests of the company's shareholders (the principals). Examples include the managers spending huge amounts of company money on executive jets and lavish offices or holding meetings at expensive resorts. These luxuries are obviously enjoyable to managers but are, of course, not in the best interest of shareholders because the money spent on them could either be reinvested back into the firm to increase future profits or paid out to shareholders immediately as dividends. But to the extent that managers are free to follow their own interests rather than those of their shareholders, they may indeed take these and other actions that are not in the better interests of their shareholders. Hence the conflicts.

In a representative democracy, principal-agent problems often arise because politicians have goals such as reelection that may be inconsistent with pursuing the best interests of their constituents. Indeed, casual reflection suggests that "sound economics" and "good politics" often differ. Sound economics calls for the public sector to pursue various programs as long as marginal benefits exceed marginal costs. Good politics, however, suggests that politicians support programs and policies that will maximize their chances of getting reelected. The result may be that the government will promote the goals of groups of voters that have special interests to the detriment of the larger public. Economic inefficiency is the likely outcome.

CONSIDER THIS . . .

Source: © Hein von Horsten/Getty Images

Mohair and the Collective-Action Problem

Smaller groups can sometimes achieve political victories against larger groups by taking advantage of the **collective-action problem**—the fact that larger groups are more difficult to organize and motivate than smaller groups.

Larger groups are harder to organize and motivate for two main reasons. First, the larger the group, the smaller each member's share of the benefits if the group gets its way. Second, the larger the group, the higher its organizing costs, as it will have to contact and recruit large numbers of strangers via e-mails, telephone calls, and mass mailings.

Smaller groups can take advantage of these difficulties and generally get their way against larger groups as long as they are pressing for policies that only cause small amounts of harm to the members of the larger groups.

Consider the infamous subsidy for mohair, the wool produced by Angora goats. Each year the federal government provides millions of dollars in subsidized loans to Angora goat farmers in Texas, Arizona, and New Mexico. The federal government began the subsidy in the late 1940s to ensure a large supply of insulation for the jackets needed to keep pilots and other crew members warm in the unheated airplanes used during that period.

The mohair subsidy should have ended in the 1950s when heated cabins were developed, but it survives because it costs taxpayers only a few cents each. This means that it would cost them more to organize and defeat the mohair subsidy than they would save by having the subsidy terminated.

More generally, the collective-action problem explains why nearly every example of the special-interest effect is characterized by "concentrated benefits and diffuse costs." Concentrated benefits make proponents easy to organize, while diffuse costs make opponents difficult to organize.

Special-Interest Effect Efficient public decision making is often impaired by the **special-interest effect.** This is any outcome of the political process whereby a small number of people obtain a government program or policy that gives them large gains at the expense of a much greater number of persons who individually suffer small losses.

The small group of potential beneficiaries is well informed and highly vocal on the issue in question, and they press politicians for approval by making campaign contributions and by hiring well-connected professional advocates known as "lobbyists" to aggressively make their case. By contrast, the large number of people facing the very small individual losses are generally unaware of the issue. So politicians feel they will lose the campaign contributions and votes of the small special-interest group that backs the issue if they legislate against it but will lose very little support from the large group of uninformed voters, who are likely to evaluate the politicians on other issues of greater importance to them.

The special-interest effect is also evident in so-called *pork-barrel politics*, a means of securing a government project that yields benefits mainly to a single political district and its political representative. In this case, the special-interest group comprises local constituents, while the larger group consists of relatively uninformed taxpayers scattered across a much larger geographic area. Politicians clearly have a strong incentive to secure government projects ("pork") for their local constituents. Such projects win political favor because they are highly valued by constituents and the costs are borne mainly by taxpayers located elsewhere.

At the federal level, pork-barrel politics often consist of congressional members inserting specific provisions that authorize spending for local projects (that will benefit only local constituents) into comprehensive legislation (that is supposed to be about making laws for the entire country). Such narrow, specifically designated authorizations of expenditure are called **earmarks.** In 2015, legislation contained 105 such earmarks, totaling $4.2 billion. These earmarks enable senators and representatives to provide benefits to in-state firms and organizations without subjecting the proposals to the usual evaluation and competitive bidding. Although some of the earmarked projects deliver benefits that exceed costs, many others are questionable, at best. These latter expenditures very likely reallocate some of society's scarce resources from higher-valued uses to lower-valued uses. Moreover, logrolling, discussed in the chapter appendix, typically enters the picture. "Vote for my special local project and I will vote for yours" becomes part of the overall strategy for securing "pork" and remaining elected.

Finally, a politician's inclination to support the smaller group of special beneficiaries is enhanced because special-interest groups are often quite willing to help finance the campaigns of "right-minded" politicians and politicians who "bring home the pork." The result is that politicians may support special-interest programs and projects that cannot be justified on economic grounds.

Rent-Seeking Behavior The appeal to government for special benefits at taxpayers' or someone else's expense is called **rent seeking.** The term "rent" in "rent seeking" is used loosely to refer to any payment in excess of the minimum amount that would be needed to keep a resource employed in its current use. Those engaged in "rent seeking" are attempting to use government influence to get themselves into a situation in which they will get paid more for providing a good or service than the minimum amount you would actually have to pay them to provide that good or service. (These excess, or surplus, payments are akin to *land rent*, which is also a surplus payment.)

Rent seeking goes beyond the usual profit seeking through which firms try to increase their profits by adjusting their output levels, improving their products, and incorporating cost-saving technologies. Rent seeking looks to obtain extra profit or income by influencing government policies. Corporations, trade associations, labor unions, and professional organizations employ vast resources to secure favorable government policies that result in rent—higher profit or income than would otherwise occur. The government is able to dispense such rent directly or indirectly through laws, rules, hiring, and purchases. Elected officials are willing to provide such rent because they want to be responsive to the key constituents who can help them remain in office.

Here are some examples of "rent-providing" legislation or policies: tariffs on foreign products that limit competition and raise prices to consumers, tax breaks that benefit specific corporations, government construction projects that create union jobs but cost more than the benefits they yield, occupational licensing that goes beyond what is needed to protect consumers, and large subsidies to farmers by taxpayers. None of these is justified by economic efficiency.

Clear Benefits, Hidden Costs

Some critics say that vote-seeking politicians will ignore economic rationality by failing to objectively weigh costs and benefits when deciding which programs to support. Because political officeholders must seek voter support every few years, they favor programs that have immediate and clear-cut benefits and vague or deferred costs. Conversely, politicians will reject programs with immediate and easily identifiable costs but with less measurable but very high long-term benefits.

Such biases may lead politicians to reject economically justifiable programs and to accept programs that are economically irrational. Example: A proposal to construct or expand mass-transit systems in large metropolitan areas may be economically rational on the basis of cost-benefit analysis. But if (1) the program is to be financed by immediate increases in highly visible income or sales taxes and (2) benefits will occur only years from now when the project is completed, then the vote-seeking politician may oppose the program.

Assume, on the other hand, that a program of federal aid to municipal police forces is not justifiable on the basis of cost-benefit analysis. But if the cost is paid for from budget surpluses, the program's modest benefits may seem so large that it will gain approval.

Unfunded Liabilities

The political tendency to favor spending priorities that have immediate payouts but deferred costs also leads to many government programs having unfunded liabilities. A government creates an **unfunded liability** when it commits to making a series of future expenditures without simultaneously committing to collect enough tax revenues to pay for those expenditures.

The most famous example of an unfunded liability belongs to the Social Security program, under which the U.S. federal government supplements the incomes of the elderly and the disabled. The government does collect Social Security taxes to help defray the expected future costs of the program, but the current tax rates will not generate nearly enough revenue to pay for all of the expected outlays. In fact, it is estimated that Social Security has an unfunded liability

(= total value of spending commitments minus expected value of tax revenues) of $20.5 trillion.

Social Security is not the only major unfunded government liability. Medicare, which provides health care to the elderly and disabled in the United States, has an unfunded liability of $4.8 trillion, while state and local governments are estimated to have $4.6 trillion in unfunded retirement and health care commitments.

Chronic Budget Deficits

A government runs an annual **budget deficit** whenever its tax revenues are less than its spending during a particular year. To make up for the shortfall, the government must borrow money, usually by issuing bonds. Whatever it borrows in a given year gets added to its overall pile of debt, which is the accumulation of all past budget deficits and budget surpluses.

Many governments run budget deficits year after year. These chronic deficits can be attributed to a pair of conflicting incentives that confront politicians. On the one hand, many government programs are highly popular with voters, so that there is almost always political pressure to either maintain or increase spending. On the other hand, hardly anyone likes paying taxes, so there is almost always political pressure to reduce taxes. Faced with those two conflicting pressures, politicians tend to opt for spending levels that exceed tax revenues.

That may be problematic because chronic deficits can pose several economic challenges, including

- ***Economic inefficiency*** Deficits may allow the government to control and direct an inefficiently large fraction of the economy's resources. To the extent that deficit spending facilitates an underallocation of resources to the private sector and an overallocation of resources to the government sector, there will be a tendency to underproduce private goods and overproduce public goods. If that occurs, the economy will experience a decrease in both allocative and productive efficiency.
- ***Debt crises*** A government's accumulated debt level may rise so high that investors lose faith in the government's ability or willingness to repay its debts. If that happens, the government will find itself in the middle of a **debt crisis,** unable to borrow any more money. Cut off from borrowing, the government will be forced to undertake some combination of drastic spending cuts or massive tax increases. Either of those actions will tend to plunge the economy into a recessionary period in which unemployment rises and output falls.

To prevent politicians from succumbing to voter preferences for deficits, many state and local governments have balanced-budget laws that make deficits illegal. No such law exists at the national level, however. As a result, federal politicians were able to run budget deficits in 51 of the 56 years between 1960 and 2015.

Misdirection of Stabilization Policy

Economies go through alternating periods of expansion and recession. Multiyear periods during which output expands, employment increases, and living standards rise alternate with periods during which output contracts, employment decreases, and living standards fall.

Governments often attempt to smooth out these so-called *business cycles* by using two types of macroeconomic stabilization policy:

- **Fiscal policy** attempts to use changes in tax rates and spending levels to offset the business cycle. For example, if the economy is going into a recessionary period with falling output and rising unemployment, the government may attempt to stimulate the economy by lowering tax rates or increasing government spending. Either action should increase spending on goods and services and consequently induce business to produce more output and hire more workers.
- **Monetary policy** attempts to use changes in interest rates to regulate the economy. In particular, the government can use its control over the money supply to lower interest rates during a recession. The lower interest rates stimulate spending by making it cheaper for individuals and businesses to borrow money to pay for capital goods such as houses, cars, and machinery. As spending on those items increases, firms are induced to produce more output and hire more workers.

Politicization of Fiscal and Monetary Policy Fiscal and monetary policy are both subject to politicization. In the case of fiscal policy, if the economy goes into recession and there are calls to stimulate the economy through lower taxes or increased spending, politicians often spend more time attempting to target any tax cuts or spending increases toward special interests than they do making sure that their fiscal policy actions will actually stimulate the overall economy. The recession also provides political cover for increasing the size of the deficit.

Monetary policy can be similarly politicized, with the biggest problem being that incumbent politicians will want to cut interest rates to boost the economy right before they are up for reelection. That is problematic because monetary stimulus is only helpful if the economy is in recession. If the economy is doing well, monetary stimulus can actually make things worse because it can raise the rate of inflation and drive up prices all over the economy.

To prevent that, most countries have put politically independent central banks in charge of monetary policy. In the

United States, the Federal Reserve serves this function. Other top central banks include the Bank of Japan, the Bank of England, and the European Central Bank. Each is run by professional economists who are insulated from political pressures so that they may use their independent expertise and judgment to decide if and when monetary stimulus should be used.

AP QUICK REVIEW 5.2

- ✓ Principal-agent problems are conflicts that occur when the agents who are supposed to be acting in the best interests of their principals instead take actions that help themselves but hurt their principals.
- ✓ Because larger groups are more difficult to organize and motivate than smaller groups, special interests can often obtain what they want politically even when what they want is opposed by a majority of voters.
- ✓ Rent seeking involves influencing government policies so that one can get paid more for providing a good or service than it costs to produce.
- ✓ Political pressures cause politicians to favor policies such as unfunded liabilities and budget deficits that have immediate benefits and delayed costs.

Limited and Bundled Choice

Economic theory points out that the political process forces citizens and their elected representatives to be less selective in choosing public goods and services than they are in choosing private goods and services.

In the marketplace, the citizen as a consumer can exactly satisfy personal preferences by buying certain goods and not buying others. However, in the public sector the citizen as a voter is confronted with, say, only two or three candidates for an office, each representing a different "bundle" of programs (public goods and services). None of these bundles of public goods is likely to fit exactly the preferences of any particular voter. Yet the voter must choose one of them. The candidate who comes closest to voter Smith's preference may endorse national health insurance, increases in Social Security benefits, subsidies to tobacco farmers, and tariffs on imported goods. Smith is likely to vote for that candidate even though Smith strongly opposes tobacco subsidies.

In other words, the voter must take the bad with the good. In the public sector, people are forced to "buy" goods and services they do not want. It is as if, in going to a sporting-goods store, you were forced to buy an unwanted pool cue to get a wanted pair of running shoes. This is a situation where resources are not being used efficiently to satisfy consumer wants. In this sense, the provision of public goods and services is inherently inefficient.

Congress is confronted with a similar limited-choice, bundled-goods problem. Appropriations legislation combines hundreds, even thousands, of spending items into a single bill. Many of these spending items may be completely unrelated to the main purpose of the legislation. Yet congressional representatives must vote on the entire package—yea or nay. Unlike consumers in the marketplace, they cannot be selective.

Bureaucracy and Inefficiency

Some economists contend that public agencies are generally less efficient than private businesses. The reason is not that lazy and incompetent workers somehow end up in the public sector while ambitious and capable people gravitate to the private sector. Rather, it is that the market system creates incentives for internal efficiency that are absent from the public sector. Private enterprises have a clear goal—profit. Whether a private firm is in a competitive or monopolistic market, efficient management means lower costs and higher profit. The higher profit not only benefits the firm's owners but enhances the promotion prospects of the firm's managers. Moreover, part of the managers' pay may be tied to profit via profit-sharing plans, bonuses, and stock options. There is no similar

CONSIDER THIS . . .

Source: © Jerry McBride/The Durango Herald/Polaris/Newscom

Government, Scofflaw

An interesting example of government failure occurs when public companies that are completely owned and operated by the government violate the law at higher rates than private companies.

A 2015 study of 1,000 hospitals, 3,000 power plants, and 4,200 water utilities found that public providers were substantially more likely than private companies to violate health and safety laws. Public hospitals and public power plants had 20 percent more high-priority violations of the Clean Air Act, while public water companies had 14 percent more health violations of the Safe Drinking Water Act as well as 29 percent more monitoring violations.

One explanation is that public companies may have difficulty getting taxpayers and politicians to approve the funding that would be needed to improve their facilities by enough to comply with the law. But the law also appears to be applied much more leniently against public companies because public power plants and public hospitals are 20 percent less likely to be fined when found to be in violation of the Clean Air Act. In addition, there is evidence that public violators are allowed to delay or avoid paying fines even when they are assessed. So they are under substantially less pressure than private firms to comply with the law.

gain to government agencies and their managers—no counterpart to profit—to create a strong incentive to achieve efficiency.

The market system imposes a very obvious test of performance on private firms: the test of profit and loss. An efficient firm is profitable and therefore successful; it survives, prospers, and grows. An inefficient firm is unprofitable and unsuccessful; it declines and in time goes out of business. But there is no similar, clear-cut test with which to assess the efficiency or inefficiency of public agencies. How can anyone determine whether a public hydroelectricity provider, a state university, a local fire department, the Department of Agriculture, or the Bureau of Indian Affairs is operating efficiently?

Cynics even argue that a public agency that inefficiently uses its resources is likely to survive and grow! In the private sector, inefficiency and monetary loss lead to the abandonment of certain activities or products or even firms. But the government, they say, does not like to abandon activities in which it has failed. Some suggest that the typical response of the government to a program's failure is to increase its budget and staff. This means that public sector inefficiency just continues on a larger scale.

Furthermore, economists assert that government employees, together with the special-interest groups they serve, often gain sufficient political clout to block attempts to pare down or eliminate their agencies. Politicians who attempt to reduce the size of huge federal bureaucracies such as those relating to agriculture, education, health and welfare, and national defense incur sizable political risk because bureaucrats and special-interest groups will team up to defeat them.

Finally, critics point out that government bureaucrats tend to justify their continued employment by looking for and eventually finding new problems to solve. It is not surprising that social "problems," as defined by government, persist or even expand.

The Last Word at the end of this chapter highlights several recent media-reported examples of the special-interest effect (including earmarks), the problem of limited and bundled choices, and problems of government bureaucracy.

Inefficient Regulation and Intervention

Governments regulate many aspects of the market economy. Examples include health and safety regulations, environmental laws, banking supervision, restrictions on monopoly power, and the imposition of wage and price controls.

These interventions are designed to improve economic outcomes, but several forms of regulation and intervention have been known to generate outcomes that are less beneficial than intended.

Regulatory Capture A government agency that is supposed to supervise a particular industry is said to have suffered from **regulatory capture** if its regulations and enforcement activities come to be heavily influenced by the industry that it is supposed to be regulating.

Regulatory capture is often facilitated by the fact that nearly everyone who knows anything about the details of a regulated industry works in the industry. So when it comes time for the regulatory agency to find qualified people to help write intelligent regulations, it ends up hiring a lot of people from regulated firms. Those individuals bring their old opinions and sympathies with them when they become bureaucrats. As a result, many regulations end up favoring the interests of the regulated firms.

Regulatory Capture in the Railroad Industry The classic example of regulatory capture is that of railroad regulation during the nineteenth and twentieth centuries. In response to public complaints that the nation's railroads were often charging exorbitant rates, the federal government established the Interstate Commerce Commission (ICC) in 1887 as the government agency charged with regulating competition and prices within the railroad industry.

Within a generation, railroad executives had achieved regulatory capture by manipulating the ICC into a policy that simultaneously fixed rates at profitable levels while also eliminating competition between different railroad companies. The public justification for these policies was that competition had to be restricted in order to prevent larger railroads from bankrupting smaller railroads and thereby becoming monopolies that could easily exploit the public. But the railroad industry's true motive was to establish a regulatory regime in which both larger and small railroads were guaranteed steady, competition-free profits.

These days, activists often complain that various government bureaucracies are subject to regulatory capture. At the federal level, complaints are voiced about the Food and Drug Administration's supervision of the pharmaceutical industry, the Securities and Exchange Commission's supervision of Wall Street financial firms, and the Bureau of Land Management's policies with respect to leasing federal lands for oil drilling, mining, and forestry.

Deregulation as an Alternative Economists are divided about the intensity and inefficiency of regulatory capture as well as what to do about it. One potential solution is for the government to engage in **deregulation** and intentionally remove most or even all of the regulations governing an industry.

Deregulation solves the problem of regulatory capture because there is no regulatory agency left to capture. But it only works well in terms of economic efficiency if the deregulated industry becomes competitive and is automatically guided toward allocative and productive efficiency by competitive forces and the invisible hand. If the deregulated industry instead tends toward monopoly or ends up generating substantial negative externalities, continued regulation might be the better option.

Proponents of deregulation often cite the deregulation of interstate trucking, railroads, and airlines in the 1970s and 1980s as examples of competition successfully replacing regulation. They do so because after regulation was removed, robust competition led to lower prices, increased output, and higher levels of productivity and efficiency.

But for government agencies tasked with environmental protection, human safety, and financial regulation, there is less confidence as to whether competitive pressures might be able to replace regulation. For those industries, regulation may always be necessary. If so, then some amount of regulatory capture may always be likely due to the fact that regulated firms will always want to capture their regulators.

Government's Poor Investment Track Record

Governments are often asked to use taxpayer money to directly invest in private businesses that have been unable to secure funding from private sources such as banks. Unfortunately, researchers have found that low and negative rates of return are the norm for government investments. In addition, government funding often allows inefficient firms to persist in operation long after competitive forces would have put them out of operation and freed up their resources for higher-valued projects elsewhere in the economy.

Critics also note that many government investments look like prime examples of rent seeking and the special-interest effect, especially when the firms receiving government investments are found to have made substantial financial contributions to influential politicians. In too many cases, the government's investment decisions appear to be based on political connections rather than on whether specific investments can produce substantial net benefits for society.

Loan Guarantees The government also tends to earn low or negative returns when it subsidizes private-sector investments with **loan guarantees.** The start-up company named Solyndra provides a good example of what can go wrong.

The Solyndra Subsidy In 2009, Solyndra was unable to convince private investors to lend it enough money to start producing solar panels with its new technology. The private investors sensibly feared that the company's new technology was too expensive and that its solar panels would not be able to compete with those made by the industry's more established firms.

At that point, Solyndra turned to a federal loan-guarantee program under which the Department of Energy told potential investors that it would cosign any loan taken out by Solyndra and thereby guarantee that if Solyndra went bankrupt, the federal government would use taxpayer money to repay the loan.

With that loan guarantee in place, the otherwise-reluctant private investors were willing to put in $535 million. After all, they had nothing to lose and everything to gain. If Solyndra went bankrupt, they would get their money back from the government. But if Solyndra somehow did well, they would collect substantial returns.

Unfortunately, the investors' original doubts proved to be well founded. Solyndra was unable to compete effectively with incumbent firms and went bankrupt in 2011, leaving taxpayers on the hook for the full $535 million.

Socializing Losses, Privatizing Gains Government loan guarantees can be socially beneficial if they help to increase the production of beneficial products that are being underproduced by the private sector—as would be the case for products that generated positive externalities. But the loan guarantees also provide an inducement toward reckless investing because they remove from private investors any consideration of losses. Indeed, loan guarantees are often criticized for "socializing losses and privatizing gains" because if things go wrong, any losses go to the taxpayer, while if things go well, any profits go to private investors.

In addition, the process by which loan guarantees are awarded is often criticized for being highly politicized and likely to award loan guarantees not to the firms whose projects are the most likely to increase economic efficiency but to those with the best political connections.

On the other hand, there may be legitimate cases where a new technology that would generate net benefits cannot be developed without government loan guarantees, so proponents of loan-guarantee programs argue that the programs should remain in place, but with tight controls against rent seeking and the special-interest effect.

Corruption

Political corruption is the unlawful misdirection of governmental resources or actions that occurs when government officials abuse their entrusted powers for personal gain. For instance, a police supervisor engages in political corruption if she accepts a bribe in exchange for illegally freeing a thief who had been lawfully arrested by another officer. Similarly, a government bureaucrat engages in political corruption if he refuses to issue a building permit to a homebuilder who is in full compliance with the law unless the homebuilder makes a "voluntary contribution" to the bureaucrat's favorite charity.

While relatively uncommon in the United States, political corruption is a daily reality in many parts of the world, as can be seen in Global Perspective 5.1, which gives the percentages of survey respondents in 10 countries who reported that they or someone else in their respective households paid a bribe during the previous 12 months.

Political corruption comes in two basic forms. In the first, a government official must be bribed to do what he should be doing as part of his job—as with the bureaucrat in our earlier example who demands a bribe to issue a

GLOBAL PERSPECTIVE 5.1

Percentage of Households Paying a Bribe in the Past Year

The Global Corruption Barometer is an international survey that asks individuals about their personal experiences with government corruption. The 2013 survey of over 114,000 people in 107 countries included a question that asked participants whether they or anyone in their respective households had paid a bribe in any form during the previous 12 months. Here are the results for 10 selected countries.

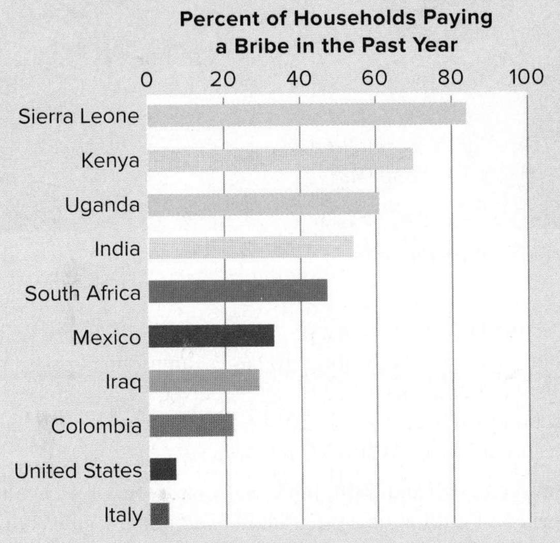

Source: Data from Transparency International, *Global Corruption Barometer,* 2013, visit **transparency.org.**

permit to a homebuilder who is in full compliance with the law. In the second, a government official demands a bribe to do something that she is not legally entitled to do—as with the police supervisor in our earlier example who illegally freed a thief.

If a candidate accepts campaign contributions from a special-interest group and then shows subsequent support for that group's legislative goals, has a subtle form of political corruption taken place? While there are strong opinions on both sides of the issue, it is often hard to tell in any particular case whether a special interest's campaign contribution amounts to a bribe. On the one hand, the special interest may indeed be trying to influence the politician's vote. On the other hand, the special interest may simply be trying to support and get elected a person who already sees things their way and who would vote the way they wanted no matter what.

That being said, the impression of impropriety lingers, and so laws have been passed in the United States limiting the amount of money that individuals can donate to specific candidates and making it illegal for certain groups such as companies to donate money directly to individual politicians (as distinct from directing funds toward supporting specific issues or advocacy groups—which is both legal and unrestricted). Proponents of these laws hope that the limitations strike a good balance—allowing contributions to be large enough that individuals and groups can meaningfully support candidates they agree with but keeping contributions small enough that no one individual or group can singlehandedly donate enough money to sway a politician's vote.

Imperfect Institutions

It is possible to argue that the wide variety of criticisms of public sector inefficiency that we have discussed in this chapter are exaggerated and cynical. Perhaps they are. Nevertheless, they do tend to shatter the concept of a benevolent government that responds with precision and efficiency to the wants of its citizens. The market system of the private sector is far from perfectly efficient, and government's economic function is mainly to correct that system's shortcomings. But the public sector is also subject to deficiencies in fulfilling its economic function. "The relevant comparison is not between perfect markets and imperfect governments, nor between faulty markets and all-knowing, rational, benevolent governments, but between inevitably imperfect institutions."[1]

Because markets and governments are both imperfect, it is sometimes difficult to determine whether a particular activity can be performed with greater success in the private sector or in the public sector. It is easy to reach agreement on opposite extremes: National defense must lie with the public sector, while automobile production can best be accomplished by the private sector. But what about health insurance? Parks and recreation areas? Fire protection? Garbage collection? Housing? Education? It is hard to assess every good or service and to say absolutely that it should be assigned to either the public sector or the private sector. Evidence: All the goods and services just mentioned are provided in part by *both* private enterprises and public agencies.

AP QUICK REVIEW 5.3

- ✓ Unlike the private sector—where the profit motive helps to ensure efficiency and variety—government lacks a strong incentive to be efficient and typically offers only limited and bundled choices.
- ✓ Regulatory capture occurs when a regulated industry can control its government regulator and get it to implement policies that favor the industry.
- ✓ Political corruption occurs when government officials abuse their powers for personal gain.

[1]Otto Eckstein, *Public Finance,* 3d ed. (Englewood Cliffs, NJ: Prentice-Hall, 1973), P. 17.

LAST WORD

"Government Failure" in the News

The Media Continually Report Government Actions That Illustrate Pork-Barrel Politics, Limited and Bundled Choices, or Bureaucratic Inefficiency.

Examples:

- The corporate tax relief bill of 2004 contained 633 pages, with 276 special provisions. Included were provisions that benefited "restaurant owners and Hollywood producers; makers of bows, arrows, tackle boxes, and sonar fish finders; NASCAR track owners; native Alaska whalers; and even importers of Chinese fans." (*The Washington Post*)
- The $878 billion American Recovery and Reinvestment Act of 2009 was laden with many dubious spending projects, including $10 million to renovate a train station in Elizabethtown, Pennsylvania, that hadn't been used in 30 years; $1.15 million to build a guardrail for an artificial lake in Woodward, Oklahoma, that had never been filled with water; and an unrequested $587,661 grant that was given to the upscale town of Union, New York, to fight a homeless problem that it didn't have. (*Lancaster Newspapers*, **newson6.com**, *Binghamton Press & Sun Union*)
- Congress funded a sanctuary for white squirrels, an antique bicycle museum, and a giant roadside coffee pot as part of 2011 federal highway spending. It also spent $765,828 to subsidize the construction of an IHOP restaurant and $113,277 to aid in the historical preservation of video games. (*Human Events, Washington Examiner, Gamasutra*)
- A 2011 audit revealed that the federal government had paid $600 million in retirement benefits to deceased federal retirees over the previous five years. Checks had been illegally cashed by living relatives. One son received cumulative payments of $515,000 over the 37 years after his father died in 1971. The fraud was only discovered after the son died in 2008. (*Associated Press*)

Source: © Royalty-Free/Corbis RF

- Despite Disney making a profit of over $2 billion per year running nine of the world's 10 largest amusement parks, two Disney contractors asked for and received $1.4 million of federal loan guarantees in 2014 to help expand the Polynesian Resort at Disney World. (*Daily Mail*)
- Between 2009 and 2014, the U.S. Department of Agriculture spent $34 million on a program to encourage Afghanis to cultivate and consume soybeans—despite soybeans growing poorly in Afghanistan and locals having no desire to eat soybeans. (*NBC News*)
- In 2014, Congress earmarked $194 million and ordered the U.S. Army to retrofit its entire fleet of M1 Abrams tanks—despite the Army stating that the tanks are obsolete for likely future conflicts. (*Fiscal Times*)

SUMMARY

LO5.1 Describe how government's power to coerce can be economically beneficial and list some of the difficulties associated with managing and directing the government.

Government's legal right to use coercion and force can help to improve economic efficiency by correcting for market failures and by enforcing laws and regulations that reduce the risk that individuals and firms will be taken advantage of.

LO5.2 Discuss "government failure" and explain why it happens.

Special interests can succeed in perpetuating policies that are opposed by the majority of voters because the costs of organizing and motivating groups to take political action increase with group size. This collective-action problem implies that special interests can perpetuate unpopular policies as long as the costs of organizing an opposition exceed the costs that the general public is currently suffering as a result of those policies.

There are powerful incentives for politicians to accommodate rent seeking and support special-interest legislation.

Because voters like receiving the benefits of government programs but do not like having to pay the taxes necessary to finance them, politicians tend to favor programs that offer easily identified immediate benefits but vague or deferred costs. This tendency helps to explain the unfunded liabilities of programs including Social Security as well as the federal government's tendency to run budget deficits.

When the economy goes into recession, politicians often use the need for fiscal policy stimulus as political cover to direct lower taxes or increased spending toward politically powerful special-interest groups. To prevent politicians from using lower interest rates and monetary stimulus as a way of increasing their reelection chances, most governments have put politically independent central banks in charge of monetary policy.

Economic theorists cite several reasons why government might be inefficient in providing public goods. (a) Citizens as voters and congressional representatives face limited and bundled choices as to public goods, whereas consumers in the private sector can be highly selective in their choices. (b) Government bureaucracies have less incentive to operate efficiently than do private businesses. (c) Regulated industries may sometimes capture their government regulatory agencies and mold government polices toward their own best interests.

Government's track record as an investor in private-sector firms is very poor, with most government investments into private sector businesses generating low or negative returns for taxpayers.

Government attempts to increase private investment by offering loan guarantees often cause resources to be misdirected toward high-risk projects that have an extremely low likelihood of success. These arrangements "socialize losses and privatize gains" because if the businesses go bankrupt, the government bears the losses, but if they do well, private individuals receive the profits.

Political corruption may cause governmental resources or actions to be misdirected.

Neither governments nor markets are perfect economic institutions. Each has its own set of shortcomings and citizens should be aware of where each is likely to fail and where each is likely to succeed.

TERMS AND CONCEPTS

government failure
principal-agent problems
special-interest effect
collective-action problem
earmarks
rent seeking
unfunded liability
budget deficit
debt crisis
fiscal policy
monetary policy
regulatory capture
deregulation
loan guarantees
political corruption

The following and additional problems can be found in connect

DISCUSSION QUESTIONS

1. Why might citizens interested in maximizing economic efficiency be happy to invest their government with the right to coerce them in at least some situations? LO5.1
2. Jean-Baptiste Colbert was the Minister of Finance under King Louis XIV of France. He famously observed, "The art of taxation consists in so plucking the goose as to obtain the largest possible amount of feathers with the smallest possible amount of hissing." How does his comment relate to special interests and the collective-action problem? LO5.2
3. What is rent seeking and how does it differ from the kinds of profit maximization and profit seeking that we discussed in previous chapters? Provide an actual or hypothetical example of rent seeking by firms in an industry. By a union. By a professional association (for example, physicians, school teachers, or lawyers). Why do elected officials often accommodate rent-seeking behavior, particularly by firms, unions, and professional groups located in their home states? LO5.2
4. How does the problem of limited and bundled choice in the public sector relate to economic efficiency? Why are public bureaucracies possibly less efficient than business firms? LO5.2
5. Discuss the political incentives that helped motivate federal politicians to approve budget deficits in all but five years between 1960 and 2015. LO5.2
6. Explain: "Politicians would make more rational economic decisions if they weren't running for reelection every few years." LO5.2
7. Critique: "Thank goodness we have so many government regulatory agencies. They keep Big Business in check." LO5.2
8. **LAST WORD** How do the concepts of pork-barrel politics and the special-interest effect relate to the items listed in the Last Word?

AP REVIEW QUESTIONS

1. Select all of the following that are true. To an economist, a coercive government can be useful in order to: LO5.1
   a. Reallocate resources in order to improve efficiency.
   b. Fight negative externalities.
   c. Ensure low gasoline prices.
   d. Provide a high-risk economic environment for individuals and firms.
   e. Provide a guaranteed economic profit for firms.
2. To an economist, a government program is too big if an analysis of that program finds that MB _______ MC. LO5.1
   a. Is greater than.
   b. Is less than.
   c. Is equal to.
   d. Is less than twice as large as.
   e. Is more than twice as large as.

3. Tammy Hall is the mayor of a large U.S. city. She has just established the Office of Window Safety. Because windows sometimes break and spray glass shards, every window in the city will now have to pass an annual safety inspection. Property owners must pay the $5-per-window cost—and by the way, Tammy has made her nephew the new head of the Office of Window Safety. This new policy is an example of: LO5.2
   a. Benevolence.
   b. Earmarks.
   c. Rent seeking.
   d. Adverse selection.
   e. Logrolling.
4. A few hundred U.S. sugar makers lobby the U.S. government each year to make sure that the government taxes imported sugar at a high rate. They do so because the policy drives up the domestic price of sugar and increases their profits. It is estimated that the policy benefits U.S. sugar producers by about $1 billion per year while costing U.S. consumers upwards of $2 billion per year. Which of the following concepts apply to the U.S. sugar tax? Select all that apply. LO5.2
   a. Political corruption.
   b. Rent-seeking behavior.
   c. The collective-action problem.
   d. The special-interest effect.
   e. Adverse selection.
5. ________________ occur when politicians commit to making a series of future expenditures without simultaneously committing to collect enough tax revenues to pay for those expenditures. LO5.2
   a. Budget deficits
   b. Debt crises
   c. Loan guarantees
   d. Unfunded liabilities
   e. Budget surpluses

PROBLEMS

1. Suppose that there are 1 million federal workers at the lowest level of the federal bureaucracy and that above them there are multiple layers of supervisors and supervisors-of-supervisors. Assume that each higher level is one-tenth the size of the one below it because the government is using a 10:1 ratio of supervisees to supervisors. That is, for every 10 workers at the bottom, there is 1 supervisor; for every 10 of those supervisors, there is 1 supervisor-of-supervisors; for every one of those supervisors-of-supervisors, there is a supervisor-of-supervisors-of-supervisors; and so on, all the way up the bureaucratic pyramid to the president. LO5.1
   a. How many supervisors will there be in each supervisory layer of the federal bureaucracy? Start with the layer of supervisors directly above the 1 million workers at the bottom.
   b. How many supervisors are there in total at all levels of the federal bureaucratic pyramid, including the president?
   c. If you count the 1 million workers at the bottom as the first layer of the federal bureaucracy, how many total layers are there, including the president?
   d. How many federal employees are there in total at all layers, including the president?
   e. What fraction of all federal employees are supervisory, including the president?
2. Consider a specific example of the special-interest effect and the collective-action problem. In 2012, it was estimated that the total value of all corn production subsidies in the United States was about $3 billion. The population of the United States was approximately 300 million people that year. LO5.2
   a. On average, how much did corn subsidies cost per person in the United States in 2012? (Hint: A billion is a 1 followed by nine zeros. A million is a 1 followed by six zeros.)
   b. If each person in the United States is only willing to spend $0.50 to support efforts to overturn the corn subsidy, and if antisubsidy advocates can only raise funds from 10 percent of the population, how much money will they be able to raise for their lobbying efforts?
   c. If the recipients of corn subsidies donate just 1 percent of the total amount that they receive in subsidies, how much could they raise to support lobbying efforts to continue the corn subsidy?
   d. By how many dollars does the amount raised by the recipients of the corn subsidy exceed the amount raised by the opponents of the corn subsidy?
3. Consider a corrupt provincial government in which each housing inspector examines two newly built structures each week. All the builders in the province are unethical and want to increase their profits by using substandard construction materials, but they can't do that unless they can bribe a housing inspector into approving a substandard building. LO5.2
   a. If bribes cost $1,000 each, how much will a housing inspector make each year in bribes? (Assume that each inspector works 52 weeks a year and gets bribed for every house he inspects.)
   b. There is a provincial construction supervisor who gets to hire all of the housing inspectors. He himself is corrupt and expects his housing inspectors to share their bribes with him. Suppose that 20 inspectors work for him and that each passes along half the bribes collected from builders. How much will the construction supervisor collect each year?
   c. Corrupt officials may have an incentive to reduce the provision of government services to help line their own pockets. Suppose that the provincial construction supervisor decides to cut the total number of housing inspectors from 20 to 10 in order to decrease the supply of new housing permits. This decrease in the supply of permits raises the equilibrium bribe from $1,000 to $2,500. How much per year will the construction supervisor now receive if he is still getting half of all the bribes collected by the 10 inspectors? How much more is the construction supervisor getting now than when he had 20 inspectors working in part *b*? Will he personally be happy with the reduction in government services?
   d. What if reducing the number of inspectors from 20 to 10 only increased the equilibrium bribe from $1,000 to $1,500? In this case, how much per year would the construction supervisor collect from his 10 inspectors? How much *less* is the construction supervisor getting than when he had 20 inspectors working in part *b*? In this case, will the construction supervisor be happy with the reduction in government services? Will he want to go back to using 20 inspectors?

Public Choice Theory and Voting Paradoxes

LO5.3 Explain the difficulties of conveying economic preferences through majority voting.

Public Choice Theory

Market failures, such as public goods and externalities, impede economic efficiency and justify government intervention in the economy.

But the government's response to market failures is not without its own problems and pitfalls. In fact, government can sometimes fail as badly or even worse than markets in terms of delivering economic efficiency and directing resources to the uses where they will bring the largest net benefits.

That is why it is important to study **public choice theory**—the economic analysis of government decision making, politics, and elections. Just as the study of *market failure* helps us to understand how regulating markets may help to improve the allocation of resources, the study of *government failure* can help us to understand how changes in the way government functions might help it to operate more efficiently.

As we will discuss shortly, many instances of government failure can be traced to incentive structures that lead political representatives to pursue policies that go against the preferences of the people that they are representing. But an even more fundamental problem exists. The majority voting systems that we rely upon may make it difficult or even impossible to correctly discern voter preferences. In such cases, it is not surprising that government fails to deliver what the voters actually want.

Revealing Preferences through Majority Voting

Through some process, society must decide which public goods it wants and in what amounts. It also must determine the extent to which it wants government to intervene in private markets to correct externalities. Decisions need to be made about the extent and type of regulation of business that is necessary, the amount of income redistribution that is desirable, what policies the government might enact to mitigate asymmetric information problems, and other such choices. Furthermore, society must determine the set of taxes it thinks is best for financing government. How should government apportion (divide) the total tax burden among the public?

Decisions such as these are made collectively in the United States through a democratic process that relies heavily on majority voting. Candidates for office offer alternative policy packages, and citizens elect people who they think will make the best decisions on their collective behalf. Voters "retire" officials who do not adequately represent their collective wishes and elect persons they think do. Also, citizens periodically have opportunities at the state and local levels to vote directly on public expenditures or new legislation.

Although the democratic process does a reasonably good job of revealing society's preferences, it is imperfect. Public choice theory demonstrates that majority voting can produce inefficiencies and inconsistencies.

Inefficient Voting Outcomes Society's well-being is enhanced when government provides a public good whose total benefit exceeds its total cost. Unfortunately, majority voting does not always deliver that outcome.

Illustration: Inefficient "No" Vote Assume that the government can provide a public good, say, national defense, at a total expense of $900. Also assume that there are only three individuals—Adams, Benson, and Conrad—in the society and that they will share the $900 tax expense equally, each being taxed $300 if the proposed public good is provided. And assume, as Figure 1a illustrates, that Adams would receive $700 worth of benefits from having this public good; Benson, $250; and Conrad, $200.

What will be the result if a majority vote determines whether or not this public good is provided? Although people do not always vote strictly according to their own economic interest, it is likely Benson and Conrad will vote "no" because they will incur tax costs of $300 each while gaining benefits of only $250 and $200, respectively. Adams will vote "yes." So the majority vote will defeat the proposal even though the total benefit of $1,150 (= $700 for Adams + $250 for Benson + $200 for Conrad) exceeds the total cost of $900. Resources should be devoted to this good, but they will not be. Too little of this public good will be produced.

Illustration: Inefficient "Yes" Vote Now consider a situation in which the majority favors a public good even though its total cost exceeds its total benefit. Figure 1b shows the details. Again, Adams, Benson, and Conrad will equally share the $900 cost of the public good; each will be taxed $300. But since Adams' benefit now is only $100 from the public good, she will vote against it. Meanwhile, Benson and Conrad will

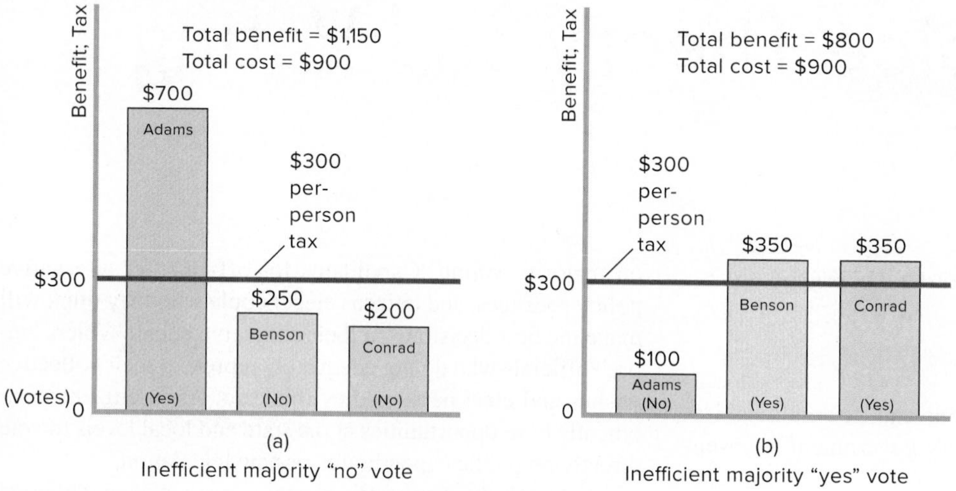

FIGURE 1 Inefficient voting outcomes. Majority voting can produce inefficient decisions. (a) Majority voting leads to rejection of a public good that would entail a greater total benefit than total cost. (b) Majority voting results in acceptance of a public good that has a higher total cost than total benefit.

benefit by $350 each. They will vote for the public good because that benefit ($350) exceeds their tax payments ($300). The majority vote will provide a public good costing $900 that produces total benefits of only $800 (= $100 for Adams + $350 for Benson + $350 for Conrad). Society's resources will be inefficiently allocated to this public good. Too much of it will be produced.

Implications The point is that an inefficient outcome may occur as either an overproduction or an underproduction of a specific public good, and therefore as an overallocation or underallocation of resources for that particular use. In Chapter 4 we saw that government can improve economic efficiency by providing public goods that the market system will not make available. Now we have extended that analysis to reveal that government may not provide some of those public goods or may provide them in the wrong amounts. In other cases, it may provide public goods that are not economically warranted.

In our examples, each person has only a single vote, no matter how much he or she might gain or lose from a public good. In the first example (inefficient "no" vote), Adams would be willing to purchase a vote from either Benson or Conrad if buying votes were legal. That way Adams could be assured of obtaining the national defense she so highly values. But since buying votes is illegal, many people with strong preferences for certain public goods may have to go without them.

When individual consumers have a strong preference for a specific *private good*, they usually can find that good in the marketplace even though it may be unpopular with the majority of consumers. A consumer can buy beef tongue, liver, and squid in some supermarkets, although it is doubtful that any of these products would be available if majority voting stocked the shelves. But a person cannot easily "buy" a *public good* such as national defense once the majority has decided against it.

Conversely, a consumer in the marketplace can decide against buying a particular product, even a popular one. But although you may not want national defense, you must "buy" it through your tax payments when the majority have decided they want it.

Conclusion: Because majority voting fails to incorporate the *strength* of the preferences of the individual voter, it may produce economically inefficient outcomes.

Interest Groups and Logrolling Some, but not all, of the inefficiencies of majority voting get resolved through the political process. Two examples follow.

Interest Groups People who share strong preferences for a public good may band together into interest groups and use advertisements, mailings, and direct persuasion to convince others of the merits of that public good. Adams might try to persuade Benson and Conrad that it is in their best interest to vote for national defense—that national defense is much more valuable to them than their $250 and $200 valuations. Such appeals are common in democratic politics. Sometimes they are successful; sometimes they are not.

Political Logrolling Perhaps surprisingly, **logrolling**—the trading of votes to secure desired outcomes—can also turn an inefficient outcome into an efficient one. In our first example (Figure 1a), suppose that Benson has a strong preference for a different public good, for example, a new road, which Adams and Conrad do not think is worth the tax expense. That would provide an opportunity for Adams and Benson to trade votes to ensure provision of both national defense and the new road. That is, Adams and Benson would each vote "yes" on both measures. Adams would get the national defense and Benson would get the road. Without the logrolling, both public goods would have been rejected. This logrolling will add to society's well-being if, as was true for national defense, the road creates a greater overall benefit than cost.

But logrolling need not increase economic efficiency. Even if national defense and the road each cost more than the total benefit each produces, both might still be provided if there is vote trading. Adams and Benson might still engage in logrolling if each expects to secure a sufficient net gain from her or his favored public good, even though the gains would come at the clear expense of Conrad.

Logrolling is very common in state legislatures and Congress. It can either increase or diminish economic efficiency, depending on the circumstances.

Paradox of Voting

Another difficulty with majority voting is the **paradox of voting,** a situation in which society may not be able to rank its preferences consistently through paired-choice majority voting.

Preferences Consider Table 1, in which we again assume a community of three voters: Adams, Benson, and Conrad. Suppose the community has three alternative public goods from which to choose: national defense, a road, and a weather warning system. We expect that each member of the community prefers the three alternatives in a certain order. For example, one person might prefer national defense to a road and a road to a weather warning system. We can attempt to determine the preferences of the community through paired-choice majority voting. Specifically, a vote can be held between any two of the public goods, and the winner of that vote can then be matched against the third public good in another vote.

The three goods and the assumed individual preferences of the three voters are listed in the top part of Table 1. The data indicate that Adams prefers national defense to the road and the road to the weather warning system. This implies also that Adams prefers national defense to the weather warning system. Benson values the road more than the weather warning system and the warning system more than national defense. Conrad's order of preference is weather warning system, national defense, and road.

TABLE 1 Paradox of Voting

	Preferences		
Public Good	**Adams**	**Benson**	**Conrad**
National defense	1st choice	3d choice	2d choice
Road	2d choice	1st choice	3d choice
Weather warning system	3d choice	2d choice	1st choice
Election	**Voting Outcomes: Winner**		
1. National defense vs. road	National defense (preferred by Adams and Conrad)		
2. Road vs. weather warning system	Road (preferred by Adams and Benson)		
3. National defense vs. weather warning system	Weather warning system (preferred by Benson and Conrad)		

Voting Outcomes The lower part of Table 1 shows the outcomes of three hypothetical elections decided through majority vote. In the first, national defense wins against the road because a majority of voters (Adams and Conrad) prefer national defense to the road. In the second election, to see whether this community wants a road or a weather warning system, a majority of voters (Adams and Benson) prefer the road.

We have determined that the majority of people in this community prefer national defense to a road and prefer a road to a weather warning system. It seems logical to conclude that the community prefers national defense to a weather warning system. But it does not!

To demonstrate this conclusion, we hold a direct election between national defense and the weather warning system. Row 3 shows that a majority of voters (Benson and Conrad) prefer the weather warning system to national defense. As listed in Table 1, then, the three paired-choice majority votes imply that this community is irrational: It seems to prefer national defense to a road and a road to a weather warning system, but would rather have a weather warning system than national defense.

The problem is not irrational community preferences but rather a flawed procedure for determining those preferences. We see that the outcome from paired-choice majority voting may depend on the order in which the votes are taken. Different sequences of majority votes can lead to different outcomes, many of which may fail to reflect the electorate's underlying preferences. As a consequence, government may find it difficult to provide the "correct" public goods by acting in accordance with majority voting. Important note: This critique is not meant to suggest that some better procedure exists. Majority voting is much more likely to reflect community preferences than decisions by, say, a dictator or a group of self-appointed leaders.

Median-Voter Model One other aspect of majority voting reveals further insights into real-world phenomena. The **median-voter model** suggests that, under majority rule and consistent voting preferences, the median voter will in a sense determine the outcomes of elections. The median voter is the person holding the middle position on an issue: Half the other voters have stronger preferences for a public good, amount of taxation, or degree of government regulation, while half have weaker or negative preferences. The extreme voters on each side of an issue prefer the median choice rather than the other extreme position, so the median voter's choice predominates.

Example Suppose a society composed of Adams, Benson, and Conrad has reached agreement that as a society it needs a weather warning system. Each person independently is to submit a total dollar amount he or she thinks should be spent on the warning system, assuming each will be taxed one-third of that amount. An election will determine the size of the

CONSIDER THIS . . .

Source: © Blend Images / Superstock RF

Voter Failure

Inefficient voting outcomes and the paradox of voting imply that governments may sometimes fail to deliver the best combination of public goods because it may be very difficult for politicians to discern what voters actually want. In other cases, though, economists worry that governments may end up failing to deliver allocative and productive efficiency not because politicians can't tell what people want—but because they *can.*

The problem is that voters sometimes support policies that reduce rather than enhance allocative and productive efficiency. Examples include several types of wage and price controls, punitive tariffs on foreign products, and various industrial and agricultural subsidies.

These policies almost always reduce economic efficiency, but they are also extremely popular with voters in many countries. Faced with that reality, a politician may well end up supporting such policies even if he personally understands that they will create more economic harm than benefit.

That behavior makes some observers wish for braver politicians who might be willing to oppose these instances of "voter failure." But others argue that it is too much to hope for braver politicians. Instead, efforts should be directed toward educating the public and convincing them to support government policies that are economically efficient.

system. Because each person can be expected to vote for his or her own proposal, no majority will occur if all the proposals are placed on the ballot at the same time. Thus, the group decides on a paired-choice vote: They will first vote between two of the proposals and then match the winner of that vote against the remaining proposal.

The three proposals are as follows: Adams desires a $400 system; Benson wants an $800 system; Conrad opts for a $300 system. Which proposal will win? The median-voter model suggests it will be the $400 proposal submitted by the median voter, Adams. Half the other voters favor a more costly system; half favor a less costly system. To understand why the $400 system will be the outcome, let's conduct the two elections.

First, suppose that the $400 proposal is matched against the $800 proposal. Adams naturally votes for her $400 proposal, and Benson votes for his own $800 proposal. Conrad, who proposed the $300 expenditure for the warning system, votes for the $400 proposal because it is closer to his own. So Adams's $400 proposal is selected by a 2-to-1 majority vote.

Next, we match the $400 proposal against the $300 proposal. Again the $400 proposal wins. It gets a vote from Adams and one from Benson, who proposed the $800 expenditure and for that reason prefers a $400 expenditure to a $300 one. Adams, the median voter in this case, is in a sense the person who has decided the level of expenditure on a weather warning system for this society.

Real-World Applicability Although our illustration is simple, it explains a great deal. We do note a tendency for public choices to match most closely the median view. Political candidates, for example, take one set of positions to win the nomination of their political parties; in so doing, they tend to appeal to the median voter within the party to get the nomination. They then shift their views more closely to the political center when they square off against opponents from the opposite political party. In effect, they redirect their appeal toward the median voter within the total population. They also try to label their opponents as being too liberal, or too conservative, and out of touch with "mainstream America." And they conduct polls and adjust their positions on issues accordingly.

Implications The median-voter model has two important implications:

- At any point in time, many people will be dissatisfied by the extent of government involvement in the economy. The size of government will largely be determined by the median preference, leaving many people desiring a much larger, or a much smaller, public sector. In the marketplace you can buy no zucchinis, 2 zucchinis, or 200 zucchinis, depending on how much you enjoy them. In the public sector you will tend to get the number of Stealth bombers and new highway projects that the median voter prefers.
- Some people may "vote with their feet" by moving into political jurisdictions where the median voter's preferences are closer to their own. They may move from the city to a suburb where the level of government services, and therefore taxes, is lower. Or they may move into an area known for its excellent, but expensive, school system. Some may move to other states; a few may even move to other countries.

For these reasons, and because our personal preferences for publicly provided goods and services are not static, the median preference shifts over time. Moreover, information about people's preferences is imperfect, leaving much room for politicians to misjudge the true median position. When they do, they may have a difficult time getting elected or reelected.

APPENDIX SUMMARY

LO5.3 Explain the difficulties of conveying economic preferences through majority voting.

Public choice theory suggests that governments may sometimes suffer from government failures because majority voting fails to correctly indicate voter preferences.

Majority voting creates the possibility of (a) underallocations or overallocations of resources to particular public goods and (b) inconsistent voting outcomes that make it impossible for a democratic political system to definitively determine the will of the people.

The median-voter model predicts that, under majority rule, the person holding the middle position on an issue will determine the outcome of an election involving that issue.

APPENDIX TERMS AND CONCEPTS

public choice theory

paradox of voting

median-voter model

logrolling

The following and additional problems can be found in connect

APPENDIX DISCUSSION QUESTIONS

1. Explain how affirmative and negative majority votes can sometimes lead to inefficient allocations of resources to public goods. Is this problem likely to be greater under a benefits-received or an ability-to-pay tax system? Use the information in Figures 1a and 1b to show how society might be better off if Adams were allowed to buy votes. LO5.3
2. "Majority voting ensures that government will produce only those public goods for which benefits exceed costs." Discuss. LO5.3
3. "The problem with our democratic institutions is that they don't correctly reflect the will of the people! If the people—rather than self-interested politicians or lobbyists—had control, we wouldn't have to worry about government taking actions that don't maximize allocative and productive efficiency." Critique. LO5.3

APPENDIX REVIEW QUESTIONS

1. Explain the paradox of voting through reference to the accompanying table, which shows the ranking of three public goods by voters Jay, Dave, and Conan: LO5.3

	Rankings		
Public Good	**Jay**	**Dave**	**Conan**
Courthouse	2nd choice	1st choice	3d choice
School	3d choice	2d choice	1st choice
Park	1st choice	3d choice	2d choice

2. We can apply voting paradoxes to the highway construction example of Chapter 4. Suppose there are only five people in a society and each favors one of the five highway construction options listed in Table 4.4 ("No new construction" is one of the five options). Explain which of these highway options will be selected using a majority paired-choice vote. Will this option be the optimal size of the project from an economic perspective? LO5.3
3. True or False: The median-voter model explains why politicians so often stake out fringe positions that appeal only to a small segment of the electorate. LO5.3

APPENDIX PROBLEMS

1. Look back at Figures 1a and 1b, which show the costs and benefits to voters Adams, Benson, and Conrad of two different public goods that the government will produce if a majority of Adams, Benson, and Conrad support them. Suppose that Adams, Benson, and Conrad have decided to have one single vote at which the funding for both of those public goods will be decided simultaneously. LO5.3
   a. Given the $300 cost per person of each public good, what are Adams's net benefits for each public good individually and for the two combined? Will he want to vote yes or no on the proposal to fund both projects simultaneously?
   b. What are Conrad's net benefits for each public good individually and for the two combined? Will he want to vote yes or no on the proposal to fund both projects simultaneously?
   c. What are Benson's net benefits for each public good individually and for the two combined? Will he want to vote yes or no on the proposal to fund both projects simultaneously—or will he be indifferent?

d. Who is the median voter here? Who will the two other voters be attempting to persuade?

2. Political advertising is often directed at winning over so-called swing voters, whose votes might go either way. Suppose that two political parties—the Freedom Party and the Liberty Party—disagree on whether to build a new road. Polling shows that of 1,000 total voters, 450 are firmly for the new road and 450 are firmly against the new road. Thus, each party will try to win over a majority of the 100 remaining swing voters. **LO5.3**

a. Suppose that each party spends $5,000 on untargeted TV, radio, and newspaper ads that are equally likely to reach any and all voters. How much per voter will be spent by both parties combined?

b. Suppose that, instead, each party could direct all of its spending toward just the swing voters by using targeted ads that exploit Internet social media. If all of the two parties' combined spending was targeted at just swing voters, how much would be spent per swing voter?

c. Suppose that only the Freedom Party knows how to target voters using social media. How much per swing voter will it be spending? If at the same time the Liberty Party is still using only untargeted TV, radio, and newspaper ads, what portion of its total spending is likely to be reaching the 100 swing voters? How much per swing voter does that portion amount to?

d. Looking at your answers to part *c*, how much more per swing voter will the Freedom Party be spending than the Liberty Party? If spending per swing voter influences elections, which party is more likely to win?

Consumer Behavior

We begin our study of the demand side of the market--the behavior of consumers--by introducing a conceptual tool of significant importance in economics: ***elasticity.*** Elasticity is useful in so many areas of life.

Essentially, it aims at explaining the extent to which one variable affects another variable. For example, if you study more, your grade should improve; but will the improvement per extra hour of study time be relatively little or a lot? Likewise, when the price of a good falls, like iPhones, will the quantity demanded increase relatively little (inelastic) or relatively a lot (elastic)? You will see in Chapter 6 that the concept of elasticity can be applied in many areas of economic life.

Next, Chapter 7 looks at how a rational consumer allocates a limited income across the many goods and services that provide satisfaction (satisfaction being called ***utility*** by economists). This study will help us derive the individual ***consumer demand curve*** for a good, and then aggregate to the ***market demand curve,*** leading to our understanding of the demand side of the market.

6 Chapter

Elasticity

Learning Objectives

LO6.1 **Discuss price elasticity of demand and how it is calculated.**

LO6.2 **Explain the usefulness of the total-revenue test for price elasticity of demand.**

LO6.3 **List the factors that affect price elasticity of demand and describe some applications of price elasticity of demand.**

LO6.4 **Describe price elasticity of supply and how it can be applied.**

LO6.5 **Apply cross elasticity of demand and income elasticity of demand.**

AP Chapter Focus

In this chapter we extend Chapter 3's discussion of demand and supply by explaining *elasticity,* an extremely important concept that helps us answer such questions as: Why do buyers of some products (for example, ocean cruises) respond to price increases by substantially reducing their purchases while buyers of other products (say, gasoline) respond by only slightly cutting back their purchases? Why do higher market prices for some products (for example, chicken) cause producers to greatly increase their output while price rises for other products (say, gold) cause only limited increases in output? Why does the demand for some products (for example, books) rise a great deal when household income increases while the demand for other products (say, milk) rises just a little?

Elasticity extends our understanding of markets by letting us know the degree to which changes in prices and incomes affect supply and demand. Sometimes the responses are substantial, and other times, minimal or even nonexistent. By knowing what to expect, businesses and the government can do a better job in deciding what to produce, how much to charge, and, surprisingly, what items to tax.

AP Price Elasticity of Demand

LO6.1 Discuss price elasticity of demand and how it is calculated.

The law of demand tells us that, other things equal, consumers will buy more of a product when its price declines and less when its price increases. But how much more or less will they buy? The amount varies from product to product and over different price ranges for the same product. It also may vary over time. And such variations matter. For example, a firm contemplating a price hike will want to know how consumers will respond. If they remain highly loyal and continue to buy, the firm's revenue will rise. But if consumers defect en masse to other sellers or other products, the firm's revenue will tumble.

The responsiveness (or sensitivity) of consumers to a price change is measured by a product's **price elasticity of demand.** For some products—for example, restaurant meals—consumers are highly responsive to price changes. Modest price changes cause very large changes in the quantity purchased. Economists say that the demand for such products is *relatively elastic* or simply *elastic.*

For other products—for example, toothpaste—consumers pay much less attention to price changes. Substantial price changes cause only small changes in the amount purchased. The demand for such products is *relatively inelastic* or simply *inelastic.*

The Price-Elasticity Coefficient and Formula

Economists measure the degree to which demand is price elastic or inelastic with the coefficient E_d, defined as

$$E_d = \frac{\text{percentage change in quantity demanded of product X}}{\text{percentage change in price of product X}}$$

The percentage changes in the equation are calculated by dividing the *change* in quantity demanded by the original quantity demanded and by dividing the *change* in price by the original price. So we can restate the formula as

$$E_d = \frac{\text{change in quantity demanded of X}}{\text{original quantity demanded of X}} \div \frac{\text{change in price of X}}{\text{original price of X}}$$

Using Averages Unfortunately, an annoying problem arises in computing the price-elasticity coefficient. A price change from, say, \$4 to \$5 along a demand curve is a 25 percent (= \$1/\$4) increase, but the opposite price change from \$5 to \$4 along the same curve is a 20 percent (= \$1/\$5) decrease. Which percentage change in price should we use in the denominator to compute the price-elasticity coefficient? And when quantity changes, for example, from 10 to 20, it is a 100 percent (= 10/10) increase. But when quantity falls from 20 to 10 along the identical demand curve, it is a 50 percent (= 10/20) decrease. Should we use 100 percent or 50 percent in the numerator of the elasticity formula? Elasticity should be the same whether price rises or falls!

The simplest solution to the problem is to use the **midpoint formula** for calculating elasticity. This formula simply averages the two prices and the two quantities as the reference points for computing the percentages. That is,

$$E_d = \frac{\text{change in quantity}}{\text{sum of quantities/2}} \div \frac{\text{change in price}}{\text{sum of prices/2}}$$

For the same \$5–\$4 price range, the price reference is \$4.50 [= (\$5 + \$4)/2], and for the same 10–20 quantity range, the quantity reference is 15 units [= (10 + 20)/2]. The percentage change in price is now \$1/\$4.50, or about 22 percent, and the percentage change in quantity is $\frac{10}{15}$, or about 67 percent. So E_d is about 3. This solution eliminates the "up versus down" problem. All the price-elasticity coefficients that follow are calculated using this midpoint formula.

Using Percentages Why use percentages rather than absolute amounts in measuring consumer responsiveness? There are two reasons.

First, if we use absolute changes, the choice of units will arbitrarily affect our impression of buyer responsiveness. To illustrate: If the price of a bag of popcorn at the local softball game is reduced from \$3 to \$2 and consumers increase their purchases from 60 to 100 bags, it will seem that consumers are quite sensitive to price changes and therefore that demand is elastic. After all, a price change of 1 unit has caused a change in the amount demanded of 40 units. But by changing the monetary unit from dollars to pennies (why not?), we find that a price change of 100 units (pennies) causes a quantity change of 40 units. This may falsely lead us to believe that demand is inelastic. We avoid this problem by using percentage changes. This particular price decline is the same whether we measure it in dollars or pennies.

Second, by using percentages, we can correctly compare consumer responsiveness to changes in the prices of different products. It makes little sense to compare the effects on quantity demanded of (1) a \$1 increase in the price of a \$10,000 used car with (2) a \$1 increase in the price of a \$1 soft drink. Here the price of the used car has increased by 0.01 percent while the price of the soft drink is up by 100 percent. We can more sensibly compare the consumer responsiveness to price increases by using some common percentage increase in price for both.

Elimination of Minus Sign We know from the downsloping demand curve that price and quantity demanded are inversely related. Thus, the price-elasticity coefficient of demand E_d will always be a negative number. As an example, if price declines, then quantity demanded will increase. This means that the numerator in our formula will be positive and the denominator negative, yielding a negative E_d. For an increase in price, the numerator will be negative but the denominator positive, again yielding a negative E_d.

Economists usually ignore the minus sign and simply present the absolute value of the elasticity coefficient to avoid an ambiguity that might otherwise arise. It can be confusing to say that an E_d of −4 is greater than one of −2. This possible confusion is avoided when we say an E_d of 4 reveals greater elasticity than one of 2. So, in what follows, we ignore the minus sign in the coefficient of price elasticity of demand

and show only the absolute value. Incidentally, the ambiguity does not arise with supply because price and quantity supplied are positively related. All elasticity of supply coefficients therefore are positive numbers.

Interpretations of E_d

We can interpret the coefficient of price elasticity of demand as follows.

Elastic Demand Demand is **elastic** if a specific percentage change in price results in a larger percentage change in quantity demanded. In such cases, E_d will be greater than 1. Example: Suppose that a 2 percent decline in the price of cut flowers results in a 4 percent increase in quantity demanded. Then demand for cut flowers is elastic and

$$E_d = \frac{.04}{.02} = 2$$

Inelastic Demand If a specific percentage change in price produces a smaller percentage change in quantity demanded, demand is **inelastic.** In such cases, E_d will be less than 1. Example: Suppose that a 2 percent decline in the price of coffee leads to only a 1 percent increase in quantity demanded. Then demand is inelastic and

$$E_d = \frac{.01}{.02} = .5$$

Unit Elasticity The case separating elastic and inelastic demands occurs where a percentage change in price and the resulting percentage change in quantity demanded are the same. Example: Suppose that a 2 percent drop in the price of chocolate causes a 2 percent increase in quantity demanded. This special case is termed **unit elasticity** because E_d is exactly 1, or unity. In this example,

$$E_d = \frac{.02}{.02} = 1$$

Extreme Cases When we say demand is "inelastic," we do not mean that consumers are completely unresponsive to a price change. In that extreme situation, where a price change results in no change whatsoever in the quantity demanded, economists say that demand is **perfectly inelastic.** The price-elasticity coefficient is zero because there is no response to a change in price. Approximate examples include an acute diabetic's demand for insulin or an addict's demand for heroin. A line parallel to the vertical axis, such as D_1 in Figure 6.1a, shows perfectly inelastic demand graphically.

Conversely, when we say demand is "elastic," we do not mean that consumers are completely responsive to a price change. In that extreme situation, where a small price reduction causes buyers to increase their purchases from zero to all they can obtain, the elasticity coefficient is infinite (= ∞) and economists say demand is **perfectly elastic.** A line parallel to the horizontal axis, such as D_2 in Figure 6.1b, shows perfectly elastic demand. You will see in Chapter 10 that such a demand applies to a firm—say, a mining firm—that is selling its output in a purely competitive market.

AP **FIGURE 6.1 Perfectly inelastic and elastic demands.** Demand curve D_1 in (a) represents perfectly inelastic demand ($E_d = 0$). A price increase will result in no change in quantity demanded. Demand curve D_2 in (b) represents perfectly elastic demand. A price increase will cause quantity demanded to decline from an infinite amount to zero ($E_d = \infty$).

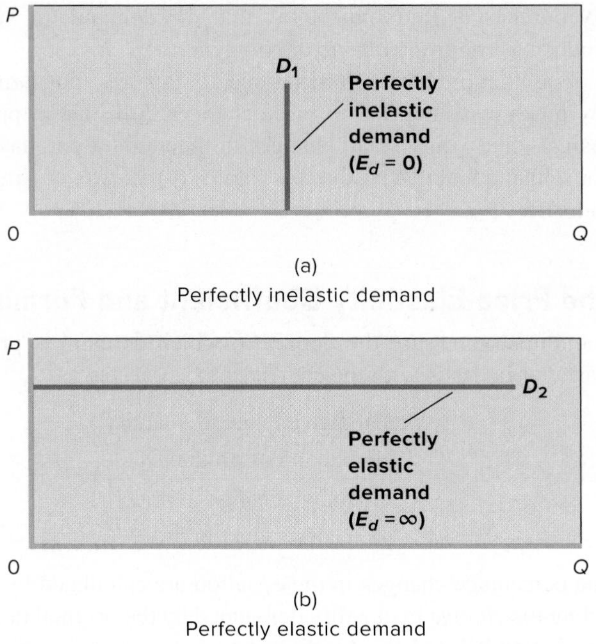

AP The Total-Revenue Test

LO6.2 Explain the usefulness of the total-revenue test for price elasticity of demand.

The importance of elasticity for firms relates to the effect of price changes on total revenue and thus on profits (= total revenue minus total costs).

Total revenue (TR) is the total amount the seller receives from the sale of a product in a particular time period; it is calculated by multiplying the product price (P) by the quantity sold (Q). In equation form:

$$TR = P \times Q$$

Graphically, total revenue is represented by the $P \times Q$ rectangle lying below a point on a demand curve. At point a in Figure 6.2a, for example, price is \$2 and quantity demanded is 10 units. So total revenue is \$20 (= \$2 × 10), shown by the rectangle composed of the yellow and green areas under the demand curve. We know from basic geometry that the area of

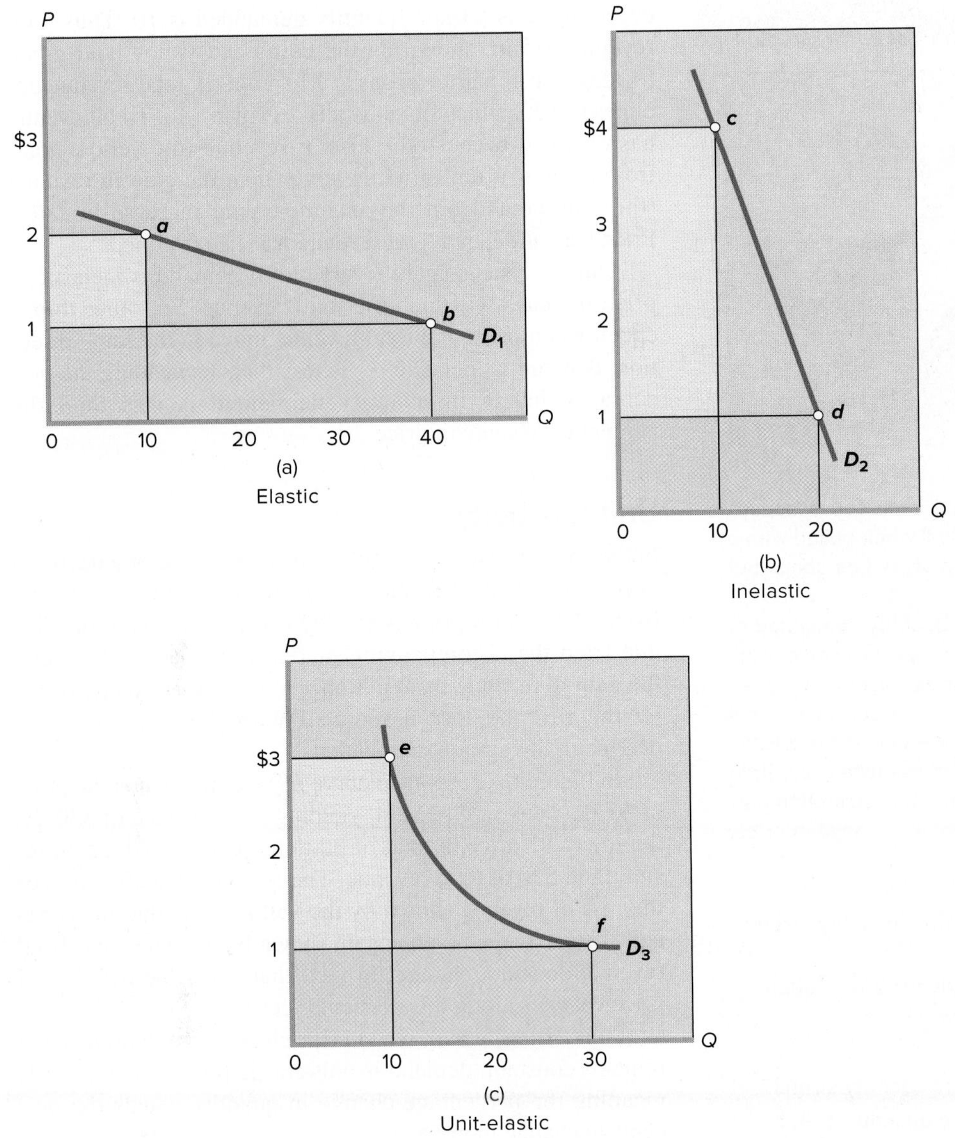

AP **FIGURE 6.2 The total-revenue test for price elasticity.** (a) Price declines from \$2 to \$1, and total revenue increases from \$20 to \$40. So demand is elastic. The gain in revenue (blue area) exceeds the loss of revenue (yellow area). (b) Price declines from \$4 to \$1, and total revenue falls from \$40 to \$20. So, demand is inelastic. The gain in revenue (blue area) is less than the loss of revenue (yellow area). (c) Price declines from \$3 to \$1, and total revenue does not change. Demand is unit-elastic. The gain in revenue (blue area) equals the loss of revenue (yellow area).

a rectangle is found by multiplying one side by the other. Here, one side is "price" (\$2) and the other is "quantity demanded" (10 units).

Total revenue and the price elasticity of demand are related. In fact, the easiest way to infer whether demand is elastic or inelastic is to employ the **total-revenue test.** Here is the test: Note what happens to total revenue when price changes. If total revenue changes in the opposite direction from price, demand is elastic. If total revenue changes in the same direction as price, demand is inelastic. If total revenue does not change when price changes, demand is unit-elastic.

Elastic Demand

If demand is elastic, a decrease in price will increase total revenue. Even though a lesser price is received per unit, enough additional units are sold to more than make up for the lower price. For an example, look at demand curve D_1 in Figure 6.2a. We have already established that at point *a*, total revenue is \$20 (= \$2 × 10), shown as the yellow plus green area. If the price declines from \$2 to \$1 (point *b*), the quantity demanded becomes 40 units and total revenue is \$40 (= \$1 × 40). As a result of the price decline, total revenue has increased from \$20 to \$40. Total revenue has increased in this case because the \$1 decline in price applies to 10 units, with a consequent revenue loss of \$10 (the yellow area). But 30 more units are sold at \$1 each, resulting in a revenue gain of \$30 (the blue area). Visually, the gain of the blue area clearly exceeds the loss of the yellow area. As indicated, the overall result is a net increase in total revenue of \$20 (= \$30 − \$10).

CONSIDER THIS . . .

A Bit of a Stretch

Source: © Nancy R. Cohen/Getty Images RF

The following analogy might help you remember the distinction between "elastic" and "inelastic." Imagine two objects—one an Ace elastic bandage used to wrap injured joints and the other a relatively firm rubber tie-down (rubber strap) used for securing items for transport. The Ace bandage stretches a great deal when pulled with a particular force; the rubber tie-down stretches some, but not a lot.

Similar differences occur for the quantity demanded of various products when their prices change. For some products, a price change causes a substantial "stretch" of quantity demanded. When this stretch in percentage terms exceeds the percentage change in price, demand is elastic. For other products, quantity demanded stretches very little in response to the price change. When this stretch in percentage terms is less than the percentage change in price, demand is inelastic.

In summary:

- Elastic demand displays considerable "quantity stretch" (as with the Ace bandage).
- Inelastic demand displays relatively little "quantity stretch" (as with the rubber tie-down).

And through extension:

- Perfectly elastic demand has infinite quantity stretch.
- Perfectly inelastic demand has zero quantity stretch.

The analysis is reversible: If demand is elastic, a price increase will reduce total revenue. The revenue gained on the higher-priced units will be more than offset by the revenue lost from the lower quantity sold. Bottom line: Other things equal, when price and total revenue move in opposite directions, demand is elastic. E_d is greater than 1, meaning the percentage change in quantity demanded is greater than the percentage change in price.

Inelastic Demand

If demand is inelastic, a price decrease will reduce total revenue. The increase in sales will not fully offset the decline in revenue per unit, and total revenue will decline. To see this, look at demand curve D_2 in Figure 6.2b. At point *c* on the curve, price is $4 and quantity demanded is 10. Thus total revenue is $40, shown by the combined yellow and green rectangle. If the price drops to $1 (point *d*), total revenue declines to $20, which obviously is less than $40. Total revenue has declined because the loss of revenue (the yellow area) from the lower unit price is larger than the gain in revenue (the blue area) from the accompanying increase in sales. Price has fallen, and total revenue has also declined.

Our analysis is again reversible: If demand is inelastic, a price increase will increase total revenue. So, other things equal, when price and total revenue move in the same direction, demand is inelastic. E_d is less than 1, meaning the percentage change in quantity demanded is less than the percentage change in price.

Unit Elasticity

In the special case of unit elasticity, an increase or a decrease in price leaves total revenue unchanged. The loss in revenue from a lower unit price is exactly offset by the gain in revenue from the accompanying increase in sales. Conversely, the gain in revenue from a higher unit price is exactly offset by the revenue loss associated with the accompanying decline in the amount demanded.

In Figure 6.2c (demand curve D_3) we find that at the price of $3, 10 units will be sold, yielding total revenue of $30. At the lower $1 price, a total of 30 units will be sold, again resulting in $30 of total revenue. The $2 price reduction causes the loss of revenue shown by the yellow area, but this is exactly offset by the revenue gain shown by the blue area. Total revenue does not change. In fact, that would be true for all price changes along this particular curve.

Other things equal, when price changes and total revenue remains constant, demand is unit-elastic (or unitary). E_d is 1, meaning the percentage change in quantity equals the percentage change in price.

Price Elasticity along a Linear Demand Curve

Now a major confession! Although the demand curves depicted in Figure 6.2 nicely illustrate the total-revenue test for elasticity, two of the graphs involve specific movements along linear (straight-line) demand curves. That presents no problem for explaining the total-revenue test. However, you need to know that elasticity typically varies over different price ranges of the same demand curve. (The exception is the curve in Figure 6.2c. Elasticity is 1 along the entire curve.)

Table 6.1 and Figure 6.3 demonstrate that elasticity typically varies over different price ranges of the same demand schedule or curve. Plotting the hypothetical data for movie tickets shown in columns 1 and 2 of Table 6.1 yields demand curve *D* in Figure 6.3. Observe that the demand curve is

TABLE 6.1 Price Elasticity of Demand for Movie Tickets as Measured by the Elasticity Coefficient and the Total-Revenue Test

(1) Total Quantity of Tickets Demanded per Week, Thousands	(2) Price per Ticket	(3) Elasticity Coefficient (E_d)	(4) Total Revenue, (1) × (2)	(5) Total-Revenue Test
1	$8		$ 8,000	
		5.00		Elastic
2	7		14,000	
		2.60		Elastic
3	6		18,000	
		1.57		Elastic
4	5		20,000	
		1.00		Unit-elastic
5	4		20,000	
		0.64		Inelastic
6	3		18,000	
		0.38		Inelastic
7	2		14,000	
		0.20		Inelastic
8	1		8,000	

linear. But we see from column 3 of the table that the price elasticity coefficient for this demand curve declines as we move from higher to lower prices. For all downsloping straight-line and most other demand curves, demand is more price-elastic toward the upper left (here, the $5–$8 price range of *D*) than toward the lower right (here, the $4–$1 price range of *D*).

This is the consequence of the arithmetic properties of the elasticity measure. Specifically, in the upper-left segment of the demand curve, the percentage change in quantity is large because the original reference quantity is small. Similarly, the percentage change in price is small in that segment because the original reference price is large. The relatively large percentage change in quantity divided by the relatively small change in price yields a large E_d—an elastic demand.

The reverse holds true for the lower-right segment of the demand curve. Here the percentage change in quantity is small because the original reference quantity is large; similarly, the percentage change in price is large because the original reference price is small. The relatively small percentage

AP **FIGURE 6.3 The relation between price elasticity of demand for movie tickets and total revenue.** (a) Demand curve *D* is based on Table 6.1 and is marked to show that the hypothetical weekly demand for movie tickets is elastic at higher price ranges and inelastic at lower price ranges. (b) The total-revenue curve TR is derived from demand curve *D*. When price falls and TR increases, demand is elastic; when price falls and TR is unchanged, demand is unit-elastic; and when price falls and TR declines, demand is inelastic.

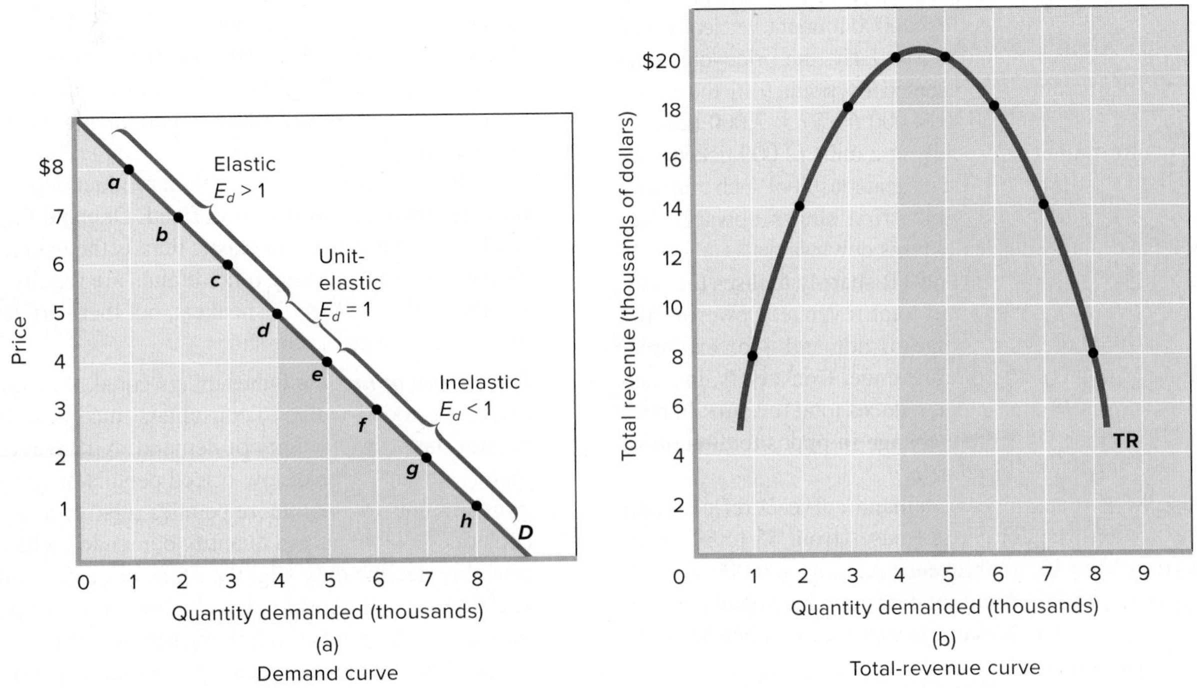

TABLE 6.2 Price Elasticity of Demand: A Summary

Absolute Value of Elasticity Coefficient	Demand Is:	Description	Impact on Total Revenue of a: Price Increase	Price Decrease
Greater than 1 ($E_d > 1$)	Elastic or relatively elastic	Quantity demanded changes by a larger percentage than does price	Total revenue decreases	Total revenue increases
Equal to 1 ($E_d = 1$)	Unit- or unitary elastic	Quantity demanded changes by the same percentage as does price	Total revenue is unchanged	Total revenue is unchanged
Less than 1 ($E_d < 1$)	Inelastic or relatively inelastic	Quantity demanded changes by a smaller percentage than does price	Total revenue increases	Total revenue decreases

change in quantity divided by the relatively large percentage change in price results in a small E_d—an inelastic demand.

The demand curve in Figure 6.3a also illustrates that the slope of a demand curve—its flatness or steepness—is not a sound basis for judging elasticity. The catch is that the slope of the curve is computed from *absolute* changes in price and quantity, while elasticity involves *relative* or *percentage* changes in price and quantity. The demand curve in Figure 6.3a is linear, which by definition means that the slope is constant throughout. But we have demonstrated that such a curve is elastic in its high-price ($8–$5) range and inelastic in its low-price ($4–$1) range.

Price Elasticity and the Total-Revenue Curve

In Figure 6.3b we plot the total revenue per week to the theater owner that corresponds to each price-quantity combination indicated along demand curve *D* in Figure 6.3a. The price–quantity-demanded combination represented by point *a* on the demand curve yields total revenue of $8,000 (= $8 × 1,000 tickets). In Figure 6.3b, we plot this $8,000 amount vertically at 1 unit (1,000 tickets) demanded. Similarly, the price–quantity-demanded combination represented by point *b* in the upper panel yields total revenue of $14,000 (= $7 × 2,000 tickets). This amount is graphed vertically at 2 units (2,000 tickets) demanded in the lower panel. The ultimate result of such graphing is total-revenue curve TR, which first slopes upward, then reaches a maximum, and finally turns downward.

Comparison of curves *D* and TR sharply focuses the relationship between elasticity and total revenue. Lowering the ticket price in the elastic range of demand—for example, from $8 to $5—increases total revenue. Conversely, increasing the ticket price in that range reduces total revenue. In both cases, price and total revenue change in opposite directions, confirming that demand is elastic.

The $5–$4 price range of demand curve *D* reflects unit elasticity. When price either decreases from $5 to $4 or increases from $4 to $5, total revenue remains $20,000. In both cases, price has changed and total revenue has remained constant, confirming that demand is unit-elastic when we consider these particular price changes.

In the inelastic range of demand curve *D,* lowering the price—for example, from $4 to $1—decreases total revenue, as shown in Figure 6.3b. Raising the price boosts total revenue. In both cases, price and total revenue move in the same direction, confirming that demand is inelastic.

Table 6.2 summarizes the characteristics of price elasticity of demand. You should review it carefully.

Determinants of Price Elasticity of Demand

LO6.3 List the factors that affect price elasticity of demand and describe some applications of price elasticity of demand.

We cannot say just what will determine the price elasticity of demand in each individual situation. However, the following generalizations are often helpful.

- ***Substitutability*** Generally, the larger the number of substitute goods that are available, the greater the price elasticity of demand. Various brands of candy bars are generally substitutable for one another, making the demand for one brand of candy bar, say Snickers, highly elastic. Toward the other extreme, the demand for tooth repair (or tooth pulling) is quite inelastic because there simply are no close substitutes when those procedures are required.

  The elasticity of demand for a product depends on how narrowly the product is defined. Demand for Reebok sneakers is more elastic than is the overall demand for shoes. Many other brands are readily substitutable for Reebok sneakers, but there are few, if any, good substitutes for shoes.

- ***Proportion of income*** Other things equal, the higher the price of a good relative to consumers' incomes, the greater the price elasticity of demand. A 10 percent increase in the price of low-priced pencils or chewing gum amounts to a few more pennies relative to a consumer's income, and quantity demanded will probably decline only slightly. Thus, price elasticity for such low-priced items tends to be low. But a 10 percent increase in the price of relatively high-priced automobiles or housing means additional expenditures

TABLE 6.3 Selected Price Elasticities of Demand

Product or Service	Coefficient of Price Elasticity of Demand (E_d)	Product or Service	Coefficient of Price Elasticity of Demand (E_d)
Newspapers	.10	Milk	.63
Electricity (household)	.13	Household appliances	.63
Bread	.15	Liquor	.70
Major League Baseball tickets	.23	Movies	.87
Cigarettes	.25	Beer	.90
Telephone service	.26	Shoes	.91
Sugar	.30	Motor vehicles	1.14
Medical care	.31	Beef	1.27
Eggs	.32	China, glassware, tableware	1.54
Legal services	.37	Residential land	1.60
Automobile repair	.40	Restaurant meals	2.27
Clothing	.49	Lamb and mutton	2.65
Gasoline	.60	Fresh peas	2.83

Source: Compiled from numerous studies and sources reporting price elasticity of demand.

of perhaps $3,000 or $20,000, respectively. These price increases are significant fractions of the annual incomes and budgets of most families, and quantities demanded will likely diminish significantly. The price elasticities for such items tend to be high.

- ***Luxuries versus necessities*** In general, the more that a good is considered to be a "luxury" rather than a "necessity," the greater is the price elasticity of demand. Electricity is generally regarded as a necessity; it is difficult to get along without it. A price increase will not significantly reduce the amount of lighting and power used in a household. (Note the very low price-elasticity coefficient of this good in Table 6.3.) An extreme case: A person does not decline an operation for acute appendicitis because the physician's fee has just gone up.

  On the other hand, vacation travel and jewelry are luxuries, which, by definition, can easily be forgone. If the prices of vacation travel and jewelry rise, a consumer need not buy them and will suffer no great hardship without them.

  What about the demand for a common product like salt? It is highly inelastic on three counts: Few good substitutes are available; salt is a negligible item in the family budget; and it is a "necessity" rather than a luxury.
- ***Time*** Generally, product demand is more elastic the longer the time period under consideration. Consumers often need time to adjust to changes in prices. For example, when the price of a product rises, time is needed to find and experiment with other products to see if they are acceptable. Consumers may not immediately reduce their purchases very much when the price of beef rises by 10 percent, but in time they may shift to chicken, pork, or fish.

Another consideration is product durability. Studies show that "short-run" demand for gasoline is more inelastic (E_d = 0.2) than is "long-run" demand (E_d = 0.7). In the short run, people are "stuck" with their present cars and trucks, but with rising gasoline prices they eventually replace them with smaller, more fuel-efficient vehicles. They also switch to mass transit where it is available.

Table 6.3 shows estimated price-elasticity coefficients for a number of products. Each reflects some combination of the elasticity determinants just discussed.

Applications of Price Elasticity of Demand

The concept of price elasticity of demand has great practical significance, as the following examples suggest.

Large Crop Yields The demand for most farm products is highly inelastic; E_d is perhaps 0.20 or 0.25. As a result, increases in the supply of farm products arising from a good growing season or from increased productivity tend to depress both the prices of farm products and the total revenues (incomes) of farmers. For farmers as a group, the inelastic demand for their products means that large crop yields may be undesirable. For policymakers it means that achieving the goal of higher total farm income requires that farm output be restricted.

Excise Taxes The government pays attention to elasticity of demand when it selects goods and services on which to levy excise taxes. If a $1 tax is levied on a product and 10,000 units are sold, tax revenue will be $10,000 (= $1 × 10,000 units sold). If the government raises the tax to $1.50, but the higher price that results reduces sales to 4,000 because of elastic demand, tax revenue will decline to $6,000 (= $1.50 × 4,000 units sold). Because a higher tax on a product with elastic demand will bring in less tax revenue, legislatures tend to seek out products that have inelastic demand—such as liquor, gasoline, and cigarettes—when levying excises.

Decriminalization of Illegal Drugs In recent years proposals to legalize drugs have been widely debated. Proponents contend that drugs should be treated like alcohol; they should be made legal for adults and regulated for purity and potency. The current war on drugs, it is argued, has been unsuccessful, and the associated costs—including enlarged police forces, the construction of more prisons, an overburdened court system, and untold human costs—have increased markedly. Legalization would allegedly reduce drug trafficking significantly by taking the profit out of it. Crack cocaine and heroin, for example, are cheap to produce and could be sold at low prices in legal markets. Because the demand of addicts is highly inelastic, the amounts consumed at the lower prices would increase only modestly. Addicts' total expenditures for cocaine and heroin would decline, and so would the street crime that finances those expenditures.

Opponents of legalization say that the overall demand for cocaine and heroin is far more elastic than proponents think. In addition to the inelastic demand of addicts, there is another market segment whose demand is relatively elastic. This segment consists of the occasional users or "dabblers," who use hard drugs when their prices are low but who abstain or substitute, say, alcohol when their prices are high. Thus, the lower prices associated with the legalization of hard drugs would increase consumption by dabblers. Also, removal of the legal prohibitions against using drugs might make drug use more socially acceptable, increasing the demand for cocaine and heroin.

Many economists predict that the legalization of cocaine and heroin would reduce street prices by up to 60 percent, depending on if and how much they were taxed. According to an important study, price declines of that size would increase the number of occasional users of heroin by 54 percent and the number of occasional users of cocaine by 33 percent. The total quantity of heroin demanded would rise by an estimated 100 percent, and the quantity of cocaine demanded would rise by 50 percent.[1] Moreover, many existing and first-time dabblers might in time become addicts. The overall result, say the opponents of legalization, would be higher social costs, possibly including an increase in street crime.

[1]Henry Saffer and Frank Chaloupka, "The Demand for Illegal Drugs," *Economic Inquiry*, July 1999, pp. 401–411.

AP QUICK REVIEW 6.1

- ✓ Price elasticity of demand measures the responsiveness (or sensitivity) of consumers to a price change. The price elasticity of demand coefficient E_d is the ratio of the percentage change in quantity demanded to the percentage change in price.
- ✓ The *averages* of the two prices and two quantities are used as the base references in calculating the percentage changes. The mid-point formula, using these averages, reduces to $[(X_2 - X_1)/(P_2 - P_1)]\ [(P_1 + P_2)/(X_1 + X_2)]$ where X = quantity and P = price. The minus sign is eliminated.
- ✓ When E_d is greater than 1, demand is elastic; when E_d is less than 1, demand is inelastic; when E_d is equal to 1, demand is of unit elasticity.
- ✓ When price changes, total revenue will change in the opposite direction if demand is price-elastic, in the same direction if demand is price-inelastic, and not at all if demand is unit-elastic.
- ✓ Along a linear demand curve, the elasticity varies. Demand is typically elastic in the high-price (low-quantity) range of the linear demand curve and inelastic in the low-price (high-quantity) range of the demand curve.

AP Price Elasticity of Supply

LO6.4 Describe price elasticity of supply and how it can be applied.

The concept of price elasticity also applies to supply. If the quantity supplied by producers is relatively responsive to price changes, supply is elastic. If it is relatively insensitive to price changes, supply is inelastic.

We measure the degree of price elasticity or inelasticity of supply with the coefficient E_s, defined almost like E_d except that we substitute "percentage change in quantity supplied" for "percentage change in quantity demanded":

$$E_s = \frac{\text{Percentage change in quantity supplied of product X}}{\text{Percentage change in price of product X}}$$

For reasons explained earlier, the averages, or midpoints, of the before and after quantities supplied and the before and after prices are used as reference points for the percentage changes. Suppose an increase in the price of a good from $4 to $6 increases the quantity supplied from 10 units to 14 units. The percentage change in price would be $\frac{2}{5}$, or 40 percent, and the percentage change in quantity would be $\frac{4}{12}$, or 33 percent. Consequently,

$$E_s = \frac{.33}{.40} = .83$$

In this case, supply is inelastic because the price-elasticity coefficient is less than 1. If E_s is greater than 1, supply is elastic. If it is equal to 1, supply is unit-elastic. Also, E_s is never negative, since price and quantity supplied are directly related. Thus, there are no minus signs to drop, as was necessary with elasticity of demand.

The degree of **price elasticity of supply** depends on how easily—and therefore quickly—producers can shift resources between alternative uses. The easier and more rapidly producers can shift resources between alternative uses, the greater the price elasticity of supply. Take the case of Christmas trees. A firm's response to, say, an increase in the price of trees depends on its ability to shift resources from the production of other products (whose prices we assume remain constant) to the production of trees. And shifting resource takes time: The longer the time, the greater the "shiftability." So we can expect a greater response, and therefore greater elasticity of supply, the longer a firm has to adjust to a price change.

In analyzing the impact of time on elasticity, economists distinguish among the immediate market period, the short run, and the long run.

CONSIDER THIS . . .

Source: © Punchstock RF

Elasticity and College Costs

Why does college cost so much? Elasticity offers some clues.

From the end of World War II through the 1970s, the supply of higher education increased massively as state and local governments spent billions of dollars expanding their higher education systems. This massive increase in supply helped to offset the huge increase in demand that took place as the large Baby Boom generation flooded the higher education system starting in the early 1960s. With supply increasing nearly as fast as demand, the equilibrium price of higher education only increased modestly.

Things changed dramatically beginning in the early 1980s. With respect to supply, state and local governments slowed the growth of higher education spending, so that many college and university systems saw only modest subsequent increases in capacity. At the same time, the federal government dramatically increased both subsidized student lending and the volume of federal student grant money. Those policy innovations were of great benefit to poor and middle-class students, but they also meant that the demand curve for higher education continued to shift to the right.

That turned out to be problematic because, with the supply of seats largely fixed by the changing priorities of state and local governments, the supply of higher education was highly inelastic even in the long run. As a result, the increases in demand caused by student loans and grant money resulted in substantially higher equilibrium prices for higher education.

Price Elasticity of Supply: The Immediate Market Period

The **immediate market period** is the length of time over which producers are unable to respond to a change in price with a change in quantity supplied. Suppose the owner of a small farm brings to market one truckload of tomatoes that is the entire season's output. The supply curve for the tomatoes is perfectly inelastic (vertical); the farmer will sell the truckload whether the price is high or low. Why? Because the farmer can offer only one truckload of tomatoes even if the price of tomatoes is much higher than anticipated. The farmer might like to offer more tomatoes, but tomatoes cannot be produced overnight. Another full growing season is needed to respond to a higher-than-expected price by producing more than one truckload. Similarly, because the product is perishable, the farmer cannot withhold it from the market. If the price is lower than anticipated, the farmer will still sell the entire truckload.

The farmer's costs of production, incidentally, will not enter into this decision to sell. Though the price of tomatoes may fall far short of production costs, the farmer will nevertheless sell everything he brought to market to avoid a total loss through spoilage. In the immediate market period, both the supply of tomatoes and the quantity of tomatoes supplied are fixed. The farmer offers only one truckload no matter how high or low the price.

Figure 6.4a shows the farmer's vertical supply curve during the immediate market period. Supply is perfectly inelastic because the farmer does not have time to respond to a change in demand, say, from D_1 to D_2. The resulting price increase from P_0 to P_m simply determines which buyers get the fixed quantity supplied; it elicits no increase in output.

However, not all supply curves are perfectly inelastic immediately after a price change. If the product is not perishable and the price rises, producers may choose to increase quantity supplied by drawing down their inventories of unsold, stored goods. This will cause the market supply curve to attain some positive slope. For our tomato farmer, the immediate market period may be a full growing season; for producers of goods that can be inexpensively stored, there may be no immediate market period at all.

Price Elasticity of Supply: The Short Run

The **short run** in microeconomics is a period of time too short to change plant capacity but long enough to use the

AP **FIGURE 6.4 Time and the elasticity of supply.** The greater the amount of time producers have to adjust to a change in demand, here from D_1 to D_2, the greater will be their output response. (a) In the immediate market period, there is insufficient time to change output, and so supply is perfectly inelastic. (b) In the short run, plant capacity is fixed, but changing the intensity of its use can alter output; supply is therefore more elastic. (c) In the long run, all desired adjustments, including changes in plant capacity, can be made, and supply becomes still more elastic.

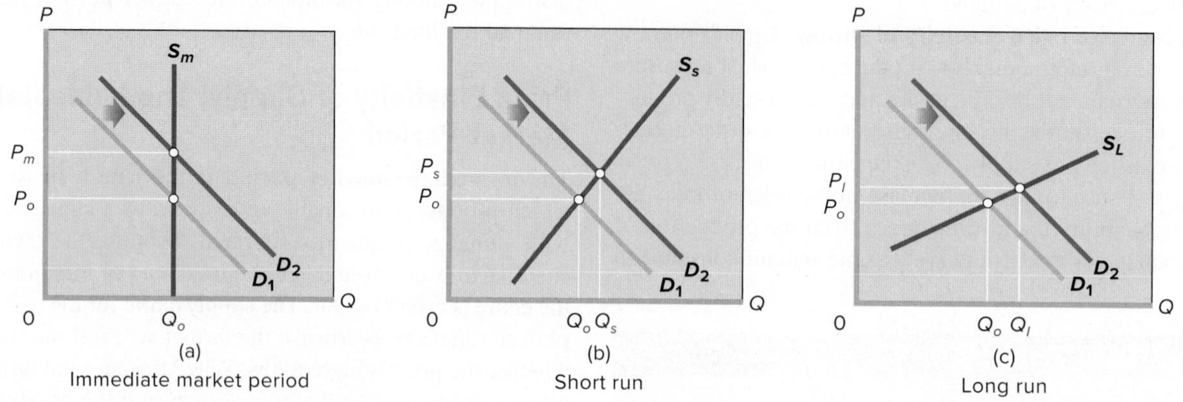

fixed-sized plant more or less intensively. In the short run, our farmer's plant (land and farm machinery) is fixed. But he does have time in the short run to cultivate tomatoes more intensively by applying more labor and more fertilizer and pesticides to the crop. The result is a somewhat greater output in response to a presumed increase in demand; this greater output is reflected in a more elastic supply of tomatoes, as shown by S_s in Figure 6.4b. Note now that the increase in demand from D_1 to D_2 is met by an increase in quantity (from Q_0 to Q_s), so there is a smaller price adjustment (from P_0 to P_s) than would be the case in the immediate market period. The equilibrium price is therefore lower in the short run than in the immediate market period.

Price Elasticity of Supply: The Long Run

The **long run** in microeconomics is a time period long enough for firms to adjust their plant sizes and for new firms to enter (or existing firms to leave) the industry. In the "tomato industry," for example, our farmer has time to acquire additional land and buy more machinery and equipment. Furthermore, other farmers may, over time, be attracted to tomato farming by the increased demand and higher price. Such adjustments create a larger supply response, as represented by the more elastic supply curve S_L in Figure 6.4c. The outcome is a smaller price rise (P_0 to P_l) and a larger output increase (Q_0 to Q_l) in response to the increase in demand from D_1 to D_2.

There is no total-revenue test for elasticity of supply. Supply shows a positive or direct relationship between price and amount supplied; the supply curve is upsloping. Regardless of the degree of elasticity or inelasticity, price and total revenue always move together.

Applications of Price Elasticity of Supply

The idea of price elasticity of supply has widespread applicability, as suggested by the following examples.

Antiques and Reproductions *Antiques Roadshow* is a popular PBS television program in which people bring antiques to a central location for appraisal by experts. Some people are pleased to learn that their old piece of furniture or funky folk art is worth a large amount, say, $30,000 or more.

The high price of an antique results from strong demand and limited, highly inelastic supply. Because a genuine antique can no longer be reproduced, its quantity supplied either does not rise or rises only slightly as price goes up. The higher price might prompt the discovery of a few more of the remaining originals and thus add to the quantity available for sale, but this quantity response is usually quite small. So the supply of antiques and other collectibles tends to be inelastic. For one-of-a-kind antiques, the supply is perfectly inelastic.

Factors such as increased population, higher income, and greater enthusiasm for collecting antiques have increased the demand for antiques over time. Because the supply of antiques is limited and inelastic, those increases in demand have greatly boosted the prices of antiques.

Contrast the inelastic supply of original antiques with the elastic supply of modern "made-to-look-old" reproductions. Such faux antiques are quite popular and widely available at furniture stores and knickknack shops. When the demand for reproductions increases, the firms making them simply boost production. Because the supply of reproductions is highly elastic, increased demand raises their prices only slightly.

Volatile Gold Prices The price of gold is quite volatile, sometimes shooting upward one period and plummeting downward the next. The main sources of these fluctuations are shifts in demand interacting with highly inelastic supply. Gold production is a costly and time-consuming process of exploration, mining, and refining. Moreover, the physical availability of gold is highly limited. For both reasons, increases in gold prices do not elicit substantial increases in quantity supplied. Conversely, gold mining is costly to shut down and existing gold bars are expensive to store. Price decreases therefore do not produce large drops in the quantity of gold supplied. In short, the supply of gold is inelastic.

The demand for gold is partly derived from the demand for its uses, such as for jewelry, dental fillings, and coins. But people also demand gold as a speculative financial investment. They increase their demand for gold when they fear general inflation or domestic or international turmoil that might undermine the value of currency and more traditional investments. They reduce their demand when events settle down. Because of the inelastic supply of gold, even relatively small changes in demand produce relatively large changes in price.

AP Cross Elasticity and Income Elasticity of Demand

LO6.5 Apply cross elasticity of demand and income elasticity of demand.

Price elasticities measure the responsiveness of the quantity of a product demanded or supplied when its price changes. The consumption of a good also is affected by a change in the price of a related product or by a change in income.

Cross Elasticity of Demand

The **cross elasticity of demand** measures how sensitive consumer purchases of one product (say, X) are to a change in the price of some other product (say, Y). We calculate the coefficient of cross elasticity of demand E_{xy} just as we do the coefficient of simple price elasticity, except that we relate the percentage change in the consumption of X to the percentage change in the price of Y:

$$E_{xy} = \frac{\text{percentage change in quantity demanded of product X}}{\text{percentage change in price of product Y}}$$

This cross-elasticity (or cross-price-elasticity) concept allows us to quantify and more fully understand substitute and complementary goods, introduced in Chapter 3. Unlike price elasticity, we allow the coefficient of cross elasticity of demand to be either positive or negative.

Substitute Goods If cross elasticity of demand is positive, meaning that sales of X move in the same direction as a change in the price of Y, then X and Y are substitute goods. An example is Evian water (X) and Dasani water (Y). An increase in the price of Evian causes consumers to buy more Dasani, resulting in a positive cross elasticity. The larger the positive cross-elasticity coefficient, the greater is the substitutability between the two products.

Complementary Goods When cross elasticity is negative, we know that X and Y "go together"; an increase in the price of one decreases the demand for the other. So the two are complementary goods. For example, a decrease in the price of digital cameras will increase the number of memory sticks purchased. The larger the negative cross-elasticity coefficient, the greater is the complementarity between the two goods.

Independent Goods A zero or near-zero cross elasticity suggests that the two products being considered are unrelated or independent goods. An example is walnuts and plums: We would not expect a change in the price of walnuts to have any effect on purchases of plums, and vice versa.

Application The degree of substitutability of products, measured by the cross-elasticity coefficient, is important to businesses and government. For example, suppose that Coca-Cola is considering whether or not to lower the price of its Sprite brand. Not only will it want to know something about the price elasticity of demand for Sprite (will the price cut increase or decrease total revenue?), but it will also be interested in knowing if the increased sales of Sprite will come at the expense of its Coke brand. How sensitive are the sales of one of its products (Coke) to a change in the price of another of its products (Sprite)? By how much will the increased sales of Sprite "cannibalize" the sales of Coke? A low cross elasticity would indicate that Coke and Sprite are weak substitutes for each other and that a lower price for Sprite would have little effect on Coke sales.

Government also implicitly uses the idea of cross elasticity of demand in assessing whether a proposed merger between two large firms will substantially reduce competition and therefore violate the antitrust laws. For example, the cross elasticity between Coke and Pepsi is high, making them strong substitutes for each other. In addition, Coke and Pepsi together sell about 70 percent of all carbonated cola drinks consumed in the United States. Taken together, the high cross elasticities and the large market shares suggest that the government would likely block a merger between Coke and Pepsi because the merger would substantially lessen competition. In contrast, the cross elasticity between cola and gasoline is low or zero. A merger between Coke and Shell oil company would have a minimal effect on competition. So government would let that merger happen.

LAST WORD

Elasticity and Pricing Power: Why Different Consumers Pay Different Prices

Firms and Nonprofit Institutions Often Recognize and Exploit Differences in Price Elasticity of Demand.

All the buyers of a product traded in a highly competitive market pay the same market price for the product, regardless of their individual price elasticities of demand. If the price rises, Jones may have an elastic demand and greatly reduce her purchases. Green may have a unit-elastic demand and reduce his purchases less than Jones. Lopez may have an inelastic demand and hardly curtail his purchases at all. But all three consumers will pay the single higher price regardless of their respective demand elasticities.

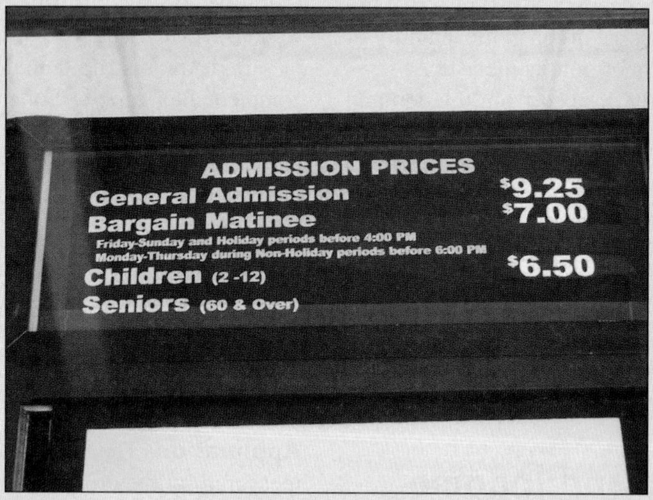

Source: © Tom Prettyman/PhotoEdit

In later chapters we will find that not all sellers must passively accept a "one-for-all" price. Some firms have "market power" or "pricing power" that allows them to set their product prices in their best interests. For some goods and services, firms may find it advantageous to determine differences in price elasticity of demand and then charge different prices to different buyers.

It is extremely difficult to tailor prices for each customer on the basis of price elasticity of demand, but it is relatively easy to

Income Elasticity of Demand

Income elasticity of demand measures the degree to which consumers respond to a change in their incomes by buying more or less of a particular good. The coefficient of income elasticity of demand E_i is determined with the formula

$$E_i = \frac{\text{percentage change in quantity demanded}}{\text{percentage change in income}}$$

Normal Goods For most goods, the income-elasticity coefficient E_i is positive, meaning that more of them are demanded as incomes rise. Such goods are called normal or superior goods (and were first described in Chapter 3). But the value of E_i varies greatly among normal goods. For example, income elasticity of demand for automobiles is about +3, while income elasticity for most farm products is only about +0.20.

Inferior Goods A negative income-elasticity coefficient designates an inferior good. Retread tires, cabbage, long-

AP TABLE 6.4 Cross and Income Elasticities of Demand

Value of Coefficient	Description	Type of Good(s)
Cross elasticity:		
Positive ($E_{wz} > 0$)	Quantity demanded of W changes in same direction as change in price of Z	Substitutes
Negative ($E_{xy} < 0$)	Quantity demanded of X changes in opposite direction from change in price of Y	Complements
Income elasticity: Positive ($E_i > 0$)	Quantity demanded of the product changes in same direction as change in income	Normal or superior
Negative ($E_i < 0$)	Quantity demanded of the product changes in opposite direction from change in income	Inferior

observe differences in group elasticities. Consider airline tickets. Business travelers generally have inelastic demand for air travel. Because their time is highly valuable, they do not see slower modes of transportation as realistic substitutes. Also, their employers pay for their tickets as part of their business expenses. In contrast, leisure travelers tend to have elastic demand. They have the option to drive rather than fly or to simply not travel at all. They also pay for their tickets out of their own pockets and thus are more sensitive to price.

Airlines recognize the difference between the groups in terms of price elasticity of demand and charge business travelers more than leisure travelers. To accomplish that, they have to dissuade business travelers from buying the less expensive round-trip tickets aimed at leisure travelers. One way to do this is by placing restrictions on the lower-priced tickets. For instance, airlines have at times made such tickets nonrefundable, required at least a 2-week advance purchase, and required Saturday-night stays. These restrictions chase off most business travelers who engage in last-minute travel and want to be home for the weekend. As a result, a business traveler often pays hundreds of dollars more for a ticket than a leisure traveler on the same plane.

Discounts for children are another example of pricing based on group differences in price elasticity of demand. For many products, children have more elastic demands than adults because children have low budgets, often financed by their parents. Sellers recognize the elasticity difference and price accordingly. The barber spends as much time cutting a child's hair as an adult's but charges the child much less. A child takes up a full seat at the baseball game but pays a lower price than an adult. A child snowboarder occupies the same space on a chairlift as an adult snowboarder but qualifies for a discounted lift ticket.

Finally, consider pricing by colleges and universities. Price elasticity of demand for higher education is greater for prospective students from low-income families than similar students from high-income families. This makes sense because tuition is a much larger proportion of household income for a low-income student or family than for his or her high-income counterpart. Desiring a diverse student body, colleges charge different *net* prices (= tuition *minus* financial aid) to the two groups on the basis of price elasticity of demand. High-income students pay full tuition, unless they receive merit-based scholarships. Low-income students receive considerable financial aid in addition to merit-based scholarships and, in effect, pay a lower *net* price.

It is common for colleges to announce a large tuition increase and immediately cushion the news by emphasizing that they also are increasing financial aid. In effect, the college is increasing the tuition for students who have inelastic demand by the full amount and raising the *net* tuition of those with elastic demand by some lesser amount or not at all. Through this strategy, colleges boost revenue to cover rising costs while maintaining affordability for a wide range of students.

There are a number of other examples of dual or multiple pricing. All relate directly to price elasticity of demand. We will revisit this topic again in Chapter 12 when we analyze *price discrimination*—charging different prices to different customers for the same product.

distance bus tickets, used clothing, and muscatel wine are likely candidates. Consumers decrease their purchases of inferior goods as incomes rise.

Insights Coefficients of income elasticity of demand provide insights into the economy. For example, when recessions (business downturns) occur and incomes fall, income elasticity of demand helps predict which products will decline in demand more rapidly than others.

Products with relatively high income-elasticity coefficients, such as automobiles ($E_i = +3$), housing ($E_i = +1.5$), and restaurant meals ($E_i = +1.4$), are generally hit hardest by recessions. Those with low or negative income-elasticity coefficients are much less affected. For example, food products prepared at home ($E_i = +0.20$) respond relatively little to income fluctuations. When incomes drop, purchases of food (and toothpaste and toilet paper) drop little compared to purchases of movie tickets, luxury vacations, and plasma screen TVs. Products we view as essential tend to have lower income-elasticity coefficients than products we view as luxuries. When our incomes fall, we cannot easily eliminate or postpone the purchase of essential products.

In Table 6.4 we provide a convenient synopsis of the cross-elasticity and income-elasticity concepts.

AP QUICK REVIEW 6.2

- ✓ Price elasticity of supply measures the sensitivity of suppliers to changes in the price of a product. The price-elasticity-of-supply coefficient E_s is the ratio of the percentage change in quantity supplied to the percentage change in price.
- ✓ The elasticity of supply varies directly with the amount of time producers have to respond to the price change. In the immediate term, firms cannot respond, so the supply curve is vertical. In the short run, firms have enough time for more or less intensive use of existing plant capacity, so the supply curve is, then, upward sloping. In the long run, firms can expand, and new firms can enter the market, and supply is more elastic.
- ✓ The cross-elasticity-of-demand coefficient E_{xy} is computed as the percentage change in the quantity demanded of product X divided by the percentage change in the price of product Y. If the cross-elasticity coefficient is positive, the two products are substitutes; if negative, they are complements.
- ✓ The income-elasticity coefficient E_i is computed as the percentage change in quantity demanded divided by the percentage change in income. A positive coefficient indicates a normal or superior good. The coefficient is negative for an inferior good.

SUMMARY

LO6.1 Discuss price elasticity of demand and how it is calculated.

Price elasticity of demand measures consumer response to price changes. If consumers are relatively sensitive to price changes, demand is elastic. If they are relatively unresponsive to price changes, demand is inelastic.

The price-elasticity coefficient E_d measures the degree of elasticity or inelasticity of demand. The coefficient is found by the formula

$$E_d = \frac{\text{percentage change in quantity demanded of X}}{\text{percentage change in price of X}}$$

Economists use the averages of prices and quantities under consideration as reference points in determining percentage changes in price and quantity. If E_d is greater than 1, demand is elastic. If E_d is less than 1, demand is inelastic. Unit elasticity is the special case in which E_d equals 1.

Perfectly inelastic demand is graphed as a line parallel to the vertical axis; perfectly elastic demand is shown by a line above and parallel to the horizontal axis.

Elasticity varies at different price ranges on a demand curve, tending to be elastic in the upper-left segment and inelastic in the lower-right segment. Elasticity cannot be judged by the steepness or flatness of a demand curve.

LO6.2 Explain the usefulness of the total-revenue test for price elasticity of demand.

If total revenue changes in the opposite direction from prices, demand is elastic. If price and total revenue change in the same direction, demand is inelastic. Where demand is of unit elasticity, a change in price leaves total revenue unchanged.

LO6.3 List the factors that affect price elasticity of demand and describe some applications of price elasticity of demand.

The number of available substitutes, the size of an item's price relative to one's budget, whether the product is a luxury or a necessity, and length of time to adjust are all determinants of elasticity of demand.

LO6.4 Describe price elasticity of supply and how it can be applied.

The elasticity concept also applies to supply. The coefficient of price elasticity of supply is found by the formula

$$E_s = \frac{\text{percentage change in quantity supplied of X}}{\text{percentage change in price of X}}$$

The averages of the prices and quantities under consideration are used as reference points for computing percentage changes. Elasticity of supply depends on the ease of shifting resources between alternative uses, which varies directly with the time producers have to adjust to a price change.

LO6.5 Apply cross elasticity of demand and income elasticity of demand.

Cross elasticity of demand indicates how sensitive the purchase of one product is to changes in the price of another product. The coefficient of cross elasticity of demand is found by the formula

$$E_{xy} = \frac{\text{percentage change in quantity demanded of X}}{\text{percentage change in price of Y}}$$

Positive cross elasticity of demand identifies substitute goods; negative cross elasticity identifies complementary goods.

Income elasticity of demand indicates the responsiveness of consumer purchases to a change in income. The coefficient of income elasticity of demand is found by the formula

$$E_i = \frac{\text{percentage change in quantity demanded of X}}{\text{percentage change in income}}$$

The coefficient is positive for normal goods and negative for inferior goods.

Industries that sell products that have high income-elasticity-of-demand coefficients are particularly hard hit by recessions. Those with products that have low or negative income-elasticity-of-demand coefficients fare much better.

TERMS AND CONCEPTS

price elasticity of demand
midpoint formula
elastic demand
inelastic demand
unit elasticity
perfectly inelastic demand
perfectly elastic demand
total revenue (TR)
total-revenue test
price elasticity of supply
immediate market period
short run
long run
cross elasticity of demand
income elasticity of demand

The following and additional problems can be found in connect

DISCUSSION QUESTIONS

1. Explain why the choice between 1, 2, 3, 4, 5, 6, 7, and 8 "units," or 1,000, 2,000, 3,000, 4,000, 5,000, 6,000, 7,000, and 8,000 movie tickets, makes no difference in determining elasticity in Table 6.1. LO6.1
2. What effect would a rule stating that university students must live in university dormitories have on the price elasticity of demand for dormitory space? What impact might this in turn have on room rates? LO6.1
3. The income elasticities of demand for movies, dental services, and clothing have been estimated to be +3.4, +1, and +0.5, respectively. Interpret these coefficients. What does it mean if an income-elasticity coefficient is negative? LO6.5
4. Research has found that an increase in the price of beer would reduce the amount of marijuana consumed. Is cross elasticity of demand between the two products positive or negative? Are these products substitutes or complements? What might be the logic behind this relationship? LO6.5
5. **LAST WORD** What is the purpose of charging different groups of customers different prices? Supplement the three broad examples in the Last Word with two additional examples of your own. Hint: Think of price discounts based on group characteristics or time of purchase.

AP REVIEW QUESTIONS

1. Suppose that the total revenue received by a company selling basketballs is $600 when the price is set at $30 per basketball and $600 when the price is set at $20 per basketball. Without using the midpoint formula, can you tell whether demand is elastic, inelastic, or unit-elastic over this price range? LO6.2
2. How would the following changes in price affect total revenue? That is, would total revenue increase, decrease, or remain unchanged? LO6.2
   a. Price falls and demand is inelastic.
   b. Price rises and demand is elastic.
   c. Price rises and demand is inelastic.
   d. Price falls and demand is elastic.
   e. Price falls and demand is of unit elasticity.
3. In 2006, Willem de Kooning's abstract painting *Woman III* sold for $137.5 million. Portray this sale in a demand and supply diagram and comment on the elasticity of supply. LO6.4
4. Suppose the cross elasticity of demand for products A and B is +3.6 and for products C and D is −5.4. What can you conclude about how products A and B are related? Products C and D? LO6.5
5. Suppose the income elasticity for product M is .5, for product R, it is 3, and for product T, it is −1.5. What can you conclude about products M, N, and T? LO6.5
6. For good X, the own price elasticity of demand is −4.2; income elasticity of demand is 3.1, and the cross-price elasticity with good Y is −2.6. Answer the following questions. LO6.1, 6.2, 6.3, 6.5
   a. At the current price for product X, is demand elastic, inelastic, or unit elastic? Explain.
   b. At the current price for product X, if price is increased, will total revenues increase, decrease, or remain the same? Explain.
   c. Is product X a normal good and income inelastic, a normal good and income elastic, or an inferior good? Explain.
   d. Are products X and Y complements or substitutes? Explain.

PROBLEMS

1. Look at the demand curve in Figure 6.2a. Use the midpoint formula and points *a* and *b* to calculate the elasticity of demand for that range of the demand curve. Do the same for the demand curves in Figures 6.2b and 6.2c using, respectively, points *c* and *d* for Figure 6.2b and points *e* and *f* for Figure 6.2c. LO6.1
2. Investigate how demand elastiticities are affected by increases in demand. Shift each of the demand curves in Figures 6.2a, 6.2b, and 6.2c to the right by 10 units. For example, point *a* in Figure 6.2a would shift rightward from location (10 units, $2) to (20 units, $2), while point *b* would shift rightward from location (40 units, $1) to (50 units, $1). After making these shifts, apply the midpoint formula to calculate the demand elasticities for the shifted points. Are they larger or smaller than the elasticities you calculated in problem 1 for the original points? In terms of the midpoint formula, what explains the change in elasticities? LO6.1
3. Graph the accompanying demand data, and then use the midpoint formula for *Ed* to determine price elasticity of demand for each of the four possible $1 price changes. What can you conclude about the relationship between the slope of a curve and its elasticity? Explain in a nontechnical way why demand is elastic in the northwest segment of the demand curve and inelastic in the southeast segment. LO6.1

Product Price	Quantity Demanded
$5	1
4	2
3	3
2	4
1	5

4. Danny "Dimes" Donahue is a neighborhood's 9-year-old entrepreneur. His most recent venture is selling homemade brownies that he bakes himself. At a price of $1.50 each, he sells 100. At a price of $1 each, he sells 300. Is demand elastic or inelastic over this price range? If demand had the same elasticity for a price decline from $1.00 to $0.50 as it does for the decline from $1.50 to $1, would cutting the price from $1.00 to $0.50 increase or decrease Danny's total revenue? **LO6.2**
5. What is the formula for measuring the price elasticity of supply? Suppose the price of apples goes up from $20 to $22 a box. In direct response, Goldsboro Farms supplies 1,200 boxes of apples instead of 1,000 boxes. Compute the coefficient of price elasticity (midpoint approach) for Goldsboro's supply. Is its supply elastic, or is it inelastic? **LO6.4**
6. **ADVANCED ANALYSIS** Currently, at a price of $1 each, 100 popsicles are sold per day in the perpetually hot town of Rostin. Consider the elasticity of supply. In the short run, a price increase from $1 to $2 is unit-elastic ($E_s$ =1.0). So how many popsicles will be sold each day in the short run if the price rises to $2 each? In the long run, a price increase from $1 to $2 has an elasticity of supply of 1.50. So how many popsicles will be sold per day in the long run if the price rises to $2 each? (Hint: Apply the midpoint approach to the elasticity of supply.) **LO6.4**
7. Lorena likes to play golf. The number of times per year that she plays depends on both the price of playing a round of golf as well as Lorena's income and the cost of other types of entertainment—in particular, how much it costs to go see a movie instead of playing golf. The three demand schedules in the following table show how many rounds of golf per year Lorena will demand at each price under three different scenarios. In scenario D_1, Lorena's income is $50,000 per year and movies cost $9 each. In scenario D_2, Lorena's income is also $50,000 per year, but the price of seeing a movie rises to $11. And in scenario D_3, Lorena's income goes up to $70,000 per year, while movies cost $11. **LO6.5**

	Quantity Demanded		
Price	D_1	D_2	D_3
$50	15	10	15
35	25	15	30
20	40	20	50

   a. Using the data under D_1 and D_2, calculate the cross elasticity of Lorena's demand for golf at all three prices. (To do this, apply the midpoints approach to the cross elasticity of demand.) Is the cross elasticity the same at all three prices? Are movies and golf substitute goods, complementary goods, or independent goods?
   b. Using the data under D_2 and D_3, calculate the income elasticity of Lorena's demand for golf at all three prices. (To do this, apply the midpoint approach to the income elasticity of demand.) Is the income elasticity the same at all three prices? Is golf an inferior good?

Chapter 7

Utility Maximization

Learning Objectives

LO7.1 **Define and explain the relationship between total utility, marginal utility, and the law of diminishing marginal utility.**

LO7.2 **Describe how rational consumers maximize utility by comparing the marginal utility-to-price ratios of all the products they could possibly purchase.**

LO7.3 **Explain how a demand curve can be derived by observing the outcomes of price changes in the utility-maximization model.**

LO7.4 **Discuss how the utility-maximization model helps highlight the income and substitution effects of a price change.**

LO7.5 **Give examples of several real-world phenomena that can be explained by applying the theory of consumer behavior.**

LO7.6 **(Appendix) Relate how the indifference curve model of consumer behavior derives demand curves from budget lines, indifference curves, and utility maximization.**

AP Chapter Focus

If you were to compare the shopping carts of almost any two consumers, you would observe striking differences. Why does Paula have potatoes, peaches, and Pepsi in her cart, while Sam has sugar, saltines, and 7-Up in his? Why didn't Paula also buy pasta and plums? Why didn't Sam have soup and spaghetti on his grocery list?

In this chapter, you will see how individual consumers allocate their incomes among the various goods and services available to them. Given a certain budget, how does a consumer decide which goods and services to buy? This chapter will develop a model to answer this question.

AP Law of Diminishing Marginal Utility

LO7.1 Define and explain the relationship between total utility, marginal utility, and the law of diminishing marginal utility.

The simplest theory of consumer behavior rests squarely on the **law of diminishing marginal utility.** This principle, first discussed in Chapter 3, is that added satisfaction declines as a consumer acquires additional units of a given product. Although consumer wants in general may be insatiable, wants for particular items can be satisfied. In a specific span of time over which consumers' tastes remain unchanged, consumers can obtain as much of a particular good or service as they can afford. But the more of that product they obtain, the less they want still more of it.

Consider durable goods, for example. A consumer's desire for an automobile, when he or she has none, may be very strong. But the desire for a second car is less intense; and for a third or fourth, weaker and weaker. Unless they are collectors, even the wealthiest families rarely have more than a half-dozen cars, although their incomes would allow them to purchase a whole fleet of vehicles.

Terminology

Evidence indicates that consumers can fulfill specific wants with succeeding units of a product but that each added unit provides less utility than the last unit purchased. Recall that a consumer derives utility from a product if it can satisfy a want: **Utility** is want-satisfying power. The utility of a good or service is the satisfaction or pleasure one gets from consuming it. Keep in mind three characteristics of this concept:

- "Utility" and "usefulness" are not synonymous. Paintings by Picasso may offer great utility to art connoisseurs but are useless functionally (other than for hiding a crack on a wall).
- Utility is subjective. The utility of a specific product may vary widely from person to person. A lifted pickup truck may have great utility to someone who drives off-road but little utility to someone unable or unwilling to climb into the rig. Eyeglasses have tremendous utility to someone who has poor eyesight but no utility to a person with 20-20 vision.
- Utility is difficult to quantify. But for purposes of illustration we assume that people can measure satisfaction with units called *utils* (units of utility). For example, a particular consumer may get 100 utils of satisfaction from a smoothie, 10 utils of satisfaction from a candy bar, and 1 util of satisfaction from a stick of gum. These imaginary units of satisfaction are convenient for quantifying consumer behavior for explanatory purposes.

Total Utility and Marginal Utility

Total utility and marginal utility are related, but different, ideas. **Total utility** is the total amount of satisfaction or pleasure a person derives from consuming some specific quantity—for example, 10 units—of a good or service. **Marginal utility** is the *extra* satisfaction a consumer realizes from an additional unit of that product—for example, from the eleventh unit. Alternatively, marginal utility is the change in total utility that results from the consumption of 1 more unit of a product.

Figure 7.1 (Key Graph) and the accompanying table demonstrate the relation between total utility and marginal utility. The curves reflect the data in the table. Column 2 shows the total utility associated with each level of consumption of tacos. Column 3 shows the marginal utility—the change in total utility—that results from the consumption of each successive taco. Starting at the origin in Figure 7.1a, observe that each of the first five units increases total utility (TU), but by a diminishing amount. Total utility reaches a maximum with the addition of the sixth unit and then declines.

So in Figure 7.1b marginal utility (MU) remains positive but diminishes through the first five units (because total utility increases at a declining rate). Marginal utility is zero for the sixth unit (because that unit doesn't change total utility). Marginal utility then becomes negative with the seventh unit and beyond (because total utility is falling). Figure 7.1b and table column 3 reveal that each successive taco yields less extra utility, meaning fewer utils, than the preceding taco.[1] That is, the table and graph illustrate the law of diminishing marginal utility.

Marginal Utility and Demand

The law of diminishing marginal utility explains why the demand curve for a given product slopes downward. If successive units of a good yield smaller and smaller amounts of marginal, or extra, utility, then the consumer will buy additional units of a product only if its price falls. The consumer for whom Figure 7.1 is relevant may buy two tacos at a price of $1 each. But because he or she obtains less marginal utility from additional tacos, the consumer will choose not to buy more at that price. The consumer would rather spend additional dollars on products that provide more utility, not less utility. Therefore, additional tacos with less utility are not worth buying unless the price declines. (When marginal utility becomes negative, Taco Bell would have to pay you to consume another taco!) Thus, diminishing marginal utility supports the idea that price must decrease in order for quantity demanded to increase. In other words, consumers behave in ways that make demand curves downsloping.

AP QUICK REVIEW 7.1

✓ Utility is the benefit or satisfaction a person receives from consuming a good or a service. *Utils* is the term used to measure satisfaction.

✓ Total Utility is the total amount of satisfaction derived from consuming a specific quantity of a product. Marginal utility is the extra satisfaction a consumer derives from an additional unit of the product.

✓ The law of diminishing marginal utility indicates that gains in satisfaction become smaller as successive units of a specific product are consumed. As the total utility reaches its peak or maximum, the marginal utility becomes zero, becoming negative as more units are consumed.

✓ The law of diminishing marginal utility provides a simple rationale for the law of demand.

---

[1]Technical footnote: In Figure 7.1b we graphed marginal utility at half-units. For example, we graphed the marginal utility of 4 utils at 3 1/2 units because "4 utils" refers neither to the third nor the fourth unit per se but to the *addition* or *subtraction* of the fourth unit.

AP KEY GRAPH

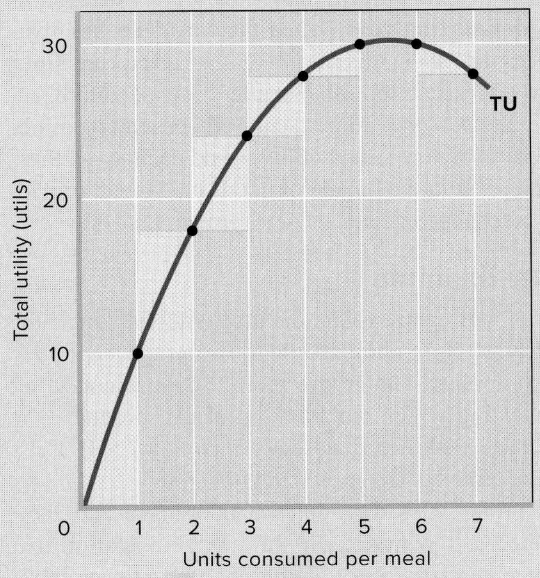

(a)
Total utility

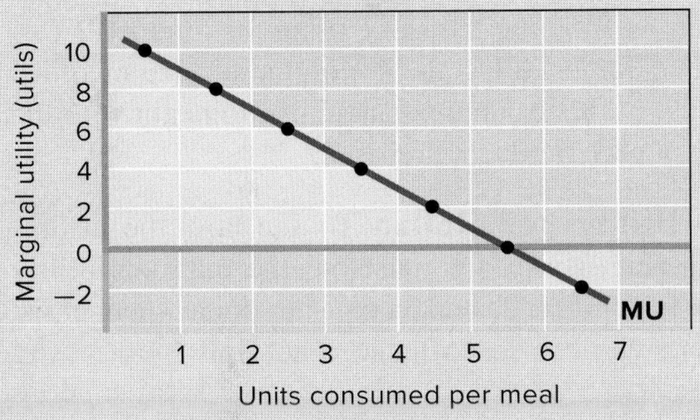

(b)
Marginal utility

FIGURE 7.1 Total and marginal utility. Curves TU and MU are graphed from the data in the table. (a) As more of a product is consumed, total utility increases at a diminishing rate, reaches a maximum, and then declines. (b) Marginal utility, by definition, reflects the changes in total utility. Thus marginal utility diminishes with increased consumption, becomes zero when total utility is at a maximum, and is negative when total utility declines. As shown by the shaded rectangles in (a) and (b), marginal utility is the change in total utility associated with each additional taco. Or, alternatively, each new level of total utility is found by adding marginal utility to the preceding level of total utility.

(1) Tacos Consumed per Meal	(2) Total Utility, Utils	(3) Marginal Utility, Utils
0	0	
1	10	10
2	18	8
3	24	6
4	28	4
5	30	2
6	30	0
7	28	−2

QUICK QUIZ FOR FIGURE 7.1

1. Marginal utility:
   a. is the extra output a firm obtains when it adds another unit of labor.
   b. explains why product supply curves slope upward.
   c. typically rises as successive units of a good are consumed.
   d. is the extra satisfaction from the consumption of 1 more unit of some good or service.
2. Marginal utility in Figure 7.1b is positive, but declining, when total utility in Figure 7.1a is positive and:
   a. rising at an increasing rate.
   b. falling at an increasing rate.
   c. rising at a decreasing rate.
   d. falling at a decreasing rate.
3. When marginal utility is zero in graph (b), total utility in graph (a) is:
   a. also zero.
   b. neither rising nor falling.
   c. negative.
   d. rising, but at a declining rate.
4. Suppose the person represented by these graphs experienced a diminished taste for tacos. As a result the:
   a. TU curve would get steeper.
   b. MU curve would get flatter.
   c. TU and MU curves would shift downward.
   d. MU curve, but not the TU curve, would collapse to the horizontal axis.

Answers: 1. d; 2. c; 3. b; 4. c

AP Theory of Consumer Behavior

LO7.2 Describe how rational consumers maximize utility by comparing the marginal utility-to-price ratios of all the products they could possibly purchase.

In addition to explaining the law of demand, the idea of diminishing marginal utility explains how consumers allocate their money incomes among the many goods and services available for purchase.

Consumer Choice and the Budget Constraint

For simplicity, we will assume that the situation for the typical consumer has the following dimensions.

- ***Rational behavior*** The consumer is a rational person, who tries to use his or her money income to derive the greatest amount of satisfaction, or utility, from it. Consumers want to get "the most for their money" or, technically, to maximize their total utility. They engage in **rational behavior.**
- ***Preferences*** Each consumer has clear-cut preferences for certain of the goods and services that are available in the market. Buyers also have a good idea of how much marginal utility they will get from successive units of the various products they might purchase.
- ***Budget constraint*** At any point in time the consumer has a fixed, limited amount of money income. Since each consumer supplies a finite amount of human and property resources to society, he or she earns only limited income. Thus, as noted in Chapter 1, every consumer faces a **budget constraint,** even consumers who earn millions of dollars a year. Of course, this budget limitation is more severe for a consumer with an average income than for a consumer with an extraordinarily high income.
- ***Prices*** Goods are scarce relative to the demand for them, so every good carries a price tag. We assume that the price of each good is unaffected by the amount of it that is bought by any particular person. After all, each person's purchase is a tiny part of total demand. Also, because the consumer has a limited number of dollars, he or she cannot buy everything wanted. This point drives home the reality of scarcity to each consumer.

So the consumer must compromise; he or she must choose the most personally satisfying mix of goods and services. Different individuals will choose different mixes.

Utility-Maximizing Rule

Of all the different combinations of goods and services a consumer can obtain within his or her budget, which specific combination will yield the maximum utility or satisfaction? *To maximize satisfaction, the consumer should allocate his or her money income so that the last dollar spent on each product yields the same amount of extra (marginal) utility.* We call this the **utility-maximizing rule.** When the consumer has "balanced his margins" using this rule, he has achieved **consumer equilibrium** and has no incentive to alter his expenditure pattern. In fact, any person who has achieved consumer equilibrium would be worse off—total utility would decline—if there were any alteration in the bundle of goods purchased, providing there is no change in taste, income, products, or prices.

Numerical Example

An illustration will help explain the utility-maximizing rule. For simplicity we limit our example to two products, but the analysis also applies if there are more. Suppose consumer Holly is analyzing which combination of two products she should purchase with her fixed daily income of $10. Let's suppose these products are apples and oranges.

Holly's preferences for apples and oranges and their prices are the basic data determining the combination that will maximize her satisfaction. Table 7.1 summarizes those data, with column 2a showing the amounts of marginal utility she will derive from each successive unit of A (apples) and with column 3a showing the same thing for product B (oranges). Both columns reflect the law of diminishing marginal utility, which, in this example, is assumed to begin with the second unit of each product purchased.

Marginal Utility per Dollar To see how the utility-maximizing rule works, we must put the marginal-utility information in columns 2a and 3a on a per-dollar-spent basis. A consumer's choices are influenced not only by the extra

AP TABLE 7.1 The Utility-Maximizing Combination of Apples and Oranges Obtainable with an Income of $10*

	(2) Apple (Product A): Price = $1		(3) Orange (Product B): Price 5 = $2	
(1) Unit of Product	(a) Marginal Utility, Utils	(b) Marginal Utility per Dollar (MU/Price)	(a) Marginal Utility, Utils	(b) Marginal Utility per Dollar (MU/Price)
First	10	10	24	12
Second	8	**8**	20	10
Third	7	7	18	9
Fourth	6	6	16	**8**
Fifth	5	5	12	6
Sixth	4	4	6	3
Seventh	3	3	4	2

*It is assumed in this table that the amount of marginal utility received from additional units of each of the two products is independent of the quantity of the other product. For example, the marginal-utility schedule for apples is independent of the number of oranges obtained by the consumer.

utility that successive apples will yield but also by how many dollars (and therefore how many oranges) she must give up to obtain additional apples.

The rational consumer must compare the extra utility from each product with its added cost (that is, its price). Switching examples for a moment, suppose that you prefer a pizza whose marginal utility is, say, 36 utils to a movie whose marginal utility is 24 utils. But if the pizza's price is $12 and the movie costs only $6, you would choose the movie rather than the pizza! Why? Because the marginal utility per dollar spent would be 4 utils for the movie (= 24 utils/$6) compared to only 3 utils for the pizza (= 36 utils/$12). You could see two movies for $12 and, assuming that the marginal utility of the second movie is, say, 16 utils, your total utility would be 40 utils. Clearly, 40 units of satisfaction (= 24 utils + 16 utils) from two movies are superior to 36 utils from the same $12 expenditure on one pizza.

To make the amounts of extra utility derived from differently priced goods comparable, marginal utilities must be put on a per-dollar-spent basis. We do this in columns 2b and 3b by dividing the marginal-utility data of columns 2a and 3a by the prices of apples and oranges—$1 and $2, respectively.

Decision-Making Process Table 7.1 shows Holly's preferences on a unit basis and a per-dollar basis as well as the price tags of apples and oranges. With $10 to spend, in what order should Holly allocate her dollars on units of apples and oranges to achieve the highest amount of utility within the $10 limit imposed by her income? And what specific combination of the two products will she have obtained at the time she uses up her $10?

Concentrating on columns 2b and 3b in Table 7.1, we find that Holly should first spend $2 on the first orange because its marginal utility per dollar of 12 utils is higher than the first apple's 10 utils. But now Holly finds herself indifferent about whether to buy a second orange or the first apple because the marginal utility per dollar of both is 10 utils per dollar. So she buys both of them. Holly now has 1 apple and 2 oranges. Also, the last dollar she spent on each good yielded the same marginal utility per dollar (10). But this combination of apples and oranges does not represent the maximum amount of utility that Holly can obtain. It cost her only $5 [= (1 × $1) + (2 × $2)], so she has $5 remaining, which she can spend to achieve a still higher level of total utility.

Examining columns 2b and 3b again, we find that Holly should spend the next $2 on a third orange because marginal utility per dollar for the third orange is 9 compared with 8 for the second apple. But now, with 1 apple and 3 oranges, she is again indifferent between a second apple and a fourth orange because both provide 8 utils per dollar. So Holly purchases 1 more of each. Now the last dollar spent on each product provides the same marginal utility per dollar (8), and Holly's money income of $10 is exhausted.

The utility-maximizing combination of goods attainable by Holly is 2 apples and 4 oranges. By summing marginal-utility information from columns 2a and 3a, we find that Holly is obtaining 18 (= 10 + 8) utils of satisfaction from the 2 apples and 78 (= 24 + 20 + 18 + 16) utils of satisfaction from the 4 oranges. Her $10, optimally spent, yields 96 (= 18 + 78) utils of satisfaction.

Table 7.2 summarizes our step-by-step process for maximizing Holly's utility. Note that we have implicitly assumed that Holly spends her entire income. She neither borrows nor saves. However, saving can be regarded as a "commodity" that yields utility and can be incorporated into our analysis. In fact, we treat it that way in problem 4 at the end of this chapter.

Inferior Options Holly can obtain other combinations of apples and oranges with $10, but none will yield as great a total utility as do 2 apples and 4 oranges. As an example, she can obtain 4 apples and 3 oranges for $10. But this combination yields only 93 utils, clearly inferior to the 96 utils provided by 2 apples and 4 oranges. True, there are other combinations of apples and oranges (such as 4 apples and 5 oranges or 1 apple and 2 oranges) in which the marginal utility of the last dollar spent is the same for both goods. But all such combinations either are unobtainable with Holly's limited money income (as 4 apples and 5 oranges) or do not exhaust her money income (as 1 apple and 2 oranges) and therefore do not yield the maximum utility attainable.

TABLE 7.2 Sequence of Purchases to Achieve Consumer Equilibrium, Given the Data in Table 7.1

Choice Number	Potential Choices	Marginal Utility per Dollar	Purchase Decision	Income Remaining
1	First apple	10	First orange for $2	$8 = $10 − $2
	First orange	12		
2	First apple	10	First apple for $1	$5 = $8 − $3
	Second orange	10	and second orange for $2	
3	Second apple	8	Third orange for $2	$3 = $5 − $2
	Third orange	9		
4	Second apple	8	Second apple for $1	$0 = $3 − $3
	Fourth orange	8	and fourth orange for $2	

CONSIDER THIS . . .

Source: © Letterberry/Shutterstock.com

There's No Accounting for Taste

In 2015, the federal government started requiring restaurants to print calorie counts next to menu items. The regulation was intended to help consumers make healthful choices. In particular, it was assumed that if they could see how many calories each item contained, consumers would consume fewer total calories. They would opt for salads instead of milkshakes.

But a funny thing happened when the new rules went into effect. Some people started consuming *more* calories. They did so because their preferences were not what policymakers expected. Instead of trying to maximize the amount of healthfulness per dollar of money spent, they instead chose to maximize the number of calories per dollar of money spent. Their preferences were such that when it came to maximizing utility, what they wanted was the maximum number of calories, not the maximum amount of health. So when the new regulations provided them with calorie counts, they went for milkshakes instead of salads and double cheeseburgers instead of chicken skewers.

The lesson learned? Know what people are trying to maximize before you attempt to alter their behavior.

Algebraic Generalization

Economists generalize the utility-maximizing rule by saying that a consumer will maximize her satisfaction when she allocates her money income so that the last dollar spent on product A, the last on product B, and so forth, yield equal amounts of additional, or marginal, utility. The marginal utility per dollar spent on A is indicated by the MU of product A divided by the price of A (column 2b in Table 7.1), and the marginal utility per dollar spent on B by the MU of product B divided by the price of B (column 3b in Table 7.1). Our utility-maximizing rule merely requires that these ratios be equal for the last dollar spent on A and the last dollar spent on B. Algebraically,

$$\frac{\text{MU of product A}}{\text{Price of A}} = \frac{\text{MU of product B}}{\text{Price of B}}$$

And, of course, the consumer must exhaust her available income. Table 7.1 shows us that the combination of 2 units of A (apples) and 4 of B (oranges) fulfills these conditions in that

$$\frac{8 \text{ utils}}{\$1} = \frac{16 \text{ utils}}{\$2}$$

and the consumer's $10 income is all spent.

If the equation is not fulfilled, then some reallocation of the consumer's expenditures between A and B (from the low to the high marginal-utility-per-dollar product) will increase the consumer's total utility. For example, if the consumer spent $10 on 4 of A (apples) and 3 of B (oranges), we would find that

$$\frac{\text{MU of A of 6 utils}}{\text{Price of A of \$1}} < \frac{\text{MU of B of 18 utils}}{\text{Price of B of \$2}}$$

Here the last dollar spent on A provides only 6 utils of satisfaction, while the last dollar spent on B provides 9 (= 18/$2). So the consumer can increase total satisfaction by purchasing more of B and less of A. As dollars are reallocated from A to B, the marginal utility per dollar of A will increase while the marginal utility per dollar of B will decrease. At some new combination of A and B the two will be equal and consumer equilibrium will be achieved. Here that combination is 2 of A (apples) and 4 of B (oranges).

AP Utility Maximization and the Demand Curve

LO7.3 Explain how a demand curve can be derived by observing the outcomes of price changes in the utility-maximization model.

Once you understand the utility-maximizing rule, you can easily see why product price and quantity demanded are inversely related. Recall that the basic determinants of an individual's demand for a specific product are (1) preferences or tastes, (2) money income, and (3) the prices of other goods. The utility data in Table 7.1 reflect our consumer's preferences. We continue to suppose that her money income is $10. And, concentrating on the construction of an individual demand curve for oranges, we assume that the price of apples, now representing all "other goods," is still $1.

Deriving the Demand Schedule and Curve

We can derive a single consumer's demand schedule for oranges by considering alternative prices at which oranges might be sold and then determining the quantity the consumer will purchase. We already know one such price-quantity combination in the utility-maximizing example: Given tastes, income, and the prices of other goods, Holly will purchase 4 oranges at $2.

Now let's assume the price of oranges falls to $1. The marginal-utility-per-dollar data of column 3b in Table 7.1 will double because the price of oranges has been halved; the new data for column 3b are (by coincidence) identical to the data in column 3a. The doubling of the MU per dollar for each successive orange means that the purchase of 2 apples and 4 oranges is no longer an equilibrium combination. By applying the same reasoning we used previously, we now find that Holly's utility-maximizing combination is 4 apples and 6 oranges. As summarized in the table in Figure 7.2, Holly will purchase

AP **FIGURE 7.2 Deriving an individual demand curve.** The consumer represented by the data in the table maximizes utility by purchasing 4 oranges at a price of \$2. The decline in the price of oranges to \$1 disrupts the consumer's initial utility-maximizing equilibrium. The consumer restores equilibrium by purchasing 6 rather than 4 oranges. Thus, a simple price-quantity schedule emerges, which locates two points on a downsloping demand curve.

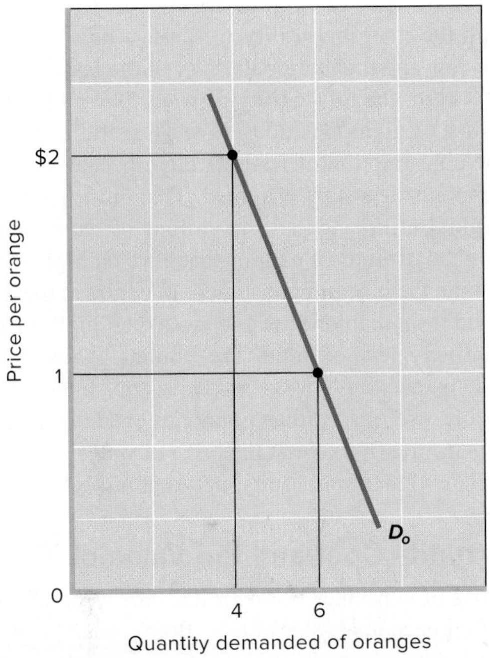

Price per Orange	Quantity Demanded
\$2	4
1	6

6 oranges when the price of oranges is \$1. Using the data in this table, we can sketch the downward-sloping demand curve for oranges, D_o, shown in Figure 7.2. This exercise, then, clearly links the utility-maximizing behavior of a consumer and that person's downsloping demand curve for a particular product.

AP Income and Substitution Effects

LO7.4 Discuss how the utility-maximization model helps highlight the income and substitution effects of a price change.

Recall from Chapter 3 that the **income effect** is the impact that a change in the price of a product has on a consumer's real income and consequently on the quantity demanded of that good. In contrast, the **substitution effect** is the impact that a change in a product's price has on its relative expensiveness and consequently on the quantity demanded. Both effects help explain why a demand curve such as that in Figure 7.2 is downsloping.

Let's first look at the substitution effect. Recall that before the price of oranges declined, Holly was in equilibrium when purchasing 2 apples and 4 oranges because

$$\frac{\text{MU of apples of 8}}{\text{Price of apples of \$1}} = \frac{\text{MU of oranges of 16}}{\text{Price of oranges of \$2}}$$

But after the price of oranges declines from \$2 to \$1,

$$\frac{\text{MU of apples of 8}}{\text{Price of apples of \$1}} < \frac{\text{MU of oranges of 16}}{\text{Price of oranges of \$1}}$$

Clearly, the last dollar spent on oranges now yields greater utility (16 utils) than does the last dollar spent on apples (8 utils). This will lead Holly to switch, or substitute, purchases away from apples and toward oranges so as to restore consumer equilibrium. This substitution effect contributes to the inverse relationship between price and quantity that is found along her demand curve for oranges: When the price of oranges declines, the substitution effect causes Holly to buy more oranges.

What about the income effect? The decline in the price of oranges from \$2 to \$1 increases Holly's real income. Before the price decline, she maximized her utility and achieved consumer equilibrium by selecting 2 apples and 4 oranges. But at the lower \$1 price for oranges, Holly would have to spend only \$6 rather than \$10 to buy that particular combination of goods. That means that the lower price of oranges has freed up \$4 that can be spent on buying more apples, more oranges, or more of both. How many more of each fruit she ends up buying will be determined by applying the utility-maximizing rule to the new situation. But it is quite likely that the increase in real income caused by the reduction in the price of oranges will cause Holly to end up buying more oranges than before the price reduction. Any such increase in orange purchases is referred to as the income effect of the reduction in the price of oranges and it, too, helps to explain why demand curves are downward sloping: When the price of oranges falls, the income effect causes Holly to buy more oranges.

AP QUICK REVIEW 7.2

- ✓ The theory of consumer behavior assumes that, with limited income and a set of product prices, consumers make rational choices on the basis of well-defined preferences.
- ✓ The Utility-Maximizing Rule states that to maximize satisfaction, a consumer should allocate income so that the last dollar spent on each product yields the same amount of extra (marginal) utility. The utility maximization rule becomes $(MU_X/P_X) = (MU_Y/P_Y)$ for goods X and Y.
- ✓ A downsloping demand curve can be derived by changing the price of one product in the consumer-behavior model and noting the change in the utility-maximizing quantity of that product demanded.
- ✓ By providing insights on the substitution and income effects of a price decline, the utility-maximization model helps explain why demand curves are downsloping.

Applications and Extensions

LO7.5 Give examples of several real-world phenomena that can be explained by applying the theory of consumer behavior.

Many real-world phenomena can be explained by applying the theory of consumer behavior.

iPads

Every so often a new product totally captures consumers' imaginations. One such product is Apple's iPad, which debuted in April 2010. Less than three years later, Apple sold its 100-millionth unit.

The swift ascendancy of the iPad resulted mainly from a leapfrog in technology. It was the first touchscreen tablet computer and became a hit because it was much better for the consumption of digital media—music, pictures, videos, and many games—than existing laptop or desktop computers. Those larger machines still held the advantage if a consumer wanted to create content or edit documents, but for consuming digital content the iPad was far superior in the eyes of millions of consumers.

In the language of our analysis, Apple's introduction of the iPad severely disrupted consumer equilibrium. Consumers en masse concluded that iPads had a higher marginal-utility-to-price ratio (= MU/*P*) than the ratios for alternative products. They therefore shifted spending away from those other products and toward iPads as a way to increase total utility. Of course, for most people the marginal utility of a second or third iPad relative to price is quite low, so most consumers purchased only a single iPad. But Apple continued to enhance the iPad, enticing some of the buyers of older models to buy new models.

This example demonstrates a simple but important point: New products succeed by enhancing consumers' total utility. This "delivery of value" generates a revenue stream. If revenues exceed production costs, substantial profits can result—as they have for Apple.

The Diamond-Water Paradox

Early economists such as Adam Smith were puzzled by the fact that some "essential" goods had much lower prices than some "unimportant" goods. Why would water, essential to life, be priced below diamonds, which have much less usefulness? The paradox is resolved when we acknowledge that water is in great supply relative to demand and thus has a very low price per gallon. Diamonds, in contrast, are rare. Their supply is small relative to demand and, as a result, they have a very high price per carat.

Moreover, the marginal utility of the last unit of water consumed is very low. The reason follows from our utility-maximizing rule. Consumers (and producers) respond to the very low price of water by using a great deal of it—for generating electricity, irrigating crops, heating buildings, watering lawns, quenching thirst, and so on. Consumption is expanded until marginal utility, which declines as more water is consumed, equals its low price. On the other hand, relatively few diamonds are purchased because of their prohibitively high price, meaning that their marginal utility remains high. In equilibrium:

$$\frac{\text{MU of water (low)}}{\text{Price of water (low)}} = \frac{\text{MU of diamonds (high)}}{\text{Price of diamonds (high)}}$$

Although the marginal utility of the last unit of water consumed is low and the marginal utility of the last diamond purchased is high, the total utility of water is very high and the total utility of diamonds quite low. The total utility derived from the consumption of water is large because of the enormous amounts of water consumed. Total utility is the sum of the marginal utilities of all the gallons of water consumed, including the trillions of gallons that have far higher marginal utilities than the last unit consumed. In contrast, the total utility derived from diamonds is low since their high price means that relatively few of them are bought. Thus the water-diamond "paradox" is solved: Water has much more total utility (roughly, usefulness) than diamonds even though the price of diamonds greatly exceeds the price of water. These relative prices relate to marginal utility, not total utility.

Opportunity Cost and the Value of Time

The theory of consumer behavior has been generalized to account for the economic value of *time*. Both consumption and production take time. Time is a valuable economic commodity; by using an hour in productive work a person can earn \$6, \$10, \$50, or more, depending on her or his education and skills. By using that hour for leisure or in consumption activities, the individual incurs the opportunity cost of forgone income; she or he sacrifices the \$6, \$10, or \$50 that could have been earned by working.

Imagine a self-employed consumer named Linden who is considering buying a round of golf, on the one hand, and a concert, on the other. The market price of the golf game is \$30 and that of the concert is \$40. But the golf game takes more time than the concert. Suppose Linden spends 4 hours on the golf course but only 2 hours at the concert. If her time is worth \$10 per hour, as evidenced by the \$10 wage she can obtain by working, then the "full price" of the golf game is \$70 (the \$30 market price plus \$40 worth of time). Similarly, the full price of the concert is \$60 (the \$40 market price plus \$20 worth of time). We find that, contrary to what market prices alone indicate, the full price of the concert is really less than the full price of the golf game.

If we now assume that the marginal utilities derived from successive golf games and concerts are identical, traditional theory would indicate that Linden should consume more golf games than concerts because the market price of the former (\$30) is lower than that of the latter (\$40). But when time is taken into account, the situation is reversed and golf games (\$70) are more expensive than concerts (\$60). So it is rational for Linden to consume more concerts than golf games.

LAST WORD

Criminal Behavior

Although Economic Analysis Is Not Particularly Relevant in Explaining Some Crimes of Passion and Violence, It Does Provide Interesting Insights on Such Property Crimes as Robbery, Burglary, and Auto Theft.

The theory of rational consumer behavior can be extended to provide some useful insights on criminal behavior. Both the lawful consumer and the criminal try to maximize their total utility (or net benefit). For example, you can remove a textbook from the campus bookstore by either purchasing it or stealing it. If you *buy* the book, your action is legal; you have fully compensated the bookstore for the product. (The bookstore would rather have your money than the book.) If you *steal* the book, you have broken the law. Theft is outlawed because it imposes uncompensated costs on others. In this case, your action reduces the bookstore's revenue and profit and also may impose costs on other buyers who now must pay higher prices for their textbooks.

Source: © Digital Vision/Getty Images RF

Why might someone engage in a criminal activity such as stealing? Just like the consumer who compares the marginal utility of a good with its price, the potential criminal compares the marginal benefit from his or her action with the "price" or cost. If the marginal benefit (to the criminal) exceeds the price or marginal cost (also to the criminal), the individual undertakes the criminal activity.

Most people, however, do not engage in theft, burglary, or fraud. Why not? The answer is that they perceive the personal price of engaging in these illegal activities to be too high relative to the marginal benefit. The price or marginal cost to the potential criminal has several facets. First, there are the "guilt costs," which for many people are substantial. Such individuals would not steal from others even if there were no penalties for doing so. Their moral sense of right and wrong would entail too great a guilt cost relative to the benefit from the stolen good. Other types of costs include the direct cost of the criminal activity (supplies and tools) and the forgone income from legitimate activities (the opportunity cost to the criminal).

Unfortunately, guilt costs, direct costs, and forgone income are not sufficient to deter some people from stealing. So society imposes other costs, mainly fines and imprisonment, on lawbreakers. The potential of being fined increases the marginal cost to the criminal. The potential of being imprisoned boosts marginal cost still further. Most people highly value their personal freedom and lose considerable legitimate earnings while incarcerated.

Given these types of costs, the potential criminal estimates the marginal cost and benefit of committing the crime. As a simple example, suppose that the direct cost and the opportunity cost of stealing an $80 textbook are both zero. The probability of getting caught is 10 percent and, if apprehended, there will be a $500 fine. The potential criminal will estimate the marginal cost of stealing the book as $50 (= $500 fine × .10 chance of apprehension). Someone who has a guilt cost of zero will choose to steal the book because the marginal benefit of $80 would exceed the marginal cost of $50. In contrast, someone having a guilt cost of, say, $40 will not steal the book. The marginal benefit of $80 will not be as great as the marginal cost of $90 (= $50 of penalty cost + $40 of guilt cost).

This perspective on illegal behavior has some interesting implications. For example, other things equal, crime will rise (more of it will be "bought") when its price falls. This explains, for instance, why some people who do not steal from stores under normal circumstances participate in looting stores during riots, when the marginal cost of being apprehended has substantially declined.

Another implication is that society can reduce unlawful behavior by increasing the "price of crime." It can nourish and increase guilt costs through family, educational, and religious efforts. It can increase the direct cost of crime by using more sophisticated security systems (locks, alarms, video surveillance) so that criminals will have to buy and use more sophisticated tools. It can undertake education and training initiatives to enhance the legitimate earnings of people who might otherwise engage in illegal activity. It can increase policing to raise the probability of being apprehended for crime. And it can impose greater penalties for those who are caught and convicted.

By accounting for the opportunity cost of a consumer's time, we can explain certain phenomena that are otherwise quite puzzling. It may be rational for the unskilled worker or retiree whose time has little market value to ride a bus from Chicago to Pittsburgh. But the corporate executive, whose time is very valuable, will find it cheaper to fly, even though bus fare is only a fraction of plane fare. It is sensible for the retiree, living on a modest company pension and a Social Security check, to spend many hours shopping for bargains at the mall or taking long trips in a motor home. It is equally intelligent for the highly paid physician, working 55 hours per week, to buy a new personal computer over the Internet and take short vacations at expensive resorts.

People in other nations often feel affluent Americans are "wasteful" of food and other material goods but "overly economical" in their use of time. Americans who visit developing countries find that time is used casually or "squandered," while material goods are very highly prized and carefully used. These differences are not a paradox or a case of radically different temperaments. The differences are primarily a rational reflection of the fact that the high productivity of labor in an industrially advanced society gives time a high market value, whereas the opposite is true in a low-income, developing country.

Medical Care Purchases

The method of payment for certain goods and services affects their prices at the time we buy them and significantly changes the amount purchased. Let's go back to Table 7.1. Suppose the \$1 price for apples is its "true" value or opportunity cost. But now, for some reason, its price is only, say, \$0.20. A rational consumer clearly would buy more apples at the \$0.20 price than at the \$1 price.

That is what happens with medical care. People in the United States who have health insurance pay a fixed premium once a month that covers, say, 80 percent of all incurred health care costs. This means that when they actually need health care, its price to them will be only 20 percent of the actual market price. How would you act in such a situation? When you are ill, you would likely purchase a great deal more medical care than you would if you were confronted with the full price. As a result, financing health care through insurance is an important factor in explaining today's high expenditures on health care and the historical growth of such spending as a percentage of domestic output.

Similar reasoning applies to purchases of buffet meals. If you buy a meal at an all-you-can-eat buffet, you will tend to eat more than if you purchased it item by item. Why not eat that second dessert? Its marginal utility is positive and its "price" is zero!

Cash and Noncash Gifts

Marginal-utility analysis also helps us understand why people generally prefer cash gifts to noncash gifts costing the same amount. The reason is simply that the noncash gifts may not match the recipient's preferences and thus may not add as much as cash to total utility. Thought of differently, consumers know their own preferences better than the gift giver does, and the \$100 cash gift provides more choices.

Look back at Table 7.1. Suppose Holly has zero earned income but is given the choice of a \$2 cash gift or a noncash gift of 2 apples. Because 2 apples can be bought with \$2, these two gifts are of equal monetary value. But by spending the \$2 cash gift on the first orange, Holly could obtain 24 utils. The noncash gift of the first 2 apples would yield only 18 (= 10 + 8) units of utility. Conclusion: The noncash gift yields less utility to the beneficiary than does the cash gift.

Since giving noncash gifts is common, a considerable value of those gifts is potentially lost because they do not match their recipients' tastes. For example, Uncle Fred may have paid \$30 for the ski goggles he gave you for the holidays, but you would pay only \$15 for them. Thus, a \$15, or 50 percent, value loss is involved. Multiplied by billions of gifts a year, the total potential loss of value is huge.

But some of that loss is avoided by the creative ways individuals handle the problem. For example, newlyweds set up gift registries for their weddings to help match up their wants to the noncash gifts received. Also, people obtain cash refunds or exchanges for gifts so they can buy goods that provide more utility. And people have even been known to "recycle gifts" by giving them to someone else at a later time. All three actions support the proposition that individuals take actions to maximize their total utility.

SUMMARY

LO7.1 Define and explain the relationship between total utility, marginal utility, and the law of diminishing marginal utility.

The law of diminishing marginal utility states that beyond a certain quantity, additional units of a specific good will yield declining amounts of extra satisfaction to a consumer.

LO7.2 Describe how rational consumers maximize utility by comparing the marginal utility-to-price ratios of all the products they could possibly purchase.

The utility-maximization model assumes that the typical consumer is rational and acts on the basis of well-defined preferences. Because income is limited and goods have prices, the consumer cannot purchase all the goods and services he or she might want. The consumer therefore selects the attainable combination of goods that maximizes his or her utility or satisfaction.

A consumer's utility is maximized when income is allocated so that the last dollar spent on each product purchased yields the same amount of extra satisfaction. Algebraically, the utility-maximizing rule is fulfilled when

$$\frac{\text{MU of product A}}{\text{Price of A}} = \frac{\text{MU of product B}}{\text{Price of B}}$$

and the consumer's total income is spent.

LO7.3 Explain how a demand curve can be derived by observing the outcomes of price changes in the utility-maximization model.

The utility-maximizing rule and the demand curve are logically consistent. Because marginal utility declines, a lower price is needed to induce the consumer to buy more of a particular product.

LO7.4 Discuss how the utility-maximization model helps highlight the income and substitution effects of a price change.

The utility-maximization model illuminates the income and substitution effects of a price change. The income effect implies that a decline in the price of a product increases the consumer's real income and enables the consumer to buy more of that product with a fixed money income. The substitution effect implies that a lower price makes a product relatively more attractive and therefore increases the consumer's willingness to substitute it for other products.

LO7.5 Give examples of several real-world phenomena that can be explained by applying the theory of consumer behavior.

The theory of consumer behavior can explain many real world phenomena, including the rapid adoption of popular consumer goods like the iPad that feature disruptive technologies, the overconsumption of products like health care that have artificially low prices, and people's preference for gifts of cash over gifts of particular items or objects of the same monetary value.

TERMS AND CONCEPTS

law of diminishing marginal utility
utility
total utility
marginal utility
rational behavior
budget constraint
utility-maximizing rule
consumer equilibrium
income effect
substitution effect

The following and additional problems can be found in connect

DISCUSSION QUESTIONS

1. Complete the following table and answer the questions below: LO7.1

Units Consumed	Total Utility	Marginal Utility
0	0	
1	10	10
2	—	8
3	25	—
4	30	—
5	—	3
6	34	—

   a. At which rate is total utility increasing: a constant rate, a decreasing rate, or an increasing rate? How do you know?
   b. "A rational consumer will purchase only 1 unit of the product represented by these data, since that amount maximizes marginal utility." Do you agree? Explain why or why not.
   c. "It is possible that a rational consumer will not purchase any units of the product represented by these data." Do you agree? Explain why or why not.

2. Mrs. Simpson buys loaves of bread and quarts of milk each week at prices of $1 and 80 cents, respectively. At present she is buying these products in amounts such that the marginal utilities from the last units purchased of the two products are 80 and 70 utils, respectively. Is she buying the utility-maximizing combination of bread and milk? If not, how should she reallocate her expenditures between the two goods? LO7.2
3. How can time be incorporated into the theory of consumer behavior? Explain the following comment: "Want to make millions of dollars? Devise a product that saves Americans lots of time." LO7.2
4. Explain: LO7.2
   a. Before economic growth, there were too few goods; after growth, there is too little time.
   b. It is irrational for an individual to take the time to be completely rational in economic decision making.
   c. Telling your spouse where you would like to go out to eat for your birthday makes sense in terms of utility maximization.
5. In the last decade or so, there has been a dramatic expansion of small retail convenience stores (such as 7-Eleven, Kwik Shop, and Circle K), although their prices are generally much higher than prices in large supermarkets. What explains the success of the convenience stores? LO7.2

6. Many apartment-complex owners are installing water meters for each apartment and billing the occupants according to the amount of water they use. This is in contrast to the former procedure of having a central meter for the entire complex and dividing up the collective water expense as part of the rent. Where individual meters have been installed, water usage has declined 10 to 40 percent. Explain that drop, referring to price and marginal utility. LO7.3
7. Using the utility-maximization rule as your point of reference, explain the income and substitution effects of an increase in the price of product B, with no change in the price of product A. LO7.4
8. **ADVANCED ANALYSIS** A "mathematically fair bet" is one in which the amount won will on average equal the amount bet, for example, when a gambler bets, say, \$100 for a 10 percent chance to win \$1,000 (\$100 = 0.10 × \$1,000). Assuming diminishing marginal utility of dollars, explain why this is not a fair bet in terms of utility. Why is it even a less fair bet when the "house" takes a cut of each dollar bet? So is gambling irrational? LO7.4
9. Rank each of the following three gift possibilities in terms of how much utility they are likely to bring and explain your reasoning. A store-specific gift card worth \$15, a \$15 item from that specific store, and \$15 of cash that can be spent anywhere. LO7.5
10. **LAST WORD** In what way is criminal behavior similar to consumer behavior? Why do most people obtain goods via legal behavior as opposed to illegal behavior? What are society's main options for reducing illegal behavior?

AP REVIEW QUESTIONS

1. True or false. The law of diminishing marginal utility predicts the consumption behavior of addicts quite well. LO7.1
2. Frank spends \$75 on 10 magazines and 25 newspapers. The magazines cost \$5 each and the newspapers cost \$2.50 each. Suppose that his MU from the final magazine is 10 utils while his MU from the final newspaper is also 10 utils. According to the utility-maximizing rule, Frank should: LO7.2
   a. Reallocate spending from magazines to newspapers.
   b. Reallocate spending from newspapers to magazines.
   c. Be satisfied because he is already maximizing his total utility.
   d. Consume more newspapers and more magazines.
   e. Reduce his total spending.
3. A consumer's demand curve for a product is downsloping because LO7.3
   a. Total utility falls below marginal utility as more of a product is consumed.
   b. Marginal utility diminishes as more of a product is consumed.
   c. Time becomes less valuable as more of a product is consumed.
   d. The income and substitution effects precisely offset each other.
   e. The income effect would cause a decrease in quantity when the price goes down.
4. Jermaine spends his money on cucumbers and lettuce. If the price of cucumbers falls, the MU per dollar of cucumbers will ____________ and Jermaine will consume ____________ cucumbers. LO7.4
   a. Fall; fewer
   b. Rise; fewer
   c. Fall; more
   d. Rise; more
   e. Remain unchanged; more
5. Tammy spends her money on lemonade and iced tea, both normal goods. If the price of lemonade falls, the income and substitution effects will lead to LO7.4

	Income effect	Substitution effect
a.	More lemonade	More lemonade
b.	More lemonade	Less lemonade
c.	Less ice tea	More ice tea
d.	More ice tea	More ice tea
e.	Less lemonade	More lemonade

6. Assume that X and Y are normal goods. Answer the following questions.
   a. A consumer spends all her income on goods X and Y. The price of good X is \$10 per unit, and the price of good Y is \$5 per unit. The marginal utility of the last unit of good X is fifty. What must the marginal utility of good Y be if the consumer is maximizing utility?
   b. Given your answer in **part a,** if the marginal utility of good Y is 10, is this consumer maximizing utility? Explain. What reallocation of purchases can this consumer do to increase total utility?
   c. Assume that the price of good Y increases and that both X and Y are normal goods. What should happen to the consumption of good X? Explain. What should happen to the consumption of good Y? Explain.

PROBLEMS

1. Mylie's total utility from singing the same song over and over is 50 utils after one repetition, 90 utils after two repetitions, 70 utils after three repetitions, 20 utils after four repetitions, −50 utils after five repetitions, and −200 utils after six repetitions. Write down her marginal utility for each repetition. Once Mylie's total utility begins to decrease, does each additional singing of the song hurt more than the previous one or less than the previous one? LO7.1
2. John likes Coca-Cola. After consuming one Coke, John has a total utility of 10 utils. After two Cokes, he has a total utility of 25 utils. After three Cokes, he has a total utility of 50 utils. Does John show diminishing marginal utility for Coke, or does he show increasing marginal utility for Coke? Suppose that John has \$3 in his pocket. If Cokes cost \$1 each and John is willing to spend one of his dollars on purchasing a first can of Coke, would he spend his second dollar on a Coke, too?

What about the third dollar? If John's marginal utility for Coke keeps on increasing no matter how many Cokes he drinks, would it be fair to say that he is addicted to Coke? LO7.1

3. Suppose that Omar's marginal utility for cups of coffee is constant at 1.5 utils per cup no matter how many cups he drinks. On the other hand, his marginal utility per doughnut is 10 for the first doughnut he eats, 9 for the second he eats, 8 for the third he eats, and so on (that is, declining by 1 util per additional doughnut). In addition, suppose that coffee costs $1 per cup, doughnuts cost $1 each, and Omar has a budget that he can spend only on doughnuts, coffee, or both. How big would that budget have to be before he would spend a dollar buying a first cup of coffee? LO7.2

4. Columns 1 through 4 in the following table show the marginal utility, measured in utils, that Ricardo would get by purchasing various amounts of products A, B, C, and D. Column 5 shows the marginal utility Ricardo gets from saving. Assume that the prices of A, B, C, and D are, respectively, $18, $6, $4, and $24 and that Ricardo has an income of $106. LO7.2
   a. What quantities of A, B, C, and D will Ricardo purchase in maximizing his utility?
   b. How many dollars will Ricardo choose to save?
   c. Check your answers by substituting them into the algebraic statement of the utility-maximizing rule.

Column 1		Column 2		Column 3		Column 4		Column 5	
Units of A	MU	Units of B	MU	Units of C	MU	Units of D	MU	Number of Dollars Saved	MU
1	72	1	24	1	15	1	36	1	5
2	54	2	15	2	12	2	30	2	4
3	45	3	12	3	8	3	24	3	3
4	36	4	9	4	7	4	18	4	2
5	27	5	7	5	5	5	13	5	1
6	18	6	5	6	4	6	7	6	$\frac{1}{2}$
7	15	7	2	7	$3\frac{1}{2}$	7	4	7	$\frac{1}{4}$
8	12	8	1	8	3	8	2	8	$\frac{1}{8}$

5. You are choosing between two goods, X and Y, and your marginal utility from each is as shown in the following table. If your income is $9 and the prices of X and Y are $2 and $1, respectively, what quantities of each will you purchase to maximize utility? What total utility will you realize? Assume that, other things remaining unchanged, the price of X falls to $1. What quantities of X and Y will you now purchase? Using the two prices and quantities for X, derive a demand schedule (a table showing prices and quantities demanded) for X. LO7.3

Units of X	MU_x	Units of Y	MU_y
1	10	1	8
2	8	2	7
3	6	3	6
4	4	4	5
5	3	5	4
6	2	6	3

6. **ADVANCED ANALYSIS** Let $MU_A = z = 10 - x$ and $MU_B = z = 21 - 2y$, where z is marginal utility per dollar measured in utils, x is the amount spent on product A, and y is the amount spent on product B. Assume that the consumer has $10 to spend on A and B—that is, $x + y = 10$. How is the $10 best allocated between A and B? How much utility will the marginal dollar yield? LO7.3

7. Suppose that with a budget of $100, Deborah spends $60 on sushi and $40 on bagels when sushi costs $2 per piece and bagels cost $2 per bagel. But then, after the price of bagels falls to $1 per bagel, she spends $50 on sushi and $50 on bagels. How many pieces of sushi and how many bagels did Deborah consume before the price change? At the new prices, how much money would it have cost Deborah to buy those same quantities (the ones that she consumed before the price change)? Given that it used to take Deborah's entire $100 to buy those quantities, how big is the income effect caused by the reduction in the price of bagels? LO7.4

Indifference Curve Analysis

LO7.6 Relate how the indifference curve model of consumer behavior derives demand curves from budget lines, indifference curves, and utility maximization.

The utility-maximization rule previously discussed requires individuals to measure and compare utility, much as a business would measure and compare costs or revenues. Such *cardinal utility* is measured in units such as 1, 2, 3, and 4 and can be added, subtracted, multiplied, and divided, just like the cardinal numbers in mathematics. More importantly, cardinal utility allows precise quantification of the marginal utilities upon which the utility-maximizing rule depends. In fact, the marginal-utility theory of consumer demand that we explained in the body of this chapter rests squarely on the assumption that economists be able to measure cardinal utility. The reality, however, is that measuring cardinal utility is highly difficult, at best. (Can you, for instance, state exactly how many utils you are getting from reading this book right now or how many utils you would get from watching a sunset?)

To avoid this measurement problem, economists have developed an alternative explanation of consumer behavior and equilibrium in which cardinal measurement is not required. In this more-advanced analysis, the consumer must simply *rank* various combinations of goods in terms of preference. For instance, Sally can simply report that she *prefers* 4 units of A to 6 units of B without having to put number values on how much she likes either option. The model of consumer behavior that is based upon such *ordinal utility* rankings is called indifference curve analysis. It has two main elements: budget lines and indifference curves.

The Budget Line: What Is Attainable

We know from Chapter 1 that a **budget line** (or, more technically, a *budget constraint*) is a schedule or curve showing various combinations of two products a consumer can purchase with a specific money income. If the price of product A is \$1.50 and the price of product B is \$1, a consumer could purchase all the combinations of A and B shown in the table in Figure 1 with \$12 of money income. At one extreme, the consumer might spend all of his or her income on 8 units of A and have nothing left to spend on B. Or, by giving up 2 units of A and thereby "freeing" \$3, the consumer could have 6 units of A and 3 of B. And so on to the other extreme, at which the consumer could buy 12 units of B at \$1 each, spending his or her entire money income on B with nothing left to spend on A.

Figure 1 also shows the budget line graphically. Note that the graph is not restricted to whole units of A and B as is the table. Every point on the graph represents a possible combination of A and B, including fractional quantities. The slope of the graphed budget line measures the ratio of the price of B to the price of A; more precisely, the absolute value of the slope is $P_B/P_A = \$1.00/\$1.50 = \frac{2}{3}$. This is the mathematical way of saying that the consumer must forgo 2 units of A (measured on the vertical axis) to buy 3 units of B (measured on the horizontal axis). In moving down the budget or price line, 2 units of A (at \$1.50 each) must be given up to obtain 3 more units of B (at \$1 each). This yields a slope of $\frac{2}{3}$.

Note that all combinations of A and B that lie on or inside the budget line are attainable from the consumer's \$12 of

FIGURE 1 A consumer's budget line. The budget line shows all the combinations of any two products that someone can purchase, given the prices of the products and the person's money income.

Units of A (Price = \$1.50)	Units of B (Price = \$1)	Total Expenditure
8	0	\$12 (= \$12 + \$0)
6	3	\$12 (= \$9 + \$3)
4	6	\$12 (= \$6 + \$6)
2	9	\$12 (= \$3 + \$9)
0	12	\$12 (= \$0 + \$12)

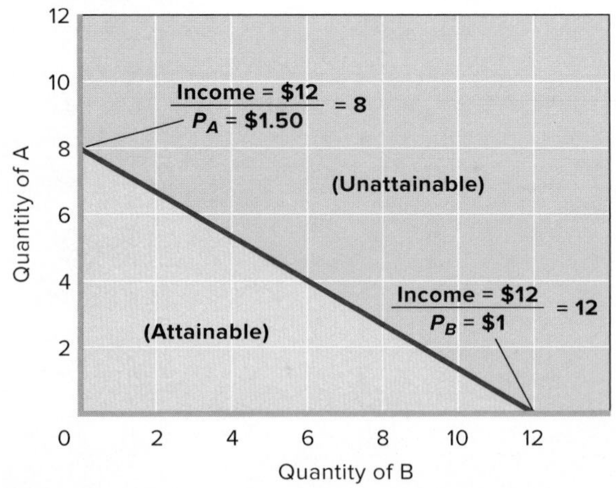

money income. He can afford to buy not only the combinations of A and B that lie along the budget line itself but also those that lie below it. He could, for instance, afford to buy 2 units of A and 4 units of B, thereby using up only \$7 (= \$3 spent on 2 units of A at a price of \$1.50 each + \$4 spent on 4 units of B at a price of \$1 each). That combination is clearly attainable because it would use up only half of the consumer's \$12 budget. But to achieve maximum utility, the consumer will want to spend the full \$12. The budget line shows all combinations that cost exactly the full \$12.

The budget line has two other significant characteristics:

- ***Income changes*** The location of the budget line varies with money income. An increase in money income shifts the budget line to the right; a decrease in money income shifts it to the left. To verify this, recalculate the table in Figure 1, assuming that money income is (a) \$24 and (b) \$6, and plot the new budget lines in Figure 1.
- ***Price changes*** A change in product prices also shifts the budget line. A decline in the prices of both products—the equivalent of an increase in real income—shifts the curve to the right. (You can verify this by recalculating the table in Figure 1 and replotting Figure 1 assuming that $P_A = \$0.75$ and $P_B = \$0.50$.) Conversely, an increase in the prices of A and B shifts the curve to the left. (Assume $P_A = \$3$ and $P_B = \$2$, and rework the table and Figure 1 to substantiate this statement.)

Note what happens if P_B changes while P_A and money income remain constant. In particular, if P_B drops, say, from \$1 to \$0.50, the lower end of the budget line fans outward to the right. Conversely, if P_B increases, say, from \$1 to \$1.50, the lower end of the line fans inward to the left. In both instances the line remains "anchored" at 8 units on the vertical axis because P_A has not changed.

Indifference Curves: What Is Preferred

Budget lines reflect "objective" market data, specifically income and prices. They reveal combinations of products A and B that can be purchased, given current money income and prices.

Indifference curves, on the other hand, reflect "subjective" information about consumer preferences for A and B. An **indifference curve** shows all the combinations of two products A and B that will yield the same total satisfaction or total utility to a consumer. The table and graph in Figure 2 present a hypothetical indifference curve for products A and B. The consumer's subjective preferences are such that he or she will realize the same total utility from each combination of A and B shown in the table or on the curve. So the consumer will be indifferent (will not care) as to which combination is actually obtained.

Indifference curves have several important characteristics.

Indifference Curves Are Downsloping An indifference curve slopes downward because more of one product means less of the other if total utility is to remain unchanged. Suppose the consumer moves from one combination of A and B to another, say, from *j* to *k* in Figure 2. In so doing, the consumer obtains more of product B, increasing his or her total utility. But because total utility is the same everywhere on the curve, the consumer must give up some of the other product, A, to reduce total utility by a precisely offsetting amount. Thus "more of B" necessitates "less of A," and the quantities of A and B are inversely related. A curve that reflects inversely related variables is downsloping.

Indifference Curves Are Convex to the Origin Recall from the appendix to Chapter 1 that the slope of a curve at a particular point is measured by drawing a straight line that is tangent to that point and then measuring the "rise over run"

FIGURE 2 A consumer's indifference curve. Every point on indifference curve *I* represents some combination of products A and B, and all those combinations are equally satisfactory to the consumer. That is, each combination of A and B on the curve yields the same total utility.

Combination	Units of A	Units of B
j	12	2
k	6	4
l	4	6
m	3	8

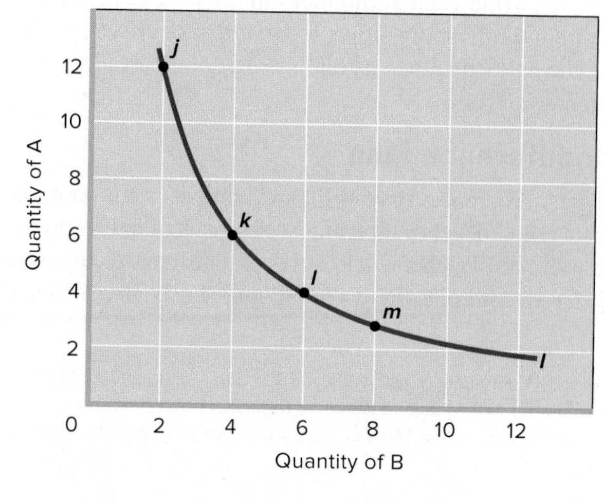

of the straight line. If you drew such straight lines for several points on the curve in Figure 2, you would find that their slopes decline (in absolute terms) as you move down the curve. An indifference curve is therefore convex (bowed inward) to the origin of the graph. Its slope diminishes or becomes flatter as we move down the curve from *j* to *k* to *l*, and so on. Technically, the slope of an indifference curve at each point measures the **marginal rate of substitution (MRS)** of the combination of two goods represented by that point. The slope or MRS shows the rate at which the consumer who possesses the combination must substitute one good for the other (say, B for A) to remain equally satisfied. The diminishing slope of the indifference curve means that the willingness to substitute B for A diminishes as more of B is obtained.

The rationale for this convexity—that is, for a diminishing MRS—is that a consumer's subjective willingness to substitute B for A (or A for B) will depend on the amounts of B and A he or she has to begin with. Consider the table and graph in Figure 2 again, beginning at point *j*. Here, in relative terms, the consumer has a substantial amount of A and very little of B. Within this combination, a unit of B is very valuable (that is, its marginal utility is high), while a unit of A is less valuable (its marginal utility is low). The consumer will then be willing to give up a substantial amount of A to get, say, 2 more units of B. In this case, the consumer is willing to forgo 6 units of A to get 2 more units of B; the MRS is $\frac{6}{2}$, or 3, for the *jk* segment of the curve.

But at point *k* the consumer has less A and more B. Here A is somewhat more valuable, and B less valuable, "at the margin." In a move from point *k* to point *l*, the consumer is willing to give up only 2 units of A to get 2 more units of B, so the MRS is only $\frac{2}{2}$, or 1. Having still less of A and more of B at point *l*, the consumer is willing to give up only 1 unit of A in return for 2 more units of B and the MRS falls to $\frac{1}{2}$ between *l* and *m*.[1]

In general, as the amount of B *increases,* the marginal utility of additional units of B *decreases*. Similarly, as the quantity of A *decreases,* its marginal utility *increases*. In Figure 2 we see that in moving down the curve, the consumer will be willing to give up smaller and smaller amounts of A to offset acquiring each additional unit of B. The result is a curve with a diminishing slope, a curve that is convex to the origin. The MRS declines as one moves southeast along the indifference curve.

The Indifference Map

The single indifference curve of Figure 2 reflects some constant (but unspecified) level of total utility or satisfaction. It is possible and useful to sketch a whole series of indifference curves or an **indifference map,** as shown in Figure 3. Each curve reflects a different level of total utility and therefore never crosses another indifference curve. Specifically, each curve to the right of our original curve (labeled I_3 in Figure 3) reflects combinations of A and B that yield more utility than I_3. Each curve to the left of I_3 reflects less total utility than I_3. As we move out from the origin, each successive indifference curve represents a higher level of utility. To demonstrate this fact, draw a line in a northeasterly direction from the origin; note that its points of intersection with successive curves entail larger amounts of both A and B and therefore higher levels of total utility.

FIGURE 3 An indifference map. An indifference map is a set of indifference curves. Curves farther from the origin indicate higher levels of total utility. Thus any combination of products A and B represented by a point on I_4 has greater total utility than any combination of A and B represented by a point on I_3, I_2, or I_1.

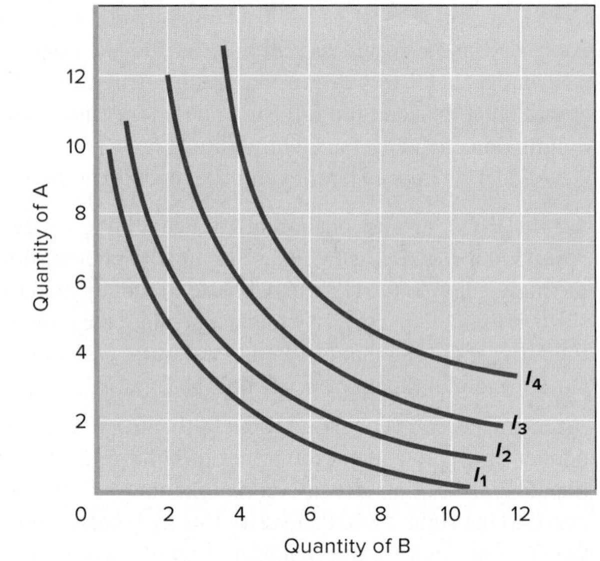

Equilibrium at Tangency

Since the axes in Figures 1 and 3 are identical, we can superimpose a budget line on the consumer's indifference map, as shown in Figure 4. By definition, the budget line indicates all the combinations of A and B that the consumer can attain with his or her money income, given the prices of A and B. Of these attainable combinations, the consumer will prefer the combination that yields the greatest satisfaction or utility. Specifically, the utility-maximizing combination will be the combination lying on the highest attainable indifference curve. It is called the consumer's **equilibrium position.**

In Figure 4 the consumer's equilibrium position is at point *X*, where the budget line is *tangent* to I_3. Why not point *Y?* Because *Y* is on a lower indifference curve, I_2. By moving "down" the budget line—by shifting dollars from purchases of A to purchases of B—the consumer can attain an indifference curve farther from the origin and thereby increase the

[1]MRS declines continuously between *j* and *k*, *k* and *l*, and *l* and *m*. Our numerical values for MRS relate to the curve segments between points and are not the actual values of the MRS at each point. For example, the MRS at point *l* is $\frac{2}{3}$.

FIGURE 4 The consumer's equilibrium position. The consumer's equilibrium position is represented by point *X*, where the black budget line is tangent to indifference curve I_3. The consumer buys 4 units of A at $1.50 per unit and 6 of B at $1 per unit with a $12 money income. Points *Z* and *Y* represent attainable combinations of A and B but yield less total utility, as is evidenced by the fact that they are on lower indifference curves. Point *W* would entail more utility than *X*, but it requires a greater income than the $12 represented by the budget line.

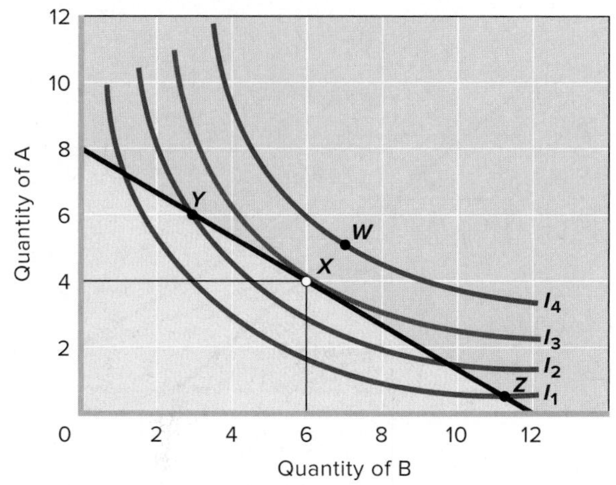

total utility derived from the same income. Why not point *Z*? For the same reason: Point *Z* is on a lower indifference curve, I_1. By moving "up" the budget line—by reallocating dollars from B to A—the consumer can get on higher indifference curve I_3 and increase total utility.

How about point *W* on indifference curve I_4? While it is true that *W* would yield a greater total utility than *X*, point *W* is beyond (outside) the budget line and hence is *not* attainable by the consumer. Point *X* represents the optimal *attainable* combination of products A and B. Note that at the equilibrium position, *X*, the definition of tangency implies that the slope of the highest attainable indifference curve equals the slope of the budget line. Because the slope of the indifference curve reflects the MRS (marginal rate of substitution) and the slope of the budget line is P_B/P_A, the consumer's optimal or equilibrium position is the point where

$$\text{MRS} = \frac{P_B}{P_A}$$

(You may benefit by trying Appendix Discussion Question 3 at this time.)

Equivalency at Equilibrium

As indicated at the beginning of this appendix, an important difference exists between the marginal-utility theory of consumer demand and the indifference curve theory. The marginal-utility theory assumes that utility is *numerically* measurable, that is, that the consumer can say how much extra utility he or she derives from each extra unit of A or B. The consumer needs that information to determine the utility-maximizing (equilibrium) position, which is defined by

$$\frac{\text{Marginal utility of A}}{\text{Price of A}} = \frac{\text{Marginal utility of B}}{\text{Price of B}}$$

The indifference curve approach imposes a less stringent requirement on the consumer. He or she need only specify whether a particular combination of A and B will yield more than, less than, or the same amount of utility as some other combination of A and B will yield. The consumer need only say, for example, that 6 of A and 7 of B will yield more (or less) satisfaction than will 4 of A and 9 of B. Indifference curve theory does not require that the consumer specify *how much* more (or less) satisfaction will be realized.

That being said, it is a remarkable mathematical fact that both models of consumer behavior will, in any given situation, point to exactly the same consumer equilibrium and, consequently, exactly the same demand behavior. This fact allows us to combine the separate pieces of information that each theory gives us about equilibrium in order to deduce an interesting property about marginal utilities that must also hold true in equilibrium. To see this, note that when we compare the equilibrium situations in the two theories, we find that in the indifference curve analysis the MRS equals P_B/P_A at equilibrium; however, in the marginal-utility approach the ratio of marginal utilities equals P_B/P_A. We therefore deduce that at equilibrium the MRS is equivalent in the marginal-utility approach to the ratio of the marginal utilities of the last purchased units of the two products.[2]

The Derivation of the Demand Curve

We noted earlier that with a fixed price for A, an increase in the price of B will cause the bottom of the budget line to fan inward to the left. We can use that fact to derive a demand curve for product B. In Figure 5a we reproduce the part of Figure 4 that shows our initial consumer equilibrium at point *X*. The budget line determining this equilibrium position assumes that money income is $12 and that P_A = $1.50 and P_B = $1. Let's see what happens to the equilibrium position when we increase P_B to $1.50 and hold both money income and the price of A constant. The result is shown in Figure 5a. The budget line fans to the left, yielding a new equilibrium point *X′* where it is tangent to lower indifference curve I_2. At *X′* the consumer buys 3 units of B and 5 of A, compared with 4 of A and 6 of B at *X*. Our interest is in B, and we now have

[2]Technical footnote: If we begin with the utility-maximizing rule, $MU_A/P_A = MU_B/P_B$, and then multiply through by P_B and divide through by MU_A, we obtain $P_B/P_A = MU_B/MU_A$. In indifference curve analysis we know that at the equilibrium position MRS = P_B/P_A. Hence, at equilibrium, MRS also equals MU_B/MU_A.

CONSIDER THIS . . .

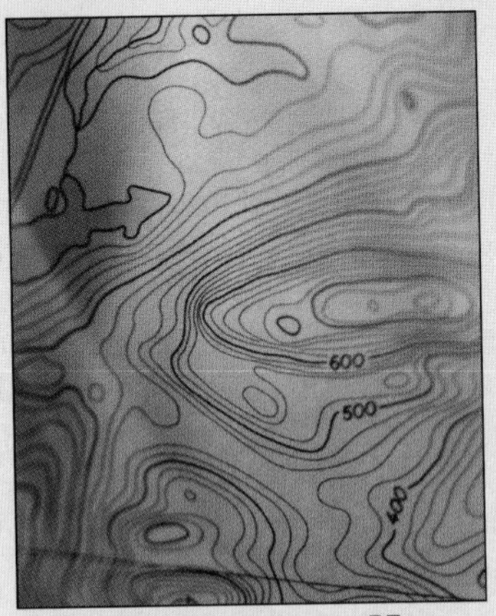

© Ryan McVay/Getty Images RF

Indifference Maps and Topographical Maps

The familiar topographical map may help you understand the idea of indifference curves and indifference maps. Each line on a topographical map represents a particular elevation above sea level, such as 500 feet. Similarly, an indifference curve represents a particular level of total utility. When you move from one point on a specific elevation line to another, the elevation remains the same. So it is with an indifference curve. A move from one position to another on the curve leaves total utility unchanged. Neither elevation lines nor indifference curves can intersect. If they did, the meaning of each line or curve would be violated. An elevation line is "an equal-elevation line"; an indifference curve is "an equal-total-utility curve."

Like the topographical map, an indifference map contains not just one line but a series of lines. That is, the topographical map may have elevation lines representing successively higher elevations of 100, 200, 300, 400, and 500 feet. Similarly, the indifference curves on the indifference map represent successively higher levels of total utility. The climber whose goal is to maximize elevation wants to get to the highest attainable elevation line; the consumer desiring to maximize total utility wants to get to the highest attainable indifference curve.

Finally, both topographical maps and indifference maps show only a few of the many such lines that could be drawn. The topographical map, for example, leaves out the elevation lines for 501 feet, 502, 503, and so on. The indifference map leaves out all the indifference curves that could be drawn between those that are displayed.

FIGURE 5 Deriving the demand curve. (a) When the price of product B is increased from \$1 to \$1.50, the equilibrium position moves from X to X', decreasing the quantity demanded of product B from 6 to 3 units. (b) The demand curve for product B is determined by plotting the \$1–6-unit and the \$1.50–3-unit price-quantity combinations for product B.

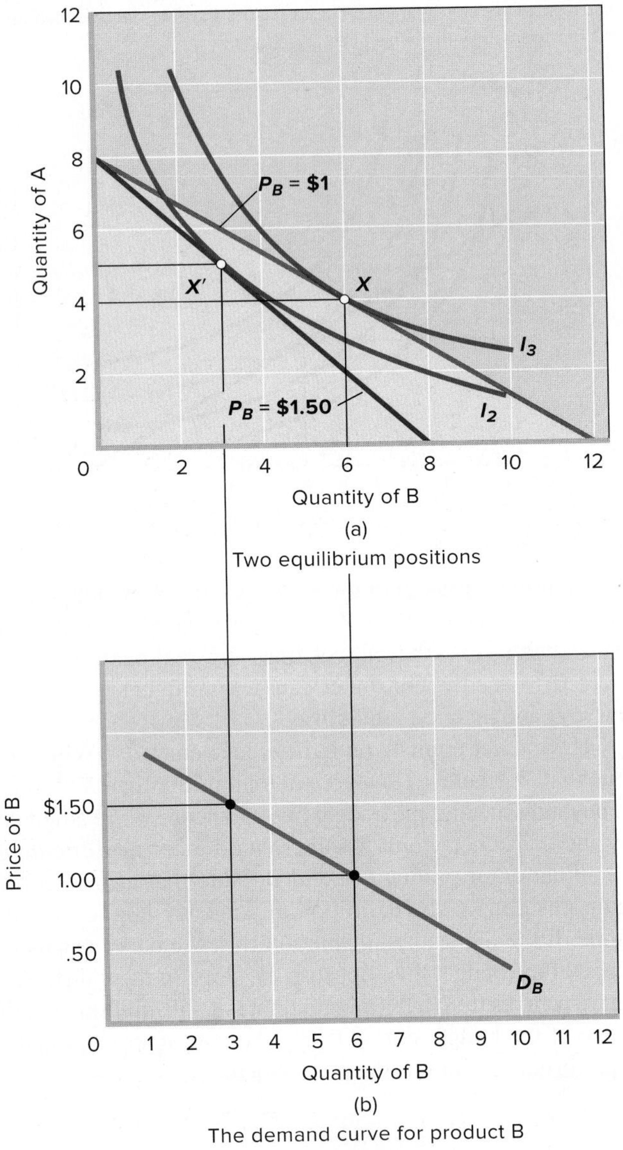

sufficient information to locate two points on the demand curve for product B. We know that at equilibrium point X the price of B is \$1 and 6 units are purchased; at equilibrium point X' the price of B is \$1.50 and 3 units are purchased.

These data are shown graphically in Figure 5b as points on the consumer's demand curve for B. Note that the horizontal axes of Figures 5a and 5b are identical; both measure the quantity demanded of B. We can therefore drop vertical reference lines from Figure 5a down to the horizontal axis of Figure 5b. On the vertical axis of Figure 5b we locate the two chosen prices of B. Knowing that these prices yield the relevant quantities demanded, we locate two points on the demand curve for B. By simple manipulation of the price of B in an indifference curve–budget line context, we have obtained a downward-sloping demand curve for B. We have thus again derived the law of demand assuming "other things equal," since only the price of B was changed (the price of A and the consumer's money income and tastes remained constant). But, in this case, we have derived the demand curve without resorting to the questionable assumption that consumers can measure utility in units called "utils." In this indifference curve approach, consumers simply compare combinations of products A and B and determine which combination they prefer, given their incomes and the prices of the two products.

APPENDIX SUMMARY

LO7.6 Relate how the indifference curve model of consumer behavior derives demand curves from budget lines, indifference curves, and utility maximization.

The indifference curve approach to consumer behavior is based on the consumer's budget line and indifference curves.

The budget line shows all combinations of two products that the consumer can purchase, given product prices and his or her money income. A change in either product prices or money income moves the budget line.

An indifference curve shows all combinations of two products that will yield the same total utility to a consumer. Indifference curves are downsloping and convex to the origin.

An indifference map consists of a number of indifference curves; the farther from the origin, the higher the total utility associated with a curve.

The consumer is in equilibrium (utility is maximized) at the point on the budget line that lies on the highest attainable indifference curve. At that point the budget line and indifference curve are tangent.

Changing the price of one product shifts the budget line and determines a new equilibrium point. A downsloping demand curve can be determined by plotting the price-quantity combinations associated with two or more equilibrium points.

APPENDIX TERMS AND CONCEPTS

budget line
indifference curve
marginal rate of substitution (MRS)
indifference map
equilibrium position

The following and additional problems can be found in connect

APPENDIX DISCUSSION QUESTIONS

1. What information is embodied in a budget line? What shifts occur in the budget line when money income (*a*) increases and (*b*) decreases? What shifts occur in the budget line when the price of the product shown on the vertical axis (*c*) increases and (*d*) decreases? LO7.6
2. What information is contained in an indifference curve? Why are such curves (*a*) downsloping and (*b*) convex to the origin? Why does total utility increase as the consumer moves to indifference curves farther from the origin? Why can't indifference curves intersect? LO7.6
3. Using Figure 4, explain why the point of tangency of the budget line with an indifference curve is the consumer's equilibrium position. Explain why any point where the budget line intersects an indifference curve is not equilibrium. Explain: "The consumer is in equilibrium where MRS = P_B/P_A." LO7.6

APPENDIX REVIEW QUESTIONS

1. Consider two bundles of coffee and chocolate and how Ted feels about them. The first bundle consists of two cups of coffee and two chocolate bars. The second bundle consists of one cup of coffee and three chocolate bars. If the first bundle gives Ted a total utility of 18 utils while the second bundle gives Ted a total utility of 19 bundles, could the two bundles be on the same indifference curve? Answer yes or no. LO7.6
2. Bill spends his money on flowers and cookies so as to maximize his total utility. Both flowers and cookies start off costing $2 each. At that price, Bill buys three flowers and two cookies. When the price of flowers is lowered to $1, Bill buys eight flowers and one cookie. Which of the following statements about Bill's reaction to the price change is **not** true? LO7.6
   a. Bill's budget line shifted outward when the price of flowers fell.
   b. Bill moved to a higher indifference curve after the price of flowers fell.
   c. Bill's demand curve for flowers shifted to the right.
   d. Bill's attainable set was smaller before the price of flowers fell.

APPENDIX PROBLEMS

1. Assume that the data in the following table give an indifference curve for Mr. Chen. Graph this curve, putting A on the vertical axis and B on the horizontal axis. Assuming that the prices of A and B are \$1.50 and \$1, respectively, and that Mr. Chen has \$24 to spend, add his budget line to your graph. What combination of A and B will Mr. Chen purchase? Does your answer meet the MRS = P_B/P_A rule for equilibrium? **LO7.6**

Units of A	Units of B
16	6
12	8
8	12
4	24

2. Explain graphically how indifference analysis can be used to derive a demand curve. **LO7.6**
3. **ADVANCED ANALYSIS** First, graphically illustrate a doubling of income without price changes in the indifference curve model. Next, on the same graph, show a situation in which the person whose indifference curves you are drawing buys considerably more of good B than good A after the income increase. What can you conclude about the relative coefficients of the income elasticity of demand for goods A and B (Chapter 6)? **LO7.6**

Part FOUR

AP

Microeconomics of Product Markets

We begin our study of the supply side of the market in Part IV. We see how businesses or firms are organized and strive to make economic profit. With Chapter 8, a firm's costs of production are analyzed, with particular attention to use of the factors of production: labor, capital (machinery), land, and other resources. We differentiate between short-run and long-run production and costs. Of particular importance is the use of opportunity costs or implicit costs for a firm in assessing performance, allowing us to differentiate between ***accounting profits*** and the more important (for decision making) ***economic profits***.

The preponderance of Part IV (Chapters 9–13) deals with how a firm operates in different types of product markets. We begin with perfect competition, with many firms and a standard product, as our reference case. The allocative and productive efficiency of perfect competition is highlighted here. Other market structures are differentiated by the number of producers (e.g., monopoly with only one firm and oligopoly with only a few firms) or by a differentiated product (e.g., monopolistic competition). The economic inefficiency and challenges of these other market structures are highlighted.

8 Chapter

Businesses and the Costs of Production

Learning Objectives

LO8.1 **Explain why economic costs include both explicit (revealed and expressed) costs and implicit (present but not obvious) costs.**

LO8.2 **Relate the law of diminishing returns to a firm's short-run production costs.**

LO8.3 **Describe the distinctions between fixed and variable costs and among total, average, and marginal costs.**

LO8.4 **Use economies of scale to link a firm's size and its average costs in the long run.**

LO8.5 **Give business examples of short-run costs, economies of scale, and minimum efficient scale (MES).**

AP Chapter Focus

Our attention now turns from the behavior of consumers to the behavior of producers. This chapter begins the discussion of a foundational set of concepts regarding production and producer costs. In market economies, a wide variety of businesses produce an even wider variety of goods and services. Firms require economic resources in order to produce products. In obtaining and using resources, a firm makes monetary payments to resource owners (for example, workers) and incurs opportunity costs when using resources it already owns (for example, entrepreneurial talent). Those payments and opportunity costs make up the firm's costs of production.

Then, in the next several chapters, the previously learned concepts of product demand, product prices, and revenue will be merged back into the analysis with the concepts discussed. We will discuss how firms compare revenues and costs in determining how much to produce. Our ultimate purpose is to show how those comparisons relate to economic efficiency, a central idea in the study of microeconomics.

AP Economic Costs

LO8.1 Explain why economic costs include both explicit (revealed and expressed) costs and implicit (present but not obvious) costs.

Firms face costs because the resources they need to produce their products are scarce and have alternative uses. Because of scarcity, firms wanting a particular resource have to bid it away from other firms. That process is costly for firms because it requires a payment to the resource owner. This reality causes economists to define an **economic cost** as the payment that must be made to obtain and retain the services of a resource. It is the income the firm must provide to resource suppliers to attract resources away from alternative uses.

This section explains how firms incorporate opportunity costs to calculate economic costs. If you need a refresher on opportunity costs, a brief review of the section on opportunity costs in Chapter 1 might be useful before continuing on with the rest of this section.

Explicit and Implicit Costs

To properly calculate a firm's economic costs, you must remember that each of the resources used by the firm has an opportunity cost. This is true both for the resources that a firm purchases from outsiders as well as for the resources that it already owns.

As an example, consider a table-making firm that starts this month with $5,000 in cash as well as ownership of a small oak forest from which it gets the oak that it turns into tables.

Suppose that during the month the firm uses the entire $5,000 of cash to pay its workers. Clearly, the $5,000 it spends purchasing their labor comes at the opportunity cost of forgoing the best alternatives that could have been bought with that money.

Less obvious, however, is the opportunity cost of the oak that the firm grows itself and which it uses to make tables. Suppose that the oak has a market value of $1,500, meaning that our table-making firm could sell it to outsiders for $1,500. This implies that using the oak to make tables has an opportunity cost of $1,500. Choosing to convert the oak into tables means giving up the best alternatives that the firm could have purchased with the $1,500.

As a result, keep in mind that *all* of the resources that a firm uses—whether purchased from outside or already owned—have opportunity costs and thus economic costs. Economists refer to these two types of economic costs as *explicit costs* and *implicit costs*:

- A firm's **explicit costs** are the monetary payments it makes to those from whom it must purchase resources that it does not own. Because these costs involve an obvious cash transaction, they are referred to as explicit costs. Be sure to remember that explicit costs are opportunity costs because every monetary payment used to purchase outside resources necessarily involves forgoing the best alternatives that could have been purchased with the money.
- A firm's **implicit costs** are the opportunity costs of using the resources that it already owns to make the firm's own product rather than selling those resources to outsiders for cash. Because these costs are present but not obvious, they are referred to as implicit costs.

A firm's economic costs are the sum of its explicit costs and its implicit costs:

$$\text{Economic costs} = \text{Explicit costs} + \text{Implicit costs}$$

The following example makes clear how both explicit costs and implicit costs affect firm profits and firm behavior.

Accounting Profit and Normal Profit

Suppose that after many years working as a sales representative for a large T-shirt manufacturer, you decide to strike out on your own. After considering many potential business ventures, you settle on opening a retail T-shirt shop. As we explain in Chapter 2, you will be providing two different economic resources to your new enterprise: labor and entrepreneurial ability. The part of your job that involves providing labor includes any of the routine tasks that are needed to help run the business—things like answering customer e-mails, taking inventory, and sweeping the floor. The part of your job that involves providing entrepreneurial ability includes any of the nonroutine tasks involved with organizing the business and directing its strategy—things like deciding on whether to use Internet ads or in-person events to promote your business, whether to include children's clothing in your product mix, and how to decorate your store to maximize its appeal to potential customers.

You begin providing entrepreneurial ability to your new firm by making some initial organizational decisions. You decide to work full time at your new business, so you quit your old job that paid you $22,000 per year. You invest $20,000 of savings that has been earning $1,000 per year. You decide that your new firm will occupy a small retail space that you own and had been previously renting out for $5,000 per year. Finally, you decide to hire one clerk to help you in the store. She agrees to work for you for $18,000 per year.

After a year in business, you total up your accounts and find the following:

Total sales revenue		$120,000
Cost of T-shirts	$40,000	
Clerk's salary	18,000	
Utilities	5,000	
Total (explicit) costs		63,000
Accounting profit		57,000

These numbers look very good. In particular, you are happy with your $57,000 **accounting profit,** the profit number that accountants calculate by subtracting total explicit costs from total sales revenue. This is the profit (or "net income") that would appear on your accounting statement and that you would report to the government for tax purposes.

But don't celebrate yet! Your $57,000 accounting profit overstates the economic success of your business because it ignores your implicit costs. Success is not defined as "having a total sales revenue that exceeds total explicit costs." Rather, the true measure of success is doing as well as you possibly can—that is, making more money in your new venture selling T-shirts than you could pursuing any other business venture.

To figure out whether you are achieving that goal, you must take into account all of your opportunity costs—both your implicit costs as well as your explicit costs. Doing so will indicate whether your new business venture is earning more money than what you could have earned in any other business venture.

To see how these calculations are made, let's continue with our example.

By providing your own financial capital, retail space, and labor, you incurred three different implicit costs during the year: $1,000 of forgone interest, $5,000 of forgone rent, and $22,000 of forgone wages. But don't forget that there is another implicit cost that you must also take account of—how much income you chose to forgo by applying your entrepreneurial abilities to your current retail T-shirt venture rather than applying them to other potential business ventures.

But what dollar value should we place on the size of the profits that you might have made if you had provided your entrepreneurial ability to one of those other ventures?

The answer is given by estimating a **normal profit,** the typical (or "normal") amount of accounting profit that you would most likely have earned in one of these other ventures. For the sake of argument, let us assume that with your particular set of skills and talents your entrepreneurial abilities would have on average yielded a normal profit of $5,000 in one of the other potential ventures. Knowing that value, we can take all of your implicit costs properly into account by subtracting them from your accounting profit:

Accounting profit		$57,000
Forgone interest	$ 1,000	
Forgone rent	5,000	
Forgone wages	22,000	
Forgone entrepreneurial income	5,000	
Total implicit costs		33,000
Economic profit		24,000

Economic Profit

After subtracting your $33,000 of implicit costs from your accounting profit of $57,000, we are left with an *economic profit* of $24,000.

Please distinguish clearly between accounting profit and economic profit. Accounting profit is the result of subtracting only explicit costs from revenue: *Accounting Profit = Revenue – Explicit Costs*. By contrast, **economic profit** is the result of subtracting all of your economic costs—both explicit costs and implicit costs—from revenue: *Economic Profit = Revenue – Explicit Costs – Implicit Costs*.

By subtracting *all* of your economic costs from your revenue, you determine how your current business venture compares with your best alternative business venture. In our example, the fact that you are generating an economic profit of $24,000 means that you are making $24,000 more than you could expect to make in your best alternative business venture.

By contrast, suppose that you had instead done poorly in business, so that this year your firm generated an economic loss (a negative economic profit) of $8,000. This would mean that you were doing worse in your current venture than you could have done in your best alternative venture. You would, as a result, wish to switch to that alternative.

Generalizing this point, we see that there is an important behavioral threshold at $0 of economic profit. If a firm is breaking even (that is, earning exactly $0 of economic profit), then its entrepreneurs know that they are doing exactly as well as they could expect to do in their best alternative business venture. They are earning enough to cover all their explicit and implicit costs, including the normal profit that they could expect to earn in other business ventures. Thus, they have no incentive to change. By contrast, anyone running a positive economic profit knows they are doing better than they could in alternative ventures and will want to continue doing what they are doing or maybe even expand their business. And anyone running an economic loss (a negative economic profit) knows that they could do better by switching to something else.

It is for this reason that economists focus on economic profits rather than accounting profits. Simply put, economic profits direct how resources are allocated in the economy. Entrepreneurs running economic losses close their current businesses, thereby liberating the land, labor, capital, and entrepreneurial ability that they had been using. These resources are freed up to be used by firms that are generating positive economic profits or that are at least breaking even. Resources thus flow from producing goods and services with lower net benefits toward producing goods and services with higher net benefits. Allocative efficiency increases as firms are led by their profit signals to produce more of what consumers want the most.

Figure 8.1 shows the relationship among the various cost and profit concepts that we have just discussed. To test

FIGURE 8.1 Economic profit versus accounting profit. Economic profit is equal to total revenue less economic costs. Economic costs are the sum of explicit and implicit costs and include a normal profit to the entrepreneur. Accounting profit is equal to total revenue less accounting (explicit) costs.

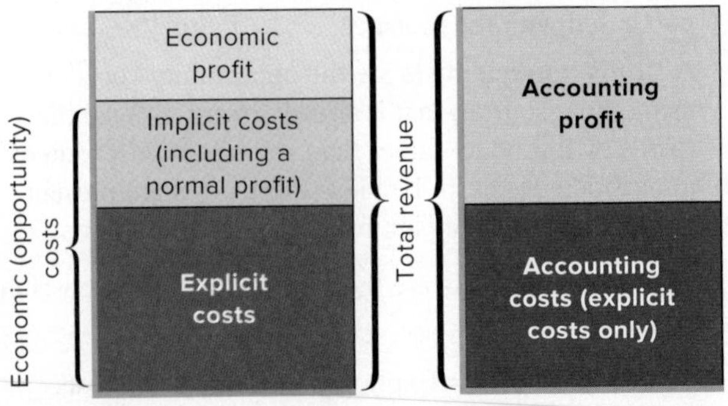

yourself, you might want to enter the cost numbers used in our example in the appropriate blocks.

Short Run and Long Run

When the demand for a firm's product changes, the firm's profitability may depend on how quickly it can adjust the amounts of the various resources it employs. It can easily and quickly adjust the quantities employed of many resources such as hourly labor, raw materials, fuel, and power. It needs much more time, however, to adjust its *plant capacity*—the size of the factory building, the amount of machinery and equipment, and other capital resources. In some heavy industries such as aircraft manufacturing, a firm may need several years to alter plant capacity. Because of these differences in adjustment time, economists find it useful to distinguish between two conceptual periods: the short run and the long run. We will discover that costs differ in these two time periods.

Short Run: Fixed Plant In microeconomics, the **short run** is a period too brief for a firm to alter its plant capacity, yet long enough to permit a change in the degree to which the plant's current capacity is used. The firm's plant capacity is fixed in the short run. However, the firm can vary its output by applying larger or smaller amounts of labor, materials, and other resources to that plant. It can use its existing plant capacity more or less intensively in the short run.

Long Run: Variable Plant In microeconomics, the **long run** is a period long enough for a firm to adjust the quantities of all the resources that it employs, including plant capacity. From the industry's viewpoint, the long run also includes enough time for existing firms to dissolve and leave the industry or for new firms to be created and enter the industry. While the short run is a "fixed-plant" period, the long run is a "variable-plant" period.

Illustrations If Boeing hires 100 extra workers for one of its commercial airline plants or adds an entire shift of workers, we are speaking of the short run. If it adds a new production facility and installs more equipment, we are referring to the long run. The first situation is a *short-run adjustment;* the second is a *long-run adjustment.*

The short run and the long run are conceptual periods rather than calendar time periods. In light-manufacturing industries, changes in plant capacity may be accomplished almost overnight. A small T-shirt manufacturer can increase its plant capacity in a matter of days by ordering and installing two or three new cutting tables and several extra sewing machines. But for heavy industry the long run is a different matter. Shell Oil may need several years to construct a new gasoline refinery.

AP QUICK REVIEW 8.1

- ✓ Explicit costs are the money payments a firm makes, such as for wages or materials. Implicit costs are the opportunity costs associated with a firm's use of resources it owns.
- ✓ Accounting profit is calculated by subtracting total explicit costs, including deprecation of capital resources, from total sales revenue. Economic profit is total revenue less all explicit and implicit costs.
- ✓ In the short run, a firm's plant capacity is fixed, and it can only vary output by adjusting one input, typically labor. In the long run, a firm can alter the use of all inputs, including capital or plant size, and firms can enter or leave the industry.

AP Short-Run Production Relationships

LO8.2 Relate the law of diminishing returns to a firm's short-run production costs.

A firm's costs of producing a specific output depend on both the prices and the quantities of the resources (inputs) needed to produce that output. Resource supply and demand determine resource prices. The technological aspects of production, specifically the relationships between inputs and output, determine the quantities of resources needed. Our focus will be on the *labor*-output relationship, given a fixed plant capacity. But before examining that relationship, we need to define three terms:

- **Total product (TP)** is the total quantity, or total output, of a particular good or service produced.
- **Marginal product (MP)** is the extra output or added product associated with adding a unit of a variable resource, in this case labor, to the production process. Thus,

$$\text{Marginal product} = \frac{\text{change in total product}}{\text{change in labor input}}$$

- **Average product (AP),** also called labor productivity, is output per unit of labor input:

$$\text{Average product} = \frac{\text{total product}}{\text{units of labor}}$$

In the short run, a firm can for a time increase its output by adding units of labor to its fixed plant. But by how much will output rise when it adds more labor? And why do we say "for a time"?

Law of Diminishing Returns

The answers are provided in general terms by the **law of diminishing returns.** This law assumes that technology is fixed and thus the techniques of production do not change. It states that as successive units of a variable resource (say, labor) are added to a fixed resource (say, capital or land), beyond some point the extra, or marginal, product that can be attributed to each additional unit of the variable resource will decline. For example, if additional workers are hired to work with a constant amount of capital equipment, output will eventually rise by smaller and smaller amounts as more workers are hired.

Rationale Suppose a farmer has a fixed resource—80 acres of land—planted in corn. If the farmer does not cultivate the cornfields (clear the weeds) at all, the yield will be 40 bushels per acre. If he cultivates the land once, output may rise to 50 bushels per acre. A second cultivation may increase output to 57 bushels per acre, a third to 61, and a fourth to 63. Succeeding cultivations will add less and less to the land's yield. If this were not so, the world's needs for corn could be fulfilled by extremely intense cultivation of this single 80-acre plot of land. Indeed, if diminishing returns did not occur, the world could be fed out of a flowerpot. Why not? Just keep adding more seed, fertilizer, and harvesters!

The law of diminishing returns also holds true in nonagricultural industries. Assume a wood shop is manufacturing furniture frames. It has a specific amount of equipment such as lathes, planes, saws, and sanders. If this shop hired just one or two workers, total output and productivity (output per worker) would be very low. The workers would have to perform many different jobs, and the advantages of specialization would not be realized. Time would be lost in switching from one job to another, and machines would stand idle much of the time. In short, the plant would be understaffed, and production would be inefficient because there would be too much capital relative to the amount of labor.

The shop could eliminate those difficulties by hiring more workers. Then the equipment would be more fully used, and workers could specialize on doing a single job. Time would no longer be lost switching from job to job. As more workers were added, production would become more efficient and the marginal product of each succeeding worker would rise.

But the rise could not go on indefinitely. Beyond a certain point, adding more workers would cause overcrowding. Since workers would then have to wait in line to use the machinery, they would be underused. Total output would increase at a diminishing rate because, given the fixed size of the plant, each worker would have less capital equipment to work with as more and more labor was hired. The marginal product of additional workers would decline because there would be more labor in proportion to the fixed amount of capital. Eventually, adding still more workers would cause so much congestion that marginal product would become negative and total product would decline. At the extreme, the addition of more and more labor would exhaust all the standing room, and total product would fall to zero.

CONSIDER THIS . . .

Source: © BananaStock/JupiterImages RF

Diminishing Returns from Study

Here is a noneconomic example of a relationship between "inputs" and "output" that may help you better understand the idea of diminishing returns. Suppose for an individual that

Total course learning = *f* (intelligence, quality of course materials, instructor effectiveness, class time, and study time)

where *f* means "function of" or "depends on." So this relationship supposes that total course learning depends on intelligence (however defined), quality of course materials such as the textbook, the effectiveness of the instructor, the amount of class time, and the amount of personal study time outside the class.

For analytical purposes, let's assume that one's intelligence, the quality of course materials, the effectiveness of the instructor, and the amount of class time are *fixed*—meaning they do not change over the length of the course. Now let's add units of study time per day over the length of the course to "produce" greater course learning. The first hour of study time per day increases total course learning. Will the second hour enhance course learning by as much as the first? By how much will the third, fourth, fifth, . . . fifteenth hour of study per day contribute to total course learning relative to the *immediate previous hour*?

We think you will agree that eventually diminishing returns to course learning will set in as successive hours of study are added each day. At some point the marginal product of an extra hour of study time will decline and, at some further point, become zero.

This is also true of production relationships within firms. As successive units of a variable input (say, labor) are added to a fixed input (say, capital), the marginal product of the variable input eventually declines. In short, diminishing returns will occur sooner or later. Total product eventually will rise at a diminishing rate, reach a maximum, and then decline.

Note that the law of diminishing returns assumes that all units of labor are of equal quality. Each successive worker is presumed to have the same innate ability, motor coordination, education, training, and work experience. Marginal product ultimately diminishes, but not because successive workers are less skilled or less energetic. It declines because the firm is using more workers relative to the amount of plant and equipment available.

TABLE 8.1 Total, Marginal, and Average Product: The Law of Diminishing Returns

(1) Units of the Variable Resource (Labor)	(2) Total Product (TP)	(3) Marginal Product (MP), Change in (2)/ Change in (1)		(4) Average Product (AP), (2)/(1)
0	0			—
1	10	10	Increasing marginal returns	10.00
2	25	15		12.50
3	45	20		15.00
4	60	15	Diminishing marginal returns	15.00
5	70	10		14.00
6	75	5		12.50
7	75	0	Negative marginal returns	10.71
8	70	−5		8.75

Tabular Example Table 8.1 is a numerical illustration of the law of diminishing returns. Column 2 shows the total product, or total output, resulting from combining each level of a variable input (labor) in column 1 with a fixed amount of capital.

Column 3 shows the marginal product (MP), the change in total product associated with each additional unit of labor. Note that with no labor input, total product is zero; a plant with no workers will produce no output. The first three units of labor generate increasing marginal returns, with marginal products of 10, 15, and 20 units, respectively. But beginning with the fourth unit of labor, marginal product diminishes continuously, becoming zero with the seventh unit of labor and negative with the eighth.

Average product, or output per labor unit, is shown in column 4. It is calculated by dividing total product (column 2) by the number of labor units needed to produce it (column 1). At 5 units of labor, for example, AP is 14 (= 70/5).

Graphical Portrayal **Figure 8.2 (Key Graph)** shows the diminishing-returns data in Table 8.1 graphically and further clarifies the relationships between total, marginal, and average products. (Marginal product in Figure 8.2b is plotted halfway between the units of labor since it applies to the addition of each labor unit.)

Note first in Figure 8.2a that total product, TP, goes through three phases: It rises initially at an increasing rate; then it increases, but at a diminishing rate; finally, after reaching a maximum, it declines.

Geometrically, marginal product—shown by the MP curve in Figure 8.2b—is the slope of the total-product curve. Marginal product measures the change in total product associated with each succeeding unit of labor. Thus, the three phases of total product are also reflected in marginal product. Where total product is increasing at an increasing rate, marginal product is rising. Here, extra units of labor are adding larger and larger amounts to total product. Similarly, where total product is increasing but at a decreasing rate, marginal product is positive but falling. Each additional unit of labor adds less to total product than did the previous unit. When total product is at a maximum, marginal product is zero. When total product declines, marginal product becomes negative.

Average product, AP (Figure 8.2b), displays the same tendencies as marginal product. It increases, reaches a maximum, and then decreases as more and more units of labor are added to the fixed plant. But note the relationship between marginal product and average product: Where marginal product exceeds average product, average product rises. And where marginal product is less than average product, average product declines. It follows that marginal product intersects average product where average product is at a maximum.

This relationship is a mathematical necessity. If you add a larger number to a total than the current average of that total, the average must rise. And if you add a smaller number to a total than the current average of that total, the average must fall. You raise your average examination grade only when your score on an additional (marginal) examination is greater than the average of all your past scores. You lower your average when your grade on an additional exam is below your current average. In our production example, when the amount an extra worker adds to total product exceeds the average product of all workers currently employed, average product will rise. Conversely, when the amount an extra worker adds to total product is less than the current average product, average product will decrease.

The law of diminishing returns is embodied in the shapes of all three curves. But, as our definition of the law of diminishing returns indicates, economists are most concerned with its effects on marginal product. The regions of increasing, diminishing, and negative marginal product (returns) are shown in Figure 8.2b.

AP KEY GRAPH

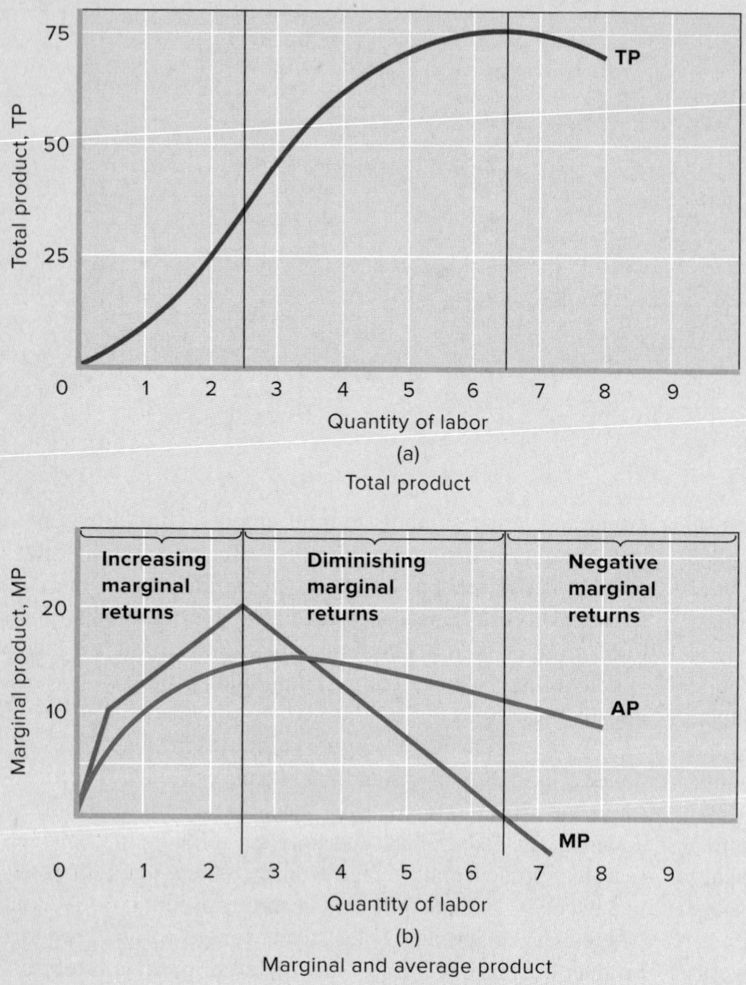

FIGURE 8.2 The law of diminishing returns. (a) As a variable resource (labor) is added to fixed amounts of other resources (land or capital), the total product that results will eventually increase by diminishing amounts, reach a maximum, and then decline. (b) Marginal product is the change in total product associated with each new unit of labor. Average product is simply output per labor unit. Note that marginal product intersects average product at the maximum average product.

QUICK QUIZ FOR FIGURE 8.2

1. Which of the following is an assumption underlying these figures?
- **a.** Firms first hire "better" workers and then hire "poorer" workers.
- **b.** Capital and labor are both variable, but labor increases more rapidly than capital.
- **c.** Consumers will buy all the output (total product) produced.
- **d.** Workers are of equal quality.

2. Marginal product is:
- **a.** the change in total product divided by the change in the quantity of labor.
- **b.** total product divided by the quantity of labor.
- **c.** always positive.
- **d.** unrelated to total product.

3. Marginal product in graph (b) is zero when:
- **a.** average product in graph (b) stops rising.
- **b.** the slope of the marginal-product curve in graph (b) is zero.
- **c.** total product in graph (a) begins to rise at a diminishing rate.
- **d.** the slope of the total-product curve in graph (a) is zero.

4. Average product in graph (b):
- **a.** rises when it is less than marginal product.
- **b.** is the change in total product divided by the change in the quantity of labor.
- **c.** can never exceed marginal product.
- **d.** falls whenever total product in graph (a) rises at a diminishing rate.

Answers: 1. d; 2. a; 3. d; 4. a

AP Short-Run Production Costs

LO8.3 Describe the distinctions between fixed and variable costs and among total, average, and marginal costs.

Production information such as that provided in Table 8.1 and Figures 8.2a and 8.2b must be coupled with resource prices to determine the total and per-unit costs of producing various levels of output. We know that in the short run, resources associated with the firm's plant are fixed. Other resources, however, are variable in the short run. As a result, short-run costs can be either fixed or variable.

Fixed, Variable, and Total Costs

Let's see what distinguishes fixed costs, variable costs, and total costs from one another.

Fixed Costs **Fixed costs** are those costs that do not vary with changes in output. Fixed costs are associated with the very existence of a firm's plant and therefore must be paid even if its output is zero. Such costs as rental payments, interest on a firm's debts, a portion of depreciation on equipment and buildings, and insurance premiums are generally fixed costs; they are fixed and do not change even if a firm produces more. In column 2 of Table 8.2 we assume that the firm's total fixed cost is $100. By definition, this fixed cost is incurred at all levels of output, including zero. The firm cannot avoid paying fixed costs in the short run.

Variable Costs **Variable costs** are those costs that change with the level of output. They include payments for materials, fuel, power, transportation services, most labor, and similar variable resources. In column 3 of Table 8.2 we find that the total of variable costs changes directly with output. But note that the increases in variable cost associated with succeeding one-unit increases in output are not equal. As production begins, variable cost will for a time increase by a decreasing amount; this is true through the fourth unit of output in Table 8.2. Beyond the fourth unit, however, variable cost rises by increasing amounts for succeeding units of output.

The reason lies in the shape of the marginal-product curve. At first, as in Figure 8.2b, marginal product is increasing, so smaller and smaller increases in the amounts of variable resources are needed to produce successive units of output. Hence the variable cost of successive units of output decreases. But when, as diminishing returns are encountered, marginal product begins to decline, larger and larger additional amounts of variable resources are needed to produce successive units of output. Total variable cost therefore increases by increasing amounts.

Total Cost **Total cost** is the sum of fixed cost and variable cost at each level of output:

$$TC = TFC + TVC$$

TC is shown in column 4 of Table 8.2. At zero units of output, total cost is equal to the firm's fixed cost. Then for each unit of the 10 units of production, total cost increases by the same amount as variable cost.

Figure 8.3 shows graphically the fixed-, variable-, and total-cost data given in Table 8.2. Observe that total variable cost, TVC, is measured vertically from the horizontal axis at each level of output. The amount of fixed cost, shown as

TABLE 8.2 Total-, Average-, and Marginal-Cost Schedules for an Individual Firm in the Short Run

	Total-Cost Data			Average-Cost Data			Marginal Cost
(1) Total Product (Q)	(2) Total Fixed Cost (TFC)	(3) Total Variable Cost (TVC)	(4) Total Cost (TC) $TC = TFC + TVC$	(5) Average Fixed Cost (AFC) $AFC = \frac{TFC}{Q}$	(6) Average Variable Cost (AVC) $AVC = \frac{TVC}{Q}$	(7) Average Total Cost (ATC) $ATC = \frac{TC}{Q}$	(8) Marginal Cost (MC) $MC = \frac{\text{change in TC}}{\text{change in Q}}$
0	$100	$ 0	$ 100				$ 90
1	100	90	190	$100.00	$90.00	$190.00	80
2	100	170	270	50.00	85.00	135.00	70
3	100	240	340	33.33	80.00	113.33	60
4	100	300	400	25.00	75.00	100.00	70
5	100	370	470	20.00	74.00	94.00	80
6	100	450	550	16.67	75.00	91.67	90
7	100	540	640	14.29	77.14	91.43	110
8	100	650	750	12.50	81.25	93.75	130
9	100	780	880	11.11	86.67	97.78	150
10	100	930	1,030	10.00	93.00	103.00	

FIGURE 8.3 Total cost is the sum of fixed cost and variable cost. Total variable cost (TVC) changes with output. Total fixed cost (TFC) is independent of the level of output. The total cost (TC) at any output is the vertical sum of the fixed cost and variable cost at that output.

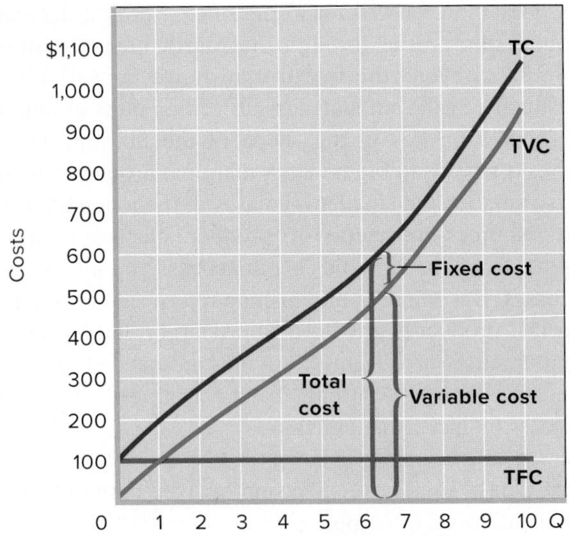

TFC, is added vertically to the total-variable-cost curve to obtain the points on the total-cost curve TC.

The distinction between fixed and variable costs is significant to the business manager. Variable costs can be controlled or altered in the short run by changing production levels. Fixed costs are beyond the business manager's current control; they are incurred in the short run and must be paid regardless of output level.

Per-Unit, or Average, Costs

Producers are certainly interested in their total costs, but they are equally concerned with per-unit, or average, costs. In particular, average-cost data are more meaningful for making comparisons with product price, which is always stated on a per-unit basis. Average fixed cost, average variable cost, and average total cost are shown in columns 5 to 7, Table 8.2.

AFC **Average fixed cost (AFC)** for any output level is found by dividing total fixed cost (TFC) by that amount of output (Q). That is,

$$\text{AFC} = \frac{\text{TFC}}{Q}$$

Because the total fixed cost is, by definition, the same regardless of output, AFC must decline as output increases. As output rises, the total fixed cost is spread over a larger and larger output. When output is just 1 unit in Table 8.2, TFC and AFC are the same at \$100. But at 2 units of output, the total fixed cost of \$100 becomes \$50 of AFC or fixed cost per unit; then it becomes \$33.33 per unit as \$100 is spread over 3 units, and \$25 per unit when spread over 4 units. This process is sometimes referred to as "spreading the overhead." Figure 8.4 shows that AFC graphs as a continuously declining curve as total output is increased.

AVC **Average variable cost (AVC)** for any output level is calculated by dividing total variable cost (TVC) by that amount of output (Q):

$$\text{AVC} = \frac{\text{TVC}}{Q}$$

Due to increasing and then diminishing returns, AVC declines initially, reaches a minimum, and then increases again. A graph of AVC is a U-shaped or saucer-shaped curve, as shown in Figure 8.4.

Because total variable cost reflects the law of diminishing returns, so must AVC, which is derived from total variable cost. Because marginal returns increase initially, fewer and fewer additional variable resources are needed to produce each of the first four units of output. As a result, variable cost per unit declines. AVC hits a minimum with the fifth unit of output, and beyond that point AVC rises as diminishing returns require more and more variable resources to produce each additional unit of output.

Rephrased, production is relatively inefficient—and therefore costly—at low levels of output. Because the firm's fixed plant is understaffed, average variable cost is relatively high. As output expands, however, greater specialization and better use of the firm's capital equipment yield more efficiency, and variable cost per unit of output declines. As still more variable resources are added, a point is reached where crowding causes diminishing returns to set in. Once diminishing returns start, each additional unit of input does not

FIGURE 8.4 The average-cost curves. AFC falls as a given amount of fixed costs is apportioned over a larger and larger output. AVC initially falls because of increasing marginal returns but then rises because of diminishing marginal returns. Average total cost (ATC) is the vertical sum of average variable cost (AVC) and average fixed cost (AFC).

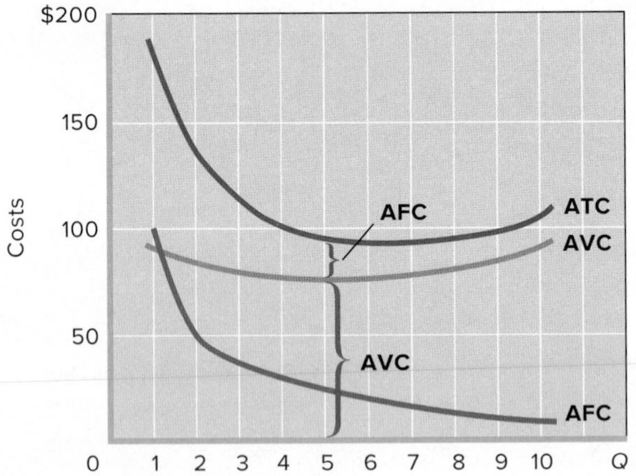

increase output by as much as preceding units did. This means that AVC eventually increases.

You can verify the U or saucer shape of the AVC curve by returning to Table 8.1. Assume the price of labor is \$10 per unit. Labor cost per unit of output is then \$10 (the price per labor unit in this example) divided by average product (output per labor unit). Because we have assumed labor to be the only variable input, the labor cost per unit of output is the variable cost per unit of output, or AVC. When average product is initially low, AVC is high. As workers are added, average product rises and AVC falls. When average product is at its maximum, AVC is at its minimum. Then, as still more workers are added and average product declines, AVC rises. The "hump" of the average-product curve is reflected in the saucer or U shape of the AVC curve. As you will soon see, the two are mirror images of each other.

ATC **Average total cost (ATC)** for any output level is found by dividing total cost (TC) by that output (Q) or by adding AFC and AVC at that output:

$$\text{ATC} = \frac{\text{TC}}{Q} = \frac{\text{TFC}}{Q} + \frac{\text{TVC}}{Q} = \text{AFC} + \text{AVC}$$

Graphically, ATC can be found by adding vertically the AFC and AVC curves, as in Figure 8.4. Thus the vertical distance between the ATC and AVC curves measures AFC at any level of output.

Marginal Cost

One final and very crucial cost concept remains: **Marginal cost (MC)** is the extra, or additional, cost of producing one more unit of output. MC can be determined for each added unit of output by noting the change in total cost entailed by that unit's production:

$$\text{MC} = \frac{\text{change in TC}}{\text{change in } Q}$$

Calculations In column 4 of Table 8.2, production of the first unit of output increases total cost from \$100 to \$190. Therefore, the additional, or marginal, cost of that first unit is \$90 (column 8). The marginal cost of the second unit is \$80 (= \$270 − \$190); the MC of the third is \$70 (= \$340 − \$270); and so forth. The MC for each of the 10 units of output is shown in column 8.

MC can also be calculated from the total-variable-cost column because the only difference between total cost and total variable cost is the constant amount of fixed costs (\$100). Thus, the change in total cost and the change in total variable cost associated with each additional unit of output are always the same.

Marginal Decisions Marginal costs are costs the firm can control directly and immediately. Specifically, MC designates all the cost incurred in producing the last unit of output. Thus, it also designates the cost that can be "saved" by not producing that last unit. Average-cost figures do not provide this information. For example, suppose the firm is undecided whether to produce 3 or 4 units of output. At 4 units Table 8.2 indicates that ATC is \$100. But the firm does not increase its total costs by \$100 by producing the fourth unit, nor does it save \$100 by not producing that unit. Rather, the change in costs involved here is only \$60, as the MC column in Table 8.2 reveals.

A firm's decisions as to what output level to produce are typically marginal decisions, that is, decisions to produce a few more or a few less units. Marginal cost is the change in costs when one more or one less unit of output is produced.

CONSIDER THIS . . .

Source: © Don Farrall/Getty Images RF

Ignoring Sunk Costs

It is a deep-seated human tendency to drag past costs—so-called sunk costs—into marginal-benefit versus marginal-cost calculations. Doing so is known as the *sunk cost fallacy.*

As an example of this error, suppose a family that's on vacation stops at a roadside stand to buy some apples. After driving a bit, the family discovers that the apples are mushy and gross. Would it be logical for the father to insist that everyone eat the apples "because we paid a premium price for them"?

Absolutely not. In making a new decision, you should ignore all costs that are not affected by that new decision. The prior bad decision (in retrospect) to buy the apples should not dictate a subsequent decision for which marginal benefit is less than marginal cost.

Consider a business example. Suppose that a firm spends \$1 million on R&D to bring out a new product, only to discover that the product sells very poorly. Should the firm continue to produce the product at a loss even when there is no realistic hope for future success? Obviously, it should not. In making this decision, the firm should realize that the amount it spent developing the product is irrelevant; it should stop production and cut its losses.

The emotional tendency that drives the sunk cost fallacy is the desire to "get one's money's worth" out of a past expenditure. But giving in to that emotion can lead to "throwing good money after bad." Instead, you should ignore all past costs and focus solely on those that depend on the decision at hand.

AP KEY GRAPH

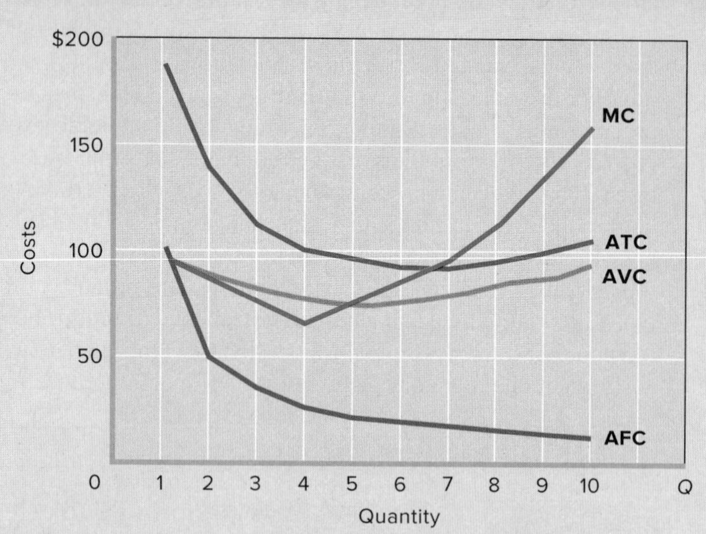

FIGURE 8.5 The relationship of the marginal-cost curve to the average-total-cost and average-variable-cost curves. The marginal-cost (MC) curve cuts through the average-total-cost (ATC) curve and the average-variable-cost (AVC) curve at their minimum points. When MC is below average total cost, ATC falls; when MC is above average total cost, ATC rises. Similarly, when MC is below average variable cost, AVC falls; when MC is above average variable cost, AVC rises.

QUICK QUIZ FOR FIGURE 8.5

1. The marginal-cost curve first declines and then increases because of:
   a. increasing, then diminishing, marginal utility.
   b. the decline in the gap between ATC and AVC as output expands.
   c. increasing, then diminishing, marginal returns.
   d. constant marginal revenue.

2. The vertical distance between ATC and AVC measures:
   a. marginal cost.
   b. total fixed cost.
   c. average fixed cost.
   d. economic profit per unit.

3. ATC is:
   a. AVC − AFC.
   b. MC + AVC.
   c. AFC + AVC.
   d. (AFC + AVC) ÷ Q.

4. When the marginal-cost curve lies:
   a. above the ATC curve, ATC rises.
   b. above the AVC curve, ATC rises.
   c. below the AVC curve, total fixed cost increases.
   d. below the ATC curve, total fixed cost falls.

Answers: 1. c; 2. c; 3. c; 4. a

When coupled with marginal revenue (which, as you will see in Chapter 9, indicates the change in revenue from one more or one less unit of output), marginal cost allows a firm to determine if it is profitable to expand or contract its production. The analysis in the next four chapters focuses on those marginal calculations.

Graphical Portrayal Marginal cost is shown graphically in **Figure 8.5 (Key Graph).** Marginal cost at first declines sharply, reaches a minimum, and then rises rather abruptly. This reflects the fact that variable cost, and therefore total cost, increase at first by decreasing amounts and then by increasing amounts (see columns 3 and 4, Table 8.2).

MC and Marginal Product The marginal-cost curve's shape is a consequence of the law of diminishing returns. Looking back at Table 8.1, we can see the relationship between marginal product and marginal cost. If all units of a variable resource (here labor) are hired at the same price, the marginal cost of each extra unit of output will fall as long as the marginal product of each additional worker is rising. This is true because marginal cost is the (constant) cost of an extra worker divided by his or her marginal product. Therefore, in Table 8.1, suppose that each worker can be hired for $10. Because the first worker's marginal product is 10 units of output, and hiring this worker increases the firm's costs by $10, the marginal cost of each of these 10 extra units of output is $1 (= $10/10 units). The second worker also increases costs by $10, but the marginal product is 15, so the marginal cost of each of these 15 extra units of output is $0.67 (= $10/15 units). Similarly, the MC of each of the 20 extra units of output contributed by the third worker is $.50 (= $10/20 units). To generalize, as long as marginal product is rising, marginal cost will fall.

But with the fourth worker diminishing returns set in and marginal cost begins to rise. For the fourth worker, marginal cost is $0.67 (= $10/15 units); for the fifth worker, MC is $1 ($10/10 units); for the sixth, MC is $2 (= $10/5 units); and so

AP **FIGURE 8.6 The relationship between productivity curves and cost curves.** The marginal-cost (MC) curve and the average-variable-cost (AVC) curve in (b) are mirror images of the marginal-product (MP) and average-product (AP) curves in (a). Assuming that labor is the only variable input and that its price (the wage rate) is constant, then when MP is rising, MC is falling, and when MP is falling, MC is rising. Under the same assumptions, when AP is rising, AVC is falling, and when AP is falling, AVC is rising.

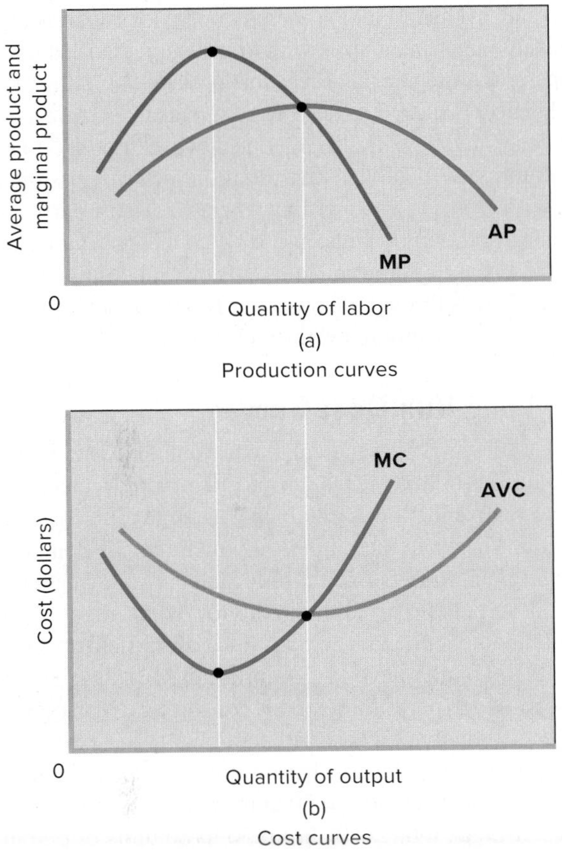

on. If the price (cost) of the variable resource remains constant, increasing marginal returns will be reflected in a declining marginal cost, and diminishing marginal returns in a rising marginal cost. The MC curve is a mirror reflection of the marginal-product curve. As you can see in Figure 8.6, when marginal product is rising, marginal cost is necessarily falling. When marginal product is at its maximum, marginal cost is at its minimum. And when marginal product is falling, marginal cost is rising.

Relation of MC to AVC and ATC Figure 8.5 shows that the marginal-cost curve MC intersects both the AVC and the ATC curves at their respective minimum points. As noted earlier, this marginal-average relationship is a mathematical necessity, which a simple illustration will reveal. Suppose an NBA basketball player has scored an average of 20 points a game over the first three games of the season. Now, whether his average rises or falls as a result of playing a fourth (marginal) game will depend on whether the additional points he scores in that game are fewer or more than his current 20-point average. If in the fourth game he scores fewer than 20 points, his average will fall. For example, if he scores 16 points in the fourth game, his total points will rise from 60 to 76 and his average will fall from 20 to 19 (= 76/4). Conversely, if in the fourth (marginal) game he scores more than 20 points, say, 24, his total will increase from 60 to 84 and his average will rise from 20 to 21 (= 84/4).

So it is with costs. When the amount (the marginal cost) added to total cost is less than the current average total cost, ATC will fall. Conversely, when the marginal cost exceeds ATC, ATC will rise. This means in Figure 8.5 that as long as MC lies below ATC, ATC will fall, and whenever MC lies above ATC, ATC will rise. Therefore, at the point of intersection where MC equals ATC, ATC has just ceased to fall but has not yet begun to rise. This, by definition, is the minimum point on the ATC curve. The marginal-cost curve intersects the average-total-cost curve at the ATC curve's minimum point.

Marginal cost can be defined as the addition either to total cost or to total variable cost resulting from one more unit of output; thus this same rationale explains why the MC curve also crosses the AVC curve at the AVC curve's minimum point. No such relationship exists between the MC curve and the average-fixed-cost curve because the two are not related; marginal cost includes only those costs that change with output, and fixed costs by definition are those that are independent of output.

Shifts of the Cost Curves

Changes in either resource prices or technology will cause costs to change and cost curves to shift. If fixed costs double from $100 to $200, the AFC curve in Figure 8.5 would be shifted upward. At each level of output, fixed costs are higher. The ATC curve would also move upward because AFC is a component of ATC. But the positions of the AVC and MC curves would be unaltered because their locations are based on the prices of variable rather than fixed resources. However, if the price (wage) of labor or some other variable input rose, AVC, ATC, and MC would rise and those cost curves would all shift upward. The AFC curve would remain in place because fixed costs have not changed. And, of course, reductions in the prices of fixed or variable resources would reduce costs and produce shifts of the cost curves exactly opposite to those just described.

The discovery of a more efficient technology would increase the productivity of all inputs. The cost figures in Table 8.2 would all be lower. To illustrate, if labor is the only variable input, if wages are $10 per hour, and if average product is 10 units, then AVC would be $1. But if a technological improvement increases the average product of labor to 20 units, then AVC will decline to $0.50. More generally, an upward shift in the productivity curves shown in Figure 8.6a means a downward shift in the cost curves portrayed in Figure 8.6b.

AP QUICK REVIEW 8.2

- ✓ The law of diminishing returns states that as more of a variable input (labor) is added to a fixed input (capital), output increases, but eventually at a diminishing rate. Additional units of the variable input have less of the fixed input to work with.
- ✓ In the short run, the total cost of any level of output is the sum of fixed and variable costs (TC = TFC + TVC).
- ✓ Average fixed, average variable, and average total costs are fixed, variable, and total costs per unit of output; marginal cost is the extra cost of producing one more unit of output.
- ✓ Average fixed cost declines continuously as output increases; the average-variable-cost curve is U-shaped, reflecting increasing and then diminishing average returns. The average total cost curve is also U-shaped, reflecting the behavior of both average variable cost and average fixed cost. Assuming increasing and then diminishing marginal product, the marginal-cost curve falls but then rises, intersecting both the average-variable-cost curve and the average-total-cost curve at their minimum points.

AP Long-Run Production Costs

LO8.4 Use economies of scale to link a firm's size and its average costs in the long run.

In the long run an industry and its individual firms can undertake all desired resource adjustments. That is, they can change the amount of all inputs used. The firm can alter its plant capacity; it can build a larger plant or revert to a smaller plant than that assumed in Table 8.2. The industry also can change its overall capacity; the long run allows sufficient time for new firms to enter or for existing firms to leave an industry. We will discuss the impact of the entry and exit of firms to and from an industry in the next chapter; here we are concerned only with changes in plant capacity made by a single firm. Let's couch our analysis in terms of average total cost (ATC), making no distinction between fixed and variable costs because all resources, and therefore all costs, are variable in the long run.

Firm Size and Costs

Suppose a manufacturer with a single plant begins on a small scale and, as the result of successful operations, expands to successively larger plant sizes with larger output capacities. What happens to average total cost as this occurs? For a time, successively larger plants will reduce average total cost. However, eventually the building of a still larger plant will cause ATC to rise.

Figure 8.7 illustrates this situation for five possible plant sizes. ATC-1 is the short-run average-total-cost curve for the smallest of the five plants, and ATC-5, the curve for the largest. Constructing larger plants will lower the minimum average total costs through plant size 3. But then larger plants will mean higher minimum average total costs.

The Long-Run Cost Curve

The vertical lines perpendicular to the output axis in Figure 8.7 indicate the outputs at which the firm should change plant size to realize the lowest attainable average total costs of production. These are the outputs at which the per-unit costs for a larger plant drop below those for the current, smaller plant. For all outputs up to 20 units, the lowest average total costs are attainable with plant size 1. However, if the firm's volume of sales expands beyond 20 units but less than 30, it can achieve lower per-unit costs by constructing a larger plant, size 2. Although total cost will be higher at the expanded levels of production, the cost per unit of output will be less. For any output between 30 and 50 units, plant size 3 will yield the lowest average total costs. From 50 to 60 units of output, the firm must build the size-4 plant to achieve the lowest unit costs. Lowest average total costs for any output over 60 units require construction of the still larger plant, size 5.

Tracing these adjustments, we find that the long-run ATC curve for the enterprise is made up of segments of the

FIGURE 8.7 The long-run average-total-cost curve: five possible plant sizes. The long-run average-total-cost curve is made up of segments of the short-run cost curves (ATC-1, ATC-2, etc.) of the various-size plants from which the firm might choose. Each point on the bumpy planning curve shows the lowest unit cost attainable for any output when the firm has had time to make all desired changes in its plant size.

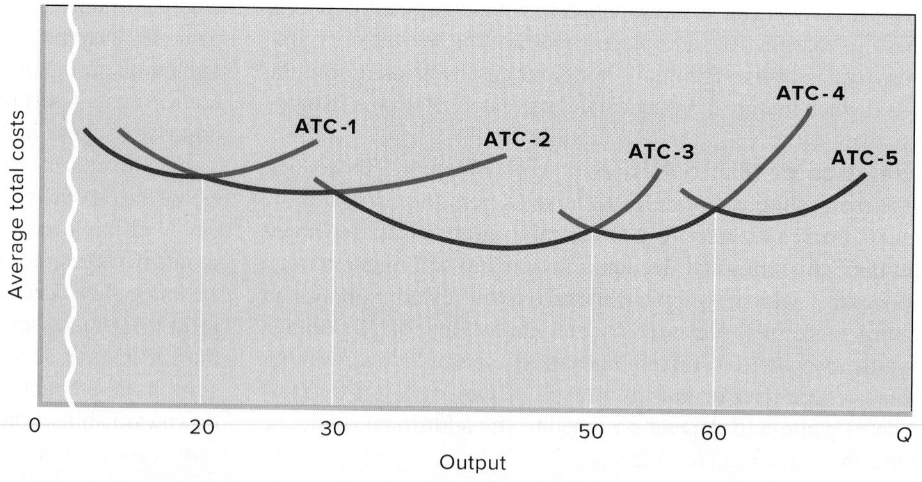

AP KEY GRAPH

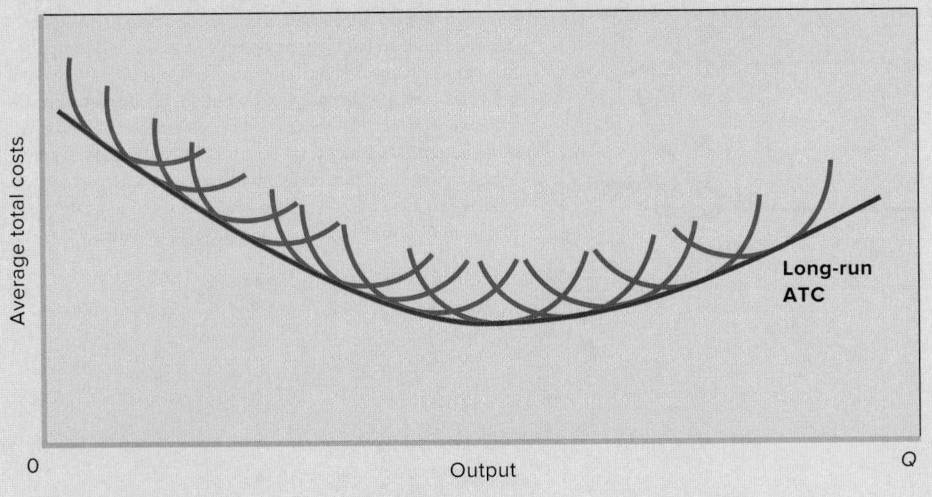

FIGURE 8.8 The long-run average-total-cost curve: unlimited number of plant sizes. If the number of possible plant sizes is very large, the long-run average-total-cost curve approximates a smooth curve. Economies of scale, followed by diseconomies of scale, cause the curve to be U-shaped.

QUICK QUIZ FOR FIGURE 8.8

1. The unlabeled red curves in this figure illustrate the:
- **a.** long-run average-total-cost curves of various firms constituting the industry.
- **b.** short-run average-total-cost curves of various firms constituting the industry.
- **c.** short-run average-total-cost curves of various plant sizes available to a particular firm.
- **d.** short-run marginal-cost curves of various plant sizes available to a particular firm.

2. The unlabeled red curves in this figure derive their shapes from:
- **a.** decreasing, then increasing, short-run returns.
- **b.** increasing, then decreasing, short-run returns.
- **c.** economies, then diseconomies, of scale.
- **d.** diseconomies, then economies, of scale.

3. The long-run ATC curve in this figure derives its shape from:
- **a.** decreasing, then increasing, short-run returns.
- **b.** increasing, then decreasing, short-run returns.
- **c.** economies, then diseconomies, of scale.
- **d.** diseconomies, then economies, of scale.

4. The long-run ATC curve is often called the firm's:
- **a.** planning curve.
- **b.** capital-expansion path.
- **c.** total-product curve.
- **d.** production possibilities curve.

Answers: 1. c; 2. b; 3. c; 4. a

short-run ATC curves for the various plant sizes that can be constructed. The long-run ATC curve shows the lowest average total cost at which *any output level* can be produced after the firm has had time to make all appropriate adjustments in its plant size. In Figure 8.7 the blue, bumpy curve is the firm's long-run ATC curve or, as it is often called, the firm's *planning curve*.

In most lines of production the choice of plant size is much wider than in our illustration. In many industries the number of possible plant sizes is virtually unlimited, and in time quite small changes in the volume of output will lead to changes in plant size. Graphically, this implies an unlimited number of short-run ATC curves, one for each output level, as suggested by **Figure 8.8 (Key Graph).** Then, rather than being made up of segments of short-run ATC curves as in Figure 8.7, the long-run ATC curve is made up of all the points of tangency of the unlimited number of short-run ATC curves from which the long-run ATC curve is derived. Therefore, the planning curve is smooth rather than bumpy. Each point on it tells us the minimum ATC of producing the corresponding level of output.

Economies and Diseconomies of Scale

We have assumed that, for a time, larger and larger plant sizes will lead to lower unit costs but that, beyond some point, successively larger plants will mean higher average total costs. That is, we have assumed the long-run ATC curve is U-shaped. But why should this be? It turns out that the U shape is caused by economies and diseconomies of large-scale production, as we explain in a moment. But before we do, please understand that the U shape of the long-run average-total-cost curve *cannot* be the result of rising resource prices or the law of diminishing returns. First, our discussion assumes that resource prices are constant. Second, the law of diminishing returns does not apply to production in the long run. This is true because the law of diminishing returns only deals with situations in which a productive resource or input is held constant. Under our definition of "long run," all resources and inputs are variable.

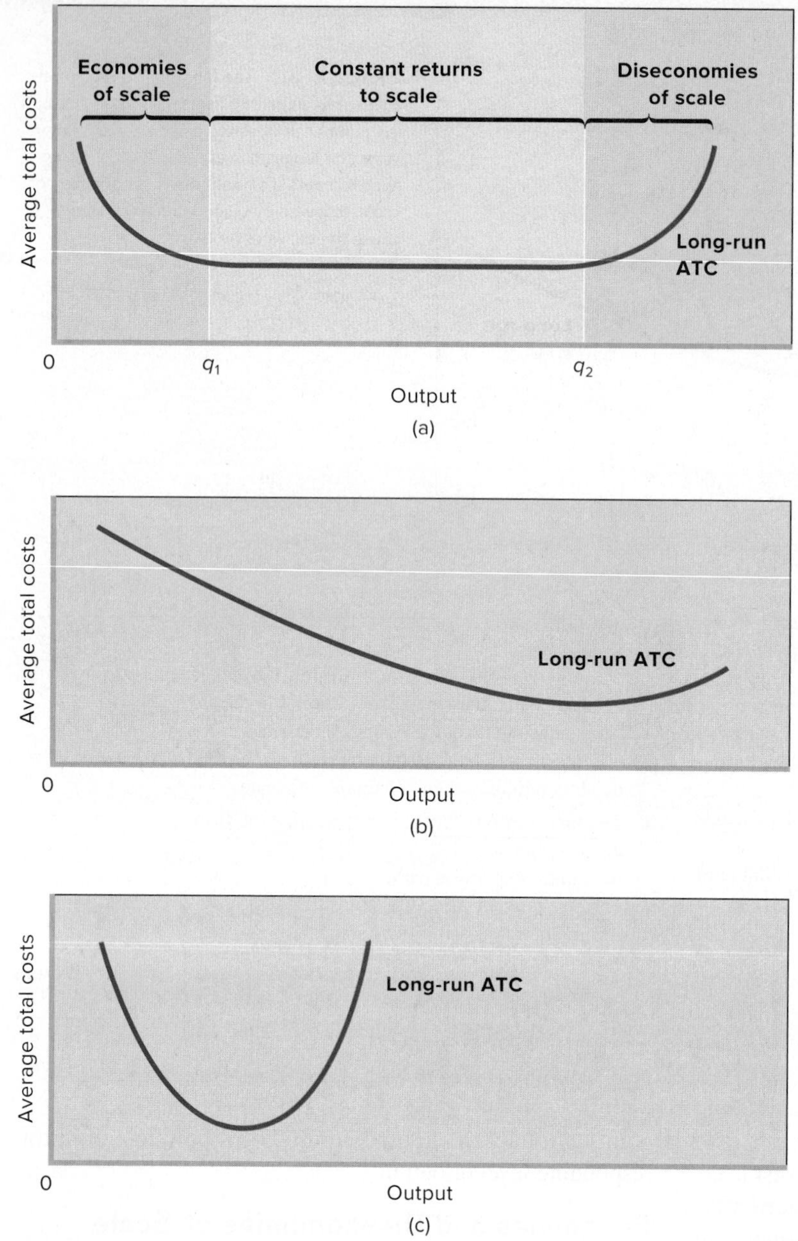

FIGURE 8.9 Various possible long-run average-total-cost curves. (a) Economies of scale are rather rapidly obtained as plant size rises, and diseconomies of scale are not encountered until a considerably large scale of output has been achieved. Thus, long-run average total cost is constant over a wide range of output. (b) Economies of scale are extensive, and diseconomies of scale occur only at very large outputs. Average total cost therefore declines over a broad range of output. (c) Economies of scale are exhausted quickly, followed immediately by diseconomies of scale. Minimum ATC thus occurs at a relatively low output.

Economies of Scale **Economies of scale,** or economies of mass production, explain the downsloping part of the long-run ATC curve, as indicated in Figure 8.9, graphs (a), (b), and (c). As plant size increases, a number of factors will for a time lead to lower average costs of production.

Labor Specialization Increased specialization in the use of labor becomes more achievable as a plant increases in size. Hiring more workers means jobs can be divided and subdivided. Each worker may now have just one task to perform instead of five or six. Workers can work full-time on the tasks for which they have special skills. By contrast, skilled machinists in a small plant may spend half their time performing unskilled tasks, leading to higher production costs.

Further, by working at fewer tasks, workers become even more proficient at those tasks. The jack-of-all-trades doing five or six jobs is not likely to be efficient in any of them. Concentrating on one task, the same worker may become highly efficient.

Finally, greater labor specialization eliminates the loss of time that occurs whenever a worker shifts from one task to another.

Managerial Specialization Large-scale production also means better use of, and greater specialization in, management. A supervisor who can handle 20 workers is underused in a small plant that employs only 10 people. The production staff could be doubled with no increase in supervisory costs.

Small firms cannot use management specialists to best advantage. For example, a marketing specialist working in a small plant may have to spend some of her time on functions outside of her area of expertise—for example, accounting, personnel, and finance. A larger scale of operations would allow her to supervise marketing full time, while other specialists perform other managerial functions. Greater productivity and efficiency, along with lower unit costs, would be the net result.

Efficient Capital Small firms often cannot afford the most efficient equipment. In many lines of production such machinery is available only in very large and extremely expensive units. Furthermore, effective use of the equipment demands a high volume of production, and that again requires large-scale producers.

In the automobile industry the most efficient fabrication method employs robotics and elaborate assembly-line equipment. Effective use of this equipment demands an annual output of several hundred thousand automobiles. Only very large-scale producers can afford to purchase and use this equipment efficiently. The small-scale producer is faced with a dilemma. To fabricate automobiles using other equipment is inefficient and therefore more costly per unit. But so, too, is buying and underutilizing the equipment used by the large manufacturers. Because it cannot spread the high equipment cost over very many units of output, the small-scale producer will be stuck with high costs per unit of output.

Other Factors Many products entail design and development costs, as well as other "start-up" costs, which must be incurred regardless of projected sales. These costs decline per unit as output is increased. Similarly, advertising costs decline per auto, per computer, per stereo system, and per box of detergent as more units are produced and sold. Also, the firm's production and marketing expertise usually rises as it produces and sells more output. This *learning by doing* is a further source of economies of scale.

All these factors contribute to lower average total costs for the firm that is able to expand its scale of operations. Where economies of scale are possible, an increase in all resources of, say, 10 percent will cause a more-than-proportionate increase in output of, say, 20 percent. The result will be a decline in ATC.

In many U.S. manufacturing industries, economies of scale have been of great significance. Firms that have expanded their scale of operations to obtain economies of mass production have survived and flourished. Those unable to expand have become relatively high-cost producers, doomed to struggle to survive.

Diseconomies of Scale In time the expansion of a firm may lead to diseconomies and therefore higher average total costs.

The main factor causing **diseconomies of scale** is the difficulty of efficiently controlling and coordinating a firm's operations as it becomes a large-scale producer. In a small plant a single key executive may make all the basic decisions for the plant's operation. Because of the firm's small size, the executive is close to the production line, understands the firm's operations, and can make efficient decisions because the small plant size requires only a relatively small amount of information to be examined and understood in order to optimize production.

This neat picture changes as a firm grows. One person cannot assemble, digest, and understand all the information essential to decision making on a large scale. Authority must be delegated to many vice presidents, second vice presidents, and so forth. This expansion of the management hierarchy leads to problems of communication and cooperation, bureaucratic red tape, and the possibility that decisions will not be coordinated. At the same time, each new manager must be paid a salary. Thus, declining efficiency in making and executing decisions goes hand-in-hand with rising average total costs as bureaucracy expands beyond a certain point.

Also, in massive production facilities workers may feel alienated from their employers and care little about working efficiently. Opportunities to shirk, by avoiding work in favor of on-the-job leisure, may be greater in large plants than in small ones. Countering worker alienation and shirking may require additional worker supervision, which increases costs.

Where diseconomies of scale are operative, an increase in all inputs of, say, 10 percent will cause a less-than-proportionate increase in output of, say, 5 percent. As a consequence, ATC will increase. The rising portion of the long-run cost curves in Figure 8.9 illustrates diseconomies of scale.

Constant Returns to Scale In some industries a rather wide range of output may exist between the output at which economies of scale end and the output at which diseconomies of scale begin. That is, there may be a range of **constant returns to scale** over which long-run average cost does not change. The q_1q_2 output range of Figure 8.9a is an example. Here a given percentage increase in all inputs of, say, 10 percent will cause a proportionate 10 percent increase in output. Thus, in this range ATC is constant.

Minimum Efficient Scale and Industry Structure

Economies and diseconomies of scale are an important determinant of an industry's structure. Here we introduce the concept of **minimum efficient scale (MES),** which is the lowest level of output at which a firm can minimize long-run average costs. In Figure 9.9a that level occurs at q_1 units of output. Because of the extended range of constant returns to scale, firms producing substantially greater outputs could also realize the minimum attainable long-run average costs. Specifically, firms within the q_1 to q_2 range would be equally efficient. So we would not be surprised to find an industry with such cost conditions to be populated by firms of quite

LAST WORD

3-D Printers

3-D Printers Are Poised to Replace Mass Production with Mass Customization.

Both a billionaire and your Average Joe can buy a pocketknife for \$10. They can also both buy an iPhone for \$199. And they can both purchase a new compact car for under \$15,000.

The fact that all of these items are affordable to both a billionaire and your Average Joe is due to mass production and economies of scale. The iPhone, for instance, is one of the most complicated devices ever made. It contains cutting-edge technologies for graphics, voice recognition, battery length, screen durability, and many other features. Most of those technologies took hundreds of millions—if not billions—of dollars to develop and the factories that manufacture the iPhone and its components themselves cost many billions of dollars to set up. Yet, the iPhone is so inexpensive that Average Joes can afford to buy one.

That mass affordability is the result of mass production coupled with mass sales. Marginal costs are typically quite low with mass production. So if manufacturers can tap mass markets and sell their products in large numbers, they can achieve low per-unit costs by spreading the massive fixed costs (for developing the new technologies and setting up the factories) over many units. Doing so results in economies of scale, low average total costs per unit, and low prices that even average folks can afford.

Mass production and mass sales first became possible during the Industrial Revolution, which began in England during the late 1700s and then spread through most of the rest of the world during the next two centuries. The Industrial Revolution occurred when steam-powered engines became powerful enough to drive factory equipment, propel ships, and pull trains. Engineers and inventors used steam power to automate factories and initiate the low-cost mass production of consumer goods. That process only accelerated when, in the late nineteenth century, the so-called Second Industrial Revolution saw electricity harnessed to drive factories and provide lighting.

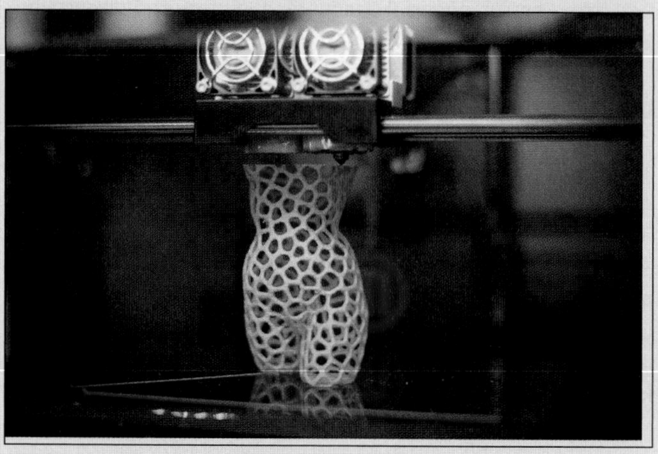

Source: © Timur Emek/Getty Images

different sizes. The apparel, food processing, furniture, wood products, snowboard, banking, and small-appliance industries are examples. With an extended range of constant returns to scale, relatively large and relatively small firms can coexist in an industry and be equally successful.

Compare this with Figure 8.9b, where economies of scale continue over a wide range of outputs and diseconomies of scale appear only at very high levels of output. This pattern of declining long-run average total cost occurs in the automobile, aluminum, steel, and other heavy industries. The same pattern holds in several of the new industries related to information technology, for example, computer microchips, operating system software, and Internet service provision.

Given consumer demand, efficient production will be achieved with a few large-scale producers. Small firms cannot realize the minimum efficient scale and will not be able to compete. In the extreme, economies of scale might extend beyond the market's size, resulting in what is termed **natural monopoly,** a relatively rare market situation in which average total cost is minimized when only one firm produces the particular good or service.

Where economies of scale are few and diseconomies come into play quickly, the minimum efficient size occurs at a low level of output, as shown in Figure 8.9c. In such industries a particular level of consumer demand will support a large number of relatively small producers. Many retail trades and some types of farming fall into this category. So do certain kinds of light manufacturing such as the baking, clothing, and shoe industries. Fairly small firms are more efficient than larger-scale producers in such industries.

Our point here is that the shape of the long-run average-total-cost curve is determined by technology and the economies and diseconomies of scale that result. The shape of the long-run ATC curve, in turn, can be significant in determining whether an industry is populated by a relatively large number of small firms or is dominated by a few large producers, or lies somewhere in between.

But we must be cautious in our assessment because industry structure does not depend on cost conditions alone.

Mass sales, however, are not easy. They require large distribution networks, massive advertising budgets, and, perhaps most important, cheap ways of shipping products from factories to consumers. Thus, it was crucially important that transportation was also vastly improved during the First and Second Industrial Revolutions. If not for better ships, smoother roads, and cheap transportation by railroad, transportation costs would have been so high that consumers would not have been able to afford mass-produced products shipped from distant factories.

Now, a new technology promises to deliver a Third Industrial Revolution that will feature not only low production costs but also zero transportation costs. Even better, both of those highly attractive features will be possible *even if you make only a single unit of a product*. In addition, each unit can be fully customized to a consumer's wants and needs. As a result, our world of affordable mass production may soon be replaced by a world of affordable mass customization.

The new technology is called additive manufacturing and it creates objects using computer-controlled devices known as "3-D printers." The 3-D (three-dimensional) printers contain a fine powder of metal or plastic particles that sit in a bin. A laser moves rapidly over the powder, the heat of its beam fusing small clumps of the powder together. Guided by a computerized blueprint, the rapidly moving laser can fuse a single layer of a complicated object together in just a few seconds.

The bin is then lowered a bit, another layer of powder is placed on top, and the laser again begins to shoot, this time fusing together both the previous layer as well as the current layer. Doing this over and over, one layer atop another, results in a solid object whose shape is limited only by the complexity of the blueprint. Any of the powder that is not struck by the laser and incorporated into the object is simply recycled for later use.

Because 3-D printers are inexpensive, they could potentially be located anywhere. Thus, there is no need to worry about transportation costs since objects could be manufactured by consumers in their own homes or in local workshops located only a short drive away. And because the powders are cheap and the machines only require a modest amount of electricity, anything that could be made using a 3-D printer would be inexpensive even if you were only making a single unit.

The First Industrial Revolution delivered low prices by spreading massive fixed costs over many units. The Third Industrial Revolution is set to deliver even lower prices by eliminating two types of costs—the massive fixed costs necessary to set up large factories and the transportation costs needed to ship resources to factories and then finished goods to consumers.

One major cost might still remain, however. That is the cost of paying people to make the blueprints that drive the 3-D printers. But just as digital file sharing has pushed the price of recorded music toward zero, many analysts suspect that digital file sharing will also drive the price of blueprints very low. If so, the cost of manufactured goods may soon plunge to levels even lower than what has been achieved through mass production.

So far, only relatively simple objects can be made with 3-D printers. But some engineers see a day in the not-so-distant future when it may be possible to create even complicated devices like an iPhone using additive manufacturing. If so, people will simply download inexpensive blueprints, make a few changes to customize the product, and then "print" what they want.

Government policies, the geographic size of markets, managerial strategy and skill, and other factors must be considered in explaining the structure of a particular industry.

AP QUICK REVIEW 8.3

- ✓ Most firms have U-shaped long-run average-total-cost curves, reflecting economies and then diseconomies of scale.
- ✓ Economies of scale are the consequence of greater specialization of labor and management, more efficient capital equipment, and the spreading of start-up costs over more units of output.
- ✓ Diseconomies of scale are caused by the problems of coordination and communication that arise in large firms.
- ✓ Minimum efficient scale (MES) is the level of output at which a firm's long-run average total cost is at its minimum.

Applications and Illustrations

LO8.5 Give business examples of short-run costs, economies of scale, and minimum efficient scale (MES).

The business world offers many examples relating to short-run costs, economies of scale, and minimum efficient scale (MES). Here are just a few.

Rising Gasoline Prices

As we discuss in the appendix to Chapter 3, changes in supply and demand often lead to rapid increases in the price of gasoline. Because gasoline is used to power the vast majority of all motor vehicles, including those used by businesses, increases in the price of gasoline lead to increases in firms' short-run variable costs, marginal costs, and average total costs. In terms of our analysis, their AVC, MC, and ATC curves all shift upward when an increase in the price of gasoline increases production costs.

The extent of these upward shifts depends upon the relative importance of gasoline as a variable input in the various firms' individual production processes. Package-delivery companies like FedEx that use a lot of gasoline-powered vehicles will see substantial upward shifts while software companies like Symantec (Norton) that mainly deliver their products through Internet downloads may see only small upward shifts.

Successful Start-Up Firms

The U.S. economy has greatly benefited over the past several decades from the explosive growth of scores of highly successful start-up firms. These firms typically reduce their costs by moving from higher to lower points on their short-run cost curves and by downward and to-the-right shifts of their short-run cost curves via economies of scale. That has certainly been the case for such former start-up firms as Intel (microchips), Starbucks (coffee), Microsoft (software), Dell (personal computers), Google (Internet searches), and Cisco Systems (Internet switching).

A major source of lower average total cost for rapidly growing firms is the ability to spread huge product development and advertising costs over a larger number of units of output. These firms also achieve economies of scale from learning by doing and through increased specialization of labor, management, and equipment. After starting up, such firms experience declining average total costs over the years or even decades it takes them to eventually reach their respective MESs.

The Verson Stamping Machine

In 1996 Verson (a U.S. firm located in Chicago) introduced a 49-foot-tall metal-stamping machine that is the size of a house and weighs as much as 12 locomotives. This $30 million machine, which cuts and sculpts raw sheets of steel into automobile hoods and fenders, enables automakers to make new parts in just 5 minutes, compared with 8 hours for older stamping presses. A single machine is designed to make 5 million auto parts per year. So, to achieve the cost saving from the machine, an auto manufacturer must have sufficient auto production to use all these parts. By allowing the use of this cost-saving piece of equipment, large firm size achieves economies of scale.

The Daily Newspaper

Daily newspapers have been going bankrupt in rapid succession over the past several years as both advertising dollars and news readership have shifted to the Internet. The falling circulation numbers have caused average fixed costs to rise significantly as newspapers are forced to spread their substantial fixed costs over fewer and fewer papers. The spike in average fixed costs has, in turn, forced newspapers to sharply increase their prices. Between July 2007 and July 2009, for instance, the *New York Times* had to raise its cover price three times as advertising revenues plunged and fixed costs had to be spread over fewer and fewer papers. Starting at $1 per copy, the cover price had to be raised to $1.25, then $1.50, and then $2.00.

With readership continuing to fall, newspapers face an average-fixed-cost death spiral. The more they raise their prices, the less they will sell. But the less their sales, the higher their average fixed costs and thus the more they must raise their prices. As a result, printed newspapers could ultimately be a thing of the past, with both advertising and news delivery shifting mainly to the Internet.

Aircraft and Concrete Plants

Why are there only two plants in the United States (both operated by Boeing) that produce large commercial aircraft and thousands of plants (owned by hundreds of firms) that produce ready-mixed concrete? The simple answer is that MES is radically different in the two industries. Why is that? First, while economies of scale are extensive in assembling large commercial aircraft, they are only very modest in mixing concrete. Manufacturing airplanes is a complex process that requires huge facilities, thousands of workers, and very expensive, specialized machinery. Economies of scale extend to huge plant sizes. But mixing portland cement, sand, gravel, and water to produce concrete requires only a handful of workers and relatively inexpensive equipment. Economies of scale are exhausted at relatively small size.

The differing MESs also derive from the vastly different sizes of the geographic markets. The market for commercial airplanes is global, and aircraft manufacturers can deliver new airplanes anywhere in the world by flying them there. In contrast, the geographic market for a concrete plant is roughly the 50-mile radius within which the concrete can be delivered before it "sets up." So thousands of small concrete plants locate close to their customers in hundreds of small and large cities in the United States.

SUMMARY

LO8.1 Explain why economic costs include both explicit (revealed and expressed) costs and implicit (present but not obvious) costs.

The economic cost of using a resource to produce a good or service is the value or worth that the resource would have had in its best alternative use. Economic costs include explicit costs, which flow to resources owned and supplied by others, and implicit costs, which are payments for the use of self-owned and self-employed resources. One implicit cost is a normal profit to the entrepreneur. Economic profit occurs when total revenue exceeds total cost (= explicit costs + implicit costs, including a normal profit).

In the short run a firm's plant capacity is fixed. The firm can use its plant more or less intensively by adding or subtracting units of variable resources, but it does not have sufficient time in the short run to alter plant size.

LO8.2 Relate the law of diminishing returns to a firm's short-run production costs.

The law of diminishing returns describes what happens to output as a fixed plant is used more intensively. As successive units of a variable resource such as labor are added to a fixed plant, beyond some point the marginal product associated with each additional unit of a resource declines.

LO8.3 Describe the distinctions between fixed and variable costs and among total, average, and marginal costs.

Because some resources are variable and others are fixed, costs can be classified as variable or fixed in the short run. Fixed costs are independent of the level of output; variable costs vary with output. The total cost of any output is the sum of fixed and variable costs at that output.

Average fixed, average variable, and average total costs are fixed, variable, and total costs per unit of output. Average fixed cost declines continuously as output increases because a fixed sum is being spread over a larger and larger number of units of production. A graph of average variable cost is U-shaped, reflecting increasing returns followed by diminishing returns. Average total cost is the sum of average fixed and average variable costs; its graph is also U-shaped.

Marginal cost is the extra, or additional, cost of producing one more unit of output. It is the amount by which total cost and total variable cost change when one more or one less unit of output is produced. Graphically, the marginal-cost curve intersects the ATC and AVC curves at their minimum points.

Lower resource prices shift cost curves downward, as does technological progress. Higher input prices shift cost curves upward.

LO8.4 Use economies of scale to link a firm's size and its average costs in the long run.

The long run is a period of time sufficiently long for a firm to vary the amounts of all resources used, including plant size. In the long run all costs are variable. The long-run ATC, or planning, curve is composed of segments of short-run ATC curves, and it represents the various plant sizes a firm can construct in the long run.

The long-run ATC curve is generally U-shaped. Economies of scale are first encountered as a small firm expands. Greater specialization in the use of labor and management, the ability to use the most efficient equipment, and the spreading of start-up costs among more units of output all contribute to economies of scale. As the firm continues to grow, it will encounter diseconomies of scale stemming from the managerial complexities that accompany large-scale production. The output ranges over which economies and diseconomies of scale occur in an industry are often an important determinant of the structure of that industry.

A firm's minimum efficient scale (MES) is the lowest level of output at which it can minimize its long-run average cost. In some industries, MES occurs at such low levels of output that numerous firms can populate the industry. In other industries, MES occurs at such high output levels that only a few firms can exist in the long run.

LO8.5 Give business examples of short-run costs, economies of scale, and minimum efficient scale (MES).

Rising gasoline prices increase (shift upward) the AVC, ATC, and MC cost curves of firms like FedEx that use gasoline as an input in their production processes.

Starbucks, Facebook, and many other successful start-up firms that experienced rapid growth reduced costs and shifted their cost curves down and to the right by spreading product-development and advertising costs over larger numbers of units and by exploiting the economies of scale that can be generated through learning by doing and increased specialization of labor, management, and equipment.

Because minimum efficient scale (MES) is extremely large for commercial aircraft, Boeing only has two production facilities in the United States. By contrast, MES is very small in concrete manufacturing. So there are thousands of concrete makers in the United States.

TERMS AND CONCEPTS

economic cost
explicit costs
implicit costs
accounting profit
normal profit
economic profit
short run
long run
total product (TP)
marginal product (MP)
average product (AP)
law of diminishing returns
fixed costs
variable costs
total cost
average fixed cost (AFC)
average variable cost (AVC)
average total cost (ATC)
marginal cost (MC)
economies of scale
diseconomies of scale
constant returns to scale
minimum efficient scale (MES)
natural monopoly

The following and additional problems can be found in connect

DISCUSSION QUESTIONS

1. Distinguish between explicit and implicit costs, giving examples of each. What are some explicit and implicit costs of attending college? LO8.1
2. Distinguish among accounting profit, economic profit, and normal profit. Does accounting profit or economic profit determine how entrepreneurs allocate resources between different business ventures? Explain. LO8.1
3. Complete the following table by calculating marginal product and average product.

Inputs of Labor	Total Product	Marginal Product	Average Product
0	0	______	
1	15	______	______
2	34	______	______
3	51	______	______
4	65	______	______
5	74	______	______
6	80	______	______
7	83	______	______
8	82		______

Plot the total, marginal, and average products and explain in detail the relationship between each pair of curves. Explain why marginal product first rises, then declines, and ultimately becomes negative. What bearing does the law of diminishing returns have on short-run costs? Be specific. "When marginal product is rising, marginal cost is falling. And when marginal product is diminishing, marginal cost is rising." Illustrate and explain graphically. LO8.2
4. Why can the distinction between fixed costs and variable costs be made in the short run? Classify the following as fixed or variable costs: advertising expenditures, fuel, interest on company-issued bonds, shipping charges, payments for raw materials, real estate taxes, executive salaries, insurance premiums, wage payments, depreciation and obsolescence charges, sales taxes, and rental payments on leased office machinery. "There are no fixed costs in the long run; all costs are variable." Explain. LO8.3
5. List several fixed and variable costs associated with owning and operating an automobile. Suppose you are considering whether to drive your car or fly 1,000 miles to Florida for spring break. Which costs—fixed, variable, or both—would you take into account in making your decision? Would any implicit costs be relevant? Explain. LO8.3
6. Use the concepts of economies and diseconomies of scale to explain the shape of a firm's long-run ATC curve. What is the concept of minimum efficient scale? What bearing can the shape of the long-run ATC curve have on the structure of an industry? LO8.4
7. **LAST WORD** Does additive manufacturing rely on economies of scale to deliver low costs? What are two ways in which additive manufacturing lowers costs? Besides what's written in the book, might there be another reason to expect 3-D blueprints to be inexpensive? (Hint: Think in terms of supply and demand.)

AP REVIEW QUESTIONS

1. Linda sells 100 bottles of homemade ketchup for $10 each. The cost of the ingredients, the bottles, and the labels was $700. In addition, it took her 20 hours to make the ketchup and to do so she took time off from a job that paid her $20 per hour. Linda's accounting profit is ______________ while her economic profit is ______________. LO8.1
   a. $700; $400
   b. $300; $100
   c. $300; negative $100
   d. $1,000; negative $100
   e. $1,000; negative $1,100
2. Which of the following is *correct*? LO8.2
   a. When total product is rising, both average product and marginal product must also be rising.
   b. When marginal product is falling, total product must be falling.
   c. When marginal product is falling, average product must also be falling.
   d. When average product is falling, marginal product must be less than average product.
   e. Marginal product becomes zero after total product reaches a peak.
3. True or False:
   If the marginal-cost curve lies below the average-variable-cost curve, the average-variable-cost curve must be falling. LO8.3
4. Which of the following are short-run and which are long-run adjustments? LO8.1
   a. Wendy's fast food chain builds a new restaurant.
   b. Harley-Davidson Corporation hires 200 more production workers.
   c. A farmer increases the amount of fertilizer used on his corn crop.
   d. An Alcoa aluminum plant adds a third shift of workers.
5. Indicate how each of the following would shift the (1) marginal-cost curve, (2) average-variable-cost curve, (3) average-fixed-cost

Total Product	Total Fixed Cost	Total Variable Cost	Total Cost	Average Fixed Cost	Average Variable Cost	Average Total Cost	Marginal Cost
0	$ _____	$ 0	$ _____			$ _____	
1	_____	45	_____	$ _____	$ _____	_____	$ _____
2	_____	85	_____	_____	_____	_____	_____
3	_____	120	_____	_____	_____	_____	_____
4	_____	150	_____	_____	_____	_____	_____
5	_____	185	_____	_____	_____	_____	_____
6	_____	225	_____	_____	_____	_____	_____
7	_____	270	_____	_____	_____	_____	_____
8	_____	325	_____	_____	_____	_____	_____
9	_____	390	_____	_____	_____	_____	_____
10	_____	465	_____	_____	_____	_____	_____

curve, and (4) average-total-cost curve of a manufacturing firm. In each case specify the direction of the shift. LO8.3

a. A reduction in business property taxes.

b. An increase in the nominal wages of production workers.

c. A decrease in the price of electricity, a variable input.

d. An increase in insurance rates on plant and equipment.

6. Complete the above table if Total Fixed Cost is equal to $100.

7. True or false. The rising portion of the short-run AVC curve is the result of diminishing returns. LO8.4

8. Suppose a firm has only three possible plant-size options, represented by the ATC curves shown in the figure to the right. What plant size will the firm choose in producing (*a*) 50, (*b*) 130, (*c*) 160, and (*d*) 250 units of output? Draw the firm's long-run average-cost curve on the diagram and describe this curve. LO8.4

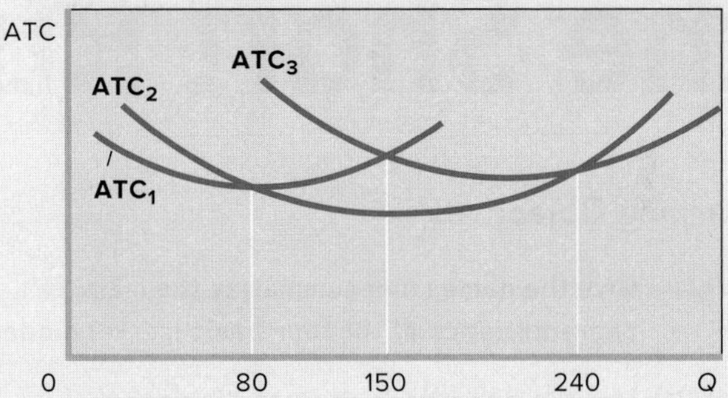

PROBLEMS

1. Gomez runs a small pottery firm. He hires one helper at $12,000 per year, pays annual rent of $5,000 for his shop, and spends $20,000 per year on materials. He has $40,000 of his own funds invested in equipment (pottery wheels, kilns, and so forth) that could earn him $4,000 per year if alternatively invested. He has been offered $15,000 per year to work as a potter for a competitor. He estimates his entrepreneurial talents are worth $3,000 per year. Total annual revenue from pottery sales is $72,000. Calculate the accounting profit and the economic profit for Gomez's pottery firm. LO8.1

2. Imagine you have some workers and some handheld computers that you can use to take inventory at a warehouse. There are diminishing returns to taking inventory. If one worker uses one computer, he can inventory 100 items per hour. Two workers sharing a computer can together inventory 150 items per hour. Three workers sharing a computer can together inventory 160 items per hour. And four or more workers sharing a computer can together inventory fewer than 160 items per hour. Computers cost $100 each and you must pay each worker $25 per hour. If you assign one worker per computer, what is the cost of inventorying a single item? What if you assign two workers per computer? Three? How many workers per computer should you assign if you wish to minimize the cost of inventorying a single item? LO8.2

3. You are a newspaper publisher. You are in the middle of a one-year rental contract for your factory that requires you to pay $500,000 per month, and you have contractual labor obligations of $1 million per month that you can't get out of. You also have a marginal printing cost of $0.25 per paper as well as a marginal delivery cost of $0.10 per paper. If sales fall by 20 percent from 1 million papers per month to 800,000 papers per month, what happens to the AFC per paper, the MC per paper, and the minimum amount that you must charge to break even on these costs? LO8.3

4. There are economies of scale in ranching, especially with regard to fencing land. Suppose that barbed-wire fencing costs $10,000 per mile to set up. How much would it cost to fence a single property whose area is one square mile if that property also happens to be perfectly square, with sides that are each one mile long? How much would it cost to fence exactly four such properties, which together would contain four square miles of area? Now, consider how much it would cost to fence in four square miles of ranch land if, instead, it comes as a single large square that is two miles long on each side. Which is more costly—fencing in the four, one-square-mile properties or the single four-square-mile property? LO8.4

9 Chapter

Pure Competition in the Short Run

Learning Objectives

LO9.1 **Give the names and summarize the main characteristics of the four basic market models.**

LO9.2 **List the conditions required for purely competitive markets.**

LO9.3 **Explain how demand is seen by a purely competitive seller.**

LO9.4 **Convey how purely competitive firms can use the total-revenue–total-cost approach to maximize profits or minimize losses in the short run.**

LO9.5 **Explain how purely competitive firms can use the marginal-revenue–marginal-cost approach to maximize profits or minimize losses in the short run.**

LO9.6 **Explain why a competitive firm's marginal cost curve is the same as its supply curve.**

AP Chapter Focus

In Chapter 6 we examined the relationship between product demand and total revenue, and in Chapter 8 we discussed production costs. Now we want to connect revenues and costs to see how a business decides what price to charge and how much output to produce. A firm's decisions concerning price and production depend greatly on the character of the industry in which it is operating. There is no "average" or "typical" industry. At one extreme is an industry in which a single producer dominates the market; at the other extreme are industries in which there are thousands of firms that each produce a tiny fraction of market supply. Between these extremes are many other types of industries.

Since we cannot examine each industry individually, we will focus on four basic *models* of **market structure.** Together, these models will help you understand how price and output are determined in the many product markets in the economy. They also will help you evaluate the efficiency or inefficiency of those markets. Finally, these four models will provide a crucial background for assessing public policies (such as antitrust policy) relating to certain firms and industries.

AP Four Market Models

LO9.1 Give the names and summarize the main characteristics of the four basic market models.

Economists group industries into four distinct market structures: pure competition, pure monopoly, monopolistic competition, and oligopoly. These four market models differ in several respects: the number of firms in the industry, whether those firms produce a standardized product or try to differentiate their products from those of other firms, and how easy or how difficult it is for firms to enter the industry.

Very briefly the four models are as follows:

- **Pure competition** involves a very large number of firms producing a standardized product (that is, a product like cotton, for which each producer's output is virtually identical to that of every other producer.) New firms can enter or exit the industry very easily.
- **Pure monopoly** is a market structure in which one firm is the sole seller of a product or service (for example, a local electric utility). Since the entry of additional firms is blocked, one firm constitutes the entire industry. The pure monopolist produces a single unique product, so product differentiation is not an issue.
- **Monopolistic competition** is characterized by a relatively large number of sellers producing differentiated products (clothing, furniture, books). Present in this model is widespread *nonprice competition,* a selling strategy in which a firm does not try to distinguish its product on the basis of price but instead on attributes like design and workmanship (an approach called *product differentiation*). Either entry to or exit from monopolistically competitive industries is quite easy.
- **Oligopoly** involves only a few sellers of a standardized or differentiated product, so each firm is affected by the decisions of its rivals and must take those decisions into account in determining its own price and output.

Table 9.1 summarizes the characteristics of the four models for easy comparison and later reference. In discussing these market models, we will occasionally distinguish the characteristics of *pure competition* from those of the three other basic market structures, which together we will designate as **imperfect competition.**

AP Pure Competition: Characteristics and Occurrence

LO9.2 List the conditions required for purely competitive markets.

Although pure competition is relatively rare in the real world, this market model is highly relevant to several industries. In particular, we can learn much about markets for agricultural goods, fish products, foreign exchange, basic metals, and stock shares by studying the pure-competition model. Also, pure competition is a meaningful starting point for any discussion of price and output determination. Moreover, the operation of a purely competitive economy provides a standard, or norm, for evaluating the efficiency of the real-world economy.

Let's take a fuller look at pure competition, the focus of the remainder of this chapter:

- ***Very large numbers*** A basic feature of a purely competitive market is the presence of a large number of independently acting sellers, often offering their products in large national or international markets. Examples: markets for farm commodities, the stock market, and the foreign exchange market.
- ***Standardized product*** Purely competitive firms produce a standardized (identical or homogeneous) product. As long as the price is the same, consumers will be indifferent about which seller to buy the product from. Buyers view the products of firms B, C, D, and E as perfect substitutes for the product of firm A. Because purely competitive firms sell standardized products,

AP TABLE 9.1 **Characteristics of the Four Basic Market Models**

	Market Model			
Characteristic	**Pure Competition**	**Monopolistic Competition**	**Oligopoly**	**Pure Monopoly**
Number of firms	A very large number	Many	Few	One
Type of product	Standardized	Differentiated	Standardized or differentiated	Unique; no close substitutes
Control over price	None	Some, but within rather narrow limits	Limited by mutual interdependence; considerable with collusion	Considerable
Conditions of entry	Very easy, no obstacles	Relatively easy	Significant obstacles	Blocked
Nonprice competition	None	Considerable emphasis on advertising, brand names, trademarks	Typically a great deal, particularly with product differentiation	Mostly public relations advertising
Examples	Agriculture	Retail trade, dresses, shoes	Steel, automobiles, farm implements, many household appliances	Local utilities

they make no attempt to differentiate their products and do not engage in other forms of nonprice competition.

- ***"Price takers"*** In a purely competitive market, individual firms do not exert control over product price. Each firm produces such a small fraction of total output that increasing or decreasing its output will not perceptibly influence total supply or, therefore, product price. In short, the competitive firm is a **price taker:** It cannot change market price; it can only adjust to it. That means that the individual competitive producer is at the mercy of the market. Asking a price higher than the market price would be futile. Consumers will not buy from firm A at \$2.05 when its 9,999 competitors are selling an identical product, and therefore a perfect substitute, at \$2 per unit. Conversely, because firm A can sell as much as it chooses at \$2 per unit, it has no reason to charge a lower price, say, \$1.95. Doing that would shrink its profit.
- ***Free entry and exit*** New firms can freely enter and existing firms can freely leave purely competitive industries. No significant legal, technological, financial, or other obstacles prohibit new firms from selling their output in any competitive market.

AP Demand as Seen by a Purely Competitive Seller

LO9.3 Explain how demand is seen by a purely competitive seller.

We begin by examining demand from a purely competitive seller's viewpoint to see how it affects revenue. This seller might be a wheat farmer, a strawberry grower, a sheep rancher, a foreign-currency broker, or some other pure competitor. Because each purely competitive firm offers only a negligible fraction of total market supply, it must accept the price determined by the market; it is a price taker, not a price maker.

Perfectly Elastic Demand

The demand schedule faced by the *individual firm* in a purely competitive industry is perfectly elastic at the market price, as demonstrated in Figure 9.1. As shown in column 1 of the table in Figure 9.1, the market price is \$131. The firm represented cannot obtain a higher price by restricting its output, nor does it need to lower its price to increase its sales volume. Columns 1 and 2 show that the firm can produce and sell as many or as few units as it likes at the market price of \$131.

We are *not* saying that *market* demand is perfectly elastic in a competitive market. Rather, market demand graphs as a downsloping curve. An entire industry (all firms producing a particular product) can affect price by changing industry output. For example, all firms, acting independently but simultaneously, can increase price by reducing output. But the individual competitive firm cannot do that because its output represents such a small fraction of its industry's total output. For the individual competitive firm, the market price is therefore a fixed value at which it can sell as many or as few units as it cares to. Graphically, this implies that the individual competitive firm's demand curve will plot as a straight, horizontal line such as *D* in Figure 9.1.

Average, Total, and Marginal Revenue

The firm's demand schedule is also its average-revenue schedule. Price per unit to the purchaser is also revenue per unit, or average revenue, to the seller. To say that all buyers must pay \$131 per unit is to say that the revenue per unit, or **average revenue** received by the seller, is \$131. Price and average revenue are the same thing.

The **total revenue** for each sales level is found by multiplying price by the corresponding quantity the firm can sell. (Column 1 multiplied by column 2 in the table in Figure 9.1 yields column 3.) In this case, total revenue increases by a constant amount, \$131, for each additional unit of sales. Each unit sold adds exactly its constant price—no more or no less—to total revenue.

When a firm is pondering a change in its output, it will consider how its total revenue will change as a result. **Marginal revenue** is the change in total revenue (or the extra revenue) that results from selling one more unit of output. In column 3 of the table in Figure 9.1, total revenue is zero when zero units are sold. The first unit of output sold increases total revenue from zero to \$131, so marginal revenue for that unit is \$131. The second unit sold increases total revenue from \$131 to \$262, and marginal revenue is again \$131. Note in column 4 that marginal revenue is a constant \$131, as is price. *In pure competition, marginal revenue and price are equal.*

Figure 9.1 shows the purely competitive firm's total-revenue, demand, marginal-revenue, and average-revenue curves. Total revenue (TR) is a straight line that slopes upward to the right. Its slope is constant because each extra unit of sales increases TR by \$131. The demand curve (*D*) is horizontal, indicating perfect price elasticity. The marginal-revenue (MR) curve coincides with the demand curve because the product price (and hence MR) is constant. The average revenue (AR) curve equals price and therefore also coincides with the demand curve.

AP QUICK REVIEW 9.1

- ✓ In a purely competitive industry a large number of relatively small firms produce a standardized product, with no significant barriers to entry.
- ✓ Purely competitive firms are "price-takers" with perfectly elastic demand (horizontal) at the competitive market equilibrium price. Having identical products, the firms can sell nothing above the prevailing equilibrium price.
- ✓ Price, marginal revenue, and average revenue for a purely competitive firm are equal and coincide with the firm's demand curve; total revenue rises by the product price for each additional unit sold.

AP **FIGURE 9.1 A purely competitive firm's demand and revenue curves.** The demand curve (*D*) of a purely competitive firm is a horizontal line (perfectly elastic) because the firm can sell as much output as it wants at the market price (here, $131). Because each additional unit sold increases total revenue by the amount of the price, the firm's total-revenue (TR) curve is a straight upsloping line and its marginal-revenue (MR) curve coincides with the firm's demand curve. The average-revenue (AR) curve also coincides with the demand curve.

Firm's Demand Schedule		Firm's Revenue Data	
(1) Product Price (*P*) (Average Revenue)	(2) Quantity Demanded (*Q*)	(3) Total Revenue (TR), (1) × (2)	(4) Marginal Revenue (MR)
$131	0	$ 0	
			$131
131	1	131	
			131
131	2	262	
			131
131	3	393	
			131
131	4	524	
			131
131	5	655	
			131
131	6	786	
			131
131	7	917	
			131
131	8	1048	
			131
131	9	1179	
			131
131	10	1310	

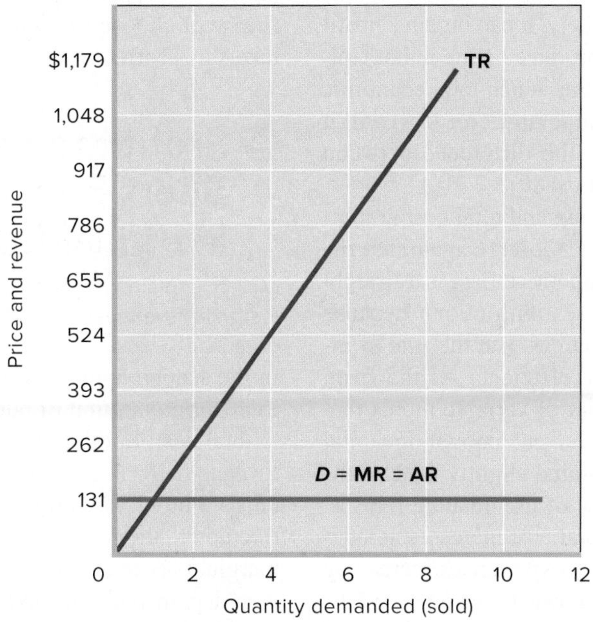

AP Profit Maximization in the Short Run: Total-Revenue–Total-Cost Approach

LO9.4 Convey how purely competitive firms can use the total-revenue–total-cost approach to maximize profits or minimize losses in the short run.

Because the purely competitive firm is a price taker, it cannot attempt to maximize its profit by raising or lowering the price it charges. With its price set by supply and demand in the overall market, the only variable that the firm can control is its output. As a result, the purely competitive firm attempts to maximize its economic profit (or minimize its economic loss) by adjusting its *output*. And, in the short run, the firm has a fixed plant. Thus it can adjust its output only through changes in the amount of variable resources (materials, labor) it uses. It adjusts its variable resources to achieve the output level that maximizes its profit or minimizes its loss.

There are two ways to determine the level of output at which a competitive firm will realize maximum profit or minimum loss. One method is to compare total revenue and total cost; the other is to compare marginal revenue and marginal cost. Both approaches apply to all firms, whether they are pure competitors, pure monopolists, monopolistic competitors, or oligopolists.[1]

We begin by examining profit maximization using the total-revenue–total-cost approach. Confronted with the market price of its product, the competitive producer will ask three questions: (1) Should we produce this product? (2) If so, in what amount? (3) What economic profit (or loss) will we realize?

Let's demonstrate how a pure competitor answers these questions, given a particular set of cost data and a specific market price. Our cost data are already familiar because they are the fixed-cost, variable-cost, and total-cost data in Table 8.2, repeated in columns 1 to 4 of the table in Figure 9.2. (Recall that these data reflect explicit and implicit costs, including a normal profit.) Assuming that the market price is $131, the total revenue for each output level is found by multiplying output (total product) by price. Total-revenue data are in column 5. Then in column 6 we find the profit or loss at each output level by subtracting total cost, TC (column 4), from total revenue, TR (column 5).

Should the firm produce? Definitely. It can obtain a profit by doing so. How much should it produce? Nine units. Column 6 tells us that this is the output at which total economic profit is at a maximum. What economic profit (or loss) will it realize? A $299 economic profit—the difference between total revenue ($1,179) and total cost ($880).

Figure 9.2a compares total revenue and total cost graphically for this profit-maximizing case. Observe again that the total-revenue curve for a purely competitive firm is a straight line (Figure 9.1). Total cost increases with output because more production requires more resources. But the *rate* of increase in total cost varies with the efficiency of the firm, which in turn varies with the amount of variable inputs that are being combined with the firm's current amount of capital (which is fixed in the short run). Stated slightly differently, the cost data reflect Chapter 8's law of diminishing returns. From zero to four units of output, total cost increases at a decreasing rate as the firm temporarily experiences increasing returns. At higher levels of output, however, efficiency falls as crowding causes diminishing returns to set in. Once that happens, the firm's total cost increases at an increasing rate because each additional unit of input yields less output than the previous unit.

Total revenue and total cost are equal where the two curves in Figure 9.2a intersect (at roughly 2 units of output). Total revenue covers all costs (including a normal profit, which is included in the cost curve), but there is no economic profit. For this reason economists call this output a **break-even point:** an output at which a firm makes a *normal profit* but not an economic profit. If we extended the data beyond 10 units of output, another break-even point would occur where total cost catches up with total revenue, somewhere between 13 and 14 units of output in Figure 9.2a. Any output within the two break-even points identified in the figure will yield an economic profit. The firm achieves maximum profit, however, where the vertical distance between the total-revenue and total-cost curves is greatest. For our particular data, this is at 9 units of output, where maximum profit is $299.

The profit-maximizing output is easier to see in Figure 9.2b, where total profit is graphed for each level of output. Where the total-revenue and total-cost curves intersect in Figure 9.2a, economic profit is zero, as shown by the total-profit line in Figure 9.2b. Where the vertical distance between TR and TC is greatest in the upper graph, economic profit is at its peak ($299), as shown in the lower graph. This firm will choose to produce 9 units since that output maximizes its profit.

AP Profit Maximization in the Short Run: Marginal-Revenue–Marginal-Cost Approach

LO9.5 Explain how purely competitive firms can use the marginal-revenue–marginal-cost approach to maximize profits or minimize losses in the short run.

In the second approach, the firm compares the amounts that each *additional* unit of output would add to total revenue and to total cost. In other words, the firm compares the *marginal revenue* (MR) and the *marginal cost* (MC) of each successive unit of output. Assuming that producing is preferable to shutting down, the firm should produce any unit of output whose marginal revenue exceeds its marginal cost because the firm would gain more in revenue from selling that unit than it would add to its costs by producing it. Conversely, if the marginal cost of a unit of output exceeds its marginal revenue, the firm should not produce that unit. Producing it would add more to costs than to revenue, and profit would decline or loss would increase.

In the initial stages of production, where output is relatively low, marginal revenue will usually (but not always) exceed marginal cost. So it is profitable to produce through this range of output. But at later stages of production, where output is relatively high, rising marginal costs will exceed marginal revenue. Obviously, a profit-maximizing firm will want to avoid output levels in that range. Separating these two production ranges is a unique point at which marginal revenue

[1]To make sure you understand these two approaches, we will apply both of them to output determination under pure competition. But since we want to emphasize the marginal approach, we will limit our graphical application of the total-revenue approach to a situation where the firm maximizes profits. We will then use the marginal approach to examine three cases: profit maximization, loss minimization, and shutdown.

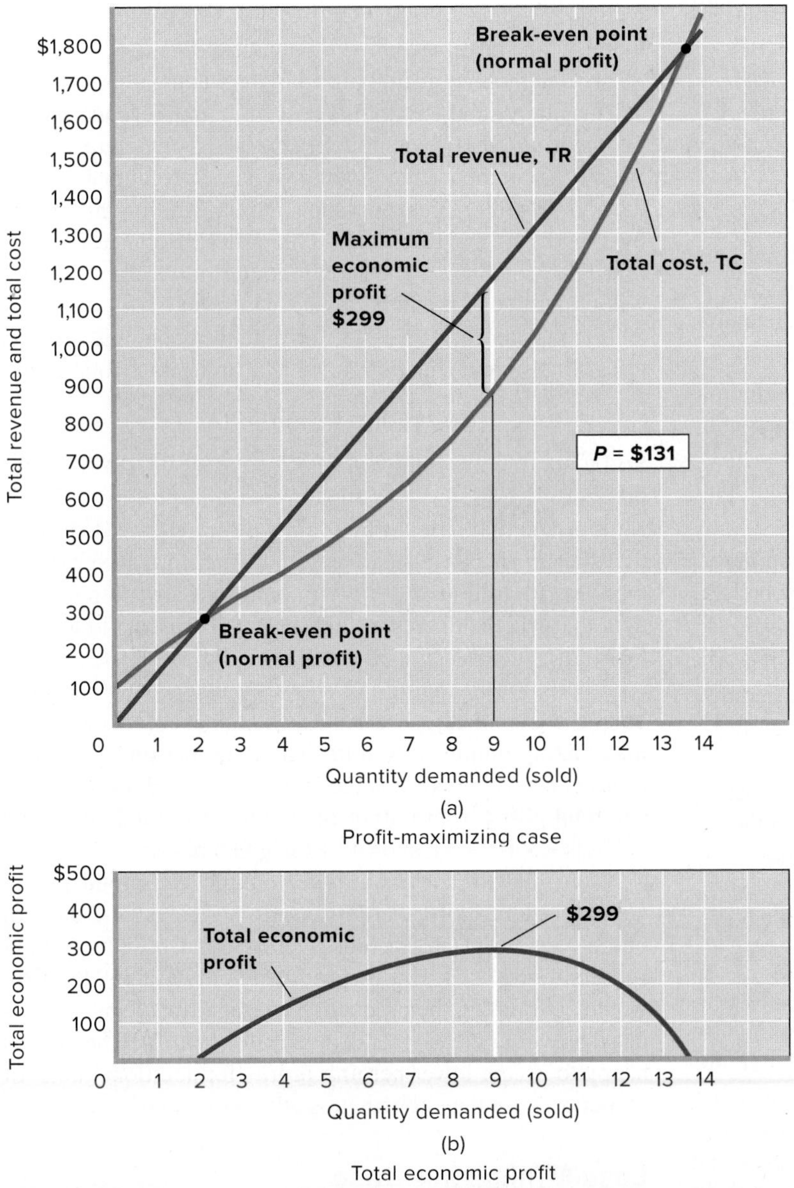

FIGURE 9.2 Total-revenue–total-cost approach to profit maximization for a purely competitive firm. (a) The firm's profit is maximized at that output (9 units) where total revenue, TR, exceeds total cost, TC, by the maximum amount. (b) The vertical distance between TR and TC in (a) is plotted as a total-economic-profit curve. Maximum economic profit is $299 at 9 units of output.

				PRICE: $131	
(1) Total Product (Output) (Q)	(2) Total Fixed Cost (TFC)	(3) Total Variable Cost (TVC)	(4) Total Cost (TC)	(5) Total Revenue (TR)	(6) Profit (+) or Loss (−)
0	$100	$ 0	$ 100	$ 0	$−100
1	100	90	190	131	−59
2	100	170	270	262	−8
3	100	240	340	393	+53
4	100	300	400	524	+124
5	100	370	470	655	+185
6	100	450	550	786	+236
7	100	540	640	917	+277
8	100	650	750	1,048	+298
9	100	780	**880**	**1,179**	**+299**
10	100	930	1,030	1,310	+280

equals marginal cost. This point is the key to the output-determining rule: *In the short run, the firm will maximize profit or minimize loss by producing the output at which marginal revenue equals marginal cost (as long as producing is preferable to shutting down).* This profit-maximizing guide is known as the **MR = MC rule.**

Keep in mind these features of the MR = MC rule:

- For most sets of MR and MC data, MR and MC will be precisely equal at a fractional level of output. In such instances the firm should produce the last complete unit of output for which MR exceeds MC.
- As noted, the rule applies only if producing is preferable to shutting down. We will show shortly that if marginal revenue does not equal or exceed average variable cost, the firm will shut down rather than produce the amount of output at which MR = MC.
- The rule is an accurate guide to profit maximization for all firms whether they are purely competitive, monopolistic, monopolistically competitive, or oligopolistic.
- The rule can be restated as P = MC when applied to a purely competitive firm. Because the demand schedule faced by a competitive seller is perfectly elastic at the going market price, product price and marginal revenue are equal. So under pure competition (and only under pure competition) we may substitute P for MR in the rule: When producing is preferable to shutting down, the competitive firm that wants to maximize its profit or minimize its loss should produce at that point where price equals marginal cost ($P = MC$).

Now let's apply the MR = MC rule or, because we are considering pure competition, the P = MC rule, first using the same price as used in our total-revenue–total-cost approach to profit maximization. Then, by considering other prices, we will demonstrate two additional cases: loss minimization and shutdown. It is crucial that you understand the MR = MC analysis that follows since it reappears in Chapters 11 through 14.

Profit-Maximizing Case

The first five columns of the table in **Figure 9.3 (Key Graph)** reproduce the AFC, AVC, ATC, and MC data derived for our product in Table 8.2. It is the marginal-cost data of column 5 that we will compare with price (equals marginal revenue) for each unit of output. Suppose first that the market price, and therefore marginal revenue, is \$131, as shown in column 6.

What is the profit-maximizing output? Every unit of output up to and including the ninth unit represents greater marginal revenue than marginal cost of output. Each of the first 9 units therefore adds to the firm's profit and should be produced. The tenth unit, however, should not be produced. It would add more to cost (\$150) than to revenue (\$131). So 9 units is the profit-maximizing output.

The economic profit realized by producing 9 units can be calculated by subtracting total cost from total revenue. Multiplying price (\$131) by output (9), we find that total revenue is \$1,179. From the average-total-cost data in column 4, we see that ATC is \$97.78 at 9 units of output. Multiplying \$97.78 by 9 gives us total cost of \$880.[2] The difference of \$299 (= \$1,179 − \$880) is the economic profit. Clearly, this firm will prefer to operate rather than shut down.

Perhaps an easier way to calculate the economic profit is to use this simple equation, in which A is average total cost:

$$\text{Profit} = (P - A) \times Q$$

So by subtracting the average total cost (\$97.78) from the product price (\$131), we obtain a per-unit profit of \$33.22. Multiplying that amount by 9 units of output, we determine that the profit is \$299. Take some time now to verify the numbers in column 7. You will find that any output other than that which adheres to the MR = MC rule will mean either profits below \$299 or losses.

The graph in Figure 9.3 shows price (= MR) and marginal cost graphically. Price equals marginal cost at the profit-maximizing output of 9 units. There the per-unit economic profit is $P - A$, where P is the market price and A is the average total cost for an output of 9 units. The total economic profit is $9 \times (P - A)$, shown by the green rectangular area.

Note that the firm wants to maximize its total profit, not its per-unit profit. Per-unit profit is greatest at 7 units of output, where price exceeds average total cost by \$39.57 (= \$131 − \$91.43). But by producing only 7 units, the firm would be forgoing the production of 2 additional units of output that would clearly contribute to total profit. The firm is happy to accept lower per-unit profits for additional units of output because they nonetheless add to total profit.

Loss-Minimizing Case

Now let's assume that the market price is \$81 rather than \$131. Should the firm still produce? If so, how much? And what will be the resulting profit or loss? The answers, respectively, are "Yes," "Six units," and "A loss of \$64."

The first five columns of the table in Figure 9.4 are the same as the first five columns of the table in Figure 9.3. But column 6 of the table in Figure 9.4 shows the new price (equal to MR), \$81. Comparing columns 5 and 6, we find that the first unit of output adds \$90 to total cost but only \$81 to total revenue. One might conclude: "Don't produce—close down!" But

[2]Most of the unit-cost data are rounded figures. Therefore, economic profits calculated from them will typically vary by a few cents from the profits determined in the total-revenue–total-cost approach. Here we simply ignore the few-cents differentials to make our answers consistent with the results of the total-revenue–total-cost approach.

AP KEY GRAPH

FIGURE 9.3 Short-run profit maximization for a purely competitive firm. The MR = MC output enables the purely competitive firm to maximize profits or to minimize losses. In this case MR (= *P* in pure competition) and MC are equal at an output *Q* of 9 units. There, *P* exceeds the average total cost *A* = \$97.78, so the firm realizes an economic profit of *P* – *A* per unit. The total economic profit is represented by the green rectangle and is 9 × (*P* – *A*).

(1) Total Product (Output)	(2) Average Fixed Cost (AFC)	(3) Average Variable Cost (AVC)	(4) Average Total Cost (ATC)	(5) Marginal Cost (MC)	(6) Price = Marginal Revenue (MR)	(7) Total Economic Profit (+) or Loss (–)
0						\$–100
1	\$100.00	\$90.00	\$190.00	\$ 90	\$131	–59
2	50.00	85.00	135.00	80	131	–8
3	33.33	80.00	113.33	70	131	+53
4	25.00	75.00	100.00	60	131	+124
5	20.00	74.00	94.00	70	131	+185
6	16.67	75.00	91.67	80	131	+236
7	14.29	77.14	91.43	90	131	+277
8	12.50	81.25	93.75	110	131	+298
9	**11.11**	**86.67**	**97.78**	**130**	**131**	**+299**
10	10.00	93.00	103.00	150	131	+280

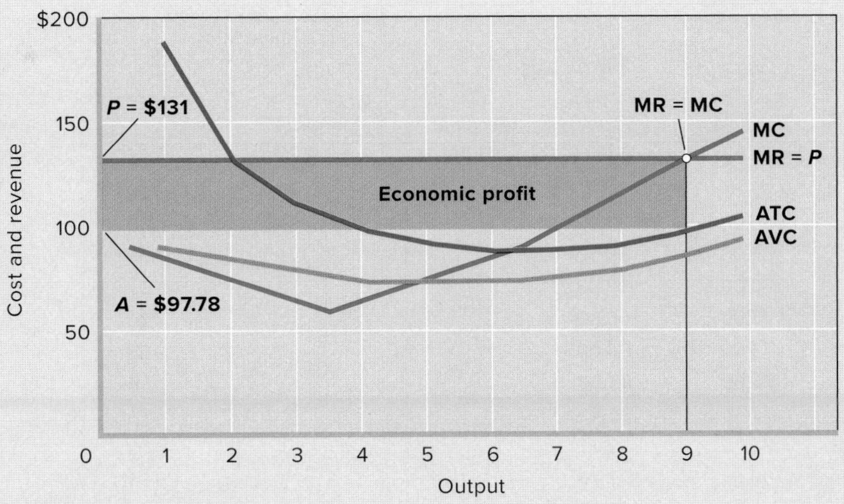

QUICK QUIZ FOR FIGURE 9.3

1. Curve MR is horizontal because:
   a. product price falls as output increases.
   b. the law of diminishing marginal utility is at work.
   c. the market demand for this product is perfectly elastic.
   d. the firm is a price taker.
2. At a price of \$131 and 7 units of output:
   a. MR exceeds MC, and the firm should expand its output.
   b. total revenue is less than total cost.
   c. AVC exceeds ATC.
   d. the firm would earn only a normal profit.
3. In maximizing profits at 9 units of output, this firm is adhering to which of the following decision rules?
   a. Produce where MR exceeds MC by the greatest amount.
   b. Produce where *P* exceeds ATC by the greatest amount.
   c. Produce where total revenue exceeds total cost by the greatest amount.
   d. Produce where average fixed costs are zero.
4. Suppose price declined from \$131 to \$100. This firm's:
   a. marginal-cost curve would shift downward.
   b. economic profit would fall to zero.
   c. profit-maximizing output would decline.
   d. total cost would fall by more than its total revenue.

Answers: 1. d; 2. a; 3. c; 4. c

AP **FIGURE 9.4 Short-run loss minimization for a purely competitive firm.** If price *P* exceeds the minimum AVC (here, $74 at *Q* = 5) but is less than ATC, the MR = MC output (here, 6 units) will permit the firm to minimize its losses. In this instance the loss is *A* – *P* per unit, where *A* is the average total cost at 6 units of output. The total loss is shown by the red area and is equal to 6 × (*A* – *P*).

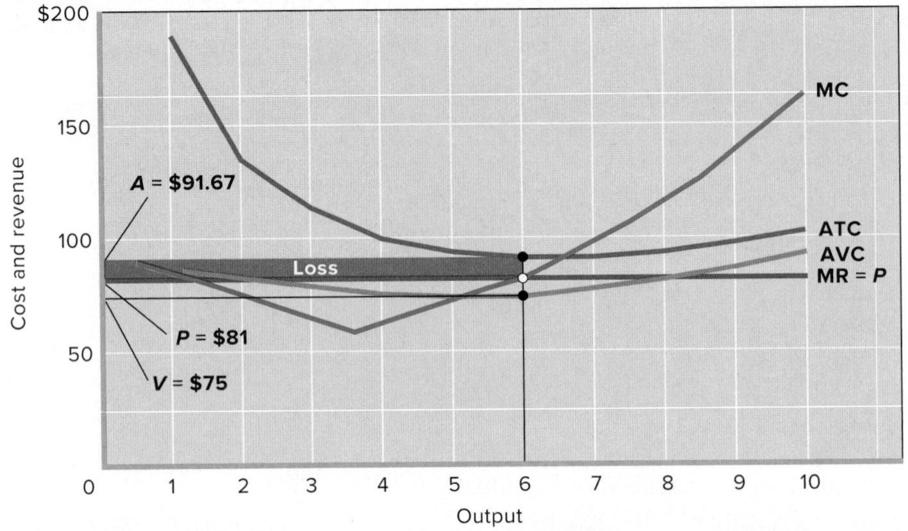

					Loss-Minimizing Case		Shutdown Case	
(1) Total Product (Output)	(2) Average Fixed Cost (AFC)	(3) Average Variable Cost (AVC)	(4) Average Total Cost (ATC)	(5) Marginal Cost (MC)	(6) $81 Price = Marginal Revenue (MR)	(7) Profit (+) or Loss (–), $81 Price	(8) $71 Price = Marginal Revenue (MR)	(9) Profit (+) or Loss (–), $71 Price
0						$–100		**$–100**
1	$100.00	$90.00	$190.00	$ 90	$81	–109	$71	–119
2	50.00	85.00	135.00	80	81	–108	71	–128
3	33.33	80.00	113.33	70	81	–97	71	–127
4	25.00	75.00	100.00	60	81	–76	71	–116
5	20.00	74.00	94.00	70	81	–65	71	–115
6	**16.67**	**75.00**	**91.67**	**80**	**81**	**–64**	71	–124
7	14.29	77.14	91.43	90	81	–73	71	–143
8	12.50	81.25	93.75	110	81	–102	71	–182
9	11.11	86.67	97.78	130	81	–151	71	–241
10	10.00	93.00	103.00	150	81	–220	71	–320

that would be hasty. Remember that in the very early stages of production, marginal product is low, making marginal cost unusually high. The price–marginal cost relationship improves with increased production. For units 2 through 6, price exceeds marginal cost. Each of these 5 units adds more to revenue than to cost, and as shown in column 7, they decrease the total loss. Together they more than compensate for the "loss" taken on the first unit. Beyond 6 units, however, MC exceeds MR (= *P*). The firm should therefore produce 6 units. In general, the profit-seeking producer should always compare marginal revenue (or price under pure competition) with the rising portion of the marginal-cost schedule or curve.

Will production be profitable? No, because at 6 units of output the average total cost of $91.67 exceeds the price of $81 by $10.67 per unit. If we multiply that by the 6 units of output, we find the firm's total loss is $64. Alternatively, comparing the total revenue of $486 (= 6 × $81) with the total cost of $550 (= 6 × $91.67), we see again that the firm's loss is $64.

Then why produce? Because this loss is less than the firm's $100 of fixed costs, which is the $100 loss the firm would incur in the short run by closing down. The firm receives enough revenue per unit ($81) to cover its average variable costs of $75 and also provide $6 per unit, or a total of $36, to apply against fixed costs. Therefore, the firm's loss is only $64 (= $100 – $36), not $100.

This loss-minimizing case is illustrated in the graph in Figure 9.4. Wherever price *P* exceeds average variable cost

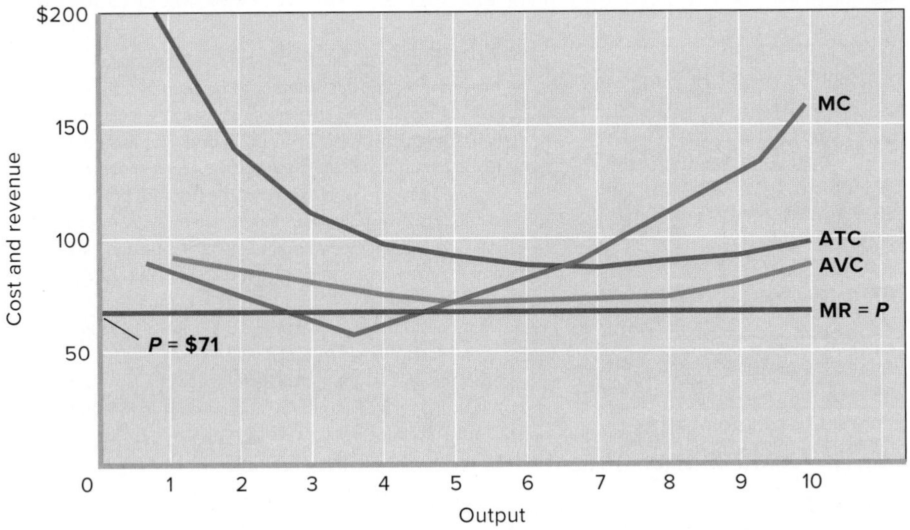

AP **FIGURE 9.5 The short-run shutdown case for a purely competitive firm.** If price P falls below the minimum AVC (here, $74 at $Q = 5$), the competitive firm will minimize its losses in the short run by shutting down. There is no level of output at which the firm can produce and incur a loss smaller than its total fixed cost.

AVC but is less than ATC, the firm can pay part, but not all, of its fixed costs by producing. The loss is minimized by producing the output at which MC = MR (here, 6 units). At that output, each unit contributes $P - V$ to covering fixed cost, where V is the AVC at 6 units of output. The per-unit loss is $A - P = \$10.67$, and the total loss is $6 \times (A - P)$, or $64, as shown by the red area.

Shutdown Case

Suppose now that the market yields a price of only $71. Should the firm produce? No, because at every output level the firm's average variable cost is greater than the price (compare columns 3 and 8 of the table in Figure 9.4). The smallest loss it can incur by producing is greater than the $100 fixed cost it will lose by shutting down (as shown by column 9). The best action is to shut down.

You can see this shutdown situation in Figure 9.5. Price comes closest to covering average variable costs at the MR (= P) = MC output of 5 units. But even here, price or revenue per unit would fall short of average variable cost by $3 (= $74 – $71). By producing at the MR (= P) = MC output, the firm would lose its $100 worth of fixed cost plus $15 ($3 of variable cost on each of the 5 units), for a total loss of $115. This compares unfavorably with the $100 fixed-cost loss the firm would incur by shutting down and producing no output. So it will make sense for the firm to shut down rather than produce at a $71 price—or at any price less than the minimum average variable cost of $74.

The shutdown case reminds us of the qualifier to our MR (= P) = MC rule. A competitive firm will maximize profit or minimize loss in the short run by producing that output at which MR (= P) = MC, *provided that market price exceeds minimum average variable cost.*

AP QUICK REVIEW 9.2

- ✓ As a price-taker, purely competitive firms need to choose the optimal output level, given that price is set in the market. The optimal decision rule is to produce to the equality of marginal revenue (or price in this competitive model) and marginal cost.
- ✓ A firm will choose to produce, if it can at least break even and generate a normal profit.
- ✓ Profit is maximized, or loss minimized, at the output at which MR = MC, provided that price exceeds average variable cost (AVC).
- ✓ If the market price is below the minimum AVC at the MR = MC profit maximizing level of output, the firm will minimize its losses by shutting down.

AP Marginal Cost and Short-Run Supply

LO9.6 Explain why a competitive firm's marginal cost curve is the same as its supply curve.

In the preceding section we simply selected three different prices and asked what quantity the profit-seeking competitive firm, faced with certain costs, would choose to offer in the market at each price. This set of product prices and corresponding quantities supplied constitutes part of the supply schedule for the competitive firm.

Table 9.2 summarizes the supply schedule data for those three prices ($131, $81, and $71) and four others. This table confirms the direct relationship between product price and quantity supplied that we identified in Chapter 3. Note first that the firm will not produce at price $61 or $71 because both are less than the $74 minimum AVC. Then note that quantity supplied increases as price increases. Observe finally that economic profit is higher at higher prices.

AP KEY GRAPH

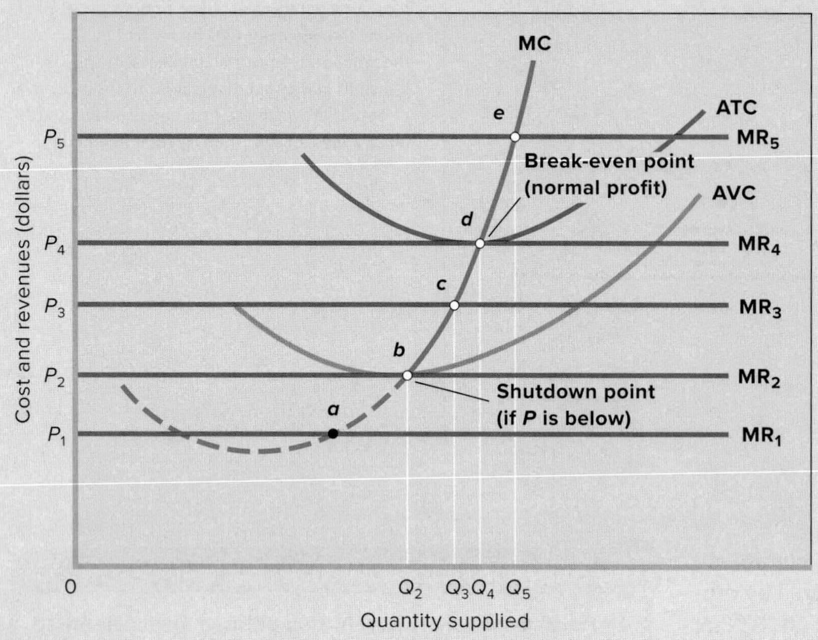

FIGURE 9.6 The $P = MC$ rule and the competitive firm's short-run supply curve. Application of the $P = MC$ rule, as modified by the shutdown case, reveals that the (solid) segment of the firm's MC curve that lies above AVC is the firm's short-run supply curve. More specifically, at price P_1, $P = MC$ at point *a*, but the firm will produce no output because P_1 is less than minimum AVC. At price P_2 the firm will operate at point *b*, where it produces Q_2 units and incurs a loss equal to its total fixed cost. At P_3 it operates at point *c*, where output is Q_3 and the loss is less than total fixed cost. With the price of P_4, the firm operates at point *d*; in this case the firm earns a normal profit because at output Q_4 price equals ATC. At price P_5 the firm operates at point *e* and maximizes its economic profit by producing Q_5 units.

QUICK QUIZ FOR FIGURE 9.6

1. Which of the following might increase product price from P_3 to P_5?
   a. An improvement in production technology.
   b. A decline in the price of a substitute good.
   c. An increase in the price of a complementary good.
   d. Rising incomes if the product is a normal good.
2. An increase in price from P_3 to P_5 would:
   a. shift this firm's MC curve to the right.
   b. mean that MR_5 exceeds MC at Q_3 units, inducing the firm to expand output to Q_5.
   c. decrease this firm's average variable costs.
   d. enable this firm to obtain a normal, but not an economic, profit.
3. At P_4:
   a. this firm has no economic profit.
   b. this firm will earn only a normal profit and thus will shut down.
   c. MR_4 will be less than MC at the profit-maximizing output.
   d. the profit-maximizing output will be Q_5.
4. Suppose P_4 is \$10, P_5 is \$15, Q_4 is 8 units, and Q_5 is 10 units. This firm's:
   a. supply curve is elastic over the Q_4–Q_5 range of output.
   b. supply curve is inelastic over the Q_4–Q_5 range of output.
   c. total revenue will decline if price rises from P_4 to P_5.
   d. marginal-cost curve will shift downward if price falls from P_5 to P_4.

Answers: 1. d; 2. b; 3. a; 4. b

TABLE 9.2 The Supply Schedule of a Competitive Firm Confronted with the Cost Data in the Table in Figure 9.3

Price	Quantity Supplied	Maximum Profit (+) or Minimum Loss (−)
\$151	10	\$+480
131	9	+299
111	8	+138
91	7	−3
81	6	−64
71	0	−100
61	0	−100

Generalized Depiction

Figure 9.6 (Key Graph) generalizes the MR = MC rule and the relationship between short-run production costs and the firm's supply behavior. The ATC, AVC, and MC curves are shown, along with several marginal-revenue lines drawn at possible market prices. Let's observe quantity supplied at each of these prices:

- Price P_1 is below the firm's minimum average variable cost, so at this price the firm won't operate at all. Quantity supplied will be zero, as it will be at all other prices below P_2.

CONSIDER THIS . . .

Source: © LWA/Getty RF

The "Still There" Motel

Have you ever driven by a poorly maintained business facility and wondered why the owner does not either fix up the property or go out of business? The somewhat surprising reason is that it may be unprofitable to improve the facility yet profitable to continue to operate the business as it deteriorates. Seeing why will aid your understanding of the "stay open or shut down" decision facing firms experiencing declining demand.

Consider the story of the Still There Motel on Old Highway North, Anytown, USA. The owner built the motel on the basis of traffic patterns and competition existing several decades ago. But as interstate highways were built, the motel found itself located on a relatively untraveled stretch of road. Also, it faced severe competition from "chain" motels located much closer to the interstate highway.

As demand and revenue fell, Still There moved from profitability to loss ($P <$ ATC). But at first its room rates and annual revenue were sufficient to cover its total variable costs and contribute some to the payment of fixed costs such as insurance and property taxes ($P >$ AVC). By staying open, Still There lost less than it would have if it shut down. But since its total revenue did not cover its total costs (or $P <$ ATC), the owner realized that something must be done in the long run. The owner decided to lower total costs by reducing annual maintenance. In effect, the owner opted to allow the motel to deteriorate as a way of temporarily regaining profitability.

This renewed profitability of Still There cannot last because in time no further reduction of maintenance costs will be possible. The deterioration of the motel structure will produce even lower room rates, and therefore even less total revenue. The owner of Still There knows that sooner or later total revenue will again fall below total cost (or P will again fall below ATC), even with an annual maintenance expense of zero. When that occurs, the owner will close down the business, tear down the structure, and sell the vacant property. But, in the meantime, the motel is still there—open, deteriorating, and profitable.

- Price P_2 is just equal to the minimum average variable cost. The firm will supply Q_2 units of output (where $MR_2 = MC$) and just cover its total variable cost. Its loss will equal its total fixed cost. (Actually, the firm would be indifferent as to shutting down or supplying Q_2 units of output, but we assume it produces.)
- At price P_3 the firm will supply Q_3 units of output to minimize its short-run losses. At any of the other prices between P_2 and P_4 the firm will also minimize its losses by producing and supplying the quantity at which MR $(= P) =$ MC.
- The firm will just break even at price P_4. There it will supply Q_4 units of output (where $MR_4 = MC$), earning a normal profit but not an economic profit. Total revenue will just cover total cost, including a normal profit, because the revenue per unit ($MR_4 = P_4$) and the total cost per unit (ATC) are the same.
- At price P_5 the firm will realize an economic profit by producing and supplying Q_5 units of output. In fact, at any price above P_4 the firm will obtain economic profit by producing to the point where MR $(= P) =$ MC.

Note that each of the MR $(= P) =$ MC intersection points labeled *b, c, d,* and *e* in Figure 10.6 indicates a possible product price (on the vertical axis) and the corresponding quantity that the firm would supply at that price (on the horizontal axis). Thus, points such as these are on the upsloping supply curve of the competitive firm. Note, too, that quantity supplied would be zero at any price below the minimum average variable cost (AVC). *We can conclude that the portion of the firm's marginal-cost curve lying above its average-variable-cost curve is its short-run supply curve.* In Figure 9.6, the solid segment of the marginal-cost curve MC is this firm's **short-run supply curve.** It tells us the amount of output the firm will supply at each price in a series of prices.

Table 9.3 summarizes the MR = MC approach to determining the competitive firm's profit-maximizing output level. It also shows the equivalent analysis in terms of total revenue and total cost.

TABLE 9.3 Output Determination in Pure Competition in the Short Run

Question	Answer
Should this firm produce?	Yes, if price is equal to, or greater than, minimum average variable cost. This means that the firm is profitable or that its losses are less than its fixed cost.
What quantity should this firm produce?	Produce where MR $(= P) =$ MC; there, profit is maximized (TR exceeds TC by a maximum amount) or loss is minimized.
Will production result in economic profit?	Yes, if price exceeds average total cost (so that TR exceeds TC). No, if average total cost exceeds price (so that TC exceeds TR).

LAST WORD

Fixed Costs: Digging Yourself Out of a Hole

For Firms Facing Losses Due to Fixed Costs, Shutting Down in the Short Run Does Not Mean Shutting Down Forever.

A firm with fixed costs starts each month standing at the bottom of a deep financial hole. The depth of that "money pit" is equal to the dollar value of all the payments that the firm is legally obligated to make even if it is producing nothing. These fixed costs include contractually guaranteed salaries, interest payments on loans, and equipment rental fees that are locked in by long-term contracts. As the firm stands at the bottom of this fixed-cost financial hole and stares upward looking for a way out, it has to ask itself the following question: Will producing output make the hole even deeper?

Naturally, the firm hopes that producing output will generate positive cash flows that will offset its fixed costs and start filling in the hole. If those positive flows are large enough, they may completely offset the firm's fixed costs and fill up the hole, thereby allowing the firm to break even. And if they are just a bit larger, they will not only fill up the hole but also accumulate a nice little pile of profits above ground.

But those are just the firm's hopes. The firm's reality may be quite unpleasant. In particular, the firm may be facing a situation in which producing output would make its financial situation worse rather than better. As explained in this chapter, if the price of the firm's output falls too low, then producing output will yield cash flows that are negative rather than positive because revenues will be less than variable costs. If that happens,

Source: © pixhook/Getty RF

Diminishing Returns, Production Costs, and Product Supply

We have now identified the links between the law of diminishing returns (Chapter 8), production costs, and product supply in the short run. Because of the law of diminishing returns, marginal costs eventually rise as more units of output are produced. And because marginal costs rise with output, a purely competitive firm must get successively higher prices to motivate it to produce additional units of output.

Viewed alternatively, higher product prices and marginal revenue encourage a purely competitive firm to expand output. As its output increases, the firm's marginal costs rise as a result of the law of diminishing returns. At some now greater output, the higher MC equals the new product price and MR. Profit once again is maximized, but at a greater total amount. Quantity supplied has increased in direct response to an increase in product price and the desire to maximize profit.

Changes in Supply

In Chapter 8 we saw that changes in such factors as the prices of variable inputs or in technology will alter costs and shift the marginal-cost or short-run supply curve to a new location. All else equal, for example, a wage increase would increase marginal cost and shift the supply curve in Figure 9.6 upward as viewed from the horizontal axis (leftward as viewed from the vertical axis). That is, supply would decrease. Similarly, technological progress that increases the productivity of labor would reduce marginal cost and shift the marginal-cost or supply curve downward as viewed from the horizontal axis (rightward as viewed from the vertical axis). This represents an increase in supply.

Firm and Industry: Equilibrium Price

In the preceding section we established the competitive firm's short-run supply curve by applying the MR (= P) = MC rule. But which of the various possible prices will actually be the market equilibrium price?

producing output will lose money for the firm so that the firm would be better off shutting down production rather than producing output. By shutting down, it will lose only its fixed costs. By shutting down, its financial hole won't get even deeper.

A crucial thing to understand, however, is that the low prices that cause firms to shut down production are often temporary—so that shutdowns are also often temporary. Just because a firm shuts down at a given moment to prevent its financial hole from getting any deeper does not mean that the firm will go out of business forever. To the contrary, many industries are characterized by firms that regularly switch production on and off depending upon the market price they can get for their output and, consequently, whether producing output will generate positive or negative cash flows.

Oil production is a good example. Different wells have different variable production costs. If the price of oil drops below a given well's variable costs, then it would be better to halt production on that well and just lose the value of its fixed costs rather than pumping oil whose variable cost exceeds the revenue that it generates when sold.

Seasonal resorts are another good example of turning production on and off depending on the price. The demand for hotel rooms near ski resorts in New Hampshire, for instance, is much higher during the winter ski season than it is during the summer. As a result, the market price of hotel rooms falls so low during the summer that many inns and resorts close during the warmer months. They have all sorts of fixed costs, but it makes more sense for them to shut down rather than remain open because operating in the summer would cost more in variable costs than it would generate in revenues. Better to lose only their fixed costs.

Numerous other examples of temporary shutdowns occur during recessions, the occasional economy-wide economic slowdowns during which demand declines for nearly all goods and services. The 2007–2009 recession in the United States, for instance, saw many manufacturing companies temporarily shut down and mothball their production facilities. The recession witnessed the mothballing of electric generating plants, factories that make fiber optic cable, automobile factories, chemical plants, textile mills, and even the plant in McIntosh, Alabama, that makes the artificial sweetener Splenda. Many other firms also shut down production to wait out the recession—so many, in fact, that there was a mini-boom for consulting firms that specialized in helping firms mothball their factories (the main problem being how to properly store idle machinery so that it will work again when it is eventually brought back into service).

Firms that mothball factories or equipment during a recession do so expecting to eventually turn them back on. But the lengths of recessions vary, as do the specific circumstances of individual firms. So while many firms shut down in the short run with the expectation of reopening as soon as their particular business conditions improve, sometimes their business conditions do not improve. Sometimes the only way to terminate fixed costs is to terminate the firm.

From Chapter 3 we know that the market equilibrium price will be the price at which the total quantity supplied of the product equals the total quantity demanded. So to determine the equilibrium price, we first need to obtain a total supply schedule and a total demand schedule. We find the total supply schedule by assuming a particular number of firms in the industry and supposing that each firm has the same individual supply schedule as the firm represented in Figure 9.6. Then we sum the quantities supplied at each price level to obtain the total (or market) supply schedule. Columns 1 and 3 in Table 9.4 repeat the supply schedule for the individual competitive firm, as derived in Table 9.2. Suppose 1,000 firms compete in this industry, all having the same total and unit costs as the single firm we discussed. This lets us calculate the market supply schedule (columns 2 and 3) by multiplying the quantity-supplied figures of the single firm (column 1) by 1,000.

TABLE 9.4 Firm and Market Supply and Market Demand

(1) Quantity Supplied, Single Firm	(2) Total Quantity Supplied, 1,000 Firms	(3) Product Price	(4) Total Quantity Demanded
10	10,000	$151	4,000
9	9,000	131	6,000
8	**8,000**	**111**	**8,000**
7	7,000	91	9,000
6	6,000	81	11,000
0	0	71	13,000
0	0	61	16,000

Market Price and Profits To determine the equilibrium price and output, these total-supply data must be compared with total-demand data. Let's assume that total demand is as shown in columns 3 and 4 in Table 9.4. By comparing the total quantity supplied and the total quantity demanded at the seven possible prices, we determine that the equilibrium price

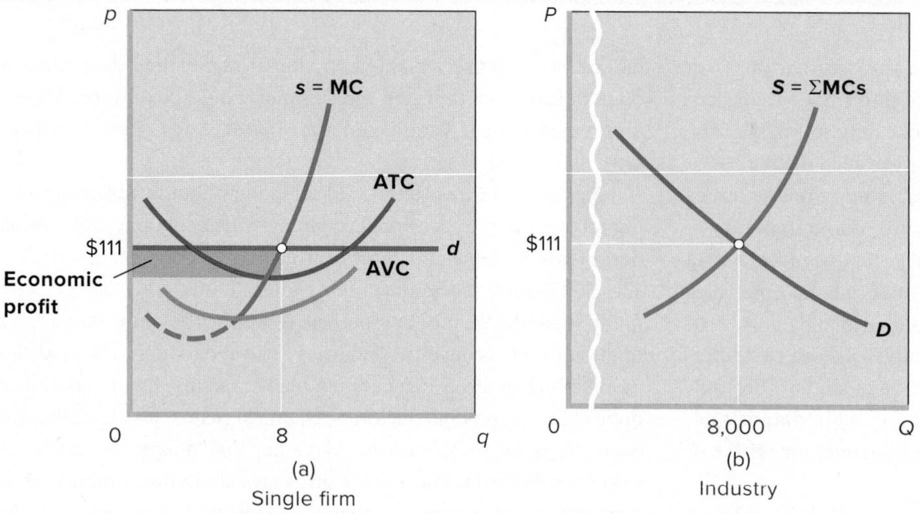

FIGURE 9.7 Short-run competitive equilibrium for (a) a firm and (b) the industry. The horizontal sum of the 1,000 firms' individual supply curves (*s*) determines the industry supply curve (*S*). Given industry demand (*D*), the short-run equilibrium price and output for the industry are $111 and 8,000 units. Taking the equilibrium price as given, the individual firm establishes its profit-maximizing output at 8 units and, in this case, realizes the economic profit represented by the green area.

is $111 and the equilibrium quantity is 8,000 units for the industry—8 units for each of the 1,000 identical firms.

Will these conditions of market supply and demand make this a profitable or unprofitable industry? Multiplying product price ($111) by output (8 units), we find that the total revenue of each firm is $888. The total cost is $750, found by looking at column 4 of the table in Figure 9.2. The $138 difference is the economic profit of each firm. For the industry, total economic profit is $138,000. This, then, is a profitable industry.

Another way of calculating economic profit is to determine per-unit profit by subtracting average total cost ($93.75) from product price ($111) and multiplying the difference (per-unit profit of $17.25) by the firm's equilibrium level of output (8). Again we obtain an economic profit of $138 per firm and $138,000 for the industry.

Figure 9.7 shows this analysis graphically. The individual supply curves of each of the 1,000 identical firms—one of which is shown as s = MC in Figure 9.7a—are summed horizontally to get the total-supply curve S = SMC of Figure 9.7b. With total-demand curve D, it yields the equilibrium price $111 and equilibrium quantity (for the industry) 8,000 units. This equilibrium price is given and unalterable to the individual firm; that is, each firm's demand curve is perfectly elastic at the equilibrium price, as indicated by d in Figure 9.7a. Because the individual firm is a price taker, the marginal-revenue curve coincides with the firm's demand curve d. This $111 price exceeds the average total cost at the firm's equilibrium MR = MC output of 8 units, so the firm earns an economic profit represented by the green area in Figure 9.7a.

Assuming no changes in costs or market demand, these diagrams reveal a genuine equilibrium in the short run. No shortages or surpluses occur in the market to cause price or total quantity to change. Nor can any firm in the industry increase its profit by altering its output. Note, too, that higher unit and marginal costs, on the one hand, or weaker market demand, on the other, could change the situation so that Figure 9.7a resembles Figure 9.4 or Figure 9.5.

Firm versus Industry Figure 9.7 underscores a point made earlier: Product price is a given fact to the *individual* competitive firm, but the supply plans of all competitive producers *as a group* are a basic determinant of product price. If we recall the fallacy of composition (Last Word, Chapter 1), we find there is no inconsistency here. Although one firm, supplying a negligible fraction of total supply, cannot affect price, the sum of the supply curves of all the firms in the industry constitutes the industry supply curve, and that curve does have an important bearing on price.

AP QUICK REVIEW 9.3

- ✓ A competitive firm's short-run supply curve is the rising portion of its marginal cost (MC) curve that lies above its average variable cost (AVC) curve.
- ✓ If price *P* is greater than minimum average variable cost, the firm will produce the amount of output where MR (= *P*) = MC in order to either maximize its profit (if price exceeds minimum ATC) or minimize its loss (if price lies between minimum AVC and minimum ATC).
- ✓ Market supply in a competitive industry is the horizontal sum of the individual supply curves of all of the firms in the industry. The market equilibrium is determined by where the industry's market supply curve intersects the industry's market demand curve, generating the competitive equilibrium price and quantity.

SUMMARY

LO9.1 Give the names and summarize the main characteristics of the four basic market models.

Economists group industries into four models based on their market structures: (*a*) pure competition, (*b*) pure monopoly, (*c*) monopolistic competition, and (*d*) oligopoly.

LO9.2 List the conditions required for purely competitive markets.

A purely competitive industry consists of a large number of independent firms producing a standardized product. Pure competition assumes that firms and resources are mobile among different industries.

LO9.3 Explain how demand is seen by a purely competitive seller.

In a competitive industry, no single firm can influence market price. This means that the firm's demand curve is perfectly elastic and price equals marginal revenue.

LO9.4 Convey how purely competitive firms can use the total-revenue–total-cost approach to maximize profits or minimize losses in the short run.

We can analyze short-run profit maximization by a competitive firm by comparing total revenue and total cost or by applying marginal analysis. A firm maximizes its short-run profit by producing the output at which total revenue exceeds total cost by the greatest amount.

LO9.5 Explain how purely competitive firms can use the marginal-revenue–marginal-cost approach to maximize profits or minimize losses in the short run.

Provided price exceeds minimum average variable cost, a competitive firm maximizes profit or minimizes loss in the short run by producing the output at which price or marginal revenue equals marginal cost.

If price is less than minimum average variable cost, a competitive firm minimizes its loss by shutting down. If price is greater than average variable cost but is less than average total cost, a competitive firm minimizes its loss by producing the P = MC amount of output. If price also exceeds average total cost, the firm maximizes its economic profit at the P = MC amount of output.

LO9.6 Explain why a competitive firm's marginal cost curve is the same as its supply curve.

Applying the MR (= P) = MC rule at various possible market prices leads to the conclusion that the segment of the firm's short-run marginal-cost curve that lies above the firm's average-variable-cost curve is its short-run supply curve.

A competitive firm shuts down production at least temporarily if price is less than minimum average variable cost because, in those situations, producing any amount of output will always result in variable costs exceeding revenues. Shutting down therefore results in a smaller loss because the firm will lose only its fixed cost, whereas, if it operated, it would lose its fixed cost plus whatever money is lost due to variable costs exceeding revenues.

Competitive firms choose to operate rather than shut down whenever price is greater than average variable cost but less than average total cost because, in those situations, revenues will always exceed variable costs. The amount by which revenues exceed variable costs can be used to help pay down some of the firm's fixed costs. Thus, the firm loses less money by operating (and paying down some of its fixed costs) than it would if it shut down (in which case it would suffer a loss equal to the full amount of its fixed costs).

TERMS AND CONCEPTS

market structure
pure competition
pure monopoly
monopolistic competition
oligopoly
imperfect competition
price taker
average revenue
total revenue
marginal revenue
break-even point
MR = MC rule
short-run supply curve

The following and additional problems can be found in connect

DISCUSSION QUESTIONS

1. Briefly state the basic characteristics of pure competition, pure monopoly, monopolistic competition, and oligopoly. Under which of these market classifications does each of the following most accurately fit? (*a*) a supermarket in your hometown; (*b*) the steel industry; (*c*) a Kansas wheat farm; (*d*) the commercial bank in which you or your family has an account; (*e*) the automobile industry. In each case, justify your classification. LO9.1
2. Strictly speaking, pure competition is relatively rare. Then why study it? LO9.2

3. "Even if a firm is losing money, it may be better to stay in business in the short run." Is this statement ever true? Under what condition(s)? LO9.5
4. Consider a firm that has no fixed costs and that is currently losing money. Are there any situations in which it would want to stay open for business in the short run? If a firm has no fixed costs, is it sensible to speak of the firm distinguishing between the short run and the long run? LO9.5
5. Why is the equality of marginal revenue and marginal cost essential for profit maximization in all market structures? Explain why price can be substituted for marginal revenue in the MR = MC rule when an industry is purely competitive. LO9.5
6. "That segment of a competitive firm's marginal-cost curve that lies above its average-variable-cost curve constitutes the short-run supply curve for the firm." Explain using a graph and words. LO9.5
7. **LAST WORD** If a firm's current revenues are less than its current variable costs, when should it shut down? If the firm decides to shut down, should we expect that decision to be final? Explain using an example that is not in the book.

AP REVIEW QUESTIONS

1. Suppose that the paper clip industry is perfectly competitive. Also assume that the market price for paper clips is 2 cents per paper clip. The demand curve faced by each firm in the industry is: LO9.3
   a. A horizontal line at 2 cents per paper clip.
   b. A vertical line at 2 cents per paper clip.
   c. The same as the market demand curve for paper clips.
   d. Always higher than the firm's MC curve.
   e. Guarantees making an economic profit.
2. Use the following demand schedule to determine total revenue and marginal revenue for each possible level of sales: LO9.3
   a. What can you conclude about the structure of the industry in which this firm is operating? Explain.

Product Price	Quantity Demanded	Total Revenue	Marginal Revenue
$2	0	$____	
			$____
2	1	____	
			____
2	2	____	
			____
2	3	____	
			____
2	4	____	
			____
2	5	____	

   b. Graph the demand, total-revenue, and marginal-revenue curves for this firm.
   c. Why do the demand and marginal-revenue curves coincide?
   d. "Marginal revenue is the change in total revenue associated with additional units of output." Explain verbally and graphically, using the data in the table.
3. A purely competitive firm whose goal is to maximize profit will choose to produce the amount of output at which: LO9.4
   a. TR and TC are equal.
   b. TR exceeds TC by as much as possible.
   c. TC exceeds TR by as much as possible.
   d. MC is greater than MR.
   e. MR is less than MC.
4. If it is possible for a perfectly competitive firm to do better economically by producing rather than shutting down, then it should produce the amount of output at which: LO9.5
   a. MR = MC where price is above the minimum variable average cost.
   b. MR < MC where price is above the minimum variable average cost.
   c. MR > MC where price is above the minimum variable average cost.
   d. P = MC and MR < MC
   e. Actually, firms would not produce unless they earn profits.
5. If a purely competitive firm is producing at some level less than the profit maximizing output, then: LO9.5
   a. Price is necessarily greater than average total cost.
   b. Fixed costs are large relative to variable costs.
   c. Price exceeds marginal revenue.
   d. Marginal revenue exceeds marginal cost.
   e. Marginal cost exceeds marginal revenue.
6. The MR = MC rule can be restated for a purely competitive seller as *P* = MC because: LO9.5
   a. Each additional unit of output adds exactly its price to total revenue.
   b. The firm's average revenue curve is downsloping.
   c. The market demand curve is downsloping.
   d. The firm's marginal revenue and total revenue curves will coincide.
   e. The firm's demand curve is perfectly inelastic at the market price.
7. Assume that the short-run market price in a competitive market for good Z is $10 per unit. Answer each of the questions below. LO9.3, 9.4, 9.5
   a. What does the marginal revenue curve for a competitive firm look like? What is the marginal revenue of the 50th unit of output for the competitive firm?
   b. Assume that firm is producing where AVC = $6.00 and MC = $8.00. Is this firm maximizing economic profits? If not, should the firm shut down, decrease its output but produce, or increase its output?
   c. At the output level that maximizes economic profits, the average total cost (ATC) for each firm is $9.00. What can you conclude about the profitability of the firm in the short run? Is there likely to be a long-run adjustment in this market?

PROBLEMS

1. A purely competitive firm finds that the market price for its product is $20. It has a fixed cost of $100 and a variable cost of $10 per unit for the first 50 units and then $25 per unit for all successive units. Does price exceed average variable cost for the first 50 units? What about for the first 100 units? What is the marginal cost per unit for the first 50 units? What about for units 51 and higher? For each of the first 50 units, does MR exceed MC? What about for units 51 and higher? What output level will yield the largest possible profit for this purely competitive firm? (Hint: Draw a graph similar to Figure 10.2 using data for this firm.) **LO9.5**
2. A purely competitive wheat farmer can sell any wheat he grows for $10 per bushel. His five acres of land show diminishing returns because some are better suited for wheat production than others. The first acre can produce 1,000 bushels of wheat, the second acre 900, the third 800, and so on. Draw a table with multiple columns to help you answer the following questions. How many bushels will each of the farmer's five acres produce? How much revenue will each acre generate? What are the TR and MR for each acre? If the marginal cost of planting and harvesting an acre is $7,000 per acre for each of the five acres, how many acres should the farmer plant and harvest? **LO9.5**
3. Karen runs a print shop that makes posters for large companies. It is a very competitive business. The market price is currently $1 per poster. She has fixed costs of $250. Her variable costs are $1,000 for the first thousand posters, $800 for the second thousand, and then $750 for each additional thousand posters. What is her AFC per poster (not per thousand!) if she prints 1,000 posters? 2,000? 10,000? What is her ATC per poster if she prints 1,000? 2,000? 10,000? If the market price fell to 70 cents per poster, would there be *any* output level at which Karen would *not* shut down production immediately? **LO9.5**
4. Assume that the cost data in the following table are for a purely competitive producer: **LO9.5**

Total Product	Average Fixed Cost	Average Variable Cost	Average Total Cost	Marginal Cost
0				
1	$60.00	$45.00	$105.00	$45
2	30.00	42.50	72.50	40
3	20.00	40.00	60.00	35
4	15.00	37.50	52.50	30
5	12.00	37.00	49.00	35
6	10.00	37.50	47.50	40
7	8.57	38.57	47.14	45
8	7.50	40.63	48.13	55
9	6.67	43.33	50.00	65
10	6.00	46.50	52.50	75

a. At a product price of $56, will this firm produce in the short run? If it is preferable to produce, what will be the profit-maximizing or loss-minimizing output? What economic profit or loss will the firm realize per unit of output?

b. Answer the questions of 4a assuming product price is $41.

c. Answer the questions of 4a assuming product price is $32.

d. In the following table, complete the short-run supply schedule for the firm (columns 1 and 2) and indicate the profit or loss incurred at each output (column 3).

(1) Price	(2) Quantity Supplied, Single Firm	(3) Profit (+) or Loss (−)	(4) Quantity Supplied 1,500 Firms
$26	______	$______	______
32	______	______	______
38	______	______	______
41	______	______	______
46	______	______	______
56	______	______	______
66	______	______	______

e. Now assume that there are 1,500 identical firms in this competitive industry; that is, there are 1,500 firms, each of which has the cost data shown in the table. Complete the industry supply schedule (column 4).

f. Suppose the market demand data for the product are as follows:

Price	Total Quantity Demanded
$26	17,000
32	15,000
38	13,500
41	12,000
46	10,500
56	9,500
66	8,000

What will be the equilibrium price? What will be the equilibrium output for the industry? For each firm? What will profit or loss be per unit? Per firm? Will this industry expand or contract in the long run?

10 Chapter

Pure Competition in the Long Run

Learning Objectives

LO10.1 **Explain how the long run differs from the short run in pure competition.**

LO10.2 **Describe how profits and losses drive the long-run adjustment process of pure competition.**

LO10.3 **Explain the differences between constant-cost, increasing-cost, and decreasing-cost industries.**

LO10.4 **Show how long-run equilibrium in pure competition produces an efficient allocation of resources.**

LO10.5 **Discuss creative destruction and the profit incentives for innovation.**

AP Chapter Focus

The previous chapter discussed how pure competition operates in the short run, the time period during which the individual firms in an industry are stuck with their current plant sizes and fixed-cost commitments. As you know, pure competitors shut down production if prices are too low or, if prices are high enough, produce where MR = MC to minimize their losses or maximize their profits. Whether they make a profit or a loss depends on how high the market price is relative to their costs.

This chapter now extends the Purely Competitive Market Model by showing the result of the freedom of firms to enter or exit an industry. We know from Chapter 2 that profits attract entry and losses prompt exit.

In this chapter, we are keenly interested in how entry and exit relate to allocative and productive efficiency. We are also interested in how continuing competition leads to new products and new business methods replacing older products and older business methods through a process aptly referred to as *creative destruction.*

The Long Run in Pure Competition

LO10.1 Explain how the long run differs from the short run in pure competition.

The entry and exit of firms in our market models can only take place in the long run. In the short run, the industry is composed of a specific number of firms, each with a plant size that is fixed and unalterable in the short run. Firms may shut down in the sense that they can produce zero units of output in the short run, but they do not have sufficient time to liquidate their assets and go out of business.

In the long run, by contrast, the firms already in an industry have sufficient time to either expand or contract their capacities. More important, the number of firms in the industry may either increase or decrease as new firms enter or existing firms leave.

The length of time constituting the long run varies substantially by industry, however, so that you should not fix in your mind any specific number of years, months, or days. Instead, focus your attention on the incentives provided by profits and losses for the entry and exit of firms into any purely competitive industry and, later in the chapter, on how those incentives lead to productive and allocative efficiency. The time horizons are far less important than the process by which profits and losses guide business managers toward the efficient use of society's resources.

Profit Maximization in the Long Run

The first part of the pure competition story (Chapter 9) was about profit, loss, and shutdown in the short run. The rest of the story (this chapter) is about entry and exit and their effects on industry size and allocative and productive efficiency in the long run.

To tell the rest of story well, we need to return to our graphical analysis and examine profit maximization by pure competitors in the long run. Several assumptions, none of which affect our conclusions, will keep things simple:

- ***Entry and exit only*** The only long-run adjustment in our graphical analysis is caused by the entry or exit of firms. Moreover, we ignore all short-run adjustments in order to concentrate on the effects of the long-run adjustments.
- ***Identical costs*** All firms in the industry have identical cost curves. This assumption lets us discuss an "average," or "representative," firm, knowing that all other firms in the industry are similarly affected by any long-run adjustments that occur.
- ***Constant-cost industry*** The industry is a constant-cost industry. This means that the entry and exit of firms does not affect resource prices or, consequently, the locations of the average-total-cost curves of individual firms.

AP The Long-Run Adjustment Process in Pure Competition

LO10.2 Describe how profits and losses drive the long-run adjustment process of pure competition.

The basic conclusion we seek to explain is this: After all long-run adjustments are completed in a purely competitive industry, product price will be exactly equal to, and production will occur at, each firm's minimum average total cost.

This conclusion follows from two basic facts: (1) Firms seek profits and shun losses, and (2) under pure competition, firms are free to enter and leave an industry. If market price initially exceeds minimum average total cost, the resulting economic profit will attract new firms to the industry. But this industry expansion will increase supply until price is brought back down to equality with minimum average total cost. Conversely, if price is initially less than minimum average total cost, the resulting loss will cause firms to leave the industry. As they leave, total supply will decline, bringing the price back up to equality with minimum average total cost.

Long-Run Equilibrium

Consider the average firm in a purely competitive industry that is initially in long-run equilibrium. This firm is represented in Figure 10.1a, where MR = MC and price and minimum average total cost are equal at \$50. Economic profit here is zero; the industry is in equilibrium or "at rest" because there is no tendency for firms to enter or to leave. The existing firms are earning normal profits, which means that their accounting profits are equal to those that the owners of these

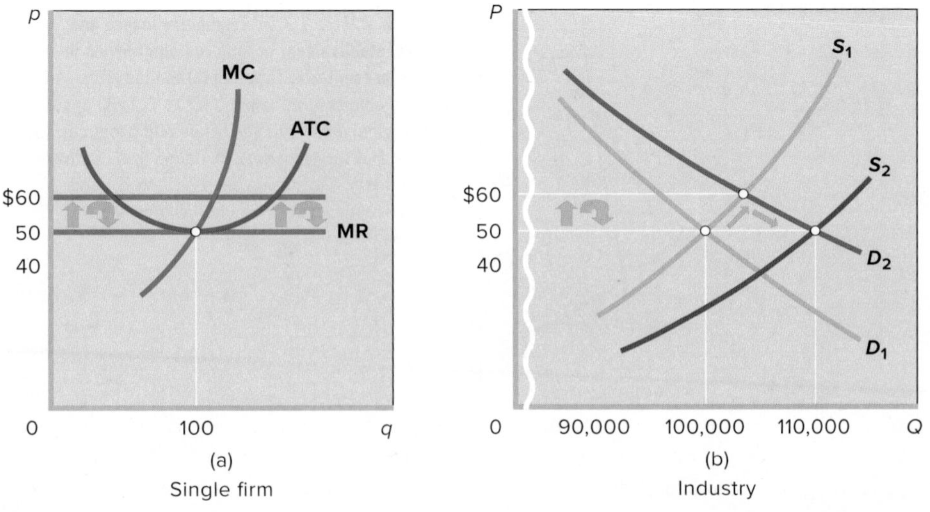

AP **FIGURE 10.1 Temporary profits and the reestablishment of long-run equilibrium in (a) a representative firm and (b) the industry.** A favorable shift in demand (D_1 to D_2) will upset the original industry equilibrium and produce economic profits. But those profits will entice new firms to enter the industry, increasing supply (S_1 to S_2) and lowering product price until economic profits are once again zero.

firms could expect to receive on average in other industries. It is because their current profits are the same as they could expect to earn elsewhere that there is no tendency for firms to enter or leave the industry. The $50 market price is determined in Figure 10.1b by market or industry demand D_1 and supply S_1. (S_1 is a short-run supply curve; we will develop the long-run industry supply curve in our discussion.) And remember that normal profits earned by these firms are considered an opportunity cost and, therefore, are included in the firms' cost curves.

As shown on the quantity axes of the two graphs, equilibrium output in the industry is 100,000 while equilibrium output for the single firm is 100. If all firms in the industry are identical, there must be 1,000 firms (= 100,000/100).

Entry Eliminates Economic Profits Let's upset the long-run equilibrium in Figure 10.1 and see what happens. Suppose a change in consumer tastes increases product demand from D_1 to D_2. Price will rise to $60, as determined at the intersection of D_2 and S_1, and the firm's marginal-revenue curve will shift upward to $60. This $60 price exceeds the firm's average total cost of $50 at output 100, creating an economic profit of $10 per unit. This economic profit will lure new firms into the industry. Some entrants will be newly created firms; others will shift from less prosperous industries.

As firms enter, the market supply of the product increases, pushing the product price below $60. Economic profits persist, and entry continues until short-run supply increases to S_2. Market price falls to $50, as does marginal revenue for the firm. Price and minimum average total cost are again equal at $50. The economic profits caused by the boost in demand have been eliminated, and, as a result, the previous incentive for more firms to enter the industry has disappeared because the firms that remain are earning only a normal profit (zero economic profit). Entry ceases and a new long-run equilibrium is reached.

Observe in Figure 10.1a and 10.1b that total quantity supplied is now 110,000 units and each firm is producing 100 units. Now 1,100 firms rather than the original 1,000 populate the industry. Economic profits have attracted 100 more firms.

Exit Eliminates Losses Now let's consider a shift in the opposite direction. We begin in Figure 10.2b with curves S_1 and D_1 setting the same initial long-run equilibrium situation as in our previous analysis, including the $50 price.

Suppose consumer demand declines from D_1 to D_3. This forces the market price and marginal revenue down to $40, making production unprofitable at the minimum ATC of $50. In time the resulting economic losses will induce firms to leave the industry. Their owners will seek a normal profit elsewhere rather than accept the below-normal profits (losses) now confronting them. As this exodus of firms proceeds, however, industry supply decreases, pushing the price up from $40 toward $50. Losses continue and more firms leave the industry until the supply curve shifts to S_3. Once this happens, price is again $50, just equal to the minimum average total cost. Losses have been eliminated so that the firms that remain are earning only a normal profit (zero economic profit). Since this is no better or worse than entrepreneurs could expect to earn in other business ventures, there is no longer any incentive to exit the industry. Long-run equilibrium is restored.

In Figure 10.2a and 10.2b, total quantity supplied is now 90,000 units and each firm is producing 100 units. Only 900 firms, not the original 1,000, populate the industry. Losses have forced 100 firms out.

You may have noted that we have sidestepped the question of which firms will leave the industry when losses occur by assuming that all firms have identical cost curves. In the real world, of course, managerial talents differ. Even if resource prices and technology are the same for all firms, less skillfully managed firms tend to incur higher

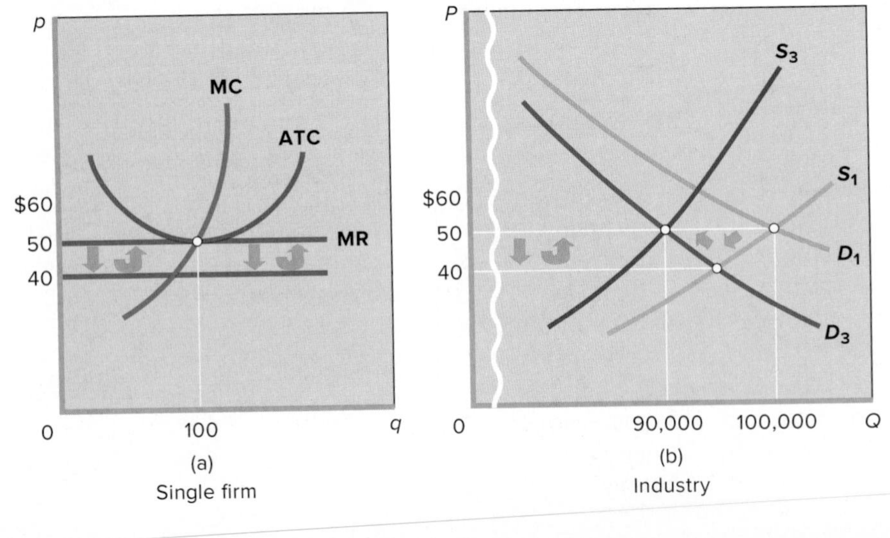

AP **FIGURE 10.2 Temporary losses and the reestablishment of long-run equilibrium in (a) a representative firm and (b) the industry.** An unfavorable shift in demand (D_1 to D_3) will upset the original industry equilibrium and produce losses. But those losses will cause firms to leave the industry, decreasing supply (S_1 to S_3) and increasing product price until all losses have disappeared.

costs and therefore are the first to leave an industry when demand declines. Similarly, firms with less productive labor forces or higher transportation costs will be higher-cost producers and likely candidates to quit an industry when demand decreases.

We have now reached an intermediate goal: Our analysis verifies that competition, reflected in the entry and exit of firms, eliminates economic profits or losses by adjusting price to equal minimum long-run average total cost. In addition, this competition forces firms to select output levels at which average total cost is minimized.

AP Long-Run Supply Curves

LO10.3 Explain the differences between constant-cost, increasing-cost, and decreasing-cost industries.

Although our analysis has dealt with the long run, we have noted that the market supply curves in Figures 10.1b and 10.2b are short-run curves. What then is the character of the **long-run supply curve** of a competitive industry? Our analysis points us toward an answer. The crucial factor here is the effect, if any, that changes in the number of firms in the industry will have on costs of the individual firms in the industry.

Long-Run Supply for a Constant-Cost Industry

In our analysis of long-run competitive equilibrium we assumed that the industry under discussion was a **constant-cost industry.** This means that industry expansion or contraction will not affect resource prices and therefore production costs. Graphically, it means that the entry or exit of firms does not shift the long-run ATC curves of individual firms. This is the case when the industry's demand for resources is small in relation to the total demand for those resources. Then the industry can expand or contract without significantly affecting resource prices and costs.

What does the long-run supply curve of a constant-cost industry look like? The answer is contained in our previous analysis. There we saw that the entry and exit of firms changes industry output but always brings the product price back to its original level, where it is just equal to the constant minimum ATC. Specifically, we discovered that the industry would supply 90,000, 100,000, or 110,000 units of output, all at a price of $50 per unit. In other words, the long-run supply curve of a constant-cost industry is perfectly elastic.

This is demonstrated graphically in Figure 10.3, which uses data from Figures 10.1 and 10.2. Suppose industry demand is originally D_1, industry output is Q_1 (100,000 units), and product price is P_1 ($50). This situation, from Figure 10.1, is one of long-run equilibrium. We saw that when

AP **FIGURE 10.3 The long-run supply curve for a constant-cost industry.** In a constant-cost industry, the entry and exit of firms do not affect resource prices, or, therefore, unit costs. So an increase in demand (D_1 to D_2) raises industry output (Q_1 to Q_2) but not price ($50). Similarly, a decrease in demand (D_1 to D_3) reduces output (Q_1 to Q_3) but not price. Thus, the long-run industry supply curve (S) is horizontal through points Z_1, Z_2, and Z_3.

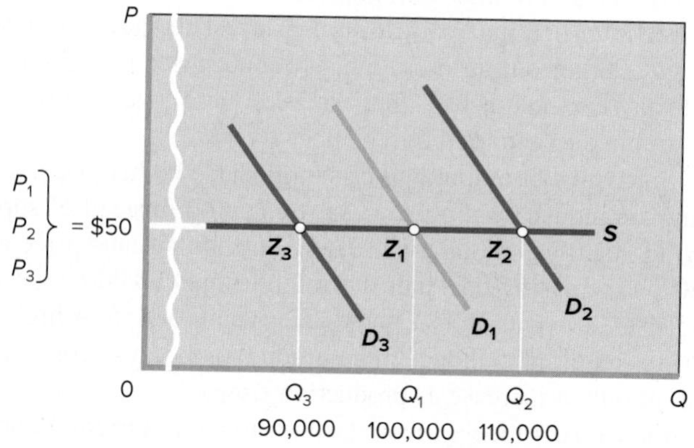

demand increases to D_2, upsetting this equilibrium, the resulting economic profits attract new firms. Because this is a constant-cost industry, entry continues and industry output expands until the price is driven back down to the level of the unchanged minimum ATC. This is at price P_2 ($50) and output Q_2 (110,000).

From Figure 10.2, we saw that a decline in market demand from D_1 to D_3 causes an exit of firms and ultimately restores equilibrium at price P_3 ($50) and output Q_3 (90,000 units). The points Z_1, Z_2, and Z_3 in Figure 10.3 represent these three price-quantity combinations. A line or curve connecting all such points shows the various price-quantity combinations that firms would produce if they had enough time to make all desired adjustments to changes in demand. This line or curve is the industry's long-run supply curve. In a constant-cost industry this curve (straight line) is horizontal, as in Figure 10.3, thus representing perfectly elastic supply.

Long-Run Supply for an Increasing-Cost Industry

Constant-cost industries are a special case. Most industries are **increasing-cost industries,** in which firms' ATC curves shift upward as the industry expands and downward as the industry contracts. Usually, the entry of new firms will increase resource prices, particularly in industries using specialized resources whose long-run supplies do not readily increase in response to increases in resource demand. Higher resource prices result in higher long-run average total costs for all firms in the industry. These higher costs cause upward shifts in each firm's long-run ATC curve.

Thus, when an increase in product demand results in economic profits and attracts new firms to an increasing-cost industry, a two-way squeeze works to eliminate those profits. As before, the entry of new firms increases market supply and lowers the market price. But now each firm's entire ATC curve also shifts upward. The overall result is a higher-than-original equilibrium price. The industry produces a larger output at a higher product price because the industry expansion has increased resource prices and the minimum average total cost.

Since greater output will be supplied at a higher price, the long-run industry supply curve is upsloping. Instead of supplying 90,000, 100,000, or 110,000 units at the same price of $50, an increasing-cost industry might supply 90,000 units at $45, 100,000 units at $50, and 110,000 units at $55. A higher price is required to induce more production because costs per unit of output increase as production rises.

Figure 10.4 nicely illustrates the situation. Original market demand is D_1 and industry price and output are P_1 ($50) and Q_1 (100,000 units), respectively, at equilibrium point Y_1. An increase in demand to D_2 upsets this equilibrium and leads to economic profits. New firms enter the industry, increasing both market supply and the production costs of individual firms. A new price is established at point Y_2, where P_2 is $55 and Q_2 is 110,000 units.

Conversely, a decline in demand from D_1 to D_3 makes production unprofitable and causes firms to leave the industry. The resulting decline in resource prices reduces the minimum average total cost of production for firms that stay. A new equilibrium price is established at some level below the original price, say, at point Y_3, where P_3 is $45 and Q_3 is 90,000 units. Connecting these three equilibrium positions, we derive the upsloping long-run supply curve S in Figure 10.4.

FIGURE 10.4 The long-run supply curve for an increasing-cost industry. In an increasing-cost industry, the entry of new firms in response to an increase in demand (D_3 to D_1 to D_2) will bid up resource prices and thereby increase unit costs. As a result, an increased industry output (Q_3 to Q_1 to Q_2) will be forthcoming only at higher prices ($45 < $50 < $55). The long-run industry supply curve (S) therefore slopes upward through points Y_3, Y_1, and Y_2.

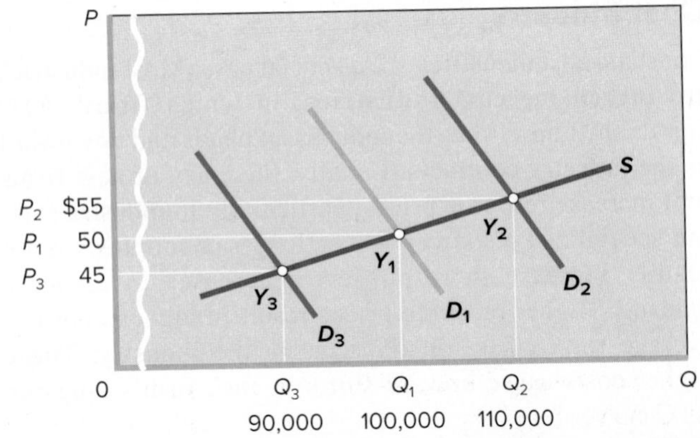

Long-Run Supply for a Decreasing-Cost Industry

In **decreasing-cost industries,** firms experience lower costs as their industry expands. The personal computer industry is an example. As demand for personal computers increased, new manufacturers of computers entered the industry and greatly increased the resource demand for the components used to build them (for example, memory chips, hard drives, monitors, and operating software). The expanded production of the components enabled the producers of those items to achieve substantial economies of scale. The decreased production costs of the components reduced their prices, which greatly lowered the computer manufacturers' average costs of production. The supply of personal computers increased by more than demand, and the price of personal computers declined.

Unfortunately, however, the industries that show decreasing costs when output expands also show increasing costs if output contracts. A good example is the American shoe-manufacturing industry as it contracted due to foreign competition. Back when the industry was doing well and there were many shoemaking firms, the cost of specialized technicians who repair shoemaking machinery could be spread across many firms. This was because the repairmen worked as independent contractors going from one firm's factory to another firm's factory on a daily basis as various pieces of equipment at different factories needed repairs. But as the demand for American footwear fell over time, there were fewer and fewer factories, so the cost of a repair technician had to be spread over fewer and fewer firms. Thus, costs per firm and per unit of output increased.

Figure 10.5 illustrates the situation. The original market demand is D_1 and industry price and output are P_1 ($50) and Q_1 (100,000 units), respectively, at equilibrium point X_1. An increase in demand to D_2 upsets this equilibrium and leads to

FIGURE 10.5 The long-run supply curve for a decreasing-cost industry. In a decreasing-cost industry, the entry of new firms in response to an increase in demand (D_3 to D_1 to D_2) will lead to decreased input prices and, consequently, decreased unit costs. As a result, an increase in industry output (Q_3 to Q_1 to Q_2) will be accompanied by lower prices ($55 > $50 > $45). The long-run industry supply curve (S) therefore slopes downward through points X_3, X_1, and X_2.

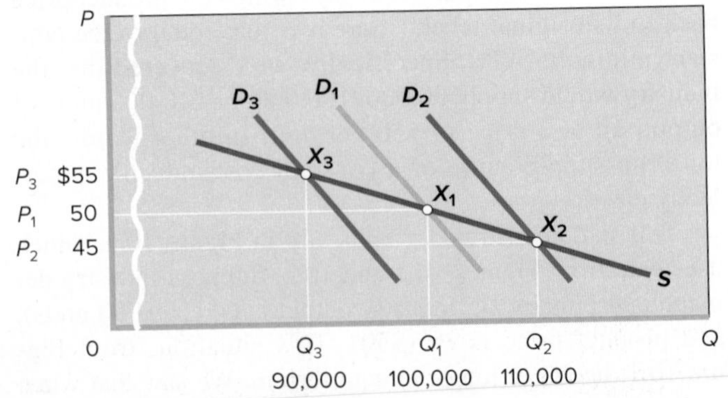

economic profits. New firms enter the industry, increasing market supply but decreasing the production costs of individual firms. A new price is established at point X_2, where P_2 is \$45 and Q_2 is 110,000 units.

Conversely, a decline in demand from D_1 to D_3 makes production unprofitable and causes firms to leave the industry. The resulting increase in input prices increases the minimum average total cost of production for the firms that remain. A new equilibrium price is established at some level above the original price, say at point X_3, where P_3 is \$55 and Q_3 is 90,000 units. Connecting these three equilibrium positions in Figure 10.5, we derive the downsloping long-run supply curve S for this decreasing-cost industry.

AP QUICK REVIEW 10.1

- ✓ In pure competition, entrepreneurs remove resources from industries and firms that are generating economic losses in order to transfer them to industries and firms that are generating economic profits.
- ✓ In the long run, the entry of firms into an industry will compete away any economic profits, and the exit of firms will eliminate economic losses, with firms earning zero economic profit. Thus, price and minimum average total cost are equal. Entry and exit cease when the firms in the industry return to making a normal profit (zero economic profit).
- ✓ The long-run supply curves of constant-, increasing-, and decreasing-cost industries are horizontal, upsloping, and downsloping, respectively.

AP Pure Competition and Efficiency

LO10.4 Show how long-run equilibrium in pure competition produces an efficient allocation of resources.

Figure 10.6 (Key Graph) demonstrates the efficiency characteristics of the individual firms (Figure 10.6a) and the market (Figure 10.6b) after long-run adjustments in pure competition. Assuming a constant- or increasing-cost industry, the final long-run equilibrium positions of all firms have the same basic efficiency characteristics. As shown in Figure 10.6a, price (and marginal revenue) will settle where it is equal to minimum average total cost: P (and MR) = minimum ATC. Moreover, since the marginal-cost curve intersects the average-total-cost curve at its minimum point, marginal cost and average total cost are equal: MC = minimum ATC. So in long-run equilibrium a triple equality occurs: P (and MR) = MC = minimum ATC. Thus, in long-run equilibrium, each firm produces at the output level Q_f that is associated with this triple equality.[1]

[1]This triple equality does not always hold for decreasing-cost industries in which individual firms produce a large fraction of the total market output. In such cases, MC may remain below ATC if average costs are decreasing. We will discuss this situation of "natural monopoly" in Chapter 11.

The triple equality tells us two very important things about long-run equilibrium. First, it tells us that although a competitive firm may realize economic profit or loss in the short run, it will earn only a normal profit by producing in accordance with the MR (= P) = MC rule in the long run. Second, the triple equality tells us that in long-run equilibrium, the profit-maximizing decision rule that leads each firm to produce the quantity at which P = MR also implies that each firm will produce at the output level Q_f that is associated with the minimum point on each identical firm's ATC curve.

This is very important because it suggests that pure competition leads to the most efficient possible use of society's resources. Indeed, subject only to Chapter 4's qualifications relating to public goods and externalities, an idealized purely competitive market economy composed of constant- or increasing-cost industries will generate both productive efficiency and allocative efficiency.

Productive Efficiency: P = Minimum ATC

Productive efficiency requires that goods be produced in the least costly way. In the long run, pure competition forces firms to produce at the minimum average total cost of production and to charge a price that is just consistent with that cost. This is true because firms that do not use the best available (least-cost) production methods and combinations of inputs will not survive.

To see why that is true, let's suppose that Figure 10.6 has to do with pure competition in the cucumber industry. In the final equilibrium position shown in Figure 10.6a, suppose each firm in the cucumber industry is producing 100 units (say, truckloads) of cucumbers by using \$5,000 (equal to average total cost of \$50 × 100 units) worth of resources. If any firm produced that same amount of output at any higher total cost, say \$7,000, it would be wasting resources because all of the other firms in the industry are able to produce that same amount of output using only \$5,000 of resources. Society would be faced with a net loss of \$2,000 worth of alternative products. But this cannot happen in pure competition; this firm would incur a loss of \$2,000, requiring it to either reduce its costs or go out of business.

Note, too, that consumers benefit from productive efficiency by paying the lowest product price possible under the prevailing technology and cost conditions. And the firm receives only a normal profit, which is part of its economic costs and thus incorporated in its ATC curve.

Allocative Efficiency: P = MC

Long-run equilibrium in pure competition guarantees productive efficiency, such that output will be produced in the least-cost way. But productive efficiency by itself does not guarantee that anyone will want to buy the items that are being produced in the least-cost manner. For all

AP KEY GRAPH

FIGURE 10.6 Long-run equilibrium: a competitive firm and market. (a) The equality of price (*P*), marginal cost (MC), and minimum average total cost (ATC) at output Q_f indicates that the firm is achieving productive efficiency and allocative efficiency. It is using the most efficient technology, charging the lowest price, and producing the greatest output consistent with its costs. It is receiving only a normal profit, which is incorporated into the ATC curve. The equality of price and marginal cost indicates that society allocated its scarce resources in accordance with consumer preferences. (b) In the purely competitive market, allocative efficiency occurs at the market equilibrium output Q_e. The sum of consumer surplus (green area) and producer surplus (blue area) is maximized.

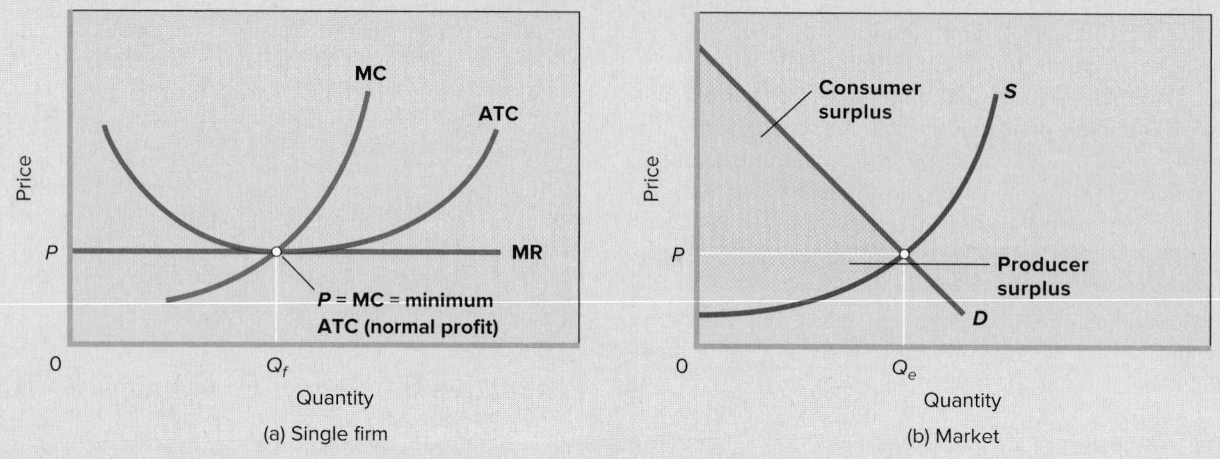

QUICK QUIZ FOR FIGURE 10.6

1. We know the firm is a price taker because:
   - **a.** its MC curve slopes upward.
   - **b.** its ATC curve is U-shaped.
   - **c.** its MR curve is horizontal.
   - **d.** MC and ATC are equal at the profit-maximizing output.
2. At this firm's profit-maximizing output:
   - **a.** total revenue equals total cost.
   - **b.** it is earning an economic profit.
   - **c.** allocative, but not necessarily productive, efficiency is achieved.
   - **d.** productive, but not necessarily allocative, efficiency is achieved.
3. The equality of *P*, MC, and minimum ATC:
   - **a.** occurs only in constant-cost industries.
   - **b.** encourages entry of new firms.
   - **c.** means that the "right goods" are being produced in the "right ways."
   - **d.** results in a zero accounting profit.
4. When *P* = MC = lowest ATC for individual firms, in the market:
   - **a.** consumer surplus necessarily exceeds producer surplus.
   - **b.** consumer surplus plus producer surplus is at a maximum.
   - **c.** producer surplus necessarily exceeds consumer surplus.
   - **d.** supply and demand are identical.

Answers: 1. c; 2. a; 3. c; 4. b

we know, consumers might prefer that the resources used to produce those items be redirected toward producing other products instead.

Fortunately, long-run equilibrium in pure competition also guarantees **allocative efficiency,** so we can be certain that society's scarce resources are directed toward producing the goods and services that people most want to consume. Stated formally, allocative efficiency occurs when it is impossible to produce any net gains for society by altering the combination of goods and services that are produced from society's limited supply of resources.

To understand how pure competition leads to allocative efficiency, recall the concept of opportunity cost while looking at Figure 10.6b, where Q_e total units are being produced in equilibrium by the firms in a purely competitive industry. For every unit up to Q_e, market demand curve *D* lies above market supply curve *S*. Recall from Chapter 4 what this means in terms of marginal benefits and marginal costs.

- For each unit of output on the horizontal axis, the point directly above it on demand curve *D* shows how many dollars' worth of other goods and services consumers are willing to give up to obtain that unit of output. Consequently, the demand curve shows the dollar value of the marginal benefit that consumers place on each unit.
- For each unit of output on the horizontal axis, the point directly above it on supply curve *S* shows how many dollars' worth of other products have to be sacrificed in order to direct the underlying resources toward producing each unit of this product. Consequently, supply curve *S* shows the dollar value of the marginal opportunity cost of each unit.

Keeping these definitions in mind, the fact that the demand curve lies above the supply curve for every unit up to Q_e means that marginal benefit exceeds marginal cost for every one of these units. Stated slightly differently, producing and consuming these units brings net benefits because consumers are willing to give up more of other goods to obtain these units than must actually be forgone to produce them. Furthermore, because the supply curve includes the opportunity cost of the other goods that must be given up when resources are directed to producing these units, we can be certain that consumers prefer to have the necessary resources directed toward producing these units rather than anything else. In other words, allocative efficiency has been achieved because redirecting the necessary resources toward producing anything else would make people less happy.

The fact that pure competition yields allocative efficiency can also be understood by looking at the situation facing each individual firm in long-run equilibrium. To see this, take the market equilibrium price P that is determined in Figure 10.6b and see how it affects the behavior of the individual firm shown in Figure 10.6a. This profit-maximizing firm takes P as fixed and produces Q_f units, the output level at which $P = \text{MC}$.

By comparing the horizontal line at P with the upsloping MC curve, it is clear that for every unit up to Q_f, the price at which each unit can be sold exceeds the marginal cost of producing it. That is equivalent to saying that these units are worth more to consumers than they cost to make. Why? Because consumers are willing to forgo P dollars' worth of other goods and services when they pay P dollars for these units, but at the same time the firm only has to use less than P dollars' worth of resources to produce them. Thus, if these units are produced and consumed, there are net benefits and society comes out ahead. And, as with our previous analysis, allocative efficiency also obtains because by spending their P dollars per unit on these units rather than anything else, consumers are indicating that they would rather have the necessary resources directed toward producing these units rather than anything else.

Maximum Consumer and Producer Surplus

We confirm the existence of allocative efficiency in Figure 10.6b, where we see that pure competition maximizes the sum of the "benefit surpluses" to consumers and producers. Recall from Chapter 4 that **consumer surplus** is the difference between the maximum prices that consumers are willing to pay for a product (as shown by the demand curve) and the market price of the product. In Figure 10.6b, consumer surplus is the green triangle, which is the sum of the vertical distances between the demand curve and equilibrium price. In contrast, **producer surplus** is the difference between the minimum prices that producers are willing to accept for a product (as shown by the supply curve) and the market price of the product. Producer surplus is the sum of the vertical distances between the equilibrium price and the supply curve. Here producer surplus is the blue area.

At the equilibrium quantity Q_e, the combined amount of consumer surplus and producer surplus is maximized. Allocative efficiency occurs because, at Q_e, marginal benefit, reflected by points on the demand curve, equals marginal cost, reflected by points on the supply curve. Alternatively, the maximum willingness of consumers to pay for unit Q_e equals the minimum acceptable price of that unit to producers. At any output less than Q_e, the sum of consumer and producer surplus—the combined size of the green and blue area—would be less than that shown. At any output greater than Q_e, an efficiency loss (deadweight loss) would subtract from the combined consumer and producer surplus shown by the green and blue area.

After long-run adjustments, pure competition produces both productive and allocative efficiency. It yields a level of output at which $P = \text{MC} =$ lowest ATC, marginal benefit = marginal cost, maximum willingness to pay for the last unit = minimum acceptable price for that unit, and combined consumer and producer surplus are maximized.

Dynamic Adjustments

A further attribute of purely competitive markets is their ability to restore the efficiency just described when disrupted by changes in the economy. A change in consumer tastes, resource supplies, or technology will automatically set in motion the appropriate realignments of resources. For example, suppose that cucumbers and pickles become dramatically more popular. First, the demand for cucumbers will increase in the market, increasing the price of cucumbers. So, at current output, the price of cucumbers will exceed their marginal cost. At this point efficiency will be lost, but the higher price will create economic profits in the cucumber industry and stimulate its expansion. The profitability of cucumbers will permit the industry to bid resources away from now-less-pressing uses, say, watermelons. Expansion of the industry will end only when the supply of cucumbers has expanded such that the price of cucumbers and their marginal cost are equal—that is, when allocative efficiency has been restored.

Similarly, a change in the supply of a particular resource—for example, the field laborers who pick cucumbers—or in a production technique will upset an existing price–marginal-cost equality by either raising or lowering marginal cost. The resulting inequality of MC and P will cause producers, in either pursuing profit or avoiding loss, to reallocate resources until product supply is such that price once again equals marginal cost. In so doing, they will correct any inefficiency in the allocation of resources

LAST WORD

A Patent Failure?

Patents May Hinder Creative Destruction. If So, Should We Consider Abolishing Patents?

Patents give inventors the sole legal right to market and sell their new ideas for a period of 20 years. So when considering the plusses and minuses of the patent system, it is important to begin with the fact that the possibility of obtaining a patent gives inventors a strong financial incentive to bear the research and development (R&D) costs necessary to come up with innovative solutions to old problems.

At the same time, however, the patent system also gives patent holders the ability to stifle the creative energies of other inventors by suing or threating to sue any individual or firm that they believe is "infringing" on their patent by producing or utilizing their invention without permission.

The problem is most acute for products like cell phones that incorporate thousands of different technologies into a single product. That's because each of those technologies might possibly infringe on one or more patents. If so, a single lawsuit filed over just one of those patents could halt the production and sale of the entire product. The alleged infringement may be totally unintentional or a matter of honest dispute. But if a patent holder believes that some part of the phone is infringing on his patent, he can threaten to sue the manufacturer and demand the shutdown of all production unless he receives royalty payments in compensation.

Consider Microsoft, which 30 years ago was a successful innovator thanks to its Windows operating system. Over the last 10 years, however, its Windows-based cell phones have been a failure. Yet Microsoft CEO Steve Balmer threatened to shut down the production of all Android phones because the Android software used to run those extremely popular phones happens to incorporate the ability to schedule a meeting. That is a feature that most Android users don't even know about. But it is a functionality over which Microsoft holds a patent for mobile devices. So to avoid a lawsuit that could have shut down the production of all Android phones, Android's parent company, Google, is now paying Microsoft a licensing fee on each and every Android phone.

That situation is very problematic for creative destruction because the patent system is being used to help an old company that hasn't had a successful product in many years to effectively tax and benefit from the successful innovations of a young rival. That ability to tax is a form of life support that allows stodgy old firms to survive longer than they should against innovative rivals and the pressures of creative destruction.

Even worse, companies known as "patent trolls" have been created to buy up patents simply for the chance to sue other companies and collect royalties. The patent trolls invent nothing and produce nothing. But they are free under the current system to make billions of dollars every year by suing innovative companies.

In response, some economists have begun to argue that the net benefits of the patent system have been overstated and that innovation might proceed faster in certain industries if patents were abolished. Their key insight is that the net benefits of patents depend upon how easy it is for rivals to successfully copy and market an innovative product.

---

that the original change may have temporarily imposed on the economy.

"Invisible Hand" Revisited

The highly efficient allocation of resources that a purely competitive economy promotes comes about because businesses and resource suppliers seek to further their self-interest. For private goods with no externalities (Chapter 4), the "invisible hand" (Chapter 2) is at work. The competitive system not only maximizes profits for individual producers but also, at the same time, creates a pattern of resource allocation that maximizes consumer satisfaction. The invisible hand thus organizes the private interests of producers in a way that is fully in sync with society's interest in using scarce resources efficiently. Striving to obtain a profit produces highly desirable economic outcomes.

AP Technological Advance and Competition

LO10.5 Discuss creative destruction and the profit incentives for innovation.

In explaining the model of pure competition, we assumed for simplicity that all the firms in an industry had the same cost curves. Competition, as a result, only involved entrepreneurs entering and exiting industries in response to changes in profits caused by changes in the market price. This form of competition is important, but it is just a game of copycat because firms entering an industry simply duplicate the production methods and cost curves of existing firms in order to duplicate their above-normal profits. In this type of competition, there is no dynamism and no innovation, just more of the same.

Consider pharmaceuticals. Once the chemical formula for a new drug becomes known, it is very easy for rivals to make chemically identical versions that will be easy to market because they will be just as effective as the version sold by the firm that invented the drug. At the same time, competition is so fierce in the pharmaceutical industry that without patent protection the price of the new drug would be driven down almost immediately to its marginal production cost. That is highly problematic because the market price would be too low to ever recoup the large R&D costs necessary to identify and develop effective new medications. Thus, without patent protection, R&D would cease and no new drugs would be developed.

So for industries like pharmaceuticals that have easy-to-copy products, patents should continue to exist as they are the only way to provide the financial incentive necessary to get firms to invest the R&D monies that must be spent if you want innovation and creative destruction.

Things are very different, however, for complicated consumer products that are made up of thousands of separate technologies that are each difficult to copy and market. As an example, even if Apple's rivals obtained the blueprints for the iPhone, it would still be extremely costly for them to build the factories necessary to make copies. And even if they did that, they would still have to convince consumers that their copycat iPhones were as good as the original. Thus, unlike pharmaceuticals, patents are not necessary to provide the firms that produce complicated consumer goods with an incentive to develop new products and invest in R&D.

On the other hand, society would likely see great benefits if patents were eliminated for complicated consumer goods like cell phones and automobiles because creative destruction would likely increase as innovative companies would no longer fear patent-infringement lawsuits and old rivals could no longer delay their own demise by taxing innovators.

Source: © Seattle Times/McClatchy-Tribune/Getty Images

As a result, some economists now argue that patents should only be available for industries with simple products that are easy to copy and market. For industries with complicated products that are hard to copy and market, patents should be eliminated.

By contrast, the most dynamic and interesting parts of competition are the fights between firms over the creation of new production technologies and new products. Firms have a strong profit incentive to develop both improved ways of making existing products as well as totally new products. To put that incentive in context, recall one fact that you just learned about long-run equilibrium in perfect competition. When each firm in a purely competitive industry has the same productive technology and therefore the same cost structure for producing output, entry and exit assure that in the long run every firm will make the exact same normal profit.

Entrepreneurs, of course, would like to earn more than a normal profit. As a result, they are constantly attempting two different strategies for increasing their profits. The first involves attempting to lower the production costs of existing products through better technology or improved business organization. Because pure competition implies that individual firms cannot affect the market price, anything that lowers an innovating firm's production costs will result in higher profits, since the innovating firm's revenues per unit (which are equal to the market price per unit) will stay the same while its costs per unit fall due to its improved production technology.

The second strategy for earning a rate of return greater than a normal profit is to try to develop a totally new product that is popular with consumers. If a firm is first-to-market with a popular new product, it will face no competition, as it is the only producer. As long as the product remains popular and the firm remains the only producer, it will be able to charge prices that are higher than production costs, thereby allowing it to earn above-normal profits. (We say much more about this in the next chapter, which covers pure monopoly.)

CONSIDER THIS . . .

Source: © Katrin Thomas/Getty Images RF

Running a Company Is Hard Business

The life expectancy of a U.S. business is just 10.2 years. About 9.5 percent of U.S. firms go out of business each year. In addition, 22 percent of new start-up firms go bankrupt within 2 years, 53 percent within 5 years, and nearly 65 percent within 10 years.

These numbers testify to the ability of competition to quickly dispose of firms that have high production costs or unpopular products. In a competitive environment, such firms quickly prove unprofitable and are shut down by their owners.

Balancing out the dying firms are start-ups that hope to use the resources freed up by the closed firms to deliver better products or lower costs. In a typical year, more than 650,000 new businesses are started in the United States. Most of these new firms will themselves eventually fall victim to creative destruction and the pressures of competition, but one of them may just be the next Google, Starbucks, or Walmart.

Notably, however, any advantages that innovative firms gain either by lowering the production costs of existing products or by introducing entirely new products will not normally persist. An innovative entrepreneur may put some of her current rivals out of business, but there are always other entrepreneurs with new ideas so that soon it may be *her* firm that is going out of business due to innovations made by others. The nearby Consider This box shows just how rapidly new firms are created and destroyed.

Creative Destruction

The innovations that firms achieve thanks to competition are considered by many economists to be the driving force behind economic growth and rising living standards. The transformative effects of competition are often referred to as **creative destruction** to capture the idea that the creation of new products and new production methods destroys the market positions of firms committed to existing products and old ways of doing business. In addition, just the *threat* that a rival may soon come out with a new technology or product can cause other firms to innovate and thereby replace or rectify their old ways of doing business. As argued decades ago by Harvard economist Joseph Schumpeter, the most important type of competition is

> competition from the new commodity, the new technology, the new source of supply, the new type of business organization—competition which commands a decisive cost or quality advantage and which strikes not at the margins of profits of the existing firms but at their foundation and their very lives. This kind of competition is . . . so . . . important that it becomes a matter of comparative indifference whether competition in the ordinary [short-run or long-run] sense functions more or less promptly. . . .
>
> . . . Competition of the kind we now have in mind acts not only when in being but also when it is merely an ever-present threat. It disciplines before it attacks. The businessman feels himself to be in a competitive situation even if he is alone in his field.[2]

There are many examples of creative destruction. In the 1800s wagons, ships, and barges were the only means of transporting freight until the railroads broke up their monopoly; the dominant market position of the railroads was, in turn, undermined by trucks and, later, by airplanes. Movies brought new competition to live theater, at one time the "only show in town." But movies were later challenged by broadcast television, which was then challenged by cable TV. Both are now challenged by Netflix, Amazon Instant Video, and other online video-on-demand services. Cassettes replaced records before being supplanted in turn by compact discs. Then compact discs were done in by iPods and MP3 players, which in turn were done in by the availability of smartphones to play music—including music streamed (instead of purchased) via services like Spotify and Pandora. Electronic communications—including faxes and e-mails—have pushed the U.S. Postal Service toward bankruptcy, including a $5.1 billion loss in 2015. And online retailers like Amazon.com have stolen substantial business away from brick-and-mortar retailers.

The "creative" part of "creative destruction" leads to new products and lower-cost production methods that are of great benefit to society because they allow for a more efficient use of society's scarce resources. Keep in mind, however, that the "destruction" part of "creative destruction" can be hard on workers in the industries being displaced by new technologies. A worker at a CD-making factory may see her job eliminated as consumers switch to online music downloads. The U.S. Postal Service cut 213,000 jobs (30 percent of its workforce) between 2005 and 2015 partly because of the impact that e-mail has had on the demand for postal services. And many jobs in retail have been eliminated due to competition with Amazon.com and other online retailers.

Normally, the process of creative destruction goes slowly enough that workers at firms being downsized can transition smoothly to jobs in firms that are expanding. But sometimes

[2]Joseph A. Schumpeter, *Capitalism, Socialism, and Democracy,* 3d ed. (New York: Harper & Row, 1950), pp. 84–85.

the change is too swift for all of them to find new jobs easily. And in other instances, such as a town with only one major employer—like a rural coal-mining town or a small town with a large auto factory—the loss of that one major employer can be devastating because there are not enough other firms in the local area to employ the workers laid off by the major employer.

While the net effects of creative destruction are indisputably positive—including ongoing economic growth and rising living standards—creative destruction involves costs as well as benefits. And while the benefits are widespread, the costs tend to be borne almost entirely by the relatively few workers in declining industries who are not positioned to make easy transitions to new jobs.

SUMMARY

LO10.1 Explain how the long run differs from the short run in pure competition.

In the short run, when plant and equipment are fixed, the firms in a purely competitive industry may earn profits or suffer losses. In the long run, when plant and equipment are adjustable, profits will attract new entrants, while losses will cause existing firms to leave the industry.

LO10.2 Describe how profits and losses drive the long-run adjustment process of pure competition.

The entry or exit of firms will change industry supply. Entry or exit will continue until the market price determined by industry supply interacting with market demand generates a normal profit for firms in the industry. With firms earning a normal profit, there will be no incentive to either enter or exit the industry. This situation constitutes long-run equilibrium in a purely competitive industry.

Entry and exit help to improve resource allocation. Firms that exit an industry due to low profits release their resources to be used more profitably in other industries. Firms that enter an industry chasing higher profits bring with them resources that were less profitably used in other industries. Both processes increase allocative efficiency.

In the long run, the market price of a product will equal the minimum average total cost of production. At a higher price, economic profits will cause firms to enter the industry until those profits have been competed away. At a lower price, losses will force the exit of firms from the industry until the product price rises to equal average total cost.

LO10.3 Explain the differences between constant-cost, increasing-cost, and decreasing-cost industries.

The long-run supply curve is horizontal for a constant-cost industry, upsloping for an increasing-cost industry, and downsloping for a decreasing-cost industry.

LO10.4 Show how long-run equilibrium in pure competition produces an efficient allocation of resources.

The long-run equality of price and minimum average total cost means that competitive firms will use the most efficient known technology and charge the lowest price consistent with their production costs. That is, the purely competitive firms will achieve productive efficiency.

The long-run equality of price and marginal cost implies that resources will be allocated in accordance with consumer tastes. Allocative efficiency will occur. In the market, the combined amount of consumer surplus and producer surplus will be at a maximum.

The competitive price system will reallocate resources in response to a change in consumer tastes, in technology, or in resource supplies and will thereby maintain allocative efficiency over time.

LO10.5 Discuss creative destruction and the profit incentives for innovation.

Competition involves never-ending attempts by entrepreneurs and managers to earn above-normal profits by either creating new products or developing lower-cost production methods for existing products. These efforts cause creative destruction, the financial undoing of the market positions of firms committed to existing products and old ways of doing business by new firms with new products and innovative ways of doing business.

TERMS AND CONCEPTS

long-run supply curve
constant-cost industry
increasing-cost industry
decreasing-cost industry
productive efficiency
allocative efficiency
consumer surplus
producer surplus
creative destruction

The following and additional problems can be found in connect

DISCUSSION QUESTIONS

1. Explain how the long run differs from the short run in pure competition. LO10.1
2. Relate opportunity costs to why profits encourage entry into purely competitive industries and how losses encourage exit from purely competitive industries. LO10.2
3. How do the entry and exit of firms in a purely competitive industry affect resource flows and long-run profits and losses? LO10.2
4. In long-run equilibrium, P = minimum ATC = MC. Of what significance for economic efficiency is the equality of P and minimum ATC? The equality of P and MC? Distinguish between productive efficiency and allocative efficiency in your answer. LO10.4
5. The basic model of pure competition reviewed in this chapter finds that in the long run all firms in a purely competitive industry will earn normal profits. If all firms will only earn a normal profit in the long run, why would any firms bother to develop new products or lower-cost production methods? Explain. LO10.5
6. "Ninety percent of new products fail within two years—so you shouldn't be so eager to innovate." Do you agree? Explain why or why not. LO10.5
7. **LAST WORD** How can patents speed up the process of creative destruction? How can patents slow down the process of creative destruction? How do differences in manufacturing costs affect which industries would be most likely to be affected by the removal of patents?

AP REVIEW QUESTIONS

1. When discussing pure competition, the term *long run* refers to a period of time long enough to allow: LO10.1
   a. Firms already in an industry to either expand or contract their capacities.
   b. New firms to enter or existing firms to leave.
   c. Only labor resources to be added to production.
   d. Firms to change their variable costs, but not their fixed costs
   e. Both a and b
2. Suppose that the pen-making industry is perfectly competitive. Also suppose that each current firm and any potential firms that might enter the industry all have identical cost curves, with minimum ATC = \$1.25 per pen. If the market equilibrium price of pens is currently \$1.50, what would you expect it to be in the long run? LO10.2
   a. \$0.25.
   b. \$1.00.
   c. \$1.25.
   d. \$1.50.
   e. \$2.75
3. Suppose that as the output of mobile phones increases, the cost per unit of touch screens and other component parts decreases. If the mobile phone industry features pure competition, we would expect the long-run supply curve for mobile phones to be: LO10.3
   a. Upward sloping.
   b. Downward sloping.
   c. Horizontal.
   d. U-shaped.
   e. Vertical.
4. Using diagrams for both the industry and a representative firm, illustrate a competitive long-run equilibrium. Assuming a constant cost industry, employ these diagrams to show how an increase in market demand will affect that long-run equilibrium. Trace graphically and describe verbally the adjustment processes by which long-run equilibrium is restored. Now rework your analysis for increasing- and decreasing-cost industries and compare the three long-run supply curves. Draw the long-run equilibrium for the competitive firm and industry. LO10.3
5. Suppose that purely competitive firms producing cashews discover that P exceeds MC and is greater than ATC. Is their combined output of cashews too little, too much, or just right to achieve allocative efficiency? In the long run, what will happen to the supply of cashews and the price of cashews? Use a supply and demand diagram to show how that response will change the combined amount of consumer surplus and producer surplus in the market for cashews. LO10.4
6. Assume a constant cost industry. LO10.2, 10.3, 10.4
   a. Draw a short-run supply curve and a demand curve. Show the equilibrium. Also, identify the area of consumer surplus and the area of producer surplus.
   b. Draw a long-run supply curve and a demand curve. Show the equilibrium. Also, identify the area of consumer surplus and the area of producer surplus.
7. Assume a constant cost industry. Consider the following six parameters: P of output, Q of output, number of firms, profits per firm, unit price of labor, and unit price of capital. LO10.2, 10.3, 10.4
   a. Along a short-run market supply curve which of the six are constant? Which of the six are variable?
   b. Along a long-run market supply curve which of the six are constant? Which of the six are variable?

PROBLEMS

1. A firm in a purely competitive industry has a typical cost structure. The normal rate of profit in the economy is 5 percent. This firm is earning \$5.50 on every \$50 invested by its founders. What is its percentage rate of return? Is the firm earning an economic profit? If so, how large? Will this industry see entry or exit? What will be the rate of return earned by firms in this industry once the industry reaches long-run equilibrium? LO10.2
2. A firm in a purely competitive industry is currently producing 1,000 units per day at a total cost of \$450. If the firm produced 800 units per day, its total cost would be \$300, and if it produced 500 units per day, its total cost would be \$275. What are the firm's ATC per unit at these three levels of production? If every firm in this industry has the same cost structure, is the industry in long-run competitive equilibrium? From what you know about these firms' cost structures, what is the highest possible price per unit that could exist as the market price in long-run equilibrium? If that price ends up being the market price and if the normal rate of profit is 10 percent, then how big will each firm's accounting profit per unit be? LO10.4
3. There are 300 purely competitive farms in the local dairy market. Of the 300 dairy farms, 298 have a cost structure that generates profits of \$24 for every \$300 invested. What is their percentage rate of return? The other two dairies have a cost structure that generates profits of \$22 for every \$200 invested. What is their percentage rate of return? Assuming that the normal rate of profit in the economy is 10 percent, will there be entry or exit? Will the change in the number of firms affect the two that earn \$22 for every \$200 invested? What will be the rate of return earned by most firms in the industry in long-run equilibrium? If firms can copy each other's technology, what will be the rate of return eventually earned by all firms? LO10.4

11 Chapter

Pure Monopoly

Learning Objectives

LO11.1 List the characteristics of pure monopoly.

LO11.2 List and explain the barriers to entry that shield pure monopolies from competition.

LO11.3 Explain how demand is seen by a pure monopoly.

LO11.4 Explain how a pure monopoly sets its profit-maximizing output and price.

LO11.5 Discuss the economic effects of monopoly.

LO11.6 Describe why a monopolist might prefer to charge different prices in different markets.

LO11.7 Distinguish among the monopoly price, the socially optimal price, and the fair-return price of a government-regulated monopoly.

AP Chapter Focus

We turn now from pure competition to pure monopoly, which is at the opposite end of the spectrum of industry structures listed in Table 9.1. You deal with monopolies more often than you might think. If you see the logo for Microsoft's Windows on your computer, you are dealing with a monopoly (or, at least, a near-monopoly). When you purchase certain prescription drugs, you are buying monopolized products. When you make a local telephone call, turn on your lights, or subscribe to cable TV, you may be patronizing a monopoly, depending on your location.

What precisely do we mean by pure monopoly, and what conditions enable it to arise and survive? How does a pure monopolist determine its profit-maximizing price and output? Does a pure monopolist achieve the efficiency associated with pure competition? If not, what, if anything, should the government do about it? Studying a simplified model of pure monopoly will help us answer these questions. It will be the first of three models of *imperfect competition,* of which pure monopoly is a type.

An Introduction to Pure Monopoly

LO11.1 List the characteristics of pure monopoly.

Pure monopoly exists when a single firm is the sole producer of a product for which there are no close substitutes. Here are the main characteristics of pure monopoly:

- ***Single seller*** A pure, or absolute, monopoly is an industry in which a single firm is the sole producer of a specific good or the sole supplier of a service; the firm and the industry are synonymous.

- ***No close substitutes*** A pure monopoly's product is unique in that there are no close substitutes. The consumer who chooses not to buy the monopolized product must do without it.
- ***Price maker*** The pure monopolist controls the total quantity supplied and thus has considerable control over price; it is a *price maker* (unlike a pure competitor, which has no such control and therefore is a *price taker*). The pure monopolist confronts the usual downsloping product demand curve. It can change its product price by changing the quantity of the product it produces. The monopolist will use this power whenever it is advantageous to do so.
- ***Blocked entry*** A pure monopolist has no immediate competitors because certain barriers keep potential competitors from entering the industry. Those barriers may be economic, technological, legal, or of some other type. But entry is totally blocked in pure monopoly.
- ***Nonprice competition*** The product produced by a pure monopolist may be either standardized (as with natural gas and electricity) or differentiated (as with Windows or Frisbees). Monopolists that have standardized products engage mainly in public relations advertising, whereas those with differentiated products sometimes advertise their products' attributes.

Examples of Monopoly

Examples of *pure* monopoly are relatively rare, but there are many examples of less pure forms. In most cities, government-owned or government-regulated public utilities—natural gas and electric companies, the water company, the cable TV company, and the local telephone company—are all monopolies or virtually so.

There are also many "near-monopolies" in which a single firm has the bulk of sales in a specific market. Intel, for example, produces 80 percent of the central microprocessors used in personal computers. First Data Corporation, via its Western Union subsidiary, accounts for 80 percent of the market for money order transfers. Brannock Device Company has an 80 percent market share of the shoe sizing devices found in shoe stores. Wham-O, through its Frisbee brand, sells 90 percent of plastic throwing disks. Google executes nearly 70 percent of all U.S. Internet searches and consequently controls nearly 75 percent of all the revenue generated by search ads in the United States.

Professional sports teams are, in a sense, monopolies because they are the sole suppliers of specific services in large geographic areas. With a few exceptions, a single major-league team in each sport serves each large American city. If you want to see a live Major League Baseball game in St. Louis or Seattle, you must patronize the Cardinals or the Mariners, respectively. Other geographic monopolies exist. For example, a small town may be served by only one airline or railroad. In a small, isolated community, the local barber shop, dry cleaner, or grocery store may approximate a monopoly. And in the skies above, airlines control the only Internet access that is available to the passengers flying on their planes.

Of course, there is almost always some competition. Satellite television is a substitute for cable, and amateur softball is a substitute for professional baseball. The Linux operating system can substitute for Windows, and so on. But such substitutes are typically either more costly or in some way less appealing.

Dual Objectives of the Study of Monopoly

Monopoly is worth studying both for its own sake and because it provides insights about the more common market structures of monopolistic competition and oligopoly (Chapters 12 and 13). These two market structures combine, in differing degrees, characteristics of pure competition and pure monopoly.

AP Barriers to Entry

LO11.2 List and explain the barriers to entry that shield pure monopolies from competition.

The factors that prohibit firms from entering an industry are called **barriers to entry.** In pure monopoly, strong barriers to entry effectively block all potential competition. Somewhat weaker barriers may permit oligopoly, a market structure dominated by a few firms. Still weaker barriers may permit the entry of a fairly large number of competing firms giving rise to monopolistic competition. And the absence of any effective entry barriers permits the entry of a very large number of firms, which provide the basis of pure competition. So barriers to entry are pertinent not only to the extreme case of pure monopoly but also to other market structures in which there are monopoly-like characteristics or monopoly-like behaviors.

We now discuss the four most prominent barriers to entry.

Economies of Scale

Modern technology in some industries is such that economies of scale—declining average total cost with added firm size—are extensive. In such cases, a firm's long-run average-cost schedule will decline over a wide range of output. Given market demand, only a few large firms or, in the extreme, only a single large firm can achieve low average total costs.

Figure 11.1 indicates economies of scale over a wide range of outputs. If total consumer demand is within that output range, then only a single producer can satisfy demand at least cost. Note, for example, that a monopolist can produce

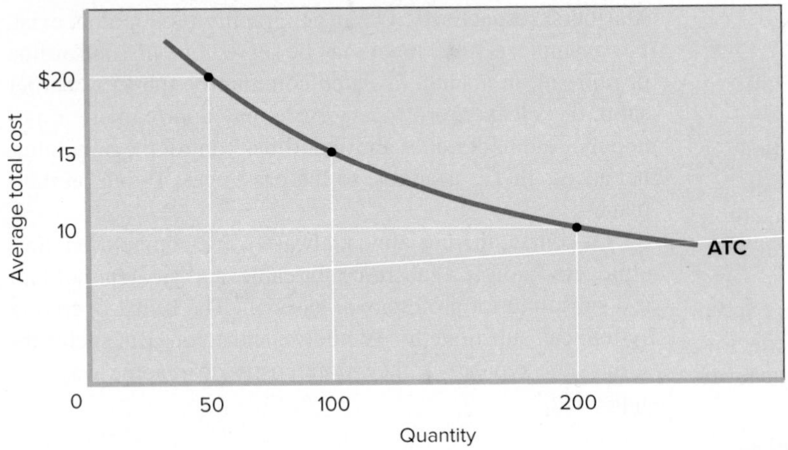

FIGURE 11.1 Economies of scale: the natural monopoly case. A declining long-run average-total-cost curve over a wide range of output quantities indicates extensive economies of scale. A single monopoly firm can produce, say, 200 units of output at lower cost ($10 each) than could two or more firms that had a combined output of 200 units.

200 units at a per-unit cost of $10 and a total cost of $2,000. If the industry has two firms and each produces 100 units, the unit cost is $15 and total cost rises to $3,000 (= 200 units × $15). A still more competitive situation with four firms each producing 50 units would boost unit and total cost to $20 and $4,000, respectively. Conclusion: When long-run ATC is declining, only a single producer, a monopolist, can produce any particular amount of output at minimum total cost.

If a pure monopoly exists in such an industry, economies of scale will serve as an entry barrier and will protect the monopolist from competition. New firms that try to enter the industry as small-scale producers cannot realize the cost economies of the monopolist. They therefore will be undercut and forced out of business by the monopolist, which can sell at a much lower price and still make a profit because of its lower per-unit cost associated with its economies of scale. A new firm might try to start out big, that is, to enter the industry as a large-scale producer so as to achieve the necessary economies of scale. But the massive expense of the plant facilities along with customer loyalty to the existing product would make the entry highly risky. Therefore, the new and untried enterprise would find it difficult to secure financing for its venture. In most cases the risks and financial obstacles to "starting big" are prohibitive. This explains why efforts to enter such industries as computer operating software, commercial aircraft, and household laundry equipment are so rare.

A monopoly firm is referred to as a *natural monopoly* if the market demand curve intersects the long-run ATC curve at any point where average total costs are declining. If a natural monopoly were to set its price where market demand intersects long-run ATC, its price would be lower than if the industry were more competitive. But it will probably set a higher price. As with any monopolist, a natural monopolist may, instead, set its price far above ATC and obtain substantial economic profit. In that event, the lowest-unit-cost advantage of a natural monopolist would accrue to the monopolist as profit and not as lower prices to consumers. That is why the government regulates some natural monopolies, specifying the price they may charge. We will say more about that later.

Legal Barriers to Entry: Patents and Licenses

Government also creates legal barriers to entry by awarding patents and licenses.

Patents A *patent* is the exclusive right of an inventor to use, or to allow another to use, her or his invention. Patents and patent laws aim to protect the inventor from rivals who would use the invention without having shared in the effort and expense of developing it. At the same time, patents provide the inventor with a monopoly position for the life of the patent. The world's nations have agreed on a uniform patent length of 20 years from the time of application. Patents have figured prominently in the growth of modern-day giants such as IBM, Pfizer, Intel, Xerox, General Electric, and DuPont.

Research and development (R&D) is what leads to most patentable inventions and products. Firms that gain monopoly power through their own research or by purchasing the patents of others can use patents to strengthen their market position. The profit from one patent can finance the research required to develop new patentable products. In the pharmaceutical industry, patents on prescription drugs have produced large monopoly profits that have helped finance the discovery of new patentable medicines. So monopoly power achieved through patents may well be self-sustaining, even though patents eventually expire and generic drugs then compete with the original brand. (Chapter 10's Last Word has more on the costs and benefits of patents.)

Licenses Government may also limit entry into an industry or occupation through *licensing*. At the national level, the Federal Communications Commission licenses only so many radio and television stations in each geographic area. In many large cities one of a limited number of municipal licenses is required to drive a taxicab. The consequent restriction of the supply of cabs creates economic profit for cab owners and drivers. New cabs cannot enter the industry to drive down prices and profits. In a few instances the government might "license" itself to provide some product and thereby create a public monopoly. For example, in some states only state-owned retail outlets can sell liquor. Similarly, many states have "licensed" themselves to run lotteries.

Ownership or Control of Essential Resources

A monopolist can use private property as an obstacle to potential rivals. For example, a firm that owns or controls a resource essential to the production process can prohibit the entry of rival firms. At one time the International Nickel Company of Canada (now called Vale Canada Limited) controlled 90 percent of the world's known nickel reserves. A local firm may own all the nearby deposits of sand and gravel. And it is very difficult for new sports leagues to be created because existing professional sports leagues have contracts with the best players and have long-term leases on the major stadiums and arenas.

Pricing and Other Strategic Barriers to Entry

Even if a firm is not protected from entry by, say, extensive economies of scale or ownership of essential resources, entry may effectively be blocked by the way the monopolist responds to attempts by rivals to enter the industry. Confronted with a new entrant, the monopolist may "create an entry barrier" by slashing its price, stepping up its advertising, or taking other strategic actions to make it difficult for the entrant to succeed.

Some examples of entry deterrence: In 2005 Dentsply, the dominant American maker of false teeth (80 percent market share) was found to have unlawfully precluded independent distributors of false teeth from carrying competing brands. The lack of access to the distributors deterred potential foreign competitors from entering the U.S. market. As another example, in 2015 American Express was found guilty of an unlawful restraint of trade because it prohibited any merchant who had signed up to accept American Express credit cards from promoting rival credit cards—such as Visa or MasterCard—to their customers.

AP Monopoly Demand

LO11.3 Explain how demand is seen by a pure monopoly.

Now that we have explained the sources of monopoly, we want to build a model of pure monopoly so that we can analyze its price and output decisions. Let's start by making three assumptions:

- Patents, economies of scale, or resource ownership secures the firm's monopoly.
- No unit of government regulates the firm.
- The firm is a single-price monopolist; it charges the same price for all units of output.

The crucial difference between a pure monopolist and a purely competitive seller lies on the demand side of the market. The purely competitive seller faces a perfectly elastic demand at the price determined by market supply and demand. It is a price taker that can sell as much or as little as it wants at the going market price. Each additional unit sold will add the amount of the constant product price to the firm's total revenue. That means that marginal revenue for the competitive seller is constant and equal to product price. (Refer to the table and graph in Figure 9.1 for price, marginal-revenue, and total-revenue relationships for the purely competitive firm.)

The demand curve for the monopolist (and for any imperfectly competitive seller) is quite different from that of the pure competitor. Because the pure monopolist *is* the industry, its demand curve *is* the market demand curve. And because market demand is not perfectly elastic, the monopolist's demand curve is downsloping. Columns 1 and 2 in Table 11.1 illustrate this concept. Note that quantity demanded increases as price decreases.

In Figure 9.7 we drew separate demand curves for the purely competitive industry and for a single firm in such an industry. But only a single demand curve is needed in pure monopoly because the firm and the industry are one and the same. We have graphed part of the demand data in Table 11.1 as demand curve *D* in Figure 11.2. This is the monopolist's demand curve *and* the market demand curve. The downsloping demand curve has three implications that are essential to understanding the monopoly model.

Marginal Revenue Is Less Than Price

With a fixed downsloping demand curve, the pure monopolist can increase sales only by charging a lower price. Consequently, marginal revenue—the change in total revenue associated with a one-unit change in output—is less than price (average revenue) for every unit of output except the first. Why so? The reason is that the lower price of the extra unit of output also applies to all prior units of output. The

AP TABLE 11.1 Revenue and Cost Data of a Pure Monopolist

Revenue Data				Cost Data			
(1) Quantity of Output	(2) Price (Average Revenue)	(3) Total Revenue, (1) × (2)	(4) Marginal Revenue	(5) Average Total Cost	(6) Total Cost, (1) × (5)	(7) Marginal Cost	(8) Profit [+] or Loss [−]
0	$172	$ 0			$ 100		$−100
1	162	162	$162	$190.00	190	$ 90	−28
2	152	304	142	135.00	270	80	+34
3	142	426	122	113.33	340	70	+86
4	132	528	102	100.00	400	60	+128
5	**122**	**610**	**82**	**94.00**	**470**	**70**	**+140**
6	112	672	62	91.67	550	80	+122
7	102	714	42	91.43	640	90	+74
8	92	736	22	93.75	750	110	−14
9	82	738	2	97.78	880	130	−142
10	72	720	−18	103.00	1030	150	−310

monopolist could have sold these prior units at a higher price if it had not produced and sold the extra output. Each additional unit of output sold increases total revenue by an amount equal to its own price less the sum of the price cuts that apply to all prior units of output.

Figure 11.2 confirms this point. There, we have highlighted two price-quantity combinations from the monopolist's demand curve. The monopolist can sell 1 more unit at $132 than it can at $142 and that way obtain $132 (the blue area) of extra revenue. But to sell that fourth unit for $132, the monopolist must also sell the first 3 units at $132 rather than $142. The $10 reduction in revenue on 3 units results in a $30 revenue loss (the red area). Thus, the net difference in total revenue from selling a fourth unit is $102: the $132 gain from the fourth unit minus the $30 forgone on the first 3 units. This net gain (marginal revenue) of $102 from the fourth unit is clearly less than the $132 price of the fourth unit.

AP FIGURE 11.2 Price and marginal revenue in pure monopoly. A pure monopolist, or any other imperfect competitor with a downsloping demand curve such as *D*, must set a lower price in order to sell more output. Here, by charging $132 rather than $142, the monopolist sells an extra unit (the fourth unit) and gains $132 from that sale. But from this gain must be subtracted $30, which reflects the $10 less the monopolist charged for each of the first 3 units. Thus, the marginal revenue of the fourth unit is $102 (= $132 − $30), considerably less than its $132 price.

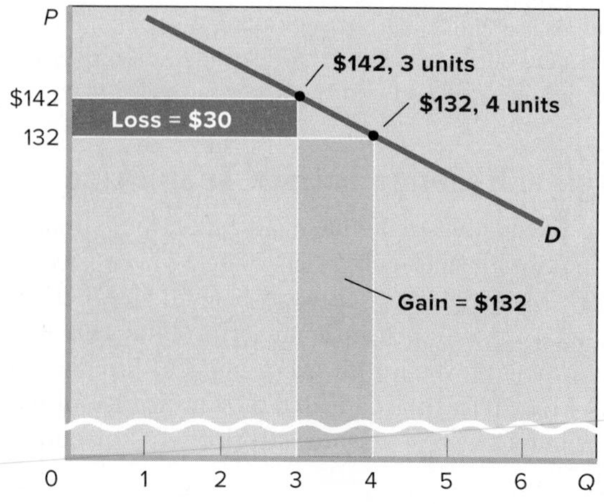

Column 4 in Table 11.1 shows that marginal revenue is always less than the corresponding product price in column 2, except for the first unit of output. Because marginal revenue is the change in total revenue associated with each additional unit of output, the declining amounts of marginal revenue in column 4 mean that total revenue increases at a diminishing rate (as shown in column 3).

We show the relationship between the monopolist's marginal-revenue curve and total-revenue curve in Figure 11.3. For this figure, we extended the demand and revenue data of columns 1 through 4 in Table 11.1, assuming that each successive $10 price cut elicits 1 additional unit of sales. That is, the monopolist can sell 11 units at $62, 12 units at $52, and so on.

Note that the monopolist's MR curve lies below the demand curve, indicating that marginal revenue is less than price at every output quantity but the very first unit. Observe also the special relationship between total revenue (shown in the lower graph) and marginal revenue (shown in the top graph). Because marginal revenue is the change in total revenue, marginal revenue is positive while total revenue is increasing. When total revenue reaches its maximum, marginal revenue is zero. When total revenue is diminishing, marginal revenue is negative.

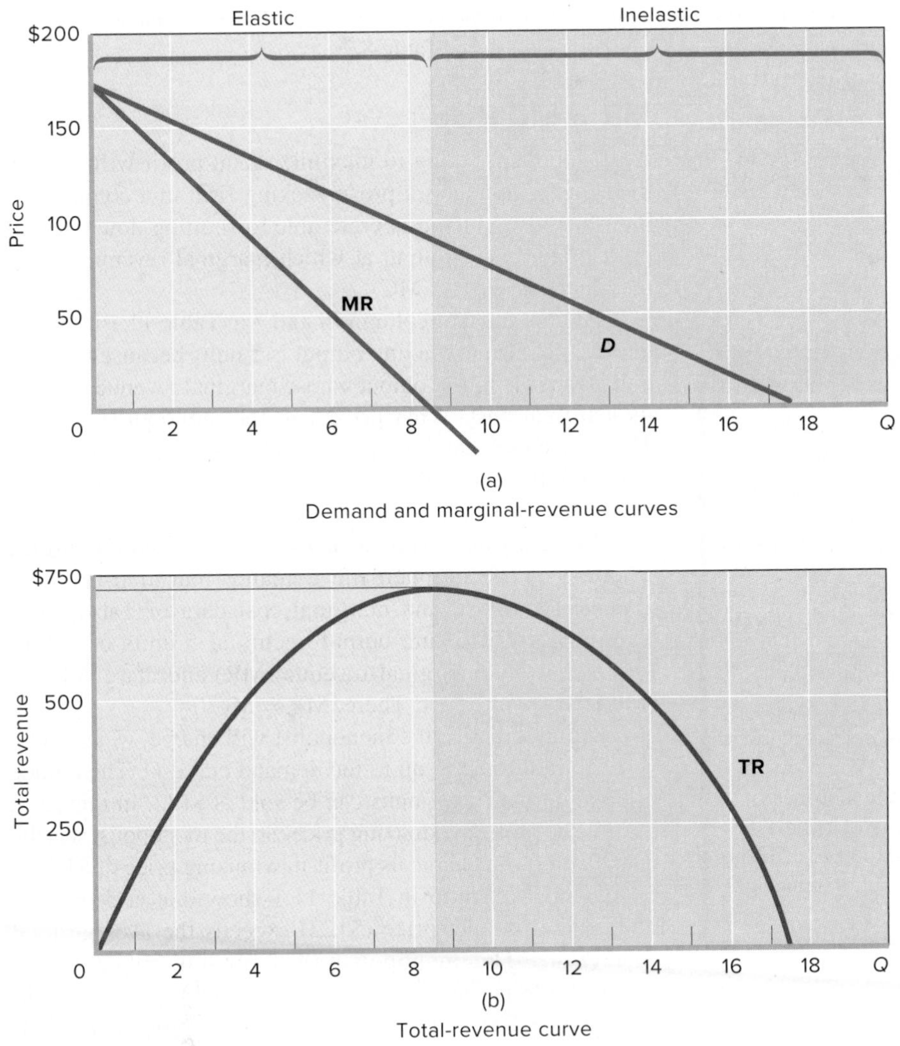

AP **FIGURE 11.3 Demand, marginal revenue, and total revenue for a pure monopolist.**
(a) Because it must lower price on all units sold in order to increase its sales, an imperfectly competitive firm's marginal-revenue curve (MR) lies below its downsloping demand curve (*D*). The elastic and inelastic regions of demand are highlighted. (b) Total revenue (TR) increases at a decreasing rate, reaches a maximum, and then declines. Note that in the elastic region, TR is increasing and hence MR is positive. When TR reaches its maximum, MR is zero. In the inelastic region of demand, TR is declining, so MR is negative.

The Monopolist Is a Price Maker

All imperfect competitors, whether pure monopolists, oligopolists, or monopolistic competitors, face downsloping demand curves. As a result, any change in quantity produced causes a movement along their respective demand curves and a change in the price they can charge for their respective products. Economists summarize this fact by saying that firms with downsloping demand curves are *price makers*.

This is most evident in pure monopoly, where an industry consists of a single monopoly firm so that total industry output is exactly equal to whatever the single monopoly firm chooses to produce. As we just mentioned, the monopolist faces a downsloping demand curve in which each amount of output is associated with some unique price. Thus, in deciding on the quantity of output to produce, the monopolist is also determining the price it will charge. Through control of output, it can "make the price." From columns 1 and 2 in Table 11.1 we find that the monopolist can charge a price of $72 if it produces and offers for sale 10 units, a price of $82 if it produces and offers for sale 9 units, and so forth.

The Monopolist Sets Prices in the Elastic Region of Demand

The total-revenue test for price elasticity of demand is the basis for our third implication. Recall from Chapter 6 that the total-revenue test reveals that when demand is elastic, a decline in price will increase total revenue. Similarly, when demand is inelastic, a decline in price will reduce total revenue. Beginning at the top of demand curve *D* in Figure 11.3a, observe that as the price declines from $172 to approximately $82, total revenue increases (and marginal revenue therefore is positive). This means that demand is elastic in this price range. Conversely, for price declines below $82, total revenue decreases (marginal revenue is negative), indicating that demand is inelastic there.

The implication is that a monopolist will never choose a price-quantity combination where price reductions cause total revenue to decrease (marginal revenue to be negative). The profit-maximizing monopolist will always want to avoid the inelastic segment of its demand curve in favor of some price-quantity combination in the elastic region. Here's why: To get into the inelastic region, the monopolist must lower price and increase output. In the inelastic region a lower price means less total revenue. And increased output always means increased total cost. Less total revenue and higher total cost yield lower profit.

AP QUICK REVIEW 11.1

- ✓ A pure monopolist is the sole supplier of a product or service for which there are no close substitutes.
- ✓ A monopoly survives because of entry barriers such as economies of scale, patents and licenses, the ownership of essential resources, and strategic actions to exclude rivals.
- ✓ The monopolist's demand curve is downsloping and its marginal-revenue curve lies below its demand curve.
- ✓ The downsloping demand curve means that the monopolist is a price maker.
- ✓ The monopolist will operate in the elastic region of demand, since moving into the inelastic region would require the monopolist to lower price and increase output; total revenues would fall, since demand is inelastic. Increased output here means increased total cost. Thus, with revenues falling and costs rising, profits unambiguously will fall.

AP Output and Price Determination

LO11.4 Explain how a pure monopoly sets its profit-maximizing output and price.

At what specific price-quantity combination will a profit-maximizing monopolist choose to operate? To answer this question, we must add production costs to our analysis.

Cost Data

On the cost side, we will assume that although the firm is a monopolist in the product market, it hires resources competitively and employs the same technology and, therefore, has the same cost structure as the purely competitive firm that we studied in Chapters 9 and 10. By using the same cost data that we developed in Chapter 8 and applied to the competitive firm in Chapters 9 and 10, we will be able to directly compare the price and output decisions of a pure monopoly with those of a pure competitor. This will help us demonstrate that the price and output differences between a pure monopolist and a pure competitor are not the result of two different sets of costs. Columns 5 through 7 in Table 11.1 restate the pertinent cost data from Table 8.2.

MR = MC Rule

A monopolist seeking to maximize total profit will employ the same rationale as a profit-seeking firm in a competitive industry. If producing is preferable to shutting down, it will produce up to the output at which marginal revenue equals marginal cost (MR = MC).

A comparison of columns 4 and 7 in Table 11.1 indicates that the profit-maximizing output is 5 units because the fifth unit is the last unit of output whose marginal revenue exceeds its marginal cost. What price will the monopolist charge? The demand schedule shown as columns 1 and 2 in Table 11.1 indicates there is only one price at which 5 units can be sold: $122.

This analysis is shown in **Figure 11.4 (Key Graph),** where we have graphed the demand, marginal-revenue, average-total-cost, and marginal-cost data of Table 11.1. The profit-maximizing output occurs at 5 units of output (Q_m), where the marginal-revenue (MR) and marginal-cost (MC) curves intersect. There, MR = MC.

To find the price the monopolist will charge, we extend a vertical line from Q_m up to the demand curve *D*. The unique price P_m at which Q_m units can be sold is $122. In this case, $122 is the profit-maximizing price. So the monopolist sets the quantity at Q_m to charge its profit-maximizing price of $122.

Columns 2 and 5 in Table 11.1 show that at 5 units of output, the product price ($122) exceeds the average total cost ($94). The monopolist thus obtains an economic profit of $28 per unit, and the total economic profit is $140 (= 5 units × $28). In Figure 11.4, per-unit profit is $P_m - A$, where *A* is the average total cost of producing Q_m units. Total economic profit—the green rectangle—is found by multiplying this per-unit profit by the profit-maximizing output Q_m.

Another way to determine the profit-maximizing output is by comparing total revenue and total cost at each possible level of production and choosing the output with the greatest positive difference. Use columns 3 and 6 in Table 11.1 to verify that 5 units is the profit-maximizing output. An accurate graphing of total revenue and total cost against output would also show the greatest difference (the maximum profit) at 5 units of output. Table 11.2 summarizes the process for determining the profit-maximizing output, profit-maximizing price, and economic profit in pure monopoly.

No Monopoly Supply Curve

Recall that MR equals *P* in pure competition and that the supply curve of a purely competitive firm is determined by applying the MR (= *P*) = MC profit-maximizing rule. At any specific market-determined price, the purely competitive seller

AP KEY GRAPH

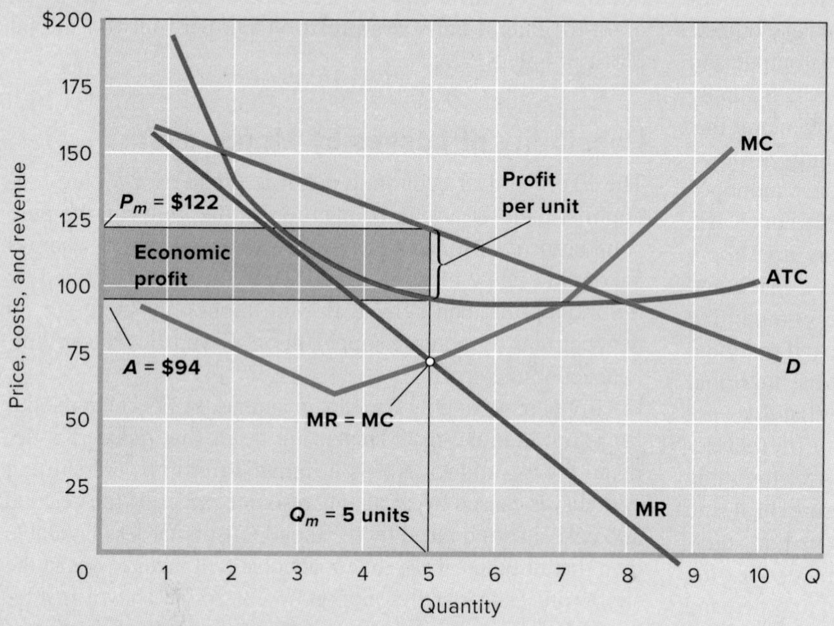

FIGURE 11.4 Profit maximization by a pure monopolist. The pure monopolist maximizes profit by producing at the MR = MC output, here $Q_m = 5$ units. Then, as seen from the demand curve, it will charge price $P_m = \$122$. Average total cost will be $A = \$94$, meaning that per-unit profit is $P_m - A$ and total profit is $5 \times (P_m - A)$. Total economic profit is thus represented by the green rectangle.

QUICK QUIZ FOR FIGURE 11.4

1. The MR curve lies below the demand curve in this figure because the:
   - **a.** demand curve is linear (a straight line).
   - **b.** demand curve is highly inelastic throughout its full length.
   - **c.** demand curve is highly elastic throughout its full length.
   - **d.** gain in revenue from an extra unit of output is less than the price charged for that unit of output.
2. The area labeled "Economic profit" can be found by multiplying the difference between *P* and ATC by quantity. It also can be found by:
   - **a.** dividing profit per unit by quantity.
   - **b.** subtracting total cost from total revenue.
   - **c.** multiplying the coefficient of demand elasticity by quantity.
   - **d.** multiplying the difference between *P* and MC by quantity.
3. This pure monopolist:
   - **a.** charges the highest price that it could achieve.
   - **b.** earns only a normal profit in the long run.
   - **c.** restricts output to create an insurmountable entry barrier.
   - **d.** restricts output to increase its price and total economic profit.
4. At this monopolist's profit-maximizing output:
   - **a.** price equals marginal revenue.
   - **b.** price equals marginal cost.
   - **c.** price exceeds marginal cost.
   - **d.** profit per unit is maximized.

Answers: 1. d; 2. b; 3. d; 4. c

TABLE 11.2 Steps for Graphically Determining the Profit-Maximizing Output, Profit-Maximizing Price, and Economic Profit (if Any) in Pure Monopoly

Step 1.	Determine the profit-maximizing output by finding where MR = MC.
Step 2.	Determine the profit-maximizing price by extending a vertical line upward from the output determined in step 1 to the pure monopolist's demand curve
Step 3.	Determine the pure monopolist's economic profit using one of two methods:
	Method 1. Find profit per unit by subtracting the average total cost of the profit-maximizing output from the profit-maximizing price. Then multiply the difference by the profit-maximizing output to determine economic profit (if any).
	Method 2. Find total cost by multiplying the average total cost of the profit-maximizing output by that output. Find total revenue by multiplying the profit-maximizing output by the profit-maximizing price. Then subtract total cost from total revenue to determine economic profit (if any).

will maximize profit by supplying the quantity at which MC is equal to that price. When the market price increases or decreases, the competitive firm produces more or less output. Each market price is thus associated with a specific output, and all such price-output pairs define the supply curve. This supply curve turns out to be the portion of the firm's MC curve that lies above the average-variable-cost curve (see Figure 9.6).

At first glance we would suspect that the pure monopolist's marginal-cost curve would also be its supply curve. But that is *not* the case. *The pure monopolist has no supply curve.* There is no unique relationship between price and quantity supplied for a monopolist. Like the competitive firm, the monopolist equates marginal revenue and marginal cost to determine output, but for the monopolist marginal revenue is less than price. Because the monopolist does not equate marginal cost to price, it is possible for different demand conditions to bring about different prices for the same output. To understand this point, refer to Figure 11.4 and pencil in a new, steeper marginal-revenue curve that intersects the marginal-cost curve at the same point as does the present marginal-revenue curve. Then draw in a new demand curve that is roughly consistent with your new marginal-revenue curve. With the new curves, the same MR = MC output of 5 units now means a higher profit-maximizing price. Conclusion: There is no single, unique price associated with each output level Q_m, and so there is no supply curve for the pure monopolist.

Misconceptions Concerning Monopoly Pricing

Our analysis exposes two fallacies concerning monopoly behavior.

Not Highest Price Because a monopolist can manipulate output and price, people often believe it "will charge the highest price possible." That is incorrect. There are many prices above P_m in Figure 11.4, but the monopolist shuns them because they yield a smaller-than-maximum total profit. The monopolist seeks maximum total profit, not maximum price. Some high prices that could be charged would reduce sales and total revenue too severely to offset any decrease in total cost.

Total, Not Unit, Profit The monopolist seeks maximum *total* profit, not maximum *unit* profit. In Figure 11.4 a careful comparison of the vertical distance between average total cost and price at various possible outputs indicates that per-unit profit is greater at a point slightly to the left of the profit-maximizing output Q_m. This is seen in Table 11.1, where the per-unit profit at 4 units of output is \$32 (= \$132 − \$100) compared with \$28 (= \$122 − \$94) at the profit-maximizing output of 5 units. Here the monopolist accepts a lower-than-maximum per-unit profit because additional sales more than compensate for the lower unit profit. A monopolist would rather sell 5 units at a profit of \$28 per unit (for a total profit of \$140) than 4 units at a profit of \$32 per unit (for a total profit of only \$128).

Possibility of Losses by Monopolist

The likelihood of economic profit is greater for a pure monopolist than for a pure competitor. In the long run the pure competitor is destined to have only a normal profit, whereas barriers to entry mean that any economic profit realized by the monopolist can persist. In pure monopoly there are no new entrants to increase supply, drive down price, and eliminate economic profit.

But pure monopoly does not guarantee profit. The monopolist is not immune from changes in tastes that reduce the demand for its product. Nor is it immune from upward-shifting cost curves caused by escalating resource prices. If the demand and cost situation faced by the monopolist is far less favorable than that in Figure 11.4, the monopolist will incur losses in the short run. Consider the monopoly enterprise shown in Figure 11.5. Despite its dominance in the market (as, say, a seller of home sewing machines), it suffers a loss, as shown, because of weak demand and relatively high costs. Yet it continues to operate for the time being because its total loss is less than its fixed cost. More precisely, at output Q_m the monopolist's price P_m exceeds its average variable cost V. Its loss per unit is $A - P_m$, and the total loss is shown by the red rectangle.

Like the pure competitor, the monopolist will not persist in operating at a loss. Faced with continuing losses, in the long run the firm's owners will move their resources to alternative industries that offer better profit opportunities. A

FIGURE 11.5 The loss-minimizing position of a pure monopolist. If demand D is weak and costs are high, the pure monopolist may be unable to make a profit. Because P_m exceeds V, the average variable cost at the MR = MC output Q_m, the monopolist will minimize losses in the short run by producing at that output. The loss per unit is $A - P_m$, and the total loss is indicated by the red rectangle.

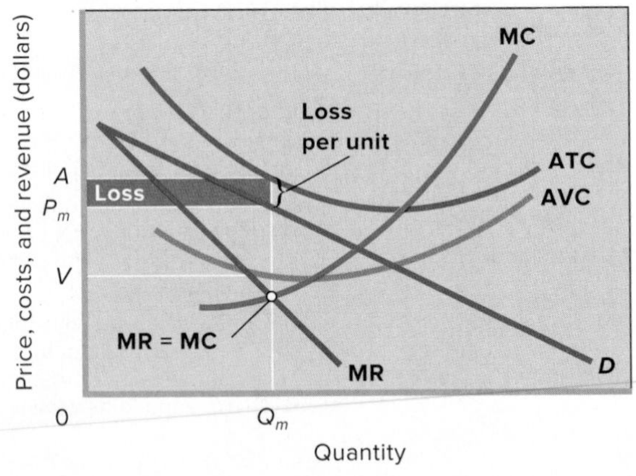

monopolist such as the one depicted in Figure 11.5 must obtain a minimum of a normal profit in the long run or it will go out of business.

AP Economic Effects of Monopoly

LO11.5 Discuss the economic effects of monopoly.

Let's now evaluate pure monopoly from the standpoint of society as a whole. Our reference for this evaluation will be the outcome of long-run efficiency in a purely competitive market, identified by the triple equality P = MC = minimum ATC.

Price, Output, and Efficiency

Figure 11.6 graphically contrasts the price, output, and efficiency outcomes of pure monopoly and a purely competitive *industry.* The S = MC curve in Figure 11.6a reminds us that the market supply curve S for a purely competitive industry is the horizontal sum of the marginal-cost curves of all the firms in the industry. Suppose there are 1,000 such firms. Comparing their combined supply curves S with market demand D, we see that the purely competitive price and output are P_c and Q_c.

Recall that this price-output combination results in both productive efficiency and allocative efficiency. *Productive efficiency* is achieved because free entry and exit force firms to operate where average total cost is at a minimum. The sum of the minimum-ATC outputs of the 1,000 pure competitors is the industry output, here, Q_c. Product price is at the lowest level consistent with minimum average total cost. The *allocative efficiency* of pure competition results because production occurs up to that output at which price (the measure of a product's value or marginal benefit to society) equals marginal cost (the worth of the alternative products forgone by society in producing any given commodity). In short: P = MC = minimum ATC.

Now let's suppose that this industry becomes a pure monopoly (Figure 11.6b) as a result of one firm acquiring all its competitors. We also assume that no changes in costs or market demand result from this dramatic change in the industry structure. What formerly were 1,000 competing firms is now a single pure monopolist consisting of 1,000 noncompeting branches.

The competitive market supply curve S has become the marginal-cost curve (MC) of the monopolist, the summation of the individual marginal-cost curves of its many branch plants. (Since the monopolist does not have a supply curve, as such, we have removed the S label.) The important change, however, is on the demand side. From the viewpoint of each of the 1,000 individual competitive firms, demand was perfectly elastic, and marginal revenue was therefore equal to the market equilibrium price P_c. So each firm equated its marginal revenue of P_c dollars per unit with its individual marginal cost curve to maximize profits. But market demand and individual demand are the same to the pure monopolist. The firm *is* the industry, and thus the monopolist sees the downsloping demand curve D shown in Figure 11.6b.

AP FIGURE 11.6 Inefficiency of pure monopoly relative to a purely competitive industry. (a) In a purely competitive industry, entry and exit of firms ensure that price (P_c) equals marginal cost (MC) and that the minimum average-total-cost output (Q_c) is produced. Both productive efficiency (P = minimum ATC) and allocative efficiency (P = MC) are obtained. (b) In pure monopoly, the MR curve lies below the demand curve. The monopolist maximizes profit at output Q_m, where MR = MC, and charges price P_m. Thus, output is lower (Q_m rather than Q_c) and price is higher (P_m rather than P_c) than they would be in a purely competitive industry. Monopoly is inefficient, since output is less than that required for achieving minimum ATC (here, at Q_c) and because the monopolist's price exceeds MC. Monopoly creates an efficiency loss (here, of triangle *abc*). There is also a transfer of income from consumers to the monopoly (here, of rectangle P_cP_mbd).

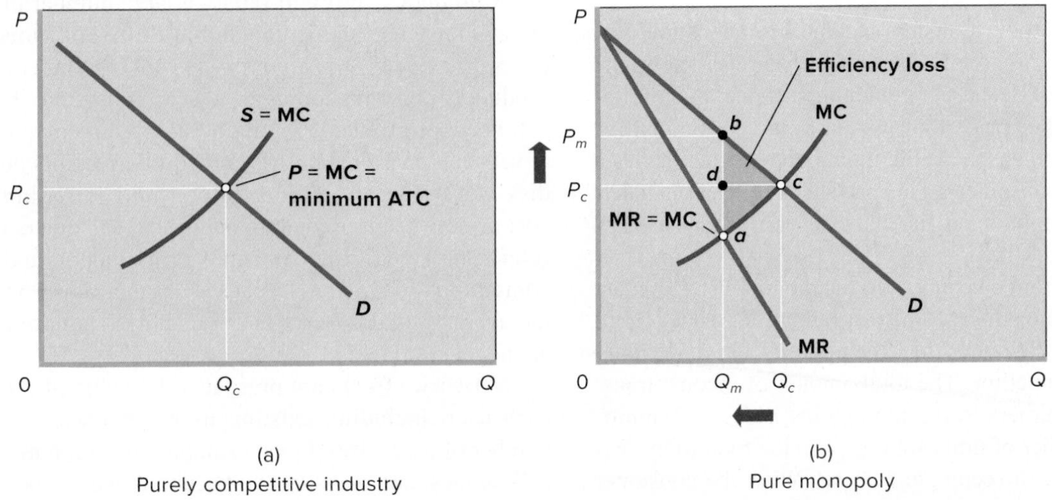

This means that marginal revenue is less than price, that graphically the MR curve lies below demand curve *D*. In using the MR = MC rule, the monopolist selects output Q_m and price P_m. A comparison of both graphs in Figure 11.6 reveals that the monopolist finds it profitable to sell a smaller output at a higher price than do the competitive producers.

Monopoly yields neither productive nor allocative efficiency. The lack of productive efficiency can be understood most directly by noting that the monopolist's output Q_m is less than Q_c, the output at which average total cost is lowest. In addition, the monopoly price P_m is higher than the competitive price P_c that we know in long-run equilibrium in pure competition equals minimum average total cost. Thus, the monopoly price exceeds minimum average total cost, thereby demonstrating in another way that the monopoly will not be productively efficient.

The monopolist's underproduction also implies allocative inefficiency. One way to see this is to note that at the monopoly output level Q_m, the monopoly price P_m that consumers are willing to pay exceeds the marginal cost of production. This means that consumers value additional units of this product more highly than they do the alternative products that could be produced from the resources that would be necessary to make more units of the monopolist's product.

The monopolist's allocative inefficiency can also be understood by noting that for every unit between Q_m and Q_c, marginal benefit exceeds marginal cost because the demand curve lies above the supply curve. By choosing not to produce these units, the monopolist reduces allocative efficiency because the resources that should have been used to make these units will be redirected instead toward producing items that bring lower net benefits to society. The total dollar value of this efficiency loss (or *deadweight loss*) is equal to the area of the gray triangle labeled *abc* in Figure 11.6b.

Income Transfer

In general, a monopoly transfers income from consumers to the owners of the monopoly. The income is received by the owners as revenue. Because a monopoly has market power, it can charge a higher price than would a purely competitive firm with the same costs. So the monopoly in effect levies a "private tax" on consumers. This private tax can often generate substantial economic profits that can persist because entry to the industry is blocked.

The transfer from consumers to the monopolist is evident in Figure 11.6b. For the Q_m units of output demanded, consumers pay price P_m rather than the price P_c that they would pay to a pure competitor. The total amount of income transferred from consumers to the monopolist is $P_m - P_c$ multiplied by the number of units sold, Q_m. So the total transfer is the dollar amount of rectangle P_cP_mbd. What the consumer loses, the monopolist gains. In contrast, the efficiency loss *abc* is a *deadweight* loss—society totally loses the net benefits of the Q_c minus Q_m units that are not produced.

Cost Complications

Our evaluation of pure monopoly has led us to conclude that, given identical costs, a purely monopolistic industry will charge a higher price, produce a smaller output, and allocate economic resources less efficiently than a purely competitive industry. These inferior results are rooted in the entry barriers characterizing monopoly.

Now we must recognize that costs may not be the same for purely competitive and monopolistic producers. The unit cost incurred by a monopolist may be either larger or smaller than that incurred by a purely competitive firm. There are four reasons costs may differ: (1) economies of scale, (2) a factor called "X-inefficiency," (3) the need for monopoly-preserving expenditures, and (4) the "very long run" perspective, which allows for technological advance.

Economies of Scale Once Again Where economies of scale are extensive, market demand may not be sufficient to support a large number of competing firms, each producing at minimum efficient scale. In such cases, an industry of one or two firms would have a lower average total cost than would the same industry made up of numerous competitive firms. At the extreme, only a single firm—a natural monopoly—might be able to achieve the lowest long-run average total cost.

Some firms relating to new information technologies—for example, computer software, Internet service, and wireless communications—have displayed extensive economies of scale. As these firms have grown, their long-run average total costs have declined because of greater use of specialized inputs, the spreading of product development costs, and learning by doing. Also, *simultaneous consumption* and *network effects* have reduced costs.

A product's ability to satisfy a large number of consumers at the same time is called **simultaneous consumption** (or *nonrivalrous consumption*). Dell Computers needs to produce a personal computer for each customer, but Microsoft needs to produce its Windows program only once. Then, at very low marginal cost, Microsoft delivers its program by disk or Internet to millions of consumers. A similarly low cost of delivering product to additional customers is true for Internet service providers, music producers, and wireless communication firms. Because marginal costs are so low, the average total cost of output declines as more customers are added.

Network effects are present if the value of a product to each user, including existing users, increases as the total number of users rises. Good examples are computer software, cell phones, and website like Facebook where the content is provided by users. When other people have Internet service and devices to access it, a person can conveniently send e-mail messages to them. And when they have similar software, various documents, spreadsheets, and photos can be attached to the e-mail messages. The greater the number of persons connected to the system, the more the benefits of the product to each person are magnified.

Such network effects may drive a market toward monopoly because consumers tend to choose standard products that everyone else is using. The focused demand for these products permits their producers to grow rapidly and thus achieve economies of scale. Smaller firms, which either have higher-cost "right" products or "wrong" products, get acquired or go out of business.

Economists generally agree that some new information firms have not yet exhausted their economies of scale. But most economists question whether such firms are truly natural monopolies. Most firms eventually achieve their minimum efficient scale at less than the full size of the market. That means competition among firms is possible.

But even if natural monopoly develops, the monopolist is unlikely to pass cost reductions along to consumers as price reductions. So, with perhaps a handful of exceptions, economies of scale do not change the general conclusion that monopoly industries are inefficient relative to competitive industries.

X-Inefficiency In constructing all the average-total-cost curves used in this book, we have assumed that the firm uses the most efficient existing technology. This assumption is only natural because firms cannot maximize profits unless they are minimizing costs. **X-inefficiency** occurs when a firm produces output at a higher cost than is necessary to produce it. In Figure 11.7 X-inefficiency is represented by operation at points X and X' above the lowest-cost ATC curve. At these points, per-unit costs are ATC_X (as opposed to ATC_1) for output Q_1 and $ATC_{X'}$ (as opposed to ATC_2) for output Q_2. Producing at any point above the average-total-cost curve in Figure 11.7 reflects inefficiency or "bad management" by the firm.

Why is X-inefficiency allowed to occur if it reduces profits? The answer is that managers may have goals, such as expanding power, an easier work life, avoiding business risk, or giving jobs to incompetent relatives, that conflict with cost minimization. Or X-inefficiency may arise because a firm's workers are poorly motivated or ineffectively supervised. Or a firm may simply become lethargic and inert, relying on rules of thumb in decision making as opposed to careful calculations of costs and revenues.

For our purposes the relevant question is whether monopolistic firms tend more toward X-inefficiency than competitive producers do. Presumably they do. Firms in competitive industries are continually under pressure from rivals, forcing them to be internally efficient to survive. But monopolists are sheltered from such competitive forces by entry barriers. That lack of pressure may lead to X-inefficiency.

Rent-Seeking Expenditures **Rent-seeking behavior** is any activity designed to transfer income or wealth to a particular firm or resource supplier at someone else's, or even society's, expense. We have seen that a monopolist can obtain an economic profit even in the long run. Therefore, it is no surprise that a firm may go to great expense to acquire or maintain a monopoly granted by government through legislation or an exclusive license. Such rent-seeking expenditures add nothing to the firm's output, but they clearly increase its costs. Taken alone, rent seeking implies that monopoly involves even higher costs and even less efficiency than suggested in Figure 11.6b.

Technological Advance In the very long run, firms can reduce their costs through the discovery and implementation of new technology. If monopolists are more likely than

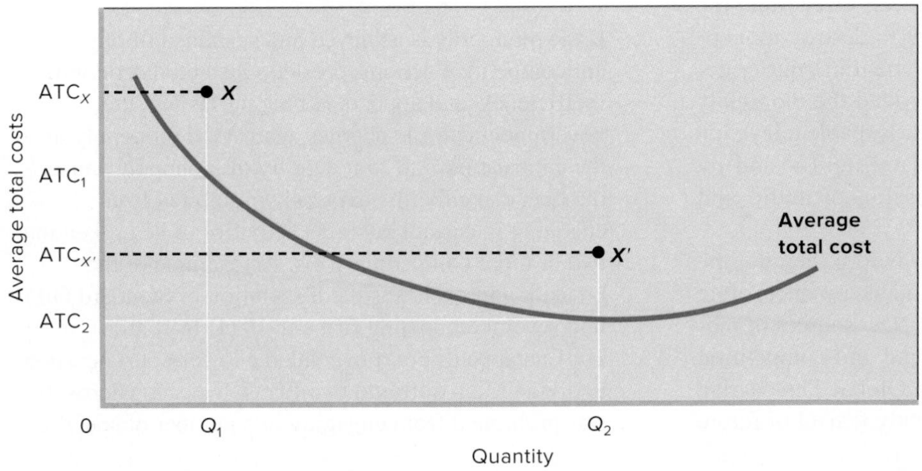

FIGURE 11.7 X-inefficiency. The average-total-cost curve (ATC) is assumed to reflect the minimum cost of producing each particular level of output. Any point above this "lowest-cost" ATC curve, such as X or X', implies X-inefficiency: operation at greater than lowest cost for a particular level of output.

competitive producers to develop more efficient production techniques over time, then the inefficiency of monopoly might be overstated. We provide a brief assessment here about research and development (R&D).

The general view of economists is that a pure monopolist will not be technologically progressive. Although its economic profit provides ample means to finance research and development, it has little incentive to implement new techniques (or products). The absence of competitors means that there is no external pressure for technological advance in a monopolized market. Because of its sheltered market position, the pure monopolist can afford to be complacent and lethargic. There simply is no major penalty for not being innovative.

One caveat: Research and technological advance may be one of the monopolist's barriers to entry. Thus, the monopolist may continue to seek technological advance to avoid falling prey to new rivals. In this case technological advance is essential to the maintenance of monopoly. But then it is *potential* competition, not the monopoly market structure, that is driving the technological advance. By assumption, no such competition exists in the pure monopoly model; entry is completely blocked.

GLOBAL PERSPECTIVE 11.1

Competition from Foreign Multinational Corporations

Competition from foreign multinational corporations diminishes the market power of firms in the United States. Here are just a few of the hundreds of foreign multinational corporations that compete strongly with U.S. firms in certain American markets.

Company (Country)	Main Products
Bayer (Germany)	chemicals
Daimler (Germany)	automobiles
Michelin (France)	tires
Lenovo (China)	electronics
Nestlé (Switzerland)	food products
Nokia (Finland)	wireless phones
Panasonic (Japan)	electronics
Petrobras (Brazil)	gasoline
Royal Dutch Shell (Netherlands)	gasoline
Samsung (South Korea)	electronics
Toyota (Japan)	automobiles

Source: Compiled from the Fortune 500 listing of the world's largest firms, "FORTUNE Global 500," 2016, **www.fortune.com.**

Assessment and Policy Options

Monopoly is a legitimate concern. Monopolists can charge higher-than-competitive prices that result in an underallocation of resources to the monopolized product. They can stifle innovation, engage in rent-seeking behavior, and foster X-inefficiency. Even when their costs are low because of economies of scale, there is no guarantee that the price they charge will reflect those low costs. The cost savings may simply accrue to the monopoly as greater economic profit.

Fortunately, however, monopoly is not widespread in the United States. Barriers to entry are seldom completely successful. Although research and technological advance may strengthen the market position of a monopoly, technology may also undermine monopoly power. Over time, the creation of new technologies may work to destroy monopoly positions. For example, the development of courier delivery, fax machines, and e-mail has eroded the monopoly power of the U.S. Postal Service. Similarly, cable television monopolies are now challenged by satellite TV and by technologies that permit the transmission of audio and video over the Internet.

Patents eventually expire; and even before they do, the development of new and distinct substitutable products often circumvents existing patent advantages. New sources of monopolized resources sometimes are found and competition from foreign firms may emerge. (See Global Perspective 11.1.) Finally, if a monopoly is sufficiently fearful of future competition from new products, it may keep its prices relatively low so as to discourage rivals from developing such products. If so, consumers may pay nearly competitive prices even though competition is currently lacking.

So what should government do about monopoly when it arises in the real world? Economists agree that government needs to look carefully at monopoly on a case-by-case basis. Three general policy options are available:

- If the monopoly is achieved and sustained through anticompetitive actions, creates substantial economic inefficiency, and appears to be long-lasting, the government can file charges against the monopoly under the antitrust laws. If found guilty of monopoly abuse, the firm can either be expressly prohibited from engaging in certain business activities or be broken into two or more competing firms. An example of the breakup approach was the dissolution of Standard Oil into several competing firms in 1911. In contrast, in 2001 an appeals court overruled a lower-court decision to divide Microsoft into two firms. Instead, Microsoft was prohibited from engaging in a number of specific anticompetitive business activities. (We discuss the antitrust laws and the Microsoft case in Chapter 18.)

- If the monopoly is a natural monopoly, society can allow it to continue to expand. If no competition emerges from new products, government may then decide to regulate its prices and operations. (We discuss this option later in this chapter and also in Chapter 18.)
- If the monopoly appears to be unsustainable because of emerging new technology, society can simply choose to ignore it. In such cases, society simply lets the process of creative destruction (discussed in Chapter 10) do its work.

AP QUICK REVIEW 11.2

✓ The monopolist maximizes profit (or minimizes loss) at the output where MR = MC and charges the price that corresponds to that output on its demand curve.

✓ The monopolist has no supply curve. As a price setter, the monopolist has a single price that maximizes economic profits for a given demand curve.

✓ A monopolist does not achieve allocative or productive efficiency, since P is greater than MC and not at the minimum average cost. Production is less than would occur in a perfectly competitive industry. There is a loss of economic surplus and an area of dead weight loss that can be identified under monopoly.

Price Discrimination

LO11.6 Describe why a monopolist might prefer to charge different prices in different markets.

We have assumed in this chapter that the monopolist charges a single price to all buyers. But under certain conditions the monopolist can increase its profit by charging different prices to different buyers. In so doing, the monopolist is engaging in **price discrimination,** the practice of selling a specific product at more than one price when the price differences are not justified by cost differences. Price discrimination can take three forms:

- Charging each customer in a single market the maximum price she or he is willing to pay.
- Charging each customer one price for the first set of units purchased and a lower price for subsequent units purchased.
- Charging some customers one price and other customers another price.

Conditions

The opportunity to engage in price discrimination is not readily available to all sellers. Price discrimination is possible when the following conditions are met:

- ***Monopoly power*** The seller must be a monopolist or, at least, must possess some degree of monopoly power, that is, some ability to control output and price.
- ***Market segregation*** At relatively low cost to itself, the seller must be able to segregate buyers into distinct classes, each of which has a different willingness or ability to pay for the product. This separation of buyers is usually based on different price elasticities of demand, as the examples below will make clear.
- ***No resale*** The original purchaser cannot resell the product or service. If buyers in the low-price segment of the market could easily resell in the high-price segment, the monopolist's price-discrimination strategy would create competition in the high-price segment. This competition would reduce the price in the high-price segment and undermine the monopolist's price-discrimination policy. This condition suggests that service industries such as the transportation industry or legal and medical services, where resale is impossible, are good candidates for price discrimination.

Examples of Price Discrimination

Price discrimination is widely practiced in the U.S. economy. For example, we noted in Chapter 6's Last Word that airlines charge high fares to business travelers, whose demand for travel is inelastic, and offer lower, highly restricted, nonrefundable fares to attract vacationers and others whose demands are more elastic.

Electric utilities frequently segment their markets by end uses, such as lighting and heating. The absence of reasonable lighting substitutes means that the demand for electricity for illumination is inelastic and that the price per kilowatt-hour for such use is high. But the availability of natural gas and petroleum for heating makes the demand for electricity for this purpose less inelastic and the price lower.

Movie theaters and golf courses vary their charges on the basis of time (for example, higher evening and weekend rates) and age (for example, lower rates for children, senior discounts). Railroads vary the rate charged per ton-mile of freight according to the market value of the product being shipped. The shipper of 10 tons of television sets or refrigerators is charged more than the shipper of 10 tons of gravel or coal.

The issuance of discount coupons, redeemable at purchase, is a form of price discrimination. It enables firms to

CONSIDER THIS . . .

Source: © Stephen Dunn/Getty Images

Some Price Differences at the Ballpark

Take me out to the ball game...

Buy me some peanuts and Cracker Jack...

Professional baseball teams earn substantial revenues through ticket sales. To maximize profit, they offer significantly lower ticket prices for children (whose demand is elastic) than for adults (whose demand is inelastic). This discount may be as much as 50 percent.

If this type of price discrimination increases revenue and profit, why don't teams also price discriminate at the concession stands? Why don't they offer half-price hot dogs, soft drinks, peanuts, and Cracker Jack to children?

The answer involves the three requirements for successful price discrimination. All three requirements are met for game tickets: (1) The team has monopoly power; (2) it can segregate ticket buyers by age group, each group having a different elasticity of demand; and (3) children cannot resell their discounted tickets to adults.

It's a different situation at the concession stands. Specifically, the third condition is *not* met. If the team had dual prices, it could not prevent the exchange or "resale" of the concession goods from children to adults. Many adults would send children to buy food and soft drinks for them: "Here's some money, Billy. Go buy *six* hot dogs." In this case, price discrimination would reduce, not increase, team profit. Thus, children and adults are charged the same high prices at the concession stands. (These prices are high relative to those for the same goods at the local convenience store because the stadium sellers have a captive audience and thus considerable monopoly power.)

give price discounts to their most price-sensitive customers who have elastic demand. Less price-sensitive consumers who have less elastic demand are not as likely to take the time to clip and redeem coupons. The firm thus makes a larger profit than if it had used a single-price, no-coupon strategy.

Finally, price discrimination often occurs in international trade. A Russian aluminum producer, for example, might sell aluminum for less in the United States than in Russia. In the United States, this seller faces an elastic demand because several substitute suppliers are available. But in Russia, where the manufacturer dominates the market and trade barriers impede imports, consumers have fewer choices and thus demand is less elastic.

Graphical Analysis

Figure 11.8 demonstrates graphically the most frequently seen form of price discrimination—charging different prices to different classes of buyers. The two side-to-side graphs are for a single pure monopolist selling its product, say, software, in two segregated parts of the market. Figure 11.8a illustrates demand for software by small-business customers; Figure 11.8b, the demand for software by students. Student versions of the software are identical to the versions sold to businesses but are available (1 per person) only to customers with a student ID. Presumably, students have lower ability to pay for the software and are charged a discounted price.

The demand curve D_b in the graph to the left indicates a relatively inelastic demand for the product on the part of business customers. The demand curve D_s in the right-hand graph reflects the more elastic demand of students. The marginal revenue curves (MR_b and MR_s) lie below their respective demand curves, reflecting the demand–marginal revenue relationship previously described.

For visual clarity we have assumed that average total cost (ATC) is constant. Therefore marginal cost (MC) equals average total cost (ATC) at all quantities of output. These costs are the same for both versions of the software and therefore appear as the identical straight lines labeled "MC = ATC."

What price will the pure monopolist charge to each set of customers? Using the MR = MC rule for profit maximization, the firm will offer Q_b units of the software for sale to small businesses. It can sell that profit-maximizing output by charging price P_b. Again using the MR = MC rule, the monopolist will offer Q_s units of software to students. To sell those Q_s units, the firm will charge students the lower price P_s.

Firms engage in price discrimination because it enhances their profit. The numbers (not shown) behind the curves in Figure 11.8 would clearly reveal that the sum of the two profit rectangles shown in green exceeds the single profit rectangle the firm would obtain from a single monopoly price. How do consumers fare? In this case, students clearly benefit by paying a lower price than they would if the firm charged a single monopoly price; in contrast, the price discrimination results in a higher price for business customers. Therefore, compared to the single-price situation, students buy more of the software and small businesses buy less.

Such price discrimination is widespread in the economy and is illegal only when it is part of a firm's strategy to lessen or eliminate competition. We will discuss illegal price discrimination in Chapter 18, which covers antitrust policy.

AP **FIGURE 11.8 Price discrimination to different groups of buyers.** The price-discriminating monopolist represented here maximizes its total profit by dividing the market into two segments based on differences in elasticity of demand. It then produces and sells the MR = MC output in each market segment. (For visual clarity, average total cost, ATC, is assumed to be constant. Therefore, MC equals ATC at all output levels.) (a) The price-discriminating monopolist charges a high price (here P_b) to small-business customers because they have a relatively inelastic demand curve for the product. (b) The firm charges a low price (here P_s) to students because their demand curve is relatively elastic. The firm's total profit from using price discrimination (here, the sum of the two green rectangles) exceeds the profit (not shown) that would have occurred if the monopolist had charged the same price to all customers.

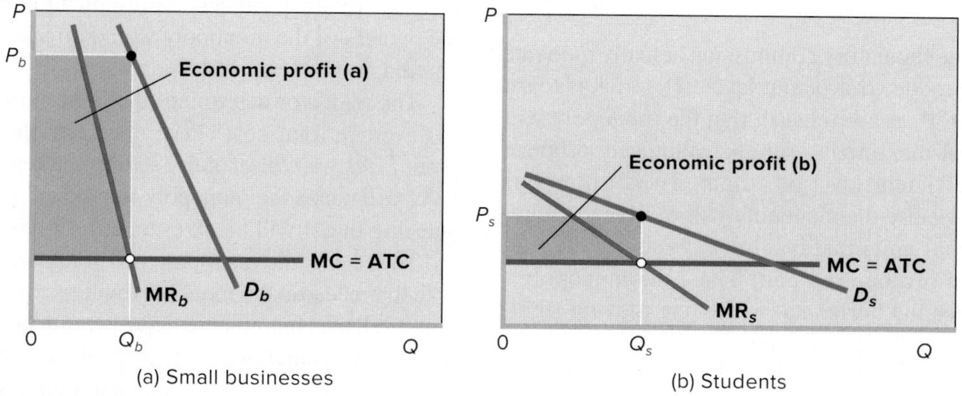

AP Regulated Monopoly

LO11.7 Distinguish among the monopoly price, the socially optimal price, and the fair-return price of a government-regulated monopoly.

Natural monopolies traditionally have been subject to *rate regulation* (price regulation), although the recent trend has been to deregulate wherever competition seems possible. For example, long-distance telephone calls, natural gas distribution, wireless communications, cable television, and long-distance electricity transmission have been, to one degree or another, deregulated over the past several decades. And regulators in some states are beginning to allow new entrants to compete with existing local telephone and electricity providers. Nevertheless, state and local regulatory commissions still regulate the prices that most local natural gas distributors, regional telephone companies, and local electricity suppliers can charge. These locally regulated monopolies are commonly called "public utilities."

Let's consider the regulation of a local natural monopoly. Our example will be a single firm that is the only seller of natural gas in the town of Springfield. Figure 11.9 shows the demand and the long-run cost curves facing our firm. Because of extensive economies of scale, the demand curve cuts the natural monopolist's long-run average-total-cost curve at a point where that curve is still falling. It would be inefficient to have several firms in this industry because each would produce a much smaller output, operating well to the left on the long-run average-total-cost curve. In short, each firm's lowest average total cost would be substantially higher than that of a single firm. So efficient, lowest-cost production requires a single seller.

We know by application of the MR = MC rule that Q_m and P_m are the profit-maximizing output and price that an unregulated monopolist would choose. Because price exceeds average total cost at output Q_m, the monopolist enjoys a substantial economic profit. Furthermore, price exceeds marginal cost, indicating an underallocation of resources to this product or service. Can government regulation bring about better results from society's point of view?

AP **FIGURE 11.9 Regulated monopoly.** The socially optimal price P_r, found where D and MC intersect, will result in an efficient allocation of resources but may entail losses to the monopoly. The fair-return price P_f will allow the monopolist to break even but will not fully correct the underallocation of resources.

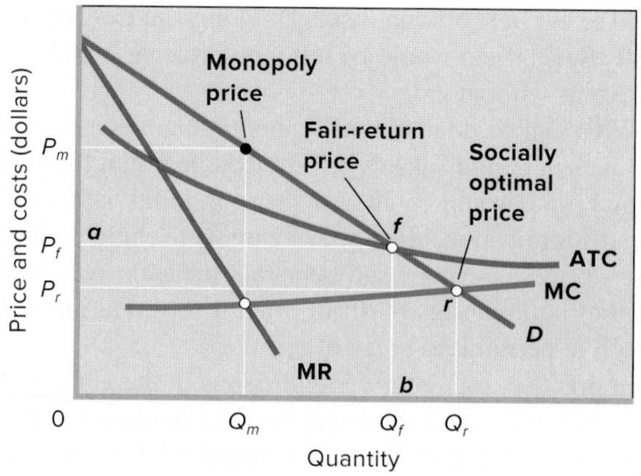

Socially Optimal Price: $P = \text{MC}$

One sensible goal for regulators would be to get the monopoly to produce the allocatively efficient output level. For our monopolist in Figure 11.9, this is output level Q_r, determined by where the demand curve D intersects the MC curve. Q_r is the allocatively efficient output level because for each unit of output up to Q_r, the demand curve lies above the MC curve, indicating that for all of these units marginal benefits exceed marginal costs.

But how can the regulatory commission actually motivate the monopoly to produce this output level? The trick is to set the regulated price P_r at a level such that the monopoly will be led by its profit-maximizing rule to voluntarily produce the allocatively efficient level of output. To see how this works, note that because the monopoly will receive the regulated price P_r for all units that it sells, P_r becomes the monopoly's marginal revenue per unit. Thus, the monopoly's MR curve becomes the horizontal white line moving rightward from price P_r on the vertical axis.

The monopoly will at this point follow its usual rule for maximizing profits or minimizing losses: It will produce where marginal revenue equals marginal cost. As a result, the monopoly will produce where the horizontal white MR ($= P_r$) line intersects the MC curve at point r. That is, the monopoly will end up producing the socially optimal output Q_r not because it is socially minded but because Q_r happens to be the output that either maximizes profits or minimizes losses when the firm is forced by the regulators to sell all units at the regulated price P_r.

The regulated price P_r that achieves allocative efficiency is called the **socially optimal price.** Because it is determined by where the MC curve intersects the demand curve, this type of regulation is often summarized by the equation $P = \text{MC}$.

Fair-Return Price: $P = \text{ATC}$

The socially optimal price suffers from a potentially fatal problem. P_r may be so low that average total costs are not covered, as is the case in Figure 11.9. In such situations, forcing the socially optimal price on the regulated monopoly would result in short-run losses and long-run exit. In our example, Springfield would be left without a gas company and its citizens without gas.

What can be done to rectify this problem? One option is to provide a public subsidy to cover the loss that the socially optimal price would entail. Another possibility is to condone price discrimination, allow the monopoly to charge some customers prices above P_r, and hope that the additional revenue that the monopoly gains from price discrimination will be enough to permit it to break even.

In practice, regulatory commissions in the United States have often pursued a third option that abandons the goal of producing every unit for which marginal benefits exceed marginal costs but that guarantees that regulated monopolies will be able to break even and continue in operation. Under this third option, regulators set a regulated price that is high enough for monopolists to break even and continue in operation. This price has come to be referred to as a **fair-return price** because of a ruling in which the Supreme Court held that regulatory agencies must permit regulated utility owners to enjoy a "fair return" on their investments.

In practice, a fair return is equal to a normal profit. That is, a fair return is an accounting profit equal in size to what the owners of the monopoly would on average receive if they entered another type of business.

The regulator determines the fair-return price P_f by where the average total cost curve intersects the demand curve at point f. As we will explain, setting the regulated price at this level will cause the monopoly to produce Q_f units while guaranteeing that it will break even and not wish to exit the industry. To see why the monopoly will voluntarily produce Q_f units, note that because the monopoly will receive P_f dollars for each unit it sells, its marginal revenue per unit becomes P_f dollars so that the horizontal line moving rightward from P_f on the vertical axis becomes the regulated monopoly's MR curve. Because this horizontal MR curve is always higher than the monopoly's MC curve, it is obvious that marginal revenues will exceed marginal costs for every possible level of output shown in Figure 11.9. Thus, the monopoly should be willing to supply whatever quantity of output is demanded by consumers at the regulated price P_f. That quantity is, of course, given by the demand curve. At price P_f consumers will demand exactly Q_f units. Thus, by setting the regulated price at P_f, the regulator gets the monopoly to voluntarily supply exactly Q_f units.

Even better, the regulator also guarantees that the monopoly firm will earn exactly a normal profit. This can be seen in Figure 11.9 by noting that the rectangle $0afb$ is equal to both the monopoly's total cost and its total revenue. Its economic profit is therefore equal to zero, implying that it must be earning a normal accounting profit for its owners.

One final point about allocative efficiency: By choosing the fair-return price P_f, the regulator leads the monopoly to produce Q_f units. This is less than the socially optimal quantity Q_r, but still more than the Q_m units that the monopolist would produce if left unregulated. So while fair-return pricing does not lead to full allocative efficiency, it is still an improvement on what the monopoly would do if left to its own devices.

Dilemma of Regulation

Comparing results of the socially optimal price ($P = \text{MC}$) and the fair-return price ($P = \text{ATC}$) suggests a policy dilemma, sometimes termed the *dilemma of regulation.* When its price is set to achieve the most efficient allocation of resources ($P = \text{MC}$), the regulated monopoly is likely to suffer losses. Survival of the firm would presumably depend on permanent public

LAST WORD

Personalized Pricing

The Potential Perils of Online Price Discrimination

Internet retailers collect vast amounts of data about their customers. They know what you buy, who your friends are, what posts you like on Facebook, what websites you visit, and—by connecting that information with other data—how old you are, where you live, your credit history, and so on.

This huge collection of "Big Data" can be used by retailers with monopoly power to engage in an individually tailored form of price discrimination known as personalized pricing. As discussed in this chapter, price discrimination involves selling the same product to different buyers at different prices when the price differences are not justified by cost differences.

Traditionally, price discrimination has operated at the group level with, for example, senior citizens getting discounts at restaurants and children under 12 getting discounts on movie tickets. Groups with relatively inelastic demand get charged higher prices while groups with relatively elastic demand get charged lower prices.

The trick behind personalized pricing is that online retailers now have the ability to set individualized prices for most patrons. When that is possible, a firm with monopoly power can set the very lowest price for the person with the most elastic demand, a slightly higher price for the person with the next-most elastic demand, and so on all the way up to the highest price being presented to the person with the most *in*elastic demand.

By proceeding in this manner, the monopoly seller can attempt to set a price for each individual that is just below his or her reservation price. Doing so allows the monopoly seller to squeeze out as much revenue as possible from each customer while still leaving him or her with a bit of consumer surplus (and thus with a motive to still buy the product).

For an offline example of how personalized pricing works, think about car dealerships, where the final price paid by a buyer is usually the result of a negotiation. In particular, keep in mind that a car salesman will negotiate much more aggressively if you drive up in a fancy BMW rather than an average Hyundai. The salesman will try to tailor the final price to your perceived ability to pay. Big Data allows the same tactic to be used online. The more online retailers know about your buying habits, background, and preferences, the more they can attempt to set a price tailored to maximize how much they think they can get from you.

But personalized pricing has its limits. Most importantly, very few firms actually have any substantial monopoly power. As just one example, car dealers have to compete with each other. So a dealership

Source: © Miss Ty/Shutterstock.com

that is driving too hard a bargain will drive customers toward rival dealers. That competitive pressure is probably even stronger online, where search engines and vast digital retail sites like eBay and Amazon often list multiple competing sellers for every item.

But even if a seller were to have monopoly power online, it would still confront another problem. Even with Big Data, it is hard for sellers to figure out what each potential buyer's reservation price is. So even if a firm with monopoly power wished to attempt personalized pricing, it probably wouldn't ever be able to figure out how to set a customized price for each individual.

On the other hand, online shoppers give up all their advantages if they fail to comparison shop. If they treat the first seller that they deal with as the only seller, they are implicitly giving that seller monopoly power over them. In those situations, online merchants can run wild with personalized pricing. In 2014, for example, Allstate Insurance admitted to Wisconsin insurance regulators that its personalized pricing computer algorithms had presented essentially identical online customers with insurance prices that varied massively, in some cased by more than 800 percent. In many instances, the differences were driven by factors as trivial as one customer having a birthdate of January 12, 1968, and another having a birthdate of April 9, 1968.

Allstate customers who failed to shop around left themselves open to paying much more than they had to. Online shopping is speedy and convenient—but it still pays to shop around.

subsidies out of tax revenues. On the other hand, although a fair-return price (P = ATC) allows the monopolist to cover costs, it only partially resolves the underallocation of resources that the unregulated monopoly price would foster. Despite this dilemma, regulation can improve on the results of monopoly from the social point of view. Price regulation (even at the fair-return price) can simultaneously reduce price, increase output, and reduce the economic profit of monopolies.

That said, we need to provide an important caution: "Fair-price" regulation of monopoly looks rather simple in theory but is amazingly complex in practice. In the actual economy, rate regulation is accompanied by large, expensive rate-setting bureaucracies and maze-like sets of procedures. Also, rate decisions require extensive public input via letters and through public hearings. Rate decisions are subject to lengthy legal challenges. Further, because regulatory commissions must set prices sufficiently above costs to create fair returns, regulated monopolists have little incentive to minimize average total costs. When these costs creep up, the regulatory commissions must set higher prices.

Regulated firms therefore are noted for higher-than-competitive wages, more managers and staff than necessary, nicer-than-typical office buildings, and other forms of X-inefficiency. These inefficiencies help explain the trend of federal, state, and local governments abandoning price regulation where the possibility of competition looks promising.

AP QUICK REVIEW 11.3

- ✓ Price discrimination occurs when a product is sold at different prices, based on willingness to pay and not based on cost differences.
- ✓ The conditions necessary for price discrimination are (a) monopoly power, (b) ability to segregate buyers on the basis of demand elasticities, and (c) the ability to stop buyers from reselling the product. Consumers with less elastic demands will pay higher prices. Examples of price discrimination include differential prices for admission to a movie (senior citizens versus others) or different prices for seats on the same flight of an airline (with early bookers typically paying less).
- ✓ Compared with a single-price monopolist, a perfectly price discriminating monopolist produces more output and gains higher profits. Many consumers pay higher prices, but other buyers pay prices below that of the single-price, profit-maximizing monopolist. Output occurs where P (or in this case MR) equals MC and the allocative efficient level of output is produced. There is no dead weight loss with perfect price discrimination. However, there is no consumer surplus, as consumers pay their full willingness to pay. All economic surplus is producer surplus.
- ✓ In some cases, a natural monopoly exists. In these cases there are significant economies of scale compared to market demand. Thus, the society only wants one producer. However, the producer needs to be regulated to avoid profit-maximizing monopoly pricing. The price can be reduced, and output increased through government regulation. In a regulated market, the socially optimal price (P = MC) achieving allocative efficiency is preferred, but results in economic losses, since the optimal price is less than average total cost. The fair-return price (P = ATC) yields a normal profit, but fails to achieve allocative efficiency.

SUMMARY

LO11.1 List the characteristics of pure monopoly.

A pure monopolist is the sole producer of a commodity for which there are no close substitutes.

LO11.2 List and explain the barriers to entry that shield pure monopolies from competition.

The existence of pure monopoly and other imperfectly competitive market structures is explained by barriers to entry in the form of (*a*) economies of scale, (*b*) patent ownership and research, (*c*) ownership or control of essential resources, and (*d*) pricing and other strategic behavior.

LO11.3 Explain how demand is seen by a pure monopoly.

The pure monopolist's market situation differs from that of a competitive firm in that the monopolist's demand curve is downsloping, causing the marginal-revenue curve to lie below the demand curve. Like the competitive seller, the pure monopolist will maximize profit by equating marginal revenue and marginal cost. Barriers to entry may permit a monopolist to acquire economic profit even in the long run. However, (*a*) the monopolist does not charge "the highest price possible," (*b*) the price that yields maximum total profit to the monopolist rarely coincides with the price that yields maximum unit profit, (*c*) high costs and a weak demand may prevent the monopolist from realizing any profit at all, and (*d*) the monopolist avoids the inelastic region of its demand curve.

LO11.4 Explain how a pure monopoly sets its profit-maximizing output and price.

With the same costs, the pure monopolist will find it profitable to restrict output and charge a higher price than would sellers in a purely competitive industry. This restriction of output causes resources to be misallocated, as is evidenced by the fact that price exceeds marginal cost in monopolized markets. Monopoly creates an efficiency loss (or deadweight loss) for society.

Monopoly transfers income from consumers to monopolists because a monopolist can charge a higher price than would a purely competitive firm with the same costs. So monopolists in effect levy a "private tax" on consumers and, if demand is strong enough, obtain substantial economic profits.

LO11.5 Discuss the economic effects of monopoly.

The costs monopolists and competitive producers face may not be the same. On the one hand, economies of scale may make lower unit costs available to monopolists but not to competitors. Also, pure monopoly may be more likely than pure competition to reduce costs via technological advance because of the monopolist's ability to realize economic profit, which can be used to finance research. On the other hand, X-inefficiency—the failure to produce with the least costly combination of inputs—is more common among monopolists than among competitive firms. Also, monopolists may make costly expenditures to maintain monopoly privileges that are conferred by government. Finally, the blocked entry of rival firms weakens the monopolist's incentive to be technologically progressive.

LO11.6 Describe why a monopolist might prefer to charge different prices in different markets.

A monopolist can increase its profit by practicing price discrimination, provided (*a*) it can segregate buyers on the basis of elasticities of demand and (*b*) its product or service cannot be readily transferred between the segregated markets.

LO11.7 Distinguish among the monopoly price, the socially optimal price, and the fair-return price of a government-regulated monopoly.

Price regulation can be invoked to eliminate wholly or partially the tendency of monopolists to underallocate resources and to earn economic profits. The socially optimal price is determined where the demand and marginal-cost curves intersect; the fair-return price is determined where the demand and average-total-cost curves intersect.

TERMS AND CONCEPTS

pure monopoly
barriers to entry
simultaneous consumption
network effects
X-inefficiency
rent-seeking behavior
price discrimination
socially optimal price
fair-return price

The following and additional problems can be found in connect

DISCUSSION QUESTIONS

1. "No firm is completely sheltered from rivals; all firms compete for consumer dollars. If that is so, then pure monopoly does not exist." Do you agree? Explain. How might you use Chapter 6's concept of cross elasticity of demand to judge whether monopoly exists? LO11.1
2. Discuss the major barriers to entry into an industry. Explain how each barrier can foster either monopoly or oligopoly. Which barriers, if any, do you feel give rise to monopoly that is socially justifiable? LO11.2
3. How does the demand curve faced by a purely monopolistic seller differ from that confronting a purely competitive firm? Why does it differ? Of what significance is the difference? Why is the pure monopolist's demand curve not perfectly inelastic? LO11.3
4. Assume that a pure monopolist and a purely competitive firm have the same unit costs. Contrast the two with respect to (*a*) price, (*b*) output, (*c*) profits, (*d*) allocation of resources, and (*e*) impact on income transfers. Since both monopolists and competitive firms follow the MC = MR rule in maximizing profits, how do you account for the different results? Why might the costs of a purely competitive firm and those of a monopolist be different? What are the implications of such a cost difference? LO11.5
5. Critically evaluate and explain each statement: LO11.5
   - **a.** Because they can control product price, monopolists are always assured of profitable production by simply charging the highest price consumers will pay.
   - **b.** The pure monopolist seeks the output that will yield the greatest per-unit profit.
   - **c.** An excess of price over marginal cost is the market's way of signaling the need for more production of a good.
   - **d.** The more profitable a firm, the greater its monopoly power.
   - **e.** The monopolist has a pricing policy; the competitive producer does not.
   - **f.** With respect to resource allocation, the interests of the seller and of society coincide in a purely competitive market but conflict in a monopolized market.
6. Assume a monopolistic publisher has agreed to pay an author 10 percent of the total revenue from the sales of a text. Will the author and the publisher want to charge the same price for the text? Explain. LO11.5
7. U.S. pharmaceutical companies charge different prices for prescription drugs to buyers in different nations, depending on elasticity of demand and government-imposed price ceilings. Explain why these companies, for profit reasons, oppose laws allowing re-importation of drugs to the United States. LO11.6
8. Explain verbally and graphically how price (rate) regulation may improve the performance of monopolies. In your answer distinguish between (*a*) socially optimal (marginal-cost) pricing and (*b*) fair-return (average-total-cost) pricing. What is the "dilemma of regulation"? LO11.7

9. It has been proposed that natural monopolists should be allowed to determine their profit-maximizing outputs and prices and then government should tax their profits away and distribute them to consumers in proportion to their purchases from the monopoly. Is this proposal as socially desirable as requiring monopolists to equate price with marginal cost or average total cost? LO11.7

10. **LAST WORD** Using Big Data to set personalized prices cannot be done with 100 percent precision. What would happen if personalized prices were set higher than customers' reservation prices? Would this possibility reduce the incentive to set the highest possible personalized prices? How can consumers protect themselves from personalized prices?

AP REVIEW QUESTIONS

1. Which of the following could explain why a firm is a monopoly? Select one or more answers from the choices shown. LO11.2
   a. Patents.
   b. Economies of scale.
   c. Inelastic product.
   d. Government licenses.
   e. Ownership or control of essential resources.
2. The MR curve of a perfectly competitive firm is horizontal. The MR curve of a monopoly firm is: LO11.3
   a. Horizontal.
   b. Upward sloping.
   c. Downward sloping.
   d. Vertical.
   e. U-shaped.
3. Use the following demand schedule to calculate total revenue and marginal revenue at each quantity. Plot the demand, total-revenue, and marginal-revenue curves, and explain the relationships between them. Explain why the marginal revenue of the fourth unit of output is $3.50, even though its price is $5. Use the total-revenue test for price elasticity to designate the elastic and inelastic segments of your graphed demand curve. What generalization can you make as to the relationship between marginal revenue and elasticity of demand? Suppose the marginal cost of successive units of output is always zero. What output would the profit-seeking firm produce? Finally, use your analysis to explain why a monopolist would never produce in the inelastic region of demand. LO11.3

Price (P)	Quantity Demanded (Q)	Price (P)	Quantity Demanded (Q)
$7.00	0	$4.50	5
6.50	1	4.00	6
6.00	2	3.50	7
5.50	3	3.00	8
5.00	4	2.50	9

4. a. Draw a graph showing a competitive market. Show the equilibrium price and quantity. Identify consumer surplus and producer surplus.
   b. Now, assume the market becomes monopolized by one firm. Show the monopolist's profit maximizing price and quantity. Identify the consumer surplus, producer surplus, and any dead weight loss. LO11.4
   c. Moving from perfect competition to monopoly, state whether each of the following increases, decreases, remains the same, or has an indeterminate change: LO11.4
      1. Price
      2. Output
      3. Producer surplus
      4. Consumer surplus
      5. Dead weight loss
5. If a monopolist engages in price discrimination, it will: LO11.6
   a. Realize a smaller profit.
   b. Charge a higher price where individual demand is less elastic, and a lower price where individual demand is more elastic.
   c. Charge a higher price where individual demand is highly elastic, and a lower price where individual demand is less elastic.
   d. Produce a smaller output than when it does not discriminate.
   e. Charge a competitive price to all its customers.
6. The socially optimal price of $P = \text{MC}$ is optimal or allocatively efficient because: LO11.7
   a. It reduces the monopolist's profit.
   b. It yields a normal profit.
   c. It minimizes ATC.
   d. It maximizes total economic surplus.
   e. It achieves productive efficiency.
7. The main problem with imposing the socially optimal price ($P = \text{MC}$) on a natural monopoly is that the socially optimal price: LO11.7
   a. May be so low that the regulated monopoly has economic losses.
   b. May cause the regulated monopoly to engage in price discrimination.
   c. May be higher than the monopoly price.
   d. May be so low that only a normal profit is earned.
   e. May be so high that economic profits will attract more firms.
8. Which of the following is true if a regulatory commission forces a natural monopoly to charge a price equal to its average total cost? LO11.7
   a. Output will decrease compared to the profit-maximizing price.
   b. The monopolist will realize only a normal profit.
   c. Resource allocation will worsen compared to the profit-maximizing price.
   d. The firm will earn economic profits.
   e. Productive efficiency is achieved.

PROBLEMS

1. Suppose a pure monopolist is faced with the following demand schedule and the same cost data as the competitive producer discussed in problem 4 at the end of Chapter 9. Calculate the missing total-revenue and marginal-revenue amounts, and determine the profit-maximizing price and profit-maximizing output for this monopolist. What is the monopolist's profit? Verify your answer graphically and by comparing total revenue and total cost. LO11.4

Price	Quantity Demanded	Total Revenue	Marginal Revenue
$115	0	$______	
100	1	______	$______
83	2	______	______
71	3	______	______
63	4	______	______
55	5	______	______
48	6	______	______
42	7	______	______
37	8	______	______
33	9	______	______
29	10	______	______

2. Suppose that a price-discriminating monopolist has segregated its market into two groups of buyers. The first group is described by the demand and revenue data that you developed for problem 1. The demand and revenue data for the second group of buyers is shown in the following table. Assume that MC is $13 in both markets and MC = ATC at all output levels. What price will the firm charge in each market? Based solely on these two prices, which market has the higher price elasticity of demand? What will be this monopolist's total economic profit? **LO11.6**

Price	Quantity Demanded	Total Revenue	Marginal Revenue
$71	0	$ 0	
63	1	63	$63
55	2	110	47
48	3	144	34
42	4	168	24
37	5	185	17
33	6	198	13
29	7	203	5

3. Assume that the most efficient production technology available for making vitamin pills has the cost structure given in the following table. Note that output is measured as the number of bottles of vitamins produced per day and that costs include a normal profit. **LO11.6**

Output	TC	MC
25,000	$100,000	$0.50
50,000	150,000	1.00
75,000	187,500	2.50
100,000	275,500	3.00

a. What is ATC per unit for each level of output listed in the table?

b. Is this a decreasing-cost industry? (Answer yes or no.)

c. Suppose that the market price for a bottle of vitamins is $2.50 and that at that price the total market quantity demanded is 75,000,000 bottles. How many firms will there be in this industry?

d. Suppose that, instead, the market quantity demanded at a price of $2.50 is only 75,000. How many firms do you expect there to be in this industry?

e. Review your answers to parts *b, c,* and *d.* Does the level of demand determine this industry's market structure?

4. A new production technology for making vitamins is invented by a college professor who decides not to patent it. Thus, it is available for anybody to copy and put into use. The TC per bottle for production up to 100,000 bottles per day is given in the following table. **LO11.6**

Output	TC
25,000	$50,000
50,000	70,000
75,000	75,000
100,000	80,000

a. What is ATC for each level of output listed in the table?

b. Suppose that for each 25,000-bottle-per-day increase in production above 100,000 bottles per day, TC increases by $5,000 (so that, for instance, 125,000 bottles per day would generate total costs of $85,000 and 150,000 bottles per day would generate total costs of $90,000). Is this a decreasing-cost industry?

c. Suppose that the price of a bottle of vitamins is $1.33 and that at that price the total quantity demanded by consumers is 75,000,000 bottles. How many firms will there be in this industry?

d. Suppose that, instead, the market quantity demanded at a price of $1.33 is only 75,000. How many firms do you expect there to be in this industry?

e. Review your answers to parts *b, c,* and *d.* Does the level of demand determine this industry's market structure?

f. Compare your answer to part *d* of this problem with your answer to part d of problem 3. Do both production technologies show constant returns to scale?

5. Suppose you have been tasked with regulating a single monopoly firm that sells 50-pound bags of concrete. The firm has fixed costs of $10 million per year and a variable cost of $1 per bag no matter how many bags are produced. **LO11.7**

a. If this firm kept on increasing its output level, would ATC per bag ever increase? Is this a decreasing-cost industry?

b. If you wished to regulate this monopoly by charging the socially optimal price, what price would you charge? At that price, what would be the size of the firm's profit or loss? Would the firm want to exit the industry?

c. You find out that if you set the price at $2 per bag, consumers will demand 10 million bags. How big will the firm's profit or loss be at that price?

d. If consumers instead demanded 20 million bags at a price of $2 per bag, how big would the firm's profit or loss be?

e. Suppose that demand is perfectly inelastic at 20 million bags, so that consumers demand 20 million bags no matter what the price is. What price should you charge if you want the firm to earn only a fair rate of return? Assume as always that TC includes a normal profit.

12 Chapter

Monopolistic Competition

Learning Objectives

LO12.1 **List the characteristics of monopolistic competition.**

LO12.2 **Explain why monopolistic competitors earn only a normal profit in the long run.**

LO12.3 **Explain why monopolistic competition delivers neither productive nor allocative efficiency.**

LO12.4 **Relate how the ability of monopolistic competition to deliver product differentiation helps to compensate for its failure to deliver economic efficiency.**

AP Chapter Focus

In the United States, most industries have a market structure that falls somewhere between the two poles of pure competition and pure monopoly. To begin with, most real-world industries have fewer than the large number of producers required for pure competition but more than the single producer that defines pure monopoly. In addition, most firms in most industries have both distinguishable rather than standardized products as well as some discretion over the prices they charge. As a result, competition often occurs on the basis of price, quality, location, service, and advertising. Finally, entry to most real-world industries ranges from easy to very difficult but is rarely completely blocked.

This chapter examines the first of two models that more closely approximate these widespread industry structures. In this chapter, you will discover that *monopolistic competition* mixes a small amount of monopoly power with a large amount of competition. In the next chapter, you will see how *oligopoly* blends a large amount of monopoly power with both considerable rivalry among existing firms and the threat of increased future competition due to foreign firms and new technologies. (You should quickly review Table 9.1, at this point.)

AP Monopolistic Competition

LO12.1 List the characteristics of monopolistic competition.

Let's begin by examining **monopolistic competition,** which is characterized by (1) a relatively large number of sellers; (2) differentiated products (often promoted by heavy advertising); and (3) easy entry to, and exit from, the industry. The first and third characteristics provide the "competitive" aspect of monopolistic competition; the second characteristic provides the "monopolistic" aspect. In general, however, monopolistically competitive industries are much more competitive than they are monopolistic.

Relatively Large Number of Sellers

Monopolistic competition is characterized by a fairly large number of firms, say, 25, 35, 60, or 70, not by the hundreds or thousands of firms in pure competition. Consequently, monopolistic competition involves:

- ***Small market shares*** Each firm has a comparatively small percentage of the total market and consequently has limited control over market price.
- ***No collusion*** The presence of a relatively large number of firms ensures that collusion by a group of firms to restrict output and set prices is unlikely.
- ***Independent action*** With numerous firms in an industry, there is no feeling of interdependence among them; each firm can determine its own pricing policy without considering the possible reactions of rival firms. A single firm may realize a modest increase in sales by cutting its price, but the effect of that action on competitors' sales will be nearly imperceptible and will probably trigger no response.

Differentiated Products

In contrast to pure competition, in which there is a standardized product, monopolistic competition is distinguished by **product differentiation.** Monopolistically competitive firms turn out variations of a particular product. They produce products with slightly different physical characteristics, offer varying degrees of customer service, provide varying amounts of locational convenience, or proclaim special qualities, real or imagined, for their products.

Let's examine these aspects of product differentiation in more detail.

Product Attributes Product differentiation may entail physical or qualitative differences in the products themselves. Real differences in functional features, materials, design, and workmanship are vital aspects of product differentiation. Personal computers, for example, differ in terms of storage capacity, speed, graphic displays, and included software. There are dozens of competing principles of economics textbooks that differ in content, organization, presentation and readability, pedagogical aids, and graphics and design. Most cities have a variety of retail stores selling men's and women's clothes that differ greatly in styling, materials, and quality of work. Similarly, one pizza place may feature thin-crust Neapolitan style pizza, while another may tout its thick-crust Chicago-style pizza.

Service Service and the conditions surrounding the sale of a product are forms of product differentiation too. One shoe store may stress the fashion knowledge and helpfulness of its clerks. A competitor may leave trying on shoes and carrying them to the register to its customers but feature lower prices. Customers may prefer one-day over three-day dry cleaning of equal quality. The prestige appeal of a store, the courteousness and helpfulness of clerks, the firm's reputation for servicing or exchanging its products, and the credit it makes available are all service aspects of product differentiation.

Location Products may also be differentiated through the location and accessibility of the stores that sell them. Small convenience stores manage to compete with large supermarkets, even though these minimarts have a more limited range of products and charge higher prices. They compete mainly on the basis of location—being close to customers and situated on busy streets. A motel's proximity to an interstate highway gives it a locational advantage that may enable it to charge a higher room rate than nearby motels in less convenient locations.

Brand Names and Packaging Product differentiation may also be created through the use of brand names and trademarks, packaging, and celebrity connections. Most aspirin tablets are very much alike, but many headache sufferers believe that one brand—for example, Bayer, Anacin, or Bufferin—is superior and worth a higher price than a generic substitute. A celebrity's name associated with watches, perfume, or athletic shoes may enhance the appeal of those products for some buyers. Many customers prefer one style of ballpoint pen to another. Packaging that touts "natural spring" bottled water may attract additional customers.

Some Control over Price Despite the relatively large number of firms, monopolistic competitors do have some control over their product prices because of product differentiation. If consumers prefer the products of specific sellers, then within limits they will pay more to satisfy their preferences. Sellers and buyers are not linked randomly, as in a purely competitive market. But the monopolistic competitor's control over price is quite limited since there are numerous potential substitutes for its product.

Easy Entry and Exit

Entry into monopolistically competitive industries is relatively easy compared to oligopoly or pure monopoly. Because monopolistic competitors are typically small firms, both absolutely and relatively, economies of scale are few and capital requirements are low. On the other hand, compared with pure competition, financial barriers may result from the need to develop and advertise a product that differs from rivals' products. Some firms have trade secrets relating to their products or hold trademarks on their brand names, making it difficult and costly for other firms to imitate them.

Exit from monopolistically competitive industries is relatively easy. Nothing prevents an unprofitable monopolistic competitor from holding a going-out-of-business sale and shutting down.

Advertising

The expense and effort involved in product differentiation would be wasted if consumers were not made aware of product differences. Thus, monopolistic competitors advertise their products, often heavily. The goal of product differentiation and advertising—so-called **nonprice competition**—is to make price less of a factor in consumer purchases and make product differences a greater factor. If successful, the firm's demand curve will shift to the right and will become less elastic.

Monopolistically Competitive Industries

Table 12.1 lists several manufacturing industries that approximate monopolistic competition. Economists measure the degree of industry concentration—the extent to which the largest firms account for the bulk of the industry's output—to identify monopolistically competitive (versus oligopolistic) industries. Two such measures are the four-firm concentration ratio and the Herfindahl index. They are listed in columns 2 and 3 of the table.

A **four-firm concentration ratio,** expressed as a percentage, is the ratio of the output (sales) of the four largest firms in an industry relative to total industry sales.

$$\text{Four-firm concentration ratio} = \frac{\text{Output of four largest firms}}{\text{Total output in the industry}}$$

Four-firm concentration ratios are very low in purely competitive industries in which there are hundreds or even thousands of firms, each with a tiny market share. In contrast, four-firm ratios are high in oligopoly and pure monopoly. Industries in which the largest four firms account for 40 percent or more of the market are generally considered to be oligopolies. If the largest four firms account for less than 40 percent, they are likely to be monopolistically competitive. Observe that the four-firm concentration ratios in Table 12.1 range from 5 percent to 32 percent.

Published concentration ratios such as those in Table 12.1 are helpful in categorizing industries but must be used cautiously because the market shares (percentage of total sales) that they list are national in scope, whereas competition in many industries is often local in scope. As a result, some industries with low national concentration ratios are in fact substantially concentrated if one focuses on local markets.

As an example, the national four-firm concentration ratio for ready-mix concrete shown in Table 12.1 is only 14 percent. This suggests that ready-mix concrete is a monopolistically competitive industry. But the sheer bulk of ready-mix concrete and the fact that it "sets up" as it dries limits the relevant market to a specific town, city, or metropolitan area. In most of these local markets, only a few firms compete, not the numerous firms needed for monopolistic competition.

Column 3 of Table 12.1 lists a second measure of concentration: the **Herfindahl index.** This index is the sum of the squared percentage market shares of all firms in the industry. In equation form:

$$\text{Herfindahl index} = (\%S_1)^2 + (\%S_2)^2 + (\%S_3)^2 + \cdots + (\%S_n)^2$$

TABLE 12.1 Percentage of Output Produced by Firms in Selected Low-Concentration U.S. Manufacturing Industries

(1) Industry	(2) Percentage of Industry Output* Produced by the Four Largest Firms	(3) Herfindahl Index for the Top 50 Firms	(1) Industry	(2) Percentage of Industry Output* Produced by the Four Largest Firms	(3) Herfindahl Index for the Top 50 Firms
Jewelry	32	550	Ready-mix concrete	14	89
Plastic pipe	31	303	Sawmills	14	93
Plastic bags	28	320	Textile bags	13	93
Asphalt paving	25	230	Wood pallets	12	55
Bolts, nuts, and rivets	23	198	Stone products	12	56
Women's dresses	22	236	Textile machinery	10	58
Wood trusses	21	158	Metal stamping	10	52
Curtains and draperies	20	172	Signs	9	36
Metal windows and doors	17	143	Sheet metal work	8	29
Quick printing	17	108	Retail bakeries	5	12

*As measured by value of shipments. Data are for 2012. See **www.census.gov/econ/manufacturing.html.**

Source: Bureau of Census, *Census of Manufacturers,* 2012.

where $\%S_1$ is the percentage market share of firm 1, $\%S_2$ is the percentage market share of firm 2, and so on for each of the n total firms in the industry. By squaring the percentage market shares of all firms in the industry, the Herfindahl index purposely gives much greater weight to larger, and thus more powerful, firms than to smaller ones. For a purely competitive industry, the index would approach zero since each firm's market share—$\%S$ in the equation—is extremely small. In the case of a single-firm industry, the index would be at its maximum of 10,000 ($= 100^2$), indicating an industry with complete monopoly power.

We will discover later in this chapter that the Herfindahl index is important for assessing oligopolistic industries. But for now, the relevant generalization is that the lower the Herfindahl index, the greater is the likelihood that an industry is monopolistically competitive rather than oligopolistic. Column 3 of Table 12.1 lists the Herfindahl index (computed for the top 50 firms, not all the industry firms) for several industries. Note that the index values are decidedly closer to the bottom limit of the Herfindahl index—0—than to its top limit—10,000.

The numbers in Table 12.1 are for manufacturing industries. In addition, many retail establishments in metropolitan areas are monopolistically competitive, including grocery stores, gasoline stations, hair salons, dry cleaners, clothing stores, and restaurants. Also, many providers of professional services such as medical care, legal assistance, real estate sales, and basic bookkeeping are monopolistic competitors.

AP Price and Output in Monopolistic Competition

LO12.2 Explain why monopolistic competitors earn only a normal profit in the long run.

How does a monopolistic competitor decide on its price and output? To explain, we initially assume that each firm in the industry is producing a specific differentiated product and engaging in a particular amount of advertising. Later we will see how changes in the product and in the amount of advertising modify our conclusions.

The Firm's Demand Curve

Our explanation is based on **Figure 12.1 (Key Graph),** which shows that the demand curve faced by a monopolistically competitive seller is highly, but not perfectly, elastic. It is precisely this feature that distinguishes monopolistic competition from both pure monopoly and pure competition. The monopolistic competitor's demand is more elastic than the demand faced by a pure monopolist because the monopolistically competitive seller has many competitors producing closely substitutable goods. The pure monopolist has no rivals at all. Yet, for two reasons, the monopolistic competitor's demand is not perfectly elastic like that of the pure competitor. First, the monopolistic competitor has fewer rivals; second, its products are differentiated, so they are not perfect substitutes.

The price elasticity of demand faced by the monopolistically competitive firm depends on the number of rivals and the degree of product differentiation. The larger the number of rivals and the weaker the product differentiation, the greater the price elasticity of each seller's demand, that is, the closer monopolistic competition will be to pure competition.

The Short Run: Profit or Loss

In the short run, monopolistically competitive firms maximize profit or minimize loss using exactly the same strategy as pure competitors and monopolists: They produce the level of output at which marginal revenue equals marginal cost (MR = MC). Thus, the monopolistically competitive firm in Figure 12.1a produces output Q_1, where MR = MC. As shown by demand curve D_1, it then can charge price P_1. It realizes an economic profit, shown by the green area $[= (P_1 - A_1) \times Q_1]$.

But with less favorable demand or costs, the firm may incur a loss in the short run. We show this possibility in Figure 12.1b, where the firm's best strategy is to minimize its loss. It does so by producing output Q_2 (where MR = MC) and, as determined by demand curve D_2, by charging price P_2. Because price P_2 is less than average total cost A_2, the firm incurs a per-unit loss of $A_2 - P_2$ and a total loss represented as the red area $[= (A_2 - P_2) \times Q_2]$.

The Long Run: Only a Normal Profit

In the long run, firms will enter a profitable monopolistically competitive industry and leave an unprofitable one. So a monopolistic competitor will earn only a normal profit in the long run or, in other words, will only break even. (Remember that the cost curves include both explicit and implicit costs, including a normal profit.)

Profits: Firms Enter In the case of short-run profit (Figure 12.1a), economic profits attract new rivals because entry to the industry is relatively easy. As new firms enter, the demand curve faced by the typical firm shifts to the left (falls). Why? Because each firm has a smaller share of total demand and now faces a larger number of close-substitute products. This decline in the firm's demand reduces its economic profit. When entry of new firms has reduced demand to the extent that the demand curve is tangent to the average-total-cost curve at the profit-maximizing output, the firm is just making a normal profit. This situation is shown in Figure 12.1c, where demand is D_3 and the firm's

AP KEY GRAPH

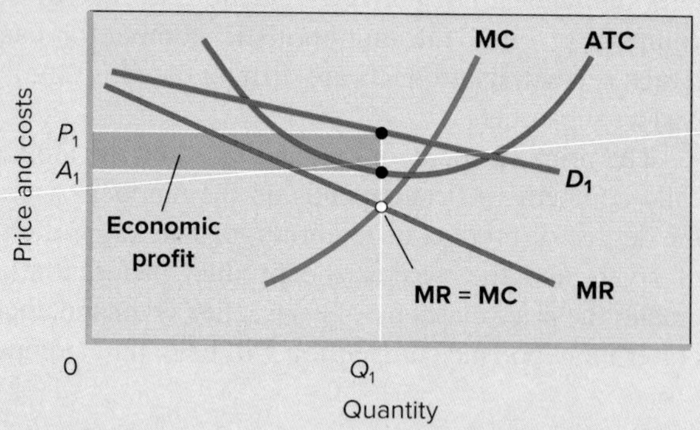

(a)
Short-run profits

FIGURE 12.1 A monopolistically competitive firm: short run and long run. The monopolistic competitor maximizes profit or minimizes loss by producing the output at which MR = MC. The economic profit shown in (a) will induce new firms to enter, eventually eliminating economic profit. The loss shown in (b) will cause an exit of firms until normal profit is restored. After such entry and exit, the price will settle in (c) to where it just equals average total cost at the MR = MC output. At this price P_3 and output Q_3, the monopolistic competitor earns only a normal profit, and the industry is in long-run equilibrium.

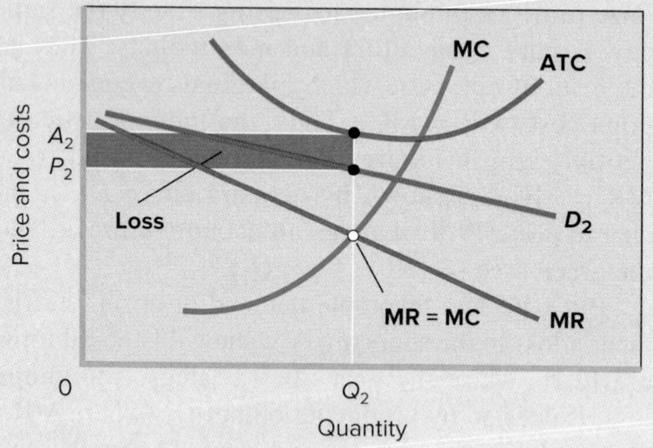

(b)
Short-run losses

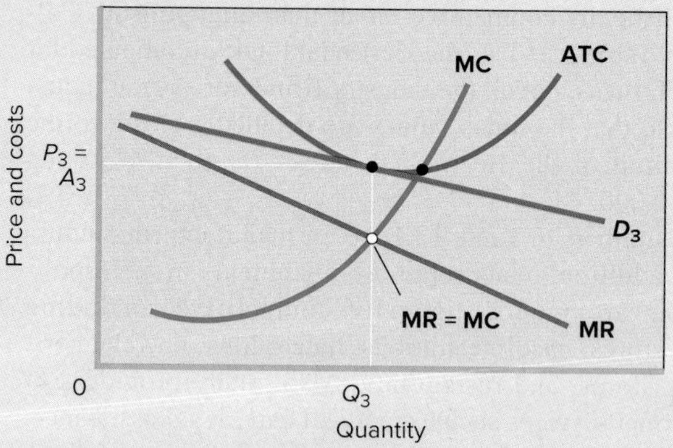

(c)
Long-run equilibrium

QUICK QUIZ FOR FIGURE 12.1

1. Price exceeds MC in:
   a. graph (a) only.
   b. graph (b) only.
   c. graphs (a) and (b) only.
   d. graphs (a), (b), and (c).
2. Price exceeds ATC in:
   a. graph (a) only.
   b. graph (b) only.
   c. graphs (a) and (b) only.
   d. graphs (a), (b), and (c).
3. The firm represented by Figure 12.1c is:
   a. making a normal profit.
   b. incurring a loss.
   c. producing at the same level of output as a purely competitive firm.
   d. producing a standardized product.
4. Which of the following pairs are both "competition-like elements" in monopolistic competition?
   a. Price exceeds MR; standardized product.
   b. Entry is relatively easy; only a normal profit in the long run.
   c. Price equals MC at the profit-maximizing output; economic profits are likely in the long run.
   d. A firm's demand curve is downsloping; differentiated products.

Answers: 1. d; 2. a; 3. a; 4. b

long-run equilibrium output is Q_3. As Figure 12.1c indicates, any greater or lesser output will entail an average total cost that exceeds product price P_3, meaning a loss for the firm. At the tangency point between the demand curve and ATC, total revenue equals total costs. With the economic profit gone, there is no further incentive for additional firms to enter.

Losses: Firms Leave When the industry suffers short-run losses, as in Figure 12.1b, some firms will exit in the long run. Faced with fewer substitute products and blessed with an expanded share of total demand, the surviving firms will see their demand curves shift to the right (rise), as to D_3. Their losses will disappear and give way to normal profits (Figure 12.1c). (For simplicity we have assumed constant costs; shifts in the cost curves as firms enter or leave would complicate our discussion slightly but would not alter our conclusions.)

Complications The representative firm in the monopolistic competition model earns only a normal profit in the long run. That outcome may not always occur, however, in the real world of small firms as opposed to the theoretical model.

- Some firms may achieve sufficient product differentiation such that other firms cannot duplicate them, even over time. One hotel in a major city may have the best location relative to business and tourist activities. Or a firm may have developed a well-known brand name that gives it a slight but very long-lasting advantage over imitators. Such firms may have sufficient monopoly power to realize modest economic profits even in the long run.
- Entry to some industries populated by small firms is not as free in reality as it is in theory. Because of product differentiation, financial barriers to entry are likely to be greater than they would be if the product were standardized. This suggests some monopoly power, with small economic profits continuing even in the long run.

With all things considered, however, the outcome that yields only a normal profit—the long-run equilibrium shown in Figure 12.1c—is a reasonable approximation of reality.

AP QUICK REVIEW 12.1

- ✓ Monopolistic competition involves a relatively large number of firms operating in a noncollusive way and producing differentiated products with easy industry entry and exit. These products are close substitutes for each other.
- ✓ In the short run, a monopolistic competitor will maximize profit or minimize loss by producing the profit maximizing level of output where MR = MC.
- ✓ In the long run, easy entry and exit of firms causes monopolistic competitors to earn only a normal profit.

AP Monopolistic Competition and Efficiency

LO12.3 Explain why monopolistic competition delivers neither productive nor allocative efficiency.

We know from Chapter 10 that economic efficiency requires each firm to produce the amount of output at which $P = \text{MC} = \text{minimum ATC}$. The equality of price and minimum average total cost yields *productive efficiency*. The good is being produced in the least costly way, and the price is just sufficient to cover average total cost, including a normal profit. The equality of price and marginal cost yields *allocative efficiency*. The right amount of output is being produced, and thus the right amount of society's scarce resources is being devoted to this specific use.

How efficient is monopolistic competition, as measured against this triple equality? In particular, do monopolistically competitive firms produce the efficient output level associated with $P = \text{MC} = \text{minimum ATC}$?

Neither Productive nor Allocative Efficiency

In monopolistic competition, neither productive nor allocative efficiency occurs in long-run equilibrium. Figure 12.2 includes an enlargement of part of Figure 12.1c and clearly shows this. First note that the profit-maximizing price P_3 slightly exceeds the lowest average total cost, A_4. In producing the profit-maximizing output Q_3, the firm's average total cost therefore is slightly higher than optimal from society's perspective—productive efficiency is not achieved. Also note that the profit-maximizing price P_3 exceeds marginal cost (here M_3), meaning that monopolistic competition causes an underallocation of resources. To measure the size of this inefficiency, note that the allocatively optimal amount of output is determined by point *c*, where demand curve *D* intersects the MC curve. So for all units between Q_3 and the level of output associated with point *c*, marginal benefits exceed marginal costs. Consequently, by producing only Q_3 units, this monopolistic competitor creates an efficiency loss (deadweight loss) equal in size to area *acd*. The total efficiency loss for the industry as a whole will be the sum of the individual efficiency losses generated by each of the firms in the industry.

Excess Capacity

In monopolistic competition, the gap between the minimum-ATC output and the profit-maximizing output identifies **excess capacity:** plant and equipment that are underused because firms are producing less than the minimum-ATC output. This gap is shown as the distance between Q_4 and Q_3 in Figure 12.2. Note in the figure that the minimum ATC is at point *b*. If each monopolistic competitor could profitably produce at this point on its ATC curve, the lower average total cost would enable a lower price than P_3. More importantly, if each firm produced at *b* rather than at *a*, fewer firms would be needed to produce the industry output. But because monopolistically competitive firms produce at *a* in long-run equilibrium, monopolistically competitive industries are overpopulated with firms, each operating below its optimal

AP **FIGURE 12.2 The inefficiency of monopolistic competition.** In long-run equilibrium a monopolistic competitor achieves neither productive nor allocative efficiency. Productive efficiency is not realized because production occurs where the average total cost A_3 exceeds the minimum average total cost A_4. Allocative efficiency is not achieved because the product price P_3 exceeds the marginal cost M_3. The results are an underallocation of resources as well as an efficiency loss and excess production capacity at every firm in the industry. This firm's efficiency loss is area *acd* and its excess production capacity is $Q_4 - Q_3$.

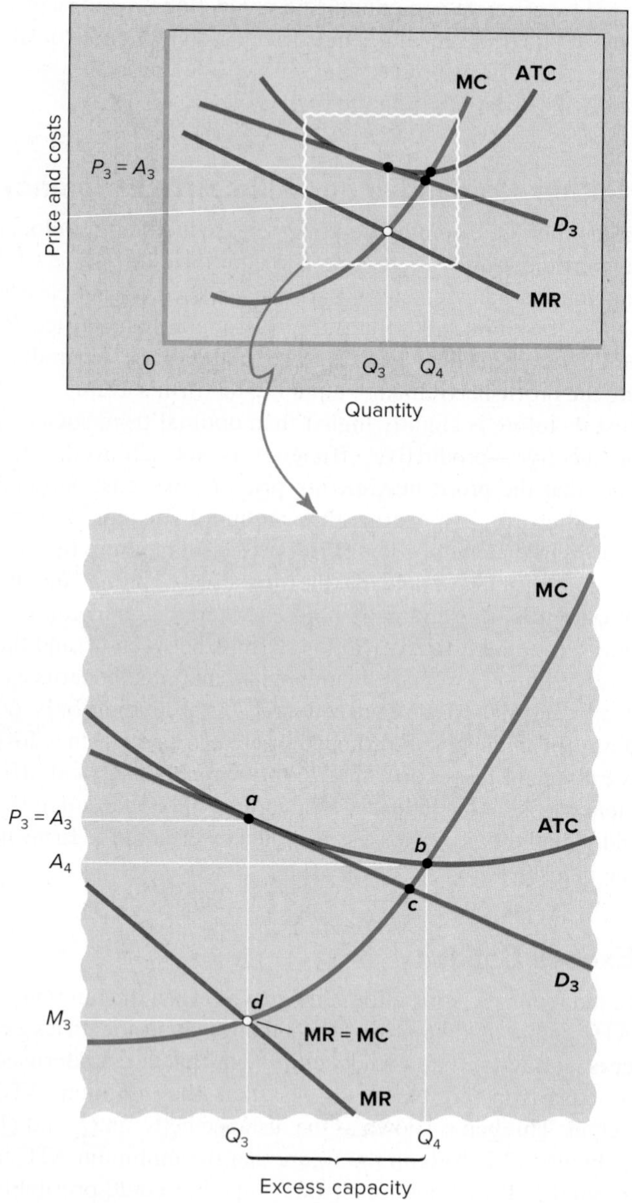

capacity. This situation is typified by many kinds of retail establishments. For example, in most cities there is an abundance of small motels and restaurants that operate well below half capacity.

Product Variety

LO12.4 Relate how the ability of monopolistic competition to deliver product differentiation helps to compensate for its failure to deliver economic efficiency.

The situation portrayed in Figures 12.1c and 12.2 is not very satisfying to monopolistic competitors, since it foretells only a normal profit. But the profit-realizing firm of Figure 12.1a need not stand by and watch new competitors eliminate its profit by imitating its product, matching its customer service, and copying its advertising. Each firm has a product that is distinguishable in some way from those of the other producers. So the firm can attempt to stay ahead of competitors and sustain its profit through further product differentiation and better advertising. By developing or improving its product, it may be able to postpone, at least for a while, the outcome of Figure 12.1c.

Although product differentiation and advertising will add to the firm's costs, they can also increase the demand for its product. If demand increases by more than enough to compensate for the added costs, the firm will have improved its profit position. As Figure 12.2 suggests, the firm has little or no prospect of increasing profit by price cutting. So why not engage in nonprice competition?

Benefits of Product Variety

The product variety and product improvement that accompany the drive to maintain economic profit in monopolistic competition are a benefit for society—one that may offset the cost of the inefficiency associated with monopolistic competition. Consumers have a wide diversity of tastes: Some like regular fries, others like curly fries; some like contemporary furniture, others like traditional furniture. If a product is differentiated, then at any time the consumer will be offered a wide range of types, styles, brands, and quality gradations of that product. Compared with pure competition, this provides an advantage to the consumer. The range of choice is widened, and producers more fully meet the wide variation in consumer tastes.

The product improvement promoted by monopolistic competition further differentiates products and expands choices. And a successful product improvement by one firm obligates rivals to imitate or improve on that firm's temporary market advantage or else lose business. So society benefits from better products.

In fact, product differentiation creates a trade-off between consumer choice and productive efficiency. The stronger the product differentiation, the greater is the excess capacity and, therefore, the greater is the productive inefficiency. But the greater the product differentiation, the more likely it is that the firms will satisfy the great diversity of consumer tastes. The greater the excess-capacity problem, the wider the range of consumer choice.

LAST WORD

Higher Wages, More McRestaurants

In the Monopolistically Competitive Restaurant Market, Higher Wages Favor Big Chain Restaurants over Small "Mom and Pop" Operations.

Source: © Sorbis/Shutterstock.com

Restaurants are monopolistic competitors. Because each one has a unique location, it has some monopoly power. Additional bits of monopoly power are generated by product differentiation. Restaurants can differ on menu items, decor, speed of service, price, drive-through convenience, and a wide variety of additional characteristics.

Restaurants also differ in their production methods. Compare a McDonald's hamburger restaurant with a small "mom and pop" hamburger stand. The McDonald's will have a huge amount of specialized equipment. There will be special machines for frying, microwaving, making milkshakes, dispensing beverages into cups automatically, and of course cooking the hamburgers.

There will also in most cases be digital touchscreen computers for taking walk-up orders; wireless headsets for taking drive-through orders, and a fully computerized register system for keeping track of cash, credit; and debit transactions. And there will be a dining area that is often tastefully decorated in modern styles at substantial expense. All these things imply that a McDonald's restaurant is capital intensive. It uses a large amount of capital equipment to produce and serve a hamburger.

By contrast, a small mom and pop hamburger stand will typically have only the bare minimum in terms of cooking equipment—a grill, a fryer, an unautomated beverage dispenser, and a refrigerator. Seating will be plain. The decor will be inexpensive and probably out of style. The mom and pop hamburger stand will use relatively little capital to produce and serve a hamburger.

In a monopolistically competitive restaurant market, equilibrium can often include both highly capitalized chain stores like McDonald's as well as lightly capitalized mom and pop operations. As long as both types of hamburger restaurant can make zero economic profits, each type will have representatives in the local restaurant market.

Economists have recently discovered, however, that wage increases can tilt the local restaurant market in favor of highly capitalized chain stores. In particular, increases in the minimum wage tend to reduce the proportion of mom and pop restaurants.

This happens because increases in the minimum wage have a relatively small impact on the cost curves of highly capitalized chain restaurants. While it is true that a highly capitalized McDonald's *does* hire minimum wage workers, the fact that it uses so much capital to produce hamburgers means that a large fraction of its costs derive from machinery and equipment. So when the minimum wage goes up, only a relatively minor part of its production costs go up.

By contrast, mom and pop restaurants use relatively little capital combined with lots of labor. After all, if you don't have much in the way of machinery and specialized equipment, you need to have lots of labor to make up for the lack of capital. So when the minimum wage is increased, the cost curves of mom and pop stores shift upward by more than the cost curves of highly capitalized chain restaurants. In both cases, economic profits will turn negative—but they will become much more negative at the mom and pop restaurants, which are heavily reliant on labor.

The result is a greater tendency on the part of mom and pop restaurants to exit the industry. Both types of restaurant will see exits. But when a new equilibrium is eventually reestablished, there will be a higher proportion of highly capitalized chain restaurants and a lower proportion of labor-intensive mom and pop restaurants.

Higher minimum wages are often promoted as a way to help low-wage workers. But they generate an unintended consequence in the restaurant market, where they favor big chain stores over small local operations. Voters and politicians need to be aware that this happens when they consider raising the minimum wage.

CONSIDER THIS . . .

Source: © Chuck Nacke/Alamy Stock Photo

The Spice of Life

The Wendy's hamburger chain debuted a hilarious TV commercial in 1987. The commercial depicts a Soviet communist fashion show. A woman walks down the runway in a drab grey factory uniform. The emcee shouts out, "Day wear!" Then she marches down the runway again in the same uniform but holding a flashlight. The emcee shouts out, "Evening wear!" She then marches out in the same uniform again but holding an inflatable beach ball. "Swimwear!"

Communist central planners didn't care about product differentiation. They typically made one design of a given product to be able to mass produce it at the lowest possible cost. The result was a society of painful sameness.

The Wendy's TV commercial hammered home a single idea—that we should embrace the fact that the food produced by Wendy's was different from that produced by its main rivals, McDonald's and Burger King. Unlike the communist central planning of the old Soviet Union, the free market system of the United States allows for huge amounts of product differentiation. If "variety is the spice of life," American capitalism is extremely well seasoned.

Source: Wendy's, "Soviet Fashion Show," 1987.

Further Complexity

Finally, the ability to engage in nonprice competition makes the market situation of a monopolistic competitor more complex than Figure 12.1 indicates. That figure assumes a given (unchanging) product and a given level of advertising expenditures. But we know that, in practice, product attributes and advertising are not fixed. The monopolistically competitive firm juggles three factors—price, product, and advertising—in seeking maximum profit. It must determine what variety of product, selling at what price, and supplemented by what level of advertising will result in the greatest profit. This complex situation is not easily expressed in a simple, meaningful economic model. At best, we can say that each possible combination of price, product, and advertising poses a different demand and cost (production cost plus advertising cost) situation for the firm and that one combination yields the maximum profit. In practice, this optimal combination cannot be readily forecast but must be found by trial and error.

AP QUICK REVIEW 12.2

- ✓ A monopolistic competitor's long-run equilibrium output is such that price exceeds the minimum average total cost (implying that consumers do not get the lowest price attainable) and price exceeds marginal cost (indicating that resources are underallocated). The productive and allocative efficiency losses are offset by the benefits to consumers from product diversity.
- ✓ The productive efficiency loss can be shown as the gap between the minimum ATC output and the profit-maximizing output that identifies excess capacity.

SUMMARY

LO12.1 List the characteristics of monopolistic competition.

The distinguishing features of monopolistic competition are (*a*) there are enough firms in the industry to ensure that each firm has only limited control over price, mutual interdependence is absent, and collusion is nearly impossible; (*b*) products are characterized by real or perceived differences so that economic rivalry entails both price and nonprice competition; and (*c*) entry to the industry is relatively easy. Many aspects of retailing, and some manufacturing industries in which economies of scale are few, approximate monopolistic competition.

The four-firm concentration ratio measures the percentage of total industry output accounted for by the largest four firms. The Herfindahl index sums the squares of the percentage market shares of all firms in the industry.

LO12.2 Explain why monopolistic competitors earn only a normal profit in the long run.

Monopolistically competitive firms may earn economic profits or incur losses in the short run. The easy entry and exit of firms results in only normal profits in the long run.

LO12.3 Explain why monopolistic competition delivers neither productive nor allocative efficiency.

The long-run equilibrium position of the monopolistically competitive producer is less efficient than that of the pure competitor. Under monopolistic competition, price exceeds marginal cost, indicating an underallocation of resources to the product, and price exceeds minimum average total cost, indicating that consumers do not get the product at the lowest price that cost conditions might allow.

LO12.4 Relate how the ability of monopolistic competition to deliver product differentiation helps to compensate for its failure to deliver economic efficiency.

Nonprice competition provides a way that monopolistically competitive firms can offset the long-run tendency for economic profit to fall to zero. Through product differentiation, product development, and advertising, a firm may strive to increase the demand for its product more than enough to cover the added cost of such nonprice competition. Consumers benefit from the wide diversity of product choice that monopolistic competition provides.

In practice, the monopolistic competitor seeks the specific combination of price, product, and advertising that will maximize profit.

TERMS AND CONCEPTS

monopolistic competition

product differentiation

nonprice competition

four-firm concentration ratio

Herfindahl index

excess capacity

The following and additional problems can be found in connect

DISCUSSION QUESTIONS

1. How does monopolistic competition differ from pure competition in its basic characteristics? From pure monopoly? Explain fully what product differentiation may involve. Explain how the entry of firms into its industry affects the demand curve facing a monopolistic competitor and how that, in turn, affects its economic profit. LO12.1
2. Compare the elasticity of a monopolistic competitor's demand with that of a pure competitor and a pure monopolist. Assuming identical long-run costs, compare graphically the prices and outputs that would result in the long run under pure competition and under monopolistic competition. Contrast the two market structures in terms of productive and allocative efficiency. Explain: "Monopolistically competitive industries are populated by too many firms, each of which produces too little." LO12.2
3. "Monopolistic competition is monopolistic up to the point at which consumers become willing to buy close substitute products and competitive beyond that point." Explain. LO12.2
4. "Competition in quality and service may be just as effective as price competition in giving buyers more for their money." Do you agree? Why? Explain why monopolistically competitive firms frequently prefer nonprice competition to price competition. LO12.2
5. Critically evaluate and explain: LO12.2
   a. In monopolistically competitive industries, economic profits are competed away in the long run; hence, there is no valid reason to criticize the performance and efficiency of such industries.
   b. In the long run, monopolistic competition leads to a monopolistic price but not to monopolistic profits.
6. **LAST WORD** What would you expect to happen to the proportion of big chain restaurants relative to mom and pop restaurants in a town that lowered its minimum wage? Will the proportion change due to exits or entrances? Which type of restaurant will see more in the way of exits or entrances? Why?

AP REVIEW QUESTIONS

1. Draw a graph of a firm in long-run equilibrium—in a monopolistically competitive market. Clearly explain and illustrate the excess capacity that arises in the long run. LO12.3
2. Industries X and Y both have four-firm concentration ratios of 65 percent, but the Herfindahl index for X is 1,500 while that for Y is 2,000. These data suggest: LO12.1, 12.5
   a. Greater market power in X than in Y.
   b. Greater market power in Y than in X.
   c. That X is more technologically progressive than Y.
   d. That price competition is stronger in Y than in X.
   e. That there is more advertising in X than in Y
3. Which of the following best describes the efficiency of monopolistically competitive firms? LO12.3
   a. Allocatively efficient but productively inefficient.
   b. Allocatively inefficient but productively efficient.
   c. Both allocatively efficient and productively efficient.
   d. Neither allocatively efficient nor productively efficient.
   e. Globally efficient with economic surplus maximized.
4. Answer the following:
   a. Graphically show a monopolistically competitive firm that is in a market where firms are experiencing losses in the short run.
   b. In the long run, what should happen in this industry? What change can firms that exist in the long run expect?
   c. Assuming the industry moves into a long-run equilibrium, show the price and quantity of an existing firm in this long-run equilibrium.

PROBLEMS

1. Suppose that a small town has seven burger shops whose respective shares of the local hamburger market are (as percentages of all hamburgers sold): 23 percent, 22 percent, 18 percent, 12 percent, 11 percent, 8 percent, and 6 percent. What is the four-firm concentration ratio of the hamburger industry in this town? What is the Herfindahl index for the hamburger industry in this town? If the top three sellers combined to form a single firm, what would happen to the four-firm concentration ratio and to the Herfindahl index? **LO12.1**
2. Suppose that the most popular car dealer in your area sells 10 percent of all vehicles. If all other car dealers sell either the same number of vehicles or fewer, what is the largest value that the Herfindahl index could possibly take for car dealers in your area? In that same situation, what would the four-firm concentration ratio be? **LO12.1**
3. Suppose that a monopolistically competitive restaurant is currently serving 230 meals per day (the output where MR = MC). At that output level, ATC per meal is $10 and consumers are willing to pay $12 per meal. What is the size of this firm's profit or loss? Will there be entry or exit? Will this restaurant's demand curve shift left or right? In long-run equilibrium, suppose that this restaurant charges $11 per meal for 180 meals and that the marginal cost of the 180th meal is $8. What is the size of the firm's profit? Suppose that the allocatively efficient output level in long-run equilibrium is 200 meals. Is the deadweight loss for this firm greater than or less than $60? **LO12.1**

Chapter 13

Oligopoly and Strategic Behavior

Learning Objectives

LO13.1 **Describe the characteristics of oligopoly.**

LO13.2 **Discuss how game theory relates to oligopoly.**

LO13.3 **Explain the three main models of oligopoly pricing and output: kinked-demand theory, collusive pricing, and price leadership.**

LO13.4 **Contrast the potential positive and negative effects of advertising.**

LO13.5 **Discuss the efficiency of oligopoly from society's standpoint and whether it is more or less efficient than monopoly.**

LO13.6 **Utilize additional game-theory terminology and demonstrate how to find Nash equilibriums in both simultaneous and sequential games.**

AP Chapter Focus

As introduced in the last chapter, in the United States, most industries have a market structure that falls somewhere between the two extremes of pure competition and pure monopoly. To review, most real-world industries have fewer than the large number of producers required for pure competition but more than the single producer that defines pure monopoly. In addition, most firms in most industries have both distinguishable (vs. standardized) products as well as some discretion over the prices they charge. As a result, for most real-world industries competition often occurs on the basis of price, quality, location, service, and advertising. Lastly, ease of entry to the market for most real-world industries ranges from easy to very difficult but is rarely completely blocked.

In this chapter, we now examine the second of two models that more closely approximate these real-world industry structures. While the *monopolistic competition* model of the previous chapter mixes a small amount of monopoly power with a large amount of competition, the *oligopoly* model covered in this chapter blends a large amount of monopoly power with both considerable rivalry among existing firms and the threat of increased future competition due to foreign firms and new technologies. (You should quickly review Table 9.1 at this point.)

AP Oligopoly

LO13.1 Describe the characteristics of oligopoly.

In terms of competitiveness, the spectrum of market structures reaches from pure competition, to monopolistic competition, to oligopoly, to pure monopoly (review Table 9.1). We now direct our attention to **oligopoly,** a market dominated by a few large producers of a homogeneous or differentiated product. Because of their "fewness," oligopolists have considerable control over their prices, but each must consider the possible reaction of rivals to its own pricing, output, and advertising decisions.

A Few Large Producers

The phrase "a few large producers" is necessarily vague because the market model of oligopoly covers much ground, ranging between pure monopoly, on the one hand, and monopolistic competition, on the other. Oligopoly encompasses the U.S. aluminum industry, in which three huge firms dominate an entire national market, and the situation in which four or five much smaller auto-parts stores enjoy roughly equal shares of the market in a medium-size town. Generally, however, when you hear a term such as "Big Three," "Big Four," or "Big Six," you can be sure it refers to an oligopolistic industry.

Homogeneous or Differentiated Products

An oligopoly may be either a **homogeneous oligopoly** or a **differentiated oligopoly,** depending on whether the firms in the oligopoly produce standardized (homogeneous) or differentiated products. Many industrial products (steel, zinc, copper, aluminum, lead, cement, industrial alcohol) are virtually standardized products that are produced in oligopolies. Alternatively, many consumer goods industries (automobiles, tires, household appliances, electronics equipment, breakfast cereals, cigarettes, and many sporting goods) are differentiated oligopolies. These differentiated oligopolies typically engage in considerable nonprice competition supported by heavy advertising.

Control over Price, but Mutual Interdependence

Because firms are few in oligopolistic industries, each firm is a "price maker"; like the monopolist, it can set its price and output levels to maximize its profit. But unlike the monopolist, which has no rivals, the oligopolist must consider how its rivals will react to any change in its price, output, product characteristics, or advertising. Oligopoly is thus characterized by *strategic behavior* and *mutual interdependence.* By **strategic behavior,** we simply mean self-interested behavior that takes into account the reactions of others. Firms develop and implement price, quality, location, service, and advertising strategies to "grow their business" and expand their profits. But because rivals are few, there is **mutual interdependence:** a situation in which each firm's profit depends not just on its own price and sales strategies but also on those of the other firms in its highly concentrated industry. So oligopolistic firms base their decisions on how they think their rivals will react. Example: In deciding whether to increase the price of its cosmetics, L'Oréal will try to predict the response of the other major producers, such as Clinique. Second example: In deciding on its advertising strategy, Burger King will take into consideration how McDonald's might react.

Entry Barriers

The same barriers to entry that create pure monopoly also contribute to the creation of oligopoly. Economies of scale are important entry barriers in a number of oligopolistic industries, such as the aircraft, rubber, and copper industries. In those industries, three or four firms might each have sufficient sales to achieve economies of scale, but new firms would have such a small market share that they could not do so. They would then be high-cost producers, and as such they could not survive. A closely related barrier is the large expenditure for capital—the cost of obtaining necessary plant and equipment—required for entering certain industries. The jet engine, automobile, commercial aircraft, and petroleum-refining industries, for example, are all characterized by very high capital requirements.

The ownership and control of raw materials help explain why oligopoly exists in many mining industries, including gold, silver, and copper. In the computer, chemicals, consumer electronics, and pharmaceutical industries, patents have served as entry barriers. Moreover, oligopolists can preclude the entry of new competitors through preemptive and retaliatory pricing and advertising strategies.

Mergers

Some oligopolies have emerged mainly through the growth of the dominant firms in a given industry (examples: breakfast cereals, chewing gum, candy bars). But for other industries the route to oligopoly has been through mergers (examples: steel, in its early history, and, more recently, airlines, banking, and entertainment). The merging, or combining, of two or more competing firms may substantially increase their market share, and this in turn may allow the new firm to achieve greater economies of scale.

Another motive underlying the "urge to merge" is the desire for monopoly power. The larger firm that results from a merger has greater control over market supply and thus the price of its product. Also, since it is a larger buyer of inputs, it may be able to demand and obtain lower prices (costs) on its production inputs.

CONSIDER THIS . . .

Creative Strategic Behavior

Source: © Richard Cummins/Corbis

The following story, offered with tongue in cheek, illustrates a localized market that exhibits some characteristics of oligopoly, including strategic behavior.

Tracy Martinez's Native American Arts and Crafts store is located in the center of a small tourist town that borders on a national park. In its early days, Tracy had a mini-monopoly. Business was brisk, and prices and profits were high.

To Tracy's annoyance, two "copycat" shops opened adjacent to her store, one on either side of her shop. Worse yet, the competitors named their shops to take advantage of Tracy's advertising. One was "Native Arts and Crafts"; the other, "Indian Arts and Crafts." These new sellers drew business away from Tracy's store, forcing her to lower her prices. The three side-by-side stores in the small, isolated town constituted a localized oligopoly for Native American arts and crafts.

Tracy began to think strategically about ways to boost profit. She decided to distinguish her shop from those on either side by offering a greater mix of high-quality, expensive products and a lesser mix of inexpensive souvenir items. The tactic worked for a while, but the other stores eventually imitated her product mix.

Then, one of the competitors next door escalated the rivalry by hanging up a large sign proclaiming: "We Sell for Less!" Shortly thereafter, the other shop put up a large sign stating: "We Won't Be Undersold!"

Not to be outdone, Tracy painted a colorful sign of her own and hung it above her door. It read: "Main Entrance."

Oligopolistic Industries

In the previous chapter, we listed the four-firm concentration ratio—the percentage of total industry sales accounted for by the four largest firms—for a number of monopolistically competitive industries (see Table 12.1). Column 2 of Table 13.1 shows the four-firm concentration ratios for 22 oligopolistic industries. For example, the four largest U.S. producers of aircraft make 80 percent of all aircraft produced in the United States.

When the largest four firms in an industry control 40 percent or more of the market (as in Table 13.1), that industry is considered oligopolistic. Using this benchmark, about one-half of all U.S. manufacturing industries are oligopolies.

Although concentration ratios help identify oligopoly, they have four shortcomings.

Localized Markets We have already noted that concentration ratios apply to the nation as a whole, whereas the markets for some products are highly localized because of high transportation costs. Local oligopolies can exist even though national concentration ratios are low.

Interindustry Competition Concentration ratios are based on somewhat arbitrary definitions of industries. In some cases, they disguise significant **interindustry competition**—competition between two products associated with different industries. The high concentration ratio for the primary aluminum industry shown in Table 13.1 understates the competition in that industry because aluminum competes with copper in many applications (for example, in the market for long-distance power lines).

World Trade The data in Table 13.1 only take account of output produced in the United States and may overstate concentration because they do not account for the **import competition** of foreign suppliers. The truck and auto tire industry is a good example. Although Table 13.1 shows that four U.S. firms produce 73 percent of the domestic output of tires, it ignores the fact that a very large portion of the truck and auto tires bought in the United States are imports. Many of the world's largest corporations are foreign, and many of them do business in the United States.

Dominant Firms The four-firm concentration ratio does not reveal the extent to which one or two firms dominate an industry. Suppose that in industry X one firm produces the entire industry output. In a second industry, Y, four firms compete, each with 25 percent of the market. The concentration ratio is 100 percent for both these industries. But industry X is a pure monopoly, while industry Y is an oligopoly that may be experiencing significant economic rivalry. Most economists would agree that monopoly power (or market power) is substantially greater in industry X than in industry Y, a fact disguised by their identical 100 percent concentration ratios.

The Herfindahl index addresses this problem. Recall that this index is the sum of the squared percentage market shares of all firms in the industry. In equation form:

$$\text{Herfindahl index} = (\%S_1)^2 + (\%S_2)^2 + (\%S_3)^2 + \cdots + (\%S_n)^2$$

where $\%S_1$ is the percentage market share of firm 1, $\%S_2$ is the percentage market share of firm 2, and so on for each firm

TABLE 13.1 Percentage of Output Produced by Firms in Selected High-Concentration U.S. Manufacturing Industries

(1) Industry	(2) Percentage of Industry Output* Produced by the Four Largest Firms	(3) Herfindahl Index for the Top 50 Firms	(1) Industry	(2) Percentage of Industry Output* Produced by the Four Largest Firms	(3) Herfindahl Index for the Top 50 Firms
Household laundry equipment	100	ND[†]	Primary aluminum	74	2,089
Household refrigerators and freezers	93	ND	Tires	73	1,531
Cigarettes	88	2,897	Bottled water	71	1,564
Beer	88	3,561	Gasoline pumps	70	1,611
Glass containers	86	ND	Bar soaps	70	2,250
Phosphate fertilizers	85	3,152	Burial caskets	69	1,699
Small-arms ammunition	84	2,848	Printer toner cartridges	67	1,449
Electric light bulbs	84	3,395	Alcohol distilleries	65	1,394
Aircraft	80	3,287	Turbines and generators	61	1,263
Breakfast cereals	79	2,333	Motor vehicles	60	1,178
Aerosol cans	75	1,667	Primary copper	50	879

*As measured by value of shipments. Data are for 2012. See **www.census.gov/econ/manufacturing.html**.

†ND = not disclosed.

Source: Bureau of Census, *Census of Manufacturers, 2012.*

in the industry. Also remember that by squaring the percentage market shares of all firms in the industry, the Herfindahl index gives much greater weight to larger, and thus more powerful, firms than to smaller ones. In the case of the single-firm industry X, the index would be at its maximum of 100^2, or 10,000, indicating an industry with complete monopoly power. For our supposed four-firm industry Y, the index would be $25^2 + 25^2 + 25^2 + 25^2$, or 2,500, indicating much less market power.

The larger the Herfindahl index, the greater the market power within an industry. Note in Table 13.1 that the four-firm concentration ratios for the gasoline pumps industry and the bar soaps industry are identical at 70 percent. But the Herfindahl index of 2,250 for the bar soaps industry suggests greater market power than the 1,611 index for the gasoline pumps industry. Also, contrast the much larger Herfindahl indexes in Table 13.1 with those for the low-concentration industries in Table 12.1.

AP Oligopoly Behavior: A Game-Theory Overview

LO13.2 Discuss how game theory relates to oligopoly.

Oligopoly pricing behavior has the characteristics of certain games of strategy such as poker, chess, and bridge. The best way to play such a game depends on the way one's opponent plays. Players (and oligopolists) must pattern their actions according to the actions and expected reactions of rivals. The study of how people behave in strategic situations is called **game theory.** A classic example of game theory is called the prisoner's dilemma, in which each of two prisoners confesses to a crime even though they might go free if neither confesses. The logic of this outcome is explained in the nearby Consider This box, which you should read now.

The "confess-confess" outcome of the prisoner's dilemma is conceptually identical to the "low price–low price" outcome in the game shown in Figure 13.1. In Figure 13.1 we assume that a duopoly, or two-firm oligopoly, is producing athletic shoes. Each of the two firms—let's call them RareAir and Uptown—has a choice of two pricing strategies: price high or price low. The profit each firm earns will depend on the strategy it chooses *and* the strategy its rival chooses.

There are four possible combinations of strategies for the two firms, and a lettered cell in Figure 13.1 represents each combination. For example, cell C represents a low-price strategy for Uptown along with a high-price strategy for RareAir. Figure 13.1 is called a *payoff matrix* because each cell shows the payoff (profit) to each firm that would result from each combination of strategies. Cell C shows that if Uptown adopts a low-price strategy and RareAir a high-price strategy, then Uptown will earn $15 million (yellow portion) and RareAir will earn $6 million (blue portion).

AP FIGURE 13.1 Profit payoff (in millions) for a two-firm oligopoly. Each firm has two possible pricing strategies. RareAir's strategies are shown in the top margin, and Uptown's in the left margin. Each lettered cell of this four-cell payoff matrix represents one combination of a RareAir strategy and an Uptown strategy and shows the profit that combination would earn for each. Assuming no collusion, the outcome of this game is Cell D, with both parties using low-price strategies and earning $8 million of profits.

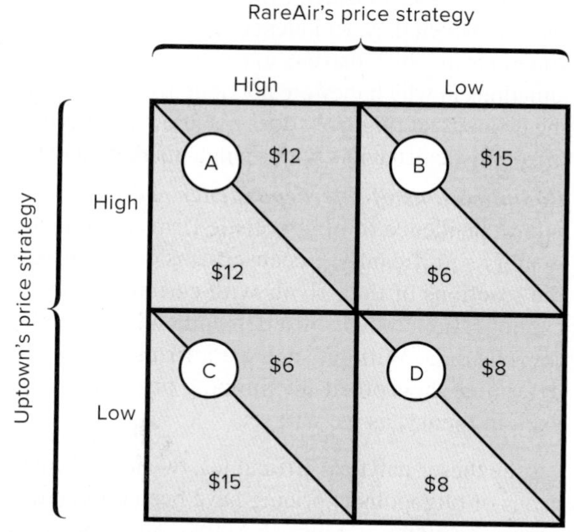

CONSIDER THIS . . .

The Prisoner's Dilemma

Source: © Brand X Pictures RF

One of the classic illustrations of game theory is the prisoner's dilemma game in which two people—let's call them Betty and Al—have committed a diamond heist and are being detained by the police as prime suspects. Unbeknownst to the two, the evidence against them is weak, so the best hope the police have for getting a conviction is if one or both of the thieves confess to the crime. The police place Betty and Al in separate holding cells and offer each the same deal: Confess to the crime and receive a lighter prison sentence.

Each detainee therefore faces a dilemma. If Betty remains silent and Al confesses, Betty will end up with a long prison sentence. If Betty confesses and Al says nothing, Al will receive a long prison sentence. What happens? Fearful that the other person will confess, both confess, even though they each would be better off saying nothing.

Mutual Interdependence Revisited

The data in Figure 13.1 are hypothetical, but their relationships are typical of real situations. Recall that oligopolistic firms can increase their profits, and influence their rivals' profits, by changing their pricing strategies. Each firm's profit depends on its own pricing strategy and that of its rivals. This mutual interdependence of oligopolists is the most obvious point demonstrated by Figure 13.1. If Uptown adopts a high-price strategy, its profit will be $12 million provided that RareAir also employs a high-price strategy (cell A). But if RareAir uses a low-price strategy against Uptown's high-price strategy (cell B), RareAir will increase its market share and boost its profit from $12 to $15 million. RareAir's higher profit will come at the expense of Uptown, whose profit will fall from $12 million to $6 million. Uptown's high-price strategy is a good strategy only if RareAir also employs a high-price strategy.

Collusion

Figure 13.1 also suggests that oligopolists often can benefit from **collusion**—that is, cooperation with rivals. To see the benefits of collusion, first suppose that both firms in Figure 13.1 are acting independently and following high-price strategies. Each realizes a $12 million profit (cell A).

Note that either RareAir or Uptown could increase its profit by switching to a low-price strategy (cell B or C). The low-price firm would increase its profit to $15 million and the high-price firm's profit would fall to $6 million. The high-price firm would be better off if it, too, adopted a low-price policy. Doing so would increase its profit from $6 million to $8 million (cell D). The effect of all this independent strategy shifting would be the reduction of both firms' profits from $12 million (cell A) to $8 million (cell D).

In real situations, too, independent action by oligopolists may lead to mutually "competitive" low-price strategies: Independent oligopolists compete with respect to price, and this leads to lower prices and lower profits. This outcome is clearly beneficial to consumers but not to the oligopolists, whose profits decrease.

How could oligopolists avoid the low-profit outcome of cell D? The answer is that they could collude, rather than establish prices competitively or independently. In our example, the two firms could agree to establish and maintain a high-price policy. So each firm will increase its profit from $8 million (cell D) to $12 million (cell A).

Incentive to Cheat

The payoff matrix also explains why an oligopolist might be strongly tempted to cheat on a collusive agreement. Suppose Uptown and RareAir agree to maintain high-price policies, with each earning $12 million in profit (cell A). Both are tempted to cheat on this collusive pricing agreement because either firm can increase its profit to $15 million by lowering its price.

For instance, if Uptown secretly cheats and sells at the low price while RareAir keeps on charging the high price, the payoff would move from cell A to cell C so that Uptown's profit would rise to $15 million while RareAir's profit would fall to $6 million. On the other hand, if RareAir cheats and sets a low price while Uptown keeps the agreement and charges the high price, the payoff matrix would move from cell A to cell B so that RareAir would get $15 million while Uptown would get only $6 million.

As you can see, cheating is both very lucrative to the cheater as well as very costly to the firm that gets cheated on. As a result, both firms will probably cheat so that the game will settle back to cell D, with each firm using its low-price strategy. (The Consider This box on the prisoner's dilemma is highly relevant, and we urge you to read it over again right now. Also, the final section in this chapter provides several additional applications of game theory.)

AP QUICK REVIEW 13.1

- ✓ Oligopolies consist of a few firms producing either homogeneous or differentiated products.
- ✓ A critical aspect of oligopoly is the interdependence of firm decision making. In decisions regarding output, price, or advertising, oligopolistic firms tend to consider the reaction of the rival firms—that is, they behave "strategically."
- ✓ Barriers to entry such as scale economies, control of patents or strategic resources, or the ability to engage in retaliatory pricing characterize oligopolies. Oligopolies may result from internal growth of firms, mergers, or both.
- ✓ In their study, economists measure the degree of market power within an oligopoly. The four-firm concentration ratio shows the percentage of an industry's sales by the four largest firms; the Herfindahl index measures the degree of market power in an industry by summing the squares of the percentage market shares held by the individual firms in the industry.

AP Three Oligopoly Models

LO13.3 Explain the three main models of oligopoly pricing and output: kinked-demand theory, collusive pricing, and price leadership.

To gain further insight into oligopolistic pricing and output behavior, we will examine three distinct pricing models: (1) the kinked-demand curve, (2) collusive pricing, and (3) price leadership.

Why not a single model, as in our discussions of the other market structures? There are two reasons:

- ***Diversity of oligopolies*** Oligopoly encompasses a greater range and diversity of market situations than do other market structures. It includes the *tight* oligopoly, in which two or three firms dominate an entire market, and the *loose* oligopoly, in which six or seven firms share, say, 70 or 80 percent of a market while a "competitive fringe" of firms shares the remainder. It includes both differentiated and standardized products. It includes cases in which firms act in collusion and those in which they act independently. It embodies situations in which barriers to entry are very strong and situations in which they are not quite so strong. In short, the diversity of oligopoly does not allow us to explain all oligopolistic behaviors with a single market model.
- ***Complications of interdependence*** The mutual interdependence of oligopolistic firms complicates matters significantly. Because firms cannot predict the reactions of their rivals with certainty, they cannot estimate their own demand and marginal-revenue data. Without such data, firms cannot determine their profit-maximizing price and output, even in theory, as we will see.

Despite these analytical difficulties, two interrelated characteristics of oligopolistic pricing have been observed. First, if the macroeconomy is generally stable, oligopolistic prices are typically inflexible (or "rigid" or "sticky"). Prices change less frequently under oligopoly than under pure competition, monopolistic competition, and, in some instances, pure monopoly. Second, when oligopolistic prices do change, firms are likely to change their prices together, suggesting that there is a tendency to act in concert, or collusively, in setting and changing prices (as we mentioned in the preceding section). The diversity of oligopolies and the presence of mutual interdependence are reflected in the models that follow.

Kinked-Demand Theory: Noncollusive Oligopoly

Imagine an oligopolistic industry made up of three hypothetical firms (Arch, King, and Dave's), each having about one-third of the total market for a differentiated product. Assume that the firms are "independent," meaning that they do not engage in collusive price practices. Assume, too, that the going price for Arch's product is P_0 and its current sales are Q_0, as shown in **Figure 13.2a (Key Graph).**

Now the question is, "What does the firm's demand curve look like?" Mutual interdependence and the uncertainty about rivals' reactions make this question hard to answer. The location and shape of an oligopolist's demand curve depend on how the firm's rivals will react to a price change introduced by Arch. There are two plausible assumptions about the reactions of Arch's rivals:

- ***Match price changes*** One possibility is that King and Dave's will exactly match any price change initiated by

KEY GRAPH

FIGURE 13.2 The kinked-demand curve. (a) The slope of a noncollusive oligopolist's demand and marginal-revenue curves depends on whether its rivals match (straight lines D_1 and MR_1) or ignore (straight lines D_2 and MR_2) any price changes that it may initiate from the current price P_0. (b) In all likelihood an oligopolist's rivals will ignore a price increase but follow a price cut. This causes the oligopolist's demand curve to be kinked (D_2eD_1) and the marginal-revenue curve to have a vertical break, or gap (fg). Because any shift in marginal costs between MC_1 and MC_2 will cut the vertical (dashed) segment of the marginal-revenue curve, no change in either price P_0 or output Q_0 will result from such a shift.

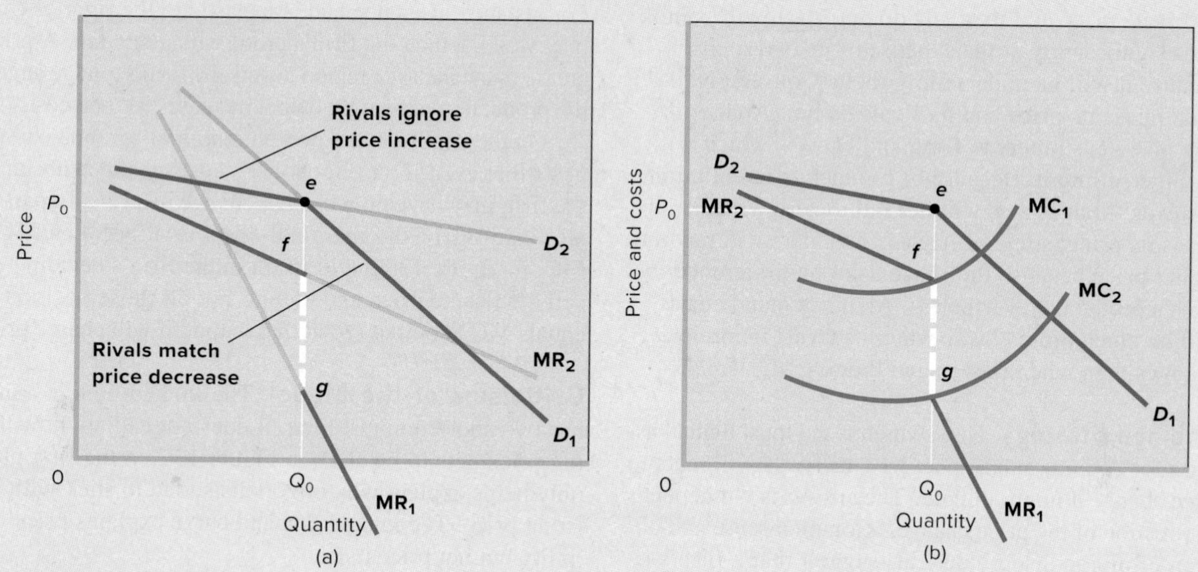

QUICK QUIZ FOR FIGURE 13.2

1. Suppose Q_0 in this figure represents annual sales of 5 million units for this firm. The other two firms in this three-firm industry sell 3 million and 2 million units, respectively. The Herfindahl index for this industry is:
   a. 100 percent.
   b. 400.
   c. 10.
   d. 3,800.
2. The D_2e segment of the demand curve D_2eD_1 in graph (b) implies that:
   a. this firm's total revenue will fall if it increases its price above P_0.
   b. other firms will match a price increase above P_0.
   c. the firm's relevant marginal-revenue curve will be MR_1 for price increases above P_0.
   d. the product in this industry is necessarily standardized.
3. By matching a price cut, this firm's rivals can:
   a. increase their market shares.
   b. increase their marginal revenues.
   c. maintain their market shares.
   d. lower their total costs.
4. A shift of the marginal-cost curve from MC_2 to MC_1 in graph (b) would:
   a. increase the "going price" above P_0.
   b. leave price at P_0 but reduce this firm's total profit.
   c. leave price at P_0 but reduce this firm's total revenue.
   d. make this firm's demand curve more elastic.

Answers: 1. d; 2. a; 3. c; 4. b

Arch. In this case, Arch's demand and marginal-revenue curves will look like the straight lines labeled D_1 and MR_1 in Figure 13.2a. Why are they so steep? Reason: If Arch cuts its price, its sales will increase only modestly because its two rivals will also cut their prices to prevent Arch from gaining an advantage over them. The small increase in sales that Arch (and its two rivals) will realize is at the expense of other industries; Arch will gain no sales from King and Dave's. In a similar fashion, if Arch raises its price, its sales will fall only modestly because King and Dave's will match its price increase. The industry will lose sales to other industries, but Arch will lose no customers to King and Dave's.

- ***Ignore price changes*** The other possibility is that King and Dave's will ignore any price change by Arch. In this case, the demand and marginal-revenue curves faced by Arch will resemble the straight lines D_2 and MR_2 in Figure 13.2a. Demand in this case is considerably more elastic than it was under the previous assumption. The reasons are clear: If Arch lowers its price and its rivals do not, Arch will gain sales significantly at the expense of its two rivals because it will be underselling them. Conversely, if Arch raises its price and its rivals do not, Arch will lose many customers to King and Dave's, which will be underselling it. Because of product differentiation, however, Arch's sales will not fall to zero when it raises its price; some of Arch's customers will pay the higher price because they have a strong preference for Arch's product. Nevertheless, Arch's demand curve will be much more elastic when its rivals ignore price changes than when they match them.

A Combined Strategy Now, which is the most logical assumption for Arch to make about how its rivals will react to any price change it might initiate? The answer is, "It depends on the direction of the price change." Common sense and observation of oligopolistic industries suggest that a firm's rivals will match price declines below P_0 as they act to prevent the price cutter from taking their customers. But they will ignore price increases above P_0 because the rivals of the price-increasing firm stand to gain the business lost by the price booster. In other words, the dark-green left-hand segment of the "rivals ignore" demand curve D_2 in Figure 13.2a seems relevant for price increases, and the dark-green right-hand segment of the "rivals match" demand curve D_1 seems relevant for price cuts. It is therefore reasonable to assume that the noncollusive oligopolist faces the **kinked-demand curve** D_2eD_1, as shown in Figure 13.2b. Demand is highly elastic above the going price P_0 but much less elastic or even inelastic below that price.

Note also that if rivals match a price cut but ignore an increase, the marginal-revenue curve of the oligopolist will also have an odd shape. It, too, will be made up of two segments: the dark gray left-hand part of marginal-revenue curve MR_2 in Figure 13.2a and the dark gray right-hand part of marginal-revenue curve MR_1. Because of the sharp difference in elasticity of demand above and below the going price, there is a gap, or what we can simply treat as a vertical segment, in the marginal-revenue curve. We show this gap as the dashed segment in the combined marginal-revenue curve MR_2fgMR_1 in Figure 13.2b.

Price Inflexibility This analysis helps explain why prices are generally stable in noncollusive oligopolistic industries. There are both demand and cost reasons.

On the demand side, the kinked-demand curve gives each oligopolist reason to believe that any change in price will be for the worse. If it raises its price, many of its customers will desert it. If it lowers its price, its sales at best will increase very modestly since rivals will match the lower price. Even if a price cut increases the oligopolist's total revenue somewhat, its costs may increase by a greater amount, depending on demand elasticity. For instance, if its demand is inelastic to the right of Q_0, as it may well be, then the firm's profit will surely fall. A price decrease in the inelastic region lowers the firm's total revenue, and the production of a larger output increases its total costs.

On the cost side, the broken marginal-revenue curve suggests that even if an oligopolist's costs change substantially, the firm may have no reason to change its price. In particular, all positions of the marginal-cost curve between MC_1 and MC_2 in Figure 13.2b will result in the firm's deciding on exactly the same price and output. For all those positions, MR equals MC at output Q_0; at that output, it will charge price P_0.

Criticisms of the Model The kinked-demand analysis has two shortcomings. First, it does not explain how the going price gets to be at P_0 in Figure 13.2 in the first place. It only helps explain why oligopolists tend to stick with an existing price. The kinked-demand curve explains price inflexibility but not price itself.

Second, when the macroeconomy is unstable, oligopoly prices are not as rigid as the kinked-demand theory implies. During inflationary periods, many oligopolists have raised their prices often and substantially. And during downturns (recessions), some oligopolists have cut prices. In some instances these price reductions have set off a **price war:** successive and continuous rounds of price cuts by rivals as they attempt to maintain their market shares.

Cartels and Other Collusion

Our game-theory model demonstrated that oligopolists might benefit from collusion. We can say that collusion occurs whenever firms in an industry reach an agreement to fix prices, divide up the market, or otherwise restrict competition among themselves. The disadvantages and uncertainties of noncollusive, kinked-demand oligopolies are obvious. There is always the danger of a price war breaking out, especially during a general business recession. Then each firm finds that, because of unsold goods and excess capacity, it can reduce per-unit costs by increasing market share. Then, too, a new firm may surmount entry barriers and initiate aggressive price cutting to gain a foothold in the market. In addition, the kinked-demand curve's tendency toward rigid prices may adversely affect profits if general inflationary pressures increase costs. However, by controlling price through collusion, oligopolists may be able to reduce uncertainty, increase profits, and perhaps even prohibit the entry of new rivals.

Price and Output Assume once again that there are three hypothetical oligopolistic firms (Gypsum, Sheetrock, and GSR) producing, in this instance, gypsum drywall panels for finishing interior walls. All three firms produce a homogeneous product and have identical cost curves. Each firm's demand curve is indeterminate unless we know how its rivals will react to any price change. Therefore, we suppose each firm assumes that its two rivals will match either a price cut or a price increase. In other words, each firm has a demand curve like the straight line D_1 in Figure 13.2a. And since they have identical cost data, and the same demand and thus marginal-revenue data, we can say that Figure 13.3 represents the position of each of our three oligopolistic firms.

What price and output combination should, say, Gypsum select? If Gypsum were a pure monopolist, the answer would be clear: Establish output at Q_0, where marginal revenue equals marginal cost, charge the corresponding price P_0, and enjoy the maximum profit attainable. However, Gypsum does have two rivals selling identical products, and if Gypsum's assumption that its rivals will match its price of P_0 proves to be incorrect, the consequences could be disastrous for Gypsum. Specifically, if Sheetrock and GSR actually charge prices below P_0, then Gypsum's demand curve D will shift sharply to the left as its potential customers turn to its rivals, which are now selling the same product at a lower price. Of course, Gypsum can retaliate by cutting its price too, but this will move all three firms down their demand curves, lowering their profits. It may even drive them to a point where average total cost exceeds price and losses are incurred.

AP **FIGURE 13.3 Collusion and the tendency toward joint-profit maximization.** If oligopolistic firms face identical or highly similar demand and cost conditions, they may collude to limit their joint output and to set a single, common price. Thus each firm acts as if it were a pure monopolist, setting output at Q_0 and charging price P_0. This price and output combination maximizes each oligopolist's profit (green area) and thus the combined or joint profit of the colluding firms.

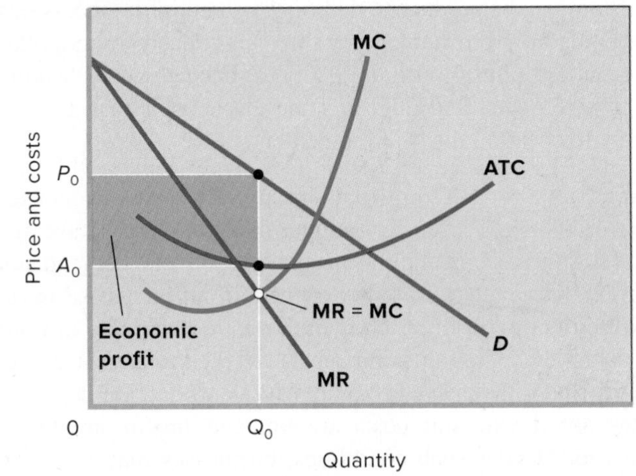

So the question becomes, "Will Sheetrock and GSR want to charge a price below P_0?" Under our assumptions, and recognizing that Gypsum has little choice except to match any price they may set below P_0, the answer is no. Faced with the same demand and cost circumstances, Sheetrock and GSR will find it in their interest to produce Q_0 and charge P_0. This is a curious situation; each firm finds it most profitable to charge the same price, P_0, but only if its rivals actually do so! How can the three firms ensure the price P_0 and quantity Q_0 solution in which each is keenly interested? How can they avoid the less profitable outcomes associated with either higher or lower prices?

The answer is evident: They can collude. They can get together, talk it over, and agree to charge the same price, P_0, and thereby enjoy the maximum profit available [$= (P_0 - A_0) \times Q_0$ units]. In addition to reducing the possibility of price wars, this will give each firm the maximum profit. (But it will also subject them to antitrust prosecution if they are caught!) For society, the result will be the same as would occur if the industry were a pure monopoly composed of three identical plants.

Overt Collusion: The OPEC Cartel Collusion may assume a variety of forms. The most comprehensive form of collusion is the **cartel,** a group of producers that typically creates a formal written agreement specifying how much each member will produce and charge. Output must be controlled—the market must be divided up—in order to maintain the agreed-upon price. The collusion is overt, or open to view.

Undoubtedly the most significant international cartel is the Organization of Petroleum Exporting Countries (OPEC), comprising 14 oil-producing nations (see Global Perspective 13.1). OPEC produces 34 percent of the world's oil and supplies 34 percent of all oil traded internationally.

OPEC has in some cases been able to drastically alter oil prices by increasing or decreasing supply. In 1973, for instance, it caused the price of oil to more than triple by getting its members to restrict output. And again, in the late 1990s it caused oil prices to rise from \$11 per barrel to \$34 per barrel over a 15-month period.

That being said, it should be kept in mind that most increases in the price of oil are not caused by OPEC. Between 2005 and 2008, for example, oil prices went from \$40 per barrel to \$140 per barrel due to rapidly rising demand from China and supply uncertainties related to armed conflict in the Middle East. But as the recession that began in December 2007 took hold, demand slumped and oil prices collapsed back down to about \$40 per barrel. OPEC was largely a nonfactor in this rise and fall in the price of oil. But in those cases where OPEC can effectively enforce its production agreements, there is little doubt that it can hold the price of oil substantially above the marginal cost of production.

Covert Collusion: Examples Cartels are illegal in the United States, and hence any collusion that exists is covert or

GLOBAL PERSPECTIVE 13.1

The 14 OPEC Nations, Daily Oil Production, December 2015

The OPEC nations produce about 34 percent of the world's oil and about 34 percent of the oil sold in world markets.

OPEC Country	Barrels of Oil
Saudi Arabia	10,088,000
Iraq	4,309,000
UAE	2,895,000
Iran	2,882,000
Kuwait	2,708,000
Venezuela	2,348,000
Nigeria	1,789,000
Angola	1,751,000
Algeria	1,103,000
Indonesia	693,000
Qatar	674,000
Ecuador	551,000
Libya	394,000
Gabon	219,000

Source: OPEC, *OPEC Monthly Oil Market Report*, January 2016.

secret. Yet there are numerous examples, as shown by evidence from antitrust (antimonopoly) cases. In 2011, U.S.-based Whirlpool, Japan-headquartered Panasonic, the Danish firm Danfoss, and the Italian company Appliance Components were fined over $200 million for attempting to run an international cartel that could rig the worldwide prices of refrigerator compressors. In 2012, several Japanese autoparts makers pleaded guilty to rigging the bids that they submitted to a major carmaker. The conspirators employed measures to keep their conduct secret, including using code names and instructing participants to destroy evidence of collusion.

In many other instances collusion is much subtler. Unwritten, informal understandings (historically called "gentlemen's agreements") are frequently made at cocktail parties, on golf courses, through phone calls, or at trade association meetings. In such agreements, executives reach verbal or even tacit (unspoken) understandings on product price, leaving market shares to be decided by nonprice competition. Although these agreements, too, violate antitrust laws—and can result in severe personal and corporate penalties—the elusive character of informal understandings makes them more difficult to detect.

Obstacles to Collusion Normally, cartels and similar collusive arrangements are difficult to establish and maintain. Here are several barriers to collusion:

Demand and Cost Differences When oligopolists face different costs and demand curves, it is difficult for them to agree on a price. This is particularly the case in industries where products are differentiated and change frequently. Even with highly standardized products, firms usually have somewhat different market shares and operate with differing degrees of productive efficiency. Thus it is unlikely that even homogeneous oligopolists would have the same demand and cost curves.

In either case, differences in costs and demand mean that the profit-maximizing price will differ among firms; no single price will be readily acceptable to all, as we assumed was true in Figure 13.3. So price collusion depends on compromises and concessions that are not always easy to obtain and hence act as an obstacle to collusion.

Number of Firms Other things equal, the larger the number of firms, the more difficult it is to create a cartel or some other form of price collusion. Agreement on price by three or four producers that control an entire market may be relatively easy to accomplish. But such agreement is more difficult to achieve where there are, say, 10 firms, each with roughly 10 percent of the market, or where the Big Three have 70 percent of the market while a competitive fringe of 8 or 10 smaller firms battles for the remainder.

Cheating As the game-theory model makes clear, collusive oligopolists are tempted to engage in secret price cutting to increase sales and profit. The difficulty with such cheating is that buyers who are paying a high price for a product may become aware of the lower-priced sales and demand similar treatment. Or buyers receiving a price concession from one producer may use the concession as a wedge to get even larger price concessions from a rival producer. Buyers' attempts to play producers against one another may precipitate price wars among the producers. Although secret price concessions are potentially profitable, they threaten collusive oligopolies over time. Collusion is more likely to succeed when cheating is easy to detect and punish. Then the conspirators are less likely to cheat on the price agreement.

Recession Long-lasting recession usually serves as an enemy of collusion because slumping markets increase average total cost. In technical terms, as the oligopolists' demand and marginal-revenue curves shift to the left in Figure 13.3 in response to a recession, each firm moves leftward and upward to a higher operating point on its average-total-cost curve. Firms find they have substantial excess production capacity, sales are down, unit costs are up, and profits are being squeezed. Under such conditions, businesses may feel they can avoid serious profit reductions (or even losses) by cutting price and thus gaining sales at the expense of rivals.

Potential Entry The greater prices and profits that result from collusion may attract new entrants, including foreign firms. Since that would increase market supply and reduce prices and profits, successful collusion requires that colluding oligopolists block the entry of new producers.

Legal Obstacles: Antitrust Law U.S. antitrust laws prohibit cartels and price-fixing collusion. So less obvious means of price control have evolved in the United States.

Price Leadership Model

Price leadership entails a type of implicit understanding by which oligopolists can coordinate prices without engaging in outright collusion based on formal agreements and secret meetings. Rather, a practice evolves whereby the "dominant firm"—usually the largest or most efficient in the industry—initiates price changes and all other firms more or less automatically follow the leader. Many industries, including farm machinery, cement, copper, newsprint, glass containers, steel, beer, fertilizer, cigarettes, and tin, are practicing, or have in the recent past practiced, price leadership.

Leadership Tactics An examination of price leadership in a variety of industries suggests that the price leader is likely to observe the following tactics.

Infrequent Price Changes Because price changes always carry the risk that rivals will not follow the lead, price adjustments are made only infrequently. The price leader does not respond to minuscule day-to-day changes in costs and demand. Price is changed only when cost and demand conditions have been altered significantly and on an industrywide basis as the result of, for example, industrywide wage increases, an increase in excise taxes, or an increase in the price of some basic input such as energy. In the automobile industry, price adjustments traditionally have been made when new models are introduced each fall.

Communications The price leader often communicates impending price adjustments to the industry through speeches by major executives, trade publication interviews, or press releases. By publicizing "the need to raise prices," the price leader seeks agreement among its competitors regarding the actual increase.

Limit Pricing The price leader does not always choose the price that maximizes short-run profits for the industry because the industry may want to discourage new firms from entering. If the cost advantages (economies of scale) of existing firms are a major barrier to entry, new entrants could surmount that barrier if the price leader and the other firms set product price high enough. New firms that are relatively inefficient because of their small size might survive and grow if the industry sets price very high. So, in order to discourage new competitors and to maintain the current oligopolistic structure of the industry, the price leader may keep price below the short-run profit-maximizing level. The strategy of establishing a price that blocks the entry of new firms is called *limit pricing*.

Breakdowns in Price Leadership: Price Wars Price leadership in oligopoly occasionally breaks down, at least temporarily, and sometimes results in a price war. An example of price leadership temporarily breaking down occurred in the breakfast cereal industry, in which Kellogg traditionally had been the price leader. General Mills countered Kellogg's leadership in 1995 by reducing the prices of its cereals by 11 percent. In 1996 Post responded with a 20 percent price cut, which Kellogg then followed. Not to be outdone, Post reduced its prices by another 11 percent.

As another example, in October 2009 with the Christmas shopping season just getting under way, Walmart cut its price on 10 highly anticipated new books to just $10 each. Within hours, Amazon.com matched the price cut. Walmart then retaliated by cutting its price for the books to just $9 each. Amazon.com matched that reduction—at which point Walmart went to $8.99! Then, out of nowhere, Target jumped in at $8.98, a price that Amazon.com and Walmart immediately matched. And that is where the price finally came to rest—at a level so low that each company was losing money on each book it sold.

Most price wars eventually run their course. After a period of low or negative profits, they again yield price leadership to one of the industry's leading firms. That firm then begins to raise prices, and the other firms willingly follow suit.

AP QUICK REVIEW 13.2

- ✓ In the kinked-demand theory of oligopoly, price is relatively inflexible because a firm contemplating a price change assumes that its rivals will follow a price cut but ignore a price increase. Thus, instead of price, firms will compete with non-price factors like advertising.
- ✓ Cartels agree on production limits and set a common price to maximize the joint profit of their members as if each were a subsidiary of a single pure monopoly.
- ✓ Collusion among oligopolists is difficult because of (a) demand and cost differences among sellers, (b) the complexity of output coordination among producers, (c) the potential for cheating, (d) a tendency for agreements to break down during recessions, (e) the potential entry of new firms, and (f) antitrust laws.
- ✓ Price leadership involves an informal understanding among oligopolists to match any price change initiated by a designated firm (often the industry's dominant firm).

Oligopoly and Advertising

LO13.4 Contrast the potential positive and negative effects of advertising.

We have noted that oligopolists would rather not compete on the basis of price and may become involved in price collusion. Nonetheless, each firm's share of the total market is typically determined through product development and advertising, for two reasons:

- Product development and advertising campaigns are less easily duplicated than price cuts. Price cuts can be quickly and easily matched by a firm's rivals to cancel any potential gain in sales derived from that strategy. Product improvements and successful advertising, however, can produce more permanent gains in market share because they cannot be duplicated as quickly and completely as price reductions.
- Oligopolists have sufficient financial resources to engage in product development and advertising. For most oligopolists, the economic profits earned in the past can help finance current advertising and product development.

Product development (or, more broadly, "research and development") is its own subject, so we will confine our present discussion to advertising. In 2014, firms spent an estimated $141 billion on advertising in the United States and $539 billion worldwide. Advertising is prevalent in both monopolistic competition and oligopoly. Table 13.2 lists the 10 leading U.S. advertisers in 2014.

Advertising may affect prices, competition, and efficiency both positively and negatively, depending on the circumstances. While our focus here is on advertising by oligopolists, the analysis is equally applicable to advertising by monopolistic competitors.

TABLE 13.2 The Largest U.S. Advertisers, 2014

Company	Advertising Spending Millions of $
Procter & Gamble	$4,607
AT&T	3,272
General Motors	3,120
Comcast	3,029
Verizon	2,526
Ford Motor	2,467
American Express	2,364
Fiat Chrysler	2,250
L'Oréal	2,158
Walt Disney	2,109

Source: Advertising Age, **www.adage.com**.

Positive Effects of Advertising

In order to make rational (efficient) decisions, consumers need information about product characteristics and prices. Media advertising may be a low-cost means for consumers to obtain that information. Suppose you are in the market for a high-quality camera that is not advertised or promoted in newspapers, in magazines, or on the Internet. To make a rational choice, you may have to spend several days visiting stores to determine the availability, prices, and features of various brands. This search entails both direct costs (gasoline, parking fees) and indirect costs (the value of your time). By providing information about the available options, advertising and Internet promotion reduce your search time and minimize these direct and indirect costs.

By providing information about the various competing goods that are available, advertising diminishes monopoly power. In fact, advertising is frequently associated with the introduction of new products designed to compete with existing brands. Could Toyota and Honda have so strongly challenged U.S. auto producers without advertising? Could FedEx have sliced market share away from UPS and the U.S. Postal Service without advertising?

Viewed this way, advertising is an efficiency-enhancing activity. It is a relatively inexpensive means of providing useful information to consumers and thus lowering their search costs. By enhancing competition, advertising results in greater economic efficiency. By facilitating the introduction of new products, advertising speeds up technological progress. By increasing sales and output, advertising can reduce long-run average total cost by enabling firms to obtain economies of scale.

Potential Negative Effects of Advertising

Not all the effects of advertising are positive, of course. Much advertising is designed simply to manipulate or persuade consumers—that is, to alter their preferences in favor of the advertiser's product. A television commercial that indicates that a popular personality drinks a particular brand of soft drink—and therefore that you should too—conveys little or no information to consumers about price or quality. In addition, advertising is sometimes based on misleading and extravagant claims that confuse consumers rather than enlighten them. Indeed, in some cases advertising may well persuade consumers to pay high prices for much-acclaimed but inferior products, forgoing better but unadvertised products selling at lower prices. Example: *Consumer Reports* has found that heavily advertised premium motor oils provide no better engine performance and longevity than do cheaper brands.

Firms often establish substantial brand-name loyalty and thus achieve monopoly power via their advertising (see Global Perspective 13.2). As a consequence, they are able to increase their sales, expand their market shares, and enjoy

GLOBAL PERSPECTIVE 13.2

The World's Top 10 Brand Names, 2015

Here are the world's top 10 brands, based on four criteria: the brand's market share within its category, the brand's world appeal across age groups and nationalities, the loyalty of customers to the brand, and the ability of the brand to "stretch" to products beyond the original product.

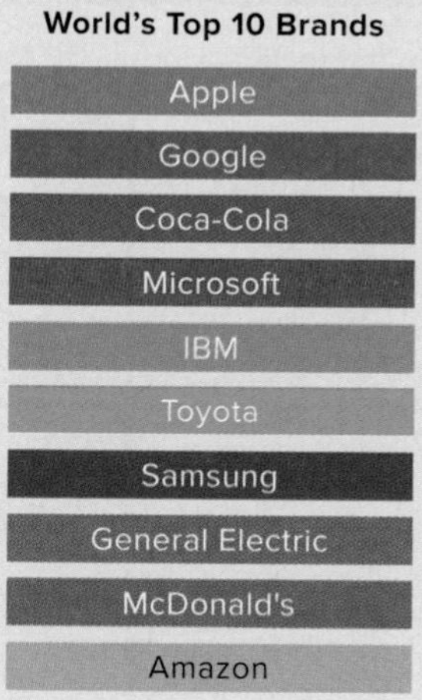

Source: Interbrand, "100 Best Global Brands, 2015," **www.interbrand.com**.

greater profits. Larger profits permit still more advertising and further enlargement of the firm's market share and profit. In time, consumers may lose the advantages of competitive markets and face the disadvantages of monopolized markets. Moreover, new entrants to the industry need to incur large advertising costs in order to establish their products in the marketplace; thus, advertising costs may be a barrier to entry.

Advertising can also be self-canceling. The advertising campaign of one fast-food hamburger chain may be offset by equally costly campaigns waged by rivals, so each firm's demand actually remains unchanged. Few, if any, extra burgers will be purchased and each firm's market share will stay the same. But because of the advertising, all firms will experience higher costs and either their profits will fall or, through successful price leadership, their product prices will rise.

When advertising either leads to increased monopoly power or is self-canceling, economic inefficiency results.

AP Oligopoly and Efficiency

LO13.5 Discuss the efficiency of oligopoly from society's standpoint and whether it is more or less efficient than monopoly.

Is oligopoly, then, an efficient market structure from society's standpoint? How do the price and output decisions of the oligopolist measure up to the triple equality $P = \text{MC} = \text{minimum ATC}$ that occurs in pure competition?

Productive and Allocative Efficiency

Many economists believe that the outcome of some oligopolistic markets is approximately as shown in Figure 13.3. This view is bolstered by evidence that many oligopolists sustain sizable economic profits year after year. In that case, the oligopolist's production occurs where price exceeds marginal cost and average total cost. Moreover, production is below the output at which average total cost is minimized. In this view, neither productive efficiency (P = minimum ATC) nor allocative efficiency (P = MC) is likely to occur under oligopoly.

A few observers assert that oligopoly is actually less desirable than pure monopoly because government usually regulates pure monopoly in the United States to guard against abuses of monopoly power. Informal collusion among oligopolists may yield price and output results similar to those under pure monopoly yet give the outward appearance of competition involving independent firms.

Qualifications

We should note, however, three qualifications to this view:

- ***Increased foreign competition*** In recent decades foreign competition has increased rivalry in a number of oligopolistic industries—steel, automobiles, video games, electric shavers, outboard motors, and copy machines, for example. This has helped to break down such cozy arrangements as price leadership and to stimulate much more competitive pricing.
- ***Limit pricing*** Recall that some oligopolists may purposely keep prices below the short-run profit-maximizing level in order to bolster entry barriers. In essence, consumers and society may get some of the benefits of competition—prices closer to marginal cost and minimum average total cost—even without the competition that free entry would provide.
- ***Technological advance*** Over time, oligopolistic industries may foster more rapid product development and greater improvement of production techniques than would be possible if they were purely competitive. Oligopolists have large economic profits from which they can fund expensive research and development (R&D). Moreover, the existence of barriers to entry may give the oligopolist some assurance that it will reap the rewards of successful R&D. Thus, the short-run economic inefficiencies of oligopolists may be partly or wholly offset by the oligopolists' contributions to better products, lower prices, and lower costs over time.

AP QUICK REVIEW 13.3

- ✓ Oligopolists emphasize nonprice competition because (a) advertising and product variations are harder to match than price changes and (b) oligopolists frequently have ample resources to fund nonprice competition.
- ✓ Advertising can help reduce monopoly power by presenting consumers with useful information about existing products and by helping to introduce new products.
- ✓ Advertising can hurt consumers and competition by promoting monopoly power and creating entry barriers.

AP Game Theory and Strategic Behavior

LO13.6 Utilize additional game-theory terminology and demonstrate how to find Nash equilibriums in both simultaneous and sequential games.

We have seen that game theory is helpful in explaining mutual interdependence and strategic behavior by oligopolists. This section provides additional oligopoly-based applications of game theory.

A One-Time Game: Strategies and Equilibrium

Consider Figure 13.4, which lists strategies and outcomes for two fictitious producers of the computer memory chips referred to as DRAMs (Dynamic Random Access Memory circuits). Chipco is the single producer of these chips in the United States and Dramco is the only producer in China. Each firm has two alternative strategies: an international strategy, in which it competes directly against the other firm in both countries; and a national strategy, in which it sells only in its home country.

The game and payoff matrix shown in Figure 13.4 is a **one-time game** because the firms select their optimal strategies in a single time period without regard to possible interactions in subsequent time periods. The game is also a **simultaneous game** because the firms choose their strategies at the same time; and a **positive-sum game,** a game in which the sum of the two firms' outcomes (here, profits) is positive. In contrast, the net gain in a **zero-sum game** is zero because one firm's gain must equal the other firm's loss, and the net gain in a **negative-sum game** is negative. In some positive-sum games, both firms may have positive outcomes. That is the case in Figure 13.4.

To determine optimal strategies, Chipco looks across the two rows in the payoff matrix (yellow portion of cells in millions of dollars) and Dramco looks down the two columns (blue portion of cells). These payoffs indicate that both firms have a **dominant strategy**—an option that is better than any alternative option *regardless of what the other firm does.* To see this, notice that Chipco's international strategy will give it a higher profit than its national strategy—regardless of whether Dramco chooses to utilize an international or a national strategy. An international strategy will produce an $11 million profit for Chipco (yellow portion of cell A) if Dramco also uses an international strategy while a national strategy will result in a $20 million profit for Chipco (yellow portion of cell B) if Dramco uses a national strategy. Chipco's possible $11 million and $20 million outcomes are clearly better than the $5 million (cell C) and $17 million (cell D) outcomes it could receive if it chose to pursue a national strategy. Chipco's international strategy is, consequently, its dominant strategy. Using similar logic, Dramco also concludes that its international strategy is its dominant strategy.

In this particular case, the outcome (cell A) of the two dominant strategies is the game's **Nash equilibrium**—an outcome from which neither rival wants to deviate.[1] At the Nash equilibrium, both rivals see their current strategy as optimal *given the other firm's strategic choice.* The Nash equilibrium is the only outcome in the payoff matrix in Figure 13.4 that, once achieved, is stable and therefore will persist.[2]

FIGURE 13.4 A one-time game. In this single-period, positive-sum game, Chipco's international strategy is its dominant strategy—the alternative that is superior to any other strategy regardless of whatever Dramco does. Similarly, Dramco's international strategy is also its dominant strategy. With both firms choosing international strategies, the outcome of the game is cell A, where each firm receives an $11 million profit. Cell A is a Nash equilibrium because neither firm will independently want to move away from it given the other firm's strategy.

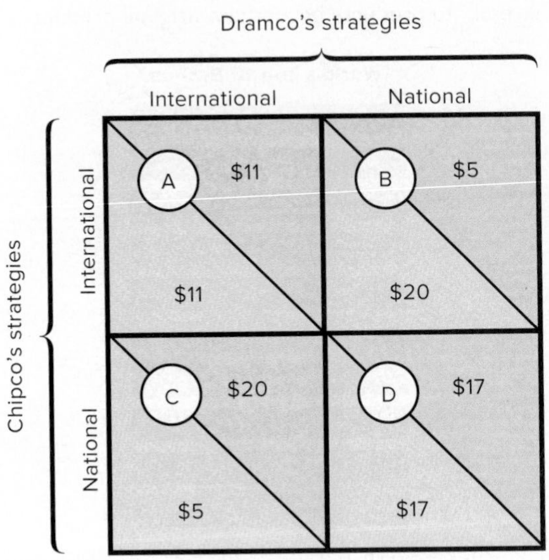

[1]The Nash equilibrium is named for its discoverer, John F. Nash. Nash's life and Nobel Prize are the subject of the motion picture A *Beautiful Mind,* directed by Ron Howard and starring Russell Crowe.

[2]Nash equilibriums can exist even in games that lack dominant strategies.

Credible and Empty Threats

In looking for optimal strategies, Chipco and Dramco both note that they could increase their profit from \$11 million to \$17 million if they could agree to jointly pursue national strategies (cell D) instead of independently pursuing international strategies (cell A). Presumably the national strategies would leave the firms as pure monopolists in their domestic economies, with each able to set higher prices and obtain greater profits as a result. But if this territorial agreement were put in place, both firms would have an incentive to cheat on the agreement by secretly selling DRAMs in the other's country. That would temporarily move the game to either cell B or cell C. Once discovered, however, such cheating would undermine the territorial agreement and return the game to the Nash equilibrium (cell A).

Now let's add a new twist—a credible threat—to the game shown in Figure 13.4. A **credible threat** is a statement of coercion (a threat!) that is believable by the other firm. Suppose that Chipco is the lower-cost producer of DRAMs because of its superior technology. Also, suppose that Chipco approaches Dramco saying that Chipco intends to use its national strategy and expects Dramco to do the same. If Dramco decides against the national strategy or agrees to the strategy and then later cheats on the agreement, Chipco will immediately drop its price to an ultra-low level equal to its average total cost (ATC). Both firms know that Chipco's ATC price is below Dramco's ATC. Although Chipco will see its economic profit fall to zero, Dramco will suffer an economic loss and possibly go out of business.

If Chipco's threat is credible, the two firms represented in Figure 13.4 will abandon the Nash equilibrium (cell A) to deploy their national strategies and achieve highly profitable cell D. In game theory, credible threats such as this can help establish and maintain collusive agreements. A strong "enforcer" can help prevent cheating and maintain the group discipline needed for cartels, price-fixing conspiracies, and territorial understandings to successfully generate high profits.

But credible threats are difficult to achieve in the actual economy. For example, Dramco might rightly wonder why Chipco had not previously driven it out of business through an ultra-low price strategy. Is Chipco fearful of the U.S. antitrust authorities?

If Dramco does not wish to participate in the proposed scheme, it might counter Chipco's threat with its own: Forget that you ever talked to us and we will not take this illegal "offer" to the U.S. Justice Department. Dramco can make this threat because strict laws are in place against attempts to restrain trade through price-fixing and territorial agreements.

So Dramco may view Chipco's threat as simply an **empty threat**—a statement of coercion that is not believable by the threatened firm. If so, the Nash equilibrium will prevail, with both firms pursuing an international strategy.

Repeated Games and Reciprocity Strategies

The Chipco-Dramco game was a one-time game, but many strategic situations are repeated by the same oligopolists over and over again. For example, Coca-Cola and Pepsi are mutually interdependent on pricing, advertising, and product development year after year, decade after decade. The same is true for Boeing and Airbus, Walmart and Target, Toyota and General Motors, Budweiser and Miller, Nike and Adidas, and numerous other dominant pairs.

In a **repeated game**—a game that recurs more than once—the optimal strategy may be to cooperate and restrain oneself from competing as hard as possible so long as the other firm reciprocates by also not competing as hard as possible.[3] To see how this works, consider two hypothetical producers of soft drinks: 2Cool and ThirstQ. If ThirstQ competes hard with 2Cool in today's situation in which 2Cool would like ThirstQ to take things easy, 2Cool will most likely retaliate against ThirstQ in any subsequent situation where the circumstances are reversed. In contrast, if ThirstQ cooperates with 2Cool in game 1, ThirstQ can expect 2Cool to reciprocate in game 2 of their repeated interaction. Both firms know full well the negative long-run consequences of ever refusing to cooperate. So the cooperation continues, not only in game 2, but in games 3, 4, 5, and beyond.

Figure 13.5 shows two side-by-side payoff matrixes for the two games. In Figure 13.5a, 2Cool and ThirstQ face a situation in which 2Cool is introducing a new cola called Cool Cola and has two advertising options: a high promotional budget to introduce the new product and a normal advertising budget. ThirstQ has the same two options: a high promotional budget to try to counter 2Cool's product introduction and a normal advertising budget.

The analysis is now familiar to you. The dominant strategies for both firms in game 1 (Figure 13.5a) are their large promotional advertising budgets and the Nash equilibrium is cell A. Both firms could do better at cell D if each agreed to use normal advertising budgets. But 2Cool could do better still. It could achieve the \$16 million of profit in cell B, but only if ThirstQ holds its advertising budget to its normal level during the introduction of Cool Cola.

ThirstQ might voluntarily do just that! It knows that game 2 (Figure 13.5b) is forthcoming in which it will be introducing its new product, Quench It. By leaving its advertising budget at its normal level during 2Cool's introduction of Cool Cola, and thereby sacrificing profit of \$2 million (= \$10 million in cell A – \$8 million in cell B), ThirstQ can expect 2Cool to reciprocate in the subsequent game in which ThirstQ introduces Quench It.

Without formally colluding—and risking antitrust penalties—game 1 ends at cell B and repeated game 2 ends at

[3]We are assuming either an infinitely repeated game or a game of unknown time horizon. Games with a known ending date undermine reciprocity strategies.

FIGURE 13.5 A repeated game with reciprocity. (a) In the first payoff matrix, 2Cool introduces its new Cool Cola with a large promotional advertising budget, but its rival ThirstQ maintains its normal advertising budget even though it could counter 2Cool with a large advertising budget of its own and drive the outcome from cell B to cell A. ThirstQ forgoes this $2 million of extra profit because it knows that it will soon be introducing its own new product (Quench It). (b) In the second payoff matrix, ThirstQ introduces Quench It with a large promotional advertising budget. Cool2 reciprocates ThirstQ's earlier accommodation by not matching ThirstQ's promotional advertising budget and instead allowing the outcome of the repeated game to be cell C. The profit of both 2Cool and ThirstQ therefore is larger over the two periods than if each firm had aggressively countered each other's single-period strategy.

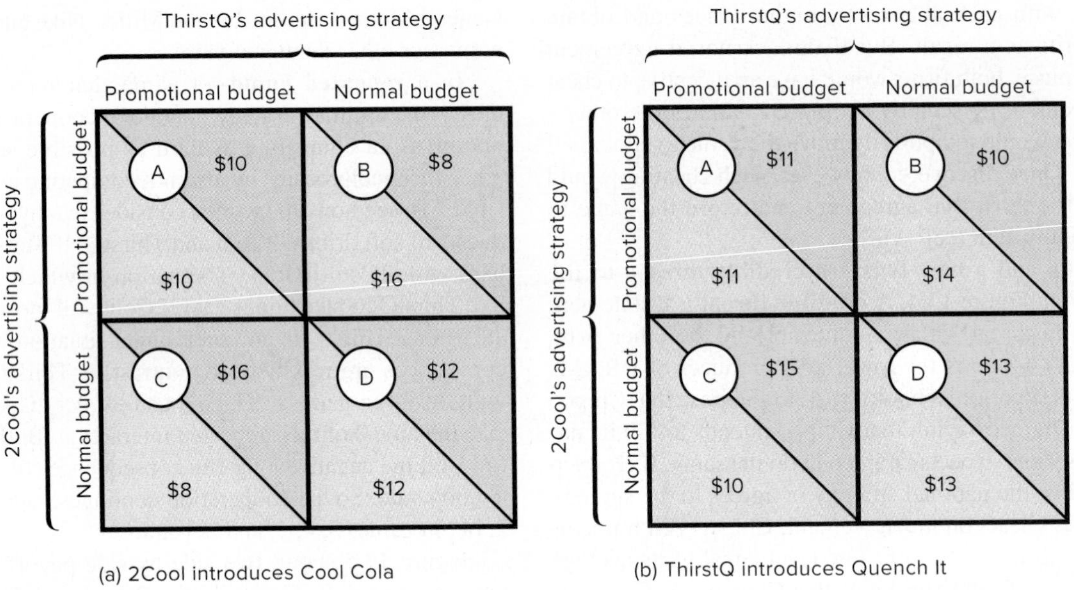

cell C. With reciprocity, 2Cool's total profit of $26 million (= $16 million in game 1 + $10 million in game 2) exceeds the $21 million (= $10 million + $11 million) it would have earned without the reciprocity. ThirstQ similarly benefits. To check your understanding, confirm this fact using the numbers in the two matrixes.

First-Mover Advantages and Preemption of Entry

The games we have highlighted thus far have been games in which the two firms simultaneously select their optimal strategies. But in some actual economic circumstances, firms apply strategies sequentially: One firm moves first and commits to a strategy to which a rival firm must subsequently respond. In such a **sequential game,** the final outcome may depend critically upon which firm moves first since the first mover may have the opportunity to establish a Nash equilibrium that works in its favor.

Consider Figure 13.6, which identifies a game in which two large retailers—let's call them Big Box and Huge Box—are each considering building a large retail store in a small rural city. As indicated in the figure, each firm has two strategies: Build or Don't Build. The payoff matrix reflects the fact that the city is not large enough to support two big box retailers profitably. If

FIGURE 13.6 A first-mover advantage and the preemption of entry. In this game in which strategies are pursued sequentially, the firm that moves first can take advantage of the particular situation represented in which only a single firm can exist profitably in some geographical market. Here, we suppose that Big Box moves first with its "Build" strategy to achieve the $12 million profit outcome in cell C. Huge Box then will find that it will lose money if it also builds because that will result in a $5 million loss, as shown in cell A.

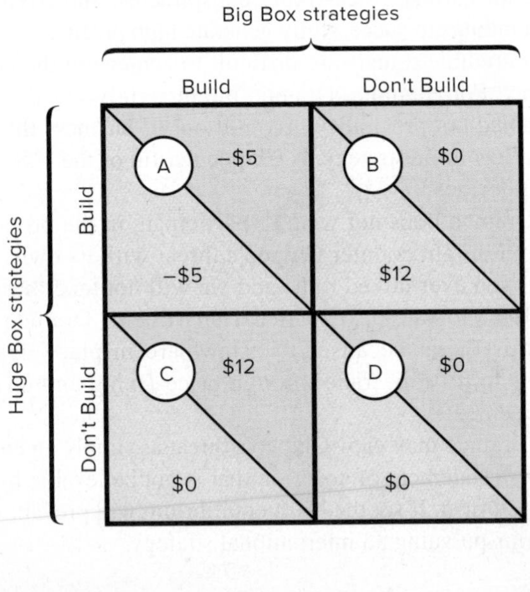

both retailers simultaneously build, the outcome will be cell A and each firm will lose $5 million. If neither firm builds, the outcome will be cell D with both firms securing zero profit. If only Big Box builds, the outcome will be cell C and Big Box will profit handsomely at $12 million. If Huge Box builds, but Big Box stays out, the outcome will be cell B and Huge Box will secure the $12 million profit. Either cell B or cell C is the possible Nash equilibrium. At either cell, both firms will have selected their best option in view of the strategy taken by the other firm.

The payoff matrix in Figure 13.6 clearly reveals that whoever builds first will preempt the other retailer from entering the market. An extremely large **first-mover advantage** exists in this particular game. Suppose that a well-thought-out strategy and adequate financing leave Big Box better prepared than Huge Box to move quickly to build a large retail store in this city. By exploiting its first-mover advantage, Big Box drives the outcome to Cell C and preempts Huge Box's entry into this market.

Many firms in the actual economy have used variations of this first-mover strategy to a greater or lesser extent to preempt major rivals, or at least greatly slow their entry. Examples are Walmart, Home Depot, Costco, Walgreens, Starbucks, and many more. The strategy, however, is highly risky because it requires the commitment of huge amounts of investment funds to saturate the market and preclude entry by other firms. Also, to be the first mover in places that are being transformed from rural land into urban areas, firms may need to build their stores many months prior to the time when the area in question becomes developed enough to provide the store with significant business. That may mean losses until the market grows sufficiently for profitability. Some firms such as Walmart have become huge, profitable international enterprises by using a first-mover strategy. Other firms, such as Krispy Kreme Donuts, have lost millions of dollars because their extremely rapid expansion turned out to be unprofitable in many of their outlets because the expected customers never materialized.

AP QUICK REVIEW 13.4

- ✓ In the basic game theory model, assume two rival firms, each with two strategies (e.g., raise or lower prices; advertise or not advertise). The outcomes, or profits, depend on what each firm does. These profits are displayed in a "pay-off matrix."
- ✓ Each firm chooses its best outcome considering what the other firm might do. When a firm has a set strategy that leads to better outcomes for it no matter what the rival firm does, then the firm is said to have a dominant strategy.
- ✓ A Nash equilibrium occurs when both firms are simultaneously playing dominant strategies, so that neither firm has any incentive to alter its behavior.
- ✓ Reciprocity can improve outcomes in repeated games.

Extensive Form Representation of Sequential Games

Summarizing a game using a payoff matrix is referred to as displaying the game in strategic form because the rows and columns of the matrix represent each firm's strategy choices (such as Build or Don't Build in Figure 13.6). But sequential games can also be displayed in an alternative format called extensive form in which an extensive (spread out) "game tree" is used to display not only which strategy choices are available but the order in which decisions are made, starting with the first mover.

Figure 13.7 presents the extensive form representation of the first-mover game that was displayed in strategic form in Figure 13.6. As you will recall, Big Box (BB) gets to move first and then Huge Box (HB) gets to move second. There are three circular **decision nodes** labeled BB, HB_1, and HB_2. Decision node BB represents the two choices that Big Box must choose between as first mover. It can either choose Build or Don't Build. If it chooses Build, we follow the upsloping path from decision node BB. But if Big Box chooses Don't Build, we take the downsloping path from decision note BB.

The upsloping path leads to decision node HB_1 while the downsloping path leads to decision node HB_2. HB_1 represents the decision that Huge Box will have to face as second mover if Big Box has chosen Build in the first stage. HB_2 represents the choice that Huge Box will have to face as second mover if Big Box has chosen Don't Build in the first stage. In either case, Huge Box must choose either Build or Don't Build. Those choices lead to the **terminal nodes** A, C, B, and D, which correspond to the identically labeled cells in the strategic form representation shown in Figure 13.6.

Associated with each terminal node is a pair of numbers representing the profits that will be earned by each firm if the sequential decisions made by Big Box and Huge Box lead to that particular terminal node. The profits are presented as a pair of numbers in the format: (Big Box profit, Huge Box profit). As an example, the profits of the two firms at terminal node C are $12 million for Big Box and $0 for Huge Box.

In Figure 13.7, two segments of the game tree have been drawn bolder to make them stand out: the upsloping segment that begins at BB and the downsloping segment that begins at HB_1. The lines are bolded because they represent the Nash equilibrium of the game. The way you determine the Nash Equilibrium when a game is displayed in extensive form is by using a two-stage process called **backward induction** that first divides the overall game tree into nested "subgames" before working backwards from right to left—from the profits shown at each terminal node on the right to the preceding decisions that are necessary to end up at any particular terminal node.

To see how this works, notice that the upsloping and downsloping choices that emanate from decision node HB_1 form a **subgame** (or mini-game) within the overall game. Starting from HB_1, Huge Box can choose either Build or

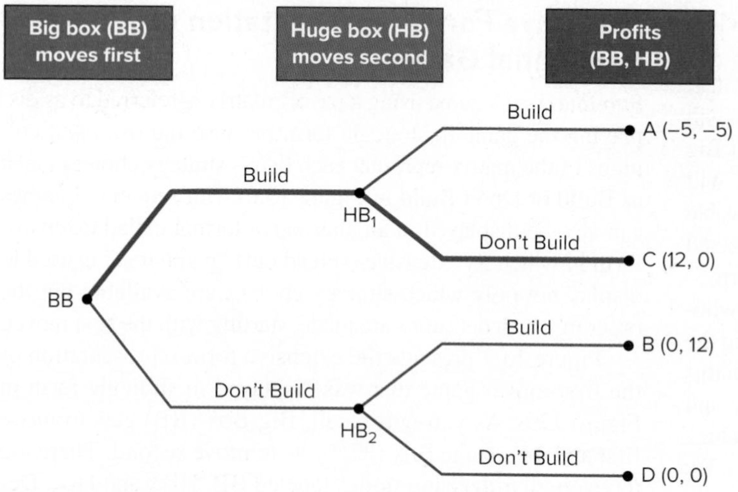

FIGURE 13.7 Extensive form representation of first-mover advantage and the preemption of entry. Here we display the game shown in Figure 13.6 in extensive form (game-tree format) rather than in strategic form (payoff-matrix format). The extensive form allows us to study the sequence in which decisions are made, moving from left to right. Big Box (BB) moves first at decision node BB. Its decision about Build or Don't Build will lead, respectively, to either decision node HB_1 or HB_2. Huge Box moves second from either HB_1 or HB_2 (depending upon what Big Box did at decision node BB). Huge Box's decision at HB_1 or HB_2 will lead to one of the four terminal nodes: A, C, B, and D (which correspond to the identically labeled cells in Figure 13.6). The bold line segments indicate the subgame perfect Nash equilibrium path that shows how the game will be played out if each company always does what is most profitable for itself given what it knows about the profit incentives facing its rival.

Don't Build. If we look at the payouts from those two choices, we see that Huge Box would prefer Don't Build so that it will receive a profit of $0 at terminal node C rather than a loss of –$5 million at terminal node A. So in the subgame that starts at decision node HB_1, Huge Box would prefer Don't Build. By contrast, in the subgame that starts at decision node HB_2, Huge box would prefer Build over Don't Build because choosing Build would lead to a profit of $12 million while choosing Don't Build would lead to a profit of $0.

We now know that if Huge Box ends up at decision node HB_1 it will choose Don't Build, so that the overall game will end at terminal node C. We also know that if Huge Box ends up at decision node HB_2 it will choose Build, thus forcing the overall game to end up at terminal node B. Those facts will be known perfectly well not only to us but to the managers of Big Box, too. So when Big Box makes its choice as the first mover at decision node BB, it will know that choosing Build will definitely lead to terminal node C because Huge Box will definitely choose Don't Build if it finds itself at decision node HB_1. Big Box will also understand that if it chooses Don't Build at decision node BB, the game will end up at terminal node B because Huge Box will definitely choose Build if it finds itself at decision node HB_2.

Thus, from Big Box's perspective, choosing Build will lead to the profits associated with C while choosing Don't Build will lead to the profits associated with B. Thus, Big Box's optimal decision at decision node BB comes down to seeing whether it will profit more highly at C than at B. If we compare Big Box's profits at C and B, we find that Big Box would prefer to end up at C rather than B because its profit at C would be $12 million while its profit at B would be $0. As a result, Big Box will choose Build at decision node BB. That choice leads upward to decision node HB_1, where Huge Box will definitely choose Don't Build. And that decision, in turn, will lead to both firms receiving the profits associated with terminal node C.

The two bold segments of the game tree show the path that results from those sequential decisions. It is a Nash equilibrium from which neither party has an incentive to deviate because by working backward from right to left through each of the subgames we have made sure that both firms will be making rational (profit-maximizing) choices at every decision node. Thus, when the game is played out in proper sequence from left to right, neither firm will want to deviate from the decisions indicated by the bold path. Economists sometimes refer to the bold path as the **subgame perfect Nash equilibrium** because the process of backward induction used to find the bold path relies on both firms having perfect information about (i.e., a complete understanding of) the decisions that will be made in each subgame.

Note that the subgame perfect Nash equilibrium path shown in Figure 13.7 implies the same outcome with regard to preemption of entry as we discovered when we studied the same game in strategic form in Figure 13.6. Along the bold equilibrium path, Big Box will choose Build as first mover and Huge Box will chose Don't Build as second mover. As a result, Big Box will be able to preempt Huge Box from entering the local market.

A Leader-Follower (Stackelberg Duopoly) Game

Extensive form representation and backward induction can also be used to solve for situations in which a leader (first mover) firm cannot preempt a follower firm from entering its industry. The subgame perfect Nash equilibrium involves both firms entering the industry and producing positive levels of output.

As an example, let us consider a duopoloy (two-firm) automobile manufacturing industry in which both firms have to make sequential decisions about factory size and output levels. In other duopoly models, both firms move simultaneously. But in this section we are assuming a Stackelberg duopoly model in which the two competitors move sequentially.

In this sequential model, an established truck maker that has political connections will get to move first and decide how big a factory it will build. Its rival will then move second and determine how big its factory will be. Both firms are aware that the more the two firms produce and supply in total, the lower will be the market price of trucks. So there is a trade-off between building higher-capacity factories on the one hand and getting less revenue per truck on the other hand.

In this strategic situation, the leader firm's choice of factory size must attempt to rationally anticipate what the follower firm's factory-size choice will be. As an example, if the leader firm anticipates that the follower firm will end up building a huge factory, the leader firm may want to build a small factory to keep total output low enough that the market price of trucks does not collapse.

In Figure 13.8, the leader firm chooses first, at decision node L. Its choices are to either set up a smaller factory that can produce 5,000 trucks per year or a larger factory that can produce 10,000 trucks per year. If the leader firm chooses the smaller factory, the upward sloping option will lead to decision node F_1, where the follower firm can either choose to set up a factory that will produce 7,000 trucks per year or a factory that can produce 12,000 trucks per year. Note that when starting at decision node F_1, both of the follower firm's factory-size options will produce more vehicles per year than the 5,000 trucks per year that the leader firm would have had to have chosen at decision node L to have moved the game to decision node F_1. This reflects the fact that the follower firm would take the leader firm's decision to produce only 5,000 cars per year as an opportunity to become the larger player in the two-firm industry. The only question for the follower firm at decision node F_1 is to decide on how much larger it will want its output of trucks to be.

By contrast, if the leader firm chooses to build the larger factory at decision node L, the game will follow the downsloping path to decision node F_2, where the follower firm can either choose to set up a factory that will produce 5,000 cars per year or a factory that will produce 7,000 cars per year. In this case, the follower firm is resigned to being the smaller firm in the industry, since both options will produce fewer cars per year than the 10,000 that the leader would have had to have chosen for the game to have ended up at decision node F_2.

We can now use subgames and backward induction to solve for the subgame perfect Nash equilibrium, which is indicated in Figure 13.8 by the bold segments of the game tree. As before, we solve the game tree backward, from right to left. Consider first the subgame that begins at decision node F_1. There, the follower firm will want to choose to produce 7,000 cars per year because the \$210 million profit it would obtain from doing so will be nearly double the \$120 million profit it would obtain if it chose to produce 12,000 cars per year. Next, consider the subgame that begins at decision node F_2. There, the follower firm will want to produce 7,000 cars per year rather than 5,000 cars per year because the former will generate a profit of \$140 million per year while the latter would generate a profit of only \$50 million per year.

The leader firm can now take into account at decision node L how the follower firm will behave if the game ends up at either decision node F_1 or decision node F_2. If the leader firm chooses to produce 5,000 cars per year at decision node L, the follower firm will choose to produce 7,000 cars at decision node F_1, thereby leading to terminal node A and a payoff of \$150 million for the leader firm. By contrast, if the leader firm chooses to produce 10,000 cars per year at decision node L, the follower firm will choose to produce 7,000 cars per year at decision node F_2, thereby leading to terminal node D and a payoff of \$200 million for the leader firm.

The leader firm can see that it would be better off ending up at terminal node D rather than at terminal node A. It will consequently choose to build a factory that can produce 10,000 cars per year. The subgame perfect Nash equilibrium therefore consists of the line segment that leads downward from decision node L followed by the line segment that leads

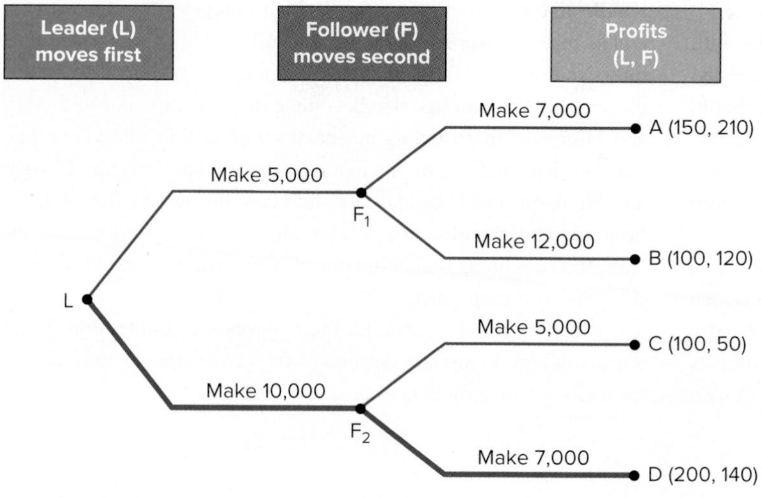

FIGURE 13.8 Extensive form representation of leader-follower (Stackelberg duopoly) game. There is a Leader firm and a Follower firm that sequentially must decide on their respective factory sizes. The Leader firm moves first at decision node L. The Follower firm moves second, starting from either decision node F_1 or decision node F_2 (depending on the Leader firm's decision at decision node L). Each firm wishes to make as much money as possible, but knows that there is a trade-off between producing more cars and reducing the market price per vehicle. Moving from right to left, backward induction indicates that the subgame perfect Nash equilibrium corresponds to the path indicated by the bold line segments.

LAST WORD

Internet Oligopolies

A Few Big Companies Dominate the Internet—and Act as Highly Competitive Oligopolists.

The Internet only became accessible to the average person in the mid-1990s. Over the past 10 years, it has evolved into a medium dominated by a few major firms. Chief among them are Google, Facebook, and Amazon. Other major players include Microsoft and Apple.

A key characteristic of each of these firms is that it holds a near-monopoly in a particular part of the tech business. Google dominates search. Facebook holds sway in social networking. Amazon rules the roost in online shopping. Microsoft holds a near-monopoly on PC operating systems and business-productivity software. And Apple became the world's most valuable company in 2012 by way of being the planet's most profitable manufacturer of computers, mobile phones, and tablets—all of which run on Apple's own operating software.

Source: © Anatolii Babii/Alamy Stock Photo

But instead of just trying to maintain dominance in its own sector, each of these Internet titans has used the profits generated by its own near-monopoly to try to steal business from one or more of the other titans. The result has been intense oligopolistic competition between a few well-funded rivals.

Consider search. Google's 64 percent share of the search market creates massive amounts of advertising revenue for Google. In fact, Google's 2015 ad revenues of $16 billion exceeded the ad revenues received by all U.S. magazines and newspapers combined. So it may not be surprising that Microsoft created its Bing search engine to compete with Google. As of late 2015, Bing held 21 percent of the search market. Along with Yahoo, which held 13 percent, Bing maintains competitive pressure on Google, forcing ad rates lower.

Facebook is by far the largest social networking website, with more than 1.8 billion regular users. But in 2011, Google succeeded in creating a large enough social network to challenge Facebook. Google did so by encouraging the users of its various free services—such as Gmail and YouTube—to join the Google+ social network. By late 2012, Google+ had 500 million total users and 235 million regular users—enough to compete credibly with Facebook.

Google+ was important for Google because Facebook had been encouraging advertisers to switch from using Google search ads to using Facebook banner ads that could be targeted at specific types of Facebook users (such as, "25–30-year-old males with pets living in Pittsburgh"). Google can now counter by offering its own social network on which advertisers can place those sorts of targeted ads.

Google has also challenged Apple by releasing its very popular Android operating system for mobile devices to compete with the iOS operating system that Apple uses on both its iPhone cell phones and its iPad tablet computers. By doing so, Google reduced the threat that Apple could at some point in the future substantially reduce Google's search revenues by directing searches done on Apple devices to a proprietary search engine of Apple's own design.

Apple's dominance in smartphones and tablets has also been challenged by some of the other Internet titans. In addition to licensing the Android operating system to any manufacturer who wants to use it on their own cell phones or tablets, Google launched its own line of Nexus mobile devices to compete with Apple's iPhone and iPad. Also seeking to challenge Apple in mobile devices, Microsoft updated its Windows operating system to handle phones and tablets, launched its Surface line of tablets to compete with the iPad, and attempted to compete with the iPhone by marketing its own Windows Phone as well as by purchasing long-time cell-phone maker Nokia.

Microsoft's fundamental problem is that smartphone and tablet sales are rising rapidly while PC sales are falling quickly. So unless Microsoft can generate revenues from smartphones, tablets, or search, it will suffer an inexorable decline as the PC sector continues to shrink.

Amazon has also made forays outside of the online retail sector that it dominates. The foray best known to the general public is its Kindle line of tablet computers, which compete directly with the tablets made by Apple, Google, Microsoft, and the various manufacturers that utilize Google's Android operating system. But behind the scenes, Amazon has also become a major competitor to Google and Microsoft in providing businesses with online "cloud computing" services that run on the massive servers that Amazon, Google, and Microsoft must maintain for their core businesses (like search). So in cloud computing, too, we see oligopoly competition resulting from Internet titans branching out of their own dominant sectors to compete with each other.

There's a simple reason for their aggressive competition. When a near-monopoly already dominates its own sector, its only chance for major profit growth is to invade a rival's sector.

downward from decision node F_2. Along that path, neither firm has any reason to change its behavior given the perfect (complete) knowledge it possesses about both its own incentives and those of the other firm.

Note that there is no preemption of entry in this game. Both firms produce, but at different levels of output. The leader firm produces more and the follower firm produces less. This intuition can be generalized from duopoly industries with just two firms to oligopoly industries with several firms. The leader goes first but the profit possibilities at the various terminal nodes imply a subgame perfect Nash equilibrium in which additional firms enter the industry as followers. The followers produce less than the leader but are still able to survive and carry on. Examples include microchips, where Intel was the leader and several other firms such as AMD became followers, and smartphones, where Apple was the leader and several other firms such as Samsung, LG, and Google became followers.

Please note, however, that once entry has occurred and competition is possible, it may be the case that one or more of the follower firms may come to dominate the industry, pushing aside the leader firm that once held sway. This happened with televisions. Early leaders such as Sylvania got pushed aside in the 1980s by Japanese brands such as Sony before Korean brands such as Samsung came to dominate in the 2000s.

SUMMARY

LO13.1 Describe the characteristics of oligopoly.

Oligopolistic industries are characterized by the presence of few firms, each having a significant fraction of the market. Firms thus situated engage in strategic behavior and are mutually interdependent: The behavior of any one firm directly affects, and is affected by, the actions of rivals. Products may be either virtually uniform or significantly differentiated. Various barriers to entry, including economies of scale, underlie and maintain oligopoly.

High concentration ratios are an indication of oligopoly (monopoly) power. By giving more weight to larger firms, the Herfindahl index is designed to measure market dominance in an industry.

LO13.2 Discuss how game theory relates to oligopoly.

Game theory (*a*) shows the interdependence of oligopolists' pricing policies, (*b*) reveals the tendency of oligopolists to collude, and (*c*) explains the temptation of oligopolists to cheat on collusive arrangements.

LO13.3 Explain the three main models of oligopoly pricing and output: kinked-demand theory, collusive pricing, and price leadership.

Noncollusive oligopolists may face a kinked-demand curve. This curve and the accompanying marginal-revenue curve help explain the price rigidity that often characterizes oligopolies; they do not, however, explain how the actual prices of products were first established.

The uncertainties inherent in oligopoly promote collusion. Collusive oligopolists such as cartels maximize joint profits—that is, they behave like pure monopolists. Demand and cost differences, a "large" number of firms, cheating through secret price concessions, recessions, and the antitrust laws are all obstacles to collusive oligopoly.

Price leadership is an informal means of collusion whereby one firm, usually the largest or most efficient, initiates price changes and the other firms in the industry follow the leader.

LO13.4 Contrast the potential positive and negative effects of advertising.

Market shares in oligopolistic industries are usually determined on the basis of product development and advertising. Oligopolists emphasize nonprice competition because (*a*) advertising and product variations are less easy for rivals to match and (*b*) oligopolists frequently have ample resources to finance nonprice competition.

Advertising may affect prices, competition, and efficiency either positively or negatively. Positive: It can provide consumers with low-cost information about competing products, help introduce new competing products into concentrated industries, and generally reduce monopoly power and its attendant inefficiencies. Negative: It can promote monopoly power via persuasion and the creation of entry barriers. Moreover, it can be self-canceling when engaged in by rivals; then it boosts costs and creates inefficiency while accomplishing little else.

LO13.5 Discuss the efficiency of oligopoly from society's standpoint and whether it is more or less efficient than monopoly.

Neither productive nor allocative efficiency is realized in oligopolistic markets, but oligopoly may be superior to pure competition in promoting research and development and technological progress.

Table 10.1 provides a concise review of the characteristics of monopolistic competition and oligopoly as they compare to those of pure competition and pure monopoly.

LO13.6 Utilize additional game-theory terminology and demonstrate how to find Nash equilibriums in both simultaneous and sequential games.

Positive-sum games are games in which the payoffs to the firms sum to a positive number; zero-sum games are games in which the payoffs sum to zero; and negative-sum games are games in which the payoffs sum to less than zero. Positive-sum games allow for "win-win" opportunities, whereas zero-sum games always feature "I win–you lose" outcomes. Games can be either one-time games or repeated games. Decisions in games may be made either simultaneously or sequentially.

When two firms are playing a strategic game, a firm is said to have a dominant strategy if there is an option that leads to better outcomes for the firm no matter what the other firm does. Not all games have dominant strategies. The Nash equilibrium is an outcome from which neither firm wants to deviate because both firms see their current strategy as optimal given the other firm's chosen strategy. The Nash equilibrium is stable and persistent. Attempts by the firms to rig games to achieve some other outcome are difficult to accomplish and maintain, although credible threats can sometimes work. In contrast, empty threats accomplish nothing and leave the outcome at the Nash equilibrium.

Reciprocity can improve outcomes for firms participating in repeated games. In such games, one firm avoids taking advantage of the other firm because it knows that the other firm can take advantage of it in subsequent games. This reciprocity increases firm profits relative to what they would have been without reciprocity.

Two possible Nash equilibriums can exist in sequential games with first-mover advantages. Which one occurs depends on which firm moves first since that firm can preempt the other firm, making it unprofitable for the other firm to match the choice made by the firm that moves first. Several real-world firms, including Walmart, have successfully used first-mover advantages to saturate markets and preempt entry by rivals.

Sequential games can be represented as game trees in extensive form. In extensive form, the order of decisions made by players is displayed in sequence from left to right. The game can be solved for a subgame perfect Nash equilibrium by using backward induction to examine each of the overall game's nested subgames from right to left.

TERMS AND CONCEPTS

oligopoly
homogeneous oligopoly
differentiated oligopoly
strategic behavior
mutual interdependence
interindustry competition
import competition
game theory
collusion
kinked-demand curve
price war
cartel
price leadership
one-time game
simultaneous game
positive-sum game
zero-sum game
negative-sum game
dominant strategy
Nash equilibrium
credible threat
empty threat
repeated game
sequential game
first-mover advantage
decision node
terminal node
backward induction
subgame
subgame perfect Nash equilibrium

The following and additional problems can be found in connect

DISCUSSION QUESTIONS

1. Why do oligopolies exist? List five or six oligopolists whose products you own or regularly purchase. What distinguishes oligopoly from monopolistic competition? LO13.1
2. Answer the following questions, which relate to measures of concentration: LO13.1
   a. What is the meaning of a four-firm concentration ratio of 60 percent? 90 percent? What are the shortcomings of concentration ratios as measures of monopoly power?
   b. Suppose that the five firms in industry A have annual sales of 30, 30, 20, 10, and 10 percent of total industry sales. For the five firms in industry B, the figures are 60, 25, 5, 5, and 5 percent. Calculate the Herfindahl index for each industry and compare their likely competitiveness.
3. Explain the general meaning of the profit payoff matrix below for oligopolists X and Y. All profit figures are in thousands. LO13.2
   a. Use the payoff matrix to explain the mutual interdependence that characterizes oligopolistic industries.
   b. Assuming no collusion between X and Y, what is the likely pricing outcome?

c. In view of your answer to 3b, explain why price collusion is mutually profitable. Why might there be a temptation to cheat on the collusive agreement?

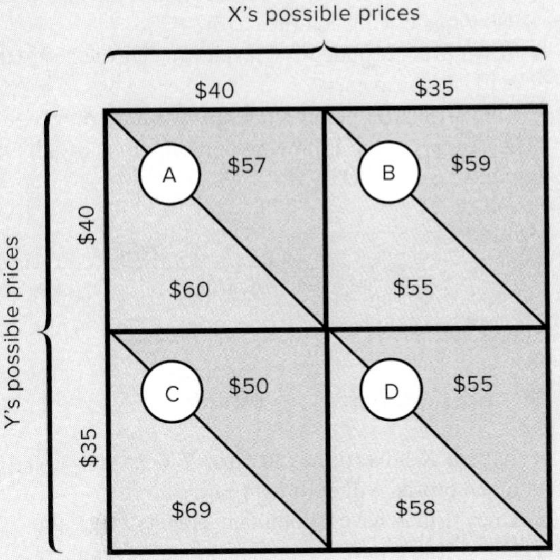

4. What assumptions about a rival's response to price changes underlie the kinked-demand curve for oligopolists? Why is there a gap in the oligopolist's marginal-revenue curve? How does the kinked-demand curve explain price rigidity in oligopoly? What are the shortcomings of the kinked-demand model? **LO13.3**

5. Why might price collusion occur in oligopolistic industries? Assess the economic desirability of collusive pricing. What are the main obstacles to collusion? Speculate as to why price leadership is legal in the United States, whereas price-fixing is not. **LO13.3**

6. Why is there so much advertising in monopolistic competition and oligopoly? How does such advertising help consumers and promote efficiency? Why might it be excessive at times? **LO13.4**

7. **ADVANCED ANALYSIS** Construct a strategic form payoff matrix involving two firms and their decisions on high versus low advertising budgets and the effects of each on profits. Show a circumstance in which both firms select high advertising budgets even though both would be more profitable with low advertising budgets. Why won't they unilaterally cut their advertising budgets? **LO13.4**

8. Is the game shown by Figure 13.1 a zero-sum game or is it a positive-sum game? How can you tell? Are there dominant strategies in this game? If so, what are they? What cell represents a Nash equilibrium and why? Explain why it is so difficult for Uptown and RareAir to achieve and maintain a more favorable cell than the Nash equilibrium in this single-period pricing game. **LO13.6**

9. Refer to the payoff matrix in discussion question 3. First, assume this is a one-time game. Explain how the $60/$57 outcome might be achieved through a credible threat. Next, assume this is a repeated game (rather than a one-time game) and that the interaction between the two firms occurs indefinitely. Why might collusion with a credible threat not be necessary to achieve the $60/$57 outcome? **LO13.6**

10. Refer to the following payoff matrix. **LO13.6**

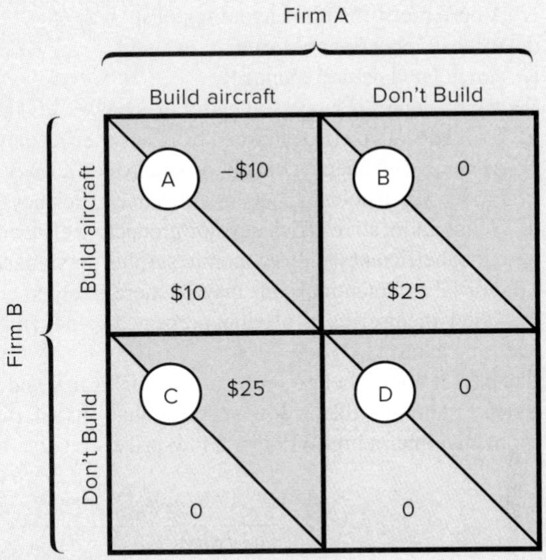

Assuming this is a sequential game with no collusion, what is the outcome if Firm A moves first to build a new type of commercial aircraft? Explain why first-mover strategies in the real world are only as good as the profit projections on which they are based. How could a supposed "win" from moving first turn out to be a big loss, whereas the "loss" of being preempted turn out to be a blessing in disguise?

11. **ADVANCED ANALYSIS** Suppose you are playing a game in which you and one other person each picks a number between 1 and 100, with the person closest to some randomly selected number between 1 and 100 winning the jackpot. (Ask your instructor to fund the jackpot.) Your opponent picks first. What number do you expect her to choose? Why? What number would you then pick? Why are the two numbers so close? How might this example relate to why Home Depot and Lowes, Walgreens and Rite-Aid, McDonald's and Burger King, and other major pairs of rivals locate so close to each other in many well-defined geographical markets that are large enough for both firms to be profitable? **LO13.6**

12. Are the subgames of a sequential game visible when the entire game is presented in strategic form? Explain. **LO13.6**

13. Can backward induction be readily applied when a sequential game is presented as a payoff matrix? Discuss. **LO13.6**

14. **LAST WORD** Why have tech firms with near monopolies in their own sectors sought to compete with tech firms that have extremely strong, near-monopoly positions in other sectors?

AP REVIEW QUESTIONS

1. Consider an oligopoly industry whose firms have identical demand and cost conditions. If the firms decide to collude, then they will want to collectively produce the amount of output that would be produced by: LO13.3
   a. A monopolistic competitor.
   b. A pure competitor.
   c. A pure profit-maximizing monopolist.
   d. Allocatively efficient firms.
   e. A regulated natural monopoly.
2. We would expect a successful cartel to achieve: LO13.3
   a. Both allocative efficiency and productive efficiency.
   b. Allocative efficiency, but not productive efficiency.
   c. Productive efficiency, but not allocative efficiency.
   d. Neither allocative efficiency nor productive efficiency.
   e. Global efficiency with economic surplus maximized.
3. True or false. Potential rivals may be more likely to collude if they view themselves as playing a repeated game rather than a one-time game. LO13.6
4. The payoff matrix below shows profits for firm X and for firm Y (X, Y) under the following combinations of the firms choosing either a high-price or a low-price strategy. LO13.6

		Firm Y	
		High Price	Low Price
Firm X	High Price	150, 150	80, 200
	Low Price	200, 90	100, 100

   a. What will be the result when each firm chooses a high-price strategy?
   b. What will be the result when Firm X chooses a low-price strategy while Firm Y maintains a high-price strategy?
   c. Does Firm X have a dominant strategy? If so, which?
   d. Does firm Y have a dominant strategy? If so, which?
   e. In the absence of any collusion what result can be expected? How much will each firm earn?
   f. If the firms collude what result can be expected? How much will each firm earn?
5. The payoff matrix below shows profits for firm X and for firm Y (X, Y) under the following combinations of advertising or not advertising. LO13.6

		Firm Y	
		Advertise	Not Advertise
Firm X	Advertise	300, 200	350, 250
	Not Advertise	200, 350	400, 400

   a. If firm X advertises and firm Y does not advertise, how much profits will each firm earn?
   b. Does firm X have a dominant strategy? Explain.
   c. Does firm Y have a dominant strategy? Explain
   d. If both firms are aware of this payoff matrix and act independently, what will be the result and the profits for each firm?
6. Look back at Figure 13.7. Suppose that the payouts at terminal node B change to (13,12) while everything else in the game stays the same. The new subgame perfect Nash equilibrium will consist of the two line segments: LO13.6
   a. Build at BB followed by Build at HB_1.
   b. Build at BB followed by Don't Build at HB_1.
   c. Don't Build at BB followed by Build at HB_2.
   d. Don't Build at BB followed by Don't Build at HB_2.
   e. Don't Build at BB followed by Don't Build at HB_1.

PROBLEMS

1. Consider a "punishment" variation of the two-firm oligopoly situation shown in Figure 13.1. Suppose that if one firm sets a low price while the other sets a high price, then the firm setting the high price can fine the firm setting the low price. Suppose that whenever a fine is imposed, *X* dollars is taken from the low-price firm and given to the high-price firm. What is the smallest amount that the fine *X* can be such that both firms will want to always set the high price? LO13.6
2. Consider whether the promises and threats made toward each other by duopolists and oligopolists are always credible (believable). Look back at Figure 13.1. Imagine that the two firms will play this game twice in sequence and that each firm claims the following policy. Each says that if both it and the other firm choose the high price in the first game, then it will also choose the high price in the second game (as a reward to the other firm for cooperating in the first game). LO13.6
   a. As a first step toward thinking about whether this policy is credible, consider the situation facing both firms in the second game. If each firm bases its decision on what to do in the second game entirely on the payouts facing the firms in the second game, which strategy will each firm choose in the second game?
   b. Now move backward in time one step. Imagine that it is the start of the first game and each firm must decide what to do during the first game. Given your answer to 2a, is the publicly stated policy credible? (Hint: No matter what happens in the first game, what will both firms do in the second game?)

c. Given your answers to 2a and 2b, what strategy will each firm choose in the first game?

3. Examine the following game tree. Fred and Sally are planning on running competing restaurants. Each must decide whether to rent space or buy space. Fred goes first at decision node F. Sally goes second at either decision node S_1 or decision node S_2 (depending on what Fred chose to do at decision node F). Note that the payoff to Sally at terminal node A is X. **LO13.6**

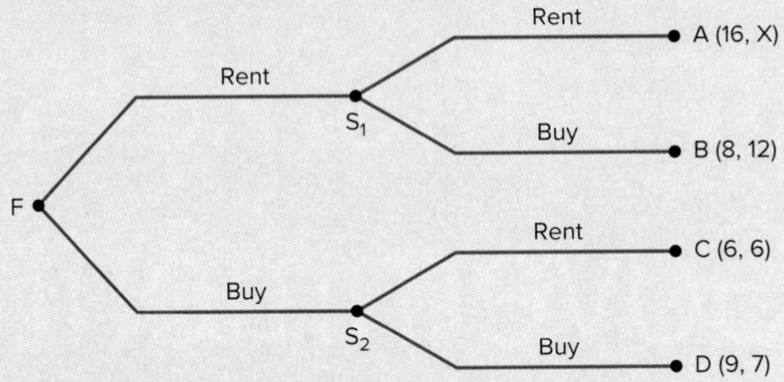

a. If $X < 12$, what terminal node will the subgame perfect Nash equilibrium path lead to?

b. If $X > 12$, what terminal node will the subgame perfect Nash Equilibrium path lead to?

c. Suppose that $X = 11$ and that it is now possible for Fred to make a side payment of value V to Sally that will boost her payout at terminal node A from $X = 11$ to $X = 11 + V$. What is the minimum amount that V can be such that the subgame perfect Nash equilibrium path will lead to terminal node A? Assume that V can take on only discrete units (0, 1, 2, 3,...).

AP Part FIVE

Microeconomics of Resource Markets and Government

Here in Part V, we turn to the input, or ***resource market.*** Remember the actual usage of resources is vital to production; the prices of resources determine the market income of individuals and households. Recall that in the resource market, the demanders of resources are the firms who wish to hire resources to produce output to earn economic profits. The suppliers of resources are the individuals who supply labor and financial capital in order earn income to buy goods and services. Even with the firms and individuals switched as demanders and sellers, competitive input markets continue to share many of the same characteristics as competitive output markets. We will look first at the firm's hiring of resources, called a ***derived demand,*** as the demand is derived from or linked to consumer demand for the goods produced by the resources, or the inputs. Then we look specifically at the labor markets and the market for capital. This part concludes with a summary of the government's role in markets.

Chapter 14

The Demand for Resources

Learning Objectives

LO14.1 **Explain the significance of resource pricing.**

LO14.2 **Convey how the marginal revenue productivity of a resource relates to a firm's demand for that resource.**

LO14.3 **List the factors that increase or decrease resource demand.**

LO14.4 **Discuss the determinants of elasticity of resource demand.**

LO14.5 **Determine how a competitive firm selects its optimal combination of resources.**

LO14.6 **Explain the marginal productivity theory of income distribution.**

AP Chapter Focus

We now turn from pricing and production of goods and services to pricing and employment of resources. In reference to the circular flow model, we shift our attention from the bottom loop of the diagram (where businesses supply products that households demand) to the top loop (where businesses demand resources that households supply).

When you finish your education and go to look for a job, why would someone want to hire you? The answer is that you have a lot to offer. Employers have a demand for educated, productive workers. Although firms come in various sizes and operate under different market conditions, each has a demand for resources in order to produce their goods or services. Firms obtain these resources from households—the direct or indirect owners of land, labor, capital, and entrepreneurial resources.

This chapter looks at the *demand* for economic resources. Although the discussion is couched in terms of labor, the principles developed also apply to land, capital, and entrepreneurial ability. In Chapter 15 we will combine resource (labor) demand with labor *supply* to analyze wage rates. In Chapter 16 we will use resource demand and resource supply to examine the prices of, and returns to, other productive resources.

Significance of Resource Pricing

LO14.1 Explain the significance of resource pricing.

Studying resource pricing is important for several reasons:

- ***Money-income determination*** Resource prices are a major factor in determining the income of households. The expenditures that firms make in acquiring economic resources flow as wage, rent, interest, and profit incomes to the households that supply those resources.
- ***Cost minimization*** To the firm, resource prices are costs. And to obtain the greatest profit, the firm must produce the profit-maximizing output with the most efficient (least costly) combination of resources. Resource prices play the main role in determining the quantities of land, labor, capital, and entrepreneurial ability that will be combined in producing each good or service (see Table 2.1).
- ***Resource allocation*** Just as product prices allocate finished goods and services to consumers, resource prices allocate resources among industries and firms. In a dynamic economy, where technology and product demand often change, the efficient allocation of resources over time calls for the continuing shift of resources from one use to another. Resource pricing is a major factor in producing those shifts.
- ***Policy issues*** Many policy issues surround the resource market. Examples: To what extent should government redistribute income through taxes and transfers? Should government do anything to discourage "excess" pay to corporate executives? Should it increase the legal minimum wage? Is the provision of subsidies to farmers efficient? Should government encourage or restrict labor unions? The facts and debates relating to these policy questions are grounded on resource pricing.

AP Marginal Productivity Theory of Resource Demand

LO14.2 Convey how the marginal revenue productivity of a resource relates to a firm's demand for that resource.

In discussing resource demand, we will first assume that a firm sells its output in a purely competitive product market and hires a certain resource in a purely competitive resource market. This assumption keeps things simple and is consistent with the model of a competitive labor market that we will develop in Chapter 15. In a competitive *product market,* the firm is a "price taker" and can dispose of as little or as much output as it chooses at the market price. The firm is selling such a negligible fraction of total output that its output decisions exert no influence on product price. Similarly, the firm also is a "price taker" (or "wage taker") in the competitive *resource market*. It purchases such a negligible fraction of the total supply of the resource that its buying (or hiring) decisions do not influence the resource price.

Resource Demand as a Derived Demand

Resource demand is the starting point for any discussion of resource prices. Resource demand is a schedule or a curve showing the amounts of a resource that buyers are willing and able to purchase at various prices over some period of time. Crucially, resource demand is a **derived demand,** meaning that the demand for a resource is derived from the demand for the products that the resource helps to produce. This is true because resources usually do not directly satisfy customer wants but do so indirectly through their use in producing goods and services. Almost nobody wants to consume an acre of land, a John Deere tractor, or the labor services of a farmer, but millions of households do want to consume the food and fiber products that these resources help produce. Similarly, the demand for airplanes generates a demand for assemblers, and the demands for such services as income-tax preparation, haircuts, and child care create derived demands for accountants, barbers, and child care workers.

Marginal Revenue Product

Because resource demand is derived from product demand, the strength of the demand for any resource will depend on:

- The productivity of the resource in helping to create a good or service.
- The market value or price of the good or service it helps produce.

Other things equal, a resource that is highly productive in turning out a highly valued commodity will be in great demand. On the other hand, a relatively unproductive resource that is capable of producing only a minimally valued commodity will be in little demand. And no demand whatsoever will exist for a resource that is phenomenally efficient in producing something that no one wants to buy.

Productivity Table 14.1 shows the roles of resource productivity and product price in determining resource demand. Here we assume that a firm adds a single variable resource, labor, to its fixed plant. Columns 1 and 2 give the number of units of the resource applied to production and the resulting total product (output). Column 3 provides the **marginal product (MP),** or additional output, resulting from using each additional unit of labor. Columns 1 through 3 remind us that the law of diminishing returns applies here, causing the marginal product of labor to fall beyond some point. For simplicity, we assume that these diminishing marginal returns—these declines in marginal product—begin with the first worker hired.

AP **TABLE 14.1 The Demand for Labor: Pure Competition in the Sale of the Product**

(1) Units of Resource	(2) Total Product (Output)	(3) Marginal Product (MP)	(4) Product Price	(5) Total Revenue, (2) × (4)	(6) Marginal Revenue Product (MRP)
0	0		$2	$ 0	
		7			$14
1	7		2	14	
		6			12
2	13		2	26	
		5			10
3	18		2	36	
		4			8
4	22		2	44	
		3			6
5	25		2	50	
		2			4
6	27		2	54	
		1			2
7	28		2	56	

Product Price But the derived demand for a resource depends also on the price of the product it produces. Column 4 in Table 14.1 adds this price information. Product price is constant, in this case at $2, because the product market is competitive. The firm is a price taker and can sell units of output only at this market price.

Multiplying column 2 by column 4 provides the total-revenue data of column 5. These are the amounts of revenue the firm realizes from the various levels of resource usage. From these total-revenue data we can compute **marginal revenue product (MRP)**—the change in total revenue resulting from the use of each additional unit of a resource (labor, in this case). In equation form,

$$\text{Marginal revenue product} = \frac{\text{Change in total revenue}}{\text{Unit change in resource quantity}}$$

The MRPs are listed in column 6 in Table 14.1.

Rule for Employing Resources: MRP = MRC

The MRP schedule, shown as columns 1 and 6, is the firm's demand schedule for labor. To understand why, you must first know the rule that guides a profit-seeking firm in hiring any resource: To maximize profit, a firm should hire additional units of a specific resource as long as each successive unit adds more to the firm's total revenue than it adds to the firm's total cost.

Economists use special terms to designate what each additional unit of labor or other variable resource adds to total cost and what it adds to total revenue. We have seen that MRP measures how much each successive unit of a resource adds to total revenue. The amount that each additional unit of a resource adds to the firm's total (resource) cost is called its **marginal resource cost (MRC).** In equation form,

$$\text{Marginal resource cost} = \frac{\text{change in total (resource) cost}}{\text{unit change in resource quantity}}$$

So we can restate our rule for hiring resources as follows: It will be profitable for a firm to hire additional units of a resource up to the point at which that resource's MRP is equal to its MRC. For example, as the rule applies to labor, if the number of workers a firm is currently hiring is such that the MRP of the last worker exceeds his or her MRC, the firm can profit by hiring more workers. But if the number being hired is such that the MRC of the last worker exceeds his or her MRP, the firm is hiring workers who are not "paying their way" and it can increase its profit by discharging some workers. You may have recognized that this **MRP = MRC rule** is similar to the MR = MC profit-maximizing rule employed throughout our discussion of price and output determination. The rationale of the two rules is the same, but the point of reference is now *inputs* of a resource, not *outputs* of a product.

MRP as Resource Demand Schedule

Let's continue with our focus on labor, knowing that the analysis also applies to other resources. In a purely competitive labor market, market supply and market demand establish the wage rate. Because each firm hires such a small fraction of market supply, it cannot influence the market wage rate; it is a wage taker, not a wage maker. This means that for each additional unit of labor hired, each firm's total resource cost increases by exactly the amount of the constant market wage rate. More specifically, the MRC of labor exactly equals the market wage rate. Thus, resource "price" (the market wage rate) and resource "cost" (marginal resource cost) are equal for a firm that hires a resource in a competitive labor market. As a result, the MRP = MRC rule tells us that, in pure competition, the firm will hire workers up to the point at which the market *wage rate* (its MRC) is equal to its MRP.

In terms of the data in columns 1 and 6 of Table 14.1, if the market wage rate is, say, $13.95, the firm will hire only one worker. This is so because only the hiring of the first worker results in an increase in profits. To see this, note that for the first worker MRP (= $14) exceeds MRC (= $13.95). Thus, hiring the first worker is profitable. For each successive worker, however, MRC (= $13.95) exceeds MRP (= $12 or less), indicating that it will not be profitable to hire any of

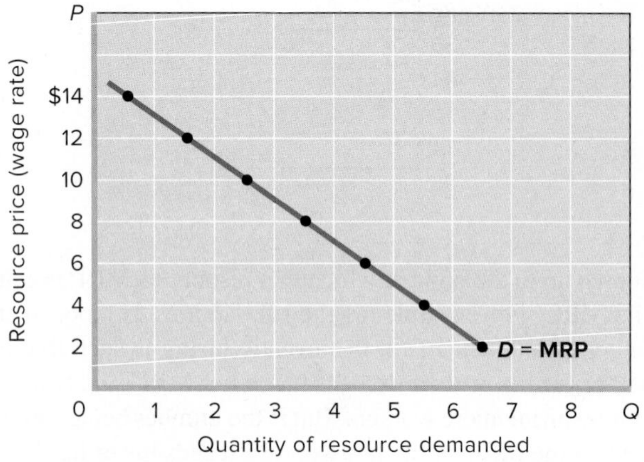

AP **FIGURE 14.1 The purely competitive seller's demand for a resource.** The MRP curve is the resource demand curve; each of its points relates a particular resource price (= MRP when profit is maximized) with a corresponding quantity of the resource demanded. Under pure competition, product price is constant; therefore, the downward slope of the $D =$ MRP curve is due solely to the decline in the resource's marginal product (law of diminishing marginal returns).

those workers. If the wage rate is $11.95, by the same reasoning we discover that it will pay the firm to hire both the first and second workers. Similarly, if the wage rate is $9.95, three workers will be hired. If it is $7.95, four. If it is $5.95, five. And so forth. So here is the key generalization: The MRP schedule constitutes the firm's demand for labor because each point on this schedule (or curve) indicates the number of workers the firm would hire at each possible wage rate.

In Figure 14.1, we show the $D =$ MRP curve based on the data in Table 14.1.[1] The competitive firm's resource demand curve identifies an inverse relationship between the wage rate and the quantity of labor demanded, other things equal. The curve slopes downward because of diminishing marginal returns.

[1]Note that we plot the points in Figure 14.1 halfway between succeeding numbers of resource units because MRP is associated with the addition of 1 more unit. Thus in Figure 14.1, for example, we plot the MRP of the second unit ($12) not at 1 or 2 but at 1½. This "smoothing" enables us to sketch a continuously downsloping curve rather than one that moves downward in discrete steps (like a staircase) as each new unit of labor is hired.

Resource Demand under Imperfect Product Market Competition

Resource demand (here, labor demand) is more complex when the firm is selling its product in an imperfectly competitive market, one in which the firm is a price maker. That is because imperfect competitors (pure monopolists, oligopolists, and monopolistic competitors) face downsloping product demand curves. As a result, whenever an imperfect competitor's product demand curve is fixed in place, the only way to increase sales is by setting a lower price (and thereby moving down along the fixed demand curve).

The productivity data in Table 14.1 are retained in columns 1 to 3 in Table 14.2. But here in Table 14.2 we show in column 4 that product price must be lowered to sell the marginal product of each successive worker. The MRP of the purely competitive seller of Table 14.1 falls for only one reason: Marginal product diminishes. But the MRP of the imperfectly competitive seller of Table 14.2 falls for two reasons: Marginal product diminishes *and* product price falls as output increases.

We emphasize that the lower price accompanying each increase in output (total product) applies not only to the marginal product of each successive worker but also to all prior output units that otherwise could have been sold at a higher price. Observe that the marginal product of the second worker is 6 units of output. These 6 units can be sold for $2.40 each, or, as a group, for $14.40. But $14.40 is not the MRP of the second worker. To sell these 6 units, the firm must take a 20-cent price cut on the 7 units produced by the first worker—units that otherwise could have been sold for $2.60 each. Thus, the MRP of the second worker is only $13 [= $14.40 – (7 × 20 cents)], as shown.

Similarly, the third worker adds 5 units to total product, and these units are worth $2.20 each, or $11 total. But to sell these 5 units, the firm must take a 20-cent price cut on the 13 units produced by the first two workers. So the third worker's

TABLE 14.2 The Demand for Labor: Imperfect Competition in the Sale of the Product

(1) Units of Resource	(2) Total Product (Output)	(3) Marginal Product (MP)	(4) Product Price	(5) Total Revenue, (2) × (4)	(6) Marginal Revenue Product (MRP)
0	0		$2.80	$ 0	
		7			$18.20
1	7		2.60	18.20	
		6			13.00
2	13		2.40	31.20	
		5			8.40
3	18		2.20	39.60	
		4			4.40
4	22		2.00	44.00	
		3			2.25
5	25		1.85	46.25	
		2			1.00
6	27		1.75	47.25	
		1			−1.05
7	28		1.65	46.20	

MRP is only \$8.40 [= \$11 − (13 × 20 cents)]. The numbers in column 6 reflect such calculations.

In Figure 14.2 we graph the MRP data from Table 14.2 and label it "*D* = MRP (imperfect competition)." The broken-line resource demand curve, in contrast, is that of the purely competitive seller represented in Figure 14.1. A comparison of the two curves demonstrates that, other things equal, the resource demand curve of an imperfectly competitive seller is less elastic than that of a purely competitive seller. Consider the effects of an identical percentage decline in the wage rate (resource price) from \$11 to \$6 in Figure 14.2. Comparison of the two curves reveals that the imperfectly competitive seller (solid curve) does not expand the quantity of labor it employs by as large a percentage as does the purely competitive seller (broken curve).

It is not surprising that the imperfectly competitive producer is less responsive to resource price cuts than the purely competitive producer. When resource prices fall, MC per unit declines for both imperfectly competitive firms as well as purely competitive firms. Because both types of firms maximize profits by producing where MR = MC, the decline in MC will cause both types of firms to produce more. But the effect will be muted for imperfectly competitive firms because their downsloping demand curves cause them to also face downsloping MR curves—so that for each additional unit sold, MR declines. By contrast, MR is constant (and equal to the market equilibrium price *P*) for competitive firms, so that they do not have to worry about MR per unit falling as they produce more units. As a result, competitive firms increase production by a larger amount than imperfectly competitive firms whenever resource prices fall.

FIGURE 14.2 The imperfectly competitive seller's demand curve for a resource. An imperfectly competitive seller's resource demand curve *D* (solid) slopes downward because both marginal product and product price fall as resource employment and output rise. This downward slope is greater than that for a purely competitive seller (dashed resource demand curve) because the pure competitor can sell the added output at a constant price.

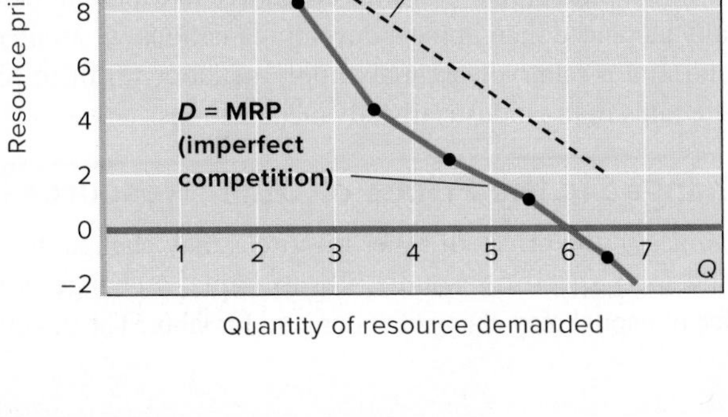

Market Demand for a Resource

The total, or market, demand curve for a specific resource shows the various total amounts of the resource that firms will purchase or hire at various resource prices, other things equal. Recall that the total, or market, demand curve for a *product* is found by summing horizontally the demand curves of all individual buyers in the market. The market demand curve for a particular *resource* is derived in essentially the same way—by summing horizontally the individual demand or MRP curves for all firms hiring that resource.

AP QUICK REVIEW 14.1

- ✓ The marginal revenue product (MRP) measures the additional contribution a firm receives from an additional unit of input (ex. labor). The marginal resource cost (MRC) is the additional cost to the firm of an additional unit of input (ex. labor). This additional cost, in the case of labor in a competitive resource market, is the competitive wage rate.
- ✓ Application of the MRP = MRC rule to a firm's MRP curve demonstrates that the MRP curve represents the firm's resource demand curve. To maximize profit, a firm will purchase or hire a resource in an amount at which MRP = MRC.
- ✓ The resource demand curve of a purely competitive seller is downsloping solely because the marginal product of the resource diminishes; the resource demand curve of an imperfectly competitive seller is downsloping because marginal product diminishes *and* product price falls as output is increased.

AP Determinants of Resource Demand

LO14.3 List the factors that increase or decrease resource demand.

What will alter the demand for a resource—that is, shift the resource demand curve? The fact that resource demand is derived from *product demand* and depends on *resource productivity* suggests two "resource demand shifters." Also, our analysis of how changes in the prices of other products can shift a product's demand curve (Chapter 3) suggests another factor: changes in the *prices of other resources*.

Changes in Product Demand

Other things equal, an increase in the demand for a product will increase the demand for a resource used in its production, whereas a decrease in product demand will decrease the demand for that resource.

Let's see how this works. The first thing to recall is that a change in the demand for a product will change its price. In

CONSIDER THIS . . .

Source: © PRNewsFoto/Diamond Information Center/AP Images

Superstars

In what economist Robert Frank calls "winner-take-all markets," a few highly talented performers have huge earnings relative to the average performers in the market. Because consumers and firms seek out "top" performers, small differences in talent or popularity get magnified into huge differences in pay.

In these markets, consumer spending gets channeled toward a few performers. The media then "hypes" these individuals, which further increases the public's awareness of their talents. Many more consumers then buy the stars' products. Although it is not easy to stay on top, several superstars emerge.

The high earnings of superstars result from the high revenues they generate from their work. Consider Beyoncé Knowles. If she sold only a few thousand songs and attracted only a few hundred fans to each concert, the revenue she would produce—her marginal revenue product—would be quite modest. So, too, would be her earnings.

But consumers have anointed Beyoncé as queen of the R&B and hip-hop portion of pop culture. The demand for her music and concerts is extraordinarily high. She sells *millions* of songs, not thousands, and draws *thousands* to her concerts, not hundreds. Her extraordinarily high net earnings derive from her extraordinarily high MRP.

So it is for the other superstars in the "winner-take-all markets." Influenced by the media, but coerced by no one, consumers direct their spending toward a select few. The resulting strong demand for these stars' services reflects their high MRP. And because top talent (by definition) is very limited, superstars receive amazingly high earnings.

Table 14.1, let's assume that an increase in product demand boosts product price from \$2 to \$3. You should calculate the new resource demand schedule (columns 1 and 6) that would result and plot it in Figure 14.1 to verify that the new resource demand curve lies to the right of the old demand curve. Similarly, a decline in the product demand (and price) will shift the resource demand curve to the left. This effect—resource demand changing along with product demand—demonstrates that resource demand is derived from product demand.

Example: Assuming no offsetting change in supply, a decrease in the demand for new houses will drive down house prices. Those lower prices will decrease the MRP of construction workers, and therefore the demand for construction workers will fall. The resource demand curve such as in Figure 14.1 or Figure 14.2 will shift to the left.

Changes in Productivity

Other things equal, an increase in the productivity of a resource will increase the demand for the resource and a decrease in productivity will reduce the demand for the resource. If we doubled the MP data of column 3 in Table 14.1, the MRP data of column 6 would also double, indicating a rightward shift of the resource demand curve.

The productivity of any resource may be altered over the long run in several ways:

- ***Quantities of other resources*** The marginal productivity of any resource will vary with the quantities of the other resources used with it. The greater the amount of capital and land resources used with, say, labor, the greater will be labor's marginal productivity and, thus, labor demand.
- ***Technological advance*** Technological improvements that increase the quality of other resources, such as capital, have the same effect. The better the *quality* of capital, the greater the productivity of labor used with it. Dockworkers employed with a specific amount of real capital in the form of unloading cranes are more productive than dockworkers with the same amount of real capital embodied in older conveyor-belt systems.
- ***Quality of the variable resource*** Improvements in the quality of the variable resource, such as labor, will increase its marginal productivity and therefore its demand. In effect, there will be a new demand curve for a different, more skilled, kind of labor.

All these considerations help explain why the average level of (real) wages is higher in industrially advanced nations (for example, the United States, Germany, Japan, and France) than in developing nations (for example, Nicaragua, Ethiopia, Angola, and Cambodia). Workers in industrially advanced nations are generally healthier, better educated, and better trained than are workers in developing countries. Also, in most industries they work with a larger and more efficient stock of capital goods and more abundant natural resources. This increases productivity and creates a strong demand for labor. On the supply side of the market, labor is scarcer relative to capital in industrially advanced than in most developing nations. A strong demand and a relatively scarce supply of labor result in high wage rates in the industrially advanced nations.

Changes in the Prices of Other Resources

Changes in the prices of other resources may change the demand for a specific resource. For example, a change in the price of capital may change the demand for labor. The direction of the change in labor demand will depend on whether labor and capital are substitutes or complements in production.

Substitute Resources Suppose the technology in a certain production process is such that labor and capital are substitutable. A firm can produce some specific amount of output using a relatively small amount of labor and a relatively large amount of capital, or vice versa. Now assume that the price of machinery (capital) falls. The effect on the demand for labor will be the net result of two opposed effects: the substitution effect and the output effect.

- ***Substitution effect*** The decline in the price of machinery prompts the firm to substitute machinery for labor. This allows the firm to produce its output at lower cost. So at the fixed wage rate, smaller quantities of labor are now employed. This **substitution effect** decreases the demand for labor. More generally, the substitution effect indicates that a firm will purchase more of an input whose relative price has declined and, conversely, use less of an input whose relative price has increased.
- ***Output effect*** Because the price of machinery has fallen, the costs of producing various outputs must also decline. With lower costs, the firm finds it profitable to produce and sell a greater output. The greater output increases the demand for all resources, including labor. So this **output effect** increases the demand for labor. More generally, the output effect means that the firm will purchase more of one particular input when the price of the other input falls and less of that particular input when the price of the other input rises.
- ***Net effect*** The substitution and output effects are both present when the price of an input changes, but they work in opposite directions. For a decline in the price of capital, the substitution effect decreases the demand for labor and the output effect increases it. The net change in labor demand depends on the relative sizes of the two effects: If the substitution effect outweighs the output effect, a decrease in the price of capital decreases the demand for labor. If the output effect exceeds the substitution effect, a decrease in the price of capital increases the demand for labor.

Complementary Resources Recall from Chapter 3 that certain products, such as computers and software, are complementary goods; they "go together" and are jointly demanded. Resources may also be complementary; an increase in the quantity of one of them used in the production process requires an increase in the amount used of the other as well, and vice versa. Suppose a small design firm does computer-assisted design (CAD) with relatively expensive personal computers as its basic piece of capital equipment. Each computer requires exactly one design engineer to operate it; the machine is not automated—it will not run itself—and a second engineer would have nothing to do.

Now assume that a technological advance in the production of these computers substantially reduces their price. There can be no substitution effect because labor and capital must be used in *fixed proportions,* one person for one machine. Capital cannot be substituted for labor. But there *is* an output effect. Other things equal, the reduction in the price of capital goods means lower production costs. Producing a larger output will therefore be profitable. In doing so, the firm will use both more capital and more labor. When labor and capital are complementary, a decline in the price of capital increases the demand for labor through the output effect.

We have cast our analysis of substitute resources and complementary resources mainly in terms of a decline in the price of capital. Table 14.3 summarizes the effects of an *increase* in the price of capital on the demand for labor. Please study it carefully.

Now that we have discussed the full list of the determinants of labor demand, let's again review their effects. Stated in terms of the labor resource, the demand for labor will increase (the labor demand curve will shift rightward) when:

- The demand for (and therefore the price of) the product produced by that labor *increases.*
- The productivity (MP) of labor *increases.*
- The price of a substitute input *decreases,* provided the output effect exceeds the substitution effect.
- The price of a substitute input *increases,* provided the substitution effect exceeds the output effect.
- The price of a complementary input *decreases.*

TABLE 14.3 The Effect of an Increase in the Price of Capital on the Demand for Labor, D_L

(1) Relationship of Inputs	(2) Increase in the Price of Capital		
	(a) Substitution Effect	(b) Output Effect	(c) Combined Effect
Substitutes in production	Labor substituted for capital	Production costs up, output down, and less of both capital and labor used	D_L increases if the substitution effect exceeds the output effect; D_L decreases if the output effect exceeds the substitution effect
Complements in production	No substitution of labor for capital	Production costs up, output down, and less of both capital and labor used	D_L decreases (because only the output effect applies)

TABLE 14.4 Determinants of Labor Demand: Factors That Shift the Labor Demand Curve

Determinant	Examples
Change in product demand	Gambling increases in popularity, increasing the demand for workers at casinos. Consumers decrease their demand for leather coats, decreasing the demand for tanners. The federal government increases spending on homeland security, increasing the demand for security personnel.
Change in productivity	An increase in the skill levels of physicians increases the demand for their services. Computer-assisted graphic design increases the productivity of, and demand for, graphic artists.
Change in the price of another resource	An increase in the price of electricity increases the cost of producing aluminum and reduces the demand for aluminum workers. The price of security equipment used by businesses to protect against illegal entry falls, decreasing the demand for night guards. The price of cell phone equipment decreases, reducing the cost of cell phone service; this in turn increases the demand for cell phone assemblers. Health-insurance premiums rise, and firms substitute part-time workers who are not covered by insurance for full-time workers who are.

Be sure that you can "reverse" these effects to explain a *decrease* in labor demand.

Table 14.4 provides several illustrations of the determinants of labor demand, listed by the categories of determinants we have discussed. You will benefit by giving them a close look.

Occupational Employment Trends

Changes in labor demand have considerable significance since they affect wage rates and employment in specific occupations. Increases in labor demand for certain occupational groups result in increases in their employment; decreases in labor demand result in decreases in their employment. For illustration, let's first look at occupations for which labor demand is growing and then examine occupations for which it is declining. (Wage rates are the subject of the next chapter.)

The Fastest-Growing Occupations Table 14.5 lists the 10 fastest-growing U.S. occupations for 2010 to 2020, as measured by percentage changes and projected by the Bureau of Labor Statistics. It is no coincidence that the service occupations dominate the list. In general, the demand for service workers in the United States is rapidly outpacing the demand for manufacturing, construction, and mining workers.

Of the 10 fastest-growing occupations in percentage terms, seven—occupational therapy assistants, physical therapist assistants, physical therapy aids, home health aides, nurse practitioners, physical therapists, and ambulance drivers—are related to the health field. The rising demand for these types of labor is derived from the growing demand for health services, caused by several factors. The aging of the U.S. population has brought with it more medical problems; the rising standard of income has led to greater expenditures on health care; and the continued presence of private and public insurance has allowed people to purchase more health care than most could afford individually.

TABLE 14.5 The 10 Fastest-Growing U.S. Occupations in Percentage Terms, 2014–2024

	Employment, Thousands of Jobs		
Occupation	2014	2024	Percentage Increase*
Wind turbine service technicians	4	9	108
Occupational therapy assistants	33	47	43
Physical therapist assistants	79	111	41
Physical therapist aides	50	70	39
Home health aides	914	1,262	38
Commercial drivers	4	6	37
Nurse practitioners	127	172	35
Physical therapists	211	283	34
Statisticians	30	40	34
Ambulance drivers and attendants, except EMTs	20	26	33

*Percentages and employment numbers may not reconcile due to rounding.

Source: Bureau of Labor Statistics, "Employment Projections," **www.bls.gov**.

The Most Rapidly Declining Occupations In contrast, Table 14.6 lists the 10 U.S. occupations with the greatest projected job loss (in percentage terms) between 2014 and 2024. Several of the occupations owe their declines mainly to "labor-saving" technological change. For example, automated or computerized equipment has greatly reduced the need for postal employees, sewing machine operators, and photographic process workers.

Two of the occupations in the declining employment list are related to textiles and apparel. The U.S. demand for these

TABLE 14.6 The 10 Most Rapidly Declining U.S. Occupations in Percentage Terms, 2014–2024

	Employment, Thousands of Jobs		
Occupation	**2014**	**2024**	**Percentage Decrease***
Locomotive firers	2	0.5	70
Electronic equipment technicians, motor vehicles	12	6	50
Telephone operators	13	8	42
Postal service mail sorters and processors	118	78	34
Switchboard operators and answering service operators	112	75	33
Photographic process workers	29	19	31
Shoe machine operators	4	3	30
Manufactured building and mobile home installers	4	3	28
Foundry mold and coremakers	12	9	27
Sewing machine operators	154	112	27

*Percentages and employment numbers may not reconcile due to rounding.

Source: Bureau of Labor Statistics, "Employment Projections," **www.bls.gov**.

goods is increasingly being filled through imports. Those jobs are therefore rapidly disappearing in the United States.

As we indicated, the "top-10" lists shown in Tables 14.5 and 14.6 are based on percentage changes. In terms of absolute job growth and loss, the greatest projected employment growth between 2014 and 2024 is for home health aides (348,000 jobs) and physical therapists (72,000 jobs). The greatest projected absolute decline in employment is for sewing machine operators (−42,000).

Elasticity of Resource Demand

LO14.4 Discuss the determinants of elasticity of resource demand.

The employment changes we have just discussed have resulted from shifts in the locations of resource demand curves. Such changes in demand must be distinguished from changes in the quantity of a resource demanded caused by a change in the price of the specific resource under consideration. Such a change is caused not by a shift of the demand curve but, rather, by a movement from one point to another on a fixed resource demand curve. Example: In Figure 14.1 we note that an increase in the wage rate from $5 to $7 will reduce the quantity of labor demanded from 5 to 4 units. This is a change in the *quantity of labor demanded* as distinct from a *change in the demand for labor*.

The sensitivity of resource quantity to changes in resource prices along a fixed resource demand curve is measured by the **elasticity of resource demand.** In coefficient form,

$$E_{rd} = \frac{\text{percentage change in resource quantity demanded}}{\text{percentage change in resource price}}$$

When E_{rd} is greater than 1, resource demand is elastic; when E_{rd} is less than 1, resource demand is inelastic; and when E_{rd} equals 1, resource demand is unit-elastic. What determines the elasticity of resource demand? Several factors are at work.

Ease of Resource Substitutability The degree to which resources are substitutable is a fundamental determinant of elasticity. More specifically, the greater the substitutability of other resources, the more elastic is the demand for a particular resource. As an example, the high degree to which computerized voice recognition systems are substitutable for human beings implies that the demand for human beings answering phone calls at call centers is quite elastic. In contrast, good substitutes for physicians are rare, so demand for them is less elastic or even inelastic. If a furniture manufacturer finds that several types of wood are equally satisfactory in making coffee tables, a rise in the price of any one type of wood may cause a sharp drop in the amount demanded as the producer substitutes some other type of wood for the type of wood whose price has gone up. At the other extreme, there may be no reasonable substitutes; bauxite is absolutely essential in the production of aluminum ingots. Thus, the demand for bauxite by aluminum producers is inelastic.

Time can play a role in the ease of input substitution. For example, a firm's truck drivers may obtain a substantial wage increase with little or no immediate decline in employment. But over time, as the firm's trucks wear out and are replaced, that wage increase may motivate the company to purchase larger trucks and in that way deliver the same total output with fewer drivers.

Elasticity of Product Demand Because the demand for labor is a derived demand, the elasticity of the demand for the output that the labor is producing will influence the elasticity of the demand for labor. Other things equal, the greater the price elasticity of product demand, the greater the elasticity of resource demand. For example, suppose that the wage rate falls. This means a decline in the cost of producing the product and a drop in the product's price. If the elasticity of product demand is great, the resulting increase in the quantity of the product demanded will be large and thus necessitate a large increase in the quantity of labor to produce the additional output. This implies an elastic demand for labor. But if the demand for the product is inelastic, the increase in the amount of the product demanded will be small, as will be the increases in the quantity of labor demanded. This suggests an inelastic demand for labor.

Remember that the resource demand curve in Figure 14.1 is more elastic than the resource demand curve shown in Figure 14.2. The difference arises because in Figure 14.1 we assume a perfectly elastic product demand curve, whereas Figure 14.2 is based on a downsloping or less than perfectly elastic product demand curve.

Ratio of Resource Cost to Total Cost The larger the proportion of total production costs accounted for by a resource, the greater the elasticity of demand for that resource. In the extreme, if labor cost is the only production cost, then a 20 percent increase in wage rates will shift all the firm's cost curves upward by 20 percent. If product demand is elastic, this substantial increase in costs will cause a relatively large decline in sales and a sharp decline in the amount of labor demanded. So labor demand is highly elastic. But if labor cost is only 50 percent of production cost, then a 20 percent increase in wage rates will increase costs by only 10 percent. With the same elasticity of product demand, this will cause a relatively small decline in sales and therefore in the amount of labor demanded. In this case the demand for labor is much less elastic.

AP QUICK REVIEW 14.2

- ✓ Recall the idea of Derived Demand, in which the demand for a resource, or input, depends on the demand for the product it produces.
- ✓ A resource demand curve will shift because of changes in product demand, changes in the productivity of the resource, and changes in the prices of other inputs.
- ✓ If resources A and B are substitutable, a decline in the price of input A will decrease the demand for B, as A is substituted for B. This substitution of inputs can only occur in the long run, when inputs are variable.
- ✓ Elasticity of resource demand measures the sensitivity of resource quantity to changes in resource prices along a fixed resource demand curve.
- ✓ For any particular resource, the elasticity of resource demand will be less elastic the greater the difficulty of substituting other resources for the resource, the smaller the elasticity of product demand, and the smaller the proportion of total cost accounted for by the resource.

AP Optimal Combination of Resources

LO14.5 Determine how a competitive firm selects its optimal combination of resources.

So far, our main focus has been on one variable input, labor. But in the long run firms can vary the amounts of all the resources they use. That's why we need to consider what combination of resources a firm will choose when *all* its inputs are variable. While our analysis is based on two resources, it can be extended to any number of inputs.

We will consider two interrelated questions:

- What combination of resources will minimize costs at a specific level of output?
- What combination of resources will maximize profit?

The Least-Cost Rule

A firm is producing a specific output with the **least-cost combination of resources** when the last dollar spent on each resource yields the same marginal product. That is, the cost of any output is minimized when the ratios of marginal product to price of the last units of resources used are the same for each resource. To see how this rule maximizes profits in a more concrete setting, consider firms that are competitive buyers in resource markets. Because each firm is too small to affect resource prices, each firm's marginal resource costs will equal market resource prices and each firm will be able to hire as many or as few units as it would like of any and all resources at their respective market prices. Thus, if there are just two resources, labor and capital, a competitive firm will minimize its total cost of a specific output when

$$\frac{\text{Marginal product of labor } (MP_L)}{\text{Price of labor } (P_L)} = \frac{\text{Marginal product of capital } (MP_C)}{\text{Price of capital } (P_C)} \quad (1)$$

Throughout, we will refer to the marginal products of labor and capital as MP_L and MP_C, respectively, and symbolize the price of labor by P_L and the price of capital by P_C.

A concrete example will show why fulfilling the condition in equation 1 leads to least-cost production. Assume that the price of both capital and labor is $1 per unit but that Siam Soups currently employs them in such amounts that the marginal product of labor is 10 and the marginal product of capital is 5. Our equation immediately tells us that this is not the least costly combination of resources:

$$\frac{MP_L = 10}{P_L = \$1} > \frac{MP_C = 5}{P_C = \$1}$$

Suppose Siam spends \$1 less on capital and shifts that dollar to labor. It loses 5 units of output produced by the last dollar's worth of capital, but it gains 10 units of output from the extra dollar's worth of labor. Net output increases by 5 (= 10 − 5) units for the same total cost. More such shifting of dollars from capital to labor will push the firm *down* along its MP curve for labor and *up* along its MP curve for capital, increasing output and moving the firm toward a position of equilibrium where equation 1 is fulfilled. At that equilibrium position, the MP per dollar for the last unit of both labor and capital might be, for example, 7. And Siam will be producing a greater output for the same (original) cost.

Whenever the same total-resource cost can result in a greater total output, the cost per unit—and therefore the total cost of any specific level of output—can be reduced. Being able to produce a *larger* output with a *specific* total cost is the same as being able to produce a *specific* output with a *smaller* total cost. If Siam buys \$1 less of capital, its output will fall by 5 units. If it spends only \$.50 of that dollar on labor, the firm will increase its output by a compensating 5 units (= $\frac{1}{2}$ of the MP per dollar). Then the firm will realize the same total output at a \$0.50 lower total cost.

The cost of producing any specific output can be reduced as long as equation 1 does not hold. But when dollars have been shifted between capital and labor to the point where equation 1 holds, no additional changes in the use of capital and labor will reduce costs further. Siam will be producing that output using the least-cost combination of capital and labor.

All the long-run cost curves developed in Chapter 8 and used thereafter assume that the least-cost combination of inputs has been realized at each level of output. Any firm that combines resources in violation of the least-cost rule would have a higher-than-necessary average total cost at each level of output. That is, it would incur *X-inefficiency,* as discussed in Figure 11.7.

The producer's least-cost rule is analogous to the consumer's utility-maximizing rule described in Chapter 7. In achieving the utility-maximizing combination of goods, the consumer considers both his or her preferences as reflected in diminishing-marginal-utility data and the prices of the various products. Similarly, in achieving the cost-minimizing combination of resources, the producer considers both the marginal-product data and the prices (costs) of the various resources.

The Profit-Maximizing Rule

Minimizing cost is not sufficient for maximizing profit. A firm can produce any level of output in the least costly way by applying equation 1. But only one unique level of output maximizes profit. Our earlier analysis of product markets showed that this profit-maximizing output occurs where marginal revenue equals marginal cost (MR = MC). Near the beginning of this chapter we determined that we could write this profit-maximizing condition as MRP = MRC as it relates to resource inputs.

In a purely competitive resource market the marginal resource cost (MRC) is equal to the resource price *P*. Thus, for any competitive resource market, we have as our profit-maximizing equation

$$\text{MRP (resource)} = P \text{ (resource)}$$

This condition must hold for every variable resource, and in the long run all resources are variable. In competitive markets, a firm will therefore achieve its **profit-maximizing combination of resources** when each resource is employed to the point at which its marginal revenue product equals its resource price. For two resources, labor and capital, we need both

$$P_L = \text{MRP}_L \qquad \text{and} \qquad P_C = \text{MRP}_C$$

We can combine these conditions by dividing both sides of each equation by their respective prices and equating the results to get

$$\frac{\text{MRP}_L}{P_L} = \frac{\text{MRP}_C}{P_C} = 1 \qquad (2)$$

Note in equation 2 that it is not sufficient that the MRPs of the two resources be *proportionate* to their prices; the MRPs must be *equal* to their prices and the ratios therefore equal to 1. For example, if MRP_L = \$15, P_L = \$5, MRP_C = \$9, and P_C = \$3, Siam is underemploying both capital and labor even though the ratios of MRP to resource price are identical for both resources. The firm can expand its profit by hiring additional amounts of both capital and labor until it moves down its downsloping MRP curves to the points at which MRP_L = \$5 and MRP_C = \$3. The ratios will then be 5/5 and 3/3 and equal to 1.

The profit-maximizing position in equation 2 includes the cost-minimizing condition of equation 1. That is, if a firm is maximizing profit according to equation 2, then it must be using the least-cost combination of inputs to do so. However, the converse is not true: A firm operating at least cost according to equation 1 may not be operating at the output that maximizes its profit.

Numerical Illustration

A numerical illustration will help you understand the least-cost and profit-maximizing rules. In columns 2, 3, 2′, and 3′ in Table 14.7 we show the total products and marginal products for various amounts of labor and capital that are assumed to be the only inputs Siam needs in producing its soup. Both inputs are subject to diminishing returns.

We also assume that labor and capital are supplied in competitive resource markets at \$8 and \$12, respectively, and that Siam's soup sells competitively at \$2 per unit. For both labor and capital we can determine the total revenue associated with each input level by multiplying total product by the

AP TABLE 14.7 Data for Finding the Least-Cost and Profit-Maximizing Combination of Labor and Capital, Siam's Soups*

Labor (Price = $8)					Capital (Price = $12)				
(1) Quantity	(2) Total Product (Output)	(3) Marginal Product	(4) Total Revenue	(5) Marginal Revenue Product	(1′) Quantity	(2′) Total Product (Output)	(3′) Marginal Product	(4′) Total Revenue	(5′) Marginal Revenue Product
0	0		$ 0		0	0		$ 0	
1	12	12	24	$24	1	13	13	26	$26
2	22	10	44	20	2	22	9	44	18
3	28	6	56	12	**3**	28	6	56	**12**
4	33	5	66	10	4	32	4	64	8
5	37	4	74	**8**	5	35	3	70	6
6	40	3	80	6	6	37	2	74	4
7	42	2	84	4	7	38	1	76	2

*To simplify, it is assumed in this table that the productivity of each resource is independent of the quantity of the other. For example, the total and marginal products of labor are assumed not to vary with the quantity of capital employed.

$2 product price. These data are shown in columns 4 and 4′. They enable us to calculate the marginal revenue product of each successive input of labor and capital as shown in columns 5 and 5′, respectively.

Producing at Least Cost What is the least-cost combination of labor and capital for Siam to use in producing, say, 50 units of output? The answer, which we can obtain by trial and error, is 3 units of labor and 2 units of capital. Columns 2 and 2′ indicate that this combination of labor and capital does, indeed, result in the required 50 (= 28 + 22) units of output. Now, note from columns 3 and 3′ that hiring 3 units of labor gives us $MP_L/P_L = \frac{6}{8} = \frac{3}{4}$ and hiring 2 units of capital gives us $MP_C/P_C = \frac{9}{12} = \frac{3}{4}$. So equation 1 is fulfilled. How can we verify that costs are actually minimized? First, we see that the total cost of employing 3 units of labor and 2 of capital is $48 [= (3 × $8) + (2 × $12)].

Other combinations of labor and capital will also yield 50 units of output, but at a higher cost than $48. For example, 5 units of labor and 1 unit of capital will produce 50 (= 37 + 13) units, but total cost is higher, at $52 [= (5 × $8) + (1 × $12)]. This comes as no surprise because 5 units of labor and 1 unit of capital violate the least-cost rule—$MP_L/P_L = \frac{4}{8}$, $MP_C/P_C = \frac{13}{12}$. Only the combination (3 units of labor and 2 units of capital) that minimizes total cost will satisfy equation 1. All other combinations capable of producing 50 units of output violate the cost-minimizing rule, and therefore cost more than $48.

Maximizing Profit Will 50 units of output maximize Siam's profit? No, because the profit-maximizing terms of equation 2 are not satisfied when the firm employs 3 units of labor and 2 of capital. To maximize profit, each input should be employed until its price equals its marginal revenue product. But for 3 units of labor, labor's MRP in column 5 is $12 while its price is only $8. This means the firm could increase its profit by hiring more labor. Similarly, for 2 units of capital, we see in column 5′ that capital's MRP is $18 and its price is only $12. This indicates that more capital should also be employed. By producing only 50 units of output (even though they are produced at least cost), labor and capital are being used in less-than-profit-maximizing amounts. The firm needs to expand its employment of labor and capital, thereby increasing its output.

Table 14.7 shows that the MRPs of labor and capital are equal to their prices, so equation 2 is fulfilled when Siam is employing 5 units of labor and 3 units of capital. So this is the profit-maximizing combination of inputs.[2] The firm's total cost will be $76, made up of $40 (= 5 × $8) of labor and $36 (= 3 × $12) of capital. Total revenue will be $130, found either by multiplying the total output of 65 (= 37 + 28) by the $2 product price or by summing the total revenues attributable to labor ($74) and to capital ($56). The difference between total revenue and total cost in this instance is $54 (= $130 − $76). Experiment with other combinations of labor and capital to demonstrate that they yield an economic profit of less than $54.

Note that the profit-maximizing combination of 5 units of labor and 3 units of capital is also a least-cost combination for this particular level of output. Using these resource amounts satisfies the least-cost requirement of equation 1 in that $MP_L/P_L = \frac{4}{8} = \frac{1}{2}$ and $MP_C/P_C = \frac{6}{12} = \frac{1}{2}$.

[2]Because we are dealing with discrete (nonfractional) units of the two outputs here, the use of 4 units of labor and 2 units of capital is equally profitable. The fifth unit of labor's MRP and its price (cost) are equal at $8, so that the fifth labor unit neither adds to nor subtracts from the firm's profit; similarly, the third unit of capital has no effect on profit.

LAST WORD

Labor and Capital: Substitutes or Complements?

Automatic Teller Machines (ATMs) Have Complemented Some Types of Labor While Substituting for Other Types of Labor.

As you have learned from this chapter, a firm achieves its least-cost combination of inputs when the last dollar it spends on each input makes the same contribution to total output. This raises an interesting real-world question: What happens when technological advance makes available a new, highly productive capital good for which MP/*P* is greater than it is for other inputs, say, a particular type of labor?

The answer is that the least-cost mix of resources abruptly changes, and the firm responds accordingly. If the new capital is a substitute for a particular type of labor, the firm will replace that particular type of labor with the new capital. But if the new capital is a complement for a particular type of labor, the firm will add additional amounts of that type of labor.

Source: © Picturenet/Getty Images RF

Consider bank tellers. One of their core functions, before ATMs became common in the 1980s, was to handle deposits and withdrawals of cash. Bank tellers had several other tasks that they needed to handle, but one particular type of labor they supplied was handling cash transactions. The task of handling cash transactions can, however, be equally well-managed by ATMs—but at one-quarter the cost. Naturally, banks responded to that cost advantage by installing more ATMs.

That might make you think that ATMs displaced tellers because it would seem natural in this scenario that ATMs were a substitute for bank tellers. But the data tells a different story! The number of human bank tellers actually *increased* over time as the number of ATMs soared. In 1985, there were 60,000 ATMs and 485,000 bank tellers. In 2015, there were 425,000 ATMs and 526,000 bank tellers. This means that over that entire time period, ATM machines must have been a complement to the labor provided by bank tellers.

To understand what happened, you have to keep in mind that bank tellers can be put to work doing many different tasks. Only one of those many possible tasks is handling cash. So while it is true that ATMs were indeed a substitute for bank tellers in terms of cash handling, ATMs did not offer a cheaper alternative for the other tasks that bank tellers could engage in. Thus, while there was a strong tendency for ATMs to substitute for the labor involved in handling cash, ATMs could not substitute for other bank teller activities. In fact, ATMs ended up becoming a complement for those other activities.

The process was not instantaneous. Eighty thousand bank teller jobs were indeed lost during the 1990s because bank managers at first *did* think of ATMs and bank tellers as substitutes. But by the early 2000s, bank managers realized that the cost savings offered by ATMs had given them the chance to operate in new ways that would actually require more tellers rather than fewer tellers.

Source: © Keith Brofsky/Getty Images RF

Before ATMs, the average branch employed 20 employees. After ATMs, the average branch employed 13 employees. That major increase in efficiency gave banks the chance to compete against one another by opening more branches—and more branches meant having to hire more human tellers. Thus, the efficiencies generated by having ATMs handle cash transactions at one-fourth the cost caused the demand for bank tellers to increase.

In addition, the banks also realized that bank tellers could be trained in more complex tasks like selling financial products and helping to issue home mortgages. Once banks figured out these new ways to employ tellers, ATMs turned from a substitute for bank teller labor into a complement for bank teller labor. By freeing human beings from having to handle cash transactions, ATMs acted as a complement for other types of human labor, such as selling financial products.

We can generalize from the history of ATMs. Capital is, overall, a complement for human labor, not a substitute for human labor. Certain types of human labor are substituted away as new technologies arrive, but humans end up being complemented by capital as they perform other tasks. Some types of work will disappear and the government may need to help displaced workers train for new jobs. But the newly deployed capital will end up increasing wages because it will increase the overall demand for human labor.

Marginal Productivity Theory of Income Distribution

LO14.6 Explain the marginal productivity theory of income distribution.

Our discussion of resource pricing is the cornerstone of the controversial view that fairness and economic justice are one of the outcomes of a competitive capitalist economy. Table 14.7 demonstrates, in effect, that workers receive income payments (wages) equal to the marginal contributions they make to their employers' outputs and revenues. In other words, workers are paid according to the value of the labor services that they contribute to production. Similarly, owners of the other resources receive income based on the value of the resources they supply in the production process.

In this **marginal productivity theory of income distribution,** income is distributed according to contribution to society's output. So, if you are willing to accept the proposition "To each according to the value of what he or she creates," income payments based on marginal revenue product provide a fair and equitable distribution of society's income.

This sounds reasonable, but you need to be aware of serious criticisms of this theory of income distribution:

- ***Inequality*** Critics argue that the distribution of income resulting from payment according to marginal productivity may be highly unequal because productive resources are very unequally distributed in the first place. Aside from their differences in mental and physical attributes, individuals encounter substantially different opportunities to enhance their productivity through education and training and the use of more and better equipment. Some people may not be able to participate in production at all because of mental or physical disabilities, and they would obtain no income under a system of distribution based solely on marginal productivity. Ownership of property resources is also highly unequal. Many owners of land and capital resources obtain their property by inheritance rather than through their own productive effort. Hence, income from inherited property resources conflicts with the "To each according to the value of what he or she creates" idea. Critics say that these inequalities call for progressive taxation and government spending programs aimed at creating an income distribution that will be more equitable than that which would occur if the income distribution were made strictly according to marginal productivity.
- ***Market imperfections*** The marginal productivity theory of income distribution rests on the assumptions of competitive markets. But, as we will see in Chapter 15, not all labor markets are highly competitive. In some labor markets employers exert their wage-setting power to pay less-than-competitive wages. And some workers, through labor unions, professional associations, and occupational licensing laws, wield wage-setting power in selling their services. Even the process of collective bargaining over wages suggests a power struggle over the division of income. In wage setting through negotiations, market forces—and income shares based on marginal productivity—may get partially pushed into the background. In addition, discrimination in the labor market can distort earnings patterns. In short, because of real-world market imperfections, wage rates and other resource prices are not always based solely on contributions to output.

AP QUICK REVIEW 14.3

- ✓ Any specific level of output, in the long run, will be produced with the least-costly combination of variable resources—at the point where the marginal product per dollar's worth of each input is equal.
- ✓ A firm is employing the profit-maximizing combination of resources when each resource is used to the point where its marginal revenue product equals its price.
- ✓ The marginal productivity theory of income distribution holds that all resources are paid according to their marginal contributions to output.

SUMMARY

LO14.1 Explain the significance of resource pricing.

Resource prices help determine money incomes, and they simultaneously ration resources to various industries and firms.

LO14.2 Convey how the marginal revenue productivity of a resource relates to a firm's demand for that resource.

The demand for any resource is derived from the product it helps produce. That means the demand for a resource will depend on its productivity and on the market value (price) of the good it is used to produce.

Marginal revenue product is the extra revenue a firm obtains when it employs 1 more unit of a resource. The marginal revenue product curve for any resource is the demand curve for that resource because the firm equates resource price and MRP in determining its profit-maximizing level of resource employment. Thus each point on the MRP curve indicates how many resource units the firm will hire at a specific resource price.

The firm's demand curve for a resource slopes downward because the marginal product of additional units declines in accordance with the law of diminishing returns. When a firm is selling in an imperfectly competitive market, the resource demand curve falls for a second reason: Product price must be reduced for the firm to sell a larger output. The market demand curve for a resource is derived by summing horizontally the demand curves of all the firms hiring that resource.

LO14.3 List the factors that increase or decrease resource demand.

The demand curve for a resource will shift as the result of (*a*) a change in the demand for, and therefore the price of, the product the resource is producing; (*b*) changes in the productivity of the resource; and (*c*) changes in the prices of other resources.

If resources A and B are substitutable for each other, a decline in the price of A will decrease the demand for B provided the substitution effect is greater than the output effect. But if the output effect *exceeds* the substitution effect, a decline in the price of A will increase the demand for B.

If resources C and D are complementary or jointly demanded, there is only an output effect; a change in the price of C will change the demand for D in the opposite direction.

The majority of the 10 fastest-growing occupations in the United States—by percentage increase—relate to health care and computers (review Table 14.5); the 10 most rapidly declining occupations by percentage decrease, however, are more mixed (review Table 14.6).

LO14.4 Discuss the determinants of elasticity of resource demand.

The elasticity of demand for a resource measures the responsiveness of producers to a change in the resource's price. The coefficient of the elasticity of resource demand is

$$E_{rd} = \frac{\text{percentage change in resource quantity demanded}}{\text{percentage change in resource price}}$$

When E_{rd} is greater than 1, resource demand is elastic; when E_{rd} is less than 1, resource demand is inelastic; and when E_{rd} equals 1, resource demand is unit-elastic.

The elasticity of demand for a resource will be greater (*a*) the greater the ease of substituting other resources for labor, (*b*) the greater the elasticity of demand for the product, and (*c*) the larger the proportion of total production costs attributable to the resource.

LO14.5 Determine how a competitive firm selects its optimal combination of resources.

Any specific level of output will be produced with the least costly combination of variable resources when the marginal product per dollar's worth of each input is the same—that is, when

$$\frac{\text{MP of labor}}{\text{Price of labor}} = \frac{\text{MP of capital}}{\text{Price of capital}}$$

A firm is employing the profit-maximizing combination of resources when each resource is used to the point where its marginal revenue product equals its price. In terms of labor and capital, that occurs when the MRP of labor equals the price of labor and the MRP of capital equals the price of capital—that is, when

$$\frac{\text{MP of labor}}{\text{Price of labor}} = \frac{\text{MP of capital}}{\text{Price of capital}} = 1$$

LO14.6 Explain the marginal productivity theory of income distribution.

The marginal productivity theory of income distribution holds that resources are paid according to their marginal contribution to output. Critics say that such an income distribution is too unequal and that real-world market imperfections result in pay above and below marginal contributions to output.

TERMS AND CONCEPTS

derived demand
marginal product (MP)
marginal revenue product (MRP)
marginal resource cost (MRC)
MRP = MRC rule
substitution effect
output effect
elasticity of resource demand
least-cost combination of resources
profit-maximizing combination of resources
marginal productivity theory of income distribution

The following and additional problems can be found in connect

DISCUSSION QUESTIONS

1. What is the significance of resource pricing? Explain how the factors determining resource demand differ from those determining product demand. Explain the meaning and significance of the fact that the demand for a resource is a derived demand. Why do resource demand curves slope downward? **LO14.1**

2. In 2009 General Motors (GM) announced that it would reduce employment by 21,000 workers. What does this decision reveal about how GM viewed its marginal revenue product (MRP) and marginal resource cost (MRC)? Why didn't GM reduce employment by more than 21,000 workers? By fewer than 21,000 workers? **LO14.3**

3. What factors determine the elasticity of resource demand? What effect will each of the following have on the elasticity or the location of the demand for resource C, which is being used to produce commodity X? Where there is any uncertainty as to the outcome, specify the causes of that uncertainty. LO14.4
   a. An increase in the demand for product X.
   b. An increase in the price of substitute resource D.
   c. An increase in the number of resources substitutable for C in producing X.
   d. A technological improvement in the capital equipment with which resource C is combined.
   e. A fall in the price of complementary resource E.
   f. A decline in the elasticity of demand for product X due to a decline in the competitiveness of product market X.
4. In each of the following four cases, MRP_L and MRP_C refer to the marginal revenue products of labor and capital, respectively, and P_L and P_C refer to their prices. Indicate in each case whether the conditions are consistent with maximum profits for the firm. If not, state which resource(s) should be used in larger amounts and which resource(s) should be used in smaller amounts. LO14.5
   a. $MRP_L = \$8$; $P_L = \$4$; $MRP_C = \$8$; $P_C = \$4$.
   b. $MRP_L = \$10$; $P_L = \$12$; $MRP_C = \$14$; $P_C = \$9$.
   c. $MRP_L = \$6$; $P_L = \$6$; $MRP_C = \$12$; $P_C = \$12$.
   d. $MRP_L = \$22$; $P_L = \$26$; $MRP_C = \$16$; $P_C = \$19$.
5. Florida citrus growers say that the recent crackdown on illegal immigration is increasing the market wage rates necessary to get their oranges picked. Some are turning to \$100,000 to \$300,000 mechanical harvesters known as "trunk, shake, and catch" pickers, which vigorously shake oranges from the trees. If widely adopted, what will be the effect on the demand for human orange pickers? What does that imply about the relative strengths of the substitution and output effects? LO14.5
6. **LAST WORD** To save money, some fast food chains are now having their customers place their orders at computer kiosks. Will the kiosks necessarily reduce the total number of workers employed in the fast food industry?

AP REVIEW QUESTIONS

1. Cindy is a baker and runs a large cupcake shop. She has already hired 11 employees and is thinking of hiring a 12th. Cindy estimates that a 12th worker would cost her \$100 per day in wages and benefits while increasing her total revenue from \$2,600 per day to \$2,750 per day. Should Cindy hire a 12th worker? Explain. LO14.2
2. Complete the following labor demand table for a firm that is hiring labor competitively and selling its product in a competitive market. LO14.2

Units of Labor	Total Product	Marginal Product	Product Price	Total Revenue	Marginal Revenue Product
0	0	______	\$2	\$______	\$______
1	17	______	2	______	______
2	31	______	2	______	______
3	43	______	2	______	______
4	53	______	2	______	______
5	60	______	2	______	______
6	65		2	______	

   a. How many workers will the firm hire if the market wage rate is \$27.95? \$19.95? Explain why the firm will not hire a larger or smaller number of units of labor at each of these wage rates.
   b. Show in schedule form and graphically the labor demand curve of this firm.
3. Indicate how the following events will shift the firm's demand curve for labor: increase it (**I**); decrease it (**D**); keep it the same (**S**). LO14.3
   ______ Technological advances increase labor's productivity.
   ______ The wage rate increases.
   ______ The demand for the product that labor produces decreases.
   ______ The wage rate decreases.
   ______ Absenteeism reduces labor's productivity.
   ______ The price of labor-saving machinery is reduced and the substitution effect is greater than the output effect.
4. FreshLeaf is a commercial salad maker that produces "salad in a bag" that is sold at many local supermarkets. Its customers like lettuce but don't care so much what type of lettuce is included in each bag of salad, so you would expect FreshLeaf's demand for iceberg lettuce to be: LO14.4
   a. Relatively elastic
   b. Relatively inelastic.
   c. Unit elastic.
   d. Vertical
   e. U-shaped.
5. Suppose the marginal product of the last unit of labor employed is 8 and the marginal product of the last unit of capital employed is 24. The firm is producing 100 units of output which sells in a purely competitive market for \$1 per unit. Both capital and labor are hired under purely competitive conditions at \$3 and \$1, respectively. LO14.5
   a. Is this firm minimizing the long run cost of producing 100 units of output? Explain.
   b. If the firm is employing 25 labor and 15 capital to produce and sell 100 units of output, what is this firm's economic profit?
6. A software company in Silicon Valley uses programmers (labor) and computers (capital) to produce 2500 apps for mobile devices. The firm estimates that when it comes to labor, $MP_L = 5$ apps per month, while $P_L = \$1{,}000$ per month. And when it comes to capital, $MP_C = 8$ apps per month, while $P_C = 1{,}000$ per month. If the company wishes to minimize

the cost of producing these 2500 apps for mobile devices, it should: LO14.5

a. Increase the use of labor while decreasing the use of capital.
b. Decrease the use of labor while increasing the use of capital.
c. Keep the current use of capital and labor.
d. Increase the use of both labor and capital.
e. Decrease the use of both labor and capital.

7. Assume that a competitive firm is producing 100 units of output in the short run, using 50 units of unskilled labor, the variable input, and 10 units of capital. Assume the market demand for this output increases. Answer the following questions?
   a. In the short run will this firm change its level of output? Explain verbally and also use correctly labeled side-by-side graphs of the output market to complete your explanation.
   b. In the short run will this firm change its use of capital, following the increase in market demand for the output? Explain.
   c. In the short run will this firm change its use of labor? Explain verbally and also use correctly labeled side-by-side graphs of the input market to complete your explanation. [Note: the wage for unskilled labor does not change in this analysis.]

PROBLEMS

1. A delivery company is considering adding another vehicle to its delivery fleet; each vehicle is rented for \$100 per day. Assume that the additional vehicle would be capable of delivering 1,500 packages per day and that each package that is delivered brings in 10 cents in revenue. Also assume that adding the delivery vehicle would not affect any other costs. LO14.2
   a. What is the MRP? What is the MRC? Should the firm add this delivery vehicle?
   b. Now suppose that the cost of renting a vehicle doubles to \$200 per day. What are the MRP and MRC? Should the firm add a delivery vehicle under these circumstances?
   c. Next suppose that the cost of renting a vehicle falls back down to \$100 per day but, due to extremely congested freeways, an additional vehicle would only be able to deliver 750 packages per day. What are the MRP and MRC in this situation? Would adding a vehicle under these circumstances increase the firm's profits?
2. Suppose that marginal product tripled while product price fell by one-half in Table 14.1. What would be the new MRP values in Table 14.1? What would be the net impact on the location of the resource demand curve in Figure 14.1? LO14.2
3. Suppose that a monopoly firm finds that its MR is \$50 for the first unit sold each day, \$49 for the second unit sold each day, \$48 for the third unit sold each day, and so on. Further suppose that the first worker hired produces 5 units per day, the second 4 units per day, the third 3 units per day, and so on. LO14.3
   a. What is the firm's MRP for each of the first five workers?
   b. Suppose that the monopolist is subjected to rate regulation and the regulator stipulates that it must charge exactly \$40 per unit for all units sold. At that price, what is the firm's MRP for each of the first five workers?
   c. If the daily wage paid to workers is \$170 per day, how many workers will the unregulated monopoly demand? How many will the regulated monopoly demand? Looking at those figures, will the regulated or the unregulated monopoly demand more workers at that wage?
   d. If the daily wage paid to workers falls to \$77 per day, how many workers will the unregulated monopoly demand? How many will the regulated monopoly demand? Looking at those figures, will the regulated or the unregulated monopoly demand more workers at that wage?
   e. Comparing your answers to parts *c* and *d*, does regulating a monopoly's output price *always* increase its demand for resources?
4. Consider a small landscaping company run by Mr. Viemeister. He is considering increasing his firm's capacity. If he adds one more worker, the firm's total monthly revenue will increase from \$50,000 to \$58,000. If he adds one more tractor, monthly revenue will increase from \$50,000 to \$62,000. Each additional worker costs \$4,000 per month, while an additional tractor would also cost \$4,000 per month. LO14.5
   a. What is the marginal product of labor? The marginal product of capital?
   b. What is the ratio of the marginal product of labor to the price of labor (MP_L/P_L)? What is the ratio of the marginal product of capital to the price of capital (MP_K/P_K)?
   c. Is the firm using the least-costly combination of inputs?
   d. Does adding an additional worker or adding an additional tractor yield a larger increase in total revenue for each dollar spent?

15 Chapter

Wage Determination

Learning Objectives

LO15.1 **Explain why labor productivity and real hourly compensation track so closely over time.**

LO15.2 **Show how wage rates and employment levels are determined in competitive labor markets.**

LO15.3 **Demonstrate how monopsony (a market with a single employer) can reduce wages below competitive levels.**

LO15.4 **Discuss how unions increase wage rates by pursuing the demand-enhancement model, the craft union model, or the industrial union model.**

LO15.5 **Explain why wages and employment are determined by collective bargaining in a situation of bilateral monopoly.**

LO15.6 **Discuss how minimum wage laws affect labor markets.**

LO15.7 **List the major causes of wage differentials.**

LO15.8 **Identify the types, benefits, and costs of "pay-for-performance" plans.**

LO15.9 **(Appendix) Relate who belongs to U.S. unions, the basics of collective bargaining, and the economic effects of unions.**

AP Chapter Focus

Roughly 150 million Americans go to work each day. We work at an amazing variety of jobs for thousands of different firms and receive considerable differences in pay. What determines our hourly wage or annual salary? Why is the salary for, say, a topflight major-league baseball player $15 million or more a year, whereas the pay for a first-rate schoolteacher is $50,000? Why are starting salaries for college graduates who major in engineering and accounting so much higher than those for graduates majoring in journalism and sociology?

Having explored the major factors that underlie labor demand, we now bring *labor supply* into our analysis to help answer these questions. Generally speaking, labor supply and labor demand interact to determine the level of hourly wage rates or annual salaries in each occupation. Collectively, those wages and salaries make up about 70 percent of all income paid to American resource suppliers.

AP Labor, Wages, and Earnings

LO15.1 Explain why labor productivity and real hourly compensation track so closely over time.

Economists use the term "labor" broadly to apply to (1) blue- and white-collar workers of all varieties; (2) professional people such as lawyers, physicians, dentists, and teachers; and (3) owners of small businesses, including barbers, plumbers, and a host of retailers who provide labor as they operate their own businesses.

Wages are the price that employers pay for labor. Wages take the form of not only direct money payments such as hourly pay, annual salaries, bonuses, commissions, and royalties, but also fringe benefits such as paid vacations, health insurance, and pensions. Unless stated otherwise, we will use the term "wages" to mean all such payments and benefits converted to an hourly basis. That will remind us that the **wage rate** is the price paid per unit of labor services, in this case an hour of work. It will also let us distinguish between the wage rate and labor earnings, the latter determined by multiplying the number of hours worked by the hourly wage rate.

We must also distinguish between nominal wages and real wages. A **nominal wage** is the amount of money received per hour, day, or year. A **real wage** is the quantity of goods and services a worker can obtain with nominal wages; real wages reveal the "purchasing power" of nominal wages.

Your real wage depends on your nominal wage and the prices of the goods and services you purchase. Suppose you receive a 5 percent increase in your nominal wage during a certain year but in that same year the price level increases by 3 percent. Then your real wage has increased by 2 percent (= 5 percent − 3 percent). Unless otherwise indicated, we will assume that the overall level of prices remains constant. In other words, we will discuss only *real* wages.

General Level of Wages

Wages differ among nations, regions, occupations, and individuals. Wage rates are much higher in the United States than in China or India. They are slightly higher in the north and east of the United States than in the south. Plumbers are paid less than NFL punters. And one physician may earn twice as much as another physician for the same number of hours of work. The average wages earned by workers also differ by gender, race, and ethnic background.

The general, or average, level of wages, like the general level of prices, includes a wide range of different wage rates. It includes the wages of bakers, barbers, brick masons, and brain surgeons. By averaging such wages, we can more easily compare wages among regions and among nations.

GLOBAL PERSPECTIVE 15.1

Hourly Wages of Production Workers, Selected Nations

Wage differences are pronounced worldwide. The data shown here indicate that hourly compensation in the United States is not as high as in some European nations. It is important to note, however, that the prices of goods and services vary greatly among nations, and the process of converting foreign wages into dollars may not accurately reflect such variations.

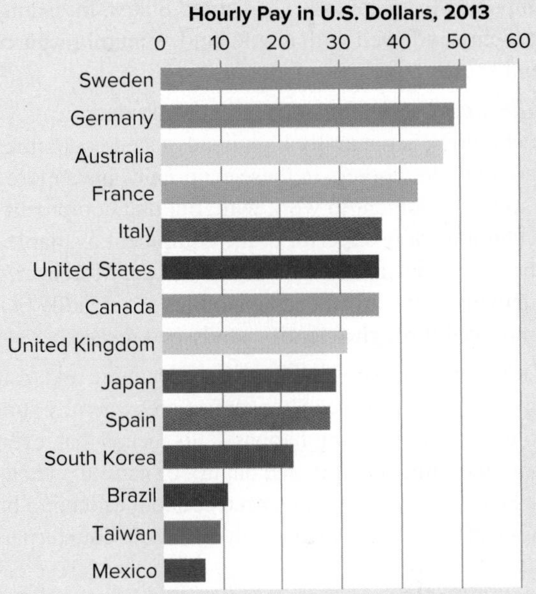

Source: The Conference Board, **www.conference-board.org**.

As Global Perspective 15.1 suggests, the general level of real wages in the United States is relatively high—although clearly not the highest in the world.

The simplest explanation for the high real wages in the United States and other industrially advanced economies (referred to hereafter as advanced economies) is that the demand for labor in those nations is relatively large compared to the supply of labor.

Role of Productivity

We know from the previous chapter that the demand for labor, or for any other resource, depends on its productivity. In general, the greater the productivity of labor, the greater is the demand for it. And if the total supply of labor is fixed, then the stronger the demand for labor, the higher is the average level of real wages. The demand for labor in the United States and the other major advanced economies is large because labor in those countries is highly productive. There are several reasons for that high productivity:

- ***Plentiful capital*** Workers in the advanced economies have access to large amounts of physical capital equipment (machinery and buildings). In the United States in 2015, $180,076 of physical capital was available, on average, for each worker.
- ***Access to abundant natural resources*** In advanced economies, natural resources tend to be abundant in relation to the size of the labor force. Some of those resources are available domestically and others are imported from abroad. The United States, for example, is richly endowed with arable land, mineral resources, and sources of energy for industry.
- ***Advanced technology*** The level of production technology is generally high in advanced economies. Not only do workers in these economies have more capital equipment to work with, but that equipment is technologically superior to the equipment available to the vast majority of workers worldwide. Moreover, work methods in the advanced economies are steadily being improved through scientific study and research.
- ***Labor quality*** The health, vigor, education, and training of workers in advanced economies are generally superior to those in developing nations. This means that, even with the same quantity and quality of natural and capital resources, workers in advanced economies tend to be more efficient than many of their foreign counterparts.
- ***Other factors*** Less obvious factors also may underlie the high productivity in some of the advanced economies. In the United States, for example, such factors include (a) the efficiency and flexibility of management; (b) a business, social, and political environment that emphasizes production and productivity; (c) the vast size of the domestic market, which enables firms to engage in mass production; and (d) the increased specialization of production enabled by free-trade agreements with other nations.

Real Wages and Productivity

Figure 15.1 shows the close long-run relationship in the United States between output per hour of work and real hourly compensation (= wages and salaries + employers' contributions to social insurance and private benefit plans). Because real income and real output are two ways of viewing the same thing, real income (compensation) per worker can increase only at about the same rate as output per worker. When workers produce more real output per hour, more real income is available to distribute to them for each hour worked.

In the actual economy, however, suppliers of land, capital, and entrepreneurial talent also share in the income from production. Real wages therefore do not always rise in lockstep with gains in productivity over short spans of time. But over long periods, productivity and real wages tend to rise together.

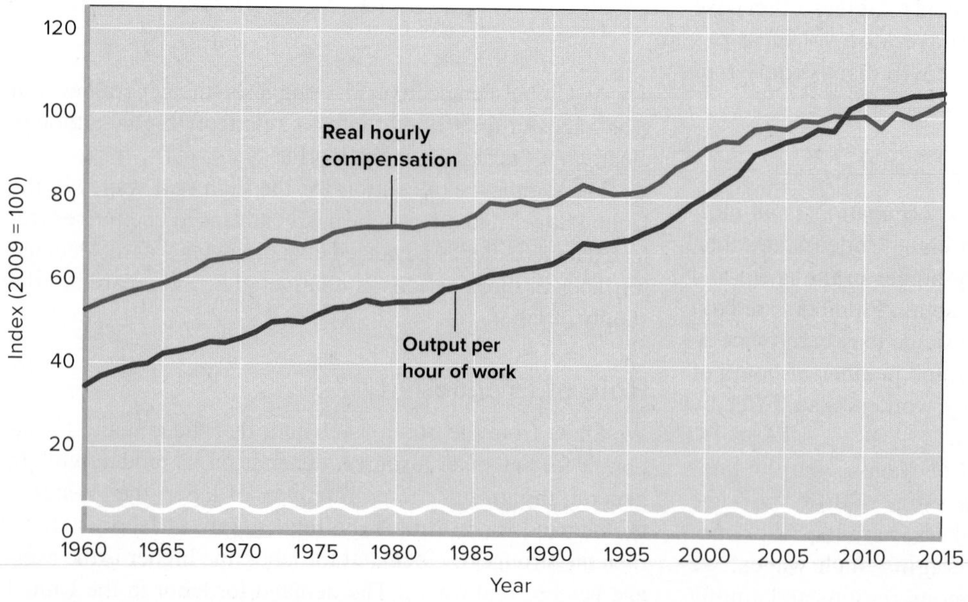

FIGURE 15.1 Output per hour and real hourly compensation in the United States, 1960–2015. Over long time periods, output per hour of work and real hourly compensation are closely related.

Source: Bureau of Labor Statistics, **www.bls.gov**.

FIGURE 15.2 **The long-run trend of real wages in the United States.** The productivity of U.S. labor has increased substantially over the long run, causing the demand for labor *D* to shift rightward (that is, to increase) more rapidly than increases in the supply of labor *S*. The result has been increases in real wages.

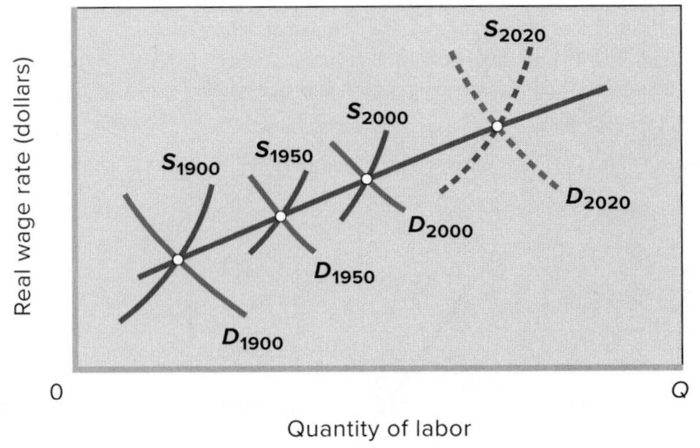

Long-Run Trend of Real Wages

Basic supply and demand analysis helps explain the long-term trend of real-wage growth in the United States. The nation's labor force has grown significantly over the decades. But as a result of the productivity-increasing factors we have mentioned, increases in labor demand have outstripped increases in labor supply. Figure 15.2 shows several such increases in labor supply and labor demand. The result has been a long-run, or secular, increase in wage rates and employment. For example, real hourly compensation in the United States has roughly doubled since 1960. Over that same period, employment has increased by about 80 million workers.

AP A Purely Competitive Labor Market

LO15.2 Show how wage rates and employment levels are determined in competitive labor markets.

Average levels of wages, however, disguise the great variation of wage rates among occupations and within occupations. What determines the wage rate paid for a specific type of labor? Demand and supply analysis again is revealing. Let's begin by examining labor demand and labor supply in a **purely competitive labor market.** In this type of market:

- Numerous firms compete with one another in hiring a specific type of labor.
- Each of many qualified workers with identical skills supplies that type of labor.
- Individual firms and individual workers are "wage takers" since neither can exert any control over the market wage rate.

Market Demand for Labor

Suppose 200 firms demand a particular type of labor, say, carpenters. These firms need not be in the same industry; industries are defined according to the products they produce and not the resources they employ. Thus, firms producing wood-framed furniture, wood windows and doors, houses and apartment buildings, and wood cabinets will demand carpenters. To find the total, or market, labor demand curve for a particular labor service, we sum horizontally the labor demand curves (the marginal revenue product curves) of the individual firms, as indicated in **Figure 15.3 (Key Graph).** The horizontal summing of the 200 labor demand curves like *d* in Figure 15.3b yields the market labor demand curve *D* in Figure 15.3a.

Market Supply of Labor

On the supply side of a purely competitive labor market, we assume that no union is present and that workers individually compete for available jobs. The supply curve for each type of labor slopes upward, indicating that employers as a group must pay higher wage rates to obtain more workers. They must do this to bid workers away from other industries, occupations, and localities. Within limits, workers have alternative job opportunities. For example, they may work in other industries in the same locality, or they may work in their present occupations in different cities or states, or they may work in other occupations.

Firms that want to hire these workers (here, carpenters) must pay higher wage rates to attract them away from the alternative job opportunities available to them. They must also pay higher wages to induce people who are not currently in the labor force—who are perhaps doing household activities or enjoying leisure—to seek employment. In short, assuming that wages are constant in other labor markets, higher wages in a particular labor market entice more workers to offer their labor services in that market—a fact expressed graphically by the upsloping market supply-of-labor curve *S* in Figure 15.3a.

Labor Market Equilibrium

The intersection of the market labor demand curve and the market labor supply curve determines the equilibrium wage rate and level of employment in a purely competitive labor market. In Figure 15.3a the equilibrium wage rate is W_c ($10) and the number of workers hired is Q_c (1,000). To the individual firm the market wage rate W_c is given. Each of the many firms employs such a small fraction of the total available supply of this type of labor that no single firm can influence the wage rate. As shown by the horizontal line *s* in Figure 15.3b, the supply of labor faced by an individual firm is perfectly elastic. It can hire as many or as few workers as it wants to at the market wage rate.

AP KEY GRAPH

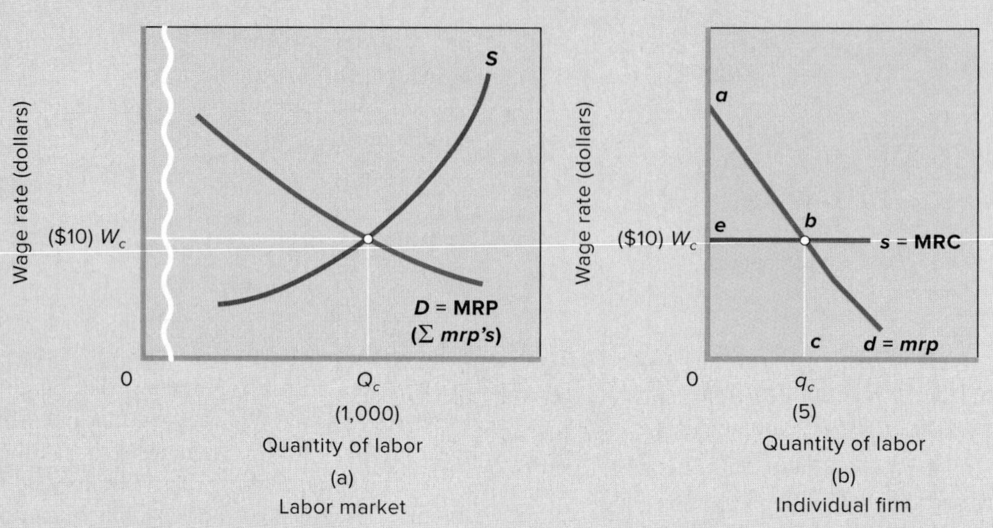

FIGURE 15.3 Labor supply and labor demand in (a) a purely competitive labor market and (b) a single competitive firm. In a purely competitive labor market (a), market labor supply *S* and market labor demand *D* determine the equilibrium wage rate W_c and the equilibrium number of workers Q_c. Each individual competitive firm (b) takes this competitive wage W_c as given. Thus, the individual firm's labor supply curve *s* = MRC is perfectly elastic at the going wage W_c. Its labor demand curve, *d*, is its MRP curve (here labeled *mrp*). The firm maximizes its profit by hiring workers up to where MRP = MRC. Area 0*abc* represents both the firm's total revenue and its total cost. The green area is its total wage cost; the blue area is its nonlabor costs, including a normal profit—that is, the firm's payments to the suppliers of land, capital, and entrepreneurship.

QUICK QUIZ FOR FIGURE 15.3

1. The supply-of-labor curve *S* slopes upward in graph (a) because:
   a. the law of diminishing marginal utility applies.
   b. the law of diminishing returns applies.
   c. workers can afford to "buy" more leisure when the wage rate increases.
   d. higher wages are needed to attract workers away from other labor markets, household activities, and leisure.
2. This firm's labor demand curve *d* in graph (b) slopes downward because:
   a. the law of diminishing marginal utility applies.
   b. the law of diminishing returns applies.
   c. the firm must lower its price to sell additional units of its product.
   d. the firm is a competitive employer, not a monopsonist.
3. In employing five workers, the firm represented in graph (b):
   a. has a total wage cost of $6,000.
   b. is adhering to the general principle of undertaking all actions for which the marginal benefit exceeds the marginal cost.
   c. uses less labor than would be ideal from society's perspective.
   d. experiences increasing marginal returns.
4. A rightward shift of the labor supply curve in graph (a) would shift curve:
   a. *d* = *mrp* leftward in graph (b).
   b. *d* = *mrp* rightward in graph (b).
   c. *s* = MRC upward in graph (b).
   d. *s* = MRC downward in graph (b).

Answers: 1. d; 2. b; 3. b; 4. d

Each individual firm will maximize its profit (or minimize its loss) by hiring this type of labor up to the point at which marginal revenue product is equal to marginal resource cost. This is merely an application of the MRP = MRC rule we developed in Chapter 14.

As Table 15.1 indicates, when an individual competitive firm faces the market price for a resource, the marginal cost of that resource (MRC) is constant and is equal to the market price for each and every unit that the competitive firm may choose to purchase. Note that MRC is constant at $10 and matches the $10 wage rate. Each additional worker hired adds precisely his or her own wage rate ($10 in this case) to the firm's total resource cost. So the firm in a purely competitive labor market maximizes its profit by hiring workers up to the point at which its wage rate equals MRP. In Figure 15.3b this firm will hire q_c (5) workers, paying each worker the market wage rate W_c ($10). The other 199 firms (not shown) that are hiring workers in this labor market will also each employ 5 workers and pay $10 per hour.

TABLE 15.1 The Supply of Labor: Pure Competition in the Hire of Labor

(1) Units of Labor	(2) Wage Rate	(3) Total Labor Cost	(4) Marginal Resource (Labor) Cost
0	$10	$ 0	
1	10	10	$10
2	10	20	10
3	10	30	10
4	10	40	10
5	10	50	10
6	10	60	10

CONSIDER THIS . . .

Source: © numbeos/E-plus /Getty Images RF

Fringe Benefits vs. Take-Home Pay

Figure 15.2 shows that total compensation has risen significantly over the past several decades. Not shown in that figure, however, is the fact that the amount of take-home pay received by middle-class American workers has increased by much less. One contributing factor has been the rise of fringe benefits.

To see why fringe benefits matter, recall that throughout this chapter we have defined the wage as the total price that employers pay to obtain labor and compensate workers for providing it. Under our definition, wages are the sum of take-home pay (such as hourly pay and annual salaries) and fringe benefits (such as paid vacations, health insurance, and pensions).

So now consider an equilibrium wage, such as W_c in Figure 15.3. If workers want higher fringe benefits, they can have them—but only if take-home pay falls by an equal amount. With the equilibrium wage fixed by supply and demand, the only way workers can get more fringe benefits is by accepting lower take-home pay.

This is an important point to understand because in recent decades, workers have received an increasing fraction of their total compensation in the form of fringe benefits—especially health insurance. Those fringe benefits are costly and in a competitive labor market, each $1 increase in fringe benefits means $1 less for paychecks.

That trade-off helps to explain why take-home pay has increased by less than total compensation in recent decades. With a rising fraction of total compensation flowing toward fringe benefits, the increase in take-home pay was much less than the overall increase in total compensation.

To determine a firm's total revenue from employing a particular number of labor units, we sum the MRPs of those units. For example, if a firm employs 3 labor units with marginal revenue products of $14, $13, and $12, respectively, then the firm's total revenue is $39 (= $14 + $13 + $12). In Figure 15.3b, where we are not restricted to whole units of labor, total revenue is represented by area 0*abc* under the MRP curve to the left of q_c. And what area represents the firm's total cost, including a normal profit? Answer: For q_c units, the same area—0*abc*. The green rectangle represents the firm's total wage cost ($0q_c \times 0W_c$). The blue triangle (total revenue minus total wage cost) represents the firm's nonlabor costs—its explicit and implicit payments to land, capital, and entrepreneurship. Thus, in this case, total cost (wages plus other income payments) equals total revenue. This firm and others like it are earning only a normal profit. So Figure 15.3b represents a long-run equilibrium for a firm that is selling its product in a purely competitive product market and hiring its labor in a purely competitive labor market.

Monopsony Model

LO15.3 Demonstrate how monopsony (a market with a single employer) can reduce wages below competitive levels.

In the purely competitive labor market described in the preceding section, each employer hires too small an amount of labor to influence the wage rate. Each firm can hire as little or as much labor as it needs, but only at the market wage rate, as reflected in its horizontal labor supply curve. The situation is quite different when the labor market is a **monopsony,** a market structure in which there is only a single buyer. A labor market monopsony has the following characteristics:

- There is only a single buyer of a particular type of labor.
- The workers providing this type of labor have few employment options other than working for the monopsony because they are either geographically immobile or because finding alternative employment would mean having to acquire new skills.
- The firm is a "wage maker" because the wage rate it must pay varies directly with the number of workers it employs.

As is true of monopoly power, there are various degrees of monopsony power. In *pure* monopsony such power is at its maximum because only a single employer hires labor in the labor market. The best real-world examples are probably the labor markets in some towns that depend almost entirely on one major firm. For example, a silver-mining company may be almost the only source of employment in a remote Idaho town. A Colorado ski resort, a Wisconsin paper mill, or an Alaskan fish processor may provide most of the employment in its geographically isolated locale.

In other cases three or four firms may each hire a large portion of the supply of labor in a certain market and therefore have some monopsony power. Moreover, if they tacitly or openly act in concert in hiring labor, they greatly enhance their monopsony power.

Upsloping Labor Supply to Firm

When a firm hires most of the available supply of a certain type of labor, its decision to employ more or fewer workers affects the wage rate it pays to those workers. Specifically, if a firm is large in relation to the size of the labor market, it will have to pay a higher wage rate to attract labor away from other employment or from leisure. Suppose that there is only one employer of a particular type of labor in a certain geographic area. In this pure monopsony situation, the labor supply curve for the *firm* and the total labor supply curve for the *labor market* are identical. The monopsonist's supply curve—represented by curve *S* in Figure 15.4—is upsloping because the firm must pay higher wage rates if it wants to attract and hire additional workers. This same curve is also the monopsonist's average-cost-of-labor curve. Each point on curve *S* indicates the wage rate (cost) per worker that must be paid to attract the corresponding number of workers.

MRC Higher Than the Wage Rate

When a monopsonist pays a higher wage to attract an additional worker, it must pay that higher wage not only to the additional worker, but to all the workers it is currently employing at a lower wage. If not, labor morale will deteriorate, and the employer will be plagued with labor unrest because of wage-rate differences existing for the same job. Paying a uniform wage to all workers means that the cost of an extra worker—the marginal resource (labor) cost (MRC)—is the sum of that

AP FIGURE 15.4 The wage rate and level of employment in a monopsonistic labor market. In a monopsonistic labor market the employer's marginal resource (labor) cost curve (MRC) lies above the labor supply curve *S*. Equating MRC with MRP at point *b*, the monopsonist hires Q_m workers (compared with Q_c under competition). As indicated by point *c* on *S*, it pays only wage rate W_m (compared with the competitive wage W_c).

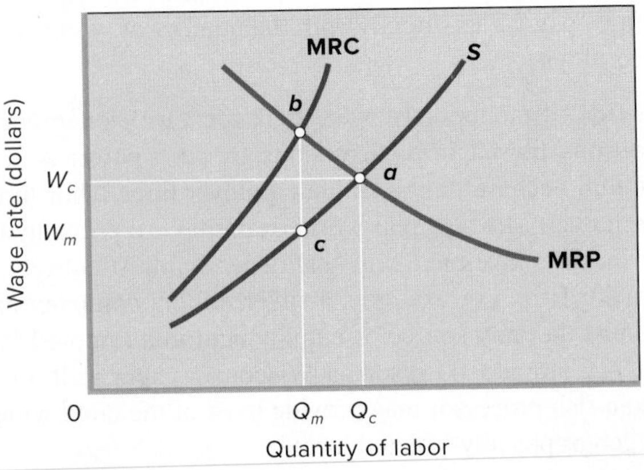

AP TABLE 15.2 The Supply of Labor: Monopsony in the Hiring of Labor

(1) Units of Labor	(2) Wage Rate	(3) Total Labor Cost	(4) Marginal Resource (Labor) Cost
0	$ 5	$ 0	
1	6	6	$ 6
2	7	14	8
3	8	24	10
4	9	36	12
5	10	50	14
6	11	66	16

worker's wage rate and the amount necessary to bring the wage rate of all current workers up to the new wage level.

Table 15.2 illustrates this point. One worker can be hired at a wage rate of $6. But hiring a second worker forces the firm to pay a higher wage rate of $7. The marginal resource (labor) cost of the second worker is $8—the $7 paid to the second worker plus a $1 raise for the first worker. From another viewpoint, total labor cost is now $14 (= 2 × $7), up from $6 (= 1 × $6). So the MRC of the second worker is $8 (= $14 – $6), not just the $7 wage rate paid to that worker. Similarly, the marginal labor cost of the third worker is $10—the $8 that must be paid to attract this worker from alternative employment plus $1 raises, from $7 to $8, for the first two workers.

Here is the key point: Because the monopsonist is the only employer in the labor market, its marginal resource (labor) cost exceeds the wage rate. Graphically, the monopsonist's MRC curve lies above the average-cost-of-labor curve, or labor supply curve *S*, as is clearly shown in Figure 15.4.

Equilibrium Wage and Employment

How many units of labor will the monopsonist hire, and what wage rate will it pay? To maximize profit, the monopsonist will employ the quantity of labor Q_m in Figure 15.4, because at that quantity MRC and MRP are equal (point *b*).[1] The

[1] The fact that MRC exceeds resource price when resources are hired or purchased under imperfectly competitive (monopsonistic) conditions calls for adjustments in Chapter 14's least-cost and profit-maximizing rules for hiring resources. (See equations 1 and 2 in the "Optimal Combination of Resources" section of Chapter 14.) Specifically, we must substitute MRC for resource price in the denominators of our two equations. That is, with imperfect competition in the hiring of both labor and capital, equation 1 becomes

$$\frac{MP_L}{MRC_L} = \frac{MP_C}{MRC_C} \qquad (1')$$

and equation 2 is restated as

$$\frac{MRP_L}{MRC_L} = \frac{MRP_C}{MRC_C} = 1 \qquad (2')$$

In fact, equations 1 and 2 can be regarded as special cases of 1′ and 2′ in which firms happen to be hiring under purely competitive conditions and resource price is therefore equal to, and can be substituted for, marginal resource cost.

monopsonist next determines how much it must pay to attract these Q_m workers. From the supply curve S, specifically point c, it sees that it must pay wage rate W_m. Clearly, it need not pay a wage equal to MRP; it can attract and hire exactly the number of workers it wants (Q_m) with wage rate W_m. And that is the wage that it will pay.

Contrast these results with those that would prevail in a competitive labor market. With competition in the hiring of labor, the level of employment would be greater (at Q_c) and the wage rate would be higher (at W_c). Other things equal, the monopsonist maximizes its profit by hiring a smaller number of workers and thereby paying a less-than-competitive wage rate. Society obtains a smaller output, and workers receive a wage rate that is less by bc than their marginal revenue product. Just as a monopolistic seller finds it profitable to restrict product output to realize an above-competitive price for its goods, the monopsonistic employer of resources finds it profitable to restrict employment in order to reduce wage rates below those that would occur under competitive conditions.

Examples of Monopsony Power

Fortunately, monopsonistic labor markets are uncommon in the United States. In most labor markets, several potential employers compete for most workers, particularly for workers who are occupationally and geographically mobile. Also, where monopsony labor market outcomes might have otherwise occurred, unions have often sprung up to counteract that power by forcing firms to negotiate wages. Nevertheless, economists have found some evidence of monopsony power in such diverse labor markets as the markets for nurses, professional athletes, public school teachers, newspaper employees, and some building-trade workers.

In the case of nurses, the major employers in most locales are a relatively small number of hospitals. Further, the highly specialized skills of nurses are not readily transferable to other occupations. It has been found, in accordance with the monopsony model, that, other things equal, the smaller the number of hospitals in a town or city (that is, the greater the degree of monopsony), the lower the beginning salaries of nurses.

Professional sports leagues also provide a good example of monopsony, particularly as it relates to the pay of first-year players. The National Football League, the National Basketball Association, and Major League Baseball assign first-year players to teams through "player drafts." That device prohibits other teams from competing for a player's services, at least for several years, until the player becomes a "free agent." In this way each league exercises monopsony power, which results in lower salaries than would occur under competitive conditions.

AP QUICK REVIEW 15.1

- ✓ Real wages have increased over time in the U.S. because labor demand has increased relative to labor supply. Principally, this relative increase results from productivity gains and technological progress.
- ✓ Over the long term, real wages per worker have increased at approximately the same rate as worker productivity.
- ✓ The competitive employer is a wage taker and employs workers at the point where the wage rate (MRC) equals MRP. The competitive employer can hire all the labor it wishes at the prevailing wage rate.
- ✓ The labor supply curve to a monopsonist is upsloping, causing MRC to exceed the wage rate for each worker. Other things equal, the monopsonist, hiring the quantity where MRC = MRP (and moving to the supply curve at that quantity for the wage rate), will employ fewer workers and pay a lower wage rate than would a purely competitive employer.

AP Three Union Models

LO15.4 Discuss how unions increase wage rates by pursuing the demand-enhancement model, the craft union model, or the industrial union model.

Our assumption thus far has been that workers compete with one another in selling their labor services. But in some labor markets workers unionize and sell their labor services collectively. (We examine union membership, collective bargaining, and union impacts in detail in an appendix to this chapter. Here our focus is on three union wage models.)

When a union is formed in an otherwise competitive labor market, it usually bargains with a relatively large number of employers. It has many goals, the most important of which is to raise wage rates. It can pursue that objective in several ways.

Demand-Enhancement Model

Unions recognize that their ability to influence the demand for labor is limited. But from the union's viewpoint, increasing the demand for union labor is highly desirable. As Figure 15.5 shows, an increase in the demand for union labor will create a higher union wage along with more jobs.

Unions can increase the demand for their labor by increasing the demand for the goods or services they help produce. Political lobbying is the main tool for increasing the demand for union-produced goods or services. For example, construction unions have lobbied for new highways, mass-transit systems, and stadium projects. Teachers' unions and associations have pushed for increased public spending on education. Unions in the aerospace industry have lobbied to increase spending on the military and on space exploration. U.S. steel unions and forest-product workers have lobbied for tariffs and quotas on foreign

FIGURE 15.5 Unions and demand enhancement. When unions can increase the demand for union labor (say, from D_1 to D_2), they can realize higher wage rates (W_c to W_u) and more jobs (Q_c to Q_u).

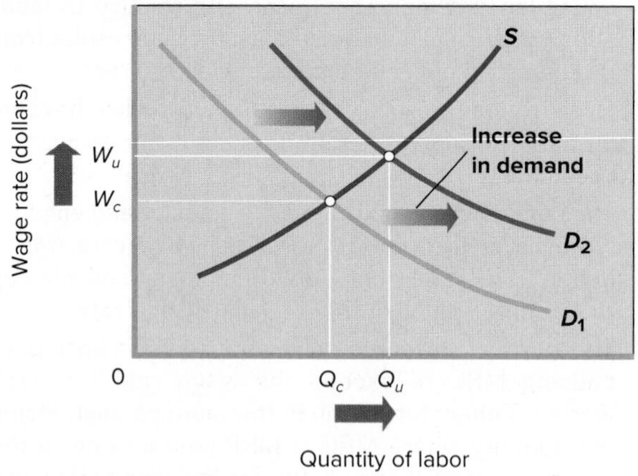

imports of steel and lumber, respectively. Such trade restrictions shift the demand for labor away from foreign countries and toward unionized U.S. labor.

Unions can also increase the demand for union labor by altering the price of other inputs. For example, although union members are generally paid significantly more than the minimum wage, unions have strongly supported increases in the minimum wage. The purpose may be to raise the price of low-wage, nonunion labor, which in some cases is substitutable for union labor. A higher minimum wage for nonunion workers will discourage employers from substituting such workers for union workers and will thereby bolster the demand for union members.

Similarly, unions have sometimes sought to increase the demand for their labor by supporting policies that will reduce or hold down the price of a complementary resource. For example, unions in industries that represent workers who transport fruits and vegetables may support legislation that allows low-wage foreign agricultural workers to temporarily work in the United States. Where union labor and another resource are complementary, a price decrease for the other resource will increase the demand for union labor through Chapter 14's output effect.

Exclusive or Craft Union Model

Unions can also boost wage rates by reducing the supply of labor, and over the years organized labor has favored policies to do just that. For example, labor unions have supported legislation that has (1) restricted permanent immigration, (2) reduced child labor, (3) encouraged compulsory retirement, and (4) enforced a shorter workweek.

Moreover, certain types of workers have adopted techniques designed to restrict the number of workers who can join their union. This is especially true of *craft unions,* whose members possess a particular skill, such as carpenters, brick masons, or plumbers. Craft unions have frequently forced employers to agree to hire only union members, thereby gaining virtually complete control of the labor supply. Then, by following restrictive membership policies—for example, long apprenticeships, very high initiation fees, and limits on the number of new members admitted—they have artificially restricted labor supply. As indicated in Figure 15.6, such practices result in higher wage rates and constitute what is called **exclusive unionism.** By excluding workers from unions and therefore from the labor supply, craft unions succeed in elevating wage rates.

This craft union model is also applicable to many professional organizations, such as the American Medical Association, the National Education Association, the American Bar Association, and hundreds of others. Such groups seek to prohibit competition for their services from less qualified labor suppliers by leveraging the special interest effect under which a small group of insiders is able to obtain favorable political treatment despite imposing substantial costs on outsiders. One way to accomplish that is through **occupational licensing.** Here a group of workers in a given occupation pressure federal, state, or municipal government to pass a law that says that some occupational group (for example, barbers, physicians, lawyers, plumbers, cosmetologists, egg graders, pest controllers) can practice their trade only if they meet certain requirements. Those requirements might include level of education, amount of work experience, the passing of an examination, and personal characteristics ("the practitioner must be of good moral character"). Members of the licensed occupation typically dominate the licensing board that administers such laws. The result is self-regulation, which often leads to policies that serve only to restrict entry to the occupation and reduce labor supply.

FIGURE 15.6 Exclusive or craft unionism. By reducing the supply of labor (say, from S_1 to S_2) through the use of restrictive membership policies, exclusive unions achieve higher wage rates (W_c to W_u). However, restriction of the labor supply also reduces the number of workers employed (Q_c to Q_u).

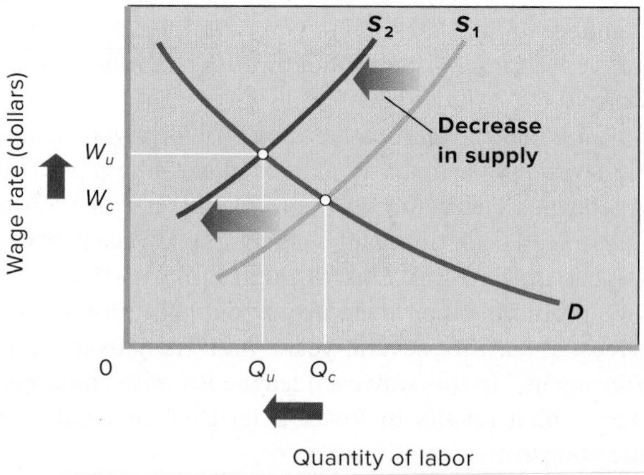

The expressed purpose of licensing is to protect consumers from incompetent practitioners—surely a worthy goal. But such licensing, if abused, results in above-competitive wages and earnings for those in the licensed occupation (Figure 15.6). Moreover, licensing requirements often include a residency requirement, which inhibits the interstate movement of qualified workers. Some 1,100 occupations are now licensed in the United States. This chapter's Last Word gives examples of excessive licensing requirements that hurt the employment prospects of lower-income workers.

Inclusive or Industrial Union Model

Instead of trying to limit their membership, however, most unions seek to organize all available workers. This is especially true of the *industrial unions,* such as those of the automobile workers and steelworkers. Such unions seek as members all available unskilled, semiskilled, and skilled workers in an industry. It makes sense for a union to be exclusive when its members are skilled craft workers for whom the employer has few substitutes. But it does not make sense for a union to be exclusive when trying to organize unskilled and semiskilled workers. To break a strike, employers could then easily substitute unskilled or semiskilled nonunion workers for the unskilled or semiskilled union workers.

By contrast, an industrial union that includes virtually all available workers in its membership can put firms under great pressure to agree to its wage demands. Because of its legal right to strike, such a union can threaten to deprive firms of their entire labor supply. And an actual strike can do just that. Further, with virtually all available workers in the union, it will be difficult in the short run for new nonunion firms to emerge and thereby undermine what the union is demanding from existing firms.

We illustrate such **inclusive unionism** in Figure 15.7. Initially, the competitive equilibrium wage rate is W_c and the level of employment is Q_c. Now suppose an industrial union is formed that demands a higher, above-equilibrium wage rate of, say, W_u. That wage rate W_u would create a perfectly elastic labor supply over the range *ae* in Figure 15.7. If firms wanted to hire any workers in this range, they would have to pay the union-imposed wage rate. If they decide against meeting this wage demand, the union will supply no labor at all, and the firms will be faced with a strike. If firms decide it is better to pay the higher wage rate than to suffer a strike, they will cut back on employment from Q_c to Q_u.

By agreeing to the union's wage demand, individual employers become wage takers at the union wage rate W_u. Because labor supply is perfectly elastic over range *ae,* the marginal resource (labor) cost is equal to the wage rate W_u over this range. The Q_u level of employment is the result of employers' equating this MRC (now equal to the union wage rate) with MRP, according to our profit-maximizing rule.

FIGURE 15.7 Inclusive or industrial unionism. By organizing virtually all available workers in order to control the supply of labor, inclusive industrial unions may impose a wage rate, such as W_u, which is above the competitive wage rate W_c. In effect, this changes the labor supply curve from *S* to *aeS*. At wage rate W_u, employers will cut employment from Q_c to Q_u.

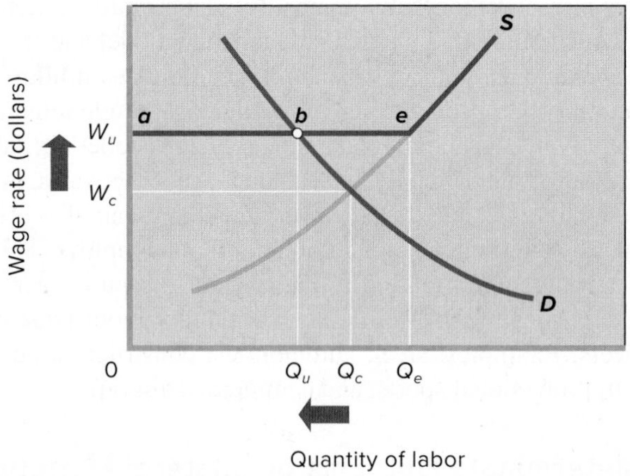

Note from point *e* on labor supply curve *S* that Q_e workers desire employment at wage W_u. But as indicated by point *b* on labor demand curve *D,* only Q_u workers are employed. The result is a surplus of labor of $Q_e - Q_u$ (also shown by distance *eb*). In a purely competitive labor market without the union, the effect of a surplus of unemployed workers would be lower wages. Specifically, the wage rate would fall to the equilibrium level W_c where the quantity of labor supplied equals the quantity of labor demanded (each Q_c). But this drop in wages does not happen because workers are acting collectively through their union. Individual workers cannot offer to work for less than W_u nor can employers pay less than that.

Wage Increases and Job Loss

Have U.S. unions been successful in raising the wages of their members? Evidence suggests that union members on average achieve a 15 percent wage advantage over nonunion workers. But when unions are successful in raising wages, their efforts also have another major effect.

As Figures 15.6 and 15.7 suggest, the wage-raising actions achieved by both exclusive and inclusive unionism reduce employment in unionized firms. Simply put, a union's success in achieving above-equilibrium wage rates tends to be accompanied by a decline in the number of workers employed. That result acts as a restraining influence on union wage demands. A union cannot expect to maintain solidarity within its ranks if it seeks a wage rate so high that 20 to 30 percent of its members lose their jobs.

AP Bilateral Monopoly Model

LO15.5 Explain why wages and employment are determined by collective bargaining in a situation of bilateral monopoly.

Suppose a strong industrial union is formed in a monopsonist labor market rather that a competitive labor market, thereby creating a combination of the monopsony model and the inclusive unionism model. Economists call the result **bilateral monopoly** because in its pure form there is a single seller and a single buyer. The union is a monopolistic "seller" of labor that controls labor supply and can influence wage rates, but it faces a monopsonistic "buyer" of labor that can also affect wages by altering the amount of labor that it employs. This is not an uncommon case, particularly in less pure forms in which a single union confronts two, three, or four large employers. Examples: steel, automobiles, construction equipment, professional sports, and commercial aircraft.

Indeterminate Outcome of Bilateral Monopoly

We show this situation in Figure 15.8, where Figure 15.7 is superimposed onto Figure 15.4. The monopsonistic employer will seek the below-competitive-equilibrium wage rate W_m, and the union will press for some above-competitive-equilibrium wage rate such as W_u. Which will be the outcome? We cannot say with certainty. The outcome is "logically indeterminate" because the bilateral monopoly model does not explain what will happen at the bargaining table. We can expect the wage outcome to lie somewhere between W_m and W_u. Beyond that, about all we can say is that the party with the greater bargaining power and the more effective bargaining strategy will probably get a wage closer to the one it seeks.

FIGURE 15.8 Bilateral monopoly in the labor market. A monopsonist seeks to hire Q_m workers (where MRC = MRP) and pay wage rate W_m corresponding to quantity Q_m on labor supply curve *S*. The inclusive union it faces seeks the above-equilibrium wage rate W_u. The actual outcome cannot be predicted by economic theory. It will result from bargaining between the two parties.

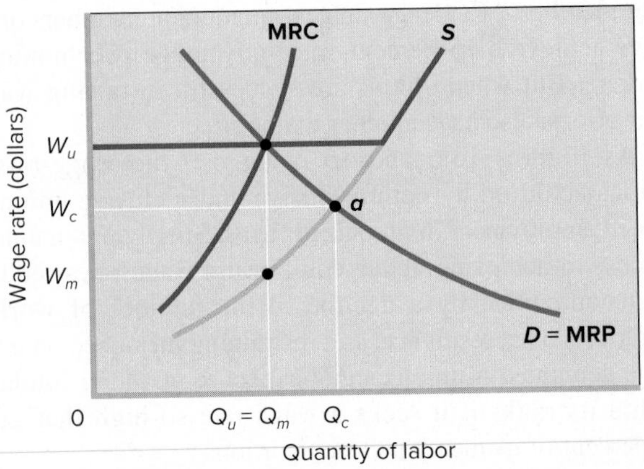

Desirability of Bilateral Monopoly

The wage and employment outcomes in this situation might be more economically desirable than the term "bilateral monopoly" implies. The monopoly on one side of the market might in effect cancel out the monopoly on the other side, yielding competitive or near-competitive results. If either the union or management prevailed in this market—that is, if the actual wage rate were either W_u or W_m—employment would be restricted to Q_m (where MRP = MRC), which is below the competitive level.

But now suppose the monopoly power of the union roughly offsets the monopsony power of management, and the union and management agree on wage rate W_c, which is the competitive wage. Once management accepts this wage rate, its incentive to restrict employment disappears; no longer can it depress wage rates by restricting employment. Instead, management hires at the most profitable resource quantity, where the bargained wage rate W_c (which is now the firm's MRC) is equal to the MRP. It hires Q_c workers. Thus, with monopoly on both sides of the labor market, the resulting wage rate and level of employment may be closer to competitive levels than would be the case if monopoly existed on only one side of the market.

AP QUICK REVIEW 15.2

- ✓ In the demand-enhancement union model, a union increases the wage rate by increasing labor demand through actions that increase product demand or alter the prices of related inputs.
- ✓ In the exclusive (craft) union model, a union increases wage rates by artificially restricting labor supply, through, say, long apprenticeships or occupational licensing.
- ✓ In the inclusive (industrial) union model, a union raises the wage rate through controlling a firm's labor supply and having the power to withhold labor via a strike unless a negotiated wage is obtained.
- ✓ Bilateral monopoly occurs in a labor market where a monopsonist bargains with an inclusive, or industrial, union. Wage and employment outcomes are determined by collective bargaining in this situation. An example would be a single employer in a town (like a textile firm) confronting a single source of labor, i.e., a union representing all the labor in the town.

The Minimum-Wage Controversy

LO15.6 Discuss how minimum wage laws affect labor markets.

Since the passage of the Fair Labor Standards Act in 1938, the United States has had a federal **minimum wage.** That wage has ranged between 30 and 50 percent of the average wage paid to manufacturing workers and was most recently raised to \$7.25 in July 2009. Numerous states, however, have minimum wages that are higher than the federal minimum wage. Some of these state minimum wages are considerably higher. For example, in 2016 the minimum wage in the state of Washington was $9.47 an hour. The purpose of the minimum wage is to provide a "wage floor" that will help less-skilled workers earn enough income to escape poverty.

Case against the Minimum Wage

Critics, reasoning in terms of Figure 15.7, contend that an above-equilibrium minimum wage (say, W_u) will simply cause employers to hire fewer workers. Downsloping labor demand curves are a reality. The higher labor costs may even force some firms out of business. Then some of the poor, low-wage workers whom the minimum wage was designed to help will find themselves out of work. Critics point out that a worker who is *unemployed* and desperate to find a job at a minimum wage of $7.25 per hour is clearly worse off than he or she would be if *employed* at a market wage rate of, say, $6.50 per hour.

A second criticism of the minimum wage is that it is "poorly targeted" to reduce household poverty. Critics point out that much of the benefit of the minimum wage accrues to workers, including many teenagers, who do not live in impoverished households.

Case for the Minimum Wage

Advocates of the minimum wage say that critics analyze its impact in an unrealistic context. Figure 15.7, advocates claim, assumes a competitive labor market. But in a less competitive, low-pay labor market where employers possess some monopsony power (Figure 15.8), the minimum wage can increase wage rates without causing significant unemployment. Indeed, a higher minimum wage may even produce more jobs by eliminating the motive that monopsonistic firms have for restricting employment. For example, a minimum-wage floor of W_c in Figure 15.8 would change the firm's labor supply curve to $W_c aS$ and prompt the firm to increase its employment from Q_m workers to Q_c workers.

Moreover, even if the labor market is competitive, the higher wage rate might prompt firms to find more productive tasks for low-paid workers, thereby raising their productivity. Alternatively, the minimum wage may reduce *labor turnover* (the rate at which workers voluntarily quit). With fewer low-productive trainees, the *average* productivity of the firm's workers would rise. In either case, the alleged negative employment effects of the minimum wage might not occur.

Evidence and Conclusions

Which view is correct? Unfortunately, there is no clear answer. All economists agree that firms will not hire workers who cost more per hour than the value of their hourly output. So there is some minimum wage sufficiently high that it would severely reduce employment. Consider $30 an hour, as an absurd example. Because the majority of U.S. workers earned barely over $20 per hour in 2015, a minimum wage of $30 per hour would render the majority of American workers unemployable because the minimum wage that they would have to be paid by potential employers would far exceed their marginal revenue products.

It has to be remembered, though, that a minimum wage will only cause unemployment in labor markets where the minimum wage is higher than the equilibrium wage. Because the current minimum wage of $7.25 per hour is much lower than the average hourly wage of about $21.04 that was earned by American workers in 2015, any unemployment caused by the $7.25 per hour minimum wage is most likely to fall on low-skilled workers who earn low wages due to their low productivity. These workers are mostly teenagers, adults who did not complete high school, and immigrants with low levels of education and poor English proficiency. For members of such groups, recent research suggests that a 10 percent increase in the minimum wage will cause a 1 to 3 percent decline in employment. However, estimates of the employment effect of minimum wage laws vary from study to study so that significant controversy remains.

The overall effect of the minimum wage is thus uncertain. On the one hand, the employment and unemployment effects of the minimum wage do not appear to be as great as many critics fear. On the other hand, because a large part of its effect is dissipated on nonpoverty families, the minimum wage is not as strong an antipoverty tool as many supporters contend.

Voting patterns and surveys make it clear, however, that the minimum wage has strong political support. Perhaps this stems from two realities: (1) More workers are believed to be helped than hurt by the minimum wage, and (2) the minimum wage gives society some assurance that employers are not "taking undue advantage" of vulnerable, low-skilled workers.

Wage Differentials

LO15.7 List the major causes of wage differentials.

Hourly wage rates and annual salaries differ greatly among occupations. In Table 15.3 we list average annual salaries for a number of occupations to illustrate such occupational **wage differentials.** For example, observe that surgeons on average earn nine times as much as retail salespersons. Not shown, there are also large wage differentials within some of the occupations listed. For example, some highly experienced surgeons earn several times as much income as surgeons just starting their careers. And although average wages for retail salespersons are relatively low, some top salespersons selling on commission make several times the average wages listed for their occupation.

TABLE 15.3 **Average Annual Wages in Selected Occupations, 2014**

Occupation	Average Annual Wages
1. Surgeons	$240,440
2. Petroleum engineers	147,520
3. Financial managers	130,320
4. Law professors	126,270
5. Pharmacists	118,470
6. Civil engineers	87,130
7. Dental hygienists	71,970
8. Registered nurses	69,790
9. Police officers	59,530
10. Electricians	54,520
11. Carpenters	45,490
12. Travel agents	37,370
13. Barbers	28,430
14. Retail salespersons	25,760
15. Janitors	25,460
16. Child care workers	21,710
17. Fast food cooks	19,030

Source: Bureau of Labor Statistics, **www.bls.gov**.

What explains wage differentials such as these? Once again, the forces of demand and supply are revealing. As we demonstrate in Figure 15.9, wage differentials can arise on either the supply or the demand side of labor markets. Figure 15.9a and Figure 15.9b represent labor markets for two occupational groups that have identical *labor supply curves*. Labor market (a) has a relatively high equilibrium wage (W_a) because labor demand is very strong. In labor market (b) the equilibrium wage is relatively low (W_b) because labor demand is weak. Clearly, the wage differential between occupations (a) and (b) results solely from differences in the magnitude of labor demand.

Contrast that situation with Figure 15.9c and 15.9d, where the *labor demand curves* are identical. In labor market (c) the equilibrium wage is relatively high (W_c) because labor supply is low. In labor market (d) labor supply is highly abundant, so the equilibrium wage (W_d) is relatively low. The wage differential between (c) and (d) results solely from the differences in the magnitude of labor supply.

Although Figure 15.9 provides a good starting point for understanding wage differentials, we need to know *why* demand and supply conditions differ in various labor markets. There are several reasons.

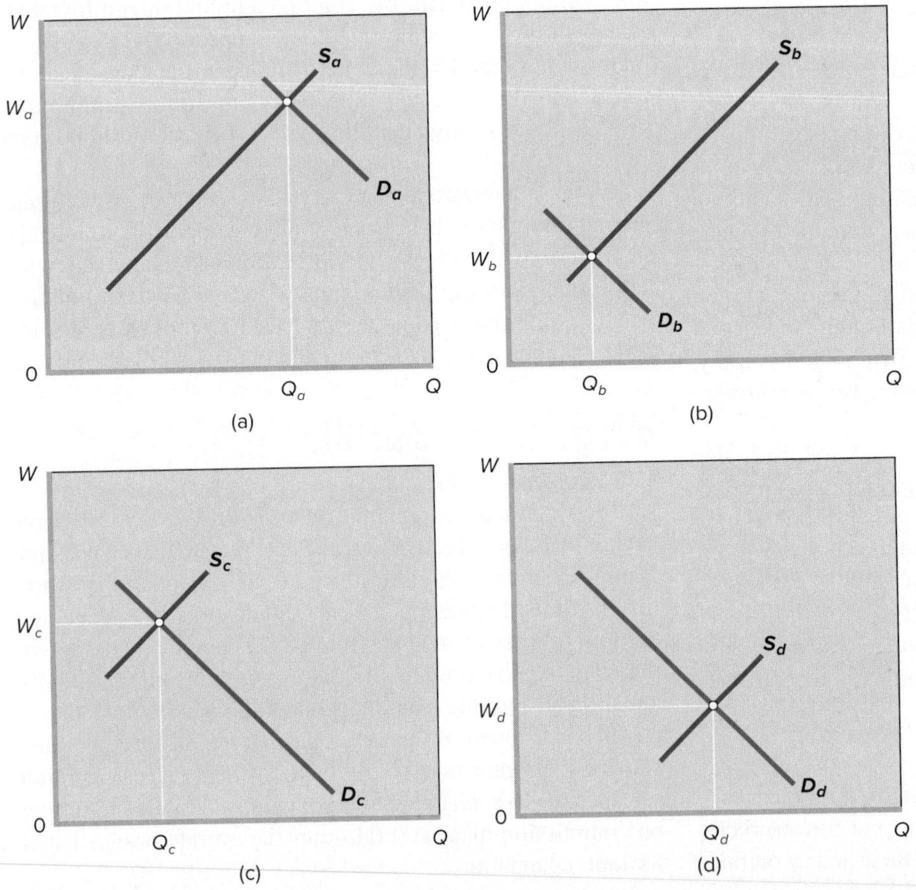

FIGURE 15.9 **Labor demand, labor supply, and wage differentials.** Wage differentials in labor markets are caused by varying supply and demand conditions (a) and (b). Because the labor supply curves S_a and S_b are identical in the labor markets depicted in the two top graphs, differences in demand are the sole cause of the W_a - W_b wage differential (c) and (d). Because the labor demand curves D_c and D_d are identical in the bottom two graphs, the W_c – W_d wage differential results solely from differences in labor supply.

Marginal Revenue Productivity

The strength of labor demand—how far rightward the labor demand curve is located—differs greatly among occupations due to differences in how much various occupational groups contribute to the revenue of their respective employers. This revenue contribution, in turn, depends on the workers' productivity and the strength of the demand for the products they are helping to produce. Where labor is highly productive and product demand is strong, labor demand also is strong and, other things equal, pay is high. Top professional athletes, for example, are highly productive at producing sports entertainment, for which millions of people are willing to pay billions of dollars over the course of a season. Because the **marginal revenue productivity** of these players is so high, they are in very high demand by sports teams. This high demand leads to their extremely high salaries (as in Figure 15.9a). In contrast, most workers generate much more modest revenue for their employers. This results in much lower demand for their labor and, consequently, much lower wages (as in Figure 15.9b).

Noncompeting Groups

On the supply side of the labor market, workers are not homogeneous; they differ in their mental and physical capacities and in their education and training. At any given time the labor force is made up of many **noncompeting groups** of workers, each representing several occupations for which the members of a particular group qualify. In some groups qualified workers are relatively few, whereas in others they are plentiful. And workers in one group do not qualify for the occupations of other groups.

Ability At any moment in time, only a few workers have the skills or physical attributes to be hired as brain surgeons, concert violinists, top fashion models, research chemists, or professional athletes. Because the supply of these particular types of labor is very small in relation to labor demand, their wages are high (as in Figure 15.9c). The members of these and similar groups do not compete with one another or with other skilled or semiskilled workers. The violinist does not compete with the surgeon, nor does the surgeon compete with the violinist or the fashion model.

The concept of noncompeting groups can be applied to various subgroups and even to specific individuals in a particular group. Some especially skilled violinists can command higher salaries than colleagues who play the same instrument. A handful of top corporate executives earn 10 to 20 times as much as the average chief executive officer. In each of these cases, the supply of top talent is highly limited since less-talented colleagues are only imperfect substitutes.

Education and Training Another source of wage differentials is differing amounts of **human capital,** which is the personal stock of knowledge, know-how, and skills that enables a person to be productive and thus to earn income. Such stocks result from investments in human capital. Like expenditures on machinery and equipment, productivity-enhancing expenditures on education or training are investments. In both cases, people incur *present costs* with the intention that those expenditures will lead to a greater flow of *future earnings.*

FIGURE 15.10 **Education levels and individual annual earnings.** Annual income by age is higher for workers with more education than less. Investment in education yields a return in the form of earnings differences enjoyed over one's work life.

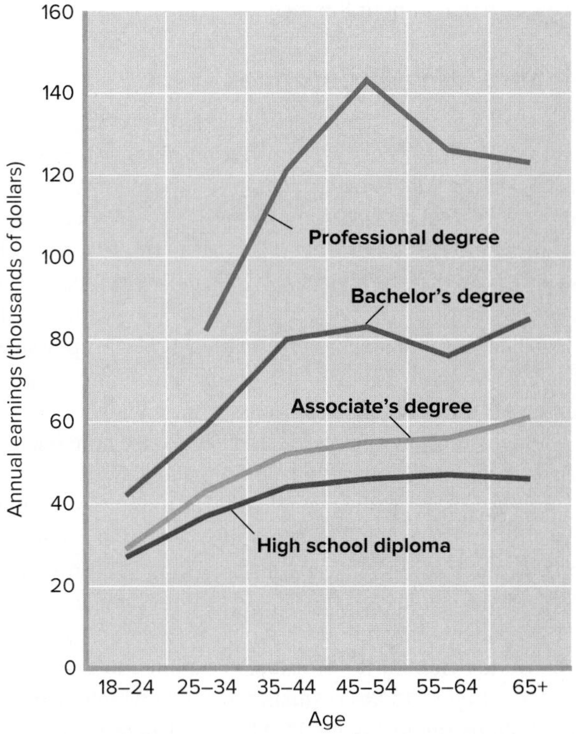

Source: U.S. Bureau of the Census. Data are for both sexes in 2014.

Figure 15.10 indicates that workers who have made greater investments in education achieve higher incomes during their careers. The reason is twofold: (1) There are fewer such workers, so their supply is limited relative to less-educated workers, and (2) more-educated workers tend to be more productive and thus in greater demand. Figure 15.10 also indicates that the earnings of better-educated workers rise more rapidly than those of poorly educated workers. The primary reason is that employers provide more on-the-job training to the better-educated workers, boosting their marginal revenue productivity and therefore their earnings.

Although education yields higher incomes, it carries substantial costs. A college education involves not only direct costs (tuition, fees, books) but indirect or opportunity costs (forgone earnings) as well. Does the higher pay received by better-educated workers compensate for these costs? The answer is yes. Rates of return are estimated to be 10 to 13 percent for investments in secondary education and 8 to 12 percent for investments in college education. One generally accepted estimate is that each year of schooling raises a worker's wage by about 8 percent.

Compensating Differences

If the workers in a particular noncompeting group are equally capable of performing several different jobs, you might expect the wage rates to be identical for all these jobs. Not so. A group of high school graduates may be equally capable of becoming salesclerks or general construction workers. But these jobs pay different wages. In virtually all locales, construction laborers receive much higher wages than salesclerks. These wage differentials are called **compensating differences** because they must be paid to compensate for nonmonetary differences in various jobs.

The construction job involves dirty hands, a sore back, the hazard of accidents, and irregular employment, both seasonally and during recessions (the economywide economic slowdowns that periodically affect the economy). The retail sales job means clean clothing, pleasant air-conditioned surroundings, and little fear of injury or layoff. Other things equal, it is easy to see why workers would rather pick up a credit card than a shovel. So the amount of labor that is supplied to construction firms (as in Figure 15.9c) is smaller than that which is supplied to retail shops (as in Figure 15.9d). Construction firms must pay higher wages than retailers to compensate for the unattractive nonmonetary aspects of construction jobs.

Such compensating differences spring up throughout the economy. Other things equal, jobs having high risk of injury or death pay more than comparable, safer jobs. Jobs lacking employer-paid health insurance, pensions, and vacation time pay more than comparable jobs that provide these "fringe benefits." Jobs with more flexible hours pay less than jobs with rigid work-hour requirements. Jobs with greater risk of unemployment pay more than comparable jobs with little unemployment risk. Entry-level jobs in occupations that provide very poor prospects for pay advancement pay more than entry-level jobs that have clearly defined "job ladders."

These and other compensating differences play an important role in allocating society's scarce labor resources. If very few workers want to be garbage collectors, then society must pay high wages to garbage collectors to get the garbage collected. If many more people want to be salesclerks, then society need not pay them as much as it pays garbage collectors to get those services performed.

Market Imperfections

Differences in marginal revenue productivity, amounts of human capital, and nonmonetary aspects of jobs explain most of the wage differentials in the economy. But some persistent differentials result from various market imperfections that impede workers from moving from lower-paying jobs to higher-paying jobs.

Lack of Job Information Workers may simply be unaware of job opportunities and wage rates in other geographic areas and in other jobs for which they qualify. Consequently, the flow of qualified labor from lower-paying to higher-paying jobs—and thus the adjustments in labor supply—may not be sufficient to equalize wages within occupations.

Geographic Immobility Workers take root geographically. Many are reluctant to move to new places. Doing so would involve leaving friends, relatives, and associates. It would mean forcing their children to change schools, having to sell their homes, and incurring the costs and inconveniences of adjusting to a new job and a new community. As Adam Smith noted over two centuries ago, "A [person] is of all sorts of luggage the most difficult to be transported." The reluctance or inability of workers to move enables geographic wage differentials within the same occupation to persist.

CONSIDER THIS . . .

Source: © Grand Palais/Art Resource, NY

My Entire Life

Human capital is the accumulation of outcomes of prior investments in education, training, and other factors that increase productivity and earnings. It is the stock of knowledge, know-how, and skills that enables individuals to be productive and thus earn income. A valuable stock of human capital, together with a strong demand for one's services, can add up to a large capacity to earn income. For some people, high earnings have little to do with actual hours of work and much to do with their tremendous skill, which reflects their accumulated stock of human capital.

The point is demonstrated in the following story: It is said that a tourist once spotted the famous Spanish artist Pablo Picasso (1881–1973) in a Paris café. The tourist asked Picasso if he would do a sketch of his wife for pay. Picasso sketched the wife in a matter of minutes and said, "That will be 10,000 francs [roughly $2,000]." Hearing the high price, the tourist became irritated, saying, "But that took you only a few minutes."

"No," replied Picasso, "it took me my entire life!"

Unions and Government Restraints Wage differentials may be reinforced by artificial restrictions on mobility imposed by unions and government. We have noted that craft unions find it to their advantage to restrict membership. After all, if carpenters and bricklayers become too plentiful, the wages they can command will decline. Thus the low-paid nonunion carpenter of Brush, Colorado, may be willing to move to Chicago in the pursuit of higher wages. But her chances for succeeding are slim. She may be unable to get a union card, and no card means no job. Similarly, an optometrist or lawyer qualified to practice in one state may not meet the licensing requirements of other states, so his or her ability to move is limited. Other artificial barriers involve pension plans, health insurance benefits, and seniority rights that might be jeopardized by moving from one job to another.

Discrimination Despite legislation to the contrary, discrimination sometimes results in lower wages being paid to women and minority workers than to white males doing very similar or even identical work. Also, women and minorities may be crowded into certain low-paying occupations, driving down wages there and raising them elsewhere. If this *occupational segregation* keeps qualified women and minorities from taking higher-paying jobs, then differences in pay will persist. (We discuss discrimination in Chapter 19.)

All four considerations—differences in marginal revenue productivity, noncompeting groups, nonmonetary differences, and market imperfections—come into play in explaining actual wage differentials. For example, the differential between the wages of a physician and those of a construction worker can be explained on the basis of marginal revenue productivity and noncompeting groups. Physicians generate considerable revenue because of their high productivity and the strong willingness of consumers (via insurance) to pay for health care. Physicians also fall into a noncompeting group where, because of stringent training requirements, only relatively few persons qualify. So the supply of labor is small in relation to demand.

In construction work, where training requirements are much less significant, the supply of labor is great relative to demand. So wages are much lower for construction workers than for physicians. However, if not for the unpleasantness of the construction worker's job and the fact that his or her craft union observes restrictive membership policies, the differential would be even greater than it is.

Pay for Performance

LO15.8 Identify the types, benefits, and costs of "pay-for-performance" plans.

The models of wage determination we have described in this chapter assume that worker pay is always a standard amount for each hour's work, for example, $15 per hour. But pay schemes are often more complex than that both in composition and in purpose. For instance, many workers receive annual salaries rather than hourly pay. And workers receive differing proportions of fringe benefits (health insurance, life insurance, paid vacations, paid sick-leave days, pension contributions, and so on) as part of their pay. Finally, some pay plans are designed to elicit a desired level of performance from workers. This last aspect of pay plans requires further elaboration.

The Principal-Agent Problem

The **principal-agent problem** is usually associated with the possible differences in the interests of corporate stockholders (principals) and the executives (agents) they hire. But this problem extends to all paid employees. Firms hire workers because they are needed to help produce the goods and services the firms sell in their attempts to turn a profit. Workers are the firms' agents; they are hired to advance the interest (profit) of the firms. The principals are the firms; they hire agents to advance their goals. Firms and workers have one interest in common: They both want the firm to survive and thrive. That will ensure profit for the firm and continued employment and wages for the workers.

But the interests of firms and workers are not identical. As a result, a principal-agent problem arises. Workers may seek to increase their utility by shirking on the job, that is, by providing less than the agreed-upon effort or by taking unauthorized breaks. They may improve their well-being by increasing their leisure during paid work hours, without forfeiting income. The night security guard in a warehouse may leave work early or spend time reading a novel rather than making the assigned rounds. A salaried manager may spend time away from the office visiting with friends rather than attending to company business.

Firms (principals) have a profit incentive to reduce or eliminate shirking. One option is to monitor workers, but monitoring is difficult and costly. Hiring another worker to supervise or monitor the security guard might double the cost of maintaining a secure warehouse. Another way of resolving a principal-agent problem is through some sort of **incentive pay plan** that ties worker compensation more closely to worker output or performance. Such incentive pay schemes include piece rates; commissions and royalties; bonuses, stock options, and profit sharing; and efficiency wages.

Piece Rates Piece rates consist of compensation paid according to the number of units of output a worker produces. If a principal pays fruit pickers by the bushel or typists by the page, it need not be concerned with shirking or with monitoring costs.

Commissions or Royalties Unlike piece rates, commissions and royalties tie compensation to the value of sales.

Employees who sell products or services—including real estate agents, insurance agents, stockbrokers, and retail salespersons—commonly receive *commissions* that are computed as a percentage of the monetary value of their sales. Recording artists and authors are paid *royalties,* computed as a certain percentage of sales revenues from their works. Such types of compensation link the financial interests of the salespeople, artists, and authors to the profit interest of the firms.

Bonuses, Stock Options, and Profit Sharing *Bonuses* are payments in addition to one's annual salary that are based on some factor such as the performance of the individual worker, or of a group of workers, or of the firm itself. A professional baseball player may receive a bonus based on a high batting average, the number of home runs hit, or the number of runs batted in. A business manager may receive a bonus based on the profitability of her or his unit. *Stock options* allow workers to buy shares of their employer's stock at a fixed, lower price when the stock price rises. Such options are part of the compensation packages of top corporate officials, as well as many workers in relatively high-technology firms. *Profit-sharing plans* allocate a percentage of a firm's profit to its employees.

Efficiency Wages The rationale behind *efficiency wages* is that employers will enjoy greater effort from their workers by paying them above-equilibrium wage rates. Glance back at Figure 15.3, which shows a competitive labor market in which the equilibrium wage rate is \$10. What if an employer decides to pay an above-equilibrium wage of \$12 per hour? Rather than putting the firm at a cost disadvantage compared with rival firms paying only \$10, the higher wage might improve worker effort and productivity so that unit labor costs actually fall. For example, if each worker produces 10 units of output per hour at the \$12 wage rate compared with only 6 units at the \$10 wage rate, unit labor costs for the high-wage firm will be only \$1.20 (= \$12/10) compared to \$1.67 (= \$10/6) for firms paying the equilibrium wage.

An above-equilibrium wage may enhance worker efficiency in several ways. It enables the firm to attract higher-quality workers. It lifts worker morale. And it lowers turnover, resulting in a more experienced workforce, greater worker productivity, and lower recruitment and training costs. Because the opportunity cost of losing a higher-wage job is greater, workers are more likely to put forth their best efforts with less supervision and monitoring. In fact, efficiency wage payments have proved effective for many employers.

Addenda: Negative Side Effects of Pay for Performance

Although pay for performance may help overcome the principal-agent problem and enhance worker productivity, such plans may have negative side effects and require careful design. Here are a few examples:

- The rapid production pace that piece rates encourage may result in poor product quality and may compromise the safety of workers. Such outcomes can be costly to the firm over the long run.
- Commissions may cause some salespeople to engage in questionable or even fraudulent sales practices, such as making exaggerated claims about products or recommending unneeded repairs. Such practices may lead to private lawsuits or government legal action.
- Bonuses based on personal performance may disrupt the close cooperation needed for maximum team production. A professional basketball player who receives a bonus for points scored may be reluctant to pass the ball to teammates.
- Since profit sharing is usually tied to the performance of the entire firm, less energetic workers can "free ride" by obtaining their profit share on the basis of the hard work by others.
- Stock options may prompt some unscrupulous executives to manipulate the cost and revenue streams of their firms to create a false appearance of rapidly rising profit. When the firm's stock value rises, the executives exercise their stock options at inflated share prices and reap a personal fortune.
- There may be a downside to the reduced turnover resulting from above-market wages: Firms that pay efficiency wages have fewer opportunities to hire new workers and suffer the loss of the creative energy that they often bring to the workplace.

AP QUICK REVIEW 15.3

- ✓ Proponents of the minimum wage argue that it is needed to assist the working poor and to counter monopsony where it might exist; critics say that it is poorly targeted to reduce poverty and that it reduces employment.
- ✓ Wage differentials are attributable in general to the forces of supply and demand, influenced by differences in workers' marginal revenue productivity, education, and skills and by nonmonetary differences in jobs. But several labor market imperfections also play a role.
- ✓ As it applies to labor, the principal-agent problem is one of workers pursuing their own interests to the detriment of the employer's profit objective.
- ✓ Pay-for-performance plans (piece rates, commissions, royalties, bonuses, stock options, profit sharing, and efficiency wages) are designed to improve worker productivity by overcoming the principal-agent problem.

LAST WORD

Occupational Licensing

Many Industries Impose Unnecessary Licensing Requirements as a Way of Restricting Competition.

Occupational licensing laws operate at the state and local level. They were originally created to protect the public from harm by ensuring that the members of licensed professions met high standards for training and expertise. This makes perfect sense for physicians and emergency medical technicians (EMTs), who are literally responsible for people's lives. But various business groups whose activities pose little or no threat to anyone have managed to get their industries covered by unnecessary licensing requirements as a way of limiting competition and driving up prices.

The most egregious example is interior design. You have probably put up a poster, painted a wall, or rearranged your furniture at least a few times in your life. These acts of interior design probably didn't strike you as requiring any particular training or being in any way a threat to the public. But the National Association of Interior Designers disagrees. They have spent decades lobbying state governments to impose occupational licensing requirements on interior designers. And they have succeeded in Florida, Maryland, and Nevada.

In those states, anyone who wishes to work as an interior designer has to complete six years of training and internships before they can even apply for a license. Those six years plus the cost of all that training limits the supply of interior designers and thereby raises the wages of the few who do obtain a license. Those few naturally lobby to maintain the licensing requirement.

Source: NSBAIDRD

The six years of training that are required to obtain an interior-design license in those three states stand in stark contrast to the average of just 33 days that are required across all 50 states to obtain an EMT license. The EMT licensing requirements are much less onerous because EMTs have not organized themselves politically the way interior designers have. So the EMT licensing requirements reflect only what is actually required for competence. There has been no attempt to artificially increase the EMT requirements in order to reduce the supply of EMTs and thereby artificially increase EMT wages.

There are dozens of examples of industries where occupational licensing is not obviously needed to protect the public or in which licensing requirements have been made artificially excessive to drive up wages. Thirty-six states "protect" the public by requiring make-up artists to spend an average of seven months earning a license. Forty-six states "safeguard" gym-goers by requiring personal trainers to take an average of four years of classes and internships. And three states "defend" the public by requiring eight months of classes and training to obtain a license to install home entertainment systems.

These examples of unnecessary licensing might be funny except for the burden they place on consumers and workers. Not only do consumers have to pay higher prices because of reduced supply, they also enjoy fewer choices because they cannot legally hire an unlicensed provider even if that person is perfectly capable of doing the job well. Even worse, unnecessary licensing requirements substantially limit job opportunities for poorer workers. Instead of being able to start working as soon as any honestly needed training is completed, they are forced to go through months or even years of costly artificial requirements whose only purpose is to limit competition for those who already have licenses.

These barriers to employment have grown more burdensome and pervasive in recent decades. Whereas only about 1 in 20 jobs required an occupational license in the 1950s, nearly 1 in 3 do today. And of the 1,100 or so occupations that require a license at either the federal or state level, over 100 are for lower-wage jobs in fields such as cosmetology, child care, floristry, barbering, bus driving, bartending, tree trimming, hair braiding, massage therapy, and travel agency. Thus, unnecessary occupational licensing presents a major impediment to millions of poorer people hoping to set up their own businesses or switch careers. If they live in a state that requires licensing, they will have to pay fees, take classes, endure internships, and pass tests to obtain jobs that many consumers would be happy to pay them to do without a license. Unfortunately, that state of affairs is likely to continue indefinitely due to the power of the *special-interest effect* under which a small group of insiders can impose large costs on outsiders.

Source: **http://www.nsbaidrd.org/?page=16**

SUMMARY

LO15.1 Explain why labor productivity and real hourly compensation track so closely over time.

The term "labor" encompasses all people who work for pay. The wage rate is the price paid per unit of time for labor. Labor earnings comprise total pay and are found by multiplying the number of hours worked by the hourly wage rate. The nominal wage rate is the amount of money received per unit of time; the real wage rate is the purchasing power of the nominal wage.

The long-run growth of real hourly compensation—the average real wage—roughly matches that of productivity, with both increasing over the long run.

Global comparisons suggest that real wages in the United States are relatively high, but not the highest, internationally. High real wages in the advanced industrial countries stem largely from high labor productivity.

LO15.2 Show how wage rates and employment levels are determined in competitive labor markets.

Specific wage rates depend on the structure of the particular labor market. In a competitive labor market the equilibrium wage rate and level of employment are determined at the intersection of the labor supply curve and labor demand curve. For the individual firm, the market wage rate establishes a horizontal labor supply curve, meaning that the wage rate equals the firm's constant marginal resource cost. The firm hires workers to the point where its MRP equals its MRC.

LO15.3 Demonstrate how monopsony (a market with a single employer) can reduce wages below competitive levels.

Under monopsony the marginal resource cost curve lies above the resource supply curve because the monopsonist must bid up the wage rate to hire extra workers and must pay that higher wage rate to all workers. The monopsonist hires fewer workers than are hired under competitive conditions, pays less-than-competitive wage rates (has lower labor costs), and thus obtains greater profit.

LO15.4 Discuss how unions increase wage rates by pursuing the demand-enhancement model, the craft union model, or the industrial union model.

A union may raise competitive wage rates by (*a*) increasing the derived demand for labor, (*b*) restricting the supply of labor through exclusive unionism, or (*c*) directly enforcing an above-equilibrium wage rate through inclusive unionism. On average, unionized workers realize wage rates 15 percent higher than those of comparable nonunion workers.

LO15.5 Explain why wages and employment are determined by collective bargaining in a situation of bilateral monopoly.

In many industries the labor market takes the form of bilateral monopoly, in which a strong union "sells" labor to a monopsonistic employer. The wage-rate outcome of this labor market model depends on union and employer bargaining power.

LO15.6 Discuss how minimum wage laws affect labor markets.

Economists disagree about the desirability of the minimum wage as an antipoverty mechanism. While it causes unemployment for some low-income workers, it raises the incomes of those who retain their jobs.

LO15.7 List the major causes of wage differentials.

Wage differentials are largely explainable in terms of (*a*) marginal revenue productivity of various groups of workers; (*b*) noncompeting groups arising from differences in the capacities and education of different groups of workers; (*c*) compensating wage differences, that is, wage differences that must be paid to offset nonmonetary differences in jobs; and (*d*) market imperfections in the form of lack of job information, geographic immobility, union and government restraints, and discrimination.

LO15.8 Identify the types, benefits, and costs of "pay-for-performance" plans.

As it a applies to labor, the principal-agent problem arises when workers provide less-than-expected effort. Firms may combat this by monitoring workers or by creating incentive pay schemes that link worker compensation to performance.

TERMS AND CONCEPTS

wage rate
nominal wage
real wage
purely competitive labor market
monopsony
exclusive unionism
occupational licensing
inclusive unionism
bilateral monopoly
minimum wage
wage differentials
marginal revenue productivity
noncompeting groups
human capital
compensating differences
principal-agent problem
incentive pay plan

The following and additional problems can be found in connect

DISCUSSION QUESTIONS

1. Explain why the general level of wages is high in the United States and other industrially advanced countries. What is the single most important factor underlying the long-run increase in average real-wage rates in the United States? LO15.1
2. Why is a firm in a purely competitive labor market a wage taker? What would happen if it decided to pay less than the going market wage rate? LO15.2
3. Describe wage determination in a labor market in which workers are unorganized and many firms actively compete for the services of labor. Show this situation graphically, using W_1 to indicate the equilibrium wage rate and Q_1 to show the number of workers hired by the firms as a group. Show the labor supply curve of the individual firm, and compare it with that of the total market. Why the differences? In the diagram representing the firm, identify total revenue, total wage cost, and revenue available for the payment of non-labor resources. LO15.2
4. Suppose the formerly competing firms in the previous question form an employers' association that hires labor as a monopsonist would. Describe verbally the effect on wage rates and employment. Adjust the graph you drew for review question 1, showing the monopsonistic wage rate and employment level as W_2 and Q_2, respectively. Using this monopsony model, explain why hospital administrators sometimes complain about a "shortage" of nurses. How might such a shortage be corrected? LO15.3
5. Assume a monopsonistic employer is paying a wage rate of W_m and hiring Q_m workers, as indicated in Figure 15.8. Now suppose an industrial union is formed that forces the employer to accept a wage rate of W_c. Explain verbally and graphically why in this instance the higher wage rate will be accompanied by an increase in the number of workers hired. LO15.5
6. Have you ever worked for the minimum wage? If so, for how long? Would you favor increasing the minimum wage by a dollar? By two dollars? By five dollars? Explain your reasoning. LO15.6
7. "Many of the lowest-paid people in society—for example, short-order cooks—also have relatively poor working conditions. Hence, the notion of compensating wage differentials is disproved." Do you agree? Explain. LO15.7
8. What is meant by investment in human capital? Use this concept to explain (*a*) wage differentials and (*b*) the long-run rise of real-wage rates in the United States. LO15.7
9. What is the principal-agent problem? Have you ever worked in a setting where this problem has arisen? If so, do you think increased monitoring would have eliminated the problem? Why don't firms simply hire more supervisors to eliminate shirking? LO15.8
10. **LAST WORD** Speculate as to why we see unnecessary occupational licensing only in some industries but not others. Consider both costs and benefits, who gets them, and how hard it would be to organize opposition to unnecessary licensing in various industries.

AP REVIEW QUESTIONS

1. Draw side-by-side graphs of the labor market and a representative firm to show how wage rates are determined in a labor market in which workers are unorganized (not in labor unions) and many firms actively compete for the services of unskilled labor. Use "Wage" to indicate the equilibrium wage rate in the market. How do we determine the wage rate for the firm? On the firm graph, indicate the quantity of workers hired using L1. How do we determine this quantity? In the graph representing the firm, identify total revenue, total wage cost, and revenue available for the payment of non-labor resources and for economic profits. LO15.2
2. Because a perfectly competitive employer's MRC curve is ____________, it will hire ____________ workers than would a monoposony employer with the same MRP curve. LO15.3
   a. Upsloping; more.
   b. Upsloping; fewer.
   c. Perfectly elastic; more.
   d. Perfectly elastic; fewer.
   e. Downsloping; more.
3. True or false. When a labor market consists of a single monopsony buyer of labor (one firm) interacting with a single monopoly seller of labor (such as a trade union), the resulting quantity of labor that is hired cannot be allocatively efficient. LO15.5
4. The market equilibrium wage is currently $12 per hour among hairdressers. At that wage, 17,323 hairdressers are currently employed in the state. The state legislature then sets a minimum wage of $11.50 per hour for hairdressers. If there are no changes to either the demand or supply for hairdressers when that minimum wage is imposed, the number of hairdressers employed in the state will be: LO15.6
   a. Fewer than 17,323.
   b. Still 17,323.
   c. More than 17,323.
   d. No longer allocatively efficient.
   e. Indeterminate.
5. On average, 50-year-old workers are paid several times more than workers in their teens and twenties. Which of the following options is the most likely explanation for that huge difference in average earnings? LO15.7
   a. Older workers have more human capital and higher MRPs.
   b. Employers engage in widespread discrimination against younger workers.

c. Young people lack information about the existence of the high-paying jobs occupied by older workers.
d. Older workers receive compensating differences because they do jobs that are more risky than the jobs done by younger workers.
e. Young workers should be paid less, since they are less likely to have families to support.

6. Manny owns a local fast-food franchise. Angel runs it for him. So in this situation, Manny is the ____________ and Angel is the ____________. LO15.8
a. Free rider; entrepreneur.
b. Agent; principal.
c. Principal; agent.
d. Producer; consumer.
e. Consumer; producer.

7. A principal is worried that her agent may not do what she wants. As a solution, she should consider: LO15.8
a. Commissions.
b. Bonuses.
c. Profit sharing.
d. Paying efficiency wages.
e. All of the above.

9. Use side-by-side graphs of the market for unskilled labor and a representative firm hiring unskilled labor in this geographic area. Assume there is an increase in the number of working age individuals into this geographic area. LO15.2
a. Show the effect on the equilibrium wage and employment in the labor market from this increase in the number of potential workers.
b. Does the wage and hiring of labor for the individual firm change? If so, show graphically and explain.
c. Will the marginal revenue product of the last worker hired by the representative firm be higher, the same, or lower following the increase in the working age population. Explain.

PROBLEMS

1. Workers are compensated by firms with "benefits" in addition to wages and salaries. The most prominent benefit offered by many firms is health insurance. Suppose that in 2000, workers at one steel plant were paid $20 per hour and in addition received health benefits at the rate of $4 per hour. Also suppose that by 2010 workers at that plant were paid $21 per hour but received $9 in health insurance benefits. LO15.1
a. By what percentage did total compensation (wages plus benefits) change at this plant from 2000 to 2010? What was the approximate average annual percentage change in total compensation?
b. By what percentage did wages change at this plant from 2000 to 2010? What was the approximate average annual percentage change in wages?
c. If workers value a dollar of health benefits as much as they value a dollar of wages, by what total percentage will they feel that their incomes have risen over this time period? What if they only consider wages when calculating their incomes?
d. Is it possible for workers to feel as though their wages are stagnating even if total compensation is rising?

2. Complete the following labor supply table for a firm hiring labor competitively: LO15.2

Units of Labor	Wage Rate	Total Labor Cost	Marginal Resource (Labor) Cost
0	$14	$ ______	
			$ ______
1	14	______	
			______
2	14	______	
			______
3	14	______	
			______
4	14	______	
			______
5	14	______	
			______
6	14	______	

a. Show graphically the labor supply and marginal resource (labor) cost curves for this firm. Are the curves the same or different? If they are different, which one is higher?
b. Plot the labor demand data of review question 2 in Chapter 16 on the graph used in part *a* above. What are the equilibrium wage rate and level of employment?

3. Assume a firm is a monopsonist that can hire its first worker for $6 but must increase the wage rate by $3 to attract each successive worker (so that the second worker must be paid $9, the third $12, and so on). LO15.3
a. Draw the firm's labor supply and marginal resource cost curves. Are the curves the same or different? If they are different, which one is higher?
b. On the same graph, plot the labor demand data of review question 2 in Chapter 14. What are the equilibrium wage rate and level of employment?
c. Compare these answers with those you found in problem 2. By how much does the monopsonist reduce wages below the competitive wage? By how much does the monopsonist reduce employment below the competitive level?

4. Suppose that low-skilled workers employed in clearing woodland can each clear one acre per month if each is equipped with a shovel, a machete, and a chainsaw. Clearing one acre brings in $1,000 in revenue. Each worker's equipment costs the worker's employer $150 per month to rent and each worker toils 40 hours per week for four weeks each month. LO15.6
a. What is the marginal revenue product of hiring one low-skilled worker to clear woodland for one month?
b. How much revenue per hour does each worker bring in?
c. If the minimum wage were $6.20, would the revenue per hour in part *b* exceed the minimum wage? If so, by how much per hour?
d. Now consider the employer's total costs. These include the equipment costs as well as a normal profit of $50 per acre. If the firm pays workers the minimum wage of

$6.20 per hour, what will the firm's economic profit or loss be per acre?

e. At what value would the minimum wage have to be set so that the firm would make zero economic profit from employing an additional low-skilled worker to clear woodland?

5. Suppose that a car dealership wishes to see if efficiency wages will help improve its salespeople's productivity. Currently, each salesperson sells an average of one car per day while being paid $20 per hour for an eight-hour day. LO15.8

a. What is the current labor cost per car sold?

b. Suppose that when the dealer raises the price of labor to $30 per hour the average number of cars sold by a salesperson increases to two per day. What is now the labor cost per car sold? By how much is it higher or lower than it was before? Has the efficiency of labor expenditures by the firm (cars sold per dollar of wages paid to salespeople) increased or decreased?

c. Suppose that if the wage is raised a second time to $40 per hour the number of cars sold rises to an average of 2.5 per day. What is now the labor cost per car sold?

d. If the firm's goal is to maximize the efficiency of its labor expenditures, which of the three hourly salary rates should it use: $20 per hour, $30 per hour, or $40 per hour?

e. By contrast, which salary maximizes the productivity of the car dealer's workers (cars sold per worker per day)?

Labor Unions and Their Impacts

LO15.9 Relate who belongs to U.S. unions, the basics of collective bargaining, and the economic effects of unions.

We have noted that unions can increase wage rates by augmenting the demand for labor (Figure 15.5) or by restricting or controlling the supply of labor (Figures 15.6 and 15.7). The purpose of this appendix is to provide some additional information about American unions, collective bargaining, and union impacts.

Union Membership

In 2015, about 16.4 million U.S. workers—11.1 percent of employed wage and salary workers—belonged to unions. Some 11.6 million of these U.S. union members belonged to one of many unions that are loosely and voluntarily affiliated with the **American Federation of Labor and the Congress of Industrial Organizations (AFL-CIO).** Examples of AFL-CIO unions are the United Autoworkers, Communications Workers, and United Steelworkers. Another 5.5 million union members belonged to one of the seven unions, including the Service Workers and Teamsters, loosely federated as **Change to Win.** The remaining union members belonged to other **independent unions** that were not affiliated with either federation.

The likelihood that any particular worker will be a union member depends mainly on the industry in which the worker is employed and his or her occupation. As shown in Figure 1a, the **unionization rate**—the percentage of workers unionized—is high in government, transportation, telecommunications, construction, and manufacturing. The unionization rate is very low in finance, agriculture, and retail trade. Figure 1b shows that unionism also varies greatly by occupation. Protective service workers (fire and police), teachers, production workers, transportation services employees, and social workers have high unionization rates; sales workers, food workers, and managers have very low rates.

Because disproportionately more men than women work in the industries and occupations with high unionization rates, men are more likely to be union members than women. Specifically, 12 percent of male wage and salary workers belong to unions compared with 11 percent of women. For the same reason, African Americans have higher unionization rates than whites: 14 percent compared with 11 percent. The unionization rate for Asians is 10 percent; Hispanics, 9 percent. Unionism in the United States is largely an urban phenomenon. Seven heavily urbanized, heavily industrialized states (New York, California, Pennsylvania, Illinois, Ohio, New Jersey, and Michigan) account for approximately half of all union members.

The Decline of Unionism

Since the mid-1950s, union membership has not kept pace with the growth of the labor force. While 25 percent of employed wage and salary workers belonged to unions in the

FIGURE 1 Union membership as a percentage of employed wage and salary workers, selected industries and occupations, 2015. In percentage terms, union membership varies greatly by (a) industry and (b) occupation.

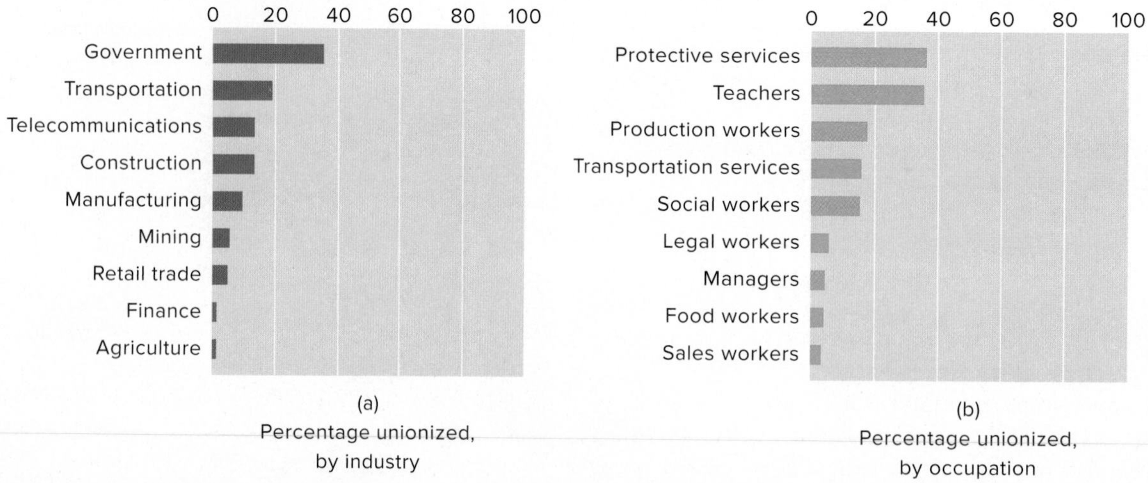

Source: Bureau of Labor Statistics, **www.bls.gov**.

mid-1950s, today only 11.1 percent are union members. Over recent years, even the absolute number of union members has declined significantly. More than 22 million workers were unionized in 1980 but only 16.4 million in 2015.

Some of the major reasons for the decline of U.S. unionism involve structural changes in the economy. Employment has shifted away from manufactured goods (where unions have been stronger) and toward services (where unions have been weaker). Consumer demand has shifted toward foreign manufactured goods and away from goods produced by union labor in the United States. Industry has shifted from the northeast and midwest, where unionism is "a way of life," to "hard-to-organize" areas of the south and southwest. These and other factors have reduced the growth of union membership.

Also, management has greatly intensified its opposition to unions and has increasingly engaged in aggressive collective bargaining, including the use of strikebreakers. Within unionized firms, employers have substituted machinery for workers, subcontracted work to nonunion suppliers, and shifted the production of components to low-wage nations. Nonunion firms have greatly improved their wage, fringe benefits, and working conditions. That has reduced the demand for unionism.

Collective Bargaining

Despite the overall decline of unionism, **collective bargaining** (the negotiation of labor contracts) remains an important feature of labor-management relations in several U.S. industries. The goal of collective bargaining is to establish a "work agreement" between the firm and the union.

Collective bargaining agreements (contracts) assume many forms, but typically cover several topics.

Union Status

Union status is the degree of security afforded a union by the work agreement. The strongest form of union security is a **closed shop,** in which a worker must be (or must become) a member of the union before being hired. Under federal labor law, such shops are illegal in industries other than transportation and construction.

In contrast, a **union shop** permits the employer to hire nonunion workers but provides that these workers must join the union within a specified period, say 30 days, or relinquish their jobs. An **agency shop** allows nonunion workers but requires nonunion workers to either pay union dues or donate an equivalent amount to charity. Union and agency shops are legal, except in the 25 states that expressly prohibit them through so-called **right-to-work laws.**

In an **open shop,** an employer may hire either union or nonunion workers. Those who are nonunion are not obligated to join the union or to pay union dues; they may continue on their jobs indefinitely as nonunion workers. Nevertheless, the wages, hours, and working conditions set forth in the work agreement apply to the nonunion workers as well as to the union workers.

Managerial Prerogatives

Most work agreements contain clauses outlining certain decisions that are reserved solely for management. These managerial prerogatives usually cover such matters as the size and location of plants, the products to be manufactured, and the types of equipment and materials to be used in production and in production scheduling.

Wages and Hours

The focal point of almost all bargaining agreements is wages (including fringe benefits) and hours. Both labor and management press for the advantage in wage bargaining. The arguments that unions use most frequently in demanding wage boosts are (1) "what others are getting"; (2) the employer's ability to pay, based on its profitability; (3) increases in the cost of living; and (4) increases in labor productivity.

Hours of work, voluntary versus mandatory overtime, holiday and vacation provisions, profit sharing, health plans, and pension benefits are other contract issues that must be addressed in the bargaining process.

Seniority and Job Protection

The uncertainty of employment in a market economy, along with the fear of antiunion discrimination on the part of employers, has made workers and their unions "job-conscious." The explicit and detailed provisions covering job opportunities that most agreements contain reflect this concern. Unions stress length of service, or *seniority,* as the basis for worker promotion and for layoff and recall. They want the worker with the longest continuous service to have the first chance at relevant promotions, to be the last one laid off, and to be the first one recalled from layoff.

In recent years, unions have become increasingly sensitive to losing jobs to nonunion subcontractors and to overseas workers. Unions sometimes seek limits on the firm's ability to subcontract out work or to relocate production facilities overseas.

Grievance Procedures

Even the most detailed and comprehensive work agreement cannot spell out all the specific issues and problems that might occur during its life. For example, suppose a particular worker gets reassigned to a less pleasant job. Was this reassignment for legitimate business reasons or, as the person suspects, because of a personality conflict with a particular manager? Labor contracts contain grievance procedures to resolve such matters.

The Bargaining Process

The date for the beginning of collective bargaining on a new contract is usually specified in the existing contract and is typically 60 days before the current one expires.

The union normally takes the initiative, presenting its demands in the form of specific wage, fringe-benefit, and other adjustments to the present union-management contract. The firm counters with an offer relating to these and other contract provisions. It is not unusual for the original union demand and the first offer by the firm to be far apart, not only because of the parties' conflicting goals but also because starting far apart leaves plenty of room for compromise and counteroffers during negotiations.

Hanging over the negotiations is the contract deadline, which occurs the moment the present contract expires. At that time there is a possibility of a **strike**—a work stoppage by the union—if it thinks its demands are not being satisfactorily met. But there is also the possibility that at the deadline the firm may engage in a **lockout,** in which it forbids the workers to return to work until a new contract is signed. In this setting of uncertainty prior to the deadline, both parties feel pressure to find mutually acceptable terms.

Although bluster and bickering often occur in collective bargaining, labor and management display a remarkable capacity for compromise and agreement. Typically they reach a compromise that is written into a new contract. Nevertheless, strikes and lockouts occasionally do occur. When they happen, workers lose income and firms lose profit. To stem their losses, both parties usually look for and eventually find ways to settle the labor dispute and get the workers back to work.

Bargaining, strikes, and lockouts occur within a framework of federal labor law, specifically the **National Labor Relations Act (NLRA).** This act was first passed as the Wagner Act of 1935 and later amended by the Taft-Hartley Act of 1947 and the Landrum-Griffin Act of 1959. The act sets forth the *dos and don'ts* of union and management labor practices. For example, while union members can picket in front of a firm's business, they cannot block access to the business by customers, coworkers, or strikebreakers hired by the firm. Another example: Firms cannot refuse to meet and talk with the union's designated representatives.

Either unions or management can file charges of unfair labor practices under the labor law. The **National Labor Relations Board (NLRB)** has the authority to investigate such charges and to issue cease-and-desist orders in the event of a violation. The board also conducts worker elections to decide which specific union, if any, a group of workers might want to have represent them in collective bargaining.

Economic Effects of Unions

The most straightforward effect of unions is an increase in the wage rates for their members. The consensus estimate is that the overall union wage premium (wage advantage) averages about 15 percent. The effects of unions on output and efficiency, however, are slightly more complicated.

Featherbedding and Work Rules

Some unions diminish output and efficiency by engaging in "make-work" or "featherbedding" practices and resisting the introduction of output-increasing machinery and equipment. These productivity-reducing practices often arise in periods of technological change. For example, in 2002 the ILWU (dockworkers' union) obtained a contract provision guaranteeing 40-hour-per-week jobs for all current ILWU clerical personnel for as long as they wish to continue working at their current jobs at West Coast ports. However, many of those workers will not be needed because the ports are rapidly moving toward labor-saving computerized systems for tracking cargo. Thus, many of the current clerical personnel will be paid for doing little or nothing. This will be very inefficient.

More generally, unions may reduce efficiency by establishing work rules and practices that impede putting the most productive workers in particular jobs. Under seniority rules, for example, workers may be promoted for their employment tenure rather than for their ability to perform the available job with the greatest efficiency. Also, unions might restrict the kinds of tasks workers may perform. Contract provisions may prohibit sheet-metal workers or bricklayers from doing the simple carpentry work often associated with their jobs. Observance of such rules means, in this instance, that firms must hire unneeded and under-used carpenters.

Finally, critics of unions contend that union contracts often chip away at managerial prerogatives to establish work schedules, determine production targets, introduce new technology, and make other decisions contributing to productive efficiency.

Output Losses from Strikes

A second way unions can impair efficiency and output is through strikes. If union and management reach an impasse during their contract negotiations, a strike may result and the firm's production may cease for the strike's duration. If so, the firm will forgo sales and profit; workers will sacrifice income; and the economy might lose output. U.S. strike activity, however, has dwindled in the past few decades. In 2015, there were 12 major work stoppages—strikes or lockouts involving 1,000 or more employees.

About 47,000 workers were idled by the 12 work stoppages in 2015, with the average length of stoppages being 26 days. It is estimated that the amount of work time lost to the stoppages was less than 0.005 percent of the total work time provided by employees that year.

But the amount of work time lost is an imprecise indicator of the potential economic costs of strikes. These costs may be greater than indicated if strikes disrupt production in nonstruck firms that either supply inputs to struck firms or buy products from them. Example: An extended strike in the auto industry might reduce output and cause layoffs in firms producing, say, glass, tires, paints, and fabrics used in producing cars. It also may reduce sales and cause layoffs in auto dealerships.

On the other hand, the costs of strikes may be less than is implied by the work time lost by strikers if nonstruck firms increase their output to offset the loss of production by struck firms. While the output of General Motors declines when its workers strike, auto buyers may shift their demand to Ford, Toyota, or Honda, which will respond by increasing their employment and output. Therefore, although GM and its employees are hurt by a strike, society as a whole may experience little or no decline in employment, real output, and income.

Efficiency Losses from Labor Misallocation

A third and more subtle way that unions might reduce efficiency and output is through the union wage advantage itself. Figure 2 splits the economy into two sectors, showing identical labor demand curves for the unionized sector and the nonunionized sector. If all markets are competitive and no union is initially present in either sector, the wage rate in both parts of the economy will be W_n and N_1 workers will be employed in each sector.

Now suppose workers form a union in one sector and succeed in increasing the wage rate from W_n to W_u. As a consequence, $N_1 - N_2$ workers lose their jobs in the union sector. Assume that they all move to the nonunion sector, where they are employed. This increase in labor supply (not shown) in the nonunion sector increases the quantity of labor supplied there from N_1 to N_3, reducing the wage rate from W_n to W_s.

Recall that the labor demand curves reflect the marginal revenue products (MRPs) of workers or, in other words, the contribution that each additional worker makes to domestic output. This means that area A + B + C in the union sector represents the sum of the MRPs—the total contributions to domestic output—of the workers displaced by the wage increase achieved by the union. The reemployment of these workers in the nonunion sector produces an increase in domestic output shown by area D + E. Because area A + B + C exceeds area D + E, a net loss of domestic output is the result.

More precisely, because A = D and C = E, the efficiency loss attributable to the union wage advantage is represented by area B. Because the same amount of employed labor is now producing a smaller output, labor is being misallocated and used inefficiently. After the shift of N_1N_2 workers to the nonunion sector has occurred, workers in both sectors will be paid wage rates according to their MRPs. But the workers who shifted sectors will be working at a lower MRP than before. An economy always obtains a larger domestic output when labor is reallocated from a low-MRP use to a high-MRP

FIGURE 2 The effects of the union wage advantage on the allocation of labor. (a) The higher wage rate W_u obtained by unions in the union sector displaces $N_1 - N_2$ workers and reduces output by area $A + B + C$. (b) The displaced workers from the union sector are reemployed in the nonunion sector, where employment increases from N_1 to N_3 and the wage rate declines from W_n to W_s. Output increases by area $D + E$ in the nonunion sector, but that increase is less than the loss of output $A + B + C$ in the union sector. The net loss of output, shown by area B in blue, means that the union wage advantage has caused a misallocation of resources and a decline in economic efficiency.

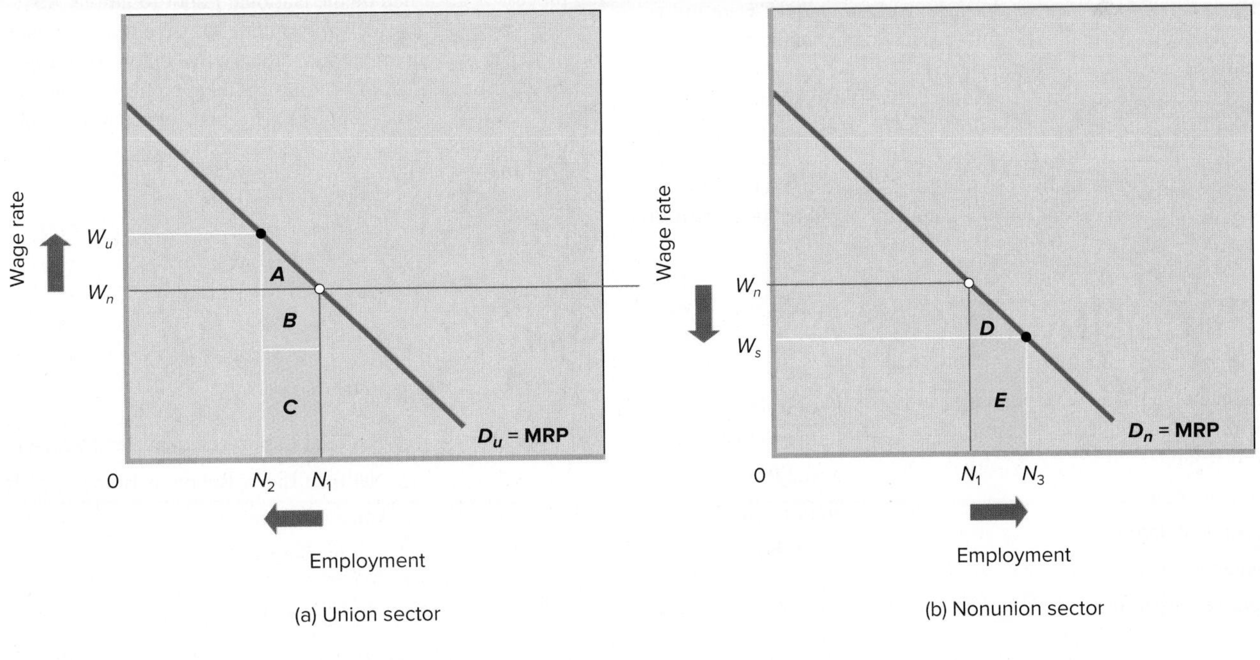

use. But here the opposite has occurred. And assuming the union can maintain the W_u wage rate in its sector, a reallocation of labor from the nonunion sector to the union sector will never occur.

Attempts to estimate the efficiency loss associated with union wage gains, however, suggest that it is very small: perhaps 0.2 to 0.4 percent (or one-fifth of 1 percent to two-fifths of 1 percent) of U.S. GDP. In 2011 this cost would have amounted to about $32 billion to $63 billion.

Offsetting Factors

Some long-run consequences of unionization may enhance productivity and reduce the efficiency loss from unions. One such impact is lower worker turnover within unionized firms. Compared with the rates at nonunion firms, the quit rates (resignation rates) for union workers are 31 to 65 percent lower, depending on the industry.

The union wage premium may reduce worker turnover by increasing the desirability of the union job relative to alternative employment. In economic terms, the higher opportunity cost of quitting reduces the frequency of quitting. Unions also may reduce turnover by using collective communication—the **voice mechanism**—to correct job dissatisfactions that otherwise would be "resolved" by workers quitting and taking other jobs—the **exit mechanism.** It might be risky for individual workers to express their dissatisfaction to employers because employers might retaliate by firing them as "troublemakers." But a union can provide workers with a collective voice to communicate problems and grievances to management and to press for satisfactory resolutions.

A lower quit rate may give a firm a more experienced, more productive workforce. Over time, that might offset a part of the higher costs and reduced profitability associated with the union premium. Also, having fewer resignations might reduce the firm's recruitment, screening, and hiring costs. Additionally, reduced turnover may encourage employers to invest more in the training (and therefore the productivity) of their workers. If a worker quits or "exits" at the end of, say, a year's training, the employer will get no return from providing that training. Lower turnover increases the likelihood that the employer will receive a return on the training it provides, thereby increasing its willingness to upgrade the skills of its workforce. All these factors may increase the long-run productivity of the unionized labor force and therefore reduce the efficiency loss caused by the union wage premium.

APPENDIX SUMMARY

LO15.9 Relate who belongs to U.S. unions, the basics of collective bargaining, and the economic effects of unions.

About 11.6 million of the 16.4 million union members in 2015 belonged to unions affiliated with the AFL-CIO; another 5.5 million belonged to 7 unions loosely federated under the name Change to Win. The rest were members of other independent unions. About 11.1 percent of U.S. wage and salary workers in 2015 were union members, with government employees having the highest unionization rates. As an occupation, protective service workers (fire and police) have the highest rate of unionization—36 percent.

Union membership has declined as a percentage of the labor force and in absolute numbers in recent decades. Some of the key causes are structural changes such as the shift from manufacturing employment to service employment. Other causes include improved wages and working conditions in nonunion firms and increased managerial opposition to unions.

Collective bargaining determines the terms of union work agreements, which typically cover (*a*) union status and managerial prerogatives; (*b*) wages, hours, and working conditions; (*c*) control over job opportunities; and (*d*) grievance procedures. The bargaining process is governed by the National Labor Relations Act.

Union wages are on average about 15 percent higher than nonunion wages in comparable jobs. Restrictive union work rules, output losses from strikes, and labor misallocation from the union wage advantage are ways that unions may reduce efficiency, output, and productivity. The efficiency losses from unions may be partially offset in the long run by union productivity advances deriving from reduced labor turnover.

APPENDIX TERMS AND CONCEPTS

American Federation of Labor and the Congress of Industrial Organizations (AFL-CIO)
Change to Win
independent unions
unionization rate
collective bargaining
closed shop
union shop
agency shop
right-to-work laws
open shop
strike
lockout
National Labor Relations Act (NLRA)
National Labor Relations Board (NLRB)
voice mechanism
exit mechanism

The following and additional problems can be found in connect

APPENDIX DISCUSSION QUESTIONS

1. Which industries and occupations have the highest rates of unionization? Which the lowest? Speculate on the reasons for such large differences. LO15.9
2. What percentage of wage and salary workers are union members? Is this percentage higher, or is it lower, than in previous decades? Which of the factors explaining the trend do you think is most dominant? LO15.9
3. Explain how featherbedding and other restrictive work practices can reduce labor productivity. Why might strikes reduce the economy's output less than the loss of production by the struck firms? LO15.9
4. What is the estimated size of the union wage advantage? How might this advantage diminish the efficiency with which labor resources are allocated in the economy? Normally, labor resources of equal potential productivity flow from low-wage employment to high-wage employment. Why does that not happen to close the union wage advantage? LO15.9
5. Contrast the voice mechanism and the exit mechanism for communicating dissatisfaction. In what two ways do labor unions reduce labor turnover? How might such reductions increase productivity? LO15.9

APPENDIX REVIEW QUESTIONS

1. True or false. In the United States, unions have been gaining in membership and power for several decades. LO15.9
2. Suppose that you are president of a newly established local union about to bargain with an employer for the first time. List the basic areas you want covered in the work agreement. Why might you begin with a larger wage demand than you actually are willing to accept? What is the logic of a union threatening an employer with a strike during the collective bargaining process? Of an employer threatening the union with a lockout? What is the role of the deadline in encouraging agreement in collective bargaining? LO15.9
3. Look back at Figure 2. In the union sector, the union's ability to raise wages from W_n to W_u decreases total employment from N_1 to N_2. Thus $N_1 - N_2$ workers are displaced from the union sector and will seek employment in the nonunion sector. But suppose that wages in the nonunion sector cannot fall (perhaps because of a minimum wage law). Suppose, more specifically, that they are fixed at W_n in the nonunion sector. If the union and nonunion sectors are the only two sectors in the economy, how many workers will become unemployed because of the union's ability to raise wages in the union sector? (Hint: $N_1 - N_2$ in the union sector is the same number of workers as $N_3 - N_1$ in the nonunion sector.) LO15.9
   a. N_1.
   b. N_2.
   c. N_3.
   d. $N_1 - N_2$.
   e. $N_1 + N_2$.
4. True or false. "To the extent that they succeed in their goals, unions only ever reduce productivity and efficiency." LO15.9

APPENDIX PROBLEMS

1. Suppose that a delivery company currently uses one employee per vehicle to deliver packages. Each driver delivers 50 packages per day, and the firm charges $20 per package for delivery. LO15.9
   a. What is the MRP per driver per day?
   b. Now suppose that a union forces the company to place a supervisor in each vehicle at a cost of $300 per supervisor per day. The presence of the supervisor causes the number of packages delivered per vehicle per day to rise to 60 packages per day. What is the MRP per supervisor per day? By how much per vehicle per day do firm profits fall after supervisors are introduced?
   c. How many packages per day would each vehicle have to deliver in order to maintain the firm's profit per vehicle after supervisors are introduced?
   d. Suppose that the number of packages delivered per day cannot be increased but that the price per delivery might potentially be raised. What price would the firm have to charge for each delivery in order to maintain the firm's profit per vehicle after supervisors are introduced?
2. Suppose that a car factory initially hires 1,500 workers at $30 per hour and that each worker works 40 hours per week. Then the factory unionizes, and the new union demands that wages be raised by 10 percent. The firm accedes to that request in collective bargaining negotiations but then decides to cut the factory's labor force by 20 percent due to the higher labor costs. LO15.9
   a. What is the new union wage? How many workers does the factory employ after the agreement goes into effect?
   b. How much in total did the factory's workers receive in wage payments each week before the agreement? How much do the factory's remaining workers receive in wage payments each week after the agreement?
   c. Suppose that the workers who lose their jobs as a result of the agreement end up unemployed. By how much do the total wages received each week by the initial 1,500 workers (both those who continue to be employed at the factory and those who lose their jobs) change from before the agreement to after the agreement?
   d. If the workers who lose their jobs as a result of the agreement end up making $15 per hour at jobs where they work 40 hours per week, by how much do the total wages received each week by the initial 1,500 workers change from before the agreement to after the agreement?

16 Chapter

Rent, Interest, and Profit

Learning Objectives

LO16.1 Explain the nature of economic rent and how it is determined.

LO16.2 Define interest and explain how interest rates vary based on risk, maturity, loan size, and taxability.

LO16.3 Explain the loanable funds theory of interest rates.

LO16.4 Demonstrate how interest rates relate to the time-value of money.

LO16.5 Explain the role of interest rates in allocating capital, modulating R&D spending, and helping to determine the economy's total output of goods and services.

LO16.6 Relate why economic profits occur and how profits, along with losses, allocate resources among alternative uses.

LO16.7 List the share of U.S. earnings received by each of the factors of production.

AP Chapter Focus

In Chapter 15, we focused on the wages and salaries paid by firms to obtain labor. Here our attention is focused on the rent, interest, and profit paid by firms to obtain, respectively, land, capital, and entrepreneurship. Our analysis will provide answers to numerous practical questions, including:

How do *land prices* and *land rents* get established, and why do they differ from property to property? For example, why do 20 acres of land in the middle of the Nevada desert sell for $5,000 while 20 acres along The Strip in Las Vegas command $500 million?

What determines *interest rates* and causes them to change? For instance, why were interest rates on 3-month bank certificates of deposit 1.3 percent in January 2003, 5.4 percent in June 2006, and 0.2 percent in November 2009? How does interest compound over time, and how does that compounding relate to the so-called present value and future value of a particular sum of money?

What are the sources of *profits* and *losses*, and why do they vary? For example, why did Walmart earn profits of nearly $17 billion in 2015 while financial firm RCS Capital went bankrupt after losing over $1.4 billion of its clients' money?

AP Economic Rent

LO16.1 Explain the nature of economic rent and how it is determined.

To most people, "rent" means the money paid for the use of an apartment or a room in a residence hall. To the business executive, "rent" is a payment made for the use of a factory building, machine, or warehouse facility owned by others. Such definitions of rent can be confusing and ambiguous, however. Residence hall room rent, for example, may include other payments as well: interest on money the university borrowed to finance the dormitory, wages for custodial services, utility payments, and so on.

Economists use "rent" in a much narrower sense. **Economic rent** is the price paid for the use of land and other natural resources that are completely fixed in total supply. As you will see, this fixed overall supply distinguishes rental payments from wage, interest, and profit payments.

Let's examine this idea and some of its implications through supply and demand analysis. We first assume that all land has a single use, for example, growing wheat. We assume, too, that all land is of the same grade or quality, meaning that each arable (tillable) acre of land is as productive as every other acre. And we suppose that land is rented or leased in a competitive market in which many producers are demanding land and many landowners are offering land in the market.

In Figure 16.1, curve S represents the supply of arable land available in the economy as a whole, and curve D_2 represents the demand of producers for use of that land. As with all economic resources, the demand for land is a derived demand, meaning that the demand for land is derived from the demand for the products that land helps to produce. Demand curves such as D_2 reflect the marginal revenue product ($MRP = MP \times P$) of land. The curve slopes downward because of diminishing returns (MP declines) and because, for producers as a group, additional units of land result in greater output and thus lower output prices (P is less).

AP **FIGURE 16.1 The determination of land rent.** Because the supply S of land (and other natural resources) is perfectly inelastic, demand is the sole active determinant of land rent. An increase in demand from D_2 to D_1 or a decrease in demand from D_2 to D_3 will cause a considerable change in rent: from R_2 to R_1 in the first instance and from R_2 to R_3 in the second. But the amount of land supplied will remain at L_0. If demand is very weak (D_4) relative to supply, land will be a "free good," commanding no rent.

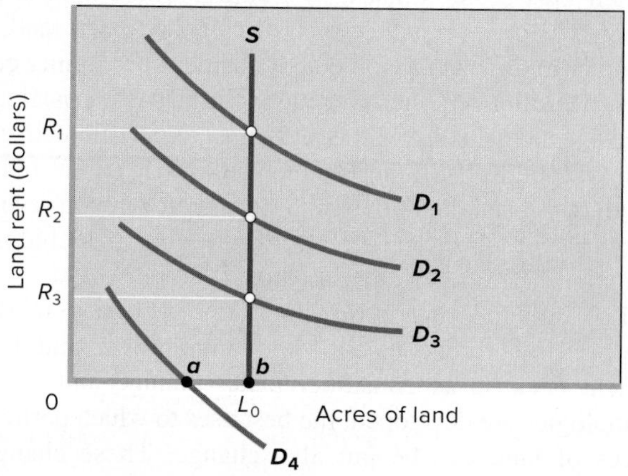

Perfectly Inelastic Supply

The unique feature of our analysis is on the supply side. For all practical purposes the supply of land is perfectly inelastic (in both the short run and the long run), as reflected in supply curve S. Land has no production cost; it is a "free and nonreproducible gift of nature." The economy has only so much land, and that's that. Of course, within limits any parcel of land can be made more usable by clearing, drainage, and irrigation. But these are capital improvements and not changes in the amount of land itself. Moreover, increases in the usability of land affect only a small fraction of the total amount of land and do not change the basic fact that land and other nonrenewable natural resources are fixed in supply.

Equilibrium Rent and Changes in Demand

Because the supply of land is fixed, demand is the only active determinant of land rent. In this case, supply is passive. And what determines the demand for land? The factors we discussed in Chapter 14: the price of the products produced on the land, the productivity of land (which depends in part on the quantity and quality of the resources with which land is combined), and the prices of the other resources that are combined with land.

If demand is D_2, as we have suggested, the equilibrium rent will be R_2. The quantity of land L_0 that producers wish to rent will equal the quantity of land available (also L_0). But if the demand for land in Figure 16.1 increased from D_2 to D_1, land rent would rise from R_2 to R_1. On the other hand, if the demand for land declined from D_2 to D_3, land rent would fall from R_2 to R_3. Finally, if the demand for land were only D_4, land rent would be zero. In this situation, land would be a *free good*—a good for which demand is so weak relative to supply that an excess supply of it occurs even if the market price is zero. In Figure 16.1, we show this excess supply as distance $b - a$ at rent of zero. This essentially was the situation in the free-land era of U.S. history.

The ideas underlying Figure 16.1 help answer one of our chapter-opening questions. Land prices and rents are so high along the Las Vegas strip because the demand for that land is tremendous. It is capable of producing exceptionally high revenue from gambling, lodging, and entertainment. In contrast, the demand for isolated land in the middle of the desert is highly limited because very little revenue can be generated from its use. (It is an entirely different matter, of course, if gold can be mined from the land, as is true of some isolated parcels in Nevada!)

Productivity Differences and Rent Differences

So far we have assumed that all land is equally productive. That assumption is unrealistic because land varies widely in terms of productivity. As an example, differences in rainfall, soil quality, and other factors imply that while land in Kansas is excellently suited to wheat production, the sagebrush plains of Wyoming are much less well suited and the desert of Arizona is practically useless. Such productivity differences are reflected in resource demands and economic rents. Competitive bidding by producers will establish a high rent for highly productive Kansas land, less productive Wyoming land will command a much lower rent, and Arizona desert land may command no rent at all.

This process whereby differences in productivity lead to differences in rents can be understood graphically if we look at Figure 16.1 from a slightly different perspective. As before, assume that land can only be used for wheat production. But this time assume that there are four different plots of land. Each plot is of the same size L_0 but differs in productivity so that different marginal revenue products emerge when each plot of land is combined with identical amounts of labor, capital, and entrepreneurial talent.

These differences in marginal revenue products lead to four different demand curves: D_1, D_2, D_3, and D_4. D_1 is the highest demand curve because plot 1 has the highest productivity. D_4 is the lowest demand curve because plot 4 has the lowest productivity. When combined with supply curve S, the different demand curves yield different equilibrium rents: R_1, R_2, R_3, and R_4. The differences in rents mirror the differences in productivity so that plot 1 commands the highest rent, while plot 4 is so poor in quality that, given supply S, farmers won't pay anything to use it. It will be a free good because it is not sufficiently scarce in relation to its demand for it to command a price above zero.

As a final point, be aware that location itself can affect productivity and rent. Other things equal, renters will pay more for a unit of land that is strategically located with respect to materials, transportation, labor, and customers than they will for a unit of land whose location is remote from these things. Examples include the enormously high land prices near major ski resorts and the high price of land that contains oil beneath it.

Land Rent: A Surplus Payment

The supply of land is perfectly inelastic both in total and with respect to individual parcels of land. Whether land prices rise or fall, a nation will have the same total area to work with and individual plots of land will stay the same size.

The perfectly inelastic supply of land must be contrasted with the relatively elastic supply of nonland resources. Consider capital, which includes apartment buildings, fiber optic networks, and machinery. When the prices of these and other capital goods rise, entrepreneurs respond by increasing the production of capital goods. Conversely, a decline in capital goods prices results in reduced production of capital goods. As a result, the supply curves of nonland resources are normally upsloping, so that the prices paid to such resources provide an **incentive function.** A high price provides an incentive to offer more of the resource, whereas a low price prompts resource suppliers to offer less.

Not so with unimproved land. Rent serves no incentive function because both the total area of land in a nation as well as the sizes of individual plots of land will always stay exactly the same no matter what land prices are. As a result, economists consider land rents to be *surplus payments* that are not necessary to ensure that land is made available for economic use. From this perspective, the sum of all the land rents paid across a nation constitutes a giant surplus payment because it has no effect on the total supply of land in the nation. And in the same way, the individual land rents paid on particular plots of land are also surplus payments because they likewise have no effect on the sizes of those individual plots.

Land Ownership: Fairness versus Allocative Efficiency

If land is a gift of nature, costs nothing to produce, and would be available even without rental payments, why should rent be paid to those who just happen to be landowners? Socialists have long argued that all land rents are unearned incomes because the act of owning land and renting it out to others produces nothing of value in and of itself. They urge that land should be nationalized (owned by the state) so that any payments for its use can be put to work by the government to further the well-being of the entire population.

Opponents of land nationalization argue that private land ownership allows Adam Smith's "invisible hand" to work its magic in terms of allocating scarce land resources to their best possible uses. In a nation where land is privately owned and rents are charged for the use of land, individuals and firms are forced to consider opportunity costs when deciding whether to secure the use of a particular piece of land. This gives them an incentive to allocate each piece of land to its highest-value use. In particular, renters will only allocate land to uses that generate enough revenue to both pay the rent and cover all other costs, including a normal profit.

Private land ownership and having to pay market-determined land rents also aid economic growth and development because as consumer tastes change and as new technologies are developed, the best uses to which particular pieces of land can be put also change. These changing opportunity costs are reflected in land rents, whose changing values thereby help to reallocate land from lower-value uses to higher-value uses as the economy evolves—thus, the often-heard remark, "The land was just too valuable for its previous use."

By contrast, if land were nationalized, government planners would have a difficult time assigning each piece of land to its best possible use and adjusting its use with changing circumstances without the guidance about opportunity costs provided by market-determined rents.

Along those lines, it is important to be clear that while economic rents are surplus payments when viewed from the perspective of society as a whole, they are most definitely costs to individual people and individual firms. To see why this is true, recall that because land is a free gift of nature, there is no cost to society as a whole for obtaining the current supply of land. Thus, economic rents are, from the perspective of society, surplus payments because they have no effect on land supply. But individuals must pay economic rents because such rents determine how society's fixed supply of land is allocated among competing potential uses. Those who are willing and able to pay the market rent get to use the land, while those who are unwilling or unable to pay the market rent do not. Put slightly differently: Economic rents do not cause land to be supplied—they cause land to be directed.

Application: A Single Tax on Land

In the United States, criticism of rental payments produced the **single-tax movement,** which gained significant support in the late nineteenth century. Spearheaded by Henry George's provocative book *Progress and Poverty* (1879), supporters of this reform movement held that economic rent could be heavily taxed without diminishing the available supply of land or reducing the efficiency with which it is allocated.

Henry George's Proposal George observed that, as population grew and the Western frontier closed, landowners enjoyed larger and larger rents (or lease incomes) from their landholdings. That increase in rents was the result of a growing demand for a resource whose supply was perfectly inelastic. Some landlords were receiving fabulously high incomes, not through any productive effort but solely through their ownership of highly prized land. George insisted that these increases in land rent belonged to society at large. Consequently, he argued that land rents should be heavily taxed and that the revenue generated by land taxes be spent for public uses. In seeking popular support for his ideas on land taxation, George proposed that a tax on rental income be the *only* tax levied by government.

George's case for taxing rental income was based not only on equity or fairness but also on efficiency. First, he wished for land to remain in private hands so that the "invisible hand" would guide private landowners to allocate their land to its best possible use. Allocative efficiency would still be achieved because the most profitable use for a particular piece of land before it is taxed remains the most profitable use for that land after it is taxed. Thus, landowners would not have any incentive to shift the use of their land from one activity to another just because it was taxed. In addition, landlords would not withdraw land from production when the tax was imposed because doing so would mean no rental income at all. Because some rental income, no matter how small, is better than no rental income, landlords would continue to supply land.

George further argued that, in addition to maintaining allocative efficiency for land, his single tax would also be much better for society in terms of productive efficiency. His argument was based on the fact that because land is in fixed supply, it does not have an incentive function. Thus, when taxed, the quantity of land supplied does not change. By contrast, because other resources have incentive functions, taxing them would likely reduce their supply—something that would cause an underproduction of output and, consequently, productive inefficiency. For instance, if workers responded to a tax on labor by supplying less labor, output would decline. Similarly, if a property tax on buildings caused builders to supply fewer buildings, there would be less capital available to produce output and, hence, less output. But because land is in fixed supply, no such reductions in output need be feared when taxing land. Thus, if only land were taxed, society would never have to worry about taxes causing productive inefficiency by reducing output.

Criticisms The single tax on land has few remaining advocates. Critics of the idea have pointed out that:

- Current levels of government spending are such that a land tax alone would not bring in enough revenue.
- Most income payments consist of a mixture of interest, rent, wages, and profits. So in practice it would be difficult to isolate how much of any specific income payment is actually derived from rent.
- So-called unearned income accrues to many people other than landowners. For example, consider the capital-gains income received by someone who many years ago purchased or inherited stock that now delivers hefty dividend payments. Is such income more "earned" than the rental income of the landowner?
- Historically, a piece of land is likely to have changed ownership many times. It would therefore be highly unfair to impose a heavy tax on recent buyers who paid a high price for their land and thus did not gain in any way from previous price increases.

AP QUICK REVIEW 16.1

- ✓ Rent is the price paid for unimproved land whose supply is perfectly inelastic.
- ✓ Rent is socially useful because it puts an opportunity cost on land parcels, thereby helping to allocate each parcel of land to its best possible use.
- ✓ Henry George proposed a single tax on land rent, noting that rent was a surplus payment and that taxing it would not distort land allocation.
- ✓ Contemporary economists dismiss George's single-tax proposal as inadequate, impractical, and unfair.

AP Interest

LO16.2 Define interest and explain how interest rates vary based on risk, maturity, loan size, and taxability.

Interest is the price paid for the use of money. It can be thought of as the amount of money that a borrower must pay a lender for the use of the lender's money over some period of time. As an example, a borrower might be required to pay $100 of interest for the use of $1,000 for one year.

Because borrowers pay for loans of money with money, interest can be stated as a percentage of the amount of money borrowed rather than as a dollar amount. This is useful because it is far less clumsy to say that interest is "12 percent annually" than to say that interest is "$120 per year per $1,000."

Stating interest as a percentage also makes it much easier to compare the interest paid on loans involving different amounts of money. By expressing interest as a percentage, we can immediately compare an interest payment of, say, $432 per year per $2,880 with one of $1,800 per year per $12,000. Both interest payments are 15 percent per year, which is not obvious from the actual dollar figures.

And to make things even simpler, an interest payment of 15 percent per year can also be referred to as a 15 percent interest rate.

Money Is Not a Resource

When considering why borrowers are willing to pay interest for the right to use borrowed money, it is important to remember that money is not itself an economic resource. Whether money comes in the form of coins, paper currency, or checking accounts, you cannot directly produce any goods and services with it.

Thus, borrowers do not value money for its own sake. Rather, they value money because of what it can purchase. Individuals and households are willing to pay interest to borrow for consumption spending because they would rather consume certain goods and services sooner rather than later. And businesses are willing to pay interest because the money that they borrow can be used to expand their businesses and increase their profits. In particular, borrowed money can be used to fund the acquisition of capital goods such as computers, machinery, and warehouses.

Interest Rates and Interest Income

The interest rate on money loans determines the *interest income* earned by households for providing capital to firms. This is true because firms have the choice of either leasing capital from households or purchasing their own capital. Because businesses have this option, households wishing to lease their capital to businesses cannot charge more for the use of their capital than what businesses would have to pay in terms of interest payments to borrow the money needed to purchase their own capital.

As an example, consider a custom T-shirt shop that needs a $10,000 embroidering machine to expand production. If the owners of the shop can borrow the money to buy such a machine at an interest rate of 8 percent per year, then anyone wishing to lease them an identical machine could charge them no more than $800 per year for it (since $800 is how much per year the shop would have to pay in interest to borrow $10,000 at an 8 percent interest rate.)

Range of Interest Rates

For convenience, economists often speak in terms of a single interest rate. However, there are actually a number of interest rates in the economy. Table 16.1 lists several interest rates often referred to in the media. On March 9, 2016, these rates ranged from 0.32 to 15.92 percent. Why the differences?

- ***Risk*** Loans to different borrowers for different purposes carry varying degrees of risk. The greater the chance that a borrower will not repay his loan, the higher the interest rate the lender will charge to compensate for that risk.
- ***Maturity*** The time length of a loan, or its *maturity* (when it needs to be paid back), also affects the interest rate. Other things equal, longer-term loans usually command higher interest rates than shorter-term loans. This is true because one function of interest rates is to compensate lenders for the inconvenience and potential financial sacrifices involved with forgoing alternative uses of their money until their loans are repaid. Longer-term loans must offer higher interest rates to compensate lenders for having to forgo alternative opportunities for longer periods of time.
- ***Loan size*** If there are two loans of equal maturity and risk, the interest rate on the smaller of the two loans usually will be higher. The administrative costs of

AP **TABLE 16.1 Selected Interest Rates, March 9, 2016**

Type of Interest Rate	Annual Percentage
20-year Treasury bond rate (interest rate on federal government securities used to finance the public debt)	2.28%
90-day Treasury Bill rate (interest rate on federal government securities used to finance the public debt)	0.32
Prime interest rate (interest rate used as a reference point for a wide range of bank loans)	3.50
30-year mortgage rate (fixed-interest rate on loans for houses)	3.78
4-year automobile loan rate (interest rate for new autos by automobile finance companies)	4.24
Tax-exempt state and municipal bond rate (interest rate paid on low-risk bonds issued by a state or local government)	3.42
Federal funds target rate (interest rate on overnight loans between banks)	0.50
Consumer credit card rate (interest rate charged for credit card purchases)	15.92

Sources: Federal Reserve, **www.federalreserve.gov**, and Bankrate.com, **www.bankrate.com**.

issuing a large loan and a small loan are about the same in dollars, but the cost is greater *as a percentage* of the smaller loan.

- ***Taxability*** Interest on certain state and municipal bonds is exempt from the federal income tax. Because lenders are interested in their after-tax rate of interest, the bonds issued by state and local governments can attract lenders even though they pay lower before-tax interest rates than other bonds of similar maturity and risk. Consider a lender who expects to pay a 35 percent federal income tax on any taxable interest payments. She may prefer a 5 percent interest rate on a tax-exempt municipal bond to a 6 percent interest rate on a taxable corporate bond because, after paying taxes on that taxable corporate bond, she will be left with an after-tax return of only 3.9 percent.

Pure Rate of Interest

When economists and financial specialists talk of "the" interest rate, they typically have in mind the **pure rate of interest.** This is the hypothetical interest rate that would serve purely and solely to compensate lenders for their willingness to patiently forgo alternative consumption and investment opportunities until their money is repaid.

The pure rate of interest is best approximated by the interest rates of long-term, virtually riskless securities, such as the 20-year Treasury bonds issued by the U.S. federal government. Because such bonds involve minimal risk and negligible administrative costs, the interest that they pay can be thought of as compensating purely and solely for the use of money over an extended period of time. In March 2016, the pure rate of interest in the United States was 2.28 percent.

AP Loanable Funds Theory of Interest Rates

LO16.3 Explain the loanable funds theory of interest rates.

Because macroeconomics deals with the entire economy, it typically focuses on the pure rate of interest and assumes that it is determined by the total supply and demand for money in the economy. But because our present focus is on microeconomics, we will focus on a more micro-based theory of interest rates. By doing so, we will be able to explain why the interest rates on different types of loans vary so greatly, as in Table 16.1.

The **loanable funds theory of interest** explains the interest rate on any particular type of loan in terms of the supply of and demand for *funds available for lending* in the loanable funds market that exists for that particular type of loan. As Figure 16.2 shows, the equilibrium interest rate (here, 8 percent) on a particular type of loan is the rate at which the quantities of loanable funds supplied and demanded are equal for that type of loan.

To gain a deeper understanding of the loanable funds theory of interest, let's focus on a simplified lending market.

AP **FIGURE 16.2 A loanable funds market.** The upsloping supply curve *S* for loanable funds in a specific lending market reflects the idea that at higher interest rates, households will defer more of their present consumption (save more), making more funds available for lending. The downsloping demand curve *D* for loanable funds in such a market indicates that businesses will borrow more at lower interest rates than at higher interest rates. At the equilibrium interest rate (here, 8 percent), the quantities of loanable funds lent and borrowed are equal (here, F_0 each).

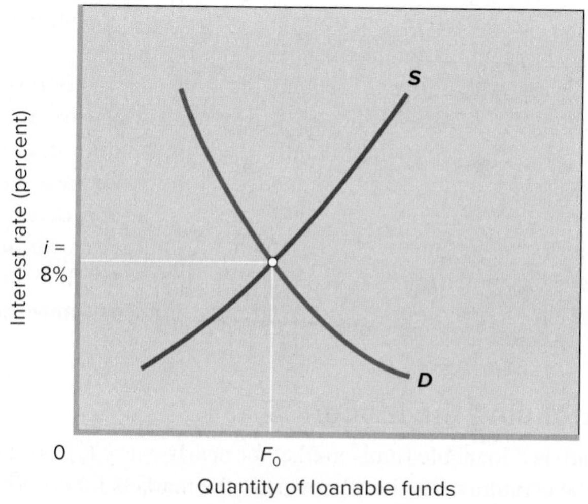

First, assume that, for a particular type of loan, households or consumers are the sole suppliers of loanable funds, while businesses are the sole demanders of loanable funds. Also assume that lending occurs directly between households and businesses so that there are no financial institutions acting as intermediaries.

Supply of Loanable Funds

The supply of loanable funds in our simplified lending market is represented by curve *S* in Figure 16.2. Its upward slope indicates that households will make available a larger quantity of funds at high interest rates than at low interest rates. Most people prefer to use their incomes to purchase goods and services *today,* rather than delay purchases to sometime in the *future*. For people to delay consumption and increase their saving, they must be "bribed" or compensated by an interest payment. The larger the amount of that payment, the greater the deferral of household consumption and thus the greater the amount of money made available for loans.

Demand for Loanable Funds

Businesses borrow loanable funds primarily to add to their stocks of capital goods, such as new plants or warehouses, machinery, and equipment. Assume that a firm wants to buy a machine that will increase output and sales such that the firm's total revenue will rise by $110 for the year. Also assume that the machine costs $100 and has a useful life of just 1 year. Comparing the $10 earned with the $100 cost of the machine, we find that the expected rate of return on this investment is 10 percent (= $10/$100) for the 1 year.

To determine whether the investment would be profitable and whether it should be made, the firm must compare the interest rate—the price of loanable funds—with the 10 percent expected rate of return. If funds can be borrowed at some rate less than the rate of return, say, at 8 percent, as in Figure 16.2, then the investment is profitable and should be made. But if funds can be borrowed only at an interest rate above the 10 percent rate of return, say, at 14 percent, the investment is unprofitable and should not be made.

Why is the demand for loanable funds downsloping, as in Figure 16.2? At higher interest rates fewer investment projects will be profitable and therefore a smaller quantity of loanable funds will be demanded. At lower interest rates, more investment projects will be profitable and therefore more loanable funds will be demanded. Indeed, as we have just seen, purchasing the $100 machine is profitable if funds can be borrowed at 8 percent but not if the firm must borrow at 14 percent.

Extending the Model

There is a loanable funds market for nearly every type of loan in the economy. The best known are the markets for corporate and government bonds. But there are also loanable funds markets for student loans, home mortgages, and car loans. Each type of loan ends up with its own equilibrium interest rate determined by the demand and supply for loanable funds in its particular market.

We now extend the simple loanable funds model to make it more realistic and better able to capture the diversity of these many lending markets.

Financial Institutions Households rarely directly lend their savings to the businesses that are borrowing funds for investment. Instead, they place their savings in banks (and other financial institutions). The banks pay interest to savers in order to attract loanable funds and in turn lend those funds to businesses. Businesses borrow the funds from the banks, paying them interest for the use of the money. Financial institutions profit by charging borrowers higher interest rates than the interest rates they pay savers. Both interest rates, however, are based on the supply of and demand for loanable funds in their respective markets.

Changes in Supply Anything that causes households to be thriftier will prompt them to save more at each interest rate, shifting the supply curve rightward. For example, if interest earned on savings were to be suddenly exempted from taxation, we would expect the supply of loanable funds to increase and the equilibrium interest rate to decrease.

Conversely, a decline in thriftiness would shift the supply-of-loanable-funds curve leftward and increase the equilibrium interest rate. Illustration: If the government expanded social insurance to cover the costs of hospitalization, prescription drugs, and retirement living more fully, the incentive of households to save might diminish.

Changes in Demand On the demand side, anything that increases the rate of return on potential investments will increase the demand for loanable funds. Let's return to our earlier example, where a firm would receive additional revenue of $110 by purchasing a $100 machine and, therefore, would realize a 10 percent return on investment. What factors might increase or decrease the rate of return? Suppose a technological advance raised the productivity of the machine such that the firm's total revenue increased by $120 rather than $110. The rate of return would then be 20 percent, not 10 percent. Before the technological advance, the firm would have demanded zero loanable funds at, say, an interest rate of 14 percent. But now it will demand $100 of loanable funds at that interest rate, meaning that the demand curve for loanable funds has been shifted to the right.

Similarly, an increase in consumer demand for the firm's product will increase the price of its product. So even though the productivity of the machine is unchanged, its potential revenue will rise from $110 to perhaps $120, increasing the firm's rate of return from 10 to 20 percent. Again the firm will be willing to borrow more than previously at our presumed 8 or 14 percent interest rate, implying that the demand curve for loanable funds has shifted rightward. This shift in demand increases the equilibrium interest rate.

Conversely, a decline in productivity or in the price of the firm's product would shift the demand curve for loanable funds leftward, reducing the equilibrium interest rate.

Other Participants We must recognize that participation in many loanable funds markets may go well beyond our simplification of households as suppliers of funds and businesses as demanders of funds. For example, while households are suppliers of loanable funds, many are also demanders of such funds. Households borrow to finance expensive purchases such as housing, automobiles, furniture, and household appliances. Governments also are on the demand side of a loanable funds market when they borrow to finance budgetary deficits. And businesses that have revenues in excess of their current expenditures may offer some of those revenues in various loanable funds markets. Thus, like households, businesses operate on both the supply and the demand sides of various loanable funds markets.

Finally, in addition to gathering and making available the savings of households, banks and other financial institutions also increase funds through the lending process and decrease funds when the money that is used to pay off loans is retained by the banks rather than being lent out again to other borrowers. The Federal Reserve (the nation's central bank) controls the amount of this bank activity and thus influences a wide variety of interest rates.

This fact helps answer one of our chapter-opening questions: Why did the interest rate on 3-month certificates of deposit in the United States fall from 5.4 percent in June 2006 to only 0.2 percent in November 2009? There are two reasons: (1) The demand for loanable funds sharply declined because businesses reduced their desire to purchase more capital goods and (2) the Federal Reserve, fighting recession and sluggish recovery, took monetary actions that greatly increased the supply of loanable funds. In contrast, between 2003 and 2006 the Federal Reserve restricted the growth of loanable funds. Because the demand for loanable funds increased more rapidly than the supply of loanable funds, interest rates such as those on 3-month certificates of deposit rose. As indicated in the chapter opening, that rate increased from 1.3 percent in January 2003 to 5.4 percent in June 2006.

AP Time-Value of Money

LO16.4 Demonstrate how interest rates relate to the time-value of money.

Interest is central to understanding the **time-value of money**—the idea that a specific amount of money is more valuable to a person the sooner it is obtained. To see where money's time value comes from, suppose that you could choose between being paid \$1,000 today or \$1,000 in a year. The fact that \$1,000 received today can be invested at interest and grow into more than \$1,000 in a year implies that it is better to receive \$1,000 today than \$1,000 in a year. By how much is it better? By the amount of interest that can be gained over the course of the year. The higher the interest rate, the greater the time-value of money.

In addition to giving money its time value, the fact that money can be invested to earn interest also implies a way in which a given amount of money today can be thought of as being equivalent to a larger amount of money in the future and how a future amount of money can be thought of as being equivalent to a smaller amount of money today. We explore this idea next.

Compound Interest

Compound interest is the total interest that cumulates over time on money that is placed into an interest-bearing account. Table 16.2 helps us explain compound interest, as well as the related ideas of future value and present value. Suppose that Max places \$1,000 into an interest-bearing account at 10 percent interest with the intent to let the *principal* (the initial deposit) and interest compound for 3 years. The first row of each column shows the beginning period sum; the second column shows the yearly computation as to how that sum grows, given a particular interest rate. That growth is found by multiplying the dollar amount at the beginning of each year by $1 + i$, where i is the interest rate expressed as a decimal.

In year 1 the 10 percent interest rate increases the money in the account from \$1,000 to \$1,100 (= \$1,000 × 1.10). So,

AP TABLE 16.2 **Compound Interest, Future Value, and Present Value, 10 Percent Interest Rate**

(1) Beginning Period Value	(2) Computation	(3) Total Interest	(4) End Period Value
\$1,000 (Year 1)	\$1,000 × 1.10 = \$1,100	\$100	\$1,100 (= \$1,000 + \$100)
\$1,100 (Year 2)	\$1,100 × 1.10 = \$1,210	\$210 (= \$100 + \$110)	\$1,210 (= \$1,000 + \$210)
\$1,210 (Year 3)	\$1,210 × 1.10 = \$1,331	\$331 (= \$100 + \$110 + \$121)	\$1,331 (= \$1,000 + \$331)

as shown in Column 3, total interest is \$100. Column 4 simply lists the \$1,100 again but reinforces that this amount consists of the original principal plus the total interest. Similarly, in year 2, the \$1,100 now in the account grows to \$1,210 (= \$1,100 × 1.10) because \$110 of new interest accrues on the \$1,100. At the end of year 2, the principal remains \$1,000, but the total interest is \$210 and the total amount in the account is \$1,210. Interest in year 3 is \$121 and total interest rises to \$331. After this \$331 of total interest is added to the \$1,000 principal, the accumulation is \$1,331. As shown in Column 3, compound interest builds and builds over time.

Future Value and Present Value

Now note from Table 16.2 that we can look at the time-value of money in two distinct ways. **Future value** is the amount to which some current amount of money will grow as interest compounds over time. In our table, the future value (FV) of \$1,000 today at 10 percent interest is \$1,331 three years from now. Future value is always forward-looking.

But we can just as easily look backward from the end value of \$1,331 and ask how much that amount is worth today, given the 10 percent interest rate. **Present value** is today's value of some amount of money to be received in the future. In terms of the table, the present value (PV) of \$1,331 is \$1,000. Here, FV is "discounted" by three years at 10 percent to remove the \$331 of compounded interest and therefore to obtain PV. (We will defer explaining the discounting procedure to our chapter on financial economics in the macro portion of *Economics*. But if you are interested in the mathematics, see the text within the footnote.)[1]

With any positive interest rate (and assuming no inflation), a person would prefer to receive \$1,000 today rather than \$1,000 at some time in the future. The higher the interest rate, the greater is the *future value* of a specific amount of money today. To confirm, substitute a 20 percent interest rate for the 10 percent rate in Table 16.2 and rework the analysis. Finally, you should know that the analysis presented in the table is extendable to any number of years.

The time-value of money is an important concept. For example, it helps explain the optimal timing of natural resource extraction. It also is critical to the entire field of financial economics (Chapter 31). In our present chapter, our goal is simply to stress that *money has time value because of the potential for compound interest.*

[1]The mathematics is as follows:

$$FV = PV(1 + i)^t \quad \text{and} \quad PV = \frac{FV}{(1 + i)^t}$$

where i is the interest rate and t is time, here the number of years of compounding.

CONSIDER THIS . . .

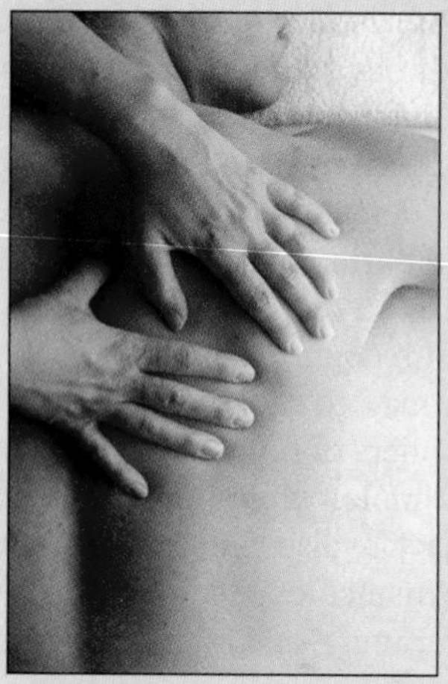

© Matthew Borkoski Photography/ Getty Images

That Is Interest

The following story told by economist Irving Fisher (1867–1947) helps illustrate the time-value of money.

In the process of a massage, a masseur informed Fisher that he was a socialist who believed that "interest is the basis of capitalism and is robbery." Following the massage, Fisher asked, "How much do I owe you?"

The masseur replied, "Thirty dollars."

"Very well," said Fisher, "I will give you a note payable a hundred years hence. I suppose you have no objections to taking this note without any interest. At the end of that time, you, or perhaps your grandchildren, can redeem it."

"But I cannot afford to wait that long," said the masseur.

"I thought you said that interest was robbery. If interest is robbery, you ought to be willing to wait indefinitely for the money. If you are willing to wait ten years, how much would you require?"

"Well, I would have to get more than thirty dollars."

His point now made, Fisher replied, "That is interest."*

*Irving Fisher, as quoted in Irving Norton Fisher, *My Father Irving Fisher* (New York: Comet Press Books, 1956), p. 77.

AP Role of Interest Rates

LO16.5 Explain the role of interest rates in allocating capital, modulating R&D spending, and helping to determine the economy's total output of goods and services.

We have already explained that interest rates on money loans determine the interest incomes earned by the owners of capital goods. This fact implies that interest rates are the critical prices determining both the *level* and *composition* of new investments in capital goods as well as the amount of research and development (R&D) spending in the economy.

Interest and Total Output

Lower equilibrium interest rates encourage businesses to borrow more for investment, other things equal. As a result, total spending in the economy rises, and if the economy has unused resources, so does total output. Conversely, higher equilibrium interest rates discourage businesses from borrowing for investment, thereby reducing investment and total spending. Such a decrease in spending may be desirable if an economy is experiencing inflation.

The Federal Reserve often manages interest rates to try to expand investment and output, on the one hand, or to reduce investment and inflation, on the other. It affects interest rates by changing the supply of money. Increases in the money supply increase the supply of loanable funds, causing equilibrium interest rates to fall. This boosts investment spending and expands the economy. In contrast, decreases in the money supply decrease the supply of loanable funds, boosting equilibrium interest rates. As a result, investment is constrained and so is the economy.

Interest and the Allocation of Capital

Prices are rationing devices. And interest rates are prices. Thus, when it comes to allocating capital in the economy, the interest rates charged on investment loans ration the available supply of loanable investment funds to investment projects that have expected rates of return at or above the interest rate cost of the borrowed funds.

If, say, the computer industry expects to earn a return of 12 percent on the money it invests in physical capital and it can secure the required funds at an interest rate of 8 percent, it can borrow and expand its physical capital. If the expected rate of return on additional capital in the steel industry is only 6 percent, that industry will find it unprofitable to expand its capital at 8 percent interest. The interest rate allocates money, and ultimately physical capital, to the industries in which it will be most productive and therefore most profitable. Such an allocation of capital goods benefits society.

But the interest rate on investment loans does not perfectly ration capital to its most productive uses. Large oligopolistic borrowers may be better able than competitive borrowers to pass interest costs on to consumers because they can change prices by controlling output. Also, the size, prestige, and monopsony power of large corporations may help them obtain funds on more favorable terms than can smaller firms, even when the smaller firms have similar rates of profitability.

Interest and R&D Spending

Similar to an investment decision, a decision on how much to spend on R&D depends on the cost of borrowing funds in relationship to the expected rate of return. Other things equal, the lower the interest rate and thus the lower the cost of borrowing funds for R&D, the greater is the amount of R&D spending that is potentially profitable. Low interest rates encourage R&D spending; high interest rates discourage it.

Also, the interest rate allocates R&D funds to firms and industries for which the expected rate of return on R&D is the greatest. Ace Microcircuits may have an expected rate of return of 16 percent on an R&D project, while Glow Paints has only a 2 percent expected rate of return on an R&D project. With the interest rate at 8 percent, loanable funds will flow to Ace, not to Glow. Society will benefit by having R&D spending allocated to projects that have high enough expected rates of return to justify using scarce resources for R&D rather than for other purposes.

Nominal and Real Interest Rates

This discussion of the role of interest in investment decisions and in R&D decisions assumes that there is no inflation. If inflation exists, we must distinguish between nominal and real interest rates, just like we needed to distinguish between nominal and real wages in Chapter 15. The **nominal interest rate** is the rate of interest expressed in dollars of current value. The **real interest rate** is the rate of interest expressed in purchasing power—dollars of inflation-adjusted value.

Example: Suppose the nominal interest rate and the rate of inflation are both 10 percent. If you borrow \$100, you must pay back \$110 a year from now. However, because of 10 percent inflation, each of these 110 dollars will be worth 10 percent less. Thus, the real value or purchasing power of your \$110 at the end of the year is only \$100. In inflation-adjusted dollars you are borrowing \$100 and at year's end you are paying back \$100. While the nominal interest rate is 10 percent, the real interest rate is zero. We determine the real interest rate by subtracting the 10 percent inflation rate from the 10 percent nominal interest rate. It is the real interest rate, not the nominal rate, that affects investment and R&D decisions.

For a comparison of nominal interest rates on bank loans in selected countries, see Global Perspective 16.1. Note that some countries now have negative nominal interest rates, meaning that a saver will get back less than the amount she invested. Negative nominal interest rates are the result of deliberate central bank monetary policies intended to get people to consume more. The central banks are hoping that consumers will save less and consume more when savings earns a negative return due to negative rates.

Application: Usury Laws

A number of states have passed **usury laws,** which specify a maximum interest rate at which loans can be made. Such rates are a special case of *price ceilings,* discussed in Chapter 3. The purpose of usury laws is to hold down the interest cost of borrowing, particularly for low-income borrowers. ("Usury" simply means exorbitant interest.)

Figure 16.2 helps us assess the impact of such legislation. The equilibrium interest rate there is 8 percent, but suppose a

GLOBAL PERSPECTIVE 16.1

Short-Term Nominal Interest Rates, Selected Nations

These data show the short-term nominal interest rates (percentage rates on 3-month loans) in various countries in 2015. Because these are nominal rates, much of the variation reflects differences in rates of inflation. But differences in central bank monetary policies and default risk also influence the variation.

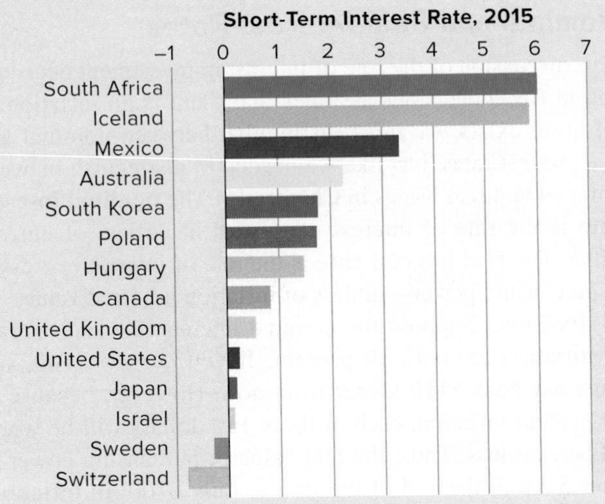

Source: OECD Economic Outlook, Organization for Economic Cooperation and Development, **www.oecd.org**.

usury law specifies that lenders cannot charge more than 6 percent. The effects are as follows:

- ***Nonmarket rationing*** At 6 percent, the quantity of loanable funds demanded exceeds the quantity supplied: There is a shortage of loanable funds. Because the market interest rate no longer can ration the available loanable funds to borrowers, lenders (banks) have to do the rationing. We can expect them to make loans only to the most creditworthy borrowers (mainly wealthy, high-income people), thus defeating the goal of the usury law. Low-income, riskier borrowers are excluded from the market and may be forced to turn to loan sharks who charge illegally high interest rates.
- ***Gainers and losers*** Creditworthy borrowers gain from usury laws because they pay below-market interest rates. Lenders (ultimately bank shareholders) are losers because they receive 6 percent rather than 8 percent on each dollar lent.
- ***Inefficiency*** We have just seen how the equilibrium interest rate allocates money to the investments and the R&D projects whose expected rates of return are greatest. Under usury laws, funds are much less likely to be allocated by banks to the most productive projects. Suppose Mendez has a project so promising she would pay 10 percent for funds to finance it. Chen has a less-promising investment, and he would be willing to pay only 7 percent for financing. If the market were rationing funds, Mendez's highly productive project would be funded and Chen's would not. That allocation of funds would be in the interest of both Mendez and society. But with a 6 percent usury rate, Chen may get to the bank before Mendez and receive the loanable funds at 6 percent. So Mendez may not get funded. Legally controlled interest rates may thus inefficiently ration funds to less-productive investments or R&D projects.

AP QUICK REVIEW 16.2

- ✓ Interest is the price paid for the use of money and determines the interest income earned by households for providing capital to banks, other financial intermediaries, or directly to firms.
- ✓ The range of interest rates is influenced by risk, maturity, loan size, and taxability.
- ✓ In the loanable funds model, the equilibrium interest rate is determined by the demand for and supply of loanable funds.
- ✓ The time-value of money is the idea that $1 can be converted into more than $1 of future value through compound interest and therefore that $1 to be received sometime in the future has less than $1 of present value.
- ✓ Interest rates on investment loans affect the total level of investment and therefore the levels of total spending and total output; they also allocate money and real capital to specific industries and firms. Similarly, interest rates also affect the level and composition of R&D spending.
- ✓ Usury laws establish an interest-rate ceiling below the market interest rate, a form of price ceiling. They may (a) deny credit to low-income people, (b) subsidize high-income borrowers and penalize lenders, and (c) diminish the efficiency with which loanable funds are allocated to investment and R&D projects.

Economic Profit

LO16.6 Relate why economic profits occur and how profits, along with losses, allocate resources among alternative uses.

Recall from previous chapters that economists define profit narrowly. To accountants, "profit" is what remains of a firm's total revenue after it has paid individuals and other firms for the materials, capital, and labor they have supplied to the firm. To the economist, these "accounting profits" overstate profit.

The reason is that the accountant's view of profit considers only **explicit costs:** payments made by the firm to outsiders. It ignores **implicit costs:** the monetary income the firm sacrifices when it uses resources that it owns, rather than supplying those resources to the market. The economist considers implicit costs to be opportunity costs that must be accounted for in determining profit. **Economic**, or **pure, profit** is what remains after all costs—both explicit and implicit costs, the latter including a normal profit—have been subtracted from a firm's total revenue. Economic profit may be either positive or negative (a loss).

Entrepreneurship and Profit

Economic profit flows to individuals to motivate them to provide the economic resource known as entrepreneurship. For illustration, let's suppose that two entrepreneurs establish a start-up company called Upside and that they are the only owners. They do not incorporate or borrow and instead use their own funds to finance the firm.

As discussed in previous chapters, the resource that these entrepreneurs provide is clearly not labor. Typical workers simply complete assigned tasks and engage in routine activities. For their labor inputs, they are compensated with wages and salaries.

Entrepreneurs, by contrast, make nonroutine decisions that involve substantial financial risk. Among other things, they (1) decide their firm's strategy for combining land, labor, and capital to produce a good or service; (2) decide whether and how to develop new products and new production processes; and (3) personally bear the financial risks associated with the success or failure of their respective firms.

With regard to bearing those financial risks, it is crucial to understand that a firm's entrepreneurs are its *residual claimants,* meaning that they only receive whatever residual revenue—if any—remains after all the other factors of production have been paid. As residual claimants, the entrepreneurs at Upside receive whatever accounting profit or accounting loss the firm generates. Thus, the financial risks of running the firm are borne by its two entrepreneurs. If Upside loses money, it loses *their* money.

Insurable and Uninsurable Risks

As residual claimants, entrepreneurs face financial risks. These fall into two categories. **Insurable risks** are those risks for which it is possible to buy insurance from an insurance company, while **uninsurable risks** are those risks for which it is not possible to buy insurance from an insurance company.

Individuals and firms who purchase insurance policies (contracts) from an insurance company are referred to as policyholders. In exchange for an annual premium (fee), the policyholders obtain the insurance company's guarantee to reimburse them for any financial losses caused by any of the risks covered under the insurance contract. In order to be able to keep that promise, the insurance company must be able to collect enough in premiums from its policyholders in the present to be able to fully reimburse the ones who eventually suffer losses in the future. This is only possible with risks like fire, flood, theft, accident, and death whose frequencies of occurrence can be predicted with relative accuracy. Risks whose frequencies of occurrence cannot be predicted with accuracy are uninsurable.

Sources of Uninsurable Risks

Because insurance is available for insurable risks, entrepreneurs only have to deal with uninsurable risks whose frequency of occurrence cannot be predicted with any accuracy. In practice, these are the result of uncontrollable and unpredictable changes in demand and supply that either reduce revenues or increase costs. These uninsurable risks fall into four main categories:

- ***Changes in the general economic environment*** An economy-wide downturn in business (a recession) can lead to greatly reduced demand, sales, and revenues, and thus to business losses. An otherwise prosperous firm may experience substantial losses through no fault of its own.
- ***Changes in the structure of the economy*** Consumer tastes, technology, resource availability, and prices change unpredictably in the real world, bringing changes in production costs and revenues. For example, an airline earning an economic profit one year may sustain substantial losses the next year as the result of a significant increase in the price of jet fuel.
- ***Changes in government policy*** A newly instituted regulation, the removal of a tariff, or a change in national defense policy may significantly alter the costs and revenues of the affected industry and firms.
- ***New products or production methods pioneered by rivals*** Any firm can suddenly find itself losing sales and revenue to popular new products brought out by rivals. Similarly, a firm may suddenly find itself having to sell its product at a loss if rival firms cut their prices after figuring out a lower-cost way to make the same product.

Profit as Compensation for Bearing Uninsurable Risks

Economists list entrepreneurship as its own economic resource—separate from land, labor, and capital—because it is not possible to run a business without somebody being willing to undertake and live with uninsurable risks. Entrepreneurs are rewarded with profit precisely to compensate them for personally taking on the uninsurable risks of running a business. Indeed, their willingness to bear those uninsurable risks means that the providers of the firm's other resource

LAST WORD

Determining the Price of Credit

A Variety of Lending Practices May Cause the Effective Interest Rate to Be Quite Different from What It Appears to Be.

Borrowing and lending—receiving and granting credit—are a way of life. Individuals receive credit when they negotiate a mortgage loan and when they use their credit cards. Individuals make loans when they open a savings account in a commercial bank or buy a government bond.

It is sometimes difficult to determine exactly how much interest we pay and receive when we borrow and lend. Let's suppose that you borrow \$10,000 that you agree to repay plus \$1,000 of interest at the end of 1 year. In this instance, the interest rate is 10 percent per year. To determine the interest rate i, we compare the interest paid with the amount borrowed:

$$i = \frac{\$1{,}000}{\$10{,}000} = 10\%$$

But in some cases a lender—say, a bank—will discount the interest payment from the loan amount at the time the loan is made. Thus, instead of giving the borrower \$10,000, the bank discounts the \$1,000 interest payment in advance, giving the borrower only \$9,000. This increases the interest rate:

$$i = \frac{\$1{,}000}{\$9{,}000} = 11\%$$

Source: © JoeFox/Radharc Images/Alamy Stock Photo

While the absolute amount of interest paid is the same, in the second case the borrower has only \$9,000 available for the year.

An even more subtle point is that, to simplify their calculations, many financial institutions assume a 360-day year (twelve 30-day months). This means the borrower has the use of the lender's funds

inputs (of land, labor, and capital) can almost completely ignore those risks.

To see why this is true, again consider our start-up company, Upside, and suppose that its two entrepreneurs used \$100,000 of their own money to fund the firm. If revenues ever run below costs, the entrepreneurs will use that pile of money to cover the losses and make sure that the firm's workers and other resource suppliers get paid on time and in full. The resource suppliers are shielded from the losses because the entrepreneurs have taken it upon themselves to bear the firm's uninsurable financial risks. In such situations, no bill is sent to the workers or other resource suppliers asking them to help make up the firm's losses. The entrepreneurs, who took on the firm's uninsurable risks, are "on the hook."

The entrepreneurs' compensation for providing entrepreneurship and shielding the other resource suppliers from uninsurable risk is the opportunity to run the business and keep the firm's profits if things go well. Thus, entrepreneurship boils down to a simple bargain: In exchange for making sure that everyone else gets paid if things go wrong, the entrepreneur gets to receive the firm's profits if things go right.

Sources of Economic Profit

For bearing a firm's uninsurable risks, its entrepreneurs receive control of the firm. This allows them to try to make as much profit as possible in exchange for taking on those risks.

Along those lines, there are three main ways in which entrepreneurs can generate economic profits (that is, accounting profits that exceed normal profits):

- ***Create popular new products*** If an entrepreneur can develop a popular new product at a sufficiently low cost, his firm will be able to generate economic profits until competitors bring out competing products.
- ***Reduce production costs below rivals' costs*** Entrepreneurs who implement more efficient production methods for existing products can generate economic

for 5 days less than the normal year. This use of a "short year" also increases the actual interest rate paid by the borrower.

The interest rate paid may change dramatically if a loan is repaid in installments. Suppose a bank lends you $10,000 and charges interest in the amount of $1,000 to be paid at the end of the year. But the loan contract requires that you repay the $10,000 loan in 12 equal monthly installments. As a result, the average amount of the loan outstanding during the year is only $5,000. Therefore:

$$i = \frac{\$1{,}000}{\$5{,}000} = 20\%$$

Here interest is paid on the total amount of the loan ($10,000) rather than on the outstanding balance (which averages $5,000 for the year), making for a much higher interest rate.

Another factor that influences the effective interest rate is whether or not interest is compounded. Suppose you deposit $10,000 in a savings account that pays a 10 percent interest rate compounded semiannually. In other words, interest is paid twice a year. At the end of the first 6 months, $500 of interest (10 percent of $10,000 for half a year) is added to your account. At the end of the year, interest is calculated on $10,500 so that the second interest payment is $525 (10 percent of $10,500 for half a year). Thus:

$$i = \frac{\$1{,}025}{\$10{,}000} = 10.25\%$$

This 10.25 percent return means that a bank offering a 10 percent interest rate compounded semiannually would pay more interest to its customers than a competitor offering a simple (noncompounded) rate of, say, 10.2 percent.

Two pieces of legislation have attempted to clarify interest charges and payments. The Truth in Lending Act of 1968 requires that lenders state the costs and terms of consumer credit in concise and uniform language, in particular, as an annual percentage rate (APR). More recently, the Truth in Savings Act of 1991 requires that all advertisements of deposit accounts by banks and other financial institutions disclose all fees connected with such accounts and the interest rates and APRs on each account. Nevertheless, some "payday" check-cashing firms that lend money to people in return for postdated personal checks have been found to receive interest payments on one- and two-week loans that are equivalent to APRs of hundreds of percent per year. These interest rates prompted calls for state legislators to protect consumers from "predatory lenders."

More recently, many banks have established fee-based "bounce (overdraft) protection" for checking accounts. The bank agrees to pay each overdraft for a flat fee of around $35. These fees are essentially interest on a loan for the amount of the overdraft. When the overdraft amount is small, the annual interest on the loan can easily exceed 1,000 percent.

Similarly, late-payment fees on credit card accounts can boost the actual interest rate paid on credit card balances to extremely high levels. Furthermore, low "teaser" rates designed to attract new customers often contain "fin e print" that raises the interest rate to 16 percent, or even 28 percent, if a payment on the account is late. Also, low initial rates on some variable rate mortgages eventually "reset" to higher rates, greatly increasing the monthly payments that are due. "Let the borrower (or depositor) beware" remains a fitting motto in the world of credit.

profits until their efficiency gains are matched or exceeded by competitors.

- ***Create and maintain a profitable monopoly*** Entrepreneurs who possess a monopoly for their product may be able to generate economic rent by restricting their outputs and raising their prices. And such economic profits may persist if entry to the industry is blocked. But remember from Chapter 11 that having a monopoly does not guarantee that a monopoly will be profitable. If demand is weak relative to production costs, monopolies can and will go bankrupt.

By reallocating resources toward the production of popular new products that consumers prefer to old products, entrepreneurs improve allocative efficiency. By reducing production costs, they improve productive efficiency. Thus, with the important exception of monopoly, the entrepreneur's pursuit of profit clearly benefits society.

With monopolies, though, things are very different, because a monopoly's profit cannot be justified as rewarding its entrepreneurs for personally taking on a firm's financial risks or for making perceptive business decisions that enhance productive or allocative efficiency. As a result, governments use antitrust laws to impede monopolies from forming or, if they arise, break them up or restrict their business behaviors. In some instances, governments also regulate away their excessive profits.

Profit Rations Entrepreneurship

Even if a firm is making an accounting profit, its entrepreneurs may decide to quit and go into another line of business. This is because they will want their accounting profit to be at least as large as the typical accounting profit that their risk taking and decision making could on average be expected to earn in other business ventures. This typical accounting profit is known as their **normal profit.**

CONSIDER THIS . . .

© E. Audras/PhotoAlto RF

Profits and Efficiency

Entrepreneurs focus on a single number: profit. That might make you think that entrepreneurs will end up neglecting the other aspects of their business. But a wonderful thing about the market system is that the only way for a firm to maximize profit is by paying close attention to *every* aspect of its operations.

This is true because entrepreneurs have to make many simultaneous decisions about how to spend their firm's limited budget. Should they allocate a little more money to research and development? Should they reduce spending on advertising? How about allocating more money for bonuses?

The only way to give one activity more resources is to give another activity fewer resources. If an entrepreneur wishes to maximize her firm's overall profit, she will have to get all of these marginal decisions right, and simultaneously. She will also have to find the correct allocation of the firm's limited resources across all possible tasks so that MB = MC for each budget item. So while profit is just a single number, focusing on profit forces entrepreneurs to be efficient in every aspect of her firm's operations.

Because entrepreneurs will be comparing their current accounting profit with the normal profit that they could be making elsewhere, profit can be thought of as the "price" that allocates the scarce resource of entrepreneurship toward different possible economic activities. Just as wages must be paid to attract and retain labor, profits must be paid to attract and retain entrepreneurial talent. And just as higher wages attract workers, higher profits attract entrepreneurs.

Entrepreneurs, Profits, and Corporate Stockholders

In the actual economy, economic profits are distributed widely beyond the entrepreneurs who first start new businesses. The corporate structure of business enterprise has allowed millions of individuals to purchase ownership shares in corporations and therefore to share in the risks and rewards of ownership.

Some of these people participate in the for-profit economy by purchasing the stock of individual firms or by investing in mutual funds, which in turn buy corporate stock. Millions of additional people share in the profits of corporations through the financial investments of their pension funds. But at their core, all of the profits that are shared with these direct and indirect corporate shareholders are made possible in the first place by the activities of entrepreneurs. For instance, without Bill Gates and Paul Allen, there would have been no Microsoft Corporation—and, consequently, no Microsoft profits (dividends) to distribute to the millions of owners of Microsoft stock.

The desire on the part of so many millions of people to own corporate stock and thereby share in the risks and rewards of business reflects the fact that economic profit is the main energizer of the capitalistic economy. It influences both the level of economic output and the allocation of resources among alternative uses. The expectation of economic profit motivates firms to innovate. Innovation stimulates new investment, thereby increasing total output and employment. Thus, the pursuit of profit enhances economic growth by promoting innovation.

Profit also helps allocate resources among alternative lines of production, distribution, and sales. Entrepreneurs seek profit and shun losses. The occurrence of continuing profits in a firm or industry is a signal that society wants that particular firm or industry to expand. It attracts resources from firms and industries that are not profitable. But the rewards of profits are more than an inducement for a firm to expand; they also attract the financing needed for expansion. In contrast, continuing losses penalize firms or industries that fail to adjust their productive efforts to match consumer wants. Such losses signal society's desire for the afflicted entities to contract.

So, in terms of our chapter-opening question, Walmart garnered large profits because it was locating its stores close to customers and delivering the mix of products many consumers wanted at exceptionally low prices. These profits signaled that society wanted more of its scarce resources allocated to Walmart stores. RCS Capital, in contrast, was not delivering products equivalent in value to the costs of the resources used to provide them—so the firm suffered losses. The losses and RCS Capital's bankrupty signaled that society would benefit from a reallocation of all or a part of those resources to some other use.

AP QUICK REVIEW 16.3

- ✓ Pure or economic profit is what remains after all explicit and implicit costs (including all opportunity costs and a normal profit) are subtracted from a firm's total revenue.
- ✓ As residual claimants, entrepreneurs receive accounting profit. They earn economic profit if their accounting profit exceeds the normal profit they could earn as entrepreneurs elsewhere.
- ✓ The corporate structure of business enables millions of individuals to share in the risks and rewards of enterprise.
- ✓ Profit and profit expectations affect the levels of investment, total spending, and domestic output; profit and loss also allocate resources among alternative uses.

Income Shares

LO16.7 List the share of U.S. earnings received by each of the factors of production.

Our discussion in this and in the preceding chapter would not be complete without a brief examination of how U.S. income is distributed among wages, rent, interest, and profit.

Figure 16.3 shows how the income generated in the United States in 2015 was distributed among the five "functional" income categories tracked by the U.S. government. These five categories do not match up perfectly with the economic definitions of wages, rent, interest, and profit. The biggest difference is "proprietors' income," which is the income received by doctors, lawyers, small-business owners, farmers, and the owners of other unincorporated enterprises. In terms of our four economic categories, proprietors' income is a combination of wages and profit. The wages compensate for labor, while the profits compensate for entrepreneurship. The economists who have looked into this combination believe that the large majority of proprietors' income is implicitly composed of wages and salaries rather than profit. That is, the large majority of proprietors' income is compensation for labor rather than compensation for entrepreneurship.

FIGURE 16.3 The functional distribution of U.S. income, 2015. Seventy percent of U.S. income is received as wages and salaries. Income to property owners—corporate profit, interest, and rents—accounts for about 20 percent of total income. The dollar amounts are in billions of dollars.

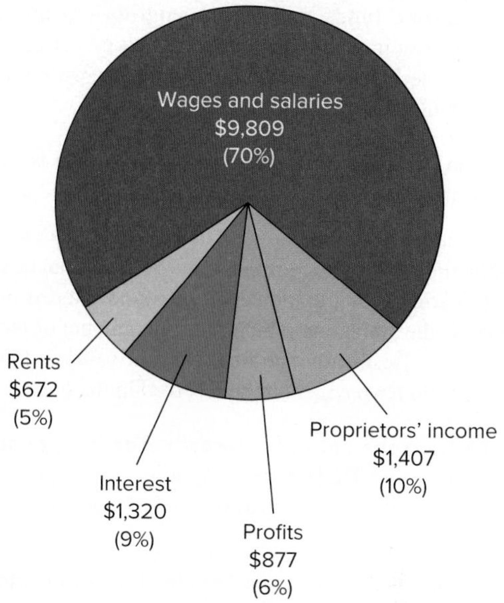

Source: Bureau of Economic Analysis, **www.bea.gov.**

Taking that into account, note the dominant role of labor income in the U.S. economy. Even with labor income narrowly defined as wages and salaries, labor receives 70 percent of all income earned by Americans in a typical year. But if we add in proprietors' income because most of it is believed to be a payment for labor, then labor's share of national income rises to almost 80 percent, a percentage that has been remarkably stable since at least 1900. That leaves about 20 percent for "capitalists" in the form of rent, income, and profit. Ironically, income from capital is a relatively small share of the U.S. economy, though we call it a capitalist system.

SUMMARY

LO16.1 Explain the nature of economic rent and how it is determined.

Economic rent is the price paid for the use of land and other natural resources whose total supplies are fixed.

Differences in land rent result from differences in demand, often stemming from differences in the fertility and climate features of the land or differences in location.

Because the supply of land is fixed by nature, rent is a surplus payment that is socially unnecessary from the viewpoint of causing land to be supplied. The idea of land rent as a surplus payment gave rise to the single-tax movement of the late 1800s.

Although land rent is a surplus payment rather than a cost to the economy as a whole, to individuals and firms, land rents are correctly regarded as costs. The payment of land rents by individuals and firms is socially useful because it puts an opportunity cost on the use of land so that people are incentivized to put each piece of land to its best possible use.

LO16.2 Define interest and explain how interest rates vary based on risk, maturity, loan size, and taxability.

Interest is the price paid for the use of money. Because money is not itself an economic resource, people do not value money for its own sake; they value it for its purchasing power.

The interest rate on money loans determines the interest income earned by households for providing capital to firms.

Interest rates vary in size because loans differ as to risk, maturity, amount, and taxability.

The pure rate of interest is the hypothetical interest rate that would serve purely and solely to compensate lenders for their willingness to patiently forgo alternative consumption and investment opportunities until their money is repaid. The pure rate is best approximated by the interest rate on long-term, virtually riskless, 20-year U.S. Treasury bonds.

LO16.3 Explain the loanable funds theory of interest rates.

In the loanable funds theory of interest, the equilibrium interest rate in a loan market is determined by the demand for and supply of loanable funds in that market. Other things equal, an increase in the supply of loanable funds reduces the equilibrium interest rate, whereas a decrease in supply increases it. And increases in the demand for loanable funds raise the equilibrium interest rate, whereas decreases in demand reduce it.

LO16.4 Demonstrate how interest rates relate to the time-value of money.

The time-value of money is the idea that $1 today has more value than $1 sometime in the future because the $1 today can be placed in an interest-bearing account and earn compound interest over time. Future value is the amount to which a current amount of money will grow through interest compounding. Present value is the current value of some money payment to be received in the future.

LO16.5 Explain the role of interest rates in allocating capital, modulating R&D spending, and helping to determine the economy's total output of goods and services.

The equilibrium interest rate influences the level of investment and helps ration financial and physical capital to specific firms and industries. Similarly, this rate influences the size and composition of R&D spending. The real interest rate, not the nominal rate, is critical to investment and R&D decisions.

Although designed to make funds available to low-income borrowers, usury laws tend to allocate credit to high-income persons, subsidize high-income borrowers at the expense of lenders, and lessen the efficiency with which loanable funds are allocated.

LO16.6 Relate why economic profits occur and how profits, along with losses, allocate resources among alternative uses.

As residual claimants, entrepreneurs receive a firm's accounting profits (total revenue minus explicit costs) in exchange for assuming the uninsurable risks associated with running a business. An entrepreneur can earn an economic profit (total revenue minus both explicit and implicit costs, including a normal profit) if her firm's accounting profit exceeds the normal profit that her entrepreneurship could on average earn in other business ventures.

The corporate form of business organization has allowed the millions who own corporate stock to share in the financial risks and economic profits engendered by entrepreneurship. Profits are the key energizer of business firms within the capitalist system. Profit expectations influence innovating and investment activities and therefore the economy's levels of employment and economic growth. The basic function of profits and losses, however, is to allocate resources in accord with consumers' preferences.

LO16.7 List the share of U.S. earnings received by each of the factors of production.

The largest share of all income earned by Americans—about 70 percent—goes to labor, a share narrowly defined as "wages and salaries." When labor's share is more broadly defined to include "proprietors' income," it rises to about 80 percent of national income, leaving about 20 percent for rent, interest, and profit payments to the providers of land, capital, and entrepreneurship.

TERMS AND CONCEPTS

economic rent	compound interest	explicit costs
incentive function	future value	implicit costs
single-tax movement	present value	economic or pure profit
pure rate of interest	nominal interest rate	insurable risks
loanable funds theory of interest	real interest rate	uninsurable risks
time-value of money	usury laws	normal profit

The following and additional problems can be found in connect

DISCUSSION QUESTIONS

1. How does the economist's use of the term "rent" differ from everyday usage? Explain: "Though rent need not be paid by society to make land available, rental payments are useful in guiding land into the most productive uses." LO16.1
2. Explain why economic rent is a surplus payment when viewed by the economy as a whole but a cost of production from the standpoint of individual firms and industries. Explain: "Land rent performs no 'incentive function' for the overall economy." LO16.1
3. How does Henry George's proposal for a single tax on land relate to the elasticity of the supply of land? Why are there so few remaining advocates of George's proposal? LO16.1
4. If money is not an economic resource, why is interest paid and received for its use? What considerations account for the fact

that interest rates differ greatly on various types of loans? Use those considerations to explain the relative sizes of the interest rates on the following: LO16.2
   a. A 10-year $1,000 government bond.
   b. A $20 pawnshop loan.
   c. A 30-year mortgage loan on a $175,000 house.
   d. A 24-month $12,000 commercial bank loan to finance the purchase of an automobile.
   e. A 60-day $100 loan from a personal finance company.
5. Why is the supply of loanable funds upsloping? Why is the demand for loanable funds downsloping? Explain the equilibrium interest rate. List some factors that might cause it to change. LO16.3
6. Here is the deal: You can pay your college tuition at the beginning of the academic year or the same amount at the end of the academic year. You either already have the money in an interest-bearing account or will have to borrow it. Deal, or no deal? Explain your financial reasoning. Relate your answer to the time-value of money, present value, and future value. LO16.4
7. What are the major economic functions of the interest rate? How might the fact that many businesses finance their investment activities internally affect the efficiency with which the interest rate performs its functions? LO16.5
8. Distinguish between nominal and real interest rates. Which is more relevant in making investment and R&D decisions? If the nominal interest rate is 12 percent and the inflation rate is 8 percent, what is the real rate of interest? LO16.5
9. Historically, usury laws that put below-equilibrium ceilings on interest rates have been used by some states to make credit available to poor people who could not otherwise afford to borrow. Critics contend that poor people are those most likely to be hurt by such laws. Which view is correct? LO16.5
10. How do the concepts of accounting profit and economic profit differ? Why is economic profit smaller than accounting profit? What are the three basic sources of economic profit? Classify each of the following according to those sources: LO16.6
    a. A firm's profit from developing and patenting a new medication that greatly reduces cholesterol and thus diminishes the likelihood of heart disease and stroke.
    b. A restaurant's profit that results from the completion of a new highway past its door.
    c. The profit received by a firm due to an unanticipated change in consumer tastes.
11. Why is the distinction between insurable and uninsurable risks significant for the theory of profit? Carefully evaluate: "All economic profit can be traced to either uncertainty or the desire to avoid it." What are the major functions of economic profit? LO16.6
12. What is the combined rent, interest, and profit share of the income earned by Americans in a typical year if proprietors' income is included within the labor (wage) share? LO16.7
13. **LAST WORD** Assume that you borrow $5,000, and you pay back the $5,000 plus $250 in interest at the end of the year. Assuming no inflation, what is the real interest rate? What would the interest rate be if the $250 of interest had been discounted at the time the loan was made? What would the interest rate be if you were required to repay the loan in 12 equal monthly installments?

AP REVIEW QUESTIONS

1. When using a supply-and-demand model to illustrate how land rents are set, economists typically draw the supply curve as a vertical line because: LO16.1
   a. The supply of land is fixed.
   b. The supply of land is perfectly inelastic.
   c. The quantity supplied of land does not increase when the rental rate increases.
   d. The quantity supplied depends on the rental rate.
   e. Answers a, b, and c are true.
2. The main argument put forth by advocates of the *single-tax movement* was that: LO16.1
   a. Taxing only income would make for a more equal society.
   b. Taxing only land would be very efficient because taxing land does not decrease its supply.
   c. Taxing only imports would help to protect local jobs and stimulate local entrepreneurs.
   d. Having only one tax would be much easier for people to understand and much less costly to administer than our current system with its wide variety of taxes.
   e. Answers a and d are true.
3. Angela puts $1,000 in a savings account that pays 3 percent per year. What is the future value of her money one year from now? LO16.4
   a. $970.
   b. $1,000.
   c. $1,003.
   d. $1,030.
   e. $1,300.
4. As shown in Table 16.2, $1,000 invested at 10 percent compound interest will grow into $1,331 after three years. What is the present value of $2,662 in three years if it is discounted back to the present at a 10 percent compound interest rate? (Hint: $2,662 is twice as much as $1,331.) LO16.4
5. Entrepreneurs are the residual claimants at their respective firms. This means that they: LO16.6
   a. Only get paid if there is any income left over after all the other factors of production have been paid.
   b. Must bear the financial risks of running their firms.
   c. Receive whatever accounting profits or losses their firms generate.
   d. Do not have any opportunity costs, only explicit costs.
   e. Answers a, b, and c are true.
6. True or false. As a capitalist economy, the vast majority of U.S. national income flows to the owners of capital. LO16.7

PROBLEMS

1. Suppose that you own a 10-acre plot of land that you would like to rent out to wheat farmers. For them, bringing in a harvest involves \$30 per acre for seed, \$80 per acre for fertilizer, and \$70 per acre for equipment rentals and labor. With these inputs, the land will yield 40 bushels of wheat per acre. If the price at which wheat can be sold is \$5 per bushel and if farmers want to earn a normal profit of \$10 per acre, what is the most that any farmer would pay to rent your 10 acres? What if the price of wheat rose to \$6 per bushel? LO16.1
2. Suppose that the demand for loanable funds for car loans in the Milwaukee area is \$10 million per month at an interest rate of 10 percent per year, \$11 million at an interest rate of 9 percent per year, \$12 million at an interest rate of 8 percent per year, and so on. If the supply of loanable funds is fixed at \$15 million, what will be the equilibrium interest rate? If the government imposes a usury law and says that car loans cannot exceed 3 percent per year, how big will the monthly shortage (or excess demand) for car loans be? What if the usury limit is raised to 7 percent per year? LO16.3
3. To fund its wars against Napoleon, the British government sold consol bonds. They were referred to as "perpetuities" because they would pay £3 every year in perpetuity (forever). If a citizen could purchase a consol for £25, what would its annual interest rate be? What if the price were £50? £100? Bonds are known as "fixed income" securities because the future payments that they will make to investors are fixed by the bond agreement in advance. Do the interest rates of bonds and other investments that offer fixed future payments vary positively or inversely with their current prices? LO16.4
4. Suppose that the interest rate is 4 percent. What is the future value of \$100 four years from now? How much of the future value is total interest? By how much would total interest be greater at a 6 percent interest rate than at a 4 percent interest rate? LO16.4
5. You are currently a worker earning \$60,000 per year but are considering becoming an entrepreneur. You will not switch unless you earn an accounting profit that is on average at least as great as your current salary. You look into opening a small grocery store. Suppose that the store has annual costs of \$150,000 for labor, \$40,000 for rent, and \$30,000 for equipment. There is a one-half probability that revenues will be \$200,000 and a one-half probability that revenues will be \$400,000. LO16.6
   a. In the low-revenue situation, what will your accounting profit or loss be? In the high-revenue situation?
   b. *On average,* how much do you expect your revenue to be? Your accounting profit? Your economic profit? Will you quit your job and try your hand at being an entrepreneur?
   c. Suppose the government imposes a 25 percent tax on accounting profits. This tax is only levied if a firm is earning positive accounting profits. What will your after-tax accounting profit be in the low-revenue case? In the high-revenue case? What will your *average* after-tax accounting profit be? What about your *average* after-tax economic profit? Will you now want to quit your job and try your hand at being an entrepreneur?
   d. Other things equal, does the imposition of the 25 percent profit tax increase or decrease the supply of entrepreneurship in the economy?

Chapter 17

Public Finance: Expenditures and Taxes

Learning Objectives

LO17.1 **Use a circular flow diagram to illustrate how the allocation of resources is affected by government's revenue and expenditure decisions.**

LO17.2 **Identify the main categories of government spending and the main sources of government revenue.**

LO17.3 **List the main categories of federal revenue and spending and describe the difference between marginal and average tax rates.**

LO17.4 **List the main categories of state and local revenue and spending.**

LO17.5 **Discuss the magnitude and distribution across job categories of government employment at the local, state, and federal levels.**

LO17.6 **Summarize the different philosophies regarding the distribution of a nation's tax burden.**

LO17.7 **Explain the principles relating to tax shifting, tax incidence, and the efficiency losses caused by taxes.**

LO17.8 **Discuss the probable incidence of U.S. taxes and how the distribution of income between rich and poor is affected by government taxes, transfers, and spending.**

AP Chapter Focus

As discussed in Chapter 2, the U.S. economy relies heavily on the private sector (households and businesses) and the market system to decide what gets produced, how it gets produced, and who gets the output. But the private sector is not the only entity in the decision process. The public sector (federal, state, and local government) also affects these economic decisions.

Government influences what gets produced and how it gets produced through laws that regulate the activities of private firms and also by directly producing certain goods and services, such as national defense and education. As discussed in Chapter 4, many of these government-produced goods and services are *public goods* that the private sector has trouble producing because of free-rider problems. Also, government influences who receives society's output of goods and services through various tax policies, welfare programs, and income-transfer payments that redistribute income.

Government-provided goods, services, and transfer payments are funded by taxes, borrowing, and *proprietary income*—the income that governments receive from running government-owned enterprises such as hospitals, utilities, toll roads, and lotteries.

Public finance is the subdiscipline of economics that studies the various ways in which governments raise and expend money. In this chapter we view the economy through the lens of public finance. Our main goal is to understand how taxes and income transfers not only pay for government-produced goods and services, but also affect the distribution of income between rich and poor.

Government and the Circular Flow

LO17.1 Use a circular flow diagram to illustrate how the allocation of resources is affected by government's revenue and expenditure decisions.

In Figure 17.1, we integrate government into the circular flow model first shown in Figure 2.2. Here flows (1) through (4) are the same as the corresponding flows in that figure. Flows (1) and (2) show business expenditures for the resources provided by households. These expenditures are costs to businesses but represent wage, rent, interest, and profit income to households. Flows (3) and (4) show household expenditures for the goods and services produced by businesses.

Now consider what happens when we add government. Flows (5) through (8) illustrate that government makes purchases in both product and resource markets. Flows (5) and (6) represent government purchases of such products as paper, computers, and military hardware from private businesses. Flows (7) and (8) represent government purchases of resources. The federal government employs and pays salaries to members of Congress, the armed forces, Justice Department lawyers, meat inspectors, and so on. State and local governments hire and pay teachers, bus drivers, police, and firefighters. The federal government might also lease or purchase land to expand a military base and a city might buy land on which to build a new elementary school.

Government then provides goods and services to both households and businesses, as shown by flows (9) and (10). Governments rely on three revenue sources to finance those

FIGURE 17.1 Government within the circular flow diagram. Government buys products from the product market and employs resources from the resource market to provide goods and services to households and businesses. Government finances its expenditures through the net taxes (taxes minus transfer payments) it receives from households and businesses.

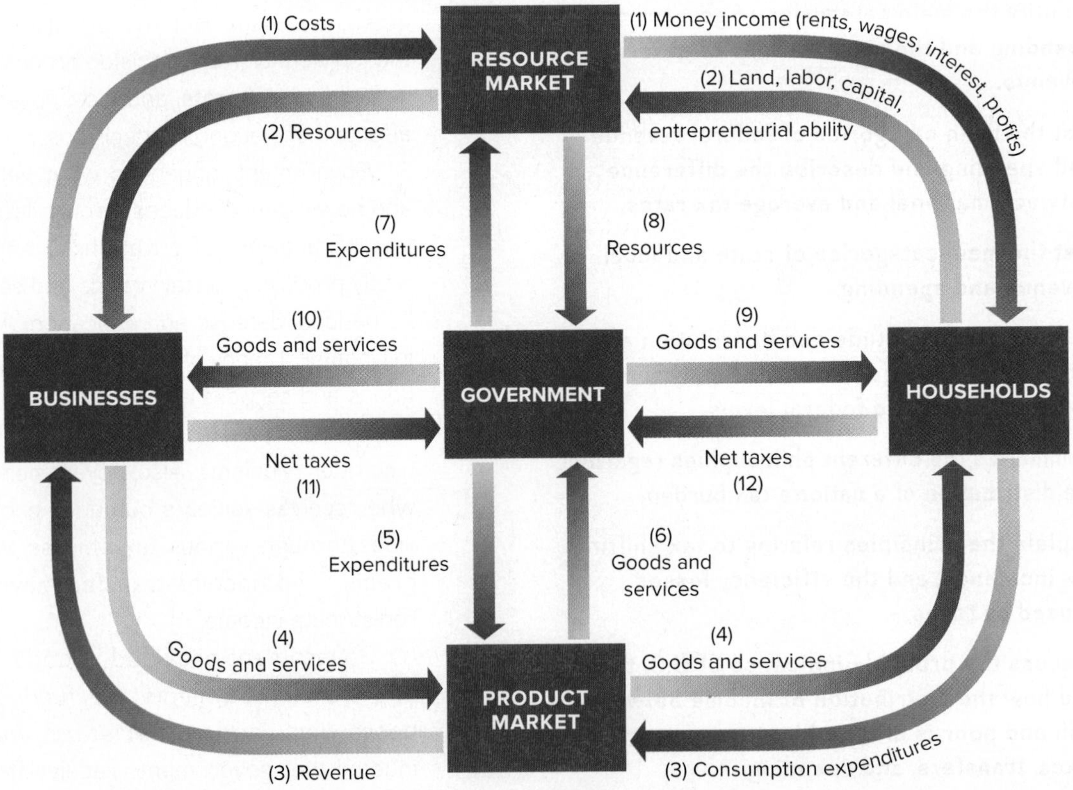

goods and services: taxes, borrowing, and the proprietary income generated by government-run or government-sponsored businesses like public utilities and state lotteries. These revenues flowing from households and businesses to government are included in flows (11) and (12), which are labeled as "net taxes" for two reasons. First, the vast majority of the money raised by these three revenue sources comes from taxes; thus, it is sensible to have these labels refer to taxes. Second, the labels refer to *net* taxes to indicate that they also include "taxes in reverse" in the form of transfer payments to households and subsidies to businesses. Thus, flow (11) entails various subsidies to farmers, shipbuilders, and airlines as well as income, sales, and excise taxes paid by businesses to government. Most subsidies to business are "concealed" in the form of low-interest loans, loan guarantees, tax concessions, or public facilities provided at prices below their cost. Similarly, flow (12) includes not only taxes (personal income taxes, payroll taxes) collected by government from households but also transfer payments made by government to households. These include welfare payments and Social Security benefits.

FIGURE 17.2 Government purchases, transfers, and total spending as percentages of U.S. output, 1960 and 2015. Government purchases have declined as a percentage of U.S. output since 1960. Transfer payments, however, have increased by more than this drop, raising total government spending (purchases plus transfers) from 27 percent of U.S. GDP in 1960 to about 33 percent today.

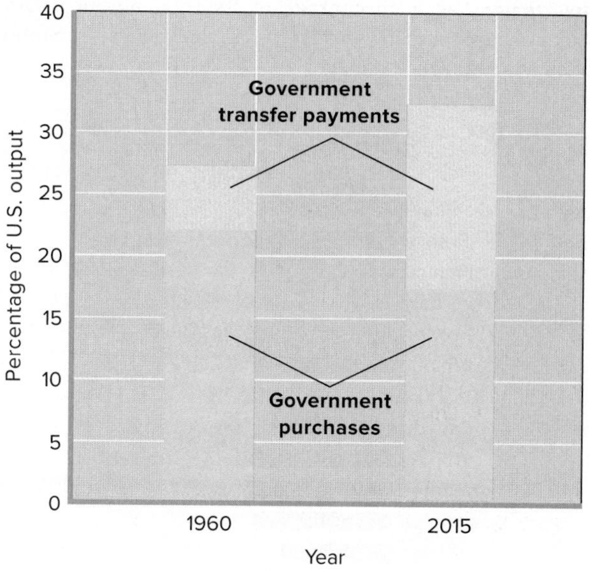

Source: Compiled from Bureau of Economic Analysis data, **www.bea.gov**.

Government Finance

LO17.2 Identify the main categories of government spending and the main sources of government revenue.

How large is the U.S. public sector? What are the main expenditure categories of federal, state, and local governments? How are these expenditures financed?

Government Purchases and Transfers

We can get an idea of the size of government's economic role by examining government purchases of goods and services and government transfer payments. There is a significant difference between these two kinds of outlays:

- **Government purchases** are *exhaustive;* the products purchased directly absorb (require the use of) resources and are part of the domestic output. For example, the purchase of a missile absorbs the labor of physicists and engineers along with steel, explosives, and a host of other inputs.
- **Transfer payments** are *nonexhaustive;* they do not directly absorb resources or create output. Social Security benefits, welfare payments, veterans' benefits, and unemployment compensation are examples of transfer payments. Their key characteristic is that recipients make no current contribution to domestic output in return for them.

Federal, state, and local governments spent $5,879 billion (roughly $5.9 trillion) in 2015. Of that total, government purchases were $3,204 billion and government transfers were $2,675 billion. Figure 17.2 shows these amounts as percentages of U.S. domestic output for 2015 and compares them to percentages for 1960. Government purchases have declined from about 22 to 18 percent of output since 1960. But transfer payments have tripled as a percentage of output—from 5 percent in 1960 to about 15 percent in 2015. Relative to U.S. output, total government spending is thus higher today than it was 55 years earlier. This means that the tax revenues required to finance government expenditures are also higher. Today, government spending and the tax revenues needed to finance it are about 33 percent of U.S. output.

In 2015, the so-called Tax Freedom Day in the United States was April 24. On that day the average worker had earned enough (from the start of the year) to pay his or her share of the taxes required to finance government spending for the year. Tax Freedom Day arrives even later in several other countries, as indicated in Global Perspective 17.1.

Government Revenues

The funds used to pay for government purchases and transfers come from three sources: taxes, proprietary income, and funds that are borrowed by selling bonds to the public.

Government Borrowing and Deficit Spending The ability to borrow allows a government to spend more in a given time period than it collects in tax revenues and proprietary

GLOBAL PERSPECTIVE 17.1

Total Tax Revenue as a Percentage of Total Output, Selected Nations, 2014*

A nation's "tax burden" is its tax revenue from all levels of government as a percentage of its total output (GDP). Among the world's industrialized nations, the United States has a very moderate tax burden.

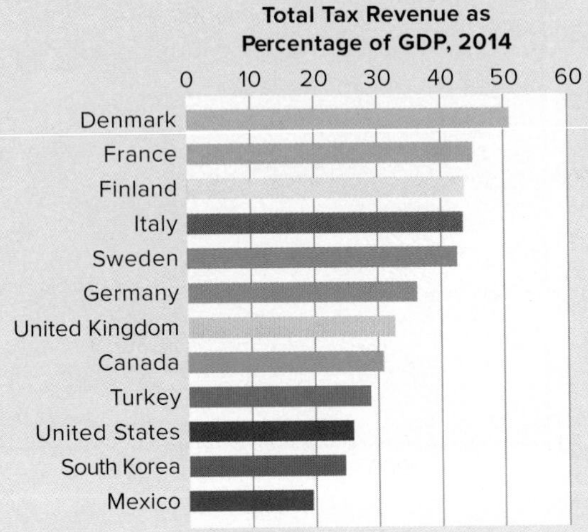

*Includes government nontax revenue from fees, charges, fines and sales of government property.

Source: OECD iLibrary, *Taxation: Key Tables from OECD*, **www.oecd-ilibrary.org**, accessed April 26, 2016. Numbers are 2014 estimates.

income during that period. This flexibility is useful during an economic downturn because a government can use borrowed funds to maintain high levels of spending on goods, services, and transfer payments even if tax revenues and proprietary income are falling due to the slowing economy.

Any money borrowed by a government, however, is money that cannot be put to other uses. During an economic downturn, this opportunity cost is likely to be small because any funds that the government does not borrow are likely to sit idle and unused by other parties due to the lack of economic activity during the downturn. But if the government borrows when the economy is doing well, many economists worry that the opportunity cost may be high. In particular, the government's borrowing may "crowd out" private-sector investment. As an example, a billion dollars borrowed and spent by the federal government on roads is a billion dollars that was not lent to private companies to fund the expansion of factories or the development of new technologies.

Government spending that is financed by borrowing is often referred to as *deficit spending* because a government's budget is said to be "in deficit" if the government's spending in a given time period exceeds the money that it collects from taxes and proprietary income during that period.

AP QUICK REVIEW 17.1

- ✓ A circular flow diagram can be used to illustrate how the government affects the allocation of resources in the economy through its revenue and expenditure decisions.
- ✓ As percentages of recent GDP, government purchases are 18 percent; government transfers, 15 percent; and the two combined are approximately 33 percent.
- ✓ The funds used to pay for government purchases and transfers come from taxes, proprietary income, and borrowing.
- ✓ The ability to borrow allows a government to maintain a high level of spending during an economic downturn even if taxes and proprietary income are falling.

AP Federal Finance

LO17.3 List the main categories of federal revenue and spending and describe the difference between marginal and average tax rates.

Now let's look separately at each of the federal, state, and local units of government in the United States and compare their expenditures and taxes. Figure 17.3 tells the story for the federal government.

Federal Expenditures

Four areas of federal spending stand out: (1) pensions and income security, (2) national defense, (3) health, and (4) interest on the public debt. The *pensions and income security* category includes the many income-maintenance programs for the aged, persons with disabilities or handicaps, the unemployed, the retired, and families with no breadwinner. This category—dominated by the $888 billion pension portion of the Social Security program—accounts for 38 percent of total federal expenditures. *National defense* accounts for about 16 percent of the federal budget, underscoring the high cost of military preparedness. *Health* reflects the cost of government health programs for the retired (Medicare) and poor (Medicaid). *Interest on the public debt* accounts for 6 percent of federal spending.

Federal Tax Revenues

The revenue side of Figure 17.3 shows that the personal income tax, payroll taxes, and the corporate income tax are the largest revenue sources, accounting respectively for 47, 33, and 11 cents of each dollar collected.

Personal Income Tax The **personal income tax** is the kingpin of the federal tax system and merits special comment. This tax is levied on *taxable income,* that is, on the

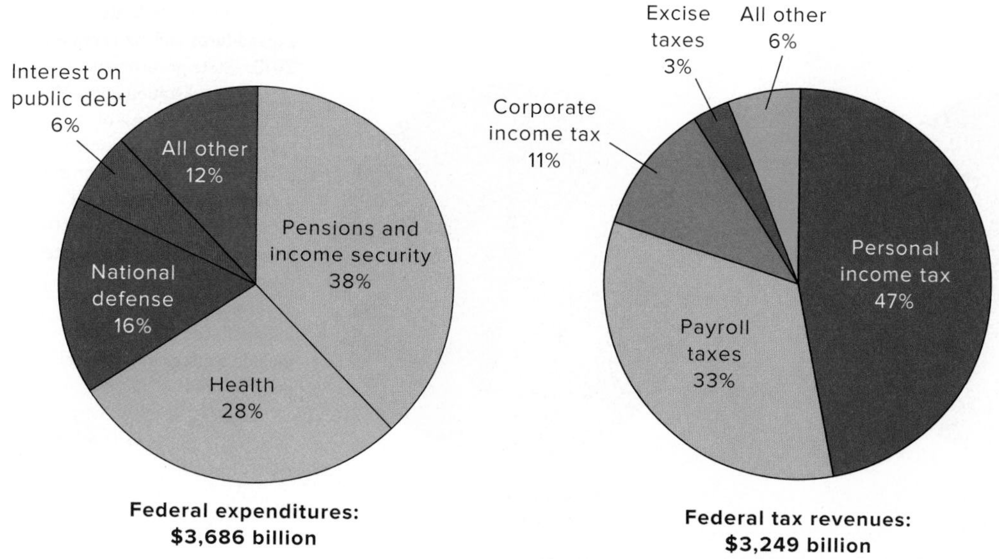

FIGURE 17.3 Federal expenditures and tax revenues, 2015. Federal expenditures are dominated by spending for pensions and income security, health, and national defense. A full 80 percent of federal tax revenue is derived from just two sources: the personal income tax and payroll taxes. The $437 billion difference between expenditures and revenues reflects a budget deficit.

Source: U.S. Treasury, *Combined Statement of Receipts, Outlays, and Balances, 2015,* **fms.treas.gov**.

incomes of households and unincorporated businesses after certain exemptions ($4,050 for each household member) and deductions (business expenses, charitable contributions, home mortgage interest payments, certain state and local taxes) are taken into account.

The federal personal income tax is a *progressive tax,* meaning that people with higher incomes pay a larger percentage of their incomes as taxes than do people with lower incomes. The progressivity is achieved by applying higher tax rates to successive layers or brackets of income.

Columns 1 and 2 in Table 17.1 show the mechanics of the income tax for a married couple filing a joint return in 2016. Note that a 10 percent tax rate applies to all taxable income up to $18,550 and a 15 percent rate applies to additional income up to $75,300. The rates on additional layers of income then go up to 25, 28, 33, 35, and 39.6 percent.

The tax rates shown in column 2 in Table 17.1 are marginal tax rates. A **marginal tax rate** is the rate at which the tax is paid on each *additional* unit of taxable income. Thus, if a couple's taxable income is $80,000, they will pay the marginal rate of 10 percent on each dollar from $1 to $18,550, 15 percent on each dollar from $18,551 to $75,300, and 25 percent on each dollar from $75,301 to $80,000. You should confirm that their total income tax is $13,398.

The marginal tax rates in column 2 overstate the personal income tax bite because the rising rates in that column apply only to the income within each successive tax bracket. To get a better idea of the tax burden, we must consider average tax rates. The **average tax rate** is the total tax paid divided by total taxable income. The couple in our previous example is in the 25 percent tax bracket because they pay a top marginal tax rate of 25 percent on the highest dollar of their income. But their *average* tax rate is 17 percent (= $13,398/$80,000).

As we will discuss in more detail shortly, a tax whose average rate rises as income increases is said to be a *progressive tax* because it claims both a progressively larger absolute amount of income as well as a progressively larger proportion of income as income rises. Thus we can say that the federal personal income tax is progressive.

Payroll Taxes Social Security contributions are **payroll taxes**—taxes based on wages and salaries—used to finance two compulsory federal programs for retired workers: Social Security (an income-enhancement program) and Medicare (which pays for medical services). Employers and employees pay these taxes equally. In 2016, employees and employers each paid 7.65 percent on the first $118,500

TABLE 17.1 Federal Personal Income Tax Rates, 2016*

(1) Total Taxable Income	(2) Marginal Tax Rate,%	(3) Total Tax on Highest Income In Bracket	(4) Average Tax Rate on Highest Income in Bracket,% (3) ÷ (1)
$0–$18,550	10	$1,855	10
$18,551–$75,300	15	10,368	14
$75,301–$151,900	25	29,518	19
$151,901–$231,450	28	51,792	22
$231,451–$413,350	33	111,819	27
$413,351–$466,950	35	130,579	28
$466,951 and above	39.6		

*For a married couple filing a joint return.

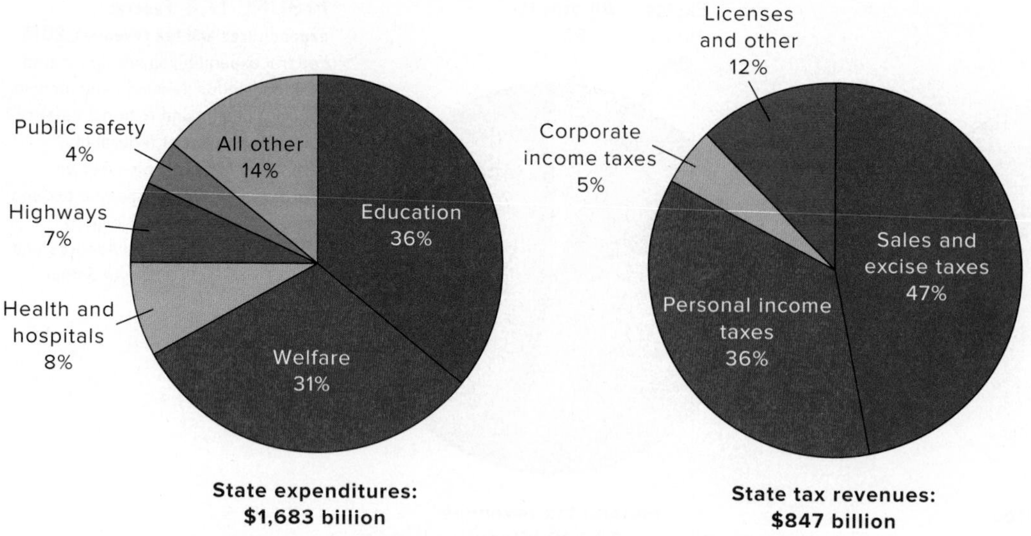

FIGURE 17.4 State expenditures and tax revenues, 2013. State governments spend largely on education and welfare. Their primary source of tax revenue is sales and excise taxes. The deficit between state expenditures and state tax revenues is filled by proprietary income and intergovernmental grants from the federal government. The state expenditures numbers here include state grants to local governments.

Source: U.S. Census Bureau, *2013 Annual Survey of State Government Finances,* **www.census.gov**.

of an employee's annual earnings and 1.45 percent on all additional earnings.

Corporate Income Tax The federal government also taxes corporate income. The **corporate income tax** is levied on a corporation's profit—the difference between its total revenue and its total expenses. For almost all corporations, the tax rate is 35 percent.

Excise Taxes Taxes on commodities or on purchases take the form of **sales** and **excise taxes.** The two differ primarily in terms of coverage. Sales taxes fall on a wide range of products, whereas excises are levied individually on a small, select list of commodities. An additional difference is that sales taxes are calculated as a percentage of the price paid for a product, whereas excise taxes are levied on a per-unit basis—for example, $2 per pack of cigarettes or $0.50 per gallon of gasoline.

As Figure 17.3 suggests, the federal government collects excise taxes of various rates (on the sale of such commodities as alcoholic beverages, tobacco, and gasoline) but does not levy a general sales tax; sales taxes are, however, the primary revenue source of most state governments.

State and Local Finance

LO17.4 List the main categories of state and local revenue and spending.

State and local governments have different mixes of revenues and expenditures than the federal government has.

State Finances

Figure 17.4 shows that the primary source of tax revenue for state governments is sales and excise taxes, which account for about 47 percent of all their tax revenue. State personal income taxes, which have much lower rates than the federal income tax, are the second most important source of state tax revenue. They bring in about 36 percent of total state tax revenue. Corporate income taxes and license fees account for most of the remainder of state tax revenue.

Education expenditures account for about 36 percent of all state spending. State expenditures on public welfare are next in relative weight, at about 31 percent of the total. States also spend heavily on health and hospitals (8 percent), highway maintenance and construction (7 percent), and public safety (4 percent). That leaves about 14 percent of all state spending for a variety of other purposes.

These tax and expenditure percentages combine data from all the states, so they reveal little about the finances of individual states. States vary significantly in the taxes levied. Thus, although personal income taxes are a major source of revenue for all state governments combined, seven states do not levy a personal income tax. Also, there are great variations in the sizes of tax revenues and disbursements among the states, both in the aggregate and as percentages of personal income.

Forty-three states augment their tax revenues with state-run lotteries to help close the gap between their tax receipts and expenditures. Individual states also receive large intergovernmental grants from the federal government. In fact, about 25 percent of their total revenue is in that form. States also take in revenue from miscellaneous sources such as state-owned utilities and liquor stores.

Local Finances

The local levels of government include counties, municipalities, townships, and school districts as well as cities and towns. Figure 17.5 shows that local governments obtain about 73 percent

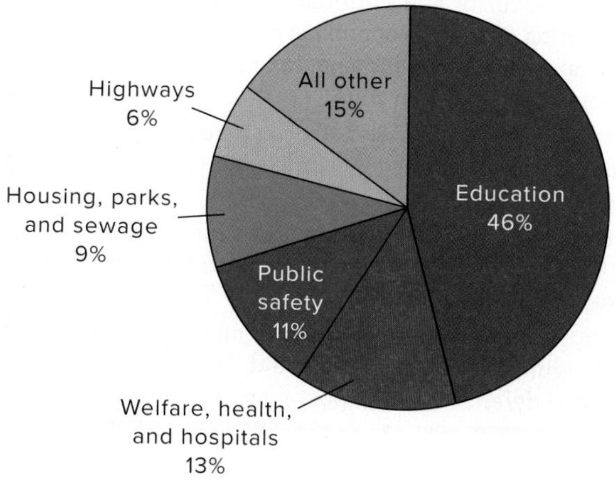

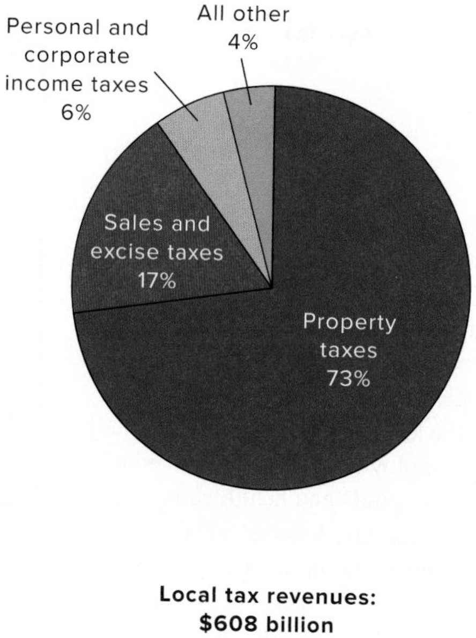

FIGURE 17.5 Local expenditures and tax revenues, 2013. The expenditures of local governments go largely to education, while a large majority of local tax collections are obtained via property taxes. The large deficit between local expenditures and local tax revenues is filled by proprietary income and federal and state intergovernmental grants.

Source: U.S. Census Bureau, *2013 Annual Surveys of State and Local Government Finances*, **www.census.gov**.

of their tax revenue from **property taxes.** Sales and excise taxes contribute about 17 percent of all local government tax revenue.

About 46 percent of local government expenditures go to education. Welfare, health, and hospitals (13 percent); public safety (11 percent); housing, parks, and sewerage (9 percent); and streets and highways (6 percent) are also major spending categories.

The tax revenues of local government cover less than one-half of their expenditures. The bulk of the remaining revenue comes from intergovernmental grants from the federal and state governments. Also, local governments receive considerable amounts of proprietary income, for example, revenue from government-owned utilities providing water, electricity, natural gas, and transportation.

CONSIDER THIS . . .

Source: © Mark Steinmetz

State Lotteries: A Good Bet?

State lotteries generated about $64.6 billion in revenue in 2014. Of that amount, $40.3 billion went to prizes and $3.1 billion went to administrative costs. That left $21.2 billion that could be spent by the states as they saw fit.

Though nowadays common, state lotteries are still controversial. Critics argue that (1) it is morally wrong for states to sponsor gambling; (2) lotteries generate compulsive gamblers who impoverish themselves and their families; (3) low-income families spend a larger portion of their incomes on lotteries than do high-income families; (4) as a cash business, lotteries attract criminals and other undesirables; and (5) lotteries send the message that luck and fate—rather than education, hard work, and saving—are the route to wealth.

Defenders contend that (1) lotteries are preferable to taxes because they are voluntary rather than compulsory; (2) they are a relatively painless way to finance government services such as education, medical care, and welfare; and (3) lotteries compete with illegal gambling and are thus socially beneficial in curtailing organized crime.

As a further point for debate, also note that state lotteries are monopolies, with states banning competing private lotteries. The resulting lack of competition allows many states to restrict prizes to only about half the money wagered. These payout rates are substantially lower than the 80–95 percent payout rates typically found in private betting operations such as casinos.

Thus, while lotteries are indeed voluntary, they are overpriced and underprovided relative to what would happen if there were a free market in lotteries. But, then again, a free market in lotteries would eliminate monopoly profits for state lotteries and possibly add government costs for regulation and oversight. Consequently, the alternative of allowing a free market in lottery tickets and then taxing the firms selling lottery tickets would probably net very little additional revenue to support state spending programs.

Local, State, and Federal Employment

LO17.5 Discuss the magnitude and distribution across job categories of government employment at the local, state, and federal levels.

In 2014, U.S. governments (local, state, and federal) employed about 21.9 million workers, or about 14 percent of the U.S. labor force. Figure 17.6 shows the percentages of these government employees assigned to different tasks at both the federal level and the state and local level.

As Figure 17.6 makes clear, the types of jobs done by government workers depend on the level of government. Over half of state and local government employment is focused on education. The next largest sector is hospitals and health care, which accounts for about 8 percent of state and local government employment. Police and corrections make up another 9 percent. Smaller categories like highways, public welfare, and judicial together combine for less than 8 percent of state and local employment. The "other" category includes workers in areas such as parks and recreation, fire fighting, transit, and libraries.

Almost half of federal government jobs are in national defense or the postal service. A further 15 percent of federal government jobs are in hospitals or health care. The natural resources, police, and financial administration categories each account for between 4 and 7 percent of federal employment. The "other" category at the federal level is composed of workers in areas such as justice and law, corrections, air transportation, and social insurance administration.

AP QUICK REVIEW 17.2

- ✓ Income security and national defense are the main categories of federal spending; personal income, payroll, and corporate income taxes are the primary sources of federal revenue.
- ✓ States rely on sales and excise taxes for revenue; their spending is largely for education and public welfare.
- ✓ Education is the main expenditure for local governments, most of whose revenue comes from property taxes.
- ✓ State and local employment is dominated by education, while federal employment is dominated by national defense and the postal service.

AP Apportioning the Tax Burden

LO17.6 Summarize the different philosophies regarding the distribution of a nation's tax burden.

Taxes are the major source of funding for the goods and services provided by government and the wages and salaries paid to government workers. Without taxes, there would be no public schools, no national defense, no public highways, no courts, no police, and no other government-provided public and quasi-public goods. As stated by Supreme Court Justice Oliver Wendell Holmes, "Taxes are the price we pay for civilization."

FIGURE 17.6 Job functions of state and local employees and federal employees, 2014. A majority of state and local workers are employed in education. Federal employment is dominated by the postal service and national defense, which together employ just over half of federal employees.

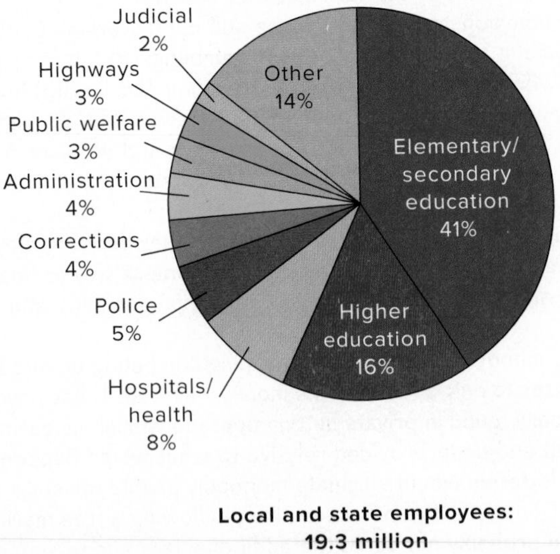

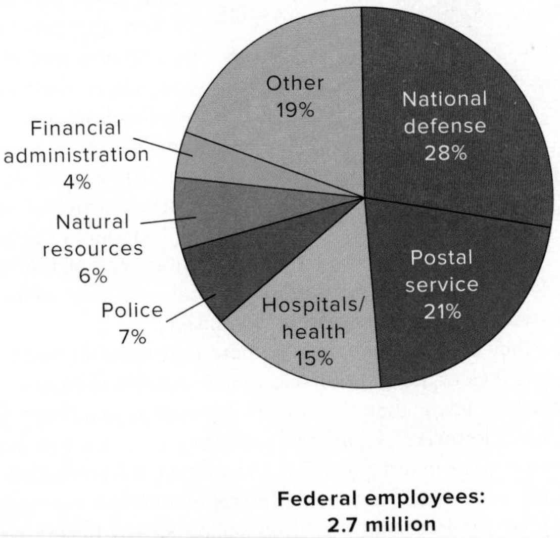

Source: U.S. Census Bureau, *State and Local Government Employment and Payroll Data, by State and Function*, and *Federal Government Employment by Function*, **www.census.gov**.

But taxes are controversial. To begin with, many people would prefer to obtain government goods and services without paying for them. Many others argue that certain taxes cause more harm than good, either by discouraging beneficial economic activity or by unfairly reducing the income flowing to workers and investors. And millions more chafe at the huge variety of taxes that governments levy, including income taxes, Social Security taxes, Medicare taxes, property taxes, sales taxes, liquor taxes, cigarette taxes, cell phone taxes, hotel taxes, gasoline taxes, profit taxes, and estate taxes.

For these and other reasons, people are intently focused on the overall level of taxes, the amount they must personally pay, and the idea of tax fairness (which is often defined in terms of their own circumstances).

The public's attention to taxes has spurred public finance economists to undertake considerable research into the size, distribution, and impact of the total costs that taxes impose on society—the so-called tax burden. Their investigations reveal with reasonable clarity both the size of the tax burden as well as how it is apportioned across the income distribution.

Whether you consider their findings to be good news or bad news, however, depends significantly on your opinion about the fairest way to allocate taxes and the tax burden. So before turning to their findings, let's first discuss some of the major philosophical viewpoints regarding taxation.

Benefits Received versus Ability to Pay

Two basic philosophies coexist on how the economy's tax burden should be apportioned.

Benefits-Received Principle The **benefits-received principle** of taxation asserts that households should purchase the goods and services of government in the same way they buy other commodities. Those who benefit most from government-supplied goods or services should pay the taxes necessary to finance them. A few public goods are now financed on this basis. For example, money collected as gasoline taxes is typically used to finance highway construction and repairs. Thus people who benefit from good roads pay the cost of those roads. Difficulties immediately arise, however, when we consider widespread application of the benefits-received principle:

- How will the government determine the benefits that individual households and businesses receive from national defense, education, the court system, and police and fire protection? Recall from Chapter 4 that public goods are characterized by nonrivalry and nonexcludability. So benefits from public goods are especially widespread and diffuse. Even in the seemingly straightforward case of highway financing it is difficult to measure benefits. Good roads benefit owners of cars in different degrees. But others also benefit. For example, businesses benefit because good roads bring them workers and customers.
- The benefits-received principle cannot logically be applied to income redistribution programs. It would be absurd and self-defeating to ask poor families to pay the taxes needed to finance their welfare payments. It would also be self-defeating to tax only unemployed workers to finance the unemployment benefits they receive.

Ability-to-Pay Principle The **ability-to-pay principle** of taxation asserts that the tax burden should be apportioned according to taxpayers' income and wealth. In practice, this means that individuals and businesses with larger incomes should pay more taxes in both absolute and relative terms than those with smaller incomes.

In justifying the ability-to-pay principle, proponents contend that each additional dollar of income received by a household yields a smaller amount of satisfaction or marginal utility when it is spent. Because consumers act rationally, the first dollars of income received in any time period will be spent on high-urgency goods that yield the greatest marginal utility. Successive dollars of income will go for less urgently needed goods and finally for trivial goods and services. This means that a dollar taken through taxes from a poor person who has few dollars represents a greater utility sacrifice than a dollar taken through taxes from a rich person who has many dollars. To balance the sacrifices that taxes impose on income receivers, taxes should be apportioned according to the amount of income a taxpayer receives.

This argument is appealing, but application problems arise here too. Although we might agree that the household earning $100,000 per year has a greater ability to pay taxes than a household receiving $10,000, we don't know exactly how much more ability to pay the first family has. Should the wealthier family pay the *same* percentage of its larger income, and hence a larger absolute amount, as taxes? Or should it be made to pay a *larger* percentage of its income as taxes? And how much larger should that percentage be? Who is to decide?

There is no scientific way of making utility comparisons among individuals and thus of measuring someone's relative ability to pay taxes. That is the main problem. In practice, the solution hinges on guesswork, the tax views of the political party in power, expediency, and how urgently the government needs revenue.

Progressive, Proportional, and Regressive Taxes

Any discussion of taxation leads ultimately to the question of tax rates. Taxes are classified as progressive, proportional, or regressive, depending on the relationship between average tax rates and taxpayer incomes. We focus on incomes because all taxes—whether on income, a product, a building, or a parcel of land—are ultimately paid out of someone's income.

- A tax is **progressive** if its average rate increases as income increases. Such a tax claims not only a larger absolute (dollar) amount but also a larger percentage of income as income increases.
- A tax is **regressive** if its average rate declines as income increases. Such a tax takes a smaller proportion of income as income increases. A regressive tax may or may not take a larger absolute amount of income as income increases. (You may want to develop an example to substantiate this fact.)
- A tax is **proportional** if its average rate *remains the same* regardless of the size of income. Proportional income taxes are often referred to as *flat taxes* or *flat-rate taxes* because their average rates do not vary with (are flat with respect to) income levels.

We can illustrate these ideas with the personal income tax. Suppose tax rates are such that a household pays 10 percent of its income in taxes regardless of the size of its income. This is a *proportional* income tax. Now suppose the rate structure is such that a household with an annual taxable income of less than $10,000 pays 5 percent in income taxes; a household with an income of $10,000 to $20,000 pays 10 percent; one with a $20,000 to $30,000 income pays 15 percent; and so forth. This is a *progressive* income tax. Finally, suppose the rate declines as taxable income rises: You pay 15 percent if you earn less than $10,000; 10 percent if you earn $10,000 to $20,000; 5 percent if you earn $20,000 to $30,000; and so forth. This is a *regressive* income tax.

In general, progressive taxes are those that fall relatively more heavily on people with high incomes; regressive taxes are those that fall relatively more heavily on the poor.

Let's examine the progressivity, or regressivity, of several taxes.

Personal Income Tax As noted earlier, the federal personal income tax is progressive, with marginal tax rates (those assessed on additional income) ranging from 10 to 39.6 percent in 2016. Rules that allow individuals to deduct from income interest on home mortgages and property taxes and that exempt interest on state and local bonds from taxation tend to make the tax less progressive than these marginal rates suggest. Nevertheless, average tax rates rise with income.

Sales Taxes At first thought, a general sales tax with, for example, a 5 percent rate would seem to be proportional. But in fact it is regressive with respect to income. A larger portion of a low-income person's income is exposed to the tax than is the case for a high-income person; the rich pay no tax on the part of income that is saved, whereas the poor are unable to save. Example: "Low-income" Smith has an income of $15,000 and spends it all. "High-income" Jones has an income of $300,000 but spends only $200,000 and saves the rest. Assuming a 5 percent sales tax applies to all expenditures of each individual, we find that Smith pays $750 (5 percent of $15,000) in sales taxes and Jones pays $10,000 (5 percent of $200,000). But Smith pays $750/$15,000, or 5 percent of income as sales taxes while Jones pays $10,000/$300,000, or 3.3 percent of income. The general sales tax therefore is regressive.

Corporate Income Tax The federal corporate income tax is essentially a proportional tax with a flat 35 percent tax rate. In the short run, the corporate owners (shareholders) bear the tax through lower dividends and share values. In the long run, workers may bear some of the tax since it reduces the return on investment and therefore slows capital accumulation. It also causes corporations to relocate to other countries that have lower tax rates. With less capital per worker, U.S. labor productivity may decline and wages may fall. To the extent this happens, the corporate income tax may be somewhat regressive.

Payroll Taxes Payroll taxes are taxes levied upon wages and salaries by certain states as well as by the federal government. The federal payroll tax is known as the FICA tax after the Federal Insurance Contributions Act, which mandated one payroll tax to fund the Social Security program and another to fund the Medicare program.

Both taxes are split equally between employer and employee. Thus, the 12.4 percent Social Security tax is split in half, with 6.2 percent paid by employees and an additional 6.2 percent paid by employers. In the same way, the 2.9 percent Medicare tax is also split in half, with 1.45 percent paid by employees and 1.45 percent paid by employers.

Crucially, however, only the Medicare tax applies to all wage and salary income without limit. The Social Security tax, by contrast, is "capped," meaning that it applies only up to a certain limit, or cap. In 2016, the cap was $118,500.

The fact that the Social Security tax applies only on income below the cap implies that the FICA tax is regressive. To see this, consider a person with $118,500 in wage income. He would pay $9,065.25, or 7.65 percent (= 6.2 percent + 1.45 percent) of his wages in FICA taxes. By contrast, someone with twice that income, or $237,000, would pay $10,783.50 (= $9,065.25 on the first $118,500 + 1,718.25 on the second $118,500), which is only 4.6 percent of his wage income. Thus the average FICA tax falls as income rises, thereby confirming that the FICA tax is regressive.

But payroll taxes are even more regressive than suggested by this example because they only apply to wage and salary income. People earning high incomes tend to derive a higher percentage of their total incomes from nonwage sources like rents and dividends than do people who have incomes below the $118,500 cap on which Social Security taxes are paid. Thus, if

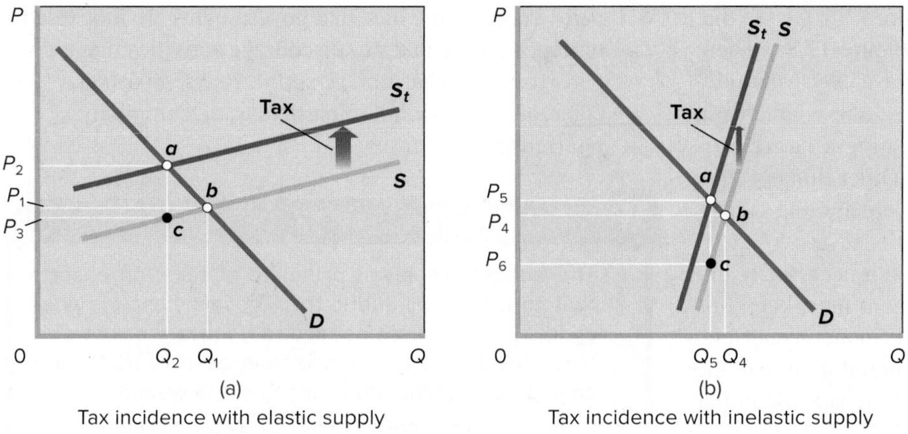

AP FIGURE 17.9 **Supply elasticity and the incidence of an excise tax.** (a) With elastic supply, an excise tax results in a large price increase (P_1 to P_2) and the tax is therefore paid mainly by consumers. (b) If supply is inelastic, the price rise is small (P_4 to P_5) and sellers bear most of the tax.

Efficiency Loss of a Tax

We just observed that producers and consumers typically each bear part of an excise tax levied on producers. Let's now look more closely at the overall economic effect of the excise tax. Consider Figure 17.10, which is identical to Figure 17.7 but contains the additional detail we need for our discussion.

Tax Revenues In our example, a $2 excise tax on wine increases its market price from $8 to $9 per bottle and reduces the equilibrium quantity from 15 million bottles to 12.5 million. Government tax revenue is $25 million (= $2 × 12.5 million bottles), an amount shown as the rectangle *efac* in Figure 17.10. The elasticities of supply and demand in this case are such that consumers and producers each pay half this total amount, or $12.5 million apiece (= $1 × 12.5 million bottles). The government uses this $25 million of tax revenue to provide public goods and services. So this transfer of dollars from consumers and producers to government involves no loss of well-being to society.

AP FIGURE 17.10 **Efficiency loss (or deadweight loss) of a tax.** The levy of a $2 tax per bottle of wine increases the price per bottle from $8 to $9 and reduces the equilibrium quantity from 15 million to 12.5 million. Tax revenue to the government is $25 million (area *efac*). The efficiency loss of the tax arises from the 2.5 million decline in output; the amount of that loss is shown as triangle *abc*.

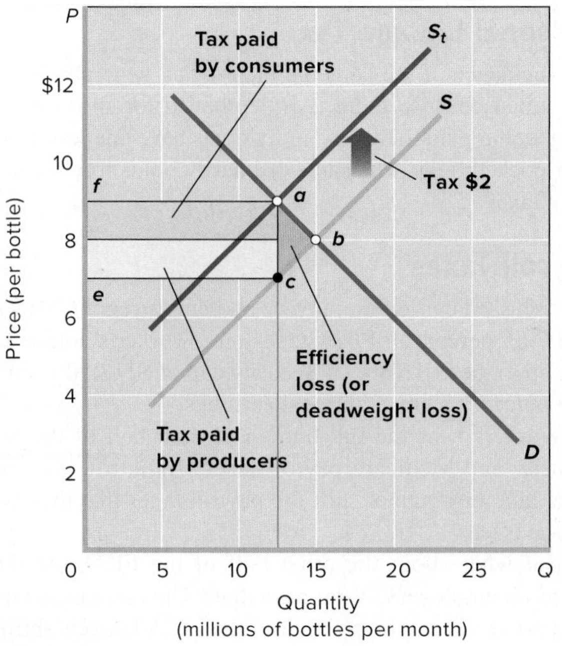

Efficiency Loss The $2 tax on wine does more than require consumers and producers to pay $25 million of taxes; it also reduces the equilibrium amount of wine produced and consumed by 2.5 million bottles. The fact that consumers and producers demanded and supplied 2.5 million more bottles of wine before the tax means that those 2.5 million bottles provided benefits in excess of their production costs. This is clear from the following analysis.

Segment *ab* of demand curve *D* in Figure 17.10 indicates the willingness to pay—the marginal benefit—associated with each of the 2.5 million bottles consumed before (but not after) the tax. Segment *cb* of supply curve *S* reflects the marginal cost of each of the bottles of wine. For all but the very last one of these 2.5 million bottles, the marginal benefit (shown by a point on *ab*) exceeds the marginal cost (shown by a point on *cb*). Not producing these 2.5 million bottles of wine reduces well-being by an amount represented by the triangle *abc*. The area of this triangle identifies the **efficiency loss of the tax** (also called the *deadweight loss of the tax*). This loss is society's sacrifice of net benefit because the tax reduces production and consumption of the product below their levels of economic efficiency, where marginal benefit and marginal cost are equal.

Role of Elasticities Most taxes create some degree of efficiency loss, but just how much depends on the supply and demand elasticities. Glancing back at Figure 17.8, we see that the efficiency loss area *abc* is greater in Figure 17.8a, where demand is relatively elastic, than in Figure 17.8b, where demand is relatively inelastic. Similarly, area *abc* is greater in Figure 17.9a than in Figure 17.9b, indicating a larger efficiency loss where supply is more elastic. Other things equal, the greater the elasticities of supply and demand, the greater the efficiency loss of a particular tax.

Two taxes yielding equal revenues do not necessarily impose equal costs on society. The government must keep this fact in mind in designing a tax system to finance beneficial public goods and services. In general, it should minimize the efficiency loss of the tax system in raising any specific dollar amount of tax revenue.

Qualifications We must acknowledge, however, that other tax goals may be as important as, or even more important than, minimizing efficiency losses from taxes. Here are two examples:

- ***Redistributive goals*** Government may wish to impose progressive taxes as a way to redistribute income. The 10 percent excise tax the federal government placed on selected luxuries in 1990 was an example. Because the demand for luxuries is elastic, substantial efficiency losses from this tax were to be expected. However, Congress apparently concluded that the benefits from the redistribution effects of the tax would exceed the efficiency losses.

  Ironically, in 1993 Congress repealed the luxury taxes on personal airplanes and yachts, mainly because the taxes had reduced quantity demanded so much that widespread layoffs of workers were occurring in those industries. But the 10 percent tax on luxury automobiles remained in place until it expired in 2003.

- ***Reducing negative externalities*** Our analysis of the efficiency loss of a tax assumes no negative externalities arising from either the production or consumption of the product in question. Where such spillover costs occur, an excise tax on producers might actually improve allocative efficiency by reducing output and thus lessening the negative externality. For example, the \$2 excise tax on wine in our example might be part of a broader set of excise taxes on alcoholic beverages. The government may have concluded that the consumption of these beverages produces certain negative externalities. Therefore, it might have purposely levied this \$2 tax to shift the market supply curve in Figure 17.10 to increase the price of wine, decrease alcohol consumption, and reduce the amount of resources devoted to wine.

  Excise taxes that are intended to reduce the production and consumption of products with negative externalities are sometimes referred to as *sin taxes*. This name captures the idea that governments are motivated to impose these taxes to discourage activities that are perceived to be harmful or sinful. Excise taxes on cigarettes and alcohol in particular are commonly referred to as sin taxes.

AP QUICK REVIEW 17.3

- ✓ The benefits-received principle of taxation asserts that those who benefit from government services should pay the taxes needed to finance them; by contrast, the ability-to-pay principle asserts that taxes should be apportioned by income and wealth.
- ✓ If the average amount taxed away (*a*) increases with income, it is *progressive*, (*b*) if it decreases with income, it is *regressive*, (c) if it remains constant as income increases, it is *proportional*.
- ✓ Given fixed demand, more elastic supply shifts tax burdens from product-specific taxes to consumers; given fixed supply, more elastic demand shifts those tax burdens to producers.
- ✓ Taxes imposed in markets raise the market equilibrium price, reduce the market equilibrium output, and normally generate efficiency losses, unless being used to address a negative externality.

Probable Incidence of U.S. Taxes

LO17.8 Discuss the probable incidence of U.S. taxes and how the distribution of income between rich and poor is affected by government taxes, transfers, and spending.

Let's look now at the probable incidence of each of the major sources of tax revenue in the United States.

Personal Income Tax

The incidence of the personal income tax generally is on the individual because there is little chance for shifting it. For every dollar paid to the tax, individuals have one less dollar in their pocketbooks. The same ordinarily holds true for inheritance taxes.

Payroll Taxes

As discussed earlier, employees and employers in 2016 *each* paid 7.65 percent in FICA taxes on a worker's annual earnings up to the 2016 Social Security cap of \$118,500 and then 1.45 percent on any additional earnings.

Workers bear the full burden of their half of the Social Security and Medicare payroll taxes. As is true for the income tax, they cannot shift the payroll taxes that they pay to anyone else.

But what about the other half of the FICA tax that is levied on employers? Who pays that? The consensus view is that part of the employers' half of the FICA tax gets shifted to workers in the form of lower before-tax wages. By making it more costly to hire workers, the payroll tax reduces the demand for labor relative to supply. That reduces the market wages that employers pay workers. In a sense, employers "collect" some of the payroll tax they owe from their workers.

Corporate Income Tax

In the short run, the incidence of the corporate income tax falls on the company's stockholders (owners), who bear the burden of the tax through lower dividends or smaller amounts of retained corporate earnings. Here is why. A firm currently charging the profit-maximizing price and producing the profit-maximizing output will have no reason to change product price, output, or wages when a tax on corporate income (profit) is imposed. The price and output combination yielding the greatest profit before the tax will still yield the greatest profit after a fixed percentage of the firm's profit is removed by a corporate income tax. So, the company's stockholders will not be able to shift the tax to consumers or workers.

As previously indicated, the situation may be different in the long run. Workers, in general, may bear a significant part of the corporate income tax in the form of lower wage growth. Because it reduces the return on investment, the corporate income tax may slow the accumulation of capital (plant and equipment). It also may prompt some U.S. firms to relocate abroad in countries that have lower corporate tax rates. In either case, the tax may slow the growth of U.S. labor productivity, which depends on American workers having access to more and better equipment. We know from Figure 15.1 that the growth of labor productivity is the main reason labor demand grows over time. If the corporate income tax reduces the growth of labor productivity, then labor demand and wages may rise less rapidly. In this indirect way—and over long periods of time—workers may bear part of the corporate income tax.

Sales and Excise Taxes

A *sales tax* is a general excise tax levied on a full range of consumer goods and services, whereas a *specific excise tax* is one levied only on a particular product. Sales taxes are usually transparent to the buyer, whereas excise taxes are often "hidden" in the price of the product. But whether they are hidden or clearly visible, both are often partly or largely shifted to consumers through higher equilibrium product prices (as in Figures 17.7 through 17.9). Sales taxes and excise taxes may get shifted to different extents, however. Because a sales tax covers a much wider range of products than an excise tax, there is little chance for consumers to avoid the price boosts that sales taxes entail. They cannot reallocate their expenditures to untaxed, lower-priced products. Therefore, sales taxes tend to be shifted in their entirety from producers to consumers.

Excise taxes, however, fall on a select list of goods. Therefore, the possibility of consumers turning to substitute goods and services is greater. An excise tax on theater tickets that does not apply to other types of entertainment might be difficult to pass on to consumers via price increases. Why? The answer is provided in Figure 17.8a, where demand is elastic. A price boost to cover the excise tax on theater tickets might cause consumers to substitute alternative types of entertainment. The higher price would reduce sales so much that a seller would be better off to bear all, or a large portion of, the excise tax.

With other products, modest price increases to cover taxes may have smaller effects on sales. The excise taxes on gasoline, cigarettes, and alcoholic beverages provide examples. Here consumers have few good substitute products to which they can turn as prices rise. For these goods, the seller is better able to shift nearly all the excise tax to consumers. Example: Prices of cigarettes have gone up nearly in lockstep with the recent, substantial increases in excise taxes on cigarettes.

As indicated in Global Perspective 17.2, the United States depends less on sales and excise taxes for tax revenue than do several other nations.

GLOBAL PERSPECTIVE 17.2

Taxes on General Consumption as a Percentage of GDP, Selected Nations

A number of advanced industrial nations rely much more heavily on consumption taxes—sales taxes, specific excise taxes, and value-added taxes—than does the United States. A value-added tax, which the United States does not have, applies only to the difference between the value of a firm's sales and the value of its purchases from other firms. As a percentage of GDP, the highest tax rates on consumption are in countries that have value-added taxes.

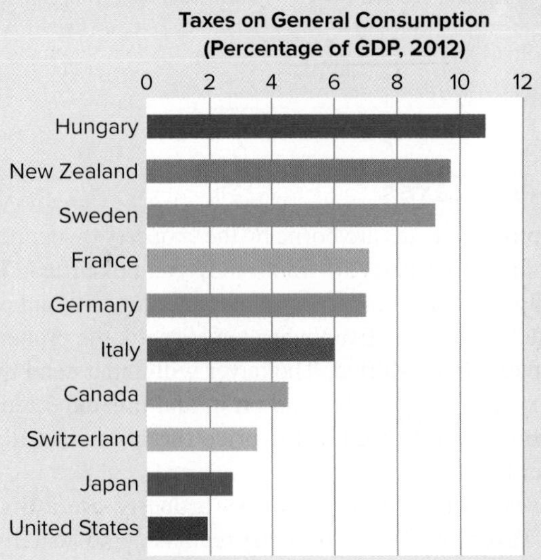

Source: Organization for Economic Cooperation and Development, *OECD Stat Extracts*, **stats.oecd.org**.

LAST WORD

Taxation and Spending: Redistribution versus Recycling

Many Think of Taxes as the Best Way to Level the Income Distribution, but the Real Action Is in Expenditures.

Modern governments face substantial political pressure to ensure a fair distribution of society's economic benefits. In most people's minds, this boils down to taxing the rich more than the poor, which is why there is such a focus on whether particular taxes are progressive or regressive.

But taxing the rich cannot by itself alter the income distribution. One other thing is needed: The taxes taken from the rich have to flow to the poor. In particular, they have to be spent on goods, services, and programs that are used mostly by the poor rather than on goods, services, and programs that are used mostly by the rich. If government doesn't do this, the tax revenues of the rich will simply be recycled back to the rich rather than being redistributed to the poor.

Until recently, however, economists had only patchy evidence about whether our system of taxation and spending actually redistributes income from the rich to the poor. The problem was that the U.S. government only publishes statistics on whether the rich are being taxed more than the poor. It does not publish statistics on who receives most of its spending.

Fortunately, two economists from the nonpartisan Tax Foundation took it upon themselves to calculate those statistics. By combining data on government spending with household questionnaire responses in which people report what goods and services they consume, economists Gerald Prante and Scott A. Hodge generated reliable estimates of whether the government transfers significant amounts of income from the rich to the poor.*

© PhotoDisc/Getty Images RF

As it turns out, the government *does* transfer an enormous amount of income from those with high incomes to those with low incomes. Not only do people with high incomes pay a much larger fraction of their incomes in taxes, it is also the case that the majority of that money gets transferred to the poor because government spending is indeed concentrated on programs that are used more by

*Gerald Prante and Scott A. Hodge, "The Distribution of Tax and Spending Policies in the United States," Tax Foundation *Special Report* No. 211, November 2013.

Property Taxes

Many property taxes are borne by the property owner because there is no other party to whom they can be shifted. This is typically true for taxes on land, personal property, and owner-occupied residences. Even when land is sold, the property tax is not likely to be shifted. The buyer will understand that future taxes will have to be paid on it, and this expected taxation would be reflected in the price the buyer is willing to offer for the land.

Taxes on rented and business property are a different story. Taxes on rented property can be, and usually are, shifted wholly or in part from the owner to the tenant by the process of boosting the rent. Business property taxes are treated as a business cost and are taken into account in establishing product price; hence such taxes are ordinarily shifted to the firm's customers.

Table 17.2 summarizes this discussion of the shifting and incidence of taxes.

The U.S. Tax Structure

Is the overall U.S. tax structure—federal, state, and local taxes combined—progressive, proportional, or regressive? The question is difficult to answer. Estimates of the distribution of the total tax burden depend on the extent to which the various taxes are shifted to others, and who bears the burden the poor than by the rich. These include welfare, subsidized health care, public education, and jobs programs. The poor also benefit from government-provided public goods that are available to everyone on an equal basis—things like public roads, clean drinking water, national defense, and so on.

The size and impact of the income transfers from rich to poor are most clearly understood by looking at the nearby figure, which groups the 133 million households living in the United States in 2012 into one of five equally sized groups (or quintiles) on the basis of household income. The quintiles are labeled Bottom 20%, Second 20%, Third 20%, Fourth 20%, and Top 20%. The yellow and blue bars above each quintile show, respectively, how much in taxes its members paid on average and how much in government spending they received on average during 2012.

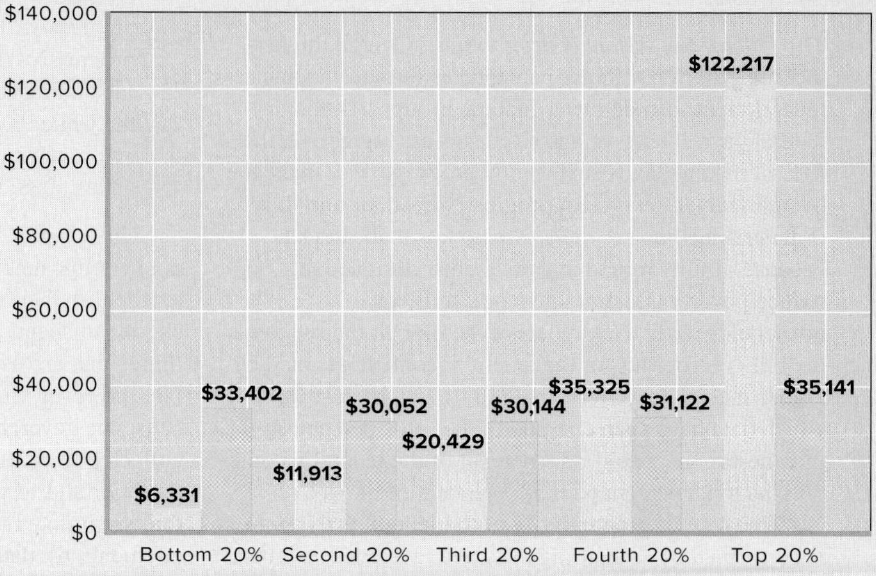

The first thing to notice is how much more money the poor received in government spending than they paid in taxes that year. A comparison of the yellow and blue bars for the bottom quintile reveals that the poorest households received $27,071 (= $33,402 in government spending – $6,331 in taxes) more in government spending than they paid in taxes in 2012. By contrast, households in the top 20 percent of the income distribution paid $87,076 more in taxes than they received in government spending that year.

This $87,076 per-household excess paid by households in the top quintile plus the $4,203 per-household excess paid by the households in the second-highest quintile provided the money that allowed the members of the lower three quintiles to receive more in government spending than they paid in taxes. In total, the transfers from the top two quintiles to the bottom three quintiles amounted to more than $1 trillion in 2012, or about 10 percent of all income earned by households that year.

The authors also found that the average tax rates paid by the five quintiles (on their total incomes, including government spending received) were, respectively, 14.7 percent for the bottom quintile, 19.5 percent for the second quintile, 23.5 percent for the third quintile, 26.9 percent for the fourth quintile, and 35.2 percent for the top quintile. Thus, the overall tax system is highly progressive (due to the federal income tax) despite many individual taxes being quite regressive.

But, more significantly, the spending made possible by taxing the rich more than the poor disproportionately flows back to the poor rather than being recycled to the rich. In fact, households in the top quintile receive back only 29 cents in government spending for each dollar they pay in taxes—which means that the remaining 71 cents are channeled to poorer households.

TABLE 17.2 The Probable Incidence of Taxes

Type of Tax	Probable Incidence
Personal income tax	The household or individual on which it is levied.
Payroll taxes	Workers pay the full tax levied on their earnings and part of the tax levied on their employers.
Corporate income tax	In the short run, the full tax falls on owners of the businesses. In the long run, some of the tax may be borne by workers through lower wages.
Sales tax	Consumers who buy the taxed products.
Specific excise taxes	Consumers, producers, or both, depending on elasticities of demand and supply.
Property taxes	Owners in the case of land and owner-occupied residences; tenants in the case of rented property; consumers in the case of business property.

is subject to dispute. But the majority view of economists who study taxes is as follows:

- ***The federal tax system is progressive.*** Overall, higher-income groups pay larger percentages of their income as federal taxes than do lower-income groups. Although federal payroll taxes and excise taxes are regressive, the federal income tax is sufficiently progressive to make the overall federal tax system progressive. About one-third of federal income tax filers owe no tax at all. In fact, because of fully refundable tax credits designed to reduce poverty and promote work, millions of households receive tax rebates even though their income tax bill is zero. Most of the federal income tax is paid by higher-income taxpayers. In 2013 (the latest year for which data have been compiled), the top 1 percent of income-tax filers paid 37.8 percent of the federal income tax; the top 5 percent paid 58.5 percent of the tax.

  The overall progressivity of the federal tax system is confirmed by comparing effective (average) tax rates, which are found by dividing the total of federal income, payroll, and excise taxes paid at various income levels by the total incomes earned by the people at those various income levels. In 2011, the 20 percent of the households with the lowest income paid an effective tax rate of 1.9 percent. The 20 percent of households with the highest income paid a 23.4 percent rate. The top 1 percent paid a 29.0 percent rate.[1]
- ***The state and local tax structures are largely regressive.*** As a percentage of income, property taxes and sales taxes fall as income rises. Also, state income taxes are generally less progressive than the federal income tax.
- ***The overall U.S. tax system is progressive.*** Higher-income people carry a substantially larger tax burden, as a percentage of their income, than do lower-income people, as discussed in this chapter's Last Word.
- ***The overall U.S. tax system is more progressive than that of other rich countries.*** A study by the Organization for Economic Cooperation and Development (OECD) concluded that the U.S. tax system is the most progressive among OECD nations and therefore more progressive than those of countries such as Canada, Japan, France, Sweden, Germany, Korea, Australia, and the United Kingdom.[2] This is because those other nations rely much more heavily on national sales taxes and value-added taxes, both of which are regressive.

This chapter's Last Word also points out that the income tax system cannot be relied upon by itself to substantially alter the distribution of income because the government might choose to spend the taxes collected from the rich to pay for things that are used more by the rich than the poor. In actual fact, however, this does not happen in the United States because the government uses a large portion of the tax revenues collected from the rich to make income transfer payments to the poor and to pay for the provision of goods and services that are utilized more by the poor than the rich. The transfer payments by themselves are so large that they almost quadruple the incomes of the poorest fifth of U.S. households. Thus, the combined tax-transfer system levels the income distribution by much more than the tax system does on its own.

AP QUICK REVIEW 17.4

- ✓ Incidence is the term to denote that some taxes are borne by those taxed while other taxes are shifted to someone else.
- ✓ The personal income tax and the corporate income tax (in the short run) are borne by those taxed.
- ✓ Sales taxes are shifted to consumers; the employer's share of the payroll tax is shifted to workers; excise taxes may be shifted to consumers; and property taxes on rental properties are shifted to tenants.
- ✓ The federal tax structure is mildly progressive. The state and local tax structures are mildly regressive. The overall U.S. tax structure is slightly progressive.

[1] *The Distribution of Household Income and Federal Taxes*, 2011, Congressional Budget Office, November 2014.

[2] *Growing Unequal? Income Distribution and Poverty in OECD Countries*, Organization for Economic Cooperation and Development, 2008.

SUMMARY

LO17.1 Use a circular flow diagram to illustrate how the allocation of resources is affected by government's revenue and expenditure decisions.

The funds used to pay for government purchases and transfers come from taxes, proprietary income, and borrowing. The ability to borrow allows governments to maintain high spending during economic downturns, but government borrowing when the economy is doing well may "crowd out" private-sector investment.

LO17.2 Identify the main categories of government spending and the main sources of government revenue.

Government purchases exhaust (use up or absorb) resources; transfer payments do not. Government purchases have declined from about 22 percent of domestic output in 1960 to about 18 percent today. Transfer payments, however, have grown rapidly. As a percentage of GDP, total government spending (purchases plus transfers) now stands at about 33 percent, up from 27 percent in 1960.

LO17.3 List the main categories of federal revenue and spending and describe the difference between marginal and average tax rates.

The main categories of federal spending are pensions and income security, national defense, health, and interest on the public debt; federal revenues come primarily from personal income taxes, payroll taxes, and corporate income taxes.

It is important to distinguish between marginal and average tax rates. An income tax system may have different rates for different ranges of income. The tax rate that applies to any particular range is that range's marginal tax rate. The average tax rate is found by dividing the total amount of taxes paid on the full value of a taxpayer's taxable income and then dividing by the amount of the taxable income.

LO17.4 List the main categories of state and local revenue and spending.

States derive their revenue primarily from sales and excise taxes and personal income taxes; major state expenditures go to education, public welfare, health and hospitals, and highways. Local communities derive most of their revenue from property taxes; education is their most important expenditure. State and local tax revenues are supplemented by sizable revenue grants from the federal government.

LO17.5 Discuss the magnitude and distribution across job categories of government employment at the local, state, and federal levels.

Slightly over half of state and local government employees work in education. Just over half of federal government employees work for either the postal service or in national defense.

LO17.6 Summarize the different philosophies regarding the distribution of a nation's tax burden.

The benefits-received principle of taxation states that those who receive the benefits of goods and services provided by government should pay the taxes required to finance them. The ability-to-pay principle states that those who have greater income should be taxed more, absolutely and relatively, than those who have less income.

LO17.7 Explain the principles relating to tax shifting, tax incidence, and the efficiency losses causes by taxes.

Excise taxes affect supply and therefore equilibrium price and quantity. The more inelastic the demand for a product, the greater is the portion of an excise tax that is borne by consumers. The greater the inelasticity of supply, the larger is the portion of the tax that is borne by the seller.

Taxation involves the loss of some output whose marginal benefit exceeds its marginal cost. The more elastic the supply and demand curves, the greater is the efficiency loss (or deadweight loss) resulting from a particular tax.

LO17.8 Discuss the probable incidence of U.S. taxes and how the distribution of income between rich and poor is affected by government taxes, transfers, and spending.

The federal personal income tax is progressive. The corporate income tax is roughly proportional. General sales, excise, payroll, and property taxes are regressive.

Some taxes are borne by those taxed; other taxes are shifted to someone else. The income tax, the payroll tax levied on workers, and the corporate income tax (in the short run) are borne by those taxed. In contrast, sales taxes are shifted to consumers, part of the payroll tax levied on employers is shifted to workers, and, in the long run, part of the corporate income tax is shifted to workers. Specific excise taxes may or may not be shifted to consumers, depending on the elasticities of demand and supply. Property taxes on owner-occupied property are borne by the owner; those on rental property are borne by tenants.

The federal tax structure is progressive; the state and local tax structures are regressive; and the overall tax structure is progressive.

As discussed in the Last Word, the overall tax-spending system in the United States redistributes significant amounts of income from high-income individuals to low-income individuals. Because of the highly progressive federal income tax, the overall tax system is progressive. In addition, spending flows disproportionately to those with lower incomes, so that the tax collections from the rich are redistributed to the poor rather than being recycled back to the rich.

TERMS AND CONCEPTS

government purchases
transfer payments
personal income tax
marginal tax rate
average tax rate
payroll taxes
corporate income tax
excise tax
sales tax
property taxes
benefits-received principle
ability-to-pay principle
progressive tax
regressive tax
proportional tax
tax incidence
efficiency loss of a tax

The following and additional problems can be found in connect

DISCUSSION QUESTIONS

1. Use a circular flow diagram to show how the allocation of resources and the distribution of income are affected by each of the following government actions. **LO17.1**
   - **a.** The construction of a new high school.
   - **b.** A 2-percentage-point reduction of the corporate income tax.
   - **c.** An expansion of preschool programs for disadvantaged children.
   - **d.** The levying of an excise tax on polluters.
2. What do economists mean when they say government purchases are "exhaustive" expenditures whereas government transfer payments are "nonexhaustive" expenditures? Cite an example of a government purchase and a government transfer payment. **LO17.1**
3. What are the main categories of government spending? What are the main categories of government revenue? **LO17.2**
4. What is the most important source of revenue and the major type of expenditure at the federal level? **LO17.3**
5. For state and local governments, what are the three most important sources of revenue and types of expenditure? **LO17.4**
6. How do the top two categories of federal employment differ from the top two categories of local and state employment? **LO17.5**
7. Distinguish between the benefits-received and the ability-to-pay principles of taxation. Which philosophy is more evident in our present tax structure? Justify your answer. To which principle of taxation do you subscribe? Why? **LO17.6**
8. What is meant by a progressive tax? A regressive tax? A proportional tax? Comment on the progressivity or regressivity of each of the following taxes, indicating in each case where you think the tax incidence lies: (*a*) the federal personal income tax, (*b*) a 4 percent state general sales tax, (*c*) a federal excise tax on automobile tires, (*d*) a municipal property tax on real estate, (*e*) the federal corporate income tax, (*f*) the portion of the payroll tax levied on employers. **LO17.6**
9. What is the tax incidence of an excise tax when demand is highly inelastic? Highly elastic? What effect does the elasticity of supply have on the incidence of an excise tax? What is the efficiency loss of a tax, and how does it relate to elasticity of demand and supply? **LO17.7**
10. Given the inelasticity of cigarette demand, discuss an excise tax on cigarettes in terms of efficiency loss and tax incidence. **LO17.7**
11. **ADVANCED ANALYSIS** Suppose the equation for the demand curve for some product X is $P = 8 - 0.6Q$ and the supply curve is $P = 2 + 0.4Q$. What are the equilibrium price and quantity? Now suppose an excise tax is imposed on X such that the new supply equation is $P = 4 + 0.4Q$. How much tax revenue will this excise tax yield the government? Graph the curves, and label the area of the graph that represents the tax collection "TC" and the area that represents the efficiency loss of the tax "EL." Briefly explain why area EL is the efficiency loss of the tax but TC is not. **LO17.7**
12. Is it possible for a country with a regressive tax system to have a tax-spending system that transfers resources from the rich to the poor? **LO17.8**
13. **LAST WORD** Does a progressive tax system by itself guarantee that resources will be redistributed from the rich to the poor? Explain. Is the *tax* system in the United States progressive, regressive, or proportional? Does the *tax-spending* system in the United States redistribute resources from higher-income earners to lower-income earners?

AP REVIEW QUESTIONS

1. Suppose George made $20,000 last year and that he lives in the country of Harmony. The way Harmony levies income taxes, each citizen must pay 10 percent in taxes on their first $10,000 in earnings and then 50 percent in taxes on anything else they might earn. So given that George earned $20,000 last year, his marginal tax rate on the last dollar he earns will be ________ and his average tax rate for his entire income will be ________. **LO17.3**
   - **a.** 50 percent; 50 percent.
   - **b.** 50 percent; less than 50 percent.
   - **c.** 10 percent; 50 percent.
   - **d.** 10 percent; less than 50 percent.
   - **e.** 10 percent; 10 percent.
2. The rationale for ability-to-pay taxation with the contention that those with large incomes should pay more taxes both absolutely and relatively is that: **LO17.6**
   - **a.** High-income receivers are generally in a better position to shift taxes than are low-income receivers.
   - **b.** The transfer system is regressive and it is therefore essential to have an offsetting progressive tax structure.
   - **c.** Rational consumers spend their first dollars of income on the most urgently desired goods and successive dollars on less essential goods. Thus, taxing high incomes imposes less reduction in total utility on the population.
   - **d.** Taxes should be paid for financing public goods in direct proportion to the satisfaction an individual derives from those goods.
   - **e.** Low-income receivers are generally in a better position to shift taxes than are high-income receivers.
3. Identify each of the following taxes as being either progressive, regressive, or proportional in the United States. **LO17.6**
   - **a.** Personal income tax.
   - **b.** Sales taxes.
   - **c.** Payroll taxes.
   - **d.** Property taxes.

4. The benefits-received principle of taxation is most evident in: LO17.6
   a. Inheritance taxes.
   b. Excise taxes on gasoline.
   c. The personal income tax.
   d. Property tax.
   e. The corporate income tax.
5. In the graph, if the government imposes a $6 per unit tax as shown, what is the amount of tax burden to the seller? What amount is the burden to the buyer? Explain. LO17.7

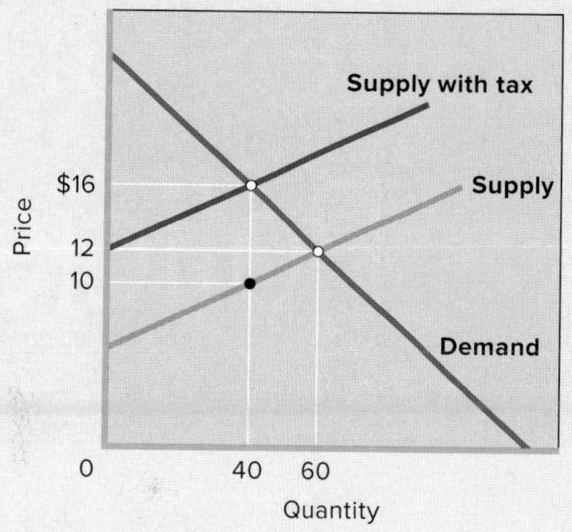

6. Assume an initial equilibrium price of $5.00 per unit of good Z. Now the government imposes a $2.00 per unit tax on good Z. Answer each of the following two questions, that are independent of each other. LO17.7
   a. Assume the demand for good Z is perfectly inelastic. Graphically, show the impact of this tax. What will be the new price for the consumer? What will be the new price for the producer? Explain whether there will be any deadweight loss.
   b. Following the imposition of the tax, the consumer price rises to $5.50. What will be the new producer price? Graphically show the new equilibrium quantity of good Z. Show any area of deadweight loss on your graph. How is this tax burden shared between the consumer and producer?
7. True or false. The incidence of property taxes that are levied on rented houses and apartments is high—meaning that they are paid almost entirely by the landlords, who are billed by the government for those taxes. LO17.8

PROBLEMS

1. Suppose a tax is such that an individual with an income of $10,000 pays $2,000 of tax, a person with an income of $20,000 pays $3,000 of tax, a person with an income of $30,000 pays $4,000 of tax, and so forth. What is each person's average tax rate? Is this tax regressive, proportional, or progressive? LO17.7
2. Suppose in Fiscalville there is no tax on the first $10,000 of income, but a 20 percent tax on earnings between $10,000 and $20,000 and a 30 percent tax on income between $20,000 and $30,000. Any income above $30,000 is taxed at 40 percent. If your income is $50,000, how much will you pay in taxes? Determine your marginal and average tax rates. Is this a progressive tax? LO17.7
3. For tax purposes, "gross income" is all the money a person receives in a given year from any source. But income taxes are levied on "taxable income" rather than gross income. The difference between the two is the result of many exemptions and deductions. To see how they work, suppose you made $50,000 last year in wages, earned $10,000 from investments, and were given $5,000 as a gift by your grandmother. Also assume that you are a single parent with one small child living with you. LO17.7
   a. What is your gross income?
   b. Gifts of up to $14,000 per year from any person are not counted as taxable income. Also, the "personal exemption" allows you to reduce your taxable income by $4,050 for each member of your household. Given these exemptions, what is your taxable income?
   c. Next, assume you paid $700 in interest on your student loans last year, put $2,000 into a health savings account (HSA), and deposited $4,000 into an individual retirement account (IRA). These expenditures are all *tax exempt*, meaning that any money spent on them reduces taxable income dollar-for-dollar. Knowing that fact, now what is your taxable income?
   d. Next, you can either take the so-called standard deduction or apply for itemized deductions (which involve a lot of tedious paperwork). You opt for the standard deduction that allows you as head of your household to exempt another $8,500 from your taxable income. Taking that into account, what is your taxable income?
   e. Apply the tax rates shown in Table 16.1 to your taxable income. How much federal income tax will you owe? What is the marginal tax rate that applies to your last dollar of taxable income?
   f. As the parent of a dependent child, you qualify for the government's $1,000 per-child "tax credit." Like all tax credits, this $1,000 credit "pays" for $1,000 of whatever amount of tax you owe. Given this credit, how much money will you actually have to pay in taxes? Using that actual amount, what is your average tax rate relative to your taxable income? What about your average tax rate relative to your gross income?

AP Part SIX

6 Microeconomic Issues and Policies

In Part VI, we look at two very specific but important microeconomic issues. The first in Chapter 18 relates to ***anti-trust policy*** with its aim of promoting effective competition in markets, on the premise that competitive markets are more efficient (and desirable) than less competitive markets that have restricted output. The second, Chapter 19, draws on our knowledge of resource markets and how different prices of different types of labor and how different personal endowments of financial capital can generate very different or unequal incomes within a society. This chapter will discuss this issue, as well as the implications from trying to change (ie. specifically, trying to make it more equal) the ***income distribution.***

Chapter 18

Antitrust Policy and Regulation

Learning Objectives

LO18.1 **List and explain the core elements of the major antitrust (antimonopoly) laws in the United States.**

LO18.2 **Describe some of the key issues relating to the interpretation and application of antitrust laws.**

LO18.3 **Identify and explain the economic principles and difficulties relating to the setting of prices (rates) charged by so-called natural monopolies.**

LO18.4 **Discuss the nature of "social regulation," its benefits and costs, and its optimal level.**

AP Chapter Focus

We now can apply the economics of product markets (Part 4) and the economics of resource markets and governments (Part 5) to selected microeconomic issues and policies.

In this chapter we look at three sets of government policies toward business: antitrust policy, industrial regulation, and social regulation.

Antitrust policy consists of laws and government actions designed to prevent monopoly and promote competition. **Industrial regulation** pertains to government regulation of firms' prices (or "rates") within selected industries. **Social regulation** is government regulation of the conditions under which goods are produced, the physical characteristics of goods, and the impact of the production and consumption of goods on society.

Then, in the remaining chapter of Part 6, we discuss issues and policies relating to income inequality.

AP The Antitrust Laws

LO18.1 List and explain the core elements of the major antitrust (antimonopoly) laws in the United States.

The underlying purpose of antitrust policy (antimonopoly policy) is to prevent monopolization, promote competition, and achieve allocative efficiency. Although all economists would agree that these are meritorious goals, there is sharp conflict of opinion about the appropriateness and effectiveness of U.S. antitrust policy. As we will see, antitrust policy over the years has been neither clear-cut nor consistent.

Historical Background

Just after the U.S. Civil War (1861–1865), local markets widened into national markets because of improved transportation facilities, mechanized production methods, and sophisticated corporate structures. In the 1870s and 1880s, dominant firms formed in several industries, including petroleum, meatpacking, railroads, sugar, lead, coal, whiskey, and tobacco. Some of these oligopolists, near-monopolists, or monopolists were known as *trusts*—business combinations that assign control to a single decision group ("trustees"). Because these trusts "monopolized" industries, the word "trust" became synonymous with "monopoly" in common usage. The public, government, and historians began to define a business monopoly as a large-scale dominant seller, even though that seller was not always "a sole seller" as specified in the model of pure monopoly.

These dominant firms often used questionable tactics in consolidating their industries and then charged high prices to customers and extracted price concessions from resource suppliers. Farmers and owners of small businesses were particularly vulnerable to the power of large corporate monopolies and were among the first to oppose them. Consumers, labor unions, and economists were not far behind in their opposition.

The main economic case against monopoly is familiar to you from Chapter 11. Monopolists tend to produce less output and charge higher prices than would be the case if their industries were competitive. With pure competition, each competitive firm maximizes profit by producing the output level at which $P = \text{MC}$. That output level generates allocative efficiency because price P measures the marginal benefit to society of an extra unit of output while marginal cost MC reflects the cost of an extra unit. When $P = \text{MC}$, society cannot gain by producing 1 more or 1 less unit of the product. In contrast, a monopolist maximizes profit by producing the lower output level at which marginal revenue (rather than price) equals marginal cost. At this $\text{MR} = \text{MC}$ point, price exceeds marginal cost, meaning that society would obtain more benefit than it would incur cost by producing extra units. An underallocation of resources to the monopolized product occurs, and the economy suffers an efficiency loss. So society's economic well-being is less than it would be with greater competition.

But an efficiency loss isn't the only consequence of the monopolist's higher-than-competitive price. The higher price also transfers income from consumers to the monopolist. This transfer causes significant resentment because it results purely from the monopolist's ability to restrict output and cannot be justified on the basis of increased production costs. Consumers consequently express their ire to elected officials to "do something about the situation."

Responding to that pressure, government officials concluded in the late 1800s and early 1900s that monopolized industries lacked enough of the beneficial market forces that in competitive industries help to protect consumers, achieve fair competition, and achieve allocative efficiency. So the government instituted two alternative means of control as substitutes for, or supplements to, market forces:

- ***Regulatory agencies*** In the few markets where the nature of the product or technology creates a *natural monopoly,* the government established public regulatory agencies to control economic behavior.
- ***Antitrust laws*** In most other markets, government control took the form of antitrust (antimonopoly) legislation designed to inhibit or prevent the growth of monopoly.

Four particular pieces of federal legislation, as refined and extended by various amendments, constitute the basic law relating to monopoly structure and conduct.

Sherman Act of 1890

The public resentment of trusts that emerged in the 1870s and 1880s culminated in the **Sherman Act** of 1890. This cornerstone of antitrust legislation is surprisingly brief and, at first glance, directly to the point. The core of the act resides in two provisions:

- ***Section 1*** "Every contract, combination in the form of a trust or otherwise, or conspiracy, in restraint of trade or commerce among the several States, or with foreign nations is declared to be illegal."
- ***Section 2*** "Every person who shall monopolize, or attempt to monopolize, or combine or conspire with any person or persons, to monopolize any part of the trade or commerce among the several states, or with foreign nations, shall be deemed guilty of a felony" (as later amended from "misdemeanor").

The Sherman Act thus outlawed *restraints of trade* (for example, collusive price-fixing and dividing up markets) as well as *monopolization.* Today, the U.S. Department of Justice, the Federal Trade Commission, injured private parties, or state attorney generals can file antitrust suits against alleged violators of the act. The courts can issue injunctions to prohibit anticompetitive practices or, if necessary, break up monopolists into competing firms. Courts can also fine and imprison violators. Further, parties injured by illegal combinations and conspiracies can sue the perpetrators for *treble damages*—awards of three times the amount of the monetary injury done to them.

The Sherman Act seemed to provide a sound foundation for positive government action against business monopolies. However, early court interpretations limited the scope of the act and created ambiguities of law. It became clear that a more explicit statement of the government's antitrust sentiments was needed. The business community itself sought a clearer statement of what was legal and what was illegal.

Clayton Act of 1914

The **Clayton Act** of 1914 contained the desired elaboration of the Sherman Act. Four sections of the act, in particular, were designed to strengthen and make explicit the intent of the Sherman Act:

- Section 2 outlaws *price discrimination* when such discrimination is not justified on the basis of cost differences and when it reduces competition.
- Section 3 prohibits **tying contracts**, in which a producer requires that a buyer purchase another (or other) of its products as a condition for obtaining a desired product.
- Section 7 prohibits the acquisition of stocks of competing corporations when the outcome would be less competition.
- Section 8 prohibits the formation of **interlocking directorates**—situations where a director of one firm is also a board member of a competing firm—in large corporations where the effect would be reduced competition.

The Clayton Act simply sharpened and clarified the general provisions of the Sherman Act. It also sought to outlaw the techniques that firms might use to develop monopoly power and, in that sense, was a preventive measure. Section 2 of the Sherman Act, by contrast, was aimed more at breaking up existing monopolies.

Federal Trade Commission Act of 1914

The **Federal Trade Commission Act** created the five-member Federal Trade Commission (FTC), which has joint federal responsibility with the U.S. Justice Department for enforcing the antitrust laws. The act gave the FTC the power to investigate unfair competitive practices on its own initiative or at the request of injured firms. It can hold public hearings on such complaints and, if necessary, issue **cease-and-desist orders** in cases where it discovers "unfair methods of competition in commerce."

The **Wheeler-Lea Act** of 1938 amended the Federal Trade Commission Act to give the FTC the additional responsibility of policing "deceptive acts or practices in commerce." In so doing, the FTC tries to protect the public against false or misleading advertising and the misrepresentation of products. So the Federal Trade Commission Act, as modified by the Wheeler-Lea Act, (1) established the FTC as an independent antitrust agency and (2) made unfair and deceptive sales practices illegal.

The FTC is highly active in enforcing the deceptive advertising statutes. As one recent example, in 2007 the FTC fined four makers of over-the-counter diet pills a collective $25 million for claiming their products produced fast and permanent weight loss.

Celler-Kefauver Act of 1950

The **Celler-Kefauver Act** amended the Clayton Act, Section 7, which prohibits a firm from merging with a competing firm (and thereby lessening competition) by acquiring its stock. However, firms could evade Section 7 by acquiring the physical assets (plant and equipment) of competing firms without formally merging. The Celler-Kefauver Act closed that loophole by prohibiting one firm from obtaining the physical assets of another firm when the effect would be reduced competition. Section 7 of the Clayton Act now prohibits anticompetitive mergers no matter how they are undertaken.

AP Antitrust Policy: Issues and Impacts

LO18.2 Describe some of the key issues relating to the interpretation and application of antitrust laws.

The effectiveness of any law depends on how the courts interpret it and on the vigor of government enforcement. The courts have been inconsistent in interpreting the antitrust laws. At times, they have applied them vigorously, adhering closely to their spirit and objectives. At other times, their interpretations have rendered certain laws nearly powerless. The federal government itself has varied considerably in its aggressiveness in enforcing the antitrust laws. Some administrations have made tough antitrust enforcement a high priority. Other administrations have taken a more laissez-faire approach, initiating few antitrust actions or even scaling back the budgets of the enforcement agencies.

Issues of Interpretation

Differences in judicial interpretations have led to vastly different applications of the antitrust laws. Two questions, in particular, have arisen: (1) Should the focus of antitrust policy be on monopoly behavior or on monopoly structure? (2) How broadly should markets be defined in antitrust cases?

Monopoly Behavior versus Monopoly Structure A comparison of three landmark Supreme Court decisions reveals two distinct interpretations of Section 2 of the Sherman Act as it relates to monopoly behavior and structure.

In the 1911 **Standard Oil case**, the Supreme Court found Standard Oil guilty of monopolizing the petroleum industry through a series of abusive and anticompetitive actions. The Court's remedy was to divide Standard Oil into several competing firms. But the Standard Oil case left open an important question: Is every monopoly in violation of Section 2 of the Sherman Act or just those created or maintained by anticompetitive actions?

In the 1920 **U.S. Steel case,** the courts established the so-called **rule of reason,** under which not every monopoly is illegal. Only monopolies that "unreasonably" restrain trade violate Section 2 of the Sherman Act and are subject to antitrust action. Size alone is not an offense. Under the rule of reason, U.S. Steel was innocent of "monopolizing" because it had not resorted to illegal acts against competitors in obtaining and then maintaining its monopoly power. Unlike Standard Oil, which was a so-called bad trust, U.S. Steel was a "good trust" and therefore not in violation of the law.

In the **Alcoa case** of 1945 the courts touched off a 20-year turnabout. The Supreme Court sent the case to the U.S. court of appeals in New York because four of the Supreme Court justices had been involved with litigation of the case before their appointments. Led by Judge Learned Hand, the court of appeals held that, even though a firm's behavior might be legal, the mere possession of monopoly power (Alcoa held 90 percent of the aluminum ingot market) violated the antitrust laws. So Alcoa was found guilty of violating the Sherman Act.

These two cases point to a controversy in antitrust policy. Should a firm be judged by its behavior (as in the U.S. Steel case) or by its structure or market share (as in the Alcoa case)?

- "Structuralists" assume that any firm with a very high market share will behave like a monopoly. As a result, they assert that any firm with a very high market share is a legitimate target for antitrust action. Structuralists argue that changes in the structure of an industry, say, by splitting the monopolist into several smaller firms, will improve behavior and performance.
- "Behavioralists" assert that the relationships among structure, behavior, and performance are tenuous and unclear. They feel a monopolized or highly concentrated industry may be technologically progressive and have a good record of providing products of increasing quality at reasonable prices. If a firm has served society well and has engaged in no anticompetitive practices, it should not be accused of antitrust violation just because it has an extraordinarily large market share. That share may be the product of superior technology, superior products, and economies of scale. "Why use antitrust laws to penalize efficient, technologically progressive, well-managed firms?" they ask.

Over the past several decades, the courts have returned to the rule of reason first established in the 1920 U.S. Steel case, and most contemporary economists and antitrust enforcers reject strict structuralism. For instance, in 1982 the government dropped its 13-year-long monopolization case against IBM on the grounds that IBM had not unreasonably restrained trade, despite having possessed extremely high market share in the market for mainframe computers. More recently, the government has made no attempt to break up Intel's near monopoly in the sale of microprocessors for personal computers. And in prosecuting the Microsoft case, the federal government made it clear that the behavior used by Microsoft to maintain and extend its monopoly, not the presence of its large market share, violated the Sherman Act. In essence, the government declared Microsoft to be "a bad monopoly" that could become a good monopoly if it stopped doing bad things.

Defining the Relevant Market Courts often decide whether or not market power exists by considering the share of the market held by the dominant firm. They have roughly adhered to a "90-60-30 rule" in defining monopoly: If a firm has a 90 percent market share, it is definitely a monopolist; if it has a 60 percent market share, it probably is a monopolist; if it has a 30 percent market share, it clearly is not a monopolist. The market share will depend on how the market is defined. If the market is defined broadly to include a wide range of somewhat similar products, the firm's market share will appear small. If the market is defined narrowly to exclude such products, the market share will seem large. The Supreme Court has the final say on how broadly to define relevant markets, but the Supreme Court has not always been consistent.

In the Alcoa case, the Court used a narrow definition of the relevant market: the aluminum ingot market. But in the **DuPont cellophane case** of 1956 the Court defined the market very broadly. The government contended that DuPont, along with a licensee, controlled 100 percent of the cellophane market. But the Court accepted DuPont's contention that the relevant market included all "flexible packaging materials"—waxed paper, aluminum foil, and so forth, in addition to cellophane. Despite DuPont's monopoly in the "cellophane market," it controlled only 20 percent of the market for "flexible wrapping materials." The Court ruled that this did not constitute a monopoly.

Issues of Enforcement

Some U.S. presidential administrations have enforced the antitrust laws more strictly than others. The degree of federal antitrust enforcement makes a difference in the overall degree of antitrust action in the economy. It is true that individual firms can sue other firms under the antitrust laws. For example, in 2005 AMD—a maker of microprocessors—filed an antitrust suit against Intel, claiming that Intel was a monopolist that used anticompetitive business practices to thwart the growth of AMD's market share. But major antitrust suits often last years and are highly expensive. Injured parties therefore often look to the federal government to initiate and litigate such cases. Once the federal government gains a conviction, the injured parties no longer need to prove guilt and can simply sue the violator to obtain treble damages. In many cases, lack of federal antitrust action therefore means diminished legal action by firms.

Why might one administration enforce the antitrust laws more or less strictly than another? The main reason is differences in political philosophies about the market economy and the wisdom of intervention by government. There are two contrasting general perspectives on antitrust policy.

The *active antitrust perspective* is that competition is insufficient in some circumstances to achieve allocative efficiency and ensure fairness to consumers and competing firms. Firms occasionally use illegal tactics against competitors to dominate markets. In other instances, competitors collude to fix prices or merge to enhance their monopoly power. Active, strict enforcement of the antitrust laws is needed to stop illegal business practices, prevent anticompetitive mergers, and remedy monopoly. This type of government intervention maintains the viability and vibrancy of the market system and thus allows society to reap its full benefits. In this view, the antitrust authorities need to act much like the officials in a football game. They must observe the players, spot infractions, and enforce the rules.

In contrast, the *laissez-faire perspective* holds that antitrust intervention is largely unnecessary, particularly as it relates to monopoly. Economists holding this position view competition as a long-run dynamic process in which firms battle against each other for dominance of markets. In some markets, a firm successfully monopolizes the market, usually because of its superior innovativeness or business skill. But in exploiting its monopoly power to raise prices, these firms inadvertently create profit incentives and profit opportunities for other entrepreneurs and firms to develop alternative technologies and new products to better serve consumers. As discussed in Chapter 2 and expanded upon in Chapter 10, a process of *creative destruction* occurs in which today's monopolies are eroded and eventually destroyed by tomorrow's technologies and products. The government therefore should not try to break up a monopoly. It should stand aside and allow the long-run competitive process to work.

The extent to which a particular administration adheres to—or leans toward—one of these contrasting antitrust perspectives usually gets reflected in the appointments to the agencies overseeing antitrust policy. Those appointees help determine how strictly the laws are enforced.

Effectiveness of Antitrust Laws

Have the antitrust laws been effective? Although this question is difficult to answer, we can at least observe how the laws have been applied to monopoly, mergers, price-fixing, price discrimination, and tying contracts.

Monopoly On the basis of the rule of reason, the government has generally been lenient in applying antitrust laws to monopolies that have developed naturally. Generally, a firm will be sued by the federal government only if it has a very high market share and there is evidence of abusive conduct in achieving, maintaining, or extending its market dominance.

But even if the federal government wins the antitrust lawsuit, there is still the matter of *remedy:* What actions should the court order to correct for the anticompetitive practices of the monopoly that lost the lawsuit?

The issue of remedy arose in two particularly noteworthy monopoly cases. The first was the AT&T (American Telephone and Telegraph) case in which the government charged AT&T with violating the Sherman Act by engaging in anticompetitive practices designed to maintain its domestic telephone monopoly. As part of an out-of-court settlement between the government and AT&T, in 1982 AT&T agreed to divest itself of its 22 regional telephone-operating companies.

A second significant monopoly case was the **Microsoft case.** In 2000 Microsoft was found guilty of violating the Sherman Act by taking several unlawful actions designed to maintain its monopoly of operating systems for personal computers. A lower court ordered that Microsoft be split into two competing firms. A court of appeals upheld the lower-court finding of abusive monopoly but rescinded the breakup of Microsoft. Instead of the structural remedy, the eventual outcome was a behavioral remedy in which Microsoft was prohibited from engaging in a set of specific anticompetitive business practices.

The antitrust agency for the European Union (EU) has generally been more aggressive than the United States in prosecuting monopolists. For example, in 2015 the EU began to prosecute Google for showing a bias in search results in favor of products being sold on the Google online marketplace rather than on other online stores. Google faced €6.6 billion in fines in the EU despite having been investigated and cleared by U.S. antitrust authorities for the same behavior. (See this chapter's Last Word for details.)

Mergers The treatment of mergers, or combinations of existing firms, varies with the type of merger and its effect on competition.

Merger Types There are three basic types of mergers, as represented in Figure 18.1. This figure shows two stages of production (the input stage and the output, or final-product, stage) for two distinct final-goods industries (autos and blue jeans). Each rectangle (A, B, C, . . . X, Y, Z) represents a particular firm.

A **horizontal merger** is a merger between two competitors that sell similar products in the same geographic market. In Figure 18.1 this type of merger is shown as a combination

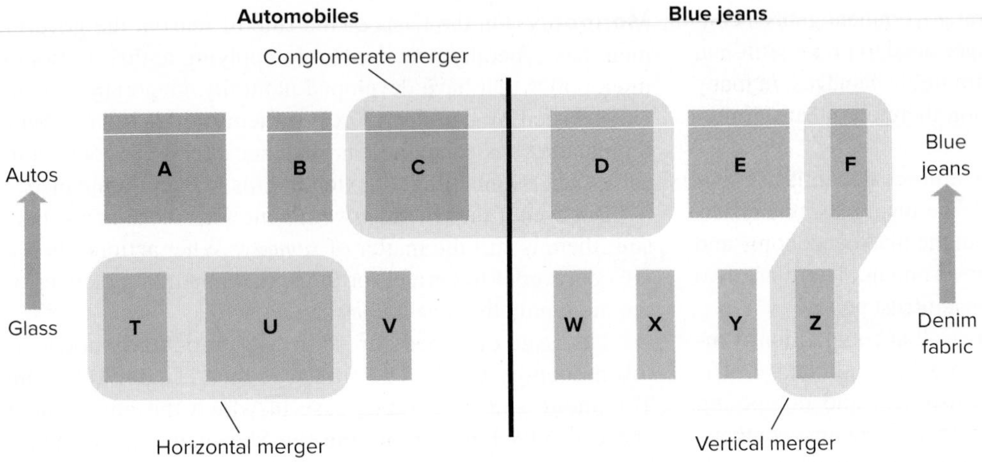

FIGURE 18.1 Types of mergers. Horizontal mergers (T + U) bring together firms selling the same product in the same geographic market; vertical mergers (F + Z) connect firms having a buyer-seller relationship; and conglomerate mergers (C + D) join firms in different industries or firms operating in different geographic areas.

of glass producers T and U. Actual examples of such mergers include Chase Manhattan's merger with Chemical Bank, Boeing's merger with McDonnell Douglas, and Exxon's merger with Mobil.

A **vertical merger** is a merger between firms at different stages of the production process. In Figure 18.1, the merger between firm Z, a producer of denim fabric, and firm F, a producer of blue jeans, is a vertical merger. Vertical mergers are mergers between firms that have buyer-seller relationships. Actual examples of such mergers are PepsiCo's mergers with Pizza Hut, Taco Bell, and Kentucky Fried Chicken. PepsiCo supplies soft drinks to each of these fast-food outlets. (In 1997, PepsiCo spun off these entities into a separate company now called Yum! Brands.)

A **conglomerate merger** is officially defined as any merger that is not horizontal or vertical; in general, it is the combination of firms in different industries or firms operating in different geographic areas. Conglomerate mergers can extend the line of products sold, extend the territory in which products are sold, or combine totally unrelated companies. In Figure 18.1, the merger between firm C, an auto manufacturer, and firm D, a blue jeans producer, is a conglomerate merger. Real-world examples of conglomerate mergers include the merger between Walt Disney Company (movies) and the American Broadcasting Company (radio and television) and the merger between America Online (Internet service provider) and Time Warner (communications).

Merger Guidelines: The Herfindahl Index The federal government has established very loose merger guidelines based on the Herfindahl index. Recall from Chapter 13 that this measure of concentration is the sum of the squared percentage market shares of the firms within an industry. An industry of only four firms, each with a 25 percent market share, has a Herfindahl index of 2,500 ($= 25^2 + 25^2 + 25^2 + 25^2$). In pure competition, where each firm's market share is minuscule, the index approaches 0 ($= 0^2 + 0^2 + \ldots + 0^2$). In pure monopoly, the index for that single firm is 10,000 ($= 100^2$).

The U.S. government uses Section 7 of the Clayton Act to block horizontal mergers that will substantially lessen competition. It is likely to challenge a horizontal merger if the post-merger Herfindahl index would be high (above 1,800) and if the merger has substantially increased the index (added 100 or more points). However, other factors, such as economies of scale, the degree of foreign competition, and the ease of entry of new firms, are also considered. Furthermore, horizontal mergers are usually allowed if one of the merging firms is suffering major and continuing losses. (This is one reason Boeing was allowed to acquire McDonnell Douglas in 1996: MD was losing money in producing its commercial airplanes.)

During the past several decades, the federal government has blocked several proposed horizontal mergers. For example, it blocked mergers between Staples and Office Depot, two major office-supply retailers; WorldCom and Sprint, two competing telecommunications firms; and Hughes (DirecTV) and Echostar (DISH Network), providers of direct-broadcast satellite television.

More recently, the federal government successfully challenged mergers between Snyder's of Hanover and Utz Quality Foods, makers of pretzels; Polypore and Microporous, battery-parts makers; and Blue Cross Blue Shield of Michigan and Physician's Health Plan of Michigan, health insurance providers.

Most *vertical mergers* escape antitrust prosecution because they do not substantially lessen competition in either of the two markets. (In Figure 18.1 neither the Herfindahl index in the industry producing denim fabric nor the index in the blue jeans industry changes when firms Z and F merge vertically.) However, a vertical merger between large firms in highly concentrated industries may be challenged. For example, in 1999 the threat of FTC action spurred Barnes & Noble to abandon its merger with Ingram Book Company, the nation's largest book wholesaler. The merger would have enabled Barnes & Noble to set the wholesale price of books charged to its direct retail competitors such as Borders and Amazon.com.

Conglomerate mergers are generally permitted. If an auto manufacturer acquires a blue jeans producer, no antitrust action is likely since neither firm has increased its own market share as a result. That means the Herfindahl index remains unchanged in each industry.

Price-Fixing Price-fixing among competitors is treated strictly. Evidence of price-fixing, even by small firms, will bring antitrust action, as will other collusive activities such as scheming to rig bids on government contracts or dividing up sales in a market. In antitrust law, these activities are known as **per se violations;** they are "in and of themselves" illegal, and therefore are *not* subject to the rule of reason. To gain a conviction, the government or other party making the charge need show only that there was a conspiracy to fix prices, rig bids, or divide up markets, not that the conspiracy succeeded or caused serious damage to other parties.

Price-fixing investigations and court actions are common. (See the Consider This box.)

Price Discrimination Price discrimination is a common business practice that rarely reduces competition and therefore is rarely challenged by government. The exception occurs when a firm engages in price discrimination as part of a strategy to block entry or drive out competitors.

Tying Contracts The federal government strictly enforces the prohibition of tying contracts, particularly when practiced by dominant firms. For example, it stopped movie distributors from forcing theaters to buy the projection rights to a full package of films as a condition of showing a blockbuster movie. Also, it prevented Kodak—the dominant maker of photographic film—from requiring that consumers process their film only through Kodak.

Conclusions So what can we conclude about the overall effectiveness of antitrust laws? Antitrust policy has not been very effective in restricting the rise of or in breaking up monopolies or oligopolies resulting from legally undertaken internal expansions of firms. But most economists do not deem that to be a flaw. The antitrust laws have been used more effectively against predatory or abusive monopoly, but that effectiveness has been diminished by the slow legal process and consequently long time between the filing of charges and the implementation of remedies. In contrast, antitrust policy *has* been effective in prosecuting price-fixing and tying contracts.

Most economists conclude that, overall, U.S. antitrust policy has been moderately effective in achieving its goal of promoting competition and efficiency. Much of the success of antitrust policy arises from its deterrent effect on price-fixing and anticompetitive mergers. Some economists, however, think that enforcement of antitrust laws has been too weak. Others believe that parts of U.S. antitrust policy are anachronistic in an era of rapidly changing technology that continuously undermines existing monopoly power.

CONSIDER THIS . . .

Of Airfare and eBooks (and Other Things in Common)

© APCortizasJr/Getty Images RF

Examples of price-fixing are numerous. Here are just a few:

- In 2007, British Airlines and Korean Air agreed to pay fines of $300 million each for conspiring to fix fuel surcharges on passenger tickets and cargo.
- Between 2008 and 2010, five manufacturers of liquid crystal displays (LCDs)—LG, Sharp, Hitachi, Chi Mei Optoelectronics, and Chunghwa Picture Tubes—were fined a total of over $860 million by the U.S. Justice Department for fixing the prices of the displays they sold to computer maker Dell Inc.
- In 2009, three international cargo airlines—Cargolux of Luxembourg, Nippon Cargo of Japan, and Asiana Airlines of South Korea—were fined $214 million by the U.S. Justice Department for conspiring to fix international airline cargo rates.
- In 2012, nine Japanese, German, and Swedish auto parts makers were fined a total of $790 million for conspiring to fix the prices of automobile heater control panels. Eleven corporate officers received jail sentences ranging from one to two years.
- In 2013, Apple was convicted along with five publishers—Harper Collins, Penguin, Simon & Schuster, Hachette, and Macmillan—of horizontal price-fixing in the market for e-books to be sold on Apple's iBook store. Apple was ordered to pay $450 million in reparations to those harmed by the scheme, which raised prices 20 percent in Apple's online bookstore.

AP QUICK REVIEW 18.1

- ✓ The Sherman Act of 1890 outlaws restraints of trade and monopolization; the Clayton Act of 1914 as amended by the Celler-Kefauver Act of 1950 outlaws price discrimination (when anticompetitive), tying contracts, anticompetitive mergers, and interlocking directorates.
- ✓ The Federal Trade Commission Act of 1914 as bolstered by the Wheeler-Lea Act of 1938 created the Federal Trade Commission (FTC) and gave it authority to investigate unfair methods of competition and deceptive acts or practices in commerce.
- ✓ Prior to World War II, the courts applied a "rule of reason" test, first established in the U.S. Steel case of 1920. Under this rule, only monopolists that achieve or maintain their status abusively are in violation of the Sherman Act. Some economists would not support this test, as it does not directly address the structural problem of monopoly.
- ✓ "Structuralists" say highly concentrated industries will behave like monopolists; "behaviorists" hold that the relationship between industry structure and firm behavior is uncertain. Behaviorists tend to assess the degree of potential competition within a market, seeking that markets are "contestable."
- ✓ The degree of strictness of enforcement of antitrust laws depends on the general antitrust philosophy of each U.S. administration and its appointees.
- ✓ Government tends to block most horizontal mergers between dominant, profitable firms in highly concentrated industries; and vigorously prosecutes price-fixing and tying contracts.

AP Industrial Regulation

LO18.3 Identify and explain the economic principles and difficulties relating to the setting of prices (rates) charged by so-called natural monopolies.

Antitrust policy assumes that society will benefit if a monopoly is prevented from evolving or if it is dissolved where it already exists. We now return to a special situation in which there is an economic reason for an industry to be organized monopolistically.

Natural Monopoly

A natural monopoly exists when economies of scale are so extensive that a single firm can supply the entire market at a lower average total cost than could a number of competing firms. Clear-cut circumstances of natural monopoly are relatively rare, but such conditions exist for many *public utilities,* such as local electricity, water, and natural gas providers. As discussed in Chapter 11, large-scale operations in some cases are necessary to obtain low unit costs and a low product price. Where natural monopoly occurs, competition is uneconomical. If the market were divided among many producers, economies of scale would not be achieved and unit costs and prices would be higher than necessary.

There are two possible alternatives for promoting better economic outcomes where natural monopoly exists. One is public ownership, and the other is public regulation.

Public ownership or some approximation of it has been established in a few instances. Examples: the Postal Service, the Tennessee Valley Authority, and Amtrak at the national level and mass transit, water supply systems, and garbage collection at the local level.

But *public regulation,* or what economists call *industrial regulation,* has been the preferred option in the United States. In this type of regulation, government commissions regulate the prices (or "rates") charged by natural monopolists. Table 18.1 lists the two major federal regulatory commissions and their jurisdictions. It also notes that all 50 states have commissions that regulate the intrastate activities and "utility rates" of local natural monopolies.

The economic objective of industrial regulation is embodied in the **public interest theory of regulation.** In that theory, industrial regulation is necessary to keep a natural monopoly from charging monopoly prices and thus harming consumers and society. The goal of such regulation is to garner for society at least part of the cost reductions associated with natural monopoly while avoiding the restrictions of output and high prices associated with unregulated monopoly. If competition is inappropriate or impractical, society should allow or even encourage a monopoly but regulate its prices. Regulation should then be structured so that ratepayers benefit from the economies of scale—the lower per-unit costs—that natural monopolists are able to achieve.

In practice, regulators seek to establish rates that will cover production costs and yield a "fair" return to the enterprise. The goal is to set price equal to average total cost so that the regulated firm receives a normal profit, as described in the "Regulated Monopoly" section of Chapter 11. In particular, you should carefully review Figure 11.9.

TABLE 18.1 The Main Regulatory Commissions Providing Industrial Regulation

Commission (Year Established)	Jurisdiction
Federal Energy Regulatory Commission (1930)*	Electricity, gas, gas pipelines, oil pipelines, water-power sites
Federal Communications Commission (1934)	Telephones, television, cable television, radio, telegraph, CB radios, ham operators
State public utility commissions (various years)	Electricity, gas, telephones

*Originally called the Federal Power Commission; renamed in 1977.

Problems with Industrial Regulation

There is considerable disagreement on the effectiveness of industrial regulation. Let's examine two criticisms.

Costs and Inefficiency An unregulated firm has a strong incentive to reduce its costs at each level of output because that will increase its profit. The regulatory commission, however, confines the regulated firm to a normal profit or a "fair return" on the value of its assets. If a regulated firm lowers its operating costs, the rising profit eventually will lead the regulatory commission to require that the firm lower its rates in order to return its profits to normal. The regulated firm therefore has little or no incentive to reduce its operating costs.

Worse yet, higher costs do not result in lower profit. Because the regulatory commission must allow the public utility a fair return, the regulated monopolist can simply pass through higher production costs to consumers by charging higher rates. A regulated firm may reason that it might as well have high salaries for its workers, opulent working conditions for management, and the like, since the "return" is the same in percentage terms whether costs are minimized or not. So, although a natural monopoly reduces costs through economies of scale, industrial regulation fosters considerable X-inefficiency (Figure 11.7). Due to the absence of competition, the potential cost savings from natural monopoly may never actually materialize.

Perpetuating Monopoly A second general problem with industrial regulation is that it sometimes perpetuates monopoly long after the conditions of natural monopoly have ended.

Technological change often creates the potential for competition in some or even all portions of the regulated industry. Examples: Trucks began competing with railroads; transmission of voice and data by microwave and satellites began competing with transmission over telephone wires; satellite television began competing with cable television; and cell phones began competing with landline phones.

But spurred by the firms they regulate, commissions often protect the regulated firms from new competition by either blocking entry or extending regulation to competitors. Industrial regulation therefore may perpetuate a monopoly that is no longer a natural monopoly and would otherwise erode. Ordinary monopoly, protected by government, may supplant natural monopoly. If so, the regulated prices may exceed those that would occur with competition. The beneficiaries of outdated regulation are the regulated firms and their employees. The losers are consumers and the potential entrants.

Example: Regulation of the railroads by the Interstate Commerce Commission (ICC) was justified in the late 1800s and early 1900s. But by the 1930s, with the emergence of a network of highways, the trucking industry had seriously undermined the monopoly power of the railroads. That is, for the transport of many goods over many routes, railroad service was no longer a natural monopoly. At that time it would have been desirable to dismantle the ICC and let railroads and truckers, along with barges and airlines, compete with one another. Instead, in the 1930s the ICC extended regulation of rates to interstate truckers. The ICC remained in place until its elimination in 1996. It was eliminated because the deregulation of railroads and trucking in the late 1970s and early 1980s had made its work irrelevant.

Second example: Until the mid-1990s, both long-distance telephone companies such as AT&T as well as cable-television providers such as Time Warner were prohibited from offering local telephone services in competition with regulated local and regional telephone companies. But the very fact that AT&T, Time Warner, and other firms wanted to compete with regulated monopolies calls into question whether those local providers are in fact natural monopolies or government-protected monopolies.

Legal Cartel Theory

In Chapter 13, we noted that a *cartel* is formed when a group of previously competing firms makes a formal agreement to cease competing. They either control the price of a product by establishing the amounts of output that each cartel member will produce or they divide up the overall market for the product geographically so that each firm becomes a monopolist within its assigned region.

Privately organized cartels are illegal in the United States. But, in some cases, government regulations can have effects on prices and competition very similar to cartels. Thus, firms may seek to be regulated if they believe that regulation will reduce competition and raise prices in the same way a private cartel would. In essence, they see regulation as a way of creating a legal, publicly sanctioned cartel.

This possibility is known as the **legal cartel theory of regulation.** In place of having socially minded officials forcing regulation on natural monopolies to protect consumers, holders of this view see practical politicians "supplying" regulation to local, regional, and national firms that fear the impact of competition on their profits or even on their long-term survival. These firms desire regulation because it yields a legal monopoly that can virtually guarantee a profit. Specifically, the regulatory commission performs such functions as blocking entry (for example, in local telephone service). Or, where there are several firms, the commission divides up the market much like an illegal cartel (for example, prior to airline deregulation, the Civil Aeronautics Board assigned routes to specific airlines). The commission may also restrict potential competition by enlarging the "cartel" (for example, the ICC's addition of trucking to its regulatory domain).

While private cartels are illegal and unstable and often break down, the special attraction of a government-sponsored cartel under the guise of regulation is that it endures. The legal cartel theory of regulation suggests that regulation is a form of regulatory capture that results from the rent-seeking activities of private firms and the desire of politicians to be responsive in order to win reelection (Chapter 5).

Proponents of the legal cartel theory of regulation note that the Interstate Commerce Commission was welcomed by the railroads and that the trucking and airline industries both supported the extension of ICC regulation to their industries, arguing that unregulated competition was severe and destructive.

Occupational licensing is a labor market application of the legal cartel theory. Certain occupational groups—barbers, dentists, hairstylists, interior designers, dietitians, lawyers—demand stringent licensing on the grounds that it protects the public from charlatans and quacks. But skeptics say the real reason may be to limit entry into the occupational group so that practitioners can receive monopoly incomes.

Deregulation

Beginning in the 1970s, evidence of inefficiency in regulated industries and the contention that the government was regulating potentially competitive industries contributed to a wave of deregulation. Since then, Congress and many state legislatures have passed legislation that has deregulated in varying degrees the airline, trucking, banking, railroad, natural gas, television, and electricity industries. Deregulation has also occurred in the telecommunications industry, where antitrust authorities dismantled the regulated monopoly known as the Bell System (AT&T). Deregulation in the 1970s and 1980s was one of the most extensive experiments in economic policy to take place during the last 50 years.

The overwhelming consensus among economists is that deregulation has produced large net benefits for consumers and society. Most of the gains from deregulation have occurred in three industries: airlines, railroads, and trucking. Airfares (adjusted for inflation) declined by about one-third, and airline safety has continued to improve. Trucking and railroad freight rates (again, adjusted for inflation) dropped by about one-half.

Significant efficiency gains were also realized in long-distance telecommunications, and there have been slight efficiency gains in cable television, stock brokerage services, and the natural gas industry. Moreover, deregulation has unleashed a wave of technological advances that have resulted in such new and improved products and services as fax machines, cellular phones, fiber-optic cable, microwave communication systems, and the Internet.

The most recent and perhaps controversial industry to be deregulated is electricity. Deregulation is relatively advanced at the wholesale level, where firms can buy and sell electricity at market prices. They are also free to build generating facilities and sell electricity to local electricity providers at unregulated prices. In addition, several states have deregulated retail prices and encouraged households and businesses to choose among available electricity suppliers. This competition has generally lowered electricity rates for consumers and enhanced allocative efficiency.

But deregulation suffered a severe setback in California, where wholesale electricity prices, but not retail rates, were deregulated. Wholesale electricity prices surged in 2001 when California experienced electricity shortages. Because they could not pass on wholesale price increases to consumers, California electric utilities suffered large financial losses. California then filed lawsuits against several energy-trading companies that allegedly manipulated electricity supplies to boost the wholesale price of electricity during the California energy crisis. One multibillion-dollar energy trader—Enron—collapsed in 2002 when federal investigators uncovered a pattern of questionable and fraudulent business and accounting practices.

The California deregulation debacle and the Enron collapse have muddied the overall assessment of electricity deregulation in the United States. California's policy of deregulating only wholesale prices clearly did not work. So, even enthusiastic supporters of deregulation are now careful to reflect on the details of how, exactly, an industry should be dergulated.

AP QUICK REVIEW 18.2

- ✓ Natural monopoly occurs where economies of scale are so extensive that only one firm can produce the product at minimum average total cost, for the quantity consumed.
- ✓ The public interest theory of regulation says that government must regulate natural monopolies to prevent abuses arising from monopoly power. Regulated firms, however, have less incentive than competitive firms to reduce costs.
- ✓ Deregulation initiated by government in the past several decades has yielded large annual efficiency gains for society.

Social Regulation

LO18.4 Discuss the nature of "social regulation," its benefits and costs, and its optimal level.

The industrial regulation discussed in the preceding section has focused on the regulation of prices (or rates) in natural monopolies. But in the early 1960s a new type of regulation began to emerge. This *social regulation* is concerned with the conditions under which goods and services are produced, the

TABLE 18.2 The Main Federal Regulatory Commissions Providing Social Regulation

Commission (Year Established)	Jurisdiction
Food and Drug Administration (1906)	Safety and effectiveness of food, drugs, and cosmetics
Equal Employment Opportunity Commission (1964)	Hiring, promotion, and discharge of workers
Occupational Safety and Health Administration (1971)	Industrial health and safety
Environmental Protection Agency (1972)	Air, water, and noise pollution
Consumer Product Safety Commission (1972)	Safety of consumer products
Consumer Financial Protection Bureau (2011)	Fairness and transparency in lending and other financial services

impact of production on society, and the physical qualities of the goods themselves.

The federal government carries out most of the social regulation, although states also play a role. In Table 18.2 we list the main federal regulatory commissions engaged in social regulation.

Distinguishing Features

Social regulation differs from industrial regulation in several ways.

First, social regulation applies to far more firms than does industrial regulation. Social regulation is often applied "across the board" to all industries and directly affects more producers than does industrial regulation. For instance, while the industrial regulation of the Federal Energy Regulatory Commission (FERC) applies to a relatively small number of firms, the rules and regulations issued by the Occupational Safety and Health Administration (OSHA) apply to firms in all industries.

Second, social regulation intrudes into the day-to-day production process to a greater extent than industrial regulation. While industrial regulation focuses on rates, costs, and profits, social regulation often dictates the design of products, the conditions of employment, and the nature of the production process. As examples, the Consumer Product Safety Commission (CPSC) regulates the design of potentially unsafe products, and the Environmental Protection Agency (EPA) regulates the amount of pollution allowed during production.

Finally, social regulation has expanded rapidly during the same period in which industrial regulation has waned. Between 1970 and 1980, the U.S. government created 20 new social regulatory agencies. More recently, Congress has established new social regulations to be enforced by existing regulatory agencies. For example, the Equal Employment Opportunity Commission, which is responsible for enforcing laws against workplace discrimination on the basis of race, gender, age, or religion, has been given the added duty of enforcing the Americans with Disabilities Act of 1990. Under this social regulation, firms must provide reasonable accommodations for qualified workers and job applicants with disabilities. Also, sellers must provide reasonable access for customers with disabilities.

The names of the regulatory agencies in Table 18.2 suggest the reasons for their creation and growth: As much of our society had achieved a fairly affluent standard of living by the 1960s, attention shifted to improvement in the nonmaterial quality of life. The new focus called for safer products, less pollution, improved working conditions, and greater equality of economic opportunity.

The Optimal Level of Social Regulation

While economists agree on the need for social regulation, they disagree on whether or not the current level of such regulation is optimal. Recall that an activity should be expanded as long as its marginal benefit (MB) exceeds its marginal cost (MC). If the MB of social regulation exceeds its MC, then there is too little social regulation. But if MC exceeds MB, there is too much (review Figure 4.9). Unfortunately, the marginal costs and benefits of social regulation are not always easy to measure. So ideology about the proper size and role of government often drives the debate over social regulation as much as, or perhaps more than, economic cost-benefit analysis.

In Support of Social Regulation Defenders of social regulation say that it has achieved notable successes and, overall, has greatly enhanced society's well-being. They point out that the problems that social regulation confronts are serious and substantial. According to the National Safety Council, about 5,000 workers die annually in job-related accidents and 3.7 million workers suffer injuries that force them to miss a day or more of work. Air pollution continues to cloud major U.S. cities, imposing large costs in terms of reduced property values and increased health care expense. Numerous children and adults die each year because of poorly designed or manufactured products (for example, car tires) or tainted food (for example, *E. coli* in beef). Discrimination against some ethnic and racial minorities, persons with disabilities, and older workers reduces their earnings and imposes heavy costs on society.

Proponents of social regulation acknowledge that social regulation is costly. But they correctly point out that a high "price" for something does not necessarily mean that it should not be purchased. They say that the appropriate economic test should be not whether the costs of social regulation are high or low but, rather, whether the benefits of social regulation exceed the costs. After decades of neglect, they further assert, society cannot expect to cleanse the environment, enhance the safety of the workplace, and promote economic opportunity for all without incurring substantial costs. So statements about the huge costs of social regulation are irrelevant, say defenders, since the benefits are even greater. The public often underestimates those benefits since they are more difficult to measure than costs and often become apparent only after some time has passed (for example, the benefits of reducing global warming).

Proponents of social regulation point to its many specific benefits. Here are just a few examples: It is estimated that highway fatalities would be 40 percent greater annually in the absence of auto safety features mandated through regulation. Compliance with child safety-seat and seat-belt laws has significantly reduced the auto fatality rate for small children. The national air quality standards set by law have been reached in nearly all parts of the nation for sulfur dioxide, nitrogen dioxide, and lead. Moreover, recent studies clearly link cleaner air, other things equal, with increases in the values of homes. Affirmative action regulations have increased the labor demand for racial and ethnic minorities and females. The use of childproof lids has resulted in a 90 percent decline in child deaths caused by accidental swallowing of poisonous substances.

Some defenders of social regulation say there are many remaining areas in which greater regulation would generate net benefits to society. For instance, some call for greater regulation of the meat, poultry, and seafood industries to improve food safety. Others favor greater regulation of health care organizations and insurance companies to ensure "patients' rights" for consumers of health care services. Still others say that more regulation is needed to ensure that violent movies, CDs, and video games are not marketed to children.

Advocates of social regulation say that the benefits of such regulation are well worth the considerable costs. The costs are simply the price we must pay to create a hospitable, sustainable, and just society.

Criticisms of Social Regulation Critics of social regulation contend that, in many instances, it has been expanded to the point where the marginal costs exceed the marginal benefits. In this view, society would achieve net benefits by cutting back on irritating social regulation. Critics say that many social regulation laws are poorly written, making regulatory objectives and standards difficult to understand. As a result, regulators pursue goals well beyond the original intent of the legislation. Businesses complain that regulators often press for additional increments of improvement, unmindful of costs.

Also, decisions must often be made and rules formed on the basis of inadequate information. Examples: CPSC officials may make decisions about certain ingredients in products on the basis of limited laboratory experiments that suggest that those ingredients might cause cancer. Or government agencies may establish costly pollution standards to attack the global-warming problem without knowing for certain whether pollution is the main cause of the problem. These efforts, say critics, lead to excessive regulation of business.

Moreover, critics argue that social regulations produce many unintended and costly side effects. For instance, the federal gas mileage standard for automobiles has been blamed for an estimated 2,000 to 3,900 traffic deaths a year because auto manufacturers have reduce d the weight of vehicles to meet the higher miles-per-gallon standards. Other things equal, drivers of lighter cars have a higher fatality rate than drivers of heavier vehicles.

Finally, opponents of social regulation say that the regulatory agencies may attract overzealous workers who are hostile toward the market system and "believe" too fervently in regulation. For example, some staff members of government agencies may see large corporations as "bad guys" who regularly cause pollution, provide inadequate safety for workers, deceive their customers, and generally abuse their power in the community. Such biases can lead to seemingly never-ending calls for still more regulation, rather than objective assessments of the costs and benefits of added regulation.

Two Reminders

The debate over the proper amount of social regulation will surely continue. By helping determine costs and benefits, economic analysis can lead to more informed discussions and to better decisions. In this regard, economic analysis provides pertinent reminders for both ardent supporters and ardent opponents of social regulation.

There Is No Free Lunch Fervent supporters of social regulation need to remember that "there is no free lunch." Social regulation can produce higher prices, stifle innovation, and reduce competition.

Social regulation raises product prices in two ways. It does so directly because compliance costs normally get passed on to consumers, and it does so indirectly by reducing labor productivity. Resources invested in making workplaces accessible to disabled workers, for example, are not available for investment in new machinery designed to increase output per worker. Where the wage rate is fixed, a drop in labor productivity increases the marginal and average total costs of production. In effect, the supply curve for the product shifts leftward, causing the price of the product to rise.

Social regulation may have a negative impact on the rate of innovation. Technological advance may be stifled by, say, the fear that a new plant will not meet EPA guidelines or that a new medicine will require years of testing before being approved by the Food and Drug Administration (FDA).

Social regulation may weaken competition since it usually places a relatively greater burden on small firms than on

LAST WORD

Antitrust Online

The Internet Has Presented Antitrust Authorities with Both Old and New Causes for Concern.

The Airline Tariff Publishing case was the first important example of how digital communication platforms could be used by businesses to engage in price-fixing. In the late 1980s, U.S. airlines began to post both current and future prices for airline tickets on a centralized computer system known as the Airline Tariff Publishing Company. The system was set up so that travel agents could comparison shop for their clients. But the airlines used the system's ability to list start dates and end dates for ticket purchases as a way of colluding.

As an example, suppose that American Airlines and Delta Airlines had both been charging $200 for a one-way ticket between New York and Chicago. American could then post a higher price of $250 for the route with the stipulation that nobody could start buying tickets at that price until the next month. Delta could then respond by also saying that it would start selling tickets at the higher price next month. In that way, the two airlines could tacitly coordinate their price setting ahead of time so as to collude on a major price increase.

The antitrust authorities at the U.S. Department of Justice stopped this practice in 1994 by getting the airlines to agree to the behavioral remedy that any fare changes would have to become immediately available to consumers. Airlines could no longer use suggested future prices as a way of signaling each other about how to collude.

The monopoly power gained during the 1990s and early 2000s by online giants such as Microsoft and Google has also led to business practices that have raised the ire of antitrust authorities. Microsoft, for example, was fined $2.7 billion after being convicted in 2000 of using the near-monopoly (95 percent market share) dominance of its Windows operating system software to coerce computer makers into favoring Microsoft's Internet Explorer web browser over rival browsers such as Netscape Navigator.

More recently, Google was indicted in 2015 by European Union antitrust officials for allegedly using its 90 percent share of the market for Internet searches in Europe to favor its Google Shopping price-comparison service over price-comparison services run by rival firms. For example, if a person in Germany types "prices for used iPhones" into Google's search bar, the top of the search results page will feature images of several used iPhones for sale on Google Shopping. By contrast, anyone wanting comparison prices for used iPhones that are listed on other price-comparison sites will have to click on links further down on the search-results page to get to those other sites and their respective lists of used iPhone prices. Google faces up to €6.6 billion in fines if convicted.

© grzegorz knec/Alamy Stock Photo

The most recent threat to competition spawned by the Internet is the rise of collusion via pieces of software that use pricing algorithms (automatically applied rules for setting prices) to constantly adjust a company's the online prices in response to seeing what rival firms are charging for similar products. The problem for regulators is that the pricing algorithms of different firms could end up interacting in ways that collusively raise prices for consumers. This is especially true for pieces of software that use artificial intelligence to learn how to achieve preset goals. Two such pieces of software could each be programmed to try to maximize profits and, as they interacted with each other, "realize" that the best way to do so is by coordinating rather than competing.

That possibility is especially challenging because, given the way antitrust laws are currently written, firms can be prosecuted for collusion only if they make an anticompetitive "agreement" with each other. If the algorithms come to collude on their own, there is no such agreement to prosecute. In fact, the behavior of the two pieces of software could just as easily be interpreted as independent parallel conduct rather than coordination since they don't even directly communicate with each other. And, in addition, should asking a piece of software to try to figure out how to maximize profits be illegal just by itself?

These issues are still very much up in the air but being faced squarely by U.S. regulators, who made their first prosecution against the collusive use of algorithmic pricing software in 2015 and who established the Office of Technology Research and Investigation as part of the Federal Trade Commission's Bureau of Consumer Protection that same year.

large ones. The costs of complying with social regulation are, in effect, fixed costs. Because smaller firms produce less output over which to distribute those costs, their compliance costs per unit of output put them at a competitive disadvantage with their larger rivals. Social regulation is more likely to force smaller firms out of business, thus contributing to the increased concentration of industry.

Finally, social regulation may prompt some U.S. firms to move their operations to countries in which the rules are not as burdensome and therefore production costs are lower.

Less Government Is Not Always Better Than More

On the opposite side of the issue, opponents of social regulation need to remember that less government is not always better than more government. While the market system is a powerful engine for producing goods and services and generating income, it has certain flaws and can camouflage certain abuses. Through appropriate amounts of social regulation, government can clearly increase economic efficiency and thus society's well-being. Ironically, by "taking the rough edges off of capitalism," social regulation may be a strong pro-capitalism force. Properly conceived and executed, social regulation helps maintain political support for the market system. Such support could quickly wane should there be a steady drumbeat of reports of unsafe workplaces, unsafe products, discriminatory hiring, choking pollution, deceived loan customers, and the like. Social regulation helps the market system deliver not only goods and services but also a "good society."

QUICK REVIEW 18.3

- ✓ Social regulation is concerned with the conditions under which goods and services are produced, the effects of production on society, and the physical characteristics of the goods themselves.
- ✓ Defenders of social regulation point to the benefits arising from policies that keep dangerous products from the marketplace, reduce workplace injuries and deaths, contribute to clean air and water, and reduce employment discrimination.
- ✓ Critics of social regulation say uneconomical policy goals, inadequate information, unintended side effects, and overzealous personnel create excessive regulation, for which regulatory costs exceed regulatory benefits.

SUMMARY

LO18.1 List and explain the core elements of the major antitrust (antimonopoly) laws in the United States.

The cornerstones of antitrust policy are the Sherman Act of 1890 and the Clayton Act of 1914. The Sherman Act specifies that "every contract, combination . . . or conspiracy in the restraint of interstate trade . . . is . . . illegal" and that any person who monopolizes or attempts to monopolize interstate trade is guilty of a felony.

If a company is found guilty of violating the antimonopoly provisions of the Sherman Act, the government can either break up the monopoly into competing firms (a structural remedy) or prohibit it from engaging in specific anticompetitive business practices (a behavioral remedy).

The Clayton Act was designed to bolster and make more explicit the provisions of the Sherman Act. It declares that price discrimination, tying contracts, intercorporate stock acquisitions, and interlocking directorates are illegal when their effect is to reduce competition.

The Federal Trade Commission Act of 1914 created the Federal Trade Commission to investigate antitrust violations and to prevent the use of "unfair methods of competition." The FTC Act was amended by the Wheeler-Lea Act of 1938 to outlaw false and deceptive representation of products to consumers. Empowered by cease-and-desist orders, the FTC serves as a watchdog agency over unfair, deceptive, or false claims made by firms about their own products or the products of their competitors.

The Celler-Kefauver Act of 1950 amended the Clayton Act of 1914 to prohibit one firm from acquiring the assets of another firm when doing so would substantially reduce competition.

LO18.2 Describe some of the key issues relating to the interpretation and application of antitrust laws.

Some of the key issues in applying antitrust laws include (a) determining whether an industry should be judged by its structure or by its behavior, (b) defining the scope and size of the dominant firm's market, and (c) deciding how strictly to enforce the antitrust laws.

The courts treat price-fixing among competitors as a *per se violation,* meaning that the conduct is illegal independently of whether the conspiracy causes harm. In contrast, a *rule of reason* is used to assess monopoly. Only monopolies that unreasonably (abusively) achieve or maintain their status violate the law. Antitrust officials are more likely to challenge price-fixing, tying contracts, and horizontal mergers than to try to break up existing monopolies. Nevertheless, antitrust suits by the federal government led to the breakup of the AT&T monopoly in the early 1980s.

LO18.3 Identify and explain the economic principles and difficulties relating to the setting of prices (rates) charged by so-called natural monopolies.

The objective of industrial regulation is to protect the public from the market power of natural monopolies by regulating prices and quality of service.

Critics of industrial regulation contend that it can lead to inefficiency and rising costs and that in many instances it constitutes a legal cartel for the regulated firms. Legislation passed in the late 1970s and the 1980s has brought about varying degrees of deregulation in the airline, trucking, banking, railroad, and television broadcasting industries.

Studies indicate that deregulation of airlines, railroads, trucking, and telecommunications is producing sizable annual gains to society through lower prices, lower costs, and increased output. Less certain is the effect of the more recent deregulation of the electricity industry.

LO18.4 Discuss the nature of "social regulation," its benefits and costs, and its optimal level.

Social regulation is concerned with product safety, working conditions, and the effects of production on society. Whereas industrial regulation is on the wane, social regulation continues to expand. The optimal amount of social regulation occurs where MB = MC.

People who support social regulation point to its numerous specific successes and assert that it has greatly enhanced society's well-being. Critics of social regulation contend that businesses are excessively regulated to the point where marginal costs exceed marginal benefits. They also say that social regulation often produces unintended and costly side effects.

TERMS AND CONCEPTS

antitrust policy
industrial regulation
social regulation
Sherman Act
Clayton Act
tying contracts
interlocking directorates
Federal Trade Commission Act
cease-and-desist order
Wheeler-Lea Act
Celler-Kefauver Act
Standard Oil case
U.S. Steel case
rule of reason
Alcoa case
DuPont cellophane case
Microsoft case
horizontal merger
vertical merger
conglomerate merger
per se violations
natural monopoly
public interest theory of regulation
legal cartel theory of regulation

The following and additional problems can be found in connect

DISCUSSION QUESTIONS

1. Both antitrust policy and industrial regulation deal with monopoly. What distinguishes the two approaches? How does government decide to use one form of remedy rather than the other? LO18.1, LO18.3
2. Describe the major provisions of the Sherman and Clayton acts. What government entities are responsible for enforcing those laws? Are firms permitted to initiate antitrust suits on their own against other firms? LO18.1
3. Contrast the outcomes of the Standard Oil and U.S. Steel cases. What was the main antitrust issue in the DuPont cellophane case? In what major way do the Microsoft and Standard Oil cases differ? LO18.2
4. Why might one administration interpret and enforce the antitrust laws more strictly than another? How might a change of administrations affect a major monopoly case in progress? LO18.2
5. Suppose a proposed merger of firms would simultaneously lessen competition and reduce unit costs through economies of scale. Do you think such a merger should be allowed? LO18.2
6. In the 1980s, PepsiCo Inc., which then had 28 percent of the soft-drink market, proposed to acquire the Seven-Up Company. Shortly thereafter, the Coca-Cola Company, with 39 percent of the market, indicated it wanted to acquire the Dr Pepper Company. Seven-Up and Dr Pepper each controlled about 7 percent of the market. In your judgment, was the government's decision to block these mergers appropriate? LO18.2
7. Why might a firm charged with violating the Clayton Act, Section 7, try arguing that the products sold by the merged firms are in separate markets? Why might a firm charged with violating Section 2 of the Sherman Act try convincing the court that none of its behavior in achieving and maintaining its monopoly was illegal? LO18.2
8. "The social desirability of any particular firm should be judged not on the basis of its market share but on the basis of its conduct and performance." Make a counterargument, referring to the monopoly model in your statement. LO18.2
9. What types of industries, if any, should be subjected to industrial regulation? What specific problems does industrial regulation entail? LO18.3

10. In view of the problems involved in regulating natural monopolies, compare socially optimal (marginal-cost) pricing and fair-return pricing by referring again to Figure 12.9. Assuming that a government subsidy might be used to cover any loss resulting from marginal-cost pricing, which pricing policy would you favor? Why? What problems might such a subsidy entail? LO18.3

11. How does social regulation differ from industrial regulation? What types of benefits and costs are associated with social regulation? LO18.4

12. Use economic analysis to explain why the optimal amount of product safety may be less than the amount that would totally eliminate the risk of accidents and deaths. Use automobiles as an example. LO18.4

13. **LAST WORD** On what basis were the airlines found guilty of violating antitrust laws in the Airline Tariff Publishing case? What was the remedy? By contrast, why might it be hard to prosecute algorithmic collusion, which also uses prices posted electronically?

AP REVIEW QUESTIONS

1. Effective anti-trust action should seek which resolution for the level of output in a market? LO18.1
   a. Zero economic profits
   b. MR = MC; as long as P > MR
   c. P > MC
   d. P = MC
   e. P = ATC

2. Allocative efficiency occurs when production is at the point where LO18.1
   a. Economic profits = 0
   b. MR = MC
   c. MSB = MSC (marginal social benefit equals marginal social cost)
   d. MR = MC and P = ATC, as long as P > MR
   e. P = LRAC

3. How would you expect antitrust authorities to react to: LO18.2
   a. A proposed merger of Ford and General Motors.
   b. Evidence of secret meetings by contractors to rig bids for highway construction projects.
   c. A proposed merger of a large shoe manufacturer and a chain of retail shoe stores.
   d. A proposed merger of a small life-insurance company and a regional candy manufacturer.
   e. An automobile rental firm that charges higher rates for last-minute rentals than for rentals reserved weeks in advance.

4. When confronted with a natural monopoly that restricts output and charges monopoly prices, the two methods that governments have for promoting better outcomes are: LO18.3
   a. Public ownership and public regulation.
   b. Encouraging effective competition and public goods.
   c. Antitrust law and horizontal mergers.
   d. Creative destruction and laissez-faire.
   e. Encouraging the entry of firms or taxing the natural monopoly

PROBLEMS

1. Suppose that there are only three types of fruit sold in the United States. Annual sales are 1 million tons of blueberries, 5 million tons of strawberries, and 10 million tons of bananas. Suppose that of those total amounts, the Sunny Valley Fruit Company sells 900,000 tons of blueberries, 900,000 tons of strawberries, and 7.9 million tons of bananas. LO18.2
   a. What is Sunny Valley's market share if the relevant market is blueberries? If a court applies the "90-60-30 rule" when considering just the blueberry market, would it rule that Sunny Valley is a monopoly?
   b. What is Sunny Valley's market share if the relevant market is all types of berries? Would the court rule Sunny Valley to be a monopolist in that market?
   c. What if the relevant market is all types of fruit? What is Sunny Valley's market share, and would the court consider Sunny Valley to be a monopolist?

2. Carrot Computers and its competitors purchase touch screens for their tablet computers from several suppliers. The six makers of touch screens have market shares of, respectively, 19 percent, 18 percent, 14 percent, 16 percent, 20 percent, and 13 percent. LO18.2
   a. What is the Herfindahl index for the touch screen manufacturing industry?
   b. By how much would a proposed merger between the two smallest touch screen makers increase the Herfindahl index? Would the government be likely to challenge that proposed merger?
   c. If Carrot Computers horizontally merges with its competitor Blueberry Handhelds, by how much would the Herfindahl index change for the touch screen industry?

Chapter 19

Income Inequality, Poverty, and Discrimination

Learning Objectives

LO19.1 **Explain how income inequality in the United States is measured and described.**

LO19.2 **Discuss the extent and sources of income inequality.**

LO19.3 **Demonstrate how income inequality has changed since 1975.**

LO19.4 **Debate the economic arguments for and against income inequality.**

LO19.5 **Relate how poverty is measured and its incidence by age, gender, ethnicity, and other characteristics.**

LO19.6 **Identify the major components of the income-maintenance program in the United States.**

LO19.7 **Discuss labor market discrimination and how it might affect hiring decisions and wages.**

AP Chapter Focus

Evidence that suggests wide income disparity in the United States is easy to find. In 2015 boxer Floyd Mayweather earned $300 million, singer Katy Perry earned $135 million, and celebrity chef Gordon Ramsay earned $60 million. In contrast, the salary of the president of the United States is $400,000, and the typical schoolteacher earns $56,000. A full-time minimum-wage worker at a fast-food restaurant makes about $15,000. Cash welfare payments to a mother with two children average $5,150 per year.

In 2014 about 46.7 million Americans—or 15.0 percent of the population—lived in poverty. An estimated 576,400 people were homeless that year. The richest fifth of American households received about 51.2 percent of total income, while the poorest fifth received about 3.1 percent.

What are the sources of income inequality? Is income inequality rising or falling? Is the United States making progress against poverty? What are the major income-maintenance programs in the United States? What role does discrimination play in reducing wages for some and increasing wages for others? These are some of the questions we will answer in this chapter.

AP Facts about Income Inequality

LO19.1 Explain how income inequality in the United States is measured and described.

Average household income in the United States is among the highest in the world; in 2014, it was $68,426 per household (one or more persons occupying a housing unit). But that average tells us nothing about income inequality. To learn about that, we must examine how income is distributed around the average.

Distribution by Income Category

One way to measure **income inequality** is to look at the percentages of households in a series of income categories. Table 19.1 shows that 23.6 percent of all households had annual before-tax incomes of less than $25,000 in 2014, while 24.7 percent had annual incomes of $100,000 or more. The data in the table suggest a wide dispersion of household income and considerable inequality of income in the United States.

Distribution by Quintiles (Fifths)

A second way to measure income inequality is to divide the total number of individuals, households, or families (two or more persons related by birth, marriage, or adoption) into five numerically equal groups, or *quintiles,* and examine the percentage of total personal (before-tax) income received by each quintile. We do this for households in the table in Figure 19.1, where we also provide the upper income limit for each quintile. Any amount of income greater than that listed in each row of column 3 would place a household into the next-higher quintile.

TABLE 19.1 The Distribution of U.S. Income by Households, 2014

(1) Personal Income Category	(2) Percentage of All Households in This Category
Under $15,000	12.6
$15,000–$24,999	11.0
$25,000–$34,999	10.1
$35,000–$49,999	13.1
$50,000–$74,999	17.0
$75,000–$99,999	11.5
$100,000 and above	24.7
Total	100.0

Source: Bureau of the Census, **www.census.gov**.

The Lorenz Curve and Gini Ratio

We can display the quintile distribution of personal income through a **Lorenz curve.** In Figure 19.1, we plot the cumulative percentage of households on the horizontal axis and the percentage of income they obtain on the vertical axis. The diagonal line 0*e* represents a *perfectly equal distribution of income* because each point along that line indicates that a particular percentage of households receive the same percentage of income. In other words, points representing 20 percent of all households receiving 20 percent of total income, 40 percent receiving 40 percent, 60 percent receiving 60 percent, and so on, all lie on the diagonal line.

By plotting the quintile data from the table in Figure 19.1, we obtain the Lorenz curve for 2014. The bottom 20 percent of all households received 3.1 percent of the income, as shown by point *a*; the bottom 40 percent received 11.3 percent (= 3.1 + 8.2), as shown by point *b*; and so forth. The blue area between the diagonal line and the Lorenz curve is determined by the extent that the Lorenz curve sags away from the diagonal and indicates the degree of income inequality. If the actual income distribution were perfectly equal, the Lorenz curve and the diagonal would coincide and the blue area would disappear.

At the opposite extreme is complete inequality, where all households but one have zero income. In that case the Lorenz curve would coincide with the horizontal axis from 0 to point *f* (at 0 percent of income) and then would move immediately up from *f* to point *e* along the vertical axis (indicating that a single household has 100 percent of the total income). The entire area below the diagonal line (triangle 0*ef*) would indicate this extreme degree of inequality. So the farther the Lorenz curve sags away from the diagonal, the greater is the degree of income inequality.

The income inequality described by the Lorenz curve can be transformed into a **Gini ratio**—a numerical measure of the overall dispersion of income:

$$\text{Gini ratio} = \frac{\text{Area between Lorenz curve and diagonal}}{\text{Total area below the diagonal}}$$

$$= \frac{A \text{ (blue are)}}{A + B \text{ (blue + green area)}}$$

The Gini ratio is 0.480 for the distribution of household income shown in Figure 19.1. As the area between the Lorenz curve and the diagonal gets larger, the Gini ratio rises to reflect greater inequality. Lower Gini ratios denote less inequality; higher ratios indicate more inequality. The Gini coefficient for complete income equality is zero and for complete inequality is 1.

Because Gini ratios are numerical, they are easier to use than Lorenz curves for comparing the income distributions of

AP **FIGURE 19.1 The Lorenz curve and Gini ratio.** The Lorenz curve is a convenient way to show the degree of income inequality (here, household income by quintile in 2014). The area between the diagonal (the line of perfect equality) and the Lorenz curve represents the degree of inequality in the distribution of total income. This inequality is measured numerically by the Gini ratio—area *A* (shown in blue) divided by area *A* + *B* (the blue + green area). The Gini ratio for the distribution shown is 0.480.

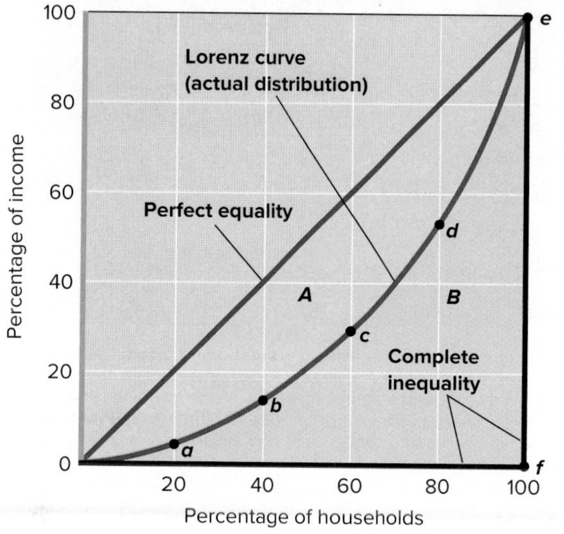

(1) Quintile (2011)	(2) Percentage of Total Income	(3) Upper Income Limit
Lowest 20 percent	3.1	$ 21,432
Second 20 percent	8.2	41,186
Third 20 percent	14.3	68,212
Fourth 20 percent	23.2	112,262
Highest 20 percent	51.2	No limit
Total	100.0	

Source: Bureau of the Census, **www.census.gov**.

different ethnic groups and countries. For example, in 2014 the Gini ratio of U.S. household income for Hispanics was 0.455; for whites, 0.472; for Asians, 0.463; and for African-Americans, 0.499.[1] In 2014, national Gini ratios ranged from a low of 0.247 in Ukraine to a high of 0.608 in Haiti. Examples within this range include Denmark, 0.291; Italy, 0.352; Mexico, 0.481; and Honduras, 0.574.[2]

Income Mobility: The Time Dimension

The income data used so far have a major limitation: The income accounting period of 1 year is too short to be very meaningful. Because the Census Bureau data portray the distribution of income in only a single year, they may conceal a more equal distribution over a few years, a decade, or even a lifetime. If Brad earns $1,000 in year 1 and $100,000 in year 2, while Jenny earns $100,000 in year 1 and only $1,000 in year 2, do we have income inequality? The answer depends on the period of measurement. Annual data would reveal great income inequality, but there would be complete equality over the 2-year period.

This point is important because evidence suggests considerable "churning around" in the distribution of income over time. Such movement of individuals or households from one income quintile to another over time is called **income mobility**. For most income receivers, income starts at a relatively low level during youth, reaches a peak during middle age, and then declines. It follows that if all people receive exactly the same stream of income over their lifetimes, considerable income inequality would still exist in any specific year because of age differences. In any single year, the young and the old would receive low incomes while the middle-aged receive high incomes.

If we change from a "snapshot" view of income distribution in a single year to a "time exposure" portraying incomes over much longer periods, we find considerable movement of income receivers among income classes. For instance, one study showed that between 1996 and 2005, half the individuals in the lowest quintile of the U.S. income distribution in 1996 were in a higher income quintile in 2005. Almost 25 percent made it to the middle fifth and 5 percent achieved the top quintile. There was income mobility in both directions. About 57 percent of the top 1 percent of income receivers in 1996 had dropped out of that category by 2005. Overall, income mobility between 1996 and 2005 was the same as it was the previous 10 years. All this correctly suggests that income is more equally distributed over a 5-, 10-, or 20-year period than in any single year.[3]

[1] U.S. Census Bureau, *Historical Income Tables*, **www.census.gov**.

[2] *CIA World Factbook*, 2014, **www.cia.gov**.

[3] U.S. Department of the Treasury, *Income Mobility in the U.S. from 1996–2005*, November 13, 2007, pp. 1–22.

FIGURE 19.2 **The impact of taxes and transfers on U.S. income inequality.** The distribution of household income is significantly more equal after taxes and transfers are taken into account than before. Transfers account for most of the lessening of inequality and provide most of the income received by the lowest quintile of households.

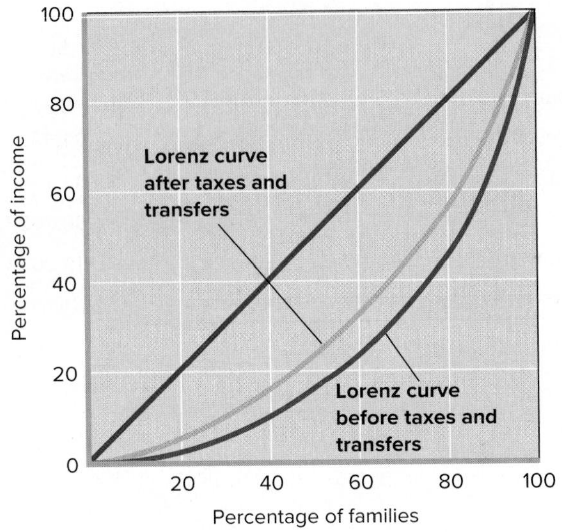

Quintile	Percentage of Total Income Received, 2013 (1) Before Taxes and Transfers	(2) After Taxes and Transfers
Lowest 20 percent	2.2	9.3
Second 20 percent	7.2	10.7
Third 20 percent	12.8	14.1
Fourth 20 percent	20.8	19.9
Highest 20 percent	57.0	46.0

Source: Congressional Budget Office, **www.cbo.gov**. Income received "before taxes and transfers" excludes government cash transfers, realized capital gains, and employer-provided health insurance. Income received "after taxes and transfers" includes both cash and noncash transfers as well as realized capital gains and employer-provided health insurance. Numbers may not add to 100 percent due to rounding.

In short, individual and family income mobility over time is significant; for many people, "low income" and "high income" are not permanent conditions. Also, the longer the time period considered, the more equal the distribution of income becomes.

Effect of Government Redistribution

The income data in Table 19.1 and Figure 19.1 include wages, salaries, dividends, and interest. They also include all cash transfer payments such as Social Security, unemployment compensation benefits, and welfare assistance to needy families. The data are before-tax data and therefore do not take into account the effects of personal income and payroll (Social Security) taxes that are levied directly on income receivers. Nor do they include in-kind or **noncash transfers,** which provide specific goods or services rather than cash. Noncash transfers include such things as Medicare, Medicaid, housing subsidies, subsidized school lunches, and food stamps. Such transfers are "incomelike," since they enable recipients to "purchase" goods and services.

One economic function of government is to redistribute income, if society so desires. Figure 19.2 and its table[4] reveal that government significantly redistributes income from higher- to lower-income households through taxes and transfers. Note that the U.S. distribution of household income before taxes and transfers are taken into account (dark red Lorenz curve) is substantially less equal than the distribution after taxes and transfers (light red Lorenz curve). Without government redistribution, the lowest 20 percent of households in 2013 would have received only 2.2 percent of total income. *With* redistribution, they received 9.3 percent, or 4.2 times as much.

Which contributes more to redistribution, government taxes or government transfers? The answer is transfers. As discussed in Chapter 17's Last Word, the combined federal, state, and local tax system in the United States is only modestly progressive. As a result, nearly all the reduction in income inequality in the United States is attributable to transfer payments. Together with job opportunities, transfer payments have been the most important means of alleviating poverty in the United States.

AP Causes of Income Inequality

LO19.2 Discuss the extent and sources of income inequality.

There are several causes of income inequality in the United States. In general, the market system is permissive of a high degree of income inequality because it rewards individuals based on the contributions that they make, or the resources that they own, in producing society's output.

More specifically, the factors that contribute to income inequality are the following.

Ability

People have different mental, physical, and aesthetic talents. Some have inherited the exceptional mental qualities that are essential to such high-paying occupations as medicine, corporate leadership, and law. Others are blessed with the physical capacity and coordination to become highly paid

[4]The "before" data in this table differ from the data in the table in Figure 19.1 because the latter include cash transfers. Also, the data in Figure 19.2 are based on a broader concept of income than are the data in Figure 19.1.

professional athletes. A few have the talent to become great artists or musicians or have the beauty to become top fashion models. Others have very weak mental endowments and may work in low-paying occupations or may be incapable of earning any income at all. The intelligence and skills of most people fall somewhere in between.

Education and Training

Native ability alone rarely produces high income; people must develop and refine their capabilities through education and training. Individuals differ significantly in the amount of education and training they obtain and thus in their capacity to earn income. Such differences may be a matter of choice: Nguyen enters the labor force after graduating from high school, while Nyberg takes a job only after earning a college degree. Other differences may be involuntary: Nguyen and her parents may simply be unable to finance a college education.

People also receive varying degrees of on-the-job training, which contributes to income inequality. Some workers learn valuable new skills each year on the job and therefore experience significant income growth over time; others receive little or no on-the-job training and earn no more at age 50 than they did at age 30. Moreover, firms tend to select for advanced on-the-job training the workers who have the most formal education. That added training magnifies the education-based income differences between less-educated and better-educated individuals.

Discrimination

Discrimination in education, hiring, training, and promotion undoubtedly causes some income inequality. If discrimination confines certain racial, ethnic, or gender groups to lower-pay occupations, the supply of labor in those occupations will increase relative to demand, and hourly wages and income in those lower-pay jobs will decline. Conversely, labor supply will be artificially reduced in the higher-pay occupations populated by "preferred" workers, raising their wage rates and income. In this way, discrimination can add to income inequality. In fact, economists cannot account for all racial, ethnic, and gender differences in work earnings on the basis of differences in years of education, quality of education, occupations, and annual hours of work. Many economists attribute the unexplained residual to discrimination.

Economists, however, do not see discrimination by race, gender, and ethnicity as a dominant factor explaining income inequality. The income distributions *within* racial or ethnic groups that historically have been targets of discrimination—for example, African Americans—are similar to the income distribution for whites. Other factors besides discrimination are obviously at work.

Nevertheless, discrimination is an important concern since it harms individuals and reduces society's overall output and income. We will discuss it in more detail later in this chapter.

Preferences and Risks

Incomes also differ because of differences in preferences for market work relative to leisure, market work relative to work in the household, and types of occupations. People who choose to stay home with children, work part-time, or retire early usually have less income than those who make the opposite choices. Those who are willing to take arduous, unpleasant jobs (for example, underground mining or heavy construction), to work long hours with great intensity, or to "moonlight" will tend to earn more.

Individuals also differ in their willingness to assume risk. We refer here not only to the race-car driver or the professional boxer but also to the entrepreneur. Although many entrepreneurs fail, many of those who develop successful new products or services realize very substantial incomes. That contributes to income inequality.

Unequal Distribution of Wealth

Income is a *flow;* it represents a stream of wage and salary earnings, along with rent, interest, and profits, as depicted in Chapter 2's circular flow diagram. In contrast, wealth is a *stock,* reflecting at a particular moment the financial and real assets an individual has accumulated over time. A retired person may have very little income and yet own a home, mutual fund shares, and a pension plan that add up to considerable wealth. A new college graduate may be earning a substantial income as an accountant, middle manager, or engineer but has yet to accumulate significant wealth.

As you will discover in this chapter's Last Word, the ownership of wealth in the United States is more unequal than the distribution of income. This inequality of wealth leads to inequality in rent, interest, and dividends, which in turn contributes to income inequality. Those who own more machinery, real estate, farmland, stocks, and bonds and who have more money in savings accounts obviously receive greater income from that ownership than people with less or no such wealth.

Market Power

The ability to "rig the market" on one's own behalf also contributes to income inequality. For example, in *resource* markets certain unions and professional groups have adopted policies that limit the supply of their services, thereby boosting the incomes of those "on the inside." Also, legislation that requires occupational licensing for, say, doctors, dentists, and lawyers can bestow market power that favors the licensed groups. In *product* markets, "rigging the market" means gaining or enhancing monopoly power, which results in greater profit and thus greater income to the firms' owners.

Luck, Connections, and Misfortune

Other forces also play a role in producing income inequality. Luck and "being in the right place at the right time" have helped individuals stumble into fortunes. Discovering oil on a ranch, owning land along a proposed freeway interchange, and hiring the right press agent have accounted for some high incomes. Personal contacts and political connections are other potential routes to attaining high income.

In contrast, economic misfortunes such as prolonged illness, serious accident, the death of the family breadwinner, or unemployment may plunge a family into the low range of income. The burden of such misfortune is borne very unevenly by the population and thus contributes to income inequality.

Income inequality of the magnitude we have described is not exclusively an American phenomenon. Global Perspective 19.1 compares income inequality (here by individuals, not by households) in the United States with that in several other nations. Income inequality tends to be greatest in South American nations, where land and capital resources are highly concentrated in the hands of a relatively small number of wealthy families.

AP QUICK REVIEW 19.1

- ✓ Data reveal considerable income inequality in the United States; in 2014 the richest fifth of all households received 51.2 percent of before-tax income, and the poorest fifth received 3.1 percent.
- ✓ The Lorenz curve depicts income inequality graphically by comparing percentages of total families and percentages of total income. The larger the gap between Lorenz curve and a line of total equality means more inequality. The Gini ratio measures of the overall dispersion of income and is found by dividing the area between the diagonal and the Lorenz curve by the total area below the diagonal. Higher ratios mean greater degrees of income inequality; the distribution of income is less unequal over longer time periods.
- ✓ Government taxes and transfers reduce income inequality by redistributing income from higher-income groups to lower-income groups.
- ✓ Differences in ability, education and training, preferences for market work versus nonmarket activities, property ownership, and market power—along with discrimination and luck—help explain income inequality.

GLOBAL PERSPECTIVE 19.1

Percentage of Total Income Received by the Top One-Tenth of Income Receivers, Selected Nations

The share of income going to the highest 10 percent of income receivers varies among nations.

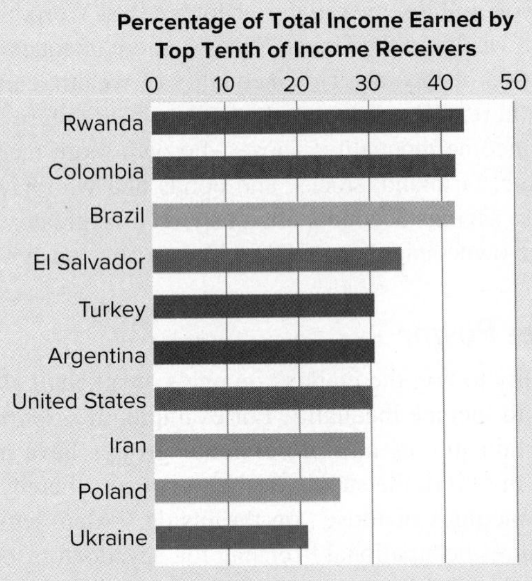

Source: Human Development Report, 2009, **hdr.undp.org**. United Nations Development Programme.

Income Inequality over Time

LO19.3 Demonstrate how income inequality has changed since 1975.

Over a period of years economic growth has raised incomes in the United States: In *absolute* dollar amounts, the entire distribution of income has been moving upward. But incomes may move up in *absolute* terms while leaving the *relative* distribution of income less equal, more equal, or unchanged. Table 19.2 shows how the distribution of household income has changed since 1975. This income is "before tax" and includes cash transfers but not noncash transfers.

Rising Income Inequality since 1975

It is clear from Table 19.2 that the distribution of income by quintiles has become more unequal since 1975. In 2014 the lowest 20 percent of households received 3.1 percent of total before-tax income, compared with 4.4 percent in 1975. Meanwhile, the income share received by the highest 20 percent rose from 43.2 in 1975 to 51.2 percent in 2014. The percentage of income received by the top 5 percent of households also rose significantly over the 1975–2014 period.

TABLE 19.2 Percentage of Total Before-Tax Income Received by Each One-Fifth, and by the Top 5 Percent, of Households, Selected Years

Quintile	1975	1980	1985	1990	1995	2000	2005	2014
Lowest 20 percent	4.4	4.3	4.0	3.7	3.6	3.4	3.4	3.1
Second 20 percent	10.5	10.3	9.7	9.1	8.9	8.6	8.6	8.2
Third 20 percent	17.1	16.9	16.3	15.2	14.8	14.6	14.6	14.3
Fourth 20 percent	24.8	24.9	24.0	23.3	23.0	23.0	23.0	23.2
Highest 20 percent	43.2	43.7	46.6	48.7	50.4	49.8	50.4	51.2
Total	100.0	100.0	100.0	100.0	100.0	100.0	100.0	100.0
Top 5 percent	15.9	15.8	17.0	18.6	21.0	22.1	22.2	21.9

Source: Bureau of the Census, **www.census.gov**. Numbers may not add to 100 percent due to rounding.

Causes of Growing Inequality

Economists suggest several major explanations for the increase in U.S. income inequality since 1975.

Greater Demand for Highly Skilled Workers Perhaps the most significant contributor to the growing income inequality has been an increasing demand by many firms for workers who are highly skilled and well-educated. Moreover, several industries requiring highly skilled workers have either recently emerged or expanded greatly, such as the computer software, business consulting, biotechnology, health care, and Internet industries. Because highly skilled workers remain relatively scarce, their wages have been bid up. Consequently, the wage differences between them and less-skilled workers have increased.

Between 1980 and 2007 the wage difference between college graduates and high school graduates rose from 28 percent to 49 percent for women and from 22 percent to 44 percent for men. And the so-called *90-10 ratio*—how many times larger the hourly wage at the 90th percentile is compared to the hourly wage at the 10th percentile—rose from 3.6 in 1980 to 4.5 in 2007.[5]

The rising demand for skill has also shown up in rapidly rising pay for chief executive officers (CEOs), sizable increases in income from stock options, substantial increases in income for professional athletes and entertainers, and huge fortunes for successful entrepreneurs. This growth of "superstar" pay has also contributed to rising income inequality.

Demographic Changes The entrance of large numbers of less-experienced and less-skilled "baby boomers" into the labor force during the 1970s and 1980s may have contributed to greater income inequality in those two decades. Because younger workers tend to earn less income than older workers, their growing numbers contributed to income inequality. There has also been a growing tendency for men and women with high earnings potential to marry each other, thus increasing household income among the highest income quintiles. Finally, the number of households headed by single or divorced women has increased greatly. That trend has increased income inequality because such households lack a second major wage earner and also because the poverty rate for female-headed households is very high.

International Trade, Immigration, and Decline in Unionism Other factors are probably at work as well. Stronger international competition from imports has reduced the demand for and employment of less-skilled (but highly paid) workers in such industries as the automobile and steel industries. The decline in such jobs has reduced the average wage for less-skilled workers. It also has swelled the ranks of workers in already low-paying industries, placing further downward pressure on wages there.

Similarly, the transfer of jobs to lower-wage workers in developing countries has exerted downward wage pressure on less-skilled workers in the United States. Also, an upsurge in the immigration of unskilled workers has increased the number of low-income households in the United States. Finally, the decline in unionism in the United States has undoubtedly contributed to wage inequality, since unions tend to equalize pay within firms and industries.

Two cautions: First, when we note growing income inequality, we are not saying that the "rich are getting richer and the poor are getting poorer" in terms of absolute income. Both the rich and the poor are experiencing rises in real income. Rather, what has happened is that, while incomes have risen in all quintiles, income growth has been fastest in the top quintile. Second, increased income inequality is not solely a U.S. phenomenon. The recent rise of inequality has also occurred in several other industrially advanced nations.

[5] Economic Policy Institute, **www.epinet.org**. The college wage premiums are adjusted for differences in earnings based on race, ethnicity, marital status, and region.

CONSIDER THIS . . .

Source: © Moviestore collection Ltd/Alamy Stock Photo

Laughing at *The Lego Movie*

Some economists say that the distribution of annual *consumption* is more meaningful for examining inequality of well-being than is the distribution of annual *income*. In a given year, people's consumption of goods and services may be above or below their income because they can save, draw down past savings, use credit cards, take out home mortgages, spend from inheritances, give money to charities, and so on.

A recent study of the distribution of consumption finds that annual consumption inequality is less than income inequality. Moreover, consumption inequality has remained relatively constant over several decades, even though income inequality has increased.*

The Economist magazine extends the argument even further, pointing out that despite the recent increase in income inequality, the products consumed by the rich and the poor are far closer in functionality today than at any other time in history.

More than 70 percent of Americans under the official poverty line own at least one car. The difference between driving a beat-up sedan and a high-end sports car is nigh undetectable when compared to the difference between driving and hiking through the mud. A flat panel television is lovely, but you do not need one to laugh at *The Lego Movie*.

The successful entrepreneurs who make fortunes by improving quality while dropping prices widen the income gap while reducing meaningful differences.†

Economists generally agree that products and experiences once reserved exclusively for the rich in the United States have, in fact, become more commonplace for nearly all income classes. But skeptics contend that *The Economist*'s argument is too simplistic. Even though both are water outings, there is a fundamental difference between sailing among the Greek isles on your private yacht and paddling on a local pond in a rented kayak.

*Dirk Krueger and Fabrizio Perri, "Does Income Inequality Lead to Consumption Inequality?" *Review of Economic Studies*, 2006, pp. 163–193.

†*The Economist*, "Economic Focus: The New (Improved) Gilded Age," December 22, 2007, p. 122.

The Lorenz curve can be used to contrast the distribution of income at different points in time. If we plotted Table 19.2's data as Lorenz curves, we would find that the curves shifted farther away from the diagonal between 1975 and 2014. The Gini ratio rose from 0.397 in 1975 to 0.480 in 2014.

AP Equality versus Efficiency

LO19.4 Debate the economic arguments for and against income inequality.

The main policy issue concerning income inequality is how much is necessary and justified. While there is no general agreement on the justifiable amount, we can gain insight by exploring the cases for and against greater equality.

The Case for Equality: Maximizing Total Utility

The basic argument for an equal distribution of income is that income equality maximizes total consumer satisfaction (utility) from any particular level of output and income. The rationale for this argument is shown in Figure 19.3, in which we assume that the money incomes of two individuals, Anderson and Brooks, are subject to diminishing marginal utility. In any time period, income receivers spend the first dollars received on the products they value most—products whose marginal utility is high. As their most pressing wants become satisfied, consumers then spend additional dollars of income on less-important, lower-marginal-utility goods. The identical diminishing-marginal-utility-from-income curves (MU_A and MU_B in the figure) reflect the assumption that Anderson and Brooks have the same capacity to derive utility from income.

Now suppose that there is $10,000 worth of income (output) to be distributed between Anderson and Brooks. According to proponents of income equality, the optimal distribution is an equal distribution, which causes the marginal utility of the last dollar spent to be the same for both persons. We can prove this by demonstrating that if the income distribution is initially unequal, then distributing income more equally can increase the combined utility of the two individuals.

Suppose that the $10,000 of income initially is distributed unequally, with Anderson getting $2,500 and Brooks $7,500. The marginal utility, a, from the last dollar received by Anderson is high, and the marginal utility, b, from Brooks's last dollar of income is low. If a single dollar of income is shifted from Brooks to Anderson—that is, toward greater equality—then Anderson's utility increases by a and Brooks's utility decreases by b. The combined utility then increases by a minus b (Anderson's large gain minus Brooks's small loss). The transfer of another dollar from Brooks to Anderson again increases their combined utility, this time by a slightly smaller amount. Continued transfer of dollars from Brooks to Anderson increases their combined utility until the income is evenly distributed and both receive $5,000. At that time their marginal utilities from the last dollar of income are equal (at a' and b'), and any further income redistribution beyond the $2,500 already transferred would begin to create inequality and decrease their combined utility.

FIGURE 19.3 The utility-maximizing distribution of income. With identical marginal-utility-of-income curves MU_A and MU_B, Anderson and Brooks will maximize their combined utility when any amount of income (say, $10,000) is equally distributed. If income is unequally distributed (say, $2,500 to Anderson and $7,500 to Brooks), the marginal utility derived from the last dollar will be greater for Anderson than for Brooks, and a redistribution of income toward equality will result in a net increase in total utility. The utility gained by equalizing income at $5,000 each, shown by the blue area below curve MU_A in panel (a), exceeds the utility lost, indicated by the red area below curve MU_B in (b).

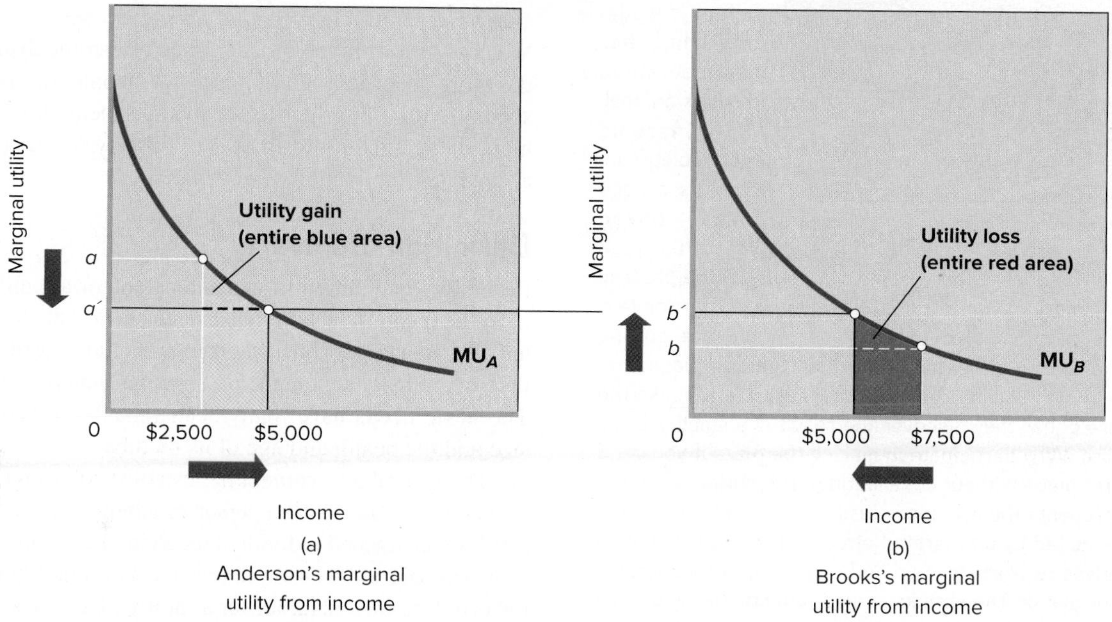

The area under the MU curve and to the left of the individual's particular level of income represents the total utility of that income. Therefore, as a result of the transfer of the $2,500, Anderson has gained utility represented by the blue area below curve MU_A, and Brooks has lost utility represented by the red area below curve MU_B. The blue area is obviously greater than the red area, so income equality yields greater combined total utility than income inequality does.

The Case for Inequality: Incentives and Efficiency

Although the logic of the argument for equality might seem solid, critics of income equality say that the transfer of income required to create income equality is both unfair and unwise. They say that income inequality largely reflects rewards to individuals for supplying their talents and resources to the economy. They conclude that it is not fair to take some of Brooks's income and give it to Anderson. Further, critics of income equality point out that proponents of income equality falsely assume that there is some fixed amount of output produced and therefore income to be distributed. These critics argue that the way in which income is distributed is an important determinant of the amount of output or income that is produced and is available for distribution.

Suppose once again in Figure 19.3 that Anderson earns $2,500 and Brooks earns $7,500. In moving toward equality, society (the government) must tax away some of Brooks's income and transfer it to Anderson. This tax and transfer process diminishes the income rewards of high-income Brooks and raises the income rewards of low-income Anderson; in so doing, it reduces the incentives of both to earn high incomes. Why should high-income Brooks work hard, save and invest, or undertake entrepreneurial risks when the rewards from such activities will be reduced by taxation? And why should low-income Anderson be motivated to increase his income through market activities when the government stands ready to transfer income to him? Taxes are a reduction in the rewards from increased productive effort; redistribution through transfers is a reward for diminished effort.

In the extreme, imagine a situation in which the government levies a 100 percent tax on income and distributes the tax revenue equally to its citizenry. Why would anyone work hard? Why would anyone work at all? Why would anyone assume business risk? Or why would anyone save (forgo current consumption) in order to invest? The economic incentives to "get ahead" will have been removed, greatly reducing society's total production and income. That is, the way income is distributed affects the size of that income. The basic argument for income inequality therefore is twofold: (1) income inequality is justified because it results from differences in

CONSIDER THIS . . .

Source: © Fuse/Getty Images RF

Slicing the Pizza

The equality-efficiency trade-off might better be understood through an analogy. Assume that society's income is a huge pizza, baked year after year, *with the sizes of the pieces going to people on the basis of their contribution to making it.* Now suppose that for fairness reasons, society decides some people are getting pieces that are too large and others are getting pieces too small. But when society redistributes the pizza to make the sizes more equal, they discover the result is a smaller pizza than before. Why participate in making the pizza if you get a decent-size piece without contributing? The shrinkage of the pizza represents the efficiency loss—the loss of output and income—caused by the harmful effects of the redistribution on incentives to work, to save and invest, and to accept entrepreneurial risk. The shrinkage also reflects the resources that society must divert to the bureaucracies that administer the redistribution system.

How much pizza shrinkage will society accept while continuing to agree to the redistribution? If redistributing pizza to make it less unequal reduces the size of the pizza, what amount of pizza loss will society tolerate? Is a loss of 10 percent acceptable? 25 percent? 75 percent? This is the basic question in any debate over the ideal size of a nation's income redistribution program.

the quantity and quality of labor and other resources supplied by individuals to the economy, and (2) it is an unavoidable consequence of maintaining the incentives needed to motivate people to produce output and income year after year.

The Equality-Efficiency Trade-off

At the essence of the income equality-inequality debate is a fundamental trade-off between equality and efficiency. In this **equality-efficiency trade-off,** greater income equality (achieved through redistribution of income) comes at the opportunity cost of reduced production and income. And greater production and income (through reduced redistribution) comes at the expense of less equality of income. The trade-off obligates society to choose how much redistribution it wants, in view of the costs. If society decides it wants to redistribute income, it needs to determine methods that minimize the adverse effects on fairness, incentives, productivity, and economic efficiency.

The Economics of Poverty

LO19.5 Relate how poverty is measured and its incidence by age, gender, ethnicity, and other characteristics.

We now turn from the broader issue of income distribution to the more specific issue of very low income, or "poverty." A society with a high degree of income inequality can have a high, moderate, or low amount of poverty. We therefore need a separate examination of poverty.

Definition of Poverty

Poverty is a condition in which a person or a family does not have the means to satisfy basic needs for food, clothing, shelter, and transportation. The means include currently earned income, transfer payments, past savings, and property owned. The basic needs have many determinants, including family size and the health and age of its members.

The federal government has established minimum income thresholds below which a person or a family is "in poverty." In 2014 an unattached individual receiving less than $12,071 per year was said to be living in poverty. For a family of four, the poverty line was $24,230; for a family of six, it was $32,473. Based on these thresholds, in 2014 about 46.7 million Americans lived in poverty. In 2014 the **poverty rate**—the percentage of the population living in poverty—was 14.8 percent.

Incidence of Poverty

The poor are heterogeneous: They can be found in all parts of the nation; they are of all races and ethnicities, rural and urban, young and old. But as Figure 19.4 indicates, poverty is far from randomly distributed. For example, the poverty rate for African Americans is above the national average, as is the rate for Hispanics, while the rates for whites and Asians are below the average. In 2014, the poverty rates for African Americans and Hispanics were 25.2 and 23.6, respectively; for whites and Asians, 12.9 and 13.1 percent, respectively.[6]

Figure 19.4 shows that female-headed households (no husband present), foreign-born noncitizens, and children under 18 years of age have very high incidences of poverty. Marriage and full-time, year-round work are associated with low poverty rates, and, because of the Social Security system, the incidence of poverty among the elderly is less than that for the population as a whole.

The high poverty rate for children is especially disturbing because poverty tends to breed poverty. Poor children are at greater risk for a range of long-term problems, including poor health and inadequate education, crime, drug use, and teenage pregnancy. Many of today's impoverished children will

[6]Bureau of the Census, **www.census.gov**.

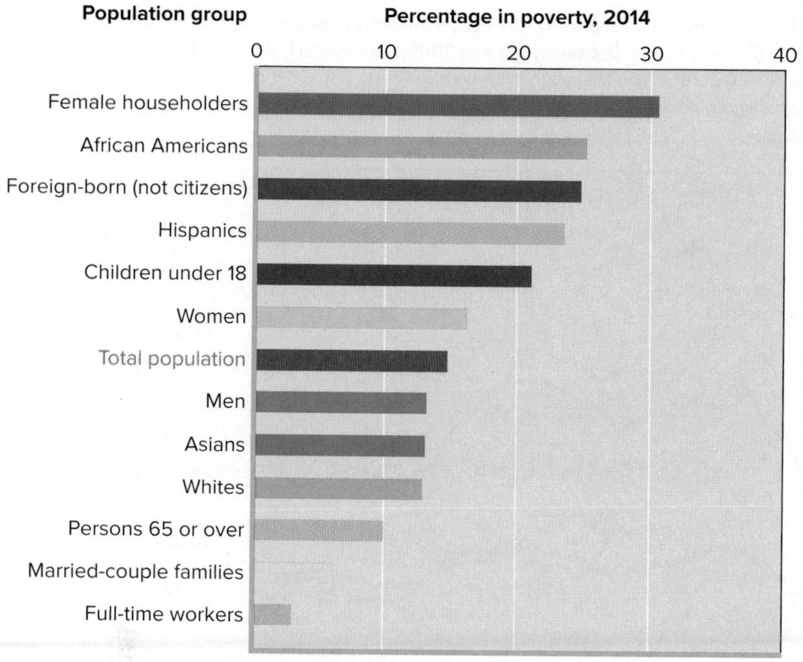

Source: Bureau of the Census, **www.census.gov**.

FIGURE 19.4 Poverty rates among selected population groups, 2014. Poverty is disproportionately borne by African Americans, Hispanics, children, foreign-born residents who are not citizens, and families headed by women. People who are employed full-time, have a college degree, or are married tend to have low poverty rates.

reach adulthood unhealthy and illiterate and unable to earn above-poverty incomes.

As many as half of people in poverty are poor for only one or two years before climbing out of poverty. But poverty is much more long-lasting among some groups than among others. In particular, African American and Hispanic families, families headed by women, persons with little education and few labor market skills, and people who are dysfunctional because of drug use, alcoholism, or mental illness are more likely than others to remain in poverty. Also, long-lasting poverty is heavily present in depressed areas of cities, parts of the Deep South, and some Indian reservations.

Poverty Trends

As Figure 19.5 shows, the total poverty rate fell significantly between 1959 and 1969, stabilized at 11 to 13 percent over the next decade, and then rose in the early 1980s. In 1993 the rate was 15.1 percent, the highest since 1983. Between 1993 and 2000 the rate turned downward, falling to 11.3 percent in 2000. Because of recession, slow employment growth, and relatively slow wage growth, the poverty rate rose from 11.7 percent in 2001 to 12.7 percent in 2004. During the second half of the 1990s, poverty rates plunged for African Americans, Hispanics, and Asians, and they have remained historically low. Nevertheless, in 2008 African Americans and Hispanics still had poverty rates that were roughly double the rate for whites.

The recession that began in December 2007 increased poverty rates for all groups with, for instance, the Asian poverty rate rising from 10.2 percent in 2007 to 11.8 percent in 2008. As data became available for the years 2009 to 2011, many economists were surprised that poverty rates appeared to level off or fall despite the widespread and lingering unemployment caused by the so-called Great Recession.

Measurement Issues

The poverty rates and trends in Figures 19.4 and 19.5 should be interpreted cautiously. The official income thresholds for defining poverty are necessarily arbitrary and therefore may inadequately measure the true extent of poverty in the United States.

Some observers say that the high cost of living in major metropolitan areas means that the official poverty thresholds exclude millions of families whose income is slightly above the poverty level but clearly inadequate to meet basic needs for food, housing, and medical care. These observers use city-by-city studies on "minimal income needs" to argue that poverty in the United States is much more widespread than officially measured and reported.

In contrast, some economists point out that using income to measure poverty understates the standard of living of many of the people who are officially poor. When individual, household, or family *consumption* is considered rather than family *income,* some of the poverty in the United States disappears. Some low-income families maintain their consumption by drawing down past savings, borrowing against future income, or selling homes. Moreover, many poor families receive substantial noncash benefits such as food stamps and rent subsidies that boost their living standards. Such "in-kind" benefits are not included in determining a family's official poverty status.

FIGURE 19.5 **Poverty-rate trends, 1959–2014.** Although the national poverty rate declined sharply between 1959 and 1969, it stabilized in the 1970s only to increase significantly in the early 1980s. Between 1993 and 2000 it substantially declined, before rising slightly again in the immediate years following the 2001 recession. Although poverty rates for African Americans and Hispanics are much higher than the average, they significantly declined during the 1990s. Poverty rates rose in 2008 in response to the recession that began in December 2007.

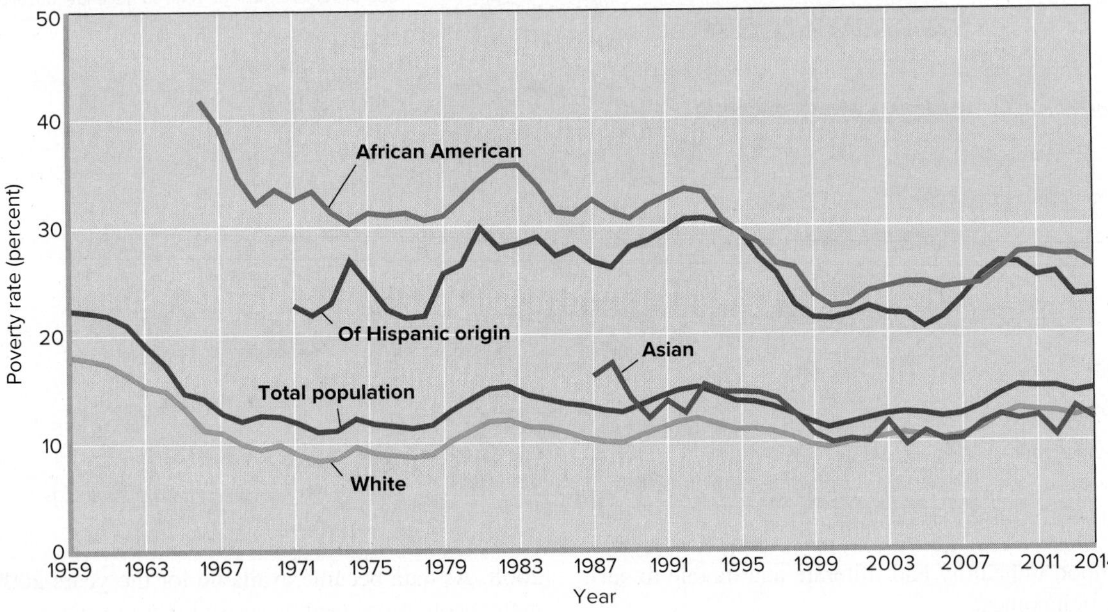

Source: Bureau of the Census, **www.census.gov**.

The U.S. Income-Maintenance System

LO19.6 Identify the major components of the income-maintenance program in the United States.

Regardless of how poverty is measured, economists agree that considerable poverty exists in the United States. Helping those who have very low income is a widely accepted goal of public policy. A wide array of antipoverty programs, including education and training programs, subsidized employment, minimum-wage laws, and antidiscrimination policies, are designed to increase the earnings of the poor. In addition, a number of income-maintenance programs were devised to reduce poverty; the most important are listed in Table 19.3. These programs involve large expenditures and have numerous beneficiaries.

The U.S. income-maintenance system consists of two kinds of programs: (1) social insurance and (2) public assistance, or "welfare." Both are known as **entitlement programs** because all eligible persons are legally entitled to receive the benefits set forth in the programs.

Social Insurance Programs

Social insurance programs partially replace earnings that have been lost due to retirement, disability, or temporary unemployment; they also provide health insurance for the elderly. The main social insurance programs are Social Security, unemployment compensation, and Medicare. Benefits are viewed as earned rights and do not carry the stigma of public charity. These programs are financed primarily out of federal payroll taxes. In these programs the entire population shares the risk of an individual's losing income because of retirement, unemployment, disability, or illness. Workers (and employers) pay a part of wages into a government fund while they are working. The workers are then entitled to benefits when they retire or when a specified misfortune occurs.

Social Security and Medicare The major social insurance program is known as **Social Security.** It is a federal pension program that replaces part of the earnings lost when workers retire, become disabled, or die. This gigantic program ($882 billion in 2014) is financed by compulsory payroll taxes levied on both employers and employees. Workers currently may retire at age 65 and receive full retirement benefits or retire early at age 62 with reduced benefits. When a worker dies, benefits accrue to his or her family survivors. Special provisions provide benefits for disabled workers.

Social Security covers over 90 percent of the workforce; some 59 million people receive Social Security benefits, with benefits for retirees averaging about $1,230 per month. In 2014, those benefits were financed with a combined Social Security and Medicare payroll tax of 15.3 percent, with both

TABLE 19.3 Characteristics of Major Income-Maintenance Programs

Program	Basis of Eligibility	Source of Funds	Form of Aid	Expenditures,* Billions	Beneficiaries, Millions
Social Insurance Programs					
Social Security	Age, disability, or death of parent or spouse; life-time work earnings	Federal payroll tax on employers and employees	Cash	$882	59
Medicare	Age or disability	Federal payroll tax on employers and employees	Subsidized health insurance	$634	54
Unemployment compensation	Unemployment	State and federal payroll taxes on employers	Cash	$32	7.4
Public Assistance Programs					
Supplemental Security Income (SSI)	Age or disability; income	Federal revenues	Cash	$55	8.3
Temporary Assistance for Needy Families (TANF)	Certain families with children; income	Federal-state-local revenues	Cash and services	$10	4
Supplemental Nutrition Assistance Program (SNAP)	Income	Federal revenues	Cash via EBT cards	$76	46
Medicaid	Persons eligible for TANF or SSI and medically indigent	Federal-state-local revenues	Subsidized medical services	$495	67
Earned-income tax credit (EITC)	Low-wage working families	Federal revenues	Refundable tax credit, cash	$61	28

*Expenditures by federal, state, and local governments; excludes administrative expenses.

Source: Social Security Administration, *Annual Statistical Supplement, 2014,* **www.socialsecurity.gov**; U.S. Department of Agriculture, **www.fns.usda.gov**; Internal Revenue Service, **www.irs.gov/taxstats**; and other government sources. Latest data.

the worker and the employer paying 7.65 percent on their first $118,500 of earnings. The 7.65 percent tax comprises 6.2 percent for Social Security and 1.45 percent for Medicare. Self-employed workers pay a tax of 15.3 percent.

Medicare is a federal insurance program that provides health insurance benefits to those 65 or older and people who are disabled. It is financed by payroll taxes on employers and employees. This overall 2.9 percent tax is paid on all work income, not just on the first $118,500. Medicare also makes available supplementary low-cost insurance programs that help pay for doctor visits and prescription drug expenses. In 2014, some 54 million people received Medicare benefits. The benefits paid to recipients totaled $634 billion.

The number of retirees drawing Social Security and Medicare benefits is rapidly rising relative to the number of workers paying payroll taxes. As a result, Social Security and Medicare face serious long-term funding problems. These fiscal imbalances have spawned calls to reform the programs.

Unemployment Compensation All 50 states sponsor unemployment insurance programs called **unemployment compensation,** a federal–state social insurance program that makes income available to workers who are unemployed. This insurance is financed by a relatively small payroll tax, paid by employers, which varies by state and by the size of the firm's payroll. Any insured worker who becomes unemployed can, after a short waiting period, become eligible for benefit payments. The program covers almost all wage and salary workers. The size of payments and the number of weeks they are made available vary considerably from state to state. Generally, benefits approximate 33 percent of a worker's wages up to a certain maximum payment. In 2014 benefits averaged about $333 weekly. The number of beneficiaries and the level of total disbursements varies with economic conditions.

Typically, unemployment compensation payments last a maximum of 26 weeks. But during recessions—when unemployment rates soar—Congress extends the benefits for additional weeks.

Public Assistance Programs

Public assistance programs (welfare) provide benefits to people who are unable to earn income because of permanent disabling conditions or who have no or very low income and also have dependent children. These programs are financed out of

CONSIDER THIS . . .

Welfare Cliffs

Source: © Christopher Kimmel/Getty Images RF

A **welfare cliff** occurs when an employed welfare recipient's overall income (= wages they earn from work + government benefits) will fall if they earn more money at work. This happens because many types of welfare benefits are withdrawn abruptly if the recipient's income rises above a particular level.

As an example, a single mother named Linda earning wages of $30,000 per year in the state of Pennsylvania would qualify for about $7,000 in housing credits, which would raise her overall income to $37,000. But the housing credits are withdrawn for anyone earning more than $30,000 per year. Thus, if Linda went out and earned an extra $1,000 per year, her overall income would actually fall by $6,000 (= $1,000 more earned income minus $7,000 of lost housing credits).

Welfare cliffs discourage welfare recipients from working more, transitioning into higher-paying jobs, or undertaking the education and training that could lead to higher income levels. One solution would be to have welfare benefits taper off gently as earned income rises. In our example, suppose that Linda's housing credit fell by only $500 (rather than $7,000) when she earned that extra $1,000. In that case, she would come out $500 ahead and thus have an incentive to work more.

general tax revenues and are regarded as public charity. They include "means tests" that require that individuals and families demonstrate low incomes in order to qualify for aid. The federal government finances about two-thirds of the welfare program expenditures, and the rest is paid for by the states.

Many needy persons who do not qualify for social insurance programs are assisted through the federal government's **Supplemental Security Income (SSI)** program. This is a federal program (financed by general tax revenues) that provides a uniform nationwide minimum income for the aged, blind, and disabled who are unable to work and who do not qualify for Social Security aid. In 2014 the average monthly payment was $733 for individuals and $1,100 for couples with both people eligible. More than half the states provide additional income supplements to the aged, blind, and disabled.

Temporary Assistance for Needy Families (TANF) is the basic welfare program for low-income families in the United States. The program is financed through general federal tax revenues and consists of lump-sum payments of federal money to states to operate their own welfare and work programs. These lump-sum payments are called TANF funds, and in 2014 about 3.5 million people (including children) received TANF assistance. TANF expenditures in 2014 were about $10 billion.

In 1996 TANF replaced the six-decade-old Aid for Families with Dependent Children (AFDC) program. Unlike that welfare program, TANF established work requirements and placed limits on the length of time a family can receive welfare payments. Specifically, the TANF program:

- Set a lifetime limit of 5 years on receiving TANF benefits and requires able-bodied adults to work after receiving assistance for 2 years.
- Ended food-stamp eligibility for able-bodied persons age 18 to 50 (with no dependent children) who are not working or engaged in job-training programs.
- Tightened the definition of "disabled children" as it applies for eligibility of low-income families for Supplemental Security Income (SSI) assistance.
- Established a 5-year waiting period on public assistance for new legal immigrants who have not become citizens.

In 1996, about 12.6 million people, or about 4.8 percent of the U.S. population, were welfare recipients. By the middle of 2007 those totals had declined to 3.9 million and 1.3 percent of the population. The recession that began in December 2007 pushed the number of welfare recipients up to about 4.4 million by December 2009. These recipients accounted for about 1.4 percent of the population in December 2009.

The welfare program has greatly increased the employment rate (= employment/population) for single mothers with children under age 6—a group particularly prone to welfare dependency. Today, that rate is about 13 percentage points higher than it was in 1996.

The **Supplemental Nutrition Assistance Program (SNAP)** was formerly known as the food-stamp program. SNAP is a federal program (financed through general tax revenues) that permits eligible low-income persons to obtain vouchers that can be used to buy food. It is designed to provide all low-income Americans with a nutritionally adequate diet. Under the program, eligible households receive monthly deposits of spendable electronic money on specialized debit cards known as Electronic Benefit Transfer (EBT) cards. The EBT cards are designed so that the deposits can be spent only on food. The amount deposited onto a family's EBT card varies inversely with the family's earned income.

Medicaid is a federal program (financed by general tax revenues) that provides medical benefits to people covered by the SSI and TANF (basic welfare) programs. It helps finance the medical expenses of individuals participating in those programs.

The **earned-income tax credit (EITC)** is a refundable federal tax credit provided to low-income wage earners to supplement their families' incomes and encourage work. It is available for low-income working families, with or without children. The credit reduces the federal income taxes that such families owe or provides them with cash payments if the credit exceeds their tax liabilities. The purpose of the credit is to offset Social Security taxes paid by low-wage earners and thus keep the federal government from "taxing families into poverty." In essence, EITC is a wage subsidy from the federal government that works out to be as much as $2 per hour for the lowest-paid workers with families. Under the program many people owe no income tax and receive direct checks from the federal government once a year. According to the Internal Revenue Service, 28 million taxpayers received $61 billion in payments from the EITC in 2014.

Several other welfare programs are not listed in Table 19.3. Some provide help in the form of noncash transfers. Head Start provides education, nutrition, and social services to economically disadvantaged 3- and 4-year-olds. Housing assistance in the form of rent subsidies and funds for construction is available to low-income families. Pell grants provide assistance to undergraduate students from low-income families. Low-income home energy assistance provides help with home heating bills. Other programs—such as veteran's assistance and black lung benefits—provide cash assistance to those eligible.

AP QUICK REVIEW 19.2

- ✓ The basic argument for income equality is that it maximizes total utility by equalizing the marginal utility of the last dollar of income received by all people.
- ✓ The basic argument for income inequality is that it is an unavoidable consequence of maintaining the economic incentives for production.
- ✓ By government standards, 46.7 million people in the United States, or 15 percent of the population, lived in poverty in 2014.
- ✓ The U.S. income-maintenance system includes both social insurance programs and public assistance (welfare) programs.

Economic Analysis of Discrimination

LO19.7 Discuss labor market discrimination and how it might affect hiring decisions and wages.

Although the majority of Americans who are in the lowest income quintile or in poverty are white, African Americans and Hispanics are in those two categories disproportionally to their total populations. For that reason, the percentages of all African Americans and Hispanics receiving public assistance from the TANF, SSI, and food stamp programs are also well above the average for the entire population. This fact raises the question of what role, if any, discrimination plays in reducing wages for some and increasing wages for others.

Discrimination is the practice of according people inferior treatment (for example, in hiring, occupational access, education and training, promotion, wage rate, or working conditions) on the basis of some factor such as race, gender, or ethnicity. People who practice discrimination are said to exhibit a prejudice or a bias against the groups they discriminate against.

Prejudice reflects complex, multifaceted, and deeply ingrained beliefs and attitudes. Thus, economics can contribute some insights into discrimination but no detailed explanations. With this caution in mind, let's look more deeply into the economics of discrimination.

Taste-for-Discrimination Model

The **taste-for-discrimination model** examines prejudice by using the emotion-free language of demand theory. It views discrimination as resulting from a preference or taste for which the discriminator is willing to pay. The model assumes that, for whatever reason, prejudiced people experience a subjective or psychic cost—a disutility—whenever they must interact with those they are biased against. Consequently, they are willing to pay a certain "price" to avoid interactions with the nonpreferred group. The size of this price depends directly on the degree of prejudice.

The taste-for-discrimination model is general, since it can be applied to race, gender, age, and religion. But our discussion focuses on employer discrimination, in which employers discriminate against nonpreferred workers. For concreteness, we will look at a white employer discriminating against African-American workers.

Discrimination Coefficient A prejudiced white employer behaves as if employing African-American workers would add a cost. The amount of this cost—this disutility—is reflected in a **discrimination coefficient**, *d*, measured in monetary units. Because the employer is not prejudiced against whites, the cost of employing a white worker is the white wage rate, W_w. However, the employer's perceived "cost" of employing an African-American worker is the African-American worker's wage rate, W_{aa}, *plus* the cost *d* involved in the employer's prejudice, or $W_{aa} + d$.

The prejudiced white employer will have no preference between African-American and white workers when the total cost per worker is the same, that is, when $W_w = W_{aa} + d$. Suppose the market wage rate for whites is $10 and the monetary value of the disutility the employer attaches to hiring African

Americans is \$2 (that is, $d = \$2$). This employer will be indifferent between hiring African Americans and whites only when the African-American wage rate is \$8, since at this wage the perceived cost of hiring either a white or an African-American worker is \$10:

$$\$10 \text{ white wage} = \$8 \text{ African-American wage} + \$2 \text{ discrimination coefficient}$$

It follows that our prejudiced white employer will hire African Americans only if their wage rate is sufficiently below that of whites. By "sufficiently" we mean at least the amount of the discrimination coefficient.

The greater a white employer's taste for discrimination as reflected in the value of *d*, the larger the difference between white wages and the lower wages at which African Americans will be hired. A "color-blind" employer whose *d* is \$0 will hire equally productive African Americans and whites impartially if their wages are the same. A blatantly prejudiced white employer whose *d* is infinity would refuse to hire African Americans even if the African-American wage were zero.

Most prejudiced white employers will not refuse to hire African Americans under all conditions. They will, in fact, *prefer* to hire African Americans if the actual white-black wage difference in the market exceeds the value of *d*. In our example, if whites can be hired at \$10 and equally productive African Americans at only \$7.50, the biased white employer will hire African Americans. That employer is willing to pay a wage difference of up to \$2 per hour for whites to satisfy his or her bias, but no more. At the \$2.50 actual difference, the employer will hire African Americans.

Conversely, if whites can be hired at \$10 and African Americans at \$8.50, whites will be hired. Again, the biased employer is willing to pay a wage difference of up to \$2 for whites; a \$1.50 actual difference means that hiring whites is a "bargain" for this employer.

Prejudice and the Market African-American–White Wage Ratio For a particular supply of African-American workers, the actual African-American–white wage ratio—the ratio determined in the labor market—will depend on the collective prejudice of white employers. To see why, consider Figure 19.6, which shows a labor market for African-American workers. Initially, suppose the relevant labor demand curve is D_1, so the equilibrium African-American wage is \$8 and the equilibrium level of African-American employment is 16 million. If we assume that the white wage (not shown) is \$10, then the initial African-American–white wage ratio is 0.8 (= \$8/\$10).

Now assume that prejudice against African-American workers increases—that is, the collective *d* of white employers rises. An increase in *d* means an increase in the perceived cost of African-American labor at each African-American wage rate, and that reduces the demand for African-American labor, say, from D_1 to D_2. The African-American wage rate falls from \$8 to \$6 in the market, and the level of African-American employment declines from 16 million to 12 million. The increase in white employer prejudice reduces the African-American wage rate and thus the actual African-American–white wage ratio. If the white wage rate remains at \$10, the new African-American–white ratio is 0.6 (= \$6/\$10).

FIGURE 19.6 The African-American wage and employment level in the taste-for-discrimination model. An increase in prejudice by white employers as reflected in higher discrimination coefficients would decrease the demand for African-American workers, here from D_1 to D_2, and reduce the African-American wage rate and level of African-American employment. Not shown, this drop in the African-American wage rate would lower the African-American–white wage ratio. In contrast, if prejudice were reduced such that discrimination coefficients of employers declined, the demand for African-American labor would increase, as from D_1 to D_3, boosting the African-American wage rate and level of employment. The higher African-American wage rate would increase the African-American–white wage ratio.

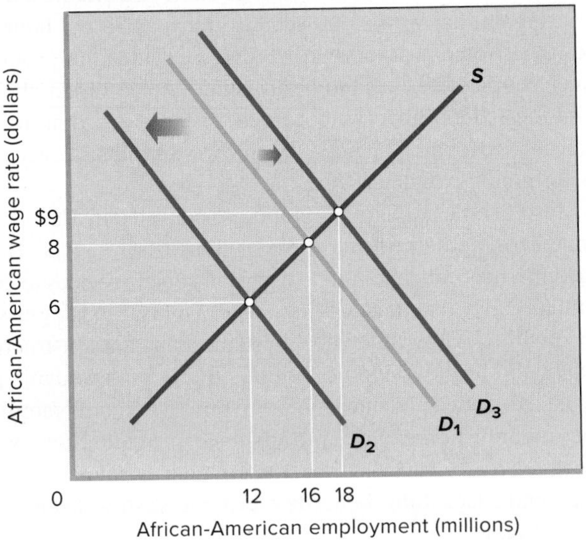

Conversely, suppose social attitudes change such that white employers become less biased and their discrimination coefficient as a group declines. This decreases the perceived cost of African-American labor at each African-American wage rate, so the demand for African-American labor increases, as from D_1 to D_3. In this case, the African-American wage rate rises to \$9, and employment of African-American workers increases to 18 million. The decrease in white employer prejudice increases the African-American wage rate and thus the actual African-American–white wage ratio. If the white wage remains at \$10, the new African-American–white wage ratio is 0.9 (= \$9/\$10).

Competition and Discrimination The taste-for-discrimination model suggests that competition will reduce discrimination in the very long run, as follows: The actual African-American–white wage difference for equally productive workers—say, $2—allows nondiscriminators to hire African Americans for less than whites. Firms that hire African-American workers will therefore have lower actual wage costs per unit of output and lower average total costs than will the firms that discriminate. These lower costs will allow nondiscriminators to underprice discriminating competitors, eventually driving them out of the market.

But critics of this implication of the taste-for-discrimination model say that it overlooks entry barriers to new firms and point out that progress in eliminating racial discrimination has been slow. Discrimination based on race has persisted in the United States and other market economies decade after decade. To explain why, economists have proposed alternative models.

Statistical Discrimination

A second theory of discrimination centers on the concept of **statistical discrimination,** in which people are judged on the basis of the average characteristics of the group to which they belong, rather than on their own personal characteristics or productivity. For example, insurance rates for teenage males are higher than those for teenage females. The difference is based on factual evidence indicating that, on average, young males are more likely than young females to be in accidents. But many young men are actually less accident-prone than the average young woman, and those men are discriminated against by having to pay higher insurance rates. The uniqueness of the theory of statistical discrimination is its suggestion that discriminatory outcomes are possible even where there is no prejudice.

Labor Market Example How does statistical discrimination show itself in labor markets? Employers with job openings want to hire the most productive workers available. They have their personnel department collect information concerning each job applicant, including age, education, and prior work experience. They may supplement that information with preemployment tests, which they feel are helpful indicators of potential job performance. But collecting detailed information about job applicants is very expensive, and predicting job performance on the basis of limited data is difficult. Consequently, some employers looking for inexpensive information may consider the *average* characteristics of women and minorities in determining whom to hire. They are in fact practicing statistical discrimination when they do so. They are using gender, race, or ethnic background as a crude indicator of production-related attributes.

Example: Suppose an employer who plans to invest heavily in training a worker knows that on average women are less likely to be career-oriented than men, more likely to quit work in order to care for young children, and more likely to refuse geographic transfers. Thus, on average, the return on the employer's investment in training is likely to be less when choosing a woman than when choosing a man. All else equal, when choosing between two job applicants, one a woman and the other a man, this employer is likely to hire the man.

Note what is happening here. Average characteristics for a *group* are being applied to *individual* members of that group. The employer is falsely assuming that *each and every* woman worker has the same employment tendencies as the *average* woman. Such stereotyping means that numerous women who are career-oriented, who do not plan on quitting work in order to care for young children, and who are flexible as to geographic transfers will be discriminated against.

Profitable, Undesirable, but Not Malicious The firm that practices statistical discrimination is not being malicious in its hiring behavior (although it may be violating antidiscrimination laws). The decisions it makes will be rational and profitable because *on average* its hiring decisions are likely to be correct. Nevertheless, many people suffer because of statistical discrimination, since it blocks the economic betterment of capable people. And since it is profitable, statistical discrimination tends to persist.

Occupational Segregation: The Crowding Model

The practice of **occupational segregation**—the crowding of women, African Americans, and certain ethnic groups into less desirable, lower-paying occupations—is still apparent in the U.S. economy. Statistics indicate that women are disproportionately concentrated in a limited number of occupations such as teaching, nursing, and secretarial and clerical jobs. African Americans and Hispanics are crowded into low-paying jobs such as those of laundry workers, cleaners and household aides, hospital orderlies, agricultural workers, and other manual laborers.

Let's look at a model of occupational segregation, using women and men as an example.

The Model The character and income consequences of occupational discrimination are revealed through a labor supply and demand model. We make the following assumptions:

- The labor force is equally divided between men and women workers. Let's say there are 6 million male and 6 million female workers.
- The economy comprises three occupations, X, Y, and Z, with identical labor demand curves, as shown in Figure 19.7.
- Men and women have the same labor-force characteristics; each of the three occupations could be filled equally well by men or by women.

FIGURE 19.7 The economics of occupational segregation. (a) Because 1 million women are excluded from occupation X, the wage rate for men in that occupation is *M* rather than *B*. (b) Because another 1 million women are excluded from occupation Y, the wage for men in occupation Y is also *M* rather than *B*. (c) Because the 2 million women excluded from occupations X and Y are crowded into occupation Z, the wage rate for women there is *W* rather *B*. The elimination of discrimination will create flows of 1 million women to occupation X and 1 million women to occupation Y. The wage rate will equalize at *B* in all three occupations and the nation's output will rise by the sum of the two blue areas minus the single green area.

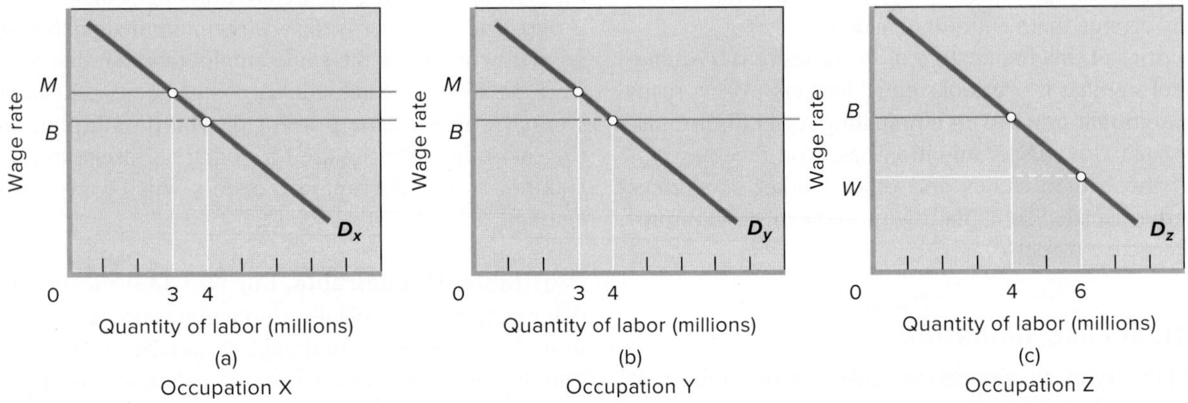

Effects of Crowding Suppose that, as a consequence of discrimination, the 6 million women are excluded from occupations X and Y and crowded into occupation Z, where they earn wage *W*. The men distribute themselves equally among occupations X and Y, meaning that 3 million male workers are in each occupation and have a common wage of *M*. (If we assume that there are no barriers to mobility between X and Y, any initially different distribution of males between X and Y would result in a wage differential between the two occupations. That would prompt labor shifts from the low- to the high-wage occupation until an equal distribution occurred.)

Because women are crowded into occupation Z, labor supply (not shown) is larger and their wage rate *W* is much lower than *M*. Because of the discrimination, this is an equilibrium situation that will persist as long as the crowding occurs. The occupational barrier means women cannot move into occupations X and Y in pursuit of a higher wage.

The result is a loss of output for society. To see why, recall again that labor demand reflects labor's marginal revenue product, which is labor's contribution to domestic output. Thus, the blue areas for occupations X and Y in Figure 19.7 show the decrease in domestic output—the market value of the marginal output—caused by subtracting 1 million women from each of these occupations. Similarly, the green area for occupation Z shows the increase in domestic output caused by moving 2 million women into occupation Z. Although society would gain the added output represented by the green area in occupation Z, it would lose the output represented by the sum of the two blue areas in occupations X and Y. That output loss exceeds the output gain, producing a net output loss for society.

Eliminating Occupational Segregation Now assume that through legislation or sweeping changes in social attitudes, discrimination disappears. Women, attracted by higher wage rates, shift from occupation Z to X and Y; 1 million women move into X and another 1 million move into Y. Now there are 4 million workers in Z, and occupational segregation is eliminated. At that point there are 4 million workers in each occupation, and wage rates in all three occupations are equal, here at *B*. That wage equality eliminates the incentive for further reallocations of labor.

The new, nondiscriminatory equilibrium clearly benefits women, who now receive higher wages; it hurts men, who now receive lower wages. But women were initially harmed and men benefited through discrimination; removing discrimination corrects that situation.

Society also gains. The elimination of occupational segregation reverses the net output loss just discussed. Adding 1 million women to each of occupations X and Y in Figure 19.7 increases domestic output by the sum of the two blue areas. The decrease in domestic output caused by losing 2 million women from occupation Z is shown by the green area. The sum of the two increases in domestic output in X and Y exceeds the decrease in domestic output in Z. With the end of the discrimination, 2 million women workers have moved from occupation Z, where their contribution to domestic output (their MRP) is low, to higher-paying occupations X and Y, where their contribution to domestic output is high. Thus society gains a more efficient allocation of resources from the removal of occupational discrimination.

Example: The easing of occupational barriers has led to a surge of women gaining advanced degrees in some high-paying professions. In recent years, for instance, the percentage of law degrees and medical degrees awarded to women has exceeded 50 percent, compared with less than 10 percent in 1970.

LAST WORD

U.S. Family Wealth and Its Distribution

Between 1995 and 2010, Family Wealth Rose Rapidly for Both the Typical Family as Well as Very Well-Off Families. But Then the Collapse of the Housing Bubble and the Recession of 2007–2009 Greatly Reduced the Typical Family's Level of Wealth.

The latest findings on U.S. family wealth (= net worth = assets *minus* liabilities) were reported in 2014. The data were obtained from the Survey of Consumer Finances and *The State of Working America*. The information includes data on median family wealth, average family wealth, and the distribution of wealth in the United States. *Median family wealth* is the wealth received by the family at the midpoint of the wealth distribution; *average family wealth* is simply total wealth divided by the number of families.

As shown in Table 1, median and average family wealth, adjusted for inflation, both grew rapidly between 1995 and 2007. But then the 2007–2009 recession caused both to drop precipitously. Median wealth, in particular, fell so far that its 2010 value of $77,300 was nearly 8 percent lower than the $84,000 value observed 15 years earlier, in 1995. Even worse, the decline continued over the next few years, with the 2013 value falling to $76,000, or about 10 percent less than the 1995 value.

Most of the decline was due to the 30 percent fall in average housing prices that took place during and after the recession. Millions of people who had taken out loans to buy houses found themselves "underwater" on their home mortgages because the market values of their homes had fallen below what they owed on their loans. That meant that they had *negative* wealth in terms of their housing purchases. As a result, overall wealth levels dropped sharply.

Table 2 looks at the distribution of family wealth for various percentile groups and reveals that the distribution of wealth is highly unequal. In 2010 the wealthiest 10 percent of families owned almost 77 percent of the total wealth and the top 1 percent owned about 35 percent. By contrast, the bottom 90 percent held only about 23 percent of the total wealth. Moreover, the general trend is toward greater inequality. The lowest 90 percent of families saw their share fall from about 32 percent of total U.S. wealth in 1995 to only about 23 percent in 2010.

Source: © Kelly Ryerson/Getty Images

Tables 1 and 2 raise many interesting questions: Will the inequality of wealth continue to grow in the future? If so, what are the implications for the future character of American society? Should government do more, or less, in the future to try to redistribute wealth? Would new government policies to redistribute wealth endanger or slow the creation of wealth and the growth of income for average Americans? As of 2016, the federal estate (inheritance) tax had a zero percent rate up to $5.43 million and then a 40 percent rate on anything above $5.43 million. There is a vigorous debate about whether this represents too much or too little in the way of estate taxation.

Sources: "Changes in U.S. Family Finances from 2004 to 2007: Evidence from the Survey of Consumer Finances," *Federal Reserve Bulletin,* vol. 95 (February 2009); "Ponds and Streams: Wealth and Income in the U.S., 1989 to 2007," Survey of Consumer Finances working paper, January 2009, p. 35; Lawrence Mishel, Josh Bivens, Elise Gould, and Heidi Shierholz, *The State of Working America,* 12th ed., Economic Policy Institute (2012).

TABLE 1 Median and Average Family Wealth, Survey Years 1995–2010 (in 2010 Dollars)

Year	Median	Average*
1995	$ 84,000	$307,900
1998	98,100	386,700
2001	106,100	487,000
2004	107,200	517,100
2007	126,400	584,600
2010	77,300	498,800
2013	76,000	500,400

*The averages greatly exceed the medians because the averages are boosted by the multibillion-dollar wealth of a relatively few families.

TABLE 2 Percentage of Total Family Wealth Held by Different Groups, Survey Years 1995–2010

	Percentage of Total Wealth by Group		
Year	Bottom 90%	Top 10%	Top 1%
1995	32.2%	67.8%	34.6%
1998	31.4	68.6	33.9
2001	30.2	69.8	32.7
2004	30.4	69.5	33.4
2007	28.5	71.5	33.8
2010	23.3	76.7	35.4

Cost to Society as Well as to Individuals

It is obvious from all three models of discrimination that discrimination by characteristics such as race, ethnicity, gender, or age imposes costs on those who are discriminated against. They have lower wages, less access to jobs, or both. Preferred workers in turn benefit from discrimination through less job competition, greater job access, and higher wages. But discrimination does more than simply transfer earnings from some people to others, thus contributing to income inequality and increasing poverty. Where it exists, discrimination also diminishes the economy's total output and income. In that regard, discrimination acts much like any other artificial barrier to free competition. By arbitrarily blocking qualified individuals from high-productivity (and thus high-wage) jobs, discrimination keeps those discriminated against from providing their maximum contribution to society's total output and total income. In terms of production possibilities analysis, discrimination locates society inside the production possibilities curve that would be available to it if there were no discrimination.

Discrimination redistributes a diminished amount of total income.

AP QUICK REVIEW 19.3

- ✓ Discrimination occurs when workers who have the same abilities, education, training, and experience as other workers receive inferior treatment with respect to hiring, occupational access, promotion, or wages.
- ✓ The taste-for-discrimination model sees discrimination as representing a preference or "taste" for which the discriminator is willing to pay.
- ✓ The theory of statistical discrimination says that employers often wrongly judge individuals on the basis of average group characteristics rather than on personal characteristics, thus harming those discriminated against.
- ✓ The crowding model of discrimination suggests that when women and minorities are systematically excluded from high-paying occupations and crowded into low-paying ones, their wages and society's domestic output are reduced.

SUMMARY

LO19.1 Explain how income inequality in the United States is measured and described.

The distribution of income in the United States reflects considerable inequality. The richest 20 percent of households receive 51.2 percent of total income, while the poorest 20 percent receive 3.1 percent.

The Lorenz curve shows the percentage of total income received by each percentage of households. The extent of the gap between the Lorenz curve and a line of total equality illustrates the degree of income inequality.

The Gini ratio measures the overall dispersion of the income distribution and is found by dividing the area between the diagonal and the Lorenz curve by the entire area below the diagonal. The Gini ratio ranges from zero to 1, with higher ratios signifying greater degrees of income inequality.

LO19.2 Discuss the extent and sources of income inequality.

Recognizing that the positions of individual families in the distribution of income change over time and incorporating the effects of noncash transfers and taxes would reveal less income inequality than do standard census data. Government transfers (cash and noncash) greatly lessen the degree of income inequality; taxes also reduce inequality, but not nearly as much as transfers.

Causes of income inequality include differences in abilities, in education and training, and in job tastes, along with discrimination, inequality in the distribution of wealth, and an unequal distribution of market power.

LO19.3 Demonstrate how income inequality has changed since 1975.

Census data show that income inequality has increased since 1975. The major cause of the recent increases in income inequality is a rising demand for highly skilled workers, which has boosted their earnings significantly.

LO19.4 Debate the economic arguments for and against income inequality.

The basic argument for income equality is that it maximizes consumer satisfaction (total utility) from a particular level of total income. The main argument for income inequality is that it provides the incentives to work, invest, and assume risk and is necessary for the production of output, which, in turn, creates income that is then available for distribution.

LO19.5 Relate how poverty is measured and its incidence by age, gender, ethnicity, and other characteristics.

Current statistics reveal that 15 percent of the U.S. population lives in poverty. Poverty rates are particularly high for female-headed families, young children, African Americans, and Hispanics.

LO19.6 Identify the major components of the income-maintenance program in the United States.

The present income-maintenance program in the United States consists of social insurance programs (Social Security, Medicare, and unemployment compensation) and public assistance programs (SSI, TANF, food stamps, Medicaid, and the earned-income tax credit).

LO19.7 Discuss labor market discrimination and how it might affect hiring decisions and wages.

Discrimination relating to the labor market occurs when women or minorities having the same abilities, education, training, and experience as men or white workers are given inferior treatment with respect to hiring, occupational choice, education and training, promotion, and wage rates. Discrimination redistributes national income and, by creating inefficiencies, diminishes its size.

In the taste-for-discrimination model, some white employers have a preference for discrimination, measured by a discrimination coefficient d. Prejudiced white employers will hire African-American workers only if their wages are at least d dollars below those of whites. The model indicates that declines in the discrimination coefficients of white employers will increase the demand for African-American workers, raising the African-American wage rate and the ratio of African-American wages to white wages. It also suggests that competition may eliminate discrimination in the long run.

Statistical discrimination occurs when employers base employment decisions about *individuals* on the average characteristics of *groups* of workers. That can lead to discrimination against individuals even in the absence of prejudice.

The crowding model of occupational segregation indicates how white males gain higher earnings at the expense of women and certain minorities who are confined to a limited number of occupations. The model shows that discrimination also causes a net loss of domestic output.

TERMS AND CONCEPTS

income inequality
Lorenz curve
Gini ratio
income mobility
noncash transfers
equality-efficiency trade-off
poverty rate
entitlement programs
social insurance programs
Social Security
Medicare
unemployment compensation
public assistance programs
welfare cliff
Supplemental Security Income (SSI)
Temporary Assistance for Needy Families (TANF)
Supplemental Nutrition Assistance Program (SNAP)
Medicaid
earned-income tax credit (EITC)
discrimination
taste-for-discrimination model
discrimination coefficient
statistical discrimination
occupational segregation

The following and additional problems can be found in connect

DISCUSSION QUESTIONS

1. Use quintiles to briefly summarize the degree of income inequality in the United States. How and to what extent does government reduce income inequality? LO19.1
2. Assume that Al, Beth, Carol, David, and Ed receive incomes of \$500, \$250, \$125, \$75, and \$50, respectively. Construct and interpret a Lorenz curve for this five-person economy. What percentage of total income is received by the richest quintile and by the poorest quintile? LO19.1
3. How does the Gini ratio relate to the Lorenz curve? Why can't the Gini ratio exceed 1? What is implied about the direction of income inequality if the Gini ratio declines from 0.42 to 0.35? How would one show that change of inequality in the Lorenz diagram? LO19.1
4. Why is the lifetime distribution of income more equal than the distribution in any specific year? LO19.1
5. Briefly discuss the major causes of income inequality. With respect to income inequality, is there any difference between inheriting property and inheriting a high IQ? Explain. LO19.2
6. What factors have contributed to increased income inequality since 1975? LO19.3
7. Should a nation's income be distributed to its members according to their contributions to the production of that total income or according to the members' needs? Should society attempt to equalize income or economic opportunities? Are the issues of equity and equality in the distribution of income synonymous? To what degree, if any, is income inequality equitable? LO19.4
8. Do you agree or disagree? Explain your reasoning. "There need be no trade-off between equality and efficiency. An 'efficient' economy that yields an income distribution that many regard as unfair may cause those with meager incomes to become discouraged and stop trying. So efficiency may be undermined. A fairer distribution of rewards may generate a higher average productive effort on the part of the population, thereby enhancing efficiency. If people think they are playing a fair economic game and this belief causes them to try harder, an economy with an equitable income distribution may be efficient as well."[7] LO19.4

[7]Paraphrased from Andrew Schotter, *Free Market Economics* (New York: St. Martin's Press, 1985), pp. 30–31.

9. Comment on or explain: LO19.4
   a. Endowing everyone with equal income will make for very unequal enjoyment and satisfaction.
   b. Equality is a "superior good"; the richer we become, the more of it we can afford.
   c. The mob goes in search of bread, and the means it employs is generally to wreck the bakeries.
   d. Some freedoms may be more important in the long run than freedom from want on the part of every individual.
   e. Capitalism and democracy are really a most improbable mixture. Maybe that is why they need each other—to put some rationality into equality and some humanity into efficiency.
   f. The incentives created by the attempt to bring about a more equal distribution of income are in conflict with the incentives needed to generate increased income.
10. How do government statisticians determine the poverty rate? How could the poverty rate fall while the number of people in poverty rises? Which group in each of the following pairs has the higher poverty rate: (*a*) children or people age 65 or over? (*b*) African Americans or foreign-born noncitizens? (*c*) Asians or Hispanics? LO19.5
11. What are the essential differences between social insurance and public assistance programs? Why is Medicare a social insurance program, whereas Medicaid is a public assistance program? Why is the earned-income tax credit considered to be a public assistance program? LO19.6
12. The labor demand and supply data in the following table relate to a single occupation. Use them to answer the questions that follow. Base your answers on the taste-for-discrimination model. LO19.7

Quantity of Hispanic Labor Demanded, Thousands	Hispanic Wage Rate	Quantity of Hispanic Labor Supplied, Thousands
24	$16	52
30	14	44
35	12	35
42	10	28
48	8	20

   a. Plot the labor demand and supply curves for Hispanic workers in this occupation.
   b. What are the equilibrium Hispanic wage rate and quantity of Hispanic employment?
   c. Suppose the white wage rate in this occupation is $16. What is the Hispanic-to-white wage ratio?
   d. Suppose a particular employer has a discrimination coefficient *d* of $5 per hour. Will that employer hire Hispanic or white workers at the Hispanic-white wage ratio indicated in part *c*? Explain.
   e. Suppose employers as a group become less prejudiced against Hispanics and demand 14 more units of Hispanic labor at each Hispanic wage rate in the table. What are the new equilibrium Hispanic wage rate and level of Hispanic employment? Does the Hispanic-white wage ratio rise or fall? Explain.
   f. Suppose Hispanics as a group increase their labor services in that occupation, collectively offering 14 more units of labor at each Hispanic wage rate. Disregarding the changes indicated in part *e*, what are the new equilibrium Hispanic wage rate and level of Hispanic employment? Does the Hispanic-white wage ratio rise, or does it fall?
13. Males under the age of 25 must pay far higher auto insurance premiums than females in this age group. How does this fact relate to statistical discrimination? Statistical discrimination implies that discrimination can persist indefinitely, while the taste-for-discrimination model suggests that competition might reduce discrimination in the long run. Explain the difference. LO19.7
14. Use a demand-and-supply model to explain the impact of occupational segregation or "crowding" on the relative wage rates and earnings of men and women. Who gains and who loses from the elimination of occupational segregation? Is there a net gain or a net loss to society? Explain. LO19.7
15. **LAST WORD** Go to Table 1 in the Last Word and compute the ratio of average wealth to median wealth for each of the 7 years. What trend do you find? What is your explanation for the trend? The federal estate tax redistributes wealth in two ways: by encouraging charitable giving, which reduces the taxable estate, and by heavily taxing extraordinarily large estates and using the proceeds to fund government programs. Do you favor repealing the estate tax? Explain.

AP REVIEW QUESTIONS

1. The greater the area between the Lorenz curve and the diagonal in the Lorenz Curve diagram, the LO19.1
   a. Smaller is the Gini ratio and the greater is the degree of income inequality.
   b. Larger is the Gini ratio and the greater is the degree of income inequality.
   c. Smaller is the Gini ratio and the greater is the percentage of the population in poverty.
   d. Larger is the Gini ratio and the greater is the percentage of the population in poverty.
   e. Larger is the Gini ratio and the lower is the degree of income inequality.
2. Some part of income inequality is likely to be the result of discrimination. But other factors responsible for inequality include (select as many as apply): LO19.2
   a. Differences in abilities and talents.
   b. Differences in education and training.
   c. Different preferences for work versus leisure.
   d. Different preferences for low-paying but safe jobs relative to high-paying but dangerous jobs.
   e. Different levels of experience.
3. The basic argument for income inequality is that LO19.4
   a. The very rich establish consumption patterns that are desirable for the rest of society to emulate.

b. The rich buy luxury goods that soon become affordable to everyone else because of economies of scale.
c. Income inequality is essential to maintain incentives to produce.
d. Income equality means less total utility for all.
e. Inequality undermines incentives and tends to reduce the size of the national income.

4. The basic economic argument for greater income equality is that LO19.4
a. An equal distribution of income is the logical outcome of any tax-transfer program.
b. Because citizens enjoy political equality, they are also entitled to economic equality.
c. A more equal distribution of income will tend to maximize incentives to work, invest, and assume risk.
d. A more equal distribution of a given amount of income will increase the total utility of consumers.
e. A more equal distribution of a given amount of income will increase the marginal utility of consumers.

5. Suppose that the last dollar that Victoria receives as income brings her a marginal utility of 10 utils while the last dollar that Fredrick receives as income brings him a marginal utility of 15 utils. If our goal is to maximize the combined total utility of Victoria and Fredrick, we should: LO19.4
a. Redistribute income from Victoria to Fredrick.
b. Redistribute income from Fredrick to Victoria.
c. Not engage in any redistribution because the current situation already maximizes total utility.
d. Provide each with less income.
e. Tax Fredrick's income, but not Victoria's income.

6. If women are crowded into elementary education and away from fire fighting, wages in fire fighting will tend to be ____________ than if women weren't crowded into elementary education. LO19.7
a. Higher.
b. Lower.

PROBLEMS

1. In 2015, *Forbes* magazine listed Bill Gates, the founder of Microsoft, as the richest person in the United States. His personal wealth was estimated to be $76 billion. Given that there were about 322 million people living in the United States that year, how much could each person have received if Gates's wealth had been divided equally among the population of the United States? (Hint: A billion is a 1 followed by 9 zeros while a million is a 1 followed by six zeros.) LO19.1

2. Imagine an economy with only two people. Larry earns $20,000 per year, while Roger earns $80,000 per year. As shown in the following figure, the Lorenz curve for this two-person economy consists of two line segments. The first runs from the origin to point *a*, while the second runs from point *a* to point *b*. LO19.1

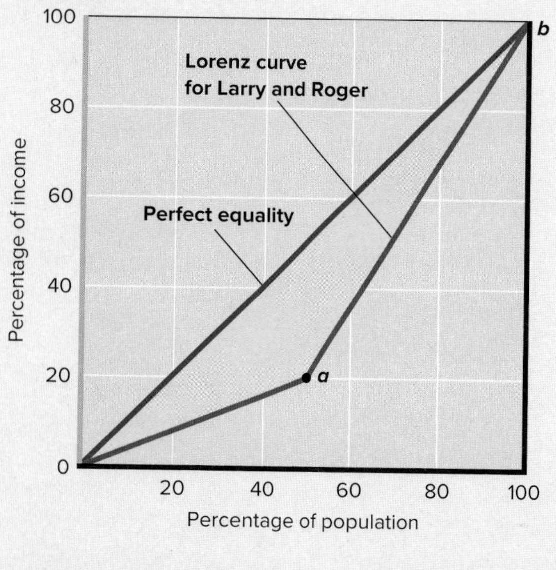

a. Calculate the Gini ratio for this two-person economy using the geometric formulas for the area of a triangle (= ½ × base × height) and the area of a rectangle (= base × height). (Hint: The area under the line segment from point *a* to point *b* can be thought of as the sum of the area of a particular triangle and the area of a particular rectangle.)
b. What would the Gini ratio be if the government taxed $20,000 away from Roger and gave it to Larry? (Hint: The figure will change.)
c. Start again with Larry earning $20,000 per year and Roger earning $80,000 per year. What would the Gini ratio be if both their incomes doubled? How much has the Gini ratio changed from before the doubling in incomes to after the doubling in incomes?

3. In 2015, many unskilled workers in the United States earned the federal minimum wage of $7.25 per hour. By contrast, average earnings in 2015 were about $23 per hour, and certain highly skilled professionals, such as doctors and lawyers, earned $100 or more per hour. LO19.6
a. If we assume that wage differences are caused solely by differences in productivity, how many times more productive was the average worker than a worker being paid the federal minimum wage? How many times more productive was a $100-per-hour lawyer compared to a worker earning minimum wage?
b. Assume that there are 20 minimum-wage workers in the economy for each $100-per-hour lawyer. Also assume that both lawyers and minimum-wage workers work the same number of hours per week. If everyone works 40 hours per week, how much does a $100-per-hour lawyer earn a week? How much does a minimum-wage worker earn a week?
c. Suppose that the government pairs each $100-per-hour lawyer with 20 nearby minimum-wage workers. If the government taxes 25 percent of each lawyer's income each

week and distributes it equally among the 20 minimum-wage workers with whom each lawyer is paired, how much will each of those minimum-wage workers receive each week? If we divide by the number of hours worked each week, how much does each minimum-wage worker's weekly transfer amount to on an hourly basis?

d. What if instead the government taxed each lawyer 100 percent before dividing the money equally among the 20 minimum-wage workers with whom each lawyer is paired—how much per week will each minimum-wage worker receive? And how much is that on an hourly basis?

4. The desire to maximize profits can work against racial and other types of discrimination. To see this, consider two equally productive accountants named Ted and Jared. Ted is black, and Jared is white. Both can complete 10 audits per month. **LO19.7**

a. Suppose that for any accounting firm that hires either Ted or Jared, all the other costs of performing an audit (besides paying either Ted or Jared) come to $1,000 per audit. If the going rate that must be paid to hire an accountant is $7,000 per month, how much will it cost an accounting firm to produce one audit if it hires either Ted or Jared to do the work?

b. If the market price that accounting firms charge their clients for an audit is $1,800, what would the accounting profit per audit be for a firm that hired either Ted or Jared? What is the profit rate as a percentage?

c. Suppose that firm *A* dislikes hiring black accountants, while firm *B* is happy to hire them. So Ted ends up working at firm *B* rather than firm *A*. If Ted works 11 months per year, how many audits will he complete for firm *B* each year? How much in accounting profits will firm *B* earn each year from those audits?

d. Because firm *A* passed on hiring Ted because he was black, firm *A* is forgoing the profits it could have earned if it had hired Ted. If the firm is willing to forgo up to $5,000 per year in profit to avoid hiring blacks, by how many dollars will firm *A* regret its decision not to hire Ted?

Part SEVEN

AP

GDP, Growth, and Instability

This part introduces macroeconomics and the measurement of macroeconomic variables. First, we look at aggregate output produced within the economy during a time period, referred to as ***Gross Domestic Product (GDP).*** While not a true measure of economic welfare, GDP is the most important indicator of the overall health of the economy. Changes in GDP track closely to changes in employment and, inversely, with changes in unemployment. Variations in GDP are referred to as ***business cycles,*** with downturns in GDP, a ***recession,*** in which people lose their jobs, being of particular concern to policy makers. We will discuss elements of ***economic growth,*** the expansion of the economy's capacity to produce. Finally, we look at how economists measure both ***employment and unemployment,*** as well as ***price level changes*** (increasing ones representing ***inflation*** and decreasing ones representing ***deflation***).

Chapter 20

An Introduction to Macroeconomics

Learning Objectives

LO20.1 **Explain why economists focus on GDP, inflation, and unemployment when assessing the health of an entire economy.**

LO20.2 **Discuss why sustained increases in living standards are a historically recent phenomenon.**

LO20.3 **Identify why saving and investment are key factors in promoting rising living standards.**

LO20.4 **Describe why economists believe that "shocks" and "sticky prices" are responsible for short-run fluctuations in output and employment.**

LO20.5 **Characterize the degree to which various prices in the economy are sticky.**

LO20.6 **Explain why the greater flexibility of prices as time passes causes economists to utilize different macroeconomic models for different time horizons.**

AP Chapter Focus

Macroeonomics focuses its attention on national economies while seeking answers to the largest of economic questions. For instance: Why are some countries really wealthy while others are really poor? Why do some countries enjoy sustained, long-run increases in living standards, while other countries simply stagnate? Why do all countries—even the richest—go through alternating boom and bust periods? And is there anything that governments can do to improve living standards or fight recessions?

This chapter provides an overview of the data that macroeconomists use to measure the status and growth of an entire economy as well as a preview of the models that they use to help explain both long-run growth and short-run fluctuations. Because it is an overview chapter, it raises many unanswered questions. Subsequent chapters will explain these topics in much greater detail.

AP Performance and Policy

LO20.1 Explain why economists focus on GDP, inflation, and unemployment when assessing the health of an entire economy.

As you know from Chapter 1, macroeconomics studies the behavior of the economy as a whole. It is primarily concerned with two topics: long-run economic growth and the short-run fluctuations in output and employment that are often referred to as the **business cycle.** These phenomena are closely related because they happen simultaneously. Economies show a distinct growth trend that leads to higher output and higher standards of living in the long run, but in the short run there is considerable variability. Sometimes growth proceeds more rapidly and sometimes it proceeds more slowly. It may even turn negative for a while so that output and living standards actually decline, a situation referred to as a **recession.** That is precisely what happened in late 2007 and continued through 2008 and into 2009. The economy experienced what has come to be called the Great Recession.

To understand how economies operate and how their performance might be improved, economists collect and analyze economic data. An almost infinite number of data items can be looked at, including the amount of new construction taking place each month, how many ships laden with cargo are arriving at our ports each year, and how many new inventions have been patented in the last few weeks. That being said, macroeconomists tend to focus on just a few statistics when trying to assess the health and development of an economy. Chief among these are real GDP, unemployment, and inflation.

- **Real GDP**, or **real gross domestic product**, measures the value of final goods and services produced within the borders of a country during a specific period of time, typically a year. This statistic is very useful because it can tell us whether an economy's output is growing. For instance, if U.S. real GDP in one year is larger than in the previous year, we know that U.S. output increased from the first year to the next. To determine real GDP, government statisticians first calculate **nominal GDP,** which totals the dollar value of all goods and services produced within the borders of a country using *their current prices during the year that they were produced.* But because nominal GDP uses the prices in place in the year the output was produced, it suffers from a major problem: It can increase from one year to the next even if there is no increase in output. To see how, consider a commercial blacksmith who produced 10 iron spiral staircases last year and 10 identical staircases this year. Clearly, the blacksmith's output did not change. But if the price of each staircase rose from $10,000 last year to $20,000 this year, nominal GDP increased from $100,000 (= 10 × $10,000) to $200,000 (= 10 × $20,000). Without knowing about the price increase, we might unwisely conclude that the output of staircases increased from 10 to 20. Real GDP statistically eliminates these kinds of price changes. As a result, we can compare real GDP numbers from one year to the next and really know if there is a change in output (rather than prices). Because more output means greater consumption possibilities—including not only the chance to consume more fun things such as movies, vacations, and video games, but also more serious things like better health care and safer roads—economists and policymakers are deeply committed to encouraging a large and growing real GDP.
- **Unemployment** is the state a person is in if he or she cannot get a job despite being willing to work and actively seeking work. High rates of unemployment are undesirable because they indicate that a nation is not using a large portion of its most important resource—the talents and skills of its people. Unemployment is a waste because we must count as a loss all the goods and services that unemployed workers could have produced if they had been working. Researchers have also drawn links between higher rates of unemployment and major social problems like higher crime rates and greater political unrest as well as higher rates of depression, heart disease, and other illnesses among unemployed individuals.
- **Inflation** is an increase in the overall level of prices. As an example, consider all the goods and services bought by a typical family over the course of one year. If the economy is experiencing inflation, it will cost the family more money to buy those goods and services this year than it cost to buy them last year. This can be troublesome for several reasons. First, if the family's income does not rise as fast as the prices of the goods and services that it consumes, it won't be able to purchase as much as it used to and its standard of living will fall. Along the same lines, a surprise jump in inflation reduces the purchasing power of people's savings. Savings that they believed would be able to buy them a specific amount of goods and services will turn out to buy them less than they expected due to the higher-than-expected prices.

Because these statistics are the standards by which economists keep track of long-run growth and short-run fluctuations, we will spend a substantial amount of time in the next few chapters examining how these statistics are computed, how well they are able to capture the well-being of actual people, and how they vary both across countries and over time. Once they are understood, we will build on them in subsequent chapters by developing macroeconomic models of both long-run growth and short-run fluctuations. These will help us understand how policymakers attempt to maximize growth while minimizing unemployment and inflation.

Macroeconomic models also clarify many important questions about the powers and limits of government economic policy. These include:

- Can governments promote long-run economic growth?
- Can they reduce the severity of recessions by smoothing out short-run fluctuations?
- Are certain government policy tools such as manipulating interest rates (monetary policy) more effective at

mitigating short-run fluctuations than other government policy tools such as changes in tax rates or levels of government spending (fiscal policy)?

- Is there a trade-off between lower rates of unemployment and higher rates of inflation?
- Does government policy work best when it is announced in advance or when it is a surprise?

The answers to these questions are of crucial importance because of the vast differences in economic performance experienced by national economies at different times. For instance, the amount of output generated by the U.S. economy grew at an average rate of 2.7 percent per year between 1995 and the start of the recession of 2007–2009, while the amount of output generated by the Japanese economy grew at an average rate of only 1.0 percent per year over the same time period. In 2008 and 2009, however, the U.S. economy lost 8 million jobs, and the unemployment rate rose from 4.6 percent to as high as 10.1 percent. In 2015, after more than a half-decade of recovery, the unemployment rate was 5.3 percent in the United States, 25.0 percent in Greece, 3.6 percent in South Korea, 10.4 percent in France, and 40.6 percent in Haiti. At the same time, the inflation rate was 0.1 percent in the United States, 2.2 percent in Norway, 2.7 percent in Mexico, 6.6 percent in Kenya, and a very high 121.7 percent in Venezuela.

Our models will help us understand why such large differences in rates of growth, unemployment, and inflation exist among countries and why those rates can change so substantially from one period to another. These models also will provide significant insights on how government policies can influence rates of growth, unemployment, and inflation.

AP QUICK REVIEW 20.1

✓ Macroeconomics is concerned with the performance of the aggregate economy. In particular, topics of importance include long-run economic growth and short-run economic fluctuations.

✓ Macroeconomists focus on three key economic statistics: real GDP, unemployment, and inflation.

✓ *Real GDP* is the value of final goods and services produced within a country over a specific time period, adjusted for price level. *Unemployment* data reflect those who want, but cannot find, a job. *Inflation* is an increase in the overall level of prices.

AP The Miracle of Modern Economic Growth

LO20.2 Discuss why sustained increases in living standards are a historically recent phenomenon.

Rapid and sustained economic growth is a modern phenomenon. Before the Industrial Revolution began in the late 1700s in England, standards of living showed virtually no growth over hundreds or even thousands of years. For instance, the standard of living of the average Roman peasant was virtually the same at the start of the Roman Empire around the year 500 B.C. as it was at the end of the Roman Empire 1,000 years later. Similarly, historians and archaeologists have estimated that the standard of living enjoyed by the average Chinese peasant was essentially the same in the year A.D. 1800 as it was in the year A.D. 100.

That is not to say that the Roman and Chinese economies did not expand over time. They did. In fact, their total outputs of goods and services increased many times over. The problem was that as they did, their populations went up by similar proportions so that the amount of output *per person* remained virtually unchanged.

This historical pattern continued until the start of the Industrial Revolution, which ushered in not only factory production and automation but also massive increases in research and development so that new and better technologies were constantly being invented. The result was that output began to grow faster than the population. This meant that living standards began to rise as the amount of output *per person* increased.

Not all countries experienced this phenomenon, but those that did were said to be experiencing **modern economic growth** (in which output per person rises) as compared with earlier times in which output (but not output per person) increased. Under modern economic growth, the annual increase in output per person is often not large, perhaps 2 percent per year in countries such as England that were the first to industrialize. But when compounded over time, an annual growth rate of 2 percent adds up very rapidly. Indeed, it implies that the standard of living will double every 35 years. So if the average citizen of a country enjoying 2 percent growth begins this year with an income of $10,000, in 35 years that person will have an income of $20,000. And 35 years after that there will be another doubling so that her income in 70 years will be $40,000. And 35 years after that, the average citizen's income will double again to $80,000. Such high rates of growth are amazing when compared to the period before modern economic growth when standards of living remained unchanged century after century.

The vast differences in living standards seen today between rich and poor countries are almost entirely the result of the fact that only some countries have experienced modern economic growth. Indeed, before the start of the Industrial Revolution in the late 1700s, living standards around the world were very similar, so much so that the average standard of living in the richest parts of the world was at most only two or three times higher than the standard of living in the poorest parts of the world. By contrast, the citizens of the richest nations today have material standards of living that are on average more than 50 times higher than those experienced by citizens of the poorest nations, as can be seen by the GDP per person data for the year 2011 given in Global Perspective 20.1.

GLOBAL PERSPECTIVE 20.1

GDP per Person, Selected Countries

Country	**GDP per Person, 2014** (U.S. dollars based on purchasing power parity)
Switzerland	$58,171
United States	54,360
Saudi Arabia	52,397
France	40,498
United Kingdom	40,163
Japan	37,442
South Korea	35,379
Russia	26,138
Mexico	17,150
China	13,131
India	5,758
Tanzania	2,742
Zimbabwe	2,067
North Korea	1,800
Burundi	865

Source: International Monetary Fund, **www.imf.org**, for all countries except for North Korea, the estimate for which is from the *CIA World Factbook*, **www.cia.gov.**

Global Perspective 20.1 facilitates international comparisons of living standards by making three adjustments to each country's GDP. First, it converts each country's GDP from its own currency into U.S. dollars so that there is no confusion about the values of different currencies. Second, it divides each country's GDP measured in dollars by the size of its population. The resulting number, *GDP per person,* is the average amount of output each person in each country could have if each country's total output were divided equally among its citizens. It is a measure of each country's average standard of living. Third, the table uses a method called *purchasing power parity* to adjust for the fact that prices are much lower in some countries than others. By making this adjustment, we can trust that $1 of GDP per person in the United States represents about the same quantity of goods and services as $1 of GDP per person in any of the other countries. The resulting numbers—GDP per person adjusted for purchasing power parity—are presented in Global Perspective 20.1.

AP QUICK REVIEW 20.2

- ✓ Before the Industrial Revolution, living standards did not show any sustained increases over time because any increase in output tended to be offset by an equally large increase in population.
- ✓ Since the Industrial Revolution, many nations have experienced *modern per capita economic growth* in which output grows faster than population—so that living standards rise over time.

Saving, Investment, and Choosing between Present and Future Consumption

LO20.3 Identify why saving and investment are key factors in promoting rising living standards.

At the heart of economic growth is the principle that to raise living standards over time, an economy must devote at least some fraction of its current output to increasing future output. As implied in Chapter 1, this process requires flows of both saving and investment, which we will define and discuss before returning to why they are so important for economic growth.

- **Saving** occurs when current consumption is less than current output (or when current spending is less than current income).
- **Investment** happens when resources are devoted to increasing future output—for instance by building a new research facility in which scientists invent the next generation of fuel-efficient automobiles or by constructing a modern, super-efficient factory. (A caution: In economics, the term "investment" differs from common usage. To understand why, be sure to read the nearby Consider This box.)

When thinking about why saving and investment are so important for economic growth, the key point is that the amount of investment is ultimately limited by the amount of saving. The only way that more output can be directed at investment activities is if saving increases. But that, in turn, implies that individuals and society as a whole must make trade-offs between current and future consumption. This is true because the only way to pay for more investment—and the higher levels of future consumption that more investment can generate—is to increase present saving. But increased saving can only come at the price of reduced current consumption. Individuals and society as a whole must therefore wrestle with a choice between present consumption and future consumption. They must decide how to balance the reductions in current consumption required to fund current investment against the increases in future consumption that the added current investment will make possible.

CONSIDER THIS . . .

Source: © Stephen Brashear/Getty Images

Economic versus Financial Investment

Economics students often are confused by how the word "investment" is used in economics. This is understandable, because economists draw a distinction between "financial investment" and "economic investment."

Financial investment captures what ordinary people mean when they say investment, namely, the purchase of assets like stocks, bonds, and real estate in the hope of reaping a financial gain. Anything of monetary value is an asset and, in everyday usage, people purchase—or "invest" in—assets hoping to receive a financial gain, either by eventually selling them at higher prices than they paid for them or by receiving a stream of payments from others who are allowed to use the asset. By contrast, when economists say "investment," they are referring to **economic investment,** which relates to the creation and expansion of business enterprises. Specifically, economic investment only includes spending on the production and accumulation of newly created capital goods such as machinery, tools, factories, and warehouses. For example, economic investment will occur when the airplane shown in the accompanying photo is purchased by a commercial airline.

For economists, purely financial transactions, such as swapping cash for a stock or a bond, are not "investment." Neither are the purchases of factories or apartment buildings built in previous years. These transactions simply transfer the ownership of financial assets or existing real assets from one party to another. They do not purchase newly created capital goods. As such, they are great examples of financial investment, but not of economic investment. So now that you know the difference, remember that purely financial transactions, like buying Google stock or a five-year-old factory, are indeed referred to as "investment"—except in economics!

Banks and Other Financial Institutions

Households are the principal source of savings. But businesses are the main economic investors. So how does the pool of savings generated by households when they spend less than they consume get transferred to businesses so that they can purchase newly created capital goods? The answer is through banks and other financial institutions such as mutual funds, pension plans, and insurance companies. These institutions collect the savings of households, rewarding savers with interest and dividends and sometimes capital gains (increases in asset values). The banks and other financial institutions then lend the funds to businesses, which invest in equipment, factories, and other capital goods.

Macroeconomics devotes considerable attention to money, banking, and financial institutions because a well-functioning financial system helps to promote economic growth and stability by encouraging saving and by properly directing that saving into the most productive possible investments. In contrast, a poorly functioning financial system can create serious problems for an economy.

AP QUICK REVIEW 20.3

- ✓ An economy grows where there are more resources or inputs available and/or when productivity increases. Savings from current output can be used for investment which increases the stock of capital and generates output growth. Thus, saving is crucial to increasing investment and, consequently, future output.
- ✓ Banks and other financial institutions channel household savings toward businesses, which invest in equipment, factories, and other capital goods.

AP Uncertainty, Expectations, and Shocks

LO20.4 Describe why economists believe that "shocks" and "sticky prices" are responsible for short-run fluctuations in output and employment.

Decisions about savings and investment are complicated by the fact that the future is uncertain. Investment projects sometimes produce disappointing results or even fail totally. As a result, firms spend considerable time trying to predict future trends so that they can, hopefully, invest only in projects that are likely to succeed. This implies that macroeconomics has to take into account **expectations** about the future.

The Importance of Expectations and Shocks

Expectations are hugely important for two reasons. The more obvious reason involves the effect that changing expectations have on current behavior. If firms grow more pessimistic about the future returns that are likely to come from current investments, they are going to invest less today than they would if they were more optimistic. Expectations therefore have a large effect on economic growth since increased pessimism will lead to less current investment and, subsequently, less future consumption.

The less-obvious reason that expectations are so important has to do with what happens when expectations are unmet. Firms are often forced to cope with **shocks**—situations in which they were expecting one thing to happen but then something else happened. For instance, consider a situation in which a firm decides to build a high-speed railroad that will shuttle passengers between Los Angeles and Las Vegas.

The firm expects it to be very popular and make a handsome profit. But if it unexpectedly turns out to be unpopular and loses money, the railroad must figure out how to respond. Should the railroad go out of business completely? Should it attempt to see if it can turn a profit by hauling cargo instead of passengers? Is there a possibility that the venture might succeed if the firm borrows $30 million from a bank to pay for a massive advertising campaign? These sorts of decisions are necessitated by the shock and surprise of having to deal with an unexpected situation.

Economies are exposed to both demand shocks and supply shocks. **Demand shocks** are unexpected changes in the demand for goods and services. **Supply shocks** are unexpected changes in the supply of goods and services. Note that the word *shock* only reveals that something unexpected has happened. It does not tell us whether what has happened is unexpectedly good or unexpectedly bad. To clarify this, economists use more specific terms. For instance, a *positive demand shock* refers to a situation in which demand turns out to be higher than expected, while a *negative demand shock* refers to a situation in which demand turns out to be lower than expected.

Demand Shocks and Sticky Prices

Economists believe that most short-run fluctuations in GDP and the business cycle are the result of demand shocks. Supply shocks do happen in some cases and are very important when they do occur. But we will focus most of our attention in this chapter and subsequent chapters on demand shocks, how they affect the economy, and how government policy may be able to help the economy adjust to them.

But why are demand shocks such a big problem? Why would we have to consider calling in the government to help deal with them? And why can't firms deal with demand shocks on their own?

The answer to these questions is that the prices of many goods and services are inflexible (slow to change, or "sticky") in the short run. As we will explain, this implies that price changes do not quickly equalize the quantities demanded of such goods and services with their respective quantities supplied. Instead, because prices are inflexible, the economy is forced to respond in the short run to demand shocks primarily through changes in output and employment rather than through changes in prices.

Example: A Single Firm Dealing with Demand Shocks and Sticky Prices

Although an economy as a whole is vastly more complex than a single firm, an analogy that uses a single car factory will be helpful in explaining why demand shocks and inflexible prices are so important to understanding most of the short-run fluctuations that affect the entire economy. Consider a car manufacturing company named Buzzer Auto. Like most companies, Buzzer Auto is in business to try to make a profit. Part of turning a profit involves trying to develop accurate expectations about future market conditions. Consequently, Buzzer constantly does market research to estimate future demand conditions so that it will, hopefully, only build cars that people are going to want to buy.

Setting Expectations After extensive market research, Buzzer concludes that it could earn a modest profit if it builds and staffs an appropriately sized factory to build an environmentally friendly SUV, which it decides to call the Prion. Buzzer's marketing economists collaborate with Buzzer's engineers and conclude that expected profits will be maximized if the firm builds a factory that has an optimal output rate of 900 cars per week. If the factory operates at this rate, it can produce Prions for only $36,500 per vehicle. This is terrific because the firm's estimates for demand indicate that a supply of 900 vehicles per week can be sold at a price of $37,000 per vehicle—meaning that if everything goes according to plan, Buzzer Auto should make an accounting profit of $500 on each Prion that it produces and sells. Expecting these future conditions, Buzzer decides to build the factory, staff it with workers, and begin making the Prion.

Look at Figure 20.1a, which shows the market for Prions when the vertical supply curve for Prions is fixed at the factory's optimal output rate of 900 cars per week. Notice that we have drawn in three possible demand curves. D_L corresponds to low demand for the Prion, D_M corresponds to the medium level of demand that Buzzer's marketing economists are expecting to materialize, and D_H corresponds to high demand for the Prion. Figure 20.1a is consistent with the marketing economists' expectations: If all goes according to plan and the actual demand that materializes is D_M, the equilibrium price will in fact be $37,000 per Prion and the equilibrium quantity demanded will be 900 cars per week. Thus, if all goes according to expectations, the factory will have exactly the right capacity to meet the expected quantity demanded at the sales price of $37,000 per vehicle. In addition, the firm's books will show a profit of $500 per vehicle on each of the 900 vehicles that it builds and expects to sell each week at that price.

Full Employment if There Are No Shocks Here is the key point. If expectations are always fulfilled, Buzzer Auto will never contribute to any of the short-run fluctuations in output and unemployment that affect real-world economies. First, if everything always goes according to plan and Buzzer Auto's expectations always come true, then the factory will always produce and sell at its optimal output rate of 900 cars per week. This would mean that it would never experience any fluctuations in output—either in the short run or in the long run.

AP FIGURE 20.1 The effect of unexpected changes in demand under flexible and fixed prices. (a) If prices are flexible, then no matter what demand turns out to be, Buzzer Auto can continue to sell its optimal output of 900 cars per week since the equilibrium price will adjust to equalize the quantity demanded with the quantity supplied. (b) By contrast, if Buzzer Auto sticks with a fixed-price policy, then the quantity demanded will vary with the level of demand. At the fixed price of $37,000 per vehicle, the quantity demanded will be 700 cars per week if demand is D_L, 900 cars per week if demand is D_M, and 1,150 cars per week if demand is D_H.

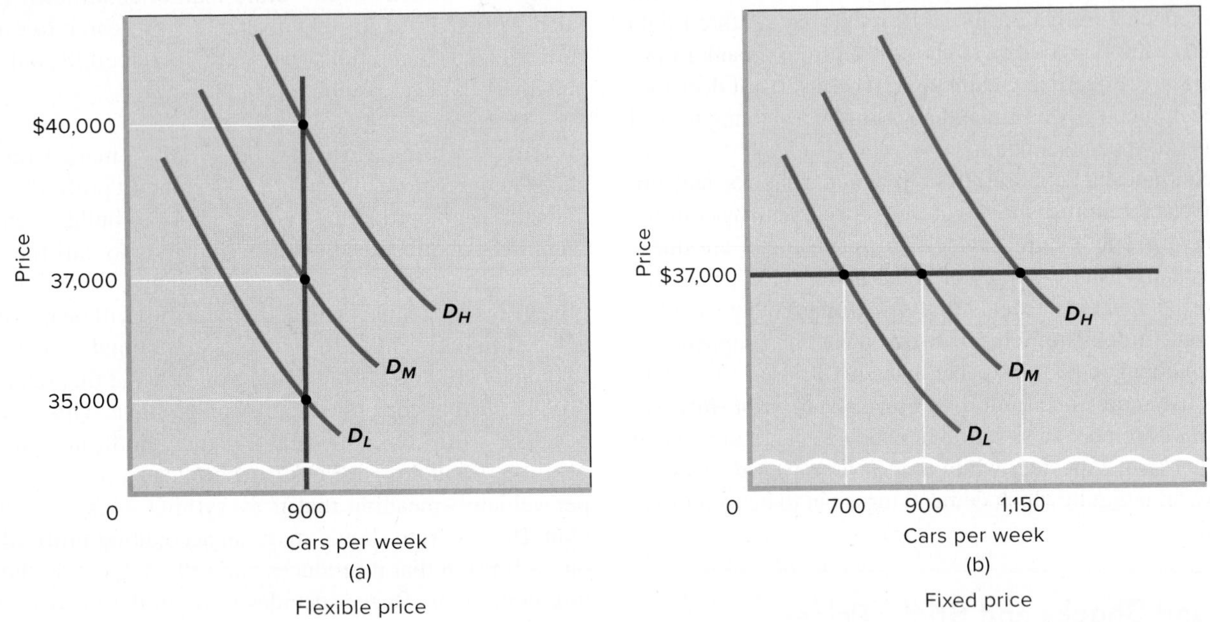

At the same time, since producing a constant output of 900 cars each week will always require the same number of workers, the factory's labor demand and employment should never vary. So if everything always goes according to plan, Buzzer Auto will never have any effect on unemployment because it will always hire a constant number of workers.

These facts imply that the short-run fluctuations in output and unemployment that we do see in the real world must be the result of shocks and things *not* going according to plan. In particular, business cycle fluctuations typically arise because the actual demand that materializes ends up being either lower or higher than what people were expecting. When this occurs, some adjustments will be necessary to bring quantity demanded and quantity supplied back into alignment. As we are about to explain, the nature of these adjustments varies hugely depending on whether prices are flexible or inflexible.

Price Changes if There Are Demand Shocks and Flexible Prices Figure 20.1a illustrates the case of adjusting to unexpected changes in demand *when prices are flexible*. Here, if demand is unexpectedly low at D_L, the market price can adjust downward to $35,000 per vehicle so that the quantity demanded at that price will still be equal to the factory's optimal output rate of 900 cars per week. On the other hand, if demand is unexpectedly high at D_H, the market price can adjust upward to $40,000 per vehicle so that the quantity demanded will still be equal to the factory's optimal output rate of 900 cars per week. These adjustments imply that *if* the price of Prions is free to quickly adjust to new equilibrium levels in response to unexpected changes in demand, the factory could always operate at its optimal output rate of 900 cars per week. Only the amount of profit or loss will vary with demand.

Applying this logic to the economy as a whole, *if* the prices of goods and services could always adjust quickly to unexpected changes in demand, then the economy could always produce at its optimal capacity since prices would adjust to ensure that the quantity demanded of each good and service would always equal the quantity supplied. Simply put, if prices were fully flexible, there would be no short-run fluctuations in output. Production levels would remain constant and unemployment levels would not change because firms would always need the same number of workers to produce the same amount of output.

Output Changes if There Are Demand Shocks and Sticky Prices In reality, many prices in the economy are inflexible and are not able to change rapidly when demand changes unexpectedly. Consider the extreme case shown in Figure 20.1b, in which the price of Prions is totally inflexible, fixed at $37,000 per Prion. Here, if demand unexpectedly falls from D_M to D_L, the quantity demanded at the fixed price of $37,000 will only be 700 cars per week, which is 200 cars fewer than the factory's optimal output of 900 cars per week. On the other hand, if demand is unexpectedly high at D_H, the quantity demanded at the fixed price of $37,000 will be 1,150 cars per week, which is 250 cars more than the factory's optimal output of 900 cars per week.

One way for companies to deal with these unexpected shifts in quantity demanded would be to try to adjust the factory's output to match them. That is, during weeks of low demand, Buzzer Auto could attempt to produce only 700 Prions, while during weeks of high demand it could try to produce 1,150 Prions. But this sort of flexible output strategy is very expensive because factories operate at their lowest costs when they are producing constantly at their optimal output levels; operating at either a higher or a lower production rate results in higher per-unit production costs.[1]

Knowing this, manufacturing firms typically attempt to deal with unexpected changes in demand by maintaining an inventory. An **inventory** is a store of output that has been produced but not yet sold. Inventories are useful because they can be allowed to grow or decline in periods when demand is unexpectedly low or high—thereby allowing production to proceed smoothly even when demand is variable. In our example, Buzzer Auto would maintain an inventory of unsold Prions. In weeks when demand is unexpectedly low, the inventory will increase by 200 Prions as the quantity demanded falls 200 vehicles short of the factory's optimal output. By contrast, during weeks when demand is unexpectedly high, the inventory will decrease as the quantity demanded exceeds the factory's optimal output by 250 cars. By allowing inventory levels to fluctuate with these unexpected shifts in demand, Buzzer Auto can respond by adjusting inventory levels rather than output levels. In addition, with any luck, the overall inventory level will stay roughly constant over time as unexpected increases and decreases in demand cancel each other out.

But consider what will happen if the firm experiences many successive weeks of unexpectedly low demand. For each such week, the firm's inventory of unsold Prions will increase by 200 cars. The firm's managers will not mind if this happens for a few weeks, but if it continues for many weeks, then the managers will be forced to cut production because, among other things, there will simply be no place to park so many unsold vehicles. More importantly, holding large numbers of unsold cars in inventory is unprofitable because while costs must be incurred to build an unsold car, an unsold car obviously brings in no revenue. Constantly rising inventories hurt firm profits and the management will want to reduce output if it sees inventories rising week after week due to unexpectedly low demand.

Generalizing from a Single Firm to the Entire Economy

This simplified story about a single car company explains why economists believe that a combination of unexpected changes in demand and inflexible prices are the key to understanding the short-run fluctuations that affect real-world economies. If prices were flexible, then the firm could always operate at the factory's optimal output level because prices would always adjust to ensure that it could sell its optimal output of 900 cars per week no matter what happens to demand. But if prices are inflexible, then an unexpected decline in demand that persists for any length of time will result in increasing inventories that will eventually force the firm's management to cut production to less than the optimal output level of 900 cars per week. When this happens, not only will output fall, but unemployment will also rise. The firm will lay off workers because fewer employees will be needed to produce fewer cars.

Generalizing this story to the economy as a whole, if demand falls off for many goods and services across the entire economy for an extended period of time, then the firms that make those goods and services will be forced to cut production. Manufacturing firms that maintain inventories will do so as they find inventories piling up due to sluggish sales. And services firms will do so as they encounter slow sales for their services. As both manufacturing and service output declines, the economy will recede, with GDP falling and unemployment rising.

On the other hand, if demand is unexpectedly high for a prolonged period of time, the economy will boom and unemployment will fall. In the case of our Prion example, for each week that demand is unexpectedly high, inventories will fall by 250 cars. If this keeps happening week after week, inventories will start to run out and the firm will have to react by increasing production to more than the optimal output rate of 900 cars per week so that orders do not go unfilled. When this happens, GDP will increase as more cars per week are produced and unemployment will fall because the factory will need to hire more workers to produce the larger number of cars.

AP QUICK REVIEW 20.4

- ✓ Economic shocks occur when events unfold in ways that people were not expecting.
- ✓ Demand shocks, such as changes in consumer expectations, are unexpected changes in the demand for goods and services; supply shocks, such as changes in input prices, are unexpected changes in the supply.
- ✓ Real-world prices are often inflexible or "sticky" (slow to change) in the short run, so the economy responds to demand shocks through changes in output and employment rather than changes in prices.

[1] If you have studied microeconomics, you will recognize that the firm's optimal output level of 900 cars per week is the level that minimizes the factory's average total cost (ATC) per vehicle of producing the Prion. Producing either more or fewer Prions will result in higher per-vehicle production costs.

CONSIDER THIS . . .

Source: © Miguel Villagran/Getty Images

The Great Recession

In 2008 and 2009, the United States encountered its worst financial and economic crisis since the Great Depression of the 1930s.

The recession was so severe that it has been dubbed the Great Recession. The recession was triggered by a steep decline in housing prices and a crisis involving mortgage loans and the financial securities built on them. Several key U.S. financial institutions collapsed or nearly failed, and lending markets largely froze. Despite government bailout efforts, the financial crisis eventually spread to the broader economy. Employment fell by 8 million workers between 2007 and the end of 2009, and the unemployment rate rose from 4.6 percent to 10.1 percent over that same period. Economic growth slumped to 0.4 percent in 2008 and to a *negative* 2.4 percent in 2009, compared with the 2.7 percent annual increases occurring between 1995 and 2007.

And this is where Buzzer Auto comes into the picture. The situation in Figure 20.1b, where the price of Buzzer's autos is inflexible, is highly relevant to the Great Recession. Like Buzzer, actual auto producers such as GM, Ford, and Chrysler, as well as thousands of producers of other products across the economy, established their production capacity and set their expectations of product demand on the basis of normal times. But demand for their goods and services fell unexpectedly because of greater consumer difficulty in getting loans, declining consumer confidence, and eventually declining income. The economy's price level (essentially a weighted average of all prices) declined only slightly, and that was after the recession was well under way. Therefore, real output (not prices) took the major brunt of the decline of total demand in the economy. Output dropped, employment plummeted, and unemployment soared.

How Sticky Are Prices?

LO20.5 Characterize the degree to which various prices in the economy are sticky.

We have just shown that **inflexible prices**—or **"sticky prices"** as economists are fond of saying—help to explain how unexpected changes in demand lead to the fluctuations in GDP and employment that occur over the course of the business cycle. Of course, not all prices are sticky. Indeed, the markets for many commodities and raw materials such as corn, oil, and natural gas feature extremely **flexible prices** that react within seconds to changes in supply and demand. By contrast, the prices of most of the final goods and services that people consume are quite sticky, with the average good or service going 4.3 months between price changes. To get a better appreciation for the fact that price stickiness varies greatly by product or service, look at Table 20.1, which gives the average number of months between price changes for various common goods and services. The prices of some products like gasoline and airline tickets change very rapidly—about once a month or even less than once a month. By contrast, haircuts and newspapers average more than two years between price changes. And coin-operated laundry machines average nearly four years between price changes!

TABLE 20.1 Average Number of Months between Price Changes for Selected Goods and Services

Item	Months
Coin-operated laundry machines	46.4
Newspapers	29.9
Haircuts	25.5
Taxi fare	19.7
Veterinary services	14.9
Magazines	11.2
Computer software	5.5
Beer	4.3
Microwave ovens	3.0
Milk	2.4
Electricity	1.8
Airline tickets	1.0
Gasoline	0.6

Source: Mark Bils and Peter J. Klenow, "Some Evidence on the Importance of Sticky Prices," *Journal of Political Economy*, October 2004, pp. 947–985. Used with permission of The University of Chicago Press via Copyright Clearance Center.

An important recent study has found that product prices are particularly sticky in response to widespread macroeconomic and monetary disturbances.[2] In later chapters, we will identify and discuss several factors that cause short-run price stickiness. But to keep the current discussion brief, let's focus on just two factors here. One factor is that companies selling final goods and services know that consumers prefer stable, predictable prices that do not fluctuate rapidly with changes in demand. Consumers would be annoyed if the same bottle of soda or shampoo cost one price one day, a different price the next day, and yet another price a week later. Volatile prices make planning more difficult, and, in addition, consumers who come in to buy the product on a day when the price happens to be high will likely feel that they are being taken advantage of. To avoid this, most firms try to maintain

[2]Jean Boivin, Marc P. Giannoni, and Illian Mihov, "Sticky Prices and Monetary Policy: Evidence from Disaggregated U.S. Data," *American Economic Review*, March 2009, pp. 350–384.

stable prices that do not change very often. Firms do have occasional sales where they lower prices, but on the whole they tend to try to keep prices stable and predictable—the result being price inflexibility.

Another factor that causes sticky prices has to do with the fact that in certain situations, a firm may be afraid that cutting its price may be counterproductive because its rivals might simply match the price cut—a situation often referred to as a "price war." This possibility is common among firms that only have one or two major rivals. Consider Coca-Cola and Pepsi. If Coca-Cola faces unexpectedly low demand for its product, it might be tempted to reduce its price in the hope that it can steal business away from Pepsi. But such a strategy would only work if Pepsi left its price alone when Coca-Cola cut its price. That, of course, is not likely. If Coca-Cola cuts its price, Pepsi will very likely cut its price in retaliation, doing its best to make sure that Coca-Cola doesn't steal away any of its customers. Thus, if Pepsi retaliates, Coca-Cola will only be made worse off by its decision to cut its price: It will not pick up much more business (because Pepsi also cut its price) and it will also be receiving less money for each bottle of Coke that it sells (because it lowered its own price.) Thus, firms that have to deal with the possibility of price wars often have sticky prices.

Categorizing Macroeconomic Models Using Price Stickiness

LO20.6 Explain why the greater flexibility of prices as time passes causes economists to utilize different macroeconomic models for different time horizons.

We have now demonstrated why price stickiness is believed to have such a large role in short-run economic fluctuations. It should be noted, however, that price stickiness moderates over time. This is true because firms that choose to use a fixed-price policy in the short run do not have to stick with that policy permanently. In particular, if unexpected changes in demand begin to look permanent, many firms will allow their prices to change so that price changes (in addition to quantity changes) can help to equalize quantities supplied with quantities demanded.

For this reason, economists speak of "sticky prices" rather than "stuck prices." Only in the very short run are prices totally inflexible. As time passes and prices are revised, the world looks much more like Figure 20.1a, in which prices are fully flexible, than Figure 20.1b, in which prices are totally inflexible. Indeed, the totally inflexible case shown in Figure 20.1b can be thought of as the extremely short-run response to an unexpected change in demand, while the fully flexible case shown in Figure 20.1a can be thought of as a longer-run response to an unexpected change in demand. In terms of time durations, the extreme short run can be thought of as the first few weeks and months after a demand shock, while the long run can be thought of as extending from many months to several years after a demand shock happens.

This realization is very useful in categorizing and understanding the differences between the various macroeconomic models that we will be presenting in subsequent chapters. For instance, the aggregate expenditures model presented in Chapter 25 assumes perfectly inflexible prices (and wages) and thus is a model in which prices are not just sticky but completely stuck. By contrast, the aggregate demand–aggregate supply model presented in Chapter 26 allows for flexible prices (with or without flexible wages) and is therefore useful for understanding how the economy behaves over longer periods of time.

As you study these various models, keep in mind that we need different models precisely because the economy behaves so differently depending on how much time has passed after a demand shock. The differences in behavior result from the fact that prices go from stuck in the extreme short run to fully flexible in the long run. Using different models for different stages in this process gives us much better insights into not only how economies actually behave but also how various government and central bank policies may have different effects in the short run when prices are fixed versus the long run when prices are flexible.

Where will we go from here? In the remainder of Part 7, we examine how economists measure GDP and why GDP has expanded over time. Then, we discuss the terminology of business cycles and explore the measurement and types of unemployment and inflation. At that point you will be well-prepared to examine the economic models, monetary considerations, and stabilization policies that lie at the heart of macroeconomics.

AP QUICK REVIEW 20.5

- ✓ Many commodity prices are extremely flexible and change constantly, but other prices in the economy change only very infrequently and are referred to as "sticky" or downward rigid.
- ✓ Some prices are inflexible in order to please retail customers, others because rival firms are afraid that price changes may trigger a price war.
- ✓ Prices tend to become more flexible over time, so that as time passes, the economy can react to demand shocks with price changes as well as with output and employment changes.
- ✓ Different macroeconomics models are used for the short run, during which prices are inflexible (such that demand shocks lead almost exclusively to output and employment changes), vs. for longer periods, during which prices become increasingly flexible (such that demand shocks lead more to price changes than to output and employment changes).

21 Chapter

Measuring Domestic Output and National Income

Learning Objectives:

LO21.1 **Explain how gross domestic product (GDP) is defined and measured.**

LO21.2 **Describe how expenditures on goods and services can be summed to determine GDP.**

LO21.3 **Explain how GDP can be determined by summing up all of the incomes that were derived from producing the economy's output of goods and services.**

LO21.4 **Describe the relationships among GDP, net domestic product, national income, personal income, and disposable income.**

LO21.5 **Discuss the nature and function of a GDP price index and describe the difference between nominal GDP and real GDP.**

LO21.6 **List and explain some limitations of the GDP measure.**

AP Chapter Focus

"Disposable Income Flat." "Personal Consumption Surges." "Investment Spending Stagnates." "GDP Up 4 Percent." These headlines, typical of those found on *Yahoo! Finance* or in *The Wall Street Journal,* give knowledgeable readers valuable information on the state of the economy. This chapter will help you interpret such headlines and understand the stories reported under them. Specifically, it will help you become familiar with the vocabulary and methods of national income accounting. Such accounting enables economists to measure the long-run rate of economic growth and identify the recessions and expansions associated with the economic ups and downs known as the business cycle. In addition, the terms and ideas that you encounter in this chapter will provide a needed foundation for the macroeconomic models found in subsequent chapters.

AP Assessing the Economy's Performance

LO21.1 Explain how gross domestic product (GDP) is defined and measured.

National income accounting measures the economy's overall performance. It does for the economy as a whole what private accounting does for the individual firm or for the individual household.

A business firm measures its flows of income and expenditures regularly—usually every 3 months or once a year. With that information in hand, the firm can gauge its

AP FIGURE 21.1 The expenditures and income approaches to GDP. There are two general approaches to measuring gross domestic product. We can determine GDP as the value of output by summing all expenditures on that output. Alternatively, with some modifications, we can determine GDP by adding up all the components of income arising from the production of that output.

Expenditures, or output, approach		Income, or allocations, approach
Consumption expenditures by households **plus** Investment expenditures by businesses **plus** Government purchases of goods and services **plus** Expenditures by foreigners	= GDP =	Wages **plus** Rents **plus** Interest **plus** Profits **plus** Statistical adjustments

The final-product approach and the value-added approach are two ways of looking at the same thing. What is spent on making a product is income to those who helped make it. If $350 is spent on manufacturing a coat, then $350 is the total income derived from its production.

We can look at GDP in the same two ways. We can view GDP as the sum of all the money spent in buying it. That is the *output approach*, or **expenditures approach.** Or we can view GDP in terms of the income derived or created from producing it. That is the *earnings* or *allocations approach*, or the **income approach.**

As illustrated in Figure 21.1, we can determine GDP for a particular year either by adding up all that was spent to buy total output or by adding up all the money that was derived as income from its production. Buying (spending money) and selling (receiving income) are two aspects of the same transaction. On the expenditures side of GDP, all final goods produced by the economy are bought either by three domestic sectors (households, businesses, and government) or by foreign buyers. On the income side (once certain statistical adjustments are made), the total receipts acquired from the sale of that total output are allocated to the suppliers of resources as wage, rent, interest, and profit.

Table 21.3 shows U.S. GDP for the year 2015 totaled up using the expenditures approach while Table 21.4 shows U.S. GDP for 2015 totaled up using the income approach. As you would expect, both methods reach the same conclusion: U.S. GDP in 2015 was $17,947 billion.

We will now go through both approaches in detail. Doing so will help you better understand both methods and, in particular, why the income accounting statement shown in Table 21.4 looks substantially more complicated than the income side of Figure 21.1.

AP The Expenditures Approach

LO21.2 Describe how expenditures on goods and services can be summed to determine GDP.

To determine GDP using the expenditures approach, we add up all the spending on final goods and services that has taken place throughout the year. National-income accountants use precise terms for the types of spending listed on the left side of Figure 21.1.

Personal Consumption Expenditures (C)

What we have called "consumption expenditures by households," the national income accountants call **personal consumption expenditures.** This term covers all expenditures by households on goods and services.

In a typical year, roughly 10 percent of these personal consumption expenditures are on **durable goods**—products that have expected lives of 3 years or more. Such goods include new automobiles, furniture, and refrigerators. Another 30 percent are on **nondurable goods**—products with less than 3 years of expected life. Included are goods like food, clothing, and gasoline. About 60 percent of personal consumption expenditures are on **services**—the work done by lawyers, hair stylists, doctors, mechanics, and other service providers. Because of this high percentage, economists sometimes refer to the U.S. economy as a *service economy*. National income accountants combine the household spending on durable goods, nondurable goods, and services and use the symbol C to designate the personal consumption expenditures component of GDP.

Gross Private Domestic Investment (I_g)

Under the heading **gross private domestic investment,** the accountants include the following items:

- All final purchases of machinery, equipment, and tools by business enterprises.
- All construction.
- Changes in inventories.
- Money spent on research and development (R&D) or for the creation of new works of art, music, writing, film, and so on.

Notice that this list, except for the first item, includes more than we have meant by "investment" so far. The second item

AP TABLE 21.3 Accounting Statement for the U.S. Economy Using the Expenditures (Receipts) Approach, 2015 (in Billions)

	Billions
Sum of:	
Personal consumption expenditures (C)	$12,272
Gross private domestic investment (I_g)	3,021
Government purchases (G)	3,183
Net exports (X_n)	−529
Equals:	
Gross domestic product	**$17,947**

Source: Bureau of Economic Analysis, **www.bea.gov**. All data are subject to government revision.

AP TABLE 21.4 Accounting Statement for the U.S. Economy Using the Income (Allocations) Approach, 2015 (in Billions)*

	Billions
Sum of:	
Compensation of employees	$9,655
Rents	657
Interest	524
Proprietors' income	1,388
Corporate profits	2,009
Taxes on production and imports	1,302
Equals:	
National income	**$15,535**
National income	$15,535
Less: Net foreign factor income	214
Plus: Consumption of fixed capital	2,821
Plus: Statistical discrepancy	−195
Equals:	
Gross domestic product	**$17,947**

*Some of the items in this table combine related categories that appear in the more detailed accounts. All data are subject to government revision.

Source: Bureau of Economic Analysis, **www.bea.gov**.

includes residential construction as well as the construction of new factories, warehouses, and stores. Why do the accountants regard residential construction as investment rather than consumption? Because apartment buildings and houses, like factories and stores, earn income when they are rented or leased. Owner-occupied houses are treated as investment goods because they *could be* rented to bring in an income return. So the national income accountants treat all residential construction as investment.

Increases in inventories (unsold goods) are considered to be investment because they represent, in effect, "unconsumed output." For economists, all new output that is not consumed is, by definition, capital. An increase in inventories is an addition (although perhaps temporary) to the stock of capital goods, and such additions are precisely how we define investment.

Starting in 2013, the NIPA accountants who compile U.S. GDP statistics began to include expenditures on R&D as well as money spent to develop new works of writing, art, music, and software as a form of investment. They did so because a country's stock of "capital goods" useful in producing output can be thought of as including not only tangible pieces of physical capital like fiber optic networks and factories but also useful ideas that increase the economy's ability to produce goods and services.

Software is a great example, as it is merely sets of instructions for telling computers what to do. But without those instructions, computers would be useless. So spending on software as well as on R&D and other intellectual activities that improve the economy's stock of "know-how" are now counted as investment.

To make it possible to compare GDP numbers across time, the accountants have gone back and applied the new, more comprehensive definition of investment all the way back to 1929. The numbers for U.S. GDP for the year 2015 that are used in this chapter incorporate the revised definition of investment.

Positive and Negative Changes in Inventories We need to look at changes in inventories more closely. Inventories can either increase or decrease over some period. Suppose they increased by $10 billion between December 31, 2015, and December 31, 2016. Therefore, in 2016 the economy produced $10 billion more output than people purchased. We need to count all output produced in 2016 as part of that year's GDP, even though some of it remained unsold at the end of the year. This is accomplished by including the $10 billion increase in inventories as investment in 2016. That way the expenditures in 2016 will correctly measure the output produced that year.

Alternatively, suppose that inventories decreased by $10 billion in 2016. This "drawing down of inventories" means that the economy sold $10 billion more of output in 2016 than it produced that year. It did this by selling goods produced in prior years—goods already counted as GDP in those years. Unless corrected, expenditures in 2016 will overstate GDP for 2016. So in 2016 we consider the $10 billion decline in inventories as "negative investment" and subtract it from total investment that year. Thus, expenditures in 2016 will correctly measure the output produced in 2016.

Noninvestment Transactions So much for what investment *is*. You also need to know what it *isn't*. For economists and NIPA accountants, investment does *not* include noninvestment transactions such as the transfer of paper assets (stocks, bonds) or the resale of tangible assets (houses, jewelry, boats). Such financial transactions merely transfer the ownership of existing assets. The investment in the GDP accounts is economic investment—the creation of *new* capital assets. The mere transfer (sale) of claims to existing capital goods does not produce new capital goods. Therefore such transactions (so-called financial investments) are not included as investment in the GDP accounts.

Gross Investment versus Net Investment As we have seen, the category gross private domestic investment includes (1) all final purchases of machinery, equipment, and tools; (2) all construction; (3) changes in inventories; and (4) spending on R&D and other activities that expand the economy's stock of technology and know-how. The words "private" and "domestic" mean that we are speaking of spending by private businesses, not by government (public) agencies, and that the investment is taking place inside the country, not abroad.

The word "gross" means that we are referring to *all* investment goods—both those that replace machinery, equipment, and buildings that were used up (worn out or made obsolete) in producing the current year's output and any net additions to the economy's stock of capital. Gross investment includes investment in replacement capital *and* in added capital.

In contrast, **net private domestic investment** includes *only* investment in the form of added capital. The amount of capital that is used up over the course of a year is called *depreciation*. So

Net investment = gross investment − depreciation

In typical years, gross investment exceeds depreciation. Thus net investment is positive and the nation's stock of capital rises by the amount of net investment. As illustrated in Figure 21.2, the stock of capital at the end of the year exceeds the stock of capital at the beginning of the year by the amount of net investment.

Gross investment need not always exceed depreciation, however. When gross investment and depreciation *are equal*, net investment is zero and there is no change in the size of the capital stock. When gross investment *is less than* depreciation, net investment is negative. The economy then is *disinvesting*—using up more capital than it is producing—and the nation's stock of capital shrinks. That happened in the Great Depression of the 1930s.

National income accountants use the symbol *I* for private domestic investment spending. To differentiate between gross investment and net investment, they add either the subscript *g* or the subscript *n*. But it is gross investment, I_g, that they use when tallying up GDP.

AP

Government Purchases (*G*)

The third category of expenditures in the national income accounts is **government purchases,** officially labeled "government consumption expenditures and gross investment." These expenditures have three components: (1) expenditures for goods and services that government consumes in providing public services; (2) expenditures for *publicly owned capital* such as schools and highways, which have long lifetimes; and (3) government expenditures on R&D and other activities that increase the economy's stock of know-how. Government purchases (federal, state, and local) include all government expenditures on final goods and all direct purchases of resources, including labor. It does *not* include government transfer payments because, as we have seen, they merely transfer government receipts to certain households and generate no production of any sort. National income accountants use the symbol *G* to signify government purchases.

Net Exports (X_n)

International trade transactions are a significant item in national income accounting. But when calculating U.S. GDP, we must keep in mind that we want to total up only those expenditures that are used to purchase goods and services produced *within the borders of the United States*. Thus, we must add in the value of exports, *X*, since exports are by definition goods and services produced within the borders of the United States. Don't be confused by the fact that the expenditures made to buy our exports are made by foreigners. The definition of GDP does not care about *who* is making expenditures on U.S.-made goods and services—only that the goods and services that they buy are made within the borders of the United States. Thus, foreign spending on our exports *must* be included in GDP.

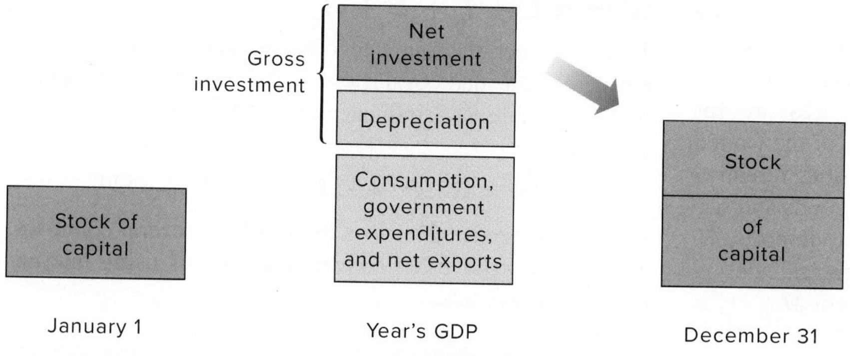

AP **FIGURE 21.2 Gross investment, depreciation, net investment, and the stock of capital.** When gross investment exceeds depreciation during a year, net investment occurs. This net investment expands the stock of private capital from the beginning of the year to the end of the year by the amount of the net investment. Other things equal, the economy's production capacity expands.

CONSIDER THIS . . .

Stocks versus Flows

Source: Lynn Betts/Natural Resources Conservation Service/U.S.Department of Agriculture (USDA)

An analogy of a reservoir is helpful in thinking about a nation's capital stock, investment, and depreciation. Picture a reservoir that has water flowing in from a river and flowing out from an outlet after it passes through turbines. The volume of water in the reservoir *at any particular point in time* is a "stock." In contrast, the inflow from the river and outflow from the outlet are "flows."

The volume or stock of water in the reservoir will rise if the weekly inflow exceeds the weekly outflow. It will fall if the inflow is less than the outflow. And it will remain constant if the two flows are equal.

Now let's apply this analogy to the stock of capital, gross investment, and depreciation. The stock of capital is the total capital in place at any point in time and is analogous to the level of water in the reservoir. Changes in this capital stock over some period, for example, 1 year, depend on *gross investment* and *depreciation*. Gross investment (analogous to the reservoir inflow) is an addition of capital goods and therefore adds to the stock of capital, while depreciation (analogous to the reservoir outflow) is the using up of capital and thus subtracts from the capital stock. The capital stock increases when gross investment exceeds depreciation, declines when gross investment is less than depreciation, and remains the same when gross investment and depreciation are equal.

Alternatively, the stock of capital increases when *net investment* (gross investment *minus* depreciation) is positive. When net investment is negative, the stock of capital declines, and when net investment is zero, the stock of capital remains constant.

At this point, you might incorrectly think that GDP should be equal to the sum of $C + I_g + G + X$. But this sum overstates GDP. The problem is that, once again, we must consider only expenditures made on *domestically produced* goods and services. As it stands, C, I_g, and G count expenditures on consumption, investment, and government purchases *regardless* of where those goods and services are made. Crucially, not all of the C, I_g, or G expenditures are for domestically produced goods and services. Some of the expenditures are for imports—goods and services produced outside of the United States. Because we wish to count *only* the part of C, I_g, and G that goes to purchasing domestically produced goods and services, we must subtract the spending that goes to imports, M. That subtraction yields the correct formula for calculating gross domestic product: GDP $= C + I_g + G + X - M$.

GLOBAL PERSPECTIVE 21.1

Comparative GDPs in Trillions of U.S. Dollars, Selected Nations, 2014

The United States, China, and Japan have the world's highest GDPs. The GDP data charted below have been converted to U.S. dollars via international exchange rates.

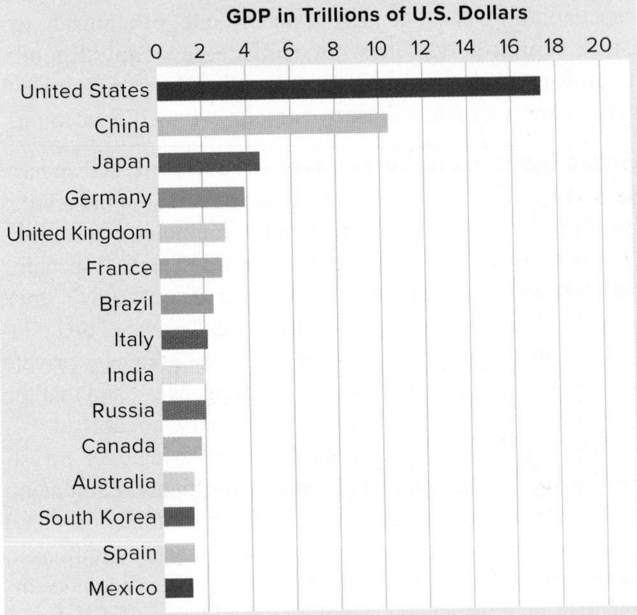

Source: International Monetary Fund, **www.imf.org**.

Accountants simplify this formula for GDP by defining **net exports,** X_n, to be equal to exports minus imports:

$$\text{Net exports } (X_n) = \text{exports } (X) - \text{imports } (M)$$

Using this definition of net exports, the formula for gross domestic product simplifies to,

$$\text{GDP} = C + I_g + G + X_n$$

Table 21.3 shows that in 2015 Americans spent \$529 billion more on imports than foreigners spent on U.S. exports. That is, net exports in 2015 were a *minus* \$529 billion.

Putting It All Together: GDP $= C + I_g + G + X_n$

Taken together, the four categories of expenditures provide a measure of the market value of a specific year's total output—its GDP. Table 21.3 indicates that 2015 U.S. GDP (in billions) totaled:

$$\text{GDP} = \$12{,}272 + \$3{,}021 + \$3{,}183 - \$529$$

Global Perspective 21.1 lists the GDPs of several countries. The values of GDP are converted to dollars using international exchange rates.

AP The Income Approach

LO21.3 Explain how GDP can be determined by summing up all of the incomes that were derived from producing the economy's output of goods and services.

Table 21.4 shows how 2015's expenditures of $17,947 billion were allocated as income to those responsible for producing the output. It would be simple if we could say that the entire amount of expenditures flowed back to them in the form of wages, rent, interest, and profit. But some expenditures flow to other recipients (such as the government) or to other uses (such as paying to replace the capital goods that have worn out while producing this year's GDP). These must be accounted for to balance the expenditures and income sides of the overall account. We will begin by looking at the items that make up *national income*.

Compensation of Employees

By far the largest share of national income—$9,655 billion in 2015—was paid as wages and salaries by business and government to their employees. That figure also includes wage and salary supplements, in particular, payments by employers into social insurance and into a variety of private pension, health, and welfare funds for workers.

Rents

Rents consist of the income received by the households and businesses that supply property resources. They include the monthly payments tenants make to landlords and the lease payments corporations pay for the use of office space. The figure used in the national accounts is *net* rent—gross rental income minus depreciation of the rental property.

Interest

Interest consists of the money paid by private businesses to the suppliers of loans used to purchase capital. It also includes such items as the interest households receive on savings deposits, certificates of deposit (CDs), and corporate bonds.

Proprietors' Income

What we have loosely termed "profits" is broken down by the national income accountants into two accounts: proprietors' income, which consists of the net income of sole proprietorships, partnerships, and other unincorporated businesses; and corporate profits. Proprietors' income flows to the proprietors.

Corporate Profits

Corporate profits are the earnings of corporations. National income accountants subdivide corporate profits into three categories:

- ***Corporate income taxes*** These taxes are levied on corporations' profits. They flow to the government.
- ***Dividends*** These are the part of after-tax profits that corporations choose to pay out, or distribute, to their stockholders. They thus flow to households—the ultimate owners of all corporations.
- ***Undistributed corporate profits*** Any after-tax profits that are not distributed to shareholders are saved, or retained, by corporations to be invested later in new plants and equipment. Undistributed corporate profits are also called *retained earnings*.

Taxes on Production and Imports

The account called **taxes on production and imports** includes general sales taxes, excise taxes, business property taxes, license fees, and customs duties. Why do national income accountants add these indirect business taxes to wages, rent, interest, and profits in determining national income? The answer is, "to account for expenditures that are diverted to the government." Consider an item that would otherwise sell for $1 but costs $1.05 because the government has imposed a 5 percent sales tax. When this item is purchased, consumers will expend $1.05 to buy it. But only $1 will go to the seller (who will then distribute it as income in the form of wages, rent, interest, and profit in order to compensate resource providers). The remaining 5 cents will flow as revenue to the government. The GDP accountants handle the extra 5 cents by placing it into the category called "Taxes on Production and Imports" and loosely consider it to be "income" to government.

From National Income to GDP

We have just shown that expenditures on final goods and services flow either as income to private citizens or as "income" to government. As a result, **national income** is the total of all sources of private income (employee compensation, rents, interest, proprietors' income, and corporate profits) plus government revenue from taxes on production and imports. National income is all the income that flows to American-supplied resources, whether here or abroad, plus taxes on production and imports. But notice that the figure for national income shown in Table 21.4—$15,535 billion—is less than GDP as reckoned by the expenditures approach shown in Table 21.3. The two versions of the accounting statement—the expenditures version and the income version—are brought into balance by subtracting one item from national income and adding two others.

Net Foreign Factor Income First, we need to make a slight adjustment in "national" income versus "domestic" income. National income includes the total income of

Americans, whether it was earned in the United States or abroad. But GDP is a measure of *domestic* output—total output produced within the United States regardless of the nationality of those who provide the resources. So in moving from national income to GDP, we must take out the income Americans gain from supplying resources abroad and add in the income that foreigners gain by supplying resources in the United States. That process provides *net foreign factor income*. In 2015, net foreign factor income was $214 billion, meaning that American-owned resources earned $214 billion more in other countries than foreign-owned resources earned in the United States. Because this $214 billion is earnings of Americans, it is included in U.S. national income. But this income is not part of U.S. domestic income because it reflects earnings from output produced in other nations. It is part of those nations' domestic income, derived from production of their domestic output. Thus, we subtract net foreign factor income from U.S. national income to stay on the correct path to use the income approach to determine the value of *U.S. domestic output* (output produced within U.S. borders).

Consumption of Fixed Capital Next, we must recognize that the useful lives of private capital equipment (such as bakery ovens or automobile assembly lines) extend far beyond the year in which they were produced. To avoid understating profit and income in the year of purchase and to avoid overstating profit and income in succeeding years, the cost of such capital must be allocated over its lifetime. The amount allocated is an estimate of how much of the capital is being used up each year. It is called *depreciation*. Accounting for depreciation results in a more accurate statement of profit and income for the economy each year. Publicly owned capital, such as courthouses and bridges, also requires a depreciation allowance in the national income accounts.

The huge depreciation charge made against private and publicly owned capital each year is called **consumption of fixed capital** because it is the allowance for capital that has been "consumed" in producing the year's GDP. It is the portion of GDP that is set aside to pay for the ultimate replacement of those capital goods.

The money allocated to consumption of fixed capital (the depreciation allowance) is a cost of production and thus included in the gross value of output. But this money is not available for other purposes, and, unlike other costs of production, it does not add to anyone's income. So it is not included in national income. We must therefore add it to national income to achieve balance with the economy's expenditures.

Statistical Discrepancy As you know, it should be possible to calculate GDP either by totaling up expenditures or by summing up incomes. Either method should give the same result.

In practice, however, it is not possible for NIPA accountants to measure every input into either set of calculations with total precision. Difficulties arise due to a wide range of factors including people misreporting their incomes on tax returns and the difficulty involved with accurately estimating depreciation. As a result, the GDP number produced by the income method always differs by a small percentage from the GDP number produced by the expenditures method.

To account for this difference, NIPA accountants add a statistical discrepancy to national income. The addition of that number equalizes the GDP totals produced by the two methods. In 2015 the discrepancy value was negative $195 billion, or about 1 percent of GDP.

Table 21.3 summarizes the expenditures approach to GDP while Table 21.4 summarizes the income approach to GDP. Table 21.3 shows how much the U.S. economy produced in 2015 by showing how much was spent to purchase that year's output of goods and services. Table 21.4 shows how those expenditures were allocated either as income to individuals, as revenue to the government, or to other uses such as paying for the replacement of depreciated capital.

AP QUICK REVIEW 21.1

- ✓ Gross domestic product (GDP) is a measure of the total market value of all final goods and services produced within the country or its economy in a specific year.
- ✓ The expenditures approach to GDP sums the total spending on final goods and services: GDP $= C + I_g + G + X_n$.
- ✓ *Net Investment* is *Gross Investment* minus *Depreciation*. The economy's stock of private capital expands when net investment is positive; stays constant when net investment is zero; and declines when net investment is negative.
- ✓ The income approach to GDP sums compensation to employees, rent, interest, proprietors' income, corporate profits, and taxes on production and imports to obtain national income, and then subtracts net foreign factor income and adds consumption of fixed capital (depreciation) and a statistical discrepancy to obtain GDP.

AP Other National Accounts

LO21.4 Describe the relationships among GDP, net domestic product, national income, personal income, and disposable income.

Several other national accounts provide additional useful information about the economy's performance. We can derive these accounts by making various adjustments to GDP.

Net Domestic Product

As a measure of total output, GDP does not make allowances for replacing the capital goods used up in each year's production. As a result, it does not tell us how much new output was available for consumption and for additions to the stock of capital. To determine that, we must subtract from GDP the capital that was consumed in producing the GDP and that had to be replaced. That is, we need to subtract consumption of fixed capital (depreciation) from GDP. The result is a measure of **net domestic product (NDP):**

$$\text{NDP} = \text{GDP} - \text{consumption of fixed capital (depreciation)}$$

For the United States in 2015:

	Billions
Gross domestic product	$17,947
Less: Consumption of fixed capital	2,821
Equals: Net domestic product	$15,126

NDP is simply GDP adjusted for depreciation. It measures the total annual output that the entire economy—households, businesses, government, and foreigners—can consume without impairing its capacity to produce in ensuing years.

National Income

Sometimes it is useful to know how much Americans earned for their contributions of land, labor, capital, and entrepreneurial talent. Recall that U.S. national income (NI) includes all income earned through the use of American-owned resources, whether they are located at home or abroad. It also includes taxes on production and imports. To derive NI from NDP, we must subtract the aforementioned statistical discrepancy from NDP and add net foreign factor income, since the latter is income earned by Americans overseas minus income earned by foreigners in the United States.

For the United States in 2015:

	Billions
Net domestic product	$15,126
Less: Statistical discrepancy	−195
Plus: Net foreign factor income	214
Equals: National income	$15,535

We know, too, that we can calculate national income through the income approach by simply adding up employee compensation, rent, interest, proprietors' income, corporate profit, and taxes on production and imports.

Personal Income

Personal income (PI) includes all income received, whether earned or unearned. It is likely to differ from national income (income earned) because some income earned—taxes on production and imports, Social Security taxes (payroll taxes), corporate income taxes, and undistributed corporate profits—is not received by households. Conversely, some income received—such as Social Security payments, unemployment compensation payments, welfare payments, disability and education payments to veterans, and private pension payments—is not earned. These transfer payments must be added to obtain PI.

In moving from national income to personal income, we must subtract the income that is earned but not received and add the income that is received but not earned. For the United States in 2015:

	Billions
National income	$15,535
Less: Taxes on production and imports	1,177
Less: Social Security contributions	1,203
Less: Corporate income taxes	530
Less: Undistributed corporate profits	591
Plus: Transfer payments	3,306*
Equals: Personal income	$15,340

*Includes statistical discrepancy and rounding error.

Disposable Income

Disposable income (DI) is personal income less personal taxes. Personal taxes include personal income taxes, personal property taxes, and inheritance taxes. Disposable income is the amount of income that households have left over after paying their personal taxes. They are free to divide that income between consumption (*C*) and saving (*S*):

$$\text{DI} = C + S$$

For the United States in 2015:

	Billions
Personal income	$15,340
Less: Personal taxes	1,945
Equals: Disposable income	$13,395

Table 21.5 summarizes the relationships among GDP, NDP, NI, PI, and DI.

The Circular Flow Revisited

Figure 21.3 is an elaborate flow diagram that shows the economy's four main sectors along with the flows of expenditures and allocations that determine GDP, NDP, NI, and PI. The orange arrows represent the spending flows—$C + I_g + G + X_n$—that together measure gross domestic product. To the right of the GDP rectangle are green arrows that show first

AP TABLE 21.5 The Relationship among GDP, NDP, NI, PI, and DI in the United States, 2015*

	Billions
Gross domestic product (GDP)	$17,947
Less: Consumption of fixed capital	2,821
Equals: Net domestic product	$15,126
Net domestic product (NDP)	$15,126
Less: Statistical discrepancy	−195
Plus: Net foreign factor income	214
Equals: National income (NI)	$15,535
National income (NI)	$15,535
Less: Taxes on production and imports	1,177
Less: Social Security contributions	1,203
Less: Corporate income taxes	530
Less: Undistributed corporate profits	591
Plus: Transfer payments	3,306
Equals: Personal income (PI)	$15,340
Personal income (PI)	$15,340
Less: Personal taxes	1,945
Equals: Disposable income (DI)	$13,395

*Some of the items combine categories that appear in the more detailed accounts.

Source: Bureau of Economic Analysis, **www.bea.gov**.

the allocations of GDP and then the adjustments needed to derive NDP, NI, PI, and DI.

The diagram illustrates the adjustments necessary to determine each of the national income accounts. For example, net domestic product is smaller than GDP because consumption of fixed capital flows away from GDP in determining NDP. Also, disposable income is smaller than personal income because personal taxes flow away from PI (to government) in deriving DI.

Note the three domestic sectors of the economy: households, government, and businesses. The household sector has an inflow of disposable income and outflows of consumption spending and savings. The government sector has an inflow of revenue in the form of types of taxes and an outflow of government disbursements in the form of purchases and transfers. The business sector has inflows from three major sources of funds for business investment and an outflow of investment expenditures.

Also, take a look at the foreign sector (all other countries) in the flow diagram. Spending by foreigners on U.S. exports adds to U.S. GDP, but some of U.S. consumption, government, and investment expenditures buys imported products. The flow from foreign markets shows that we handle this complication by calculating net exports (U.S. exports minus U.S. imports). The net export flow may be a positive or negative amount, adding to or subtracting from U.S. GDP.

Finally, you need to be aware that the flows shown in Figure 21.3 are dynamic entities and generally expand in size over time as the economy grows. But not always! Case in point: The Great Recession of 2007–2009—which is described in a Consider This box in Chapter 20—produced a pronounced slowing of the main spending and income flows. Specifically, U.S. businesses greatly reduced investment expenditures and households initially reduced personal consumption expenditures. Consequently, GDP, NDP, NI, and PI all significantly declined.

AP QUICK REVIEW 21.2

- ✓ Net domestic product (NDP) is the market value of GDP minus consumption of fixed capital (depreciation).
- ✓ National income (NI) is all income earned through the use of American-owned resources, whether located at home or abroad. NI also includes taxes on production and imports.
- ✓ Personal income (PI) is all income received by households, whether earned or not. Thus, personal income includes transfer payments.
- ✓ Disposable income (DI) is all income received by households minus personal taxes. Disposable income measures the income that is available for a household to either spend or save.

AP Nominal GDP versus Real GDP

LO21.5 Discuss the nature and function of a GDP price index, and describe the difference between nominal GDP and real GDP.

Recall that GDP is a measure of the market or money value of all final goods and services produced by the economy in a given year. We use money or nominal values as a common denominator to sum that heterogeneous output into a meaningful total. But, as alluded to in Chapter 20, that creates a problem: How can we compare the market values of GDP from year to year if the value of money itself changes in response to inflation (rising prices) or deflation (falling prices)? After all, we determine the value of GDP by multiplying total output by market prices.

Whether there is a 5 percent increase in output with no change in prices or a 5 percent increase in prices with no change in output, the change in the value of GDP will be the same. And yet it is the *quantity* of goods and services that get produced and distributed to households that affects our standard of living, not the price of those goods and services. For instance, the McDonald's hamburger that sold for $1.29 in 2015 yields the same satisfaction as a nearly identical McDonald's hamburger that sold for 18 cents in 1967.

The way around this problem is to *deflate* GDP when prices rise and to *inflate* GDP when prices fall. These adjustments

FIGURE 21.3 U.S. domestic output and the flows of expenditure and income. This figure is an elaborate circular flow diagram that fits the expenditures and allocations sides of GDP to one another. The expenditures flows are shown in orange; the allocations or income flows are shown in green. You should trace through the income and expenditures flows, relating them to the five basic national income accounting measures.

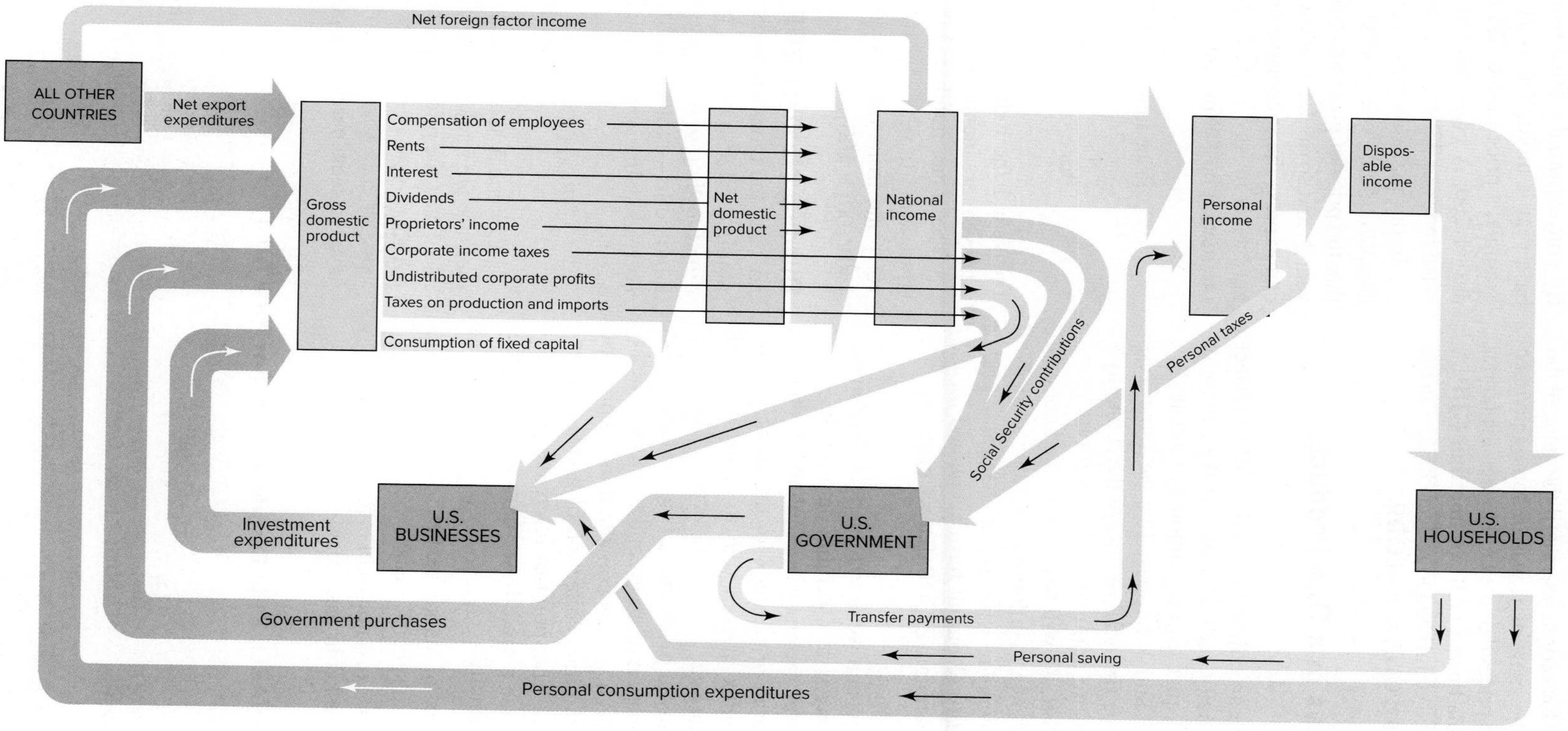

give us a measure of GDP for various years as if the value of the dollar had always been the same as it was in some reference year. A GDP based on the prices that prevailed when the output was produced is called unadjusted GDP, or **nominal GDP.** A GDP that has been deflated or inflated to reflect changes in the price level is called adjusted GDP, or **real GDP.**

Adjustment Process in a One-Product Economy

There are two ways we can adjust nominal GDP to reflect price changes. For simplicity, let's assume that the economy produces only one good, pizza, in the amounts indicated in Table 21.6 for years 1, 2, and 3. Suppose that we gather revenue data directly from the financial reports of the economy's pizza businesses to measure nominal GDP in various years. After completing our effort, we will have determined nominal GDP for each year, as shown in column 4 of Table 21.6. We will have no way of knowing to what extent changes in price and/or changes in quantity of output have accounted for the increases or decreases in nominal GDP that we observe.

GDP Price Index How can we determine real GDP in our pizza economy? One way is to assemble data on the price changes that occurred over various years (column 2) and use them to establish an overall price index for the entire period. Then we can use the index in each year to adjust nominal GDP to real GDP for that year.

In the actual economy, a **price index** is a measure of the price of a specified collection of goods and services, called a "market basket," in a given year as compared to the price of an identical (or highly similar) collection of goods and services in a reference year. That point of reference, or benchmark, is known as the base period, **base year,** or, simply, the reference year. More formally,

$$\text{Price index in given year} = \frac{\text{price of market basket in specific year}}{\text{price of same market basket in base year}} \times 100 \qquad (1)$$

By convention, the price ratio between a given year and the base year is multiplied by 100 to facilitate computation. For example, a price ratio of 2/1 (= 2) is expressed as a price index of 200. A price ratio of 1/3 (= 0.33) is expressed as a price index of 33.

In our pizza-only example, of course, our market basket consists of only one product. Column 2 of Table 21.6 reveals that the price of pizza was \$10 in year 1, \$20 in year 2, \$25 in year 3, and so on. Let's select year 1 as our base year. Now we can express the successive prices of the contents of our market basket in, say, years 2 and 3 as compared to the price of the market basket in year 1:

$$\text{Price index, year 2} = \frac{\$20}{\$10} \times 100 = 200$$

$$\text{Price index, year 3} = \frac{\$25}{\$10} \times 100 = 250$$

For year 1 the index has to be 100, since that year and the base year are identical.

The index numbers tell us that the price of pizza rose from year 1 to year 2 by 100 percent {= [(200 − 100)/100] × 100} and from year 1 to year 3 by 150 percent {= [(250 − 100)/100] × 100}.

Dividing Nominal GDP by the Price Index We can now use the index numbers shown in column 3 to deflate the nominal GDP figures in column 4. The simplest and most direct method of deflating is to express the index numbers as hundredths—in decimal form—and then to divide them into corresponding nominal GDP. That gives us real GDP:

$$\text{Real GDP} = \frac{\text{nominal GDP}}{\text{price index (in hundredths)}} \qquad (2)$$

Column 5 shows the results. These figures for real GDP measure the market value of the output of pizza in years 1, 2, and 3 as if the price of pizza had been a constant \$10 throughout the 3-year period. In short, real GDP reveals the market value of each year's output measured in terms of dollars that have the same purchasing power as dollars had in the base year.

AP **TABLE 21.6 Calculating Real GDP (Base Year = Year 1)**

Year	(1) Units of Output	(2) Price of Pizza per Unit	(3) Price Index (Year 1 = 100)	(4) Unadjusted, or Nominal, GDP, (1) × (2)	(5) Adjusted, or Real, GDP
1	5	\$10	100	\$ 50	\$50
2	7	20	200	140	70
3	8	25	250	200	80
4	10	30	___	___	___
5	11	28	___	___	___

To test your understanding, extend Table 21.6 to years 4 and 5, using equations 1 and 2. Then run through the entire deflating procedure, using year 3 as the base period. This time you will have to inflate some of the nominal GDP data, using the same procedure as we used in the examples.

An Alternative Method

Another way to calculate real GDP is to gather separate data on physical outputs (as in column 1) and their prices (as in column 2) of Table 21.6. We could then determine the market value of outputs in successive years *if the base-year price ($10) had prevailed.* In year 2, the 7 units of pizza would have a value of $70 (= 7 units × $10). As column 5 confirms, that $70 worth of output is year 2's real GDP. Similarly, we could determine the real GDP for year 3 by multiplying the 8 units of output that year by the $10 price in the base year.

Once we have determined real GDP through this method, we can identify the price index for a given year simply by dividing the nominal GDP by the real GDP for that year:

$$\begin{array}{c}\text{Price index}\\ \text{(in hundredths)}\end{array} = \frac{\text{nominal GDP}}{\text{real GDP}} \qquad (3)$$

Example: In year 2 we get a price index of 200—or, in hundredths, 2.00—which equals the nominal GDP of $140 divided by the real GDP of $70. Note that equation 3 is simply a rearrangement of equation 2. Table 21.7 summarizes the two methods of determining real GDP in our single-good economy.

Real-World Considerations and Data

In the real world of many goods and services, of course, determining GDP and constructing a reliable price index are far more complex matters than in our pizza-only economy. The government accountants must assign a "weight" to each of several categories of goods and services based on the relative proportion of each category in total output. They update the weights annually as expenditure patterns change and roll the base year forward year by year using a moving average of expenditure patterns. The GDP price index used in the United States is called the *chain-type annual-weights price index*—which hints at its complexity. We spare you the details.

Table 21.8 shows some of the relationships among nominal GDP, real GDP, and the GDP price index for the U.S. economy. Here the base year is 2009, where the value of the index is set at 100. Because the U.S. price level has been rising over the long run, the pre-2009 values of real GDP (column 3) are higher than the nominal values of GDP for those years (column 2). This upward adjustment acknowledges that prices were lower in the years before 2009, and thus nominal GDP understated the real output of those years in 2009 prices and must be inflated to show the correct relationship to other years.

Conversely, the rising price level of the post-2009 years caused nominal GDP figures for those years to overstate real output. So the statisticians deflate those figures to determine what real GDP would have been in other years if 2009 prices had prevailed. Doing so reveals that real GDP has been less than nominal GDP since 2009.

By inflating the nominal pre-2009 GDP data and deflating the post-2009 data, government accountants determine annual real GDP, which can then be compared with the real GDP of any other year in the series of years. So the real GDP values in column 3 are directly comparable with one another.

Once we have determined nominal GDP and real GDP, we can compute the price index. And once we have determined nominal GDP and the price index, we can calculate real GDP. Example: Nominal GDP in 2015 was $17,947.0

AP TABLE 21.7 Steps for Deriving Real GDP from Nominal GDP

Method 1

1. Find nominal GDP for each year.
2. Compute a GDP price index.
3. Divide each year's nominal GDP by that year's price index (in hundredths) to determine real GDP.

Method 2

1. Break down nominal GDP into physical quantities of output and prices for each year.
2. Find real GDP for each year by determining the dollar amount that each year's physical output would have sold for if base-year prices had prevailed. (The GDP price index can then be found by dividing nominal GDP by real GDP.)

AP TABLE 21.8 Nominal GDP, Real GDP, and GDP Price Index for the United States, Selected Years

(1) Year	(2) Nominal GDP, Billions	(3) Real GDP, Billions	(4) GDP Price Index (2009 = 100)
1995	$ 7,664.0	$10,167.3	____
2000	10,289.7	____	81.9
2005	13,095.4	14,235.6	92.0
2009	14,417.9	____	100.0
2010	14,958.3	14,779.4	101.2
2015	17,947.0	16,348.9	109.8

Source: Bureau of Economic Analysis, **www.bea.gov**. All data are subject to government revision.

billion and real GDP was $16,348.9 billion. So the price level in 2015 was 109.8 (= [$17,947.0/$16,348.9] × 100), or 9.8 percent higher than in 2009. If we knew the nominal GDP and the price level only, we could find the real GDP for 2015 by dividing the nominal GDP of $17,947.0 by the 2015 price index, expressed in hundredths (1.098).

To test your understanding of the relationships between nominal GDP, real GDP, and the price level, determine the values of the price index for 1995 in Table 21.8 and determine real GDP for 2000 and 2009. We have left those figures out on purpose.

AP QUICK REVIEW 21.3

- ✓ Nominal GDP is output valued at current prices. Real GDP is output valued at constant base-year prices.
- ✓ The GDP price index compares the prices of a "market basket" of the goods and services included in GDP in a given year to the price of the same "market basket" prices in a reference year.
- ✓ Nominal GDP can be transformed into real GDP by dividing the nominal GDP by the GDP price index expressed in hundredths.

AP Shortcomings of GDP

LO21.6 List and explain some limitations of the GDP measure.

GDP is a reasonably accurate and highly useful measure of how well or how poorly the economy is performing. But it has several shortcomings as a measure of both total output and well-being (total utility).

Nonmarket Activities

Certain productive activities do not take place in any market—the services of stay-at-home parents, for example, and the labor of carpenters who repair their own homes. Such activities never show up in GDP because the accountants who tally up GDP only get data on economic transactions involving *market activities*—that is, transactions in which output or resources are traded for money. Consequently, GDP understates a nation's total output because it does not count *unpaid work*. There is one exception: The portion of farmers' output that farmers consume themselves *is* estimated and included in GDP.

Leisure

The average workweek (excluding overtime) in the United States has declined since the beginning of the 1900s—from about 53 hours to about 35 hours. Moreover, the greater frequency of paid vacations, holidays, and leave time has shortened the work year itself. This increase in leisure time has clearly had a positive effect on overall well-being. But our system of national income accounting understates well-being by ignoring leisure's value. Nor does the system accommodate the satisfaction—the "psychic income"—that many people derive from their work.

Improved Product Quality

Because GDP is a quantitative measure rather than a qualitative measure, it fails to capture the full value of improvements in product quality. A $200 cell phone purchased today is of very different quality than a cell phone that cost $200 just a decade ago. Today's cell phone is digital and has greater memory capacity, a viewing screen, and quite likely a camera and a music player.

Obviously quality improvement has a great effect on economic well-being, as does the quantity of goods produced. Although the BEA adjusts GDP for quality improvement for selected items, the vast majority of such improvement for the entire range of goods and services does not get reflected in GDP.

The Underground Economy

Embedded in our economy is a flourishing, productive underground sector. Some of the people who conduct business there are gamblers, smugglers, prostitutes, "fences" of stolen goods, drug growers, and drug dealers. They have good reason to conceal their incomes.

Most participants in the underground economy, however, engage in perfectly legal activities but choose illegally not to report their full incomes to the Internal Revenue Service (IRS). A barista at a coffee shop may report just a portion of the tips received from customers. Storekeepers may report only a portion of their sales receipts. Workers who want to hold on to their unemployment compensation benefits may take an "off-the-books" or "cash-only" job. A brick mason may agree to rebuild a neighbor's fireplace in exchange for the neighbor's repairing his boat engine. The value of none of these transactions shows up in GDP.

The value of underground transactions is estimated to be about 8 percent of the recorded GDP in the United States. That would mean that GDP in 2015 was understated by about $1.4 trillion. Global Perspective 21.2 shows estimates of the relative sizes of underground economies in selected nations.

GDP and the Environment

The growth of GDP is inevitably accompanied by "gross domestic by-products," including dirty air and polluted water,

GLOBAL PERSPECTIVE 21.2

The Underground Economy as a Percentage of GDP, Selected Nations

Underground economies vary in size worldwide. Three factors that help explain the variation are (1) the extent and complexity of regulation, (2) the type and degree of taxation, and (3) the effectiveness of law enforcement.

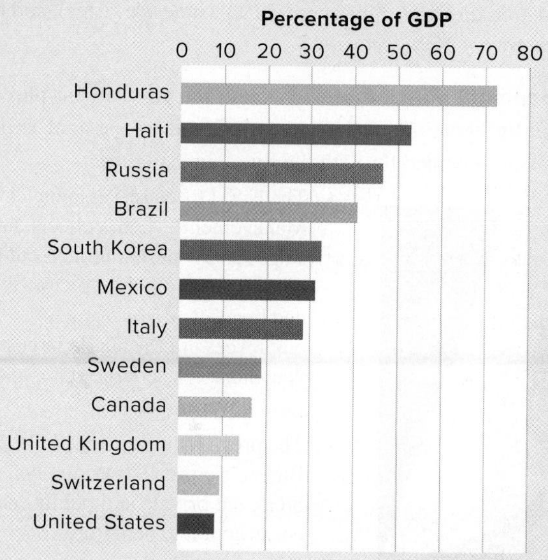

Source: Mai Hassan and Friedrich Schneider, "Size and Development of the Shadow Economies of 157 Countries Worldwide: Updated and New Measures from 1999 to 2013," IZA Discussion Paper No. 10281, October 2016, Institute for the Study of Labor (IZA).

toxic waste, congestion, and noise. The social costs of the negative by-products reduce our economic well-being. And since those costs are not deducted from total output, GDP overstates our national well-being. Ironically, when money is spent to clean up pollution and reduce congestion, those expenses are added to GDP!

Composition and Distribution of Output

The composition of output is undoubtedly important for well-being. But GDP does not tell us whether the currently produced mix of goods and services is enriching or potentially detrimental to society. GDP assigns equal weight to an assault rifle and a set of encyclopedias, as long as both sell for the same price. Moreover, GDP reveals nothing about the way output is distributed. Does 90 percent of the output go to 10 percent of the households, for example, or is the output more evenly distributed? The distribution of output may make a big difference for society's overall well-being.

Noneconomic Sources of Well-Being

Finally, the connection between GDP and well-being is problematic for another reason. Just as a household's income does not measure its total happiness, a nation's GDP does not measure its total well-being. Many things could make a society better off without necessarily raising GDP: a reduction of crime and violence, peaceful relations with other countries, people's greater civility toward one another, better understanding between parents and children, and a reduction of drug and alcohol abuse.

The Importance of Intermediate Output

GDP's focus on final output means that it ignores all of the "business to business" economic activity that takes place in the economy at earlier stages of production and distribution. That omission is worrisome because many people's jobs and many firms' profitability depend on economic activity at earlier stages.

Fortunately, a statistic called **gross output (GO)** sums together the dollar value of the economic activity that takes place at each of four stages into which all economic activity can be grouped: resource extraction, production, distribution, and final output (GDP).

Because GO includes GDP (the final stage) as well as the three earlier stages, GO is always larger than GDP. Thus, in 2015, GO was $31.5 trillion while GDP was $17.9 trillion.

Because GO takes into account every stage of economic activity, it reflects the overall status of the productive side of the economy better than GDP does. GO is particularly useful when attempting to gauge the magnitude of business cycle fluctuations. During the 2007-2009 recession, real GDP fell 4.2 percent, while real GO fell 8.6 percent. Thus, total economic activity fell by more than twice as much as final output. That substantial difference goes some way toward explaining why employment fell so dramatically during and after the Great Recession.

AP QUICK REVIEW 21.4

- ✓ GDP is a reasonably accurate and very useful indicator of a nation's economic performance but should not be interpreted as a comprehensive measure of well-being.
- ✓ The major limitations of GDP as an indicator of well-being are that it fails to account for nonmarket and illegal transactions, changes in leisure and in product quality, the composition and distribution of output (or income), the environmental effects of pollution, and economic activity at earlier stages of production and distribution.

LAST WORD

Magical Mystery Tour

The Bureau of Economic Analysis (BEA), an Agency of the Department of Commerce, Compiles the NIPA Tables. Where Does It Get the Actual Data?

Discussions of national income accounting often leave the impression that the data for the National Income and Product Accounts magically appear from some mysterious place. Let's take a tour to see where economists get their data.

Consumption The BEA derives the data for the consumption component of the GDP accounts from four main sources:

- The Census Bureau's *Retail Trade Survey*, which gains sales information from a sample of 22,000 firms.
- The Census Bureau's *Survey of Manufacturers*, which gathers information on shipments of consumer goods from 50,000 establishments.
- The Census Bureau's *Service Survey*, which collects sales data from 30,000 service businesses.
- Industry trade sources. For example, data on auto sales and aircraft are collected directly from auto and aircraft manufacturers.

Source: © Hill Street Studios/Getty Images RF

Investment The sources of the data for the investment component of GDP include:

- All the sources above used to determine consumption. Purchases of capital goods are separated from purchases of consumer goods. For example, estimates of investment in equipment and software are based on manufacturers' shipments reported in the *Survey of Manufacturers*, the *Service Survey*, and industry sources.
- Census construction surveys. The Census Bureau's *Housing Starts Survey* and *Housing Sales Survey* produce the data used to measure the amount of housing construction, and the *Construction Progress Reporting Survey* is the source of data on nonresidential construction. The BEA determines changes in business inventories through the *Retail Trade Survey*, the *Wholesale Trade Survey* (of 7,100 wholesale firms), and the *Survey of Manufacturing*.

Government Purchases The data for government purchases (officially "government consumption and investment expenditures") are obtained through the following sources:

- The U.S. Office of Personnel Management, which collects data on wages and benefits, broken out by the private and public sector. Wages and benefits of government employees are the single largest "purchase" by federal, state, and local government.
- The previously mentioned Census Bureau's construction surveys, which break out private and public sector construction expenditures.
- The Census Bureau's *Survey of Government Finance,* which provides data on government consumption and investment expenditures.

Net Exports The BEA determines net exports through two main sources:

- The U.S. Customs Service, which collects data on exports and imports of goods.
- BEA surveys of potential domestic exporters and importers of services, which collect data on exports and imports of services.

So there you have it. Not so magical after all!

Source: Based on Joseph A. Ritter, "Feeding the National Accounts," Federal Reserve Bank of St. Louis *Review*, March–April 2000, pp. 11–20. For those interested, this article also provides information on the sources of data for the income side of the national accounts.

SUMMARY

LO21.1 Explain how gross domestic product (GDP) is defined and measured.

Gross domestic product (GDP), a basic measure of an economy's economic performance, is the market value of all final goods and services produced within the borders of a nation in a year.

Final goods are those purchased by end users, whereas intermediate goods are those purchased for resale or for further processing or manufacturing. Intermediate goods, nonproduction transactions, and secondhand sales are purposely excluded in calculating GDP.

LO21.2 Describe how expenditures on goods and services can be summed to determine GDP.

GDP may be calculated by summing total expenditures on all final output or by summing the income derived from the production of that output.

By the expenditures approach, GDP is determined by adding consumer purchases of goods and services, gross investment spending by businesses, government purchases, and net exports: GDP = $C + I_g + G + X_n$.

Personal consumption expenditures consist of expenditures on goods (durable goods and nondurable goods) and services. About 60 percent of consumer expenditures in the United States are on services, leading economists to refer to the U.S. economy as a *service economy*.

Gross investment is divided into (*a*) replacement investment (required to maintain the nation's stock of capital at its existing level) and (*b*) net investment (the net increase in the stock of capital). In most years, net investment is positive and therefore the economy's stock of capital and production capacity increase.

LO21.3 Explain how GDP can be determined by summing up all of the incomes that were derived from producing the economy's output of goods and services.

By the income or allocations approach, GDP is calculated as the sum of compensation to employees, rents, interest, proprietors' income, corporate profits, taxes on production and imports *minus* net foreign factor income, *plus* consumption of fixed capital and a statistical discrepancy.

LO21.4 Describe the relationships among GDP, net domestic product, national income, personal income, and disposable income.

Other national accounts are derived from GDP. Net domestic product (NDP) is GDP less the consumption of fixed capital. National income (NI) is total income earned by a nation's resource suppliers plus taxes on production and imports; it is found by subtracting a statistical discrepancy from NDP and adding net foreign factor income to NDP. Personal income (PI) is the total income paid to households prior to any allowance for personal taxes. Disposable income (DI) is personal income after personal taxes have been paid. DI measures the amount of income available to households to consume or save.

LO21.5 Discuss the nature and function of a GDP price index and describe the difference between nominal GDP and real GDP.

Price indexes are computed by dividing the price of a specific collection or market basket of output in a particular period by the price of the same market basket in a base period and multiplying the result (the quotient) by 100. The GDP price index is used to adjust nominal GDP for inflation or deflation and thereby obtain real GDP.

Nominal (current-dollar) GDP measures each year's output valued in terms of the prices prevailing in that year. Real (constant-dollar) GDP measures each year's output in terms of the prices that prevailed in a selected base year. Because real GDP is adjusted for price-level changes, differences in real GDP are due only to differences in production activity.

LO21.6 List and explain some limitations of the GDP measure.

GDP is a reasonably accurate and very useful indicator of a nation's economic performance, but it has its limitations. It fails to account for nonmarket and illegal transactions, changes in leisure and in product quality, the composition and distribution of output, the environmental effects of pollution, and economic activity at earlier stages of production and distribution. GDP should not be interpreted as a complete measure of well-being.

TERMS AND CONCEPTS

national income accounting
gross domestic product (GDP)
intermediate goods
final goods
multiple counting
value added
expenditures approach
income approach
personal consumption expenditures (C)
durable goods
nondurable goods
services
gross private domestic investment (I_g)
net private domestic investment
government purchases (G)
net exports (X_n)
taxes on production and imports
national income
consumption of fixed capital
net domestic product (NDP)
personal income (PI)
disposable income (DI)
nominal GDP
real GDP
price index
base year
gross output (GO)

The following and additional problems can be found in connect

DISCUSSION QUESTIONS

1. In what ways are national income statistics useful? LO21.1
2. Why do national income accountants compare the market value of the total outputs in various years rather than actual physical volumes of production? What problem is posed by any comparison over time of the market values of various total outputs? How is this problem resolved? LO21.1
3. Which of the following goods are usually intermediate goods and which are usually final goods: running shoes, cotton fibers, watches, textbooks, coal, sunscreen lotion, lumber? LO21.1
4. Why do economists include only final goods and services when measuring GDP for a particular year? Why don't they include the value of the stocks and bonds bought and sold? Why don't they include the value of the used furniture bought and sold? LO21.1
5. Explain why an economy's output, in essence, is also its income. LO21.1
6. Provide three examples of each: consumer durable goods, consumer nondurable goods, and services. LO21.2
7. Why are changes in inventories included as part of investment spending? Suppose inventories declined by $1 billion during 2014. How would this affect the size of gross private domestic investment and gross domestic product in 2014? Explain. LO21.2
8. What is the difference between gross private domestic investment and net private domestic investment? If you were to determine net domestic product (NDP) through the expenditures approach, which of these two measures of investment spending would be appropriate? Explain. LO21.2
9. Use the concepts of gross investment and net investment to distinguish between an economy that has a rising stock of capital and one that has a falling stock of capital. Explain: "Though net investment can be positive, negative, or zero, it is impossible for gross investment to be less than zero." LO21.2
10. Define net exports. Explain how U.S. exports and imports each affects domestic production. How are net exports determined? Explain how net exports might be a negative amount. LO21.2
11. Contrast the ideas of nominal GDP and real GDP. Why is one more reliable than the other for comparing changes in the standard of living over a series of years? What is the GDP price index and what is its role in differentiating nominal GDP and real GDP? LO21.5
12. Which of the following are included or excluded in this year's GDP? Explain your answer in each case. LO21.6
    a. Interest received on an AT&T corporate bond.
    b. Social Security payments received by a retired factory worker.
    c. Unpaid services of a family member in painting the family home.
    d. Income of a dentist from the dental services provided.
    e. A monthly allowance a college student receives from home.
    f. Money received by Josh when he resells his nearly brand-new Honda automobile to Kim.
    g. The publication and sale of a new college textbook.
    h. An increase in leisure resulting from a 2-hour decrease in the length of the workweek, with no reduction in pay.
    i. A $2 billion increase in business inventories.
    j. The purchase of 100 shares of Google stock.
13. Why does gross output do a better job than GDP of measuring overall economic activity? How could you construct a new statistic that focused only on non-final economic activity? Given what you know about the behavior of GO and GDP during the Great Recession, would you expect your new statistic to show more or less volatility than GO and GDP? Why? How would you rank the three in terms of volatility? LO21.6
14. **LAST WORD** What government agency compiles the U.S. NIPA tables? In what U.S. department is it located? Of the several specific sources of information, name one source for each of the four components of GDP: consumption, investment, government purchases, and net exports.

AP REVIEW QUESTIONS

1. Tina walks into Ted's sporting goods store and buys a punching bag for $100. That $100 payment counts as ____________ for Tina and ____________ for Ted. LO21.1
    a. Income; expenditure.
    b. Value added; multiple counting.
    c. Expenditure; income.
    d. Expenditures; profits.
    e. Rents; profits.
2. Classify each of these statements as C (consumption) I (gross private domestic investment) G (government) X (exports) and M (imports). Use N for not counted as GDP. LO21.1
    a. You spend $5 to see a movie.
    b. You pay $100,000 to a contractor for a home built this year.
    c. You pay the bank the remaining amount of your mortgage for a home constructed 15 years ago.
    d. The Pentagon budget increases by $3 billion for military expenditures.
    e. The government makes a $200 Social Security payment to a retired person.
    f. U.S. farmers ship 2 million tons of almonds to China.
    g. You buy 100 shares of General Motors stock for $5300.
    h. At the end of the year, a flour-milling firm finds that its inventories of grain and flour are valued at $10,000 above the amounts of its inventories at the beginning of the year.
    i. Your mother does many tasks caring for all of your family.
    j. General Motors buys new robots for a truck assembly plant.
    k. You pay $300 a month to rent a house.
    l. Your family takes a vacation to France.
    m. The R. J. Reynolds company buys control of the Nabisco company.
    n. You buy a new Toyota that was built in Ohio.

3. A small economy starts the year with $1 million in physical capital. During the course of the year, gross investment is $150,000 and depreciation is $50,000. What is the value of the the economy's stock of physical capital at the end of the year? LO21.2
   a. $1,150,000.
   b. $1,100,000.
   c. $1,000,000.
   d. $850,000.
   e. $800,000.
4. Suppose that this year a small country has a GDP of $100 billion. Also assume that I_g = $30 billion, C = $60 billion, and X_n = – $10 billion. How big is G? LO21.3
   a. $0.
   b. $10 billion.
   c. $20 billion.
   d. $30 billion.
   e. Not enough information to answer.
5. If intermediate goods and services were included in GDP: LO21.3
   a. The GDP would then have to be deflated for changes in the price level.
   b. Nominal GDP would exceed real GDP.
   c. The GDP would be overstated.
   d. The GDP would be understated.
   e. The GDP would be the same.
6. Suppose GDP is $16 trillion, with $10 trillion coming from consumption, $2 trillion coming from gross investment, $3.5 trillion coming from government expenditures, and $500 billion coming from net exports. Also suppose that across the whole economy, depreciation (consumption of fixed capital) totals $1 trillion. From these figures, we see that net domestic product equals: LO21.4
   a. $2.0 trillion.
   b. $17.0 trillion.
   c. $16.0 trillion.
   d. $15.0 trillion.
   e. None of the above.
7. Suppose that across the whole economy, personal income is $12 trillion. If the government collects $1.5 trillion in personal taxes, then disposable income will be: LO21.4
   a. $13.5 trillion.
   b. $12.0 trillion.
   c. $10.5 trillion.
   d. $8.0 trillion.
   e. None of the above.
8. As defined in national income accounting, investment refers to LO21.1
   a. Business expenditures on machinery and equipment.
   b. All construction—residential and non-residential.
   c. Changes in business inventories.
   d. Purchases of a company's corporate bonds.
   e. Answers a, b, and c.
9. Net exports are a negative figure when: LO21.1
   a. The economy's stock of capital goods is declining.
   b. The economy's stock of capital goods is rising.
   c. Depreciation exceeds gross private domestic investment.
   d. A nation's exports of goods and services exceeds its imports.
   e. A nation's imports of goods and services exceed its exports.
10. Suppose that this year's nominal GDP is $16 trillion. To account for the effects of inflation, we construct a price-level index in which an index value of 100 represents the price level five years ago. Using that index, we find that this year's real GDP is $15 trillion. Given those numbers, we can conclude that the current value of the index is: LO21.5
    a. Higher than 100.
    b. Lower than 100.
    c. Still 100.
    d. Zero.
    e. Not calculable.
11. Which of the following items will be included in official U.S. GDP statistics? LO21.6
    *Select **one or more** answers from the choices shown.*
    a. Revenue generated by illegal marijuana growers in Oregon.
    b. Money spent to clean up a local toxic waste site in Ohio.
    c. Revenue generated by legal medical marijuana sales in California.
    d. The dollar value of the annoyance felt by local citizens living near a noisy airport in Georgia.
    e. Robert paying Ted for a haircut in Chicago.
    f. Emily and Rhonda trading an hour of dance lessons for a haircut in Dallas.
12. Which of the following six statements are true? LO21.1–LO21.6
    a. The sum of the value added of each firm will equal the current GDP.
    b. Subtracting depreciation from personal income will equal disposable income.
    c. If a firm has an economic loss, it cannot have a positive value added.
    d. When a can of soup is sold from inventory; there is no net change in GDP. The increase in consumption is just offset by a decrease gross investment.
    e. An increase in imports, *ceteris parabis*, will reduce nominal GDP.
    f. Gross domestic product minus taxes equals net domestic product.

PROBLEMS

1. Suppose that annual output in year 1 in a 3-good economy is 3 quarts of ice cream, 1 bottle of shampoo, and 3 jars of peanut butter. In year 2, the output mix changes to 5 quarts of ice cream, 2 bottles of shampoo, and 2 jars of peanut butter. If the prices in both years are $4 per quart for ice cream, $3 per bottle of shampoo, and $2 per jar of peanut butter, what was the economy's GDP in year 1? What was its GDP in year 2? LO21.1
2. Assume that a grower of flower bulbs sells its annual output of bulbs to an Internet retailer for $70,000. The retailer, in turn, brings in $160,000 from selling the bulbs directly to final customers. What amount would these two transactions add to personal consumption expenditures and thus to GDP during the year? LO21.1

3. If in some country personal consumption expenditures in a specific year are $50 billion, purchases of stocks and bonds are $30 billion, net exports are − $10 billion, government purchases are $20 billion, sales of secondhand items are $8 billion, and gross investment is $25 billion, what is the country's GDP for the year? **LO21.2**

4. Below is a list of domestic output and national income figures for a certain year. All figures are in billions. The questions that follow ask you to determine the major national income measures by both the expenditures and the income approaches. The results you obtain with the different methods should be the same. **LO21.4**

Personal consumption expenditures	$245
Net foreign factor income	4
Transfer payments	12
Rents	14
Consumption of fixed capital (depreciation)	27
Statistical discrepancy	8
Social Security contributions	20
Interest	13
Proprietors' income	33
Net exports	11
Dividends	16
Compensation of employees	223
Taxes on production and imports	18
Undistributed corporate profits	21
Personal taxes	26
Corporate income taxes	19
Corporate profits	56
Government purchases	72
Net private domestic investment	33
Personal saving	20

a. Using the above data, determine GDP by both the expenditures and the income approaches. Then determine NDP.

b. Now determine NI in two ways: first, by making the required additions or subtractions from NDP; and second, by adding up the types of income and taxes that make up NI.

c. Adjust NI (from part *b*) as required to obtain PI.

d. Adjust PI (from part *c*) as required to obtain DI.

5. Using the following national income accounting data, compute (*a*) GDP, (*b*) NDP, and (*c*) NI. All figures are in billions. **LO21.4**

Compensation of employees	$194.2
U.S. exports of goods and services	17.8
Consumption of fixed capital	11.8
Government purchases	59.4
Taxes on production and imports	14.4
Net private domestic investment	52.1
Transfer payments	13.9
U.S. imports of goods and services	16.5
Personal taxes	40.5
Net foreign factor income	2.2
Personal consumption expenditures	219.1
Statistical discrepancy	0.0

6. Suppose that in 1984 the total output in a single-good economy was 7,000 buckets of chicken. Also suppose that in 1984 each bucket of chicken was priced at $10. Finally, assume that in 2005 the price per bucket of chicken was $16 and that 22,000 buckets were produced. Determine the GDP price index for 1984, using 2005 as the base year. By what percentage did the price level, as measured by this index, rise between 1984 and 2005? What were the amounts of real GDP in 1984 and 2005? **LO21.5**

7. The following table shows nominal GDP and an appropriate price index for a group of selected years. Compute real GDP. Indicate in each calculation whether you are inflating or deflating the nominal GDP data. **LO21.5**

Year	Nominal GDP, Billions	Price Index (2005 = 100)	Real GDP, Billions
1968	$ 909.8	22.01	$______
1978	2,293.8	40.40	$______
1988	5,100.4	66.98	$______
1998	8,793.5	85.51	$______
2008	14,441.4	108.48	$______

8. Assume that the total value of the following items is $600 billion in a specific year for Upper Mongoose: net exports = $50 billion; value of new goods and services produced in the underground economy = $75 billion; personal consumption expenditures = $300 billion; value of the services of stay-at-home parents = $25 billion; gross domestic investment = $100 billion; government purchases = $50 billion. What is Upper Mongoose's GDP for the year? What is the size of the underground economy as a percentage of GDP? By what percentage would GDP be boosted if the value of the services of stay-at-home spouses were included in GDP? **LO21.6**

Chapter 22

Economic Growth

Learning Objectives

LO22.1 **List two ways that economic growth is measured.**

LO22.2 **Define "modern economic growth" and explain the institutional structures needed for an economy to experience it.**

LO22.3 **Identify the general supply, demand, and efficiency forces that give rise to economic growth.**

LO22.4 **Describe "growth accounting" and the specific factors accounting for economic growth in the United States.**

LO22.5 **Explain how the average rate of U.S. productivity growth has fluctuated since 1973.**

LO22.6 **Discuss differing perspectives as to whether growth is desirable and sustainable.**

AP Chapter Focus

People living in rich countries tend to take economic growth and rising standards of living for granted. Recessions—periods during which output declines—are normally infrequent and temporary, usually lasting less than a year. Once they pass, modern capitalistic economies return to growing, and living standards continue their seemingly inexorable rise.

But a look back at history or a look around the world today quickly dispels any confidence that economic growth and rising standards of living are automatic or routine. Historically, continually rising living standards are a recent phenomenon, seen only during the last century or two. Before that time, living standards barely rose—if at all—from one generation to the next. And a look around the world today reveals huge differences in standards of living resulting from the disturbing fact that, although some countries have enjoyed decades or even centuries of steadily rising per capita income levels, other countries have experienced hardly any economic growth at all.

This chapter investigates the causes of economic growth, what institutional structures appear to promote economic growth, and the controversies surrounding the benefits and costs of economic growth. We will learn, specifically the definition of economic growth, discuss its determinants, and explore growth policy. As you will see, economic growth has been perhaps the most revolutionary and powerful force in history. No study of economics is complete without a thorough understanding of the causes and consequences of economic growth.

AP Economic Growth

LO22.1 List two ways that economic growth is measured.

Economists define and measure **economic growth** as either:

- An increase in real GDP occurring over some time period.
- An increase in real GDP per capita occurring over some time period.

With either definition, economic growth is calculated as a percentage rate of growth per quarter (3-month period) or per year. For the first definition, for example, real GDP in the United States was \$15,961.7 billion in 2014 and \$16,348.9 in 2015. So the U.S. economic growth rate for 2015 was 2.4 percent {= [(16,348.9 billion − \$15,961.7 billion)/\$15,961.7 billion] × 100}. Growth rates normally are positive, but not always. In recession year 2009, for instance, the U.S. rate of economic growth was a *minus* 2.4 percent.

The second definition of economic growth in the bulleted list takes into consideration the size of the population. **Real GDP per capita** (or per capita output) is the amount of real output per person in a country. It is calculated, as follows.

$$\text{Real GDP per capita} = \frac{\text{Real GDP}}{\text{Population}}$$

For example, in 2014 the real GDP in the United States was \$15,961.7 billion and population was 319.4 million. Therefore, real GDP per capita in that year was \$49,974. In 2015 real GDP per capita increased to \$50,820. So the growth rate of real GDP per capita in 2015 was 1.7 percent {= [(\$50,820 − \$49,974)/\$49,974] × 100}. In contrast, real GDP per capita fell by 3.3 percent in recession year 2009.

For measuring expansion of military potential or political preeminence, the growth of real GDP is more useful. Unless specified otherwise, growth rates reported in the news and by international agencies use this definition of economic growth. For comparing living standards, however, the second definition is superior. While China's GDP in 2015 was \$10,983 billion compared with Denmark's \$295 billion, Denmark's real GDP per capita was \$64,186 compared with China's strikingly lower \$8,211. And in some cases real GDP growth statistics can be misleading, even when accurate. The African nation of Eritrea had real GDP growth of 1.3 percent per year from 2000–2008. But over the same period its annual growth of population was 3.8 percent, resulting in a decline in real GDP per capita of roughly 2.5 percent per year.

Growth as a Goal

Growth is a widely held economic goal. The expansion of total output relative to population results in rising real wages and incomes and thus higher standards of living. An economy that is experiencing economic growth is better able to meet people's wants and resolve socioeconomic problems. Rising real wages and income provide richer opportunities to individuals and families—a vacation trip, a personal computer, a higher education—without sacrificing other opportunities and pleasures. A growing economy can undertake new programs to alleviate poverty, embrace diversity, cultivate the arts, and protect the environment without impairing existing levels of consumption, investment, and public goods production.

In short, *growth lessens the burden of scarcity*. A growing economy, unlike a static economy, can consume more today while increasing its capacity to produce more in the future. By easing the burden of scarcity—by relaxing society's constraints on production—economic growth enables a nation to attain its economic goals more readily and to undertake new endeavors that require the use of goods and services to be accomplished.

Arithmetic of Growth

Why do economists pay so much attention to small changes in the rate of economic growth? Because those changes really matter! For the United States, with a current nominal GDP of about \$17.9 trillion, the difference between a 3 percent and a 4 percent rate of growth is about \$179 billion of output each year. For a poor country, a difference of one-half of a percentage point in the rate of growth may mean the difference between starvation and mere hunger.

The mathematical approximation called the **rule of 70** provides a quantitative grasp of the effect of economic growth. The rule of 70 tells us that we can find the number of years it will take for some measure to double, given its annual percentage increase, by dividing that percentage increase into the number 70:

$$\begin{array}{c}\text{Approximate}\\ \text{number of years}\\ \text{required to double}\\ \text{real GDP}\end{array} = \frac{70}{\begin{array}{c}\text{annual percentage rate}\\ \text{of growth}\end{array}}$$

Examples: A 3 percent annual rate of growth will double real GDP in about 23 (= 70 ÷ 3) years. Growth of 8 percent per year will double real GDP in about 9 (= 70 ÷ 8) years. The rule of 70 is applicable generally. For example, it works for estimating how long it will take the price level or a savings account to double at various percentage rates of inflation or interest. When compounded over many years, an apparently small difference in the rate of growth thus becomes highly significant. Suppose China and Italy start with identical GDPs, but then China grows at an 8 percent yearly rate, while Italy grows at 2 percent. China's GDP would double in about 9 years, while Italy's GDP would double in 35 years.

Growth in the United States

Table 22.1 gives an overview of economic growth in the United States since 1950. Column 2 reveals strong growth as

AP TABLE 22.1 Real GDP and Real GDP per Capita, Selected Years, 1950–2015

(1) Year	(2) Real GDP, Billions of 2009 $	(3) Population, Millions	(4) Real GDP, per Capita, 2009 $ (2) ÷ (3)
1950	$ 2,184	152	$14,638
1960	3,109	181	17,177
1970	4,722	205	23,034
1980	6,450	228	28,289
1990	8,955	250	35,830
2000	12,560	282	44,539
2010	14,784	309	47,845
2015	16,349	321	50,820

Source: Data are from the Bureau of Economic Analysis, **www.bea.gov**, and the U.S. Census Bureau, **www.census.gov**. All data are subject to government revision.

measured by increases in real GDP. Note that between 1950 and 2015 real GDP increased more than sevenfold. But the U.S. population also increased. Nevertheless, in column 4 we find that real GDP per capita rose more than threefold over these years.

What has been the *rate* of U.S. growth? Real GDP grew at an annual rate of about 3.1 percent between 1950 and 2015. Real GDP per capita increased at roughly 2.0 percent per year over that time. But we must qualify these raw numbers in several ways:

- ***Improved products and services*** Since the numbers in Table 22.1 do not fully account for improvements in products and services, they understate the growth of economic well-being. Such purely quantitative data do not fully compare an era of vacuum tube computers and low-efficiency V8 hot rods with an era of digital cell phone networks and fuel-sipping, hybrid-drive vehicles.
- ***Added leisure*** The increases in real GDP and per capita GDP identified in Table 22.1 were accomplished despite increases in leisure. The average workweek, once 50 hours, is now about 35 hours (excluding overtime hours). Again the raw growth numbers understate the gain in economic well-being.
- ***Other impacts*** These measures of growth do not account for any effects growth may have had on the environment and the quality of life. If growth debases the physical environment, excessively warms the planet, and creates a stressful work environment, the bare growth numbers will overstate the gains in well-being that result from growth. On the other hand, if growth leads to stronger environmental protections or a more secure and stress-free lifestyle, these numbers will understate the gains in well-being.

In Chapter 20, we made two other key points about U.S. growth rates. First, they are not constant or smooth over time. Like those of other countries, U.S. growth rates vary quarterly and annually depending on a variety of factors such as the introduction of major new inventions and the economy's current position in the business cycle. Second, many countries share the U.S. experience of positive and ongoing economic growth. But sustained growth is both a historically new occurrence and also one that is not shared equally by all countries.

AP QUICK REVIEW 22.1

✓ Economists measure economic growth as either (a) an increase in real GDP over time or (b) an increase in real GDP per capita over time.

✓ Real GDP in the United States has grown at an average annual rate of about 3.1 percent since 1950; real GDP per capita has grown at roughly a 2 percent annual rate over that same period.

AP Modern Economic Growth

LO22.2 Define "modern economic growth" and explain the institutional structures needed for an economy to experience it.

We now live in an era of wireless high-speed Internet connections, genetic engineering, and space exploration. New inventions and new technologies drive continual economic growth and ongoing increases in living standards. But it wasn't always like this. Economic growth and sustained increases in living standards are a historically recent phenomenon that started with the Industrial Revolution of the late 1700s. Before the Industrial Revolution, living standards were basically flat over long periods of time so that, for instance, Greek peasants living in the year 300 B.C. had about the same material standard of living as Greek peasants living in the year A.D. 1500. By contrast, our current era of **modern economic growth** is characterized by sustained and ongoing increases in living standards that can cause dramatic increases in the standard of living within less than a single human lifetime.

Economic historians informally date the start of the Industrial Revolution to the year 1776, when the Scottish inventor James Watt perfected a powerful and efficient steam engine. This steam engine inaugurated the modern era since the device could be used to drive industrial factory equipment, steamships, and steam locomotives.

The new industrial factories mass-produced goods for the first time. This meant that nearly all manufacturing shifted from items produced by hand by local craftsmen to items mass-produced in distant factories. The new steamships and steam locomotives meant that resources could easily flow to factories and that the products of factories could be shipped to distant consumers at low cost. The result was a huge increase in long-distance trade and a major population shift as people left farms to go work in the towns and cities where the new industrial factories were concentrated.

Steam power would later be largely replaced by electric power, and many more inventions would follow the steam engine that started the Industrial Revolution. These included railroads, motorized vehicles, telephones, airplanes, container ships, computers, the Internet, and many more. But the key point is that the last 200 or so years of history have been fundamentally different from anything that went before.

The biggest change has been change itself. Whereas in earlier times material standards of living and the goods and services that people produced and consumed changed very little even over the course of an entire human life span, today people living in countries experiencing modern economic growth are constantly exposed to new technologies, new products, and new services.

What is more, modern economic growth has vastly affected cultural, social, and political arrangements.

- Culturally, the vast increases in wealth and living standards have allowed ordinary people for the first time in history to have significant time for leisure activities and the arts.
- Socially, countries experiencing modern economic growth have abolished feudalism, instituted universal public education, and largely eliminated ancient social norms and legal restrictions against women and minorities doing certain jobs or holding certain positions.
- Politically, countries experiencing modern economic growth have tended to move toward democracy, a form of government that was extremely rare before the start of the Industrial Revolution.

In addition, the average human lifespan has more than doubled, from an average of less than 30 years before modern economic growth began in the late 1700s to a worldwide average of over 71 years today. Thus, for the first time in world history, the average person can expect to live into old age. These and other changes speak to the truly revolutionary power of economic growth and naturally lead economists to consider the causes of economic growth and what policies could be pursued to sustain and promote it. Their desire is intensified by the reality that economic growth is distributed so unevenly around the world.

The Uneven Distribution of Growth

Modern economic growth has spread only slowly from its British birthplace. It first advanced to France, Germany, and other parts of western Europe in the early 1800s before spreading to the United States, Canada, and Australia by the mid-1800s. Japan began to industrialize in the 1870s, but the rest of Asia did not follow until the early to mid-1900s, at which time large parts of Central and South America as well as the Middle East also began to experience modern economic growth. Most recent has been Africa, which for the most part did not experience modern economic growth until the last few decades. Notably, some parts of the world have yet to experience modern economic growth at all.

The different starting dates for modern economic growth in various parts of the world are the main cause of the vast differences in per capita GDP levels seen today. The current huge gaps between rich countries like the United States and Japan and poor countries like North Korea and Burundi were shown previously in Global Perspective 20.1. But the huge divergence in living standards caused by the fact that different countries started modern economic growth at different times is best seen in Figure 22.1, which shows how GDP per capita has evolved since 1820 in the United States, western Europe, Latin America, Asia, and Africa.

To make the comparison of living standards easier, income levels in all places and at all times have been converted into 1990 U.S. dollars. Using this convention, it is clear that in 1820 per capita incomes in all areas were quite similar, with the richest area in the world in 1820, western Europe, having an average per capita income of $1,232, while the poorest area of the world at that time, Africa, had an average per capita income of $418. Thus, in 1820, average incomes in the richest area were only about three times larger than those in the poorest area.

But because western Europe and the United States started experiencing modern economic growth earlier than other areas, they have now ended up vastly richer than other areas, despite the fact that per capita incomes in nearly all places have increased at least a bit. For instance, per capita GDP in the United States in 1998 was $27,331 while it was only $1,368 in Africa. Thus, because modern economic growth has occurred for nearly two centuries in the United States compared to a few decades in Africa, average living standards in the United States in 1998 were nearly 20 times higher than those in Africa.

Catching Up Is Possible

Do not get the wrong impression looking at Figure 22.1. Countries that began modern economic growth more recently are *not* doomed to be permanently poorer than the countries that began modern economic growth at an earlier date. This is true because people can adopt technology more quickly than they can invent it. Broadly speaking, the richest countries today have achieved that status because they have the most advanced technology. But because they already have the most advanced technology, they must invent new technology to get

AP FIGURE 22.1 The great divergence in standards of living. Income levels around the world were very similar in 1820. But they are now very different because certain areas, including the United States and western Europe, began experiencing modern economic growth much earlier than other areas.

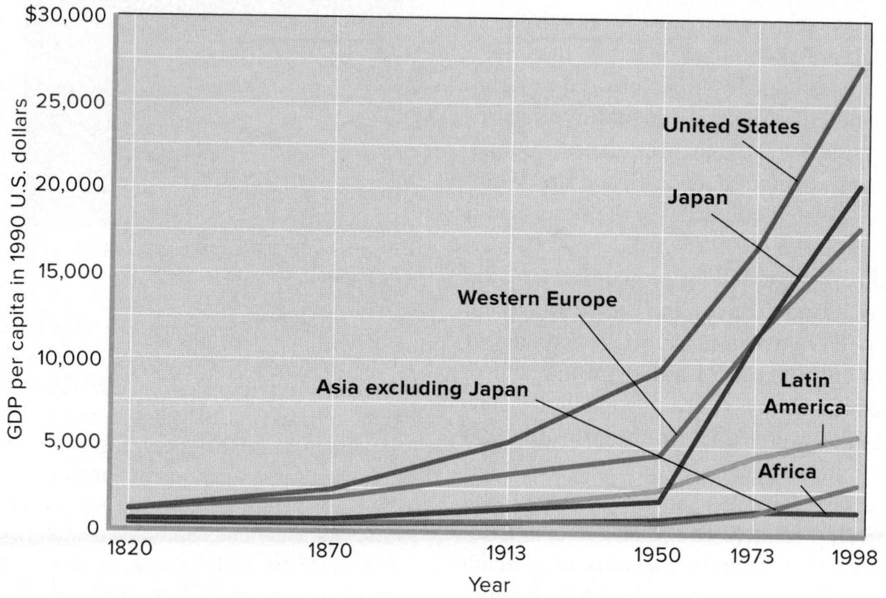

Source: Angus Maddison, *The World Economy: A Millennial Perspective* (Paris: OECD, 2001), p. 264.

even richer. Because inventing and implementing new technology is slow and costly, real GDP per capita in the richest **leader countries** typically grows by an average annual rate of just 2 or 3 percent per year.

By contrast, poorer **follower countries** can grow much faster because they can simply adopt existing technologies from rich leader countries. For instance, in many places in Africa today, the first telephones most people have ever been able to use are cell phones. That is, these countries have not even bothered to install the copper wires necessary for landline telephones, which are basically a nineteenth-century technology. Instead, they have gone directly for Internet-capable mobile phone networks, a twenty-first-century technology. By doing so, they skip past many stages of technology and development that the United States and other currently rich countries had to pass through. In effect, they jump directly to the most modern, most highly productive technology. The result is that, under the right circumstances, it is possible for poorer countries to experience extremely rapid increases in living standards. This can continue until they have caught up with the leader countries and become leader countries themselves. Once that happens, their growth rates fall down to the 2 or 3 percent rate typical of leader countries. This happens because once they are also rich and using the latest technology, their growth rates are limited by the rate at which new technology can be invented and applied.

Table 22.2 shows both how the growth rates of leader countries are constrained by the rate of technological progress as well as how certain follower countries have been able to catch up by adopting more advanced technologies and growing rapidly. Table 22.2 shows real GDP per capita in 1960 and 2010 as well as the average annual growth rate of

AP TABLE 22.2 Real GDP per Capita in 1960 and 2010 plus Average Annual Growth Rates of Real GDP per Capita from 1960–2010 for Selected Countries. (Figures are in 2005 dollars.)

Country	Real GDP per Capita, 1960	Real GDP per Capita, 2010	Average Annual Growth Rate, 1960–2010
United States	$14,766	$41,365	2.1
United Kingdom	11,257	34,268	2.2
France	9,347	31,299	2.4
Ireland	6,666	34,877	3.3
Japan	5,472	31,477	3.5
Singapore	4,149	55,862	5.2
Hong Kong	3,849	38,865	4.6
South Korea	1,765	26,609	5.4

Note: GDP figures for all countries are measured in "international dollars" of equal value to U.S. dollars in 2005.

Source: Alan Heston, Robert Summers, and Bettina Aten, Penn World Table Version 6.3, Center for International Comparisons of Production, Income and Prices at the University of Pennsylvania, August 2009.

real GDP per capita between 1960 and 2010 for three countries—the United States, the United Kingdom, and France—that were already rich leader countries in 1960 as well as for five other nations that were relatively poor follower countries at that time. To make comparisons easy, the GDPs and GDPs per capita for all countries are expressed in terms of 2005 U.S. dollars. The countries are ordered by their respective GDPs per capita in 1960, so that the richest country in the world at the time, the United States, is listed first while the poorest of the eight selected countries at the time, South Korea, is listed last.

First, notice that the average annual growth rates of the three leader countries—the United States, the United Kingdom, and France—have all been between 2.1 and 2.5 percent per year because their growth rates are limited by the rate at which new technologies can be invented and applied. By contrast, the five countries that were follower countries in 1960 have been able to grow much faster, between 3.3 percent per year and 5.4 percent per year. This has had remarkable effects on their standards of living relative to the leader countries. For instance, Ireland's GDP per capita was only 60 percent that of its neighbor, the United Kingdom, in 1960. But because Ireland grew at a 3.3 percent rate for the next 50 years while the United Kingdom grew at only a 2.2 percent rate over that time period, by 2010 Ireland's GDP per capita was actually higher than the United Kingdom's GDP per capita. Ireland had become a leader country, too.

The growth experiences of the other four nations that were poor in 1960 have been even more dramatic. Hong Kong, for instance, moved from a GDP per capita that was less than one-third of that enjoyed by the United Kingdom in 1960 to a GDP per capita 13 percent higher than that of the United Kingdom in 2010. The Consider This box emphasizes both how quickly small differences in growth rates can change the level of real GDP per capita and how countries stand in relation to each other in terms of real GDP per capita.

Finally, you may be puzzled as to why the GDP per capita of the United States in 2010 in Table 22.2 is so much higher than that of other rich leader countries. Why, for instance, is U.S. GDP per capita 32 percent higher than French GDP per capita? One important reason is that U.S. citizens put in substantially more labor time than do the citizens of most other leader countries. First, a much larger fraction of the U.S. population is employed than in other rich leader countries. Second, U.S. employees work many more hours per year than do employees in other rich leader countries. For example, 58 percent of the working-age population of the United States was employed in 2010 compared to 51 percent in France. That's a difference of about 14 percent. And American employees worked an average of 1,778 total hours during 2010, compared to an average of 1,478 total hours for French workers. That's a difference of about 20 percent. Added together, these two differences between U.S. and French labor supply imply about a 34 percent difference in the total number of hours worked in the French and American economies. Thus, differences in labor supply help explain differences between rich leader countries in terms of their differing levels of GDP per person.

Buy why do Americans supply so much more labor than workers in France and some of the other rich leader countries? Explanations put forth by economists include cultural differences regarding the proper balance between work and leisure, stronger unions in France and other rich leader countries, and more generous unemployment and welfare programs in France and other rich leader countries. France and other rich leader countries also tend to have higher tax rates than the United States—something that may significantly discourage employment. And, finally, the legal workweek is shorter in some countries than it is in the United States.

CONSIDER THIS . . .

Economic Growth Rates Matter!

Source: © Todd Warshaw/Getty Images Sport/Getty Images

When compounded over many decades, small absolute differences in rates of economic growth add up to substantial differences in real GDP and standards of living. Consider three hypothetical countries—Slogo, Sumgo, and Speedo. Suppose that in 2014 these countries have identical levels of real GDP ($6 trillion), population (200 million), and real GDP per capita ($30,000). Also, assume that annual real GDP growth is 2 percent in Slogo, 3 percent in Sumgo, and 4 percent in Speedo.

How will these alternative growth rates affect real GDP and real GDP per capita over a long period, say, a 70-year life-span? By 2084 the 2, 3, and 4 percent growth rates would boost real GDP from $6 trillion to:

- $24 trillion in Slogo.
- $47 trillion in Sumgo.
- $93 trillion in Speedo.

For illustration, let's assume that each country experienced an average annual population growth of 1 percent over the 70 years. Then, in 2084 real GDP per capita would be about:

- $60,000 in Slogo.
- $118,000 in Sumgo.
- $233,000 in Speedo.

Even small differences in growth rates matter!

AP QUICK REVIEW 22.2

- ✓ Before the advent of modern economic growth starting in England in the late 1700s, living standards showed no sustained increases over time.
- ✓ Modern economic growth is characterized by sustained and ongoing increases in living standards that can cause dramatic increases in the standard of living within less than a single human lifetime.
- ✓ Poor follower countries can catch up with and even surpass the living standards of rich leader countries by adopting the cutting-edge technologies and institutions already developed by rich leader countries.
- ✓ Substantial differences in GDP per capita among technologically advanced leader countries can be caused by differences in the amount of labor supplied.

Institutional Structures That Promote Modern Economic Growth

Table 22.2 demonstrates that poor follower countries can catch up and become rich leader countries by growing rapidly. But how does a country start that process and enter into modern economic growth? And once it has started modern economic growth, how does it keep the process going?

Economic historians have identified several institutional structures that promote and sustain modern economic growth. Some structures increase the savings and investment that are needed to fund the construction and maintenance of the huge amounts of infrastructure required to run modern economies. Other institutional structures promote the development of new technologies. And still others act to ensure that resources flow efficiently to their most productive uses. These growth-promoting institutional structures include:

- ***Strong property rights*** These appear to be absolutely necessary for rapid and sustained economic growth. People will not invest if they believe that thieves, bandits, or a rapacious and tyrannical government will steal their investments or their expected returns.
- ***Patents and copyrights*** Before patents and copyrights were first issued and enforced, inventors and authors usually saw their ideas stolen before they could profit from them. By giving inventors and authors the exclusive right to market and sell their creations, patents and copyrights give a strong financial incentive to invent and create.
- ***Efficient financial institutions*** These are needed to channel the savings generated by households toward the businesses, entrepreneurs, and inventors that do most of society's investing and inventing. Banks as well as stock and bond markets appear to be institutions crucial to modern economic growth.
- ***Literacy and widespread education*** Without highly educated inventors, new technologies do not get developed. And without a highly educated workforce, it is impossible to implement those technologies and put them to productive use.
- ***Free trade*** Free trade promotes economic growth by allowing countries to specialize so that different types of output can be produced in the countries where they can be made at the lowest opportunity cost. In addition, free trade promotes the rapid spread of new ideas so that innovations made in one country quickly spread to other countries.
- ***A competitive market system*** Under a market system, prices and profits serve as the signals that tell firms what to make and how much of it to make. Rich leader countries vary substantially in terms of how much government regulation they impose on markets, but in all cases, firms have substantial autonomy to follow market signals in deciding on current production and in making investments to produce what they believe consumers will demand in the future.

Several other difficult-to-measure factors also influence a nation's capacity for economic growth. The overall social-cultural-political environment of the United States, for example, has encouraged economic growth. Beyond the market system that has prevailed in the United States, the United States also has had a stable political system characterized by democratic principles, internal order, the right of property ownership, the legal status of enterprise, and the enforcement of contracts. Economic freedom and political freedom have been "growth-friendly."

In addition, and unlike some nations, there are virtually no social or moral taboos on production and material progress in the United States. The nation's social philosophy has embraced wealth creation as an attainable and desirable goal and the inventor, the innovator, and the businessperson are accorded high degrees of prestige and respect in American society. Finally, Americans have a positive attitude toward work and risk taking, resulting in an ample supply of willing workers and innovative entrepreneurs. A flow of energetic immigrants has greatly augmented that supply.

The following Consider This box deals with how fast-growing follower countries such as India sometimes alter their growth-related institutional structures as they grow richer. This course's online Enrichment Chapter 7 looks at the special problems of economic growth in developing nations.

CONSIDER THIS . . .

Source: © Stockbyte/Getty Images RF

Patents and Innovation

It costs U.S. and European drug companies about $1 billion to research, patent, and safety-test a new drug because literally thousands of candidate drugs fail for each drug that succeeds. The only way to cover these costs is by relying on patent protections that give a drug's developer the exclusive monopoly right to market and sell the new drug for 20 years following the patent application. The revenues over that time period will hopefully be enough to cover the drug's development costs and—if the drug is popular—generate a profit for the drug company.

Leader and follower countries have gotten into heated disputes over patented drugs, however, because the follower countries have often refused to recognize the patents granted to pharmaceutical companies in rich countries. India, for instance, has allowed local drug companies to copy and sell drugs that were developed by U.S. companies and are still under patent protection in the United States.

That policy benefits Indian consumers because competition among the local drug companies drives down the price to below the monopoly price that would be charged by the patent owner. But the weak patent protections in India have a side effect. They make it completely unprofitable for local drug producers to try to develop innovative new drugs. Local rivals would simply copy the new drugs and sell them at very low prices. So India has recently moved to strengthen its patent protections to try to provide financial incentives to transform its local drug companies from copycats into innovators. But note that the innovative new drugs that may result from the increased patent protections are not without a cost. As patent protections in India are improved, inexpensive local drugs copied from the leader countries will no longer be available to Indian consumers.

AP Determinants of Growth

LO22.3 Identify the general supply, demand, and efficiency forces that give rise to economic growth.

Our discussion of modern economic growth and the institutional structures that promote it has purposely been general. We now want to focus our discussion on six factors that directly affect the *rate* and quality of economic growth. These determinants of economic growth can be grouped into four supply factors, one demand factor, and one efficiency factor.

Supply Factors

The first four determinants of economic growth relate to the physical ability of the economy to expand. They are:

- Increases in the quantity and quality of natural resources.
- Increases in the quantity and quality of human resources.
- Increases in the supply (or stock) of capital goods.
- Improvements in technology.

Any increases or improvements in these **supply factors** will increase the *potential* size of an economy's GDP. The remaining two factors are necessary for that potential to be fulfilled not just in terms of the overall quantity of output but also in terms of the quality of that output and whether it is properly directed toward producing the items most highly valued by society.

Demand Factor

The fifth determinant of economic growth is the **demand factor:**

- To actually achieve the higher production potential created when the supply factors increase or improve, households, businesses, and the government must also expand their purchases of goods and services so as to provide a market for all the new output that can potentially be produced.

If that occurs, there will be no unplanned increases in inventories and resources will remain fully employed. The demand factor acknowledges that economic growth requires that increases in total spending must occur if we are to actually realize the output gains made available by increased production capacity.

Efficiency Factor

The sixth determinant of economic growth is the **efficiency factor:**

- To reach its full production potential, an economy must achieve economic efficiency as well as full employment.

The economy must use its resources in the least costly way (productive efficiency) to produce the specific mix of goods and services that maximizes people's well-being (allocative efficiency). The ability to expand production, together with the full use of available resources, is not sufficient for achieving maximum possible growth. Also required is the efficient use of those resources.

The supply, demand, and efficiency factors in economic growth are related. Unemployment caused by insufficient total spending (the demand factor) may lower the rate of new capital accumulation (a supply factor) and delay expenditures on research (also a supply factor). Conversely, low spending on investment (a supply factor) may cause insufficient spending (the demand factor) and unemployment. Widespread inefficiency in the use of resources (the efficiency factor) may translate into higher costs of goods and services and thus lower profits, which in turn may slow innovation and reduce the accumulation of capital (supply factors). Economic growth is a dynamic process in which the supply, demand, and efficiency factors all interact.

Production Possibilities Analysis

To put the six factors affecting the rate of economic growth into better perspective, let's use the production possibilities analysis introduced in Chapter 1.

Growth and Production Possibilities Recall that a curve like *AB* in Figure 22.2 is a production possibilities curve. It indicates the various *maximum* combinations of products an economy can produce with its fixed quantity and quality of natural, human, and capital resources and its stock of technological knowledge. An improvement in any of the supply factors will push the production possibilities curve outward, as from *AB* to *CD*.

But the demand factor reminds us that an increase in total spending is needed to move the economy from a point like *a* on curve *AB* to any of the points on the higher curve *CD*. And the efficiency factor reminds us that we need least-cost production and an optimal location on *CD* for the resources to make their maximum possible dollar contribution to total output. You will recall from Chapter 1 that this "best allocation" is determined by expanding the production of each good until its marginal benefit equals its marginal cost. Here, we assume that this optimal combination of capital and consumer goods occurs at point *b*. If the efficiency factor is in full effect, then the economy will produce at point *b* rather than at any other point along curve *CD*.

Example: The net increase in the size of the labor force in the United States in recent years has been 1.5 to 2 million workers per year. That increment raises the economy's production capacity. But obtaining the extra output that these added workers could produce depends on their success in finding jobs. It also depends on whether or not the jobs are in firms and industries where the workers' talents are fully and optimally used. Society does not want new labor-force entrants to be unemployed. Nor does it want pediatricians working as plumbers or pediatricians producing pediatric services for which marginal costs exceed marginal benefits.

Normally, increases in total spending match increases in production capacity, and the economy moves from a point on the previous production possibilities curve to a point on the expanded curve. Moreover, the competitive market system tends to drive the economy toward productive and allocative efficiency. Occasionally, however, the economy may end up at some point such as *c* in Figure 22.2. That kind of outcome occurred in the United States during the severe recession of 2007–2009. Real output fell far below the amount of output that the economy could have produced if it had achieved full employment and operated on its production possibilities curve.

AP FIGURE 22.2 Economic growth and the production possibilities curve. Economic growth is made possible by the four supply factors that shift the production possibilities curve outward, as from *AB* to *CD*. Economic growth is realized when the demand factor and the efficiency factor move the economy from points such as *a* and *c* that are inside *CD* to the optimal output point, which is assumed to be point *b* in this figure.

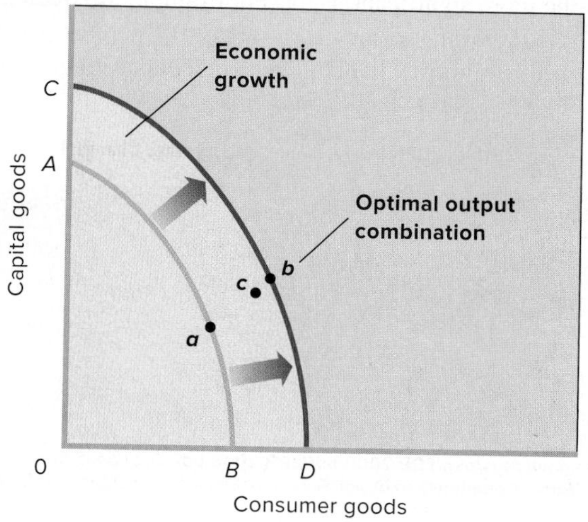

Labor and Productivity Although the demand and efficiency factors are important, discussions of economic growth focus primarily on supply factors. Society can increase its real output and income in two fundamental ways: (1) by increasing its inputs of resources and (2) by raising the productivity of those inputs. Figure 22.3 concentrates on the input of *labor* and provides a useful framework for discussing the role of supply factors in growth. A nation's real GDP in any year depends on the input of labor (measured in hours of work) multiplied by **labor productivity** (measured as real output per hour of work):

$$\text{Real GDP} = \text{hours of work} \times \text{labor productivity}$$

Thought of this way, a nation's economic growth from one year to the next depends on its *increase* in labor inputs (if any) and its *increase* in labor productivity (if any).

Illustration: Assume that the hypothetical economy of Ziam has 10 workers in year 1, each working 2,000 hours per year (50 weeks at 40 hours per week). The total input of labor therefore is 20,000 hours. If productivity (average real output per hour of work) is $10, then real GDP in Ziam will be $200,000

AP **FIGURE 22.3 The supply determinants of real output.** Real GDP is usefully viewed as the product of the quantity of labor inputs (hours of work) multiplied by labor productivity.

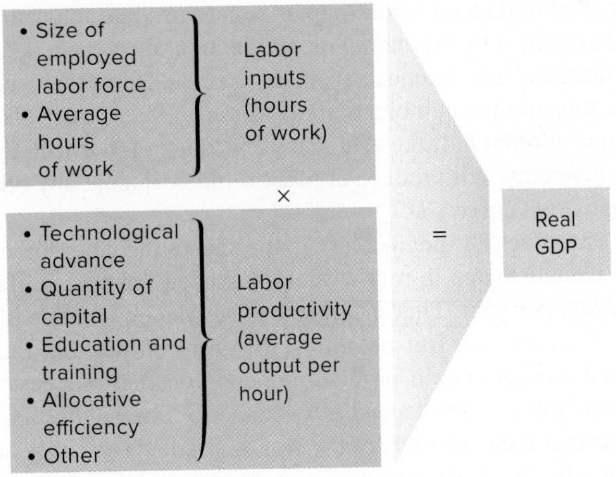

(= 20,000 × $10). If work hours rise to 20,200 and labor productivity rises to $10.40, Ziam's real GDP will increase to $210,080 in year 2. Ziam's rate of economic growth will be about 5 percent [= ($210,080 – $200,000)/$200,000] for the year.

Hours of Work What determines the number of hours worked each year? As shown in Figure 22.3, the hours of labor input depend on the size of the employed labor force and the length of the average workweek. Labor-force size depends on the size of the working-age population and the **labor-force participation rate**—the percentage of the working-age population actually in the labor force. The length of the average workweek is governed by legal and institutional considerations and by collective bargaining agreements negotiated between unions and employers.

Labor Productivity Figure 22.3 tells us that labor productivity is determined by technological progress, the quantity of capital goods available to workers, the quality of labor itself, and the efficiency with which inputs are allocated, combined, and managed. Productivity rises when the health, training, education, and motivation of workers improve; when workers have more and better machinery and natural resources with which to work; when production is better organized and managed; and when labor is reallocated from less-efficient industries to more-efficient industries.

AP Accounting for Growth

LO22.4 Describe "growth accounting" and the specific factors accounting for economic growth in the United States.

The president's Council of Economic Advisers uses a system called **growth accounting** to assess the relative importance of the supply-side elements that contribute to changes in real GDP. This system groups these elements into two main categories:

- Increases in hours of work.
- Increases in labor productivity.

Labor Inputs versus Labor Productivity

Table 22.3 provides the relevant data for the United States for five periods. The symbol "Q" in the table stands for "quarter" of the year. The beginning points for the first four periods are business-cycle peaks, and the last period includes future projections by the Council of Economic Advisers. It is clear from the table that both increases in the quantity of labor and increases in labor productivity are important sources of economic growth. Between 1953 and 2015, the labor force increased from 63 million to 158 million workers. Over that period the average length of the workweek remained relatively stable. Falling birthrates slowed the growth of the native population, but increased immigration partly offset that slowdown. As indicated in the nearby Consider This box, of particular significance was a surge of women's participation in the labor force. Partly as a result, U.S. labor-force growth averaged 1.5 million workers per year over those 62 years.

The growth of labor productivity also has been important to economic growth. In fact, productivity growth has usually been the more significant factor. For example, between 2007 and 2015, labor inputs increased by just 0.1 percent per year. As a result, almost all of the 1.2 percent average annual

TABLE 22.3 Accounting for the Growth of U.S. Real GDP, 1953–2015 plus Projection from 2015 to 2026 (Average Annual Percentage Changes)

	Actual				Projected
Item	1953 Q2 to 1973 Q4	1973 Q4 to 1995 Q2	1995 Q2 to 2007 Q3	2007 Q3 to 2015 Q3	2015 Q3 to 2026 Q4
Increase in real GDP	3.6	2.8	3.2	1.2	2.4
Increase in quantity of labor	1.1	1.3	0.5	0.1	0.3
Increase in labor productivity	2.5	1.5	2.7	1.1	2.1

Source: Derived from *Economic Report of the President, 2008,* p. 45, **https://www.gpo.gov/fdsys/pkg/ERP-2008/pdf/ERP-2008.pdf**; *Economic Report of the President 2016,* p. 113, **https://www.whitehouse.gov/sites/default/files/docs/ERP_2016_Book_Complete%20JA.pdf**; Bureau of Economic Analysis; and Bureau of Labor Statistics.

growth rate of GDP over that time period was due to increases in labor productivity. As can be calculated from the data in the far right column of Table 22.3, productivity growth is projected to account for 88 percent of the growth of real GDP between 2015 and 2026.

Because increases in labor productivity are so important to economic growth, economists go to the trouble of investigating and assessing the relative importance of the factors that contribute to productivity growth. There are five factors that, together, appear to explain changes in productivity growth rates: technological advance, the amount of capital each worker has to work with, education and training, economies of scale, and resource allocation. We will examine each factor in turn, noting how much each factor contributes to productivity growth.

Technological Advance

The largest contributor to productivity growth is technological advance, which is thought to account for about 40 percent of productivity growth. As economist Paul Romer stated, "Human history teaches us that economic growth springs from better recipes, not just from more cooking."

Technological advance includes not only innovative production techniques but new managerial methods and new forms of business organization that improve the process of production. Generally, technological advance is generated by the discovery of new knowledge, which allows resources to be combined in improved ways that increase output. Once discovered and implemented, new knowledge soon becomes available to entrepreneurs and firms at relatively low cost. Technological advance therefore eventually spreads through the entire economy, boosting productivity and economic growth.

Technological advance and capital formation (investment) are closely related, since technological advance usually promotes investment in new machinery and equipment. In fact, technological advance is often *embodied* within new capital. For example, the purchase of new computers brings into industry speedier, more powerful computers that incorporate new technology.

Technological advance has been both rapid and profound. Gas and diesel engines, conveyor belts, and assembly lines are significant developments of the past. So, too, are fuel-efficient commercial aircraft, integrated microcircuits, personal computers, digital photography, and containerized shipping. More recently, technological advance has exploded, particularly in the areas of computers, photography, wireless communications, and the Internet. Other fertile areas of recent innovation are medicine and biotechnology.

Quantity of Capital

A second major contributor to productivity growth is increased capital, which explains roughly 30 percent of productivity growth. More and better plant and equipment make workers more productive. And a nation acquires more capital by saving some of its income and using that savings to invest in plant and equipment.

Although some capital substitutes for labor, most capital is complementary to labor—it makes labor more productive. A key determinant of labor productivity is the amount of capital goods available *per worker*. If both the aggregate stock of capital goods and the size of the labor force increase over a given period, the individual worker is not necessarily better equipped and productivity will not necessarily rise. But the quantity of

CONSIDER THIS . . .

Source: © Dynamic Graphics/JupiterImages RF

Women, the Labor Force, and Economic Growth

The substantial rise in the number of women working in the paid workforce in the United States has been one of the major labor market trends of the last 50 years. In 1960, about 40 percent of women worked full-time or part-time in paid jobs. Today, that number is about 60 percent.

Women have greatly increased their productivity in the workplace, mostly by becoming better educated and professionally trained. Rising productivity has increased women's wage rates. Those higher wages have raised the opportunity costs—the forgone wage earnings—of staying at home. Women have therefore substituted employment in the labor market for traditional home activities. This substitution has been particularly pronounced among married women. (Single women have always had high labor-force participation rates.)

Furthermore, changing lifestyles and the widespread availability of birth control have freed up time for greater labor-force participation by women. Women not only have fewer children, but those children are spaced closer together in age. Thus women who leave their jobs during their children's early years return to the labor force sooner.

Greater access to jobs by women also has raised the labor-force participation of women. Service industries—teaching, nursing, and office work, for instance—that traditionally have employed many women have expanded rapidly in the past several decades. Also, the population in general has shifted from farms and rural regions to urban areas, where jobs for women are more abundant and more geographically accessible. Additionally, occupational barriers to professions have greatly eroded, resulting in many more women becoming business managers, lawyers, professors, and physicians.

In summary, women in the United States are better educated, more productive, and more efficiently employed than ever before. Their greater presence in the labor force has contributed greatly to U.S. economic growth.

FIGURE 22.4 Changes in the educational attainment of the U.S. adult population. The percentage of the U.S. adult population, age 25 or older, completing high school and college has been rising over recent decades.

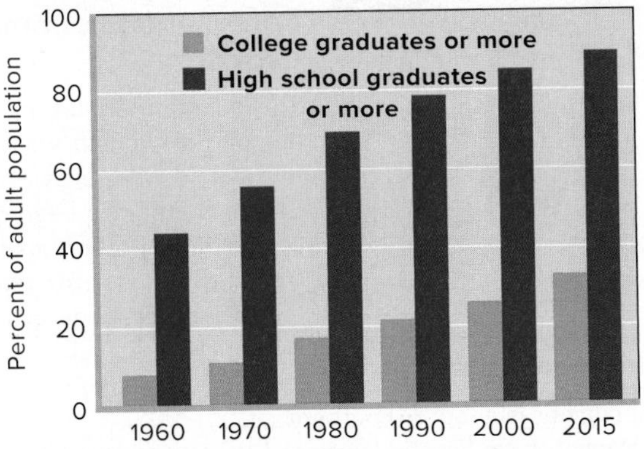

Source: U.S. Census Bureau, www.census.gov

capital equipment available per U.S. worker has increased greatly over time. (In 2014 it was about $149,286 per worker.)

Public investment in the U.S. **infrastructure** (highways and bridges, public transit systems, wastewater treatment facilities, water systems, airports, educational facilities, and so on) has also grown over the years. This publicly owned capital complements private capital. Investments in new highways promote private investment in new factories and retail stores along their routes. Industrial parks developed by local governments attract manufacturing and distribution firms.

Private investment in infrastructure also plays a large role in economic growth. One example is the tremendous growth of private capital relating to communications systems over the years.

Education and Training

Ben Franklin once said, "He that hath a trade hath an estate," meaning that education and training contribute to a worker's stock of **human capital**—the knowledge and skills that make a worker productive. Investment in human capital includes not only formal education but also on-the-job training. Like investment in physical capital, investment in human capital is an important means of increasing labor productivity and earnings. An estimated 15 percent of productivity growth derives from investments in people's education and skills.

One measure of a nation's quality of labor is its level of educational attainment. Figure 22.4 shows large gains in education attainment over the past several decades. In 1960 only 41 percent of the U.S. population age 25 or older had at least a high school education, and only 8 percent had a college or post-college education. By 2015, those numbers had increased to 88 and 33 percent, respectively. Clearly, more people are receiving more education than ever before.

But all is not upbeat with education in the United States. Many observers think that the quality of education in the United States has declined. For example, U.S. students perform poorly on science and math tests relative to students in many other nations (see Global Perspective 22.1). And the United States has been producing fewer engineers and scientists, a problem that may trace back to inadequate training in math and science in elementary and high schools. For these reasons, much recent public policy discussion and legislation have been directed toward improving the quality of the U.S. education and training system.

GLOBAL PERSPECTIVE 22.1

Average Test Scores of Eighth-Grade Students in Math and Science, Top 10 Test-Taking Countries

The test performance of U.S. eighth-grade students did not compare favorably with that of eighth-graders in several other nations in the Fifth International Math and Science Study (2011).

Mathematics

Rank	Score
1 South Korea	613
2 Singapore	611
3 Taiwan	609
4 Hong Kong	586
5 Japan	570
6 Russia	539
7 Israel	516
8 Finland	514
9 United States	509
10 Great Britain	507

Science

Rank	Score
1 Singapore	590
2 Taiwan	564
3 South Korea	560
4 Japan	558
5 Finland	552
6 Slovenia	543
7 Russia	542
8 Hong Kong	535
9 Great Britain	533
10 United States	525

Source: US Department of Education, *Fifth International Math and Science Study* (2011).

Economies of Scale and Resource Allocation

Economies of scale and improved resource allocation are a fourth and fifth source of productivity growth, and together they explain about 15 percent of productivity growth.

Economies of Scale Reductions in per-unit production costs that result from increases in output levels are called **economies of scale**. Markets have increased in size over time, allowing firms to increase output levels and thereby achieve production advantages associated with greater size. As firms expand their size and output, they are able to use larger, more productive equipment and employ methods of manufacturing and delivery that increase productivity. They also are better able to recoup substantial investments in developing new products and production methods. Examples: A large manufacturer of autos can use elaborate assembly lines with computerization and robotics, while smaller producers must settle for less-advanced technologies using more labor inputs. Large pharmaceutical firms greatly reduce the average amount of labor (researchers, production workers) needed to produce each pill as they increase the number of pills produced. Accordingly, economies of scale result in greater real GDP and thus contribute to economic growth.

Improved Resource Allocation Improved resource allocation means that workers over time have moved from low-productivity employment to high-productivity employment. Historically, many workers have shifted from agriculture, where labor productivity is low, to manufacturing, where it is quite high. More recently, labor has shifted away from some manufacturing industries to even higher-productivity industries such as computer software, business consulting, and pharmaceuticals. As a result of such shifts, the average productivity of U.S. workers has increased.

Also, discrimination in education and the labor market has historically deterred some women and minorities from entering high-productivity jobs. With the decline of such discrimination over time, many members of those groups have shifted from lower-productivity jobs to higher-productivity jobs. The result has been higher overall labor productivity and real GDP.

Finally, things such as tariffs, import quotas, and other barriers to international trade tend to relegate resources to relatively unproductive pursuits. The long-run movement toward liberalized international trade through international agreements has improved the allocation of resources, increased labor productivity, and expanded real output, both here and abroad.

AP QUICK REVIEW 22.3

- ✓ Institutional structures that promote growth include strong property rights, patents, efficient financial institutions, education, and a competitive market system.
- ✓ The principal determinants of economic growth include four supply factors (increases in the quantity and quality of natural resources, increases in the quantity and quality of human resources, increases in the stock of capital goods, and improvements in technology).
- ✓ Improvements in labor productivity accounted for about two-thirds of the increase in U.S. real GDP between 1990 and 2012; the use of more labor inputs accounted for the remainder.
- ✓ Improved technology, more capital (public and private), greater education and training, economies of scale, and better resource allocation have been the main contributors to U.S. productivity growth and, thus, to U.S. economic growth.

Recent Fluctuations in the Average Rate of Productivity Growth

LO22.5 Explain how the average rate of U.S. productivity growth has fluctuated since 1973.

Figure 22.5 shows the growth of labor productivity (as measured by changes in the index of labor productivity) in the United States from 1973 to 2015, along with separate trend lines for 1973–1995, 1995–2010, and 2010–2015. Labor productivity in the business sector grew by an average of only 1.5 percent yearly over the 1973–1995 period. But productivity growth averaged a much higher 2.6 percent per year between 1995 and 2010 before plummeting to just 0.4 percent between 2010 and 2015. Many economists believe that the rapid productivity growth experienced between 1995 and 2010 resulted from a significant new wave of technological advances, coupled with global competition. By contrast, the dramatic decline in productivity growth that followed the Great Recession of 2007–2009 was perhaps due to a slowdown in the rate at which productive new technologies were being implemented by businesses.

Robust productivity growth is important because real output, real income, and real wages are linked to labor productivity. To see why, suppose you are alone on an uninhabited island. The number of fish you can catch or coconuts you can pick per hour—your productivity—is your real wage (or real income) per hour. By *increasing* your productivity, you can improve your standard of living because you can gather more fish and more coconuts (goods) for each hour of work.

AP **FIGURE 22.5 Growth of labor productivity in the United States, 1973–2012.** U.S. labor productivity (here, for the business sector) increased at an average annual rate of only 1.5 percent from 1973 to 1995. But between 1995 and 2010, it rose at an annual rate of 2.6 percent before decreasing to just 0.4 percent per year after the Great Recession of 2007–2009.

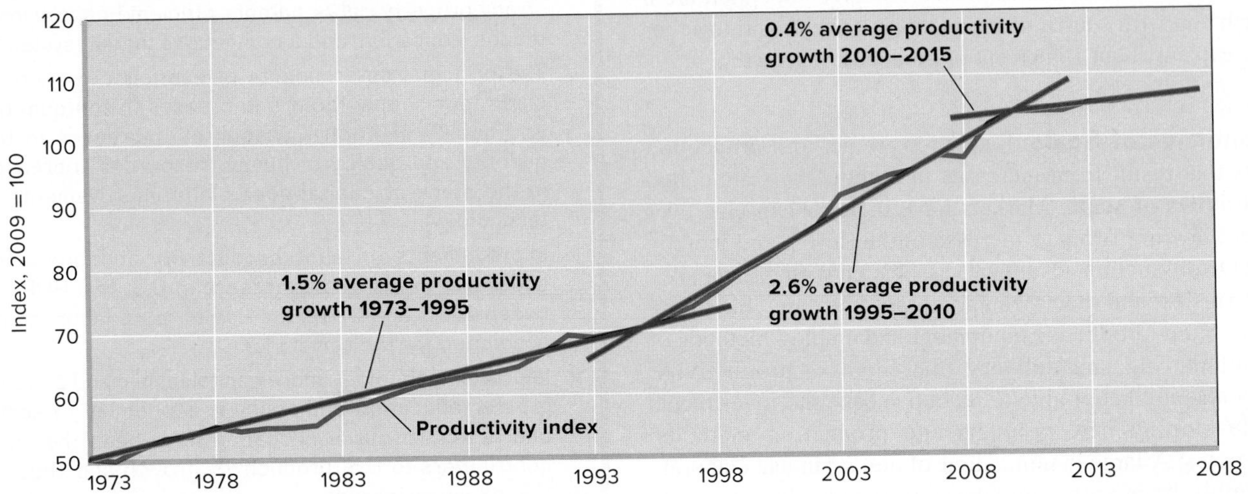

Source: U.S. Bureau of Labor Statistics, **www.bls.gov**.

So it is for the economy as a whole: Over long periods, the economy's labor productivity determines its average real hourly wage, which includes fringe benefits such as health care insurance and contributions to pensions. The economy's income per hour is equal to its output per hour. So productivity growth is the economy's main route for improving the living standards for its workers. It allows firms to pay higher wages without lowering their business profits.

Reasons for the Rise in the Average Rate of Productivity Growth between 1995 and 2010

Why did productivity growth increase rapidly between 1995 and 2010?

The Microchip and Information Technology The core element of the productivity speedup between 1995 and 2010 was an explosion of entrepreneurship and innovation based on the microprocessor, or *microchip*, which bundles transistors on a piece of silicon. Some observers liken the invention of the microchip to that of electricity, the automobile, air travel, the telephone, and television in importance and scope.

The microchip has found its way into thousands of applications. It has helped create a wide array of new products and services and new ways of doing business. Its immediate results were the pocket calculator, the bar-code scanner, the personal computer, the laptop computer, and more powerful business computers. But the miniaturization of electronic circuits also advanced the development of many other products such as cell phones and pagers, computer-guided lasers, global positioning equipment, energy conservation systems, Doppler radar, digital cameras, and machines to decipher the human genome.

Perhaps of greatest significance, the widespread availability of personal and laptop computers stimulated the desire to tie them together. That desire promoted rapid development of the Internet and all its many manifestations, such as business-to-household and business-to-business electronic commerce (e-commerce). The combination of the computer, fiber-optic cable, wireless technology, and the Internet constitutes a spectacular advance in **information technology,** which has been used to connect all parts of the world.

New Firms and Increasing Returns Hundreds of new **start-up firms** advanced various aspects of the new information technology. Many of these firms created more "hype" than goods and services and quickly fell by the wayside. But a number of firms flourished, eventually to take their places among the nation's largest firms. Examples of those firms include Intel (microchips); Apple and Dell (personal computers); Microsoft and Oracle (computer software); Cisco Systems (Internet switching systems); America Online (Internet service provision); Yahoo and Google (Internet search engines); and eBay, PayPal, and Amazon.com (electronic commerce). There are scores more! Most of these firms were either "not on the radar" or "a small blip on the radar" 30 years ago. Today each of them has large annual revenue and employs thousands of workers.

Successful new firms often experience **increasing returns,** a situation in which a given percentage increase in the amount of inputs a firm uses leads to an even larger percentage increase in the amount of output the firm produces. For example, suppose that a company called Techco decides to double the size of its operations to meet the growing demand for its services. After doubling its plant and equipment and doubling its workforce, say, from 100 workers to 200 workers, it finds that its total output has tripled from 8,000 units to 24,000 units. Techco has experienced increasing returns; its output has increased by 200 percent, while its inputs have increased by only 100 percent. That is, its labor productivity has gone up from 80 units per worker (= 8,000 units/100 workers) to 120 units per worker (= 24,000 units/200 workers). Increasing returns boost labor productivity and reduce per-unit production costs. Since these cost reductions result from increases in output levels, they are examples of *economies of scale*.

Both emerging firms as well as established firms can exploit several different sources of increasing returns and economies of scale:

- ***More specialized inputs*** Firms can use more specialized and thus more productive capital and workers as they expand their operations. A growing new e-commerce business, for example, can purchase highly specialized inventory management systems and hire specialized personnel such as accountants, marketing managers, and system maintenance experts.
- ***Spreading of development costs*** Firms can spread high product development costs over greater output. For example, suppose that a new software product costs $100,000 to develop and only $2 per unit to manufacture and sell. If the firm sells 1,000 units of the software, its per-unit cost will be $102 [= ($100,000 + $2,000)/1,000], but if it sells 500,000 units, that cost will drop to only $2.20 [= ($100,000 + $1 million)/500,000].
- ***Simultaneous consumption*** Many recently developed products and services can satisfy large numbers of customers at the same time. Unlike a gallon of gas that needs to be produced for each buyer, a software program needs to be produced only once. It then becomes available at very low expense to thousands or even millions of buyers. The same is true of books delivered to electronic reading devices, movies distributed on DVDs, and information disseminated through the Internet.
- ***Network effects*** Software and Internet service become more beneficial to a buyer the greater the number of households and businesses that also buy them. When others have Internet service, you can send e-mail messages to them. And when they also have software that allows display of documents and photos, you can attach those items to your e-mail messages. These interconnectivity advantages are called **network effects,** which are increases in the value of a product to each user, including existing users, as the total number of users rises. The domestic and global expansion of the Internet in particular has produced network effects, as have cell phones, pagers, tablet computers, and other aspects of wireless communication. Network effects magnify the value of output well beyond the costs of inputs.
- ***Learning by doing*** Finally, firms that produce new products or pioneer new ways of doing business experience increasing returns through **learning by doing.** Tasks that initially may have taken firms hours may take them only minutes once the methods are perfected.

Whatever the particular source of increasing returns, the result is higher productivity, which tends to reduce the per-unit cost of producing and delivering products.

Global Competition The recent economy is characterized not only by information technology and increasing returns but also by heightened global competition. The collapse of the socialist economies in the late 1980s and early 1990s, together with the success of market systems, has led to a reawakening of capitalism throughout the world. The new information technologies have "shrunk the globe" and made it imperative for all firms to lower their costs and prices and to innovate in order to remain competitive. Free-trade zones such as NAFTA and the European Union (EU), along with trade liberalization through the World Trade Organization (WTO), have also heightened competition internationally by removing trade protection from domestic firms. The larger geographic markets, in turn, have enabled firms to expand beyond their national borders.

Implications for Economic Growth

Other things equal, stronger productivity growth and heightened global competition allow the economy to achieve a higher rate of economic growth. A glance back at Figure 22.2 will help make this point. Suppose that the shift of the production possibilities curve from *AB* to *CD* reflects annual changes in potential output levels before the recent increase in growth rates. Then the higher growth rates of the more recent period of accelerated productivity growth would be depicted by a *larger* outward shift of the economy's production possibilities from *AB* to a curve beyond *CD*. When coupled with economic efficiency and increased total spending, the economy's real GDP would rise by even more than what is shown.

The Recent Productivity Slowdown

It is not clear whether the dramatic slowdown in productivity growth that took place after the Great Recession is permanent or transitory. Some economists have argued that the high productivity growth rates observed between 1995 and 2010 were a one-time anomaly due to the information technology revolution. But even if information technology caused an unusual

GLOBAL PERSPECTIVE 22.2

Global Competitiveness Index

The Global Competitiveness Index, published annually by the World Economic Forum, measures each country's potential for economic growth. The index uses various factors—such as innovativeness, the capability to transfer technology among sectors, the efficiency of the financial system, rates of investment, and the degree of economic integration with the rest of the world—to measure a country's ability to achieve economic growth over time. Here is the top 10 list for 2015–2016.

Country	Global Competitiveness Ranking, 2015–2016
Switzerland	1
Singapore	2
United States	3
Germany	4
Netherlands	5
Japan	6
Hong Kong	7
Finland	8
Sweden	9
United Kingdom	10

Source: World Economic Forum, **www.weforum.org**.

burst of growth for 15 years, it is still surprising that post-2010 productivity growth rates have been so very low, much lower in fact than the rates that prevailed before the information technology revolution.

By the mid-2010s, several possible explanations had been put forward to explain why productivity growth rates had fallen so low. One possible culprit is the high debt levels that accumulated before the Great Recession. Under this hypothesis, individuals and firms are now too busy paying down debts to make productive investments. At the same time, entrepreneurs who might be able to improve productivity may be unable to obtain loans because banks are reluctant to lend after having made so many bad loans prior to the Great Recession.

Overcapacity may be another possible explanation for the productivity slowdown. During the boom that preceded the Great Recession, worldwide productive capacity increased massively as many new factories were built. But the additional capacity may have exceeded the amount of consumer demand that would have been necessary to purchase the additional output made possible by the additional capacity. If so, firms would have been reluctant to install newer, more productive equipment or build newer, more productive factories after the Great Recession because they already had more than enough production capacity. Under this hypothesis, productivity stagnated because producers continued to rely on aging machinery and equipment.

Another possible explanation for the slowdown in measured productivity has to do with the fact that many recent products—especially Internet apps—do not generate much of a measurable effect on GDP. Consider Facebook, YouTube, and Instagram. They are for the most part totally free to consumers. So even if billions of people are using these products, measured output won't go up very much because there is no monetary payment being made by users. Under this hypothesis, things aren't so bad. *Measured* productivity growth is low, but the new products are in fact innovative and bring with them a huge amount of consumer surplus; we just can't discern those benefits in the GDP and productivity statistics.

Finally, it is also possible that technological progress itself may have stalled. Under this hypothesis, productivity growth will remain slow until invention and innovation speed up again.

AP QUICK REVIEW 22.4

- ✓ Over long time periods, labor productivity growth determines an economy's growth of real wages and its standard of living.
- ✓ Labor productivity grew at an average rate of 1.5 percent from 1973 to 1995, 2.6 percent from 1995 to 2010, and 0.4 percent from 2010 to 2015.
- ✓ The high productivity growth rate observed between 1995 and 2010 is attributed to the information technology revolution, increasing returns and lower per-unit costs, and heightened global competition that helps hold down prices.
- ✓ Possible explanations for the low productivity growth rate after 2010 include high debt levels, overcapacity, the rise of "free" Internet products, and a slowdown in technological progress.

Is Growth Desirable and Sustainable?

LO22.6 Discuss differing perspectives as to whether growth is desirable and sustainable.

Economists usually take for granted that economic growth is desirable and sustainable. But not everyone agrees.

The Antigrowth View

Critics of growth say industrialization and growth result in pollution, climate change, ozone depletion, and other environmental problems. These adverse negative externalities occur because inputs in the production process reenter the environment as some form of waste. The more rapid our growth and the higher our standard of living, the more waste the environment must absorb—or attempt to absorb. In an already wealthy society,

LAST WORD

Can Economic Growth Survive Population Decline?

The Demographic Transition Is Causing Greying Populations, Shrinking Labor Forces, and Overall Population Decreases in Many Nations. Can Economic Growth Survive?

Source: © Agencja Fotograficzna Caro/Alamy Stock Photo

As you know from this chapter, Real GDP = hours of work × labor productivity. The number of *hours of work* depends heavily, however, on the size of the working-age population. If it begins to shrink, the number of *hours of work* almost always falls. In such cases, the only way real GDP can rise is if *labor productivity* increases faster than *hours of work* decreases. The world is about to see if that can happen in countries that have populations that are greying and shrinking.

The historical background has to do with the fact that as nations industrialize, their economies shift from agriculture to industry. As that happens, fertility levels plummet because the shift to modern technology transforms children from being economically essential farm hands that can contribute to their families' incomes from a young age to expensive investment goods that require many years of costly schooling before they can support themselves.

As people react to this change, birthrates tend to fall quite dramatically. The key statistic is the *total fertility rate* that keeps track of the average number of births that women have during their lifetimes. To keep the population stable in modern societies, the total fertility rate must be about 2.1 births per woman per lifetime (= 1 child to replace mom, 1 child to replace dad, and 0.1 child to compensate for those people who never end up reproducing as adults).

Every rich industrial nation has now seen its total fertility rate drop below the replacement level of 2.1 births per woman per lifetime. In Japan and many eastern European countries, the number has been so low for so long that there are no longer enough children being born each year to replace the old folks who are dying. As a result, their overall populations are shrinking.

Economists only expect that pattern to become more common and more rapid, so that by the year 2050 the majority of nations will have decreasing populations. But decades before a nation's overall population begins to decrease, it faces a situation in which the labor force shrinks while the elderly population swells.

That pattern is the result of each generation being smaller than the one before. As an example, the baby boom generation born between 1946 and 1964 is much larger than the "baby bust" generation that followed it. So as the boomers retire over the next two decades, there will be a lot of retirees as compared to working-age adults.

This trend can be quantified by the *inverse dependency ratio*, which is defined as the number of people of working age (ages 20 to 64) divided by the number of dependents (seniors over age 65 plus youths under age 20). In the United States, the inverse dependency ratio is set to fall from 1.5 people of working age per dependent in 2010 to just 1.16 people of working age per dependent in 2050. That is extremely problematic because it implies that worker productivity will have to rise dramatically just to make up for the relative decline in the number of workers as compared to dependents. If productivity doesn't keep up with the fall in the inverse dependency ratio, living standards will have to decline because there will simply be too many nonworking consumers relative to working-age producers.

The place where this problem is likely to show up first is Social Security. There are currently 2.9 workers paying into the Social Security system for each retiree receiving Social Security benefits. But that number is set to fall to just 2.0 workers per retiree in 2030. So worker productivity would have to increase by almost a third in under 20 years just to keep up with the decline in the number of workers relative to retirees.

Economists are uncertain about whether such large productivity increases will be forthcoming. The problem is that consumption competes with investment. A society with a larger fraction of dependents is a society that is likely to devote an increasingly high fraction of total output toward consumption rather than investment. If so, productivity growth may slow considerably.

Another possible problem is that, historically, most transformative new technologies and businesses have been created by energetic young people under the age of 40. With each generation getting smaller, there will be fewer people in that age range and thus, possibly, less innovation and slower productivity growth.

Other economists are more hopeful, however. They view old people as consumers and demanders. As their numbers swell, inventors may simply switch from inventing products for young people to inventing products for old people. If so, productivity growth and living standards could keep on rising at the rates we have come to expect.

further growth usually means satisfying increasingly trivial wants at the cost of mounting threats to the ecological system.

Critics of growth also argue that there is little compelling evidence that economic growth has solved sociological problems such as poverty, homelessness, and discrimination. Consider poverty: In the antigrowth view, American poverty is a problem of distribution, not production. The requisite for solving the problem is a firm commitment to redistribute wealth and income, not further increases in output.

Antigrowth sentiment also says that while growth may permit us to "make a better living," it does not give us "the good life." We may be producing more and enjoying it less. Growth means frantic paces on jobs, worker burnout, and alienated employees who have little or no control over decisions affecting their lives. The changing technology at the core of growth poses new anxieties and new sources of insecurity for workers. Both high-level and low-level workers face the prospect of having their hard-earned skills and experience rendered obsolete by onrushing technology. High-growth economies are high-stress economies, which may impair our physical and mental health.

Finally, critics of high rates of growth doubt that they are sustainable. The planet Earth has finite amounts of natural resources available, and they are being consumed at alarming rates. Higher rates of economic growth simply speed up the degradation and exhaustion of the earth's resources. In this view, slower economic growth that is environmentally sustainable is preferable to faster growth.

In Defense of Economic Growth

The primary defense of growth is that it is the path to the greater material abundance and higher living standards desired by the vast majority of people. Rising output and incomes allow people to buy

> more education, recreation, and travel, more medical care, closer communications, more skilled personal and professional services, and better-designed as well as more numerous products. It also means more art, music, and poetry, theater, and drama. It can even mean more time and resources devoted to spiritual growth and human development.[1]

Growth also enables society to improve the nation's infrastructure, enhance the care of the sick and elderly, provide greater access for the disabled, and provide more police and fire protection. Economic growth may be the only realistic way to reduce poverty, since there is only limited political support for greater redistribution of income. The way to improve the economic position of the poor is to increase household incomes through higher productivity and economic growth. Also, a no-growth policy among industrial nations might severely limit growth in poor nations. Foreign investment and development assistance in those nations would fall, keeping the world's poor in poverty longer.

Economic growth has not made labor more unpleasant or hazardous, as critics suggest. New machinery is usually less taxing and less dangerous than the machinery it replaces. Air-conditioned workplaces are more pleasant than steamy workshops. Furthermore, why would an end to economic growth reduce materialism or alienation? The loudest protests against materialism are heard in those nations and groups that now enjoy the highest levels of material abundance! The high standard of living that growth provides has increased our leisure and given us more time for reflection and self-fulfillment.

Does growth threaten the environment? The connection between growth and environment is tenuous, say growth proponents. Increases in economic growth need not mean increases in pollution. Pollution is not so much a by-product of growth as it is a "problem of the commons." Much of the environment—streams, lakes, oceans, and the air—is treated as common property, with insufficient or no restrictions on its use. The commons have become our dumping grounds; we have overused and debased them. Environmental pollution is a case of negative externalities, and correcting this problem involves regulatory legislation, specific taxes ("effluent charges"), or market-based incentives to remedy misuse of the environment.

Those who support growth admit there are serious environmental problems. But they say that limiting growth is the wrong solution. Growth has allowed economies to reduce pollution, be more sensitive to environmental considerations, set aside wilderness, create national parks and monuments, and clean up hazardous waste, while still enabling rising household incomes. (See the Last Word in Enrichment Chapter 3 available online.)

Is growth sustainable? Yes, say the proponents of growth. If we were depleting natural resources faster than their discovery, we would see the prices of those resources rise. That has not been the case for most natural resources; in fact, the prices of most of them have declined (see Figure E3.1). And if one natural resource becomes too expensive, another resource will be substituted for it. Moreover, say economists, economic growth has to do with the expansion and application of human knowledge and information, not of extractable natural resources. In this view, economic growth is limited only by human imagination.

AP QUICK REVIEW 22.5

- ✓ Critics of growth argue that it adds to environmental degradation, increases human stress, and exhausts the earth's finite supply of natural resources.
- ✓ Defenders of growth say that it is the primary path to the rising living standards, that it need not debase the environment, and that there are no indications that we are running out of resources.
- ✓ Defenders of growth argue that growth is sustainable because it is based on the expansion and application of human knowledge, which is limited only by human imagination.

[1]Alice M. Rivlin, *Reviving the American Dream* (Washington, D.C.: Brookings Institution, 1992), p. 36.

SUMMARY

LO22.1 List two ways that economic growth is measured.

A nation's economic growth can be measured either as an increase in real GDP over time or as an increase in real GDP per capita over time. Real GDP in the United States has grown at an average annual rate of about 3.2 percent since 1950; real GDP per capita has grown at roughly a 2 percent annual rate over that same period.

LO22.2 Define "modern economic growth" and explain the institutional structures needed for an economy to experience it.

Sustained increases in real GDP per capita did not happen until the past two centuries, when England and then other countries began to experience modern economic growth, which is characterized by institutional structures that encourage savings, investment, and the development of new technologies. Institutional structures that promote growth include strong property rights, patents, efficient financial institutions, education, and a competitive market system.

Because some nations have experienced nearly two centuries of modern economic growth while others have only recently begun to experience modern economic growth, some countries today are much richer than other countries.

It is possible, however, for countries that are currently poor to grow faster than countries that are currently rich because the growth of real GDP per capita for rich countries is limited to about 2 percent per year. To continue growing, rich countries must invent and apply new technologies. By contrast, poor countries can grow much faster because they can simply adopt the institutions and cutting-edge technologies already developed by the rich countries.

LO22.3 Identify the general supply, demand, and efficiency forces that give rise to economic growth.

The determinants of economic growth to which we can attribute changes in growth rates include four supply factors (changes in the quantity and quality of natural resources, changes in the quantity and quality of human resources, changes in the stock of capital goods, and improvements in technology), one demand factor (changes in total spending), and one efficiency factor (changes in how well an economy achieves allocative and productive efficiency).

The growth of a nation's capacity to produce output can be illustrated graphically by an outward shift of its production possibilities curve.

LO22.4 Describe "growth accounting" and the specific factors accounting for economic growth in the United States.

Growth accounting attributes increases in real GDP either to increases in the amount of labor being employed or to increases in the productivity of the labor being employed. Increases in U.S. real GDP are mostly the result of increases in labor productivity. The increases in labor productivity can be attributed to technological progress, increases in the quantity of capital per worker, improvements in the education and training of workers, the exploitation of economies of scale, and improvements in the allocation of labor across different industries.

LO22.5 Explain how the average rate of U.S. productivity growth has fluctuated since 1973.

Over long time periods, the growth of labor productivity underlies an economy's growth of real wages and its standard of living. U.S. productivity rose by 1.5 percent annually between 1973 and 1995, 2.6 percent annually between 1995 and 2010, and just 0.4 percent annually from 2010 to 2015.

The 1995 to 2010 increase in the average rate of productivity growth was based on (*a*) rapid technological change in the form of the microchip and information technology, (*b*) increasing returns and lower per-unit costs, and (*c*) heightened global competition that holds down prices.

The main sources of increasing returns are (*a*) the use of more specialized inputs as firms grow, (*b*) the spreading of development costs, (*c*) simultaneous consumption by consumers, (*d*) network effects, and (*e*) learning by doing. Increasing returns mean higher productivity and lower per-unit production costs.

Possible explanations for the slow productivity growth rate after the Great Recession of 2007–2008 include high debt levels, overcapacity, the rise of "free" Internet products, and a slowdown in technological innovation.

LO22.6 Discuss differing perspectives as to whether growth is desirable and sustainable.

Skeptics wonder if the recent rise in the average rate of productivity growth is permanent, and suggest a wait-and-see approach. They point out that surges in productivity and real GDP growth have previously occurred but do not necessarily represent long-lived trends.

Critics of rapid growth say that it adds to environmental degradation, increases human stress, and exhausts the earth's finite supply of natural resources. Defenders of rapid growth say that it is the primary path to the rising living standards nearly universally desired by people, that it need not debase the environment, and that there are no indications that we are running out of resources. Growth is based on the expansion and application of human knowledge, which is limited only by human imagination.

TERMS AND CONCEPTS

economic growth
real GDP per capita
rule of 70
modern economic growth
leader countries
follower countries

supply factors	growth accounting	start-up firms
demand factor	infrastructure	increasing returns
efficiency factor	human capital	network effects
labor productivity	economies of scale	learning by doing
labor-force participation rate	information technology	

The following and additional problems can be found in connect

DISCUSSION QUESTIONS

1. How is economic growth measured? Why is economic growth important? Why could the difference between a 2.5 percent and a 3 percent annual growth rate be of great significance over several decades? **LO22.1**
2. When and where did modern economic growth first happen? What are the major institutional factors that form the foundation for modern economic growth? What do they have in common? **LO22.2**
3. Why are some countries today much poorer than other countries? Are today's poor countries destined to always be poorer than today's rich countries? If so, explain why. If not, explain how today's poor countries can catch or even pass today's rich countries. **LO22.2**
4. What are the four supply factors of economic growth? What is the demand factor? What is the efficiency factor? Illustrate these factors in terms of the production possibilities curve. **LO22.3**
5. Suppose that Alpha and Omega have identically sized working-age populations but that total annual hours of work are much greater in Alpha than in Omega. Provide two possible reasons for this difference. **LO22.3**
6. What is growth accounting? To what extent have increases in U.S. real GDP resulted from more labor inputs? From greater labor productivity? Rearrange the following contributors to the growth of productivity in order of their quantitative importance: economies of scale, quantity of capital, improved resource allocation, education and training, and technological advance. **LO22.4**
7. True or False: If false, explain why. **LO22.4**
   a. Technological advance, which to date has played a relatively small role in U.S. economic growth, is destined to play a more important role in the future.
   b. Many public capital goods are complementary to private capital goods.
   c. Immigration has slowed economic growth in the United States.
8. Explain why there is such a close relationship between changes in a nation's rate of productivity growth and changes in its average real hourly wage. **LO22.5**
9. Relate each of the following to the 1995 to 2010 increase in the trend rate of productivity growth: **LO22.5**
   a. Information technology.
   b. Increasing returns.
   c. Network effects.
   d. Global competition.
10. What, if any, are the benefits and costs of economic growth, particularly as measured by real GDP per capita? **LO22.6**
11. **LAST WORD** Would you expect a country with a total fertility rate of 2.7 to have a growing or a shrinking population over the long run? What about a country with a total fertility rate of 1.2? In 20 years, will America have more or fewer workers per retiree than it does today? Why does a falling inverse dependency ratio make it harder for real GDP to continue growing?

AP REVIEW QUESTIONS

1. If real GDP grows at 7 percent per year, then real GDP will double in approximately ________ years. **LO22.1**
   a. 70. **d.** 7.
   b. 14. **e.** 5.
   c. 10.
2. Economic growth can be shown by: **LO22.1**
   a. Outward shift of the production possibilities curve.
   b. Inward shift of the production possibilities curve.
   c. Movement from a point *on* to a point *inside* a production possibilities curve.
   d. Movement from one point to another point on a fixed production possibilities curve.
   e. Fewer resources producing less output.
3. Identify each of the following situations as something that either promotes growth or retards growth. **LO22.2**
   a. Increasing corruption allows government officials to steal people's homes.
   b. A nation introduces patent laws for the first time.
   c. A court order shuts down all banks permanently.
   d. A poor country extends free public schooling from 8 years to 12 years.
   e. A nation adopts a free-trade policy.
   f. A formerly communist country adopts free markets.
4. How does investment in capital goods and infrastructure contribute to economic growth? **LO22.3**
5. Suppose that just by doubling the amount of output that it produces each year, a firm's per-unit production costs fall by 30 percent. This is an example of: **LO22.4**
   a. Economies of scale.
   b. Improved resource allocation.
   c. Technological advance.
   d. The demand factor.
   e. Efficiency factor.

6. Which of the following is *correct*? LO22.5
   a. An increase in the availability of labor increases labor productivity per hour and grows the economy.
   b. With technological progress the same number of workers will produce less total output.
   c. A move from inside the production possibilities curve onto the curve shows economic growth.
   d. Greater availability of inputs and technological progress are the primary determinants of economic growth.
   e. Once a given level of output has been achieved, it will always be possible to reach this output level.

7. Identify the following arguments about economic growth as being either anti-growth or pro-growth. LO22.6
   a. Growth means worker burnout and frantic schedules.
   b. Rising incomes allow people to buy more education, medical care, and recreation.
   c. Earth has only finite amounts of natural resources.
   d. We still have poverty, homelessness, and discrimination even in the richest countries.
   e. Richer countries spend more money protecting the environment.
   f. Natural resource prices have fallen rather than increased over time.

PROBLEMS

1. Suppose an economy's real GDP is $30,000 in year 1 and $31,200 in year 2. What is the growth rate of its real GDP? Assume that population is 100 in year 1 and 102 in year 2. What is the growth rate of real GDP per capita? LO22.1
2. What annual growth rate is needed for a country to double its output in 7 years? In 35 years? In 70 years? In 140 years? LO22.1
3. Assume that a "leader country" has real GDP per capita of $40,000, whereas a "follower country" has real GDP per capita of $20,000. Next suppose that the growth of real GDP per capita falls to zero percent in the leader country and rises to 7 percent in the follower country. If these rates continue for long periods of time, how many years will it take for the follower country to catch up to the living standard of the leader country? LO22.2
4. Refer to Figure 22.2 and assume that the values for points *a*, *b*, and *c* are $10 billion, $20 billion, and $18 billion, respectively. If the economy moves from point *a* to point *b* over a 10-year period, what must have been its annual rate of economic growth? If, instead, the economy was at point *c* at the end of the 10-year period, by what percentage did it fall short of its production capacity? LO22.3
5. Suppose that work hours in New Zombie are 200 in year 1 and productivity is $8 per hour worked. What is New Zombie's real GDP? If work hours increase to 210 in year 2 and productivity rises to $10 per hour, what is New Zombie's rate of economic growth? LO22.4
6. The per-unit cost of an item is its average total cost (= total cost/quantity). Suppose that a new cell phone application costs $100,000 to develop and only $0.50 per unit to deliver to each cell phone customer. What will be the per-unit cost of the application if it sells 100 units? 1,000 units? 1 million units? LO22.5

Chapter 23

Business Cycles, Unemployment, and Inflation

Learning Objectives

LO23.1 Describe the business cycle and its primary phases.

LO23.2 Illustrate how unemployment is measured and explain the different types of unemployment.

LO23.3 Explain how inflation is measured and distinguish between cost-push inflation and demand-pull inflation.

LO23.4 Relate how unanticipated inflation can redistribute real income.

LO23.5 Discuss how inflation may affect the economy's level of real output.

AP Chapter Focus

As indicated in Chapter 22, the United States has experienced remarkable economic growth over time. But this growth has not been smooth, steady, and predictable from year to year. At various times the United States has experienced recessions, high unemployment rates, or high inflation rates. For example, U.S. unemployment rose by 8 million workers and the unemployment rate increased from 4.7 percent to 10.1 percent during the 2007–2009 recession. Other nations have also suffered high unemployment rates at times. As just one example, the Greek unemployment rate exceeded 25 percent in 2015. Also, inflation has occasionally plagued the United States and other nations. For instance, the U.S. inflation rate in 1980 was 13.5 percent. Zimbabwe's inflation rate soared to 26,000 percent in 2007!

Our goal in this chapter is to examine the concepts, terminology, and facts relating to macroeconomic instability. Specifically, we want to discuss the business cycle, unemployment, and inflation. The concepts discussed are extremely important for understanding subsequent chapters on economic theory and economic policy in the study of macroeconomics.

AP The Business Cycle

LO23.1 Describe the business cycle and its primary phases.

The long-run trend of the U.S. economy is one of economic growth, as stylized by the upsloping line labeled "Growth Trend" in Figure 23.1. But growth has been interrupted by periods of economic instability usually associated with **business cycles.** Business cycles are alternating rises and declines in the level of economic activity, sometimes over several years. Individual cycles (one "up" followed by one "down") vary substantially in duration and intensity.

AP FIGURE 23.1 The business cycle. Economists distinguish four phases of the business cycle; the duration and strength of each phase may vary.

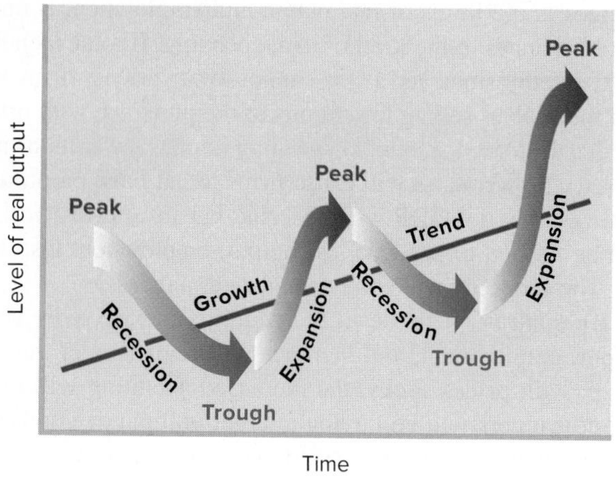

Phases of the Business Cycle

Figure 23.1 shows the four phases of a generalized business cycle:

- At a **peak,** such as the middle peak shown in Figure 23.1, business activity has reached a temporary maximum. Here the economy is near or at full employment and the level of real output is at or very close to the economy's capacity. The price level is likely to rise during this phase.
- A **recession** is a period of decline in total output, income, and employment. This downturn, which lasts 6 months or more, is marked by the widespread contraction of business activity in many sectors of the economy. Along with declines in real GDP, significant increases in unemployment occur. Table 23.1 documents the 10 recessions in the United States since 1950.
- In the **trough** of the recession or depression, output and employment "bottom out" at their lowest levels. The trough phase may be either short-lived or quite long.
- A recession is usually followed by a recovery and **expansion,** a period in which real GDP, income, and employment rise. At some point, the economy again approaches full employment. If spending then expands more rapidly than does production capacity, prices of nearly all goods and services will rise. In other words, inflation will occur.

Although business cycles all pass through the same phases, they vary greatly in duration and intensity. Many economists prefer to talk of business "fluctuations" rather than cycles because cycles imply regularity while fluctuations do not. The Great Depression of the 1930s resulted in a 27 percent decline in real GDP over a 3-year period in the United States and seriously impaired business activity for a decade. By comparison, the U.S. recessions detailed in Table 23.1 were less severe in both intensity and duration.

AP TABLE 23.1 U.S. Recessions since 1950

Period	Duration, Months	Depth (Decline in Real Output)
1953–54	10	−2.6%
1957–58	8	−3.7
1960–61	10	−1.1
1969–70	11	−0.2
1973–75	16	−3.2
1980	6	−2.2
1981–82	16	−2.9
1990–91	8	−1.4
2001	8	−0.4
2007–09	18	−4.3

Source: National Bureau of Economic Research, **www.nber.org**, Bureau of Economic Analysis, **www.bea.gov**, and Minneapolis Federal Reserve Bank, "The Recession and Recovery in Perspective," **www.minneapolisfed.gov**. Output data are in 2000 dollars.

The Business Cycle Dating Committee of the National Bureau of Economic Research (NBER), a nonprofit economic research organization, declares the start and end of recessions in the United States. Citing evidence of declining real output and falling employment, the NBER officially declared that the latest recession began in December 2007. The NBER subsequently declared that the Great Recession ended in June 2009, 18 months after it began. In making this announcement, the NBER pointed out that its declaration was not a forecast for the future path of the economy.

Recessions, of course, occur in other countries, too. For example, nearly all industrial nations and many developing nations have suffered recessions in the past several years.

Causation: A First Glance

The long-run trend of the U.S. economy is expansion and growth. That is why the business cycles in Figure 23.1 are drawn against a trend of economic growth. A key issue in macroeconomics is why the economy sees business cycle fluctuations rather than slow, smooth growth. In terms of Figure 23.1, why does output move up and down rather than just staying on the smooth growth trend line?

Economists have developed several possible explanations. But before turning to them, recall that in Chapter 20 we explained that these theories are founded on the idea that fluctuations are driven by shocks—unexpected events that individuals and firms may have trouble adjusting to. Also recall that short-run price stickiness is widely believed to be a major factor preventing the economy from rapidly adjusting to shocks. With prices sticky in the short run, price changes cannot quickly equalize the quantities demanded of goods and services with their respective quantities supplied after a shock has happened. Instead, the economy is forced to respond to shocks in the short run primarily through changes in output and employment rather than through changes in prices.

Economists cite several possible general sources of shocks that can cause business cycles.

- ***Irregular innovation*** Significant new products or production methods, such as those associated with the railroad, automobile, computer, and Internet, can rapidly spread through the economy, sparking sizable increases in investment, consumption, output, and employment. After the economy has largely absorbed the new innovation, the economy may for a time slow down or possibly decline. Because such innovations occur irregularly and unexpectedly, they may contribute to the variability of economic activity.
- ***Productivity changes*** When productivity—output per unit of input—unexpectedly increases, the economy booms; when productivity unexpectedly decreases, the economy recedes. Such changes in productivity can result from unexpected changes in resource availability (of, say, oil or agricultural commodities) or from unexpected changes in the general rate of technological advance.
- ***Monetary factors*** Some economists see business cycles as purely monetary phenomena. When a nation's central bank shocks the economy by creating more money than people were expecting, an inflationary boom in output occurs. By contrast, printing less money than people were expecting triggers an output decline and, eventually, a price-level fall.
- ***Political events*** Unexpected political events, such as peace treaties, new wars, or the 9/11 terrorist attacks, can create economic opportunities or strains. In adjusting to these shocks, the economy may experience upswings or downswings.
- ***Financial instability*** Unexpected financial bubbles (rapid asset price increases) or bursts (abrupt asset price decreases) can spill over to the general economy by expanding or contracting lending, and boosting or eroding the confidence of consumers and businesses. Booms and busts in the rest of the economy may follow.

The severe recession of 2007–2009 was precipitated by a combination of excessive money and a financial frenzy that led to overvalued real estate and unsustainable mortgage debt. Institutions bundled this debt into new securities ("derivatives") that were sold to financial investors. Some of the investors, in turn, bought insurance against losses that might arise from the securities. As real estate prices plummeted and mortgage defaults unexpectedly rocketed, the securitization and insurance structure buckled and nearly collapsed. Credit markets froze, pessimism prevailed, and spending by businesses and households declined.

Whatever the source of economic shocks, most economists agree that the *immediate* cause of the large majority of cyclical changes in the levels of real output and employment is unexpected changes in the level of total spending. If total spending unexpectedly sinks and firms cannot lower prices, firms will find themselves selling fewer units of output (since with prices fixed, a decreased amount of spending implies fewer items purchased). Slower sales will cause firms to cut back on production. As they do, GDP will fall. And because fewer workers will be needed to produce less output, employment also will fall. The economy will contract and enter a recession.

By contrast, if the level of spending unexpectedly rises, output, employment, and incomes will rise. This is true because, with prices sticky, the increased spending will mean that consumers will be buying a larger volume of goods and services (since, with prices fixed, more spending means more items purchased). Firms will respond by increasing output. This will increase GDP. And because firms will need to hire more workers to produce the larger volume of output, employment also will increase. The economy will boom and enjoy an expansion. Eventually, as time passes and prices become more flexible, prices are also likely to rise as a result of the increased spending.

Cyclical Impact: Durables and Nondurables

Although the business cycle is felt everywhere in the economy, it affects different segments in different ways and to different degrees.

Firms and industries producing *capital goods* (for example, housing, commercial buildings, heavy equipment, and farm implements) and *consumer durables* (for example, automobiles, personal computers, and refrigerators) are affected most by the business cycle. Within limits, firms can postpone the purchase of capital goods. For instance, when the economy goes into recession, producers frequently delay the purchase of new equipment and the construction of new plants. The business outlook simply does not warrant increases in the stock of capital goods. In good times, capital goods are usually replaced before they depreciate completely. But when recession strikes, firms patch up their old equipment and make do. As a result, investment in capital goods declines sharply. Firms that have excess plant capacity may not even bother to replace all the capital that is depreciating. For them, net investment may be negative. The pattern is much the same for consumer durables such as automobiles and major appliances. When recession occurs and households must trim their budgets, purchases of these goods are often deferred. Families repair their old cars and appliances rather than buy new ones, and the firms producing these products suffer. (Of course, producers of capital goods and consumer durables also benefit most from expansions.)

In contrast, *service* industries and industries that produce *nondurable consumer goods* are somewhat insulated from the most severe effects of recession. People find it difficult to cut back on needed medical and legal services, for example. And a recession actually helps some service firms, such as pawnbrokers and law firms that specialize in bankruptcies. Nor are the purchases of many nondurable goods such as food and clothing easy to postpone. The quantity and quality of purchases of nondurables will decline, but not so much as will purchases of capital goods and consumer durables.

AP QUICK REVIEW 23.1

- ✓ The typical business cycle goes through four phases: peak, recession, trough, and expansion, followed by a peak and a recurring recession.
- ✓ Fluctuations in output and employment are caused by economic shocks combining with sticky wages and prices.
- ✓ Sources of shocks that cause recessions include irregular innovation, productivity changes, monetary factors, input price shocks, political events, and financial instability.
- ✓ During a recession, industries that produce capital goods and consumer durables normally suffer greater output and employment declines than do service and nondurable consumer goods industries.

AP Unemployment

LO23.2 Illustrate how unemployment is measured and explain the different types of unemployment.

Two problems that arise over the course of the business cycle are unemployment and inflation. Let's look at unemployment first.

Measurement of Unemployment

The U.S. Bureau of Labor Statistics (BLS) conducts a nationwide random survey of some 60,000 households each month to determine who is employed and who is not employed. In a series of questions, it asks which members of the household are working, unemployed and looking for work, not looking for work, and so on. From the answers, it determines an unemployment rate for the entire nation.

Figure 23.2 helps explain the mathematics. The BLS divides the total U.S. population into three groups. One group is made up of people under 16 years of age and people who are institutionalized, for example, in mental hospitals or correctional institutions. Such people are not considered potential members of the labor force.

A second group, labeled "Not in labor force," is composed of adults who are potential workers but are not employed and are not seeking work. For example, they are stay-at-home parents, full-time students, or retirees.

The third group is the **labor force,** which constituted slightly more than 50 percent of the total population in 2009.

AP FIGURE 23.2 The U.S. labor force, employment, and unemployment, 2015.* The labor force consists of persons 16 years of age or older who are not in institutions and who are (1) employed or (2) unemployed but seeking employment.

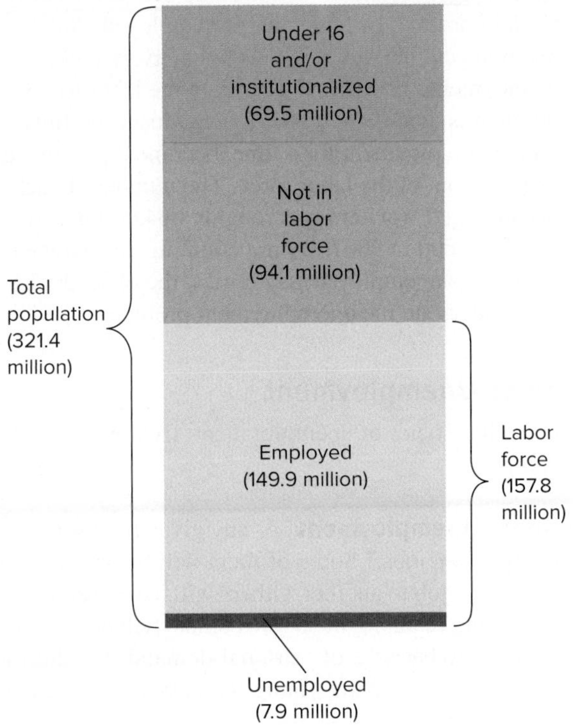

*Civilian labor-force data, which excludes military employment.

Source: Bureau of Labor Statistics, **www.bls.gov**.

The labor force consists of people who are able and willing to work. Both those who are employed and those who are unemployed but actively seeking work are counted as being in the labor force. The **unemployment rate** is the percentage of the labor force unemployed:

$$\text{Unemployment rate} = \frac{\text{unemployed}}{\text{labor force}} \times 100$$

The statistics underlying the rounded numbers in Figure 23.2 show that in 2015 the unemployment rate averaged

$$\frac{7{,}900{,}000}{157{,}800{,}000} \times 100 = 5.0\%$$

Despite the use of scientific sampling and interviewing techniques, the data collected in this survey are subject to criticism:

- ***Part-time employment*** The BLS lists all part-time workers as fully employed. In 2015 about 30 million people worked part-time as a result of personal choice. But another 6 million part-time workers either wanted to work full-time and could not find suitable full-time work or worked fewer hours because of a temporary slack in consumer demand. These last two groups were, in effect, partially employed and partially unemployed. By counting them as fully employed, say critics, the official BLS data understate the unemployment rate.

- ***Discouraged workers*** You must be actively seeking work in order to be counted as unemployed. An unemployed individual who is not actively seeking employment is classified as "not in the labor force." The problem is that many workers, after unsuccessfully seeking employment for a time, become discouraged and drop out of the labor force. The number of such **discouraged workers** was roughly 664,000 in 2015, up from 396,000 in 2007. By not counting discouraged workers as unemployed, say critics, the official BLS data understate the unemployment problem.

Types of Unemployment

There are three *types* of unemployment: frictional, structural, and cyclical.

Frictional Unemployment At any given time some workers are "between jobs." Some of them will be moving voluntarily from one job to another. Others will have been fired and will be seeking reemployment. Still others will have been laid off temporarily because of seasonal demand. In addition to those between jobs, many young workers will be searching for their first jobs.

As these unemployed people find jobs or are called back from temporary layoffs, other job seekers and laid-off workers will replace them in the "unemployment pool." It is important to keep in mind that while the pool itself persists because there are always newly unemployed workers flowing into it, most workers do *not* stay in the unemployment pool for very long. Indeed, when the economy is strong, the majority of unemployed workers find new jobs within a couple of months. One should be careful not to make the mistake of confusing the permanence of the pool itself with the false idea that the pool's membership is permanent, too. On the other hand, there are workers who do remain unemployed and in the pool for very long periods of time—sometimes for many years. As we discuss the different types of unemployment below, notice that certain types tend to be transitory while others are associated with much longer spells of unemployment.

Economists use the term **frictional unemployment**—consisting of *search unemployment* and *wait unemployment*—for workers who are either searching for jobs or waiting to take jobs in the near future. The word "frictional" implies that the labor market does not operate perfectly and instantaneously (without friction) in matching workers and jobs.

Frictional unemployment is inevitable and, at least in part, desirable. Many workers who are voluntarily between jobs are moving from low-paying, low-productivity jobs to higher-paying, higher-productivity positions. That means greater income for the workers, a better allocation of labor resources, and a larger real GDP for the economy.

Structural Unemployment Frictional unemployment blurs into a category called **structural unemployment.** Here, economists use "structural" in the sense of "compositional." Changes over time in consumer demand and in technology alter the "structure" of the total demand for labor, both occupationally and geographically.

CONSIDER THIS . . .

Source: © JGI/Jamie Grill/Getty Images RF

Downwardly Sticky Wages and Unemployment

Labor markets have an important quirk that helps to explain why unemployment goes up so much during a recession.

The quirk is that wages are flexible upward but sticky downward.

On the one hand, workers are perfectly happy to accept wage increases. So when the economy is booming and firms start bidding for the limited supply of labor, wages rise—often quite rapidly.

On the other hand, workers deeply resent pay cuts. So if the economy goes into a recession and firms need to reduce labor costs, managers almost never cut wages because doing so would only lead to disgruntled employees, low productivity, and—in extreme cases—workers stealing supplies or actively sabotaging their own firms.

Instead, managers usually opt for layoffs. The workers who are let go obviously don't like being unemployed. But those who remain get to keep their old wages and, consequently, keep on being as productive and cooperative as they were before.

This preference that firms show for layoffs over wage cuts results in downwardly sticky wages and an informal price floor that helps to explain why unemployment goes up so much during a recession. The problem is that when the demand for labor falls during a recession, the informal price floor prevents wages from falling. As a result, there is no way for falling wages to help entice at least some firms to hire a few more workers. Thus, when a recession hits, employment falls more precipitously than it would if wages were downwardly flexible and falling wages could help to increase hiring.

Occupationally, the demand for certain skills (for example, sewing clothes or working on farms) may decline or even vanish. The demand for other skills (for example, designing software or maintaining computer systems) will intensify. Unemployment results because the composition of the labor force does not respond immediately or completely to the new structure of job opportunities. Workers who find that their skills and experience have become obsolete or unneeded thus find that they have no marketable talents. They are structurally unemployed until they adapt or develop skills that employers want.

Geographically, the demand for labor also changes over time. An example: the migration of industry and thus of employment opportunities from the Snowbelt to the Sunbelt over the past few decades. Another example is the movement of jobs from inner-city factories to suburban industrial parks. And a final example is the so-called *offshoring* of jobs that occurs when the demand for a particular type of labor shifts from domestic firms to foreign firms. As job opportunities shift from one place to another, some workers become structurally unemployed.

The distinction between frictional and structural unemployment is hazy at best. The key difference is that *frictionally* unemployed workers have marketable skills and either live in areas where jobs exist or are able to move to areas where they do. *Structurally* unemployed workers find it hard to obtain new jobs without retraining, gaining additional education, or relocating. Frictional unemployment is short-term; structural unemployment is more likely to be long-term and consequently more serious.

Cyclical Unemployment Unemployment that is caused by a decline in total spending is called **cyclical unemployment** and typically begins in the recession phase of the business cycle. As the demand for goods and services decreases, employment falls and unemployment rises. Cyclical unemployment results from insufficient demand for goods and services. The 25 percent unemployment rate in the depth of the Great Depression in 1933 reflected mainly cyclical unemployment, as did significant parts of the 9.7 percent unemployment rate in 1982, the 7.5 percent rate in 1992, the 5.8 percent rate in 2002, and the 9.3 percent rate in 2009.

Cyclical unemployment is a very serious problem when it occurs. We will say more about its high costs later, but first we need to define "full employment."

Definition of Full Employment

Because frictional and structural unemployment are largely unavoidable in a dynamic economy, *full employment* is something less than 100 percent employment of the labor force. Economists say that the economy is "fully employed" when it is experiencing only frictional and structural unemployment. That is, full employment occurs when there is no cyclical unemployment.

Economists describe the unemployment rate that is consistent with full employment as the **full-employment rate of unemployment,** or the **natural rate of unemployment (NRU).** At the NRU, the economy is said to be producing its **potential output.** This is the real GDP that occurs when the economy is "fully employed."

Note that a fully employed economy does not mean zero unemployment. Even when the economy is fully employed, the NRU is some positive percentage because it takes time for frictionally unemployed job seekers to find open jobs they can fill. Also, it takes time for the structurally unemployed to achieve the skills and geographic relocation needed for reemployment.

"Natural" does not mean, however, that the economy will always operate at this rate and thus realize its potential output. When cyclical unemployment occurs, the economy has much more unemployment than that which would occur at the NRU. Moreover, the economy can operate for a while at an unemployment rate *below* the NRU. At times, the demand for labor may be so great that firms take a stronger initiative to hire and train the structurally unemployed. Also, some parents, teenagers, college students, and retirees who were casually looking for just the right part-time or full-time jobs may quickly find them. Thus the unemployment rate temporarily falls below the natural rate.

Also, the NRU can vary over time as demographic factors, job-search methods, and public policies change. In the 1980s, the NRU was about 6 percent. Today, it is 5 to 6 percent.

Economic Cost of Unemployment

Unemployment that is excessive involves great economic and social costs.

GDP Gap and Okun's Law The basic economic cost of unemployment is forgone output. When the economy fails to create enough jobs for all who are able and willing to work, potential production of goods and services is irretrievably lost. In terms of Chapter 1's analysis, unemployment above the natural rate means that society is operating at some point inside its production possibilities curve. Economists call this sacrifice of output a **GDP gap**—the difference between actual and potential GDP. That is:

$$\text{GDP gap} = \text{actual GDP} - \text{potential GDP}$$

The GDP gap can be either negative (actual GDP < potential GDP) or positive (actual GDP > potential GDP). In the case of unemployment above the natural rate, it is negative because actual GDP falls short of potential GDP.

Potential GDP is determined by assuming that the natural rate of unemployment prevails. The growth of potential GDP is simply projected forward on the basis of the economy's "normal" growth rate of real GDP. Figure 23.3 shows the GDP gap for recent years in the United States. It also

AP FIGURE 23.3 Actual and potential real GDP and the unemployment rate. (a) The difference between actual and potential GDP is the GDP gap. A negative GDP gap measures the output the economy sacrifices when actual GDP falls short of potential GDP. A positive GDP gap indicates that actual GDP is above potential GDP. (b) A high unemployment rate means a large GDP gap (negative), and a low unemployment rate means a small or even positive GDP gap.

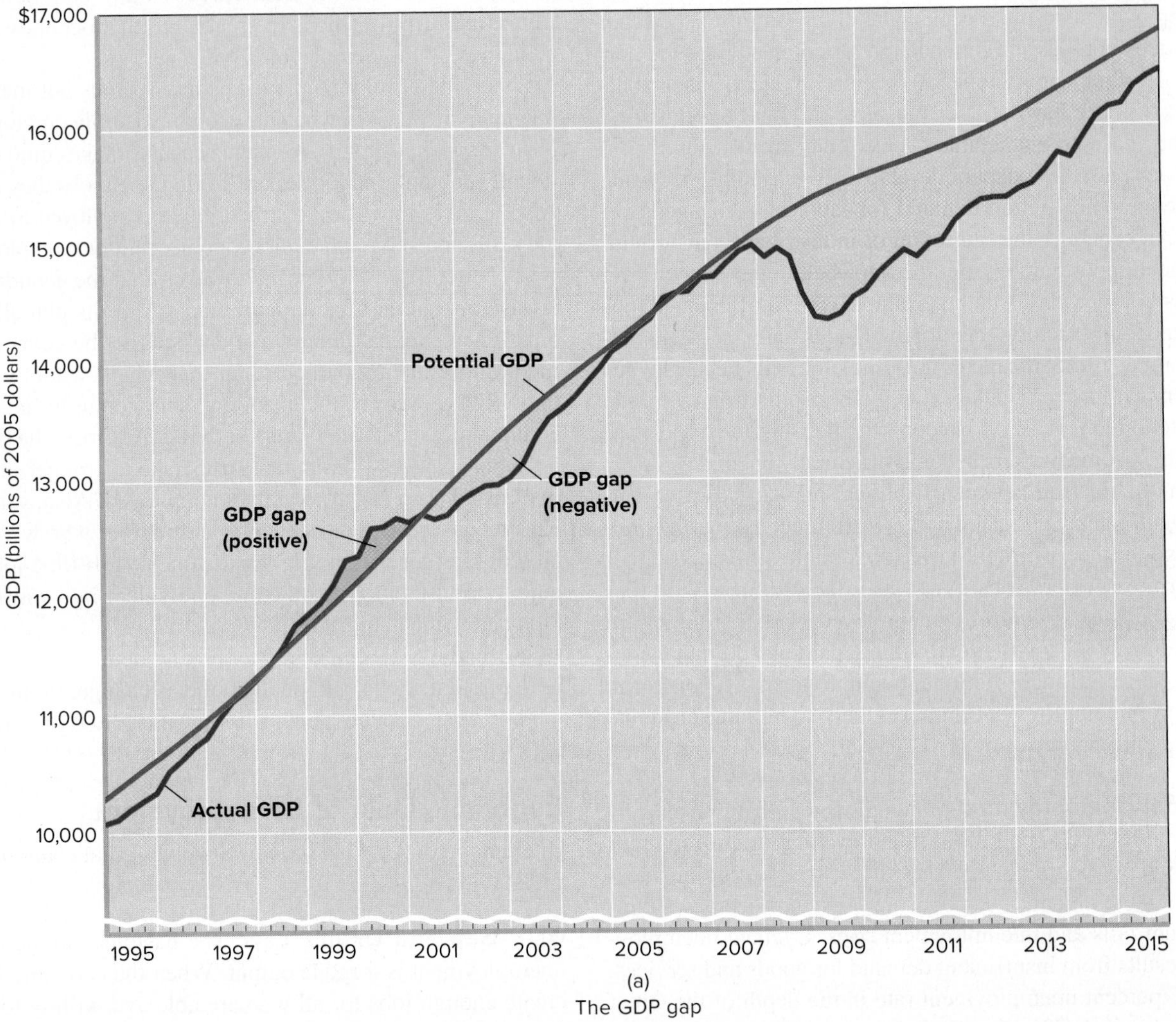

(a)
The GDP gap

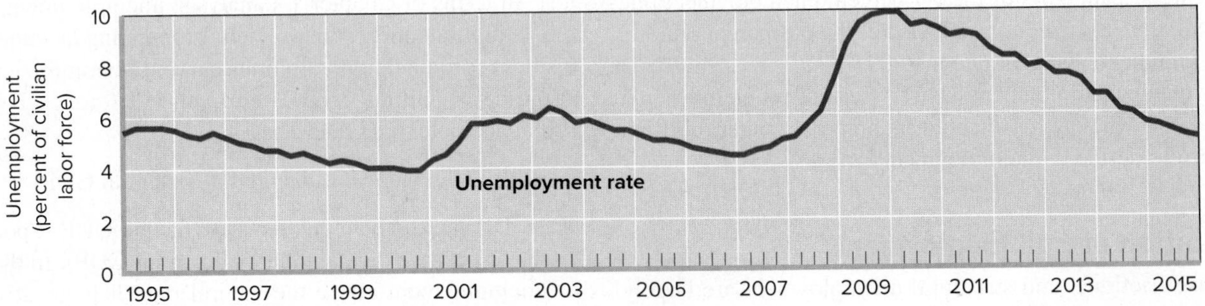

(b)
Unemployment rate

Source: Congressional Budget Office, **www.cbo.gov**; Bureau of Economic Analysis, **www.bea.gov**; and the Bureau of Labor Statistics, **www.bls.gov**. Note that the data for actual real GDP and potential real GDP above differ from the real GDP data in the previous two chapters. The data above are in 2009 dollars, but do not reflect the 2013 redefinition of investment expenditures in the National Income and Product Accounts to include research and development spending.

indicates the close correlation between the actual unemployment rate (Figure 23.3b) and the GDP gap (Figure 23.3a). The higher the unemployment rate, the larger is the GDP gap.

Macroeconomist Arthur Okun was the first to quantify the relationship between the unemployment rate and the GDP gap. **Okun's law** indicates that for every 1 percentage point by which the actual unemployment rate exceeds the natural rate, a negative GDP gap of about 2 percent occurs. With this information, we can calculate the absolute loss of output associated with any above-natural unemployment rate. For example, in 2009 the unemployment rate was 9.3 percent, or 4.3 percentage points above that period's 5.0 percent natural rate of unemployment. Multiplying this 4.3 percent by Okun's 2 indicates that 2009's GDP gap was 8.6 percent of potential GDP (in real terms). By applying this 8.6 percent loss to 2009's potential GDP of $13,894 billion, we find that the economy sacrificed $1,195 billion of real output because the natural rate of unemployment was not achieved.

As you can see in Figure 23.3, sometimes the economy's actual output will exceed its potential or full-employment output. Figure 23.3 reveals that an economic expansion in 1999 and 2000, for example, caused actual GDP to exceed potential GDP in those years. There was a positive GDP gap in 1999 and 2000. Actual GDP for a time can exceed potential GDP, but positive GDP gaps create inflationary pressures and cannot be sustained indefinitely.

Unequal Burdens An increase in the unemployment rate from 5 to, say, 9 or 10 percent might be more tolerable to society if every worker's hours of work and wage income were reduced proportionally. But this is not the case. Part of the burden of unemployment is that its cost is unequally distributed.

Table 23.2 examines unemployment rates for various labor market groups for 2 periods. In 2007, the economy achieved full employment, with a 4.6 percent unemployment rate. The economy receded in December 2007 and two years later was feeling the full unemployment impact of the Great Recession. By observing the large variance in unemployment rates for the different groups within each period and comparing the rates between the 2 periods, we can generalize as follows:

- ***Occupation*** Workers in lower-skilled occupations (for example, laborers) have higher unemployment rates than workers in higher-skilled occupations (for example, professionals). Lower-skilled workers have more and longer spells of structural unemployment than higher-skilled workers. They also are less likely to be self-employed than are higher-skilled workers. Moreover, lower-skilled workers usually bear the brunt of recessions. Manufacturing, construction, and mining tend to be particularly hard-hit, and businesses generally retain most of their higher-skilled workers, in whom they have invested the expense of training.
- ***Age*** Teenagers have much higher unemployment rates than adults. Teenagers have lower skill levels, quit their jobs more frequently, are more frequently fired, and have less geographic mobility than adults. Many unemployed teenagers are new in the labor market, searching for their first jobs. Male African-American teenagers, in particular, have very high unemployment rates. The unemployment rate for all teenagers rises during recessions.

TABLE 23.2 Unemployment Rates by Demographic Group: Full Employment Year (2007) and Recession Year (2009)*

	Unemployment Rate	
Demographic Group	**2007**	**2009**
Overall	4.6%	9.3%
Occupation:		
Managerial and professional	2.1	4.6
Construction and extraction	7.6	19.7
Age:		
16–19	15.7	24.3
African American, 16–19	29.4	39.5
White, 16–19	13.9	21.8
Male, 20+	4.1	9.6
Female, 20+	4.0	7.5
Race and ethnicity:		
African American	8.3	14.8
Hispanic	5.6	12.1
White	4.1	8.5
Gender:		
Women	4.5	8.1
Men	4.7	10.3
Education:†		
Less than high school diploma	7.1	14.6
High school diploma only	4.4	9.7
College degree or more	2.0	4.6
Duration:		
15 or more weeks	1.5	4.7

*Civilian labor-force data.

†People age 25 or over.

Source: Economic Report of the President; Bureau of Labor Statistics, **www.bls.gov**; Census Bureau, **www.census.gov**.

- ***Race and ethnicity*** The unemployment rates for African Americans and Hispanics are higher than that for whites. The causes of the higher rates include lower rates of educational attainment, greater concentration in lower-skilled occupations, and discrimination in the labor market. In general, the unemployment rate for African Americans is twice that of whites and rises by more percentage points than for whites during recessions.
- ***Gender*** The unemployment rates for men and women normally are very similar. But in the recent recession, the unemployment rate for men significantly exceeded that for women.
- ***Education*** Less-educated workers, on average, have higher unemployment rates than workers with more education. Less education is usually associated with lower-skilled, less-permanent jobs; more time between jobs; and jobs that are more vulnerable to cyclical layoff.
- ***Duration*** The number of persons unemployed for long periods—15 weeks or more—as a percentage of the labor force is much lower than the overall unemployment rate. But that percentage rises significantly during recessions. Notice from Table 23.2 that it rose from 1.5 percent of the labor force in 2007 to 4.7 percent in 2009.

Noneconomic Costs

Severe cyclical unemployment is more than an economic malady; it is a social catastrophe. Unemployment means idleness. And idleness means loss of skills, loss of self-respect, plummeting morale, family disintegration, and sociopolitical unrest. Widespread joblessness increases poverty, heightens racial and ethnic tensions, and reduces hope for material advancement.

History demonstrates that severe unemployment can lead to rapid and sometimes violent social and political change. Witness Hitler's ascent to power against a background of unemployment in Germany. Furthermore, relatively high unemployment among some racial and ethnic minorities has contributed to the unrest and violence that has periodically plagued some cities in the United States and abroad. At the individual level, research links increases in suicide, homicide, fatal heart attacks and strokes, and mental illness to high unemployment.

International Comparisons

Unemployment rates differ greatly among nations at any given time. One reason is that nations have different natural rates of unemployment. Another is that nations may be in different phases of their business cycles. Global Perspective 23.1 shows unemployment rates for five industrialized nations for the years 2004 through 2014. Between 2004 and 2008, the U.S. unemployment rate was considerably lower than the rates in Italy, France, and Germany. But during the Great Recession, U.S. unemployment spiked to the highest level among the five countries before declining significantly over the following five years.

GLOBAL PERSPECTIVE 23.1

Unemployment Rates in Five Industrial Nations, 2004–2014

Compared with Italy, France, and Germany, the United States had a relatively low unemployment rate until the start of the 2007–2009 Great Recession, when the U.S. rate shot up to become the highest among the five nations in 2010 before declining substantially over the next few years while the unemployment rates in Italy and France continued to rise.

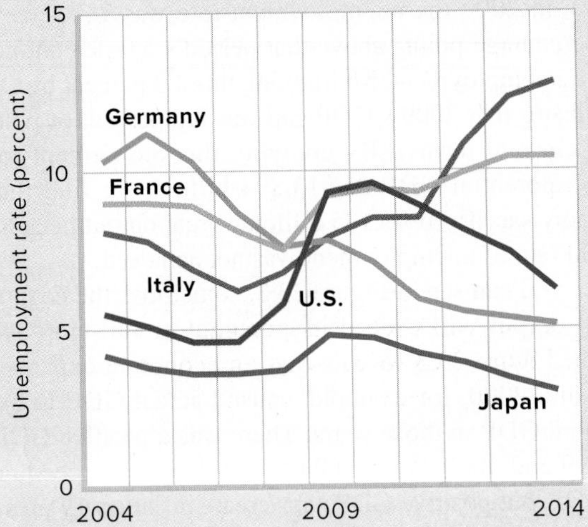

Source: Bureau of Labor Statistics, **www.bls.gov**. Based on U.S. unemployment concepts.

AP QUICK REVIEW 23.2

- ✓ Unemployment is of three general types: frictional, structural, and cyclical.
- ✓ The natural unemployment rate (frictional plus structural) is presently 5 to 6 percent in the United States.
- ✓ A positive (inflationary) GDP gap occurs when actual GDP exceeds potential GDP; a negative (recessionary) GDP gap occurs when actual GDP falls short of potential GDP.
- ✓ Society loses real GDP when cyclical unemployment occurs; according to Okun's law, for each 1 percentage point of unemployment above the natural rate, the U.S. economy suffers a 2 percent decline in real GDP below its potential GDP.
- ✓ Lower-skilled workers, teenagers, African Americans and Hispanics, and less-educated workers frequently bear a disproportionate burden of unemployment.

AP Inflation

LO23.3 Explain how inflation is measured and distinguish between cost-push inflation and demand-pull inflation.

We now turn to inflation, another aspect of macroeconomic instability. The problems inflation poses are subtler than those posed by unemployment.

Meaning of Inflation

Inflation is a rise in the general level of prices. When inflation occurs, each dollar of income will buy fewer goods and services than before. Inflation reduces the "purchasing power" of money. But inflation does not mean that *all* prices are rising. Even during periods of rapid inflation, some prices may be relatively constant and others may even fall. For example, although the United States experienced high rates of inflation in the 1970s and early 1980s, the prices of video recorders, digital watches, and personal computers declined.

Measurement of Inflation

The main measure of inflation in the United States is the **Consumer Price Index (CPI),** compiled by the BLS. The government uses this index to report inflation rates each month and each year. It also uses the CPI to adjust Social Security benefits and income tax brackets for inflation. The CPI reports the price of a "market basket" of some 300 consumer goods and services that are purchased by a typical urban consumer. (The GDP price index of Chapter 21 is a much broader measure of inflation since it includes not only consumer goods and services but also capital goods, goods and services purchased by government, and goods and services that enter world trade.)

The composition of the market basket for the CPI is based on spending patterns of urban consumers in a specific period, presently 2009–2010. The BLS updates the composition of the market basket every 2 years so that it reflects the most recent patterns of consumer purchases and captures the inflation that consumers are currently experiencing. The BLS arbitrarily sets the CPI equal to 100 for 1982–1984. So the CPI for any particular year is found as follows:

$$\text{CPI} = \frac{\text{price of the most recent market basket in the particular year}}{\text{price estimate of the market basket in 1982–1984}} \times 100$$

The rate of inflation is equal to the percentage growth of CPI from one year to the next. For example, the CPI was 236.7 in 2014, up from 233.0 in 2013. So the rate of inflation for 2014 is calculated as follows:

$$\text{Rate of inflation} = \frac{236.7 - 233.0}{233.0} \times 100 = 1.6\%$$

In rare cases, the CPI declines from one year to the next. For example, the CPI fell from 215.3 in 2008 to 214.5 in 2009. The rate of inflation for 2009 therefore was −0.4 percent. Such price level declines are called **deflation.**

In Chapter 22, we discussed the mathematical approximation called *the rule of 70*, which tells us that we can find the number of years it will take for some measure to double, given its annual percentage increase, by dividing that percentage increase into the number 70. So a 3 percent annual rate of inflation will double the price level in about 23 (= 70 ÷ 3) years. Inflation of 8 percent per year will double the price level in about 9 (= 70 ÷ 8) years.

Facts of Inflation

Figure 23.4 shows December-to-December rates of annual inflation in the United States between 1960 and 2015. Observe that inflation reached double-digit rates in the 1970s and early 1980s but has since declined and has been relatively mild recently.

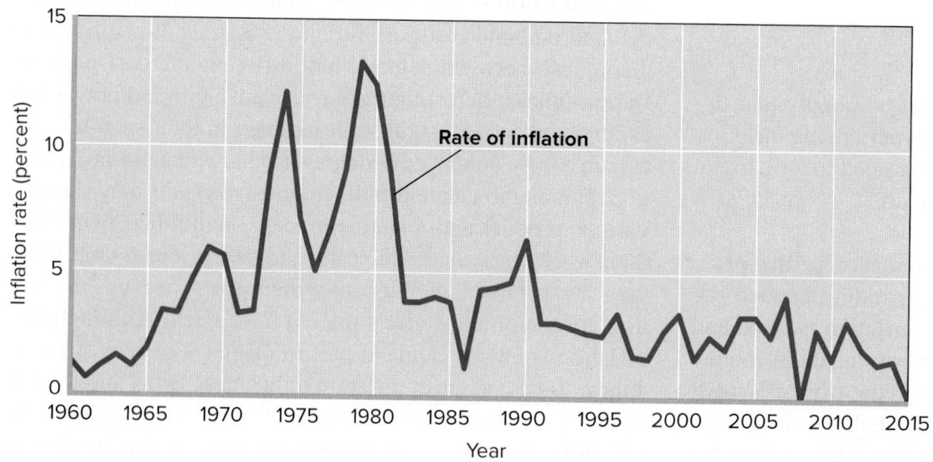

Source: Bureau of Labor Statistics, **www.bls.gov**.

AP **FIGURE 23.4 Annual inflation rates in the United States, 1960–2015 (December-to-December changes in the CPI).** The major periods of inflation in the United States in the past 56 years were in the 1970s and 1980s.

GLOBAL PERSPECTIVE 23.2

Inflation Rates in Five Industrial Nations, 2005–2015

Inflation rates in the United States in recent years were neither extraordinarily high nor extraordinarily low relative to rates in other industrial nations.

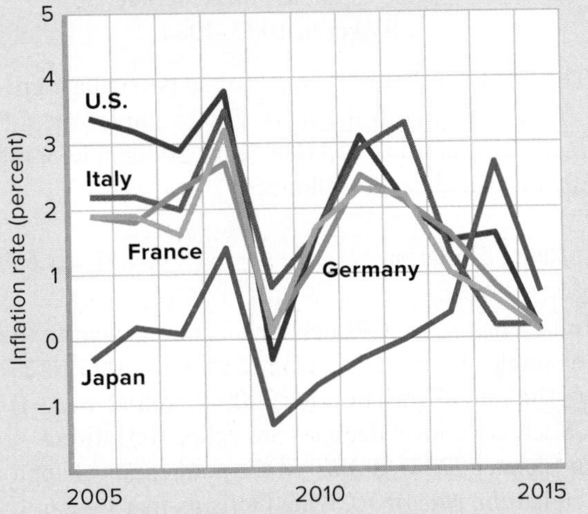

Source: World Economic Outlook Database, April 2016, International Monetary Fund, **www.imf.org**.

In recent years U.S. inflation has been neither unusually high nor low relative to inflation in several other industrial countries (see Global Perspective 23.2). Some nations (not shown) have had double-digit or even higher annual rates of inflation in recent years. In 2015, for example, the annual inflation rate in Argentina was 28 percent; Yemen, 30 percent; Syria, 34 percent; Ukraine, 49 percent; and Venezuela, 275 percent. Zimbabwe's inflation rate was 14.9 billion percent in 2008 before Zimbabwe reformed its currency the following year.

Types of Inflation

Nearly all prices in the economy are set by supply and demand. Consequently, if the economy is experiencing inflation and the overall level of prices is rising, we need to look for an explanation in terms of supply and demand.

Demand-Pull Inflation Usually, increases in the price level are caused by an excess of total spending beyond the economy's capacity to produce. Where inflation is rapid and sustained, the cause invariably is an overissuance of money by the central bank (the Federal Reserve in the United States). When resources are already fully employed, the business sector cannot respond to excess demand by expanding output. So the excess demand bids up the prices of the limited output, producing **demand-pull inflation.** The essence of this type of inflation is "too much spending chasing too few goods."

Cost-Push Inflation Inflation also may arise on the supply, or cost, side of the economy. During some periods in U.S. economic history, including the mid-1970s, the price level increased even though total spending was not excessive. These were periods when output and employment were both *declining* (evidence that total spending was not excessive) while the general price level was *rising*.

The theory of **cost-push inflation** explains rising prices in terms of factors that raise **per-unit production costs** at each level of spending. A per-unit production cost is the average cost of a particular level of output. This average cost is found by dividing the total cost of all resource inputs by the amount of output produced. That is,

$$\text{Per-unit production cost} = \frac{\text{total input cost}}{\text{units of output}}$$

Rising per-unit production costs squeeze profits and reduce the amount of output firms are willing to supply at the existing price level. As a result, the economy's supply of goods and services declines and the price level rises. In this scenario, costs are *pushing* the price level upward, whereas in demand-pull inflation demand is *pulling* it upward.

The major source of cost-push inflation has been so-called *supply shocks*. Specifically, abrupt increases in the costs of raw materials or energy inputs have on occasion driven up per-unit production costs and thus product prices. The rocketing prices of imported oil in 1973–1974 and again in 1979–1980 are good illustrations. As energy prices surged upward during these periods, the costs of producing and transporting virtually every product in the economy rose. Cost-push inflation ensued.

Complexities

The real world is more complex than the distinction between demand-pull and cost-push inflation suggests. It is difficult to distinguish between demand-pull inflation and cost-push inflation unless the original source of inflation is known. For example, suppose a significant increase in total spending occurs in a fully employed economy, causing demand-pull inflation. But as the demand-pull stimulus works its way through various product and resource markets, individual firms find their wage costs, material costs, and fuel prices rising. From their perspective they must raise their prices because production costs (someone else's prices) have risen. Although this inflation is clearly demand-pull in origin, it may mistakenly appear to be cost-push inflation to business firms and to government. Without proper identification of the source of the inflation, government and the Federal Reserve may be slow to undertake policies to reduce excessive total spending.

Another complexity is that cost-push inflation and demand-pull inflation differ in their sustainability. Demand-pull inflation will continue as long as there is excess total spending. Cost-push inflation is automatically self-limiting; it will die out by itself. Increased per-unit costs will reduce supply, and this means lower real output and employment. Those decreases will constrain further per-unit cost increases. In other words, cost-push inflation generates a recession. And in a recession, households and businesses concentrate on keeping their resources employed, not on pushing up the prices of those resources.

CONSIDER THIS . . .

Source: © Royalty-Free/Corbis RF

Clipping Coins

Some interesting early episodes of demand-pull inflation occurred in Europe from the ninth century to the fifteenth century under feudalism. In that economic system, *lords* (or *princes*) ruled individual fiefdoms and their *vassals* (or *peasants*) worked the fields. The peasants initially paid parts of their harvest as taxes to the princes. Later, when the princes began issuing "coins of the realm," peasants began paying their taxes with gold coins.

Some princes soon discovered a way to transfer purchasing power from their vassals to themselves without explicitly increasing taxes. As coins came into the treasury, princes clipped off parts of the gold coins, making them slightly smaller. From the clippings they minted new coins and used them to buy more goods for themselves.

This practice of clipping coins was a subtle form of taxation. The quantity of goods being produced in the fiefdom remained the same, but the number of gold coins increased. With "too much money chasing too few goods," inflation occurred. Each gold coin earned by the peasants therefore had less purchasing power than previously because prices were higher. The increase of the money supply shifted purchasing power away from the peasants and toward the princes just as surely as if the princes had increased taxation of the peasants.

In more recent eras some dictators have simply printed money to buy more goods for themselves, their relatives, and their key loyalists. These dictators, too, have levied hidden taxes on their population by creating inflation.

The moral of the story is quite simple: A society that values price-level stability should not entrust the control of its money supply to people who benefit from inflation.

Core Inflation

Another complication relating to inflation (regardless of type) is noteworthy. Some price-flexible items within the consumer price index—particularly, food and energy—experience rapid changes in supply and demand and therefore considerable price volatility from month to month and year to year. For example, the prices of grain, fruit, vegetables, and livestock sometimes move rapidly in one direction or the other, leading to sizable changes in the prices of food items such as bread, oranges, lettuce, and beef. Also, energy items such as gasoline and natural gas can rise or fall rapidly from period to period. These ups and downs of food and energy prices usually are temporary and often cancel each other out over longer periods.

In tracking inflation, policymakers want to avoid being misled by rapid but temporary price changes that may distort the inflation picture. They mainly are interested in how rapidly the prices of the typically more stable components of the CPI are rising. By stripping volatile food and energy prices from the CPI, policymakers isolate so-called **core inflation,** the underlying increases in the CPI after volatile food and energy prices are removed.

If core inflation is low and stable, policymakers may be satisfied with current policy even though changes in the overall CPI index may be suggesting a rising rate of inflation. But policymakers become greatly concerned when core inflation is high and rising and take deliberate measures to try to halt it. We discuss these policies in later chapters.

AP QUICK REVIEW 23.3

- ✓ Inflation is a rising general level of prices and is measured as a percentage change in a price index such as the CPI; deflation is a decline in the general level of prices.
- ✓ For the past several years, the U.S. inflation rate has been within the general range of the rates of other advanced industrial nations and far below the rates experienced by some nations.
- ✓ Demand-pull inflation occurs when total spending exceeds the economy's ability to provide goods and services at the existing price level; total spending *pulls* the price level upward.
- ✓ Cost-push inflation occurs when factors such as rapid increases in the prices of imported raw materials drive up per-unit production costs at each level of output; higher costs *push* the price level upward.
- ✓ Core inflation is the underlying inflation rate after volatile food and energy prices have been removed.

AP Redistribution Effects of Inflation

LO23.4 Relate how unanticipated inflation can redistribute real income.

Inflation redistributes real income. This redistribution helps some people and hurts some others while leaving many people largely unaffected. Who gets hurt? Who benefits? Before we can answer, we need some terminology.

Nominal and Real Income

There is a difference between money (or nominal) income and real income. **Nominal income** is the number of dollars received as wages, rent, interest, or profit. **Real income** is a measure of the amount of goods and services nominal income can buy; it is the purchasing power of nominal income, or income adjusted for inflation. That is,

$$\text{Real income} = \frac{\text{nominal income}}{\text{price index (in hundredths)}}$$

Inflation need not alter an economy's overall real income—its total purchasing power. It is evident from the above equation that real income will remain the same when nominal income rises at the same percentage rate as does the price index.

But when inflation occurs, not everyone's nominal income rises at the same pace as the price level. Therein lies the potential for redistribution of real income from some to others. If the change in the price level differs from the change in a person's nominal income, his or her real income will be affected. The following approximation (shown by the $\cong$ sign) tells us roughly how much real income will change:

$$\begin{array}{lll}\text{Percentage} & \text{percentage} & \text{percentage} \\ \text{change in} & \cong \text{change in} & - \text{change in} \\ \text{real income} & \text{nominal income} & \text{price level}\end{array}$$

For example, suppose that the price level rises by 6 percent in some period. If Bob's nominal income rises by 6 percent, his real income will *remain unchanged*. But if his nominal income instead rises by 10 percent, his real income will *increase* by about 4 percent. And if Bob's nominal income rises by only 2 percent, his real income will *decline* by about 4 percent.[1]

[1] A more precise calculation uses our equation for real income. In our first illustration above, if nominal income rises by 10 percent from \$100 to \$110 and the price level (index) rises by 6 percent from 100 to 106, then real income has increased as follows:

$$\frac{\$110}{1.06} = \$103.77$$

The 4 percent increase in real income shown by the simple formula in the text is a reasonable approximation of the 3.77 percent yielded by our more precise formula.

Anticipations

The redistribution effects of inflation depend upon whether or not it is expected. We will first discuss situations involving **unanticipated inflation.** As you will see, these cause real income and wealth to be redistributed, harming some and benefiting others. We will then discuss situations involving **anticipated inflation.** These are situations in which people see an inflation coming in advance. With the ability to plan ahead, people are able to avoid or lessen the redistribution effects associated with inflation.

Who Is Hurt by Inflation?

Unanticipated inflation hurts fixed-income recipients, savers, and creditors. It redistributes real income away from them and toward others.

Fixed-Income Receivers People whose incomes are fixed see their real incomes fall when inflation occurs. The classic case is the elderly couple living on a private pension or annuity that provides a fixed amount of nominal income each month. They may have retired in, say, 1993 on what appeared to be an adequate pension. However, by 2009 they would have discovered that inflation had cut the annual purchasing power of that pension—their real income—by one-third.

Similarly, landlords who receive lease payments of fixed dollar amounts will be hurt by inflation as they receive dollars of declining value over time. Likewise, public sector workers whose incomes are dictated by fixed pay schedules may suffer from inflation. The fixed "steps" (the upward yearly increases) in their pay schedules may not keep up with inflation. Minimum-wage workers and families living on fixed welfare incomes also will be hurt by inflation.

Savers Unanticipated inflation hurts savers. As prices rise, the real value, or purchasing power, of an accumulation of savings deteriorates. Paper assets such as savings accounts, insurance policies, and annuities that were once adequate to meet rainy-day contingencies or provide for a comfortable retirement decline in real value during inflation. The simplest case is the person who hoards money as a cash balance. A \$1,000 cash balance would have lost one-third its real value between 1995 and 2015. Of course, most forms of savings earn interest. But the value of savings will still decline if the rate of inflation exceeds the rate of interest.

Example: Suppose that a household saves \$1,000 in a certificate of deposit (CD) in a commercial bank or savings and loan association at 6 percent annual interest. But if inflation is 13 percent (as it was in 1980), the real value or purchasing power of that $1,000 will be cut to about $938 by the end of the year. Although the saver will receive $1,060 (equal to $1,000 plus $60 of interest), deflating that $1,060 for 13 percent inflation means that its real value is only about $938 (= $1,060 ÷ 1.13).

Creditors Unanticipated inflation harms creditors (lenders). Suppose Chase Bank lends Bob $1,000, to be repaid in 2 years. If in that time the price level doubles, the $1,000 that Bob repays will have only half the purchasing power of the $1,000 he borrowed. True, if we ignore interest charges, the same number of dollars will be repaid as was borrowed. But because of inflation, each of those dollars will buy only half as much as it did when the loan was negotiated. As prices go up, the purchasing power of the dollar goes down. So the borrower pays back less-valuable dollars than those received from the lender. The owners of Chase Bank suffer a loss of real income.

Who Is Unaffected or Helped by Inflation?

Some people are unaffected by inflation and others are actually helped by it. For the second group, inflation redistributes real income toward them and away from others.

Flexible-Income Receivers People who have flexible incomes may escape inflation's harm or even benefit from it. For example, individuals who derive their incomes solely from Social Security are largely unaffected by inflation because Social Security payments are *indexed* to the CPI. Benefits automatically increase when the CPI increases, preventing erosion of benefits from inflation. Some union workers also get automatic **cost-of-living adjustments (COLAs)** in their pay when the CPI rises, although such increases rarely equal the full percentage rise in inflation.

Some flexible-income receivers and all borrowers are helped by unanticipated inflation. The strong product demand and labor shortages implied by rapid demand-pull inflation may cause some nominal incomes to spurt ahead of the price level, thereby enhancing real incomes. For some, the 3 percent increase in nominal income that occurs when inflation is 2 percent may become a 7 percent increase when inflation is 5 percent. As an example, property owners faced with an inflation-induced real estate boom may be able to boost rents more rapidly than the rate of inflation. Also, some business owners may benefit from inflation. If product prices rise faster than resource prices, business revenues will increase more rapidly than costs. In those cases, the growth rate of profit incomes will outpace the rate of inflation.

Debtors Unanticipated inflation benefits debtors (borrowers). In our earlier example, Chase Bank's loss of real income from inflation is Bob's gain of real income. Debtor Bob borrows "dear" dollars but, because of inflation, pays back the principal and interest with "cheap" dollars whose purchasing power has been eroded by inflation. Real income is redistributed away from the owners of Chase Bank toward borrowers such as Bob.

The federal government, which had amassed $18.2 trillion of public debt through 2015, has also benefited from inflation. Historically, the federal government regularly paid off its loans by taking out new ones. Inflation permitted the Treasury to pay off its loans with dollars of less purchasing power than the dollars originally borrowed. Nominal national income and therefore tax collections rise with inflation; the amount of public debt owed does not. Thus, inflation reduces the real burden of the public debt to the federal government.

Anticipated Inflation

The redistribution effects of inflation are less severe or are eliminated altogether if people anticipate inflation and can adjust their nominal incomes to reflect the expected price-level rises. The prolonged inflation that began in the late 1960s prompted many labor unions in the 1970s to insist on labor contracts with cost-of-living adjustment clauses.

Similarly, if inflation is anticipated, the redistribution of income from lender to borrower may be altered. Suppose a lender (perhaps a commercial bank or a savings and loan institution) and a borrower (a household) both agree that 5 percent is a fair rate of interest on a 1-year loan provided the price level is stable. But assume that inflation has been occurring and is expected to be 6 percent over the next year. If the bank lends the household $100 at 5 percent interest, the bank will be paid back $105 at the end of the year. But if 6 percent inflation does occur during that year, the purchasing power of the $105 will have been reduced to about $99. The lender will, in effect, have paid the borrower $1 for the use of the lender's money for a year.

The lender can avoid this subsidy by charging an *inflation premium*—that is, by raising the interest rate by 6 percent, the amount of the anticipated inflation. By charging 11 percent, the lender will receive back $111 at the end of the year. Adjusted for the 6 percent inflation, that amount will have roughly the purchasing power of $105 worth of today's money. The result then will be a mutually agreeable transfer of purchasing power from borrower to lender of $5, or 5 percent, for the use of $100 for 1 year. Financial institutions have also developed variable-interest-rate mortgages to protect themselves from the adverse effects of inflation. (Incidentally, this example points out that, rather than being a *cause* of inflation, high nominal interest rates are a *consequence* of inflation.)

AP **FIGURE 23.5 The inflation premium and nominal and real interest rates.** The inflation premium—the expected rate of inflation—gets built into the nominal interest rate. Here, the nominal interest rate of 11 percent comprises the real interest rate of 5 percent plus the inflation premium of 6 percent.

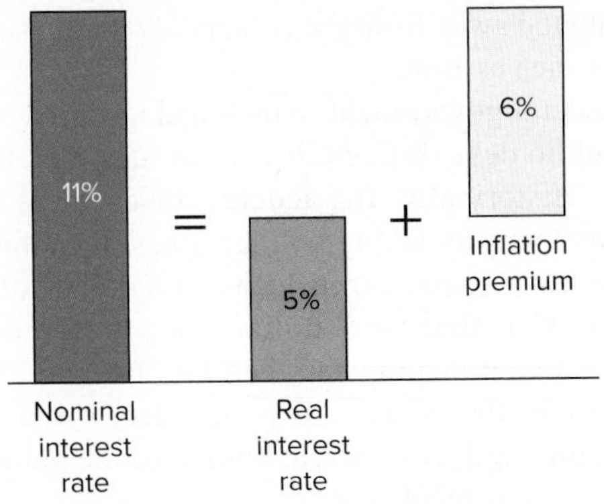

Our example reveals the difference between the real rate of interest and the nominal rate of interest. The **real interest rate** is the percentage increase in *purchasing power* that the borrower pays the lender. In our example the real interest rate is 5 percent. The **nominal interest rate** is the percentage increase in *money* that the borrower pays the lender, including that resulting from the built-in expectation of inflation, if any. In equation form:

Nominal interest rate = real interest rate + inflation premium (the expected rate of inflation)

As illustrated in Figure 23.5, the nominal interest rate in our example is 11 percent.

Negative Nominal Interest Rates

In response to slow recoveries after the Great Recession, many nations attempted to stimulate their economies by intentionally forcing the nominal interest rate on short-term loans to become negative. By early 2016, a negative short-term interest rate had been engineered by Denmark, Japan, Switzerland, Sweden, and the 19 European countries that use the euro as their currency.

In terms of the equation illustrated in Figure 23.5, a negative nominal interest rate on the left side of the equals sign implies that the real interest rate and the inflation premium must sum to a number less than zero on the right side of the equals sign. Either the real interest rate or the inflation premium (or both!) have to be negative for the nominal interest rate to be negative.

In the countries where a negative nominal interest rate was imposed, the inflation rate was positive and expected to remain positive. As a result, the inflation premium was positive. We can therefore conclude that the short-term real interest rate must have been negative (because the only way that the real interest rate and the inflation premium can sum to a negative nominal interest rate when the inflation premium is positive is if the real interest rate is negative).

A negative real interest rate implies that savers lose purchasing power over time. The governments that opted for negative nominal interest rates hoped that this penalty against saving would result in consumers deciding to consume more today rather than lose purchasing power over time by saving. The governments hoped that higher consumption expenditures would boost economic activity.

But a negative real interest rate might also produce the opposite effect and reduce consumption spending. That's because anybody who is saving with a future goal in mind will have to save more today to make up for the negative rates that will erode the future value of any money saved today. Thus, the governments that opted for negative rates may have been shooting themselves in the foot. As this edition went to print, it was unclear whether negative interest rates would actually boost economic activity as intended.

Other Redistribution Issues

We end our discussion of the redistribution effects of inflation by making three final points:

- ***Deflation*** The effects of unanticipated deflation—declines in the price level—are the reverse of those of inflation. People with fixed nominal incomes will find their real incomes enhanced. Creditors will benefit at the expense of debtors. And savers will discover that the purchasing power of their savings has grown because of the falling prices.
- ***Mixed effects*** A person who is simultaneously an income earner, a holder of financial assets, and a debtor will probably find that the redistribution impact of unanticipated inflation is cushioned. If the person owns fixed-value monetary assets (savings accounts, bonds, and insurance policies), inflation will lessen their real value. But that same inflation may produce an increase in the person's nominal wage. Also, if the person holds a fixed-interest-rate mortgage, the real burden of that debt will decline. In short, many individuals are simultaneously hurt and helped by inflation. All these effects must be considered before we can conclude that any particular person's net position is better or worse because of inflation.
- ***Arbitrariness*** The redistribution effects of inflation occur regardless of society's goals and values. Inflation lacks a social conscience and takes from some and gives to others, whether they are rich, poor, young, old, healthy, or infirm.

CONSIDER THIS . . .

Source: © Simon Dawson/Bloomberg/Getty Images

The Specter of Deflation

Inflation rates typically rise during the expansion phase of the business cycle as demand increases faster than supply throughout the economy. But when the peak has past and the recession phase of the business cycle begins, the inflation rate will tend to decline as unemployment rises and the demand for goods and services declines. In some cases, the decrease in demand may be so precipitous that deflation (a falling price level) becomes a possibility.

Economists fear deflation because it can lead to a wave of bankruptcies among firms that owe money. When prices fall, firms have a hard time making enough revenue to pay back their loans. They may be selling just as much stuff as before, but will now receive less money for it due to falling prices. That reduction in revenue can lead to bankruptcy. If enough bankruptcies occur, deflation may accelerate as workers are laid off and demand decreases even more. The downward spiral may be further exacerbated if consumers delay purchases in anticipation of lower future prices. After all, why buy something today if its price is expected to be substantially lower in a month?

To prevent the downward spiral of deflation, central banks use monetary policy to try to always maintain a positive inflation rate. They are almost always successful, so that deflation hardly ever takes hold, even after severe recessions like the Great Recession of 2007–2009. That's good news because with inflation always at least a little bit positive, a downward deflationary spiral can't get started.

AP QUICK REVIEW 23.4

- ✓ Nominal income is the income from wages and other sources, measured in current values. The **real** value, however, is the measure of the amount of goods and services that the nominal income can buy—that is, it is income adjusted for inflation.
- ✓ Inflation harms those with fixed nominal incomes and either leaves unaffected or helps those with flexible nominal incomes. Unanticipated inflation hurts savers and creditors, but benefits debtors.
- ✓ The nominal interest rate equals the real interest rate plus the inflation premium (the expected rate of inflation).

Does Inflation Affect Output?

LO23.5 Discuss how inflation may affect the economy's level of real output.

Thus far, our discussion has focused on how inflation redistributes a specific level of total real income. But inflation also may affect an economy's level of real output (and thus its level of real income). The direction and significance of this effect on output depend on the type of inflation and its severity.

Cost-Push Inflation and Real Output

Recall that abrupt and unexpected rises in key resource prices such as oil can sufficiently drive up overall production costs to cause cost-push inflation. As prices rise, the quantity demanded of goods and services falls. So firms respond by producing less output, and unemployment goes up.

Economic events of the 1970s provide an example of how inflation can reduce real output. In late 1973 the Organization of Petroleum Exporting Countries (OPEC), by exerting its market power, managed to quadruple the price of oil. The cost-push inflationary effects generated rapid price-level increases in the 1973–1975 period. At the same time, the U.S. unemployment rate rose from slightly less than 5 percent in 1973 to 8.5 percent in 1975. Similar outcomes occurred in 1979–1980 in response to a second OPEC oil supply shock.

In short, cost-push inflation reduces real output. It redistributes a decreased level of real income.

Demand-Pull Inflation and Real Output

Economists do not fully agree on the effects of mild inflation (less than 3 percent) on real output. One perspective is that even low levels of inflation reduce real output because inflation diverts time and effort toward activities designed to hedge against inflation. Here are some examples of this:

- Businesses must incur the cost of changing thousands of prices on their shelves and in their computers simply to reflect inflation.
- Households and businesses must spend considerable time and effort obtaining the information they need to distinguish between real and nominal values such as prices, wages, and interest rates.
- To limit the loss of purchasing power from inflation, people try to limit the amount of money they hold in their billfolds and checking accounts at any one time and instead put more money into interest-bearing accounts and stock and bond funds. But cash and checks are needed in even greater amounts to buy the higher-priced goods and services. So more frequent trips, phone calls, or Internet visits to financial institutions are required to transfer funds to checking accounts and billfolds, when needed.

Without inflation, these uses of resources, time, and effort would not be needed, and they could be diverted toward producing more valuable goods and services. Proponents of "zero inflation" bolster their case by pointing to cross-country studies that indicate that lower rates of inflation are associated with higher rates of economic growth. Even mild inflation, say these economists, is detrimental to economic growth.

LAST WORD

Employment after the Great Recession

Employment Growth Has Been Slow and Weak Since the Great Recession.

Soon after the Great Recession ended, some economists warned that the economy would grow only very slowly as it came out of the downturn. They pointed out that not all recessions are created equal. Recessions that follow credit (lending) bubbles usually take from between 7 and 15 years to recover from, rather than the 2 or 3 years that is typical for a normal recession. Since the Great Recession had been preceded by history's largest credit bubble, they were expecting very slow growth.

Their worries were well founded. It was slow going not only for GDP growth but also employment growth. Employment peaked at a high of 139.5 million (part-time plus full-time) jobs in November 2007 before falling to a low of 127.8 million jobs in January 2010. It then 4.5 years before the economy was able to once again provide employment to 139.5 million people.

The recovery in overall employment was in some sense illusory, however. The composition of jobs had changed, with millions transitioning from full-time employment to part-time employment as full-time jobs became relatively scarce. The number of full-time employees declined from 121.8 million in December 2007 to 110.5 million in December 2009. At the same time, the number of part-time employees rose from 24.7 million in December 2007 to 27.4 million in December 2009. So 11.3 million full-time jobs were lost while 2.7 million part-time jobs were gained. The gain in part-time work helped to disguise the decline in full-time work because when anybody looked at total employment (the sum of full-time and part-time jobs) the decline was "only" 8.6 million jobs.

Another troubling pattern was that employment growth mostly went to older workers. Between December 2007 and December 2009, the number of jobs held by people age 54 or younger fell by 6.5 percent (from 100.5 million jobs to 94.0 million jobs). By contrast, the number of jobs held by people 55 or older increased by 4.2 percent (from 26.2 million jobs to 27.3 million jobs) over the same time period.

Economists believe that this age-related difference in employment was due to employers favoring experienced workers in tough times. Why hire someone with only 5 years of work experience when you can get someone with 30 years of work experience for the same salary? That sort of thinking may also explain why the recovery period after the Great Recession also favored older workers. The number of older employees increased from 28.2 million to 34.2 million (or by 21.2 percent) between December 2009 and March 2016. By contrast, the number of jobs held by people age 54 or younger increased from 94.0 million to 98.0 million (or just 4.3 percent) over the same time period. Even worse, the number of jobs for people age 54 and younger was still 2.5 million lower in March 2016 than it had been in December 2007.

Source: © Ingram Publishing/SuperStock RF

The weakness of employment growth after the Great Recession was also evident when looking at the employment-population ratio, which is the percentage of people age 16 or older who have either a full-time job or a part-time job. The employment-population ratio fell from a pre-recession peak of 63.4 percent in December 2006 to a post-recession low of 58.2 percent in November 2010. Recovery in the employment-population ratio was slow and in March 2016 the statistic remained at just 59.9 percent, meaning that the number of occupied jobs relative to the number of people 16 and older was still 3.5 percent less than when the Great Recession began. New jobs were being created, but not quickly enough to keep up with population growth.

These facts should be kept in mind when considering the most commonly referenced employment statistic, the unemployment rate. By March 2016 the unemployment rate had declined to 5.0 percent, the same level it had been at when the Great Recession started in late 2007. If one had only looked at the unemployment rate, one might have concluded that things had returned to normal. But the data on part-time versus full-time jobs, age-related employment growth, and the employment-population ratio indicated that the jobs market was still struggling almost 7 years after the Great Recession ended.

In contrast, other economists point out that full employment and economic growth depend on strong levels of total spending. Such spending creates high profits, strong demand for labor, and a powerful incentive for firms to expand their plants and equipment. In this view, the mild inflation that is a by-product of strong spending is a small price to pay for full employment and continued economic growth.

Moreover, a little inflation may have positive effects because it makes it easier for firms to adjust real wages downward when the demands for their products fall. With mild inflation, firms can reduce real wages by holding nominal wages steady. With zero inflation firms would need to cut nominal wages to reduce real wages. Such cuts in nominal wages are highly visible and may cause considerable worker resistance and labor strife.

Finally, defenders of mild inflation say that it is much better for an economy to err on the side of strong spending, full employment, economic growth, and mild inflation than on the side of weak spending, unemployment, recession, and deflation.

Hyperinflation

All economists agree that **hyperinflation,** which is extraordinarily rapid inflation, can have a devastating impact on real output and employment.

As prices shoot up sharply and unevenly during hyperinflation, people begin to anticipate even more rapid inflation and normal economic relationships are disrupted. Business owners do not know what to charge for their products. Consumers do not know what to pay. Resource suppliers want to be paid with actual output, rather than with rapidly depreciating money. Money eventually becomes almost worthless and ceases to do its job as a medium of exchange. Businesses, anticipating further price increases, may find that hoarding both materials and finished products is profitable. Individual savers may decide to buy nonproductive wealth—jewels, gold and other precious metals, real estate, and so forth—rather than providing funds that can be borrowed to purchase capital equipment. The economy may be thrown into a state of barter, and production and exchange drop further. The net result is economic collapse and, often, political chaos.

Examples of hyperinflation are Germany after the First World War and Japan after the Second World War. In Germany, "prices increased so rapidly that waiters changed the prices on the menu several times during the course of a lunch. Sometimes customers had to pay double the price listed on the menu when they ordered."[2] In postwar Japan in 1947, "fisherman and farmers . . . used scales to weigh currency and change, rather than bothering to count it."[3]

There are also more recent examples: Between June 1986 and March 1991 the cumulative inflation in Nicaragua was 11,895,866,143 percent. From November 1993 to December 1994 the cumulative inflation rate in the Democratic Republic of Congo was 69,502 percent. From February 1993 to January 1994 the cumulative inflation rate in Serbia was 156,312,790 percent.[4]

Such dramatic hyperinflations are always the consequence of highly imprudent expansions of the money supply by government. The rocketing money supply produces frenzied total spending and severe demand-pull inflation. Zimbabwe's 14.9 billion percent inflation in 2008 is just the latest example.

AP QUICK REVIEW 23.5

- ✓ Cost-push inflation reduces real output and employment.
- ✓ Economists argue about the effects of demand-pull inflation. Some argue that even mild demand-pull inflation (1 to 3 percent) reduces the economy's real output over time. Others say that mild inflation may be a necessary by-product of the high and growing spending that produces high levels of output, full employment, and economic growth.
- ✓ Hyperinflation, caused by highly imprudent expansions of the money supply, may undermine the monetary system and cause severe declines in real output.

[2]Theodore Morgan, *Income and Employment,* 2nd ed. (Englewood Cliffs, NJ: Prentice Hall, 1952), p. 361.

[3]Raburn M. Williams, *Inflation! Money, Jobs, and Politicians* (Arlington Heights, IL: AHM Publishing, 1980), p. 2.

[4]Stanley Fischer, Ratna Sahay, and Carlos Végh, "Modern Hyper- and High Inflations," *Journal of Economic Literature,* September 2002, p. 840.

SUMMARY

LO23.1 Describe the business cycle and its primary phases.

The United States and other industrial economies have gone through periods of fluctuations in real GDP, employment, and the price level. Although they have certain phases in common—peak, recession, trough, expansion—business cycles vary greatly in duration and intensity.

Although economists explain the business cycle in terms of underlying causal factors such as major innovations, productivity shocks, money creation, and financial crises, they generally agree that changes in the level of total spending are the immediate causes of fluctuating real output and employment.

The business cycle affects all sectors of the economy, though in varying ways and degrees. The cycle has greater effects on output and employment in the capital goods and durable consumer goods industries than in the services and nondurable goods industries.

LO23.2 Illustrate how unemployment is measured and explain the different types of unemployment.

Economists distinguish between frictional, structural, and cyclical unemployment. The full-employment or natural rate of unemployment, which is made up of frictional and structural unemployment, is currently between 5 and 6 percent. The presence of part-time and discouraged workers makes it difficult to measure unemployment accurately.

The GDP gap, which can be either a positive or a negative value, is found by subtracting potential GDP from actual GDP. The economic cost of unemployment, as measured by the GDP gap, consists of the goods and services forgone by society when its resources are involuntarily idle. Okun's law suggests that every 1-percentage-point increase in unemployment above the natural rate causes an additional 2 percent negative GDP gap.

LO23.3 Explain how inflation is measured and distinguish between cost-push inflation and demand-pull inflation.

Inflation is a rise in the general price level and is measured in the United States by the Consumer Price Index (CPI). When inflation occurs, each dollar of income will buy fewer goods and services than before. That is, inflation reduces the purchasing power of money. Deflation is a decline in the general price level.

Unemployment rates and inflation rates vary widely globally. Unemployment rates differ because nations have different natural rates of unemployment and often are in different phases of their business cycles. Inflation and unemployment rates in the United States recently have been in the middle to low range compared with rates in other industrial nations.

Economists discern both demand-pull and cost-push (supply-side) inflation. Demand-pull inflation results from an excess of total spending relative to the economy's capacity to produce. The main source of cost-push inflation is abrupt and rapid increases in the prices of key resources. These supply shocks push up per-unit production costs and ultimately raise the prices of consumer goods.

LO23.4 Relate how unanticipated inflation can redistribute real income.

Unanticipated inflation arbitrarily redistributes real income at the expense of fixed-income receivers, creditors, and savers. If inflation is anticipated, individuals and businesses may be able to take steps to lessen or eliminate adverse redistribution effects.

When inflation is anticipated, lenders add an inflation premium to the interest rate charged on loans. The nominal interest rate thus reflects the real interest rate plus the inflation premium (the expected rate of inflation).

LO23.5 Discuss how inflation may affect the economy's level of real output.

Cost-push inflation reduces real output and employment. Proponents of zero inflation argue that even mild demand-pull inflation (1 to 3 percent) reduces the economy's real output. Other economists say that mild inflation may be a necessary by-product of the high and growing spending that produces high levels of output, full employment, and economic growth.

Hyperinflation, caused by highly imprudent expansions of the money supply, may undermine the monetary system and cause severe declines in real output.

TERMS AND CONCEPTS

business cycles
peak
recession
trough
expansion
labor force
unemployment rate
discouraged workers
frictional unemployment
structural unemployment
cyclical unemployment
full-employment rate of unemployment
natural rate of unemployment (NRU)
potential output
GDP gap
Okun's law
inflation
Consumer Price Index (CPI)
deflation
demand-pull inflation
cost-push inflation
per-unit production costs
core inflation
nominal income
real income
unanticipated inflation
anticipated inflation
cost-of-living adjustments (COLAs)
real interest rate
nominal interest rate
hyperinflation

The following and additional problems can be found in connect

DISCUSSION QUESTIONS

1. What are the four phases of the business cycle? How long do business cycles last? Why does the business cycle affect output and employment in capital goods industries and consumer durable goods industries more severely than in industries producing consumer nondurables? LO23.1
2. How, in general, can a financial crisis lead to a recession? How, in general, can a major new invention lead to an expansion? LO23.1
3. How is the labor force defined and who measures it? How is the unemployment rate calculated? Does an increase in the unemployment rate necessarily mean a decline in the size of the labor force? Why is a positive unemployment rate—one more than zero percent—fully compatible with full employment? LO23.2
4. How, in general, do unemployment rates vary by race and ethnicity, gender, occupation, and education? Why does the average length of time people are unemployed rise during a recession? LO23.2
5. Why is it difficult to distinguish among frictional, structural, and cyclical unemployment? Why is unemployment an economic problem? What are the consequences of a negative GDP gap? What are the noneconomic effects of unemployment? LO23.2
6. Because the United States has an unemployment compensation program that provides income for those out of work, why should we worry about unemployment? LO23.2
7. What is the Consumer Price Index (CPI) and how is it determined each month? How does the Bureau of Labor Statistics calculate the rate of inflation from one year to the next? What effect does inflation have on the purchasing power of a dollar? How does it explain differences between nominal and real interest rates? How does deflation differ from inflation? LO23.3
8. Distinguish between demand-pull inflation and cost-push inflation. Which of the two types is most likely to be associated with a negative GDP gap? Which with a positive GDP gap, in which actual GDP exceeds potential GDP? What is core inflation? Why is it calculated? LO23.3
9. Explain how an increase in your nominal income and a decrease in your real income might occur simultaneously. Who loses from inflation? Who gains? LO23.4
10. Explain how hyperinflation might lead to a severe decline in total output. LO23.5
11. **LAST WORD** Did the eventual recovery of the unemployment rate after the Great Recession indicate recovery in all aspects of employment? Explain and give examples.

AP REVIEW QUESTIONS

1. Which of the following statements relating to price level changes is true? LO23.3–23.5
   a. If nominal income exceeds real income, then there has been deflation.
   b. Deflation is very harmful to individuals on fixed incomes.
   c. Debtors tend to benefit from inflation, with the real value of their debt falling.
   d. Sustained inflation tends to be caused by continual increases in productivity.
   e. Deflation is frequently caused by sustained increases in the money supply.
2. Most economists agree that the immediate cause of the large majority of cyclical changes in the levels of real output and employment is unexpected changes in ________________. LO23.1
   a. The level of total spending.
   b. The level of the stock market.
   c. The level of the trade deficit.
   d. The level of unemployment.
   e. The level of inflation.
3. Suppose that an economy has 9 million people working full-time. It also has 1 million people who are actively seeking work but currently unemployed as well as 2 million discouraged workers who have given up looking for work and are currently unemployed. What is this economy's unemployment rate? LO23.2
   a. 10 percent.
   b. 15 percent.
   c. 20 percent.
   d. 25 percent.
   e. 33 percent.
4. Label each of the following scenarios as either frictional unemployment, structural unemployment, or cyclical unemployment. LO23.2
   a. Tim just graduated and is looking for a job.
   b. A recession causes a local factory to lay off 30 workers.
   c. Thousands of bus and truck drivers permanently lose their jobs when driverless, computer-driven vehicles make human drivers redundant.
   d. Hundreds of New York legal jobs permanently disappear when a lot of legal work gets outsourced to lawyers in India.
   e. A waiter at a Wall Street restaurant loses his job as the number of lunch-time customers falls during a recession.
5. The unemployment rate that is consistent with full employment is known as ________________. LO23.2
   a. The natural rate of unemployment.
   b. The unnatural rate of unemployment.
   c. The status quo rate of unemployment.
   d. Cyclical unemployment.
   e. Okun's rate of unemployment.
6. A country's current unemployment rate is 11 percent. Economists estimate that its natural rate of unemployment is 6 percent. About how large is this economy's negative GDP gap? LO23.2
   a. 1 percent.
   b. 3 percent.
   c. 6 percent.
   d. 10 percent.
   e. 11 percent.

7. Cost-push inflation occurs when there is ________________. LO23.3

a. Excess inventory.
b. A trade deficit.
c. Rising per-unit production costs.
d. Excess demand for goods and services.
e. High unemployment.

8. In 2005 Tatum's nominal income rose by 4.6 percent and the price level rose by 1.6 percent. We can conclude that Tatum's real income: LO23.3

a. May have either increased or decreased.
b. Rose by 6.2 percent.
c. Rose by 3 percent.
d. Fell by 3 percent.
e. Fell by 13 percent.

9. Kaitlin has $10,000 of savings that she may deposit with her local bank. Kaitlin wants to earn a real rate of return of at least 4 percent and she is expecting inflation to be exactly 3 percent. What is the lowest nominal interest rate that Kaitlin would be willing to accept from her local bank? LO23.4

a. 3 percent.
b. 4 percent.
c. 5 percent.
d. 6 percent.
e. 7 percent.

10. Real income is found by: LO23.3

a. Dividing nominal income by 70.
b. Multiplying nominal income by 1.03.
c. Dividing the price index (in hundredths) by nominal income.
d. Dividing nominal income by the price index (in hundredths).
e. Dividing the nominal income by the expected rate of inflation.

11. Demand-pull inflation: LO23.3

a. Occurs when prices of resources rise, pushing up costs and the price level.
b. Occurs when total spending exceeds the economy's ability to provide output at the existing price level.
c. Occurs only when the economy has reached its absolute production capacity.
d. Is also called cost-push inflation.
e. Increases real income.

12. The population of Norta is 1200, of whom 1000 people are 16 years of age or over. In Norta there are 750 workers employed, of whom 700 are full-time and 50 are part-time. One hundred (100) people are without jobs and looking, and one hundred fifty (150) people are either retired, in school, or at home not looking for work. Answer the following questions: LO23.2

a. What is the size of Norta's potential labor force?
b. What is the size of Norta's current labor force?
c. What is the labor force participation rate (percentage) in Norta?
d. What is the unemployment rate in Norta?

PROBLEMS

1. Suppose that a country's annual growth rates were 5, 3, 4, −1, −2, 2, 3, 4, 6, and 3 in yearly sequence over a 10-year period. What was the country's trend rate of growth over this period? Which set of years most clearly demonstrates an expansionary phase of the business cycle? Which set of years best illustrates a recessionary phase of the business cycle? LO23.1

2. Assume the following data for a country: total population, 500; population under 16 years of age or institutionalized, 120; not in labor force, 150; unemployed, 23; part-time workers looking for full-time jobs, 10. What is the size of the labor force? What is the official unemployment rate? LO23.2

3. Suppose that the natural rate of unemployment in a particular year is 5 percent and the actual rate of unemployment is 9 percent. Use Okun's law to determine the size of the GDP gap in percentage-point terms. If the potential GDP is $500 billion in that year, how much output is being forgone because of cyclical unemployment? LO23.2

4. If the CPI was 110 last year and is 121 this year, what is this year's rate of inflation? In contrast, suppose that the CPI was 110 last year and is 108 this year. What is this year's rate of inflation? What term do economists use to describe this second outcome? LO23.3

5. How long would it take for the price level to double if inflation persisted at (*a*) 2 percent per year, (*b*) 5 percent per year, and (*c*) 10 percent per year? LO23.3

6. If your nominal income rose by 5.3 percent and the price level rose by 3.8 percent in some year, by what percentage would your real income (approximately) increase? If your nominal income rose by 2.8 percent and your real income rose by 1.1 percent in some year, what must have been the (approximate) rate of inflation? LO23.4

7. Suppose that the nominal rate of inflation is 4 percent and the inflation premium is 2 percent. What is the real interest rate? Alternatively, assume that the real interest rate is 1 percent and the nominal interest rate is 6 percent. What is the inflation premium? LO23.4

8. If the inflation premium is 2 percent and the nominal interest rate is 1 percent, what is the real interest rate? What if the inflation premium is 3 percent while the nominal interest rate is 0.5 percent? LO23.4

Part EIGHT AP

Macroeconomic Models and Fiscal Policy

In this part, using the tools of ***aggregate demand and aggregate supply,*** we will introduce a modeling of the aggregate economy, permitting us to look at possible outcomes for economic activity from a ***full employment, long-run equilibrium*** to serious recession or inflation. In comparing these outcomes, we can introduce elements of a ***Classical, competitive market*** macro analysis with a more ***Keynesian, sticky or rigid price*** model. These are different and competing schools of economic analysis, around which much of the macroeconomic policy debate is centered. Finally, one of the principal tools of economic policy is studied—elements of ***fiscal policy,*** which include tax changes and expenditures changes. Economists are not in full agreement concerning the appropriate use of fiscal policy to stabilize the economy or in pursuit of other economic goals. A particular feature of the Keynesian view of the world is the beneficial effect that expansionary fiscal policy can have in leading the economy to full employment.

Chapter 24

Basic Macroeconomic Relationships*

Learning Objectives

LO24.1 Describe how changes in income affect consumption (and saving).

LO24.2 List and explain factors other than income that can affect consumption.

LO24.3 Explain how changes in real interest rates affect investment.

LO24.4 Identify and explain factors other than the real interest rate that can affect investment.

LO24.5 Illustrate how changes in investment (or one of the other components of total spending) can increase or decrease real GDP by a multiple amount.

AP Chapter Focus

In Chapter 23 we discussed the business cycle, unemployment, and inflation. Our eventual goal is to build economic models that can explain these phenomena. This chapter begins that process by examining the basic relationships that exist between three different pairs of economic aggregates. (Recall that to economists "aggregate" means "total" or "combined.") Specifically, this chapter looks at the relationships between:

- Income and consumption (and income and saving).
- The interest rate and investment.
- Changes in spending and changes in output.

What explains the trends in consumption (consumer spending) and saving reported in the news? How do changes in interest rates affect investment? How can initial changes in spending ultimately produce multiplied changes in GDP? The basic macroeconomic relationships discussed in this chapter answer these questions, and the concepts of the average and marginal propensities to consume and save and the multiplier effect will be introduced.

AP The Income-Consumption and Income-Saving Relationships

LO24.1 Describe how changes in income affect consumption (and saving).

The other-things-equal relationship between income and consumption is one of the best-established relationships in macroeconomics. In examining that relationship, we are also exploring the relationship between income and saving.

*Note to the Instructor: If you wish to bypass the aggregate expenditures model (Keynesian cross model) covered in full in Chapter 25, assigning the present chapter will provide a seamless transition to the AD-AS model of Chapter 26 and the chapters beyond. If you want to cover the aggregate expenditures model, this present chapter provides the necessary building blocks.

Recall that economists define *personal saving* as "not spending" or as "that part of disposable (after-tax) income not consumed." Saving (S) equals disposable income (DI) *minus* consumption (C).

Many factors determine a nation's levels of consumption and saving, but the most significant is disposable income. Consider some recent historical data for the United States. In Figure 24.1 each dot represents consumption and disposable income for 1 year since 1993. The line C that is loosely fitted to these points shows that consumption is directly (positively) related to disposable income; moreover, households spend most of their income.

But we can say more. The **45°(degree) line** is a reference line. Because it bisects the 90° angle formed by the two axes of the graph, each point on it is equidistant from the two axes. At each point on the 45° line, consumption would equal disposable income, or C = DI. Therefore, the vertical distance between the 45° line and any point on the horizontal axis measures either consumption *or* disposable income. If we let it measure disposable income, the vertical distance between it and the consumption line labeled C represents the amount of saving (S) in that year. Saving is the amount by which actual consumption in any year falls short of the 45° line—(S = DI − C). For example, in 2005 disposable income was $9,401 billion and consumption was $9,158 billion, so saving was $243 billion. Observe that the vertical distance between the 45° line and line C increases as we move rightward along the horizontal axis and decreases as we move leftward. Like consumption, saving typically varies directly with the level of disposable income. However, that historical pattern broke down somewhat in several years preceding the recession of 2007–2009.

The Consumption Schedule

The dots in Figure 24.1 represent historical data—the actual amounts of DI, C, and S in the United States over a period of years. But because we want to understand how the economy would behave under different possible scenarios, we need a schedule showing the various amounts that households would *plan* to consume at each of the various levels of disposable income that might prevail at some specific time. Columns 1 and 2 of Table 24.1, represented in **Figure 24.2a (Key Graph),** show the hypothetical consumption schedule that we

AP FIGURE 24.1 Consumption and disposable income, 1993–2015. Each dot in this figure shows consumption and disposable income in a specific year. The line *C*, which generalizes the relationship between consumption and disposable income, indicates a direct relationship and shows that households consume most of their after-tax incomes.

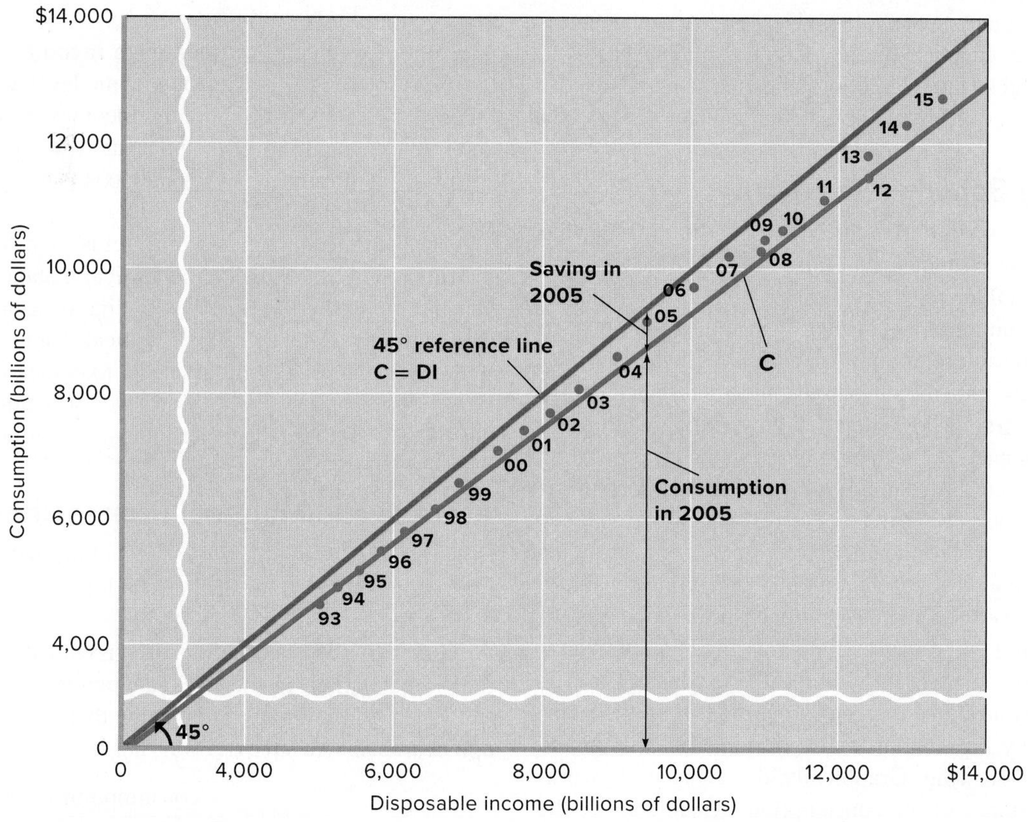

Source: Bureau of Economic Analysis, **www.bea.gov**.

AP TABLE 24.1 Consumption and Saving Schedules (in Billions) and Propensities to Consume and Save

(1) Level of Output and Income (GDP = DI)	(2) Consumption (C)	(3) Saving (S), (1) − (2)	(4) Average Propensity to Consume (APC), (2)/(1)	(5) Average Propensity to Save (APS), (3)/(1)	(6) Marginal Propensity to Consume (MPC), Δ(2)/Δ(1)*	(7) Marginal Propensity to Save (MPS), Δ(3)/Δ(1)*
(1) $370	$375	$−5	1.01	−.01		
					.75	.25
(2) 390	390	0	1.00	.00		
					.75	.25
(3) 410	405	5	.99	.01		
					.75	.25
(4) 430	420	10	.98	.02		
					.75	.25
(5) 450	435	15	.97	.03		
					.75	.25
(6) 470	450	20	.96	.04		
					.75	.25
(7) 490	465	25	.95	.05		
					.75	.25
(8) 510	480	30	.94	.06		
					.75	.25
(9) 530	495	35	.93	.07		
					.75	.25
(10) 550	510	40	.93	.07		

*The Greek letter Δ, delta, means "the change in."

require. This **consumption schedule** (or "consumption function") reflects the direct consumption–disposable income relationship suggested by the data in Figure 24.1, and it is consistent with many household budget studies. In the aggregate, households increase their spending as their disposable income rises and spend a larger proportion of a small disposable income than of a large disposable income.

The Saving Schedule

It is relatively easy to derive a **saving schedule** (or "saving function"). Because saving equals disposable income less consumption ($S = \text{DI} - C$), we need only subtract consumption (Table 24.1, column 2) from disposable income (column 1) to find the amount saved (column 3) at each DI. Thus, columns 1 and 3 in Table 24.1 are the saving schedule, represented in Figure 24.2b. The graph shows that there is a direct relationship between saving and DI but that saving is a smaller proportion of a small DI than of a large DI. If households consume a smaller and smaller proportion of DI as DI increases, then they must be saving a larger and larger proportion.

Remembering that at each point on the 45° line consumption equals DI, we see that *dissaving* (consuming in excess of after-tax income) will occur at relatively low DIs. For example, at $370 billion (row 1, Table 24.1), consumption is $375 billion. Households can consume more than their current incomes by liquidating (selling for cash) accumulated wealth or by borrowing. Graphically, dissaving is shown as the vertical distance of the consumption schedule above the 45° line or as the vertical distance of the saving schedule below the horizontal axis. We have marked the dissaving at the $370 billion level of income in Figure 24.2a and 24.2b. Both vertical distances measure the $5 billion of dissaving that occurs at $370 billion of income.

In our example, the **break-even income** is $390 billion (row 2, Table 24.1). This is the income level at which households plan to consume their entire incomes ($C = \text{DI}$). Graphically, the consumption schedule cuts the 45° line, and the saving schedule cuts the horizontal axis (saving is zero) at the break-even income level.

At all higher incomes, households plan to save part of their incomes. Graphically, the vertical distance between the consumption schedule and the 45° line measures this saving (see Figure 24.2a), as does the vertical distance between the saving schedule and the horizontal axis (see Figure 24.2b). For example, at the $410 billion level of income (row 3, Table 24.1), both these distances indicate $5 billion of saving.

Average and Marginal Propensities

Columns 4 to 7 in Table 24.1 show additional characteristics of the consumption and saving schedules.

APC and APS The fraction, or percentage, of total income that is consumed is the **average propensity to consume (APC)**. The fraction of total income that is saved is the **average propensity to save (APS).** That is,

$$\text{APC} = \frac{\text{consumption}}{\text{income}}$$

AP KEY GRAPH

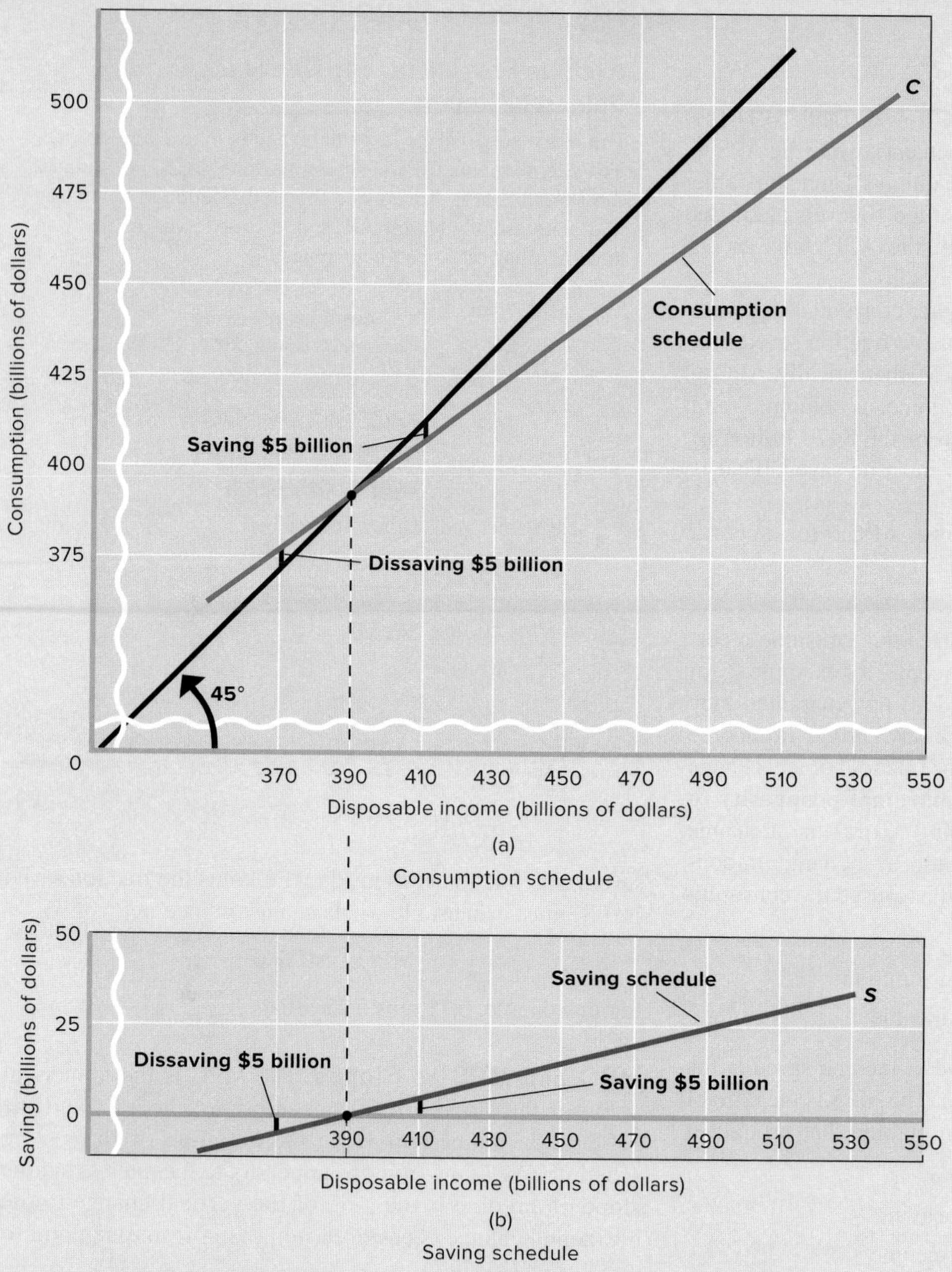

FIGURE 24.2 Consumption and saving schedules. The two parts of this figure show the income-consumption and income-saving relationships in Table 24.1 graphically. (a) Consumption rises as income increases. Saving is negative (dissaving occurs) when the consumption schedule is above the 45° line, and saving is positive when the consumption schedule is below the 45° line. (b) Like consumption, saving increases as income goes up. The saving schedule is found by subtracting the consumption schedule in the top graph vertically from the 45° line. For these hypothetical data, saving is −$5 billion at $370 billion of income, zero at $390 billion of income, and $5 billion at $410 billion of income. Saving is zero where consumption equals disposable income.

QUICK QUIZ FOR FIGURE 24.2

1. The slope of the consumption schedule in this figure is 0.75. Thus, the:
   - **a.** slope of the saving schedule is 1.33.
   - **b.** marginal propensity to consume is 0.75.
   - **c.** average propensity to consume is 0.25.
   - **d.** slope of the saving schedule is also 0.75.
2. In this figure, when consumption is a positive amount, saving:
   - **a.** must be a negative amount.
   - **b.** must also be a positive amount.
   - **c.** can be either a positive or a negative amount.
   - **d.** is zero.
3. In this figure:
   - **a.** the marginal propensity to consume is constant at all levels of income.
   - **b.** the marginal propensity to save rises as disposable income rises.
   - **c.** consumption is inversely (negatively) related to disposable income.
   - **c.** saving is inversely (negatively) related to disposable income.
4. When consumption equals disposable income:
   - **a.** the marginal propensity to consume is zero.
   - **b.** the average propensity to consume is zero.
   - **c.** consumption and saving must be equal.
   - **d.** saving must be zero.

Answers: 1. b; 2. c; 3. a; 4. d

and

$$APS = \frac{\text{saving}}{\text{income}}$$

For example, at \$470 billion of income (row 6, Table 24.1), the APC is $\frac{450}{470} = \frac{45}{47}$, or about 0.96 (= 96 percent), while the APS is $\frac{20}{470} = \frac{2}{47}$, or about 0.04 (= 4 percent). Columns 4 and 5 in Table 24.1 show the APC and APS at each of the 10 levels of DI. As implied by our previous discussion, the APC falls as DI increases, while the APS rises as DI goes up.

Because disposable income is either consumed or saved, the fraction of any DI consumed plus the fraction saved (not consumed) must exhaust that income. Mathematically, APC + APS = 1 at any level of disposable income, as columns 4 and 5 in Table 24.1 illustrate. So if 0.96 of the \$470 billion of income in row 6 in consumed, 0.04 must be saved. That is why APC + APS = 1.

Global Perspective 24.1 shows APCs for several countries.

GLOBAL PERSPECTIVE 24.1

Average Propensities to Consume, Selected Nations

There are surprisingly large differences in average propensities to consume (APCs) among nations. In 2014, Canada, the United States, Korea, and the Netherlands in particular had substantially higher APCs, and thus lower APSs, than several other advanced economies.

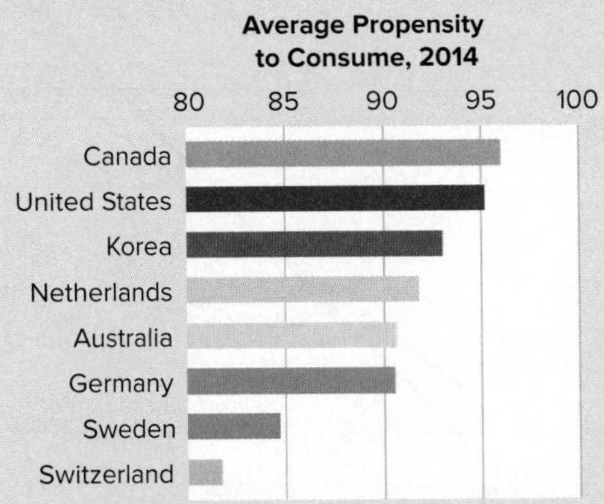

Source: Organization for Economic Cooperation and Development, OECD, **www.oecd.org**. Derived from OECD household saving rates as percentages of disposable income. *Econ Outlook 98*, Annex Table 23, extracted April 2016.

MPC and MPS The fact that households consume a certain proportion of a particular total income, for example, $\frac{45}{47}$ of a \$470 billion disposable income, does not guarantee they will consume the same proportion of any *change* in income they might receive. The proportion, or fraction, of any change in income consumed is called the **marginal propensity to consume (MPC),** "marginal" meaning "extra" or "a change in." Equivalently, the MPC is the ratio of a change in consumption to a change in the income that caused the consumption change:

$$MPC = \frac{\text{change in consumption}}{\text{change in income}}$$

Similarly, the fraction of any change in income saved is the **marginal propensity to save (MPS)**. The MPS is the ratio of a change in saving to the change in income that brought it about:

$$MPS = \frac{\text{change in saving}}{\text{change in income}}$$

If disposable income is \$470 billion (row 6 horizontally in Table 24.1) and household income rises by \$20 billion to \$490 billion (row 7), households will consume $\frac{15}{20}$, or $\frac{3}{4}$, and save $\frac{5}{20}$, or $\frac{1}{4}$, of that increase in income. In other words, the MPC is $\frac{3}{4}$ or 0.75, and the MPS is $\frac{1}{4}$ or 0.25, as shown in columns 6 and 7.

The sum of the MPC and the MPS for any change in disposable income must always be 1. Consuming or saving out of extra income is an either-or proposition; the fraction of any change in income not consumed is, by definition, saved. If 0.75 of extra disposable income is consumed, 0.25 must be saved. The fraction consumed (MPC) plus the fraction saved (MPS) must exhaust the whole change in income:

$$MPC + MPS = 1$$

In our example, 0.75 plus 0.25 equals 1.

MPC and MPS as Slopes The MPC is the numerical value of the slope of the consumption schedule, and the MPS is the numerical value of the slope of the saving schedule. We know from the appendix to Chapter 1 that the slope of any line is the ratio of the vertical change to the horizontal change occasioned in moving from one point to another on that line.

Figure 24.3 measures the slopes of the consumption and saving lines, using enlarged portions of Figure 24.2a and 24.2b. Observe that consumption changes by \$15 billion (the vertical change) for each \$20 billion change in disposable income (the horizontal change). The slope of the consumption line is thus 0.75 (= \$15/\$20), which is the value of the MPC. Saving changes by \$5 billion (shown as the vertical change) for every \$20 billion change in disposable income (shown as the horizontal change). The slope of the saving line therefore is 0.25 (= \$5/\$20), which is the value of the MPS.

FIGURE 24.3 The marginal propensity to consume and the marginal propensity to save. In the two parts of this figure, the Greek letter delta (Δ) means "the change in." (a) The MPC is the slope ($\Delta C/\Delta DI$) of the consumption schedule. (b) The MPS is the slope ($\Delta S/\Delta DI$) of the saving schedule.

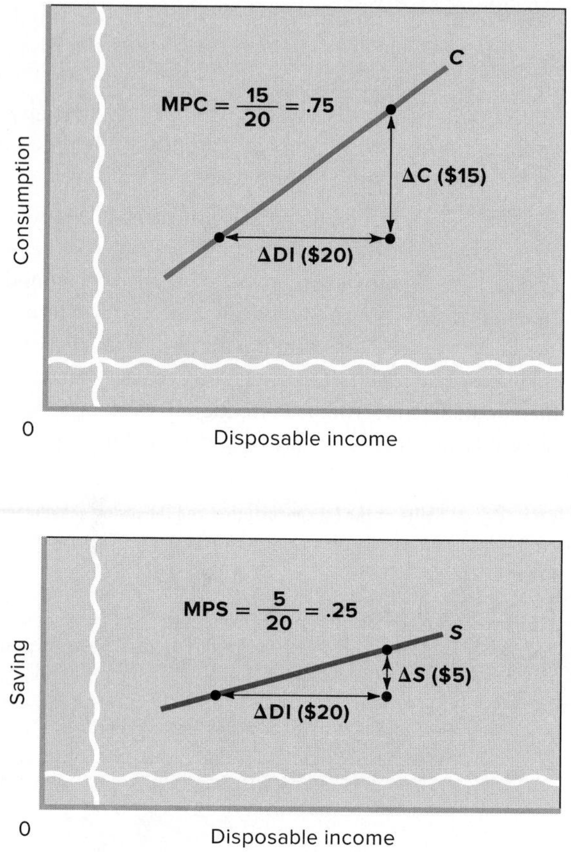

Nonincome Determinants of Consumption and Saving

LO24.2 List and explain factors other than income that can affect consumption.

The amount of disposable income is the basic determinant of the amounts households will consume and save. But certain determinants other than income might prompt households to consume more or less at each possible level of income and thereby change the locations of the consumption and saving schedules. Those other determinants are wealth, borrowing, expectations, and interest rates.

- ***Wealth*** A household's wealth is the dollar amount of all the assets that it owns minus the dollar amount of its liabilities (all the debt that it owes). Households build wealth by saving money out of current income. The point of building wealth is to increase consumption possibilities. The larger the stock of wealth that a household can build up, the larger will be its present and future consumption possibilities.

  Events sometimes suddenly boost the value of existing wealth. When this happens, households tend to increase their spending and reduce their saving. This so-called **wealth effect** shifts the consumption schedule upward and the saving schedule downward. They move in response to households taking advantage of the increased consumption possibilities afforded by the sudden increase in wealth. Examples: In the late 1990s, skyrocketing U.S. stock values expanded the value of household wealth by increasing the value of household assets. Predictably, households spent more and saved less. In contrast, a strong "reverse wealth effect" occurred in 2008. Plunging real estate and stock market prices joined together to erase $11.2 trillion (yes, trillion) of household wealth. Consumers quickly reacted by reducing their consumption spending. The consumption schedule shifted downward.

- ***Borrowing*** Household borrowing also affects consumption. When a household borrows, it can increase current consumption beyond what would be possible if its spending were limited to its disposable income. By allowing households to spend more, borrowing shifts the current consumption schedule upward.

  But note that there is no "free lunch." While borrowing in the present allows for higher consumption in the present, it necessitates lower consumption in the future when the debts that are incurred due to the borrowing must be repaid. Stated a bit differently, increased borrowing increases debt (liabilities), which in turn reduces household wealth (since *wealth* = *assets* – *liabilities*). This reduction in wealth reduces future consumption possibilities in much the same way that a decline in asset values would. But note that the term "reverse wealth effect" is reserved for situations in which wealth unexpectedly changes because asset values unexpectedly change. It is not used to refer to situations such as the one being discussed here where wealth is intentionally reduced by households through borrowing and piling up debt to increase current consumption.

- ***Expectations*** Household expectations about future prices and income may affect current spending and saving. For example, the expectation of higher prices tomorrow may cause households to buy more today while prices are still low. Thus, the current consumption schedule shifts up and the current saving schedule shifts down. Or expectations of a recession and thus lower income in the future may lead households to reduce consumption and save more today. Their greater present saving will help build wealth that will help them ride out the expected bad times. The consumption schedule therefore will shift down and the saving schedule will shift up.

- ***Real interest rates*** When real interest rates (those adjusted for inflation) fall, households tend to borrow more, consume more, and save less. A lower interest rate, for example, decreases monthly loan payments and induces consumers to purchase automobiles and other goods bought on credit. A lower interest rate also diminishes the incentive to save because of the reduced interest "payment" to the saver. These effects on consumption and saving, however, are very modest. They mainly shift consumption toward some products (those bought on credit) and away from others. At best, lower interest rates shift the consumption schedule slightly upward and the saving schedule slightly downward. Higher interest rates do the opposite.

Other Important Considerations

There are several additional important points regarding the consumption and saving schedules:

- ***Switching to real GDP*** When developing macroeconomic models, economists change their focus from the relationship between consumption (and saving) and *disposable income* to the relationship between consumption (and saving) and *real domestic output (real GDP)*. This modification is reflected in Figure 24.4a and 24.4b, where the horizontal axes measure real GDP.
- ***Changes along schedules*** The movement from one point to another on a consumption schedule (for example, from *a* to *b* on C_0 in Figure 24.4a) is a *change in the amount consumed* and is solely caused by a change in real GDP. On the other hand, an upward or downward shift of the entire schedule, for example, a shift from C_0 to C_1 or C_2 in Figure 24.4a, is a *shift of the consumption schedule* and is caused by changes in any one or more of the *nonincome* determinants of consumption just discussed.

  A similar distinction in terminology applies to the saving schedule in Figure 24.4b.
- ***Simultaneous shifts*** Changes in wealth, expectations, interest rates, and household debt will shift the consumption schedule in one direction and the saving schedule in the opposite direction. If households decide to consume more at each possible level of real GDP, they must save less, and vice versa. (Even when they spend more by borrowing, they are, in effect, reducing their current saving by the amount borrowed since borrowing is, effectively, "negative saving.") Graphically, if the consumption schedule shifts upward from C_0 to C_1 in Figure 24.4a, the saving schedule shifts downward, from S_0 to S_1 in Figure 24.4b. Similarly, a downward shift of the consumption schedule from C_0 to C_2 means an upward shift of the saving schedule from S_0 to S_2.
- ***Taxation*** In contrast, a change in taxes shifts the consumption and saving schedules in the same direction. Taxes are paid partly at the expense of consumption and partly at the expense of saving. So an increase in taxes will reduce both consumption and saving, shifting the consumption schedule in Figure 24.4a and the saving schedule in Figure 24.4b downward. Conversely, households will partly consume and partly save any decrease in taxes. Both the consumption schedule and saving schedule will shift upward.
- ***Stability*** The consumption and saving schedules usually are relatively stable unless altered by major tax increases or decreases. Their stability may be because consumption-saving decisions are strongly influenced by long-term considerations such as saving to meet emergencies or saving for retirement. It may also be because changes in the nonincome determinants frequently work in opposite directions and therefore may be self-canceling.

FIGURE 24.4 Shifts of the (a) consumption and (b) saving schedules. Normally, if households consume more at each level of real GDP, they are necessarily saving less. Graphically this means that an upward shift of the consumption schedule (C_0 to C_1) entails a downward shift of the saving schedule (S_0 to S_1). If households consume less at each level of real GDP, they are saving more. A downward shift of the consumption schedule (C_0 to C_2) is reflected in an upward shift of the saving schedule (S_0 to S_2). This pattern breaks down, however, when taxes change; then the consumption and saving schedules move in the *same* direction—opposite to the direction of the tax change.

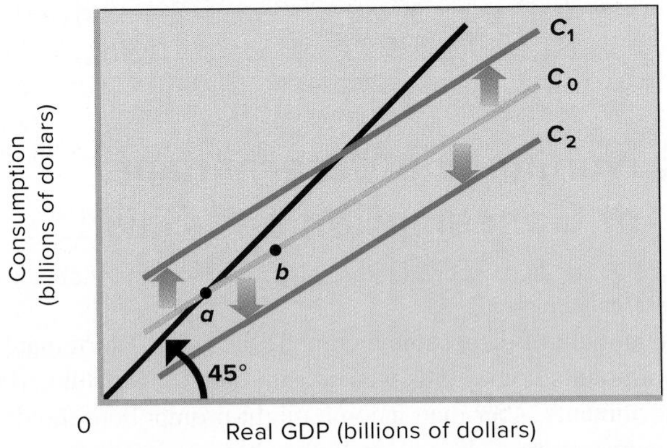

(a)
Consumption schedule

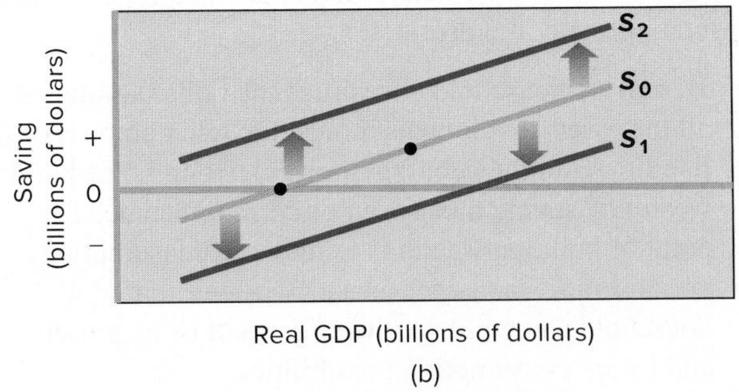

(b)
Saving schedule

CONSIDER THIS . . .

Source: © Digital Vision/Getty Images RF

The Great Recession and the Paradox of Thrift

The Great Recession of 2007–2009 altered the prior consumption and saving behavior in the economy. Concerned about reduced wealth, high debt, and potential job losses, households increased their saving and reduced their consumption at each level of after-tax income (or each level of GDP). In Figure 24.4, this outcome is illustrated as the downward *shift* of the consumption schedule in the top graph and the upward *shift* of the saving schedule in the lower graph.

This change of behavior illustrates the so-called **paradox of thrift,** which refers to the possibility that a recession can be made worse when households become more thrifty and save in response to the downturn. The paradox of thrift rests on two major ironies. One irony is that saving more is *good* for the economy in the long run, as noted in Chapter 1 and Chapter 20. It finances investment and therefore fuels subsequent economic growth. But saving more can be *bad* for the economy during a recession. Because firms are pessimistic about future sales, the increased saving is not likely to be matched by an equal amount of added investment. The extra saving simply reduces spending on currently produced goods and services. That means that even more businesses suffer, more layoffs occur, and people's incomes decline even more.

The paradox of thrift has a second irony related to the *fallacy of composition* (Chapter 1, Last Word): Households as a group may inadvertently end up saving less when each individual household tries to save more during a recession. This is because each household's attempt to save more implies that it is also attempting to spend less. Across all households, that collective reduction in total spending in the economy creates additional job losses and further drives down total income. The decline in total income reduces the ability of households as a group to save as much as they did before their spending reduction and subsequent income decline.

AP QUICK REVIEW 24.1

- ✓ Disposable income (DI) equals Consumption (C) plus Saving (S). Both consumption spending and saving rise when disposable income increases; both fall when disposable income decreases.
- ✓ The average propensity to consume (APC) is the fraction of any specific level of disposable income that is spent on consumer goods; the average propensity to save (APS) is the fraction of any specific level of disposable income that is saved. The APC falls and the APS rises as disposable income increases. Since income must be spent or saved, APC + APS = 1.
- ✓ The marginal propensity to consume (MPC) is the fraction of a change in disposable income that is consumed and it is the slope of the consumption schedule; the marginal propensity to save (MPS) is the fraction of a change in disposable income that is saved and it is the slope of the saving schedule. MPS + MPC = 1.
- ✓ Changes in consumer wealth, consumer expectations, interest rates, household debt, and taxes can shift the consumption and saving schedules (as they relate to real GDP).

AP The Interest-Rate–Investment Relationship

LO24.3 Explain how changes in real interest rates affect investment.

In our consideration of major macro relationships, we next turn to the relationship between the real interest rate and investment. Recall that investment consists of expenditures on new plants, capital equipment, machinery, inventories, and so on. The investment decision is a marginal-benefit–marginal-cost decision: The marginal benefit from investment is the expected rate of return businesses hope to realize. The marginal cost is the interest rate that must be paid for borrowed funds. Businesses will invest in all projects for which the expected rate of return exceeds the interest rate. Expected returns (profits) and the interest rate therefore are the two basic determinants of investment spending.

Expected Rate of Return

Investment spending is guided by the profit motive; businesses buy capital goods only when they think such purchases will be profitable. Suppose the owner of a small cabinetmaking shop is considering whether to invest in a new sanding machine that costs $1,000 and has a useful life of only 1 year. (Extending the life of the machine beyond 1 year complicates the economic decision but does not change the fundamental analysis. We discuss the valuation of returns beyond 1 year in Chapter 31.) The new machine will increase the firm's output and sales revenue. Suppose the net expected revenue from the machine (that is, after such operating costs as power, lumber, labor, and certain taxes have been subtracted) is $1,100. Then, after the $1,000 cost of the machine is subtracted from the net expected revenue of $1,100, the firm will have an expected profit of $100. Dividing this $100 profit by the $1,000 cost of the machine, we find that the **expected rate of return,** *r*, on the machine is 10 percent (= $100/$1,000). It is important to note that this is an *expected* rate of return, not a *guaranteed* rate of return. The investment may or may not generate as much revenue or as much profit as anticipated. Investment involves risk.

The Real Interest Rate

One important cost associated with investing that our example has ignored is interest, which is the financial cost of borrowing the $1,000 of *money* "capital" to purchase the $1,000 of *real* capital (the sanding machine).

The interest cost of the investment is computed by multiplying the interest rate, *i*, by the $1,000 borrowed to buy the machine. If the interest rate is, say, 7 percent, the total interest cost will be $70. This compares favorably with the net expected return of $100, which produced the 10 percent expected rate of return. If the investment works out as expected, it will add $30 to the firm's profit.

We can generalize as follows: If the expected rate of return (10 percent) exceeds the interest rate (here, 7 percent), the investment should be undertaken. The firm expects the investment to be profitable. But if the interest rate (say, 12 percent) exceeds the expected rate of return (10 percent), the investment should not be undertaken. The firm expects the investment to be unprofitable. The firm should undertake all investment projects it thinks will be profitable. This means that the firm should array its prospective investment projects from the highest expected rate of return, *r*, downward and then invest in all projects for which *r* exceeds *i*. The firm therefore should invest to the point where $r = i$ because then it will have undertaken all investments for which *r* is greater than *i*.

This guideline applies even if a firm finances the investment internally out of funds saved from past profit rather than borrowing the funds. The role of the interest rate in the investment decision does not change. When the firm uses money from savings to invest in the sander, it incurs an opportunity cost because it forgoes the interest income it could have earned by lending the funds to someone else. That interest cost, converted to percentage terms, needs to be weighed against the expected rate of return.

The *real* rate of interest, rather than the *nominal* rate, is crucial in making investment decisions. Recall from Chapter 23 that the nominal interest rate is expressed in dollars of current value, while the real interest rate is stated in dollars of constant or inflation-adjusted value. Recall that the real interest rate is the nominal rate less the rate of inflation. In our sanding machine illustration, our implicit assumption of a constant price level ensures that all our data, including the interest rate, are in real terms.

But what if inflation *is* occurring? Suppose a $1,000 investment is expected to yield a real (inflation-adjusted) rate of return of 10 percent and the nominal interest rate is 15 percent. At first, we would say the investment would be unprofitable. But assume there is ongoing inflation of 10 percent per year. This means the investing firm will pay back dollars with approximately 10 percent less in purchasing power. While the nominal interest rate is 15 percent, the real rate is only 5 percent (= 15 percent − 10 percent). By comparing this 5 percent real interest rate with the 10 percent expected real rate of return, we find that the investment is potentially profitable and should be undertaken.

Investment Demand Curve

We now move from a single firm's investment decision to total demand for investment goods by the entire business sector. Assume that every firm has estimated the expected rates of return from all investment projects and has recorded those data. We can cumulate (successively sum) these data by asking: How many dollars' worth of investment projects have an expected rate of return of, say, 16 percent or more? How many have 14 percent or more? How many have 12 percent or more? And so on.

Suppose no prospective investments yield an expected return of 16 percent or more. But suppose there are $5 billion of investment opportunities with expected rates of return between 14 and 16 percent; an additional $5 billion yielding between 12 and 14 percent; still an additional $5 billion yielding between 10 and 12 percent; and an additional $5 billion in each successive 2 percent range of yield down to and including the 0 to 2 percent range.

To cumulate these figures for each rate of return, *r*, we add the amounts of investment that will yield each particular rate of return *r* or higher. This provides the data in the table in **Figure 24.5 (Key Graph).** The data are shown graphically in Figure 24.5. In the table, the number opposite 12 percent, for example, means there are $10 billion of investment opportunities that will yield an expected rate of return of 12 percent or more. The $10 billion includes the $5 billion of investment expected to yield a return of 14 percent or more plus the $5 billion expected to yield between 12 and 14 percent.

We know from our example of the sanding machine that an investment project will be undertaken if its expected rate of return, *r*, exceeds the real interest rate, *i*. Let's first suppose *i* is 12 percent. Businesses will undertake all investments for which *r* exceeds 12 percent. That is, they will invest until the 12 percent rate of return equals the 12 percent interest rate. Figure 24.5 reveals that $10 billion of investment spending will be undertaken at a 12 percent interest rate; that means $10 billion of investment projects have an expected rate of return of 12 percent or more.

AP KEY GRAPH

FIGURE 24.5 The investment demand curve. The investment demand curve is constructed by arraying all potential investment projects in descending order of their expected rates of return. The curve slopes downward, reflecting an inverse relationship between the real interest rate (the financial "price" of each dollar of investing) and the quantity of investment demanded.

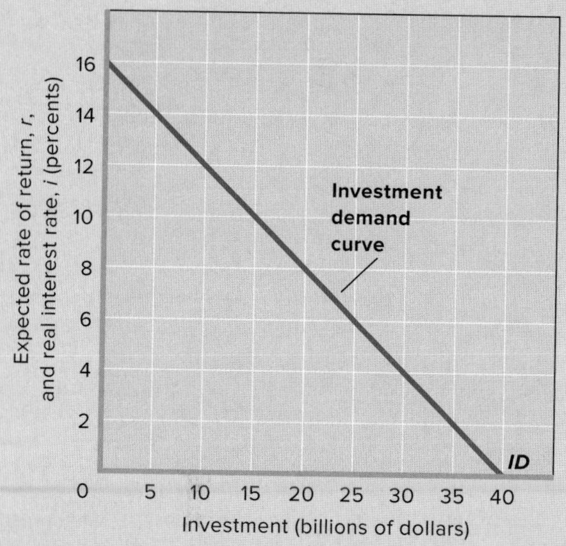

Real Interest Rate (*i*) and Expected Rate of Return (*r*)	Cumulative Amount of Investment Having this Rate of Return or Higher, Billions per Year
16%	$ 0
14	5
12	10
10	15
8	20
6	25
4	30
2	35
0	40

QUICK QUIZ FOR FIGURE 24.5

1. The investment demand curve:
a. reflects a direct (positive) relationship between the real interest rate and investment.
b. reflects an inverse (negative) relationship between the real interest rate and investment.
c. shifts to the right when the real interest rate rises.
d. shifts to the left when the real interest rate rises.

2. In this figure:
a. greater cumulative amounts of investment are associated with lower real interest rates.
b. lesser cumulative amounts of investment are associated with lower expected rates of return on investment.
c. higher interest rates are associated with higher expected rates of return on investment, and therefore greater amounts of investment.
d. interest rates and investment move in the same direction.

3. In this figure, if the real interest rate falls from 6 to 4 percent:
a. investment will increase from 0 to $30 billion.
b. investment will decrease by $5 billion.
c. the expected rate of return will rise by $5 billion.
d. investment will increase from $25 billion to $30 billion.

4. In this figure, investment will be:
a. zero if the real interest rate is zero.
b. $40 billion if the real interest rate is 16 percent.
c. $30 billion if the real interest rate is 4 percent.
d. $20 billion if the real interest rate is 12 percent.

Answers: 1. b; 2. a; 3. d; 4. c

Put another way: At a financial "price" of 12 percent, $10 billion of investment goods will be demanded. If the interest rate is lower, say, 8 percent, the amount of investment for which r equals or exceeds i is $20 billion. Thus, firms will demand $20 billion of investment goods at an 8 percent real interest rate. At 6 percent, they will demand $25 billion of investment goods.

By applying the marginal-benefit–marginal-cost rule that investment projects should be undertaken up to the point where $r = i$, we see that we can add the real interest rate to the vertical axis in Figure 24.5. The curve in Figure 24.5 not only shows rates of return; it shows the quantity of investment demanded at each "price" i (interest rate) of investment. The vertical axis in Figure 24.5 shows the various possible real interest rates, and the horizontal axis shows the corresponding quantities of investment demanded. The inverse (downsloping) relationship between the interest rate (price) and dollar quantity of investment demanded conforms to the law of demand discussed in Chapter 3. The curve *ID* in Figure 24.5 is the economy's **investment demand curve.** It shows the amount of investment forthcoming at each real interest rate. The level of investment depends on the expected rate of return and the real interest rate.

AP Shifts of the Investment Demand Curve

LO24.4 Identify and explain factors other than the real interest rate that can affect investment.

Figure 24.5 shows the relationship between the interest rate and the amount of investment demanded, other things equal. When other things change, the investment demand curve shifts. In general, any factor that leads businesses collectively to expect greater rates of return on their investments increases investment demand. That factor shifts the investment demand curve to the right, as from ID_0 to ID_1 in Figure 24.6. Any factor that leads businesses collectively to expect lower rates of return on their investments shifts the curve to the left, as from ID_0 to ID_2. What are those non-interest-rate determinants of investment demand?

- ***Acquisition, maintenance, and operating costs*** The initial costs of capital goods, and the estimated costs of operating and maintaining those goods, affect the expected rate of return on investment. When these costs rise, the expected rate of return from prospective investment projects falls and the investment demand curve shifts to the left. Example: Higher electricity costs associated with operating tools and machinery shifts the investment demand curve to the left. Lower costs, in contrast, shift it to the right.
- ***Business taxes*** When government is considered, firms look to expected returns *after taxes* in making their investment decisions. An increase in business taxes lowers the expected profitability of investments and shifts the investment demand curve to the left; a reduction of business taxes shifts it to the right.

AP **FIGURE 24.6** **Shifts of the investment demand curve.** Increases in investment demand are shown as rightward shifts of the investment demand curve; decreases in investment demand are shown as leftward shifts of the investment demand curve.

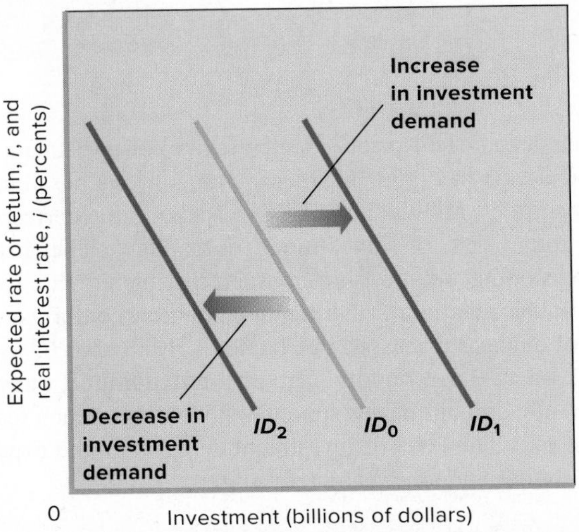

- ***Technological change*** Technological progress—the development of new products, improvements in existing products, and the creation of new machinery and production processes—stimulates investment. The development of a more efficient machine, for example, lowers production costs or improves product quality and increases the expected rate of return from investing in the machine. Profitable new products (cholesterol medications, Internet services, high-definition televisions, cellular phones, and so on) induce a flurry of investment as businesses tool up for expanded production. A rapid rate of technological progress shifts the investment demand curve to the right.
- ***Stock of capital goods on hand*** The stock of capital goods on hand, relative to output and sales, influences investment decisions by firms. When the economy is overstocked with production facilities and when firms have excessive inventories of finished goods, the expected rate of return on new investment declines. Firms with excess production capacity have little incentive to invest in new capital. Therefore, less investment is forthcoming at each real interest rate; the investment demand curve shifts leftward.

  When the economy is understocked with production facilities and when firms are selling their output as fast as they can produce it, the expected rate of return on new investment increases and the investment demand curve shifts rightward.
- ***Planned inventory changes*** Recall from Chapter 21 that the definition of investment includes changes in inventories of unsold goods. An increase in inventories is counted as positive investment while a decrease in inventories is counted as negative investment. It is important to remember that some inventory changes are planned, while others are unplanned. Since the investment demand curve deals only with *planned* investment, it is only affected by *planned* changes that firms desire to make to their inventory levels. If firms are planning to increase their inventories, the investment demand curve shifts to the right. If firms are planning on decreasing their inventories, the investment demand curve shifts to the left.

  Firms make planned changes to their inventory levels mostly because they are expecting either faster or slower sales. A firm that expects its sales to double in the next year will want to keep more inventory in stock, thereby increasing its investment demand. By contrast, a firm that is expecting slower sales will plan on reducing its inventory, thereby reducing its overall investment demand. But because life often does not turn out as expected, firms often find that the actual amount of inventory investment that they end up making is either more or less than what they had planned. The size of the gap is, naturally, the dollar amount of their *unplanned* inventory changes. These unplanned inventory adjustments will play a large role in the aggregate expenditures model studied in Chapter 25.

- ***Expectations*** We noted that business investment is based on expected returns (expected additions to profit). Most capital goods are durable, with a life expectancy of 10 or 20 years. Thus, the expected rate of return on capital investment depends on the firm's expectations of future sales, future operating costs, and future profitability of the product that the capital helps produce. These expectations are based on forecasts of future business conditions as well as on such elusive and difficult-to-predict factors as changes in the domestic political climate, international relations, population growth, and consumer tastes. If executives become more optimistic about future sales, costs, and profits, the investment demand curve will shift to the right; a pessimistic outlook will shift the curve to the left.

Global Perspective 24.2 compares investment spending relative to GDP for several nations in a recent year. Domestic real interest rates and investment demand determine the levels of investment relative to GDP.

GLOBAL PERSPECTIVE 24.2

Gross Investment Expenditures as a Percentage of GDP, Selected Nations

As a percentage of GDP, investment varies widely by nation. These differences, of course, can change from year to year.

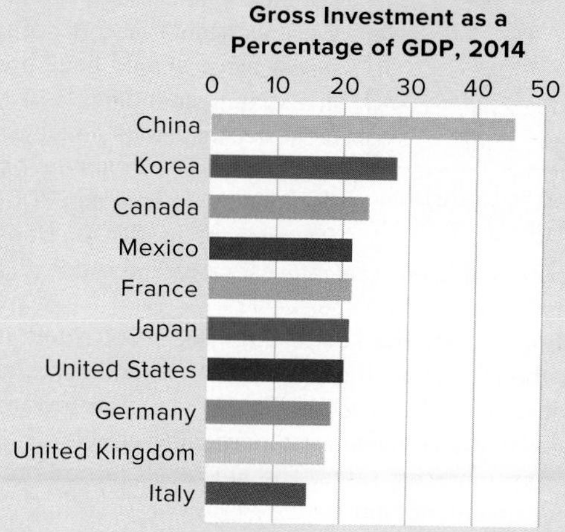

Source: Gross fixed capital formation data from International Financial Statistics, International Monetary Fund, **www.imf.org**.

Instability of Investment

In contrast to consumption, investment is unstable; it rises and falls quite often. Investment, in fact, is the most volatile component of total spending—so much so that most of the fluctuations in output and employment that happen over the course of the business cycle can be attributed to demand shocks relating to unexpected increases and decreases in investment. Figure 24.7 shows just how volatile investment in the United States has been. Notice that the percentage swings in investment in real terms are greater than the percentage

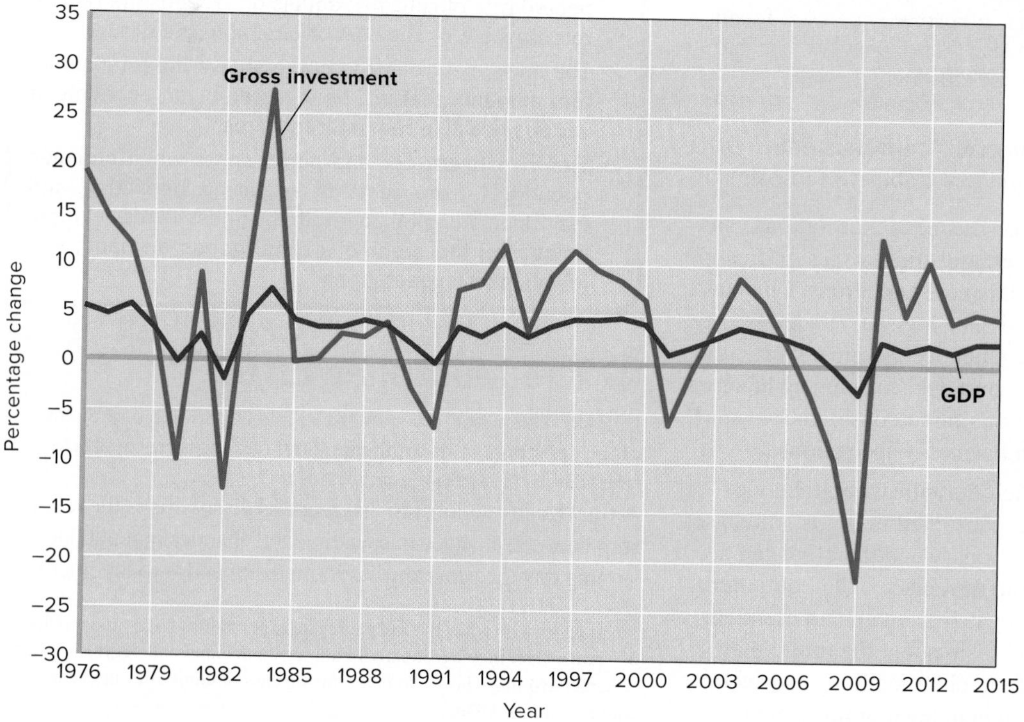

Source: Bureau of Economic Analysis, **www.bea.gov**.

FIGURE 24.7 The volatility of investment, 1976–2015. Annual percentage changes in investment spending are often several times greater than the percentage changes in GDP. (Data are in real terms. Investment is gross private domestic investment.)

CONSIDER THIS . . .

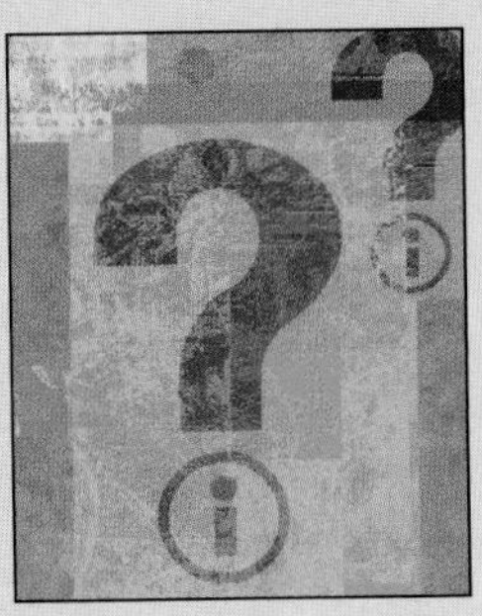

Source: © Stephanie Dalton Cowan/Getty Images RF

The Great Recession and the Investment Riddle

During the severe recession of 2007–2009, real interest rates essentially declined to zero. Figure 24.5 suggests that this drop in interest rates should have boosted investment spending. But investment declined substantially during this period. On an annual basis, it declined by 9 percent in 2008 and 26 percent in 2009. Does this combination of lower real interest rates and reduced investment make Figure 24.5 irrelevant?

Definitely not! The key to the investment riddle is that during the recession, the investment demand curve shifted inward, as from ID_0 to ID_2 in Figure 24.6. This inward shift overwhelmed any investment-increasing effects of the decline of real interest rates. The net result turned out to be less investment, not more.

The leftward shift of the investment demand reflected a decline in the expected returns from investment. Firms envisioned zero or negative returns on investment in new capital because they were facing an overstock of existing capital relative to their current sales. Understandably, they therefore were not inclined to invest. Also, firms were extremely pessimistic about when the economy would regain its strength. This pessimism also contributed to low expected rates of return on investment and thus to exceptionally weak investment demand. Further, even though the interest rate was so low, firms that wanted to borrow and invest found that lenders were reluctant to lend them money for fear that they would not be able to pay back the loans.

swings in real GDP. Several interrelated factors drawn from our previous discussion explain the variability of investment.

- ***Variability of expectations*** Business expectations can change quickly when some event suggests a significant possible change in future business conditions. Changes in exchange rates, trade barriers, legislative actions, stock market prices, government economic policies, the outlook for war or peace, court decisions in key labor or antitrust cases, and a host of similar considerations may cause substantial shifts in business expectations.
- ***Durability*** Because of their durability, capital goods have indefinite useful lifespans. Within limits, purchases of capital goods are discretionary and therefore can be postponed. Firms can scrap or replace older equipment and buildings, or they can patch them up and use them for a few more years. Optimism about the future may prompt firms to replace their older facilities and such modernizing will call for a high level of investment. A less optimistic view, however, may lead to smaller amounts of investment as firms repair older facilities and keep them in use.
- ***Irregularity of innovation*** New products and processes stimulate investment. Major innovations such as railroads, electricity, airplanes, automobiles, computers, the Internet, and cell phones induce vast upsurges or "waves" of investment spending that in time recede. But such innovations occur quite irregularly, adding to the volatility of investment.
- ***Variability of profits*** High current profits often generate optimism about the future profitability of new investments, whereas low current profits or losses spawn considerable doubt about the wisdom of new investments. Additionally, firms often save a portion of current profits as retained earnings and use these funds (as well as borrowed funds) to finance new investments. So current profits affect both the incentive and ability to invest. But profits themselves are highly variable from year to year, contributing to the volatility of investment.

In terms of our previous analysis, we would represent volatility of investment as occasional and substantial unexpected shifts of the investment demand curve (as in Figure 24.6), which cause significant changes in investment spending (as in Figure 24.7). These demand shocks can contribute to cyclical instability.

AP QUICK REVIEW 24.2

- ✓ A specific investment will be undertaken if the expected rate of return, r, equals or exceeds the real interest rate, i, or the cost of capital to the firm.
- ✓ The investment demand curve shows the total monetary amounts that will be invested by an economy at various possible real interest rates.
- ✓ The investment demand curve shifts when changes occur in (a) the costs of acquiring, operating, and maintaining capital goods, (b) business taxes, (c) technology, (d) the stock of capital goods on hand, and (e) business expectations.

AP The Multiplier Effect*

LO24.5 Illustrate how changes in investment (or one of the other components of total spending) can increase or decrease real GDP by a multiple amount.

A final basic relationship that requires discussion is the relationship between changes in spending and changes in real GDP. Assuming that the economy has room to expand—so that increases

*Instructors who cover the full aggregate expenditures (AE) model (Chapter 25) rather than moving directly to aggregate demand and aggregate supply (Chapter 26) may choose to defer this discussion until after the analysis of equilibrium real GDP.

in spending do not lead to increases in prices—there is a direct relationship between these two aggregates. More spending results in a higher GDP; less spending results in a lower GDP. But there is much more to this relationship. A change in spending, say, investment, ultimately changes output and income by more than the initial change in investment spending. That surprising result is called the *multiplier effect:* a change in a component of total spending leads to a larger change in GDP. The **multiplier** determines how much larger that change will be; it is the ratio of a change in GDP to the initial change in spending (in this case, investment). Stated generally,

$$\text{Multiplier} = \frac{\text{change in real GDP}}{\text{initial change in spending}}$$

By rearranging this equation, we can also say that Change in GDP = multiplier × initial change in spending.

So if investment in an economy rises by $30 billion and GDP increases by $90 billion as a result, we then know from our first equation that the multiplier is 3 (= $90/$30).

Note these three points about the multiplier:

- The "initial change in spending" is usually associated with investment spending because of investment's volatility. But changes in consumption (unrelated to changes in income), net exports, and government purchases also lead to the multiplier effect.
- The "initial change in spending" associated with investment spending results from a change in the real interest rate and/or a shift of the investment demand curve.
- Implicit in the preceding point is that the multiplier works in both directions. An increase in initial spending will create a multiple increase in GDP, while a decrease in spending will create a multiple decrease in GDP.

Rationale

The multiplier effect follows from two facts. First, the economy supports repetitive, continuous flows of expenditures and income through which dollars spent by Smith are received as income by Chin and then spent by Chin and received as income by Gonzales, and so on. (This chapter's Last Word presents this idea in a humorous way.) Second, any change in income will change both consumption and saving in the same direction as, and by a fraction of, the change in income.

It follows that an initial change in spending will set off a spending chain throughout the economy. That chain of spending, although of diminishing importance at each successive step, will cumulate to a multiple change in GDP. Initial changes in spending produce magnified changes in output and income.

The table in Figure 24.8 illustrates the rationale underlying the multiplier effect. Suppose that a $5 billion increase in investment spending occurs. We assume that the MPC is 0.75, the MPS is 0.25, and prices remain constant. That is, neither the initial increase in spending nor any of the subsequent increases in spending will cause prices to rise.

The initial $5 billion increase in investment generates an equal amount of wage, rent, interest, and profit income because spending and receiving income are two sides of the same transaction. How much consumption will be induced by this $5 billion increase in the incomes of households? We find the answer by applying the marginal propensity to consume of 0.75 to this change in income. Thus, the $5 billion increase in income initially raises consumption by $3.75 (= 0.75 × $5) billion and saving by $1.25 (= 0.25 × $5) billion, as shown in columns 2 and 3 in the table.

Other households receive as income (second round) the $3.75 billion of consumption spending. Those households consume 0.75 of this $3.75 billion, or $2.81 billion, and save 0.25 of it, or $0.94 billion. The $2.81 billion that is consumed flows to still other households as income to be spent or saved (third round). And the process continues, with the added consumption and income becoming less in each round. The process ends when there is no more additional income to spend.

The bar chart in Figure 24.8 shows several rounds of the multiplier process of the table graphically. As shown by rounds 1 to 5, each round adds a smaller and smaller blue block to national income and GDP. The process, of course, continues beyond the five rounds shown (for convenience we have simply cumulated the subsequent declining blocks into a single block labeled "All other"). The accumulation of the additional income in each round—the sum of the blue blocks—is the total change in income or GDP resulting from the initial $5 billion change in spending. Because the spending and respending effects of the increase in investment diminish with each successive round of spending, the cumulative increase in output and income eventually ends. In this case, the ending occurs when $20 billion of additional income accumulates. Thus, the multiplier is 4 (= $20 billion/$5 billion).

The Multiplier and the Marginal Propensities

You may have sensed from the table in Figure 24.8 that the fractions of an increase in income consumed (MPC) and saved (MPS) determine the cumulative respending effects of any initial change in spending and therefore determine the size of the multiplier. The MPC and the multiplier are directly related and the MPS and the multiplier are inversely related. The precise formulas are as shown in the next two equations:

$$\text{Multiplier} = \frac{1}{1 - \text{MPC}}$$

Recall, too, that MPC + MPS = 1. Therefore MPS = 1 − MPC, which means we can also write the multiplier formula as

$$\text{Multiplier} = \frac{1}{\text{MPC}}$$

LAST WORD

Toppling Dominoes

A Humorous Look at the Multiplier

CLEVELAND—Yesterday, the local economy was plunged into a recession in less than 6 hours.

Many people are trying to explain the sudden change in local prospects. Here's one conjecture.

At precisely 9 a.m., Humbug, the Ford dealer, called Mr. Ajani, of Ajani's Men's Wear. "It's a great day, Mr. Ajani! The new models are in. Per your request, I've put in an order for you."

Source: © Tim Boyle/Getty Images

Agitated, Mr. Ajani responded, "That's not going to work Mr. Humbug. I just got hit with an unexpected tax bill. It's huge and I can't afford a new car right now. Sorry."

Humbug hung up. Two minutes later, his cell phone rang.

"This is Tanaka the landscaper. When do you want us to start working on your yard?"

"I'm sorry, Tanaka, but I can't do that right now," said Humbug.

Perplexed, Tanaka responded, "You were so excited about your new yard. What happened?"

"It's one of my customers. He canceled an order because he got hit with an unexpected tax bill."

Two hours later, Tanaka received a call from his wife, Samantha. "I'm so excited! Goldman's Electronics just received our new TV. They said they can install it tomorrow."

"We're going to have to send it back."

	(1) Change in Income	(2) Change in Consumption (MPC = 0.75)	(3) Change in Saving (MPS = 0.25)
Increase in investment of **$5.00**	$5.00	$ 3.75	$1.25
Second round	3.75	2.81	0.94
Third round	2.81	2.11	0.70
Fourth round	2.11	1.58	0.53
Fifth round	1.58	1.19	0.39
All other rounds	4.75	3.56	1.19
Total	**$20.00**	$15.00	$5.00

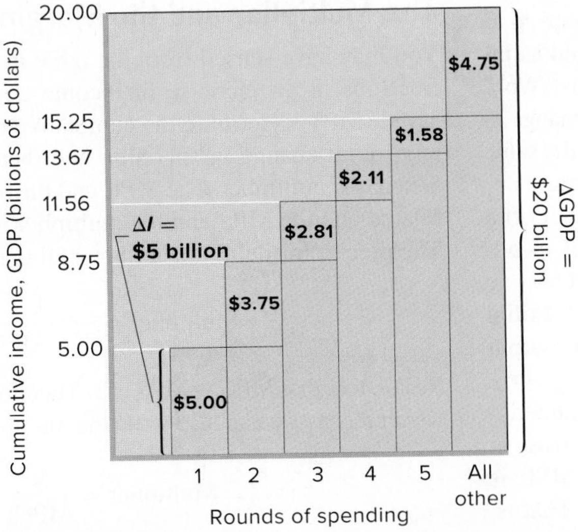

FIGURE 24.8 The multiplier process (MPC = 0.75). An initial change in investment spending of $5 billion creates an equal $5 billion of new income in round 1. Households spend $3.75 (= 0.75 × $5) billion of this new income, creating $3.75 billion of added income in round 2. Of this $3.75 billion of new income, households spend $2.81 (= 0.75 × $3.75) billion, and income rises by that amount in round 3. Such income increments over the entire process get successively smaller but eventually produce a total change of income and GDP of $20 billion. The multiplier therefore is 4 (= $20 billion/$5 billion).

"Why?"

"Because Humbug isn't going to have that yard put in now that his customer Ajani can't buy a new car due to an unexpected tax assessment."

Ten minutes later, Samantha called Goldman's Electronics. "We don't need the TV."

Goldman frowned. He immediately called his travel agent, Gonzales. "Remember that trip to Spain that you scheduled for me?"

"Yes, everything is ready to go. We just need to run your credit card."

"It's impossible now. Mrs. Tanaka just sent back an entertainment center because Humbug didn't sell a car to Ajani because Ajani can't figure out how to pay his taxes."

Gonzalez got online and canceled Goldman's trip to Spain. He also went over to his local bank to talk to the lending officer, Tommy Tightfist. "I can't make this month's loan payment because Goldman canceled his trip to Spain."

Tightfist got upset. When Kozysic the baker came into the bank a bit later to ask for a loan, Tightfist shouted no. "How can I loan you money, Ms. Kozysic, when Gonzalez can't repay what he owes me?"

Dejected, Kozysic phoned up her general contractor, Bill Johnson, and said she couldn't remodel her storefront. Johnson laid off seven workers. It was a tough thing to tell them right after lunch.

At 2 p.m., Ford announced that it would be offering big rebates on all its new models.

Humbug phoned Ajani immediately, "I have great news. Unless that unexpected tax bill is massive, you are still going to be able to afford the car you wanted!"

"I don't have an expected tax bill," Ajani said. "My accountant made an error. It was all a mistake."

"Excellent!" exclaimed Humbug. "Now you can afford that lovely new car."

"Not possible," replied Ajani in a grim tone. "Business has been lousy."

"I'm sorry to hear that. What's going on?"

"I haven't seen Tanaka, Goldman, Gonzalez, Tightfist, or Kozysic for over a month. How can I survive if they don't patronize my shop?"

Source: Adapted from Art Buchwald, "Squaring the Economic Circle," *Cleveland Plain Dealer*, February 22, 1975.

This latter formula is a quick way to determine the multiplier. All you need to know is the MPS.

The smaller the fraction of any change in income saved, the greater the respending at each round and, therefore, the greater the multiplier. When the MPS is 0.25, as in our example, the multiplier is 4. If the MPS were 0.2, the multiplier would be 5. If the MPS were 0.33, the multiplier would be 3. Let's see why.

Suppose the MPS is 0.2 and businesses increase investment by $5 billion. In the first round of the table in Figure 24.8, consumption will rise by $4 billion (= MPC of 0.8 × $5 billion) rather than by $3.75 billion because saving will increase by $1 billion (= MPS of 0.2 × $5 billion) rather than $1.25 billion. The greater rise in consumption in round 1 will produce a greater increase in income in round 2. The same will be true for all successive rounds. If we worked through all rounds of the multiplier, we would find that the process ends when income has cumulatively increased by $25 billion, not the $20 billion shown in the table. When the MPS is 0.2 rather than 0.25, the multiplier is 5 (= $25 billion/$5 billion) as opposed to 4 (= $20 billion/$5 billion).

If the MPS were 0.33 rather than 0.25, the successive increases in consumption and income would be less than those in the table in Figure 24.8. We would discover that the process ended with a $15 billion increase in income rather than the $20 billion shown. When the MPS is 0.33, the multiplier is 3 (= $15 billion/$5 billion). The mathematics works such that the multiplier is equal to the reciprocal of the MPS. The reciprocal of any number is the quotient you obtain by dividing 1 by that number.

A large MPC (small MPS) means the succeeding rounds of consumption spending shown in Figure 24.8 diminish slowly and thereby cumulate to a large change in income. Conversely, a small MPC (a large MPS) causes the increases in consumption to decline quickly, so the cumulative change in income is small. The relationship between the MPC (and thus the MPS) and the multiplier is summarized in Figure 24.9.

How Large Is the Actual Multiplier Effect?

The multiplier we have just described is based on simplifying assumptions. Consumption of domestic output rises by the increases in income minus the increases in saving. But in reality, consumption of domestic output increases in each round by a lesser amount than implied by the MPS alone. In addition to saving, households use some of the extra income in each round to purchase additional goods from abroad (imports) and pay additional taxes. Buying imports and paying taxes drains off some of the additional consumption spending (on domestic output) created by the increases in income. So the multiplier effect is reduced and the 1/MPS formula for the multiplier overstates the actual outcome. To correct that problem, we would need to change the multiplier equation to read "1 divided by the fraction of the change in income that is not spent on domestic output." Also, we will find in later chapters that an increase in spending may be partly dissipated

FIGURE 24.9 The MPC and the multiplier. The larger the MPC (the smaller the MPS), the greater the size of the multiplier.

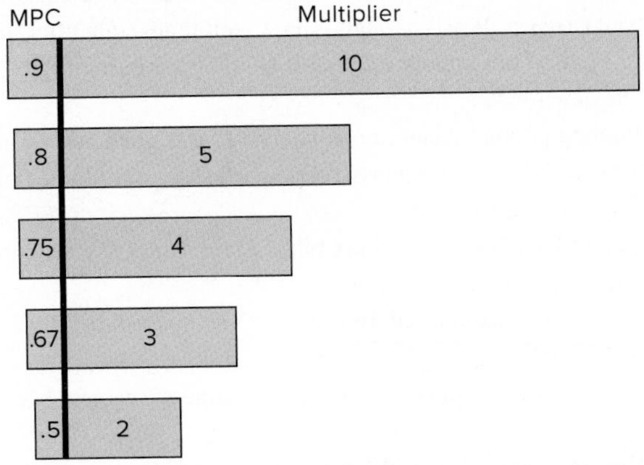

as inflation rather than realized fully as an increase in real GDP. This happens when increases in spending drive up prices. The multiplier process still happens, but it induces a much smaller change in real output because, at higher prices, any given amount of spending buys less real output. Economists disagree on the size of the actual multiplier in the United States. Estimates range from as high as 2.5 to as low as zero. So keep in mind throughout later discussions that the actual multiplier is much lower than the multipliers in our simple explanatory examples.

AP QUICK REVIEW 24.3

- ✓ The multiplier effect reveals that an initial change in spending can cause a larger change in domestic income and output. The multiplier shows the maximum change in total spending or aggregate demand from an initial change in autonomous spending, like an increase in government spending or an increase in autonomous consumption.
- ✓ The MPC and the multiplier are directly related and the MPS and the multiplier are inversely related. The higher the marginal propensity to consume (the lower the marginal propensity to save), the larger the multiplier: multiplier = 1/(1 − MPC) or 1/MPS. For instance, if the marginal propensity to consumer is .8 or 4/5, the multiplier is equal to 5. If the marginal propensity to consume is .9 or 9/10, the multiplier is 10.
- ✓ With a multiplier of 5, a $1,000 increase in government spending can increase total spending or aggregate demand by a maximum of $5,000 ($1,000 × 5).

SUMMARY

LO24.1 Describe how changes in income affect consumption (and saving).

Other things equal, a direct (positive) relationship exists between income and consumption and income and saving. The consumption and saving schedules show the various amounts that households intend to consume and save at the various income and output levels, assuming a fixed price level.

The *average* propensities to consume and save show the fractions of any total income that are consumed and saved; APC + APS = 1. The *marginal* propensities to consume and save show the fractions of any change in total income that are consumed and saved; MPC + MPS = 1.

LO24.2 List and explain factors other than income that can affect consumption.

The locations of the consumption and saving schedules (as they relate to real GDP) are determined by (*a*) the amount of wealth owned by households, (*b*) expectations of future prices and incomes, (*c*) real interest rates, (*d*) household debt, and (*e*) tax levels. The consumption and saving schedules are relatively stable.

LO24.3 Explain how changes in real interest rates affect investment.

The immediate determinants of investment are (*a*) the expected rate of return and (*b*) the real rate of interest. The economy's investment demand curve is found by cumulating investment projects, arraying them in descending order according to their expected rates of return, graphing the result, and applying the rule that investment should be undertaken up to the point at which the real interest rate, i, equals the expected rate of return, r. The investment demand curve reveals an inverse (negative) relationship between the interest rate and the level of aggregate investment.

Shifts of the investment demand curve can occur as the result of changes in (*a*) the acquisition, maintenance, and operating costs of capital goods; (*b*) business taxes; (*c*) technology; (*d*) the stocks of capital goods on hand; and (*e*) expectations.

Either changes in interest rates or shifts of the investment demand curve can change the level of investment.

LO24.4 Identify and explain factors other than the real interest rate that can affect investment.

The durability of capital goods, the irregular occurrence of major innovations, profit volatility, and the variability of expectations all contribute to the instability of investment spending.

LO24.5 Illustrate how changes in investment (or one of the other components of total spending) can increase or decrease real GDP by a multiple amount.

Through the multiplier effect, an increase in investment spending (or consumption spending, government purchases, or net export spending) ripples through the economy, ultimately creating a magnified increase in real GDP. The multiplier is the ultimate change in GDP divided by the initiating change in investment or some other component of spending.

The multiplier is equal to the reciprocal of the marginal propensity to save: The greater is the marginal propensity to save, the smaller is the multiplier. Also, the greater is the marginal propensity to consume, the larger is the multiplier.

Economists disagree on the size of the actual multiplier in the United States, with estimates ranging all the way from 2.5 to 0. But all estimates of actual-economy multipliers are less than the multiplier in our purposefully simple text illustrations.

TERMS AND CONCEPTS

45° (degree) line
consumption schedule
saving schedule
break-even income
average propensity to consume (APC)
average propensity to save (APS)
marginal propensity to consume (MPC)
marginal propensity to save (MPS)
wealth effect
paradox of thrift
expected rate of return
investment demand curve
multiplier

The following and additional problems can be found in connect

DISCUSSION QUESTIONS

1. Precisely how do the MPC and the APC differ? How does the MPC differ from the MPS? Why must the sum of the MPC and the MPS equal 1? LO24.1
2. Why does a downshift of the consumption schedule typically involve an equal upshift of the saving schedule? What is the exception to this relationship? LO24.2
3. Why will a reduction in the real interest rate increase investment spending, other things equal? LO24.3
4. In what direction will each of the following occurrences shift the investment demand curve, other things equal? LO24.4
   a. An increase in unused production capacity occurs.
   b. Business taxes decline.
   c. The costs of acquiring equipment fall.
   d. Widespread pessimism arises about future business conditions and sales revenues.
   e. A major new technological breakthrough creates prospects for a wide range of profitable new products.
5. How is it possible for investment spending to increase even in a period in which the real interest rate rises? LO24.4
6. Why is investment spending unstable? LO24.4
7. Is the relationship between changes in spending and changes in real GDP in the multiplier effect a direct (positive) relationship or is it an inverse (negative) relationship? How does the size of the multiplier relate to the size of the MPC? The MPS? What is the logic of the multiplier-MPC relationship? LO24.5
8. Why is the actual multiplier in the U.S. economy less than the multiplier in this chapter's example? LO24.5
9. **LAST WORD** What is the central economic idea humorously illustrated in the Last Word "Toppling Dominoes"? How does the central idea relate to economic recessions, on the one hand, and vigorous economic expansions, on the other?

AP REVIEW QUESTIONS

1. Which statement about the multiplier is true? LO24.5
   a. The larger the marginal propensity to save, the larger the multiplier.
   b. If the MPS is .2, then a $1000 increase in government spending would increase aggregate demand or income by a maximum of $4000.
   c. If the marginal propensity to consume falls, the multiplier increases.
   d. A spending multiplier of 10 is associated with a MPC of .9
   e. The value of the multiplier is equal to 1/APS, where APS is the average propensity to save.
2. In year 1, Adam earns $1,000 and saves $100. In year 2, Adam gets a $500 raise so that he earns a total of $1,500. Out of that $1,500, he saves $200. What is Adam's MPC out of his $500 raise? LO24.1
   a. 0.50.
   b. 0.75.
   c. 0.80.
   d. 0.90.
   e. 1.00.
3. If the MPS rises to .2, then the MPC will: LO24.1
   a. Fall by 20%
   b. Fall to .2
   c. Fall to .8
   d. Fall below .2
   e. Will not change

4. In what direction will each of the following occurrences shift the consumption and saving schedules, other things equal? LO24.2
   a. A large decrease in real estate values, including private homes.
   b. A sharp, sustained increase in stock prices.
   c. A 5-year increase in the minimum age for collecting Social Security benefits.
   d. An economywide expectation that a recession is over and that a robust expansion will occur.
5. Irving owns a chain of movie theaters. He is considering whether he should build a new theater downtown. The expected rate of return is 15 percent per year. He can borrow money at a 12 percent interest rate to finance the project. Should Irving proceed with this project? Explain your answer. LO24.3
6. Which of the following scenarios will shift the investment demand curve right? LO24.4
   *Select **one or more** answers from the choices shown.*
   a. Business taxes increase.
   b. The expected return on capital increases.
   c. Firms have a lot of unused production capacity.
   d. Firms are planning on increasing their inventories.
   e. Consumer incomes are increasing in a sustained manner.
7. Calculate the simple spending multiplier when the MPC is .5, .75, and .90. What is the relationship between MPC and the multiplier? LO24.5
8. If a $50 billion increase in government spending leads to a $250 billion change in aggregate demand or income, how big is the multiplier from this change in government spending? LO24.5
   a. 1.0.
   b. 2.5.
   c. 4.0.
   d. 5.0.
   e. 10.00.
9. If the marginal propensity to consume is .75 and government spending increases by $500, then which of the following shows the correct marginal propensity to save, spending multiplier, and maximum increase in aggregate demand from this spending increase. LO24.5

	Marginal Propensity to save	Spending Multiplier	Maximum change in Income
a.	.2	5	$2500
b.	.25	4	2000
c.	.25	5	2500
d.	.75	1.33	667
e.	.75	4	2000

10. Assume that higher income households have a higher marginal propensity to save than lower income households. In this case, would a transfer of income from high income to lower income households, *a*) change the simple spending multiplier and *b*) change the maximum impact of a $200 increase in government spending on aggregate demand or income? Explain. LO24.5

PROBLEMS

1. Refer to the table below. LO24.1
   a. Fill in the missing numbers in the table.
   b. What is the break-even level of income in the table? What is the term that economists use for the saving situation shown at the $240 level of income?
   c. For each of the following items, indicate whether the value in the table is either constant or variable as income changes: the MPS, the APC, the MPC, the APS.

Level of Output and Income (GDP = DI)	Consumption	Saving	APC	APS	MPC	MPS
$240	$____	$ −4	___	___		
					___	___
260	____	0	___	___		
					___	___
280	____	4	___	___		
					___	___
300	____	8	___	___		
					___	___
320	____	12	___	___		
					___	___
340	____	16	___	___		
					___	___
360	____	20	___	___		
					___	___
380	____	24	___	___		
					___	___
400	____	28	___	___		

2. Suppose that disposable income, consumption, and saving in some country are $200 billion, $150 billion, and $50 billion, respectively. Next, assume that disposable income increases by $20 billion, consumption rises by $18 billion, and saving goes up by $2 billion. What is the economy's MPC? Its MPS? What was the APC before the increase in disposable income? After the increase? LO24.1
3. **ADVANCED ANALYSIS** Suppose that the linear equation for consumption in a hypothetical economy is $C = 40 + 0.8Y$. Also suppose that income (Y) is $400. Determine (*a*) the marginal propensity to consume, (*b*) the marginal propensity to save, (*c*) the level of consumption, (*d*) the average propensity to consume, (*e*) the level of saving, and (*f*) the average propensity to save. LO24.1

4. **ADVANCED ANALYSIS** Linear equations for the consumption and saving schedules take the general form $C = a + bY$ and $S = -a + (1 - b)Y$, where C, S, and Y are consumption, saving, and national income, respectively. The constant a represents the vertical intercept, and b represents the slope of the consumption schedule. **LO24.1, LO24.2**
   a. Use the following data to substitute numerical values for a and b in the consumption and saving equations.

National Income (*Y*)	Consumption (*C*)
$ 0	$ 80
100	140
200	200
300	260
400	320

   b. What is the economic meaning of b? Of $(1 - b)$?
   c. Suppose that the amount of saving that occurs at each level of national income falls by $20 but that the values of b and $(1 - b)$ remain unchanged. Restate the saving and consumption equations inserting the new numerical values, and cite a factor that might have caused the change.
5. Use your completed table for problem 1 to solve this problem. Suppose the wealth effect is such that $10 changes in wealth produce $1 changes in consumption at each level of income. If real estate prices tumble such that wealth declines by $80, what will be the new level of consumption and saving at the $340 billion level of disposable income? The new level of saving? **LO24.2**
6. Suppose a handbill publisher can buy a new duplicating machine for $500 and the duplicator has a 1-year life. The machine is expected to contribute $550 to the year's net revenue. What is the expected rate of return? If the real interest rate at which funds can be borrowed to purchase the machine is 8 percent, will the publisher choose to invest in the machine? Will it invest in the machine if the real interest rate is 9 percent? If it is 11 percent? **LO24.3**
7. Assume there are no investment projects in the economy that yield an expected rate of return of 25 percent or more. But suppose there are $10 billion of investment projects yielding expected returns of between 20 and 25 percent; another $10 billion yielding between 15 and 20 percent; another $10 billion between 10 and 15 percent; and so forth. Cumulate these data and present them graphically, putting the expected rate of return (and the real interest rate) on the vertical axis and the amount of investment on the horizontal axis. What will be the equilibrium level of aggregate investment if the real interest rate is (*a*) 15 percent, (*b*) 10 percent, and (*c*) 5 percent? **LO24.3**
8. Refer to the table in Figure 24.5 and suppose that the real interest rate is 6 percent. Next, assume that some factor changes such that the expected rate of return declines by 2 percentage points at each prospective level of investment. Assuming no change in the real interest rate, by how much and in what direction will investment change? Which of the following might cause this change: (*a*) a decision to increase inventories; (*b*) an increase in excess production capacity? **LO24.4**
9. What will the multiplier be when the MPS is 0, 0.4, 0.6, and 1? What will it be when the MPC is 1, 0.90, 0.67, 0.50, and 0? How much of a change in GDP will result if firms increase their level of investment by $8 billion and the MPC is 0.80? If the MPC instead is 0.67? **LO24.5**
10. Suppose that an initial $10 billion increase in investment spending expands GDP by $10 billion in the first round of the multiplier process. If GDP and consumption both rise by $6 billion in the second round of the process, what is the MPC in this economy? What is the size of the multiplier? If, instead, GDP and consumption both rose by $8 billion in the second round, what would have been the size of the multiplier? **LO24.5**

Chapter 25

The Aggregate Expenditures Model

Learning Objectives

LO25.1 **Explain how sticky prices relate to the aggregate expenditures model.**

LO25.2 **Explain how an economy's investment schedule is derived from the investment demand curve and an interest rate.**

LO25.3 **Illustrate how economists combine consumption and investment to depict an aggregate expenditures schedule for a private closed economy and how that schedule can be used to demonstrate the economy's equilibrium level of output (where the total quantity of goods produced equals the total quantity of goods purchased).**

LO25.4 **Discuss the two other ways to characterize the equilibrium level of real GDP in a private closed economy: saving = investment and no unplanned changes in inventories.**

LO25.5 **Analyze how changes in equilibrium real GDP can occur in the aggregate expenditures model and describe how those changes relate to the multiplier.**

LO25.6 **Explain how economists integrate the international sector (exports and imports) into the aggregate expenditures model.**

LO25.7 **Explain how economists integrate the public sector (government expenditures and taxes) into the aggregate expenditures model.**

LO25.8 **Differentiate between equilibrium GDP and full-employment GDP and identify and describe the nature and causes of "recessionary expenditure gaps" and "inflationary expenditure gaps."**

AP Chapter Focus

In previous chapters we answered in detail two of the most critical questions in macroeconomics: How is an economy's output measured? Why does an economy grow? But we have been relatively general in addressing two other important questions: What determines the level of GDP, given a nation's production capacity? What causes real GDP to rise in one period and to fall in another? To provide more thorough answers to these two questions, we construct the aggregate expenditures model, which has its origins in 1936 in the writings of British economist John Maynard Keynes (pronounced "Caines"). The basic premise of the aggregate expenditures model—also known as the "Keynesian cross" model—is that the amount of goods and services produced and therefore the level of employment depend directly on the level of aggregate expenditures (total spending). Businesses will produce only a level of output that they think they can profitably sell. They will idle their workers and machinery when there are no markets for their goods and services.

AP Assumptions and Simplifications

LO25.1 Explain how sticky prices relate to the aggregate expenditures model.

The simplifying assumptions underpinning the aggregate expenditures model reflect the economic conditions that were prevalent during the Great Depression. As discussed in this chapter's Last Word, Keynes created the model during the middle of the Great Depression in the hopes of understanding both why the Great Depression had happened as well as how it might be ended.

The most fundamental assumption behind the aggregate expenditures model is that prices in the economy are fixed. In the terminology of Chapter 20, the aggregate expenditures model is an extreme version of a sticky price model. In fact, it is a stuck-price model because the price level cannot change at all.

Keynes made this simplifying assumption because he had observed that prices had not declined sufficiently during the Great Depression to boost spending and maintain output and employment at their pre-Depression levels. Such price declines had been predicted by macroeconomic theories that were popular before the Great Depression. But actual prices did not fall sufficiently during the Great Depression, and the economy sank far below its potential output. Real GDP in the United States declined by 27 percent from 1929 to 1933, and the unemployment rate rose to 25 percent. Thousands of factories sat idle, gathering dust and producing nothing, because nobody wanted to buy their output.

To Keynes, this massive unemployment of labor and capital resulted from firms reacting to information about how much they should produce. As households and businesses greatly reduced their spending, inventories of unsold goods rocketed. Unable or unwilling to slash their prices, firms could not sell all the goods they had already produced. So they greatly reduced their current production. This meant discharging workers, idling production lines, and even closing entire factories. Keynes thought that a new economic model was needed to show how all this could have happened and how it might be reversed.

The Keynesian aggregate expenditures model is not just of historical interest. It is still insightful even today because many prices in the modern economy are inflexible downward over relatively short periods of time. The aggregate expenditures model therefore can help us understand how the modern economy is likely to initially adjust to various economic shocks over shorter periods of time. For example, it clarifies aspects of the severe 2007–2009 recession, such as why unexpected initial declines in spending caused even larger declines in real GDP. It also illuminates the thinking underlying the stimulus programs (tax cuts, government spending increases) enacted by the government during the recession.

We will build up the aggregate expenditures model in simple stages. Let's first look at aggregate expenditures and equilibrium GDP in a *private closed economy*—one without international trade or government. Then we will "open" the "closed" economy to exports and imports and also convert our "private" economy to a more realistic "mixed" economy that includes government purchases (or, more loosely, "government spending") and taxes.

In addition, until we introduce taxes into the model, we will assume that real GDP equals disposable income (DI). For instance, if $500 billion of output is produced as GDP, households will receive exactly $500 billion of disposable income that they can then consume or save. And finally, unless specified otherwise, we will assume (as Keynes did) that the presence of excess production capacity and unemployed labor implies that an increase in aggregate expenditures will increase real output and employment without raising the price level.

AP Consumption and Investment Schedules

LO25.2 Explain how an economy's investment schedule is derived from the investment demand curve and an interest rate.

In the private closed economy, the two components of aggregate expenditures are consumption, C, and gross investment, I_g. Because we examined the *consumption schedule* (Figure 25.2a) in the previous chapter, there is no need to repeat that analysis here. But to add the investment decisions of businesses to the consumption plans of households, we need to construct an investment schedule showing the amounts business firms collectively intend to invest—their **planned investment**—at each possible level of GDP. Such a schedule represents the investment plans of businesses in the same way the consumption schedule represents the consumption plans of households. In developing the investment schedule, we will assume that this planned investment is independent of the level of current disposable income or real output.

AP FIGURE 25.1 (a) The investment demand curve and (b) the investment schedule. (a) The level of investment spending (here, $20 billion) is determined by the real interest rate (here, 8 percent) together with the investment demand curve *ID*. (b) The investment schedule I_g relates the amount of investment ($20 billion) determined in (a) to the various levels of GDP.

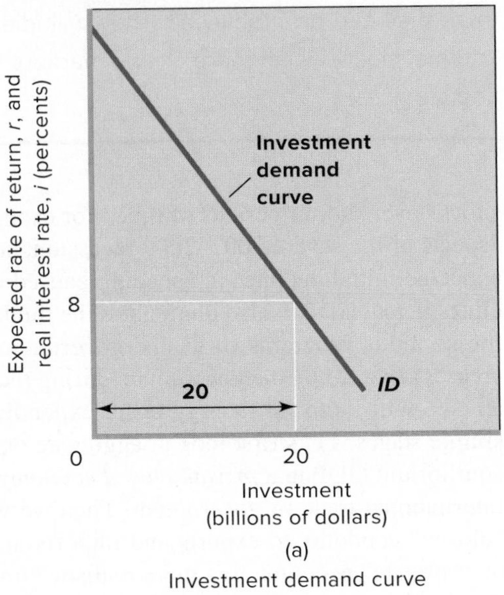

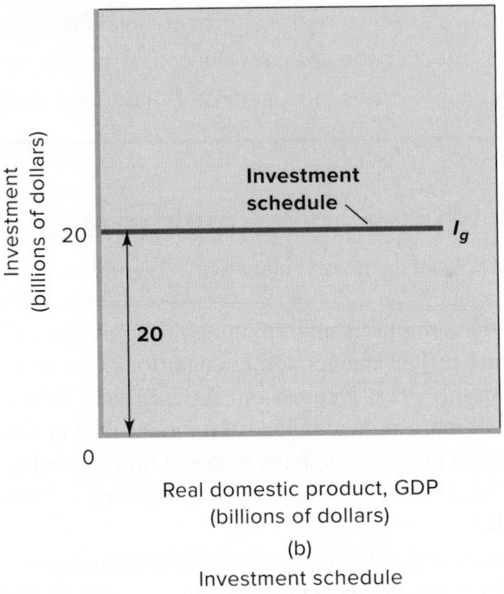

Suppose the investment demand curve is as shown in Figure 25.1a and the current real interest rate is 8 percent. This means that firms will spend $20 billion on investment goods. Our assumption tells us that this $20 billion of investment will occur at both low and high levels of GDP. The line I_g in Figure 25.1b shows this graphically; it is the economy's **investment schedule.** You should not confuse this investment schedule I_g with the investment demand curve *ID* in Figure 25.1a. The investment schedule shows the amount of investment forthcoming at each level of GDP. As indicated in Figure 25.1b, the interest rate and investment demand curve together determine this amount ($20 billion). Table 25.1 shows the investment schedule in tabular form. Note that investment (I_g) in column 2 is $20 billion at all levels of real GDP.

AP TABLE 25.1 The Investment Schedule (in Billions)

(1) Level of Real Output and Income	(2) Investment (I_g)
$370	$20
390	20
410	20
430	20
450	20
470	20
490	20
510	20
530	20
550	20

AP Equilibrium GDP: $C + I_g = \text{GDP}$

LO25.3 Illustrate how economists combine consumption and investment to depict an aggregate expenditures schedule for a private closed economy and how that schedule can be used to demonstrate the economy's equilibrium level of output (where the total quantity of goods produced equals the total quantity of goods purchased).

Now let's combine the consumption schedule of Chapter 24 and the investment schedule here to explain the equilibrium levels of output, income, and employment in the private closed economy.

Tabular Analysis

Columns 2 through 5 in Table 25.2 repeat the consumption and saving schedules of Table 24.1 and the investment schedule of Table 25.1.

Real Domestic Output Column 2 in Table 25.2 lists the various possible levels of total output—of real GDP—that the private sector might produce. Firms would be willing to produce any one of these 10 levels of output just as long as the revenue that they receive from selling any particular level equals or exceeds the costs they would incur to produce it. Those costs are the factor payments needed to obtain the required amounts of land, labor, capital, and entrepreneurship. For example, firms would be willing to produce $370 billion of output if the costs of production (wages, rents, interest, and the normal profit needed to attract entrepreneurship) are less than or equal to the $370 billion in revenue that they would get from selling the output.

AP TABLE 25.2 Determination of the Equilibrium Levels of Employment, Output, and Income: A Private Closed Economy

(1) Possible Levels of Employment, Millions	(2) Real Domestic Output (and Income) (GDP = DI),* Billions	(3) Consumption (C), Billions	(4) Saving (S), Billions	(5) Investment (I_g), Billions	(6) Aggregate Expenditures ($C + I_g$), Billions	(7) Unplanned Changes in Inventories, (+ or −)	(8) Tendency of Employment, Output, and Income
(1) 40	$370	$375	$−5	$20	$395	$−25	Increase
(2) 45	390	390	0	20	410	−20	Increase
(3) 50	410	405	5	20	425	−15	Increase
(4) 55	430	420	10	20	440	−10	Increase
(5) 60	450	435	15	20	455	−5	Increase
(6) 65	**470**	**450**	**20**	**20**	**470**	**0**	**Equilibrium**
(7) 70	490	465	25	20	485	+5	Decrease
(8) 75	510	480	30	20	500	+10	Decrease
(9) 80	530	495	35	20	515	+15	Decrease
(10) 85	550	510	40	20	530	+20	Decrease

*If depreciation and net foreign factor income are zero, government is ignored, and it is assumed that all saving occurs in the household sector of the economy, then GDP as a measure of domestic output is equal to NI, PI, and DI. This means that households receive a DI equal to the value of total output.

Aggregate Expenditures In the private closed economy of Table 25.2, aggregate expenditures consist of consumption (column 3) plus investment (column 5). Their sum is shown in column 6, which along with column 2 makes up the **aggregate expenditures schedule** for the private closed economy. This schedule shows the amount ($C + I_g$) that will be spent at each possible output or income level.

At this point we are working with *planned investment*—the data in column 5, Table 25.2. These data show the amounts firms plan or intend to invest, not the amounts they actually will invest if there are unplanned changes in inventories. More about that shortly.

Equilibrium GDP Of the 10 possible levels of GDP in Table 25.2, which is the equilibrium level? Which total output is the economy capable of sustaining?

The equilibrium output is that output whose production creates total spending just sufficient to purchase that output. So the equilibrium level of GDP is the level at which the total quantity of goods produced (GDP) equals the total quantity of goods purchased ($C + I_g$). In the private closed economy, the **equilibrium GDP** is where

$$C + I_g = \text{GDP}$$

If you look at the domestic output levels in column 2 and the aggregate expenditures levels in column 6, you will see that this equality exists only at $470 billion of GDP (row 6). That is the only output at which economywide spending is precisely equal to the amount needed to move that output off the shelves. At $470 billion of GDP, the annual rates of production and spending are in balance. There is no overproduction, which would result in a piling up of unsold goods and consequently cutbacks in the production rate. Nor is there an excess of total spending, which would draw down inventories of goods and prompt increases in the rate of production. In short, there is no reason for businesses to alter this rate of production; $470 billion is the equilibrium GDP.

Disequilibrium No level of GDP other than the equilibrium level of GDP can be sustained. At levels of GDP *less than* equilibrium, spending always exceeds GDP. If, for example, firms produced $410 billion of GDP (row 3 in Table 25.2), they would find it would yield $405 billion in consumer spending. Supplemented by $20 billion of planned investment, aggregate expenditures ($C + I_g$) would be $425 billion, as shown in column 6. The economy would provide an annual rate of spending more than sufficient to purchase the $410 billion of annual production. Because buyers would be taking goods off the shelves faster than firms could produce them, an unplanned decline in business inventories of $15 billion would occur (column 7) if this situation continued. But businesses can adjust to such an imbalance between aggregate expenditures and real output by stepping up production. Greater output will increase employment and total income. This process will continue until the equilibrium level of GDP is reached ($470 billion).

The reverse is true at all levels of GDP *greater than* the $470 billion equilibrium level. Businesses will find that these total outputs fail to generate the spending needed to clear the shelves of goods. Being unable to recover their costs, businesses will cut back on production. To illustrate: At the $510 billion output (row 8), business managers would find spending is insufficient to permit the sale of all that output. Of the $510 billion of income that this output creates, $480 billion would be received back by businesses as consumption

KEY GRAPH

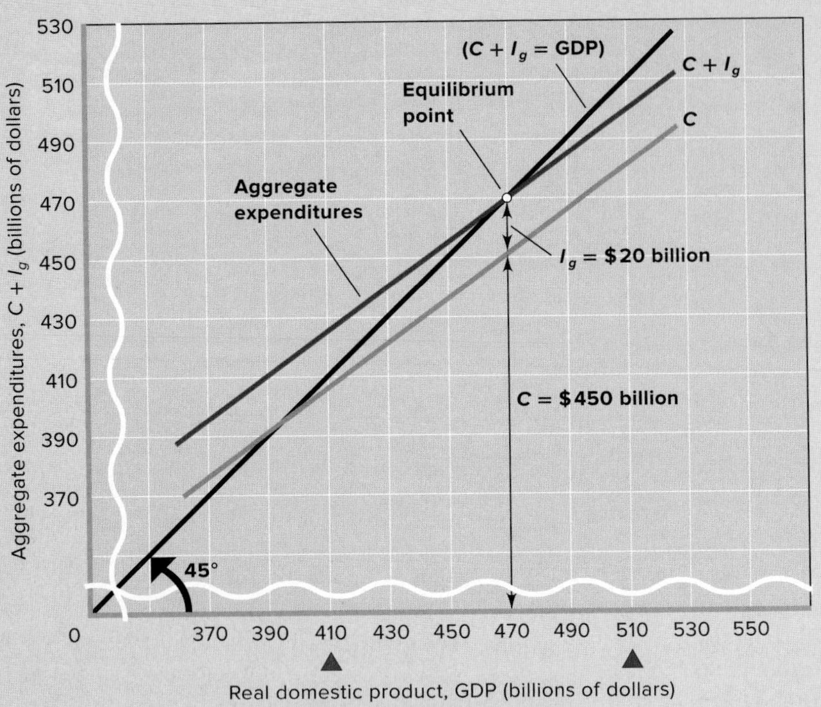

FIGURE 25.2 Equilibrium GDP in a private closed economy. The aggregate expenditures schedule, $C + I_g$, is determined by adding the investment schedule I_g to the upsloping consumption schedule C. Since investment is assumed to be the same at each level of GDP, the vertical distances between C and $C + I_g$ do not change. Equilibrium GDP is determined where the aggregate expenditures schedule intersects the 45° line, in this case at $470 billion.

QUICK QUIZ FOR FIGURE 25.2

1. In this figure, the slope of the aggregate expenditures schedule $C + I_g$:
   - **a.** increases as real GDP increases.
   - **b.** falls as real GDP increases.
   - **c.** is constant and equals the MPC.
   - **d.** is constant and equals the MPS.
2. At all points on the 45° line:
   - **a.** equilibrium GDP is possible.
   - **b.** aggregate expenditures exceed real GDP.
   - **c.** consumption exceeds investment.
   - **d.** aggregate expenditures are less than real GDP.
3. The $490 billion level of real GDP is not at equilibrium because:
   - **a.** investment exceeds consumption.
   - **b.** consumption exceeds investment.
   - **c.** planned $C + I_g$ exceeds real GDP.
   - **d.** planned $C + I_g$ is less than real GDP.
4. The $430 billion level of real GDP is not at equilibrium because:
   - **a.** investment exceeds consumption.
   - **b.** consumption exceeds investment.
   - **c.** planned $C + I_g$ exceeds real GDP.
   - **d.** planned $C + I_g$ is less than real GDP.

Answers: 1. c; 2. a; 3. d; 4. c

spending. Though supplemented by $20 billion of planned investment spending, total expenditures ($500 billion) would still be $10 billion below the $510 billion quantity produced. If this imbalance persisted, $10 billion of inventories would pile up (column 7). But businesses can adjust to this unintended accumulation of unsold goods by cutting back on the rate of production. The resulting decline in output would mean fewer jobs and a decline in total income.

Graphical Analysis

We can demonstrate the same analysis graphically. In **Figure 25.2 (Key Graph)** the 45° line developed in Chapter 24 now takes on increased significance. Recall that at any point on this line, the value of what is being measured on the horizontal axis (here, GDP) is equal to the value of what is being measured on the vertical axis (here, aggregate expenditures, or $C + I_g$). Having discovered in our tabular analysis that the equilibrium level of domestic output is determined where $C + I_g$ equals GDP, we can say that the 45° line in Figure 25.2 is a graphical statement of that equilibrium condition.

Now we must graph the aggregate expenditures schedule onto Figure 25.2. To do this, we duplicate the consumption schedule C in Figure 25.2a and add to it vertically the constant $20 billion amount of investment I_g from Figure 25.1b. This $20 billion is the amount we assumed firms plan to invest at all levels of GDP. Or, more directly, we can plot the $C + I_g$ data in column 6, Table 25.2.

Observe in Figure 25.2 that the aggregate expenditures line $C + I_g$ shows that total spending rises with income and output (GDP), but not as much as income rises. That is true because the marginal propensity to consume—the slope of line C—is less than 1. A part of any increase in income will be saved rather than spent. And because the aggregate expenditures line $C + I_g$ is parallel to the consumption line C, the slope of the aggregate expenditures line also equals the MPC for the economy and is less than 1. For our particular data, aggregate expenditures rise by \$15 billion for every \$20 billion increase in real output and income because \$5 billion of each \$20 billion increment is saved. Therefore, the slope of the aggregate expenditures line is 0.75 ($= \Delta\$15/\Delta\$20$).

The equilibrium level of GDP is determined by the intersection of the aggregate expenditures schedule and the 45° line. This intersection locates the only point at which aggregate expenditures (on the vertical axis) are equal to GDP (on the horizontal axis). Because Figure 25.2 is based on the data in Table 25.2, we once again find that equilibrium output is \$470 billion. Observe that consumption at this output is \$450 billion and investment is \$20 billion.

It is evident from Figure 25.2 that no levels of GDP *above* the equilibrium level are sustainable because at those levels $C + I_g$ falls short of GDP. Graphically, the aggregate expenditures schedule lies below the 45° line in those situations. At the \$510 billion GDP level, for example, $C + I_g$ is only \$500 billion. This underspending causes inventories to rise, prompting firms to readjust production downward, in the direction of the \$470 billion output level.

Conversely, at levels of GDP *below* \$470 billion, the economy wants to spend in excess of what businesses are producing. Then $C + I_g$ exceeds total output. Graphically, the aggregate expenditures schedule lies above the 45° line. At the \$410 billion GDP level, for example, $C + I_g$ totals \$425 billion. This excess spending causes inventories to fall below their planned level, prompting firms to adjust production upward, in the direction of the \$470 billion output level. Once production reaches that level, it will be sustained there indefinitely unless there is some change in the location of the aggregate expenditures line.

Other Features of Equilibrium GDP

LO25.4 Discuss the two other ways to characterize the equilibrium level of real GDP in a private closed economy: saving = investment and no unplanned changes in inventories.

We have seen that $C + I_g =$ GDP at equilibrium in the private closed economy. A closer look at Table 25.2 reveals two more characteristics of equilibrium GDP:

- Saving and *planned* investment are equal ($S = I_g$).
- There are no *unplanned* changes in inventories.

Saving Equals Planned Investment

As shown by row 6 in Table 25.2, saving and planned investment are both \$20 billion at the \$470 billion equilibrium level of GDP.

Saving is a **leakage** or withdrawal of spending from the economy's circular flow of income and expenditures. Saving is what causes consumption to be less than total output or GDP. Because of saving, consumption by itself is insufficient to remove domestic output from the shelves, apparently setting the stage for a decline in total output.

However, firms do not intend to sell their entire output to consumers. Some of that output will be capital goods sold to other businesses. Investment—the purchases of capital goods—is therefore an **injection** of spending into the income-expenditures stream. As an adjunct to consumption, investment is thus a potential replacement for the leakage of saving.

If the leakage of saving at a certain level of GDP exceeds the injection of investment, then $C + I_g$ will be less than GDP and that level of GDP cannot be sustained. Any GDP for which saving exceeds investment is an above-equilibrium GDP. Consider GDP of \$510 billion (row 8 in Table 25.2). Households will save \$30 billion, but firms will plan to invest only \$20 billion. This \$10 billion excess of saving over planned investment will reduce total spending to \$10 billion below the value of total output. Specifically, aggregate expenditures will be \$500 billion while real GDP is \$510 billion. This spending deficiency will reduce real GDP.

Conversely, if the injection of investment exceeds the leakage of saving, then $C + I_g$ will be greater than GDP and drive GDP upward. Any GDP for which investment exceeds saving is a below-equilibrium GDP. For example, at a GDP of \$410 billion (row 3 in Table 25.2), households will save only \$5 billion, but firms will invest \$20 billion. So investment exceeds saving by \$15 billion. The small leakage of saving at this relatively low GDP level is more than compensated for by the larger injection of investment spending. That causes $C + I_g$ to exceed GDP and drives GDP higher.

Only where $S = I_g$—where the leakage of saving of \$20 billion is exactly offset by the injection of planned investment of \$20 billion—will aggregate expenditures ($C + I_g$) equal real output (GDP). That $C + I_g =$ GDP equality is what defines the equilibrium GDP.

No Unplanned Changes in Inventories

As part of their investment plans, firms may decide to increase or decrease their inventories. But, as confirmed in line 6 of Table 25.2, there are no **unplanned changes in inventories** at equilibrium GDP. This fact, along with $C + I_g =$ GDP, and $S = I_g$ is a characteristic of equilibrium GDP in the private closed economy.

Unplanned changes in inventories play a major role in achieving equilibrium GDP. Consider, as an example, the \$490 billion *above-equilibrium* GDP shown in row 7 of Table 25.2. What happens if firms produce that output, thinking they can sell it? Households save $25 billion of their $490 billion DI, so consumption is only $465 billion. Planned investment—which includes *planned* changes in inventories—is $20 billion (column 5). So aggregate expenditures ($C + I_g$) are $485 billion and sales fall short of production by $5 billion. Firms retain that extra $5 billion of goods as an *unplanned* increase in inventories (column 7). It results from the failure of total spending to remove total output from the shelves.

Because changes in inventories are a part of investment, we note that *actual investment* is $25 billion. It consists of $20 billion of planned investment *plus* the $5 billion unplanned increase in inventories. Actual investment equals the saving of $25 billion, even though saving exceeds planned investment by $5 billion. Because firms cannot earn profits by accumulating unwanted inventories, the $5 billion unplanned increase in inventories will prompt them to cut back employment and production. GDP will fall to its equilibrium level of $470 billion, at which unplanned changes in inventories are zero.

Now look at the *below-equilibrium* $450 billion output (row 5, Table 25.2). Because households save only $15 billion of their $450 billion DI, consumption is $435 billion. Planned investment by firms is $20 billion, so aggregate expenditures are $455 billion. Sales exceed production by $5 billion. This is so only because a $5 billion unplanned decrease in business inventories has occurred. Firms must *disinvest* $5 billion in inventories (column 7). Note again that actual investment is $15 billion ($20 billion planned *minus* the $5 billion decline in inventory investment) and is equal to saving of $15 billion, even though planned investment exceeds saving by $5 billion. The unplanned decline in inventories, resulting from the excess of sales over production, will encourage firms to expand production. GDP will rise to $470 billion, at which unplanned changes in inventories are zero.

When economists say differences between investment and saving can occur and bring about changes in equilibrium GDP, they are referring to planned investment and saving. Equilibrium occurs only when planned investment and saving are equal. But when unplanned changes in inventories are considered, investment and saving are always equal, regardless of the level of GDP. That is true because actual investment consists of planned investment and unplanned investment (unplanned changes in inventories). Unplanned changes in inventories act as a balancing item that equates the actual amounts saved and invested in any period.

AP Changes in Equilibrium GDP and the Multiplier

LO25.5 Analyze how changes in equilibrium real GDP can occur in the aggregate expenditures model and describe how those changes relate to the multiplier.

In the previous chapter, we established that an initial change in spending can cause a greater change in real output through the multiplier effect. In equation form,

$$\text{Multiplier} = \frac{\text{change in real GDP}}{\text{initial change in spending}}$$

Further, we discovered that the size of the multiplier depends on the size of the MPS in the economy:

$$\text{Multiplier} = \frac{1}{\text{MPS}}$$

(Because the multiplier is such an important element of the aggregate expenditures model, we highly recommend that you quickly review Figure 24.8 at this time.)

In a private closed economy, the equilibrium GDP will change in response to changes in either the investment schedule or the consumption schedule. Because changes in the investment schedule are the main sources of instability, we will direct our attention toward them.

Figure 25.3 shows the effect of changes in investment spending on the equilibrium real GDP. Suppose that the expected rate of return on investment rises or that the real interest rate falls such that investment spending increases by $5 billion. That would be shown as an upward shift of the investment schedule in Figure 25.1b. In Figure 25.3, the $5 billion increase of investment spending will increase aggregate expenditures from $(C + I_g)_0$ to $(C + I_g)_1$ and raise equilibrium real GDP from $470 billion to $490 billion.

If the expected rate of return on investment decreases or if the real interest rate rises, investment spending will decline by, say, $5 billion. That would be shown as a downward shift of the investment schedule in Figure 25.1b and a downward shift of the aggregate expenditures schedule from $(C + I_g)_0$ to $(C + I_g)_2$ in Figure 25.3. Equilibrium GDP will fall from $470 billion to $450 billion.

In our examples, a $5 billion change in investment spending leads to a $20 billion change in output and income. So the *multiplier* is 4 (= $20/$5). The MPS is 0.25, meaning that for every $1 billion of new income, $0.25 billion of new saving occurs. Therefore, $20 billion of new income is needed to generate $5 billion of new saving. Once that increase in income and saving occurs, the economy is back in equilibrium—$C + I_g = \text{GDP}$; saving and investment are equal; and there are no unplanned changes in inventories. You can see, then, why the multiplier is equal to 1/MPS and that the multiplier process is an integral part of the aggregate expenditures model.

AP QUICK REVIEW 25.1

- ✓ In a private closed economy, equilibrium GDP occurs where aggregate expenditures equal real domestic output ($C + I_g = \text{GDP}$).
- ✓ At equilibrium GDP, saving equals planned investment ($S = I_g$) and unplanned changes in inventories are zero.
- ✓ Actual investment consists of planned investment plus unplanned changes in inventories (+ or −) and is always equal to saving in a private closed economy.
- ✓ Through the multiplier effect, an initial change in investment spending can cause a magnified change in domestic output and income. Recall the value of the multiplier is 1/(1-MPC) or 1/MPS.

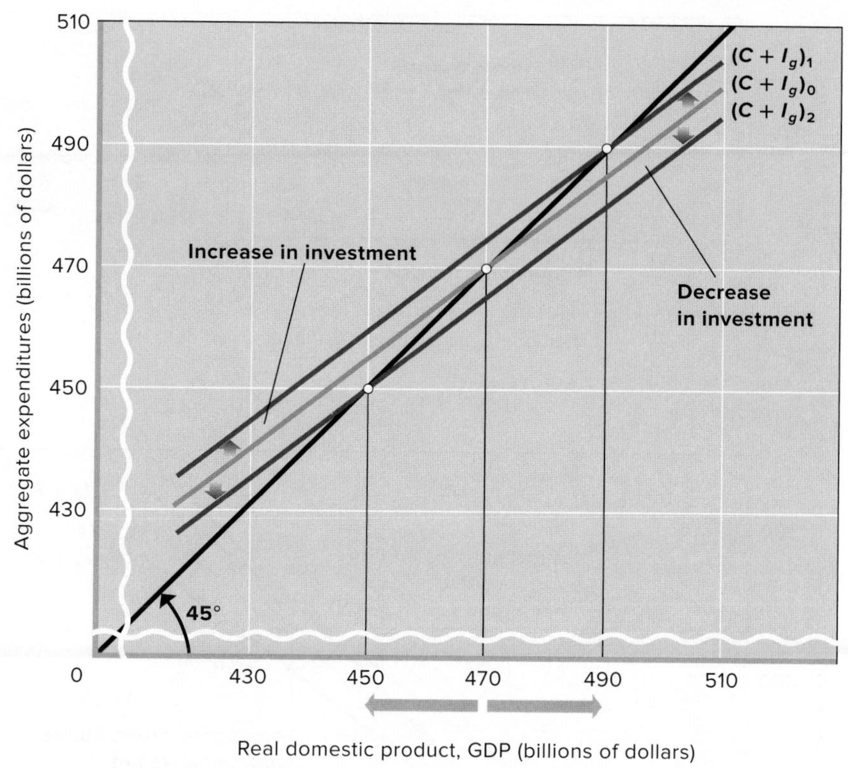

FIGURE 25.3 Changes in the aggregate expenditures schedule and the multiplier effect. An upward shift of the aggregate expenditures schedule from $(C + I_g)_0$ to $(C + I_g)_1$ will increase the equilibrium GDP. Conversely, a downward shift from $(C + I_g)_0$ to $(C + I_g)_2$ will lower the equilibrium GDP. The extent of the changes in equilibrium GDP will depend on the size of the multiplier, which in this case is 4 (= 20/5). The multiplier is equal to 1/MPS (here, 4 = 1/.25).

AP Adding International Trade

LO25.6 Explain how economists integrate the international sector (exports and imports) into the aggregate expenditures model.

We next move from a private closed economy to a private open economy that incorporates exports (X) and imports (M). Our focus will be on **net exports** (exports minus imports), which may be either positive or negative.

Net Exports and Aggregate Expenditures

Like consumption and investment, exports create domestic production, income, and employment for a nation. Although U.S. goods and services produced for export are sent abroad, foreign spending on those goods and services increases production and creates jobs and incomes in the United States. We must therefore include exports as a component of U.S. aggregate expenditures.

Conversely, when an economy is open to international trade, it will spend part of its income on imports—goods and services produced abroad. To avoid overstating the value of domestic production, we must subtract the amount spent on imported goods because such spending generates production and income abroad rather than at home. So, to correctly measure aggregate expenditures for domestic goods and services, we must subtract expenditures on imports from total spending.

In short, for a private closed economy, aggregate expenditures are $C + I_g$. But for an open economy, aggregate expenditures are $C + I_g + (X - M)$. Or, recalling that net exports (X_n) equal ($X - M$), we can say that aggregate expenditures for a private open economy are $C + I_g + X_n$.

The Net Export Schedule

A net export schedule lists the amount of net exports that will occur at each level of GDP. Table 25.3 shows two possible net export schedules for the hypothetical economy represented in Table 25.2. In net export schedule X_{n1} (columns 1 and 2), exports exceed imports by $5 billion at each level of GDP. Perhaps exports are $15 billion while imports are $10 billion. In schedule X_{n2} (columns 1 and 3), imports are $5 billion higher than exports. Perhaps imports are $20 billion while exports

TABLE 25.3 Two Net Export Schedules (in Billions)

(1) Level of GDP	(2) Net Exports, X_{n1} $(X > M)$	(3) Net Exports, X_{n2} $(X < M)$
$370	$+5	$−5
390	+5	−5
410	+5	−5
430	+5	−5
450	+5	−5
470	+5	−5
490	+5	−5
510	+5	−5
530	+5	−5
550	+5	−5

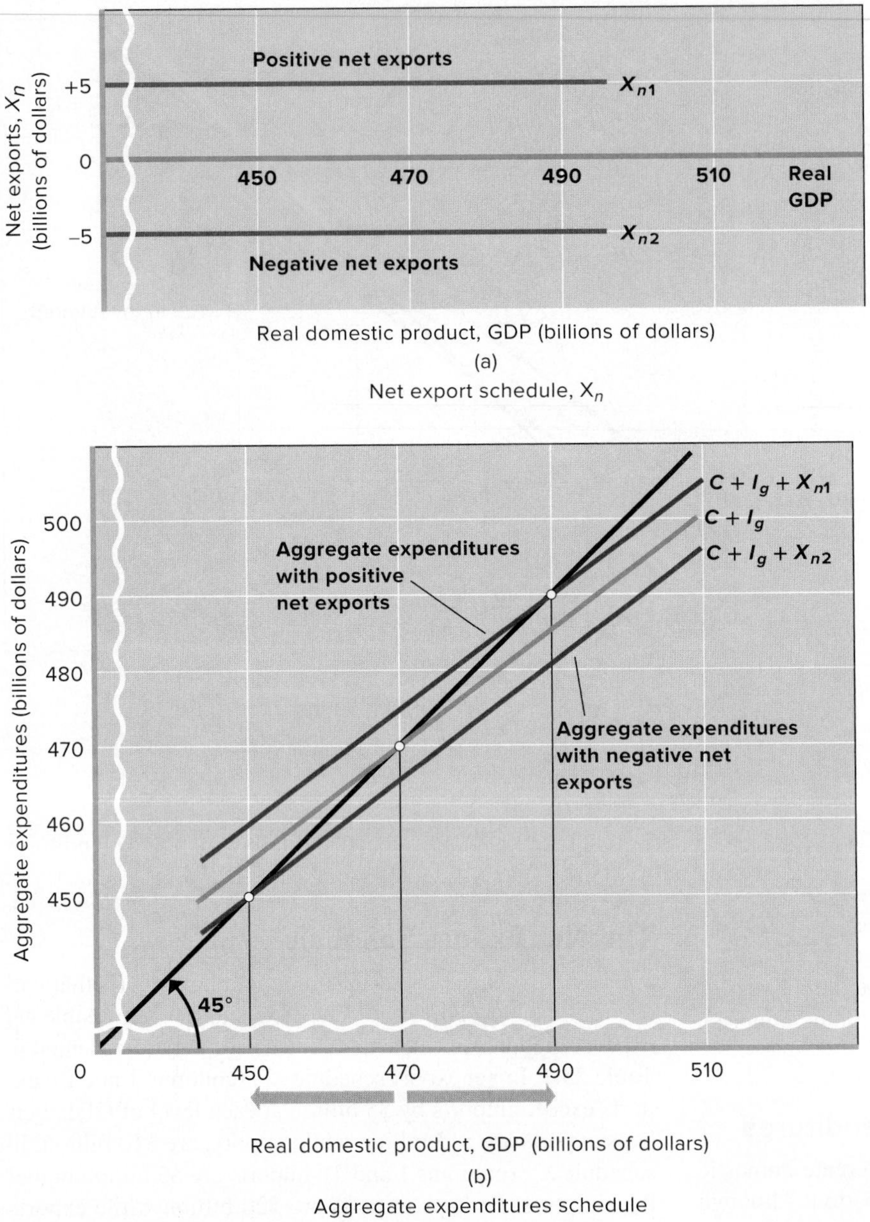

FIGURE 25.4 Net exports and equilibrium GDP. (a) Net exports can be either positive, as shown by the net export schedule X_{n1} or negative, as depicted by net export schedule X_{n2}. (b) Positive net exports elevate the aggregate expenditure schedule from the closed-economy level of $C + I_g$ to the open-economy level of $C + I_g + X_{n1}$. Negative net exports lower the aggregate expenditures schedule from the closed-economy level of $C + I_g$ to the open-economy level of $C + I_g + X_{n2}$.

are $15 billion. To simplify our discussion, we assume in both schedules that net exports are independent of GDP.[1]

Figure 25.4a represents the two net export schedules in Table 25.3. Schedule X_{n1} is above the horizontal axis and depicts positive net exports of $5 billion at all levels of GDP. Schedule X_{n2}, which is below the horizontal axis, shows negative net exports of $5 billion at all levels of GDP.

Net Exports and Equilibrium GDP

The aggregate expenditures schedule labeled $C + I_g$ in Figure 25.4b reflects the private closed economy. It shows the combined consumption and gross investment expenditures occurring at each level of GDP. With no foreign sector, the equilibrium GDP is $470 billion.

But in the private open economy, net exports can be either positive or negative. Let's see how each of the net export schedules in Figure 25.4a affects equilibrium GDP.

Positive Net Exports Suppose the net export schedule is X_{n1}. The $5 billion of additional net export expenditures by the rest of the world is accounted for by adding that $5 billion to the $C + I_g$ schedule in Figure 25.4b. Aggregate expenditures at

[1] In reality, although our exports depend on foreign incomes and are thus independent of U.S. GDP, our imports do vary directly with our own domestic national income. Just as our domestic consumption varies directly with our GDP, so do our purchases of foreign goods. As our GDP rises, U.S. households buy not only more Cadillacs and Harleys, but also more Mercedes and Kawasakis. However, for now we will ignore the complications of the positive relationship between imports and U.S. GDP.

each level of GDP are then $5 billion higher than $C + I_g$ alone. The aggregate expenditures schedule for the open economy thus becomes $C + I_g + X_{n1}$. In this case, international trade increases equilibrium GDP from $470 billion in the private closed economy to $490 billion in the private open economy. Adding net exports of $5 billion has increased GDP by $20 billion, in this case implying a multiplier of 4.

Generalization: Other things equal, positive net exports increase aggregate expenditures and GDP beyond what they would be in a closed economy. Be careful to notice that this increase is the result of exports being larger than imports. This is true because exports and imports have opposite effects on the measurement of domestically produced output. Exports increase real GDP by increasing expenditures on domestically produced output. Imports, by contrast, must be subtracted when calculating real GDP because they are expenditures directed toward output produced abroad. It is only because net exports are positive in this example—so that the expansionary effect of exports outweighs the reductions caused by imports—that we get the overall increase in real GDP. As the next section shows, if net exports are negative, then the reductions caused by imports will outweigh the expansionary effect of exports so that domestic real GDP will decrease.

Negative Net Exports Suppose that net exports are a negative $5 billion as shown by X_{n2} in Figure 25.4a. This means that our hypothetical economy is importing $5 billion more of goods than it is exporting. The aggregate expenditures schedule shown as $C + I_g$ in Figure 25.4b therefore overstates the expenditures on domestic output at each level of GDP. We must reduce the sum of expenditures by the $5 billion net amount spent on imported goods. We do that by subtracting the $5 billion of net imports from $C + I_g$.

The relevant aggregate expenditures schedule in Figure 25.4b becomes $C + I_g + X_{n2}$ and equilibrium GDP falls from $470 billion to $450 billion. Again, a change in net exports of $5 billion has produced a fourfold change in GDP, reminding us that the multiplier in this example is 4.

This gives us a corollary to our first generalization: Other things equal, negative net exports reduce aggregate expenditures and GDP below what they would be in a closed economy. When imports exceed exports, the contractionary effect of the larger amount of imports outweighs the expansionary effect of the smaller amount of exports, and equilibrium real GDP decreases.

Our generalizations of the effects of net exports on GDP mean that a decline in X_n—a decrease in exports or an increase in imports—reduces aggregate expenditures and contracts a nation's GDP. Conversely, an increase in X_n—the result of either an increase in exports or a decrease in imports—increases aggregate expenditures and expands GDP.

As is shown in Global Perspective 25.1, net exports vary greatly among the major industrial nations.

GLOBAL PERSPECTIVE 25.1

Net Exports of Goods, Selected Nations, 2015

Some nations, such as China and Germany, have positive net exports; other countries, such as the United States and the United Kingdom, have negative net exports.

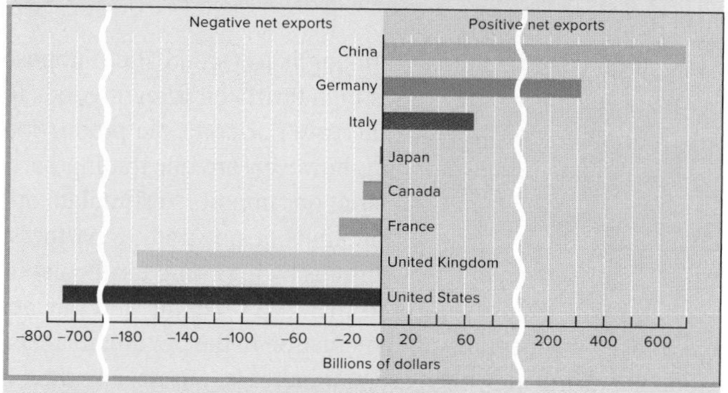

Source: The World Factbook, CIA, **www.cia.gov**.

International Economic Linkages

Our analysis of net exports and real GDP suggests how circumstances or policies abroad can affect U.S. GDP.

Prosperity Abroad A rising level of real output and income among U.S. foreign trading partners enables the United States to sell more goods abroad, thus raising U.S. net exports and increasing U.S. real GDP (assuming initially there is excess capacity). There is good reason for Americans to be interested in the prosperity of our trading partners. Their good fortune enables them to buy more of our exports, increasing our income and enabling us in turn to buy more foreign imports. These imported goods are the ultimate benefit of international trade. Prosperity abroad transfers some of that prosperity to Americans.

Exchange Rates Depreciation of the dollar relative to other currencies enables people abroad to obtain more dollars with each unit of their own currencies. The price of U.S. goods in terms of those currencies will fall, stimulating purchases of U.S. exports. Also, U.S. customers will find they need more dollars to buy foreign goods and, consequently, will reduce their spending on imports. If the economy has available capacity, the increased exports and decreased imports will increase U.S. net exports and expand the nation's GDP.

This last example has been cast only in terms of depreciation of the dollar. You should think through the impact that appreciation of the dollar would have on net exports and equilibrium GDP.

A Caution on Tariffs and Devaluations Because higher net exports increase real GDP, countries often look for ways to reduce imports and increase exports during recessions or depressions. Thus, a recession might tempt the U.S. federal government to increase tariffs and devalue the international value of the dollar (say, by supplying massive amounts of dollars in the foreign exchange market) to try to increase net exports. Such an increase of net exports would expand domestic production, reduce domestic unemployment, and help the economy recover.

But this interventionist thinking is too simplistic. Suppose that the United States imposes high tariffs on foreign goods to reduce our imports and thus increase our domestic production and employment. Our imports, however, are our trading partners' exports. So when we restrict our imports to stimulate our economy, we depress the economies of our trading partners. They are likely to retaliate against us by imposing tariffs on our products. If so, our exports to them will decline and our net exports may in fact fall. With retaliation in the picture, it is possible that tariffs may decrease, not increase, our net exports.

That unfortunate possibility became a sad reality during the Great Depression of the 1930s, when various nations, including the United States, imposed trade barriers as a way of reducing domestic unemployment. The result was many rounds of retaliation that simply throttled world trade, worsened the depression, and increased unemployment. Abetting the problem were attempts by some nations to increase their net exports by devaluing their currencies. Other nations simply retaliated by devaluing their own currencies. The international exchange rate system collapsed, and world trade spiraled downward. Economic historians agree that tariffs and devaluations during the 1930s were huge policy mistakes!

Nations are tempted to use tariffs and currency devaluations because, *other things equal*, these policies *do* increase net exports and real GDP. But keep in mind that other things aren't likely to stay equal. In particular, other nations will almost certainly retaliate with their own tariffs and devaluations—the final result being lower net exports and lower GDP for those countries and for our own.

AP QUICK REVIEW 25.2

- ✓ Exports increase aggregate expenditures relative to the closed economy and, other things equal, increase equilibrium GDP.
- ✓ Imports decrease aggregate expenditures relative to the closed economy and, other things equal, reduce equilibrium GDP.
- ✓ In the open economy, changes in (a) prosperity abroad, (b) tariffs, and (c) exchange rates can affect U.S. net exports and therefore U.S. aggregate expenditures and equilibrium GDP.
- ✓ Tariffs and deliberate currency depreciations are unlikely to increase net exports because other nations will likely retaliate.

AP Adding the Public Sector

LO25.7 Explain how economists integrate the public sector (government expenditures and taxes) into the aggregate expenditures model.

Our final step in constructing the full aggregate expenditures model is to move the analysis from a private (no-government) open economy to an economy with a public sector (sometimes called a "mixed economy"). This means adding government purchases and taxes to the model.

For simplicity, we will assume that government purchases are independent of the level of GDP and do not alter the consumption and investment schedules. Also, government's net tax revenues—total tax revenues less "negative taxes" in the form of transfer payments—are derived entirely from personal taxes. Finally, a fixed amount of taxes is collected regardless of the level of GDP.

Government Purchases and Equilibrium GDP

Suppose the government decides to purchase $20 billion of goods and services regardless of the level of GDP and tax collections.

Tabular Example Table 25.4 shows the impact of this purchase on the equilibrium GDP. Columns 1 through 4 are carried over from Table 25.2 for the private closed economy, in which the equilibrium GDP was $470 billion. The only new items are exports and imports in column 5 and government purchases in column 6. (Observe in column 5 that net exports are zero.) As shown in column 7, the addition of government purchases to private spending ($C + I_g + X_n$) yields a new, higher level of aggregate expenditures ($C + I_g + X_n + G$). Comparing columns 1 and 7, we find that aggregate expenditures and real output are equal at a higher level of GDP. Without government purchases, equilibrium GDP was $470 billion (row 6); *with* government purchases, aggregate expenditures and real output are equal at $550 billion (row 10). Increases in public spending, like increases in private spending, shift the aggregate expenditures schedule upward and produce a higher equilibrium GDP.

Note, too, that government spending is subject to the multiplier. A $20 billion increase in government purchases has increased equilibrium GDP by $80 billion (from $470 billion to $550 billion). The multiplier in this example is 4.

This $20 billion increase in government spending is *not* financed by increased taxes. Shortly, we will demonstrate that increased taxes *reduce* equilibrium GDP.

Graphical Analysis In Figure 25.5, we vertically add $20 billion of government purchases, G, to the level of private spending, $C + I_g + X_n$. That added $20 billion raises the aggregate expenditures schedule (private plus public) to $C + I_g + X_n + G$, resulting in an $80 billion increase in equilibrium GDP, from $470 to $550 billion.

AP **TABLE 25.4 The Impact of Government Purchases on Equilibrium GDP**

(1) Real Domestic Output and Income (GDP = DI), Billions	(2) Consumption (C), Billions	(3) Savings (S), Billions	(4) Investment (I_g), Billions	(5) Net Exports (X_n), Billions: Exports (X)	(5) Net Exports (X_n), Billions: Imports (M)	(6) Government Purchases (G), Billions	(7) Aggregate Expenditures ($C + I_g + X_n + G$), Billions (2) + (4) + (5) + (6)
(1) $370	$375	$–5	$20	$10	$10	$20	$415
(2) 390	390	0	20	10	10	20	430
(3) 410	405	5	20	10	10	20	445
(4) 430	420	10	20	10	10	20	460
(5) 450	435	15	20	10	10	20	475
(6) 470	450	20	20	10	10	20	490
(7) 490	465	25	20	10	10	20	505
(8) 510	480	30	20	10	10	20	520
(9) 530	495	35	20	10	10	20	535
(10) **550**	**510**	**40**	**20**	**10**	**10**	**20**	**550**

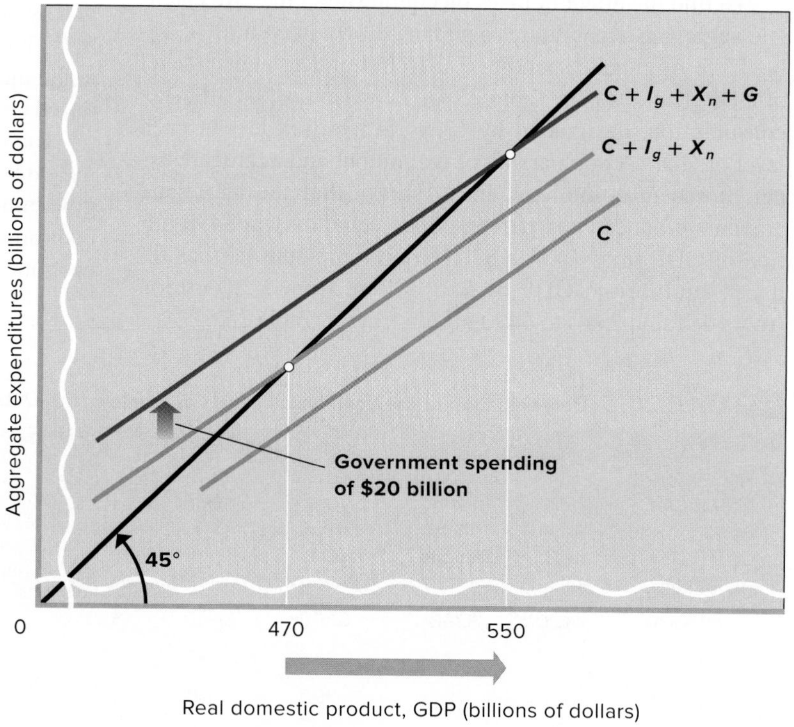

FIGURE 25.5 Government spending and equilibrium GDP. The addition of government expenditures of G to our analysis raises the aggregate expenditures ($C + I_g + X_n + G$) schedule and increases the equilibrium level of GDP, as would an increase in C, I_g, or X_n.

A decline in government purchases G will lower the aggregate expenditures schedule in Figure 25.5 and result in a multiplied decline in the equilibrium GDP. Verify in Table 25.4 that if government purchases were to decline from $20 billion to $10 billion, the equilibrium GDP would fall by $40 billion.

Taxation and Equilibrium GDP

The government not only spends but also collects taxes. Suppose it imposes a **lump-sum tax,** which is a tax of a constant amount or, more precisely, a tax yielding the same amount of tax revenue at each level of GDP. Let's assume this tax is $20 billion, so that the government obtains $20 billion of tax revenue at each level of GDP regardless of the level of government purchases.

Tabular Example In Table 25.5, which continues our example, we find taxes in column 2, and we see in column 3 that disposable (after-tax) income is lower than GDP (column 1) by the $20 billion amount of the tax. Because households use disposable income both to consume and to save, the tax lowers both consumption and saving. The MPC and MPS tell us how much consumption and saving will decline as a result of the $20 billion in taxes. Because the MPC is 0.75, the government tax collection of $20 billion will reduce consumption by $15 billion (= 0.75 × $20 billion). Since the MPS is 0.25, saving will drop by $5 billion (= 0.25 × $20 billion).

Columns 4 and 5 in Table 25.5 list the amounts of consumption and saving *at each level of GDP*. Note they are $15 billion and $5 billion smaller than those in Table 25.4. Taxes reduce disposable income relative to GDP by the amount of the taxes. This decline in DI reduces both consumption and saving at each level of GDP. The extent of the *C* and *S* reductions depends on the MPC and the MPS.

To find the effect of taxes on equilibrium GDP, we calculate aggregate expenditures again, as shown in column 9, Table 25.5. Aggregate spending is $15 billion less at each level of GDP than it was in Table 25.4. The reason is that after-tax consumption, designated by C_a, is $15 billion less at each level of GDP. A comparison of real output and aggregate expenditures in columns 1 and 9 shows that the aggregate amounts produced and purchased are equal only at $490 billion of GDP (row 7). The $20 billion lump-sum tax has reduced equilibrium GDP by $60 billion, from $550 billion (row 10, Table 25.4) to $490 billion (row 7, Table 25.5).

Graphical Analysis In Figure 25.6, the $20 billion increase in taxes shows up as a $15 (not $20) billion decline in the aggregate expenditures ($C_a + I_g + X_n + G$) schedule. This decline in the schedule results solely from a decline in the consumption *C* component of aggregate expenditures. The equilibrium GDP falls from $550 billion to $490 billion because of this tax-caused drop in consumption. With no change in government expenditures, tax increases lower the aggregate expenditures schedule relative to the 45° line and reduce the equilibrium GDP.

In contrast to our previous case, a *decrease* in existing taxes will raise the aggregate expenditures schedule in Figure 25.6 as a result of an increase in consumption at all GDP levels. You should confirm that a tax reduction of $10 billion (from the present $20 billion to $10 billion) would increase the equilibrium GDP from $490 billion to $520 billion.

Differential Impacts You may have noted that equal changes in *G* and *T* do not have equivalent impacts on GDP. The $20 billion increase in *G* in our illustration, subject to the multiplier of 4, produced an $80 billion increase in real GDP. But the $20 billion increase in taxes reduced GDP by only $60 billion. Given an MPC of 0.75, the tax increase of $20 billion reduced consumption by only $15 billion (not $20 billion) because saving also fell by $5 billion. Subjecting the $15 billion decline in consumption to the multiplier of 4, we find the tax increase of $20 billion reduced GDP by $60 billion (not $80 billion).

Table 25.5 and Figure 25.6 constitute the complete aggregate expenditures model for an open economy with government. When total spending equals total production, the economy's output is in equilibrium. In the open mixed economy, equilibrium GDP occurs where

$$C_a + I_g + X_n + G = \text{GDP}$$

AP **TABLE 25.5** **Determination of the Equilibrium Levels of Employment, Output, and Income: Private and Public Sectors**

(1) Real Domestic Output and Income (GDP = NI = DI), Billions	(2) Taxes (*T*), Billions	(3) Disposable Income (DI), Billions (1) − (2)	(4) Consumption (C_a), Billions	(5) Savings (S_a), Billions (3) − (4)	(6) Investment (I_g), Billions	(7) Net Exports (X_n), Billions: Exports (*X*)	(7) Net Exports (X_n), Billions: Imports (*M*)	(8) Government Purchases (*G*), Billions	(9) Aggregate Expenditures ($C_a + I_g + X_n + G$), Billions, (4) + (6) + (7) + (8)
(1) $370	$20	$350	$360	$−10	$20	$10	$10	$20	$400
(2) 390	20	370	375	−5	20	10	10	20	415
(3) 410	20	390	390	0	20	10	10	20	430
(4) 430	20	410	405	5	20	10	10	20	445
(5) 450	20	430	420	10	20	10	10	20	460
(6) 470	20	450	435	15	20	10	10	20	475
(7) **490**	**20**	**470**	**450**	**20**	**20**	**10**	**10**	**20**	**490**
(8) 510	20	490	465	25	20	10	10	20	505
(9) 530	20	510	480	30	20	10	10	20	520
(10) 550	20	530	495	35	20	10	10	20	535

FIGURE 25.6 Taxes and equilibrium GDP. If the MPC is 0.75, the $20 billion of taxes will lower the consumption schedule by $15 billion and cause a $60 billion decline in the equilibrium GDP. In the open economy with government, equilibrium GDP occurs where C_a (after-tax income) + $I_g + X_n + G$ = GDP. Here that equilibrium is $490 billion.

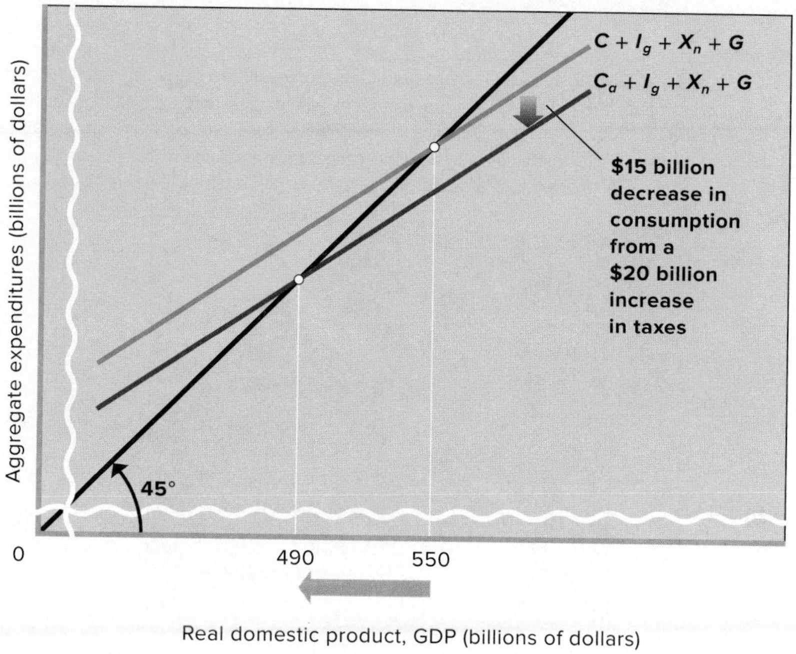

Injections, Leakages, and Unplanned Changes in Inventories The related characteristics of equilibrium noted for the private closed economy also apply to the full model. In particular, it is still the case that injections into the income-expenditures stream equal leakages from the income stream. For the private closed economy, $S = I_g$. For the expanded economy, imports and taxes are added leakages. Saving, importing, and paying taxes are all uses of income that subtract from potential consumption. Consumption will now be less than GDP—creating a potential spending gap—in the amount of after-tax saving (S_a), imports (M), and taxes (T). But exports (X) and government purchases (G), along with investment (I_g), are injections into the income-expenditures stream. At the equilibrium GDP, the sum of the leakages equals the sum of injections. In symbols:

$$S_a + M + T = I_g X + G$$

You should use the data in Table 25.5 to confirm this equality between leakages and injections at the equilibrium GDP of $490 billion. Also, substantiate that a lack of such equality exists at all other possible levels of GDP.

Although not directly shown in Table 25.5, the equilibrium characteristic of "no unplanned changes in inventories" will also be fulfilled at the $490 billion GDP. Because aggregate expenditures equal GDP, all the goods and services produced will be purchased. There will be no unplanned increase in inventories, so firms will have no incentive to reduce their employment and production. Nor will they experience an unplanned decline in their inventories, which would prompt them to expand their employment and output to replenish their inventories.

AP Equilibrium versus Full-Employment GDP

LO25.8 Differentiate between equilibrium GDP and full-employment GDP and identify and describe the nature and causes of "recessionary expenditure gaps" and "inflationary expenditure gaps."

A key point about the equilibrium GDP of the aggregate expenditures model is that it need not equal the economy's full-employment GDP. In fact, Keynes specifically designed the model so that it could explain situations like the Great Depression, during which the economy was seemingly stuck at a bad equilibrium in which real GDP was far below potential output. As we will show you in a moment, Keynes also used the model to suggest policy recommendations for moving the economy back toward potential output and full employment.

The fact that equilibrium and potential GDP in the aggregate expenditure model need not match also reveals critical insights about the causes of demand-pull inflation. We will first examine the "expenditure gaps" that give rise to differences between equilibrium and potential GDP and then see how the model helps to explain the recession of 2007–2009 and preview the policies used by the federal government to try to halt and reverse it.

Recessionary Expenditure Gap

Suppose in **Figure 25.7 (Key Graph),** panel (a), that the full-employment level of GDP is $510 billion and the aggregate expenditures schedule is AE_1. (For simplicity, we will now dispense with the $C_a + I_g + X_n + G$ labeling.) This schedule intersects the

KEY GRAPH

FIGURE 25.7 **Recessionary and inflationary expenditure gaps.** The equilibrium and full-employment GDPs may not coincide. (a) A recessionary expenditure gap is the amount by which aggregate expenditures at the full-employment GDP fall short of those needed to achieve the full-employment GDP. Here, the $5 billion recessionary expenditure gap causes a $20 billion negative GDP gap. (b) An inflationary expenditure gap is the amount by which aggregate expenditures at the full-employment GDP exceed those just sufficient to achieve the full-employment GDP. Here, the inflationary expenditure gap is $5 billion; this overspending produces demand-pull inflation.

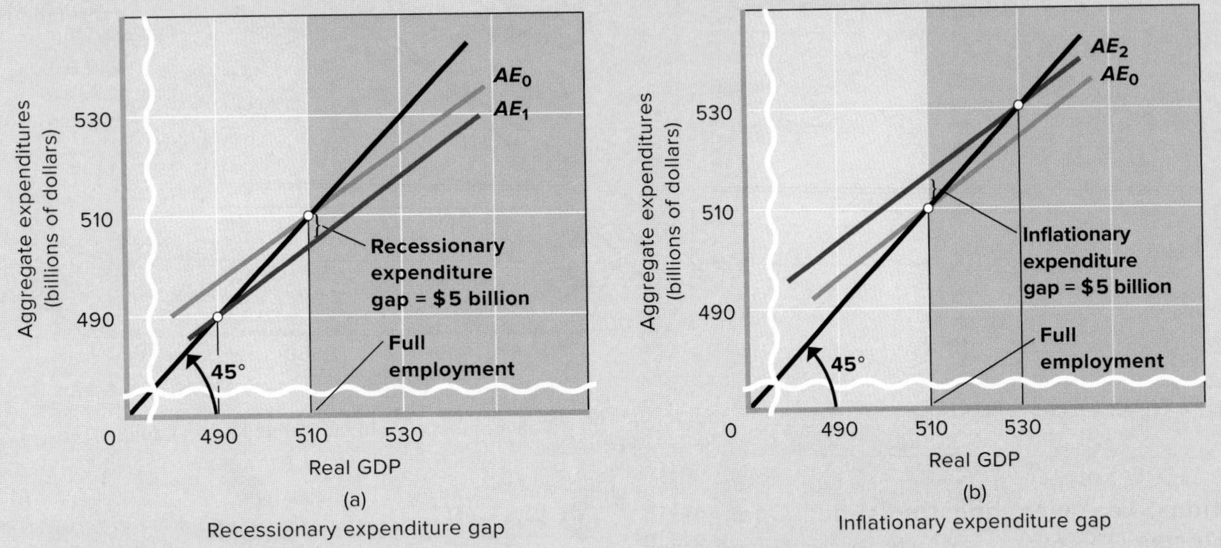

QUICK QUIZ FOR FIGURE 25.7

1. In the economy depicted:
   - **a.** the MPS is 0.50.
   - **b.** the MPC is 0.75.
   - **c.** the full-employment level of real GDP is $530 billion.
   - **d.** nominal GDP always equals real GDP.
2. The inflationary expenditure gap depicted will cause:
   - **a.** demand-pull inflation.
   - **b.** cost-push inflation.
   - **c.** cyclical unemployment.
   - **d.** frictional unemployment.
3. The recessionary expenditure gap depicted will cause:
   - **a.** demand-pull inflation.
   - **b.** cost-push inflation.
   - **c.** cyclical unemployment.
   - **d.** frictional unemployment.
4. In the economy depicted, the $5 billion inflationary expenditure gap:
   - **a.** expands real GDP to $530 billion.
   - **b.** leaves real GDP at $510 billion but causes inflation.
   - **c.** could be remedied by equal $5 billion increases in taxes and government spending.
   - **d.** implies that real GDP exceeds nominal GDP.

Answers: 1. b; 2. a; 3. c; 4. b

45° line to the left of the economy's full-employment output, so the economy's equilibrium GDP of $490 billion is $20 billion short of its full-employment output of $510 billion. According to column 1 in Table 25.2, total employment at the full-employment GDP is 75 million workers. But the economy depicted in Figure 25.7a is employing only 70 million workers; 5 million available workers are not employed. For that reason, the economy is sacrificing $20 billion of output.

A **recessionary expenditure gap** is the amount by which aggregate expenditures *at the full-employment GDP* fall short of those required to achieve the full-employment GDP. Insufficient total spending contracts or depresses the economy. Table 25.5 shows that at the full-employment level of $510 billion (column 1), the corresponding level of aggregate expenditures is only $505 billion (column 9). The recessionary expenditure gap is thus $5 billion, the amount by which the aggregate expenditures curve would have to shift upward to realize equilibrium at the full-employment GDP. Graphically, the recessionary expenditure gap is the *vertical* distance (measured at the full-employment GDP) by which the actual aggregate expenditures schedule AE_1 lies below the hypothetical full-employment aggregate expenditures schedule AE_0. In Figure 25.7a, this recessionary expenditure gap is $5 billion. Because the multiplier is 4, there is a $20 billion differential (the recessionary expenditure gap of $5 billion times the multiplier of 4) between the equilibrium GDP and the full-employment GDP. This $20 billion difference is a negative *GDP gap*—an idea we first developed when discussing cyclical unemployment in Chapter 23.

Keynes's Solution to a Recessionary Expenditure Gap

Keynes pointed to two different policies that a government might pursue to close a recessionary expenditure gap and achieve full employment. The first is to increase government spending. The second is to lower taxes. Both work by increasing aggregate expenditures.

Look back at Figure 25.5. There we showed how an increase in government expenditures *G* will increase overall aggregate expenditures and, consequently, the equilibrium real GDP. Applying this strategy to the situation in Figure 25.7a, government could completely close the $20 billion negative GDP gap between the initial equilibrium of $490 billion and the economy's potential output of $510 billion if it increased spending by the $5 billion amount of the recessionary expenditure gap. Given the economy's multiplier of 4, the $5 billion increase in *G* would create a $20 billion increase in equilibrium real GDP, thereby bringing the economy to full employment.

Government also could lower taxes to close the recessionary expenditure gap and thus eliminate the negative GDP gap. Look back at Figure 25.6 in which an increase in taxes resulted in lower after-tax consumption spending and a smaller equilibrium real GDP. Keynes simply suggested a reversal of this process: Since an increase in taxes lowers equilibrium real GDP, a decrease in taxes will raise equilibrium GDP. The decrease in taxes will leave consumers with higher after-tax income. That will lead to higher consumption expenditures and an increase in equilibrium real GDP.

But by how much should the government cut taxes? By exactly $6.67 billion. That is because the MPC is 0.75. The tax cut of $6.67 billion will increase consumers' after-tax income by $6.67 billion. They will then increase consumption spending by 0.75 of that amount, or $5 billion. This will increase aggregate expenditures by the $5 billion needed to close the recessionary expenditure gap. The economy's equilibrium real GDP will rise to its potential output of $510 billion.

But a big warning is needed here: As the economy moves closer to its potential output, it becomes harder to justify Keynes's assumption that prices are stuck. As the economy closes its negative GDP gap, nearly all workers are employed and nearly all factories are operating at or near full capacity. In such a situation, there is no massive oversupply of productive resources to keep prices from rising. In fact, economists know from real-world experience that in such situations prices are not fully stuck. Instead, they become increasingly flexible as the economy moves nearer to potential output.

This fact is one of the major limitations of the aggregate expenditures model and is the reason why we will develop a different model that can handle inflation in the next chapter. That being said, it is nevertheless true that the aggregate expenditures model is still very useful despite its inability to handle flexible prices. For instance, as we explained in Chapter 20, even an economy operating near full employment will show sticky or even stuck prices in the short run. In such situations, the intuitions of the aggregate expenditures model will still hold true. The benefit of the aggregate demand–aggregate supply model that we develop in the next chapter is that it also can show us what happens over longer periods, as prices (and wages) become more flexible and are increasingly able to adjust.

Inflationary Expenditure Gap

Economists use the term **inflationary expenditure gap** to describe the amount by which an economy's aggregate expenditures *at the full-employment GDP* exceed those just necessary to achieve the full-employment level of GDP. In Figure 25.7b, there is a $5 billion inflationary expenditure gap at the $510 billion full-employment GDP. This is shown by the vertical distance between the actual aggregate expenditures schedule AE_2 and the hypothetical schedule AE_0 that would be just sufficient to achieve the $510 billion full-employment GDP. Thus, the inflationary expenditure gap is the amount by which the aggregate expenditures schedule would have to shift downward to realize equilibrium at the full-employment GDP.

But why does the name "inflationary expenditure gap" contain the word *inflationary*? In particular, what does the situation depicted in Figure 25.7b have to do with inflation? The answer lies in the answer to a different question: *Could the economy actually achieve and maintain an equilibrium real GDP that is substantially above the full-employment output level?*

The unfortunate answer is no. It is unfortunate because if such a thing were possible, then the government could make real GDP as high as it wanted by simply increasing *G* to an arbitrarily high number. Graphically, it could raise the AE_2 curve in Figure 25.7b as far up as it wanted, thereby increasing equilibrium real GDP as high as it wanted. Living standards would skyrocket! But this is not possible because, by definition, all the available workers in the economy are fully employed at the full-employment output level. Producing slightly more than the full-employment output level for a few months might be possible if you could convince all the workers to work overtime day after day. But there simply is not enough labor to have the economy produce at much more than potential output for any extended period of time.

So what *does* happen in situations in which aggregate expenditures are so high that the model predicts an equilibrium level of GDP beyond potential output? The answer is twofold. First, the economy ends up producing either at potential output or just above potential output due to the limited supply of labor. Second, the economy experiences demand-pull inflation. With the supply of output limited by the supply of labor, high levels of aggregate expenditures simply drive up prices.

LAST WORD

Say's Law, the Great Depression, and Keynes

The Aggregate Expenditure Theory Emerged as a Critique of Classical Economics and as a Response to the Great Depression.

Until the Great Depression of the 1930s, many prominent economists, including David Ricardo (1772–1823) and John Stuart Mill (1806–1873), believed that the market system would ensure full employment of an economy's resources. These so-called *classical economists* acknowledged that now and then abnormal circumstances such as wars, political upheavals, droughts, speculative crises, and gold rushes would occur, deflecting the economy from full-employment status. But when such deviations occurred, the economy would automatically adjust and soon return to full-employment output. For example, a slump in output and employment would result in lower prices, wages, and interest rates, which in turn would increase consumer spending, employment, and investment spending. Any excess supply of goods and workers would soon be eliminated.

Classical macroeconomists denied that the level of spending in an economy could be too low to bring about the purchase of the entire full-employment output. They based their denial of inadequate spending in part on *Say's law*, attributed to the nineteenth-century French economist J. B. Say (1767–1832). This law is the disarmingly simple idea that the very act of producing goods generates income equal to the value of the goods produced. The production of any output automatically provides the income needed to buy that output. More succinctly stated, *supply creates its own demand.*

Say's law can best be understood in terms of a barter economy. A woodworker, for example, produces or supplies furniture as a means of buying or demanding the food and clothing produced by other workers. The woodworker's supply of furniture is the income that he will "spend" to satisfy his demand for other goods. The goods he buys (demands) will have a total value exactly equal to the goods he produces (supplies). And so it is for other producers and for the entire economy. Demand must be the same as supply!

Assuming that the composition of output is in accord with consumer preferences, all markets would be cleared of their outputs. It would seem that all firms need to do to sell a full-employment output is to produce that level of output. Say's law guarantees there will be sufficient spending to purchase it all.

The Great Depression of the 1930s called into question the theory that supply creates its own demand (Say's law). In the United States, real GDP declined by 27 percent and the unemployment rate rocketed to nearly 25 percent. Other nations experienced similar impacts. And cyclical unemployment lingered for a decade. An obvious inconsistency exists between a theory that says that unemployment is virtually impossible and the actual occurrence of a 10-year siege of substantial unemployment.

In 1936 British economist John Maynard Keynes (1883–1946) explained why cyclical unemployment could occur in a market economy. In his *General Theory of Employment, Interest, and Money*, Keynes attacked the foundations of classical theory and developed the ideas underlying the aggregate expenditures model. Keynes disputed Say's law, pointing out that not all income need be spent in the same period that it is produced. In fact, some income is always saved. In normal times, that saving is borrowed by businesses to buy capital goods—thereby boosting total spending in the economy. But if expectations about the future grow pessimistic, businesses will slash investment spending and a lot of that saving will not be put to use. The result will be insufficient total spending. Unsold goods will accumulate in producers' warehouses, and producers will respond by reducing their output and discharging workers. A recession or depression will result, and widespread cyclical unemployment will occur. Moreover, said Keynes, recessions or depressions are not likely to correct themselves. In contrast to the more laissez-faire view of the classical economists, Keynes argued that government should play an active role in stabilizing the economy.

Source: Cover image from *The General Theory of Employment, Interest, and Money,* by John Maynard Keynes (Amherst, NY: Prometheus Books, 1997).

Nominal GDP will increase because of the higher price level, but real GDP will not.

Application: The Recession of 2007–2009

In December 2007 the U.S. economy entered the longest and one of the deepest recessions since the Great Depression of the 1930s. We will defer discussion of the underlying financial crisis until later chapters, but the ultimate effect of the crisis is easily portrayed through the aggregate expenditures model. We know that the AE_0 line in Figure 25.7a consists of the combined amount of after-tax consumption expenditures (C_a), gross investment expenditures (I_g), net export expenditures (X_n), and government purchases (G) planned at each level of real GDP. During the recession, both after-tax consumption and investment expenditures declined, with planned investment expenditures suffering the largest drop by far.

Aggregate expenditures thus declined, as from AE_0 to AE_1 in Figure 25.7a. This set off a multiple decline in real GDP, illustrated in the figure by the decline from $510 billion to $490 billion. In the language of the aggregate expenditures model, a recessionary expenditure gap produced one of the largest negative GDP gaps since the Great Depression. Employment sank by more than 8 million people, and the unemployment rate jumped above 10 percent. As recessions go, this was a big one!

The federal government undertook various Keynesian policies in 2008 and 2009 to try to eliminate the recessionary expenditure gap facing the economy. In 2008, the government provided $100 billion of tax rebate checks to taxpayers, hoping that recipients would use most of their checks to buy goods and services. (They didn't! Instead, they used substantial portions of their checks to pay off credit cards and reduce other debt.) In 2009, the federal government enacted a $787 billion stimulus package designed to boost aggregate expenditures, reduce the recessionary expenditure gap, and, through the multiplier effect, increase real GDP and employment.

We will defer discussion and further assessment of these stimulus attempts until Chapter 27, but Figure 25.7a clearly illuminates their purpose. If the government could drive up aggregate expenditures, such as from AE_1 to AE_0, the recession would come to an end and the recovery phase of the business cycle would begin.

AP QUICK REVIEW 25.3

- ✓ Government purchases shift the aggregate expenditures schedule upward and raise equilibrium GDP. Aggregate expenditures will increase by the increase in government spending multiplied by the spending multiplier. Conversely, decreases in government spending will reduce aggregate expenditures by a multiplied amount.
- ✓ Taxes reduce disposable income, lower consumption spending and saving, shift the aggregate expenditures schedule downward, and reduce equilibrium GDP.
- ✓ A recessionary expenditure gap is the amount by which an economy's aggregate expenditures schedule must shift upward to achieve the full-employment GDP; an inflationary expenditure gap is the amount by which the economy's aggregate expenditures schedule must shift downward to achieve full-employment GDP and eliminate demand-pull inflation.

SUMMARY

LO25.1 Explain how sticky prices relate to the aggregate expenditures model.

The aggregate expenditures model views the total amount of spending in the economy as the primary factor determining the level of real GDP that the economy will produce. The model assumes that the price level is fixed. Keynes made this assumption to reflect the general circumstances of the Great Depression, in which declines in output and employment, rather than declines in prices, were the dominant adjustments made by firms when they faced huge declines in their sales.

LO25.2 Explain how an economy's investment schedule is derived from the investment demand curve and an interest rate.

An investment schedule shows how much investment the firms in an economy are collectively planning to make at each possible level of GDP. In this chapter, we utilize a simple investment schedule in which investment is a constant value and therefore the same at all levels of GDP. That constant value is derived from the investment demand curve by determining what quantity of investment will be demanded at the economy's current real interest rate.

LO25.3 Illustrate how economists combine consumption and investment to depict an aggregate expenditures schedule for a private closed economy and how that schedule can be used to demonstrate the economy's equilibrium level of output (where the total quantity of goods produced equals the total quantity of goods purchased).

For a private closed economy the equilibrium level of GDP occurs when aggregate expenditures and real output are equal or, graphically, where the $C + I_g$ line intersects the 45° line. At any GDP greater than equilibrium GDP, real output will exceed aggregate spending, resulting in unplanned investment in inventories and eventual declines in output and income (GDP). At any below-equilibrium GDP, aggregate expenditures will exceed real output, resulting in unplanned disinvestment in inventories and eventual increases in GDP.

LO25.4 Discuss the two other ways to characterize the equilibrium level of real GDP in a private closed economy: saving = investment and no unplanned changes in inventories.

At equilibrium GDP, the amount households save (leakages) and the amount businesses plan to invest (injections) are equal. Any excess of saving over planned investment will cause a shortage of total spending, forcing GDP to fall. Any excess of planned investment over saving will cause an excess of total spending, inducing GDP to rise. The change in GDP will in both cases correct the discrepancy between saving and planned investment.

At equilibrium GDP, there are no unplanned changes in inventories. When aggregate expenditures diverge from real GDP, an unplanned change in inventories occurs. Unplanned increases in inventories are followed by a cutback in production and a decline of real GDP. Unplanned decreases in inventories result in an increase in production and a rise of GDP.

Actual investment consists of planned investment plus unplanned changes in inventories and is always equal to saving.

LO25.5 Analyze how changes in equilibrium real GDP can occur in the aggregate expenditures model and describe how those changes relate to the multiplier.

A shift in the investment schedule (caused by changes in expected rates of return or changes in interest rates) shifts the aggregate expenditures curve and causes a new equilibrium level of real GDP. Real GDP changes by more than the amount of the initial change in investment. This multiplier effect ($\Delta GDP/\Delta I_g$) accompanies both increases and decreases in aggregate expenditures and also applies to changes in net exports (X_n) and government purchases (G).

LO25.6 Explain how economists integrate the international sector (exports and imports) into the aggregate expenditures model.

The net export schedule in the model of the open economy relates net exports (exports minus imports) to levels of real GDP. For simplicity, we assume that the level of net exports is the same at all levels of real GDP.

Positive net exports increase aggregate expenditures to a higher level than they would if the economy were "closed" to international trade. Negative net exports decrease aggregate expenditures relative to those in a closed economy, decreasing equilibrium real GDP by a multiple of their amount. Increases in exports or decreases in imports have an expansionary effect on real GDP, while decreases in exports or increases in imports have a contractionary effect.

LO25.7 Explain how economists integrate the public sector (government expenditures and taxes) into the aggregate expenditures model.

Government purchases in the model of the mixed economy shift the aggregate expenditures schedule upward and raise GDP.

Taxation reduces disposable income, lowers consumption and saving, shifts the aggregate expenditures curve downward, and reduces equilibrium GDP.

In the complete aggregate expenditures model, equilibrium GDP occurs where $C_a + I_g + X_n + G =$ GDP. At the equilibrium GDP, *leakages* of after-tax saving (S_a), imports (M), and taxes (T) equal *injections* of investment (I_g), exports (X), and government purchases (G): $S_a + M + T = I_g + X_n + G$. Also, there are no unplanned changes in inventories.

LO25.8 Differentiate between equilibrium GDP and full-employment GDP and identify and describe the nature and causes of "recessionary expenditure gaps" and "inflationary expenditure gaps."

The equilibrium GDP and the full-employment GDP may differ. A recessionary expenditure gap is the amount by which aggregate expenditures at the full-employment GDP fall short of those needed to achieve the full-employment GDP. This gap produces a negative GDP gap (actual GDP minus potential GDP). An inflationary expenditure gap is the amount by which aggregate expenditures at the full-employment GDP exceed those just sufficient to achieve the full-employment GDP. This gap causes demand-pull inflation.

Keynes suggested that the solution to the large negative GDP gap that occurred during the Great Depression was for government to increase aggregate expenditures. It could do this by increasing its own expenditures (G) or by lowering taxes (T) to increase after-tax consumption expenditures (C_a) by households. Because the economy had millions of unemployed workers and massive amounts of unused production capacity, government could boost aggregate expenditures without worrying about creating inflation.

The stuck-price assumption of the aggregate expenditures model is not credible when the economy approaches or attains its full-employment output. With unemployment low and excess production capacity small or nonexistent, an increase in aggregate expenditures will cause inflation along with any increase in real GDP.

TERMS AND CONCEPTS

planned investment
investment schedule
aggregate expenditures schedule
equilibrium GDP
leakage
injection
unplanned changes in inventories
net exports
lump-sum tax
recessionary expenditure gap
inflationary expenditure gap

The following and additional problems can be found in connect

DISCUSSION QUESTIONS

1. What is an investment schedule and how does it differ from an investment demand curve? LO25.2
2. Why does equilibrium real GDP occur where $C + I_g$ = GDP in a private closed economy? What happens to real GDP when $C + I_g$ exceeds GDP? When $C + I_g$ is less than GDP? What two expenditure components of real GDP are purposely excluded in a private closed economy? LO25.3
3. Why is saving called a *leakage*? Why is planned investment called an *injection*? Why must saving equal planned investment at equilibrium GDP in the private closed economy? Are unplanned changes in inventories rising, falling, or constant at equilibrium GDP? Explain. LO25.4
4. Other things equal, what effect will each of the following changes independently have on the equilibrium level of real GDP in the private closed economy? LO25.5
   a. A decline in the real interest rate.
   b. An overall decrease in the expected rate of return on investment.
   c. A sizable, sustained increase in stock prices.
5. Depict graphically the aggregate expenditures model for a private closed economy. Now show a decrease in the aggregate expenditures schedule and explain why the decline in real GDP in your diagram is greater than the decline in the aggregate expenditures schedule. What is the term used for the ratio of a decline in real GDP to the initial drop in aggregate expenditures? LO25.5
6. Assuming the economy is operating below its potential output, what is the impact of an increase in net exports on real GDP? Why is it difficult, if not impossible, for a country to boost its net exports by increasing its tariffs during a global recession? LO25.6
7. What is a recessionary expenditure gap? An inflationary expenditure gap? Which is associated with a positive GDP gap? A negative GDP gap? LO25.8
8. **LAST WORD** What is Say's law? How does it relate to the view held by classical economists that the economy generally will operate at a position on its production possibilities curve (Chapter 1)? Use production possibilities analysis to demonstrate Keynes's view on this matter.

AP REVIEW QUESTIONS

1. True or False: The aggregate expenditures model assumes flexible prices. LO25.1
2. If total spending is just sufficient to purchase an economy's output, then the economy is in LO25.3
   a. Short-run equilibrium.
   b. Recession.
   c. Debt.
   d. Expansion.
   e. Full employment equilibrium.
3. True or False: If spending exceeds output, real GDP will decline as firms cut back on production. LO25.3
4. If the marginal propensity to consume is .2 and investment increases by \$3 billion, equilibrium real GDP will increase by a maximum of: LO25.5
   a. \$2 billion.
   b. \$3 billion.
   c. \$8 billion.
   d. \$15 billion.
   e. \$30 billion.
5. A depression abroad will tend to ________ our exports, which in turn will ________ net exports, which in turn will ________ equilibrium real GDP. LO25.6
   a. Reduce; reduce; reduce.
   b. Increase; increase; increase.
   c. Reduce; increase; increase.
   d. Increase; reduce; reduce.
   e. Reduce, reduce, increase.
6. Explain graphically the determination of equilibrium GDP for a private economy through the aggregate expenditures model, including consumption and investment. Now add government purchases (any amount you choose) to your graph, showing its impact on equilibrium GDP. Finally, add taxation (any amount of lump-sum tax that is equal to or less than the increase in government expenditures) to your graph and show its effect on equilibrium GDP. Looking at your graph, determine whether equilibrium GDP has increased, decreased, or stayed the same given the sizes of the government purchases and taxes that you selected. LO25.7
7. The economy's current level of equilibrium GDP is \$780 billion. The full employment level of GDP is \$800 billion. The multiplier is 4. Given those facts, we know that the economy faces LO25.8
   a. An inflationary gap of \$5 billion.
   b. An inflationary gap of \$10 billion.
   c. An inflationary gap of \$20 billion.
   d. A recessionary gap of \$10 billion.
   e. A recessionary gap of \$20 billion.
8. If an economy has an inflationary expenditure gap, the government could attempt to bring the economy back toward the full-employment level of GDP by ________ taxes or ________ government expenditures. LO25.8
   a. Increasing; increasing.
   b. Increasing; decreasing.
   c. Decreasing; not changing.
   d. Decreasing; decreasing.
   e. Not changing, increasing.
9. If produced output exceeds the sum of desired consumption, investment, and government expenditures in a closed economy, which of the following will occur with inventories and future GDP? LO25.3

	Inventories	Future GDP
a.	Decrease	Increase
b.	No change	No change
c.	Increase	Decrease
d.	Increase	Increase
e.	Decrease	No change

10. For each of the following changes in the aggregate expenditure model, indicate whether equilibrium GDP will increase, decrease, or remain the same. LO25.5–25.7
    a. Increase in lump sum taxes
    b. Increase in government spending
    c. Increase in imports
    d. Increase in the marginal propensity to consume
    e. Increase in autonomous consumption
    f. Increase in desired investment

PROBLEMS

1. Assuming the level of investment is $16 billion and independent of the level of total output, complete the following table and determine the equilibrium levels of output and employment in this private closed economy. What are the sizes of the MPC and MPS? **LO25.3**

Possible Levels of Employment, Millions	Real Domestic Output (GDP = DI), Billions	Consumption, Billions	Saving, Billions
40	$240	$244	$ ____
45	260	260	____
50	280	276	____
55	300	292	____
60	320	308	____
65	340	324	____
70	360	340	____
75	380	356	____
80	400	372	____

2. Using the consumption and saving data in problem 1 and assuming investment is $16 billion, what are saving and planned investment at the $380 billion level of domestic output? What are saving and actual investment at that level? What are saving and planned investment at the $300 billion level of domestic output? What are the levels of saving and actual investment? In which direction and by what amount will unplanned investment change as the economy moves from the $380 billion level of GDP to the equilibrium level of real GDP? From the $300 billion level of real GDP to the equilibrium level of GDP? **LO25.4**
3. By how much will GDP change if firms increase their investment by $8 billion and the MPC is 0.80? If the MPC is 0.67? **LO25.5**
4. Suppose that a certain country has an MPC of 0.9 and a real GDP of $400 billion. If its investment spending decreases by $4 billion, what will be its new level of real GDP? **LO25.5**
5. The data in columns 1 and 2 in the table below are for a private closed economy. **LO25.6**
   a. Use columns 1 and 2 to determine the equilibrium GDP for this hypothetical economy.
   b. Now open up this economy to international trade by including the export and import figures of columns 3 and 4. Fill in columns 5 and 6 and determine the equilibrium GDP for the open economy. What is the change in equilibrium GDP caused by the addition of net exports?
   c. Given the original $20 billion level of exports, what would be net exports and the equilibrium GDP if imports were $10 billion greater at each level of GDP?
   d. What is the multiplier in this example?
6. Assume that, without taxes, the consumption schedule of an economy is as follows. **LO25.7**

GDP, Billions	Consumption, Billions
$100	$120
200	200
300	280
400	360
500	440
600	520
700	600

   a. Graph this consumption schedule and determine the MPC.
   b. Assume now that a lump-sum tax is imposed such that the government collects $10 billion in taxes at all levels of GDP. Graph the resulting consumption schedule and compare the MPC and the multiplier with those of the pretax consumption schedule.
7. Refer to columns 1 and 6 in the table for problem 5. Incorporate government into the table by assuming that it plans to tax and spend $20 billion at each possible level of GDP. Also assume that the tax is a personal tax and that government spending does not induce a shift in the private aggregate expenditures schedule. What is the change in equilibrium GDP caused by the addition of government? **LO25.7**
8. **ADVANCED ANALYSIS** Assume that the consumption schedule for a private open economy is such that consumption $C = 50 + 0.8Y$. Assume further that planned investment I_g and net exports X_n are independent of the level of real GDP and constant at $I_g = 30$ and $X_n = 10$. Recall also that, in equilibrium, the

(1) Real Domestic Output (GDP = DI), Billions	(2) Aggregate Expenditures, Private Closed Economy, Billions	(3) Exports, Billions	(4) Imports, Billions	(5) Net Exports, Billions	(6) Aggregate Expenditures, Private Open Economy, Billions
$200	$240	$20	$30	$ ____	$ ____
250	280	20	30	____	____
300	320	20	30	____	____
350	360	20	30	____	____
400	400	20	30	____	____
450	440	20	30	____	____
500	480	20	30	____	____
550	520	20	30	____	____

real output produced (Y) is equal to aggregate expenditures: $Y = C + I_g + X_n$. **LO25.7**

a. Calculate the equilibrium level of income or real GDP for this economy.1

b. What happens to equilibrium Y if I_g changes to 10? What does this outcome reveal about the size of the multiplier?

9. Refer to the accompanying table in answering the questions that follow: **LO25.8**

(1) Possible Levels of Employment, Millions	(2) Real Domestic Output, Millions	(3) Aggregate Expenditures ($C_a + I_g + X_n + G$), Millions
90	$500	$520
100	550	560
110	600	600
120	650	640
130	700	680

a. If full employment in this economy is 130 million, will there be an inflationary expenditure gap or a recessionary expenditure gap? What will be the consequence of this gap? By how much would aggregate expenditures in column 3 have to change at each level of GDP to eliminate the inflationary expenditure gap or the recessionary expenditure gap? What is the multiplier in this example?

b. Will there be an inflationary expenditure gap or a recessionary expenditure gap if the full-employment level of output is $500 billion? By how much would aggregate expenditures in column 3 have to change at each level of GDP to eliminate the gap? What is the multiplier in this example?

c. Assuming that investment, net exports, and government expenditures do not change with changes in real GDP, what are the sizes of the MPC, the MPS, and the multiplier?

10. Answer the following questions, which relate to the aggregate expenditures model: **LO25.8**

a. If C_a is $100, I_g is $50, X_n is −$10, and G is $30, what is the economy's equilibrium GDP?

b. If real GDP in an economy is currently $200, C_a is $100, I_g is $50, X_n is −$10, and G is $30, will the economy's real GDP rise, fall, or stay the same?

c. Suppose that full-employment (and full-capacity) output in an economy is $200. If C_a is $150, I_g is $50, X_n is −$10, and G is $30, what will be the macroeconomic result?

26 Chapter

Aggregate Demand and Aggregate Supply

Learning Objectives

LO26.1 Define aggregate demand (AD) and explain how its downward slope is the result of the real-balances effect, the interest-rate effect, and the foreign purchases effect.

LO26.2 Explain the factors that cause changes (shifts) in AD.

LO26.3 Define aggregate supply (AS) and explain how it differs in the immediate short run, the short run, and the long run.

LO26.4 Explain the factors that cause changes (shifts) in AS.

LO26.5 Discuss how AD and AS determine an economy's equilibrium price level and level of real GDP.

LO26.6 Describe how the AD-AS model explains periods of demand-pull inflation, cost-push inflation, and recession.

LO26.7 (Appendix) Identify how the aggregate demand curve relates to the aggregate expenditures model.

AP Chapter Focus

During the recession of 2007–2009, the economic terms *aggregate demand* and *aggregate supply* moved from the obscurity of economic journals and textbooks to the spotlight of national newspapers, websites, radio, and television.

The media and public asked: Why had *aggregate demand* declined, producing the deepest recession and highest rate of unemployment since 1982? Why hadn't the reductions in interest rates by the Federal Reserve boosted *aggregate demand*? Would the federal government's $787 billion stimulus package increase *aggregate demand* and reduce unemployment, as intended? Would a resurgence of oil prices and other energy prices reduce *aggregate supply*, choking off an economic expansion?

Aggregate demand and aggregate supply are the featured elements of the **aggregate demand–aggregate supply model (AD-AS model)**, the focus of this chapter. The aggregate expenditures model of the previous chapter is an immediate-short-run model, in which prices are assumed to be fixed. In contrast, the AD-AS model in this chapter is a "variable price–variable output" model that allows both the price level and level of real GDP to change. It can also show longer time horizons, distinguishing between the immediate short run, the short run, and the long run. Further, in subsequent chapters, we will see that the AD-AS model easily depicts fiscal and monetary policies such as those used in 2008 and 2009 to try to halt the downward slide of the economy and promote its recovery.

AP Aggregate Demand

LO26.1 Define aggregate demand (AD) and explain how its downward slope is the result of the real-balances effect, the interest-rate effect, and the foreign purchases effect.

Aggregate demand is a schedule or curve that shows the amount of a nation's output (real GDP) that buyers collectively desire to purchase at each possible price level. These buyers include the nation's households, businesses, and government along with consumers located abroad (households, businesses, and governments in other nations). The relationship between the price level (as measured by the GDP price index) and the amount of real GDP demanded is inverse or negative: When the price level rises, the quantity of real GDP demanded decreases; when the price level falls, the quantity of real GDP demanded increases.

Aggregate Demand Curve

The inverse relationship between the price level and real GDP is shown in Figure 26.1, where the aggregate demand curve AD slopes downward, as does the demand curve for an individual product.

Why the downward slope? The explanation is *not* the same as that for why the demand for a single product slopes downward. That explanation centered on the income effect and the substitution effect. When the price of an *individual* product falls, the consumer's (constant) nominal income allows a larger purchase of the product (the income effect). And, as price falls, the consumer wants to buy more of the product because it becomes relatively less expensive than other goods (the substitution effect).

But these explanations do not work for aggregates. In Figure 26.1, when the economy moves down its aggregate demand curve, it moves to a lower general price level. But our circular flow model tells us that when consumers pay lower prices for goods and services, less nominal income flows to resource suppliers in the form of wages, rents, interest, and profits. As a result, a decline in the price level does not necessarily mean an increase in the nominal income of the economy as a whole. Thus, a decline in the price level need not produce an income effect, where more output is purchased because lower nominal prices leave buyers with greater real income.

Similarly, in Figure 26.1, prices in general are falling as we move down the aggregate demand curve, so the rationale for the substitution effect (where more of a specific product is purchased because it becomes cheaper relative to all other products) is not applicable. There is no *overall* substitution effect among domestically produced goods when the price level falls.

If the conventional substitution and income effects do not explain the downward slope of the aggregate demand curve, what does? The explanation rests on three effects of a price-level change.

AP FIGURE 26.1 **The aggregate demand curve.** The downsloping aggregate demand curve AD indicates an inverse (or negative) relationship between the price level and the amount of real output purchased.

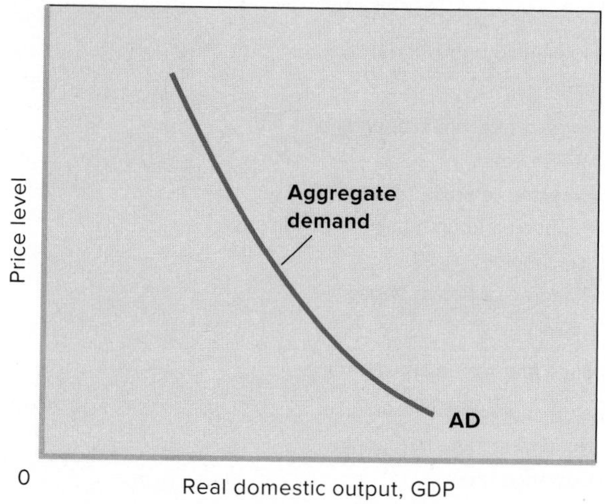

Real-Balances Effect A change in the price level produces a **real-balances effect.** Here is how it works: A higher price level reduces the real value or purchasing power of the public's accumulated savings balances. In particular, the real value of assets with fixed money values, such as savings accounts or bonds, diminishes. Because a higher price level erodes the purchasing power of such assets, the public is poorer in real terms and will reduce its spending. A household might buy a new car or a plasma TV if the purchasing power of its financial asset balances is, say, \$50,000. But if inflation erodes the purchasing power of its asset balances to \$30,000, the household may defer its purchase. So a higher price level means less consumption spending.

Interest-Rate Effect The aggregate demand curve also slopes downward because of the **interest-rate effect.** When we draw an aggregate demand curve, we assume that the supply of money in the economy is fixed. But when the price level rises, consumers need more money for purchases and businesses need more money to meet their payrolls and to buy other resources.

A $10 bill will do when the price of an item is $10, but a $10 bill plus a $1 bill is needed when the item costs $11. In short, a higher price level increases the demand for money. So, given a fixed supply of money, an increase in money demand will drive up the price paid for its use. That price is the interest rate.

Higher interest rates curtail investment spending and interest-sensitive consumption spending. Firms that expect a 6 percent rate of return on a potential purchase of capital will find that investment potentially profitable when the interest rate is, say, 5 percent. But the investment will be unprofitable and will not be made when the interest rate has risen to 7 percent. Similarly, consumers may decide not to purchase a new house or new automobile when the interest rate on loans goes up. So, by increasing the demand for money and consequently the interest rate, a higher price level reduces the amount of real output demanded.

Foreign Purchases Effect The final reason why the aggregate demand curve slopes downward is the **foreign purchases effect.** When the U.S. price level rises relative to foreign price levels (and exchange rates do not respond quickly or completely), foreigners buy fewer U.S. goods and Americans buy more foreign goods. Therefore, U.S. exports fall and U.S. imports rise. In short, the rise in the price level reduces the quantity of U.S. goods demanded as net exports.

These three effects, of course, work in the opposite direction for a decline in the price level. A decline in the price level increases consumption through the real-balances effect and interest-rate effect, increases investment through the interest-rate effect, and raises net exports by increasing exports and decreasing imports through the foreign purchases effect.

AP Changes in Aggregate Demand

LO26.2 Explain the factors that cause changes (shifts) in AD.

Other things equal, a change in the price level will change the amount of aggregate spending and therefore change the amount of real GDP demanded by the economy. Movements along a fixed aggregate demand curve represent these changes in real GDP. However, if one or more of those "other things" change, the entire aggregate demand curve will shift. We call these other things **determinants of aggregate demand** or, less formally, *aggregate demand shifters*. They are listed in Figure 26.2.

Changes in aggregate demand involve two components:

- A change in one of the determinants of aggregate demand that directly changes the amount of real GDP demanded.
- A multiplier effect that produces a greater ultimate change in aggregate demand than the initiating change in spending.

In Figure 26.2, the full rightward shift of the curve from AD_1 to AD_2 shows an increase in aggregate demand, separated into these two components. The horizontal distance between AD_1 and the broken curve to its right illustrates an initial increase in spending, say, $5 billion of added investment. If the economy's MPC is 0.75, for example, then the simple multiplier

AP **FIGURE 26.2 Changes in aggregate demand.** A change in one or more of the listed determinants of aggregate demand will shift the aggregate demand curve. The rightward shift from AD_1 to AD_2 represents an increase in aggregate demand; the leftward shift from AD_1 to AD_3 shows a decrease in aggregate demand. The vertical distances between AD_1 and the dashed lines represent the initial changes in spending. Through the multiplier effect, that spending produces the full shifts of the curves.

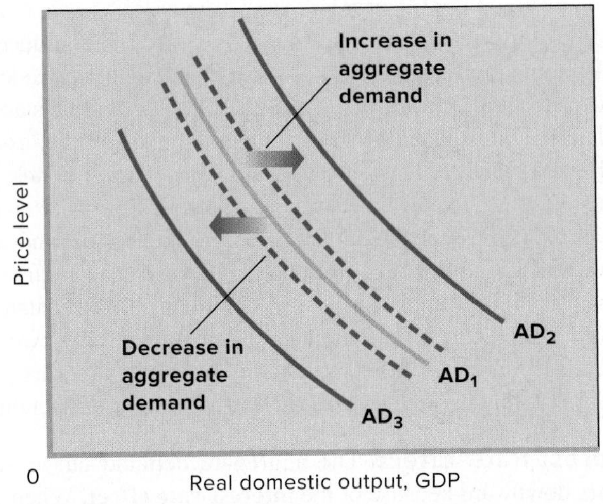

Determinants of Aggregate Demand: Factors That Shift the Aggregate Demand Curve

1. Change in consumer spending
   a. Consumer wealth
   b. Consumer expectations
   c. Household borrowing
   d. Taxes
2. Change in investment spending
   a. Interest rates
   b. Expected returns
      - Expected future business conditions
      - Technology
      - Degree of excess capacity
      - Business taxes
3. Change in government spending
4. Change in net export spending
   a. National income abroad
   b. Exchange rates

is 4. So the aggregate demand curve shifts rightward from AD_1 to AD_2—four times the distance between AD_1 and the broken line. The multiplier process magnifies the initial change in spending into successive rounds of new consumption spending. After the shift, \$20 billion (= \$5 × 4) of additional real goods and services are demanded at each price level.

Similarly, the leftward shift of the curve from AD_1 to AD_3 shows a decrease in aggregate demand, the lesser amount of real GDP demanded at each price level. It also involves the initial decline in spending (shown as the horizontal distance between AD_1 and the dashed line to its left), followed by multiplied declines in consumption spending and the ultimate leftward shift to AD_3.

Let's examine each of the determinants of aggregate demand listed in Figure 26.2.

Consumer Spending

Even when the U.S. price level is constant, domestic consumers may alter their purchases of U.S.-produced real output. If those consumers decide to buy more output at each price level, the aggregate demand curve will shift to the right, as from AD_1 to AD_2 in Figure 26.2. If they decide to buy less output, the aggregate demand curve will shift to the left, as from AD_1 to AD_3.

Several factors other than a change in the price level may change consumer spending and therefore shift the aggregate demand curve. As Figure 26.2 shows, those factors are real consumer wealth, consumer expectations, household debt, and taxes. Because our discussion here parallels that of Chapter 24, we will be brief.

Consumer Wealth Consumer wealth is the total dollar value of all assets owned by consumers in the economy less the dollar value of their liabilities (debts). Assets include stocks, bonds, and real estate. Liabilities include mortgages, car loans, and credit card balances.

Consumer wealth sometimes changes suddenly and unexpectedly due to surprising changes in asset values. An unforeseen increase in the stock market is a good example. The increase in wealth prompts pleasantly surprised consumers to save less and buy more out of their current incomes than they had previously been planning. The resulting increase in consumer spending—the so-called *wealth effect*—shifts the aggregate demand curve to the right. In contrast, an unexpected decline in asset values will cause an unanticipated reduction in consumer wealth at each price level. As consumers tighten their belts in response to the bad news, a "reverse wealth effect" sets in. Unpleasantly surprised consumers increase savings and reduce consumption, thereby shifting the aggregate demand curve to the left.

Household Borrowing Consumers can increase their consumption spending by borrowing. Doing so shifts the aggregate demand curve to the right. By contrast, a decrease in borrowing for consumption purposes shifts the aggregate demand curve to the left. The aggregate demand curve will also shift to the left if consumers increase their savings rates to pay off their debts. With more money flowing to debt repayment, consumption expenditures decline and the AD curve shifts left.

Consumer Expectations Changes in expectations about the future may alter consumer spending. When people expect their future real incomes to rise, they tend to spend more of their current incomes. Thus, current consumption spending increases (current saving falls) and the aggregate demand curve shifts to the right. Similarly, a widely held expectation of surging inflation in the near future may increase aggregate demand today because consumers will want to buy products before their prices escalate. Conversely, expectations of lower future income or lower future prices may reduce current consumption and shift the aggregate demand curve to the left.

Personal Taxes A reduction in personal income tax rates raises take-home income and increases consumer purchases at each possible price level. Tax cuts shift the aggregate demand curve to the right. Tax increases reduce consumption spending and shift the curve to the left.

Investment Spending

Investment spending (the purchase of capital goods) is a second major determinant of aggregate demand. A decline in investment spending at each price level will shift the aggregate demand curve to the left. An increase in investment spending will shift it to the right. In Chapter 24 we saw that investment spending depends on the real interest rate and the expected return from investment.

Real Interest Rates Other things equal, an increase in real interest rates will raise borrowing costs, lower investment spending, and reduce aggregate demand. We are not referring here to the "interest-rate effect" that results from a change in the price level. Instead, we are identifying a change in the real interest rate resulting from, say, a change in a nation's money supply. An increase in the money supply lowers the interest rate, thereby increasing investment and aggregate demand. A decrease in the money supply raises the interest rate, reducing investment and decreasing aggregate demand.

Expected Returns Higher expected returns on investment projects will increase the demand for capital goods and shift the aggregate demand curve to the right. Alternatively, declines in expected returns will decrease investment and shift the curve to the left. Expected returns, in turn, are influenced by several factors:

- ***Expectations about future business conditions*** If firms are optimistic about future business conditions, they are more likely to forecast high rates of return on current investment and therefore may invest more today. On the other hand, if they think the economy will deteriorate in the future, they will forecast low rates of return and perhaps will invest less today.

- ***Technology*** New and improved technologies enhance expected returns on investment and thus increase aggregate demand. For example, recent advances in microbiology have motivated pharmaceutical companies to establish new labs and production facilities.
- ***Degree of excess capacity*** A rise in excess capacity—unused capital—will reduce the expected return on new investment and hence decrease aggregate demand. Other things equal, firms operating factories at well below capacity have little incentive to build new factories. But when firms discover that their excess capacity is dwindling or has completely disappeared, their expected returns on new investment in factories and capital equipment rise. Thus, they increase their investment spending, and the aggregate demand curve shifts to the right.
- ***Business taxes*** An increase in business taxes will reduce after-tax profits from capital investment and lower expected returns. So investment and aggregate demand will decline. A decrease in business taxes will have the opposite effects.

The variability of interest rates and expected returns makes investment highly volatile. In contrast to consumption, investment spending rises and falls often, independent of changes in total income. Investment, in fact, is the least stable component of aggregate demand.

Government Spending

Government purchases are the third determinant of aggregate demand. An increase in government purchases (for example, more transportation projects) will shift the aggregate demand curve to the right, as long as tax collections and interest rates do not change as a result. In contrast, a reduction in government spending (for example, less military equipment) will shift the curve to the left.

Net Export Spending

The final determinant of aggregate demand is net export spending. Other things equal, higher U.S. *exports* mean an increased foreign demand for U.S. goods. So a rise in net exports (higher exports relative to imports) shifts the aggregate demand curve to the right. In contrast, a decrease in U.S. net exports shifts the aggregate demand curve leftward. (These changes in net exports are *not* those prompted by a change in the U.S. price level—those associated with the foreign purchases effect. The changes here are shifts of the AD curve, not movements along the AD curve.)

What might cause net exports to change, other than the price level? Two possibilities are changes in national income abroad and changes in exchange rates.

National Income Abroad Rising national income abroad encourages foreigners to buy more products, some of which are made in the United States. U.S. net exports thus rise, and the U.S. aggregate demand curve shifts to the right. Declines in national income abroad do the opposite: They reduce U.S. net exports and shift the U.S. aggregate demand curve to the left.

Exchange Rates Changes in the dollar's exchange rate—the price of foreign currencies in terms of the U.S. dollar—may affect U.S. exports and therefore aggregate demand. Suppose the dollar depreciates in terms of the euro (meaning the euro appreciates in terms of the dollar). The new, relatively lower value of dollars and higher value of euros enables European consumers to obtain more dollars with each euro. From their perspective, U.S. goods are now less expensive; it takes fewer euros to obtain them. So European consumers buy more U.S. goods, and U.S. exports rise. But American consumers can now obtain fewer euros for each dollar. Because they must pay more dollars to buy European goods, Americans reduce their imports. U.S. exports rise and U.S. imports fall. Conclusion: Dollar depreciation increases net exports (imports go down; exports go up) and therefore increases aggregate demand.

Dollar appreciation has the opposite effects: Net exports fall (imports go up; exports go down) and aggregate demand declines.

AP QUICK REVIEW 26.1

- ✓ Aggregate demand is a schedule or curve that shows the amount of a nation's output (real GDP) that buyers collectively desire to purchase at each possible price level. The components of aggregate demand are consumption, investment, government expenditures, and net exports.
- ✓ The aggregate demand curve is downward sloping for three reasons. First, a decrease in the price level creates a "real balance effect" that increases real wealth and personal consumption. Second, a lower price level tends to be associated with lower interest rates that increase desired investment and other interest-sensitive expenditures. Finally, a lower price level increases net exports as a country's goods are more attractive to foreigners and the country imports less of the relatively expensive foreign goods.
- ✓ Changes in one or more of the determinants of aggregate demand (Figure 26.2) alter the amounts of real GDP demanded at each price level; they shift the aggregate demand curve. The multiplier effect magnifies initial changes in spending into larger changes in aggregate demand. These determinants can include government spending, taxes, interest rate changes at all price levels.
- ✓ An increase in aggregate demand is shown as a rightward shift of the aggregate demand curve; a decrease, as a leftward shift of the curve.

AP Aggregate Supply

LO26.3 Define aggregate supply (AS) and explain how it differs in the immediate short run, the short run, and the long run.

Aggregate supply is a schedule or curve showing the relationship between a nation's price level and the amount of real domestic output that firms in the economy produce. This relationship varies depending on the time horizon and how quickly output prices and input prices can change. We will define three time horizons:

- In the *immediate short run*, both input prices as well as output prices are fixed.
- In the *short run*, input prices are fixed, but output prices can vary.
- In the *long run*, input prices as well as output prices can vary.

In Chapter 20, we discussed both the immediate short run and the long run in terms of how an automobile maker named Buzzer Auto responds to changes in the demand for its new car, the Prion. Here we extend the logic of that chapter to the economy as a whole to discuss how total output varies with the price level in the immediate short run, the short run, and the long run. As you will see, the relationship between the price level and total output is different in each of the three time horizons because input prices are stickier than output prices. Although both sets of prices become more flexible as time passes, output prices usually adjust more rapidly.

Aggregate Supply in the Immediate Short Run

Depending on the type of firm, the immediate short run can last anywhere from a few days to a few months. It lasts as long as *both* input prices and output prices stay fixed. Input prices are fixed in both the immediate short run and the short run by contractual agreements. In particular, 75 percent of the average firm's costs are wages and salaries—and these are almost always fixed by labor contracts for months or years at a time. As a result, they are usually fixed for a much longer duration than output prices, which can begin to change within a few days or a few months depending on the type of firm.

That being said, output prices are also typically fixed in the immediate short run. This is most often caused by firms setting fixed prices for their customers and then agreeing to supply whatever quantity demanded results at those fixed prices. For instance, once an appliance manufacturer sets its annual list prices for refrigerators, stoves, ovens, and microwaves, it is obligated to supply however many or few appliances customers want to buy at those prices. Similarly, a catalog company is obliged to sell however much customers want to buy of its products at the prices listed in its current catalog. And it is obligated to supply those quantities demanded until it sends out its next catalog.

With output prices fixed and firms selling however much customers want to purchase at those fixed prices, the **immediate-short-run aggregate supply curve** AS_{ISR} is a horizontal line, as shown in Figure 26.3. The AS_{ISR} curve is horizontal at the overall price level P_1, which is calculated from all of the individual prices set by the various firms in the economy. Its horizontal shape implies that the total amount of output supplied in the economy depends directly on the volume of spending that results at price level P_1. If total spending is low at price level P_1, firms will supply a small amount of output to match the low level of spending. If total spending is high at price level P_1, they will supply a high level of output to match the high level of spending. The amount of output that results may be higher than or lower than the economy's full-employment output level Q_f.

Notice, however, that firms will respond in this manner to changes in total spending only as long as output prices remain fixed. As soon as firms are able to change their product prices, they can respond to changes in aggregate spending not only by increasing or decreasing output but also by raising or lowering prices. This is the situation that leads to the upsloping short-run aggregate supply curve that we discuss next.

Aggregate Supply in the Short Run

The short run begins after the immediate short run ends. As it relates to macroeconomics, the short run is a period of time during which output prices are flexible, but input prices are either totally fixed or highly inflexible.

These assumptions about output prices and input prices are general—they relate to the economy in the aggregate. Naturally, some input prices are more flexible than others.

AP **FIGURE 26.3** **Aggregate supply in the immediate short run.** In the immediate short run, the aggregate supply curve AS_{ISR} is horizontal at the economy's current price level, P_1. With output prices fixed, firms collectively supply the level of output that is demanded at those prices.

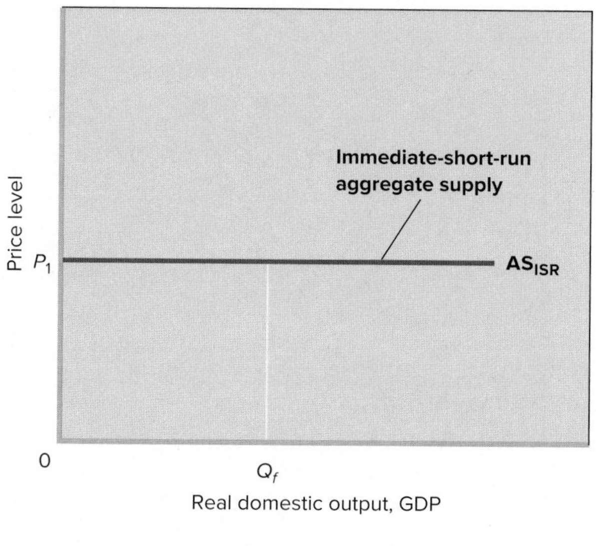

Since gasoline prices are quite flexible, a package delivery firm like UPS that uses gasoline as an input will have at least one very flexible input price. On the other hand, wages at UPS are set by five-year labor contracts negotiated with its drivers' union, the Teamsters. Because wages are the firm's largest and most important input cost, UPS faces overall input prices that are inflexible for several years at a time. Thus, its "short run"—the period when it can change its shipping prices but not its substantially fixed input prices—is actually quite long. Keep this example in mind as we derive the short-run aggregate supply for the entire economy. Its applicability does not depend on some arbitrary definition of how long the "short run" should be. Instead, the short run for which the model is relevant is any period of time during which output prices are flexible, but input prices are fixed or nearly fixed.

As illustrated in Figure 26.4, the **short-run aggregate supply curve** AS slopes upward because, with input prices fixed, changes in the price level will raise or lower real firm profits. To see how this works, consider an economy that has only a single multiproduct firm called Mega Buzzer and in which the firm's owners must receive a real profit of \$20 to produce the full-employment output of 100 units. Assume the owner's only input (aside from entrepreneurial talent) is 10 units of hired labor at \$8 per worker, for a total wage cost of \$80. Also, assume that the 100 units of output sell for \$1 per unit, so total revenue is \$100. Mega Buzzer's nominal profit is \$20 (= \$100 − \$80), and using the \$1 price to designate the base-price index of 100, its real profit is also \$20 (= \$20/1.00). Well and good; the full-employment output is produced.

FIGURE 26.4 The aggregate supply curve (short run). The upsloping aggregate supply curve AS indicates a direct (or positive) relationship between the price level and the amount of real output that firms will offer for sale. The AS curve is relatively flat below the full-employment output because unemployed resources and unused capacity allow firms to respond to price-level rises with large increases in real output. It is relatively steep beyond the full-employment output because resource shortages and capacity limitations make it difficult to expand real output as the price level rises.

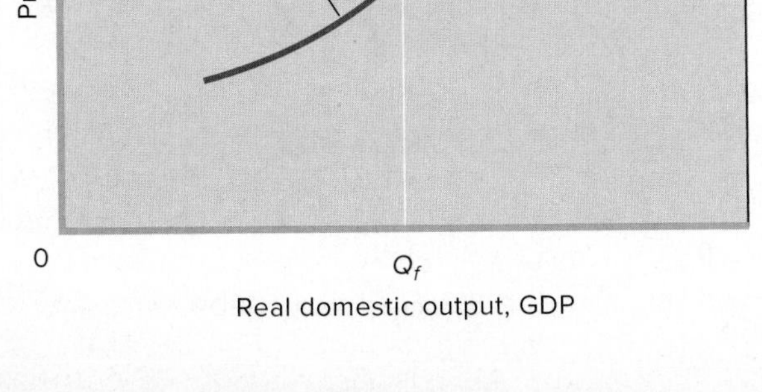

Next consider what will happen if the price of Mega Buzzer's output doubles. The doubling of the price level will boost total revenue from \$100 to \$200, but since we are discussing the short run during which input prices are fixed, the \$8 nominal wage for each of the 10 workers will remain unchanged so that total costs stay at \$80. Nominal profit will rise from \$20 (= \$100 − \$80) to \$120 (= \$200 − \$80). Dividing that \$120 profit by the new price index of 200 (= 2.0 in hundredths), we find that Mega Buzzer's real profit is now \$60. The rise in the real reward from \$20 to \$60 prompts the firm (economy) to produce more output. Conversely, price-level declines reduce real profits and cause the firm (economy) to reduce its output. So, in the short run, there is a direct, or positive, relationship between the price level and real output. When the price level rises, real output rises and when the price level falls, real output falls. The result is an upsloping short-run aggregate supply curve.

Notice, however, that the upslope of the short-run aggregate supply curve is not constant. It is flatter at outputs below the full-employment output level Q_f and steeper at outputs above it. This has to do with the fact that per-unit production costs underlie the short-run aggregate supply curve. Recall from Chapter 23 that

$$\text{Per-unit production cost} = \frac{\text{total input cost}}{\text{units of output}}$$

The per-unit production cost of any specific level of output establishes that output's price level because the associated price level must cover all the costs of production, including profit "costs."

As the economy expands in the short run, per-unit production costs generally rise because of reduced efficiency. But the extent of that rise depends on where the economy is operating relative to its capacity. When the economy is operating below its full-employment output, it has large amounts of unused machinery and equipment and large numbers of unemployed workers. Firms can put these idle human and property resources back to work with little upward pressure on per-unit production costs. And as output expands, few if any shortages of inputs or production bottlenecks will arise to raise per-unit production costs. That is why the slope of the short-run aggregate supply curve increases only slowly at output levels below the full-employment output level Q_f.

On the other hand, when the economy is operating beyond Q_f, the vast majority of its available resources are already employed. Adding more workers to a relatively fixed number of highly used capital resources such as plant and equipment creates congestion in the workplace and reduces the efficiency (on average) of workers. Adding more capital, given the limited number of available workers, leaves equipment idle and reduces the efficiency of capital. Adding more land resources when capital and labor are highly constrained reduces the efficiency of land resources. Under these circumstances, total input costs rise more rapidly than total output. The result is rapidly rising per-unit production costs that give the short-run aggregate supply curve its rapidly increasing slope at output levels beyond Q_f.

Aggregate Supply in the Long Run

In macroeconomics, the long run is the time horizon over which both input prices as well as output prices are flexible. It begins after the short run ends. Depending on the type of firm and industry, this may be from a couple of weeks to several years in the future. But for the economy as a whole, it is the time horizon over which all output and input prices—including wage rates—are fully flexible.

The **long-run aggregate supply curve** AS_{LR} is vertical at the economy's full-employment output Q_f, as shown in Figure 26.5. The vertical curve means that in the long run the economy will produce the full-employment output level no matter what the price level is. How can this be? Shouldn't higher prices cause firms to increase output? The explanation lies in the fact that in the long run when both input prices as well as output prices are flexible, profit levels will always adjust to give firms exactly the right profit incentive to produce exactly the full-employment output level, Q_f.

To see why this is true, look back at the short-run aggregate supply curve AS shown in Figure 26.4. Suppose that the economy starts out producing at the full-employment output level Q_f and that the price level at that moment has an index value of $P = 100$. Now suppose that output prices double, so that the price index goes to $P = 200$. We previously demonstrated for our single-firm economy that this doubling of the price level would cause profits to rise in the short run and that the higher profits would motivate the firm to increase output.

This outcome, however, is totally dependent on the fact that input prices are fixed in the short run. Consider what will happen in the long run when they are free to change. Firms can only produce beyond the full-employment output level by running factories and businesses at extremely high rates. This creates a great deal of demand for the economy's limited supply of productive resources. In particular, labor is in great demand because the only way to produce beyond full employment is if workers are working overtime.

As time passes and input prices are free to change, the high demand will start to raise input prices. In particular, overworked employees will demand and receive raises as employers scramble to deal with the labor shortages that arise when the economy is producing at above its full-employment output level. As input prices increase, firm profits will begin to fall. And as they decline, so does the motive firms have to produce more than the full-employment output level. This process of rising input prices and falling profits continues until the rise in input prices exactly matches the initial change in output prices (in our example, they both double). When that happens, firm profits in real terms return to their original level so that firms are once again motivated to produce at exactly the full-employment output level. This adjustment process means that in the long run the economy will produce at full employment regardless of the price level (in our example, at either $P = 100$ or $P = 200$). That is why the long-run aggregate supply curve AS_{LR} is vertical above the full-employment output level. Every possible price level on the vertical axis is associated with the economy producing at the full-employment output level in the long run once input prices adjust to exactly match changes in output prices.

AP **FIGURE 26.5** **Aggregate supply in the long run.** The long-run aggregate supply curve AS_{LR} is vertical at the full-employment level of real GDP (Q_f) because in the long run wages and other input prices rise and fall to match changes in the price level. So price-level changes do not affect firms' profits and thus they create no incentive for firms to alter their output.

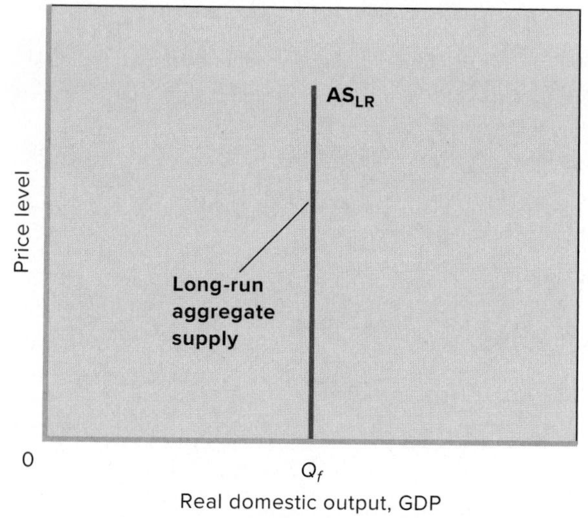

Focusing on the Short Run

The immediate-short-run aggregate supply curve, the short-run aggregate supply curve, and the long-run aggregate supply curve are all important. Each curve is appropriate to situations that match their respective assumptions about the flexibility of input and output prices. In the remainder of the book, we will have several different opportunities to refer to each curve. But our focus in the rest of this chapter and the several chapters that immediately follow will be on short-run aggregate supply curves, such as the AS curve shown in Figure 26.4. Indeed, unless explicitly stated otherwise, all references to "aggregate supply" are to the AS curve and to aggregate supply in the short run.

Our emphasis on the short-run aggregate supply curve AS stems from out interest in understanding the business cycle in the simplest possible way. It is a fact that real-world economies typically manifest simultaneous changes in both their price levels and their levels of real output. The upsloping short-run AS curve is the only version of aggregate supply that can handle simultaneous movements in both of these variables. By contrast, the price level is assumed fixed in the immediate-short-run version of aggregate supply illustrated in Figure 26.3 and the economy's output is always equal to the full-employment output level in the long-run version of aggregate supply shown in Figure 26.5. This renders these versions of the aggregate supply curve less useful as part of a core model for analyzing business cycles and demonstrating the short-run government policies designed to deal with them. In our current discussion, we will reserve use of the immediate short run and the long run for specific, clearly identified situations. Later in the book we will explore how the short-run and long-run AS curves are linked, and how that linkage adds several additional insights about business cycles and policy.

AP Changes in Aggregate Supply

LO26.4 Explain the factors that cause changes (shifts) in AS.

An existing aggregate supply curve identifies the relationship between the price level and real output, other things equal. But when one or more of these other things change, the curve itself shifts. The rightward shift of the curve from AS_1 to AS_2 in Figure 26.6 represents an increase in aggregate supply, indicating that firms are willing to produce and sell more real output at each price level. The leftward shift of the curve from AS_1 to AS_3 represents a decrease in aggregate supply. At each price level, firms produce less output than before.

Figure 26.6 lists the other things that cause a shift of the aggregate supply curve. Called the **determinants of aggregate supply** or *aggregate supply shifters*, they collectively position the aggregate supply curve and shift the curve when they change. Changes in these determinants raise or lower per-unit production costs *at each price level (or each level of output)*. These changes in per-unit production cost affect profits, thereby leading firms to alter the amount of output they are willing to produce *at each price level*. For example, firms may collectively offer \$9 trillion of real output at a price level of 1.0 (100 in index value), rather than \$8.8 trillion. Or they may offer \$7.5 trillion rather than \$8 trillion. The point is that when one of the determinants listed in Figure 26.6 changes, the aggregate supply curve shifts to the right or left. Changes that reduce per-unit production costs shift the aggregate supply curve to the right, as from AS_1 to AS_2; changes that increase per-unit production costs shift it to the left, as from AS_1 to AS_3. When per-unit production costs change for reasons other than changes in real output, the aggregate supply curve shifts.

The three aggregate supply determinants listed in Figure 26.6 require more discussion.

Input Prices

Input or resource prices—to be distinguished from the output prices that make up the price level—are a major ingredient of per-unit production costs and therefore a key determinant of aggregate supply. These resources can be either domestic or imported.

Domestic Resource Prices As stated earlier, wages and salaries make up about 75 percent of all business costs. Other things equal, decreases in wages reduce per-unit production costs. So when wages fall, the aggregate supply curve shifts to the right. Increases in wages shift the curve to the left. Examples:

- Labor supply increases because of substantial immigration. Wages and per-unit production costs fall, shifting the AS curve to the right.

AP **FIGURE 26.6** **Changes in aggregate supply.** A change in one or more of the listed determinants of aggregate supply will shift the aggregate supply curve. The rightward shift of the aggregate supply curve from AS_1 to AS_2 represents an increase in aggregate supply; the leftward shift of the curve from AS_1 to AS_3 shows a decrease in aggregate supply.

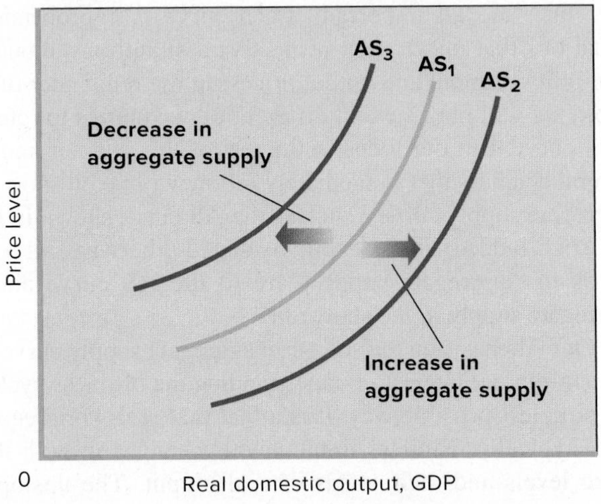

Determinants of Aggregate Supply: Factors That Shift the Aggregate Supply Curve
1. Change in input prices
a. Domestic resource prices
b. Prices of imported resources
2. Change in productivity
3. Change in legal-institutional environment
a. Business taxes and subsidies
b. Government regulations

- Labor supply decreases because a rapid increase in pension income causes many older workers to opt for early retirement. Wage rates and per-unit production costs rise, shifting the AS curve to the left.

Similarly, the aggregate supply curve shifts when the prices of land and capital inputs change. Examples:

- The price of machinery and equipment falls because of declines in the prices of steel and electronic components. Per-unit production costs decline, and the AS curve shifts to the right.
- The supply of available land resources expands through discoveries of mineral deposits, irrigation of land, or technical innovations that transform "nonresources" (say, vast desert lands) into valuable resources (productive lands). The price of land declines, per-unit production costs fall, and the AS curve shifts to the right.

Prices of Imported Resources Just as foreign demand for U.S. goods contributes to U.S. aggregate demand, resources imported from abroad (such as oil, tin, and copper) add to U.S. aggregate supply. Added supplies of resources—whether domestic or imported—typically reduce per-unit production costs. A decrease in the price of imported resources increases U.S. aggregate supply, while an increase in their price reduces U.S. aggregate supply.

A good example of the major effect that changing resource prices can have on aggregate supply is the oil price hikes of the 1970s. At that time, a group of oil-producing nations called the Organization of Petroleum Exporting Countries (OPEC) worked in concert to decrease oil production in order to raise the price of oil. The 10-fold increase in the price of oil that OPEC achieved during the 1970s drove per-unit production costs up and jolted the U.S. aggregate supply curve leftward. By contrast, a sharp decline in oil prices in the mid-1980s resulted in a rightward shift of the U.S. aggregate supply curve. In 1999 OPEC again reasserted itself, raising oil prices and therefore per-unit production costs for some U.S. producers including airlines and shipping companies like FedEx and UPS. In 2007 the price of oil shot upward, but this increase was attributed to greater demand rather than to decreases in supply caused by OPEC. But keep in mind that no matter what their cause, increases in the price of oil and other resources raise production costs and decrease aggregate supply.

Exchange-rate fluctuations are another factor that may alter the price of imported resources. Suppose that the dollar appreciates, enabling U.S. firms to obtain more foreign currency with each dollar. This means that domestic producers face a lower *dollar* price of imported resources. U.S. firms will respond by increasing their imports of foreign resources, thereby lowering their per-unit production costs at each level of output. Falling per-unit production costs will shift the U.S. aggregate supply curve to the right.

A depreciation of the dollar will have the opposite set of effects and will shift the aggregate supply curve to the left.

Productivity

The second major determinant of aggregate supply is **productivity,** which is a measure of the relationship between a nation's level of real output and the amount of resources used to produce that output. Productivity is a measure of average real output, or of real output per unit of input:

$$\text{Productivity} = \frac{\text{total output}}{\text{total inputs}}$$

An increase in productivity enables the economy to obtain more real output from its limited resources. An increase in productivity affects aggregate supply by reducing the per-unit cost of output (per-unit production cost). Suppose, for example, that real output is 10 units, that 5 units of input are needed to produce that quantity, and that the price of each input unit is \$2. Then

$$\text{Productivity} = \frac{\text{total output}}{\text{total inputs}} = \frac{10}{5} = 2$$

and

$$\text{Per-unit production cost} = \frac{\text{total input cost}}{\text{total output}}$$

$$= \frac{\$2 \times 5}{10} = \$1$$

Note that we obtain the total input cost by multiplying the unit input cost by the number of inputs used.

Now suppose productivity increases so that real output doubles to 20 units, while the price and quantity of the input remain constant at \$2 and 5 units. Using the above equations, we see that productivity rises from 2 to 4 and that the per-unit production cost of the output falls from \$1 to \$0.50. The doubled productivity has reduced the per-unit production cost by half.

By reducing the per-unit production cost, an increase in productivity shifts the aggregate supply curve to the right. The main source of productivity advance is improved production technology, often embodied within new plant and equipment that replaces old plant and equipment. Other sources of productivity increases are a better-educated and better-trained workforce, improved forms of business enterprises, and the reallocation of labor resources from lower-productivity to higher-productivity uses.

Much rarer, decreases in productivity increase per-unit production costs and therefore reduce aggregate supply (shift the curve to the left).

Legal-Institutional Environment

Changes in the legal-institutional setting in which businesses operate are the final determinant of aggregate supply. Such changes may alter the per-unit costs of output and, if so, shift the aggregate supply curve. Two changes of this type are (1) changes in taxes and subsidies and (2) changes in the extent of regulation.

Business Taxes and Subsidies Higher business taxes, such as sales, excise, and payroll taxes, increase per-unit costs and reduce short-run aggregate supply in much the same way as a wage increase does. An increase in such taxes paid by businesses will increase per-unit production costs and shift aggregate supply to the left.

Similarly, a business subsidy—a payment or tax break by government to producers—lowers production costs and increases short-run aggregate supply. For example, the federal government subsidizes firms that blend ethanol (derived from corn) with gasoline to increase the U.S. gasoline supply. This reduces the per-unit production cost of making blended gasoline. To the extent that this and other subsidies are successful, the aggregate supply curve shifts rightward.

Government Regulation It is usually costly for businesses to comply with government regulations. More regulation therefore tends to increase per-unit production costs and shift the aggregate supply curve to the left. "Supply-side" proponents of deregulation of the economy have argued forcefully that, by increasing efficiency and reducing the paperwork associated with complex regulations, deregulation will reduce per-unit costs and shift the aggregate supply curve to the right. Other economists are less certain. Deregulation that results in accounting manipulations, monopolization, and business failures is likely to shift the AS curve to the left rather than to the right.

AP QUICK REVIEW 26.2

- ✓ Aggregate supply (AS) is a schedule or curve showing the relationship between a nation's price level and the amount of real domestic output that firms in the economy will produce.
- ✓ The short-run AS curve (or simply the "aggregate supply curve") is upsloping; given fixed resource prices, higher output prices raise firm profits and encourage them to increase their output levels.
- ✓ The long run is the time horizon over which both input and output prices are flexible. The long-run AS curve is vertical at the full-employment level of real GDP. Given sufficient time, wages and other input, prices rise or fall to match any change in the price level.
- ✓ By altering per-unit production costs independent of changes in the level of output, changes in one or more of the determinants of AS (Figure 26.6) shift the AS curve.
- ✓ An increase in short-run AS is shown as a rightward shift; a decrease is shown as a leftward shift of the curve.

AP Equilibrium in the AD-AS Model

LO26.5 Discuss how AD and AS determine an economy's equilibrium price level and level of real GDP.

Of all the possible combinations of price levels and levels of real GDP, which combination will the economy gravitate toward, at least in the short run? **Figure 26.7 (Key Graph)** and its accompanying table provide the answer. Equilibrium occurs at the price level that equalizes the amounts of real output demanded and supplied. The intersection of the aggregate demand curve AD and the aggregate supply curve AS establishes the economy's **equilibrium price level** and **equilibrium real output.** So aggregate demand and aggregate supply *jointly* establish the price level and level of real GDP.

In Figure 26.7, the equilibrium price level and level of real output are 100 and $510 billion, respectively. To illustrate why, suppose the price level is 92 rather than 100. We see from the table that the lower price level will encourage businesses to produce real output of $502 billion. This is shown by point *a* on the AS curve in the graph. But as revealed by the table and point *b* on the aggregate demand curve, buyers will want to purchase $514 billion of real output at price level 92. Competition among buyers to purchase the lesser available real output of $502 billion will eliminate the $12 billion (= $514 billion − $502 billion) shortage and pull up the price level to 100.

As the table and graph show, the rise in the price level from 92 to 100 encourages producers to increase their real output from $502 billion to $510 billion and causes buyers to scale back their purchases from $514 billion to $510 billion. When equality occurs between the amounts of real output produced and purchased, as it does at price level 100, the economy has achieved equilibrium (here, at $510 billion of real GDP).

A final note: Although the equilibrium price level happens to be 100 in our example, nothing special is implied by that. Any price level can be an equilibrium price level.

AP Changes in Equilibrium

LO26.6 Describe how the AD-AS model explains periods of demand-pull inflation, cost-push inflation, and recession.

Now let's apply the AD-AS model to various situations that can confront the economy. For simplicity we will use *P* and *Q* symbols, rather than actual numbers. Remember that these symbols represent, respectively, price index values and amounts of real GDP.

Increases in AD: Demand-Pull Inflation

Suppose the economy is operating at its full-employment output and businesses and government decide to increase their spending—actions that shift the aggregate demand curve to the right. Our list of determinants of aggregate demand (Figure 26.2) provides several reasons why this shift might occur. Perhaps

AP KEY GRAPH

FIGURE 26.7 The equilibrium price level and equilibrium real GDP. The intersection of the aggregate demand curve and the aggregate supply curve determines the economy's equilibrium price level. At the equilibrium price level of 100 (in index-value terms), the $510 billion of real output demanded matches the $510 billion of real output supplied. So the equilibrium GDP is $510 billion.

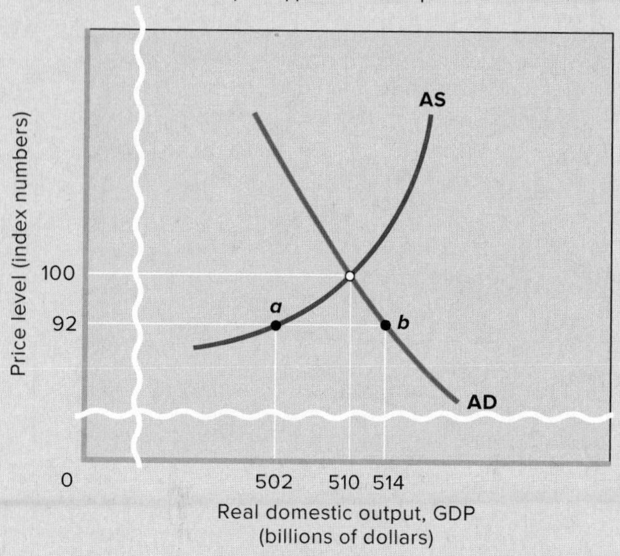

Real Output Demanded (Billions)	Price Level (Index Number)	Real Output Supplied (Billions)
$506	108	$513
508	104	512
510	**100**	**510**
512	96	507
514	92	502

QUICK QUIZ FOR FIGURE 26.7

1. The AD curve slopes downward because:
- **a.** per-unit production costs fall as real GDP increases.
- **b.** the income and substitution effects are at work.
- **c.** changes in the determinants of AD alter the amounts of real GDP demanded at each price level.
- **d.** decreases in the price level give rise to real-balances effects, interest-rate effects, and foreign purchases effects that increase the amount of real GDP demanded.

2. The AS curve slopes upward because:
- **a.** per-unit production costs rise as real GDP expands toward and beyond its full-employment level.
- **b.** the income and substitution effects are at work.
- **c.** changes in the determinants of AS alter the amounts of real GDP supplied at each price level.
- **d.** increases in the price level give rise to real-balances effects, interest-rate effects, and foreign purchases effects that increase the amounts of real GDP supplied.

3. At price level 92:
- **a.** a GDP surplus of $12 billion occurs that drives the price level up to 100.
- **b.** a GDP shortage of $12 billion occurs that drives the price level up to 100.
- **c.** the aggregate amount of real GDP demanded is less than the aggregate amount of real GDP supplied.
- **d.** the economy is operating beyond its capacity to produce.

4. Suppose real output demanded rises by $4 billion at each price level. The new equilibrium price level will be:
- **a.** 108.
- **b.** 104.
- **c.** 96.
- **d.** 92.

Answers: 1. d; 2. a; 3. b; 4. b

firms boost their investment spending because they anticipate higher future profits from investments in new capital. Those profits are predicated on having new equipment and facilities that incorporate a number of new technologies. And perhaps government increases spending to expand national defense.

As shown by the rise in the price level from P_1 to P_2 in Figure 26.8, the increase in aggregate demand beyond the full-employment level of output causes inflation. This is *demand-pull inflation* because the price level is being pulled up by the increase in aggregate demand. Also, observe that the increase in demand expands real output from the full-employment level Q_f to Q_1. The distance between Q_1 and Q_f is a positive, or "inflationary," GDP gap. Actual GDP exceeds potential GDP.

The classic American example of demand-pull inflation occurred in the late 1960s. The escalation of the war in Vietnam resulted in a 40 percent increase in defense spending between 1965 and 1967 and another 15 percent increase in 1968. The rise in government spending, imposed on an already growing economy, shifted the economy's aggregate

FIGURE 26.8 An increase in aggregate demand that causes demand-pull inflation. The increase of aggregate demand from AD_1 to AD_2 causes demand-pull inflation, shown as the rise in the price level from P_1 to P_2. It also causes an inflationary GDP gap of Q_1 minus Q_f. The rise of the price level reduces the size of the multiplier effect. If the price level had remained at P_1, the increase in aggregate demand from AD_1 to AD_2 would increase output from Q_f to Q_2 and the multiplier would have been at full strength. But because of the increase in the price level, real output increases only from Q_f to Q_1 and the multiplier effect is reduced.

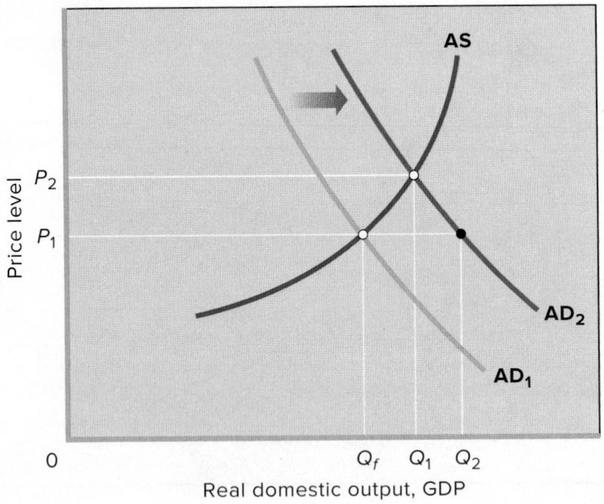

FIGURE 26.9 A decrease in aggregate demand that causes a recession. If the price level is downwardly inflexible at P_1, a decline of aggregate demand from AD_1 to AD_2 will move the economy leftward from *a* to *b* along the horizontal broken-line segment and reduce real GDP from Q_f to Q_1. Idle production capacity, cyclical unemployment, and a recessionary GDP gap (of Q_1 minus Q_f) will result. If the price level were flexible downward, the decline in aggregate demand would move the economy depicted from *a* to *c* instead of from *a* to *b*.

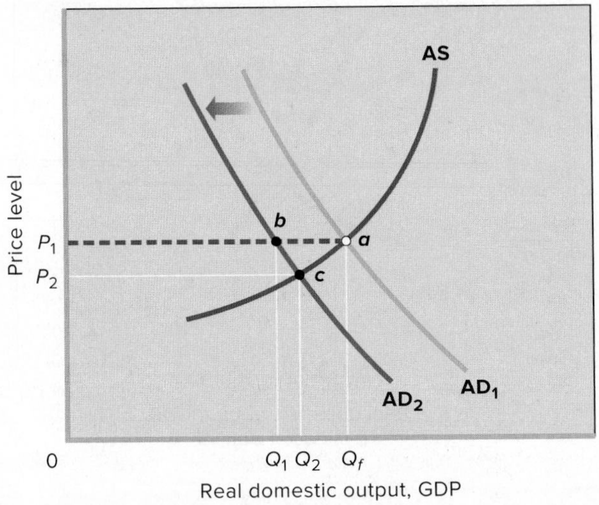

demand curve to the right, producing the worst inflation in two decades. Actual GDP exceeded potential GDP, thereby creating an inflationary GDP gap. Inflation jumped from 1.6 percent in 1965 to 5.7 percent by 1970.

A careful examination of Figure 26.8 reveals an interesting point concerning the multiplier effect. The increase in aggregate demand from AD_1 to AD_2 increases real output only to Q_1, not to Q_2, because part of the increase in aggregate demand is absorbed as inflation as the price level rises from P_1 to P_2. Had the price level remained at P_1, the shift of aggregate demand from AD_1 to AD_2 would have increased real output to Q_2. The full-strength multiplier effect of Chapters 24 and 25 would have occurred. But in Figure 26.8, inflation reduced the increase in real output—and thus the multiplier effect—by about one-half. For any initial increase in aggregate demand, the resulting increase in real output will be smaller the greater is the increase in the price level. Price-level flexibility weakens the realized multiplier effect.

Decreases in AD: Recession and Cyclical Unemployment

Decreases in aggregate demand describe the opposite end of the business cycle: recession and cyclical unemployment (rather than above-full employment and demand-pull inflation). For example, in 2008 investment spending in the United States greatly declined because of sharply lower expected returns on investment. These lower expectations resulted from the prospects of poor future business conditions and high degrees of current unused production capacity. In Figure 26.9, we show the resulting decline in aggregate demand as a leftward shift from AD_1 to AD_2.

But we now add an important twist to the analysis: *Deflation*—a decline in the price level—is not the norm in the American economy. We discussed "sticky prices" in Chapter 20 and previously explained how fixed prices lead to horizontal immediate-short-run aggregate supply curves. For reasons we will examine soon, many important prices in the U.S. economy are downwardly inflexible such that the price level is sticky downward even when aggregate demand substantially declines. Consider Figure 26.9, where the aggregate demand declines from AD_1 to AD_2. If the price level is stuck at P_1, the economy moves from *a* to *b* along the broken horizontal line rather than from *a* to *c* along the short-run aggregate supply curve AS. The outcome is a decline of real output from Q_f to Q_1, with *no* change in the price level. In this case, it is as if the aggregate supply curve in Figure 26.9 is horizontal at P_1, to the left of Q_f, as indicated by the dashed line. This decline of real output from Q_f to Q_1 constitutes a *recession*, and since fewer workers are needed to produce the lower output, *cyclical unemployment* arises. The distance between Q_1 and Q_f is a negative, or "recessionary," GDP gap—the amount by which actual output falls short of potential output.

Close inspection of Figure 26.9 also reveals that without a fall in the price level, the multiplier is at full strength. With the price level stuck at P_1, real GDP decreases by $Q_f - Q_1$, which matches the full leftward shift of the AD curve. The multiplier of Chapters 24 and 25 is at full strength when changes in aggregate demand occur along what, in effect, is a horizontal segment of the AS curve. This full-strength multiplier would also exist for an increase in aggregate demand from AD_2 to AD_1 along this broken line, since none of the increase in output would be dissipated as inflation. We will say more about that in Chapter 27.

All recent recessions in the United States have generally mimicked the "GDP gap but no deflation" scenario shown in Figure 26.9. Consider the recession of 2007–2009, which resulted from chaos in the financial markets that quickly led to significant declines in spending by businesses and households. Because of the resulting decline in aggregate demand, real GDP fell short of potential real GDP by roughly $300 billion in 2008 and $1 trillion in 2009. The nation's unemployment rate rose from 4.7 percent in December 2007 to 10.1 percent in October 2009. The price level fell in some months and the rate of inflation declined—meaning that *disinflation* occurred. Considering the full period, however, *deflation* did not occur.

Real output takes the brunt of declines in aggregate demand in the U.S. economy because the price level tends to be downwardly rigid in the immediate short run. There are several reasons for this downward price stickiness.

- ***Fear of price wars*** Some large firms may be concerned that if they reduce their prices, rivals not only will match their price cuts but may retaliate by making even deeper cuts. An initial price cut may touch off an unwanted *price war:* successively deeper and deeper rounds of price cuts. In such a situation, each firm eventually ends up with far less profit or higher losses than would be the case if each had simply maintained its prices. For this reason, each firm may resist making the initial price cut, choosing instead to reduce production and lay off workers.
- ***Menu costs*** Firms that think a recession will be relatively short-lived may be reluctant to cut their prices. One reason is what economists metaphorically call **menu costs**, named after their most obvious example: the cost of printing new menus when a restaurant decides to reduce its prices. But lowering prices also creates other costs. Additional costs derive from (1) estimating the magnitude and duration of the shift in demand to determine whether prices should be lowered; (2) repricing items held in inventory; (3) printing and mailing new catalogs; and (4) communicating new prices to customers, perhaps through advertising. When menu costs are present, firms may choose to avoid them by retaining current prices. That is, they may wait to see if the decline in aggregate demand is permanent.

CONSIDER THIS . . .

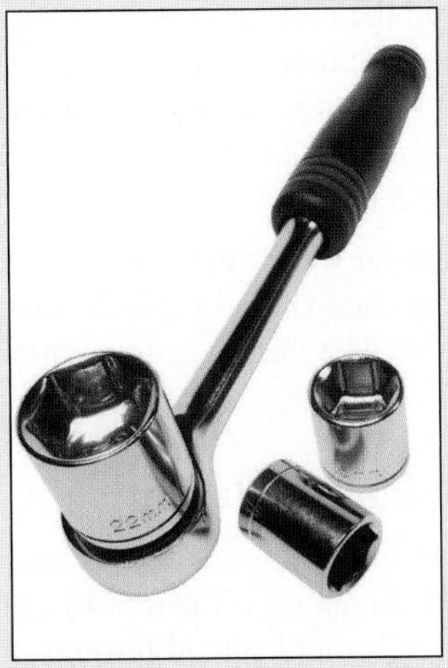

Source: © Royalty-Free/Corbis RF

Ratchet Effect

A *ratchet analogy* is a good way to think about the effects of changes in aggregate demand on the price level. A ratchet is a tool or mechanism such as a winch, car jack, or socket wrench that cranks a wheel forward but does not allow it to go backward. Properly set, each allows the operator to move an object (boat, car, or nut) in one direction while preventing it from moving in the opposite direction.

Product prices, wage rates, and per-unit production costs are highly flexible upward when aggregate demand increases along the aggregate supply curve. In the United States, the price level has increased in 60 of the 62 years since 1950.

But when aggregate demand decreases, product prices, wage rates, and per-unit production costs are inflexible downward. The U.S. price level has declined in only two years (1955 and 2009) since 1950, even though aggregate demand and real output have declined in a number of years.

In terms of our analogy, increases in aggregate demand ratchet the U.S. price level upward. Once in place, the higher price level remains until it is ratcheted up again. The higher price level tends to remain even with declines in aggregate demand.

- ***Wage contracts*** Firms rarely profit from cutting their product prices if they cannot also cut their wage rates. Wages are usually inflexible downward because large parts of the labor force work under contracts prohibiting wage cuts for the duration of the contract. (Collective bargaining agreements in major industries frequently run for 3 years. Similarly, the wages and salaries of nonunion workers are usually adjusted once a year, rather than quarterly or monthly.)
- ***Morale, effort, and productivity*** Wage inflexibility downward is reinforced by the reluctance of many employers to reduce wage rates. Some current wages may be so-called **efficiency wages**—wages that elicit maximum work effort and thus minimize labor costs per unit of output. If worker productivity (output per hour of work) remains constant, lower wages *do* reduce labor costs per unit of output. But lower wages might impair worker morale and work effort, thereby reducing productivity. Considered alone, lower productivity

raises labor costs per unit of output because less output is produced. If the higher labor costs resulting from reduced productivity exceed the cost savings from the lower wage, then wage cuts will increase rather than reduce labor costs per unit of output. In such situations, firms will resist lowering wages when they are faced with a decline in aggregate demand.

- ***Minimum wage*** The minimum wage imposes a legal floor under the wages of the least-skilled workers. Firms paying those wages cannot reduce that wage rate when aggregate demand declines.

Decreases in AS: Cost-Push Inflation

Suppose that a major terrorist attack on oil facilities severely disrupts world oil supplies and drives up oil prices by, say, 300 percent. Higher energy prices would spread through the economy, driving up production and distribution costs on a wide variety of goods. The U.S. aggregate supply curve would shift to the left, say, from AS_1 to AS_2 in Figure 26.10. The resulting increase in the price level would be *cost-push inflation.*

The effects of a leftward shift in aggregate supply are doubly bad. When aggregate supply shifts from AS_1 to AS_2, the economy moves from *a* to *b*. The price level rises from P_1 to P_2 and real output declines from Q_f to Q_1. Along with the cost-push inflation, a recession (and negative GDP gap) occurs. That is exactly what happened in the United States in the mid-1970s when the price of oil rocketed upward. Then, oil expenditures were about 10 percent of U.S. GDP, compared to only 3 percent today. So the U.S. economy is now less vulnerable to cost-push inflation arising from such "aggregate supply shocks." That said, it is not *immune* from such shocks.

AP **FIGURE 26.10 A decrease in aggregate supply that causes cost-push inflation.** A leftward shift of aggregate supply from AS_1 to AS_2 raises the price level from P_1 to P_2 and produces cost-push inflation. Real output declines and a recessionary GDP gap (of Q_1 minus Q_f) occurs.

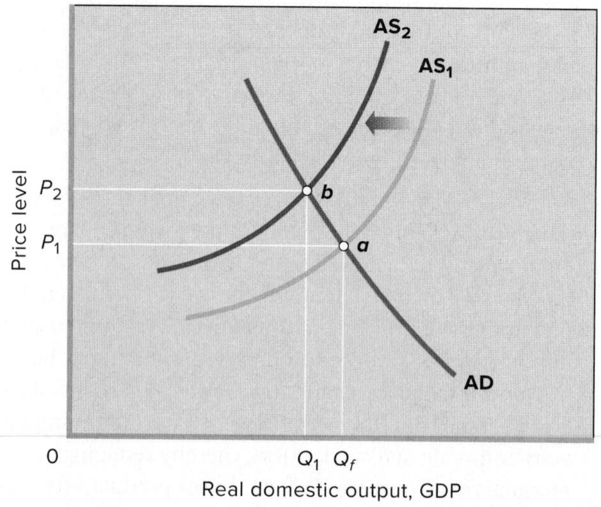

Increases in AS: Full Employment with Price-Level Stability

Between 1996 and 2000, the United States experienced a combination of full employment, strong economic growth, and very low inflation. Specifically, the unemployment rate fell to 4 percent and real GDP grew nearly 4 percent annually, *without igniting inflation*. At first thought, this "macroeconomic bliss" seems to be incompatible with the AD-AS model. The aggregate supply curve suggests that increases in aggregate demand that are sufficient for over-full employment will raise the price level (see Figure 26.8). Higher inflation, so it would seem, is the inevitable price paid for expanding output beyond the full-employment level.

But inflation remained very mild in the late 1990s. Figure 26.11 helps explain why. Let's first suppose that aggregate demand increased from AD_1 to AD_2 along aggregate supply curve AS_1. Taken alone, that increase in aggregate demand would move the economy from *a* to *b*. Real output would rise from full-employment output Q_1 to beyond-full-employment output Q_2. The economy would experience inflation, as shown by the increase in the price level from P_1 to P_3. Such inflation had occurred at the end of previous vigorous expansions of aggregate demand, including the expansion of the late 1980s.

Between 1990 and 2000, however, larger-than-usual increases in productivity occurred because of a burst of new technology relating to computers, the Internet, inventory management systems, electronic commerce, and so on. We represent this higher-than-usual productivity growth as the

AP **FIGURE 26.11 Growth, full employment, and relative price stability.** Normally, an increase in aggregate demand from AD_1 to AD_2 would move the economy from *a* to *b* along AS_1. Real output would expand to Q_2, and inflation would result (P_1 to P_3). But in the late 1990s, significant increases in productivity shifted the aggregate supply curve, as from AS_1 to AS_2. The economy moved from *a* to *c* rather than from *a* to *b*. It experienced strong economic growth (Q_1 to Q_3), full employment, and only very mild inflation (P_1 to P_2) before receding in March 2001.

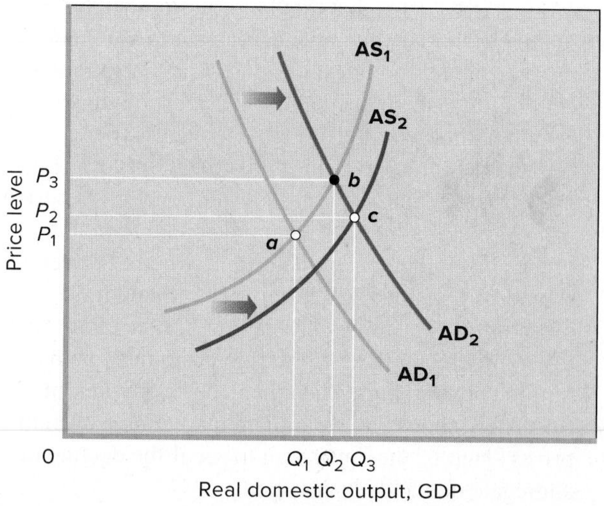

LAST WORD

Stimulus and the Great Recession

Aggregate Demand Stimulus Helped to Prevent the 2007–2009 Downturn from Becoming Another Great Depression. But Why Was the Stimulus-Fueled Recovery Substantially Weaker Than Expected?

In retrospect, it is clear that the U.S. economy was in a precarious position in 2006. Trillions of dollars had been borrowed to buy housing on the expectation that home prices would keep on rising. That expectation made borrowing seem like a "no brainer" as a potential buyer could anticipate that if she borrowed $200,000 to buy a house in one year, she would be able to sell it the next year for, say, $215,000. Selling at a higher price would allow her to pay off the $200,000 loan and keep the rest as pure profit.

Unfortunately, home prices started to fall in 2006. When they did, many people who had borrowed to buy houses found themselves unable to pay off their loans. That in turn meant that many banks found themselves holding loans that would never be paid back. Soon, many banks teetered on bankruptcy, the financial markets began to freeze up, and it became clear by late 2007 that the overall economy would probably enter a recession as the result of the housing collapse.

When it was widely recognized in late 2008 that the downturn was going to be unusually severe, public officials took extraordinarily strong steps to stimulate aggregate demand. In terms of monetary policy, the Federal Reserve lowered short-term interest rates to nearly zero in order to shift AD to the right by stimulating investment and consumption. In terms of fiscal policy, the federal government began the country's largest peacetime program of deficit-funded spending increases. Those spending increases also shifted AD to the right by increasing the total amount of government expenditures.

Those actions were widely credited with preventing a much worse downturn. Real GDP did fall by 4.7 percent and the unemployment rate did rise from 4.6 to 10.1 percent. But those negative changes were much less severe than what had happened during the Great Depression of the 1930s, when real GDP fell by nearly 27 percent and the unemployment rate rose to nearly 25 percent.

As time passed, however, it became clear that the stimulus was having less of an effect than many economists had anticipated. White House economists, for instance, had predicted that the stimulus begun in 2009 would reduce the unemployment rate to 5.2 percent by 2012. But three years later the unemployment rate was still at 8.1 percent despite the Federal Reserve continuing to keep interest rates extremely low and despite the federal government continuing to run massive deficits to fund huge amounts of government expenditures. It took until late 2014 before the unemployment rate fell below 6 percent again.

GDP growth was also disappointing. Real GDP expanded by only 2.4 percent in 2010, 1.8 percent in 2011, and 1.6 percent in 2012. Through the end of 2015, real GDP growth never exceeded 2.5 percent per year. By contrast, the period after the early 1980s recession had seen annual growth rates as high as 7.2 percent per year.

One explanation for the disappointing unemployment and GDP numbers was that it was hard for the stimulus to be very effective given

Source: © rumal/Alamy Stock Photo

the high debt levels that were built up during the bubble years. The lower interest rates engineered by the Federal Reserve, for instance, were probably not much of an inducement for consumers to increase their borrowing when so many of them were already heavily in debt.

A related problem was that savings rates had risen. When the government attempted to use deficit spending and fiscal policy to stimulate the economy, policymakers were hoping that each dollar of government spending would induce many dollars of consumer spending. But debt-strapped consumers were devoting large parts of their income to making interest payments on debt or paying off loans. So, when stimulus dollars came their way, they often short-circuited the spending process by saving a lot rather than spending a lot.

Another issue was that the stimulus was diffuse while the sectors of the economy in greatest need of stimulus were focused. In particular, the government's stimulus efforts shifted *aggregate* demand to the right. But not all sectors had been hit equally hard by the recession. Thus, when AD shifted right, a lot of the effect was felt in business sectors that hadn't been hurt that badly during the recession. Meanwhile, many sectors that had been hit hard only received a small portion of the total amount of stimulus that they would have needed to see a full recovery.

A related problem was that in some sectors of the economy, the government's stimulus may have resulted mostly in price increases rather than output gains. That is because the supply curves for many industries are steep. Consider dentists and jewelers. It takes many years to train competent dentists or skilled jewelers. So even if the demand for their services shifts right, there is a nearly fixed supply of dental services and jewelry services in the short run—meaning that any increase in demand will mostly cause higher prices rather than higher output. So when the government shifted *aggregate* demand to the right, certain sectors probably saw mostly price increases rather than output gains.

rightward shift from AS_1 to AS_2 in Figure 26.11. The relevant aggregate demand and aggregate supply curves thus became AD_2 and AS_2, not AD_2 and AS_1. Instead of moving from *a* to *b*, the economy moved from *a* to *c*. Real output increased from Q_1 to Q_3, and the price level rose only modestly (from P_1 to P_2). The shift of the aggregate supply curve from AS_1 to AS_2 accommodated the rapid increase in aggregate demand and kept inflation mild. This remarkable combination of rapid productivity growth, rapid real GDP growth, full employment, and relative price-level stability led some observers to proclaim that the United States was experiencing a "new era" or a New Economy.

But in 2001 the New Economy came face-to-face with the old economic principles. Aggregate demand declined because of a substantial fall in investment spending, and in March 2001 the economy experienced a recession. The terrorist attacks of September 11, 2001, further dampened private spending and prolonged the recession throughout 2001. The unemployment rate rose from 4.2 percent in January 2001 to 6 percent in December 2002.

The economy rebounded between 2002 and 2007, eventually reachieving its earlier strong economic growth, low inflation, and low unemployment. Some economists began to refer to the period after 1982 as "The Great Moderation" because recessions were farther apart and relatively mild. They drew the implication that businesses and government had smoothed out the business cycle. Wrong! The severity of the recession of 2007–2009 was a huge surprise to most economists. And so was the weakness of the subsequent recovery, as discussed in this chapter's Last Word.

AP QUICK REVIEW 26.3

- ✓ The equilibrium price level and amount of real output are determined at the intersection of the aggregate demand curve and the aggregate supply curve.
- ✓ Increases in aggregate demand beyond the full-employment level of real GDP cause demand-pull inflation.
- ✓ Decreases in aggregate demand below the full-employment level of real GDP cause recessions and cyclical unemployment, partly because the price level and wages tend to be inflexible in a downward direction.
- ✓ Decreases in aggregate supply cause cost-push inflation.
- ✓ Full employment, high economic growth, and price stability are compatible with one another if productivity-driven increases in aggregate supply are sufficient to balance growing aggregate demand.

SUMMARY

LO26.1 Define aggregate demand (AD) and explain how its downward slope is the result of the real-balances effect, the interest-rate effect, and the foreign purchases effect.

The aggregate demand–aggregate supply model (AD-AS model) is a flexible-price model that enables analysis of simultaneous changes of real GDP and the price level.

The aggregate demand curve shows the level of real output that the economy demands at each price level.

The aggregate demand curve is downsloping because of the real-balances effect, the interest-rate effect, and the foreign purchases effect. The real-balances effect indicates that inflation reduces the real value or purchasing power of fixed-value financial assets held by households, causing cutbacks in consumer spending. The interest-rate effect means that, with a specific supply of money, a higher price level increases the demand for money, thereby raising the interest rate and reducing investment purchases. The foreign purchases effect suggests that an increase in one country's price level relative to the price levels in other countries reduces the net export component of that nation's aggregate demand.

LO26.2 Explain the factors that cause changes (shifts) in AD.

The determinants of aggregate demand consist of spending by domestic consumers, by businesses, by government, and by foreign buyers. Changes in the factors listed in Figure 26.2 alter the spending by these groups and shift the aggregate demand curve. The extent of the shift is determined by the size of the initial change in spending and the strength of the economy's multiplier.

LO26.3 Define aggregate supply (AS) and explain how it differs in the immediate short run, the short run, and the long run.

The aggregate supply curve shows the levels of real output that businesses will produce at various possible price levels. The slope of the aggregate supply curve depends upon the flexibility of input and output prices. Since these vary over time, aggregate supply curves are categorized into three time horizons, each having different underlying assumptions about the flexibility of input and output prices.

The *immediate-short-run aggregate supply curve* assumes that both input prices and output prices are fixed. With output prices fixed, the aggregate supply curve is a horizontal line at the current price level. The *short-run aggregate supply curve* assumes nominal wages and other input prices remain fixed while output prices vary. The aggregate supply curve is generally upsloping because per-unit production costs, and hence the prices that firms must receive, rise as real output expands. The aggregate supply curve is relatively steep to the right of the full-employment output level and relatively flat to the left of it. The *long-run aggregate supply curve* assumes that nominal wages and other input prices fully match any change in the price level. The curve is vertical at the full-employment output level.

Because the short-run aggregate supply curve is the only version of aggregate supply that can handle simultaneous changes in the price level and real output, it serves well as the core aggregate supply curve for analyzing the business cycle and economic policy. Unless stated otherwise, all references to "aggregate supply" refer to short-run aggregate supply and the short-run aggregate supply curve.

LO26.4 Explain the factors that cause changes (shifts) in AS.

Figure 26.6 lists the determinants of aggregate supply: input prices, productivity, and the legal-institutional environment. A change in any one of these factors will change per-unit production costs at each level of output and therefore will shift the aggregate supply curve.

LO26.5 Discuss how AD and AS determine an economy's equilibrium price level and level of real GDP.

The intersection of the aggregate demand and aggregate supply curves determines an economy's equilibrium price level and real GDP. At the intersection, the quantity of real GDP demanded equals the quantity of real GDP supplied.

LO26.6 Describe how the AD-AS model explains periods of demand-pull inflation, cost-push inflation, and recession.

Increases in aggregate demand to the right of the full-employment output cause inflation and positive GDP gaps (actual GDP exceeds potential GDP). An upsloping aggregate supply curve weakens the multiplier effect of an increase in aggregate demand because a portion of the increase in aggregate demand is dissipated in inflation.

Shifts of the aggregate demand curve to the left of the full-employment output cause recession, negative GDP gaps, and cyclical unemployment. The price level may not fall during recessions because of downwardly inflexible prices and wages. This inflexibility results from fear of price wars, menu costs, wage contracts, efficiency wages, and minimum wages. When the price level is fixed, changes in aggregate demand produce full-strength multiplier effects.

Leftward shifts of the aggregate supply curve reflect increases in per-unit production costs and cause cost-push inflation, with accompanying negative GDP gaps.

Rightward shifts of the aggregate supply curve, caused by large improvements in productivity, help explain the simultaneous achievement of full employment, economic growth, and price stability that occurred in the United States between 1996 and 2000. The recession of 2001, however, ended the expansionary phase of the business cycle. Expansion resumed in the 2002–2007 period, before giving way to the severe recession of 2007–2009. The subsequent recovery was unexpectedly slow despite major amounts of monetary and fiscal stimuli.

TERMS AND CONCEPTS

aggregate demand–aggregate supply (AD-AS) model
aggregate demand
real-balances effect
interest-rate effect
foreign purchases effect
determinants of aggregate demand
aggregate supply
immediate-short-run aggregate supply curve
short-run aggregate supply curve
long-run aggregate supply curve
determinants of aggregate supply
productivity
equilibrium price level
equilibrium real output
menu costs
efficiency wages

The following and additional problems can be found in connect

DISCUSSION QUESTIONS

1. Why is the aggregate demand curve downsloping? Specify how your explanation differs from the explanation for the downsloping demand curve for a single product. What role does the multiplier play in shifts of the aggregate demand curve? **LO26.1**
2. Distinguish between "real-balances effect" and "wealth effect," as the terms are used in this chapter. How does each relate to the aggregate demand curve? **LO26.1**
3. What assumptions cause the immediate-short-run aggregate supply curve to be horizontal? Why is the long-run aggregate supply curve vertical? Explain the shape of the short-run aggregate supply curve. Why is the short-run aggregate supply curve relatively flat to the left of the full-employment output and relatively steep to the right? **LO26.3**
4. Explain how an upsloping aggregate supply curve weakens the realized multiplier effect from an initial change in investment spending. **LO26.6**
5. Why does a reduction in aggregate demand in the actual economy reduce real output, rather than the price level? Why might a full-strength multiplier apply to a decrease in aggregate demand? **LO26.6**
6. Explain: "Unemployment can be caused by a decrease of aggregate demand or a decrease of aggregate supply." In each case, specify the price-level outcomes. **LO26.6**

7. Use shifts of the AD and AS curves to explain (*a*) the U.S. experience of strong economic growth, full employment, and price stability in the late 1990s and early 2000s and (*b*) how a strong negative wealth effect from, say, a precipitous drop in house prices could cause a recession even though productivity is surging. **LO26.6**
8. In early 2001 investment spending sharply declined in the United States. In the two months following the September 11, 2001, attacks on the United States, consumption also declined. Use AD-AS analysis to show the two impacts on real GDP. **LO26.6**
9. **LAST WORD** What were the monetary and fiscal policy responses to the Great Recession? What were some of the reasons suggested for why those policy responses didn't seem to have as large an effect as anticipated on unemployment and GDP growth?

AP REVIEW QUESTIONS

1. Which of the following explains why the aggregate demand curve slopes downward? **LO26.1**
   - **a.** When the domestic price level rises, our goods and services become more expensive to foreigners, so net exports fall.
   - **b.** When government spending rises, the price level falls.
   - **c.** There is an inverse relationship between consumer expectations and personal taxes.
   - **d.** When the price level rises, the real value of financial assets (like stocks, bonds, and savings account balances) increases.
   - **e.** An increase in the price level will decrease the demand for money, reduce interest rates, and increase consumption and investment spending.
2. Which of the following will shift the aggregate demand curve to the left? **LO26.2**
   - **a.** The government reduces personal income taxes.
   - **b.** The nominal interest rate rises.
   - **c.** The government lowers corporate profit taxes.
   - **d.** There is an economic boom overseas that raises the incomes of foreign households.
   - **e.** Consumers take on more debt to increase spending for many goods and services across the economy.
3. Label each of the following descriptions as being either an immediate-short-run aggregate supply curve, a short-run aggregate supply curve, or a long-run aggregate supply curve. **LO26.3**
   - **a.** A vertical line at full employment real GDP.
   - **b.** The price level is fixed.
   - **c.** Output prices are flexible, but input prices are fixed.
   - **d.** A horizontal line.
   - **e.** An upsloping curve.
   - **f.** Output is fixed with unemployment equaling the natural rate of unemployment.
4. Which of the following will shift the aggregate supply curve to the right? **LO26.4**
   - **a.** A new networking technology increases productivity throughout the economy.
   - **b.** The price of oil rises substantially.
   - **c.** Foreign demand for domestic made goods increases.
   - **d.** The government passes a law increasing the minimum wage.
   - **e.** New regulations from the EPA mean higher costs of production.
5. At the current price level, producers supply $375 billion of final goods and services while consumers purchase $355 billion of final goods and services. In the short-run the price level is: **LO26.5**
   - **a.** Above the equilibrium level.
   - **b.** At the equilibrium level.
   - **c.** Below the equilibrium level.
   - **d.** Should not change.
   - **e.** Should tend to increase.
6. What effects would each of the following have on aggregate demand or aggregate supply, other things equal, in the short run? In each case, use a diagram to show the expected effects on the equilibrium price level and the level of real output, assuming that the price level is flexible both upward and downward. **LO26.5**
   - **a.** A widespread fear by consumers of an impending economic depression.
   - **b.** A new national tax on producers based on the value added between the costs of intermediate goods and the revenue received from their output.
   - **c.** A reduction in nominal interest rates at each price level.
   - **d.** A major increase in spending for health care by the federal government.
   - **e.** The general expectation of coming rapid inflation.
   - **f.** The complete disintegration of OPEC, causing oil prices to fall by one-half.
   - **g.** A 10 percent across-the-board reduction in personal income tax rates.
   - **h.** A sizable increase in labor productivity (with no change in nominal wages).
   - **i.** A 12 percent increase in nominal wages (with no change in productivity).
   - **j.** An increase in exports that exceeds an increase in imports (not due to tariffs).
7. True or False: Decreases in AD always lead to decreases in both output and the price level. **LO26.6**
8. Assume that (*a*) the price level is flexible upward but not downward and (*b*) the economy is currently operating at full-employment. Other things equal, how will each of the following affect the equilibrium price level and equilibrium level of real output in the short run? **LO26.6**
   - **a.** An increase in aggregate demand.
   - **b.** A decrease in short-run aggregate supply, with no change in aggregate demand.
   - **c.** Equal increases in aggregate demand and short-run aggregate supply.
   - **d.** A decrease in aggregate demand.
   - **e.** An increase in aggregate demand that exceeds an increase in aggregate supply.
9. True or False: If the price of oil suddenly increases by a large amount, AS will shift left (or decrease), real GDP will fall, but the price level will not rise thanks to price inflexibility. **LO26.6**

10. For each of the following changes, explain what should happen to real GDP and the price level in the short run (increase, decrease, indeterminate change, no change). Graphically show each of the following, as independent events: **LO26.5**
   a. With the economy at full employment, there is an increase in transfer payments.
   b. With the economy below full employment, there is an increase in the minimum wage.
   c. With the economy below full employment, there is an increase in the population's desire to import goods from foreign nations.
   d. With economy above full employment, there is an increase in the nominal interest rate.
   e. With the economy at full employment there is an equal increase in both government expenditures and in taxes.
   f. With the economy below full employment there is an increase in government expenditure and a decrease in a key input price, like oil.
   g. With the economy below full employment there is an increase in the nominal interest rate and an increase in foreign demand for the exports of this country.

PROBLEMS

1. Suppose that consumer spending initially rises by $5 billion for every 1 percent rise in household wealth and that investment spending initially rises by $20 billion for every 1 percentage point fall in the real interest rate. Also assume that the economy's multiplier is 4. If household wealth falls by 5 percent because of declining house values, and the real interest rate falls by 2 percentage points, in what direction and by how much will the aggregate demand curve initially shift at each price level? In what direction and by how much will it eventually shift? **LO26.2**
2. Answer the following questions on the basis of the following three sets of data for the country of North Vaudeville: **LO26.4**

(A)		(B)		(C)	
Price Level	Real GDP	Price Level	Real GDP	Price Level	Real GDP
110	275	100	200	110	225
100	250	100	225	100	225
95	225	100	250	95	225
90	200	100	275	90	225

   a. Which set of data illustrates aggregate supply in the immediate short run in North Vaudeville? The short run? The long run?
   b. Assuming no change in hours of work, if real output per hour of work increases by 10 percent, what will be the new levels of real GDP in the right column of A? Do the new data reflect an increase in aggregate supply or do they indicate a decrease in aggregate supply?
3. Suppose that the aggregate demand and aggregate supply schedules for a hypothetical economy are as shown in the following table. **LO26.5**

Amount of Real GDP Demanded, Billions	Price Level (Price Index)	Amount of Real GDP Supplied, Billions
$100	300	$450
200	250	400
300	200	300
400	150	200
500	100	100

   a. Use the data above to graph the aggregate demand and aggregate supply curves. What are the equilibrium price level and the equilibrium level of real output in this hypothetical economy? Is the equilibrium real output also necessarily the full-employment real output?
   b. If the price level in this economy is 150, will quantity demanded equal, exceed, or fall short of quantity supplied? By what amount? If the price level is 250, will quantity demanded equal, exceed, or fall short of quantity supplied? By what amount?
   c. Suppose that buyers desire to purchase $200 billion of extra real output at each price level. Sketch in the new aggregate demand curve as AD_1. What are the new equilibrium price level and level of real output?
4. Suppose that the table presented below shows an economy's relationship between real output and the inputs needed to produce that output: **LO26.4**

Input Quantity	Real GDP
150.0	$400
112.5	300
75.0	200

   a. What is productivity in this economy?
   b. What is the per-unit cost of production if the price of each input unit is $2?
   c. Assume that the input price increases from $2 to $3 with no accompanying change in productivity. What is the new per-unit cost of production? In what direction would the $1 increase in input price push the economy's aggregate supply curve? What effect would this shift of aggregate supply have on the price level and the level of real output?
   d. Suppose that the increase in input price does not occur but, instead, that productivity increases by 100 percent. What would be the new per-unit cost of production? What effect would this change in per-unit production cost have on the economy's aggregate supply curve? What effect would this shift of aggregate supply have on the price level and the level of real output?
5. Refer to the data in the table that accompanies problem 2. Suppose that the present equilibrium price level and level of real GDP are 100 and $225, and that data set B represents the relevant aggregate supply schedule for the economy. **LO26.6**
   a. What must be the current amount of real output demanded at the 100 price level?
   b. If the amount of output demanded declined by $25 at the 100 price levels shown in B, what would be the new equilibrium real GDP? In business cycle terminology, what would economists call this change in real GDP?

The Relationship of the Aggregate Demand Curve to the Aggregate Expenditures Model*

LO26.7 Identify how the aggregate demand curve relates to the aggregate expenditures model.

The aggregate demand curve of this chapter and the aggregate expenditures model of Chapter 25 are intricately related.

Derivation of the Aggregate Demand Curve from the Aggregate Expenditures Model

We can directly connect the downsloping aggregate demand curve to the aggregate expenditures model by relating various possible price levels to corresponding equilibrium GDPs. In Figure 1 we have stacked the aggregate expenditures model (Figure 1a) and the aggregate demand curve (Figure 1b) vertically. This is possible because the horizontal axes of both models measure real GDP. Now let's derive the AD curve in three distinct steps. (Throughout this discussion, keep in mind that price level P_1 is lower than price level P_2, which is lower than price level P_3.)

- First suppose that the economy's price level is P_1 and its aggregate expenditures schedule is AE_1, the top schedule in Figure 1a. The equilibrium GDP is then Q_1 at point 1. So, in Figure 1b, we can plot the equilibrium real output Q_1 and the corresponding price level P_1. This gives us point 1′ in Figure 1b.
- Now assume the price level rises from P_1 to P_2. Other things equal, this higher price level will (1) decrease the value of real balances (wealth), decreasing consumption expenditures; (2) increase the interest rate, reducing investment and interest-sensitive consumption expenditures; and (3) increase imports and decrease exports, reducing net export

*This appendix presumes knowledge of the aggregate expenditures model discussed in Chapter 25 and should be skipped if Chapter 25 was not assigned.

FIGURE 1 Deriving the aggregate demand curve from the aggregate expenditures model. (a) Rising price levels from P_1 to P_2 to P_3 shift the aggregate expenditures curve downward from AE_1 to AE_2 to AE_3 and reduce real GDP from Q_1 to Q_2 to Q_3. (b) The aggregate demand curve AD is derived by plotting the successively lower real GDPs from the upper graph against the P_1, P_2, and P_3 price levels.

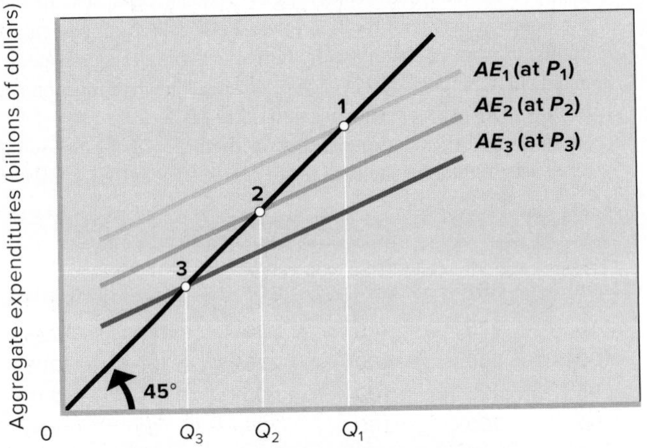

(a)
Aggregate expenditures model

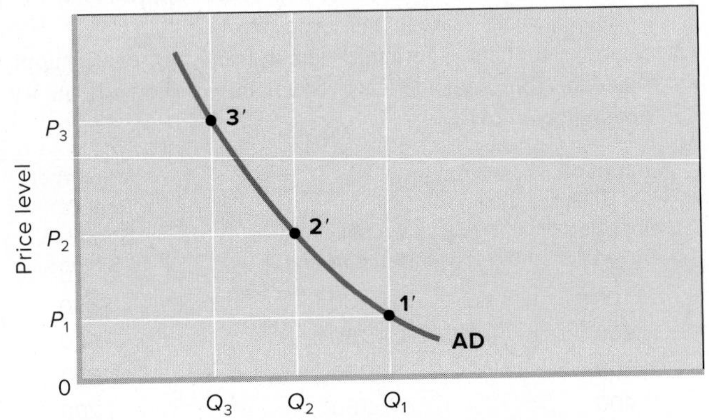

(b)
Aggregate demand–aggregate supply model

expenditures. The aggregate expenditures schedule will fall from AE_1 to, say, AE_2 in Figure 1a, giving us equilibrium Q_2 at point 2. In Figure 1b we plot this new price-level–real-output combination, P_2 and Q_2, as point 2′.

- Finally, suppose the price level rises from P_2 to P_3. The value of real balances falls, the interest rate rises, exports fall, and imports rise. Consequently, the consumption, investment, and net export schedules fall, shifting the aggregate expenditures schedule downward from AE_2 to AE_3, which gives us equilibrium Q_3 at point 3. In Figure 1b, this enables us to locate point 3′, where the price level is P_3 and real output is Q_3.

In summary, increases in the economy's price level will successively shift its aggregate expenditures schedule downward and will reduce real GDP. The resulting price-level–real-GDP combinations will yield various points such as 1′, 2′, and 3′ in Figure 1b. Together, such points locate the downsloping aggregate demand curve for the economy.

Aggregate Demand Shifts and the Aggregate Expenditures Model

The determinants of aggregate demand listed in Figure 26.2 are the components of the aggregate expenditures model discussed in Chapter 25. When one of the determinants of aggregate demand changes, the aggregate expenditures schedule shifts upward or downward. We can easily link such shifts of the aggregate expenditures schedule to shifts of the aggregate demand curve.

Let's suppose that the price level is constant. In Figure 2 we begin with the aggregate expenditures schedule at AE_1 in the top diagram, yielding equilibrium real output Q_1. Assume now that investment increases in response to more optimistic business expectations, so the aggregate expenditures schedule rises from AE_1 to AE_2. (The notation "at P_1" reminds us that the price level is assumed constant.) The result will be a multiplied increase in equilibrium real output from Q_1 to Q_2.

In Figure 2b the increase in investment spending is reflected in the horizontal distance between AD_1 and the broken curve to its right. The immediate effect of the increase in investment is an increase in aggregate demand by the exact amount of the new spending. But then the multiplier process magnifies the initial increase in investment into successive rounds of consumption spending and an ultimate multiplied increase in aggregate demand from AD_1 to AD_2. Equilibrium

FIGURE 2 Shifts of the aggregate expenditures schedule and of the aggregate demand curve. (a) A change in some determinant of consumption, investment, or net exports (other than the price level) shifts the aggregate expenditures schedule upward from AE_1 to AE_2. The multiplier increases real output from Q_1 to Q_2. (b) The counterpart of this change is an initial rightward shift of the aggregate demand curve by the amount of initial new spending (from AD_1 to the broken curve). This leads to a multiplied rightward shift of the curve to AD_2, which is just sufficient to show the same increase of real output as that in the aggregate expenditures model.

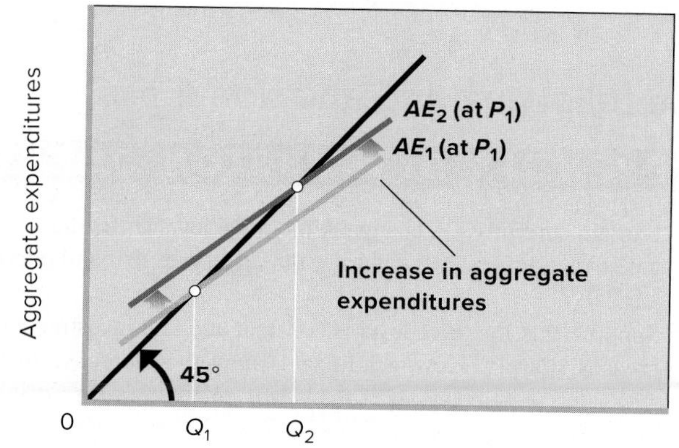

(a)
Aggregate expenditures model

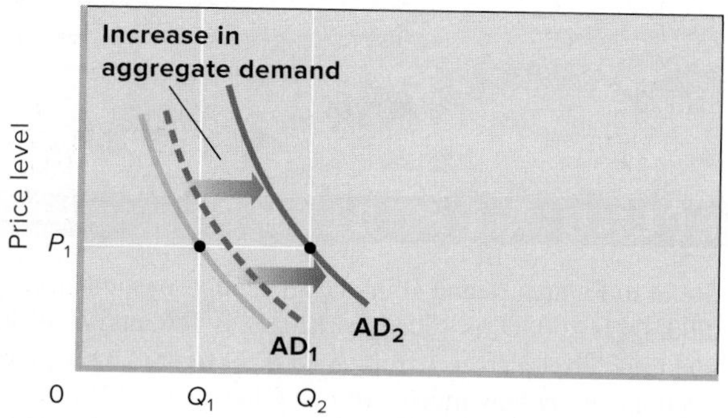

(b)
Aggregate demand–aggregate supply model

real output rises from Q_1 to Q_2, the same multiplied increase in real GDP as that in the top graph. The initial increase in investment in the top graph has shifted the AD curve in the lower graph by a horizontal distance equal to the change in investment times the multiplier. This particular change in real GDP is still associated with the constant price level P_1. To generalize,

$$\text{Shift of AD curve} = \text{initial change in spending} \times \text{multiplier}$$

APPENDIX SUMMARY

LO26.7 Identify how the aggregate demand curve relates to the aggregate expenditures model.

A change in the price level alters the location of the aggregate expenditures schedule through the real-balances, interest-rate, and foreign purchases effects. The aggregate demand curve is derived from the aggregate expenditures model by allowing the price level to change and observing the effect on the aggregate expenditures schedule and thus on equilibrium GDP.

With the price level held constant, increases in consumption, investment, government, and net export expenditures shift the aggregate expenditures schedule upward and the aggregate demand curve to the right. Decreases in these spending components produce the opposite effects.

The following and additional problems can be found in connect

APPENDIX DISCUSSION QUESTIONS

1. Explain carefully: "A change in the price level shifts the aggregate expenditures curve but not the aggregate demand curve." LO26.7
2. Suppose that the price level is constant and that investment decreases sharply. How would you show this decrease in the aggregate expenditures model? What would be the outcome for real GDP? How would you show this fall in investment in the aggregate demand–aggregate supply model, assuming the economy is operating in what, in effect, is a horizontal section of the aggregate supply curve? LO26.7

APPENDIX REVIEW QUESTIONS

1. True or False: A higher price level increases aggregate expenditures. LO26.7
2. If the government decreases expenditures, the *AE* curve will shift ________ and the AD curve will shift ________. LO26.7
   - **a.** Down; left.
   - **b.** Down; right.
   - **c.** Up; left.
   - **d.** Up; right.

APPENDIX PROBLEMS

1. Refer to Figures 1a and 1b in the Appendix. Assume that Q_1 is 300, Q_2 is 200, Q_3 is 100, P_3 is 120, P_2 is 100, and P_1 is 80. If the price level increases from P_1 to P_3 in figure 1b, in what direction and by how much will real GDP change? If the slopes of the *AE* lines in Figure 1a are 0.8 and equal to the MPC, in what direction will the aggregate expenditures schedule in Figure 1a need to shift to produce the previously determined change in real GDP? What is the size of the multiplier in this example? LO26.7
2. Refer to Figure 2 in the Appendix and assume that Q_1 is \$400 and Q_2 is \$500, the price level is stuck at P_1, and the slopes of the *AE* lines in Figure 2a are 0.75 and equal to the MPC. In what direction and by how much does the aggregate expenditures schedule in Figure 2a need to shift to move the aggregate demand curve in Figure 2b from AD_1 to AD_2? What is the multiplier in this example? Given the multiplier, what must be the distance between AD_1 and the broken line to its right at P_1? LO26.7

Chapter 27

Fiscal Policy, Deficits, and Debt

Learning Objectives

LO27.1 Identify and explain the purposes, tools, and limitations of fiscal policy.

LO27.2 Explain the role of built-in stabilizers in moderating business cycles.

LO27.3 Describe how the cyclically adjusted budget reveals the status of U.S. fiscal policy.

LO27.4 Summarize recent U.S. fiscal policy and the projections for U.S. fiscal policy over the next few years.

LO27.5 Discuss the problems that governments may encounter in enacting and applying fiscal policy.

LO27.6 Discuss the size, composition, and consequences of the U.S. public debt.

AP Chapter Focus

In the previous chapter we saw that an excessive increase in aggregate demand can cause demand-pull inflation and that a significant decline in aggregate demand can cause recession and cyclical unemployment. For these reasons, the federal government sometimes uses budgetary actions to try to "stimulate the economy" or "rein in inflation." Such countercyclical **fiscal policy** consists of deliberate changes in government spending and tax collections designed to achieve full employment, control inflation, and encourage economic growth. (The adjective "fiscal" simply means "financial.")

We begin this chapter by examining the logic behind fiscal policy, its current status, and its limitations. Then we examine a closely related topic: the U.S. public debt.

Our discussion of fiscal policy and public debt is very timely. In 2009, Congress and the Obama administration began a $787 billion stimulus program designed to help lift the U.S. economy out of deep recession. This fiscal policy contributed to a $1.4 trillion federal budget deficit in 2009, which increased the size of the U.S. public debt to $11.9 trillion. Large deficits continued in subsequent years, so that the U.S. public debt passed $19.0 trillion in 2016.

AP Fiscal Policy and the AD-AS Model

LO27.1 Identify and explain the purposes, tools, and limitations of fiscal policy.

The fiscal policy just defined is *discretionary* (or "active"). It is often initiated on the advice of the president's **Council of Economic Advisers (CEA),** a group of three economists appointed by the president to provide expertise and assistance on economic matters. Discretionary changes in government spending and taxes are *at the option* of the federal government. They do not occur automatically. Changes that occur without congressional action are *nondiscretionary* (or "passive" or "automatic"), and we will examine them later in this chapter.

Expansionary Fiscal Policy

When recession occurs, an **expansionary fiscal policy** may be in order. This policy consists of government spending increases, tax reductions, or both, designed to increase aggregate demand and therefore raise real GDP. Consider Figure 27.1, where we suppose that a sharp decline in investment spending has shifted the economy's aggregate demand curve to the left from AD_1 to AD_2. (Disregard the arrows and dashed downsloping line for now.) The cause of the recession may be that profit expectations on investment projects have dimmed, curtailing investment spending and reducing aggregate demand.

Suppose the economy's potential or full-employment output is $510 billion in Figure 27.1. If the price level is inflexible downward at P_1, the broken horizontal line becomes relevant to the analysis. The aggregate demand curve moves leftward and reduces real GDP from $510 billion to $490 billion. A negative GDP gap of $20 billion (= $490 billion − $510 billion) arises. An increase in unemployment accompanies this negative GDP gap because fewer workers are needed to produce the reduced output. In short, the economy depicted is suffering both recession and cyclical unemployment.

What fiscal policy should the federal government adopt to try to stimulate the economy? It has three main options: (1) increase government spending, (2) reduce taxes, or (3) use some combination of the two. If the federal budget is balanced at the outset, expansionary fiscal policy will create a government **budget deficit**—government spending in excess of tax revenues.

Increased Government Spending Other things equal, a sufficient increase in government spending will shift an economy's aggregate demand curve to the right, from AD_2 to AD_1 in Figure 27.1. To see why, suppose that the recession prompts the government to initiate $5 billion of new spending on highways, education, and health care. We represent this new $5 billion of government spending as the horizontal distance between AD_2 and the dashed downsloping line immediately to its right. At each price level, the amount of real output that is demanded is now $5 billion greater than that demanded before the expansion of government spending.

But the initial increase in aggregate demand is not the end of the story. Through the multiplier effect, the aggregate demand curve shifts to AD_1, a distance that exceeds that represented by the originating $5 billion increase in government purchases. This greater shift occurs because the multiplier process magnifies the initial change in spending into successive rounds of new consumption spending. If the economy's MPC is 0.75, then the simple multiplier is 4. So the aggregate demand curve shifts rightward by four times the distance between AD_2 and the broken downsloping line. Because this *particular* increase in aggregate demand occurs along the horizontal broken-line segment, real output rises by the full extent of the multiplier. Observe that real output rises to $510 billion, up $20 billion from its recessionary level of $490 billion. Concurrently, unemployment falls as firms increase their employment to the full-employment level that existed before the recession.

Tax Reductions Alternatively, the government could reduce taxes to shift the aggregate demand curve rightward, as from AD_2 to AD_1. Suppose the government cuts personal income taxes by $6.67 billion, which increases disposable income by the same amount. Consumption will rise by $5 billion (= MPC of 0.75 × $6.67 billion) and saving will go up by $1.67 billion (= MPS of 0.25 × $6.67 billion). In this case

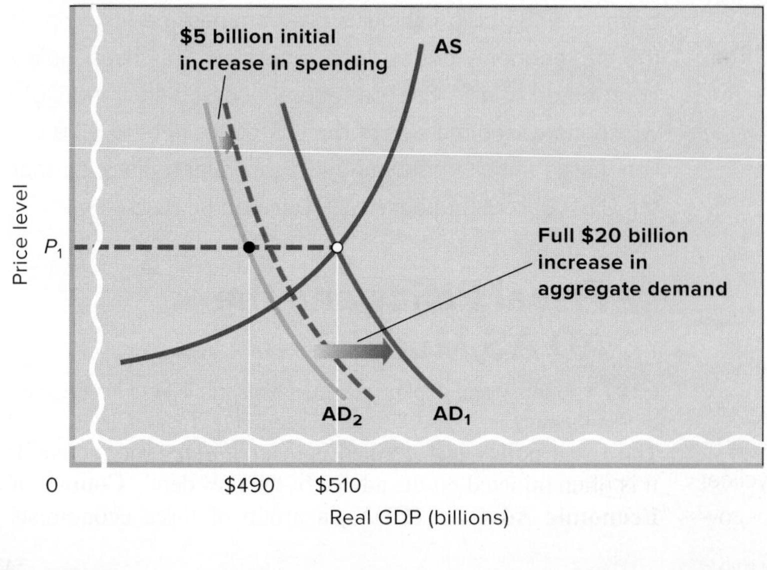

FIGURE 27.1 Expansionary fiscal policy. Expansionary fiscal policy uses increases in government spending or tax cuts to push the economy out of recession. In an economy with an MPC of 0.75, a $5 billion increase in government spending or a $6.67 billion decrease in personal taxes (producing a $5 billion initial increase in consumption) expands aggregate demand from AD_2 to the downsloping dashed curve. The multiplier then magnifies this initial increase in spending to AD_1. So real GDP rises along the broken horizontal line by $20 billion.

the horizontal distance between AD_2 and the dashed downsloping line in Figure 27.1 represents only the $5 billion initial increase in consumption spending. Again, we call it "initial" consumption spending because the multiplier process yields successive rounds of increased consumption spending. The aggregate demand curve eventually shifts rightward by four times the $5 billion initial increase in consumption produced by the tax cut. Real GDP rises by $20 billion, from $490 billion to $510 billion, implying a multiplier of 4. Employment increases accordingly.

You may have noted that a tax cut must be somewhat larger than the proposed increase in government spending if it is to achieve the same amount of rightward shift in the aggregate demand curve. This is because part of a tax reduction increases saving, rather than consumption. To increase initial consumption by a specific amount, the government must reduce taxes by more than that amount. With an MPC of 0.75, taxes must fall by $6.67 billion for $5 billion of new consumption to be forthcoming because $1.67 billion is saved (not consumed). If the MPC had instead been, say, 0.6, an $8.33 billion reduction in tax collections would have been necessary to increase initial consumption by $5 billion. The smaller the MPC, the greater the tax cut needed to accomplish a specific initial increase in consumption and a specific shift in the aggregate demand curve.

Combined Government Spending Increases and Tax Reductions The government may combine spending increases and tax cuts to produce the desired initial increase in spending and the eventual increase in aggregate demand and real GDP. In the economy depicted in Figure 27.1, the government might increase its spending by $1.25 billion while reducing taxes by $5 billion. As an exercise, you should explain why this combination will produce the targeted $5 billion initial increase in new spending.

If you were assigned Chapter 25, think through these three fiscal policy options in terms of the recessionary-expenditure-gap analysis associated with the aggregate expenditures model (Figure 25.7). And recall from the appendix to Chapter 26 that rightward shifts of the aggregate demand curve relate directly to upward shifts of the aggregate expenditures schedule.

Contractionary Fiscal Policy

When demand-pull inflation occurs, a restrictive or **contractionary fiscal policy** may help control it. This policy consists of government spending reductions, tax increases, or both, designed to decrease aggregate demand and therefore lower or eliminate inflation. Look at Figure 27.2, where the full-employment level of real GDP is $510 billion. The economy starts at equilibrium at point *a*, where the initial aggregate demand curve AD_3 intersects aggregate supply curve AS. Suppose that after going through the multiplier process, a $5 billion initial increase in investment and net export spending shifts the aggregate demand curve to the right by $20 billion, from AD_3 to AD_4. (Ignore the downsloping dashed line for now.) Given the upsloping AS curve, however, the equilibrium GDP does not rise by the full $20 billion. It only rises by $12 billion, to $522 billion, thereby creating an inflationary GDP gap of $12 billion ($522 billion − $510 billion). The upslope of the AS curve means that some of the rightward movement of the AD curve ends up causing demand-pull inflation rather than increased output. As a result, the price level rises from P_1 to P_2 and the equilibrium moves to point *b*.

Without a government response, the inflationary GDP gap will cause further inflation (as input prices rise in the long run to meet the increase in output prices). If the government looks to fiscal policy to eliminate the inflationary GDP gap, its options are the opposite of those used to combat recession. It can (1) decrease government spending, (2) raise

AP **FIGURE 27.2 Contractionary fiscal policy.** Contractionary fiscal policy uses decreases in government spending, increases in taxes, or both, to reduce demand-pull inflation. Here, an increase in aggregate demand from AD_3 to AD_4 has driven the economy to point *b* and ratcheted the price level up to P_2, where it becomes inflexible downward. If the economy's MPC is 0.75 and the multiplier therefore is 4, the government can either reduce its spending by $3 billion or increase its taxes by $4 billion (which will decrease consumption by $3 billion) to eliminate the inflationary GDP gap of $12 billion (= $522 billion − $510 billion). Aggregate demand will shift leftward, first from AD_4 to the dashed downsloping curve to its left, and then to AD_5. With the price level remaining at P_2, the economy will move from point *b* to point *c* and the inflationary GDP gap will disappear.

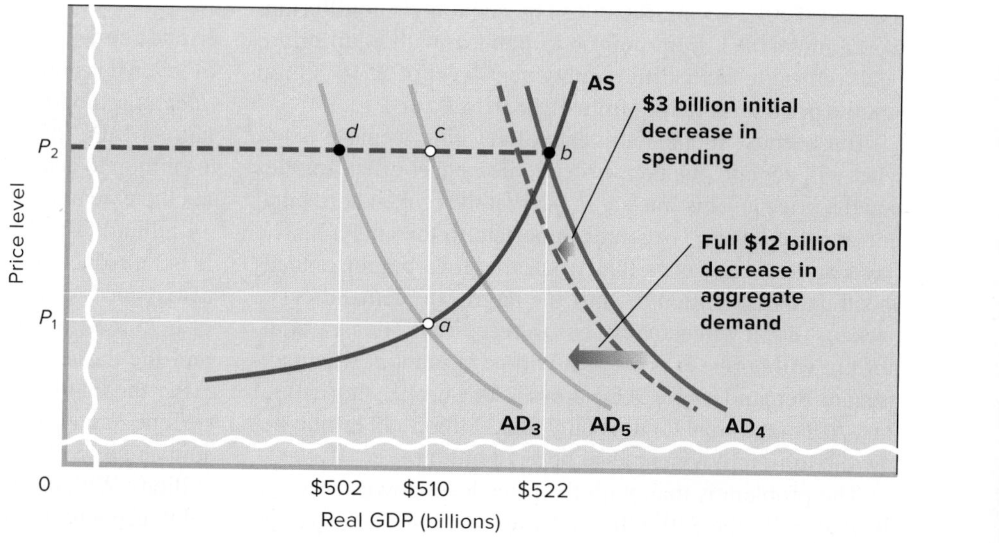

taxes, or (3) use some combination of those two policies. When the economy faces demand-pull inflation, fiscal policy should move toward a government **budget surplus**—tax revenues in excess of government spending.

But before discussing how the government can either decrease government spending or increase taxes to move toward a government budget surplus and control inflation, we have to keep in mind that the price level is like a ratchet. While increases in aggregate demand that expand real output beyond the full-employment level tend to ratchet the price level upward, declines in aggregate demand do not seem to push the price level downward. This means that stopping inflation is a matter of halting the rise of the price level, not trying to lower it to the previous level. It also means that the government must take the ratchet effect into account when deciding how big a cut in spending or an increase in taxes it should undertake.

Decreased Government Spending To control demand-pull inflation, the government can decrease aggregate demand by reducing government spending. To see why the ratchet effect matters so much, look at Figure 27.2 and consider what would happen if the government ignored the ratchet effect and attempted to design a spending-reduction policy to eliminate the inflationary GDP gap. Since the $12 billion gap was caused by the $20 billion rightward movement of the aggregate demand curve from AD_3 to AD_4, the government might naively think that it could solve the problem by causing a $20 billion leftward shift of the aggregate demand curve to move it back to where it originally was. It could attempt to do so by reducing government spending by $5 billion and then allowing the multiplier effect to expand that initial decrease into a $20 billion decline in aggregate demand. That would shift the aggregate demand curve leftward by $20 billion, putting it back at AD_3.

This policy would work fine if there were no ratchet effect and if prices were flexible. The economy's equilibrium would move back from point *b* to point *a*, with equilibrium GDP returning to the full-employment level of $510 billion and the price level falling from P_2 back to P_1.

But because there *is* a ratchet effect, this scenario is not what will actually happen. Instead, the ratchet effect implies that the price level is stuck at P_2, so that the broken horizontal line at price level P_2 becomes important to the analysis. The fixed price level means that when the government reduces spending by $5 billion to shift the aggregate demand curve back to AD_3, it will actually cause a recession! The new equilibrium will not be at point *a*. It will be at point *d*, where aggregate demand curve AD_3 crosses the broken horizontal line. At point *d*, real GDP is only $502 billion, $8 billion below the full-employment level of $510 billion.

The problem is that, with the price level downwardly inflexible at P_2, the $20 billion leftward shift of the aggregate demand curve causes a full $20 billion decline in real GDP. None of the change in aggregate demand can be dissipated as a decline in the price level. As a result, equilibrium GDP declines by the full $20 billion, falling from $522 billion to $502 billion and putting it $8 billion below potential output. By not taking the ratchet effect into account, the government has overdone the decrease in government spending, replacing a $12 billion inflationary GDP gap with an $8 billion recessionary GDP gap. This is clearly not what it had in mind.

Here's how it can avoid this scenario. First, the government takes account of the size of the inflationary GDP gap. It is $12 billion. Second, it knows that with the price level fixed, the multiplier will be in full effect. Thus, it knows that any decline in government spending will be multiplied by a factor of 4. It then reasons that government spending will have to decline by only $3 billion rather than $5 billion. Why? Because the $3 billion initial decline in government spending will be multiplied by 4, creating a $12 billion decline in aggregate demand. Under the circumstances, a $3 billion decline in government spending is the correct amount to exactly offset the $12 billion GDP gap. This inflationary GDP gap is the problem that government wants to eliminate. To succeed, it need not undo the full increase in aggregate demand that caused the inflation in the first place.

Graphically, the horizontal distance between AD_4 and the dashed downsloping line to its left represents the $3 billion decrease in government spending. Once the multiplier process is complete, this spending cut will shift the aggregate demand curve leftward from AD_4 to AD_5. With the price level fixed at P_2, the economy will come to equilibrium at point *c*. The economy will operate at its potential output of $510 billion, and the inflationary GDP gap will be eliminated. Furthermore, because the government took the ratchet effect correctly into account, the government will not accidentally push the economy into a recession by making an overly large initial decrease in government spending.

Increased Taxes Just as government can use tax cuts to increase consumption spending, it can use tax *increases* to *reduce* consumption spending. If the economy in Figure 27.2 has an MPC of 0.75, the government must raise taxes by $4 billion to achieve its fiscal policy objective. The $4 billion tax increase reduces saving by $1 billion (= the MPS of 0.25 × $4 billion). This $1 billion reduction in saving, by definition, is not a reduction in spending. But the $4 billion tax increase also reduces consumption spending by $3 billion (= the MPC of 0.75 × $4 billion), as shown by the distance between AD_4 and the dashed downsloping line to its left in Figure 27.2. After the multiplier process is complete, this initial $3 billion decline in consumption will cause aggregate demand to shift leftward by $12 billion at each price level (multiplier of 4 × $3 billion). With the economy moving to point *c*, the inflationary GDP gap will be closed and the inflation will be halted.

Combined Government Spending Decreases and Tax Increases The government may choose to combine spending decreases and tax increases in order to reduce aggregate demand and check inflation. To check your understanding, determine why a $1.5 billion decline in government spending combined with a $2 billion increase in taxes would shift the aggregate demand curve from AD_4 to AD_5. Also, if you were assigned Chapter 25, explain the three fiscal policy options for fighting inflation by referring to the inflationary-expenditure-gap concept developed with the aggregate expenditures model (Figure 25.7). And recall from the appendix to Chapter 26 that leftward shifts of the aggregate demand curve are associated with downshifts of the aggregate expenditures schedule.

Policy Options: *G* or *T*?

Which is preferable as a means of eliminating recession and inflation? The use of government spending or the use of taxes? The answer depends largely on one's view as to whether the government is too large or too small.

Economists who believe there are many unmet social and infrastructure needs usually recommend that government spending be increased during recessions. In times of demand-pull inflation, they usually recommend tax increases. Both actions either expand or preserve the size of government.

Economists who think that the government is too large and inefficient usually advocate tax cuts during recessions and cuts in government spending during times of demand-pull inflation. Both actions either restrain the growth of government or reduce its size.

The point is that discretionary fiscal policy designed to stabilize the economy can be associated with either an expanding government or a contracting government.

AP QUICK REVIEW 27.1

- ✓ Discretionary fiscal policy is the purposeful change of government expenditures and tax collections by government to promote full employment, price stability, and economic growth—that is, to stabliize the economy.
- ✓ Expansionary fiscal policy consists of increases in government spending, reductions in taxes, or both, and is designed to expand real GDP by increasing aggregate demand. These actions can create a budget deficit.
- ✓ Contractionary fiscal policy entails decreases in government spending, increases in taxes, or both, and is designed to reduce aggregate demand and slow or halt demand-pull inflation.
- ✓ To be implemented correctly, contractionary fiscal policy must properly account for the ratchet effect and the fact that the price level will not fall immediately as the government shifts the aggregate demand curve leftward.

AP Built-In Stability

LO27.2 Explain the role of built-in stabilizers in moderating business cycles.

To some degree, government tax revenues change automatically over the course of the business cycle and in ways that stabilize the economy. This automatic response, or built-in stability, constitutes nondiscretionary (or "passive" or "automatic") budgetary policy and results from the makeup of most tax systems. We did not include this built-in stability in our discussion of fiscal policy over the last few pages because we implicitly assumed that the same amount of tax revenue was being collected at each level of GDP. But the actual U.S. tax system is such that *net tax revenues* vary directly with GDP. (Net taxes are tax revenues less transfers and subsidies. From here on, we will use the simpler "taxes" to mean "net taxes.")

Virtually any tax will yield more tax revenue as GDP rises. In particular, personal income taxes have progressive rates and thus generate more-than-proportionate increases in tax revenues as GDP expands. Furthermore, as GDP rises and more goods and services are purchased, revenues from corporate income taxes and from sales taxes and excise taxes also increase. And, similarly, revenues from payroll taxes rise as economic expansion creates more jobs. Conversely, when GDP declines, tax receipts from all these sources also decline.

Transfer payments (or "negative taxes") behave in the opposite way from tax revenues. Unemployment compensation payments and welfare payments decrease during economic expansion and increase during economic contraction.

Automatic or Built-In Stabilizers

A **built-in stabilizer** is anything that increases the government's budget deficit (or reduces its budget surplus) during a recession and increases its budget surplus (or reduces its budget deficit) during an expansion without requiring explicit action by policymakers. As Figure 27.3 reveals, this is precisely what the U.S. tax system does. Government expenditures *G* are fixed and assumed to be independent of the level of GDP. Congress decides on a particular level of spending, but it does not determine the magnitude of tax revenues. Instead, it establishes tax rates, and the tax revenues then vary directly with the level of GDP that the economy achieves. Line *T* represents that direct relationship between tax revenues and GDP.

Economic Importance The economic importance of the direct relationship between tax receipts and GDP becomes apparent when we consider that:

- Taxes reduce spending and aggregate demand.
- Reductions in spending are desirable when the economy is moving toward inflation, whereas increases in spending are desirable when the economy is slumping.

FIGURE 27.3 Built-in stability. Tax revenues, *T*, vary directly with GDP, and government spending, *G*, is assumed to be independent of GDP. As GDP falls in a recession, deficits occur automatically and help alleviate the recession. As GDP rises during expansion, surpluses occur automatically and help offset possible inflation.

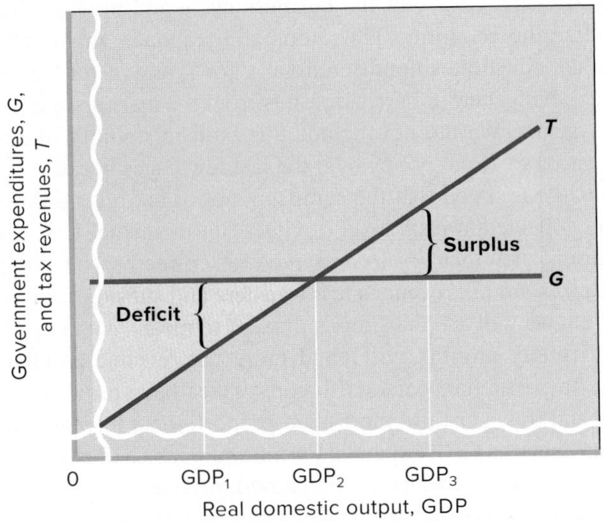

As shown in Figure 27.3, tax revenues automatically increase as GDP rises during prosperity, and since taxes reduce household and business spending, they restrain the economic expansion. That is, as the economy moves toward a higher GDP, tax revenues automatically rise and move the budget from deficit toward surplus. In Figure 27.3, observe that the high and perhaps inflationary income level GDP_3 automatically generates a contractionary budget surplus.

Conversely, as GDP falls during recession, tax revenues automatically decline, increasing spending by households and businesses and thus cushioning the economic contraction. With a falling GDP, tax receipts decline and move the government's budget from surplus toward deficit. In Figure 27.3, the low level of income GDP_1 will automatically yield an expansionary budget deficit.

Tax Progressivity Figure 27.3 reveals that the size of the automatic budget deficits or surpluses—and therefore built-in stability—depends on the responsiveness of tax revenues to changes in GDP. If tax revenues change sharply as GDP changes, the slope of line *T* in the figure will be steep and the vertical distances between *T* and *G* (the deficits or surpluses) will be large. If tax revenues change very little when GDP changes, the slope will be gentle and built-in stability will be low.

The steepness of *T* in Figure 27.3 depends on the tax system itself. In a **progressive tax system,** the average tax rate (= tax revenue/GDP) rises with GDP. In a **proportional tax system,** the average tax rate remains constant as GDP rises. In a **regressive tax system,** the average tax rate falls as GDP rises. The progressive tax system has the steepest tax line *T* of the three. However, tax revenues will rise with GDP under both the progressive and the proportional tax systems, and they may rise, fall, or stay the same under a regressive tax system. The main point is this: The more progressive the tax system, the greater the economy's built-in stability.

The built-in stability provided by the U.S. tax system has reduced the severity of business fluctuations, perhaps by as much as 8 to 10 percent of the change in GDP that otherwise would have occurred.[1] In recession-year 2009, for example, revenues from the individual income tax fell by a staggering 22 percent. This decline helped keep household spending and real GDP from falling even more than they did. But built-in stabilizers can only dampen, not counteract, swings in real GDP. Discretionary fiscal policy (changes in tax rates and expenditures) or monetary policy (central bank–caused changes in interest rates) therefore may be needed to try to counter a recession or inflation of any appreciable magnitude.

Evaluating How Expansionary or Contractionary Fiscal Policy Is Determined

LO27.3 Describe how the cyclically adjusted budget reveals the status of U.S. fiscal policy.

How can we determine whether a government's discretionary fiscal policy is expansionary, neutral, or contractionary? We cannot simply examine the actual budget deficits or surpluses that take place under the current policy because they will necessarily include the automatic changes in tax revenues that accompany every change in GDP. In addition, the expansionary or contractionary strength of any change in discretionary fiscal policy depends not on its absolute size but on how large it is relative to the size of the economy. So, in evaluating the status of fiscal policy, we must adjust deficits and surpluses to eliminate automatic changes in tax revenues and also compare the sizes of the adjusted budget deficits and surpluses to the level of potential GDP.

Cyclically Adjusted Budget

Economists use the **cyclically adjusted budget** (also called the *full-employment budget*) to adjust actual federal budget deficits and surpluses to account for the changes in tax revenues that happen automatically whenever GDP changes. The cyclically adjusted budget measures what the federal budget deficit or surplus would have been under existing tax rates and government spending levels if the economy had achieved its full-employment level of GDP (its potential output). The idea

[1] Alan J. Auerbach and Daniel Feenberg, "The Significance of Federal Taxes as Automatic Stabilizers," *Journal of Economic Perspectives*, Summer 2000, p. 54.

essentially is to compare *actual* government expenditures with the tax revenues *that would have occurred* if the economy had achieved full-employment GDP. That procedure removes budget deficits or surpluses that arise simply because of cyclical changes in GDP and thus tell us nothing about whether the government's current discretionary fiscal policy is fundamentally expansionary, contractionary, or neutral.

Consider Figure 27.4a, where line *G* represents government expenditures and line *T* represents tax revenues. In full-employment year 1, government expenditures of $500 billion equal tax revenues of $500 billion, as indicated by the intersection of lines *G* and *T* at point *a*. The cyclically adjusted budget deficit in year 1 is zero—government expenditures equal the tax revenues forthcoming at the full-employment output GDP_1. Obviously, the cyclically adjusted deficit *as a percentage of potential GDP* is also zero. The government's fiscal policy is neutral.

Now suppose that a recession occurs and GDP falls from GDP_1 to GDP_2, as shown in Figure 27.4a. Let's also assume that the government takes no discretionary action, so lines *G* and *T* remain as shown in the figure. Tax revenues automatically fall to $450 billion (point *c*) at GDP_2, while government spending remains unaltered at $500 billion (point *b*). A $50 billion budget deficit (represented by distance *bc*) arises. But this **cyclical deficit** is simply a by-product of the economy's slide into recession, not the result of discretionary fiscal actions by the government. We would be wrong to conclude from this deficit that the government is engaging in an expansionary fiscal policy. The government's fiscal policy has not changed. It is still neutral.

That fact is highlighted when we remove the cyclical part of the deficit and thus consider the cyclically adjusted budget deficit for year 2 in Figure 27.4a. The $500 billion of government expenditures in year 2 is shown by *b* on line *G*. And, as shown by *a* on line *T*, $500 billion of tax revenues would have occurred if the economy had achieved its full-employment GDP. Because both *b* and *a* represent $500 billion, the cyclically adjusted budget deficit in year 2 is zero, as is this deficit as a percentage of potential GDP. Since the cyclically adjusted deficits are zero in both years, we know that government did not change its discretionary fiscal policy, even though a recession occurred and an actual deficit of $50 billion resulted.

Next, consider Figure 27.4b. Suppose that real output declined from full-employment GDP_3 in year 3 to GDP_4 in year 4. Also suppose that government responded to the recession by reducing tax rates in year 4, as represented by the downward shift of the tax line from T_1 to T_2. What has happened to the size of the cyclically adjusted deficit? Government expenditures in year 4 are $500 billion, as shown by *e*. Compare that amount with the $475 billion of tax revenues that would occur

FIGURE 27.4 Cyclically adjusted deficits. (a) In the left-hand graph, the cyclically adjusted deficit is zero at the full-employment output GDP_1. But it is also zero at the recessionary output GDP_2 because the $500 billion of government expenditures at GDP_2 equals the $500 billion of tax revenues that would be forthcoming at the full-employment GDP_1. There has been no change in fiscal policy. (b) In the right-hand graph, discretionary fiscal policy, as reflected in the downward shift of the tax line from T_1 to T_2, has increased the cyclically adjusted budget deficit from zero in year 3 (before the tax cut) to $25 billion in year 4 (after the tax cut). This is found by comparing the $500 billion of government spending in year 4 with the $475 billion of taxes that would accrue at the full-employment GDP_3. Such a rise in the cyclically adjusted deficit (as a percentage of potential GDP) identifies an expansionary fiscal policy.

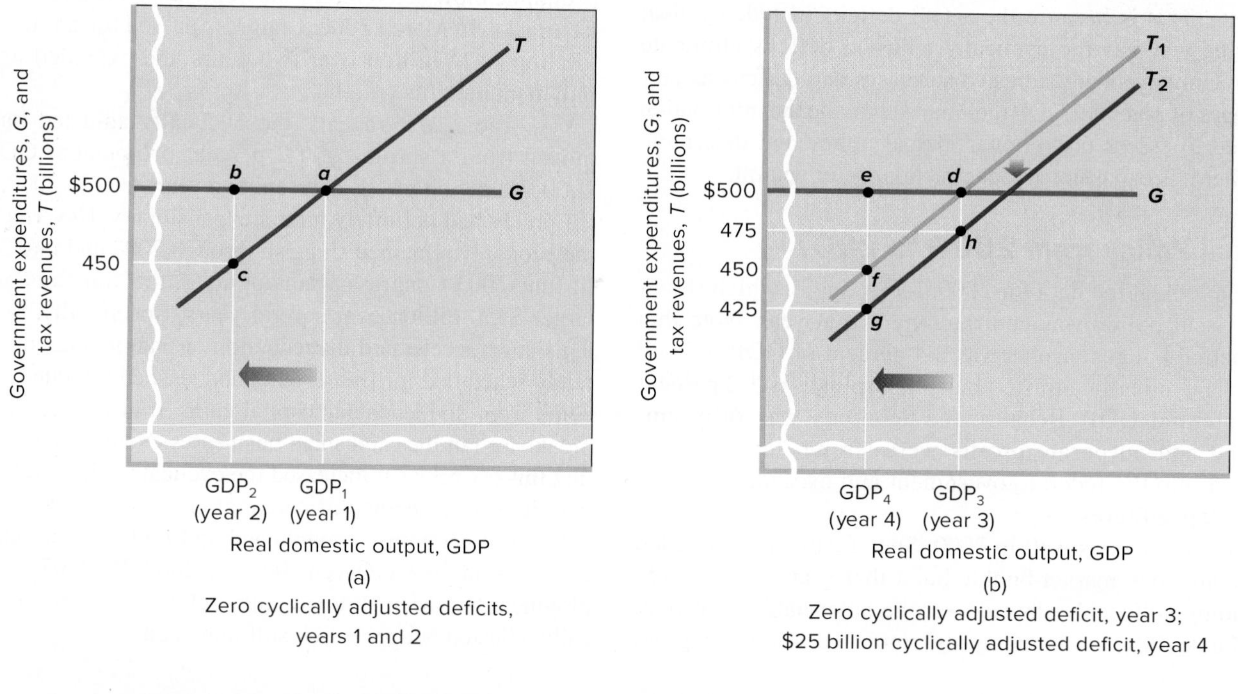

if the economy achieved its full-employment GDP. That is, compare position e on line G with position h on line T_2. The $25 billion of tax revenues by which e exceeds h is the cyclically adjusted budget deficit for year 4. As a percentage of potential GDP, the cyclically adjusted budget deficit has increased from zero in year 3 (before the tax-rate cut) to some positive percent [$= (\$25 \text{ billion}/GDP_3) \times 100$] in year 4. This increase in the relative size of the full-employment deficit between the two years reveals that the new fiscal policy is *expansionary*.

In contrast, if we observed a cyclically adjusted deficit (as a percentage of potential GDP) of zero in one year, followed by a cyclically adjusted budget surplus in the next, we could conclude that fiscal policy has changed from being neutral to being contractionary. Because the cyclically adjusted budget adjusts for automatic changes in tax revenues, the increase in the cyclically adjusted budget surplus reveals that government either decreased its spending (G) or increased tax rates such that tax revenues (T) increased. These changes in G and T are precisely the discretionary actions that we have identified as elements of a *contractionary* fiscal policy.

TABLE 27.1 Federal Deficits (−) and Surpluses (+) as Percentages of GDP, 2000–2015

(1) Year	(2) Actual Deficit − or Surplus +	(3) Cyclically Adjusted Deficit − or Surplus +*
2000	+2.4	+1.2
2001	+1.3	+0.6
2002	−1.5	−1.2
2003	−3.4	−2.7
2004	−3.5	−3.2
2005	−2.6	−2.6
2006	−1.9	−2.2
2007	−1.2	−1.3
2008	−3.2	−2.9
2009	−10.1	−7.1
2010	−9.0	−5.7
2011	−8.7	−5.6
2012	−7.0	−4.3
2013	−4.1	−2.6
2014	−2.8	−1.6
2015	−2.4	−1.6

*As a percentage of potential GDP.

Source: Congressional Budget Office, **www.cbo.gov**.

Recent and Projected U.S. Fiscal Policy

LO27.4 Summarize recent U.S. fiscal policy and the projections for U.S. fiscal policy over the next few years.

Table 27.1 lists the actual federal budget deficits and surpluses (column 2) and the cyclically adjusted deficits and surpluses (column 3), as percentages of actual GDP and potential GDP, respectively, between 2000 and 2015. Observe that the cyclically adjusted deficits are generally smaller than the actual deficits. This is because the actual deficits include cyclical deficits, whereas the cyclically adjusted deficits eliminate them. Only cyclically adjusted surpluses and deficits as percentages of potential GDP (column 3) provide the information needed to assess discretionary fiscal policy and determine whether it is expansionary, contractionary, or neutral.

Fiscal Policy from 2000 to 2007

Take a look at the data for 2000, for example, which shows that fiscal policy was contractionary that year. Note that the actual budget surplus was 2.4 percent of GDP in 2000 and the cyclically adjusted budget surplus was 1.2 percent of potential GDP. Because the economy was fully employed and corporate profits were strong, tax revenues poured into the federal government and exceeded government expenditures.

But not all was well in 2000. Specifically, the so-called dot-com stock market bubble burst that year, and the U.S. economy noticeably slowed over the latter half of the year. In March 2001, the economy slid into a recession. Congress and the Bush administration responded by cutting taxes by $44 billion in 2001 and scheduling an additional $52 billion of cuts for 2002. These stimulus policies helped boost the economy and offset the recession as well as cushion the economic blow delivered by the September 11, 2001, terrorist attacks. In March 2002, Congress passed further tax cuts totaling $122 billion over two years and extended unemployment benefits.

As Table 27.1 reveals, the cyclically adjusted budget moved from a surplus of 1.2 percent of potential GDP in 2000 to a deficit of −1.2 percent two years later in 2002. Fiscal policy had definitely turned expansionary. Nevertheless, the economy remained sluggish through 2002 and into 2003. In June 2003 Congress again cut taxes, this time by a much larger $350 billion over several years. Specifically, the tax legislation accelerated the reduction of marginal tax rates already scheduled for future years and slashed tax rates on income from dividends and capital gains. It also increased tax breaks for families and small businesses. Note from the table that this tax package increased the cyclically adjusted budget deficit as a percentage of potential GDP to −2.7 percent in 2003. The economy strengthened and both real output and employment grew between 2003 and 2007. By 2007 full employment had been restored, although a −1.3 percent cyclically adjusted budget deficit still remained.

Fiscal Policy during and after the Great Recession

As pointed out in previous chapters, major economic trouble began in 2007. In the summer of 2007, a crisis in the market for mortgage loans flared up. Later in 2007, that crisis spread rapidly to other financial markets, threatened the survival of several major U.S. financial institutions, and severely disrupted the entire financial system. As credit markets began to freeze, general pessimism spread beyond the financial markets to the overall economy. Businesses and households retrenched on their borrowing and spending, and in December 2007, the economy entered a recession. Over the following two years, it became known as the Great Recession—one of the steepest and longest economic downturns since the 1930s.

In 2008 Congress acted rapidly to pass an economic stimulus package. This law provided a total of $152 billion in stimulus, with some of it coming as tax breaks for businesses, but most of it delivered as checks of up to $600 each to taxpayers, veterans, and Social Security recipients.

As a percentage of GDP, the *actual* federal budget deficit jumped from −1.2 percent in 2007 to −3.2 percent in 2008. This increase resulted from an automatic drop-off of tax revenues during the recession, along with the tax rebates (fiscal stimulus checks) paid out in 2008. As shown in Table 27.1, the *cyclically adjusted* budget deficit rose from −1.3 percent of potential GDP in 2007 to −2.9 percent in 2008. This increase in the cyclically adjusted budget reveals that fiscal policy in 2008 was expansionary.

The government hoped that those receiving checks would spend the money and thus boost consumption and aggregate demand. But households instead saved substantial parts of the money from the checks or used some of the money to pay down credit card loans. Although this stimulus plan boosted output somewhat in mid-2008, it was neither as expansionary nor as long-lasting as policymakers had hoped. The continuing forces of the Great Recession simply overwhelmed the policy.

With the economy continuing its precipitous slide, the Obama administration and Congress enacted the American Recovery and Reinvestment Act of 2009. This gigantic $787 billion program—coming on top of a $700 billion rescue package for financial institutions—consisted of low- and middle-income tax rebates, plus large increases in expenditures on infrastructure, education, and health care. The idea was to flood the economy with additional spending to try to boost aggregate demand and get people back to work.

The tax cuts in the package were aimed at lower- and middle-income individuals and households, who were thought to be more likely than high-income people to spend (rather than save) the extra income from the tax rebates. Rather than sending out lump-sum stimulus checks as in 2008, the new tax rebates showed up as small increases in workers' monthly payroll checks. With smaller amounts per month rather than a single large check, the government hoped that people would spend the bulk of their enhanced income—rather than save it as they had done with the one-time-only, lump-sum checks received in 2008. The second part of the fiscal policy (60 percent of the funding) consisted of increases in government expenditures on a wide assortment of programs, including transportation, education, and aid to state governments. The highly stimulative fiscal policy for 2009 is fully reflected in column 3 of Table 27.1. The cyclically adjusted budget deficit rose dramatically from −2.9 percent of potential GDP in 2008 to a very high −7.1 percent of potential GDP in 2009.

The recession officially ended during the summer of 2009, but the economy did not rebound vigorously. Unemployment remained elevated and tax collections were low due to a stagnant economy. As a result, policymakers decided to continue with large amounts of fiscal stimulus. Annual actual (not cyclically adjusted) budget deficits amounted to −4.1, −2.8, and −2.4 percent of GDP, respectively, in years 2013, 2014, and 2015. The cyclically adjusted budget deficits for those years were, respectively, −2.6, −1.6, and −1.6 percent of potential GDP. Thus, while the intensity of fiscal stimulus was gradually diminishing, it remained substantially stimulatory. The

GLOBAL PERSPECTIVE 27.1

Cyclically Adjusted Budget Deficits or Surpluses as a Percentage of Potential GDP, Selected Nations

In 2014, five years after the end of the global recession, about half of the countries in the developed world had cyclically adjusted budget deficits that reflected some degree of expansionary fiscal policy.

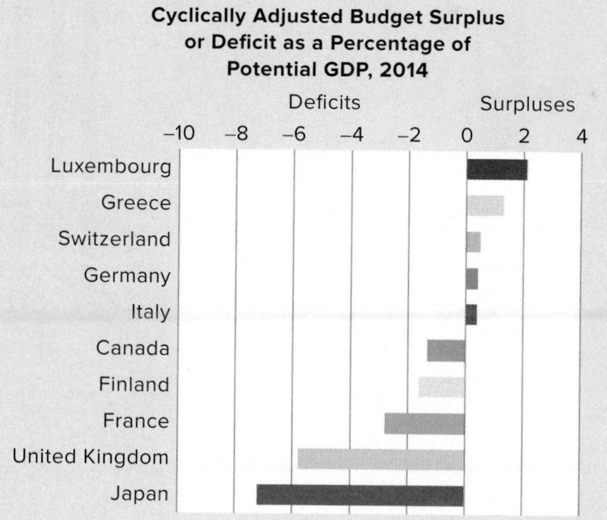

Source: OECD, *Government at a Glance*, 2015, **http://www.oecd.org/eco/economicoutlook.htm.**

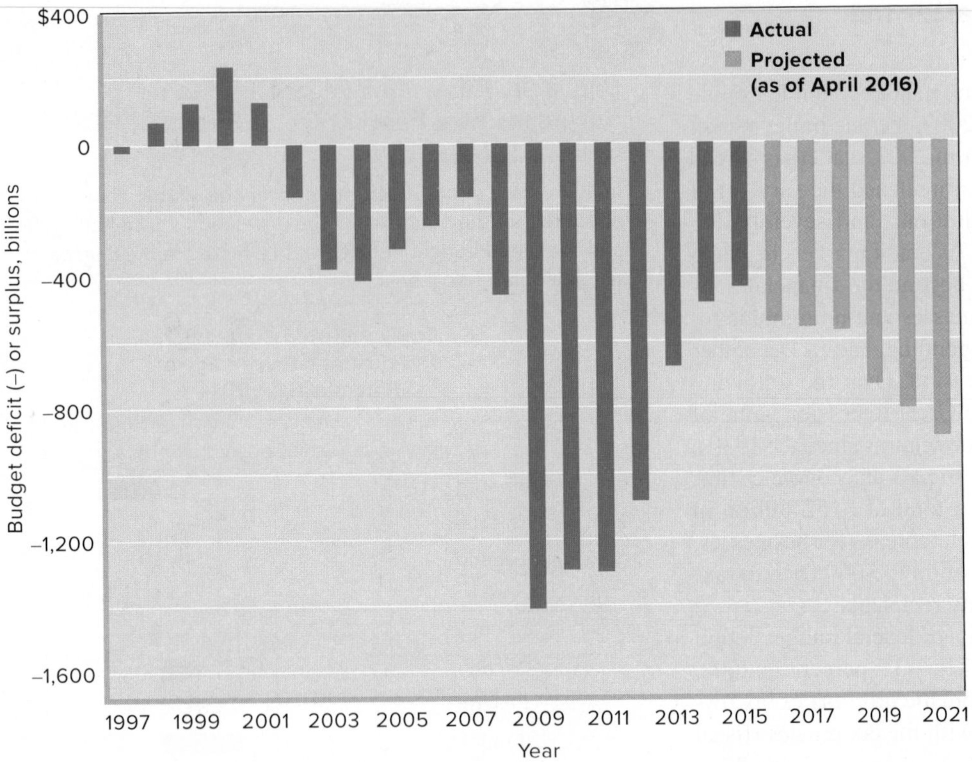

Source: Congressional Budget Office, **www.cbo.gov.**

AP **FIGURE 27.5 Federal budget deficits and surpluses, actual and projected, fiscal years 1997–2021 (in billions of nominal dollars).** The budget surpluses of 1998 through 2001 were the first budget surpluses since 1969. Deficits reemerged after the 2001 recession and then ballooned massively with the Great Recession of 2007–2009. Deficits are projected to remain high for many years to come, though not nearly as high as in the years immediately following the Great Recession.

recession had been exceptionally strong; so was the ongoing fiscal response.

Other nations also experienced recessions and also responded with expansionary fiscal policies. Global Perspective 27.1 shows the magnitudes of the cyclically adjusted surpluses and deficits of a number of countries in 2014.

Past and Projected Budget Deficits and Surpluses

Figure 27.5 shows the absolute magnitudes of actual (not cyclically adjusted) U.S. budget surpluses and deficits, from 1997 through 2015. It also shows the projected future deficits through 2021, as estimated by the Congressional Budget Office (CBO). In recession year 2009, the federal budget deficit reached $1,413 billion, mainly but not totally due to reduced tax revenues from lower income and record amounts of stimulus spending. The CBO projects high deficits for several years to come. But projected deficits and surpluses are subject to large and frequent changes, as government alters its fiscal policy and GDP growth accelerates or slows. So we suggest that you update this figure by going to the Congressional Budget Office website, **www.cbo.gov,** and finding the document titled *The Budget and Economic Outlook*. Near the start of that document, you should find Summary Table 1. The numbers are in the row labeled "Deficit (–) or Surplus."

AP Problems, Criticisms, and Complications of Implementing Fiscal Policy

LO27.5 Discuss the problems that governments may encounter in enacting and applying fiscal policy.

Economists recognize that governments may encounter a number of significant problems in enacting and applying fiscal policy.

Problems of Timing

Several problems of timing may arise in connection with fiscal policy:

- ***Recognition lag*** The recognition lag is the time between the beginning of recession or inflation and the certain awareness that it is actually happening. This lag arises because the economy does not move smoothly through the business cycle. Even during good times, the economy has slow months interspersed with months of rapid growth and expansion. This makes recognizing a recession difficult since several slow months will have to happen in succession before people can conclude with any confidence that the good times are over and a recession has begun.

The same is true with inflation. Even periods of moderate inflation have months of high inflation—so that several high-inflation months must come in sequence before people can confidently conclude that inflation has moved to a higher level.

Attempts to reduce the length of the recognition lag by trying to predict the future course of the economy also have proven to be highly difficult, at best. As a result, the economy is often 4 to 6 months into a recession or inflation before the situation is clearly discernible in the relevant statistics. Due to this recognition lag, the economic downslide or the inflation may become more serious than it would have if the situation had been identified and acted on sooner.

- ***Administrative lag*** The wheels of democratic government turn slowly. There will typically be a significant lag between the time the need for fiscal action is recognized and the time action is taken. Following the terrorist attacks of September 11, 2001, the U.S. Congress was stalemated for 5 months before passing a compromise economic stimulus law in March 2002. (In contrast, the Federal Reserve began lowering interest rates the week after the attacks.)
- ***Operational lag*** A lag also occurs between the time fiscal action is taken and the time that action affects output, employment, or the price level. Although changes in tax rates can be put into effect relatively quickly once new laws are passed, government spending on public works—new dams, interstate highways, and so on—requires long planning periods and even longer periods of construction. Such spending is of questionable use in offsetting short (for example, 6- to 12-month) periods of recession. Consequently, discretionary fiscal policy has increasingly relied on tax changes rather than on changes in spending as its main tool.

Political Considerations

Fiscal policy is conducted in a political arena. That reality not only may slow the enactment of fiscal policy but also may create the potential for political considerations swamping economic considerations in its formulation. It is a human trait to rationalize actions and policies that are in one's self-interest. Politicians are very human—they want to get reelected. A strong economy at election time will certainly help them. So they may favor large tax cuts under the guise of expansionary fiscal policy even though that policy is economically inappropriate. Similarly, they may rationalize increased government spending on popular items such as farm subsidies, health care, highways, education, and homeland security.

At the extreme, elected officials and political parties might collectively "hijack" fiscal policy for political purposes, cause inappropriate changes in aggregate demand, and thereby cause (rather than avert) economic fluctuations. For instance, before an election, they may try to stimulate the economy to improve their reelection hopes. And then after the election, they may try to use contractionary fiscal policy to dampen the excessive aggregate demand that they caused with their preelection stimulus. In short, elected officials may cause so-called **political business cycles**—swings in overall economic activity and real GDP resulting from election-motivated fiscal policy, rather than from inherent instability in the private sector. Political business cycles are difficult to document and prove, but there is little doubt that political considerations weigh heavily in the formulation of fiscal policy. The question is how often those political considerations run counter to "sound economics."

Future Policy Reversals

Fiscal policy may fail to achieve its intended objectives if households expect future reversals of policy. Consider a tax cut, for example. If taxpayers believe the tax reduction is temporary, they may save a large portion of their tax cut, reasoning that rates will return to their previous level in the future. They save more now so that they will be able to draw on this extra savings to maintain their future consumption levels if taxes do indeed rise again in the future. So a tax reduction thought to be temporary may not increase present consumption spending and aggregate demand by as much as our simple model (Figure 27.1) suggests.

The opposite may be true for a tax increase. If taxpayers think it is temporary, they may reduce their saving to pay the tax while maintaining their present consumption. They may reason they can restore their saving when the tax rate again falls. So the tax increase may not reduce current consumption and aggregate demand by as much as policymakers intended.

To the extent that this so-called *consumption smoothing* occurs over time, fiscal policy will lose some of its strength. The lesson is that tax-rate changes that households view as permanent are more likely to alter consumption and aggregate demand than tax changes they view as temporary.

Offsetting State and Local Finance

The fiscal policies of state and local governments are frequently *pro-cyclical*, meaning that they worsen rather than correct recession or inflation. Unlike the federal government, most state and local governments face constitutional or other legal requirements to balance their budgets. Like households and private businesses, state and local governments increase their expenditures during prosperity and cut them during recession.

During the Great Depression of the 1930s, most of the increase in federal spending was offset by decreases in state and local spending. During and immediately following the recession of 2001, many state and local governments had to offset lower tax revenues resulting from the reduced personal income and spending of their citizens. They offset the decline in revenues by raising tax rates, imposing new taxes, and reducing spending.

In view of these past experiences, the $787 billion fiscal package of 2009 made a special effort to reduce this problem by giving substantial aid dollars to state governments. Because of the sizable federal aid, the states did not have to increase taxes and reduce expenditure by as much as otherwise. So their collective fiscal actions did not fight as much against the increase in aggregate demand that the federal government wanted to achieve with its tax cuts and expenditure increases.

Crowding-Out Effect

Another potential flaw of fiscal policy is the so-called **crowding-out effect:** An expansionary fiscal policy (deficit spending) may increase the interest rate and reduce investment spending, thereby weakening or canceling the stimulus of the expansionary policy. The rising interest rate might also potentially crowd out interest-sensitive consumption spending (such as purchasing automobiles on credit). But since investment is the most volatile component of GDP, the crowding-out effect focuses its attention on investment and whether the stimulus provided by deficit spending may be partly or even fully neutralized by an offsetting reduction in investment spending.

To see the potential problem, realize that whenever the government borrows money (as it must if it is deficit spending), it increases the overall demand for money. If the monetary authorities are holding the money supply constant, this increase in demand will raise the price paid for borrowing money: the interest rate. Because investment spending varies inversely with the interest rate, some investment will be choked off or "crowded out."

Economists vary in their opinions about the strength of the crowding-out effect. An important thing to keep in mind is that crowding out is likely to be less of a problem when the economy is in recession because investment demand tends to be weak. Why? Because output purchases slow during recessions and therefore most businesses end up with substantial excess capacity. As a result, they do not have much incentive to add new machinery or build new factories. After all, why should they add capacity when some of the capacity they already have is lying idle?

With investment demand weak during a recession, the crowding-out effect is likely to be very small. Simply put, there is not much investment for the government to crowd out. Even if deficit spending does increase the interest rate, the effect on investment may be fully offset by the improved investment prospects that businesses expect from the fiscal stimulus.

By contrast, when the economy is operating at or near full capacity, investment demand is likely to be quite strong so that crowding out will probably be a much more serious problem. When the economy is booming, factories will be running at or near full capacity and firms will have high investment demand for two reasons. First, equipment running at full capacity wears out fast, so firms will be investing substantial amounts just to replace machinery and equipment that wears out and depreciates. Second, the economy is likely to be growing overall so that firms will be heavily investing to *add* to their production capacity to take advantage of the greater anticipated demand for their outputs.

Current Thinking on Fiscal Policy

Where do these complications leave us as to the advisability and effectiveness of discretionary fiscal policy? In view of the complications and uncertain outcomes of fiscal policy, some economists argue that it is better not to engage in it at all. Those holding that viewpoint to the superiority of monetary policy (changes in interest rates engineered by the Federal Reserve) as a stabilizing device or believe that most economic fluctuations tend to be mild and self-correcting.

But most economists believe that fiscal policy remains an important, useful policy lever in the government's macroeconomic toolkit. The current popular view is that fiscal policy can help push the economy in a particular direction but cannot fine-tune it to a precise macroeconomic outcome. Mainstream economists generally agree that monetary policy is the best month-to-month stabilization tool for the U.S. economy. If monetary policy is doing its job, the government should maintain a relatively neutral fiscal policy, with a cyclically adjusted budget deficit or surplus of no more than 2 percent of potential GDP. It should hold major discretionary fiscal policy in reserve to help counter situations where recession threatens to be deep and long lasting, as in 2008 and 2009, or where a substantial reduction in aggregate demand might help the Federal Reserve to quell a major bout of inflation.

Finally, economists agree that any proposed fiscal policy should be evaluated for its potential positive and negative impacts on long-run productivity growth. The short-run policy tools used for conducting active fiscal policy often have long-run impacts. Countercyclical fiscal policy should be shaped to strengthen, or at least not impede, the growth of long-run aggregate supply (which would be shown in Figure 26.5 as a rightward shift of the long-run aggregate supply curve). For example, a tax cut might be structured to enhance work effort, strengthen investment, and encourage innovation. Alternatively, an increase in government spending might center on preplanned projects for public capital (highways, mass transit, ports, airports), which are complementary to private investment and thus support long-term economic growth.

AP QUICK REVIEW 27.2

- ✓ Automatic changes in net taxes (taxes minus transfers) add a degree of built-in stability to the economy. For instance, as real GDP falls, tax payments automatically fall and help cushion the decrease in aggregate demand.
- ✓ The cyclically adjusted budget eliminates cyclical effects on net tax revenues; it compares actual levels of government spending to the projected levels of net taxes that would occur if the economy were achieving its full-employment output.
- ✓ Time lags, political problems, expectations, and state and local finances complicate fiscal policy.
- ✓ The crowding-out effect indicates that an expansionary fiscal policy may increase interest rates and reduce investment spending, thus maybe weakening the stimulus of the expansionary policy.

AP The U.S. Public Debt

LO27.6 Discuss the size, composition, and consequences of the U.S. public debt.

The U.S. national debt, or **public debt,** is essentially the accumulation of all past federal deficits and surpluses. The deficits have greatly exceeded the surpluses and have emerged mainly from war financing, recessions, and fiscal policy. In 2015, the total public debt was $18.2 trillion—$10.7 trillion held by the public, excluding the Federal Reserve; and $7.5 trillion held by federal agencies and the Federal Reserve. Between 2007 and 2009, the total public debt expanded by a huge $2.9 trillion. During the Great Recession, federal tax revenues plummeted because incomes and profit fell, and federal expenditures jumped because of huge spending to rescue failing financial institutions and to stimulate the shrinking economy.

Because large annual deficits continued over the next several years, the total public debt grew past $18.2 trillion in late 2015. The debt had more than doubled in just over nine years, growing from $8.5 trillion in late 2006 to $18.2 trillion in late 2015. You can find the current size of the public debt at the website of the Department of Treasury, Bureau of the Fiscal Service, or at **http://treasurydirect.gov/NP/debt/current.** At this site, you will see that the U.S. Treasury defines "the public" to include the Federal Reserve. But because the Federal Reserve is the nation's central bank, economists view it as essentially part of the federal government and not part of the public. Economists typically focus on the part of the debt that is not owned by the federal government and the Federal Reserve.

Ownership

The total public debt of $18.2 trillion represents the total amount of money owed by the federal government to the holders of **U.S. government securities:** financial instruments issued by the federal government to borrow money to finance expenditures that exceed tax revenues. U.S. government securities (loan instruments) are of four types: *Treasury bills* (short-term securities), *Treasury notes* (medium-term securities), *Treasury bonds* (long-term securities), and *U.S. savings bonds* (long-term, nonmarketable bonds).

Figure 27.6 shows that the public, sans the Federal Reserve, held 59 percent of the federal debt in 2015 and that federal government agencies and the Federal Reserve held the remaining 41 percent. The federal agencies hold U.S. government securities as risk-free assets that they can cash in as needed to make future payments. The Federal Reserve holds these securities to facilitate the "open-market operations" that it uses to control the nation's money supply (Chapter 30). Observe that "the public" in the pie chart consists of individuals here and abroad, state and local governments, and U.S. financial institutions. Foreigners held about 34 percent of the total U.S. public debt in 2015, meaning that most of the U.S. public debt is held internally and not externally. Americans owed 66 percent of the public debt to Americans. Of the $6.1 trillion

AP FIGURE 27.6 Ownership of the total public debt, 2015. The $18.2 trillion public debt can be divided into the 59 percent held by the public (excluding the Federal Reserve), and the proportion held by federal agencies and the Federal Reserve System (41 percent). Of the total debt, 34 percent is foreign-owned.

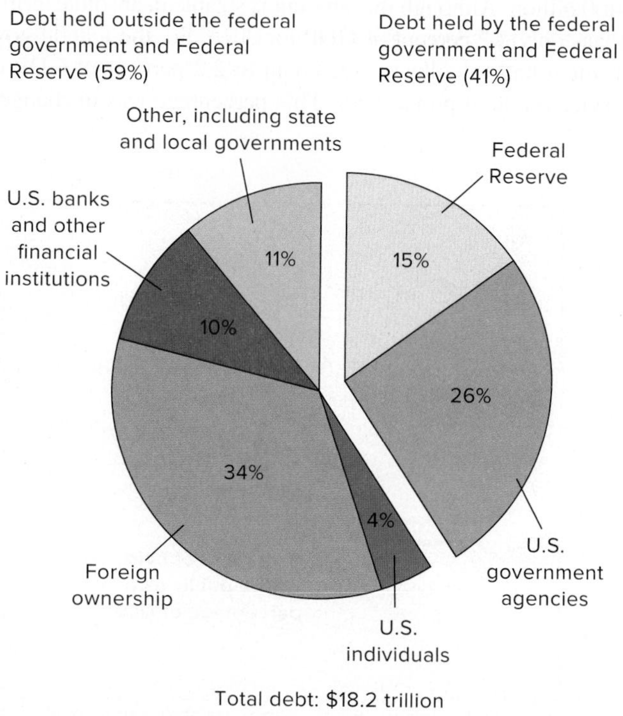

Source: Economic Report of the President, 2016, **www.whitehouse.gov/sites/default/files/docs/ERP_2016_Book_Complete%20JA.pdf**; authors' derivation from Table B-89, September 2015 data. Federal Reserve percentage is from the U.S. Treasury, **www.fiscal.treasury.gov/fsreports/rpt/treasBulletin/treasBulletin_home.htm.**

of debt held by foreigners, China held 20 percent, Japan held 18 percent, and oil-exporting nations held 5 percent.

Debt and GDP

A simple statement of the absolute size of the debt ignores the fact that the wealth and productive ability of the U.S. economy is also vast. A wealthy, highly productive nation can incur and carry a large public debt much more easily than a poor nation can. A more meaningful measure of the public debt relates it to an economy's GDP. Figure 27.7 shows the yearly relative sizes of the U.S. public debt held outside the Federal Reserve and federal agencies. In 2015 the percentage was 75 percent. Most noticeably, the percentage rose dramatically starting in 2008 because of massive annual budget deficits.

International Comparisons

It is not uncommon for countries to have sizable public debts. As shown in Global Perspective 27.2, the public debt as a percentage of real GDP in the United States is neither particularly high nor low relative to such debt percentages in other advanced industrial nations.

Interest Charges

Many economists conclude that the primary burden of the debt is the annual interest charge accruing on the bonds sold to finance the debt. In 2015 interest on the total public debt was $400 billion. Although this amount is sizable in absolute terms, it was only 2.2 percent of GDP for 2015. So, the federal government had to collect taxes equal to 2.2 percent of GDP to service the total public debt. This percentage was unchanged from 2000 despite the much higher total public debt. That was possible because interest rates were being kept extremely low

GLOBAL PERSPECTIVE 27.2

Publicly Held Debt: International Comparisons

Although the United States has the world's largest public debt, a number of other nations have larger debts as percentages of their GDPs.

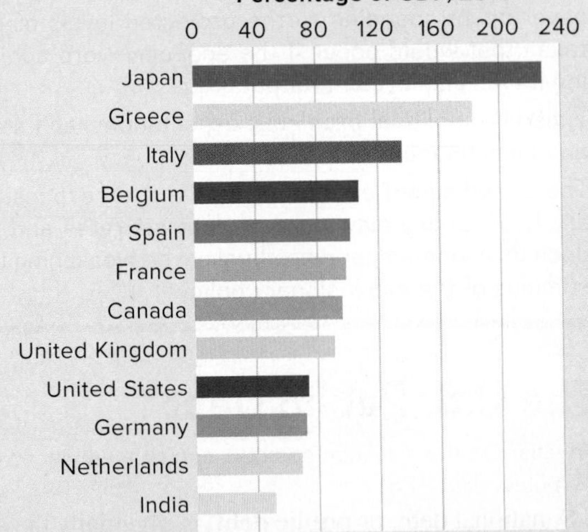

Source: The World Factbook, CIA, **www.cia.gov/library/publications/the-world-factbook/**. These debt calculations encompass federal, state, and local debt, including the debt of government-owned enterprises (not just federal debt as in Figure 27.7) and are 2015 estimates.

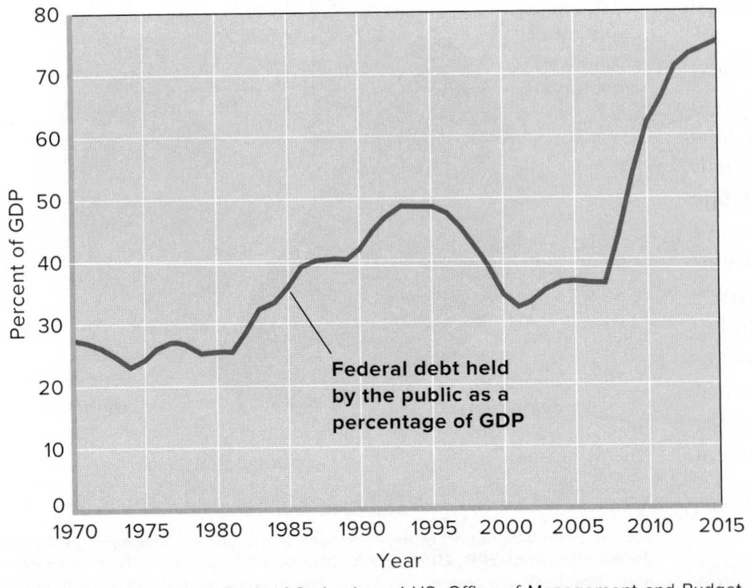

Source: Federal Reserve Bank of St. Louis and US. Office of Management and Budget, Federal Debt Held by the Public as Percent of Gross Domestic Product [FYGFGDQ188S], retrieved from FRED, Federal Reserve Bank of St. Louis **https://research.stlouisfed.org/fred2/series/FYGFGDQ188S, May 3, 2016.**

FIGURE 27.7 **Federal debt held by the public, excluding the Federal Reserve, as a percentage of GDP, 1970–2015.** As a percentage of GDP, the federal debt held by the public (held outside the Federal Reserve and federal government agencies) increased sharply over the 1980–1995 period and declined significantly between 1995 and 2001. Since 2001, the percentage has gone up again, jumping sharply after 2008.

by the Federal Reserve in order to help stimulate the economy in the wake of the Great Recession (Chapter 30).

False Concerns

You may wonder if the large public debt might bankrupt the United States or at least place a tremendous burden on your children and grandchildren. Fortunately, these are largely false concerns. People were wondering the same things 50 years ago!

Bankruptcy

The large U.S. public debt does not threaten to bankrupt the federal government, leaving it unable to meet its financial obligations. There are two main reasons: refinancing and taxation.

Refinancing As long as the U.S. public debt is viewed by lenders as manageable and sustainable, the public debt is easily refinanced. As portions of the debt come due on maturing Treasury bills, notes, and bonds each month, the government does not cut expenditures or raise taxes to provide the funds required. Rather, it refinances the debt by selling new bonds and using the proceeds to pay holders of the maturing bonds. The new bonds are in strong demand because lenders can obtain a market-determined interest return with no risk of default by the federal government.

Of course, refinancing could become an issue with a high enough debt-to-GDP ratio. Some countries such as Greece have run into this problem. High and rising ratios in the United States might raise fears that the U.S. government might be unable to pay back loans as they come due. But, with the present U.S. debt-to-GDP ratio and the prospects of long-term economic growth, this is a false concern for the United States.

Taxation The federal government has the constitutional authority to levy and collect taxes. A tax increase is a government option for gaining sufficient revenue to pay interest and principal on the public debt. Financially distressed private households and corporations cannot extract themselves from their financial difficulties by taxing the public. If their incomes or sales revenues fall short of their expenses, they can indeed go bankrupt. But the federal government does have the option to impose new taxes or increase existing tax rates if necessary to finance its debt. Such tax hikes may be politically unpopular and may weaken incentives to work and invest, but they *are* a means of raising funds to finance the debt.

Burdening Future Generations

In 2015 public debt per capita was $56,368. Was each child born in 2015 handed a $56,368 bill from the federal government? Not really. The public debt does not impose as much of a burden on future generations as commonly thought.

The United States owes a substantial portion of the public debt to itself. U.S. citizens and institutions (banks, businesses, insurance companies, governmental agencies, and trust funds) own about 66 percent of the U.S. government securities. Although that part of the public debt is a liability to Americans (as taxpayers), it is simultaneously an asset to Americans (as holders of Treasury bills, Treasury notes, Treasury bonds, and U.S. savings bonds).

To eliminate the American-owned part of the public debt would require a gigantic transfer payment from Americans to Americans. Taxpayers would pay higher taxes, and holders of the debt would receive an equal amount for their U.S. government securities. Purchasing power in the United States would not change. Only the repayment of the 34 percent of the public debt owned by foreigners would negatively impact U.S. purchasing power.

The public debt increased sharply during the Second World War. But the decision to finance military purchases through the sale of government bonds did not shift the economic burden of the war to future generations. The economic cost of the Second World War consisted of the civilian goods society had to forgo in shifting scarce resources to war goods production (recall production possibilities analysis). Regardless of whether society financed this reallocation through higher taxes or through borrowing, the real economic burden of the war would have been the same. That burden was borne almost entirely by those who lived during the war. They were the ones who did without a multitude of consumer goods to enable the United States to arm itself and its allies.

The next generation inherited the debt from the war but also an equal amount of government bonds that would pay them cash in future years. It also inherited the enormous benefits from the victory—namely, preserved political and economic systems at home and the "export" of those systems to Germany, Italy, and Japan. Those outcomes enhanced postwar U.S. economic growth and helped raise the standard of living of future generations of Americans.

Substantive Issues

Although the preceding issues relating to the public debt are false concerns, a number of substantive issues are not. Economists, however, attach varying degrees of importance to them.

Income Distribution

The distribution of ownership of government securities is highly uneven. Some people own much more than the $56,368-per-person portion of government securities; other people own less or none at all. In general, the ownership of the public debt is concentrated among wealthier groups, who own a large percentage of all stocks and bonds. Because the overall federal tax system is only slightly progressive, payment of interest on the public debt mildly increases income inequality. Income is transferred from people who, on average, have lower incomes to the higher-income bondholders. If greater income equality is one of society's goals, then this redistribution is undesirable.

LAST WORD

The Social Security and Medicare Shortfalls

Social Security and Medicare Face Gigantic Future Funding Shortfalls. Metaphorically Speaking, Some Economists See These Programs as Financial and Political Time Bombs.

Source: © Royalty-Free/Corbis RF

The American population, on average, is getting decidedly older. The percentage of the population age 62 or older will rise substantially over the next several decades, with the greatest increases for people age 75 and above. In the future, more people will be receiving Social Security benefits (income during retirement) and Medicare (medical care during retirement) for longer periods. Each person's benefits will be paid for by fewer workers. The number of workers per Social Security and Medicare beneficiary was roughly 5:1 in 1960. Today it is 3:1, and by 2040 it will be only 2:1.

The combined cost of the Social Security and Medicare programs was 8.5 percent of GDP in 2014, and that percentage is projected to grow to 11.4 percent of GDP in 2035 and 12.2 percent of GDP in 2086.*

The Social Security Shortfall Social Security is the major public retirement program in the United States. The program costs $888 billion annually and is financed by a 12.4 percent tax on earnings up to a set level of earnings ($118,500 in 2016). Half the tax (6.2 percent) is paid by the worker; the other half by the employer. Social Security is largely an annual "pay-as-you-go" plan, meaning that most of the current revenues from the Social Security tax are paid to current Social Security retirees. Through the start of 2009, Social Security revenues exceeded Social Security payouts in anticipation of the large benefits promised to the baby boomers when they retire. That excess inflow was used to buy U.S. Treasury securities that were credited to a government account called the Social Security Trust Fund. But the combined accumulation of money in the trust fund through 2009 plus the projected future revenues from the payroll tax in later years was expected to be greatly inadequate for paying the promised retirement benefits to all future retirees.

This underfunding of future retirement promises was brought into sharper focus in the latter half of 2009 when, for the first time, Social Security revenues fell below Social Security retirement payouts and the system started shifting money from the trust fund to make up the difference. The trust fund is expected to be exhausted in 2033. For each year thereafter, annual tax revenues will cover only 75 percent of the promised benefits.

*Social Security and Medicare Board of Trustees, "Status of the Social Security and Medicare Programs: A Summary of the 2015 Annual Reports," **www.ssa.gov.** This publication is also the source of most of the statistical information that follows.

Incentives

The current public debt necessitates annual interest payments of $400 billion. With no increase in the size of the debt, that interest charge must be paid out of tax revenues. Higher taxes may dampen incentives to bear risk, to innovate, to invest, and to work. So, in this indirect way, a large public debt may impair economic growth and therefore impose a burden of reduced output (and income) on future generations.

Foreign-Owned Public Debt

The 34 percent of the U.S. debt held by citizens and institutions of foreign countries *is* an economic burden to Americans. Because we do not owe that portion of the debt "to ourselves," the payment of interest and principal on this **external public debt** enables foreigners to buy some of our output. In return for the benefits derived from the borrowed funds, the United States transfers goods and services to foreign lenders. Of course, Americans also own debt issued by foreign governments, so payment of principal and interest by those governments transfers some of their goods and services to Americans.

Crowding-Out Effect Revisited

A potentially more serious problem is the financing (and continual refinancing) of the large public debt, which can transfer a real economic burden to future generations by passing on to them a smaller stock of capital goods. This possibility involves the previously discussed crowding-out effect: the idea that public borrowing drives up real interest rates, which reduces private investment spending. If public borrowing only happened during recessions, crowding out would not likely be much of a problem. Because private investment demand tends to be weak during recessions, any increase in interest

The Medicare Shortfall The Medicare program is the U.S. health care program for people age 65 and older in the United States. The program costs $510 billion per year and has been growing at about 9 percent annually. Like Social Security, it also is a pay-as-you-go plan, meaning that current medical benefits for people age 65 or older are being funded by current tax revenues from the 2.9 percent Medicare tax on earnings and the 3.8 percent investment surtax on wealthier investors that was instituted in 2013 as part of Obamacare. Like the Social Security tax, half the Medicare earnings tax is paid by the employer (1.45 percent) and half the by the employee. But the 2.9 percent Medicare tax is applied to all earnings.

The financial status of Medicare is much worse than that of Social Security. To begin with, the Medicare Trust Fund will be depleted in 2024, 9 years before the Social Security Trust Fund is expected to be depleted. Then, in subsequent years, the percentage of scheduled Medicare benefits covered by the Medicare tax will decline from 97 percent in 2025 to 72 percent in 2035 and 69 percent in 2080.

The Unpleasant Options To restore long-run balance to Social Security and Medicare, the federal government must either reduce benefits or increase revenues. It's as simple—and as complicated—as that! The Social Security Administration concludes that bringing projected Social Security revenues and payments into balance over the next 75 years would require a 16 percent permanent reduction in Social Security benefits, a 13 percent permanent increase in tax revenues, or some combination of the two. To bring projected Medicare revenues and expenses into long-run balance would require an increase in the Medicare payroll tax by 122 percent, a 51 percent reduction of Medicare payments from their projected levels, or some combination of each.

All the general options for closing all or part of the Social Security and Medicare gaps involve difficult economic trade-offs and dangerous political risks because one group or another will strongly oppose them. Here are just a few examples:

- Increasing the retirement age for collecting Social Security or Medicare benefits will upset preretirement workers who have been paying into the system and will receive their benefits later than they expected.
- Subjecting a larger portion of total earnings to the Social Security tax would constitute a gigantic tax increase on the earnings of the country's highest trained and educated individuals. This might reduce the incentive of younger people to obtain education and advance in their careers.
- Disqualifying wealthy individuals from receiving Social Security and Medicare benefits would tilt the programs toward welfare and redistribution, rather than insurance programs. This would undermine the broad existing political support for the programs.
- Redirecting legal immigration toward high-skilled, high-earning entrants and away from low-skilled, low-earning immigrants to raise Social Security and Medicare revenues would also raise the ire of some native-born high-skilled workers and the proponents of immigration based on family reunification.
- Placing the payroll tax revenues into accounts that individuals, not the government, would own, maintain, and bequeath would transform the Social Security and Medicare programs from guaranteed "defined benefit plans" into much riskier "defined contribution plans." The extreme short-run volatility of the stock market might leave some unlucky people destitute in old age.

The problem is huge and will not go away. One recent attempt to add up the underfunding of all the promised Social Security and Medicare benefits finds that the total underfunding greatly exceeds the combined current wealth (net worth) of everyone in the United States today.† Even if this estimate is somewhat extreme, the fact remains: The federal government and American people eventually will have to face up to the overpromising-underfunding problem and find ways to resolve it.

†Bruce Bartlett, "The 81% Tax Increase," Forbes.com, August 8, 2009, **www.forbes.com.**

rates caused by public borrowing will at most cause a small reduction in investment spending.

In contrast, the need to continuously finance a large public debt may be more troublesome. At times, that financing requires borrowing large amounts of money when the economy is near or at its full-employment output. Because this usually is when private demand is strong, any increase in interest rates caused by the borrowing necessary to refinance the debt may result in a substantial decline in investment spending. If the amount of current investment crowded out is extensive, future generations will inherit an economy with a smaller production capacity and, other things equal, a lower standard of living.

A Graphical Look at Crowding Out We know from Chapter 24 that the amount of investment spending is inversely related to the real interest rate. When graphed, that relationship is shown as a downsloping investment demand curve, such as either ID_1 or ID_2 in Figure 27.8. Let's first consider curve ID_1. (Ignore curve ID_2 for now.) Suppose that government borrowing increases the real interest rate from 6 percent to 10 percent. Investment spending will then fall from $25 billion to $15 billion, as shown by the economy's move from *a* to *b*. That is, the financing of the debt will compete with the financing of private investment projects and crowd out $10 billion of private investment. So the stock of private capital handed down to future generations will be $10 billion less than it would have been without the need to finance the public debt.

Public Investments and Public-Private Complementarities But even with crowding out, two factors could partly or fully offset the net economic burden shifted to future generations. First, just as private expenditures may involve either consumption or investment, so it is with public goods. Part of the government spending enabled by the public debt is

FIGURE 27.8 The investment demand curve and the crowding-out effect. If the investment demand curve (ID_1) is fixed, the increase in the interest rate from 6 percent to 10 percent caused by financing a large public debt will move the economy from *a* to *b*, crowding out $10 billion of private investment and decreasing the size of the capital stock inherited by future generations. However, if the public goods enabled by the debt improve the investment prospects of businesses, the private investment demand curve will shift rightward, as from ID_1 to ID_2. That shift may offset the crowding-out effect wholly or in part. In this case, it moves the economy from *a* to *c*.

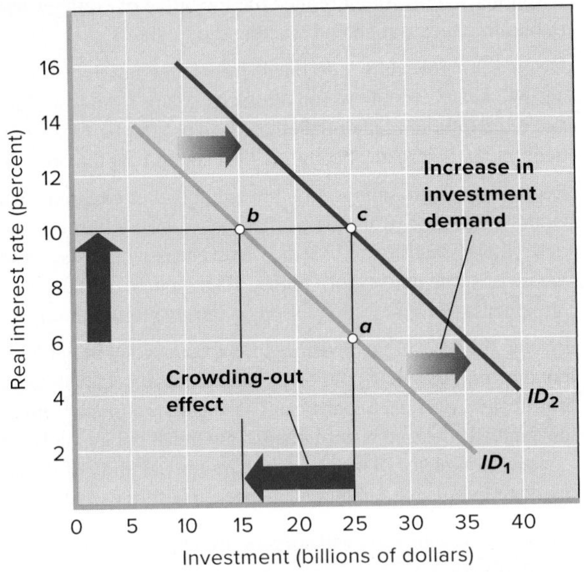

for public investment outlays (for example, highways, mass transit systems, and electric power facilities) and "human capital" (for example, investments in education, job training, and health). Like private expenditures on machinery and equipment, those **public investments** increase the economy's future production capacity. Because of the financing through debt, the stock of public capital passed on to future generations may be higher than otherwise. That greater stock of public capital may offset the diminished stock of private capital resulting from the crowding-out effect, leaving overall production capacity unimpaired.

So-called public-private complementarities are a second factor that could reduce the crowding-out effect. Some public and private investments are complementary. Thus, the public investment financed through debt could spur some private-sector investment by increasing its expected rate of return. For example, a federal building in a city may encourage private investment in the form of nearby office buildings, shops, and restaurants. Through its complementary effect, the spending on public capital may shift the private investment demand curve to the right, as from ID_1 to ID_2 in Figure 27.8. Even though the government borrowing boosts the interest rate from 6 percent to 10 percent, total private investment need not fall. In the case shown as the move from *a* to *c* in Figure 27.8, it remains at $25 billion. Of course, the increase in investment demand might be smaller than that shown. If it were smaller, the crowding-out effect would not be fully offset. But the point is that an increase in investment demand may counter the decline in investment that would otherwise result from the higher interest rate.

AP QUICK REVIEW 27.3

- ✓ The U.S. public debt is the total accumulation of all past federal budget deficits and surpluses; about 34 percent of the U.S. public debt is held by foreigners.
- ✓ The U.S. public debt held by the public (excluding the Federal Reserve) was 75 percent of GDP in 2015, up from 33 percent in 2000.
- ✓ The federal government won't go bankrupt because it needs only to refinance (not retire) the public debt and it can raise revenues, if needed, through higher taxes.
- ✓ The borrowing and interest payments associated with the public debt may (a) increase income inequality; (b) require higher taxes, which may dampen incentives; (c) reduce the flexibility of future discretionary government spending; and (d) impede the growth of the nation's stock of capital through crowding out of private investment.

SUMMARY

LO27.1 Identify and explain the purposes, tools, and limitations of fiscal policy.

Fiscal policy consists of deliberate changes in government spending, taxes, or some combination of both to promote full employment, price-level stability, and economic growth. Fiscal policy requires increases in government spending, decreases in taxes, or both—a budget deficit—to increase aggregate demand and push an economy from a recession. Decreases in government spending, increases in taxes, or both—a budget surplus—are appropriate fiscal policy for decreasing aggregate demand to try to slow or halt demand-pull inflation.

LO27.2 Explain the role of built-in stabilizers in moderating business cycles.

Built-in stability arises from net tax revenues, which vary directly with the level of GDP. During recession, the federal budget automatically moves toward a stabilizing deficit; during expansion, the budget automatically moves toward an anti-inflationary surplus. Built-in stability lessens, but does not fully correct, undesired changes in real GDP.

LO27.3 Describe how the cyclically adjusted budget reveals the status of U.S. fiscal policy.

Actual federal budget deficits can go up or down because of changes in GDP, changes in fiscal policy, or both. Deficits caused by changes in GDP are called cyclical deficits. The cyclically adjusted budget removes cyclical deficits from the budget and therefore measures the budget deficit or surplus that would occur if the economy operated at its full-employment output throughout the year. Changes in the cyclical budget deficit or surplus provide meaningful information as to whether the government's fiscal policy is expansionary, neutral, or contractionary. Changes in the actual budget deficit or surplus do not, since such deficits or surpluses can include cyclical deficits or surpluses.

LO27.4 Summarize recent U.S. fiscal policy and the projections for U.S. fiscal policy over the next few years.

In 2001 the Bush administration and Congress chose to reduce marginal tax rates and phase out the federal estate tax. A recession occurred in 2001, and federal spending for the war on terrorism rocketed. The federal budget swung from a surplus of $128 billion in 2001 to a deficit of $158 billion in 2002. In 2003 the Bush administration and Congress accelerated the tax reductions scheduled under the 2001 tax law and cut tax rates on capital gains and dividends. The purposes were to stimulate a sluggish economy. By 2007 the economy had reached its full employment level of output.

The federal government responded to the deep recession of 2007–2009 by implementing highly expansionary fiscal policy. In 2008 the federal government passed a tax rebate program that sent $600 checks to qualified individuals. Later that year, it created a $700 billion emergency fund to keep key financial institutions from failing. These and other programs increased the cyclically adjusted budget deficit from −1.3 percent of potential GDP in 2007 to −2.9 percent in 2008. When the economy continued to plunge, the Obama administration and Congress enacted a massive $787 billion stimulus program to be implemented over 2½ years. The cyclically adjusted budget deficit shot up from −2.9 percent of potential GDP in 2008 to −7.1 percent in 2009, but then decreased to −1.6 percent in 2015.

LO27.5 Discuss the problems that governments may encounter in enacting and applying fiscal policy.

Certain problems complicate the enactment and implementation of fiscal policy. They include (*a*) timing problems associated with recognition, administrative, and operational lags; (*b*) the potential for misuse of fiscal policy for political rather than economic purposes; (*c*) the fact that state and local finances tend to be pro-cyclical; (*d*) potential ineffectiveness if households expect future policy reversals; and (*e*) the possibility of fiscal policy crowding out private investment.

Most economists believe that fiscal policy can help move the economy in a desired direction but cannot reliably be used to fine-tune the economy to a position of price stability and full employment. Nevertheless, fiscal policy is a valuable backup tool for aiding monetary policy in fighting significant recession or inflation.

LO27.6 Discuss the size, composition, and consequences of the U.S. public debt.

The public debt is the total accumulation of all past federal government deficits and surpluses and consists of Treasury bills, Treasury notes, Treasury bonds, and U.S. savings bonds. In 2015 the U.S. public debt was $18.2 trillion, or $56,368 per person. The public (which here includes banks and state and local governments) holds 59 percent of that federal debt; the Federal Reserve and federal agencies hold the other 41 percent. Foreigners hold 34 percent of the federal debt. Interest payments as a percentage of GDP were about 2.2 percent in 2015.

Because of large deficits during the Great Recession and in subsequent years, the total U.S. public debt more than doubled between 2005 and 2015.

The concern that a large public debt may bankrupt the U.S. government is generally a false worry because (*a*) the debt needs only to be refinanced rather than refunded and (*b*) the federal government has the power to increase taxes to make interest payments on the debt.

In general, the public debt is not a vehicle for shifting economic burdens to future generations. Americans inherit not only most of the public debt (a liability) but also most of the U.S. government securities (an asset) that finance the debt.

More substantive problems associated with public debt include the following: (*a*) Payment of interest on the debt may increase income inequality. (*b*) Interest payments on the debt require higher taxes, which may impair incentives. (*c*) Paying interest or principal on the portion of the debt held by foreigners means a transfer of real output abroad. (*d*) Government borrowing to refinance or pay interest on the debt may increase interest rates and crowd out private investment spending, leaving future generations with a smaller stock of capital than they would have had otherwise.

The increase in investment in public capital that may result from debt financing may partly or wholly offset the crowding-out effect of the public debt on private investment. Also, the added public investment may stimulate private investment, where the two are complements.

TERMS AND CONCEPTS

fiscal policy
Council of Economic Advisers (CEA)
expansionary fiscal policy
budget deficit
contractionary fiscal policy
budget surplus
built-in stabilizer
progressive tax system
proportional tax system
regressive tax system
cyclically adjusted budget
cyclical deficit
political business cycle
crowding-out effect
public debt
U.S. government securities
external public debt
public investments

The following and additional problems can be found in connect

DISCUSSION QUESTIONS

1. What is the role of the Council of Economic Advisers (CEA) as it relates to fiscal policy? Use an Internet search to find the names and university affiliations of the present members of the CEA. **LO27.1**
2. What are government's fiscal policy options for ending severe demand-pull inflation? Which of these fiscal options do you think might be favored by a person who wants to preserve the size of government? A person who thinks the public sector is too large? How does the "ratchet effect" affect anti-inflationary fiscal policy? **LO27.1**
3. (For students who were assigned Chapter 25) Use the aggregate expenditures model to show how government fiscal policy could eliminate either a recessionary expenditure gap or an inflationary expenditure gap (Figure 25.7). Explain how equal-size increases in *G* and *T* could eliminate a recessionary gap and how equal-size decreases in *G* and *T* could eliminate an inflationary gap. **LO27.1**
4. Some politicians have suggested that the United States enact a constitutional amendment requiring that the federal government balance its budget annually. Explain why such an amendment, if strictly enforced, would force the government to enact a contractionary fiscal policy whenever the economy experienced a severe recession. **LO27.1**
5. Explain how built-in (or automatic) stabilizers work. What are the differences between proportional, progressive, and regressive tax systems as they relate to an economy's built-in stability? **LO27.2**
6. Define the cyclically adjusted budget, explain its significance, and state why it may differ from the actual budget. Suppose the full-employment, noninflationary level of real output is GDP_3 (not GDP_2) in the economy depicted in Figure 27.3. If the economy is operating at GDP_2, instead of GDP_3, what is the status of its cyclically adjusted budget? The status of its current fiscal policy? What change in fiscal policy would you recommend? How would you accomplish that in terms of the *G* and *T* lines in the figure? **LO27.3**
7. Briefly state and evaluate the problem of time lags in enacting and applying fiscal policy. Explain the idea of a political business cycle. How might expectations of a near-term policy reversal weaken fiscal policy based on changes in tax rates? What is the crowding-out effect, and why might it be relevant to fiscal policy? In view of your answers, explain the following statement: "Although fiscal policy clearly is useful in combating the extremes of severe recession and demand-pull inflation, it is impossible to use fiscal policy to fine-tune the economy to the full-employment, noninflationary level of real GDP and keep the economy there indefinitely." **LO27.5**
8. How do economists distinguish between the absolute and relative sizes of the public debt? Why is the distinction important? Distinguish between refinancing the debt and retiring the debt. How does an internally held public debt differ from an externally held public debt? Contrast the effects of retiring an internally held debt and retiring an externally held debt. **LO27.6**
9. True or false? If false, explain why. **LO27.6**
   a. The total public debt is more relevant to an economy than the public debt as a percentage of GDP.
   b. An internally held public debt is like a debt of the left hand owed to the right hand.
   c. The Federal Reserve and federal government agencies hold more than three-fourths of the public debt.
   d. The portion of the U.S. debt held by the public (and not by government entities) was larger as a percentage of GDP in 2015 than it was in 2000.
   e. As a percentage of GDP, the total U.S. public debt is the highest such debt among the world's advanced industrial nations.
10. Why might economists be quite concerned if the annual interest payments on the U.S. public debt sharply increased as a percentage of GDP? **LO27.6**
11. Trace the cause-and-effect chain through which financing and refinancing of the public debt might affect real interest rates, private investment, the stock of capital, and economic growth. How might investment in public capital and complementarities between public capital and private capital alter the outcome of the cause-effect chain? **LO27.6**
12. **LAST WORD** What do economists mean when they say Social Security and Medicare are "pay-as-you-go" plans? What are the Social Security and Medicare trust funds, and how long will they have money left in them? What is the key long-run problem of both Social Security and Medicare? Do you favor increasing taxes or do you prefer reducing benefits to fix the problem?

AP REVIEW QUESTIONS

1. Explain the maximum effect of a discretionary cut in taxes of $40 billion on real GDP, when the economy's marginal propensity to consume is .75. How does this discretionary fiscal policy differ from a discretionary increase in government spending of $40 billion? **LO27.1**
2. Suppose that the economy is in the midst of a recession. Which of the following policies would most likely end the recession and stimulate output growth? **LO27.1**
   a. A Congressional proposal to incur a Federal surplus to be used for the retirement of public debt.
   b. A reduction in agricultural subsidies and veterans' benefits.
   c. A postponement of a highway construction program.
   d. A reduction in Federal tax rates on personal and corporate income.
   e. An decrease in Social Security payments to the elderly and disabled.

3. Which of the following best describes the built-in stabilizers as they function in the United States? LO27.2
   a. Incurring deficit spending causes the crowding out effect.
   b. Personal and corporate income tax collections automatically fall and transfers and subsidies automatically rise as GDP rises.
   c. Taxes become more progressive as income falls, with the wealthy paying more in taxes
   d. Personal and corporate income tax collections automatically rise and transfers and subsidies automatically decline as GDP rises.
   e. Members of Congress vote for government spending in their districts to bolster their reelection chances.
4. Last year, while an economy was in a recession, government spending was $595 billion and government revenue was $505 billion. Economists estimate that if the economy had been at its full-employment level of GDP last year, government spending would have been $555 billion and government revenue would have been $550 billion. Which of the following statements about this government's fiscal situation are true? LO27.3
   a. The government has a non–cyclically adjusted budget deficit of $595 billion.
   b. The government has a non–cyclically adjusted budget deficit of $90 billion.
   c. The government has a cyclically adjusted budget deficit of $555 billion.
   d. The government has a cyclically adjusted budget deficit of $5 billion.
   e. The government has a cyclically adjusted budget surplus of $5 billion.
5. Label each of the following scenarios in which there are problems enacting and applying fiscal policy as being an example of either recognition lag, administrative lag, or operational lag. LO27.5
   a. To fight a recession, Congress has passed a bill to increase infrastructure spending—but the legally required environmental-impact statement for each new project will take at least two years to complete before any building can begin.
   b. Distracted by a war that is going badly, politicians take no notice until inflation reaches 8 percent.
   c. A sudden recession is recognized by politicians, but it takes many months of political deal making before a stimulus bill is finally approved.
   d. To fight a recession, the president orders federal agencies to get rid of petty regulations that burden private businesses—but the federal agencies begin by spending a year developing a set of regulations on how to remove petty regulations.
6. The crowding-out effect of expansionary fiscal policy suggests that: LO27.6
   a. Tax increases are paid primarily out of saving and therefore are not an effective fiscal device.
   b. Increases in government spending financed through borrowing will increase the interest rate and thereby reduce investment.
   c. Decreases in government spending financed through borrowing will decrease the interest rate and thereby reduce investment.
   d. It is very difficult to have excessive aggregate spending in the U.S. economy.
   e. Consumer and investment spending always vary inversely.
7. Assume that the full-employment level of GDP is $10,000. The current level of GDP is $8,000. Answer the following questions. LO27.1, LO27.3
   a. Does this economy have any cyclical unemployment? Explain.
   b. If the MPC is .8, what minimum decrease in taxes is needed to reach full employment?
   c. If the MPC is .8 what minimum increase in government spending is needed to reach full employment?
   d. Are your answers to questions b and c numerically identical? If not, explain why?
   e. Could an equal increase in government spending and in taxes be used to reach full employment GDP? If so, what amount?
8. Assume an economy is operating above full employment. LO27.1, LO27.3, LO27.5
   a. Using aggregate demand and aggregate supply analysis, show this equilibrium.
   b. What problem is this economy likely to confront: unemployment, slow growth, or inflation? Explain.
   c. What fiscal policy remedies would you propose?

PROBLEMS

1. Assume that a hypothetical economy with an MPC of .8 is experiencing severe recession. By how much would government spending have to rise to shift the aggregate demand curve rightward by $25 billion? How large a tax cut would be needed to achieve the same increase in aggregate demand? Determine one possible combination of government spending increases and tax decreases that would accomplish the same goal. LO27.1
2. Refer back to the table in Figure 26.7 in the previous chapter. Suppose that aggregate demand increases such that the amount of real output demanded rises by $7 billion at each price level. By what percentage will the price level increase? Will this inflation be demand-pull inflation or will it be cost-push inflation? If potential real GDP (that is, full-employment GDP) is $510 billion, what will be the size of the positive GDP gap after the change in aggregate demand? If government wants to use fiscal policy to counter the resulting inflation without changing tax rates, would it increase government spending or decrease it? LO27.1
3. (For students who were assigned Chapter 25) Assume that, without taxes, the consumption schedule for an economy is as shown below: LO27.1

GDP, Billions	Consumption, Billions
$100	$120
200	200
300	280
400	360
500	440
600	520
700	600

a. Graph this consumption schedule. What is the size of the MPC?

b. Assume that a lump-sum (regressive) tax of $10 billion is imposed at all levels of GDP. Calculate the tax rate at each level of GDP. Graph the resulting consumption schedule and compare the MPC and the multiplier with those of the pretax consumption schedule.

c. Now suppose a proportional tax with a 10 percent tax rate is imposed instead of the regressive tax. Calculate and graph the new consumption schedule and note the MPC and the multiplier.

d. Finally, impose a progressive tax such that the tax rate is 0 percent when GDP is $100, 5 percent at $200, 10 percent at $300, 15 percent at $400, and so forth. Determine and graph the new consumption schedule, noting the effect of this tax system on the MPC and the multiplier.

e. Use a graph similar to Figure 27.3 to show why proportional and progressive taxes contribute to greater economic stability, while a regressive tax does not.

4. Refer to the following table for Waxwania: **LO27.2**

Government Expenditures, *G*	Tax Revenues, *T*	Real GDP
$160	$100	$500
160	120	600
160	140	700
160	160	800
160	180	900

What is the marginal tax rate in Waxwania? The average tax rate? Which of the following describes the tax system: proportional, progressive, regressive?

5. Refer to the table for Waxwania in problem 4. Suppose that Waxwania is producing $600 of real GDP, whereas the potential real GDP (or full-employment real GDP) is $700. How large is its budget deficit? Its cyclically adjusted budget deficit? Its cyclically adjusted budget deficit as a percentage of potential real GDP? Is Waxwania's fiscal policy expansionary or is it contractionary? **LO27.3**

6. Suppose that a country has no public debt in year 1 but experiences a budget deficit of $40 billion in year 2, a budget surplus of $10 billion in year 3, and a budget deficit of $2 billion in year 4. What is the absolute size of its public debt in year 4? If its real GDP in year 4 is $104 billion, what is this country's public debt as a percentage of real GDP in year 4? **LO27.6**

7. Suppose that the investment demand curve in a certain economy is such that investment declines by $100 billion for every 1 percentage point increase in the real interest rate. Also, suppose that the investment demand curve shifts rightward by $150 billion at each real interest rate for every 1 percentage point increase in the expected rate of return from investment. If stimulus spending (an expansionary fiscal policy) by government increases the real interest rate by 2 percentage points, but also raises the expected rate of return on investment by 1 percentage point, how much investment, if any, will be crowded out? **LO27.6**

AP The Loanable Funds Market

LO27.7 Understand the Loanable Funds Market model and the relationship between the supply and demand for loanable funds and real interest rates on loans.

The loanable funds market represents the market where savers meet borrowers. The interaction of the supply and demand for loanable funds determines the real interest rate for loans in the economy. For borrowers, interest is the price to borrow money; for savers, interest is the return on loaned money.

A few caveats are necessary at the start of this discussion. First, there is no single "the interest rate." Interest rates differ due to the type of instrument, lending risk, the length of the loan, the purpose of the loan, location, and a host of other factors in a variety of markets. To simplify the issue, this hypothetical loanable funds market represents all of the markets for the varying interest rates, to show how interest rates are determined in each individual market. In addition, this model assumes that prices are not changing during the analysis, so the real interest rate, rather than the nominal interest rate, is used for this market.

It is important to make the distinction between nominal and real interest rates, in the same way economists distinguish nominal and real incomes. The nominal interest rate is the rate expressed in the current value of dollars. The real interest rate is the rate expressed in the purchasing power of dollars which are adjusted for inflation. Inflation erodes the purchasing power of dollars, so a dollar saved this year will not buy as much next year. The real interest rate is the nominal interest rate minus the expected inflation rate. A saver may earn a 6% nominal interest rate on a bond, but if the inflation rate is 2%, the real interest rate is only 4%. The loanable funds market assumes no inflation, so the real interest rate is used in this analysis.

The Private Sector Loanable Funds Market

In a closed private economy with no government or foreign sectors, savings equals investment. In the macroeconomic loanable funds market graph (Figure 1, Figure 2), what was originally labeled "investment" is represented by a demand for loanable funds, while "savings" are represented as a supply of loanable funds. The equilibrium interest rate is determined at the point where the quantity of loanable funds demanded equals the quantity of loanable funds supplied.

The demand for loanable funds in the private market comes from households and firms. Consumers borrow to pay for houses, cars, and college tuition. Firms borrow to buy capital, expand factories, and start entirely new businesses. Firms will only invest if the return on their investment (increased profit as a percentage of the cost) is greater than the interest rate charged for the loan. As a result, at low interest rates, firms are more willing to borrow, and at higher interest rates, firms are less willing to borrow. This relationship is also true for consumers. Therefore, the demand for loanable funds is a downward-sloping curve.

The supply of loanable funds comes from households who are saving money for future purchases or for retirement

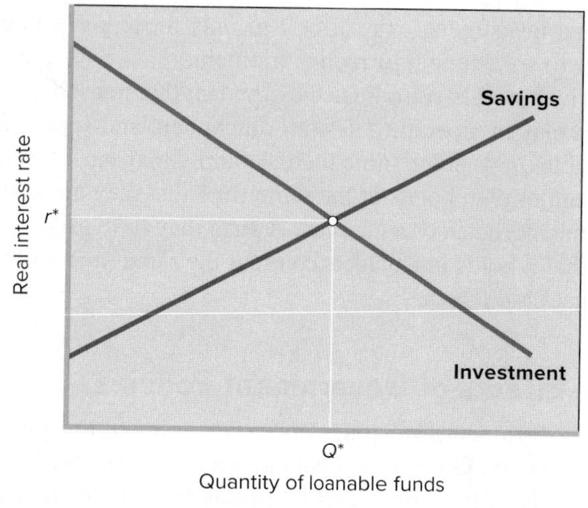

FIGURE 1 The Loanable Funds Market

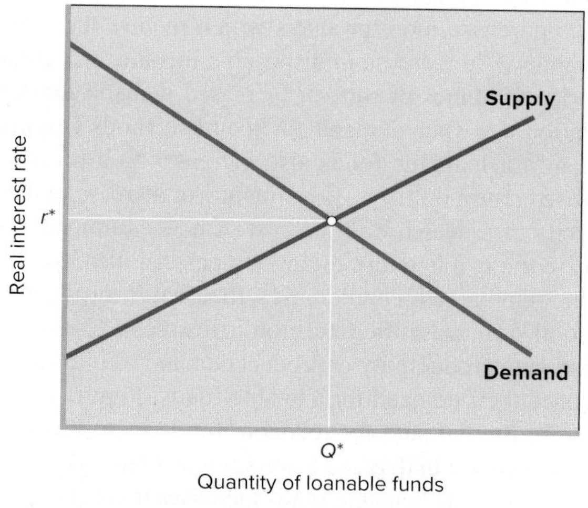

FIGURE 2 The Private Sectior Loanable Funds Market

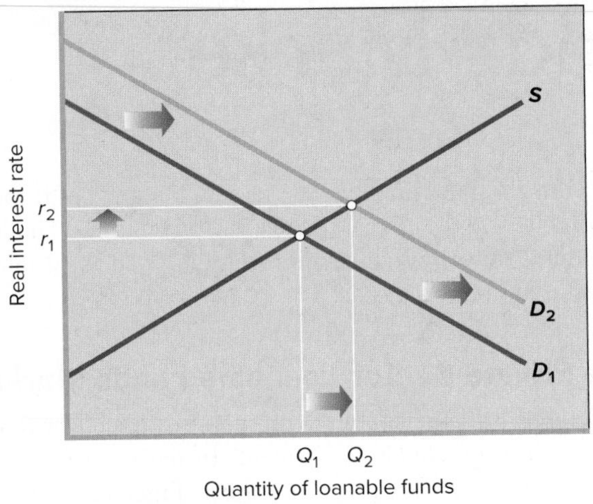

FIGURE 3 **Increase in Demand**

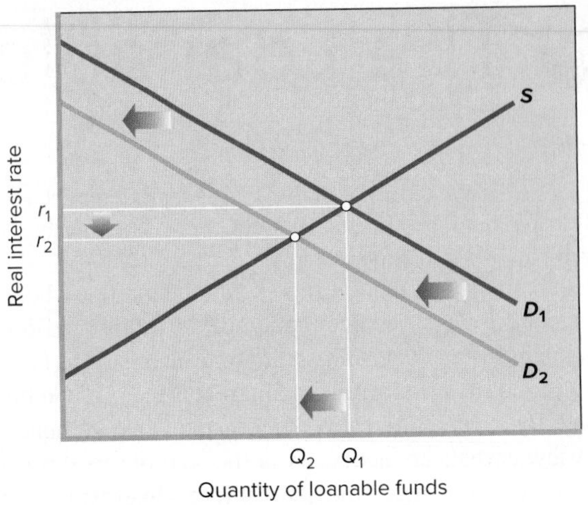

FIGURE 4 **Decrease in Demand**

and are willing to loan it to others, often through banks or bonds. Interest serves as an incentive for people to forego the present use of money in order to have even more money in the future. When interest rates are low, people incur little opportunity cost for holding money in cash, so they have little incentive to put savings in a bank or buy a bond. They would rather consume products or invest that money in commodities or other investments. But as interest rates rise, people are more willing to save, making that money available for loans to others. Therefore, the supply curve for loanable funds is upward-sloping. Because many people save for large purchases, retirement, or economic security regardless of interest rates, the supply curve may be fairly inelastic (fairly vertical).

Changes in Supply and Demand for Loanable Funds

Private sector demand for loanable funds increases when consumers purchase more products which require them to borrow money. An increase in disposable income, a decrease in the price of homes or cars, or increased demand for college education can spur demand for loanable funds (Figure 3). Demand for loanable funds also increases as a result of an increased return on firms' investment. An increase in the productivity or a decrease in the cost of new equipment would increase the firm's return on investment. An increase in consumer demand which increases the firm's product price would also increase the return on investment. Conversely, a reduction in productivity or product demand would lead firms to reduce their demand for loanable funds (Figure 4). An increase in the demand for loanable funds increases interest rates; a decrease in demand lowers interest rates.

The supply of loanable funds increases if consumers have an incentive to save more. Concerns about rising retirement or college tuition costs lead people to save more for future expenses, increasing the supply of loanable funds. The supply of loanable funds can decrease if significant numbers of savers lose jobs or real income and households have to dip into their savings to afford current consumption (Figure 5). An increase in the supply of loanable funds lowers interest rates; a decrease in the supply of loanable funds increases interest rates.

Changes in interest rates have implications far beyond the individual firm or household. If interest rates rise significantly, firms will be less willing to borrow for investment, slowing total spending in the economy and potentially leading to a recession. Conversely, interest rates that fall significantly can create inflation. Further, lower interest rates make it more profitable for firms to borrow to finance research and development, which can spur innovation and significantly increase long-run economic growth. High interest rates can deter that investment, or restrict it to only those projects most likely to see a high return on investment.

The model is complicated by the fact that households and firms may be operating as both demanders and suppliers of loanable funds at the same time. A family may have a savings account or own bonds at the same time that they are seeking a home mortgage or a car loan. A firm may have excess revenue that it holds in a bank account at the same time it obtains a construction loan.

The Effects of Government Policies

The government also plays important roles in the loanable funds market. Government policies can affect the private sector supply of loanable funds by giving households an incentive to save more, such as a tax break for interest earned on

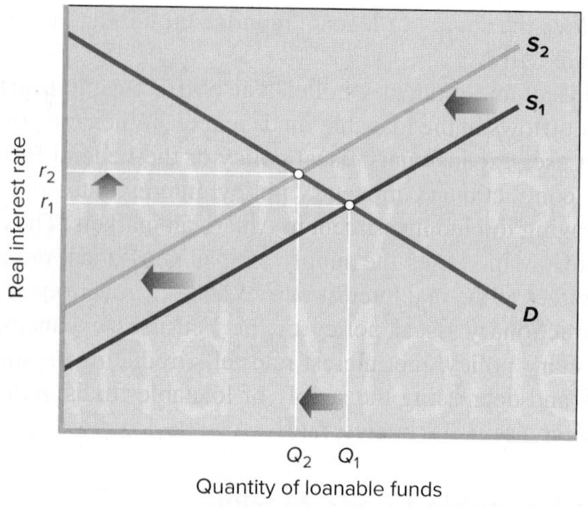

FIGURE 5 **Decrease in Supply**

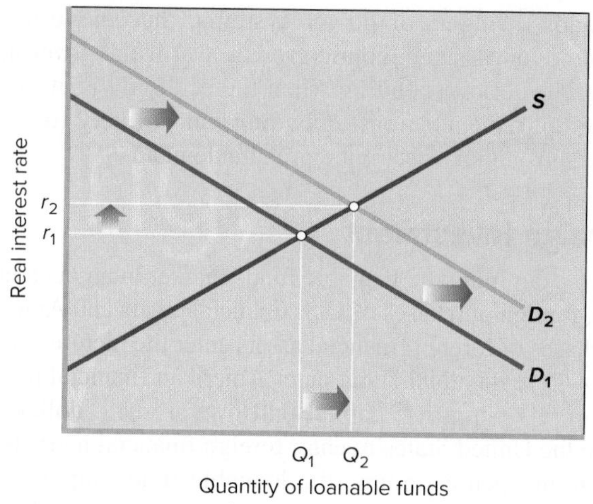

FIGURE 6 **Crowding Out**

savings accounts or bonds. In addition to private market actions, the Federal Reserve can use monetary policy to directly increase or reduce the supply of loanable funds available through banks as a means of stabilizing the economy.

The federal government acts directly as a demander of loanable funds when it borrows money to finance the national debt. Although government borrowing is not affected by interest rates, the overall demand curve remains downward-sloping. Government policies can also affect private sector demand for loanable funds. Business tax deductions and credits for investment increase the return on investment, increasing the demand for loanable funds. Tax deductions for mortgage interest and rebate programs such as the "cash for clunkers" program can entice consumers to buy hoU.S.es and cars, increasing demand for loanable funds.

One problem of fiscal policy is that when the federal government attempts to resolve a recession, it creates the potential for crowding out in the loanable funds market. When the government uses expansionary fiscal policy to increase spending and reduce taxes, a budget deficit develops. Government must borrow money to finance the deficit. As government demand for money in the loanable funds market increases, interest rates rise. Because investment spending is the most volatile of the four sectors, when interest rates increase, firms can significantly reduce investment spending, crowding firms out of the loanable funds market.

As illustrated in the graph (Figure 6), the increase in demand for loanable funds due to government borrowing increases the total quantity of loanable funds. However, assume that D_1 represents the private loanable funds market, while D_2 represents the private loanable funds plus government borrowing. As a result of higher interest rates, the quantity of loanable funds borrowed by firms in private markets would actually fall, from Q_1 to where the higher interest rate (r_2) intersects the original D_1 curve. So while the total amount of borrowing has increased (Q_1 to Q_2), borrowing in the private sector has decreased. (Note: Some economists prefer to view the loanable funds market as a purely private market without including government borrowing. In their view, crowding out occurs as a result of a decrease in supply of private market loanable funds, as some households withdraw their supply of loanable funds from the private sector market and instead invest those funds in government bonds. The interest rate in the loanable funds market increases in either approach.)

While the government is using expansionary fiscal policy and borrowing money in order to increase aggregate demand, crowding out reduces the effectiveness of the fiscal policy by offsetting part of that increase in aggregate demand. The higher interest rate can also reduce interest-sensitive consumption spending, such as consumer purchases of homes, cars, and durable goods, further reducing the effectiveness of expansionary fiscal policy.

The crowding out effect, if it occurs at all, has less impact during a time of recession (when expansionary fiscal policy is most likely to be used), because consumer and investment sector demand for loans has already decreased due to the recession. Consumers tend to buy fewer homes, cars, and expensive items, and firms reduce investment as product demand falls. So the increased government demand for loanable funds may replace decreased private sector demand for those same funds. In addition, if the increased government spending is used for infrastructure projects such

28 Chapter

Money, Banking, and Financial Institutions

Learning Objectives

LO28.1 **Identify and explain the functions of money.**

LO28.2 **List and describe the components of the U.S. money supply.**

LO28.3 **Describe what "backs" the money supply, making us willing to accept it as payment.**

LO28.4 **Discuss the makeup of the Federal Reserve and its relationship to banks and thrifts.**

LO28.5 **Identify the functions and responsibilities of the Federal Reserve and explain why Fed independence is important.**

LO28.6 **Identify and explain the main factors that contributed to the financial crisis of 2007–2008.**

LO28.7 **Discuss the actions of the U.S. Treasury and the Federal Reserve that helped keep the banking and financial crisis of 2007–2008 from worsening.**

LO28.8 **Identify the main subsets of the financial services industry in the United States and provide examples of some firms in each category.**

AP Chapter Focus

Money is a fascinating aspect of the economy:

> Money bewitches people. They fret for it, and they sweat for it. They devise most ingenious ways to get it, and most ingenuous ways to get rid of it. Money is the only commodity that is good for nothing but to be gotten rid of. It will not feed you, clothe you, shelter you, or amuse you unless you spend it or invest it. It imparts value only in parting. People will do almost anything for money, and money will do almost anything for people. Money is a captivating, circulating, masquerading puzzle.[1]

In this chapter and the three chapters that follow, the foundational theories that help us to understand the Financial Sector of our economy is examined. When the monetary system is working properly, it provides the lifeblood of the circular

[1]"Creeping Inflation," *Business Review*, August 1957, p. 3. Federal Reserve Bank of Philadelphia. Used with permission.

flows of income and expenditure. A well-operating monetary system helps the economy achieve both full employment and the efficient use of resources. A malfunctioning monetary system distorts the allocation of resources and creates severe fluctuations in the economy's levels of output, employment, and prices.

AP The Functions of Money

LO28.1 Identify and explain the functions of money.

Just what is money? There is an old saying that "money *is* what money *does*." In a general sense, anything that performs the functions of money *is* money. Here are those functions:

- ***Medium of exchange*** First and foremost, money is a **medium of exchange** that is usable for buying and selling goods and services. A bakery worker does not want to be paid 200 bagels per week. Nor does the bakery owner want to receive, say, halibut in exchange for bagels. Money, however, is readily acceptable as payment. As we saw in Chapter 2, money is a social invention with which resource suppliers and producers can be paid and that can be used to buy any of the full range of items available in the marketplace. As a medium of exchange, money allows society to escape the complications of barter. And because it provides a convenient way of exchanging goods, money enables society to gain the advantages of geographic and human specialization.
- ***Unit of account*** Money is also a **unit of account.** Society uses monetary units—dollars, in the United States—as a yardstick for measuring the relative worth of a wide variety of goods, services, and resources. Just as we measure distance in miles or kilometers, we gauge the value of goods in dollars.

  With money as an acceptable unit of account, the price of each item need be stated only in terms of the monetary unit. We need not state the price of cows in terms of corn, crayons, and cranberries. Money aids rational decision making by enabling buyers and sellers to easily compare the prices of various goods, services, and resources. It also permits us to define debt obligations, determine taxes owed, and calculate the nation's GDP.
- ***Store of value*** Money also serves as a **store of value** that enables people to transfer purchasing power from the present to the future. People normally do not spend all their incomes on the day they receive them. To buy things later, they store some of their wealth as money. The money you place in a safe or a checking account will still be available to you a few weeks or months from now. When inflation is nonexistent or mild, holding money is a relatively risk-free way to store your wealth for later use.

People can, of course, choose to hold some or all of their wealth in a wide variety of assets besides money. These include real estate, stocks, bonds, precious metals such as gold, and even collectible items like fine art or comic books. But a key advantage that money has over all other assets is that it has the most *liquidity*, or spendability.

An asset's **liquidity** is the ease with which it can be converted quickly into the most widely accepted and easily spent form of money, cash, with little or no loss of purchasing power. The more liquid an asset is, the more quickly it can be converted into cash and used for either purchases of goods and services or purchases of other assets.

Levels of liquidity vary radically. By definition, cash is perfectly liquid. By contrast, a house is highly illiquid for two reasons. First, it may take several months before a willing buyer can be found and a sale negotiated so that its value can be converted into cash. Second, there is a loss of purchasing power when the house is sold because numerous fees have to be paid to real estate agents and other individuals to complete the sale.

As we are about to discuss, our economy uses several different types of money including cash, coins, checking account deposits, savings account deposits, and even more exotic things like deposits in money market mutual funds. As we describe the various forms of money in detail, take the time to compare their relative levels of liquidity—both with each other and as compared to other assets like stocks, bonds, and real estate. Cash is perfectly liquid. Other forms of money are highly liquid, but less liquid than cash.

AP The Components of the Money Supply

LO28.2 List and describe the components of the U.S. money supply.

Money is a "stock" of some item or group of items (unlike income, for example, which is a "flow"). Societies have used many items as money, including whales' teeth, circular stones, elephant-tail bristles, gold coins, furs, and pieces of paper. Anything that is widely accepted as a medium of exchange can serve as money. In the United States, currency is not the only form of money. As you will see, certain debts of government and financial institutions also are used as money.

Money Definition *M*1

The narrowest definition of the U.S. money supply is called ***M*1.** It consists of two components:

- Currency (coins and paper money) in the hands of the public.

- All checkable deposits (all deposits in commercial banks and "thrift" or savings institutions on which checks of any size can be drawn).[2]

Government and government agencies supply coins and paper money. Commercial banks ("banks") and savings institutions ("thrifts") provide checkable deposits. Figure 28.1a shows that *M*1 is about equally divided between the two components.

Currency: Coins + Paper Money The currency of the United States consists of metal coins and paper money. The coins are issued by the U.S. Treasury while the paper money consists of **Federal Reserve Notes** issued by the Federal Reserve System (the U.S. central bank). The coins are minted by the U.S. Mint, while the paper money is printed by the Bureau of Engraving and Printing. Both the U.S. Mint and the Bureau of Engraving and Printing are part of the U.S. Department of the Treasury.

As with the currencies of other countries, the currency of the United States is **token money.** This means that the face value of any piece of currency is unrelated to its *intrinsic value*—the value of the physical material (metal or paper and ink) out of which that piece of currency is constructed. Governments make sure that face values exceed intrinsic values to discourage people from destroying coins and bills to resell the material that they are made out of. For instance, if 50-cent pieces each contained 75 cents' worth of metal, then it would be profitable to melt them down and sell the metal. Fifty-cent pieces would disappear from circulation very quickly!

Figure 28.1a shows that currency (coins and paper money) constitutes 43 percent of the *M*1 money supply in the United States.

Checkable Deposits The safety and convenience of checks has made **checkable deposits** a large component of the *M*1 money supply. You would not think of stuffing $4,896 in bills in an envelope and dropping it in a mailbox to pay a debt. But writing and mailing a check for a large sum is commonplace. The person cashing a check must endorse it (sign it on the reverse side); the writer of the check subsequently receives a record of the cashed check as a receipt attesting to the fulfillment of the obligation. Similarly, because the writing of a check requires endorsement, the theft or loss of your checkbook is not nearly as calamitous as losing an identical amount of currency. Finally, it is more convenient to write a

[2]In the ensuing discussion, we do not discuss several of the quantitatively less significant components of the definitions of money to avoid a maze of details. For example, traveler's checks are included in the *M*1 money supply. The statistical appendix of any recent *Federal Reserve Bulletin* provides more comprehensive definitions.

AP **FIGURE 28.1 Components of money supply *M*1 and money supply *M*2, in the United States.** (a) *M*1 is a narrow definition of the money supply that includes currency (in circulation) and checkable deposits. (b) *M*2 is a broader definition that includes *M*1 along with several other relatively liquid account balances.

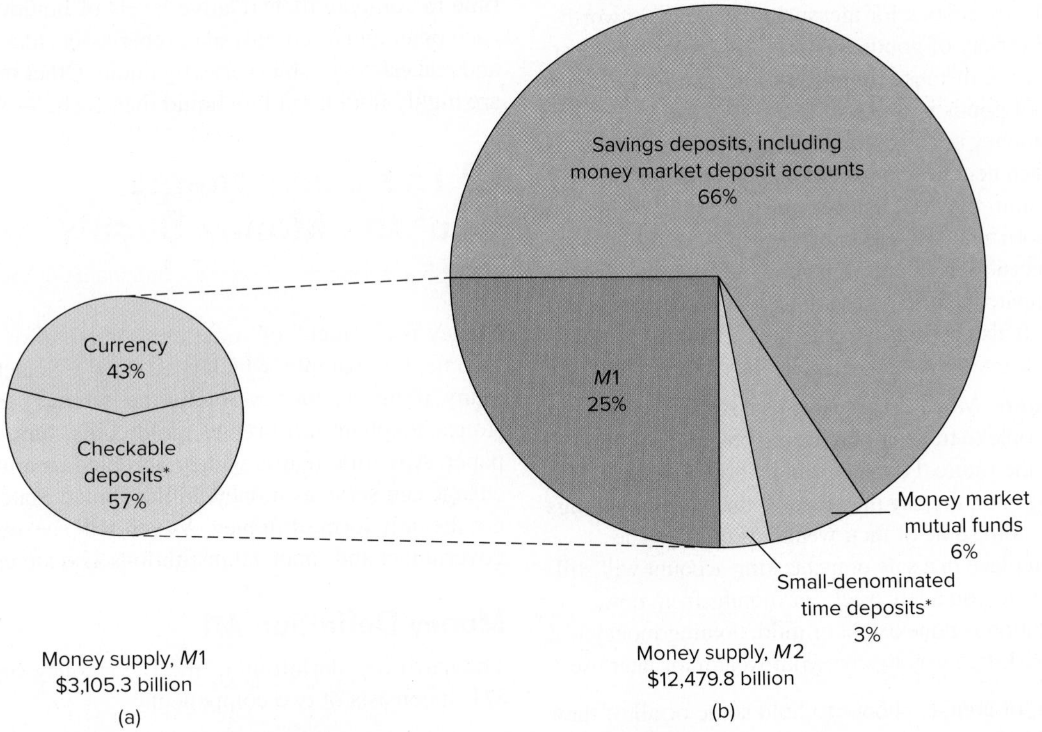

*These categories include other, quantitatively smaller components such as traveler's checks.

Source: Federal Reserve System, **www.federalreserve.gov**. Data are for February 2016.

check than to transport and count out a large sum of currency. For all these reasons, checkable deposits (checkbook money) are a large component of the stock of money in the United States. About 57 percent of *M*1 is in the form of checkable deposits, on which checks can be drawn.

It might seem strange that checking account balances are regarded as part of the money supply. But the reason is clear: Checks are nothing more than a way to transfer the ownership of deposits in banks and other financial institutions and are generally acceptable as a medium of exchange. Although checks are less generally accepted than currency for small purchases, for major purchases most sellers willingly accept checks as payment. Moreover, people can convert checkable deposits into paper money and coins on demand; checks drawn on those deposits are thus the equivalent of currency.

To summarize:

$$\text{Money, } M1 = \text{currency} + \text{checkable deposits}$$

Institutions That Offer Checkable Deposits In the United States, a variety of financial institutions allow customers to write checks in any amount on the funds they have deposited. **Commercial banks** are the primary depository institutions. They accept the deposits of households and businesses, keep the money safe until it is demanded via checks, and in the meantime use it to make available a wide variety of loans. Commercial bank loans provide short-term financial capital to businesses, and they finance consumer purchases of automobiles and other durable goods.

Savings and loan associations (S&Ls), mutual savings banks, and credit unions supplement the commercial banks and are known collectively as savings or **thrift institutions**, or simply "thrifts." *Savings and loan associations* and *mutual savings banks* accept the deposits of households and businesses and then use the funds to finance housing mortgages and to provide other loans. *Credit unions* accept deposits from and lend to "members," who usually are a group of people who work for the same company.

The checkable deposits of banks and thrifts are known variously as demand deposits, NOW (negotiable order of withdrawal) accounts, ATS (automatic transfer service) accounts, and share draft accounts. Their commonality is that depositors can write checks on them whenever, and in whatever amount, they choose.

Two Qualifications We must qualify our discussion in two important ways. First, currency held by the U.S. Treasury, the Federal Reserve banks, commercial banks, and thrift institutions is *excluded* from *M*1 and other measures of the money supply. A paper dollar or four quarters in the billfold of, say, Emma Buck obviously constitutes just $1 of the money supply. But if we counted currency held by banks as part of the money supply, the same $1 would count for $2 of money supply when Emma deposited the currency into her checkable deposit in her bank. It would count for $1 of checkable deposit owned by Buck and also $1 of currency in the bank's cash drawer or vault. By excluding currency held by banks when determining the total supply of money, we avoid this problem of double counting.

Also *excluded* from the money supply are any checkable deposits of the government (specifically, the U.S. Treasury) or the Federal Reserve that are held by commercial banks or thrift institutions. This exclusion is designed to enable a better assessment of the amount of money available *to the private sector* for potential spending. The amount of money available to households and businesses is of keen interest to the Federal Reserve in conducting its monetary policy (a topic we cover in detail in Chapter 30).

Money Definition *M*2

A second and broader definition of money includes *M*1 plus several near-monies. **Near-monies** are certain highly liquid financial assets that do not function directly or fully as a medium of exchange but can be readily converted into currency or checkable deposits. The ***M*2** definition of money includes three categories of near-monies.

- ***Savings deposits, including money market deposit accounts*** A depositor can easily withdraw funds from a **savings account** at a bank or thrift or simply request that the funds be transferred from a savings account to a checkable account. A person can also withdraw funds from a **money market deposit account (MMDA),** which is an interest-bearing account containing a variety of interest-bearing short-term securities. MMDAs, however, have a minimum-balance requirement and a limit on how often a person can withdraw funds.
- ***Small-denominated (less than $100,000) time deposits*** Funds from **time deposits** become available at their maturity. For example, a person can convert a 6-month time deposit ("certificate of deposit," or "CD") to currency without penalty 6 months or more after it has been deposited. In return for this withdrawal limitation, the financial institution pays a higher interest rate on such deposits than it does on its MMDAs. Also, a person can "cash in" a CD at any time but must pay a severe penalty.
- ***Money market mutual funds held by individuals*** By making a telephone call, using the Internet, or writing a check for $500 or more, a depositor can redeem shares in a **money market mutual fund (MMMF)** offered by a mutual fund company. Such companies use the combined funds of individual shareholders to buy interest-bearing short-term credit instruments such as certificates of deposit and U.S. government securities. Then they can offer interest on the MMMF accounts of the shareholders (depositors) who jointly own those financial assets. The MMMFs in *M*2 include only the MMMF accounts held by individuals; those held by businesses and other institutions are excluded.

CONSIDER THIS . . .

Source: © Adam Crowley/Getty Images RF

Are Credit Cards Money?

You may wonder why we have ignored credit cards such as Visa and MasterCard in our discussion of how the money supply is defined. After all, credit cards are a convenient way to buy things and account for about 25 percent of the dollar value of all transactions in the United States. The answer is that a credit card is not money. Rather, it is a convenient means of obtaining a short-term loan from the financial institution that issued the card.

What happens when you purchase an item with a credit card? The bank that issued the card will reimburse the seller by making a money payment and charging the establishment a transaction fee, and later you will reimburse the bank for its loan to you by also making a money payment. Rather than reduce your cash or checking account with each purchase, you bunch your payments once a month. You may have to pay an annual fee for the services provided, and if you pay the bank in installments, you will pay a sizable interest charge on the loan. Credit cards are merely a means of deferring or postponing payment for a short period. Your checking account balance that you use to pay your credit card bill *is* money; the credit card is *not* money.*

Although credit cards are not money, they allow individuals and businesses to "economize" in the use of money. Credit cards enable people to hold less currency in their billfolds and, prior to payment due dates, fewer checkable deposits in their bank accounts. Credit cards also help people coordinate the timing of their expenditures with their receipt of income.

*A bank debit card, however, is very similar to a check in your checkbook. Unlike a purchase with a credit card, a purchase with a debit card creates a direct "debit" (a subtraction) from your checking account balance. That checking account balance is money—it is part of *M*1.

All three categories of near-monies imply substantial liquidity. Thus, in equation form,

$$\text{Money, } M2 = \begin{array}{l} M1 + \text{savings deposits, including} \\ \text{MMDAs} + \text{small-denominated} \\ \text{(less than \$100,000) time deposits} \\ + \text{MMMFs held by individuals} \end{array}$$

In summary, *M*2 includes the immediate medium-of-exchange items (currency and checkable deposits) that constitute *M*1 plus certain near-monies that can be easily converted into currency and checkable deposits. In Figure 28.1b, we see that the addition of all these items yields an *M*2 money supply that is about five times larger than the narrower *M*1 money supply.

AP QUICK REVIEW 28.1

- ✓ Money serves as a medium of exchange, a unit of account, and a store of value.
- ✓ The narrow *M*1 definition of money includes currency held by the public plus checkable deposits in commercial banks and thrift institutions.
- ✓ Thrift institutions, as well as commercial banks, offer accounts on which checks can be written.
- ✓ The *M*2 definition of money includes *M*1 plus savings deposits, including money market deposit accounts, small-denominated (less than $100,000) time deposits, and money market mutual fund balances held by individuals.

What "Backs" the Money Supply?

LO28.3 Describe what "backs" the money supply, making us willing to accept it as payment.

The money supply in the United States essentially is "backed" (guaranteed) by the government's ability to keep the value of money relatively stable. Nothing more!

Money as Debt

The major components of the money supply—paper money and checkable deposits—are debts, or promises to pay. In the United States, paper money is the circulating debt of the Federal Reserve Banks. Checkable deposits are the debts of commercial banks and thrift institutions.

Paper currency and checkable deposits have no intrinsic value. A $5 bill is just an inscribed piece of paper. A checkable deposit is merely a bookkeeping entry. And coins, we know, have less intrinsic value than their face value. Nor will government redeem the paper money you hold for anything tangible, such as gold. To many people, the fact that the government does not back the currency with anything tangible seems implausible and insecure. But the decision not to back the currency with anything tangible was made for a very good reason. If the government backed the currency with something tangible like gold, then the supply of money would vary with how much gold was available. By not backing the currency, the government avoids this constraint and indeed receives a key freedom—the ability to provide as much or as little money as needed to maintain the value of money and to best suit the economic needs of the country. In effect, by choosing not to back the currency, the government has chosen to give itself the ability to freely "manage" the nation's money supply. Its monetary authorities attempt to provide the amount of money needed for the particular volume of business activity that will promote full employment, price-level stability, and economic growth.

Nearly all today's economists agree that managing the money supply is more sensible than linking it to gold or to some other commodity whose supply might change arbitrarily and capriciously. For instance, if we used gold to back the money supply so that gold was redeemable for money and vice versa, then a large increase in the nation's gold stock as the result of a new gold discovery might increase the money supply too rapidly and thereby trigger rapid inflation. Or a long-lasting decline in gold production might reduce the money supply to the point where recession and unemployment resulted.

In short, people cannot convert paper money into a fixed amount of gold or any other precious commodity. Money is exchangeable only for paper money. If you ask the government to redeem $5 of your paper money, it will swap one paper $5 bill for another bearing a different serial number. That is all you can get. Similarly, checkable deposits can be redeemed not for gold but only for paper money, which, as we have just seen, the government will not redeem for anything tangible.

Value of Money

So why are currency and checkable deposits money, whereas, say, Monopoly (the game) money is not? What gives a $20 bill or a $100 checking account entry its value? The answer to these questions has three parts.

Acceptability Currency and checkable deposits are money because people accept them as money. By virtue of long-standing business practice, currency and checkable deposits perform the basic function of money: They are acceptable as a medium of exchange. We accept paper money in exchange because we are confident it will be exchangeable for real goods, services, and resources when we spend it.

Legal Tender Our confidence in the acceptability of paper money is strengthened because the government has designated currency as **legal tender.** Specifically, each bill contains the statement "This note is legal tender for all debts, public and private." That means paper money is a valid and legal means of payment of any debt that was contracted in dollars. (But private firms and government are not mandated to accept cash. It is not illegal for them to specify payment in noncash forms such as checks, cashier's checks, money orders, or credit cards.)

The general acceptance of paper currency in exchange is more important than the government's decree that money is legal tender, however. The government has never decreed checks to be legal tender, and yet they serve as such in many of the economy's exchanges of goods, services, and resources. But it is true that government agencies—the Federal Deposit Insurance Corporation (FDIC) and the National Credit Union Administration (NCUA)—insure individual deposits of up to $250,000 at commercial banks and thrifts. That fact enhances our willingness to use checkable deposits as a medium of exchange.

Relative Scarcity The value of money, like the economic value of anything else, depends on its supply and demand. Money derives its value from its scarcity relative to its utility (its want-satisfying power). The utility of money lies in its capacity to be exchanged for goods and services, now or in the future. The economy's demand for money thus depends on the total dollar volume of transactions in any period plus the amount of money individuals and businesses want to hold for future transactions. With a reasonably constant demand for money, the supply of money provided by the monetary authorities will determine the domestic value or "purchasing power" of the monetary unit (dollar, yen, peso, or whatever).

Money and Prices

The purchasing power of money is the amount of goods and services a unit of money will buy. When money rapidly loses its purchasing power, it loses its role as money.

The Purchasing Power of the Dollar The amount a dollar will buy varies inversely with the price level; that is, a reciprocal relationship exists between the general price level and the purchasing power of the dollar. When the consumer price index or "cost-of-living" index goes up, the value of the dollar goes down, and vice versa. Higher prices lower the value of the dollar because more dollars are needed to buy a particular amount of goods, services, or resources. For example, if the price level doubles, the value of the dollar declines by one-half, or 50 percent.

Conversely, lower prices increase the purchasing power of the dollar because fewer dollars are needed to obtain a specific quantity of goods and services. If the price level falls by, say, one-half, or 50 percent, the purchasing power of the dollar doubles.

In equation form, the relationship looks like this:

$$\$V = 1/P$$

To find the value of the dollar $\$V$, divide 1 by the price level P expressed as an index number (in hundredths). If the price level is 1, then the value of the dollar is 1. If the price level rises to, say, 1.20, $\$V$ falls to 0.833; a 20 percent increase in the price level reduces the value of the dollar by 16.67 percent. Check your understanding of this reciprocal relationship by determining the value of $\$V$ and its percentage rise when P falls by 20 percent from $1 to 0.80.

Inflation and Acceptability In Chapter 23 we noted situations in which a nation's currency became worthless and unacceptable in exchange. These instances of runaway inflation, or *hyperinflation*, happened when the government issued so many pieces of paper currency that the purchasing power of each of those units of money was almost totally undermined. The infamous post–World War I hyperinflation in Germany is an example. In December 1919 there were about 50 billion marks in circulation. Four years later there were 496,585,345,900 billion marks in circulation! The result? The German mark in 1923 was worth an infinitesimal fraction of its 1919 value.[3]

Runaway inflation may significantly depreciate the value of money between the time it is received and the time it is spent. Rapid declines in the value of a currency may cause it to cease being used as a medium of exchange. Businesses and households may refuse to accept paper money in exchange because they do not want to bear the loss in its value that will occur while it is in their possession. (All this despite the fact that the government says that paper currency is legal tender!) Without an acceptable domestic medium of exchange, the economy may simply revert to barter. Alternatively, more stable currencies such as the U.S. dollar or European euro may come into widespread use. At the extreme, a country may adopt a foreign currency as its own official currency as a way to counter hyperinflation.

Similarly, people will use money as a store of value only as long as there is no sizable deterioration in the value of that money because of inflation. And an economy can effectively employ money as a unit of account only when its purchasing power is relatively stable. A monetary yardstick that no longer measures a yard (in terms of purchasing power) does not permit buyers and sellers to establish the terms of trade clearly. When the value of the dollar is declining rapidly, sellers do not know what to charge and buyers do not know what to pay.

Stabilizing Money's Purchasing Power

Rapidly rising price levels (rapid inflation) and the consequent erosion of the purchasing power of money typically result from imprudent economic policies. Since the purchasing power of money and the price level vary inversely, stabilization of the purchasing power of a nation's money requires stabilization of the nation's price level. Such price-level stability (2 to 3 percent annual inflation) mainly necessitates intelligent management or regulation of the nation's money supply and interest rates *(monetary policy)*. It also requires appropriate *fiscal policy* supportive of the efforts of the nation's monetary authorities to hold down inflation. In the United States, a combination of legislation, government policy, and social practice inhibits imprudent expansion of the money supply that might jeopardize money's purchasing power. The critical role of the U.S. monetary authorities (the Federal Reserve) in maintaining the purchasing power of the dollar is the subject of Chapter 30. For now, simply note that they make available a particular quantity of money, such as *M*2 in Figure 28.1, and can change that amount through their policy tools.

AP QUICK REVIEW 28.2

- ✓ In the U.S., all money consists basically of the debts of government, commercial banks, and thrift institutions.
- ✓ These debts efficiently perform the functions of money as long as their value, or purchasing power, is relatively stable and are tied to the government's ability to keep the purchasing power of money steady.
- ✓ The value of money is rooted not in precious metals but in the amounts of goods, services, and resources it will purchase.
- ✓ The value of the dollar (its domestic purchasing power) is inversely related to the price level. Rising inflation can erode the functions of money.
- ✓ Government's responsibility in stabilizing the purchasing power of the monetary unit calls for (a) effective control over the supply of money by the monetary authorities and (b) the application of appropriate fiscal policies by the president and Congress.

AP The Federal Reserve and the Banking System

LO28.4 Discuss the makeup of the Federal Reserve and its relationship to banks and thrifts.

In the United States, the "monetary authorities" we have been referring to are the members of the Board of Governors of the **Federal Reserve System** (the "Fed"). As shown in Figure 28.2, the Board directs the activities of the 12 Federal Reserve Banks, which in turn control the lending activity of the nation's banks and thrift institutions. The Fed's major goal is to control the money supply. But since checkable deposits in banks are such a large part of the money supply, an important part of its duties involves assuring the stability of the banking system.

Historical Background

Early in the twentieth century, Congress decided that centralization and public control were essential for an efficient banking system. Decentralized, unregulated banking had fostered the inconvenience and confusion of numerous private bank notes being used as currency. It also had resulted in occasional episodes of monetary mismanagement such that the money supply was inappropriate to the needs of the economy. Sometimes "too much" money precipitated rapid inflation; other times "too little money" stunted the economy's growth by hindering the production and exchange of goods and services. No single entity was charged with creating and implementing nationally consistent banking policies.

[3]Frank G. Graham, *Exchange, Prices, and Production in Hyperinflation Germany, 1920–1923* (Princeton, NJ: Princeton University Press, 1930), p. 13.

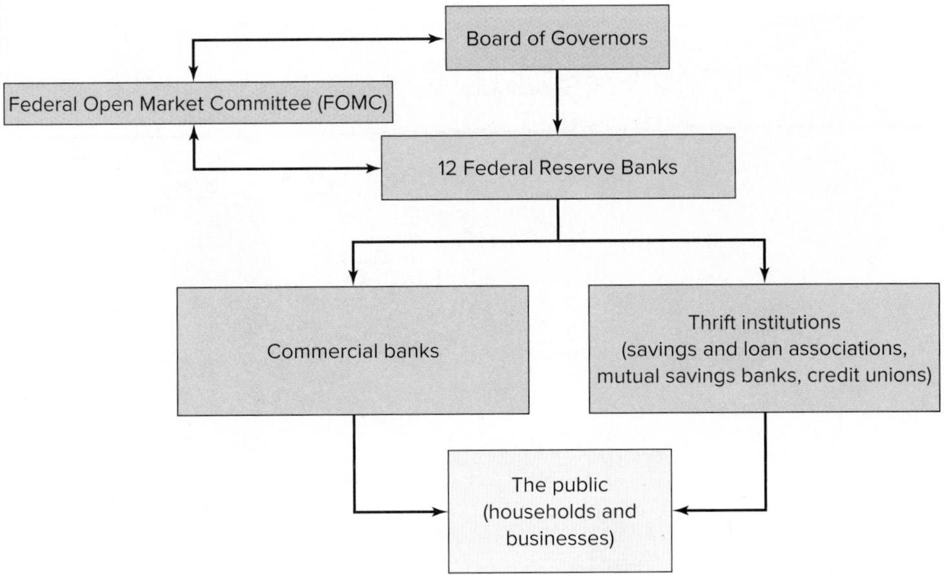

AP **FIGURE 28.2 Framework of the Federal Reserve System and its relationship to the public.** The Board of Governors makes the basic policy decisions that provide monetary control of the U.S. money and banking systems. The 12 Federal Reserve Banks implement these decisions. Both the Board of Governors and the 12 Federal Reserve Banks are aided by the Federal Open Market Committee (FOMC).

Furthermore, acute problems in the banking system occasionally erupted when banks either closed down or insisted on immediate repayment of loans to prevent their own failure. At such times, a banking crisis could emerge, with individuals and businesses who had lost confidence in their banks attempting to simultaneously withdraw all of their money—thereby further crippling the already weakened banks.

An unusually acute banking crisis in 1907 motivated Congress to appoint the National Monetary Commission to study the monetary and banking problems of the economy and to outline a course of action for Congress. The result was the Federal Reserve Act of 1913.

Let's examine the various parts of the Federal Reserve System and their relationship to one another.

Board of Governors

The central authority of the U.S. money and banking system is the **Board of Governors** of the Federal Reserve System. The U.S. president, with the confirmation of the Senate, appoints the seven Board members. Terms are 14 years and staggered so that one member is replaced every 2 years. In addition, new members are appointed when resignations occur. The president selects the chairperson and vice chairperson of the Board from among the members. Those officers serve 4-year terms and can be reappointed to new 4-year terms by the president. The long-term appointments provide the Board with continuity, experienced membership, and independence from political pressures that could result in inflation.

The 12 Federal Reserve Banks

The 12 **Federal Reserve Banks,** which blend private and public control, collectively serve as the nation's "central bank." These banks also serve as bankers' banks.

Central Bank Most nations have a single central bank—for example, Britain's Bank of England or Japan's Bank of Japan. The United States' central bank consists of 12 banks whose policies are coordinated by the Fed's Board of Governors. The 12 Federal Reserve Banks accommodate the geographic size and economic diversity of the United States and the nation's large number of commercial banks and thrifts.

Figure 28.3 locates the 12 Federal Reserve Banks and indicates the district that each serves. These banks implement the basic policy of the Board of Governors.

Quasi-Public Banks The 12 Federal Reserve Banks are quasi-public banks, which blend private ownership and public control. Each Federal Reserve Bank is owned by the private commercial banks in its district. (Federally chartered banks are required to purchase shares of stock in the Federal Reserve Bank in their district.) But the Board of Governors, a government body, sets the basic policies that the Federal Reserve Banks pursue.

Despite their private ownership, the Federal Reserve Banks are in practice public institutions. Unlike private firms, they are not motivated by profit. The policies they follow are designed by the Board of Governors to promote the well-being of the economy as a whole. Thus, the activities of the Federal Reserve Banks are frequently at odds with the profit motive.[4] Also, the Federal Reserve Banks do not compete with commercial banks. In general, they do not deal with the public; rather, they interact with the government and commercial banks and thrifts.

[4]Although it is not their goal, the Federal Reserve Banks have actually operated profitably, largely as a result of the Treasury debts they hold. Part of the profit is used to pay 6 percent annual dividends to the commercial banks that hold stock in the Federal Reserve Banks; the remaining profit is usually turned over to the U.S. Treasury.

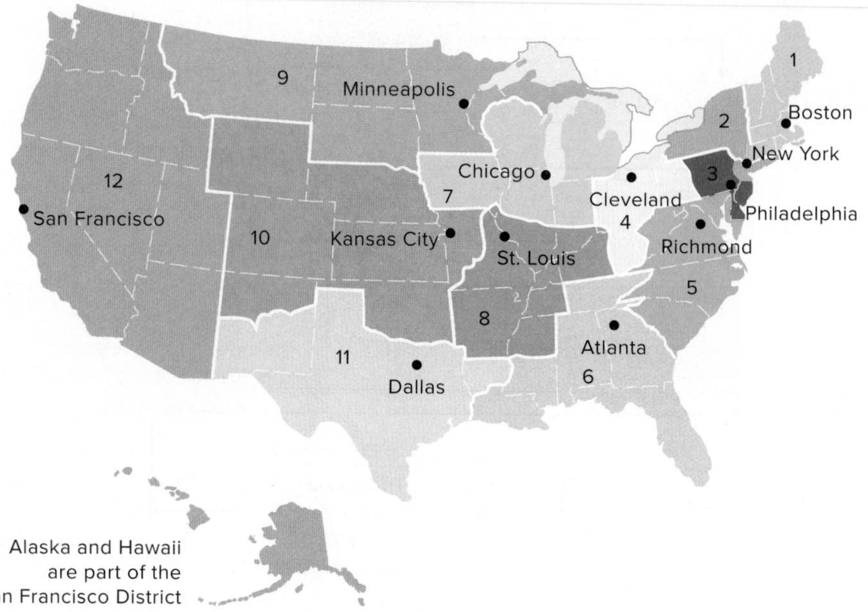

FIGURE 28.3 The 12 Federal Reserve Districts. The Federal Reserve System divides the United States into 12 districts, each having one central bank and, in some instances, one or more branches of the central bank.

Source: "The Twelve Federal Reserve Districts," *Federal Reserve Bulletin*, **www.federalreserve.gov/pubs/bulletin.**

Bankers' Banks The Federal Reserve Banks are "bankers' banks." They perform essentially the same functions for banks and thrifts as those institutions perform for the public. Just as banks and thrifts accept the deposits of and make loans to the public, so the central banks accept the deposits of and make loans to banks and thrifts. Normally, these loans average only about $150 million a day. But in emergency circumstances the Federal Reserve Banks become the "lender of last resort" to the banking system and can lend out as much as needed to ensure that banks and thrifts can meet their cash obligations. On the day after terrorists attacked the United States on September 11, 2001, the Fed lent $45 *billion* to U.S. banks and thrifts. The Fed wanted to make sure that the destruction and disruption in New York City and the Washington, D.C., area did not precipitate a nationwide banking crisis.

The Fed assumed an even greater role as a lender of last resort during the financial crisis of 2007–2008. We discuss that crisis and the Fed's emergency response to the crisis later in this chapter.

But the Federal Reserve Banks have a third function, which banks and thrifts do not perform: They issue currency. Congress has authorized the Federal Reserve Banks to put into circulation Federal Reserve Notes, which constitute the economy's paper money supply.

FOMC

The **Federal Open Market Committee (FOMC)** aids the Board of Governors in conducting monetary policy. The FOMC is made up of 12 individuals:

- The seven members of the Board of Governors.
- The president of the New York Federal Reserve Bank.
- Four of the remaining presidents of Federal Reserve Banks on a 1-year rotating basis.

The FOMC meets regularly to direct the purchase and sale of government securities (bills, notes, bonds) in the open market in which such securities are bought and sold on a daily basis. The FOMC also makes decisions about borrowing and lending government securities in the open market. We will find in Chapter 30 that the purpose of these aptly named *open-market operations* is to control the nation's money supply and influence interest rates. The Federal Reserve Bank in New York City conducts most of the Fed's open-market operations.

Commercial Banks and Thrifts

There are about 6,000 commercial banks. Roughly three-fourths are state banks. These are private banks chartered (authorized) by the individual states to operate within those states. One-fourth are private banks chartered by the federal government to operate nationally; these are national banks. Some of the U.S. national banks are very large, ranking among the world's largest financial institutions (see Global Perspective 28.1).

The 8,500 thrift institutions—most of which are credit unions—are regulated by agencies in addition to the Board of Governors and the Federal Reserve Banks. For example, credit unions are regulated and monitored by the National Credit Union Administration (NCUA). But the thrifts *are* subject to monetary control by the Federal Reserve System. In particular, like the banks, thrifts are required to keep a certain percentage of their checkable deposits as "reserves."

GLOBAL PERSPECTIVE 28.1

The World's 12 Largest Financial Institutions

The world's 12 largest private sector financial institutions are headquartered in Europe, Japan, and the United States (2015 data).

Source: "The World's Biggest Public Companies 2015 RANKING, " *Forbes*, **http://www.forbes.com/global2000/list/.**

In Figure 28.2, we use arrows to indicate that the thrift institutions are subject to the control of the Board of Governors and the central banks. Decisions concerning monetary policy affect the thrifts along with the commercial banks.

Fed Functions, Responsibilities, and Independence

LO28.5 Identify the functions and responsibilities of the Federal Reserve and explain why Fed independence is important.

The Fed performs several functions, some of which we have already identified, but they are worth repeating:

- ***Issuing currency*** The Federal Reserve Banks issue Federal Reserve Notes, the paper currency used in the U.S. monetary system. (The Federal Reserve Bank that issued a particular bill is identified in black in the upper left of the front of the newly designed bills. "A1," for example, identifies the Boston bank, "B2" the New York bank, and so on.)
- ***Setting reserve requirements and holding reserves*** The Fed sets reserve requirements, which are the fractions of checking account balances that banks must maintain as currency reserves. The central banks accept as deposits from the banks and thrifts any portion of their mandated reserves not held as vault cash.
- ***Lending to financial institutions and serving as an emergency lender of last resort*** The Fed makes routine short-term loans to banks and thrifts and charges them an interest rate called the *discount rate*. It also occasionally auctions off loans to banks and thrifts through its *Term Auction Facility*, discussed in Chapter 30. In times of financial emergencies, the Fed serves as a lender of last resort to critical parts of the U.S. financial industry.
- ***Providing for check collection*** The Fed provides the banking system with a means for collecting on checks. If Sue writes a check on her Miami bank or thrift to Joe, who deposits it in his Dallas bank or thrift, how does the Dallas bank collect the money represented by the check drawn against the Miami bank? Answer: The Fed handles it by adjusting the reserves (deposits) of the two banks.
- ***Acting as fiscal agent*** The Fed acts as the fiscal agent (provider of financial services) for the federal government. The government collects huge sums through taxation, spends equally large amounts, and sells and redeems bonds. To carry out these activities, the government uses the Fed's facilities.
- ***Supervising banks*** The Fed supervises the operations of banks. It makes periodic examinations to assess bank profitability, to ascertain that banks perform in accordance with the many regulations to which they are subject, and to uncover questionable practices or fraud. Following the financial crisis of 2007–2008, Congress expanded the Fed's supervisory powers over banks.[5]
- ***Controlling the money supply*** Finally, the Fed has ultimate responsibility for regulating the supply of money, and this enables it to influence interest rates. The major task of the Fed under usual economic circumstances is to manage the money supply (and thus interest rates) according to the needs of the economy. This involves making an amount of money available that is consistent with high and rising levels of output and employment *and* a relatively stable price level. While most of the other functions of the Fed are routine activities or have a service nature, managing the nation's money supply requires making basic, but unique, policy decisions. (We discuss those decisions in detail in Chapter 30.)

[5]The Fed is not alone in this task of supervision. The individual states supervise the banks that they charter. The Office of the Comptroller of the Currency has separate supervisory authority over the banks and the thrifts. Also, the Federal Deposit Insurance Corporation supervises the banks and thrifts whose deposits it insures.

Federal Reserve Independence

Congress purposely established the Fed as an independent agency of government. The objective was to protect the Fed from political pressures so that it could effectively control the money supply and maintain price stability. Political pressures on Congress and the executive branch may at times result in inflationary fiscal policies, including tax cuts and special-interest spending. If Congress and the executive branch also controlled the nation's monetary policy, citizens and lobbying groups undoubtedly would pressure elected officials to keep interest rates low even though at times high interest rates are necessary to reduce aggregate demand and thus control inflation. An independent monetary authority (the Fed) can take actions to increase interest rates when higher rates are needed to stem inflation. Studies show that countries that have independent central banks like the Fed have lower rates of inflation, on average, than countries that have little or no central bank independence.

AP QUICK REVIEW 28.3

- ✓ The U.S. banking system consists of (a) the Board of Governors of the Federal Reserve System, (b) the 12 Federal Reserve Banks, and (c) some 6,000 commercial banks and 8,500 thrift institutions (mainly credit unions).
- ✓ The 12 Federal Reserve Banks are simultaneously (a) central banks, (b) quasi-public banks, and (c) bankers' banks.
- ✓ The major functions of the Fed are to (a) issue Federal Reserve Notes, (b) set reserve requirements and hold reserves deposited by banks and thrifts, (c) lend money to financial institutions and serve as the lender of last resort in national financial emergencies, (d) provide for the rapid collection of checks, (e) act as the fiscal agent for the federal government, (f) supervise the operations of the banks, and (g) regulate the supply of money in the best interests of the economy.

The Financial Crisis of 2007 and 2008

LO28.6 Identify and explain the main factors that contributed to the financial crisis of 2007–2008.

As previously noted, a properly functioning monetary system supports the continuous circular flows of income and expenditures in the economy. In contrast, a malfunctioning monetary system causes major problems in credit markets and can cause severe fluctuations in the economy's levels of output, employment, and prices.

"Malfunctioning" is too gentle an adjective to describe the monetary system in late 2007 and 2008. In that period, the U.S. financial system faced its most serious crisis since the Great Depression of the 1930s. The financial crisis soon spread to the entire economy, culminating in the severe recession of 2007–2009. We discussed the recession in detail in previous chapters, and we now want to examine the financial crisis that led up to it. What was the nature of the financial crisis? What caused it? How has it changed the structure of the U.S. financial services industry?

The Mortgage Default Crisis

In 2007 a major wave of defaults on home mortgage loans threatened the health of not only the original mortgage lenders but of any financial institution that had made such loans or invested in such loans either directly or indirectly. A majority of these mortgage defaults were on **subprime mortgage loans**—high-interest-rate loans to home buyers with higher-than-average credit risk. Ironically, the federal government had encouraged banks to make these types of loans as part of an effort to broaden home ownership to more Americans. But more directly to the point, several of the biggest indirect investors in these subprime loans had been banks. The banks had lent money to investment companies that had purchased many of the mortgages from mortgage lenders. When the mortgages started to go bad, many investment funds "blew up" and could not repay the loans they had taken out from the banks. The banks thus had to "write off" (declare unrecoverable) the loans they had made to the investment companies, but doing that meant reducing their banks' reserves and limiting their ability to generate new loans. This greatly threatened the economy because both consumers and businesses rely on loans to finance consumption and investment expenditures.

A strange thing about the crisis was that before it happened, banks and government regulators had mistakenly believed that an innovation known as the "mortgage-backed security" had eliminated most of the bank exposure to mortgage defaults. **Mortgage-backed securities** are bonds backed by mortgage payments. To create them, banks and other mortgage lenders first made mortgage loans. But then instead of holding all of those loans as assets on their balance sheets and collecting the monthly mortgage payments, the banks and other mortgage lenders bundled hundreds or thousands of them together and sold them off as bonds—in essence selling the right to collect all the future mortgage payments. The banks obtained a single, up-front cash payment for the bond and the bond buyer started to collect the mortgage payments as the return on the investment.

From the banks' perspective, this seemed like a smart business decision because it transferred any future default risk on those mortgages to the buyer of the bond. The banks thought that they were off the hook for these mortgages. Unfortunately for them, however, they lent a substantial portion of the money they received from selling the bonds to investment funds that invested in mortgage-backed bonds. They also purchased large amounts of mortgage-backed securities as financial investments to help meet bank capital requirements set by bank regulators. So while the banks were no longer directly exposed to major portions of the mortgage default risk, they were still indirectly exposed to it. When many homebuyers started to default on their mortgages, the banks lost money on the mortgages they still held. The banks also lost money on the loans they had made to the investors who had purchased mortgage-backed securities, and also on the mortgage-backed securities the banks had purchased from investment firms.

But what had caused the skyrocketing mortgage default rates in the first place? There were many causes, including certain government programs that greatly encouraged and subsidized home ownership for former renters. Also contributing were declining real estate values that arrived at the end of a long housing boom during which house prices had greatly increased. But an equally important factor was the bad incentives provided by the previously discussed mortgage-backed bonds. Because the banks and other mortgage lenders thought that they were no longer exposed to large portions of their mortgage default risk, they became lax in their lending practices—so much so that people were granted subprime mortgage loans that they were unlikely to be able to repay. Some mortgage companies were so eager to sign up new homebuyers (in order to bundle their loans together to sell bonds) that they stopped running credit checks and even allowed applicants to claim higher incomes than they were actually earning in order to qualify them for big loans. The natural result was that many people took on "too much mortgage" and were soon failing to make their monthly payments.

Securitization

The problems just described relate to **securitization**—the process of slicing up and bundling groups of loans, mortgages, corporate bonds, or other financial debts into distinct new securities. This process was not new and was viewed favorably by government regulators, who thought securitization made the banking system safer by allowing banks to shed risk. As noted in our discussion of mortgages, these securities were sold to financial investors, who purchased them to obtain the interest payments and the eventual return of principal generated by the underlying securities. For example, the mortgage loans provided to the subprime borrowers were bundled together as mortgage-backed securities and sold to private investors, mutual fund firms, and pension funds. These securities were attractive to many private investors and financial institutions alike because they offered higher-interest returns than securities backed by less-risky mortgages or other safer investments.

Once created, loan-backed securities are bought and sold in financial markets just like other securities such as stocks and bonds. These sorts of securities can therefore end up worldwide in the investment portfolios of banks, thrifts, insurance companies, and pensions, as well as in personal accounts.

To reduce the risk for holders of these securities, a few large insurance companies developed other securities that the holders of loan-backed securities could purchase to insure against losses from defaults. American International Group (AIG), in particular, issued billions of dollars of *collateralized default swaps*—essentially insurance policies—that were designed to compensate the holders of loan-backed securities if the loans underlying these investments went into default and did not pay off. Thus, collateralized default swaps became yet another category of investment security that was highly exposed to mortgage-loan risk.

Securitization is so widespread and so critical to the modern financial system that economists sometimes refer to it as the *shadow banking system*. All sorts of securities backed by loans or other securities are issued, bought, sold, and resold each day in a process that helps to keep credit flowing to the households and firms that rely on it for their personal and business needs. In general, securitization therefore is a positive financial innovation. But mortgage-backed securities, in particular, turned out to contain much more risk than most people thought.

Investors and government regulators failed to ask three related questions about mortgage-backed securities: What would happen if the value of one of the types of loans (say, mortgages) that underlies part of the securitization process unexpectedly plunged? And what then would happen if some of the largest holders of the securities based on these mortgages were major U.S. financial institutions that are vitally important to the day-to-day financing of the credit needed to keep the American economy running smoothly? And what would happen after that if the main insurer of these securities not only was the largest insurance company in the United States but in the world?

All three seemingly improbable "what ifs?" occurred! As previously explained, interest rates on adjustable-rate mortgages increased and house prices fell. Borrowers who had made relatively small down payments on home purchases or had previously cashed out home equity through refinancing discovered that they owed more on their mortgages than their properties were worth. Their loans were said to be "underwater." As interest rates adjusted upward and the economy slowed, borrowers began falling behind on their monthly mortgage payments. Lenders began to foreclose on many houses, while other borrowers literally handed in their house keys and walked away from their houses *and* their mortgages.

Failures and Near-Failures of Financial Firms

When the mortgage loan "card" underpinning mortgage-based securitization fell, the securitization layers above it collapsed like a house of cards. First, the big mortgage lenders faced demise because they still held large amounts of the bad debt. Three huge mortgage lenders collapsed or nearly collapsed. Countrywide, the second largest mortgage lender, was saved from bankruptcy by Bank of America. Regulators also seized Washington Mutual bank, the nation's largest mortgage lender, and arranged a quick takeover by JPMorgan Chase. Wachovia bank's heavy exposure to mortgages through its Golden West subsidiary resulted in near bankruptcy, and it was rescued through acquisition by Wells Fargo.

The exposure to the growing problem of loan defaults quickly jumped from direct mortgage lenders to other financial institutions. Securities firms and investment banks that held large amounts of loan-backed securities began to suffer huge losses. Merrill Lynch lost more in two years than it made in the prior decade and was acquired at a fire-sale price by Bank of America. Lehman Brothers, a major holder of mortgage-backed securities, declared bankruptcy. Goldman Sachs, Morgan Stanley, and other financial firms that had heavy exposures to mortgage-backed securities and collateralized default swaps rushed to become bank holding companies so they could qualify for the massive emergency loans that the Federal Reserve was making available to banks and bank holding companies. Citibank survived through infusions of federal government loans. Insurance company AIG suffered enormous losses because it had not set aside sufficient reserves to pay off the unexpectedly large losses that accrued on the insurance policies that it had sold to holders of mortgage-backed securities. The nightmarish thought of a total collapse of the U.S. financial system suddenly became a realistic possibility.

AP QUICK REVIEW 28.4

- ✓ The financial crisis of 2007–2008 consisted of an unprecedented rise in mortgage loan defaults, the collapse or near collapse of several major financial institutions, and the generalized freezing up of credit availability.
- ✓ The crisis resulted partially from the sale of bad mortgage loans together with declining real estate prices.
- ✓ The crisis exposed the underestimation of risk by holders of mortgage-backed securities as well as faulty insurance securities that had been designed to protect holders of mortgage-backed securities from the risk of default.

The Policy Response to the Financial Crisis

LO28.7 Discuss the actions of the U.S. Treasury and the Federal Reserve that helped keep the banking and financial crisis of 2007–2008 from worsening.

The U.S. government responded to the financial crisis with historically unprecedented fiscal policy actions while the Fed acted aggressively as a lender of last resort.

The Treasury Bailout: TARP

In late 2008, Congress passed the **Troubled Asset Relief Program (TARP),** which allocated $700 billion—yes, billion—to the U.S. Treasury to make emergency loans to critical financial and other U.S. firms. Most of this "bailout" money eventually was lent out. In fact, as of March 2009, the federal government and Federal Reserve had spent $170 billion just keeping insurer AIG afloat. Other major recipients of TARP funds included Citibank, Bank of America, JPMorgan Chase, and Goldman Sachs. Later, nonfinancial firms such as General Motors and Chrysler also received several billion dollars of TARP loans.

TARP indeed saved several financial institutions whose bankruptcy would have caused a tsunami of secondary effects that probably would have brought down other financial firms and frozen credit throughout the economy. But this very fact demonstrates the problem of **moral hazard.** As it relates to financial investment, moral hazard is the tendency for financial investors and financial services firms to take on greater risks because they assume they are at least partially insured against losses. Without TARP, several firms would have gone bankrupt and their stockholders, bondholders, and executives all would have suffered large personal losses. With TARP, those outcomes were at least partially avoided. TARP and similar government bailouts were essentially government-provided insurance payouts to financial firms that never had to pay a single cent in insurance premiums for the massive bailouts that kept them afloat.

The correct assumption by large firms that they were simply too big for government to let them fail may have given them an incentive to make riskier investments than if no government bailouts were likely to be forthcoming.

The Fed's Lender-of-Last-Resort Activities

As noted in our previous list of Fed functions, one of the roles of the Federal Reserve is to serve as the lender of last resort to financial institutions in times of financial emergencies. The Fed performed this vital function well following the 9/11 terrorist attacks. The financial crisis of 2007–2008 presented another, broader-based financial emergency. Under Fed Chair Ben Bernanke, the Fed designed and implemented several highly creative new lender-of-last-resort facilities to pump liquidity into the financial system. These facilities, procedures, and capabilities were in addition to both the TARP efforts by the U.S. Treasury and the Fed's use of standard tools of monetary policy (the subject of Chapter 30) designed to reduce interest rates. All the new Fed facilities had the single purpose and desired outcome of keeping credit flowing.

Total Fed assets rose from $885 billion in February 2008 to $1,903 billion in March 2009. This increase reflected a huge rise in the amount of securities (U.S. securities, mortgage-backed securities, and others) owned by the Fed. In undertaking its lender-of-last-resort functions, the Fed bought these securities from financial institutions. The purpose was to increase liquidity in the financial system by exchanging illiquid bonds (that the firms could not easily sell during the crisis) for cash, the most liquid of all assets.

Many economists believe that TARP and the Fed's actions helped to avert a second Great Depression. But they also intensified the moral hazard problem by greatly limiting the losses that otherwise would have resulted from bad financial assumptions and decisions. See this chapter's Last Word for more.

AP QUICK REVIEW 28.5

- ✓ The Troubled Asset Relief Program (TARP) authorized the U.S. Treasury to spend up to $700 billion to make emergency loans and guarantees to failing financial firms.
- ✓ The Treasury rescue, or bailout, was aided by lender-of-last-resort loans provided by the Federal Reserve to financial institutions through a series of newly established Fed facilities.
- ✓ The TARP loans and the Fed's lender-of-last-resort actions intensified the moral hazard problem which is the idea that financial investors and financial firms take on greater risk because they assume that the government will bail them out if they lose money.

The Postcrisis U.S. Financial Services Industry

LO28.8 Identify the main subsets of the financial services industry in the United States and provide examples of some firms in each category.

Table 28.1 lists the major categories of firms within the U.S. financial services industry and gives examples of firms in each category. Note that the main categories of the **financial services industry** are commercial banks, thrifts, insurance companies, mutual fund companies, pension funds, security firms, and investment banks. Even before the financial crisis of 2007–2008, the financial services industry was consolidating into fewer, larger firms, each offering a wider spectrum of services. In 1999, Congress ended the Depression-era prohibition against banks selling stocks, bonds, and mutual funds. Thus, the lines between the subsets of the financial industry began to blur. Many banks acquired stock brokerage firms and, in a few cases, insurance companies. For example, Citigroup, which was once only into banking, now owns Smith Barney, a large securities firm. Many large banks (for example, Wells Fargo) and pension funds (for example, TIAA-CREF) now provide mutual funds, including money market mutual funds that pay relatively high interest and on which checks of $500 or more can be written.

The upheaval in the financial markets caused by the financial crisis of 2007–2008 further consolidated the industry and further blurred the lines between its segments. Between September 2007 and September 2009, the FDIC shut down more than 200 U.S. banks and transferred their bank deposits to other, usually larger, banks. In 2009, the three largest U.S. banks (JPMorgan Chase, Bank of America, and Wells Fargo) held roughly $3 of every $10 on deposit in the United States.

Also, during the financial crisis of 2007–2008, major investment banks Goldman Sachs and Morgan Stanley opted to become commercial banks to gain access to emergency Federal Reserve loans. The nation's largest thrift—Washington Mutual—was absorbed by commercial bank JPMorgan Chase. But even with all this blending, the categories in Table 28.1 remain helpful. The main lines of a firm's businesses often are in one category or another. For example, even though Goldman Sachs is licensed and regulated as a bank, it is first and foremost an investment company. And the insurance companies and pension funds do most of their business as such.

The financial crisis of 2007–2008 generated much introspection about what went wrong and how to prevent anything like it from happening again. Politicians and financial regulators tightened lending rules to offset the "pass the buck" incentives created by mortgage-backed securities and prevent loans from being issued to people who are unlikely to be able to make the required monthly payments. They also passed legislation to help homeowners who were "underwater" on mortgage loans remain in their homes.

In mid-2010 Congress passed and the president signed the **Wall Street Reform and Consumer Protection Act.** This sweeping law includes provisions that:

- Eliminate the Office of Thrift Supervision and give broader authority to the Federal Reserve to regulate all large financial institutions.
- Create a Financial Stability Oversight Council to be on the lookout for risks to the financial system.
- Establish a process for the federal government to liquidate (sell off) the assets of failing nonbank financial institutions, much like the FDIC does with failing banks.

TABLE 28.1 Major Categories of Financial Institutions within the U.S. Financial Services Industry

Institution	Description	Examples
Commercial banks	State and national banks that provide checking and savings accounts, sell certificates of deposit, and make loans. The Federal Deposit Insurance Corporation (FDIC) insures checking and savings accounts up to $250,000.	JPMorgan Chase, Bank of America, Citibank, Wells Fargo
Thrifts	Savings and loan associations (S&Ls), mutual saving banks, and credit unions that offer checking and savings accounts and make loans. Historically, S&Ls made mortgage loans for houses while mutual savings banks and credit unions made small personal loans, such as automobile loans. Today, major thrifts offer the same range of banking services as commercial banks. The Federal Deposit Insurance Corporation and the National Credit Union Administration insure checking and savings deposits up to $250,000.	Charter One, New York Community Bank, Pentagon Federal Credit Union, Boeing Employees Credit Union (BECU)
Insurance companies	Firms that offer policies (contracts) through which individuals pay premiums to insure against some loss, say, disability or death. In some life insurance policies and annuities, the funds are invested for the client in stocks and bonds and paid back after a specified number of years. Thus, insurance sometimes has a saving or financial-investment element.	Prudential, New York Life, Northwestern Mutual, Hartford, MetLife
Mutual fund companies	Firms that pool deposits by customers to purchase stocks or bonds (or both). Customers thus indirectly own a part of a particular set of stocks or bonds, say stocks in companies expected to grow rapidly (a growth fund) or bonds issued by state governments (a municipal bond fund).	Fidelity, Vanguard, Putnam, Janus, T. Rowe Price
Pension funds	For-profit or nonprofit institutions that collect savings from workers (or from employers on their behalf) throughout their working years and then buy stocks and bonds with the proceeds and make monthly retirement payments.	TIAA-CREF, Teamsters' Union, CalPERs
Securities firms	Firms that offer security advice and buy and sell stocks and bonds for clients. More generally known as *stock brokerage firms*.	Merrill Lynch, TD Ameritrade, Charles Schwab
Investment banks	Firms that help corporations and governments raise money by selling stocks and bonds. They also typically offer advisory services for corporate mergers and acquisitions as well as brokerage services and advice.	Goldman Sachs, Morgan Stanley, Deutsche Bank, Credit Suisse

- Provide federal regulatory oversight of mortgage-backed securities and other derivatives and require that they be traded on public exchanges.
- Require companies selling asset-backed securities to retain a portion of those securities so the sellers share part of the risk.
- Establish a stronger consumer financial protection role for the Fed through creation of the Bureau of Consumer Financial Protection.

Proponents of the new law say that it will help prevent many of the practices that led up to the financial crisis of 2007–2008. They also contend that the law will send a strong message to stockholders, bondholders, and executives of large financial firms that they will suffer unavoidable and extremely high personal financial losses if they allow their firms to ever again get into serious financial trouble.

Skeptics of the new law say that regulators already had all the tools they needed to prevent the financial crisis. They also point out that the government's own efforts to promote home ownership, via quasi-government institutions that purchased mortgage-backed securities, greatly contributed to the financial crisis. Critics of the new law say that it will simply impose heavy new regulatory costs on the financial industry while doing little to prevent future government bailouts. This chapter's Last Word considers those suspicions.

AP QUICK REVIEW 28.6

- ✓ The main categories of the U.S. financial services industry are commercial banks, thrifts, insurance companies, mutual fund companies, pension funds, securities firms, and investment banks.
- ✓ The reassembly of the wreckage from the financial crisis of 2007–2008 has further consolidated the already-consolidating financial services industry and has further blurred some of the lines between the subsets of the industry.
- ✓ The Wall Street Reform and Consumer Financial Protection Act of 2010 responded to the financial crisis by consolidating financial regulation, providing federal oversight of mortgage-backed securities, and creating the Bureau of Consumer Financial Protection.

LAST WORD

Extend and Pretend

To Prevent a Total Meltdown During the Financial Crisis of 2007–2008, the Fed Had to Act as a Lender of Last Resort to Both Solvent and Insolvent Firms.

An individual or firm is said to be solvent if the value of its assets exceeds the value of its debts. By contrast, an individual or firm is said to be insolvent if the value of its assets is less than the value of its debts.

A firm that is solvent can be illiquid, meaning that its assets are hard to sell in a hurry. A large factory is a good example. It's hard to find a buyer for a billion-dollar factory quickly. Finding a buyer can take many months or even many years. So a firm whose primary asset is a large factory will be illiquid.

A firm that is solvent but illiquid can be threatened by bankruptcy if it has borrowed money and ends up in a situation in which it can't make timely debt payments. This situation is tricky because if the firm had liquid assets, it could sell those assets quickly to raise the cash that it needs to make timely debt payments. But because its assets are illiquid, the firm will go bankrupt despite being solvent; it won't be able to sell assets fast enough to keep current on its debt obligations.

Source: © Caroline Purser/Getty Images

During a financial crisis, the Fed is supposed to act as a lender of last resort to banks and other financial firms that are solvent but illiquid. The financial firms pledge some of their illiquid assets as collateral in exchange for cash loans issued by the Fed. The firms get the liquidity they need to make timely payments on their loans while the Fed receives collateral that it can sell off later (if necessary) to ensure repayment.

Because the Fed itself is never in a bankruptcy crisis (because it can always print more money to pay off any of its obligations), it can take a leisurely approach to selling off illiquid assets. It is consequently immune to financial crises and thus in a position to lend freely to help calm financial crises.

During a financial crisis, the Fed and other central banks will typically make loans to insolvent firms as well as solvent firms. The insolvent firms also have to pledge assets to obtain loans from the Fed, but the fact that they are insolvent means that they are not capable of paying back all of their creditors—including the Fed, now that it has lent them money.

So why would the Fed put itself in that situation? Why would the Fed extend loans to firms that may lack the financial resources to pay the Fed back?

The answer is that during a financial crisis the Fed is worried that if it does not extend credit to insolvent firms, the insolvent firms will go bankrupt and cease to make timely debt payments to solvent firms, something that could then drive the solvent firms into bankruptcy, too.

The Fed is consequently under pressure during major a financial crisis to extend emergency loans to *any* firm that can post assets as collateral. By not discriminating between solvent and insolvent firms, the Fed is in essence pretending that all firms are just in need of a little liquidity to get them through the crisis. The hope is that once the crisis is over, the insolvent firms will be able to either go quietly into bankruptcy or find another company that is willing to buy them or invest in them (for a low enough price).

During the financial crisis of 2007–2008, the Fed extended loans to both solvent and insolvent firms. This policy of "extend and pretend" was both widely praised and widely criticized. On the one hand, the Fed prevented the financial meltdown that would have occurred if the bankruptcies of insolvent firms had also taken down solvent firms. On the other hand, many poorly managed firms that had become insolvent due to making bad investments avoided well-deserved bankruptcies. Not only was this unfair to well-managed firms, it increased moral hazard going forward. Banks and other financial companies will be more likely to engage in risky behavior because they will expect both solvent and insolvent firms to have equal access to emergency loans when the next crisis hits.

SUMMARY

LO28.1 Identify and explain the functions of money.

Anything that is accepted as (*a*) a medium of exchange, (*b*) a unit of monetary account, and (*c*) a store of value can be used as money.

LO28.2 List and describe the components of the U.S. money supply.

There are two major definitions of the money supply. *M*1 consists of currency and checkable deposits; *M*2 consists of *M*1 plus savings deposits, including money market deposit accounts, small-denominated (less than $100,000) time deposits, and money market mutual fund balances held by individuals.

LO28.3 Describe what "backs" the money supply, making us willing to accept it as payment.

Money represents the debts of government and institutions offering checkable deposits (commercial banks and thrift institutions) and has value because of the goods, services, and resources it will command in the market. Maintaining the purchasing power of money depends largely on the government's effectiveness in managing the money supply.

LO28.4 Discuss the makeup of the Federal Reserve and its relationship to banks and thrifts.

The U.S. banking system consists of (*a*) the Board of Governors of the Federal Reserve System, (*b*) the 12 Federal Reserve Banks, and (*c*) some 6,000 commercial banks and 8,500 thrift institutions (mainly credit unions). The Board of Governors is the basic policymaking body for the entire banking system. The directives of the Board and the Federal Open Market Committee (FOMC) are made effective through the 12 Federal Reserve Banks, which are simultaneously (*a*) central banks, (*b*) quasi-public banks, and (*c*) bankers' banks.

LO28.5 Identify the functions and responsibilities of the Federal Reserve and explain why Fed independence is important.

The major functions of the Fed are to (*a*) issue Federal Reserve Notes, (*b*) set reserve requirements and hold reserves deposited by banks and thrifts, (*c*) lend money to financial institutions and serve as the lender of last resort in national financial emergencies, (*d*) provide for the rapid collection of checks, (*e*) act as the fiscal agent for the federal government, (*f*) supervise the operations of the banks, and (*g*) regulate the supply of money in the best interests of the economy.

The Fed is essentially an independent institution, controlled neither by the president of the United States nor by Congress. This independence shields the Fed from political pressure and allows it to raise and lower interest rates (via changes in the money supply) as needed to promote full employment, price stability, and economic growth.

LO28.6 Identify and explain the main factors that contributed to the financial crisis of 2007–2008.

The financial crisis of 2007–2008 consisted of an unprecedented rise in mortgage loan defaults, the collapse or near-collapse of several major financial institutions, and the generalized freezing up of credit availability. The crisis resulted from bad mortgage loans together with declining real estate prices. It also resulted from underestimation of risk by holders of mortgage-backed securities and faulty insurance securities designed to protect holders of mortgage-backed securities from the risk of default.

LO28.7 Discuss the actions of the U.S. Treasury and the Federal Reserve that helped keep the banking and financial crisis of 2007–2008 from worsening.

In 2008 Congress passed the Troubled Asset Relief Program (TARP), which authorized the U.S. Treasury to spend up to $700 billion to make emergency loans and guarantees to failing financial firms. The Treasury rescue, or bailout, was aided by lender-of-last-resort loans provided by the Federal Reserve to financial institutions through a series of newly established Fed facilities.

The TARP loans and the Fed's lender-of-last-resort actions intensify the moral hazard problem. This is the tendency of financial investors and financial firms to take on greater risk when they assume they are at least partially insured against loss.

LO28.8 Identify the main subsets of the financial services industry in the United States and provide examples of some firms in each category.

The main categories of the U.S. financial services industry are commercial banks, thrifts, insurance companies, mutual fund companies, pension funds, securities firms, and investment banks. The reassembly of the wreckage from the financial crisis of 2007–2008 has further consolidated the already-consolidating financial services industry and has further blurred some of the lines between the subsets of the industry.

In response to the financial crisis, Congress passed the Wall Street Reform and Consumer Financial Protection Act of 2010.

TERMS AND CONCEPTS

medium of exchange
unit of account
store of value
liquidity
*M*1
Federal Reserve Notes
token money
checkable deposits
commercial banks
thrift institutions
near-monies
*M*2
savings account
money market deposit account (MMDA)
time deposits
money market mutual fund (MMMF)
legal tender
Federal Reserve System

Board of Governors
Federal Reserve Banks
Federal Open Market Committee (FOMC)
subprime mortgage loans
mortgage-backed securities
securitization
Troubled Asset Relief Program (TARP)
moral hazard
financial services industry
Wall Street Reform and Consumer Protection Act

The following and additional problems can be found in connect

DISCUSSION QUESTIONS

1. What are the three basic functions of money? Describe how rapid inflation can undermine money's ability to perform each of the three functions. LO28.1
2. Which two of the following financial institutions offer checkable deposits included within the *M*1 money supply: mutual fund companies; insurance companies; commercial banks; securities firms; thrift institutions? Which of the following items is *not* included in either *M*1 or *M*2: currency held by the public; checkable deposits; money market mutual fund balances; small-denominated (less than $100,000) time deposits; currency held by banks; savings deposits? LO28.2
3. What are the components of the *M*1 money supply? What is the largest component? Which of the components of *M*1 is legal tender? Why is the face value of a coin greater than its intrinsic value? What near-monies are included in the *M*2 money supply? LO28.2
4. Explain and evaluate the following statements: LO28.2
   a. The invention of money is one of the great achievements of humankind, for without it the enrichment that comes from broadening trade would have been impossible.
   b. Money is whatever society says it is.
   c. In the United States, the debts of government and commercial banks are used as money.
   d. People often say they would like to have more money, but what they usually mean is that they would like to have more goods and services.
   e. When the price of everything goes up, it is not because everything is worth more but because the currency is worth less.
   f. Any central bank can create money; the trick is to create enough, but not too much, of it.
5. What "backs" the money supply in the United States? What determines the value (domestic purchasing power) of money? How does the purchasing power of money relate to the price level? Who in the United States is responsible for maintaining money's purchasing power? LO28.3
6. How is the chairperson of the Federal Reserve System selected? Describe the relationship between the Board of Governors of the Federal Reserve System and the 12 Federal Reserve Banks. What is the purpose of the Federal Open Market Committee (FOMC)? What is its makeup? LO28.4
7. The following are two hypothetical ways in which the Federal Reserve Board might be appointed. Would you favor either of these two methods over the present method? Why or why not? LO28.4
   a. Upon taking office, the U.S. president appoints seven people to the Federal Reserve Board, including a chair. Each appointee must be confirmed by a majority vote of the Senate, and each serves the same 4-year term as the president.
   b. Congress selects seven members from its ranks (four from the House of Representatives and three from the Senate) to serve at congressional pleasure as the Board of Governors of the Federal Reserve System.
8. What is meant when economists say that the Federal Reserve Banks are central banks, quasi-public banks, and bankers' banks? LO28.4
9. Why do economists nearly uniformly support an independent Fed rather than one beholden directly to either the president or Congress? LO28.5
10. Identify three functions of the Federal Reserve of your choice, other than its main role of controlling the supply of money. LO28.5
11. How does each of the following relate to the financial crisis of 2007–2008: declines in real estate values, subprime mortgage loans, mortgage-backed securities, AIG. LO28.6
12. What is TARP and how was it funded? What is meant by the term "lender of last resort" and how does it relate to the financial crisis of 2007–2008? How do government and Federal Reserve emergency loans relate to the concept of moral hazard? LO28.7
13. What are the major categories of firms that make up the U.S. financial services industry? Are there more or fewer banks today than before the start of the financial crisis of 2007–2008? Why are the lines between the categories of financial firms even more blurred than they were before the crisis? How did the Wall Street Reform and Consumer Protection Act of 2010 try to address some of the problems that helped cause the crisis? LO28.8
14. **LAST WORD** A firm enters bankruptcy when it misses a debt payment. So does being insolvent imply being bankrupt? Explain. And why is the Fed reluctant to distinguish between solvent and insolvent firms during a financial crisis?

AP REVIEW QUESTIONS

1. Explain why debit cards are part of the money supply, while credit cards are not. LO28.1
2. Suppose that a small country currently has $4 million of currency in circulation, $6 million of checkable deposits, $200 million of savings deposits, $40 million of small-denominated time deposits, and $30 million of money market mutual fund deposits. From these numbers we see that this small country's M_1 money supply is ________, while its M_2 money supply is ________. LO28.2

a. $10 million; $200 million.
b. $10 million; $280 million.
c. $10 million; $270 million.
d. $210 million; $280 million.
e. $250 million; $270 million.

3. Which group votes on the open-market operations that are used to control the U.S. money supply and interest rates? LO28.4
a. The member banks of the Federal Reserve System.
b. The presidents of the 12 Federal Reserve Banks.
c. The Board of Governors of the Federal Reserve System.
d. The Federal Open Market Committee (FOMC).
e. The current and past chairpersons of the Federal Reserve System.

4. Which of the following is ***not*** a function of the Fed? LO28.5
a. Setting reserve requirements for commercial banks and thrift institutions.
b. Advising Congress on fiscal policy.
c. Regulating the supply of money.
d. Serving as a lender of last resort.
e. Serving as the clearinghouse for checking transactions.

5. City Bank is considering making a $50 million loan to a company named SheetOil that wants to commercialize a process for turning used blankets, pillowcases, and sheets into oil. This company's chances for success are dubious, but City Bank makes the loan anyway because it believes that the government will bail it out if SheetOil goes bankrupt and cannot repay the loan. City Bank's decision to make the loan has been affected by: LO28.7
a. Liquidity.
b. Moral hazard.
c. Token money.
d. Securitization.
e. Inflation

6. Assume Mary deposits $100 of her cash into her checking account. Which of the following is true? LO28.2
a. The M1 component falls by $100, given the reduction in circulating cash.
b. The M1 component does not change but M2 increases by $200.
c. Both the M1 and M2 components remain unchanged.
d. With more dollars in the checking account, M1 must increase in this example.
e. Both M1 and M2 increase by $100.

7. The following values exist in an economy: LO28.2
Circulating cash $200
Cash held by banks $50
Checking account balances $300
Savings accounts $600
Value of government bonds held by the public $150
Credit card debt $100
a. What is the value of M1 in this society?
b. What is value of M2 in this society?

8. Assume Charles goes into his bank and transfers $150 from his checking account to his savings account. Which of the following is true? LO28.2
a. M1 decreases by $150 and M2 increases by $150.
b. M1 decreases by $150 and there is no change to M2
c. M1 does not change but M2 increases by $150.
d. M1 and M2 increase by $150.
e. Neither M1 nor M2 changes in value.

9. Assume Martha goes into her bank and transfers $500 from her savings account to her checking account. Which of the following is true? LO28.2
a. M1 decreases by $500 and M2 increases by $500.
b. M1 decreases by $500 and M2 falls by $
c. M1 increases by $500 while M2 does not change.
d. M1 and M2 increase by $500.
e. Neither M1 nor M2 changes in value.

PROBLEMS

1. Assume that the following asset values (in millions of dollars) exist in Ironmania: Federal Reserve Notes in circulation = $700; Money market mutual funds (MMMFs) held by individuals = $400; Corporate bonds = $300; Iron ore deposits = $50; Currency in commercial banks = $100; Savings deposits, including money market deposit accounts (MMDAs) = $140; Checkable deposits = $1,500; Small-denominated (less than $100,000) time deposits = $100; Coins in circulation = $40. LO28.1
a. What is *M1* in Ironmania?
b. What is *M2* in Ironmania?

2. Assume that Jimmy Cash has $2,000 in his checking account at Folsom Bank and uses his checking account card to withdraw $200 of cash from the bank's ATM machine. By what dollar amount did the *M1* money supply change as a result of this single, isolated transaction? LO28.2

3. Suppose the price level and value of the U.S. dollar in year 1 are 1 and $1, respectively. If the price level rises to 1.25 in year 2, what is the new value of the dollar? If, instead, the price level falls to 0.50, what is the value of the dollar? LO28.3

4. Assume that securitization combined with borrowing and irrational exuberance in Hyperville have driven up the value of existing financial securities at a geometric rate, specifically from $2 to $4 to $8 to $16 to $32 to $64 over a 6-year time period. Over the same period, the value of the assets underlying the securities rose at an arithmetic rate from $2 to $3 to $4 to $5 to $6 to $7. If these patterns hold for decreases as well as for increases, by how much would the value of the financial securities decline if the value of the underlying asset suddenly and unexpectedly fell by $5? LO28.6

5. Suppose that Lady Gaga goes to Las Vegas to play poker and at the last minute her record company says it will reimburse her for 50 percent of any gambling losses that she incurs. Will Lady Gaga wager more or less as a result of the reimbursement offer? What economic concept does your answer illustrate? LO28.7

Chapter 29

Money Creation

Learning Objectives

LO29.1 **Discuss why the U.S. banking system is called a "fractional reserve" system.**

LO29.2 **Explain the basics of a bank's balance sheet and the distinction between a bank's actual reserves and its required reserves.**

LO29.3 **Describe how a bank can create money.**

LO29.4 **Describe the multiple expansion of loans and money by the entire banking system.**

LO29.5 **Define the monetary multiplier, explain how to calculate it, and demonstrate its relevance.**

AP Chapter Focus

We have seen that the *M*1 money supply consists of currency (coins and Federal Reserve Notes) and checkable deposits and that *M*1 is a base component of *M*2, a broader measure of the money supply that also includes savings deposits, small-denominated time deposits, and balances in money market mutual funds. The U.S. Mint produces the coins, and the U.S. Bureau of Engraving and Printing creates the Federal Reserve Notes. So who creates the checkable deposits? Surprisingly, it is loan officers! Although that may sound like something a congressional committee should investigate, the monetary authorities are well aware that banks and thrifts create checkable deposits. In fact, the Federal Reserve relies on these institutions to create this vital component of the nation's money supply.

AP The Fractional Reserve System

LO29.1 Discuss why the U.S. banking system is called a "fractional reserve" system.

The United States, like most other countries today, has a **fractional reserve banking system** in which only a portion (fraction) of checkable deposits are backed up by reserves of currency in bank vaults or deposits at the central bank. Our goal is to explain this system and show how commercial banks can create checkable deposits by issuing loans. Our examples will involve commercial banks, but remember that thrift institutions also provide checkable deposits. So the analysis applies to banks and thrifts alike.

Illustrating the Idea: The Goldsmiths

Here is the history behind the idea of the fractional reserve system.

When early traders began to use gold in making transactions, they soon realized that it was both unsafe and inconvenient to carry gold and to have it weighed and assayed (judged for purity) every time they negotiated a transaction. So by the sixteenth century they had begun to deposit their gold with goldsmiths, who would store it in vaults for a fee. On receiving a gold deposit, the goldsmith would issue a receipt to the depositor. Soon people were paying for goods with goldsmiths' receipts, which served as one of the first types of paper money.

At this point the goldsmiths—embryonic bankers—used a 100 percent reserve system; they backed their circulating paper money receipts fully with the gold that they held "in reserve" in their vaults. But because of the public's acceptance of the goldsmiths' receipts as paper money, the goldsmiths soon realized that owners rarely redeemed the gold they had in storage. In fact, the goldsmiths observed that the amount of gold being deposited with them in any week or month was likely to exceed the amount that was being withdrawn.

Then some clever goldsmith hit on the idea that paper "receipts" could be issued in excess of the amount of gold held. Goldsmiths would put these receipts, which were redeemable in gold, into circulation by making interest-earning loans to merchants, producers, and consumers. A borrower might, for instance, borrow $10,000 worth of gold receipts today with the promise to repay $10,500 worth of gold receipts in one year (a 5 percent interest rate). Borrowers were willing to accept loans in the form of gold receipts because the receipts were accepted as a medium of exchange in the marketplace.

This was the beginning of the fractional reserve system of banking, in which reserves in bank vaults are a fraction of the total money supply. If, for example, the goldsmith issued $1 million in receipts for actual gold in storage and another $1 million in receipts as loans, then the total value of paper money in circulation would be $2 million—twice the value of the gold. Gold reserves would be a fraction (one-half) of outstanding paper money.

Significant Characteristics of Fractional Reserve Banking

The goldsmith story highlights two significant characteristics of fractional reserve banking. First, banks can create money through lending. In fact, goldsmiths created money when they made loans by giving borrowers paper money that was not fully backed by gold reserves. The quantity of such money goldsmiths could create depended on the amount of reserves they deemed prudent to have available. The smaller the amount of reserves thought necessary, the larger the amount of paper money the goldsmiths could create. Today, gold is no longer used as bank reserves. Instead, currency itself serves as bank reserves so that the creation of checkable-deposit money by banks (via their lending) is limited by the amount of *currency reserves* that the banks feel obligated, or are required by law, to keep.

A second reality is that banks operating on the basis of fractional reserves are vulnerable to "panics" or "runs." A goldsmith who issued paper money equal to twice the value of his gold reserves would be unable to convert all that paper money into gold in the event that all the holders of that money appeared at his door at the same time demanding their gold. In fact, many European and U.S. banks were once ruined by this unfortunate circumstance. However, a bank panic is highly unlikely if the banker's reserve and lending policies are prudent. Indeed, one reason why banking systems are highly regulated industries is to prevent runs on banks.

This is also why the United States has the system of deposit insurance that we discussed in the last chapter. By guaranteeing deposits, deposit insurance helps to prevent the sort of bank runs that used to happen so often before deposit insurance was available. In those situations, rumors would spread that a bank was about to go bankrupt and that it only had a small amount of reserves left in its vaults. Bank runs are called "bank runs" because depositors would run to the bank trying to be one of the lucky few to withdraw their money while the bank had any reserves left. The rumors were usually totally unfounded. But, unfortunately, the bank would still go bankrupt even if it began the day with its normal amount of reserves. With so many customers withdrawing money simultaneously, it would run out of reserves and be forced to default on its obligations to its remaining depositors. By guaranteeing depositors that they will always get their money, deposit insurance removes the incentive to try to withdraw one's deposit before anyone else can. It thus stops most bank runs.

AP A Single Commercial Bank

LO29.2 Explain the basics of a bank's balance sheet and the distinction between a bank's actual reserves and its required reserves.

To illustrate the workings of the modern fractional reserve banking system, we need to examine a commercial bank's balance sheet.

The **balance sheet** of a commercial bank (or thrift) is a statement of assets—things owned by the bank or owed to the bank—and claims on those assets. A bank balance sheet summarizes the financial position of the bank at a certain time. Every balance sheet must balance; this means that the value of *assets* must equal the amount of claims against those assets. The claims shown on a balance sheet are divided into two groups: the claims of nonowners of the bank against the firm's assets, called *liabilities*, and the claims of the owners of the firm against the firm's assets, called *net worth*. Liabilities are things owed by the bank to depositors or others. A balance sheet is balanced because

$$\text{Assets} = \text{liabilities} + \text{net worth}$$

Every $1 change in assets must be offset by a $1 change in liabilities + net worth. Every $1 change in liabilities + net worth must be offset by a $1 change in assets.

Now let's work through a series of bank transactions involving balance sheets to establish how individual banks can create money.

Transaction 1: Creating a Bank

Suppose some far-sighted citizens of the town of Wahoo, Nebraska (yes, there is such a place), decide their town needs a new commercial bank to provide banking services for that growing community. Once they have secured a state or national charter for their bank, they turn to the task of selling, say, $250,000 worth of stock (equity shares) to buyers, both in and out of the community. Their efforts meet with success and the Bank of Wahoo comes into existence—at least on paper. What does its balance sheet look like at this stage?

The founders of the bank have sold $250,000 worth of shares of stock in the bank—some to themselves, some to other people. As a result, the bank now has $250,000 in cash on hand and $250,000 worth of stock shares outstanding. The cash is an asset to the bank. Cash held by a bank is sometimes called **vault cash** or till money. The shares of stock outstanding constitute an equal amount of claims that the owners have against the bank's assets. Those shares of stock constitute the net worth of the bank. The bank's balance sheet reads:

Creating a Bank
Balance Sheet 1: Wahoo Bank

Assets		Liabilities and net worth	
Cash	$250,000	Stock shares	$250,000

Each item listed in a balance sheet such as this is called an *account.*

Transaction 2: Acquiring Property and Equipment

The board of directors (who represent the bank's owners) must now get the new bank off the drawing board and make it a reality. First, property and equipment must be acquired. Suppose the directors, confident of the success of their venture, purchase a building for $220,000 and pay $20,000 for office equipment. This simple transaction changes the composition of the bank's assets. The bank now has $240,000 less in cash and $240,000 of new property assets. Using blue to denote accounts affected by each transaction, we find that the bank's balance sheet at the end of transaction 2 appears as follows:

Acquiring Property and Equipment
Balance Sheet 2: Wahoo Bank

Assets		Liabilities and net worth	
Cash	$ 10,000	Stock shares	$250,000
Property	240,000		

Note that the balance sheet still balances, as it must.

Transaction 3: Accepting Deposits

Commercial banks have two basic functions: to accept deposits of money and to make loans. Now that the bank is operating, suppose that the citizens and businesses of Wahoo decide to deposit $100,000 in the Wahoo bank. What happens to the bank's balance sheet?

The bank receives cash, which is an asset to the bank. Suppose this money is deposited in the bank as checkable deposits (checking account entries), rather than as savings accounts or time deposits. These newly created *checkable deposits* constitute claims that the depositors have against the assets of the Wahoo bank and thus are a new liability account. The bank's balance sheet now looks like this:

Accepting Deposits
Balance Sheet 3: Wahoo Bank

Assets		Liabilities and net worth	
Cash	$110,000	Checkable deposits	$100,000
Property	240,000	Stock shares	250,000

There has been no change in the economy's total supply of money as a result of transaction 3, but a change has occurred in the composition of the money supply. Bank money, or checkable deposits, has increased by $100,000, and currency held by the public has decreased by $100,000. As explained in the previous chapter, currency held in a bank is not part of the economy's money supply.

A withdrawal of cash will reduce the bank's checkable-deposit liabilities and its holdings of cash by the amount of the withdrawal. This, too, changes the composition, but not the total supply, of money in the economy.

Transaction 4: Depositing Reserves in a Federal Reserve Bank

All commercial banks and thrift institutions that provide checkable deposits must by law keep **required reserves.** Required reserves are an amount of funds equal to a specified percentage of the bank's own deposit liabilities. A bank must keep these reserves on deposit with the Federal Reserve Bank in its district or as cash in the bank's vault. To simplify, we suppose the Bank of Wahoo keeps its required reserves entirely as deposits in the Federal Reserve Bank of its district. But remember that vault cash is counted as reserves and real-world banks keep a significant portion of their own reserves in their vaults.

The "specified percentage" of checkable-deposit liabilities that a commercial bank must keep as reserves is known as the **reserve ratio**—the ratio of the required reserves the commercial bank must keep to the bank's own outstanding checkable-deposit liabilities:

$$\text{Reserve ratio} = \frac{\text{commercial bank's required reserves}}{\text{commercial bank's checkable-deposit liabilities}}$$

If the reserve ratio is $\frac{1}{10}$, or 10 percent, the Wahoo bank, having accepted \$100,000 in deposits from the public, would have to keep \$10,000 as reserves. If the ratio is $\frac{1}{5}$, or 20 percent, \$20,000 of reserves would be required. If $\frac{1}{2}$, or 50 percent, \$50,000 would be required.

The Fed has the authority to establish and vary the reserve ratio within limits legislated by Congress. The limits now prevailing are shown in Table 29.1. The first \$15.2 million of checkable deposits held by a commercial bank or thrift is exempt from reserve requirements. A 3 percent reserve is required on checkable deposits of between \$15.2 million and \$110.2 million. A 10 percent reserve is required on checkable deposits over \$110.2 million, although the Fed can vary that percentage between 8 and 14 percent. Currently, no reserves are required against noncheckable nonpersonal (business) savings or time deposits, although up to 9 percent can be required. Also, after consultation with appropriate Congressional committees, the Fed for 180 days may impose reserve requirements outside the 8 to 14 percent range specified in Table 29.1. Beginning in late 2008, the Fed began paying banks interest on both required reserves as well as excess reserves held at Federal Reserve Banks.

In order to simplify, we will suppose that the reserve ratio for checkable deposits in commercial banks is $\frac{1}{5}$ or 20 percent. Although 20 percent obviously is higher than the requirement really is, the figure is convenient for calculations. Because we are concerned only with checkable (spendable) deposits, we ignore reserves on noncheckable savings and time deposits. The main point is that reserve requirements are fractional, meaning that they are less than 100 percent. This point is critical in our analysis of the lending ability of the banking system.

TABLE 29.1 Reserve Requirements (Reserve Ratios) for Banks and Thrifts, 2016

Type of Deposit	Current Requirement	Statutory Limits
Checkable deposits:		
\$0–\$15.2 million	0%	3%
\$15.2–\$110.2 million	3	3
Over \$110.2 million	10	8–14
Noncheckable nonpersonal savings and time deposits	0	0–9

Source: Federal Reserve, Regulation D, **www.federalreserve.gov**.

By depositing \$20,000 in the Federal Reserve Bank, the Wahoo bank will just be meeting the required 20 percent ratio between its reserves and its own deposit liabilities. We will use "reserves" to mean the funds commercial banks deposit in the Federal Reserve Banks to distinguish those funds from the public's deposits in commercial banks.

But suppose the Wahoo bank anticipates that its holdings of checkable deposits will grow in the future. Then, instead of sending just the minimum amount, \$20,000, it sends an extra \$90,000, for a total of \$110,000. In so doing, the bank will avoid the inconvenience of sending additional reserves to the Federal Reserve Bank each time its own checkable-deposit liabilities increase. And, as you will see, it is these extra reserves that enable banks to lend money and earn interest income.

Actually, a real-world bank would not deposit *all* its cash in the Federal Reserve Bank. However, because (1) banks as a rule hold vault cash only in the amount of $1\frac{1}{2}$ or 2 percent of their total assets and (2) vault cash can be counted as reserves, we will assume for simplicity that all of Wahoo's cash is deposited in the Federal Reserve Bank and therefore constitutes the commercial bank's actual reserves. By making this simplifying assumption, we do not need to bother adding two assets—"cash" and "deposits in the Federal Reserve Bank"—to determine "reserves."

After the Wahoo bank deposits \$110,000 of reserves at the Fed, its balance sheet becomes:

Depositing Reserves at the Fed
Balance Sheet 4: Wahoo Bank

Assets		Liabilities and net worth	
Cash	\$ 0	Checkable deposits	\$110,000
Reserves	110,000		
Property	240,000	Stock shares	250,000

There are three things to note about this latest transaction.

Excess Reserves A bank's **excess reserves** are found by subtracting its *required reserves* from its **actual reserves:**

$$\text{Excess reserves} = \text{actual reserves} - \text{required reserves}$$

In this case,

Actual reserves	\$110,000
Required reserves	−20,000
Excess reserves	\$ 90,000

The only reliable way of computing excess reserves is to multiply the bank's checkable-deposit liabilities by the reserve ratio to obtain required reserves (\$100,000 × 20 percent = \$20,000) and then to subtract the required reserves from the actual reserves listed on the asset side of the bank's balance sheet.

To test your understanding, compute the bank's excess reserves from Balance Sheet 4, assuming that the reserve ratio is (1) 10 percent, (2) $33\frac{1}{3}$ percent, and (3) 50 percent.

We will soon demonstrate that the ability of a commercial bank to make loans depends on the existence of excess reserves. Understanding this concept is crucial in seeing how the banking system creates money.

Control You might think the basic purpose of reserves is to enhance the liquidity of a bank and protect commercial bank depositors from losses. Reserves would constitute a ready source of funds from which commercial banks could meet large, unexpected cash withdrawals by depositors.

But this reasoning breaks down under scrutiny. Although historically reserves have been seen as a source of liquidity and therefore as protection for depositors, a bank's required reserves are not great enough to meet sudden, massive cash withdrawals. If the banker's nightmare should materialize—everyone with checkable deposits appearing at once to demand those deposits in cash—the actual reserves held as vault cash or at the Federal Reserve Bank would be insufficient. The banker simply could not meet this "bank panic." Because reserves are fractional, checkable deposits may be much greater than a bank's required reserves.

So commercial bank deposits must be protected by other means. Periodic bank examinations are one way of promoting prudent commercial banking practices. Furthermore, insurance funds administered by the Federal Deposit Insurance Corporation (FDIC) and the National Credit Union Administration (NCUA) insure individual deposits in banks and thrifts up to $250,000.

If it is not the purpose of reserves to provide for commercial bank liquidity, then what is their function? *Control* is the answer. Required reserves help the Fed control the lending ability of commercial banks. The Fed can take certain actions that either increase or decrease commercial bank reserves and affect the ability of banks to grant credit. The objective is to prevent banks from overextending or underextending bank credit. To the degree that these policies successfully influence the volume of commercial bank credit, the Fed can help the economy avoid business fluctuations. Another function of reserves is to facilitate the collection or "clearing" of checks.

Asset and Liability Transaction 4 brings up another matter. Specifically, the reserves created in transaction 4 are an asset to the depositing commercial bank because they are a claim this bank has against the assets of another institution—the Federal Reserve Bank. The checkable deposit you get by depositing money in a commercial bank is an asset to you and a liability to the bank (since the bank is liable for repaying you whenever you choose to withdraw your deposit). In the same way, the reserves that a commercial bank establishes by depositing money in a bankers' bank are an asset to the commercial bank and a liability to the Federal Reserve Bank.

Transaction 5: Clearing a Check Drawn against the Bank

Assume that Fred Bradshaw, a Wahoo farmer, deposited a substantial portion of the $100,000 in checkable deposits that the Wahoo bank received in transaction 3. Now suppose that Fred buys $50,000 of farm machinery from the Ajax Farm Implement Company of Surprise, Nebraska. Bradshaw pays for this machinery by writing a $50,000 check against his deposit in the Wahoo bank. He gives the check to the Ajax Company. What are the results?

Ajax deposits the check in its account with the Surprise bank. The Surprise bank increases Ajax's checkable deposits by $50,000 when Ajax deposits the check. Ajax is now paid in full. Bradshaw is pleased with his new machinery.

Now the Surprise bank has Bradshaw's check. This check is simply a claim against the assets of the Wahoo bank. The Surprise bank will collect this claim by sending the check (along with checks drawn on other banks) to the regional Federal Reserve Bank. Here a bank employee will clear, or collect, the check for the Surprise bank by increasing Surprise's reserve in the Federal Reserve Bank by $50,000 and decreasing the Wahoo bank's reserve by that same amount. The check is "collected" merely by making bookkeeping notations to the effect that Wahoo's claim against the Federal Reserve Bank is reduced by $50,000 and Surprise's claim is increased by $50,000.

Finally, the Federal Reserve Bank sends the cleared check back to the Wahoo bank, and for the first time the Wahoo bank discovers that one of its depositors has drawn a check for $50,000 against his checkable deposit. Accordingly, the Wahoo bank reduces Bradshaw's checkable deposit by $50,000 and notes that the collection of this check has caused a $50,000 decline in its reserves at the Federal Reserve Bank. All the balance sheets balance: The Wahoo bank has reduced both its assets (reserves) and its liabilities (checkable deposits) by $50,000. The Surprise bank has $50,000 more in both assets (reserves) and liabilities (checkable deposits). Ownership of reserves at the Federal Reserve Bank has changed—with Wahoo owning $50,000 less and Surprise owning $50,000 more—but total reserves stay the same.

Whenever a check is drawn against one bank and deposited in another bank, collection of that check will reduce both the reserves and the checkable deposits of the bank on which the check is drawn. Conversely, if a bank receives a check drawn on another bank, the bank receiving the check will, in the process of collecting it, have its reserves and deposits increased by the amount of the check. In our example, the Wahoo bank loses $50,000 in both reserves and deposits to the Surprise bank. But there is no loss of reserves or deposits for the banking system as a whole. What one bank loses, another bank gains.

If we bring all the other assets and liabilities back into the picture, the Wahoo bank's balance sheet looks like this at the end of transaction 5:

Clearing a Check
Balance Sheet 5: Wahoo Bank

Assets		Liabilities and net worth	
Reserves	$ 60,000	Checkable deposits	$ 50,000
Property	240,000	Stock shares	250,000

Verify that with a 20 percent reserve requirement, the bank's excess reserves now stand at $50,000.

AP QUICK REVIEW 29.1

- ✓ The United States has a fractional reserve banking system, in which the collective reserves of the banks usually are considerably less than 100 percent of their checkable deposit liabilities.
- ✓ When a bank or thrift accepts deposits of cash, the composition of the money supply is changed, but the total supply of money is not immediately altered.
- ✓ Commercial banks and thrifts are obliged to keep required reserves equal to a specified percentage of their own checkable-deposit liabilities as cash or on deposit with the Federal Reserve Bank of their district.
- ✓ The amount by which a bank's actual reserves exceed its required reserves is called excess reserves.
- ✓ A bank that has a check drawn and collected against it will lose to the recipient bank both reserves and deposits equal to the value of the check.

AP Money-Creating Transactions of a Commercial Bank

LO29.3 Describe how a bank can create money.

The next two transactions are crucial because they explain (1) how a commercial bank can literally create money by making loans and (2) how banks create money by purchasing government bonds from the public.

Transaction 6: Granting a Loan

In addition to accepting deposits, commercial banks grant loans to borrowers. What effect does lending by a commercial bank have on its balance sheet?

Suppose the Gristly Meat Packing Company of Wahoo decides it is time to expand its facilities. Suppose, too, that the company needs exactly $50,000—which just happens to be equal to the Wahoo bank's excess reserves—to finance this project.

Gristly goes to the Wahoo bank and requests a loan for this amount. The Wahoo bank knows the Gristly Company's fine reputation and financial soundness and is convinced of its ability to repay the loan. So the loan is granted. In return, the president of Gristly hands a promissory note—a fancy IOU—to the Wahoo bank. Gristly wants the convenience and safety of paying its obligations by check. So, instead of receiving a basket full of currency from the bank, Gristly gets a $50,000 increase in its checkable-deposit account in the Wahoo bank.

The Wahoo bank has acquired an interest-earning asset (the promissory note, which it files under "Loans") and has created checkable deposits (a liability) to "pay" for this asset. Gristly has swapped an IOU for the right to draw an additional $50,000 worth of checks against its checkable deposit in the Wahoo bank. Both parties are pleased.

At the moment the loan is completed, the Wahoo bank's position is shown by Balance Sheet 6a:

When a Loan Is Negotiated
Balance Sheet 6a: Wahoo Bank

Assets		Liabilities and net worth	
Reserves	$ 60,000	Checkable deposits	$100,000
Loans	50,000		
Property	240,000	Stock shares	250,000

All this looks simple enough. But a close examination of the Wahoo bank's balance statement reveals a startling fact: When a bank makes loans, it creates money. The president of Gristly went to the bank with something that is *not* money—her IOU—and walked out with something that *is* money—a checkable deposit.

Contrast Balance Sheet 6a with transaction 3, in which checkable deposits were created but only as a result of currency having been taken out of circulation. There was a change in the *composition* of the money supply in that situation but no change in the *total supply* of money. But when banks lend, they create checkable deposits that *are* money. By extending credit, the Wahoo bank has "monetized" an IOU. Gristly and the Wahoo bank have created and then swapped claims. The claim created by Gristly and given to the bank is not money; an individual's IOU is not acceptable as a medium of exchange. But the claim created by the bank and given to Gristly *is* money; checks drawn against a checkable deposit are acceptable as a medium of exchange. Checkable-deposit money like this constitutes about one-half the quantity of $M1$ money in the United States and about 10 percent of $M2$.

Much of the money used in the United States therefore is created through the extension of credit by commercial banks. This checkable-deposit money may be thought of as "debts" of commercial banks and thrift institutions. Checkable deposits are bank debts in the sense that they are claims that banks and thrifts promise to pay "on demand."

But certain factors limit the ability of a commercial bank to create checkable deposits ("bank money") by lending. The Wahoo bank can expect the newly created checkable deposit of $50,000 to be a very active account. Gristly would not borrow $50,000 at, say, 7, 10, or 12 percent interest for the sheer joy of knowing that funds were available if needed.

Assume that Gristly awards a $50,000 building contract to the Quickbuck Construction Company of Omaha. Quickbuck, true to its name, completes the expansion promptly and is paid with a check for $50,000 drawn by Gristly against its checkable deposit in the Wahoo bank. Quickbuck, with headquarters in Omaha, does not deposit this check in the Wahoo bank but instead deposits it in the Fourth National Bank of Omaha. Fourth National now has a $50,000 claim against the Wahoo bank. The check is collected in the manner described in Balance Sheet 5. As a result, the Wahoo bank loses both reserves and deposits equal to the amount of the check; Fourth National acquires $50,000 of reserves and deposits.

In summary, assuming a check is drawn by the borrower for the entire amount of the loan ($50,000) and is given to a firm that deposits it in some other bank, the Wahoo bank's balance sheet will read as follows after the check has been cleared against it:

After a Check Is Drawn on the Loan
Balance Sheet 6b: Wahoo Bank

Assets		Liabilities and net worth	
Reserves	$ 10,000	Checkable deposits	$ 50,000
Loans	50,000		
Property	240,000	Stock shares	250,000

After the check has been collected, the Wahoo bank just meets the required reserve ratio of 20 percent (= $10,000/$50,000). The bank has *no* excess reserves. This poses a question: Could the Wahoo bank have lent more than $50,000—an amount greater than its excess reserves—and still have met the 20 percent reserve requirement when a check for the full amount of the loan was cleared against it? The answer is no; the bank is "fully loaned up."

Here is why: Suppose the Wahoo bank had lent $55,000 to the Gristly company and that the Gristly company had spent all of that money by writing a $55,000 check to Quickbuck Construction. Collection of the check against the Wahoo bank would have lowered its reserves to $5,000 (= $60,000 − $55,000), and checkable deposits would once again stand at $50,000 (= $105,000 − $55,000). The ratio of actual reserves to checkable deposits would then be $5,000/$50,000, or only 10 percent. Because the reserve requirement is 20 percent, the Wahoo bank could not have lent $55,000.

By experimenting with other amounts over $50,000, you will find that the maximum amount the Wahoo bank could lend at the outset of Balance Sheet 6 is $50,000. This amount is identical to the amount of excess reserves the bank had available when the loan was negotiated.

A single commercial bank in a multibank banking system can lend only an amount equal to its initial preloan excess reserves. When it lends, the lending bank faces the possibility that checks for the entire amount of the loan will be drawn and cleared against it. If that happens, it will lose (to other banks) reserves equal to the amount it lends. So, to be safe, it limits its lending to the amount of its excess reserves.

Bank creation of money raises an interesting question: If a bank creates checkable-deposit money when it lends its excess reserves, is money destroyed when borrowers pay off loans? The answer is yes. When loans are paid off, the process works in reverse. The bank's checkable deposits decline by the amount of the loan repayment.

Transaction 7: Buying Government Securities

When a commercial bank buys government bonds from the public, the effect is substantially the same as lending. New money is created.

Assume that the Wahoo bank's balance sheet initially stands as it did at the end of transaction 5. Now suppose that instead of making a $50,000 loan, the bank buys $50,000 of government securities from a securities dealer. The bank receives the interest-bearing bonds, which appear on its balance statement as the asset "Securities," and gives the dealer an increase in its checkable-deposit account. The Wahoo bank's balance sheet appears as follows:

Buying Government Securities
Balance Sheet 7: Wahoo Bank

Assets		Liabilities and net worth	
Reserves	$ 60,000	Checkable deposits	$100,000
Securities	50,000		
Property	240,000	Stock shares	250,000

Checkable deposits, that is, the supply of money, have been increased by $50,000, as in Balance Sheet 6. Bond purchases from the public by commercial banks increase the supply of money in the same way as lending to the public does. The bank accepts government bonds (which are not money) and gives the securities dealer an increase in its checkable deposits (which *are* money).

Of course, when the securities dealer draws and clears a check for $50,000 against the Wahoo bank, the bank loses both reserves and deposits in that amount and then just meets the legal reserve requirement. Its balance sheet now reads precisely as in Balance Sheet 6b except that "Securities" is substituted for "Loans" on the asset side.

Finally, the *selling* of government bonds to the public by a commercial bank—like the repayment of a loan—reduces the supply of money. The securities buyer pays by check, and both "Securities" and "Checkable deposits" (the latter being money) decline by the amount of the sale.

Profits, Liquidity, and the Federal Funds Market

The asset items on a commercial bank's balance sheet reflect the banker's pursuit of two conflicting goals:

- ***Profit*** One goal is profit. Commercial banks, like any other businesses, seek profits, which is why the bank makes loans and buys securities—the two major earning assets of commercial banks.
- ***Liquidity*** The other goal is safety. For a bank, safety lies in liquidity, specifically such liquid assets as cash and excess reserves. A bank must be on guard for depositors who want to transform their checkable deposits into cash. Similarly, it must guard against more checks clearing against it than are cleared in its favor, causing a net outflow of reserves. Bankers thus seek a balance between prudence and profit. The compromise is between assets that earn higher returns and highly liquid assets that earn no returns.

Before the financial crisis of 2007–2008, there was an interesting way in which banks could partly reconcile the goals of profit and liquidity: they could lend any temporary excess reserves that they had on deposit at the Fed to other commercial banks.

Before the crisis, normal day-to-day flows of funds to and between banks rarely left all banks with their exact levels of required reserves. Some banks had reserves in excess while others found themselves running short. There was thus an incentive for the banks that had excess reserves to lend them overnight to the banks that were deficient. These loans allowed the banks that were deficient to meet their reserve requirements while also allowing the banks making the loans to earn a little interest.

The market in which these loans were made is referred to as the federal funds market because it was the market for borrowing immediately available reserve balances at the Federal Reserve. The interest rate paid on these overnight loans is called the **federal funds rate.**

Lending excess reserves at the federal funds rate was also attractive to banks before the Financial Crisis because the Fed did not begin paying interest on excess reserves until 2008. So whatever interest could be earned by lending excess reserves at the federal funds rate exceeded the zero percent interest that banks would get from the Fed on reserves held on deposit overnight at a Federal Reserve Bank.

As the result of policy actions taken by the Federal Reserve during the Financial Crisis, nearly every bank in the United States ended up with a massive amount of excess reserves. This happened because the Fed wanted to increase liquidity in the financial system during the crisis. To do so, it purchased trillions of dollars' worth of financial assets from banks.

The banks then placed the large majority of the proceeds from selling securities to the Fed into their respective reserve accounts at the Fed. They did so to make sure that other banks, other financial firms, and their own clients all understood that they (the banks) were liquid and thus capable of honoring debt payments and withdrawal requests.

The reserves of commercial banks increased from $43 billion in February 2008 to $1,148 billion in March 2010. Total bank reserves held at the Fed exceeded total checkable deposits held by the banks. The severe distress in the financial system had turned the fractional reserve system into a 100-percent-plus reserve system!

The amount of money held as reserves overnight at the Fed remained massive through 2016. As a result, there were almost never any instances after 2010 where a bank needed to borrow reserves in the federal funds market. At the same time, nearly every bank had massive excess reserves. Those two factors implied a situation of low demand and large supply in the federal funds market. As a result, the equilibrium federal funds rate plunged to nearly zero while the volume of lending in the federal funds market shrank drastically due to there being hardly any demand for reserves.

It is possible that the federal funds market may some day revive if the volume of reserves fall. But as of the mid-2010s, the federal funds market appeared likely to remain a shadow of its previous self for many years to come.

It is still interesting, however, to give an example of how a federal funds loan affects banks' balance sheets. We would show an overnight loan of reserves from the Surprise bank to the Wahoo bank as a decrease in reserves at the Surprise bank and an increase in reserves at the Wahoo bank. Ownership of reserves at the Federal Reserve Bank of Kansas City would change, but total reserves would not be affected. Exercise: Determine what other changes would be required on the Wahoo and Surprise banks' balance sheets as a result of an overnight loan.

AP QUICK REVIEW 29.2

- ✓ Banks create money when they make loans; money vanishes when bank loans are repaid.
- ✓ A single bank can only make loans equal to its excess reserves. The loan given in the form of a new checkable deposit increases the money supply.
- ✓ The money supply is increased when banks buy government bonds from the public; money supply decreases when banks sell government bonds to the public.
- ✓ Although the Fed pays interest on excess reserves, banks may be able to obtain higher interest rates by temporarily lending the reserves to other banks in the federal funds market; the interest rate on such loans is the federal funds rate.

AP The Banking System: Multiple-Deposit Expansion

LO29.4 Describe the multiple expansion of loans and money by the entire banking system.

Thus far we have seen that a single bank in a banking system can lend one dollar for each dollar of its excess reserves. The situation is different for all commercial banks as a group. We will find that the commercial banking system can lend—that is, can create money—by a multiple of its excess reserves. This multiple lending is accomplished even though each bank in the system can lend only "dollar for dollar" with its excess reserves.

How do these seemingly paradoxical results come about? To answer this question succinctly, we will make three simplifying assumptions:

- The reserve ratio for all commercial banks is 20 percent.
- Initially all banks are meeting this 20 percent reserve requirement exactly. No excess reserves exist; or, in the parlance of banking, they are "loaned up" (or "loaned out") fully in terms of the reserve requirement.
- If any bank can increase its loans as a result of acquiring excess reserves, an amount equal to those excess reserves will be lent to one borrower, who will write a check for the entire amount of the loan and give it to someone else, who will deposit the check in another bank. This third assumption means that the worst thing possible happens to every lending bank—a check for the entire amount of the loan is drawn and cleared against it in favor of another bank.

The Banking System's Lending Potential

Suppose a junkyard owner finds a $100 bill while dismantling a car that has been on the lot for years. He deposits the $100 in bank A, which adds the $100 to its reserves. We will record only changes in the balance sheets of the various commercial banks. The deposit changes bank A's balance sheet as shown by entries (a_1):

Multiple-Deposit Expansion Process
Balance Sheet: Commercial Bank A

Assets		Liabilities and net worth	
Reserves	$+100 ($a_1$) −80 ($a_3$)	Checkable deposits	$+100 ($a_1$) +80 ($a_2$) −80 ($a_3$)
Loans	+80 (a_2)		

Recall from transaction 3 that this $100 deposit of currency does not alter the money supply. While $100 of checkable-deposit money comes into being, it is offset by the $100 of currency no longer in the hands of the public (the junkyard owner). But bank A *has* acquired excess reserves of $80. Of the newly acquired $100 in currency, 20 percent, or $20, must be earmarked for the required reserves on the new $100 checkable deposit, and the remaining $80 goes to excess reserves. Remembering that a single commercial bank can lend only an amount equal to its excess reserves, we conclude that bank A can lend a maximum of $80. When a loan for this amount is made, bank A's loans increase by $80 and the borrower gets an $80 checkable deposit. We add these figures—entries (a_2)—to bank A's balance sheet.

But now we make our third assumption: The borrower uses the full amount of the loan ($80) to write a check ($80) to someone else, and that person deposits the amount in bank B, a different bank. As we saw in transaction 6, bank A loses both reserves and deposits equal to the amount of the loan, as indicated in entries (a_3). The net result of these transactions is that bank A's reserves now stand at +$20 (= $100 − $80), loans at +$80, and checkable deposits at +$100 (= $100 + $80 − $80). When the dust has settled, bank A is just meeting the 20 percent reserve ratio.

Recalling our previous discussion, we know that bank B acquires both the reserves and the deposits that bank A has lost. Bank B's balance sheet is changed as in entries (b_1):

Multiple-Deposit Expansion Process
Balance Sheet: Commercial Bank B

Assets		Liabilities and net worth	
Reserves	$+80 ($b_1$) −64 ($b_3$)	Checkable deposits	$+80 ($b_1$) +64 ($b_2$) −64 ($b_3$)
Loans	+64 (b_2)		

When the borrower's check is drawn and cleared, bank A loses $80 in reserves and deposits and bank B gains $80 in reserves and deposits. But 20 percent, or $16, of bank B's new reserves must be kept as required reserves against the new $80 in checkable deposits. This means that bank B has $64 (= $80 − $16) in excess reserves. It can therefore lend $64 [entries ($b_2$)]. When the new borrower writes a check for $64 to buy a product, and the seller deposits the check in bank C, the reserves and deposits of bank B both fall by $64 [entries ($b_3$)]. As a result of these transactions, bank B's reserves now stand at +$16 (= $80 − $64), loans at +$64, and checkable deposits at +$80 (= $80 + $64 − $64). After all this, bank B is just meeting the 20 percent reserve requirement.

We are off and running again. Bank C acquires the $64 in reserves and deposits lost by bank B. Its balance sheet changes as in entries (c_1):

Multiple-Deposit Expansion Process Balance Sheet: Commercial Bank C			
Assets		**Liabilities and net worth**	
Reserves	$+64.00 ($c_1$) −52.20 ($c_3$)	Checkable deposits	$+64.00 ($c_1$) +51.20 ($c_2$) −51.20 ($c_3$)
Loans	+51.20 (c_2)		

Exactly 20 percent, or $12.80, of these new reserves will be required reserves, the remaining $51.20 being excess reserves. Hence, bank C can safely lend a maximum of $51.20. Suppose it does [entries (c_2)]. And suppose the borrower writes a check for the entire amount ($51.20) to a merchant who deposits it in another bank [entries (c_3)].

We could go ahead with this procedure by bringing banks D, E, F, G, . . . , N, and so on into the picture. In fact, the process will go on almost indefinitely, just as long as banks further down the line receive at least one penny in new reserves that they can use to back another round of lending and money creation. But we suggest that you work through the computations for banks D, E, and F to be sure you understand the procedure.

The entire analysis is summarized in Table 29.2. Data for banks D through N are supplied on their own rows so that you may check your computations. The last row of the table consolidates into one row everything that happens for all banks down the line after bank N. Our conclusion is startling: On the basis of only $80 in excess reserves (acquired by the banking system when someone deposited $100 of currency in bank A), the entire commercial banking system is able to lend $400, the sum of the amounts in column 4. The banking system can lend excess reserves by a multiple of 5 (= $400/$80) when the reserve ratio is 20 percent. Yet each single bank in the banking system is lending only an amount equal to its own excess reserves. How do we explain this? How can the banking system as a whole lend by a multiple of its excess reserves, when each individual bank can lend only dollar for dollar with its excess reserves?

The answer is that reserves lost by a single bank are not lost to the banking system as a whole. The reserves lost by bank A are acquired by bank B. Those lost by B are gained by C. C loses to D, D to E, E to F, and so forth. Although reserves can be, and are, lost by individual banks in the banking system, there is no loss of reserves for the banking system as a whole.

An individual bank can safely lend only an amount equal to its excess reserves, *but the commercial banking system can lend by a multiple of its collective excess reserves*. This contrast, incidentally, is an illustration of why it is imperative that we keep the fallacy of composition (Last Word, Chapter 1) firmly in mind. Commercial banks as a group can create money by lending in a manner much different from that of the individual banks in the group.

AP **TABLE 29.2 Expansion of the Money Supply by the Commercial Banking System**

Bank	(1) Acquired Reserves and Deposits	(2) Required Reserves (Reserve Ratio = .2)	(3) Excess Reserves, (1) − (2)	(4) Amount Bank Can Lend; New Money Created = (3)
Bank A	$100.00 ($a_1$)	$20.00	**$80.00**	$ 80.00 (a_2)
Bank B	80.00 (a_3, b_1)	16.00	64.00	64.00 (b_2)
Bank C	64.00 (b_3, c_1)	12.80	51.20	51.20 (c_2)
Bank D	51.20	10.24	40.96	40.96
Bank E	40.96	8.19	32.77	32.77
Bank F	32.77	6.55	26.21	26.21
Bank G	26.21	5.24	20.97	20.97
Bank H	20.97	4.20	16.78	16.78
Bank I	16.78	3.36	13.42	13.42
Bank J	13.42	2.68	10.74	10.74
Bank K	10.74	2.15	8.59	8.59
Bank L	8.59	1.72	6.87	6.87
Bank M	6.87	1.37	5.50	5.50
Bank N	5.50	1.10	4.40	4.40
Other banks	21.99	4.40	17.59	17.59
Total amount of money created (sum of the amounts in column 4)				**$400.00**

AP The Monetary Multiplier

LO29.5 Define the monetary multiplier, explain how to calculate it, and demonstrate its relevance.

The **monetary multiplier** (or, less commonly, the *checkable deposit multiplier*) defines the relationship between any new excess reserves in the banking system and the magnified creation of new checkable-deposit money by banks as a group. It is a separate idea from the spending-income multiplier of Chapter 24 but shares some mathematical similarities. The spending-income multiplier exists because the expenditures of one household become some other household's income; the multiplier magnifies a change in initial spending into a larger change in GDP. The spending-income multiplier is the reciprocal of the MPS (the leakage into saving that occurs at each round of spending).

Similarly, the monetary multiplier exists because the reserves and deposits lost by one bank become reserves of another bank. It magnifies excess reserves into a larger creation of checkable-deposit money. The monetary multiplier m is the reciprocal of the required reserve ratio R (the leakage into required reserves that occurs at each step in the lending process). In short,

$$\text{Monetary multiplier} = \frac{1}{\text{required reserve ratio}}$$

or, in symbols,

$$m = \frac{1}{R}$$

In this formula, m represents the maximum amount of new checkable-deposit money that can be created by a single dollar of excess reserves, given the value of R. By multiplying the excess reserves E by m, we can find the maximum amount of new checkable-deposit money, D, that can be created by the banking system. That is,

$$\text{Maximum checkable-deposit creation} = \text{excess reserves} \times \text{monetary multiplier}$$

or, more simply,

$$D = E \times m$$

In our example in Table 29.2, R is 0.20, so m is 5 (= 1/0.20). This implies that

$$D = \$80 \times 5 = \$400$$

Figure 29.1 depicts the final outcome of our example of a multiple-deposit expansion of the money supply. The initial deposit of $100 of currency into the bank (lower right-hand box) creates new reserves of an equal amount (upper box). With a 20 percent reserve ratio, however, only $20 of reserves are needed to "back up" this $100 checkable deposit. The excess reserves of $80 permit the creation of $400 of new checkable deposits via the making of loans, confirming a monetary multiplier of 5. The $100 of new reserves supports a total supply of money of $500, consisting of the $100 initial checkable deposit plus $400 of checkable deposits created through lending.

Higher reserve ratios mean lower monetary multipliers and therefore less creation of new checkable-deposit money via loans; smaller reserve ratios mean higher monetary multipliers and thus more creation of new checkable-deposit money via loans. With a high reserve ratio, say, 50 percent, the monetary multiplier would be 2 (= 1/0.5), and in our example the banking system could create only $100 (= $50 of excess reserves × 2) of new checkable deposits. With a low reserve ratio, say, 5 percent, the monetary multiplier would be 20 (= 1/0.05), and the banking system could create $1,900 (= $95 of excess reserves × 20) of new checkable deposits.

You might experiment with the following two brainteasers to test your understanding of multiple credit expansion by the banking system:

- Rework the analysis in Table 29.2 (at least three or four steps of it) assuming the reserve ratio is 10 percent. What is the maximum amount of money the banking system can create upon acquiring $100 in new reserves and deposits? (The answer is not $800!)
- Suppose the banking system is loaned up and faces a 20 percent reserve ratio. Explain how it might have to reduce its outstanding loans by $400 when a $100 cash withdrawal from a checkable-deposit account forces one bank to draw down its reserves by $100.

AP **FIGURE 29.1 The outcome of the money expansion process.** A deposit of $100 of currency into a checking account creates an initial checkable deposit of $100. If the reserve ratio is 20 percent, only $20 of reserves is legally required to support the $100 checkable deposit. The $80 of excess reserves allows the banking system to create $400 of checkable deposits through making loans. The $100 of reserves supports a total of $500 of money ($100 + $400).

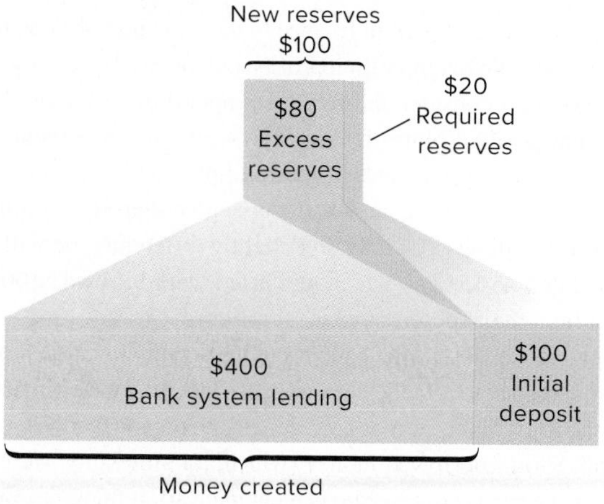

LAST WORD

Banking, Leverage, and Financial Instability

Leverage Boosts Banking Profits but Makes the Banking System Less Stable. Time to Reduce Leverage?

The term *leverage* is used in finance to describe how the use of borrowed money can magnify both profits and losses. To see how leverage works, first consider an investment opportunity that produces a 10 percent positive return if things go well but a 5 percent loss if things go poorly. Those rates of return imply that if a person invests \$100 of his own savings, he will end up with either \$110 if things go well or \$95 if things go badly. Put slightly differently, he will either gain \$10 or lose \$5 from where he started, with his own \$100 being used to fund the \$100 investment.

But now consider what happens to his potential returns if he uses borrowed money to provide "leverage." In fact, let's have him use a lot of leverage. To make the \$100 investment, he uses \$10 of his own savings and \$90 of borrowed money (which, for simplicity, we will assume that he can borrow at zero percent interest). If things go well, the investment will return \$110. He then must repay the \$90 loan. That will leave him with \$20 (= \$110 of investment return if things go well minus \$90 to repay the loan). That means that he will end up with \$20 if things go well and he uses leverage. Notice that this implies that if he uses leverage, he will get a 100 percent (= \$20 divided by \$10) return on the \$10 of his own savings that he himself invested. That, of course, is much nicer than a 10 percent return. In fact, it is 10 times as large—hence the term *leverage*. The use of borrowed money has massively increased the percentage rate of return if things go well.

Unfortunately, however, nothing in life is free. Leverage also magnifies the investor's losses if things go wrong. To see this, note that if things go wrong in this example, the investor will end up turning \$100 into \$95. But then he has to pay back the \$90 that he borrowed. That will leave him with only \$5 (= \$95 investment return if things go badly minus \$90 to repay the loan). That implies that the investor will lose \$5 off of the \$10 of his own savings that he himself originally put into the investment. That is a 50 percent loss—10 times as much as the 5 percent loss that he would have sustained if he had used only his own money to make the \$100 investment. Thus, you can see that leverage increases both profits if things go well and losses if things go badly.

A modern bank uses a lot of leverage. In fact, only about 5 percent of the money that it invests comes from its shareholders and the money they paid to purchase ownership shares in the bank. The other 95 percent comes from borrowing, either by issuing bonds (about 25 percent) or by taking in checking and savings deposits (about 70 percent). It surprises many people, but checking and savings deposits are technically a type of loan made by depositors to their banks. So banks get 70 percent of their leverage and funding from money borrowed from depositors.

The problem with that much leverage is that it takes only very small losses to drive the bank into insolvency and a situation in which it cannot repay all of the money that it has borrowed because

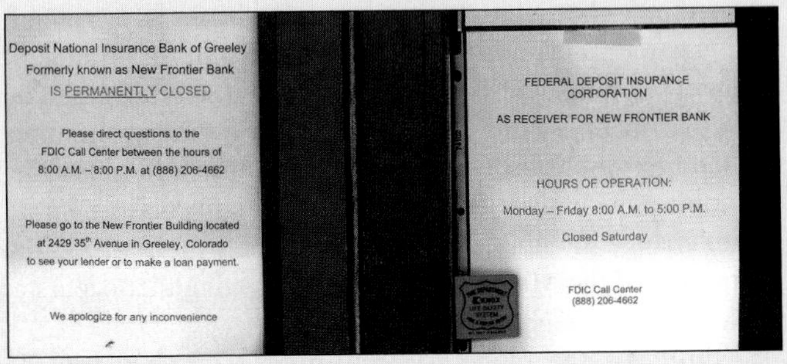

© Bloomberg/Getty Images

the value of the bank's assets has fallen below the value of the bank's liabilities. Consider what would happen if for every \$100 invested by the bank, only \$94 returned. That by itself is a 6 percent rate of loss. But because the bank is borrowing \$95 of every \$100 that it invests, it will be driven into insolvency by that 6 percent loss because it is getting back less than the amount that it borrowed to fund the investment. With the investment returning only \$94, there won't be enough money to pay off the \$95 that the bank borrowed!

So why do banks use this much leverage? Because it is very profitable for the bankers who run the banks. If things are going well, the leverage massively increases the banks' profit rates—and bankers get paid bonuses based on those profit rates. On the other hand, if things go badly, bankers have come to expect bailouts in which the government uses taxpayer money to ensure that all of a bank's liabilities are repaid. So from the perspective of the bankers, it's "heads I win, tails you lose."

One solution to these problems would be to require banks to use much less leverage. For every \$100 that a bank wants to invest, the bank could be required to raise \$30 from its shareholder owners so that it would only be borrowing the other \$70 through issuing bonds or by taking in checking and savings deposits. That would make the entire banking system much more stable because it would be very unlikely that for any \$100 invested into projects by the bank, less than \$70 would come back. Even if only \$71 came back, there would still be enough money to pay back the \$70 of borrowed money—and thus no need for the bank to go bankrupt or require a government bailout via the deposit insurance system.

Unfortunately, however, bankers have lobbied strongly and successfully against any legal attempts to require lower leverage levels. So the current regulatory system relies instead on bank supervisors who attempt to prevent the banks from making bad loans. That system was unable to prevent the 2007–2008 financial crisis and a number of economists argue that until leverage is reduced, no amount of bank supervision will be sufficient to prevent another financial crisis because with massive leverage, even a small loss can destroy a bank.

Reversibility: The Multiple Destruction of Money

The process we have described is reversible. Just as checkable-deposit money is created when banks make loans, checkable-deposit money is destroyed when loans are paid off. Loan repayment, in effect, sets off a process of multiple destruction of money the opposite of the multiple creation process. Because loans are both made and paid off in any period, the direction of the loans, checkable deposits, and money supply in a given period will depend on the net effect of the two processes. If the dollar amount of loans made in some period exceeds the dollar amount of loans paid off, checkable deposits will expand and the money supply will increase. But if the dollar amount of loans is less than the dollar amount of loans paid off, checkable deposits will contract and the money supply will decline.

Historically, one of the Fed's main ways of influencing the economy was by changing the supply of bank money. But the Fed has other ways, as well, which we will explore in the next chapter.

AP QUICK REVIEW 29.3

- ✓ A single bank in a multibank system can safely lend (create money) by an amount equal to its excess reserves; the banking system can lend (create money) by a multiple of its excess reserves. As a loan generates new economic activity and a redepositing of funds into a bank, additional loans can be made. This process creates new demand deposits and leads to the multiple creation of money (monetary multiplier).
- ✓ The monetary multiplier is the reciprocal of the required reserve ratio; it is the multiple by which the banking system can expand the money supply for each dollar of excess reserves.
- ✓ The monetary multiplier works in both directions; it applies to money destruction from the payback of loans as well as the money creation from the making of loans.

SUMMARY

LO29.1 Discuss why the U.S. banking system is called a "fractional reserve" system.

Modern banking systems are fractional reserve systems: Only a fraction of checkable deposits is backed by currency.

LO29.2 Explain the basics of a bank's balance sheet and the distinction between a bank's actual reserves and its required reserves.

The operation of a commercial bank can be understood through its balance sheet, where assets equal liabilities plus net worth.

Commercial banks keep required reserves on deposit in a Federal Reserve Bank or as vault cash. These required reserves are equal to a specified percentage of the commercial bank's checkable-deposit liabilities. Excess reserves are equal to actual reserves minus required reserves.

Banks lose both reserves and checkable deposits when checks are drawn against them.

LO29.3 Describe how a bank can create money.

Commercial banks create money—checkable deposits, or checkable-deposit money—when they make loans. They convert IOUs, which are *not* money, into checkable-deposits, which *are* money. Money is destroyed when lenders repay bank loans.

The ability of a single commercial bank to create money by lending depends on the size of its excess reserves. Generally speaking, a commercial bank can lend only an amount equal to its excess reserves. Money creation is thus limited because, in all likelihood, checks drawn by borrowers will be deposited in other banks, causing a loss of reserves and deposits to the lending bank equal to the amount of money that it has lent.

Rather than making loans, banks may decide to use excess reserves to buy bonds from the public. In doing so, banks merely credit the checkable-deposit accounts of the bond sellers, thus creating checkable-deposit money. Money vanishes when banks sell bonds to the public because bond buyers must draw down their checkable-deposit balances to pay for the bonds.

Banks earn interest by making loans and by purchasing bonds; they maintain liquidity by holding cash and excess reserves. The Fed currently pays interest on excess reserves. But prior to the financial crisis of 2007–2008, banks could obtain a higher interest rate by lending excess reserves on an overnight basis to banks that were short of required reserves. Those loans were made in the federal funds market, and the interest rate on those loans was called the federal funds rate. But policy actions during the crisis left virtually every bank in the United States with large amounts of excess reserves and thus no need to borrow any from another bank. The federal funds market has consequently shriveled in size and the federal funds rate has plunged to nearly zero due to low demand for excess reserves interacting with a massive supply of excess reserves.

LO29.4 Describe the multiple expansion of loans and money by the entire banking system.

The commercial banking system as a whole can lend by a multiple of its excess reserves because the system as a whole cannot lose reserves. Individual banks, however, can lose reserves to other banks in the system.

LO29.5 Define the monetary multiplier, explain how to calculate it, and demonstrate its relevance.

The multiple by which the banking system can lend on the basis of each dollar of excess reserves is the reciprocal of the reserve ratio. This multiple credit expansion process is reversible.

TERMS AND CONCEPTS

fractional reserve banking system
balance sheet
vault cash
required reserves
reserve ratio
excess reserves
actual reserves
federal funds rate
monetary multiplier

The following and additional problems can be found in connect

DISCUSSION QUESTIONS

1. Explain why merchants accepted gold receipts as a means of payment even though the receipts were issued by goldsmiths, not the government. What risk did goldsmiths introduce into the payments system by issuing loans in the form of gold receipts? LO29.1
2. Why is the banking system in the United States referred to as a fractional reserve bank system? What is the role of deposit insurance in a fractional reserve system? LO29.1
3. What is the difference between an asset and a liability on a bank's balance sheet? How does net worth relate to each? Why must a balance sheet always balance? What are the major assets and claims on a commercial bank's balance sheet? LO29.2
4. Why does the Federal Reserve require commercial banks to have reserves? Explain why reserves are an asset to commercial banks but a liability to the Federal Reserve Banks. What are excess reserves? How do you calculate the amount of excess reserves held by a bank? What is the significance of excess reserves ? LO29.2
5. "Whenever currency is deposited in a commercial bank, cash goes out of circulation and, as a result, the supply of money is reduced." Do you agree? Explain why or why not. LO29.2
6. "When a commercial bank makes loans, it creates money; when loans are repaid, money is destroyed." Explain. LO29.3
7. Suppose that Mountain Star Bank discovers that its reserves will temporarily fall slightly below those legally required. How might it temporarily remedy this situation through the federal funds market? Now assume Mountain Star finds that its reserves will be substantially and permanently deficient. What remedy is available to this bank? (Hint: Recall your answer to discussion question 6.) LO29.3
8. Explain why a single commercial bank can safely lend only an amount equal to its excess reserves, but the commercial banking system as a whole can lend by a multiple of its excess reserves. What is the monetary multiplier, and how does it relate to the reserve ratio? LO29.4, LO29.5
9. How would a decrease in the reserve requirement affect the (*a*) size of the monetary multiplier, (*b*) amount of excess reserves in the banking system, and (*c*) extent to which the system could expand the money supply through the creation of checkable deposits via loans? LO29.5
10. **LAST WORD** Does leverage increase the total size of the gain or loss from an investment, or just the percentage rate of return on the part of the investment amount that was not borrowed? How would lowering leverage make the financial system more stable?

AP REVIEW QUESTIONS

1. A bank that has liabilities of $150 billion and a net worth (or shareholders equity) of $20 billion must have: LO29.2
   a. Excess reserves of $130 billion.
   b. Assets of $150 billion.
   c. Excess reserves of $150 billion.
   d. Assets of $170 billion.
   e. Excess reserves of $170 billion.
2. Banks create money when they: LO29.3
   a. Add to their reserves in the Federal Reserve Bank.
   b. Withdraw reserves from the Federal Bank.
   c. Accept deposits of cash.
   d. Sell government bonds.
   e. Make loans to businesses and individuals in exchange for new checkable deposits.
3. The primary purpose of the legal reserve requirement is to: LO29.2
   a. Prevent banks from hoarding too much vault cash.
   b. Provide a means by which the monetary authorities can influence the lending ability of commercial banks.
   c. Prevent commercial banks from earning excess profits.
   d. Provide a dependable source of interest income for commercial banks.
   e. Prevent "runs and panics."
4. A single commercial bank in a multibank banking system can lend only an amount equal to its initial pre-loan ____________. LO29.3
   a. Total reserves.
   b. Excess reserves.
   c. Total deposits.
   d. Excess deposits.
   e. Total assets.
5. Assume a commercial bank uses excess reserves to buy government securities from the public. Which of the following happens immediately, as a result of that transaction? LO29.3
   a. The money supply increases.
   b. The money supply decreases.
   c. Commercial bank reserves increase.
   d. Checkable deposits decline.
   e. Excess reserves increase.
6. The Federal funds market is the market in which: LO29.3
   a. Banks borrow from the Federal Reserve Banks.
   b. U.S. securities are bought and sold.
   c. Banks borrow reserves from one another on an overnight basis.
   d. Federal Reserve Banks borrow from one another.
   e. The public can borrow at a discounted rate from the Federal Reserve Banks.
7. Suppose that the Fed has set the reserve ratio at .1 and that banks collectively have $2 billion in excess reserves. What is

the maximum amount of new checkable-deposit money that can be created by the banking system? LO29.5

a. $0. **d.** $20 billion.
b. $2 million. **e.** $200 million.
c. $2 billion.

8. Assume the required reserve ratio is 20%, and Mary brings in $100 cash and deposits it in her checking account at Bank Z which had no excess reserves. Answer the following questions. LO29.3–29.5

a. Initially by what amount does the money supply change? Explain.
b. Does bank Z now have excess reserves? If so, how much?
c. By what amount can bank Z increase its loans?
d. For the entire banking system what is the maximum change in each of the following?
1. Cash reserves by the banks 3. Demand Deposits
2. Loans 4. Money supply
e. What could prevent the banking system from having the maximum change in loans and demand deposits?

9. Charles withdraws $500 from his checking account. If the required reserve ratio is 10 percent. What is the maximum change (in absolute value) to demand deposits and the money supply for the entire banking system? LO29.3–29.5

	Demand Deposits	Money Supply
a.	−$500	−500
b.	−500	0
c.	−5000	−4500
d.	−5000	−5000
e.	+5000	+4500

10. Jane brings into her bank $300 of cash to be deposited in her checking account. After all adjustment have been made the money supply increases by $2250. Assuming that the required reserve ratio is 10 percent, which of the following is true? LO29.3–29.5

a. The money supply increase of $2250 is the maximum increase that could be expected.
b. The maximum increase that could be expected is $3000; this increase is $750 below the maximum.
c. This increase is above the maximum legal increase, so banks must have made new loans which value exceeded that which is legally permitted.
d. The maximum increase in the money supply that could occur is $2700. Thus, in this case, banks may have kept some excess reserves.
e. Jane must have taken back $150 of her initial deposit, reducing the reserves in the banking system by $150.

PROBLEMS

1. Suppose the assets of the Silver Lode Bank are $100,000 higher than on the previous day and its net worth is up $20,000. By how much and in what direction must its liabilities have changed from the day before? LO29.2

2. Suppose that Serendipity Bank has excess reserves of $8,000 and checkable deposits of $150,000. If the reserve ratio is 20 percent, what is the size of the bank's actual reserves? LO29.2

3. Third National Bank has reserves of $20,000 and checkable deposits of $100,000. The reserve ratio is 20 percent. Households deposit $5,000 in currency into the bank and that currency is added to reserves. What level of excess reserves does the bank now have? LO29.3

4. Suppose again that Third National Bank has reserves of $20,000 and checkable deposits of $100,000. The reserve ratio is 20 percent. The bank now sells $5,000 in securities to the Federal Reserve Bank in its district, receiving a $5,000 increase in reserves in return. What level of excess reserves does the bank now have? By what amount does your answer differ (yes, it does!) from the answer to problem 3? LO29.3

5. The following balance sheet is for Big Bucks Bank. The reserve ratio is 20 percent. LO29.3

Assets		(1)	(2)	Liabilities and net worth		(1′)	(2′)
Reserves	$22,000	____	____	Checkable deposits	$100,000	____	____
Securities	38,000	____	____				
Loans	40,000	____	____				

a. What is the maximum amount of new loans that Big Bucks Bank can make? Show in columns 1 and 1′ how the bank's balance sheet will appear after the bank has lent this additional amount.
b. By how much has the supply of money changed?
c. How will the bank's balance sheet appear after checks drawn for the entire amount of the new loans have been cleared against the bank? Show the new balance sheet in columns 2 and 2′.
d. Answer questions *a*, *b*, and *c* on the assumption that the reserve ratio is 15 percent.

6. Suppose the following simplified consolidated balance sheet is for the entire commercial banking system and that all figures are in billions of dollars. The reserve ratio is 25 percent. LO29.5

Assets		(1)	Liabilities and net worth		(1′)
Reserves	$ 52	____	Checkable deposits	$200	____
Securities	48	____			
Loans	100	____			

a. What is the amount of excess reserves in this commercial banking system? What is the maximum amount the banking system might lend? Show in columns 1 and 1′ how the consolidated balance sheet would look after this amount has been lent. What is the size of the monetary multiplier?
b. Answer the questions in part *a* assuming the reserve ratio is 20 percent. What is the resulting difference in the amount that the commercial banking system can lend?

7. If the required reserve ratio is 10 percent, what is the monetary multiplier? If the monetary multiplier is 4, what is the required reserve ratio? LO29.5

30 Chapter

Interest Rates and Monetary Policy

Learning Objectives

LO30.1 Discuss how the equilibrium interest rate is determined in the market for money.

LO30.2 Describe the balance sheet of the Federal Reserve and the meaning of its major items.

LO30.3 List and explain the goals and tools of monetary policy.

LO30.4 Describe the federal funds rate and how the Fed directly influences it.

LO30.5 Identify the mechanisms by which monetary policy affects GDP and the price level.

LO30.6 Explain the effectiveness of monetary policy and its shortcomings.

AP Chapter Focus

Some newspaper commentators have stated that the chairperson of the Federal Reserve Board (currently Janet Yellen) is the second most powerful person in the United States, after the U.S. president. That is undoubtedly an exaggeration because the chair has only a single vote on the 7-person Federal Reserve Board and 12-person Federal Open Market Committee. But there can be no doubt about the chair's influence as well as the overall importance of the Federal Reserve and the **monetary policy** that it conducts. Such policy consists of deliberate changes in the money supply to influence interest rates and thus the total level of spending in the economy. The goal of monetary policy is to achieve and maintain price-level stability, full employment, and economic growth. This chapter now connects the ideas of the previous two and explains the tool of monetary policy as a stabilizing influence in our economy.

AP Interest Rates

LO30.1 Discuss how the equilibrium interest rate is determined in the market for money.

The Fed's primary influence on the economy in normal economic times is through its ability to change the money supply (M_1 and M_2) and therefore affect interest rates. Interest rates can be thought of in several ways. Most basically, **interest** is the price paid for the use of money. It is also the price that borrowers need to pay lenders for transferring purchasing power to the future. And it can be thought of as the amount of money that must be paid for the use of $1 for 1 year. Although there are many different interest rates that vary by purpose, size, risk, maturity, and taxability, we will simply speak of *the* interest rate unless stated otherwise.

Let's see how the interest rate is determined. Because it is a "price," we again turn to demand and supply analysis for the answer.

The Demand for Money

Why does the public want to hold some of its wealth as *money?* There are two main reasons: to make purchases with it and to hold it as an asset.

Transactions Demand, D_t People hold money because it is convenient for purchasing goods and services. Households usually are paid once a week, every 2 weeks, or monthly, whereas their expenditures are less predictable and typically more frequent. So households must have enough money on hand to buy groceries and pay mortgage and utility bills. Nor are business revenues and expenditures simultaneous. Businesses need to have money available to pay for labor, materials, power, and other inputs. The demand for money as a medium of exchange is called the **transactions demand for money.**

The level of nominal GDP is the main determinant of the amount of money demanded for transactions. The larger the total money value of all goods and services exchanged in the economy, the larger the amount of money needed to negotiate those transactions. The transactions demand for money varies directly with nominal GDP. We specify *nominal* GDP because households and firms will want more money for transactions if prices rise or if real output increases. In both instances a larger dollar volume will be needed to accomplish the desired transactions.

In **Figure 30.1a (Key Graph),** we graph the quantity of money demanded for transactions against the interest rate. For simplicity, let's assume that the amount demanded depends exclusively on the level of nominal GDP and is independent of the interest rate. (In reality, higher interest rates are associated with slightly lower volumes of money demanded for transactions.) Our simplifying assumption allows us to graph the transactions demand, D_t, as a vertical line. This demand curve is positioned at $100 billion, on the assumption that each dollar held for transactions purposes is spent an average of three times per year and that nominal GDP is $300 billion. Thus the public needs $100 billion (= $300 billion/3) to purchase that GDP.

Asset Demand, D_a The second reason for holding money derives from money's function as a store of value. People may hold their financial assets in many forms, including corporate stocks, corporate or government bonds, or money. To the extent they want to hold money as an asset, there is an **asset demand for money.**

People like to hold some of their financial assets as money (apart from using it to buy goods and services) because money is the most liquid of all financial assets; it is immediately usable for purchasing other assets when opportunities arise. Money is also an attractive asset to hold when the prices of other assets such as bonds are expected to decline. For example, when the price of a bond falls, the bondholder who sells the bond prior to the payback date of the full principal will suffer a loss (called a *capital loss*). That loss will partially or fully offset the interest received on the bond. Holding money presents no such risk of capital loss from changes in interest rates.

The disadvantage of holding money as an asset is that it earns no or very little interest. Checkable deposits pay either no interest or lower interest rates than bonds. Currency itself earns no interest at all.

Knowing these advantages and disadvantages, the public must decide how much of its financial assets to hold as money, rather than other assets such as bonds. The answer depends primarily on the rate of interest. A household or a business incurs an opportunity cost when it holds money; in both cases, interest income is forgone or sacrificed. If a bond pays 6 percent interest, for example, holding $100 as cash or in a noninterest checkable account costs $6 per year of forgone income.

The amount of money demanded as an asset therefore varies inversely with the rate of interest (which is the opportunity cost of holding money as an asset). When the interest rate rises, being liquid and avoiding capital losses becomes more costly. The public reacts by reducing its holdings of money as an asset. When the interest rate falls, the cost of being liquid and avoiding capital losses also declines. The public therefore increases the amount of financial assets that it wants to hold as money. This inverse relationship just described is shown by D_a in Figure 30.1b.

Total Money Demand, D_m As shown in Figure 30.1, we find the **total demand for money,** D_m, by horizontally adding the asset demand to the transactions demand. The resulting downsloping line in Figure 30.1c represents the total amount of money the public wants to hold, both for transactions and as an asset, at each possible interest rate.

Recall that the transactions demand for money depends on the nominal GDP. A change in the nominal GDP—working through the transactions demand for money—will shift the total money demand curve. Specifically, an increase in nominal GDP means that the public wants to hold a larger amount of money for transactions, and that extra demand will shift the total money demand curve to the right. In contrast, a decline in the nominal GDP will shift the total money demand curve to the left. As an example, suppose nominal GDP increases from $300 billion to $450 billion and the average dollar held for transactions is still spent three times per year. Then the transactions demand curve will shift from $100 billion (= $300 billion/3) to $150 billion (= $450 billion/3). The total money demand curve will then lie $50 billion farther to the right at each possible interest rate.

The Equilibrium Interest Rate

We can combine the demand for money with the supply of money to determine the equilibrium rate of interest. In Figure 30.1c, the vertical line, S_m, represents the money

AP KEY GRAPH

FIGURE 30.1 **The demand for money, the supply of money, and the equilibrium interest rate.** The total demand for money D_m is determined by horizontally adding the asset demand for money D_a to the transactions demand D_t. The transactions demand is vertical because it is assumed to depend on nominal GDP rather than on the interest rate. The asset demand varies inversely with the interest rate because of the opportunity cost involved in holding currency and checkable deposits that pay no interest or very low interest. Combining the money supply (stock) S_m with the total money demand D_m portrays the market for money and determines the equilibrium interest rate i_e.

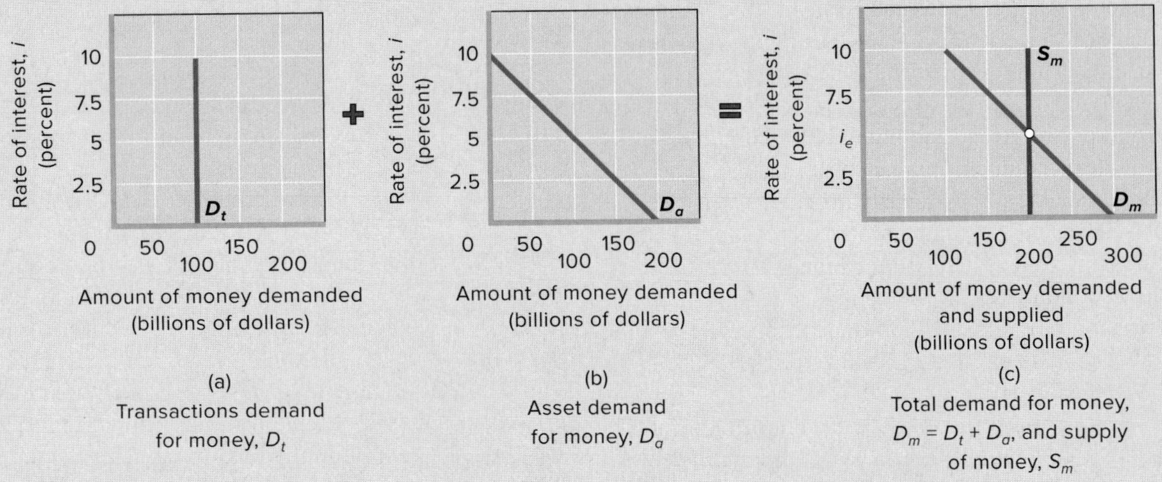

QUICK QUIZ FOR FIGURE 30.1

1. In this graph, at the interest rate i_e (5 percent):
   a. the amount of money demanded as an asset is $50 billion.
   b. the amount of money demanded for transactions is $200 billion.
   c. bond prices will decline.
   d. $100 billion is demanded for transactions, $100 billion is demanded as an asset, and the money supply is $200 billion.
2. In this graph, at an interest rate of 10 percent:
   a. no money will be demanded as an asset.
   b. total money demanded will be $200 billion.
   c. the Federal Reserve will supply $100 billion of money.
   d. there will be a $100 billion shortage of money.
3. Curve D_a slopes downward because:
   a. lower interest rates increase the opportunity cost of holding money.
   b. lower interest rates reduce the opportunity cost of holding money.
   c. the asset demand for money varies directly (positively) with the interest rate.
   d. the transactions-demand-for-money curve is perfectly vertical.
4. Suppose the supply of money declines to $100 billion. The equilibrium interest rate would:
   a. fall, the amount of money demanded for transactions would rise, and the amount of money demanded as an asset would decline.
   b. rise, and the amounts of money demanded both for transactions and as an asset would fall.
   c. fall, and the amounts of money demanded both for transactions and as an asset would increase.
   d. rise, the amount of money demanded for transactions would be unchanged, and the amount of money demanded as an asset would decline.

Answers: 1. d; 2. a; 3. b; 4. d

supply. It is a vertical line because the monetary authorities and financial institutions have provided the economy with some particular stock of money. Here it is $200 billion.

Just as in a product market or a resource market, the intersection of demand and supply determines the equilibrium price in the market for money. In Figure 30.1, this equilibrium price is the equilibrium interest rate, i_e. At this interest rate, the quantity of money demanded (= $200 billion) equals the quantity of money supplied (= $200 billion). The equilibrium interest rate can be thought of as the market-determined price that borrowers must pay for using someone else's money over some period of time.

Changes in the demand for money, the supply of money, or both can change the equilibrium interest rate. For reasons that will soon become apparent, we are most interested in changes in the supply of money. The important generalization is this: An increase in the supply of money will lower the equilibrium interest rate; a decrease in the supply of money will raise the equilibrium interest rate.

Interest Rates and Bond Prices

Interest rates and bond prices are inversely related. When the interest rate increases, bond prices fall; when the interest rate falls, bond prices rise. Why so? First understand that bonds are bought and sold in financial markets and that the price of bonds is determined by bond demand and bond supply.

Suppose that a bond with no expiration date pays a fixed \$50 annual interest payment and is selling for its face value of \$1,000. The interest yield on this bond is 5 percent:

$$\frac{\$50}{\$1{,}000} = 5\% \text{ interest yield}$$

Now suppose the interest rate in the economy rises to $7\frac{1}{2}$ percent from 5 percent. Newly issued bonds will pay \$75 per \$1,000 lent. Older bonds paying only \$50 will not be salable at their \$1,000 face value. To compete with the $7\frac{1}{2}$ percent bond, the price of this bond will need to fall to \$667 to remain competitive. The \$50 fixed annual interest payment will then yield $7\frac{1}{2}$ percent to whoever buys the bond:

$$\frac{\$50}{\$667} = 7\tfrac{1}{2}\%$$

Next suppose that the interest rate falls to $2\frac{1}{2}$ percent from the original 5 percent. Newly issued bonds will pay \$25 on \$1,000 loaned. A bond paying \$50 will be highly attractive. Bond buyers will bid up its price to \$2,000, where the yield will equal $2\frac{1}{2}$ percent:

$$\frac{\$50}{\$2{,}000} = 2\tfrac{1}{2}\%$$

The point is that bond prices fall when the interest rate rises and rise when the interest rate falls. There is an inverse relationship between the interest rate and bond prices.

AP QUICK REVIEW 30.1

- ✓ People demand money for transaction and asset purposes. Interest is the price paid for the use of money.
- ✓ The total demand for money is the sum of the transactions and asset demands; it is graphed as an inverse relationship (downsloping line) between the interest rate and the quantity of money demanded.
- ✓ The equilibrium interest rate is determined by money demand and supply; it occurs when people are willing to hold the exact amount of money being supplied by the monetary authorities.
- ✓ Interest rates and bond prices are inversely related.

GLOBAL PERSPECTIVE 30.1

Central Banks, Selected Nations

The monetary policies of the world's major central banks are often in the international news. Here are some of their official names, along with a few of their popular nicknames.

- Australia: Reserve Bank of Australia (RBA)
- Canada: Bank of Canada
- Euro Zone: European Central Bank (ECB)
- Japan: The Bank of Japan (BOJ)
- Mexico: Banco de Mexico (Mex Bank)
- Russia: Central Bank of Russia
- Sweden: Sveriges Riksbank
- United Kingdom: Bank of England
- United States: Federal Reserve System (the Fed)

The Consolidated Balance Sheet of the Federal Reserve Banks

LO30.2 Describe the balance sheet of the Federal Reserve and the meaning of its major items.

With this basic understanding of interest rates, we can turn to monetary policy, which relies on changes in interest rates to be effective. The 12 Federal Reserve Banks together constitute the U.S. "central bank," nicknamed the "Fed." (Global Perspective 30.1 also lists some of the other central banks in the world, along with their nicknames.)

The Fed's balance sheet helps us consider how the Fed conducts monetary policy. Table 30.1 consolidates the pertinent assets and liabilities of the 12 Federal Reserve Banks as of April 6, 2016. You will see that some of the Fed's assets and liabilities differ from those found on the balance sheet of a commercial bank.

Assets

The two main assets of the Federal Reserve Banks are securities and loans to commercial banks. (Again, we will simplify by referring only to *commercial banks*, even though the analysis also applies to *thrifts*—savings and loans, mutual savings banks, and credit unions.)

Securities The securities shown in Table 30.1 are bonds that have been purchased by the Federal Reserve Banks. The majority (\$2,341 billion) consists of Treasury bills (short-term securities), Treasury notes (mid-term securities), and Treasury bonds (long-term securities) issued by the U.S. government to finance past budget deficits. These securities are part of the public debt—the money borrowed by the federal government. The Federal Reserve Banks bought these securities from commercial banks and the public through open-market operations. Although they are an important source of interest income to the Federal Reserve Banks, they are mainly bought and sold to influence the size of commercial bank reserves and, therefore, the ability of those banks to create

AP TABLE 30.1 Consolidated Balance Sheet of the 12 Federal Reserve Banks, April 6, 2016 (in Millions)

Assets		Liabilities and net worth	
Securities	$4,243,689	Reserves of commercial banks	$2,467,091
Loans to commercial banks	37	Treasury deposits	263,537
All other assets	240,343	Federal Reserve Notes (outstanding)	1,400,041
		All other liabilities and net worth	353,400
Total	$4,484,069	Total	$4,484,069

Source: Federal Reserve Statistical Release, H.4.1, April 6, 2016, **www.federalreserve.gov.**

money by lending. The Fed's securities holdings also include a large amount ($1,753 billion) of mortgage-backed securities purchased during and after the mortgaged debt crisis to bail out mortgage lenders.

Loans to Commercial Banks For reasons that will soon become clear, commercial banks occasionally borrow from Federal Reserve Banks. The IOUs that commercial banks give these "bankers' banks" in return for loans are listed on the Federal Reserve balance sheet as "Loans to commercial banks." They are assets to the Fed because they are claims against the commercial banks. To commercial banks, of course, these loans are liabilities in that they must be repaid. Through borrowing in this way, commercial banks can increase their reserves.

Liabilities

On the "liabilities and net worth" side of the Fed's consolidated balance sheet, three entries are noteworthy: reserves, Treasury deposits, and Federal Reserve Notes.

Reserves of Commercial Banks The Fed requires that the commercial banks hold reserves against their checkable deposits. The Fed pays interest on these required reserves and also on the excess reserves that banks choose to hold at the Fed. Banks held a huge amount of these excess reserves at the Fed during the severe recession of 2007–2009 and on through 2016 as the economy recovered only sluggishly after the Great Recession. Banks simply were highly concerned that loans to some private borrowers might not get paid back. When held in the Federal Reserve Banks, these reserves are listed as a liability on the Fed's balance sheet. They are assets on the books of the commercial banks, which still own them even though they are deposited at the Federal Reserve Banks.

Treasury Deposits The U.S. Treasury keeps deposits in the Federal Reserve Banks and draws checks on them to pay its obligations. To the Treasury these deposits are assets; to the Federal Reserve Banks they are liabilities. The Treasury creates and replenishes these deposits by depositing tax receipts and money borrowed from the public or from the commercial banks through the sale of bonds.

Federal Reserve Notes Outstanding As we have seen, the supply of paper money in the United States consists of Federal Reserve Notes issued by the Federal Reserve Banks. When this money is circulating outside the Federal Reserve Banks, it constitutes claims against the assets of the Federal Reserve Banks. The Fed thus treats these notes as a liability.

AP QUICK REVIEW 30.2

- ✓ The two main assets of the Federal Reserve Banks are securities (U.S. government bonds previously issued) and loans to commercial banks and thrifts. Most of the securities are bills, notes, and bonds issued by the U.S. Treasury to finance past federal budget deficits.
- ✓ The three major liabilities of the Federal Reserve Banks are reserves of commercial banks, Treasury deposits, and outstanding Federal Reserve notes (or cash).

AP Tools of Monetary Policy

LO30.3 List and explain the goals and tools of monetary policy.

With this look at the Federal Reserve Banks' consolidated balance sheet, we can now explore how the Fed can influence the money-creating abilities of the commercial banking system. The Fed has four main tools of monetary control it can use to alter the reserves of commercial banks:

- Open-market operations
- The reserve ratio
- The discount rate
- Interest on reserves

Open-Market Operations

Bond markets are "open" to all buyers and sellers of corporate and government bonds (securities). The Federal Reserve is the largest single holder of U.S. government securities. The U.S. government, not the Fed, issued these Treasury bills, Treasury notes, and Treasury bonds to finance past budget deficits. Over the decades, the Fed has purchased these securities from major financial institutions that buy and sell government and corporate securities for themselves or their customers.

The Fed's **open-market operations** consist of bond market transactions in which the Fed either buys or sells government bonds (U.S. securities) outright, or uses them as collateral on loans of money. Assets—in this case, government bonds—serve as **collateral** when they are pledged by a borrower to a lender with the understanding that the lender will get to keep the assets if the borrower fails to repay the loan. Until the mortgage debt crisis of 2008, the Fed only bought or sold government bonds outright when conducting open-market operations. But in recent years it has added loans of money collateralized with government bonds to its open-market operations policy arsenal.

The conduit for the Fed's open-market operations is the trading desk of the New York Federal Reserve bank. When the Fed buys or sells government bonds, the trading desk at the New York Fed interacts exclusively with a group of 23 or so large financial firms called "primary dealers." When the Fed borrow or lends money via collateralized transactions known as *repos* and *reverse repos*, the trading desk at the New York Fed interacts with a much larger group of financial institutions that consists of 20 commercial banks (such as Bank of America and Goldman Sachs) plus 41 nonbank financial institutions: 28 investment management companies (such as Fidelity and Vanguard) plus 13 government-sponsored financial entities (such as the Federal Home Loan Bank of Boston and the Federal National Mortgage Association, or Fannie Mae).

Buying Securities Suppose that the Fed decides to have the Federal Reserve Banks buy government bonds. They can purchase these bonds either from commercial banks or from the public. In both cases the reserves of the commercial banks will increase.

From Commercial Banks When Federal Reserve Banks buy government bonds *from commercial banks*,

(*a*) The commercial banks give up part of their holdings of securities (the government bonds) to the Federal Reserve Banks.

(*b*) The Federal Reserve Banks, in paying for these securities, place newly created reserves in the accounts of the commercial banks at the Fed. (These reserves are created "out of thin air," so to speak!) The reserves of the commercial banks go up by the amount of the purchase of the securities.

We show these outcomes as (*a*) and (*b*) on the following consolidated balance sheets of the commercial banks and the Federal Reserve Banks:

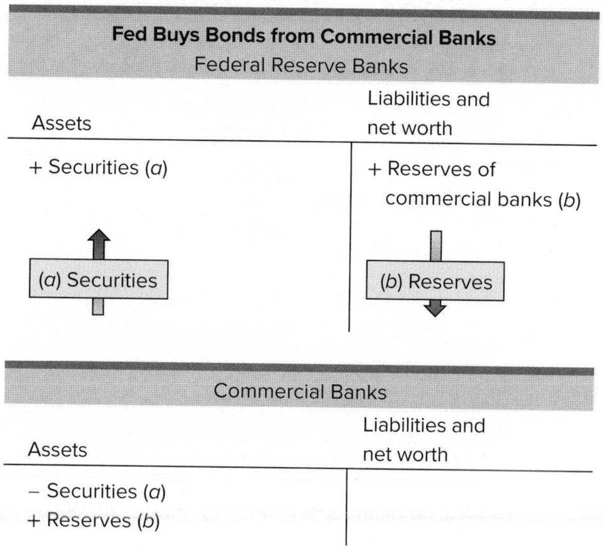

The upward arrow shows that securities have moved from the commercial banks to the Federal Reserve Banks. So we enter "– Securities" (minus securities) in the asset column of the balance sheet of the commercial banks. For the same reason, we enter "+ Securities" in the asset column of the balance sheet of the Federal Reserve Banks.

The downward arrow indicates that the Federal Reserve Banks have provided reserves to the commercial banks. So we enter "+ Reserves" in the asset column of the balance sheet for the commercial banks. In the liability column of the balance sheet of the Federal Reserve Banks, the plus sign indicates that although commercial bank reserves have increased, they are a liability to the Federal Reserve Banks because the reserves are owned by the commercial banks.

What is most important about this transaction is that when Federal Reserve Banks purchase securities from commercial banks, they increase the reserves in the banking system, which then increases the lending ability of the commercial banks.

From the Public The effect on commercial bank reserves is much the same when Federal Reserve Banks purchase securities from the general public. Suppose the Gristly Meat Packing Company has government bonds that it sells in the open market to the Federal Reserve Banks. The transaction has several elements:

(*a*) Gristly gives up securities to the Federal Reserve Banks and gets in payment a check drawn by the Federal Reserve Banks on themselves.

(*b*) Gristly promptly deposits the check in its account with the Wahoo bank.

AP FIGURE 30.2 The Federal Reserve's purchase of bonds and the expansion of the money supply. Assuming all banks are loaned up initially, a Federal Reserve purchase of a $1,000 bond from either a commercial bank or the public can increase the money supply by $5,000 when the reserve ratio is 20 percent. In the upper panel of the diagram, the purchase of a $1,000 bond from a commercial bank creates $1,000 of excess reserves that support a $5,000 expansion of checkable deposits through loans. In the lower panel, the purchase of a $1,000 bond from the public creates a $1,000 checkable deposit but only $800 of excess reserves because $200 of reserves is required to "back up" the $1,000 new checkable deposit. The commercial banks can therefore expand the money supply by only $4,000 by making loans. This $4,000 of checkable-deposit money plus the new checkable deposit of $1,000 equals $5,000 of new money.

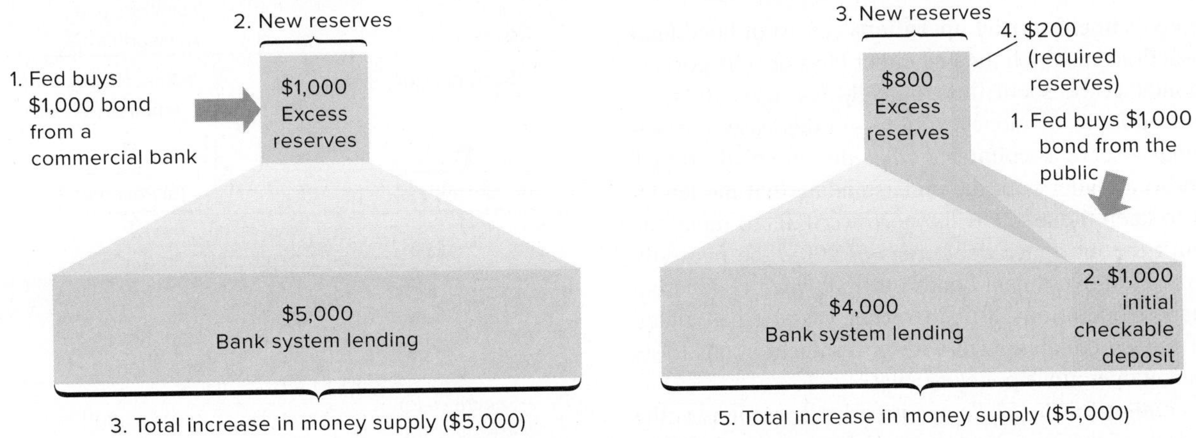

(*c*) The Wahoo bank sends this check against the Federal Reserve Banks to a Federal Reserve Bank for collection. As a result, the Wahoo bank enjoys an increase in its reserves.

To keep things simple, we will dispense with showing the balance sheet changes resulting from the Fed's sale or purchase of bonds from the public. But two aspects of this transaction are particularly important. First, as with Federal Reserve purchases of securities directly from commercial banks, the purchases of securities from the public increase the lending ability of the commercial banking system. Second, the supply of money is directly increased by the Federal Reserve Banks' purchase of government bonds (aside from any expansion of the money supply that may occur from the increase in commercial bank reserves). This direct increase in the money supply has taken the form of an increased amount of checkable deposits in the economy as a result of Gristly's deposit.

The Federal Reserve Banks' purchases of securities from the commercial banking system differ slightly from their purchases of securities from the public. If we assume that all commercial banks are loaned up initially, Federal Reserve bond purchases *from commercial banks* increase the actual reserves and excess reserves of commercial banks by the entire amount of the bond purchases. As shown in the left panel in Figure 30.2, a $1,000 bond purchase from a commercial bank increases both the actual and the excess reserves of the commercial bank by $1,000.

In contrast, Federal Reserve Bank purchases of bonds from the public increase actual reserves but also increase checkable deposits when the sellers place the Fed's check into their personal checking accounts. As shown in the right panel of Figure 30.2, a $1,000 bond purchase from the public would increase checkable deposits by $1,000 and hence the actual reserves of the loaned-up banking system by the same amount. But with a 20 percent reserve ratio applied to the $1,000 checkable deposit, the excess reserves of the banking system would be only $800 since $200 of the $1,000 would have to be held as reserves.

However, in both transactions the end result is the same: When Federal Reserve Banks buy securities in the open market, commercial banks' reserves are increased. When the banks lend out an amount equal to their excess reserves, the nation's money supply will rise. Observe in Figure 30.2 that a $1,000 purchase of bonds by the Federal Reserve results in a potential of $5,000 of additional money, regardless of whether the purchase was made from commercial banks (left panel) or from the general public (right panel).

Selling Securities As you may suspect, when the Federal Reserve Banks sell government bonds, commercial banks' reserves are reduced. Let's see why.

To Commercial Banks When the Federal Reserve Banks sell securities in the open market to commercial banks,

(*a*) The Federal Reserve Banks give up securities that the commercial banks acquire.

(*b*) The commercial banks pay for those securities by drawing checks against their deposits—that is, against their reserves—in Federal Reserve Banks. The Fed collects on those checks by reducing the commercial banks' reserves accordingly.

The balance-sheet changes—again identified by (*a*) and (*b*)—appear as shown in the following balance sheets. The reduction in commercial bank reserves is indicated by the minus signs before the appropriate entries.

Fed Sells Bonds to Commercial Banks

Federal Reserve Banks

Assets	Liabilities and net worth
− Securities (*a*)	− Reserves of commercial banks (*b*)
↓ (*a*) Securities	↑ (*b*) Reserves

Commercial Banks

Assets	Liabilities and net worth
− Reserves (*b*) + Securities (*a*)	

To the Public When the Federal Reserve Banks sell securities to the public, the outcome is much the same. Let's put the Gristly Company on the buying end of government bonds that the Federal Reserve Banks are selling:

(*a*) The Federal Reserve Banks sell government bonds to Gristly, which pays with a check drawn on the Wahoo bank.

(*b*) The Federal Reserve Banks clear this check against the Wahoo bank by reducing Wahoo's reserves.

(*c*) The Wahoo bank returns the canceled check to Gristly, reducing Gristly's checkable deposit accordingly.

Federal Reserve bond sales of $1,000 to the commercial banking system reduce the system's actual and excess reserves by $1,000. But a $1,000 bond sale to the public reduces excess reserves by $800 because the public's checkable-deposit money is also reduced by $1,000 by the sale. Since the commercial banking system's outstanding checkable deposits are reduced by $1,000, banks need to keep $200 less in reserves.

Whether the Fed sells bonds to the public or to commercial banks, the result is the same: When Federal Reserve Banks sell securities in the open market, commercial bank reserves are reduced. If all excess reserves are already lent out, this decline in commercial bank reserves produces a decline in the nation's money supply. In our example, a $1,000 sale of government securities results in a $5,000 decline in the money supply whether the sale is made to commercial banks or to the general public. You can verify this by reexamining Figure 30.2 and tracing the effects of a *sale* of a $1,000 bond by the Fed either to commercial banks or to the public.

What makes commercial banks and the public willing to sell government securities to, or buy them from, Federal Reserve Banks? The answer lies in the price of bonds and their interest yields. We know that bond prices and interest rates are inversely related. When the Fed buys government bonds, the demand for them increases. Government bond prices rise, and their interest yields decline. The higher bond prices and their lower interest yields prompt banks, securities firms, and individual holders of government bonds to sell them to the Federal Reserve Banks.

When the Fed sells government bonds, the additional supply of bonds in the bond market lowers bond prices and raises their interest yields, making government bonds attractive purchases for banks and the public.

Repos and Reverse Repos In addition to bond purchases and sales, the Fed can also alter the supply of money through collateralized loans known as repos and reverse repos.

A money loan is said to be collateralized when an asset is pledged by the borrower to reduce the financial risk of default (failure to repay) that has to be borne by the lender. As an example, consider home mortgages. If Paul takes out a home mortgage, the home that he is buying will serve as collateral for his home mortgage loan. If Paul fails to repay the loan, ownership of the home will pass to the lender, who can then sell the home to get back most or all of the money that it lent to Paul.

Because the use of collateral greatly reduces the financial consequences of default for lenders, interest rates on collateralized loans such as home mortgages and auto loans are much lower than on uncollateralized loans such as credit card debt (where if a person defaults, there is no collateral that the lender can claim to help offset the loss).

Repos and reverse repos are short-hand names for repurchase agreements, discussed in the nearby Consider This box. In essence, repos and reverse repos are collateralized loans in which government securities serve as collateral. When the Fed undertakes a **repo** transaction, it makes a loan of money in exchange for government bonds being posted as collateral. The Fed's repo loans are normally overnight loans but can last as long as 65 business days. The Fed holds the bonds posted as collateral until the loan is either repaid or goes into default. If the money is repaid on time, the Fed returns the bonds to the borrower. If the money is not repaid on time, the Fed keeps the bonds.

Reverse repo transactions are repos in reverse. Instead of the Fed lending money against bond collateral, it is the Fed that posts government bonds as collateral when borrowing money from financial institutions.

The key point is that repos involve the Fed lending money into the financial system whereas reverse repos involve the Fed borrowing money out of the financial system. That means that repos are like open-market purchases of bonds (because both increase the money supply) while reverse repos are like open-market sales of bonds (because both decrease

CONSIDER THIS . . .

Source: © John Moore/Getty Images

Repo, Man

While *repos* refer to repurchase agreements, not repossessions, they are similar to repossessions because they also involve collateralized loans. Consider car loans, which are collateralized with cars. You get your car; your lender gets your payments. If you stop making your payments, your lender will send out a repo man to collect the collateral.

A repurchase agreement consists of two successive asset transactions—an initial sale followed by a repurchase—that together are equivalent to a collateralized loan. As an example, suppose Bank A wants to enter into a repurchase agreement with the Fed. Bank A would sell, for instance, $10 million of Treasury bonds to the Fed with the stipulation that it will repurchase those bonds from the Fed the next day. The repurchase price will be $10 million plus a small additional amount of money, say $50, that is equivalent to an interest payment on what amounts to an overnight collateralized loan.

To see why the repo is equivalent to an overnight collateralized loan, note that while the repurchase agreement is in effect overnight, the Fed owns the bonds. And the Fed will get to keep them if Bank A does not follow through on its promise to repurchase the bonds the next day. Thus, the entire repo process of a sale of bonds followed by a repurchase of bonds is equivalent to the Fed loaning $10 million to Bank A in exchange for collateral worth $10 million plus the promise to pay $50 worth of interest. It is for this reason that repos are usually thought of as collateralized loans rather than as two successive asset transactions.

A reverse repo ("reverse repurchase agreement") switches the roles of the Fed and the bank. The Fed sells bonds to the bank with the promise to buy them back the next day. The bank holds the bonds as collateral. And the bank will get to keep the collateral if the Fed does not honor its promise to repurchase the bonds the next day.

the money supply). Repos increase the money supply while reverse repos decrease the money supply.

The Reserve Ratio

The Fed also can manipulate the **reserve ratio** in order to influence the ability of commercial banks to lend. Suppose a commercial bank's balance sheet shows that reserves are $5,000 and checkable deposits are $20,000. If the legal reserve ratio is 20 percent (row 2, Table 30.2), the bank's required reserves are $4,000. Since actual reserves are $5,000, the excess reserves of this bank are $1,000. On the basis of $1,000 of excess reserves, this one bank can lend $1,000; however, the banking system as a whole can create a maximum of $5,000 of new checkable-deposit money by lending (column 7).

Raising the Reserve Ratio Now, what if the Fed raised the reserve ratio from 20 to 25 percent? (See row 3.) Required reserves would jump from $4,000 to $5,000, shrinking excess reserves from $1,000 to zero. Raising the reserve ratio increases the amount of required reserves banks must keep. As a consequence, either banks lose excess reserves, diminishing their ability to create money by lending, or they find their reserves deficient and are forced to contract checkable deposits and therefore the money supply. In the example in Table 30.2, excess reserves are transformed into required reserves, and the money-creating potential of our single bank is reduced from $1,000 to zero (column 6). Moreover, the banking system's money-creating capacity declines from $5,000 to zero (column 7).

What if the Fed increases the reserve requirement to 30 percent? (See row 4.) The commercial bank, to protect itself against the prospect of failing to meet this requirement, would be forced to lower its checkable deposits and at the same time increase its reserves. To reduce its checkable deposits, the bank could let outstanding loans mature and be repaid without extending new credit. To increase reserves, the bank might sell some of its bonds, adding the proceeds to its reserves. Both actions would reduce the supply of money.

Lowering the Reserve Ratio What would happen if the Fed lowered the reserve ratio from the original 20 percent to 10 percent? (See row 1.) In this case, required reserves would decline from $4,000 to $2,000, and excess reserves would jump from $1,000 to $3,000. The single bank's lending (money-creating) ability would increase from $1,000 to $3,000 (column 6), and the banking system's money-creating potential would expand from $5,000 to $30,000 (column 7). Lowering the reserve ratio transforms required reserves into excess reserves and enhances the ability of banks to create new money by lending.

The examples in Table 30.2 show that a change in the reserve ratio affects the money-creating ability of the *banking system* in two ways:

- It changes the amount of excess reserves.
- It changes the size of the monetary multiplier.

For example, when the legal reserve ratio is raised from 10 to 20 percent, excess reserves are reduced from $3,000 to $1,000 and the checkable-deposit multiplier is reduced from 10 to 5. The money-creating potential of the banking system declines from $30,000 (= $3,000 × 10) to $5,000 (= $1,000 × 5). Raising the reserve ratio forces banks to reduce the amount of checkable deposits they create through lending.

TABLE 30.2 The Effects of Changes in the Reserve Ratio on the Lending Ability of Commercial Banks

(1) Reserve Ratio, %	(2) Checkable Deposits	(3) Actual Reserves	(4) Required Reserves	(5) Excess Reserves, (3) − (4)	(6) Money-Creating Potential of Single Bank, = (5)	(7) Money-Creating Potential of Banking System
(1) 10	$20,000	$5,000	$2,000	$3,000	$3,000	$30,000
(2) 20	20,000	5,000	4,000	1,000	1,000	5,000
(3) 25	20,000	5,000	5,000	0	0	0
(4) 30	20,000	5,000	6,000	−1,000	−1,000	−3,333

The Discount Rate

One of the functions of a central bank is to be a "lender of last resort." Occasionally, commercial banks have unexpected and immediate needs for additional funds. In such cases, each Federal Reserve Bank will make short-term loans to commercial banks in its district.

When a commercial bank borrows, it gives the Federal Reserve Bank a promissory note (IOU) drawn against itself and secured by acceptable collateral—typically U.S. government securities. Just as commercial banks charge interest on the loans they make to their clients, so too Federal Reserve Banks charge interest on loans they grant to commercial banks. The interest rate they charge is called the **discount rate.**

As a claim against the commercial bank, the borrowing bank's promissory note is an asset to the lending Federal Reserve Bank and appears on its balance sheet as "Loans to commercial banks." To the commercial bank, the IOU is a liability, appearing as "Loans from the Federal Reserve Banks" on the commercial bank's balance sheet. [See the two (*a*) entries on the balance sheets that follow.]

Commercial Bank Borrowing from the Fed

Federal Reserve Banks

Assets	Liabilities and net worth
+ Loans to commercial banks (*a*)	+ Reserves of commercial banks (*b*)
IOUs	+ Reserves

Commercial Banks

Assets	Liabilities and net worth
+ Reserves (*b*)	+ Loans from the Federal Reserve Banks (*a*)

In providing the loan, the Federal Reserve Bank increases the reserves of the borrowing commercial bank. Since no required reserves need be kept against loans from Federal Reserve Banks, all new reserves acquired by borrowing from Federal Reserve Banks are excess reserves. [These changes are reflected in the two (*b*) entries on the balance sheets.]

In short, borrowing from the Federal Reserve Banks by commercial banks increases the reserves of the commercial banks and enhances their ability to extend credit.

The Fed has the power to set the discount rate at which commercial banks borrow from Federal Reserve Banks. From the commercial banks' point of view, the discount rate is a cost of acquiring reserves. A lowering of the discount rate encourages commercial banks to obtain additional reserves by borrowing from Federal Reserve Banks. When the commercial banks lend new reserves, the money supply increases.

An increase in the discount rate discourages commercial banks from obtaining additional reserves through borrowing from the Federal Reserve Banks. So the Fed may raise the discount rate when it wants to restrict the money supply.

Interest on Reserves

In 2008, federal law was changed so that the Federal Reserve could for the first time pay banks interest on reserves held at the Fed. Before that time, any reserves held on deposit at the Federal Reserve were paid zero interest. Thus, before 2008, banks had an incentive to keep their reserves as small as possible because any money kept on reserve at the Fed was money earning a zero percent rate of return.

The new law allowed the Fed to set separate rates for required reserves and excess reserves. These are known, respectively, as interest on required reserves (IORR) and **interest on excess reserves (IOER).** In practice, however, the IORR rate and the IOER rate have been set at equal values, first at 0.25 percent per year from 2008 through December 2015, and then at 0.50 percent per year starting in December 2015.

The Fed's newfound ability to pay interest on excess reserves provided the Fed with a fourth policy tool by which it can implement monetary policy and either increase or decrease the amount of monetary stimulus in the economy. As an example, suppose that the Fed wishes to *reduce* the amount of bank lending and, consequently, the amount of money circulating in the economy. It can do so by increasing the rate of interest that it pays on excess reserves held at the Fed. The higher that interest rate, the more of an incentive banks will have to reduce their risky commercial lending for car, mortgage, and business loans in order to instead increase the reserves that they hold at the Fed and thereby earn the risk-free interest rate that the Fed is paying on reserves.

By contrast, if the Fed wishes to *increase* the amount of money that banks lend into the economy, the Fed can lower the interest rate that it pays on excess reserves. The lower rate will make it less attractive for banks to keep reserves, and, consequently, banks will be incentivized to increase consumer and commercial lending and thereby stimulate the economy.

For almost all of 2015, the rate of interest on excess reserves was 0.25 percent per year. Given that banks held about \$2.5 trillion in excess reserves at the Fed that year, the Fed paid a total of about \$6.25 billion (= 0.0025 times \$2.5 trillion) in interest payments to banks for excess reserves held at the Fed in 2015.

Relative Importance

All four of the Fed's instruments of monetary control are useful in particular economic circumstances, but open-market operations are clearly the most important of the four tools over the course of the business cycle. The buying, selling, or pledging as collateral of securities in the open market has the advantage of flexibility—government securities can be purchased, sold, or collateralized daily in large or small amounts—and the impact on bank reserves is prompt. And, compared with reserve-requirement changes, open-market operations work subtly and less directly. Furthermore, the ability of the Federal Reserve Banks to affect commercial bank reserves through open-market bond transactions is virtually unquestionable. The Federal Reserve Banks have very large holdings of government securities (\$2,341 billion in early 2016, for example). The sale of those securities could theoretically reduce commercial bank reserves to zero.

Changing the reserve requirement is a potentially powerful instrument of monetary control, but the Fed has used this technique only sparingly. Normally, it can accomplish its monetary goals more easily through open-market operations. The last change in the reserve requirement was in 1992, when the Fed reduced the requirement from 12 percent to 10 percent. The main purpose was to shore up the profitability of banks and thrifts in the aftermath of the 1990–1991 recession rather than to reduce interest rates by increasing reserves and expanding the money supply.

Until recently, the discount rate was mainly a passive tool of monetary control, with the Fed raising and lowering the rate simply to keep it in line with other interest rates. However, during the financial crisis of 2007–2008, the Fed aggressively lowered the discount rate independently of other interest rates to provide a cheap and plentiful source of reserves to banks whose reserves were being sharply reduced by unexpectedly high default rates on home mortgage loans. Banks borrowed billions at the lower discount rate. This allowed them to meet reserve ratio requirements and thereby preserved their ability to keep extending loans.

AP QUICK REVIEW 30.3

- ✓ The Fed has four main tools of monetary control, each of which works by changing the amount of reserves in the banking system: (a) conducting open-market operations (the Fed's buying and selling of government bonds to the banks and the public as well as the use of government bonds as collateral for repo and reverse repo loans), (b) changing the reserve ratio (the percentage of commercial bank deposit liabilities required as reserves), (c) changing the discount rate (the interest rate the Federal Reserve Banks charge on loans to banks and thrifts), and (d) changing the interest rate that it pays on reserves held at the Fed.
- ✓ Open-market operations are the Fed's monetary control mechanism of choice for routine increases or decreases in bank reserves over the business cycle; in contrast, changes in reserve requirements are used only in special situations.

AP Targeting the Federal Funds Rate

LO30.4 Describe the federal funds rate and how the Fed directly influences it.

The Federal Reserve focuses monetary policy on the federal funds rate, which is the short-term interest rate that the Fed can most directly influence. From the previous chapter, you know that the federal funds rate is the rate of interest that banks pay to borrow excess bank reserves overnight from another financial institution. Recall that the Federal Reserve requires banks (and thrifts) to deposit in their regional Federal Reserve Bank a certain percentage of their checkable deposits as reserves. At the end of any business day, some banks may have reserve deficiencies (fewer reserves than required). The Fed allows any such deficiency to be cured through overnight borrowing. Any bank that is deficient in reserves can borrow the amount by which it is deficient from other financial institutions that happen to have excess amounts of reserves.

Before the financial crisis of 2007–2008, excess reserves held overnight at the Federal Reserve earned zero percent interest. By contrast, banks with excess reserves could obtain a positive interest rate by making overnight loans to banks that had reserve deficiencies. The transactions took place in the federal funds market and an equilibrium interest rate—the **federal funds rate**—was determined by the demand and supply for reserves. (The reserves being lent and borrowed overnight were called "federal funds" because they were funds that were required by the Federal Reserve to meet reserve requirements.)

Before the financial crisis, the Federal Reserve adjusted monetary policy by manipulating the supply of reserves that were offered in the federal funds market. As explained earlier, the Fed could increase or decrease the overall amount of reserves in the banking system by buying and selling government bonds in open-market operations. These changes in the total amount of reserves held by banks in turn affected the amount of excess reserves that banks were willing to supply in the federal funds market—and thus the equilibrium federal funds rate. Under that system, the Federal Open Market Committee (FOMC) met regularly to set a target value (such as 3.75 percent) for the federal funds rate. The trading desk at the New York Fed would then undertake whatever open-market operations were necessary to achieve and maintain the target rate.

The system had to be adjusted in 2008, during the crisis. The FOMC has continued to meet regularly to choose a target for the federal funds rate. But the target has been a range (such as 0.25 percent to 0.50 percent) rather than a value (such as 3.75 percent).

The setting of a target range rather than a target value was a consequence of policy actions that the Fed pursued to contain the mortgage debt crisis of 2008. The Fed purchased so many bonds from banks through open-market operations that nearly every bank in the country ended up with a huge amount of excess reserves. Systemwide, the total amount of excess reserves skyrocketed from $1.9 billion in August 2008 to $796.8 billion in January 2009 before continuing to grow steadily over the following years. By early 2016, the U.S. banking system had $2,267 billion in excess reserves.

This massive increase in excess reserves meant that there were hardly ever any instances where a bank needed to borrow excess reserves overnight in the federal funds market. That lack of demand coupled with the massive increase in the supply of excess reserves had two significant effects:

- The federal funds rate (the equilibrium price of borrowing money in the federal funds market) plunged to nearly zero due to high supply coupled with low demand.
- The number of bank-to-bank transactions in the federal funds market collapsed because there were hardly any instances in which a bank found itself deficient in reserves.

In addition, the massive amount of excess reserves in the banking system meant that the Fed could no longer expect to affect the federal funds rate by using open-market operations to alter the overall amount of excess reserves in the banking system. A $50 billion or even a $100 billion change in the overall amount of excess reserves wouldn't matter when compared to the existing stockpile of $2,267 billion in excess reserves. The total amount of excess reserves would still be so large that the federal funds rate would remain stuck stubbornly near zero.

That situation forced the Fed to conduct monetary policy very differently after the mortgage debt crisis as compared with before the mortgage debt crisis. In particular, the Fed had to figure out how to conduct monetary policy when the federal funds rate was stuck near zero. To gain a strong understanding of what the Fed came up with, let's compare how the Fed conducted expansionary and restrictive monetary policy before 2008 versus after 2008.

Expansionary Monetary Policy

Suppose that the economy faces a recession and rising unemployment. How will the Fed respond? It will initiate **expansionary monetary policy** (or "easy money policy") to increase the supply of credit in the economy and, hopefully, aggregate demand and real output, too.

Expansionary Monetary Policy before the Mortgage Debt Crisis Before the mortgage debt crisis, excess reserves were low in the banking system and the federal funds rate tended to be in the 3 to 10 percent range. The low volume of excess reserves implied that the Fed could manipulate interest rates by altering bank reserves, while the fact that the federal funds rate was 3 percent or higher meant that the Fed always had room to maneuver short-term interest rates lower to stimulate the economy. The Fed also paid zero interest on excess reserves before the crisis, thereby giving banks an incentive to always try to lend out their excess reserves. Earning a 3 percent or higher federal funds rate by lending excess reserves was better than earning a zero percent return by leaving those reserves on deposit at the Fed.

Given that situation, the Fed's approach to expansionary monetary policy involved lowering the federal funds rate to boost borrowing and spending (and thereby increase aggregate demand and expand real output). The Fed would initiate an expansionary monetary policy by setting a lower target for the federal funds rate. It would then have three options for reducing the interest rate. The Fed could lower the reserve requirement, lower the discount rate, or use open-market operations to alter the amount of reserves in the banking system. In actual practice, the Fed relied almost exclusively on open-market operations to buy bonds and thereby increase the supply of reserves in the banking system.

AP **FIGURE 30.3 The prime interest rate and the federal funds rate in the United States, 1998–2016.** The prime interest rate rises and falls with changes in the federal funds rate.

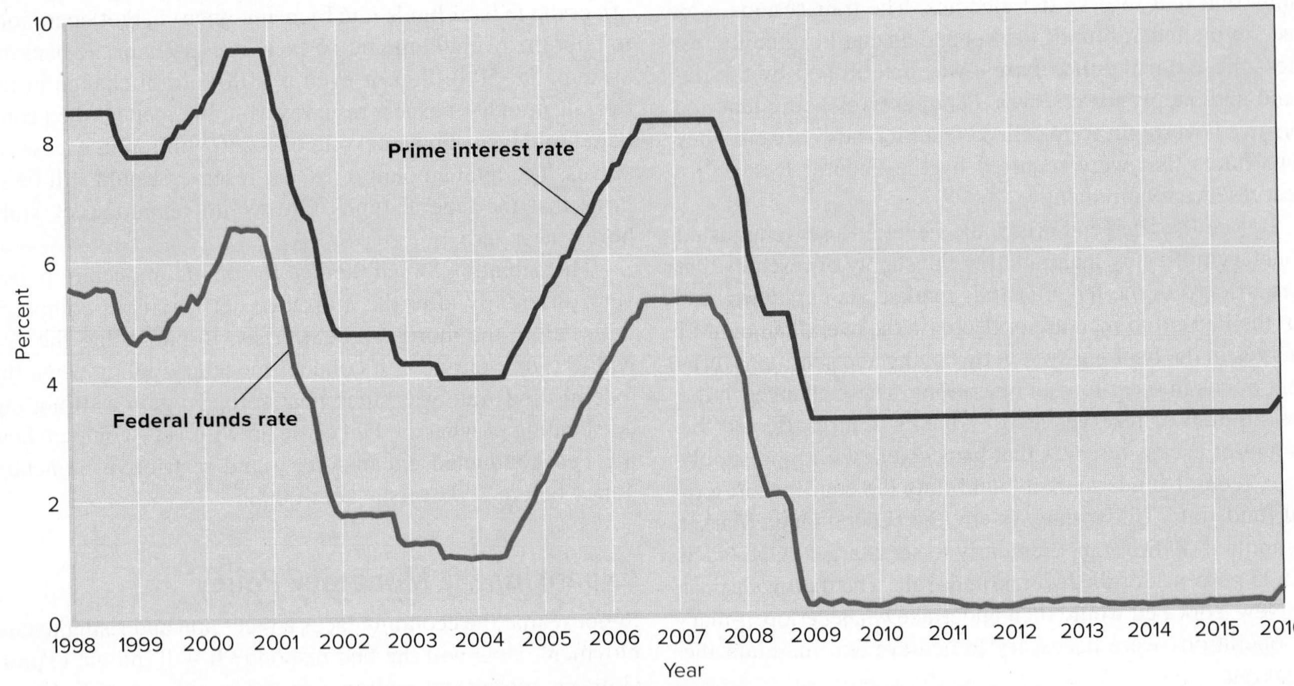

Source: Federal Reserve Statistical Release, Historical Data, H.15, **www.federalreserve.gov**.

This increase in reserves had two important effects:

- It increased the supply of excess reserves offered in the federal funds market, thereby lowering the federal funds rate.
- It initiated a multiple expansion of the nation's money supply. Given the demand for money, the larger supply of money would stimulate aggregate demand and real output by putting downward pressure on other interest rates.

One such rate is the **prime interest rate**—the benchmark interest rate used by banks as a reference point for a wide range of interest rates charged on loans to businesses and individuals. The prime interest rate is higher than the federal funds rate because the prime rate involves longer, riskier loans than the overnight loans extended between banks in the federal funds market.

The federal funds rate and the prime interest rate closely track one another, as is evident in Figure 30.3. Also evident is the plunge in both the federal funds rate and the prime rate during the height of the mortgage debt crisis in 2008.

Expansionary Monetary Policy after the Mortgage Debt Crisis The massive increase in excess reserves that took place during the mortgage debt crisis forced the Fed to conduct expansionary monetary policy in a different way.

The post-crisis Fed had two problems when it came to expansionary monetary policy:

- Open-market operations had become ineffective in moving the federal funds rate because even billion-dollar purchases and sales of bonds in the open market left a massive oversupply of excess reserves—and thus a federal funds rate stuck near zero.
- The **zero lower bound problem,** under which a central bank is constrained in its ability to stimulate the economy through lower interest rates because interest rates less than zero (that is, negative interest rates) encourage consumers to withdraw money from banks, thereby reducing the lending capacity of the banking system.

To understand the second problem, suppose that interest rates were forced into negative territory by the Fed. Many people would not want to leave their money in checking accounts because doing so would mean that their balances would shrink over time (rather than grow over time, as they do when interest rates are positive). Thus, any central bank that attempted to impose negative nominal interest rates would see deposits withdrawn from banks. That could be economically catastrophic because the withdrawals would imply that banks would have less money to lend out to consumers and entrepreneurs. The monetary multiplier of Chapter 29 would work in reverse, and the supply of lending and credit in the economy would decrease precipitously, thereby negatively affecting aggregate demand.

The Fed's response to the zero lower bound problem was **quantative easing,** or QE. In terms of mechanics, quantitative easing looks exactly like the open-market purchases of bonds that the Fed made before 2008 to lower the federal funds rate. But the Fed's goal when pursuing QE starting in 2008 was not to use open market purchases to lower the federal funds rate (because lowering it when it was already near zero might have caused negative interest rates and a rush to withdraw checking deposits in favor of cash). Rather, the Fed's goal when pursuing QE after 2008 was to buy bonds solely with the intention of increasing the quantity of reserves in the banking system. Interest rates would remain where they were—low but positive—but the larger quantity of excess reserves would hopefully spur banks to lend more and thereby stimulate aggregate demand.

Another difference between QE and regular open-market operations is that QE can involve the purchase of not only U.S. government bonds but also debt issued by U.S. government agencies or government-backed corporations (which are known as government-sponsored entities, or GSEs).

The first round of quantitative easing began in March 2009 and involved the Fed purchasing $1.75 trillion worth of bonds. The bonds consisted of $300 billion worth of Treasury bonds and $1.45 trillion worth of bonds issued by either U.S. government agencies or the two GSE mortgage lenders, Freddie Mac and Fannie Mae. The second round of quantitative easing ("QE2") began in November 2010 and involved the Fed purchasing $600 billion of U.S. Treasury bonds. A third and final round ("QE3") ran from 2012 to 2014 and involved the purchase of an additional $1.6 trillion worth of securities. Quantitative easing was the Fed's strategy for expansionary monetary policy in a world already awash with excess reserves.

AP QUICK REVIEW 30.4

- ✓ The Fed conducts its monetary policy by establishing a targeted federal funds interest rate—the rate that commercial banks charge one another for overnight loans of reserves.
- ✓ An expansionary monetary policy (loose money policy), with the Federal Reserve buying government bonds, lowers the federal funds rate by increasing the money supply. This operation also lowers other interest rates.
- ✓ Policy actions taken by the Fed, including to aggressively lower interest rates, in response to the mortgage debt crisis resulted in a massive increase in excess reserves, a federal funds rate near zero, and much less activity in the federal funds market.
- ✓ Expansionary monetary policy after 2008 consisted of quantitative easing (QE), or massive open-market bond purchases undertaken to increase bank reserves. The Fed kept the federal funds rate low but positive during QE to avoid the zero lower bound problem.

Restrictive Monetary Policy

Suppose that the economy is overheating and inflation is rising. How will the Fed respond? It will initiate a **restrictive monetary policy** (or "tight money policy") designed to reduce aggregate demand and lower the rate of inflation.

Restrictive Monetary Policy after the Mortgage Debt Crisis The mortgage debt crisis and the Great Recession of 2007–2009 were so severe that the Fed continued with expansionary monetary policy through the end of 2015, at which point it announced how it would attempt to "normalize" monetary policy by returning short-term interest rates to their historically normal range of 3 percent or higher. The plan also laid out how the Fed could engage in restrictive monetary policy in the face of massive amounts of excess reserves and a federal funds market that continued to be little used.

The Fed's normalization plan had two prongs. The first was to utilize the fact that starting in 2008 the Fed had begun paying interest on excess reserves (IOER) on any excess reserve balances held by member banks. The IOER rate was set at 0.25 percent in 2008 and was unchanged until the end of 2015, when it was raised to 0.50 percent.

The normalization process would involve raising the IOER rate even further in order to get banks to raise other interest rates. To see why raising the IOER rate could be expected to cause other interest rates to rise, suppose that banks could get an IOER of 1 percent by parking excess reserves at the Fed. Under that circumstance, they would not want to lend to anybody else at an interest rate lower than 1 percent. After all, why would the banks want to lend to businesses or individuals for less than 1 percent when they could get 1 percent simply by parking excess reserves at the Fed?

The same would be true for higher IOER rates, such as 2 percent or 3 percent. The higher the IOER rate, the higher the opportunity cost of lending to businesses or individuals; the higher the IOER rate, the more banks would charge to lend money. Thus, the Fed concluded that it could use increases in the IOER rate to help normalize interest rates throughout the economy.

The second prong of the normalization process would be to use reverse repos as a way of making sure that the Fed could raise the federal funds rate, too. The problem that the Fed faced was that after 2008 the federal funds market had come to be dominated not by bank-to-bank lending (as was the case before the mortgage debt crisis) but by nonbank-to-bank lending. In particular, many large financial firms that were not banks (such as mutual funds and government-sponsored entities) were lending excess cash (that is, potential bank reserves) to banks in the federal funds market.

The banks were willing to borrow that money at any rate below the IOER rate of 0.25 percent because they could immediately deposit the borrowed money at the Fed, increase their excess reserves, and earn the IOER rate of 0.25 percent on whatever they had borrowed from the nonbanks. The difference between the lower rate (of, say, 0.14 percent) that banks borrowed at in the federal funds market and the IOER rate of 0.25 percent that they would receive from the Fed would be pure profit.

The underlying problem was that by law the Fed could only pay IOER to banks. It could not pay IOER to nonbank financial firms. That was problematic because if the Fed had had the ability to pay IOER to nonbanks, too, the Fed could have also gotten the nonbanks to want to lend only at rates higher than the IOER rate by simply offering them the IOER rate on any cash that they wished to lend to the Fed. It was only because the Fed was banned from paying IOER to nonbanks that the nonbanks were willing to lend cash to banks in the federal funds market at less than the IOER rate that banks could get from the Fed.

The federal funds rate averaged just 0.12 percent between the summer of 2009 and December 2015. That was less than half of the upper end of the 0 to 0.25 percent target range that the Fed had set for the federal funds rate. The fact that nonbanks could not access the IOER rate meant that they were willing to lend at an average rate of just 0.12 percent in the federal funds market.

That was extremely problematic because it meant that the Fed could not fully control the federal funds rate. If the Fed was going to raise the federal funds rate as part of normalization, it would have to figure out how to deal with nonbank-to-bank lending in the federal funds market. Its proposed solution was to use reserve repo transactions to soak up the money that the nonbanks were lending to banks in the federal funds market. The Fed would perform a reverse repo with nonbanks, thereby effectively borrowing away the cash that the nonbanks would have otherwise lent to banks in the federal funds market. If the Fed did enough reverse repos with nonbanks while it raised the interest rate on excess reserves, it could make sure that the federal funds rate would always rise up all the way to the IOER rate. The Fed could therefore be confident that it could truly control short-term interests rates and thus all of the other interest rates in the economy, too.

The combination of higher IOER and reverse repo transactions could also be used by the Fed to conduct restrictive monetary policy in the post-crisis economy. A higher interest rate on excess reserves coupled with more reverse repo borrowing would reduce the supply of money and credit to the economy, reduce aggregate demand, and lower inflation.

As of 2016, however, there was no need for tight money. The rate of inflation had remained at or below the Fed's target rate of 2 percent from the start of the mortgage debt crisis through 2016. The Fed was still intending to use higher IOER and reverse repos going forward, but its goal was to use them in moderation, reducing the money supply by just enough to return interest rates to normal levels, but not so much as to slow the growth of real GDP.

AP QUICK REVIEW 30.5

- ✓ A restrictive monetary policy (tight money policy), with the Federal Reserve selling government bonds, increases the federal funds rate by reducing the money supply. This operation also increases other interest rates.
- ✓ Restrictive monetary policy before 2008 involved the Fed raising the target for the federal funds rate and then using open-market operations to sell bonds as necessary to adjust bank reserves to hit the target.
- ✓ By 2015, after the mortgage debt crisis, the Fed felt the economy was strong enough to start normalizing short-term interest rates. Its plan involved raising the interest rate that it pays banks on excess reserves (IOER) while simultaneously using reverse repos to raise the federal funds rate.
- ✓ Pursued aggressively, the combination of higher IOER and reverse repos could also be used by the Fed to engage in a restrictive monetary policy in the post-2008 world of massive excess bank reserves.

The Taylor Rule

The proper federal funds target rate (or target range) for a certain period is a matter of policy discretion by the members of the FOMC. At each of their meetings, committee members assess whether the current target for the federal funds rate remains appropriate for achieving the twin goals of low inflation and full employment. If the majority of the FOMC members conclude that a change is needed, the FOMC sets a new target. This new target is established without adhering to any particular "inflationary target" or "monetary policy rule." Instead, the committee targets the federal funds rate at the level or range most appropriate for the current underlying economic conditions.

A rule of thumb suggested by economist John Taylor, however, roughly matches the actual policy of the Fed over many time periods. This rule of thumb builds on the belief held by many economists that central banks are willing to tolerate a small positive rate of inflation if doing so will help the economy to produce at potential output. The **Taylor rule** assumes that the Fed has a 2 percent "target rate of inflation" that it is willing to tolerate and that the FOMC follows three rules when setting its target for the federal funds rate:

- When real GDP equals potential GDP and inflation is at its target rate of 2 percent, the federal funds target rate should be 4 percent, implying a real federal funds rate of 2 percent (= 4 percent nominal federal funds rate minus 2 percent inflation rate).

- For each 1 percent increase of real GDP above potential GDP, the Fed should raise the real federal funds rate by $\frac{1}{2}$ percentage point.
- For each 1 percent increase in the inflation rate above its 2 percent target rate, the Fed should raise the *real* federal funds rate by $\frac{1}{2}$ percentage point. (Note, though, that in this case each $\frac{1}{2}$ percentage point increase in the real rate will require a 1.5 percentage point increase in the nominal rate to account for the underlying 1 percent increase in the inflation rate.)

The last two rules are applied independently of each other so that if real GDP is above potential output and at the same time inflation is above the 2 percent target rate, the Fed will apply both rules and raise real interest rates in response to both factors. For instance, if real GDP is 1 percent above potential output and inflation is simultaneously 1 percent above the 2 percent target rate, then the Fed will raise the *real* federal funds rate by 1 percentage point (= $\frac{1}{2}$ percentage point for the excessive GDP + $\frac{1}{2}$ percentage point for the excessive inflation).

Also notice that the last two rules are reversed for situations in which real GDP falls below potential GDP or inflation falls below 2 percent. Each 1 percent decline in real GDP below potential GDP or fall in inflation below 2 percent calls for a decline of the real federal funds rate by $\frac{1}{2}$ percentage point.

We emphasize that the Fed has no official allegiance to the Taylor rule. It changes the federal funds rate to any level (or range) that it deems appropriate. During some periods, its policy has diverged significantly from the Taylor rule.

QUICK REVIEW 30.6

✓ The Taylor rule is a mathematical formula that stipulates how the Fed should change real interest rates in response to divergences in real GPD from potential GDP and divergences of actual rates of inflation from the Fed's target rate of inflation.

✓ The Fed uses its discretion in setting the federal funds target range, but its decisions regarding monetary policy and the target range appear to be broadly consistent with the Taylor rule over many time periods.

AP Monetary Policy, Real GDP, and the Price Level

LO30.5 Identify the mechanisms by which monetary policy affects GDP and the price level.

We have identified and explained the tools of expansionary and contractionary monetary policy. We now want to emphasize how monetary policy affects the economy's levels of investment, aggregate demand, real GDP, and prices.

Cause-Effect Chain

The four diagrams in **Figure 30.4 (Key Graph)** will help you understand how monetary policy works toward achieving its goals.

Market for Money Figure 30.4a represents the market for money, in which the demand curve for money and the supply curve of money are brought together. Recall that the total demand for money is made up of the transactions and asset demands.

This figure also shows three potential money supply curves, S_{m1}, S_{m2}, and S_{m3}. In each case, the money supply is shown as a vertical line representing some fixed amount of money determined by the Fed.

The equilibrium interest rate is the rate at which the amount of money demanded and the amount supplied are equal. With money demand D_m in Figure 30.4a, if the supply of money is \$125 billion (S_{m1}), the equilibrium interest rate is 10 percent. With a money supply of \$150 billion (S_{m2}), the equilibrium interest rate is 8 percent; with a money supply of \$175 billion (S_{m3}), it is 6 percent.

You know from Chapter 24 that the real, not the nominal, rate of interest is critical for investment decisions. So here we assume that Figure 30.4a portrays real interest rates.

Investment These 10, 8, and 6 percent real interest rates are carried rightward to the investment demand curve in Figure 30.4b. This curve shows the inverse relationship between the interest rate—the cost of borrowing to invest—and the amount of investment spending. At the 10 percent interest rate, it will be profitable for the nation's businesses to invest \$15 billion; at 8 percent, \$20 billion; at 6 percent, \$25 billion.

Changes in the interest rate mainly affect the investment component of total spending, although they also affect spending on durable consumer goods (such as autos) that are purchased on credit. The impact of changing interest rates on investment spending is great because of the large cost and long-term nature of capital purchases. Capital equipment, factory buildings, and warehouses are tremendously expensive. In absolute terms, interest charges on funds borrowed for these purchases are considerable.

Similarly, the interest cost on a house purchased on a long-term contract is very large: A $\frac{1}{2}$-percentage-point change in the interest rate could amount to thousands of dollars in the total cost of buying a home.

In brief, the impact of changing interest rates is mainly on investment (and, through that, on aggregate demand, output, employment, and the price level). Moreover, as Figure 30.4b shows, investment spending varies inversely with the real interest rate.

Equilibrium GDP Figure 30.4c shows the impact of our three real interest rates and corresponding levels of investment spending on aggregate demand. (Ignore Figure 30.4d for the time being. We will return to it shortly.) As noted,

AP KEY GRAPH

FIGURE 30.4 Monetary policy and equilibrium GDP. An expansionary monetary policy that shifts the money supply curve rightward from S_{m1} to S_{m2} in (a) lowers the interest rate from 10 to 8 percent in (b). As a result, investment spending increases from $15 billion to $20 billion, shifting the aggregate demand curve rightward from AD_1 to AD_2 in (c) so that real output rises from the recessionary level of $880 billion to the full employment level Q_f = $900 billion along the horizontal dashed line. In (d), the economy at point *a* has an inflationary output gap of $10 billion because it is producing at $910 billion, $10 billion above potential output. A restrictive monetary policy that shifts the money supply curve leftward from S_{m3} = $175 billion to just $162.5 billion in (a) will increase the interest rate from 6 percent to 7 percent. Investment spending thus falls by $2.5 billion from $25 billion to $22.5 billion in (b). This initial decline is multiplied by 4 by the multiplier process so that the aggregate demand curve shifts leftward in (d) by $10 billion from AD_3 to AD_4, moving the economy along the horizontal dashed line to equilibrium *b*. This returns the economy to full employment output and eliminates the inflationary output gap.

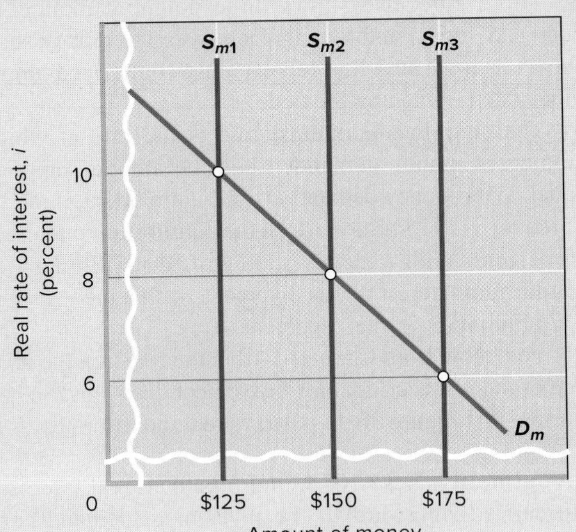

(a)
The market for money

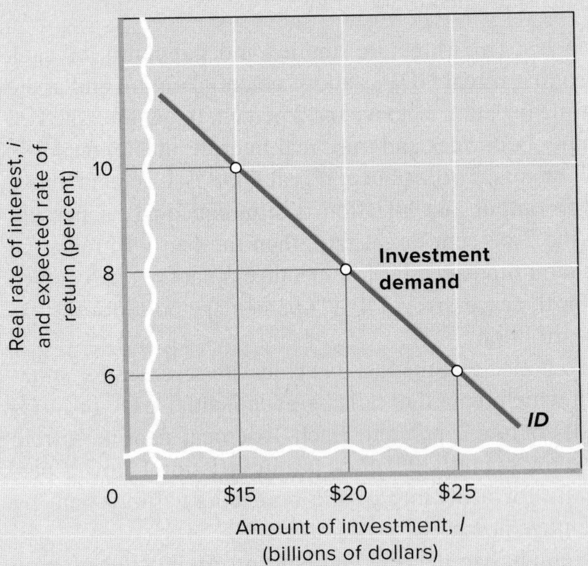

(b)
Investment demand

QUICK QUIZ FOR FIGURE 30.4

1. The ultimate objective of an expansionary monetary policy is depicted by:
   a. a decrease in the money supply from S_{m3} to S_{m2}.
   b. a reduction of the interest rate from 8 to 6 percent.
   c. an increase in investment from $20 billion to $25 billion.
   d. an increase in real GDP from Q_1 to Q_f.

aggregate demand curve AD_1 is associated with the $15 billion level of investment, AD_2 with investment of $20 billion, and AD_3 with investment of $25 billion. That is, investment spending is one of the determinants of aggregate demand. Other things equal, the greater the investment spending, the farther to the right lies the aggregate demand curve.

Suppose the money supply in Figure 30.4a is $150 billion ($S_{m2}$), producing an equilibrium interest rate of 8 percent. In Figure 30.4b we see that this 8 percent interest rate will bring forth $20 billion of investment spending. This $20 billion of investment spending joins with consumption spending, net exports, and government spending to yield aggregate demand curve AD_2 in Figure 30.4c. The equilibrium levels of real output and prices are Q_f = $900 billion and P_2, as determined by the intersection of AD_2 and the aggregate supply curve AS.

To test your understanding of these relationships, explain why each of the other two levels of money supply in Figure 30.4a results in a different interest rate, level of investment, aggregate demand curve, and equilibrium real output.

Effects of an Expansionary Monetary Policy

Recall that the inflationary ratchet effect discussed in Chapter 26 describes the fact that real-world price levels tend to be downwardly inflexible. Thus, with our economy starting from the initial equilibrium where AD_2 intersects AS, the price level will be downwardly inflexible at P_2 so that aggregate supply

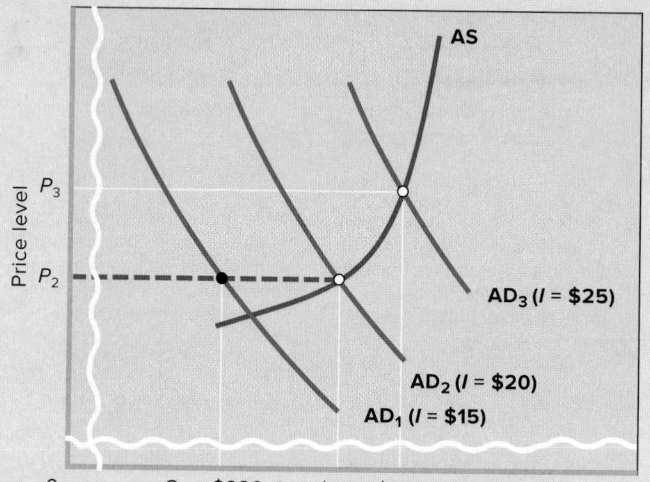

(c)
Equilibrium real GDP
and the price level

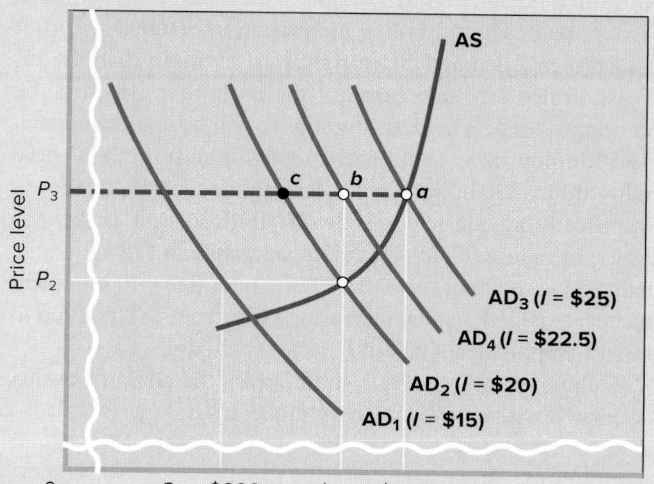

(d)
Equilibrium real GDP
and the price level

2. A successful restrictive monetary policy is evidenced by a shift in the money supply curve from:
- **a.** S_{m3} to a point halfway between S_{m2} and S_{m3}, a decrease in investment from $25 billion to $22.5 billion, and a decline in aggregate demand from AD_3 to AD_4.
- **b.** S_{m1} to S_{m2}, an increase in investment from $20 billion to $25 billion, and an increase in real GDP from Q_1 to Q_f.
- **c.** S_{m3} to S_{m2}, a decrease in investment from $25 billion to $20 billion, and a decline in the price level from P_3 to P_2.
- **d.** S_{m3} to S_{m2}, a decrease in investment from $25 billion to $20 billion, and an increase in aggregate demand from AD_2 to AD_3.

3. The Federal Reserve could increase the money supply from S_{m1} to S_{m2} by:
- **a.** increasing the discount rate.
- **b.** reducing taxes.
- **c.** buying government securities in the open market.
- **d.** increasing the reserve requirement.

4. If the spending-income multiplier is 4 in the economy depicted, an increase in the money supply from $125 billion to $150 billion will:
- **a.** shift the aggregate demand curve rightward by $20 billion.
- **b.** increase real GDP by $25 billion.
- **c.** increase real GDP by $100 billion.
- **d.** shift the aggregate demand curve leftward by $5 billion.

Answers: 1.d; 2. a; 3. c; 4. a

will be horizontal to the left of Q_f. This means that if aggregate demand decreases, the economy's equilibrium will move leftward along the dashed horizontal line shown in Figure 30.4c.

Just such a decline would happen if the money supply fell to $125 billion ($S_{m1}$), shifting the aggregate demand curve leftward to AD_1 in Figure 30.4c. This results in a real output of $880 billion, $20 billion less than the economy's full-employment output level of $900 billion. The economy will be experiencing recession, a negative GDP gap, and substantial unemployment. The Fed therefore should institute an expansionary monetary policy.

To increase the money supply, the Fed will take some combination of the following actions: (1) buy or initiate repos of government securities from banks and the public in the open market, (2) lower the legal reserve ratio, (3) lower the discount rate, and (4) reduce the interest rate that it pays on reserves. The intended outcome will be an increase in excess reserves in the commercial banking system and a decline in the federal funds rate. Because excess reserves are the basis on which commercial banks and thrifts can earn profit by lending and thus creating checkable-deposit money, the nation's money supply will rise. An increase in the money supply will lower the interest rate, increasing investment, aggregate demand, and equilibrium GDP.

For example, an increase in the money supply from $125 billion to $150 billion ($S_{m1}$ to S_{m2}) will reduce the interest rate from 10 to 8 percent, as indicated in Figure 30.4a, and will boost investment from $15 billion to $20 billion, as shown in Figure 30.4b. This $5 billion increase in investment will shift the aggregate demand curve rightward by more than the increase in investment because of the multiplier effect. If the economy's MPC is 0.75, the multiplier will be 4, meaning that the $5 billion increase in investment will shift the AD curve rightward by $20 billion (= 4 × $5 billion) at each price level. Specifically, aggregate demand will shift from AD_1 to AD_2, as shown in Figure 30.4c. This rightward shift in the aggregate demand curve along the dashed horizontal line will eliminate the negative GDP gap by increasing GDP from $880 billion to the full-employment GDP of Q_f = $900 billion.[1]

Column 1 in Table 30.3 summarizes the chain of events associated with an expansionary monetary policy.

AP TABLE 30.3 Monetary Policies for Recession and Inflation

(1) Expansionary Monetary Policy	(2) Restrictive Monetary Policy
Problem: unemployment and recession	*Problem:* inflation
↓	↓
Federal Reserve buys bonds, lowers reserve ratio, lowers the discount rate, reduces the interest rate on excess reserves, or initiates repos	Federal Reserve sells bonds, increases reserve ratio, raises the discount rate, increases the interest rate on excess reserves, or initiates reverse repos
↓	↓
Excess reserves increase	Excess reserves decrease
↓	↓
Federal funds rate falls	Federal funds rate rises
↓	↓
Money supply rises	Money supply falls
↓	↓
Interest rate falls	Interest rate rises
↓	↓
Investment spending increases	Investment spending decreases
↓	↓
Aggregate demand increases	Aggregate demand decreases
↓	↓
Real GDP rises	Inflation declines

Effects of a Restrictive Monetary Policy

Next we consider restrictive monetary policy. To prevent overcrowding, we will use graphs *a*, *b*, and *d* (not *c*) in Figure 30.4 to demonstrate the effects of a restrictive monetary policy on the economy. Figure 30.4d represents exactly the same economy as Figure 30.4c but adds some extra curves that relate only to our explanation of restrictive monetary policy.

To see how restrictive monetary policy works, first consider a situation in which the economy moves from a full-employment equilibrium to operating at more than full employment so that inflation is a problem and restrictive monetary policy would be appropriate. Assume that the economy begins at the full-employment equilibrium where AD_2 and AS intersect. At this equilibrium, Q_f = $900 billion and the price level is P_2.

Next, assume that the money supply expands from $150 billion to $175 billion ($S_{m3}$) in Figure 30.4a. This results in an interest rate of 6 percent, investment spending of $25 billion rather than $20 billion, and aggregate demand AD_3. As the AD curve shifts to the right from AD_2 to AD_3 in Figure 30.4d, the economy will move along the upsloping AS curve until it comes to an equilibrium at point *a*, where AD_3 intersects AS. At the new equilibrium, the price level has risen to P_3 and the equilibrium level of real GDP has risen to $910 billion, indicating an inflationary GDP gap of $10 billion (= $910 billion − $900 billion). Aggregate demand AD_3 is excessive relative to the economy's full-employment level of real output Q_f = $900 billion. To rein in spending, the Fed will institute a restrictive monetary policy.

The Federal Reserve Board will direct Federal Reserve Banks to undertake some combination of the following actions: (1) sell or initiate reverse repos of government securities to banks and the public in the open market, (2) increase the legal reserve ratio, (3) increase the discount rate, and (4) increase the interest rate that it pays on reserves. Banks then will discover that their reserves are below those required and that the federal funds rate has increased. So they will need to reduce their checkable deposits by refraining from issuing new loans as old loans are paid back. This will shrink the money supply and increase the interest rate. The higher interest rate will discourage investment, lowering aggregate demand and restraining demand-pull inflation.

But the Fed must be careful about just how much to decrease the money supply. The problem is that the inflation ratchet will take effect at the new equilibrium point *a*, such that prices will be inflexible at price level P_3. As a result, the dashed horizontal line to the left of point *a* in Figure 30.4d will become relevant. This means that the Fed

[1]To keep things simple, we assume that the increase in real GDP does not increase the demand for money. In reality, the transactions demand for money would rise, slightly dampening the decline in the interest rate shown in Figure 30.4a.

cannot simply lower the money supply to S_{m2} in Figure 30.4a. If it were to do that, investment demand would fall to \$20 billion in Figure 30.4b, and the AD curve would shift to the left from AD_3 back to AD_2. But because of inflexible prices, the economy's equilibrium would move to point *c*, where AD_2 intersects the horizontal dashed line to the left of point *a*. This would put the economy into a recession, with equilibrium output below the full-employment output level of Q_f = \$900 billion.

What the Fed needs to do to achieve full employment is to move the AD curve back only from AD_3 to AD_4 so that the economy will come to equilibrium at point *b*. This will require a \$10 billion decrease in aggregate demand so that equilibrium output falls from \$910 billion at point *a* to Q_f = \$900 billion at point *b*. The Fed can achieve this shift by setting the supply of money in Figure 30.4a at \$162.5 billion. To see how this works, draw in a vertical money supply curve in Figure 30.4a at \$162.5 billion and label it as S_{m4}. It will be exactly halfway between money supply curves S_{m2} and S_{m3}. Notice that the intersection of S_{m4} with the money demand curve D_m will result in an interest rate of 7 percent. In Figure 30.4b, this interest rate of 7 percent will result in investment spending of \$22.5 billion (halfway between \$20 billion and \$25 billion). Thus, by setting the money supply at \$162.5 billion, the Fed can reduce investment spending by \$2.5 billion, lowering it from the \$25 billion associated with AD_3 down to only \$22.5 billion. This decline in investment spending will initially shift the AD curve only \$2.5 billion to the left of AD_3. But then the multiplier process will work its magic. Since the multiplier is 4 in our model, the AD curve will end up moving by a full \$10 billion (= 4 × \$2.5 billion) to the left, to AD_4. This shift will move the economy to equilibrium *b*, returning output to the full employment level and eliminating the inflationary GDP gap.[2]

Column 2 in Table 30.3 summarizes the cause-effect chain of a tight money policy.

AP QUICK REVIEW 30.7

- ✓ The Fed is engaging in an expansionary monetary policy when it increases the money supply to reduce interest rates and increase investment spending and real GDP, lowering the rate of unemployment.
- ✓ The Fed is engaging in a restrictive monetary policy when it reduces the money supply to increase interest rates and reduce investment spending, lowering the rate of inflation.

[2]Again, we assume for simplicity that the decrease in nominal GDP does not feed back to reduce the demand for money and thus the interest rate. In reality, this would occur, slightly dampening the increase in the interest rate shown in Figure 30.4a.

AP Monetary Policy: Evaluation and Issues

LO30.6 Explain the effectiveness of monetary policy and its shortcomings.

Monetary policy has become the dominant component of U.S. national stabilization policy. It has two key advantages over fiscal policy:

- Speed and flexibility.
- Isolation from political pressure.

Compared with fiscal policy, monetary policy can be quickly altered. Recall that congressional deliberations may delay the application of fiscal policy for months. In contrast, the Fed can buy or sell securities from day to day and thus affect the money supply and interest rates almost immediately.

Also, because members of the Fed's Board of Governors are appointed and serve 14-year terms, they are relatively isolated from lobbying and need not worry about retaining their popularity with voters. Thus, the Board, more readily than Congress, can engage in politically unpopular policies (higher interest rates) that may be necessary for the long-term health of the economy. Moreover, monetary policy is a subtler and more politically neutral measure than fiscal policy. Changes in government spending directly affect the allocation of resources, and changes in taxes can have extensive political ramifications. Because monetary policy works more subtly, it is more politically palatable.

Recent U.S. Monetary Policy

The Fed has been highly active in its use of monetary policy in recent decades.

The 2007–2009 Recession The mortgage default crisis (discussed in Chapter 28) began during the late summer of 2007 and posed a grave threat to the financial system and the economy. In response, the Fed took several actions. In August it lowered the discount rate by half a percentage point. Then, between September 2007 and April 2008, it lowered the target for the federal funds rate from 5.25 percent to 2 percent. And as discussed in Chapter 28, the Fed also took a series of extraordinary actions to prevent the failure of key financial firms.

In October 2008, the Fed first reduced the federal funds target rate to 1.5 percent and then later that same month to 1 percent. In December 2008, the Fed lowered it further to a targeted range of 0 percent to 0.25 percent. That near-zero targeted range was by far the lowest in history. All these monetary actions and lender-of-last-resort functions helped to stabilize the banking sector and keep credit flowing—thereby offsetting at least some of the damage done by the financial crisis.

The decline in the federal funds rate to near zero during the financial and economic crisis dropped the prime interest rate (review Figure 30.4). In December 2007, the prime interest rate stood at 7.3 percent. By January 2009, it had declined to 3.25 percent, where it remained through December 2015.

The Federal Reserve is lauded by most observers for its quick and innovative actions during the financial crisis and severe recession. Nevertheless, some economists contend that the Fed contributed to the financial crisis by holding the federal funds interest rate too low for too long during the recovery from the 2001 recession. These critics say that the artificially low interest rates made mortgage and other loans too inexpensive and therefore contributed to the borrowing frenzy by homeowners and other financial investors. Other economists counter that the low mortgage interest rates resulted from huge inflows of savings from abroad to a wide variety of U.S. financial markets.

After the Great Recession The U.S. economy recovered very slowly from the Great Recession of 2007–2009, especially in terms of employment. The Federal Reserve understood the depth of the economy's problems early on and responded with a series of innovative monetary policy initiatives designed to stimulate GDP and employment growth.

The Fed began by moving toward a **zero interest rate policy,** or **ZIRP,** in December 2008. Under ZIRP, the Fed aimed to keep short-term interest rates near zero to stimulate the economy. The federal funds rate was lowered rapidly, as can be seen in Figure 30.4, and the Fed also acted as a lender of last resort, purchasing securities from banks and other financial institutions in order to provide them with liquidity and the ability to make timely debt payments.

Many of the Fed's lender-of-last-resort securities purchases were from banks. The purchases were so massive that the banking system's excess reserves skyrocketed. This left the Fed in a quandary. It wanted to continue to simulate the economy, but traditional monetary policy was made difficult by the already-low interest rates and the difficulties associated with the zero lower bound problem. The Fed did not want to risk negative interest rates, so reductions in the the federal funds rate (which low but positive) were off the table. Another method had to be found to stimulate the economy.

The Fed's solution was *quantitative easing*, or QE. Under QE, the Fed bought bonds solely with the intention of increasing the quantity of reserves in the banking system. Interest rates remained at the same (low but positive) levels to avoid the zero lower bound problem, but with excess reserves increasing thanks to QE, banks would hopefully lend more and thereby stimulate the economy.

The first round of QE began in March 2009, the second in November 2010, and the third and final round in 2012. They involved securities purchases of, respectively, $1.75 trillion, $600 billion, and $1.61 trillion.

The economy mended slowly, but by the end of 2015, the Fed felt that various economic indicators were signaling that monetary stimulus could end. The unemployment rate, in particular, had fallen back to just 5 percent after reaching 10 percent in 2009. The FOMC decided that the Fed could abandon ZIRP while attempting to raise interest rates back up to normal levels.

The Fed's first step was to raise the IOER rate from 0.25 percent to 0.50 percent in December 2015 while simultaneously raising the target range for the federal funds rate from 0 to 0.25 percent up to 0.25 to 0.50 percent. At the same time, the Fed began reverse repo transactions with nonbanks to push the equilibrium federal funds rate up toward the top end of the 0.25 percent to 0.50 percent target range. By doing so, the Fed could guarantee that the short-term interest rate facing nonbanks would be nearly the same as the 0.50 IOER rate facing banks. In this way, the Fed could ensure that it had control over short-term interest rates throughout the financial sector and not just with banks. That would preserve the Fed's ability to tighten or loosen credit throughout the economy going forward.

Problems and Complications

Despite its recent successes in the United States, monetary policy has certain limitations and faces actual-economy complications.

Lags Recall that fiscal policy is hindered by three delays, or lags—a recognition lag, an administrative lag, and an operational lag. Monetary policy also faces a recognition lag and an operational lag, but because the Fed can decide and implement policy changes within days, it avoids the long administrative lag that hinders fiscal policy.

A recognition lag affects monetary policy because normal monthly variations in economic activity and the price level mean that the Fed may not be able to quickly recognize when the economy is truly starting to recede or when inflation is really starting to rise. Once the Fed acts, an operation lag of 3 to 6 months affects monetary policy because that much time is typically required for interest-rate changes to have their full impacts on investment, aggregate demand, real GDP, and the price level. These two lags complicate the timing of monetary policy.

Cyclical Asymmetry and the Liquidity Trap Monetary policy may be highly effective in slowing expansions and controlling inflation but may be much less reliable in pushing the economy from a severe recession. Economists say that monetary policy may suffer from **cyclical asymmetry.** The metaphor of "pushing on a string" is often invoked to capture this problem. Imagine the Fed standing on the left-hand side of Figure 30.4d, holding one end of a "monetary-policy string." And imagine that the other end of the monetary-policy string is tied to the AD curve. Because the string would go taut if pulled on, monetary policy may be useful in *pulling* aggregate demand to the left. But because the string would go limp if pushed on, monetary policy will be rather ineffective at *pushing* aggregate demand to the right.

The reason for this asymmetry has to do with the asymmetric way in which people may act in response to changes in bank reserves. If pursued vigorously, a restrictive monetary policy can deplete commercial banking reserves to the point where banks are forced to reduce the volume of loans. That means a contraction of the money supply, higher interest rates, and reduced aggregate demand. The Fed can absorb sufficient reserves and eventually achieve its goal.

But the Fed cannot be certain of achieving its goal when it adds reserves to the banking system because of the so-called **liquidity trap,** in which adding more liquidity to banks has little or no additional positive effect on lending, borrowing, investment, or aggregate demand. For example, during the recent recession, the Fed created billions of dollars of excess reserves that drove down the federal funds rate to as low as 0.2 percent. The prime interest rate fell from 7.3 percent (December 2007) to 3.25 percent (March 2009). Nevertheless, lending by banks stalled throughout the first 15 months of the recession and remained weak even after the Fed implemented ZIRP and QE, over the following five years. The banks were fearful that the loans they would make to households, businesses, and other financial institutions would not be paid back. Consequently, they were content to hold reserves at the Federal Reserve Banks.

To switch analogies, an expansionary monetary policy can suffer from a "you can lead a horse to water, but you can't make it drink" problem. The Fed can create excess reserves, but it cannot guarantee that the banks will actually make additional loans and thus promote spending. If commercial banks seek liquidity and are unwilling to lend, the efforts of the Fed will be of little avail. Similarly, households and businesses can frustrate the intentions of the Fed by not borrowing excess reserves being made available as loans. And when the Fed buys securities from the public, people may choose to pay off existing loans with the money received, rather than increase their spending on goods and services.

Furthermore, a severe recession may so undermine business confidence that the investment demand curve shifts to the left and overwhelms the lower interest rates associated with an expansionary monetary policy. That is what happened in the most recent recession. Although the Fed drove the real interest rate down to zero percent, investment spending remained low and the economy remained mired in recession. The recent U.S. experience reminds us that active monetary policy certainly is not a cure-all for the business cycle. Under some circumstances, monetary policy may be like "pushing on a string."

The liquidity trap that occurred during the severe recession was a primary reason why public policy in the United States turned so significantly and forcefully toward fiscal policy in 2009. Recall our discussion of the American Recovery and Redevelopment Act of 2009, which authorized the infusion of $787 billion of new tax cuts and government spending in 2009 and 2010.

AP QUICK REVIEW 30.8

- ✓ The Fed aggressively lowered the federal funds interest rate during the severe recession of 2007–2009.
- ✓ To help stimulate the economy after the Great Recession, the Fed implemented some different and original monetary policy measures, including the zero interest rate policy (ZIRP) and quantitative easing (QE).
- ✓ The main strengths of monetary policy are (a) speed and flexibility and (b) political acceptability. The main challenges with monetary policy are (a) time lags and (b) and the liquidity trap.

The "Big Picture"

Figure 30.5 (Key Graph) brings together the analytical and policy aspects of macroeconomics discussed in this and the eight preceding chapters. This "big picture" shows how the many concepts and principles discussed relate to one another and how they constitute a coherent theory of the price level and real output in a market economy.

Study this diagram and you will see that the levels of output, employment, income, and prices all result from the interaction of aggregate supply and aggregate demand. The items shown in red relate to public policy.

AP KEY GRAPH

FIGURE 30.5 The AD-AS theory of the price level, real output, and stabilization policy. This figure integrates the various components of macroeconomic theory and stabilization policy. Determinants that either constitute public policy or are strongly influenced by public policy are shown in red.

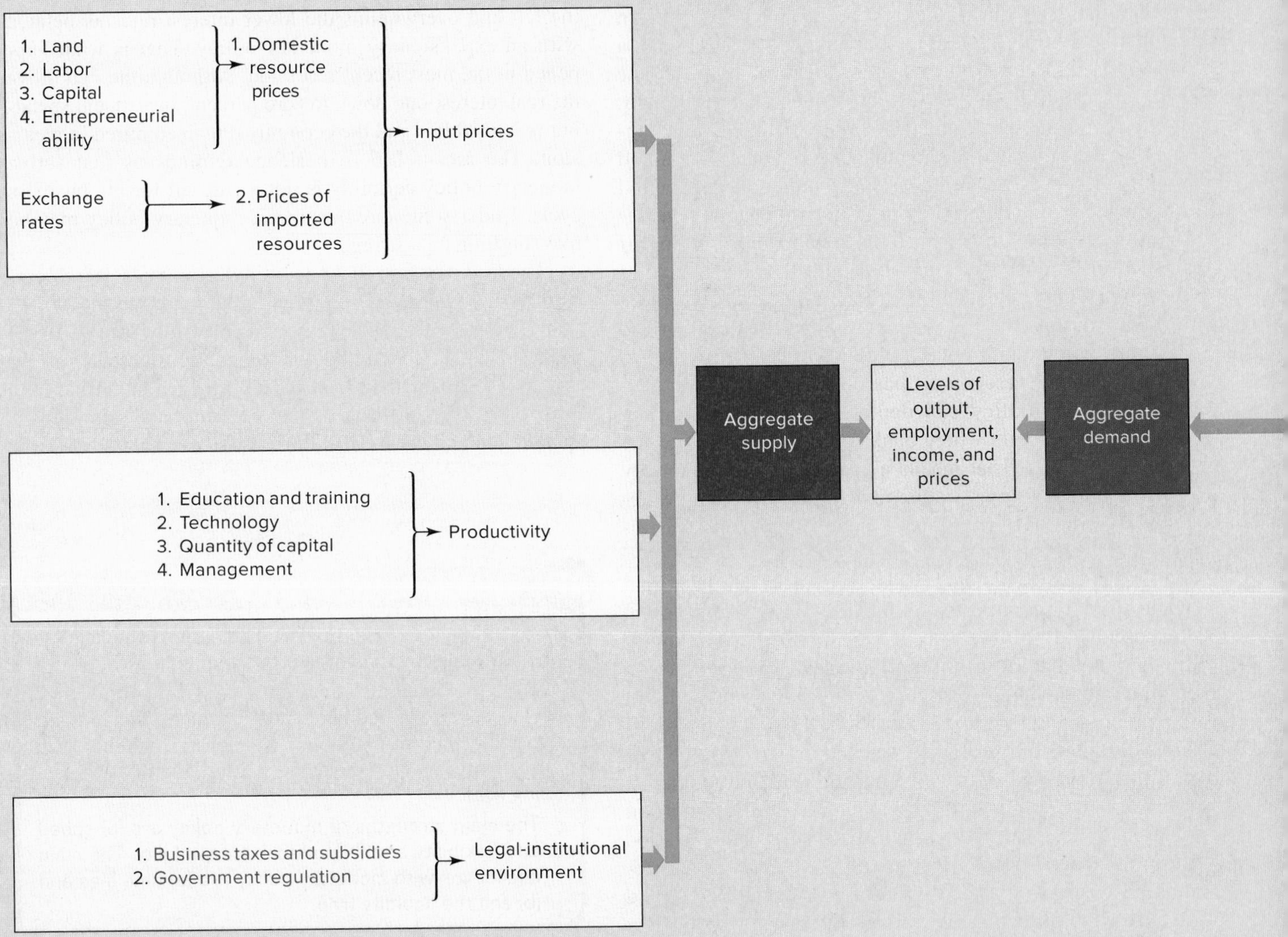

QUICK QUIZ FOR FIGURE 30.5

1. All else equal, an increase in domestic resource availability will:
   - **a.** increase input prices, reduce aggregate supply, and increase real output.
   - **b.** raise labor productivity, reduce interest rates, and lower the international value of the dollar.
   - **c.** increase net exports, increase investment, and reduce aggregate demand.
   - **d.** reduce input prices, increase aggregate supply, and increase real output.

2. All else equal, an expansionary monetary policy during a recession will:
   - **a.** lower the interest rate, increase investment, and reduce net exports.
   - **b.** lower the interest rate, increase investment, and increase aggregate demand.
   - **c.** increase the interest rate, increase investment, and reduce net exports.
   - **d.** reduce productivity, aggregate supply, and real output.

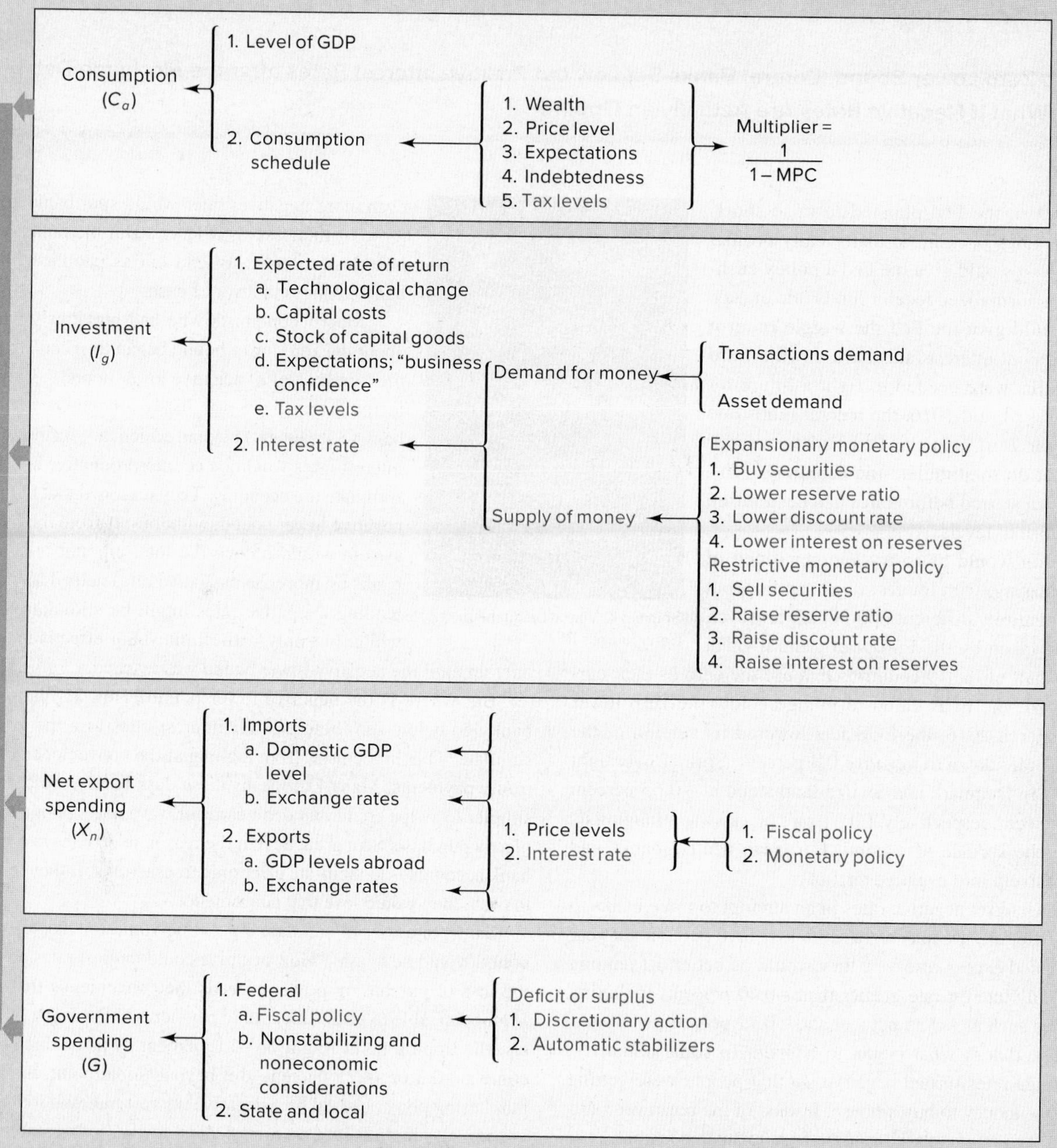

3. A personal income tax cut, combined with a reduction in corporate income and excise taxes, would:

a. increase consumption, investment, aggregate demand, and aggregate supply.

b. reduce productivity, raise input prices, and reduce aggregate supply.

c. increase government spending, reduce net exports, and increase aggregate demand.

d. increase the supply of money, reduce interest rates, increase investment, and expand real output.

4. An appreciation of the dollar would:

a. reduce the price of imported resources, lower input prices, and increase aggregate supply.

b. increase net exports and aggregate demand.

c. increase aggregate supply and aggregate demand.

d. reduce consumption, investment, net export spending, and government spending.

Answers: 1.d; 2. b; 3. a; 4. a

LAST WORD

Less Than Zero

Fearing the Zero Lower Bound, Central Banks Set Low but Positive Interest Rates after the Mortgage Debt Crisis. But What if Negative Rates Are Actually an Option?

As of mid-2016, the Fed planned to raise short-term interest rates back up to historically normal levels. Doing so would give the Fed a policy cushion because a normalized federal funds rate of, say, 5 percent would give the Fed the wiggle room it would need to cut interest rates back down toward zero if stimulus were needed to fight a future recession. But as of mid-2016, the federal funds rate remained near zero, and the Fed had to wonder what it might do to stimulate the economy if another recession started before rates had been raised back up to normal levels.

Source: © Viktor Lyagushkin/Getty Images RF

One option would be to try another round of quantitative easing, with interest rates kept low but positive. An entirely different option had, however, already been taken by the European Central Bank (ECB) on behalf of the 19 countries that use the euro as their currency. In 2014, the ECB dared to plunge below the zero lower bound. By March 2016, the ECB had lowered its version of the federal funds rate down to *negative* 0.4 percent. Similar overnight lending rates in Denmark and Switzerland stood at −0.65 percent and −0.75 percent, respectively. Like a rare black swan plunging its head below the surface of a pond, European central banks had plunged decisively into negative territory.

The ECB had set negative rates in an attempt to force banks to lend more. After all, if banks were set to lose 0.40 percent per year on any unloaned excess reserves, they would be better off lending them out at any interest rate greater than −0.40 percent, including negative rates such as −0.35 percent and −0.12 percent.

Strangely, that is what began to happen. In some countries, home mortgage rates turned negative, so that people were getting paid to borrow money to buy a house. Instead of the borrower mailing in a mortgage payment each month, the bank mailed the borrower a check for the negative interest they were earning by borrowing.

Checking and savings account rates also turned negative. As they did, the incentives generated by negative interest rates began to affect behavior. People began to withdraw money from banks, turning electronic bank balances into physical cash. They did so because they understood opportunity cost. Why get a negative rate on a bank balance when you could hold cash and lose nothing?

With people withdrawing money in the face of negative rates, the various European central banks were in a pickle. Lower (i.e., even more negative) rates would spur banks to lend more of their excess reserves. But the banks would have less reserves to lend out as people withdrew bank balances in favor of cash.

Macroeconomists who had previously worried about the zero lower bound began to speculate about the existence of a "negative lower bound." They conjectured that there was likely a negative rate (perhaps −3.0 percent) beyond which any further cuts in interest rates would be counterproductive and fail to stimulate the economy. They reasoned that below the negative lower bound, withdrawals from the banking system would reduce the total amount lent out by banks by more than negative rates helped to increase lending. Negative rates might be stimulatory for a while, but only with diminishing effectiveness and only up until the negative lower bound was reached.

But where is the negative lower bound? How far can central banks go below zero before lower interest rates lose the power to simulate? One hint comes from looking at the convenience of electronic payments. Many Europeans these days barely use cash. It is simpler to swipe credit and debit cards or wave one's phone to complete a purchase. So a great deal of the reason people leave money in bank accounts is to facilitate electronic transactions. If they switched to cash, they would lose that convenience.

Thus, one way to estimate a possible value for the zero lower bound would be to ask: "How negative could interest rates go before the loss of purchasing power exceeds the convenience that comes from being able to utilize electronic payments?" For some individuals, the tipping point might be −1.0 percent. For others, it might come at −2.5 or −4.25 percent. But beyond some point, the loss of purchasing power caused by a negative interest rate will loom larger in people's minds as interest rates decline further into negative territory. The lower the rate, the less people will want to hold electronic bank balances. The lower the rate, the more people will convert electronic bank balances into physical cash. The lower the rate, the smaller excess reserves will be.

The Fed will have to consider those trade-offs if the United States enters a recession before the Fed has had a chance to raise short-term interest rates back up to historical levels. If stimulus proves necessary, will the Fed stick with quantitative easing—or will it dare to follow the ECB into negative territory?

SUMMARY

LO30.1 Discuss how the equilibrium interest rate is determined in the market for money.

The total demand for money consists of the transactions demand for money plus the asset demand for money. The amount of money demanded for transactions varies directly with the nominal GDP; the amount of money demanded as an asset varies inversely with the interest rate. The market for money combines the total demand for money with the money supply to determine equilibrium interest rates.

Interest rates and bond prices are inversely related.

LO30.2 Describe the balance sheet of the Federal Reserve and the meaning of its major items.

The consolidated balance sheet of the Federal Reserve System lists the collective assets and liabilities of the 12 Federal Reserve banks. The assets consist largely of Treasury notes, Treasury bills, and Treasury bonds. The major liabilities are reserves of commercial banks, Treasury deposits, and Federal Reserve notes outstanding. The balance sheet is useful in understanding monetary policy because open-market operations increase or decrease the Fed's assets and liabilities.

LO30.3 List and explain the goals and tools of monetary policy.

The goal of monetary policy is to help the economy achieve price stability, full employment, and economic growth.

The four main instruments of monetary policy are (*a*) open-market operations, (*b*) the reserve ratio, (*c*) the discount rate, and (*d*) interest on reserves.

LO30.4 Describe the federal funds rate and how the Fed directly influences it.

The federal funds rate is the interest rate that banks charge one another for overnight loans of excess reserves. The prime interest rate is the benchmark rate that banks use as a reference rate for a wide range of interest rates on short-term loans to businesses and individuals.

The Fed adjusts the federal funds rate to a level deemed appropriate for economic conditions. Before the mortgage debt crisis, the Fed would engage in expansionary or restrictive monetary policy by announcing a new target for the federal funds rate and then using open-market operations to buy or sell government bonds in whatever amounts were necessary to achieve the target rate.

This policy no longer worked after the mortgage debt crisis because the banking system had ended up with a massive surplus of excess reserves. That massive surplus forced the federal funds rate to nearly zero, so that the Fed could no longer pursue its traditional stimulatory strategy of lowering interests rates to boost bank lending. That strategy was now problematic due to the zero lower bound problem and the fact that negative interest rates might reduce rather than increase the total volume of bank lending.

With the Fed unwilling to lower interest rates due to the zero lower bound problem, the Fed left the federal funds rate alone and instead concentrated on a policy of quantitative easing (QE) in which it purchased bonds not to lower interest rates but to increase reserves in the banking system and thereby spur lending and aggregate demand (it being hoped that additional reserves would lead to additional lending).

By late 2015, the Fed felt that the economy was recovering strongly enough to try to begin raising interest rates back up to their pre-crisis levels. The method chosen was to raise the interest rate on excess reserves (IOER) while simultaneously using reverse repo transactions to raise the federal funds rate. While this policy was being pursued in a gradual fashion starting in 2015 as part of the Fed's attempt to slowly normalize interest rates, a more rapid version could be used to reduce lending and thereby engage in a restrictive monetary policy if the economy were to overheat at a later date.

LO30.5 Identify the mechanisms by which monetary policy affects GDP and the price level.

Monetary policy affects the economy through a complex cause-effect chain: (a) policy decisions affect commercial bank reserves; (*b*) changes in reserves affect the money supply; (*c*) changes in the money supply alter the interest rate; (*d*) changes in the interest rate affect investment; (*e*) changes in investment affect aggregate demand; (*f*) changes in aggregate demand affect the equilibrium real GDP and the price level. Table 30.3 draws together all the basic ideas relevant to the use of monetary policy.

LO30.6 Explain the effectiveness of monetary policy and its shortcomings.

The advantages of monetary policy include its flexibility and political acceptability. In recent years, the Fed has used monetary policy to help stabilize the banking sector in the wake of the mortgage debt crisis and to promote recovery from the severe recession of 2007–2009. Today, nearly all economists view monetary policy as a significant stabilization tool.

Monetary policy has two major limitations and potential problems: (*a*) recognition and operation lags complicate the timing of monetary policy; (*b*) in a severe recession, the reluctance of banks to lend excess reserves and firms to borrow money to spend on capital goods may contribute to a liquidity trap that limits the effectiveness of an expansionary monetary policy.

TERMS AND CONCEPTS

monetary policy
interest
transactions demand for money
asset demand for money
total demand for money
open-market operations
collateral
repos
reverse repos

reserve ratio	prime interest rate	zero interest rate policy (ZIRP)
discount rate	zero lower bound problem	cyclical asymmetry
interest on excess reserves (IOER)	quantitative easing (QE)	liquidity trap
federal funds rate	restrictive monetary policy	
expansionary monetary policy	Taylor rule	

The following and additional problems can be found in connect

DISCUSSION QUESTIONS

1. What is the basic determinant of (*a*) the transactions demand and (*b*) the asset demand for money? Explain how these two demands can be combined graphically to determine total money demand. How is the equilibrium interest rate in the money market determined? Use a graph to show the effect of an increase in the total demand for money on the equilibrium interest rate (no change in money supply). Use your general knowledge of equilibrium prices to explain why the previous interest rate is no longer sustainable. LO30.1
2. What is the basic objective of monetary policy? What are the major strengths of monetary policy? Why is monetary policy easier to conduct than fiscal policy ? LO30.3
3. Distinguish between the federal funds rate and the prime interest rate. Why is one higher than the other? Why do changes in the two rates closely track one another? LO30.4
4. Distinguish between how the Fed would have to undertake restrictive monetary policy today versus before the mortgage-debt crisis. What actions would it need to take in each case? LO30.4
5. Suppose that you are a member of the Board of Governors of the Federal Reserve System. The post-2008 economy is experiencing a sharp rise in the inflation rate. What change in the federal funds rate would you recommend? How would your recommended change get accomplished? What impact would the actions have on the lending ability of the banking system, the real interest rate, investment spending, aggregate demand, and inflation? LO30.5
6. Explain the links between changes in the nation's money supply, the interest rate, investment spending, aggregate demand, real GDP, and the price level. LO30.5
7. What do economists mean when they say that monetary policy can exhibit cyclical asymmetry? How does the idea of a liquidity trap relate to cyclical asymmetry? Why is this possibility of a liquidity trap significant to policymakers? LO30.6
8. **LAST WORD** By what chain of causation does the ECB think negative interest rates will stimulate the economy? If the Fed manages to raise interest rates up to historical levels before the next recession, will it have to consider negative interest rates as a first course of action in terms of stimulating the economy? Explain.

AP REVIEW QUESTIONS

1. Other things equal, if there is an increase in nominal GDP: LO30.1
   - **a.** The demand for money will decrease.
   - **b.** The interest rate will rise and bond prices fall.
   - **c.** The interest rate will fall and bond prices rise.
   - **d.** Consumption spending will fall.
   - **e.** Tax revenues should fall.
2. Which of the following will increase commercial bank reserves? LO30.3
   - **a.** The purchase of government bonds in the open market by the Fed.
   - **b.** A increase in the required reserve ratio.
   - **c.** An increase in the discount rate.
   - **d.** The sale of government bonds in the open market by the Fed.
   - **e.** An increase in the interest rate on banks' reserves held by the Fed.
3. Use commercial bank and Federal Reserve Bank balance sheets to demonstrate the effect of each of the following transactions on commercial bank reserves: LO30.3
   - **a.** Federal Reserve Banks purchase securities from banks.
   - **b.** Commercial banks borrow from Federal Reserve Banks at the discount rate.
   - **c.** The Fed reduces the reserve ratio.
   - **d.** Commercial banks increase their reserves held by the Fed, after the Fed increases the interest rate that it pays on reserves.
4. A bank currently has $100,000 in checkable deposits and $15,000 in actual reserves. If the reserve ratio is 20 percent, the bank has ________ in money-creating potential. If the reserve ratio is 14 percent, the bank has ________ in money-creating potential. LO30.3
   - **a.** $20,000; $14,000.
   - **b.** $3,000; $2,100.
   - **c.** –$5,000; $1,000.
   - **d.** –$5,000; –$1,000.
   - **e.** $5,000; $1,000.
5. When a commercial bank borrows from a Federal Reserve Bank: LO30.3
   - **a.** The supply of money automatically increases.
   - **b.** It indicates that the commercial bank is unsound financially.
   - **c.** The commercial bank's lending ability is increased.
   - **d.** The commercial bank's reserves are reduced.
   - **e.** The size of the money multiplier increases.
6. Explain how each of the following Fed actions will impact bank lending and the money supply. LO30.3
   - **a.** The Fed raises the discount rate from 5 percent to 6 percent.
   - **b.** The Fed raises the reserve ratio from 10 percent to 11 percent.
   - **c.** The Fed buys $400 million worth of Treasury bonds from commercial banks.
   - **d.** The Fed lowers the interest rate on bank reserves at the Fed from 4 percent to 2 percent.

7. Which of the following will likely accompany an expansionary money policy? LO30.3
   a. A higher prime interest rate.
   b. A lower Federal funds rate.
   c. A higher discount rate.
   d. Higher income tax rates.
   e. A decrease in the money supply.
8. When the required reserve ratio is increased, the excess reserves of member banks are: LO30.3
   a. Reduced, but the demand-deposit multiplier is unaffected.
   b. Reduced and the demand deposit multiplier is increased.
   c. Increased and the demand deposit multiplier is increased.
   d. Reduced and the demand deposit multiplier is reduced.
   e. Unaffected since excess reserves are not dependent on the required reserve ratio.
9. True or False: A liquidity trap occurs when expansionary monetary policy fails to work because an increase in bank reserves by the Fed does not lead to an increase in bank lending. LO30.6
10. Using a simple graph of the money market, show the effect of each of the following on the equilibrium rate of interest and on the quantity of money. [Treat each of these as independent questions.] LO30.1, LO30.3
    a. A decrease in nominal income.
    b. A decrease in the riskiness of stocks and other equity-type assets.
    c. An open-market sale of government bonds by the Federal Reserve.
    d. An increase in the real GDP, with no change in the price level.
    e. A decrease in the discount rate.

PROBLEMS

1. Assume that the following data characterize the hypothetical economy of Trance: money supply = \$200 billion; quantity of money demanded for transactions = \$150 billion; quantity of money demanded as an asset = \$10 billion at 12 percent interest, increasing by \$10 billion for each 2-percentage-point fall in the interest rate. LO30.1
   a. What is the equilibrium interest rate in Trance?
   b. At the equilibrium interest rate, what are the quantity of money supplied, the total quantity of money demanded, the amount of money demanded for transactions, and the amount of money demanded as an asset in Trance?
2. Suppose a bond with no expiration date has a face value of \$10,000 and annually pays a fixed amount of interest of \$800. In the table provided below, calculate and enter either the interest rate that the bond would yield to a bond buyer at each of the bond prices listed or the bond price at each of the interest yields shown. What generalization can be drawn from the completed table? LO30.1

Bond Price	Interest Yield, %
\$ 8,000	______
______	8.9
\$10,000	______
\$11,000	______
______	6.2

3. In the tables that follow you will find consolidated balance sheets for the commercial banking system and the 12 Federal Reserve Banks. Use columns 1 through 3 to indicate how the balance sheets would read after each of transactions a to c is completed. Do not cumulate your answers; that is, analyze each transaction separately, starting in each case from the numbers provided. All accounts are in billions of dollars. LO30.3
   a. A decline in the discount rate prompts commercial banks to borrow an additional \$1 billion from the Federal Reserve Banks. Show the new balance-sheet numbers in column 1 of each table.
   b. The Federal Reserve Banks sell \$3 billion in securities to members of the public, who pay for the bonds with checks. Show the new balance-sheet numbers in column 2 of each table.
   c. The Federal Reserve Banks buy \$2 billion of securities from commercial banks. Show the new balance-sheet numbers in column 3 of each table.
   d. Now review each of the previous three transactions, asking yourself these three questions: (1) What change, if any, took place in the money supply as a direct and immediate result of each transaction? (2) What increase or decrease in the commercial banks' reserves took place in each transaction? (3) Assuming a reserve ratio of 20 percent, what change in the money-creating potential of the commercial banking system occurred as a result of each transaction?

		Consolidated Balance Sheet: All Commercial Banks		
		(1)	(2)	(3)
Assets:				
Reserves	\$33	______	______	______
Securities	60	______	______	______
Loans	60	______	______	______
Liabilities and net worth:				
Checkable deposits	\$150	______	______	______
Loans from the Federal Reserve Banks	3	______	______	______

		Consolidated Balance Sheet: The 12 Federal Reserve Banks		
		(1)	(2)	(3)
Assets:				
Securities	$60	______	______	______
Loans to commercial banks	3	______	______	______
Liabilities and net worth:				
Reserves of commercial banks	$33			
Treasury deposits	3	______	______	______
Federal Reserve Notes	27	______	______	______

4. Refer to Table 30.2 and assume that the Fed's reserve ratio is 10 percent and the economy is in a severe recession. Also suppose that the commercial banks are hoarding all excess reserves (not lending them out) because of their fear of loan defaults. Finally, suppose that the Fed is highly concerned that the banks will suddenly lend out these excess reserves and possibly contribute to inflation once the economy begins to recover and confidence is restored. By how many percentage points would the Fed need to increase the reserve ratio to eliminate one-third of the excess reserves? What would be the size of the monetary multiplier before and after the change in the reserve ratio? By how much would the lending potential of the banks decline as a result of the increase in the reserve ratio? **LO30.3**
5. Suppose that the target range for the federal funds rate is 1.5 to 2.0 percent but that the equilibrium federal funds rate is currently 1.70 percent. Assume that the equilibrium federal funds rate falls (rises) by 1 percent for each $120 billion in repo (reverse repo) bond transactions the Fed undertakes. If the Fed wishes to raise the equilibrium federal funds rate up to the top end of the target range, will it initiate repos or reverse repos of bonds to nonbank financial firms? How much will it have to repo or reverse repo? **LO30.4**
6. Suppose that inflation is 2 percent, the federal funds rate is 4 percent, and real GDP falls 2 percent below potential GDP. According to the Taylor rule, in what direction and by how much should the Fed change the real federal funds rate? **LO30.4**
7. Refer to the table for Moola below to answer the following questions. What is the equilibrium interest rate in Moola? What is the level of investment at the equilibrium interest rate? Is there either a recessionary output gap (negative GDP gap) or an inflationary output gap (positive GDP gap) at the equilibrium interest rate and, if either, what is the amount? Given money demand, by how much would the Moola central bank need to change the money supply to close the output gap? What is the expenditure multiplier in Moola? **LO30.5**

Money Supply	Money Demand	Interest Rate	Investment at Interest (Rate Shown)	Potential Real GDP	Actual Real GDP at Interest (Rate Shown)
$500	$800	2%	$50	$350	$390
500	700	3	40	350	370
500	600	4	30	350	350
500	500	5	20	350	330
500	400	6	10	350	310

AP The Federal Reserve's Control over Nominal and Real Interest Rates

Investment and aggregate demand are affected by the real interest rate, not the nominal interest rate. So when the Federal Reserve wishes to alter monetary policy, its ultimate goal is to change the real interest rate and thereby affect the amount of investment and aggregate demand in the economy.

It is the case, though, that the Federal Reserve cannot target the real interest rate directly. That's because each of the interest rates that the Fed targets is nominal. That is true for the Federal Funds rate, the discount rate, and the interest rate paid on reserves. Each is a nominal interest rate. In addition, the various government and GSE bonds that the Fed purchases when engaging in quantitative easing also has its own nominal interest rate. So while the Fed's ultimate goal is to change the real interest rate, it has to do so by manipulating nominal interest rates.

The Fisher Equation

The Fed is able to affect the real interest rate via the various nominal interest rates because there is a simple equation that relates nominal and real interest rates. As we first explained in Chapter 23:

Nominal interest rate = real interest rate + inflation premium (the expected rate of inflation)

This equation is sometimes referred to as the **Fisher equation** in honor of Irving Fisher, the Yale economics professor who first described it in the early 20th century. The equation posits that in the various markets where demand and supply set a nominal interest rate, market participants will set it so that it is equal to the real interest rate plus an inflation premium that reflects what market participants believe the future inflation rate will be. The real interest rate compensates lenders for giving up the use of their money for the length of the loan. The inflation premium compensates lenders for the anticipated erosion in the purchasing power of money that will occur over the length of the loan if there is inflation and a rising price level.

Two Possibilities for Adjusting Real Interest Rates

Because the nominal interest rate is the sum of the real interest rate and the inflation premium, the Fed can use the Fisher equation to target the real interest rate in two ways. To see them, rearrange the Fisher equation so that it is solved for the real interest rate:

Real interest rate = nominal interest rate − inflation premium (the expected rate of inflation)

This version of the Fisher equation tells us that if the Fed wants to achieve a particular value for the real interest rate, it has to change either the nominal interest rate or the inflation premium or both. One or the other or both have to be manipulated until their difference equals the desired real interest rate.

Targeting the Inflation Premium It is the case, however, that the Fed and other central banks have not found any surefire methods for influencing the inflation premium. Expected inflation is in large measure beyond the control of policy makers. It is for all intents and purposes a number that they cannot manipulate and which they must take as a given.

Targeting the Nominal Interest Rate With expected inflation beyond the reach of policy makers, the only remaining way for the Fed to adjust the real interest rate is by manipulating the nominal interest rate. To do that, the Fed will utilize the Fisher equation to determine the nominal interest rate that it should target.

Determining the Nominal Interest Rate Target To see what the Fed has to do in a specific case, look back at the first version of the Fisher equation, the one that has the nominal interest rate on the left-hand side. If the Fed wants to achieve a 1 percent real interest rate when expected inflation is running at 2 percent, that first version of the Fisher equation tells us that the Fed must take whatever policy actions are necessary to get the nominal interest rate to be 3 percent (= 1 percent real interest rate + 2 percent expected rate of inflation).

In a similar fashion, imagine that expected inflation is 0 percent and the Fed wants a real interest rate of 2 percent. In that case, the Fed would have to adjust the nominal interest rate to 2 percent (= 2 percent real interest rate + 0 percent expected rate of inflation).

Try another scenario for yourself. Suppose that expected inflation is −2 percent (there is a deflation) and the Fed wants to set a real interest rate of 3 percent. What will the nominal rate have to be if the Fed wants to achieve that real interest rate?

Adjusting the Money Supply to Achieve the Nominal Interest Rate Target The Fed's manipulation of the nominal interest rate in order to achieve a particular real interest rate can be seen graphically in Figures 1(c) and 2. In Figure 1(c), the Fed can adjust the equilibrium nominal interest rate by shifting the supply of money to the left or the right. In this way, the Fed can achieve whatever nominal interest rate is needed in order to get to whatever real interest rate the Fed wishes to set.

FIGURE 1

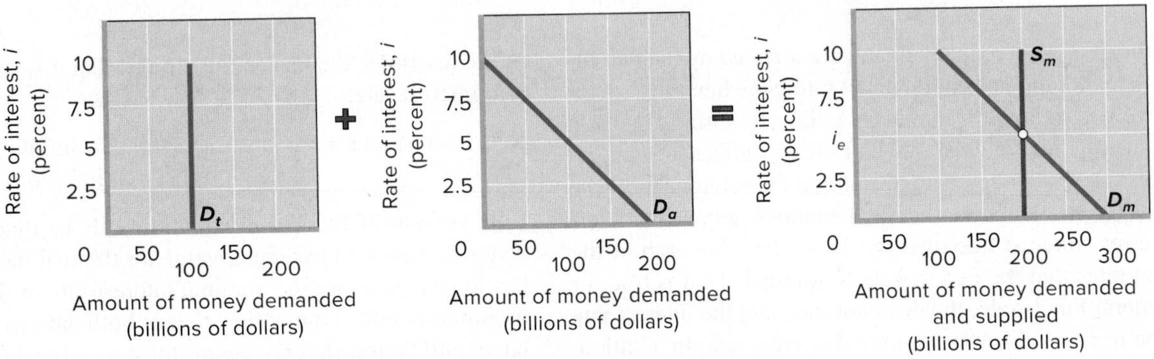

(a) Transactions demand for money, D_t

(b) Asset demand for money, D_a

(c) Total demand for money, $D_m = D_t + D_a$, and supply of money, S_m

FIGURE 2

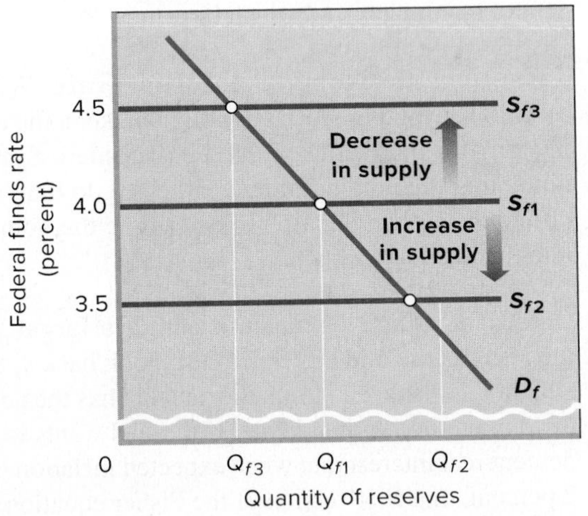

A specific instance of the Fed adjusting a nominal interest rate can be seen in Figure 2. There, the Fed uses open market operations to adjust the supply of bank reserves that are made available in the federal funds market. By doing so, the Fed can achieve its desired value for the (nominal) federal funds rate.

Next, consider Figure 3, which explains how Fed policy actions lead to changes in investment and AD. In Figure 3(a), we are implicitly assuming (for simplicity) that expected inflation equals zero. With expected inflation equal to zero, we know from the Fisher equation that the real interest rate will always equal the nominal interest rate. Thus, in Figure 3(a), any change in the money supply engineered by the Fed can be thought of as directly affecting the real interest rate. Those changes in the real interest rate then go on to affect the quantity of investment and AD in Figures 3(b) and 3(c), respectively.

FIGURE 3

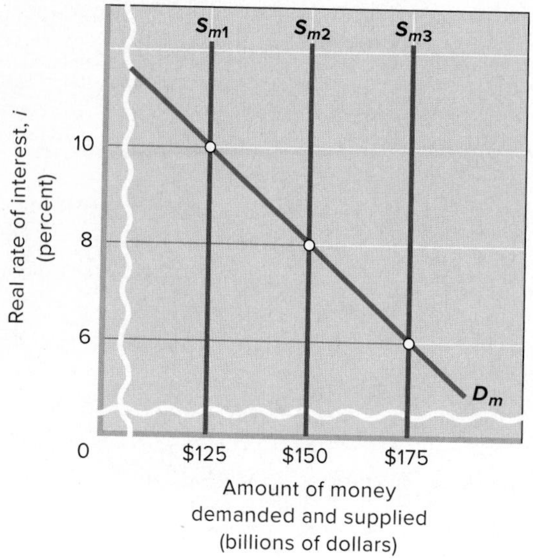

(a)
The market for money

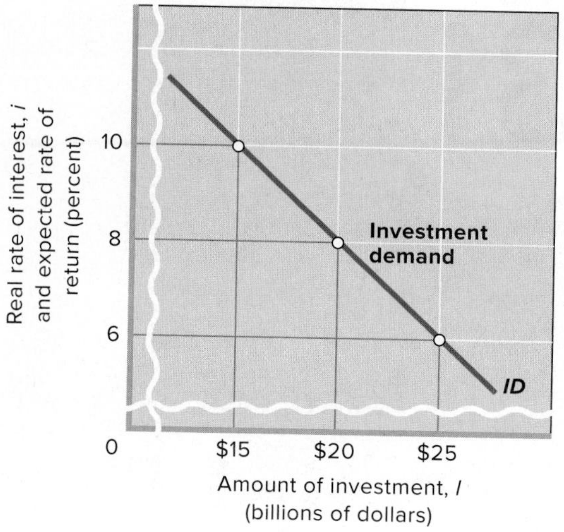

(b)
Investment demand

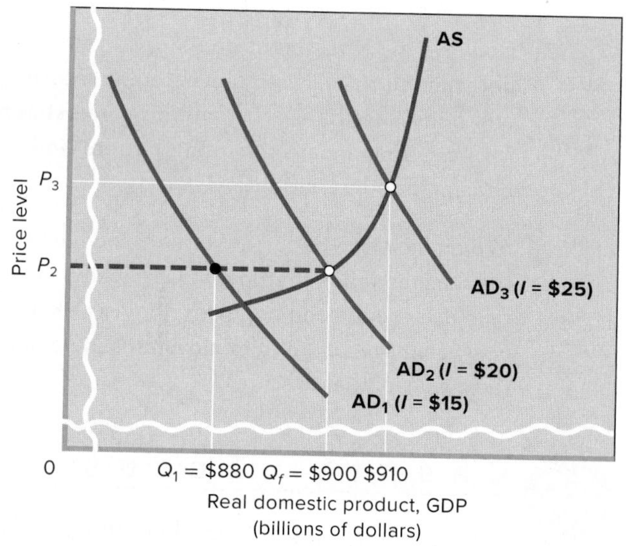

(c)
Equilibrium real GDP and the price level

In nearly all real-economy situations, however, expected inflation is not zero. As a result, the Fed can't think of its expansionary or contractionary policy actions as directly affecting the real interest rate. Whenever the expected rate of inflation deviates from zero, the Fed must use the Fisher equation to adjust the nominal interest rate as necessary until it equals the desired real interest rate plus the expected rate of inflation.

Difficulties Estimating Expected Inflation

There is one additional complication. It is not easy to know precisely what people expect future inflation to be. The Fed has to rely on estimates. To the extent that those estimates are incorrect, the nominal interest rate that the Fed sets will be either higher or lower than it should be in order to achieve the desired real interest rate.

In order to minimize this problem as much as possible, economists at the Federal Reserve spend a great deal of time attempting to come up with the best possible estimates of expected inflation: they monitor polling data on inflation expectations; they closely examine the prices of assets like gold whose values have historically reflected inflation expectations; and they also keep track of currency exchange rates because the currencies of countries with higher rates of inflation are believed to be likely to fall in value relative to the currencies of countries with lower rates of inflation.

31 Chapter

Financial Economics

Learning Objectives

LO31.1 Define *financial economics* and distinguish between economic investment and financial investment.

LO31.2 Explain the time value of money and how compound interest can be used to calculate the present value of any future amount of money.

LO31.3 Identify and distinguish among the most common financial investments: stocks, bonds, and mutual funds.

LO31.4 Relate how percentage rates of return provide a common framework for comparing assets and explain why asset prices and rates of return are inversely related.

LO31.5 Define and utilize the concept of arbitrage.

LO31.6 Describe how the word *risk* is used in financial economics and explain the difference between diversifiable and nondiversifiable risk.

LO31.7 Convey why investment decisions are determined primarily by investment returns and nondiversifiable risk and how investment returns compensate for being patient and for bearing nondiversifiable risk.

LO31.8 Explain how the Security Market Line illustrates the compensation that investors receive for time preference and nondiversifiable risk and why arbitrage will tend to move all assets onto the Security Market Line.

AP Chapter Focus

In this chapter you will learn about the time value of money and about financial assets. Financial economics studies investor preferences and how they affect the trading and pricing of financial assets like stocks, bonds, and real estate. The two most important investor preferences are a desire for high rates of return and a dislike of risk and uncertainty. This chapter will explain how these preferences interact to produce a strong positive relationship between risk and return: the riskier an investment, the higher its rate of return. This positive relationship compensates investors for bearing risk. And it is enforced by a powerful set of buying and selling pressures known as arbitrage, which ensures consistency across investments so that assets with identical levels of risk generate identical rates of return. As we will demonstrate, this consistency makes it extremely difficult for anyone to "beat the market" by finding a set of investments that can generate high rates of return at low levels of risk. Instead, investors are stuck with a trade-off: If they want higher rates of return, they must accept higher levels of risk. On average, higher risk results in higher returns. But it can also result in large losses, as it did for many investors who held risky assets during the financial crisis of 2007–2008.

AP Financial Investment

LO31.1 Define *financial economics* and distinguish between economic investment and financial investment.

Financial economics focuses its attention on the investments that individuals and firms make in the wide variety of assets available to them in our modern economy. But before proceeding, it is important for you to recall the difference between economic investment and financial investment.

Economic investment refers either to paying for *new* additions to the capital stock or *new* replacements for capital stock that has worn out. Thus, *new* factories, houses, retail stores, construction equipment, and wireless networks are all good examples of economic investments. And so are purchases of office computers to replace computers that have become obsolete as well as purchases of new commercial airplanes to replace planes that have served out their useful lives.

In contrast, financial investment is a far broader, much more inclusive concept. It includes economic investment and a whole lot more. **Financial investment** refers to either buying an asset or building an asset in the expectation of financial gain. It does not distinguish between *new* assets and *old* assets. Purchasing an old house or an old factory is just as much a financial investment as purchasing a new house or a new factory. For financial investment, it does not matter if the purchase of an asset adds to the capital stock, replaces the capital stock, or does neither. Investing in old comic books is just as much a financial investment as building a new refinery. Finally, unlike economic investment, financial investment can involve either *financial assets* (such as stocks, bonds, and futures contracts) or *real assets* (such as land, factories, and retail stores).

When bankers, entrepreneurs, corporate executives, retirement planners, and ordinary people use the word *investment,* they almost always mean financial investment. In fact, the ordinary meaning of the word *investment* is financial investment. So for this chapter, we will use the word *investment* in its ordinary sense of "financial investment" rather than in the far narrower sense of "economic investment," which is used throughout the rest of this book.

AP Present Value

LO31.2 Explain the time value of money and how compound interest can be used to calculate the present value of any future amount of money.

Money has "time value" because current dollars can be converted into a larger amount of future dollars through compound interest. The *time-value of money* is the idea that a specific amount of money is more valuable to a person the sooner it is received, and a person will need to be compensated for waiting to obtain it later. The time-value of money can also be thought of as the opportunity cost of receiving a sum of money later rather than earlier.

The time-value of money underlies one of the most fundamental ideas in financial economics: **present value,** which is the present-day value, or worth, of returns or costs that are expected to arrive in the future. The ability to calculate present values is especially useful when investors wish to determine the proper current price to pay for an asset. In fact, the proper current price for any risk-free investment *is* the present value of its expected future returns. And while some adjustments have to be made when determining the proper price of a risky investment, the process is entirely based on the logic of present value. So we begin our study of finance by explaining present value and how it can be used to price risk-free assets. Once that is accomplished, we will turn our attention to risk and how the financial markets determine the prices of risky assets by taking into account investor preferences regarding the trade-off between potential return and potential risk.

Compound Interest

The best way to understand present value is by first understanding compound interest. **Compound interest** describes how quickly an investment increases in value when interest is paid, or compounded, not only on the original amount invested but also on all interest payments that have been previously made.

As an example of compound interest in action, consider Table 31.1, which shows the amount of money that \$100 invested today becomes if it increases, or compounds, at an 8 percent annual interest rate, *i*, for various numbers of years.

AP TABLE 31.1 Compounding: $100 at 8 Percent Interest

(1) Years of Compounding	(2) Compounding Computation	(3) Value at Year's End
1	$100 (1.08)	$108.00
2	100 $(1.08)^2$	116.64
3	100 $(1.08)^3$	125.97
4	100 $(1.08)^4$	136.05
5	100 $(1.08)^5$	146.93
17	100 $(1.08)^{17}$	370.00

To simplify, let's express the 8 percent annual interest rate as a decimal so that it becomes $i = 0.08$. The key to understanding compound interest is to realize that 1 year's worth of growth at interest rate i will always result in $(1 + i)$ times as much money at the end of a year as there was at the beginning of the year. Consequently, if the first year begins with $100 and if $i = 0.08$, then $(1 + 0.08)$ or 1.08 times as much money—$108—will be available at the end of the year. We show the computation for the first year in column 2 of Table 31.1 and display the $108 outcome in column 3. The same logic would also apply with other initial amounts. If a year begins with $500, there will be 1.08 times more money after 1 year, or $540. Algebraically, let X_0 denote the amount of money at the start of the first year and X_1 the amount after 1 year's worth of growth. Then we see that any given number of dollars X_0 at the start of the first year grows into $X_1 = (1 + i)X_0$ dollars after one year's worth of growth.

Next, consider what happens if the initial investment of $100 that grew into $108 after 1 year continues to grow at 8 percent interest for a second year. The $108 available at the beginning of the second year will grow into an amount of money that is 1.08 times larger by the end of the second year. That amount, as shown in Table 31.1, is $116.64. Notice that the computation in the table is made by multiplying the initial $100 by $(1.08)^2$. That is because the original $100 is compounded by 1.08 into $108 and then the $108 is again compounded by 1.08. More generally, since the second year begins with $(1 + i)X_0$ dollars, it will grow to $(1 + i)(1 + i)X_0 = (1 + i)^2X_0$ dollars by the end of the second year.

Similar reasoning shows that the amount of money at the end of 3 years has to be $(1 + i)^3X_0$ since the amount of money at the beginning of the third year, $(1 + i)^2X_0$, gets multiplied by $(1 + i)$ to convert it into the amount of money at the end of the third year. In terms of Table 31.1, that amount is $125.97, which is $(1.08)^3$\$100.

As you can see, we now have a fixed pattern. The $100 that is invested at the beginning of the first year becomes $(1 + i)$\$100 after 1 year, $(1 + i)^2$\$100 after 2 years, $(1 + i)^3$\$100 after 3 years, and so on. It therefore is clear that the amount of money after t years will be $(1 + i)^t$\$100. This pattern always holds true, regardless of the size of the initial investment.

Thus, investors know that if X_0 dollars is invested today and earns compound interest at the rate i, it will grow into exactly $(1 + i)^tX_0$ dollars after t years. Economists express that fact with the following formula:

$$X_t = (1 + i)^tX_0 \qquad (1)$$

Equation 1 captures the idea that if investors have the opportunity to invest X_0 dollars today at interest rate i, then they have the ability to transform X_0 dollars today into $(1 + i)^tX_0$ dollars in t years.

But notice that the logic of the equality also works in reverse, so that it can also be thought of as showing that $(1 + i)^tX_0$ dollars in t years can be transformed into X_0 dollars today. That may seem very odd, but it is exactly what happens when people take out loans. For instance, consider a situation where an investor named Roberto takes out a loan for $100 dollars today, a loan that will accumulate interest at 8 percent per year for 5 years. Under such an arrangement, the amount Roberto owes will grow with compound interest into $(1.08)^5$\$100 = \$146.93 dollars in 5 years. This means that Roberto can convert $146.93 dollars in 5 years (the amount required to pay off the loan) into $100 dollars today (the amount he borrows).

Consequently, the compound interest formula given in equation 1 defines not only the rate at which present amounts of money can be converted to future amounts of money but also the rate at which future amounts of money can be converted into present amounts of money.

The Present Value Model

The present value model simply rearranges equation 1 to make it easier to transform future amounts of money into present amounts of money. To derive the formula used to calculate the present value of a future amount of money, we divide both sides of equation 1 by $(1 + i)^t$ to obtain

$$\frac{X_t}{(1 + i)^t} = X_0 \qquad (2)$$

The logic of equation 2 is identical to that of equation 1. Both allow investors to convert present amounts of money into future amounts of money and vice versa. However, equation 2 makes it much more intuitive to convert a given number of dollars in the future into their present-day equivalent. In fact, it says that X_t dollars in t years converts into exactly $X_t/(1 + i)^t$ dollars today. This may not seem important, but it is actually very powerful because it allows investors to easily calculate how much they should pay for any given asset.

To see why this is true, understand that an asset's owner obtains the right to receive one or more future payments. If an investor is considering buying an asset, her problem is to try to determine how much she should pay today to buy the asset and receive those future payments. Equation 2 makes this task very easy. If she knows how large a future payment will be (X_t dollars), when it will arrive (in t years), and what the interest rate (i) is, then she can apply equation 2 to determine the payment's present value: its value in present-day dollars. If she does this for each of the future payments that the asset in question is expected to make, she will be able to calculate the overall present value of all the asset's future payments by simply summing together the present values of each of the individual payments. This will allow her to determine the price she should pay for the asset. In particular, *the asset's price should exactly equal the sum of the present values of all of the asset's future payments.*

As a simple example, suppose that Cecilia has the chance to buy an asset that is guaranteed to return a single payment of exactly \$370.00 in 17 years. Again let's assume the interest rate is 8 percent per year. Then the present value of that future payment can be determined using equation 2 to equal precisely $\$370.00/(1 + 0.08)^{17} = \$370.00/(1.08)^{17} = \$100$ today. This is confirmed in the row for year 17 in Table 31.1.

To see why Cecilia should be willing to pay a price that is *exactly* equal to the \$100 present value of the asset's single future payment of \$370.00 in 17 years, consider the following thought experiment. What would happen if she were to invest \$100 today in an alternative investment that is guaranteed to compound her money for 17 years at 8 percent per year? How large would her investment in this alternative become? Equation 1 and Table 31.1 tell us that the answer is exactly \$370.00 in 17 years.

This is very important because it shows that Cecilia and other investors have two different possible ways of purchasing the right to receive \$370.00 in 17 years. They can either:

- Purchase the asset in question for \$100.
- Invest \$100 in the alternative asset that pays 8 percent per year.

Because either investment will deliver the same future benefit, both investments are in fact identical. Consequently, they should have identical prices—meaning that each will cost precisely \$100 today.

A good way to see why this must be the case is by considering how the presence of the alternative investment affects the behavior of both the potential buyers and the potential sellers of the asset in question. First, notice that Cecilia and other potential buyers would never pay more than \$100 for the asset in question because they know that they could get the same future return of \$370.00 in 17 years by investing \$100 in the alternative investment. At the same time, people selling the asset in question would not sell it to Cecilia or other potential buyers for anything less than \$100 since they know that the only other way for Cecilia and other potential buyers to get a future return of \$370.00 in 17 years is by paying \$100 for the alternative investment. Since Cecilia and the other potential buyers will not pay more than \$100 for the asset in question and its sellers will not accept less than \$100 for the asset in question, the result will be that the asset in question and the alternative investment will have the exact same price of \$100 today.

AP QUICK REVIEW 31.1

- ✓ Financial investment refers to buying an asset with the hope of financial gain.
- ✓ The time-value of money is the idea that a specific amount of money is more valuable to a person the sooner it is received because of the potential for compound interest.
- ✓ Compound interest is the payment of interest not only on the original amount invested but also on any interest payments previously made; X_0 dollars today growing at interest rate i will become $(1 + i)^t X_0$ dollars in t years.
- ✓ The present value formula facilitates transforming future amounts of money into present-day amounts of money; X_t dollars in t years converts into exactly $X_t/(1 + i)^t$ dollars today.
- ✓ An investment's proper current price is equal to the sum of the present values of all the future payments that it is expected to make.

Applications

Present value is not only an important idea for understanding investment, but it has many everyday applications. Let's examine two of them.

Take the Money and Run? The winners of state lotteries are typically paid their winnings in equal installments spread out over 20 years. For instance, suppose that Zoe gets lucky one week and wins a \$100 million jackpot. She will not be paid \$100 million all at once. Rather, she will receive \$5 million per year for 20 years, for a total of \$100 million.

Zoe may object to this installment payment system for a variety of reasons. For one thing, she may be very old, so that she is not likely to live long enough to collect all of the payments. Alternatively, she might prefer to receive her winnings immediately so that she could make large immediate donations to her favorite charities or large immediate investments in a business project that she would like to get started. And, of course, she may just be impatient and want to buy a lot of really expensive consumption goods sooner rather than later.

Fortunately for Zoe, if she does have a desire to receive her winnings sooner rather than later, several private financial companies are ready and willing to help her. They do this by arranging swaps. Lottery winners sell the right to receive their installment payments in exchange for a single lump sum that they get immediately. The people who hand over the lump sum receive the right to collect the installment payments.

Present value is crucial to arranging these swaps since it is used to determine the value of the lump sum that lottery winners like Zoe will receive in exchange for giving up their installment payments. In any case, the lump sum is simply equal to the sum of the present values of each of the future payments. Assuming an interest rate of 5 percent per year, the sum of the present values of each of Zoe's 20 installment payments of $5 million is $62,311,051.71. So, depending on her preferences, Zoe can either receive that amount immediately or $100 million spread out over 20 years.

Salary Caps and Deferred Compensation Another example of present value comes directly from the sporting news. Many professional sports leagues worry that richer teams, if not held in check, would outbid poorer teams for the best players. The result would be a situation in which only the richer teams have any real chance of doing well and winning championships.

To prevent this from happening, many leagues have instituted salary caps. These are upper limits on the total amount of money that each team can spend on salaries during a given season. For instance, one popular basketball league has a salary cap of about $58 million per season, so that the combined value of the salaries that each team pays its players can be no more than $58 million.

Typically, however, the salary contracts that are negotiated between individual players and their teams are for multiple seasons. This means that during negotiations, players are often asked to help their team stay under the current season's salary cap by agreeing to receive more compensation in later years. For instance, suppose that a team's current payroll is $53 million but that it would like to sign a superstar nicknamed HiTop to a two-year contract. HiTop, however, is used to earning $10 million per year. This is a major problem for the team because the $58 million salary cap means that the most that the team can pay HiTop for the current season is $5 million.

A common solution is for HiTop to agree to receive only $5 million the first season in order to help the team stay under the salary cap. In exchange for this concession, the team agrees to pay HiTop more than the $10 million he would normally demand for the second season. The present value formula is used to figure out how large his second-season salary should be. In particular, the player can use the present value formula to figure out that if the interest rate is 8 percent per year, he should be paid a total of $15,400,000 during his second season, since this amount will equal the $10 million he wants for the second season plus $5.4 million to make up for the $5 million reduction in his salary during the first season. That is, the present value of the $5.4 million that he will receive during the second season precisely equals the $5 million that he agrees to give up during the first season.

AP Some Popular Investments

LO31.3 Identify and distinguish among the most common financial investments: stocks, bonds, and mutual funds.

The number and types of financial "instruments" in which one can invest are very numerous, amazingly creative, and highly varied. Most are much more complicated than the investments we used to explain compounding and present value. But, fortunately, all investments share three features:

- They require that investors pay some price—determined in the market—to acquire them.
- They give their owners the chance to receive future payments.
- The future payments are typically risky.

These features allow us to treat all assets in a unified way. Three of the more popular investments are stocks, bonds, and mutual funds. In 2013, the median value of stock holdings for U.S. families that held stocks was $27,000; the median value for bonds, $94,500; and the median value for "pooled funds" (mainly mutual funds) was $80,000.[1]

Stocks

Recall that **stocks** are ownership shares in a corporation. If an investor owns 1 percent of a corporation's shares, she gets 1 percent of the votes at the shareholder meetings that select the company's managers and she is also entitled to 1 percent of any future profit distributions. There is no guarantee, however, that a company will be profitable.

Firms often lose money and sometimes even go **bankrupt,** meaning that they are unable to make timely payments on their debts. In the event of a bankruptcy, control of a corporation's assets is given to a bankruptcy judge, whose job is to enforce the legal rights of the people who lent the company money by doing what he can to see that they are repaid. Typically, this involves selling off the corporation's assets (factories, real estate, patents, etc.) to raise the money necessary to pay off the company's debts. The money raised by selling the assets may be greater than or less than what is needed to fully pay off the firm's debts. If it is more than what is necessary, any remaining money is divided equally among shareholders. If it is less than what is necessary, then the lenders do not get repaid in full and have to suffer a loss.

A key point, however, is that the maximum amount of money that shareholders can lose is what they pay for their shares. If the company goes bankrupt owing more than the value of the firm's assets, shareholders do not have to make up the difference. This **limited liability rule** limits the risks involved in investing in corporations and encourages investors

[1]Federal Reserve, "Changes in U.S. Family Finances from 2010–2013; Evidence from the Survey of Consumer Finances," p. 16.

to invest in stocks by capping their potential losses at the amount that they paid for their shares.

When firms are profitable, however, investors can look forward to gaining financially in either or both of two possible ways. The first is through **capital gains,** meaning that they sell their shares in the corporation for more money than they paid for them. The second is by receiving **dividends,** which are equal shares of the corporation's profits. As we will soon explain, a corporation's current share price is determined by the size of the capital gains and dividends that investors expect the corporation to generate in the future.

Bonds

Bonds are debt contracts that are issued most frequently by governments and corporations. They typically work as follows: An initial investor lends the government or the corporation a certain amount of money, say $1,000, for a certain period of time, say 10 years. In exchange, the government or corporation promises to make a series of semiannual payments in addition to returning the $1,000 at the end of the 10 years. The semiannual payments constitute interest on the loan. For instance, the bond agreement may specify that the borrower will pay $30 every six months. This means that the bond will pay $60 per year in payments, which is equivalent to a 6 percent rate of interest on the initial $1,000 loan.

The initial investor is free, however, to sell the bond at any time to other investors, who then gain the right to receive any of the remaining semiannual payments as well as the final $1,000 payment when the bond expires after 10 years. As we will soon demonstrate, the price at which the bond will sell if it is indeed sold to another investor will depend on the current rates of return available on other investments offering a similar stream of future payments and facing a similar level of risk.

The primary risk a bondholder faces is the possibility that the corporation or government that issues his bond will **default** on, or fail to make, the bond's promised payments. This risk is much greater for corporations, but it also faces local and state governments in situations where they cannot raise enough tax revenue to make their bond payments or where defaulting on bond payments is politically easier than reducing spending on other items in the government's budget to raise the money needed to keep making bond payments. The U.S. federal government, however, has never defaulted on its bond payments and is very unlikely to ever default because it has access to huge amounts of current and potential tax revenue and can sell U.S. securities to the Fed as a way to obtain money.

A key difference between bonds and stocks is that bonds are much more predictable. Unless a bond goes into default, its owner knows both how big its future payments will be and exactly when they will arrive. By contrast, stock prices and dividends are highly volatile because they depend on profits, which vary greatly depending on the overall business cycle and on factors specific to individual firms and industries—things such as changing consumer preferences, variations in the costs of inputs, and changes in the tax code. As we will demonstrate later, the fact that bonds are typically more predictable (and thus less risky) than stocks explains why they generate lower average rates of return than stocks. Indeed, this difference in rates of return has been very large historically. From 1926 to 2015, stocks on average returned about 11 percent per year worldwide, while bonds on average returned only roughly 6 percent per year worldwide.

Mutual Funds

A **mutual fund** is a company that maintains a professionally managed **portfolio,** or collection, of either stocks or bonds. The portfolio is purchased by pooling the money of many investors. Since these investors provide the money to purchase the portfolio, they own it and any gains or losses generated by the portfolio flow directly to them. Table 31.2 lists the 10 largest U.S. mutual funds based on their assets.

Most of the more than 8,000 mutual funds currently operating in the United States choose to maintain portfolios that invest in specific categories of bonds or stocks. For instance, some fill their portfolios exclusively with the stocks of small tech companies, while others buy only bonds issued by certain state or local governments. In addition, there are **index funds,** whose portfolios are selected to exactly match a stock or bond index. Indexes follow the performance of a particular group of stocks or bonds to gauge how well a particular category of investments is doing. For instance, the Standard & Poor's 500 Index contains the 500 largest stocks trading in the United States to capture how the stocks of large corporations vary over time.

TABLE 31.2 The 10 Largest Mutual Funds, April 2016

Fund Name*	Assets under Management, Billions
SPDR S&P 500 ETF	$170.8
Vanguard 500 Index Admiral Shares	147.1
Vanguard Total Stock Index Admiral Shares	121.4
Vanguard Institutional Index	100.8
Vanguard Total Stock Index Investor	92.5
Vanguard Institutional Index	85.5
Vanguard Total International Stock Index Fund Investor	73.7
Fidelity Contrafund	72.1
American Funds Income A	68.5
American Funds Growth A	67.3

Source: Thomson Reuters, *Lipper Performance Report,* March 31, 2016.

*The letter *A* indicates funds that have sales commissions and are generally purchased by individuals through their financial advisors.

An important distinction must be drawn between actively managed and passively managed mutual funds. **Actively managed funds** have portfolio managers who constantly buy and sell assets in an attempt to generate high returns. By contrast, index funds are **passively managed funds** because the assets in their portfolios are chosen to exactly match whatever stocks or bonds are contained in their respective underlying indexes.

Later in the chapter, we will discuss the relative merits of actively managed funds and index funds, but for now we merely point out that both types are very popular and that, overall, U.S. households and nonprofit organizations held $8.1 trillion in mutual funds at the end of 2015. By way of comparison, U.S. GDP in 2015 was $17.9 trillion and the estimated value of all the financial assets held by households and nonprofit organizations in 2015 (including everything from individual stocks and bonds to checking account deposits) was about $70 trillion.

AP QUICK REVIEW 31.2

- ✓ Three popular forms of financial investments are stocks, bonds, and mutual funds.
- ✓ Stocks are ownership shares in corporations and bestow upon their owners a proportional share of any future profit. There is no guaranteed payment to owners.
- ✓ Bonds are debt contracts that promise to pay a fixed series of payments in the future. Bonds are issued with a payment of interest that is tied to the interest rate at the time of issue.
- ✓ Mutual funds are pools of investor money used to buy a portfolio of stocks or bonds.

AP Calculating Investment Returns

LO31.4 Relate how percentage rates of return provide a common framework for comparing assets and explain why asset prices and rates of return are inversely related.

Investors buy assets to obtain one or more future payments. The simplest case is purchasing an asset for resale. For instance, an investor may buy a house for $300,000 with the hope of selling it for $360,000 in one year. On the other hand, he could also rent out the house for $3,000 per month and thereby receive a stream of future payments. And he, of course, could do a little of both, paying $300,000 for the house now to rent it out for five years and then sell it. In that case, he is expecting a stream of smaller payments followed by a large one.

Percentage Rates of Return

Economists have developed a common framework for evaluating the gains or losses of assets that only make one future payment as well as those that make many future payments. They state the gain or loss as a **percentage rate of return,** by which they mean the percentage gain or loss (relative to the buying price) over a given period of time, typically a year. For instance, if Noelle buys a rare comic book today for $100 and sells it in 1 year for $125, she is said to make a 25 percent per year rate of return because she would divide the gain of $25 by the purchase price of $100. By contrast, if she were only able to sell it for $92, then she would be said to have made a loss of 8 percent per year since she would divide the $8 loss by the purchase price of $100.

A similar calculation is made for assets that deliver a series of payments. For instance, an investor who buys a house for $300,000 and expects to rent it out for $3,000 per month would be expecting to make a 12 percent per year rate of return because he would divide his $36,000 per year of rent by the $300,000 purchase price of the house.

CONSIDER THIS . . .

Corporate Ownership

Source: © Chris Stein/Getty Images

The rise of mutual funds has radically changed the way corporations are controlled. Before the 1970s, corporations knew that the vast majority of their shares were owned by individuals, the large majority of whom were interested in holding their shares for the long run. Those long-run individual investors paid close attention to what corporate officers were doing and would reprimand bad decisions at annual shareholder meetings.

By contrast, neither actively nor passively managed funds have much incentive to care about the long-run success of the companies whose shares they buy and sell. Consider actively managed funds. Their managers lack an incentive to care about long-term performance because they are paid bonuses that depend almost entirely on quarterly performance rather than long-term performance. At the same time, the managers of passively managed funds have no incentive to care about corporate management or policy initiatives because they simply buy whatever stocks are included in their funds' respective underlying indexes.

Critics worry that the decline of close scrutiny by individual shareholders has helped to exacerbate a variety of problems, including corporate managers being paid excessive salaries and CEOs being overly focused on accounting gimmicks that offer a short-run boost to company share prices rather than good management decisions that will pay off only after many years have passed.

The Inverse Relationship between Asset Prices and Rates of Return

A fundamental concept in financial economics is that, other things equal, *an investment's rate of return is inversely related to its price*. The higher the price paid for a fixed-return asset, the lower the rate of return on the investment. To see why, consider a bond that pays $24,000 of interest each year. If an investor pays $100,000 for the bond, he will earn a 24 percent per year rate of return because the $24,000 annual interest payment will be divided by the $100,000 purchase price of the bond.

But suppose that the purchase price of the bond rises to $200,000. In that case, the investor would earn only a 12 percent per year rate of return, since the $24,000 annual interest payment would be divided by the much larger purchase price of $200,000. Consequently, as the price of the bond goes up, the rate of return from buying it goes down.

The same relationship holds for other fixed-return investments, such as rental property. The higher the price of the property, given its monthly rent, the lower the rate of return. The underlying cause of this general relationship is the fact that the annual payments are fixed in value so that there is an upper limit to the financial rewards of owning the asset. As a result, the more an investor pays for the asset, the lower the asset's rate of return.

Arbitrage

LO31.5 Define and utilize the concept of arbitrage.

Arbitrage is the name that financial economists give to the buying and selling process that leads profit-seeking investors to equalize the average expected rates of return generated by identical or nearly identical assets. Arbitrage happens when investors try to take advantage and profit from situations where two identical or nearly identical assets have different rates of return. They do so by simultaneously selling the asset with the lower rate of return and buying the asset with the higher rate of return. For instance, consider what would happen in a case where two very similar T-shirt companies start with different rates of return despite the fact that they are equally profitable and have equally good future prospects. To make things concrete, suppose that a company called T4me starts out with a rate of return of 10 percent per year while TSTG (T-Shirts to Go) starts out with a rate of return of 15 percent per year.

Since both companies are basically identical and have equally good prospects, investors in T4me will want to shift over to TSTG, which offers higher rates of return for the same amount of risk. As they begin to shift over, however, the prices of the two companies will change—and with them, the rates of return on the two companies. In particular, since so many investors will be selling the shares of the lower-return company, T4me, the supply of its shares trading on the stock market will rise so that its share price will fall. But since asset prices and rates of return are inversely related, this will cause its rate of return to rise.

At the same time, however, the rate of return on the higher-return company, TSTG, will begin to fall. This has to be the case because, as investors switch from T4me to TSTG, the increased demand for TSTG's shares will drive up their price. And as the price of TSTG goes up, its rate of return must fall.

The interesting thing is that this arbitrage process will continue—with the rate of return on the higher-return company falling and the rate of return on the lower-return company rising—until both companies have the same rate of return. This convergence must happen because as long as the rates of return on the two companies are not identical, there will always be some investors who will want to sell the shares of the lower-return company so they can buy the shares of the higher-return company. As a result, arbitrage will continue until the rates of return are equal.

What is even more impressive, however, is that generally only a very short while is needed for prices to equalize. In fact, for highly traded assets like stocks and bonds, arbitrage will often force the rates of return on identical or nearly identical investments to converge within a matter of minutes or sometimes even within a matter of seconds. This is very helpful to small investors who do not have a large amount of time to study the thousands of potential investment opportunities available in the financial markets. Thanks to arbitrage, they can invest with the confidence that assets with similar characteristics will have similar rates of return. As we discuss in the next section, this is especially important when it comes to risk—a characteristic that financial economists believe investors care about very deeply.

AP QUICK REVIEW 31.3

- ✓ Stating gains or losses as percentage rates of return provides a common framework for comparing different assets.
- ✓ Asset prices and percentage rates of return are inversely related.
- ✓ Arbitrage refers to the buying and selling that takes place to equalize the percentage rates of return on identical or nearly identical assets.

Risk

LO31.6 Describe how the word *risk* is used in financial economics and explain the difference between diversifiable and nondiversifiable risk.

Investors purchase assets to obtain one or more future payments. As used by financial economists, the word **risk** refers to the fact that investors never know with total certainty what those future payments will turn out to be.

The underlying problem is that the future is uncertain. Many factors affect an investment's future payments, and each of these may turn out better or worse than expected. As a simple example, consider buying a farm. Suppose that in an average year, the farm will generate a profit of $100,000. But if a freak hailstorm damages the crops, the profit will fall to only $60,000. On the other hand, if weather conditions turn out to be perfect, the profit will rise to $120,000. Since there is no way to tell in advance what will happen, investing in the farm is risky.

Also notice that when financial economists use the word *risk,* they do not use it in the casual way that refers only to potentially bad outcomes (as in, "there is a risk that this experimental medicine may kill you"). In financial economics, the word *risk* means only that an outcome—good or bad, major or minor, likely or unlikely—lacks total certainty. Some outcome will occur, but you cannot be sure what it will be. For instance, suppose that you are gifted a raffle ticket that will pay you $10, $100, or $1,000 when a drawing is made in one month. There are no bad outcomes in this particular case, only good ones. But because you do not know with certainty which outcome will occur, the situation is, by definition, risky. On the other hand, the word *risk* in financial economics certainly does not preclude negative outcomes. If you buy shares of common stock in some company, your stock may go up in value. But the company could also go bankrupt, in which case you would lose your entire investment.

Diversification

Investors have many options regarding their portfolios, or collections of investments. Among other things, they can choose to concentrate their wealth in just one or two investments or spread it out over a large number of investments. **Diversification** is the name given to the strategy of investing in a large number of investments to reduce the overall risk to the entire portfolio.

The underlying reason that diversification generally succeeds in reducing risk is best summarized by the old saying, "Don't put all your eggs in one basket." If an investor's portfolio consists of only one investment—say, one stock—then if anything awful happens to that stock, the investor's entire portfolio will suffer greatly. By contrast, if the investor spreads his wealth over many stocks, then a bad outcome for any one particular stock will cause only a small amount of damage to the overall portfolio. In addition, it will typically be the case that if something bad is happening to one part of the portfolio, something good will be happening to another part of the portfolio and the two effects will tend to offset each other. Thus, the risk to the overall portfolio is reduced by diversification.

It must be stressed, however, that while diversification can reduce a portfolio's risks, it cannot eliminate them entirely. The problem is that even if an investor has placed each of his eggs into a different basket, all of the eggs may still end up broken if all of the different baskets somehow happen to get dropped simultaneously. That is, even if an investor has created a well-diversified portfolio, all of the investments still have a chance to do badly simultaneously. As an example, consider the early portion of the severe recession of 2007–2009: With economic activity declining and consumer spending falling, nearly all companies faced reduced sales and lowered profits, a fact that caused their stock prices to decline simultaneously. Consequently, even if investors had diversified their portfolios across numerous stocks, their overall wealth portfolios would have still declined because nearly all of their many investments simultaneously performed poorly.

Financial economists build on the intuition behind the benefits and limits to diversification to divide an individual investment's overall risk into two components, diversifiable risk and nondiversifiable risk. **Diversifiable risk** (or "idiosyncratic risk") is the risk that is specific to a given investment and that can be eliminated by diversification. For instance, a soda pop maker faces the risk that the demand for its product may suddenly decline because people will want to drink mineral water instead of soda pop. But this risk does not matter if an investor has a diversified portfolio that contains stock in the soda pop maker as well as stock in a mineral water maker. This is true because when the stock price of the soda pop maker falls due to the change in consumer preferences, the stock price of the mineral water maker will go up—so that, as far as the overall portfolio is concerned, the two effects will offset each other.

By contrast, **nondiversifiable risk** (or "systemic risk") pushes all investments in the same direction at the same time so that there is no possibility of using good effects to offset bad effects. The best example of a nondiversifiable risk is the business cycle. If the economy does well, then corporate profits rise and nearly every stock does well. But if the economy does badly, then corporate profits fall and nearly every stock does badly. As a result, even if one were to build a well-diversified portfolio, it would still be affected by the business cycle because nearly every asset contained in the portfolio would move in the same direction at the same time whenever the economy improved or worsened.

That being said, creating a diversified portfolio is still an investor's best strategy because doing so at least eliminates diversifiable risk. Indeed, it should be emphasized that for investors who have created diversified portfolios, all diversifiable risks will be eliminated, so that the only remaining source of risk will be nondiversifiable risk.

A significant implication of this fact is that when investors consider whether to add any particular investment to a portfolio that is already diversified, they can ignore the investment's diversifiable risk. They can ignore it because, as part of a diversified portfolio, the investment's diversifiable risk will be "diversified away." Indeed, the only risk left will be the

GLOBAL PERSPECTIVE 31.1

Investment Risks Vary across Different Countries

The International Country Risk Guide is a monthly publication that attempts to distill the political, economic, and financial risks facing 140 countries into a single "composite risk rating" number for each country, with higher numbers indicating less risk and more safety. The table below presents the January 2016 ranks and rating numbers for 15 countries including the three least risky (ranked 1 through 3) and the three most risky (ranked 138 through 140). Risk ratings numbers above 80 are considered *very low risk;* 70–80 are considered *low risk;* 60–70 *moderate risk;* 50–60 *high risk;* and below 50 *very high risk.*

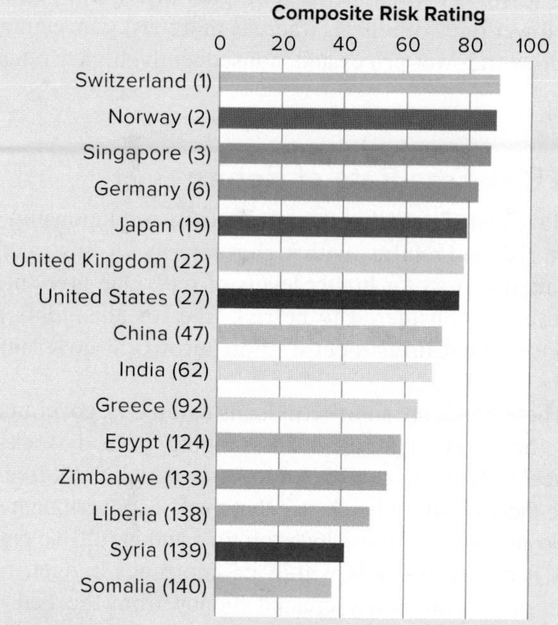

Source: The PRS Group, *International Country Risk Guide,* 2016. **www.prsgroup.com.**

amount of nondiversifiable risk that the investment carries with it. This is crucial because it means that investors can base their decisions about whether to add a potential new investment to their portfolios on a comparison between the potential investment's level of nondiversifiable risk and its potential returns. If they find this trade-off attractive, they will add the investment, whereas if it seems unattractive, they will not.

The next section shows how investors can measure each asset's level of nondiversifiable risk as well as its potential returns to facilitate such comparisons. Global Perspective 31.1 shows how investment risk varies significantly across countries due to underlying differences in political, economic, and financial risks.

AP QUICK REVIEW 31.4

- ✓ An asset is risky if its future payments are uncertain.
- ✓ Diversification is an investment strategy in which an investor invests in a large number of different investments in order to reduce the overall risk to his or her entire portfolio.
- ✓ Risks that can be canceled out by diversification are called diversifiable risks; risks that cannot be canceled out by diversification are called nondiversifiable risks.

Comparing Risky Investments

LO31.7 Convey why investment decisions are determined primarily by investment returns and nondiversifiable risk and how investment returns compensate for being patient and for bearing nondiversifiable risk.

Economists believe that the two most important factors affecting investment decisions are returns and risk—specifically nondiversifiable risk. But for investors to properly compare different investments on the basis of returns and risk, they need ways to measure returns and risk. The two standard measures are, respectively, the average expected rate of return and the beta statistic.

Average Expected Rate of Return

Each investment's **average expected rate of return** is the probability-weighted average of the investment's possible future rates of return. The term **probability-weighted average** simply means that each of the possible future rates of return is multiplied by its probability expressed as a decimal (so that a 50 percent probability is 0.5 and a 23 percent probability is 0.23) before being added together to obtain the average. For instance, if an investment has a 75 percent probability of generating 11 percent per year and a 25 percent probability of generating 15 percent per year, then its average expected rate of return will be 12 percent = (0.75 × 11 percent) + (0.25 × 15 percent). By weighting each possible outcome by its probability, this process ensures that the resulting average gives more weight to those outcomes that are more likely to happen (unlike the normal averaging process that would treat every outcome the same).

Once investors have calculated the average expected rates of return for all the assets they are interested in, there will naturally be some impulse to simply invest in those assets having the highest average expected rates of return. But while this might satisfy investor cravings for higher rates of return, it would not take proper account of the fact that investors dislike risk and uncertainty. To quantify their dislike, investors require a statistic that can measure each investment's risk level.

Beta

One popular statistic that measures risk is called beta. **Beta** is a *relative* measure of nondiversifiable risk. It measures how the nondiversifiable risk of a given asset or portfolio of assets compares with that of the **market portfolio,** which is the name given to a portfolio that contains every asset available in the financial markets. The market portfolio is a useful standard of comparison because it is as diversified as possible. In fact, since it contains every possible asset, every possible diversifiable risk will be diversified away—meaning that it will be exposed *only* to nondiversifiable risk. Consequently, it can serve as a useful benchmark against which to measure the levels of nondiversifiable risk to which individual assets are exposed.

Such comparisons are very simple because the beta statistic is standardized such that the market portfolio's level of nondiversifiable risk is set equal to 1.0. Consequently, an asset with beta = 0.5 has a level of nondiversifiable risk that is one-half of that possessed by the market portfolio, while an asset with beta = 2.0 has twice as much nondiversifiable risk as the market portfolio. In addition, the beta numbers of various assets also can be used to compare them with each other. For instance, an asset with beta = 2.0 has four times as much exposure to nondiversifiable risk as does an asset with beta = 0.5.

Another useful feature of beta is that it can be calculated not only for individual assets but also for portfolios. Indeed, it can be calculated for portfolios no matter how many or how few assets they contain and no matter what those assets happen to be. This fact is very convenient for mutual fund investors because it means that they can use beta to quickly see how the nondiversifiable risk of any given fund's portfolio compares with that of other potential investments that they may be considering.

The beta statistic is used along with average expected rates of return to give investors standard measures of risk and return that can be used to sensibly compare different investment opportunities. As we will discuss in the next section, this leads to one of the most fundamental relationships in financial economics: riskier assets have higher rates of return.

Relationship of Risk and Average Expected Rates of Return

The fact that investors dislike risk has a profound effect on asset prices and average expected rates of return. In particular, their dislike of risk and uncertainty causes investors to pay higher prices for less-risky assets and lower prices for more-risky assets. But since asset prices and average expected rates of return are inversely related, this implies that less-risky assets will have lower average expected rates of return than more-risky assets.

Stated a bit more clearly: *Risk levels and average expected rates of return are positively related.* The more risky an investment is, the higher its average expected rate of return will be. A great way to understand this relationship is to think of higher average expected rates of return as being a form of compensation. Since investors dislike risk, they demand higher levels of compensation the more risky an asset is. The higher levels of compensation come in the form of higher average expected rates of return.

Be sure to note that this phenomenon affects all assets. Regardless of whether the assets are stocks or bonds or real estate or anything else, assets with higher levels of risk always end up with higher average expected rates of return to compensate investors for the higher levels of risk involved. No matter what the investment opportunity is, investors examine its possible future payments, determine how risky they are, and then select a price that reflects those risks. Since less-risky investments get higher prices, they end up with lower rates of return, whereas more-risky investments end up with lower prices and, consequently, higher rates of return.

The Risk-Free Rate of Return

We have just shown that there is a positive relationship between risk and returns, with higher returns serving to compensate investors for higher levels of risk. One investment, however, is considered to be risk-free for all intents and purposes. That investment is short-term U.S. government bonds.

These bonds are short-term loans to the U.S. government, with the duration of the loans ranging from 4 weeks to 26 weeks. They are considered to be essentially risk-free because there is almost no chance that the U.S. government will not be able to repay these loans on time and in full. To pay its debt, it can shift funds within its enormous budget, raise taxes, or borrow newly created money from the Fed. Although it is true that the U.S. government may eventually be destroyed or disabled to such an extent that it will not be able to repay some of its loans, the chances of such a calamity happening within 4 or even 26 weeks are essentially zero. Consequently, because it is a near certainty that the bonds will be repaid in full and on time, they are considered by investors to be risk-free.

Since higher levels of risk lead to higher rates of return, a person might be tempted to assume—incorrectly—that since government bonds are risk-free, they should earn a zero percent rate of return. The problem with this line of thinking is that it mistakenly assumes that risk is the *only* thing that rates of return compensate for. The truth is that rates of return compensate not only for risk but also for something that economists call time preference.

Time preference refers to the fact that because people tend to be impatient, they typically prefer to consume things in the present rather than in the future. Stated more concretely, most people, if given the choice between a serving of their favorite dessert immediately or a serving of their favorite dessert in five years, will choose to consume their favorite dessert immediately.

This time preference for consuming sooner rather than later affects the financial markets because people want to be compensated for delayed consumption. In particular, if Dave asks Oprah to lend him \$1 million for one year, he is implicitly asking Oprah to delay consumption for a year because if she lends Dave the \$1 million, she will not be able to spend that money herself for at least a year. If Oprah is like most people and has a preference for spending her \$1 million sooner rather than later, the only way Dave will be able to convince Oprah to let him borrow \$1 million is to offer her some form of compensation. The compensation comes in the form of an interest payment that will allow Oprah to consume more in the future than she can now. For instance, Dave can offer to pay Oprah \$1.1 million in one year in exchange for \$1 million today. That is, Oprah will get back the \$1 million she lends to Dave today as well as an extra \$100,000 to compensate her for being patient.

Notice the very important fact that this type of interest payment has nothing to do with risk. It is purely compensation for being patient and must be paid even if there is no risk involved and 100 percent certainty that Dave will fulfill his promise to repay.

Since short-term U.S. government bonds are for all intents and purposes completely risk-free and 100 percent likely to repay as promised, their rates of return are *purely* compensation for time preference and the fact that people must be compensated for delaying their own consumption opportunities when they lend money to the government. One consequence of this fact is that the rate of return earned by short-term U.S. government bonds is often referred to as the **risk-free interest rate,** or i^f, to clearly indicate that the rate of return that they generate is not in any way a compensation for risk.

It should be kept in mind, however, that the Federal Reserve has the power to change the risk-free interest rate generated by short-term U.S. government bonds. As discussed in Chapter 30, the Federal Reserve can use open-market operations to lower or raise the federal funds interest rate by making large purchases or sales of U.S. securities in the bond market. These open-market operations affect the money supply, which affects all interest rates, including the rates on short-term U.S. government bonds. This means that the Federal Reserve indirectly determines the risk-free interest rate and, consequently, the compensation that investors receive for being patient. As we will soon demonstrate, this fact is very important because by manipulating the reward for being patient, the Federal Reserve can affect the rate of return and prices of not only government bonds but all assets.

AP QUICK REVIEW 31.5

- ✓ The average expected rate of return is the probability-weighted average of an investment's possible future returns.
- ✓ Because investors dislike risk, riskier investments must offer higher rates of return to compensate investors for bearing more risk.
- ✓ Average expected rates of return compensate investors for both risk and time preference, which is the preference most people have to consume sooner rather than later.

The Security Market Line

LO31.8 Explain how the Security Market Line illustrates the compensation that investors receive for time preference and nondiversifiable risk and why arbitrage will tend to move all assets onto the Security Market Line.

Investors must be compensated for time preference as well as for the amount of nondiversifiable risk that an investment carries with it. This section introduces a simple model called the **Security Market Line,** which indicates how this compensation is determined for all assets no matter what their respective risk levels happen to be.

The underlying logic of the model is this: Any investment's average expected rate of return has to be the sum of two parts—one that compensates for time preference and another that compensates for risk. That is,

$$\begin{aligned}\text{Average expected rate of return} &= \text{rate that compensates for time preference}\\ &\quad + \text{rate that compensates for risk}\end{aligned}$$

As we explained, the compensation for time preference is equal to the risk-free interest rate, i^f, that is paid on short-term government bonds. As a result, this equation can be simplified to

$$\text{Average expected rate of return} = i^f + \text{rate that compensates for risk}$$

Finally, because economists typically refer to the rate that compensates for risk as the **risk premium,** this equation can be simplified even further to

$$\text{Average expected rate of return} = i^f + \text{risk premium}$$

Naturally, the size of the risk premium that compensates for risk will vary depending on how risky an investment happens to be. In particular, it will depend on how big or small the investment's beta is. Investments with large

FIGURE 31.1 The Security Market Line. The Security Market Line shows the relationship between average expected rates of return and risk levels that must hold for every asset or portfolio trading in the financial markets. Each investment's average expected rate of return is the sum of the risk-free interest rate that compensates for time preference as well as a risk premium that compensates for the investment's level of risk. The Security Market Line's upward slope reflects the fact that investors must be compensated for higher levels of risk with higher average expected rates of return.

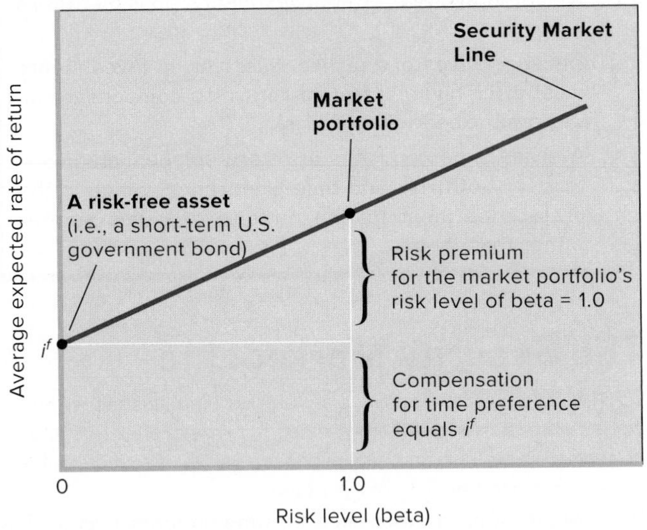

betas and lots of nondiversifiable risk will require larger risk premiums than investments that have small betas and low levels of nondiversifiable risk. And, in the most extreme case, risk-free assets that have betas equal to zero will require no compensation for risk at all since they have no risk to compensate for.

This logic is translated into the graph presented in Figure 31.1. The horizontal axis of Figure 31.1 measures risk levels using beta; the vertical axis measures average expected rates of return. As a result, any investment can be plotted on Figure 31.1 just as long as we know its beta and its average expected rate of return. We have plotted two investments in Figure 31.1. The first is a risk-free short-term U.S. government bond, which is indicated by the lower-left dot in the figure. The second is the market portfolio, which is indicated by the upper-right dot in the figure.

The lower dot marking the position of the risk-free bond is located where it is because it is a risk-free asset having a beta = 0 and because its average expected rate of return is given by i^f. These values place the lower dot i^f percentage points up the vertical axis, as shown in Figure 31.1. Note that this location conveys the logic that because this asset has no risk, its average expected rate of return only has to compensate investors for time preference—which is why its average expected rate of return is equal to precisely i^f and no more.

The market portfolio, by contrast, is risky so that its average expected rate of return must compensate investors not only for time preference but also for the level of risk to which the market portfolio is exposed, which by definition is beta = 1.0. This implies that the vertical distance from the horizontal axis to the upper dot is equal to the sum of i^f and the market portfolio's risk premium.

The straight line connecting the risk-free asset's lower dot and the market portfolio's upper dot is called the Security Market Line, or SML. The SML is extremely important because it defines the relationship between average expected rates of return and risk levels that must hold for all assets and all portfolios trading in the financial markets. The SML illustrates the idea that every asset's average expected rate of return is the sum of a rate of return that compensates for time preference and a rate of return that compensates for risk. More specifically, the SML has a vertical intercept equal to the rate of interest earned by short-term U.S. government bonds and a positive slope that compensates investors for risk.

As we explained earlier, the precise location of the intercept at any given time is determined by the Federal Reserve's monetary policy and how it affects the rate of return on short-term U.S. government bonds. The slope of the SML, however, is determined by investors' feelings about risk and how much compensation they require for dealing with it. If investors greatly dislike risk, then the SML will have to be very steep, so that any given increase in risk on the horizontal axis will result in a very large increase in compensation as measured by average expected rates of return on the vertical axis. On the other hand, if investors dislike risk only moderately, then the SML will be relatively flat since any given increase in risk on the horizontal axis would require only a moderate increase in compensation as measured by average expected rates of return on the vertical axis.

It is important to realize that once investor preferences about risk have determined the slope of the SML and monetary policy has determined its vertical intercept, the SML plots out the precise relationship between risk levels and average expected rates of return *that should hold for every asset.* For instance, consider Figure 31.2, where there is an asset whose risk level on the horizontal axis is beta = X. The SML tells us that every asset with that risk level should have an average expected rate of return equal to Y on the vertical axis. This average expected rate of return exactly compensates for both time preference and the fact that the asset in question is exposed to a risk level of beta = X.

Finally, it should be pointed out that arbitrage will ensure that all investments having an identical level of risk also will have an identical rate of return—the return given by the SML. This is illustrated in Figure 31.3, where the three assets A, B, and C all share the same risk level of beta = X but initially have three different average expected rates of return. Since asset B lies on the SML, it has the average expected rate of return Y that precisely compensates investors for time preference and risk level X. Asset A, however, has a higher average expected rate of return that overcompensates investors while

FIGURE 31.2 Risk levels determine average expected rates of return. The Security Market Line can be used to determine an investment's average expected rate of return based on its risk level. In this figure, investments having a risk level of beta = X will have an average expected rate of return of Y percent per year. This average expected rate of return will compensate investors for time preference in addition to providing them exactly the right-sized risk premium to compensate them for dealing with a risk level of beta = X.

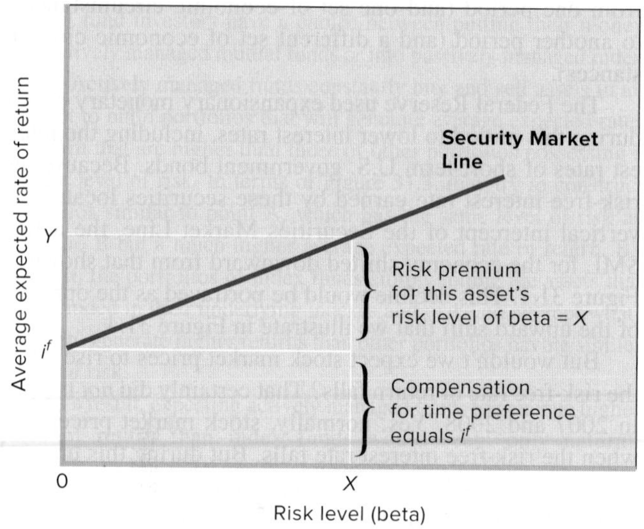

FIGURE 31.3 Arbitrage and the Security Market Line. Arbitrage pressures will tend to move any asset or portfolio that lies off the Security Market Line back onto the line. Investors will increase their purchases of asset A, driving up its price and decreasing its average expected rate of return. They will decrease their purchases of asset C, reducing its price and raising its return. Therefore, assets A, B, and C will all end up on the Security Market Line with each having the same average expected rate of return, Y, at risk level (beta) X. This average expected rate of return will fully compensate the investors for time preference plus nondiversifiable risk as measured by beta.

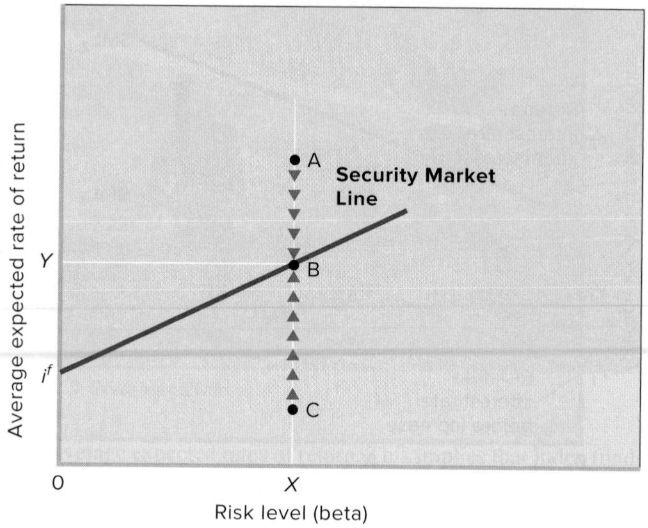

asset C has a lower average expected rate of return that undercompensates investors.

Arbitrage pressures will quickly eliminate these over- and undercompensations. For instance, consider what will happen to asset A. Investors will be hugely attracted to its overly high rate of return and will rush to buy it. That will drive up its price. But because average expected rates of return and prices are inversely related, the increase in price will cause its average expected rate of return to fall. Graphically, this means that asset A will move vertically downward as illustrated in Figure 31.3. And it will continue to move vertically downward until it reaches the SML since only then will it have the average expected rate of return Y that properly compensates investors for time preference and risk level X.

A similar process also will move asset C back to the SML. Investors will dislike the fact that its average expected rate of return is so low. This will cause them to sell it, driving down its price. Since average expected rates of return and prices are inversely related, this will cause its average expected rate of return to rise, thereby causing C to rise vertically as illustrated in Figure 31.3. And as with point A, point C will continue to rise until it reaches the SML, since only then will it have the average expected rate of return Y that properly compensates investors for time preference and risk level X.

Security Market Line: Applications

The SML analysis is highly useful in clarifying why investors scrutinize the intentions and actions of the Federal Reserve and change their behaviors during financial crises.

An Increase in the Risk-Free Rate by the Fed We have just explained how the position of the Security Market Line is fixed by two factors. The vertical intercept is set by the risk-free interest rate while the slope is determined by the amount of compensation investors demand for bearing nondiversifiable risk. As a result, changes in either one of these factors can shift the SML and thereby cause large changes in both average expected rates of return and asset prices.

As an example, consider what happens to the SML if the Federal Reserve changes policy and uses open-market operations (described in Chapter 30) to reduce the money supply, raise the federal funds rate, and increase other interest rates such as those on short-term U.S. government bonds. Since the risk-free interest rate earned by these bonds is also the SML's vertical intercept, an increase in their interest rate will move the SML's vertical intercept upward, as illustrated in Figure 31.4. The result is a parallel upward shift of the SML from SML_1 to SML_2. (The shift is parallel because nothing has happened that would affect the SML's slope, which is determined by the amount of compensation that investors demand for bearing risk.)

Notice what this upward shift implies. Not only does the rate of return on short-term U.S. government bonds increase when the Federal Reserve changes policy, but the rate of return on risky assets increases as well. For instance, consider asset A, which originally has rate of return Y_1. After the SML shifts upward, asset A ends up with the higher rate of return Y_2. There is a simple intuition behind this increase. Risky assets must

AP From Short Run to Long Run

LO32.1 Explain the relationship between short-run aggregate supply and long-run aggregate supply.

In Chapter 26, we noted that in macroeconomics the difference between the **short run** and the **long run** has to do with the flexibility of input prices. Input prices are inflexible or even totally fixed in the short run but fully flexible in the long run. (By contrast, output prices are assumed under these definitions to be fully flexible in both the short run and the long run.)

The assumption that input prices are flexible only in the long run leads to large differences in the shape and position of the short-run aggregate supply curve and the long-run aggregate supply curve. As explained in Chapter 26, the short-run aggregate supply curve is an upsloping line, whereas the long-run aggregate supply curve is a vertical line situated directly above the economy's full-employment output level, Q_f.

We will begin this chapter by discussing how aggregate supply transitions *from* the short run *to* the long run. Once that is done, we will combine the long-run and short-run aggregate supply curves with the aggregate demand curve to form a single model that can provide insights into how the economy adjusts to economic shocks as well as changes in monetary and fiscal policy in both the short run and the long run. That will lead us to discuss how economic growth relates to long-run aggregate supply and how inflation and aggregate supply are related in the long run and the short run. We will conclude with a discussion of a particular set of economic policies that may help increase both short-run aggregate supply and long-run aggregate supply.

Short-Run Aggregate Supply

Our immediate objective is to demonstrate the relationship between short-run aggregate supply and long-run aggregate supply. We begin by briefly reviewing short-run aggregate supply.

Consider the short-run aggregate supply curve AS_1 in Figure 32.1a. This curve is based on three assumptions: (1) The initial price level is P_1, (2) firms and workers have established nominal wages on the expectation that this price level will persist, and (3) the price level is flexible both upward and downward. Observe from point a_1 that at price level P_1 the economy is operating at its full-employment output Q_f. This output is the real production forthcoming when the economy is operating at its natural rate of unemployment (or potential output).

Now let's review the short-run effects of changes in the price level, say, from P_1 to P_2 in Figure 32.1a. The higher prices associated with price level P_2 increase firms' revenues, and because their nominal wages and other input prices remain unchanged, their profits rise. Those higher profits lead firms to increase their output from Q_f to Q_2, and the economy moves from a_1 to a_2 on aggregate supply AS_1. At output Q_2 the economy is operating beyond its full-employment output. The firms make this possible by extending the work hours of part-time and full-time workers, enticing new workers such as homemakers and retirees into the labor force, and hiring and training the structurally unemployed. Thus, the nation's unemployment rate declines below its natural rate.

How will the firms respond when the price level *falls*, say, from P_1 to P_3 in Figure 32.1a? Because the prices they receive

AP FIGURE 32.1 Short-run and long-run aggregate supply. (a) In the short run, nominal wages and other input prices do not respond to price-level changes and are based on the expectation that price level P_1 will continue. An increase in the price level from P_1 to P_2 increases profits and output, moving the economy from a_1 to a_2; a decrease in the price level from P_1 to P_3 reduces profits and real output, moving the economy from a_1 to a_3. The short-run aggregate supply curve therefore slopes upward. (b) In the long run, a rise in the price level results in higher nominal wages and other input prices and thus shifts the short-run aggregate supply curve to the left. Conversely, a decrease in the price level reduces nominal wages and shifts the short-run aggregate supply curve to the right. After such adjustments, the economy obtains equilibrium of points such as b_1 and c_1. Thus, the long-run aggregate supply curve is vertical at the full-employment output.

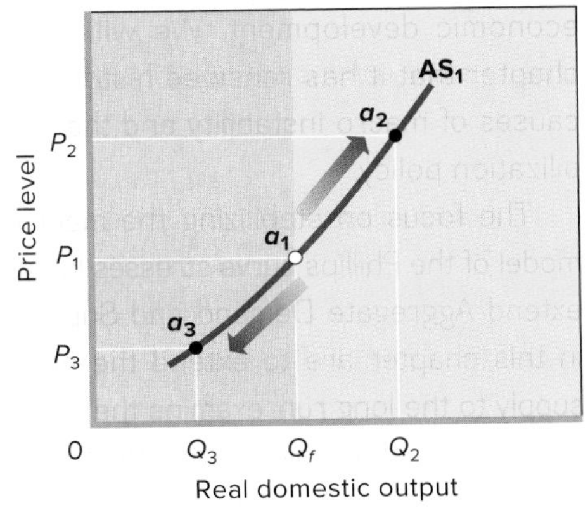

(a)
Short-run aggregate supply

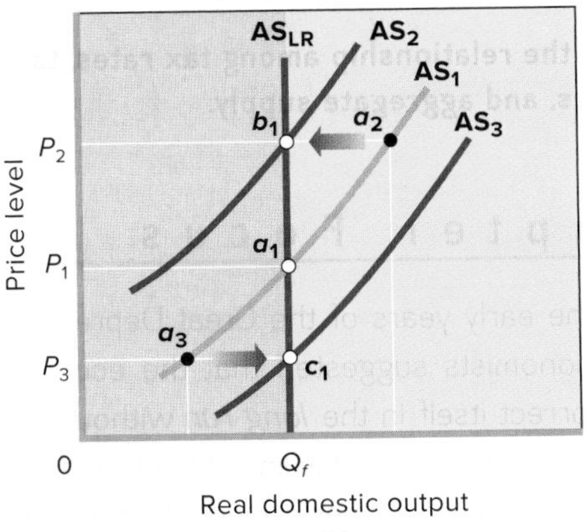

(b)
Long-run aggregate supply

for their products are lower while the nominal wages they pay workers remain unchanged, firms discover that their revenues and profits have diminished or disappeared. So they reduce their production and employment, and, as shown by the movement from a_1 to a_3, real output falls to Q_3. Increased unemployment and a higher unemployment rate accompany the decline in real output. At output Q_3 the unemployment rate is greater than the natural rate of unemployment associated with output Q_f.

Long-Run Aggregate Supply

The outcomes are different in the long run. To see why, we need to extend the analysis of aggregate supply to account for changes in nominal wages that occur in response to changes in the price level. That will enable us to derive the economy's long-run aggregate supply curve.

We illustrate the implications for aggregate supply in Figure 32.1b. Again, suppose that the economy is initially at point a_1 (P_1 and Q_f). As we just demonstrated, an increase in the price level from P_1 to P_2 will move the economy from point a_1 to a_2 along the short-run aggregate supply curve AS_1. At a_2, the economy is producing at more than its potential output. This implies very high demand for productive inputs, so that input prices will begin to rise. In particular, the high demand for labor will drive up nominal wages, which will increase per unit production costs. As a result, the short-run supply curve shifts leftward from AS_1 to AS_2, which now reflects the higher price level P_2 and the new expectation that P_2, not P_1, will continue. The leftward shift in the short-run aggregate supply curve to AS_2 moves the economy from a_2 to b_1. Real output falls back to its full-employment level Q_f, and the unemployment rate rises to its natural rate.

What is the long-run outcome of a *decrease* in the price level? Assuming eventual downward wage flexibility, a decline in the price level from P_1 to P_3 in Figure 32.1b works in the opposite way from a price-level increase. At first the economy moves from point a_1 to a_3 on AS_1. Profits are squeezed or eliminated because prices have fallen and nominal wages have not. But this movement along AS_1 is the short-run supply response that results only while input prices remain constant. As time passes, input prices will begin to fall because the economy is producing at below its full-employment output level. With so little output being produced, the demand for inputs will be low and their prices will begin to decline. In particular, the low demand for labor will drive down nominal wages and reduce per-unit production costs. Lower nominal wages therefore shift the short-run aggregate supply curve rightward from AS_1 to AS_3, and real output returns to its full-employment level of Q_f at point c_1.

By tracing a line between the long-run equilibrium points b_1, a_1, and c_1, we obtain a long-run aggregate supply curve. Observe that it is vertical at the full-employment level of real GDP. After long-run adjustments in nominal wages and other nominal input prices, real output is Q_f regardless of the specific price level.

Long-Run Equilibrium in the AD-AS Model

Figure 32.2 helps us understand the long-run equilibrium in the AD-AS model, now extended to include the distinction between short-run and long-run aggregate supply. (Hereafter, we will refer to this model as the extended AD-AS model, with "extended" referring to the inclusion of both the short-run and the long-run aggregate supply curves.)

In the short run, equilibrium occurs wherever the downsloping aggregate demand curve and upsloping short-run aggregate supply curve intersect. This can be at any level of output, not simply the full-employment level. Either a negative GDP gap or a positive GDP gap is possible in the short run.

But in the long run, the short-run aggregate supply curve adjusts as we just described. After those adjustments, long-run equilibrium occurs where the aggregate demand curve, vertical long-run aggregate supply curve, and short-run aggregate supply curve all intersect. Figure 32.2 shows the long-run outcome. Equilibrium occurs at point a, where AD_1 intersects both AS_{LR} and AS_1, and the economy achieves its full-employment (or potential) output, Q_f. At long-run equilibrium price level P_1 and output level Q_f, neither a negative GDP gap nor a positive GDP gap occurs. The economy's *natural rate of unemployment* prevails, meaning that the economy achieves full employment.

In the United States, output Q_f in Figure 32.2 implies a 4 to 5 percent unemployment rate. The natural rate of unemployment can vary from one time period to another and can differ between countries. But whatever the rate happens to be, it defines the level of potential output and establishes the location of the long-run AS curve.

AP **FIGURE 32.2 Equilibrium in the long-run AD-AS model.** The long-run equilibrium price level P_1 and level of real output Q_f occur at the intersection of the aggregate demand curve AD_1, the long-run aggregate supply curve AS_{LR}, and the short-run aggregate supply curve AS_1.

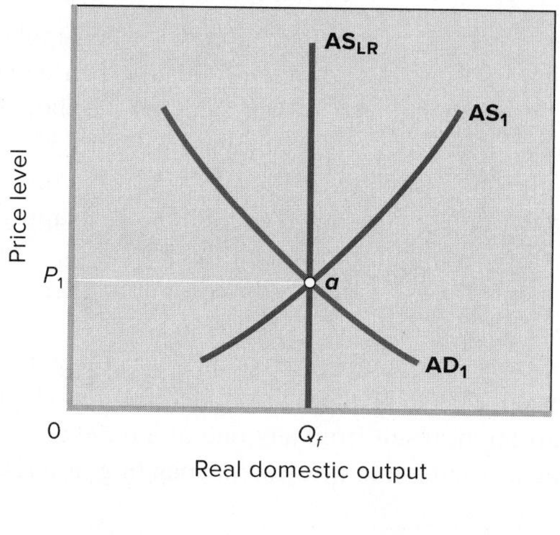

AP QUICK REVIEW 32.1

- ✓ The short-run aggregate supply curve slopes upward, because nominal wages and other input prices are fixed. With diminishing marginal product of labor, firms require higher output prices to increase the quantity of real output supplied.
- ✓ The long-run aggregate supply curve is vertical. All wages and prices are flexible. Over time, the economy should move to the full-employment level of real GDP. Thus, the long-run supply curve is vertical at the full-employment real GDP.
- ✓ The short-run equilibrium RGDP and price level occur where aggregate demand and short-run aggregate supply intersect; this short-run RGPD may be equal to the full-employment output, less than, or greater than the full employment output. Thus, a negative or positive GDP gap is possible in the short run.
- ✓ In long-run equilibrium, the economy achieves its natural rate of unemployment and its full potential real output. The natural rate of unemployment or the full-employment, unemployment rate is estimated as between 4.5 and 5.5 percent.

AP Applying the Extended AD-AS Model

LO32.2 Explain how to apply the "extended" (short-run/long-run) AD-AS model to inflation, recessions, and economic growth.

The extended AD-AS model helps clarify the long-run aspects of demand-pull inflation, cost-push inflation, and recession.

Demand-Pull Inflation in the Extended AD-AS Model

Recall that demand-pull inflation occurs when an increase in aggregate demand pulls up the price level. Earlier, we depicted this inflation by shifting an aggregate demand curve rightward along a stable aggregate supply curve (see Figure 26.8).

In our more complex version of aggregate supply, an increase in the price level eventually leads to an increase in nominal wages and thus a leftward shift of the short-run aggregate supply curve. This is shown in Figure 32.3, where we initially suppose the price level is P_1 at the intersection of aggregate demand curve AD_1, short-run supply curve AS_1, and long-run aggregate supply curve AS_{LR}. Observe that the economy is achieving its full-employment real output Q_f at point *a*.

Now consider the effects of an increase in aggregate demand as represented by the rightward shift from AD_1 to AD_2. This shift might result from any one of a number of factors, including an increase in investment spending or a rise in net exports. Whatever its cause, the increase in aggregate demand boosts the price level from P_1 to P_2 and expands real output from Q_f to Q_2 at point *b*. There, a positive GDP gap of $Q_2 - Q_f$ occurs.

AP FIGURE 32.3 Demand-pull inflation in the extended AD-AS model. An increase in aggregate demand from AD_1 to AD_2 drives up the price level and increases real output in the short run. But in the long run, nominal wages rise and the short-run aggregate supply curve shifts leftward, as from AS_1 to AS_2. Real output then returns to its prior level, and the price level rises even more. In this scenario, the economy moves from *a* to *b* and then eventually to *c*.

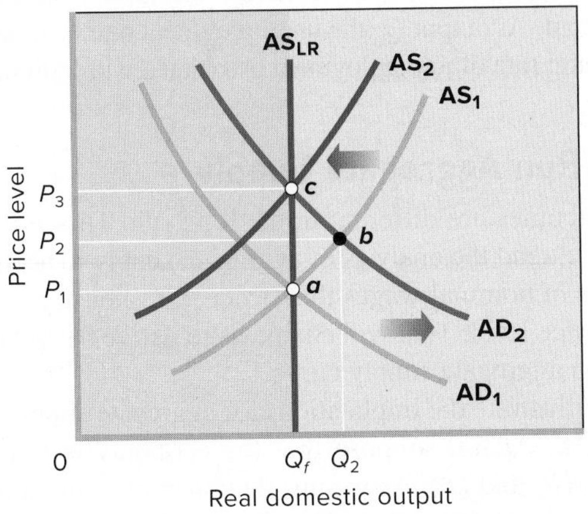

So far, none of this is new to you. But now the distinction between short-run aggregate supply and long-run aggregate supply becomes important. With the economy producing above potential output, inputs will be in high demand. Input prices including nominal wages will rise. As they do, the short-run aggregate supply curve will ultimately shift leftward such that it intersects long-run aggregate supply at point *c*.[1] There, the economy has reestablished long-run equilibrium, with the price level and real output now P_3 and Q_f, respectively. Only at point *c* does the new aggregate demand curve AD_2 intersect both the short-run aggregate supply curve AS_2 and the long-run aggregate supply curve AS_{LR}.

In the short run, demand-pull inflation drives up the price level and increases real output; in the long run, only the price level rises. In the long run, the initial increase in aggregate demand moves the economy along its vertical aggregate supply curve AS_{LR}. For a while, an economy can operate beyond its full-employment level of output. But the demand-pull inflation eventually causes adjustments of nominal wages that return the economy to its full-employment output Q_f.

[1]We say "ultimately" because the initial leftward shift in short-run aggregate supply will intersect the long-run aggregate supply curve AS_{LR} at price level P_2 (review Figure 32.1b). But the intersection of AD_2 and this new short-run aggregate supply curve (that is not shown in Figure 32.3) will produce a price level above P_2. (You may want to pencil this in to make sure that you understand this point.) Again nominal wages will rise, shifting the short-run aggregate supply curve farther leftward. The process will continue until the economy moves to point *c*, where the short-run aggregate supply curve is AS_2, the price level is P_3, and real output is Q_f.

Cost-Push Inflation in the Extended AD-AS Model

Cost-push inflation arises from factors that increase the cost of production at each price level, shifting the aggregate supply curve leftward and raising the equilibrium price level. Previously (Figure 26.10), we considered cost-push inflation using only the short-run aggregate supply curve. Now we want to analyze that type of inflation in its long-run context.

Analysis Look at Figure 32.4, in which we again assume that the economy is initially operating at price level P_1 and output level Q_f (point *a*). Suppose that international oil producers agree to reduce the supply of oil to boost its price by, say, 100 percent. As a result, the per-unit production cost of producing and transporting goods and services rises substantially in the economy represented by Figure 32.4. This increase in per-unit production costs shifts the short-run aggregate supply curve to the left, as from AS_1 to AS_2, and the price level rises from P_1 to P_2 (as seen by comparing points *a* and *b*). In this case, the leftward shift of the aggregate supply curve is *not a response* to a price-level increase, as it was in our previous discussions of demand-pull inflation; it is the *initiating cause* of the price-level increase.

Policy Dilemma Cost-push inflation creates a dilemma for policymakers. Without some expansionary stabilization policy, aggregate demand in Figure 32.4 remains in place at AD_1 and real output declines from Q_f to Q_2. Government can counter this recession, negative GDP gap, and attendant high unemployment by using fiscal policy and monetary policy to increase aggregate demand to AD_2. But there is a potential policy trap here: An increase in aggregate demand to AD_2 will further raise inflation by increasing the price level from P_2 to P_3 (a move from point *b* to point *c*).

Suppose the government recognizes this policy trap and decides not to increase aggregate demand from AD_1 to AD_2 (you can now disregard the dashed AD_2 curve) and instead decides to allow a cost-push-created recession to run its course. How will that happen? Widespread layoffs, plant shutdowns, and business failures eventually occur. At some point the demand for oil, labor, and other inputs will decline so much that oil prices and nominal wages will decline. When that happens, the initial leftward shift of the short-run aggregate supply curve will reverse itself. That is, the declining per-unit production costs caused by the recession will shift the short-run aggregate supply curve rightward from AS_2 to AS_1. The price level will return to P_1, and the full-employment level of output will be restored at Q_f (point *a* on the long-run aggregate supply curve AS_{LR}).

This analysis yields two generalizations:

- If the government attempts to maintain full employment when there is cost-push inflation, even more inflation will occur.
- If the government takes a hands-off approach to cost-push inflation, the recession will linger. Although falling input prices will eventually undo the initial rise in per-unit production costs, the economy in the meantime will experience high unemployment and a loss of real output.

AP **FIGURE 32.4 Cost-push inflation in the extended AD-AS model.** Cost-push inflation occurs when the short-run aggregate supply curve shifts leftward, as from AS_1 to AS_2. If government counters the decline in real output by increasing aggregate demand to the broken line, the price level rises even more. That is, the economy moves in steps from *a* to *b* to *c*. In contrast, if government allows a recession to occur, nominal wages eventually fall and the aggregate supply curve shifts back rightward to its original location. The economy moves from *a* to *b* and eventually back to *a*.

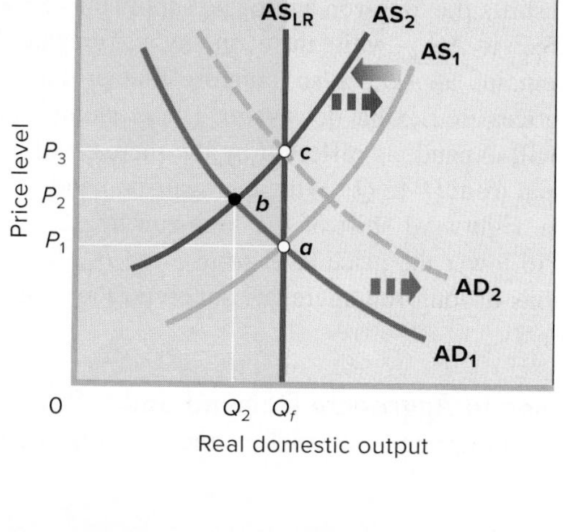

Recession and the Extended AD-AS Model

By far the most controversial application of the extended AD-AS model is its application to recession (or depression) caused by decreases in aggregate demand. We will look at this controversy in detail in Chapter 33; here we simply identify the key point of contention.

Suppose in Figure 32.5 that aggregate demand initially is AD_1 and that the short-run and long-run aggregate supply curves are AS_1 and AS_{LR}, respectively. Therefore, as shown by point *a*, the price level is P_1 and output is Q_f. Now suppose that investment spending declines dramatically, reducing aggregate demand to AD_2. Observe that real output declines from Q_f to Q_1, indicating that a recession has occurred. But if we make the controversial assumption that prices and wages are flexible downward, the price level falls from P_1 to P_2. With the economy producing below potential output at point *b*, demand for inputs will be low. Eventually, nominal wages themselves fall to restore the previous real wage; when that happens, the short-run aggregate supply curve shifts rightward from AS_1 to AS_2. The negative GDP

AP FIGURE 32.5 Recession in the extended AD-AS model. A recession occurs when aggregate demand shifts leftward, as from AD_1 to AD_2. If prices and wages are downwardly flexible, the price level falls from P_1 to P_2 as the economy moves from point *a* to point *b*. With the economy in recession at point *b*, wages eventually fall, shifting the aggregate supply curve from AS_1 to AS_2. The price level declines to P_3, and real output returns to Q_f. The economy moves from *a* to *b* to *c*.

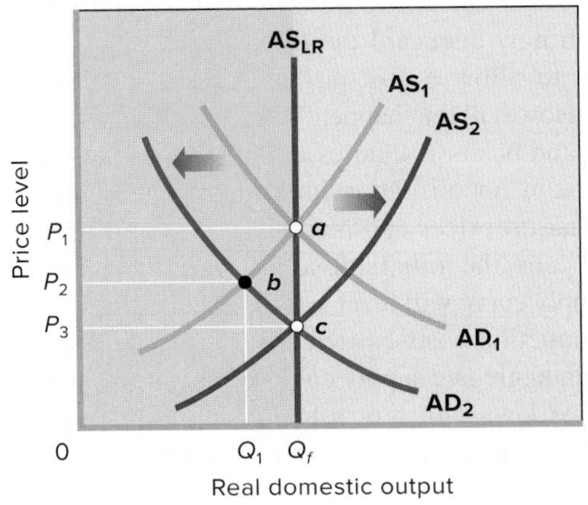

gap evaporates without the need for expansionary fiscal or monetary policy since real output expands from Q_1 (point *b*) back to Q_f (point *c*). The economy is again located on its long-run aggregate supply curve AS_{LR}, but now at lower price level P_3.

There is much disagreement about this hypothetical scenario. The key point of dispute revolves around the degree to which both input and output prices may be downwardly inflexible and how long it would take in the actual economy for the necessary downward price and wage adjustments to occur to regain the full-employment level of output. For now, suffice it to say that most economists believe that if such adjustments are forthcoming, they will occur only after the economy has experienced a relatively long-lasting recession with its accompanying high unemployment and large loss of output. The severity and length of the major recession of 2007–2009 has strengthened this view. Therefore, economists recommend active monetary policy, and perhaps fiscal policy, to counteract recessions.

Economic Growth with Ongoing Inflation

In our analysis so far, we have seen how demand and supply shocks can cause, respectively, demand-push inflation and cost-push inflation. But in these previous cases, the extent of the inflation was *finite* because the size of the initial movement in either the AD curve or the AS curve was *limited*. For instance, in Figure 32.3, the aggregate demand curve shifts right by a limited amount, from AD_1 to AD_2. As the economy's equilibrium moves from *a* to *b* to *c*, the price level rises from P_1 to P_2 to P_3. During this transition, inflation obviously occurs because the price level is rising. But once the economy reaches its new equilibrium at point *c*, the price level remains constant at P_3 and no further inflation takes place. That is, the limited movement in aggregate demand causes a limited amount of inflation that ends when the economy returns to full employment.

But the modern economy almost always experiences continuous, but usually mild, positive rates of inflation. That can only happen with ongoing shifts in either the aggregate demand or long-run aggregate supply curves because any single, finite shift will only cause inflation of limited duration. This insight is crucial to understanding why modern economies usually experience ongoing inflation while achieving economic growth. Both aggregate demand and long-run aggregate supply increase over time in the actual economy, and inflation occurs because the increases in aggregate demand generally exceed the increases in long-run aggregate supply. It will be helpful to examine this point graphically.

Increases in Long-Run Aggregate Supply As discussed in Chapter 22, economic growth is driven by supply factors such as improved technologies and access to more or better resources. Economists illustrate economic growth as either an outward shift of an economy's production possibilities curve or as a rightward shift of its long-run aggregate supply curve. As shown in Figure 32.6, the outward shift of the production possibilities curve from *AB* to *CD* in graph *a* is equivalent to the rightward shift of the economy's long-run aggregate supply curve from AS_{LR1} to AS_{LR2} in graph *b*.

Let's simply transfer this rightward shift of the economy's long-run aggregate supply curve to Figure 32.7, which depicts economic growth in the United States in the context of the extended aggregate demand–aggregate supply model. Suppose the economy's long-run aggregate supply curve initially is AS_{LR1}, while its aggregate demand curve and short-run aggregate supply curve are AD_1 and AS_1, as shown. The equilibrium price level is P_1 and the equilibrium level of real output is Q_1.

Now let's assume that economic growth driven by changes in supply factors (quantity and quality of resources and technology) shifts the long-run aggregate supply curve rightward from AS_{LR1} to AS_{LR2} while the economy's aggregate demand curve remains at AD_1. Also, suppose that product and resource prices are flexible downward. The economy's potential output will expand, as reflected by the increase of available real output from Q_1 to Q_2. With aggregate demand constant at AD_1, the rightward shift of the long-run aggregate supply curve will lower the price level from P_1 to P_3. Taken alone, expansions of long-run aggregate supply in the economy are deflationary.

Increases in Aggregate Demand and Inflation But a decline in the price level, such as the one from P_1 to P_3 in

AP FIGURE 32.6 Production possibilities and long-run aggregate supply. (a) Economic growth driven by supply factors (such as improved technologies or the use of more or better resources) shifts an economy's production possibilities curve outward, as from *AB* to *CD*. (b) The same factors shift the economy's long-run aggregate supply curve to the right, as from AS_{LR1} to AS_{LR2}.

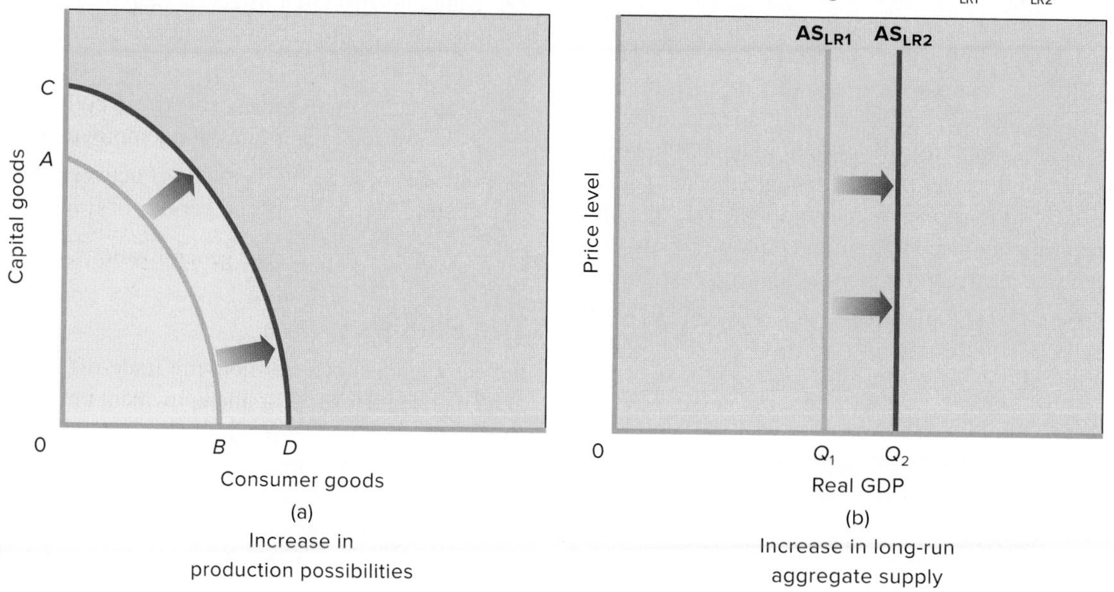

Figure 32.7, is not part of the long-run U.S. growth experience. Why not? The answer is that the nation's central bank—the Federal Reserve—engineers ongoing increases in the nation's money supply to create rightward shifts of the aggregate demand curve. These increases in aggregate demand would be highly inflationary absent the increases in long-run aggregate supply. But because the Fed usually makes sure that the inflationary rightward shifts of the aggregate demand curve proceed only slightly faster than the deflationary rightward shifts of the aggregate supply curve, only mild inflation occurs along with economic growth.

We illustrate this outcome in Figure 32.7, where aggregate demand shifts to the right from AD_1 to AD_2 at the same time long-run aggregate supply shifts rightward from AS_{LR1} to AS_{LR2}. Real output expands from Q_1 to Q_2 and the price level increases from P_1 to P_2. At the higher price level P_2, the

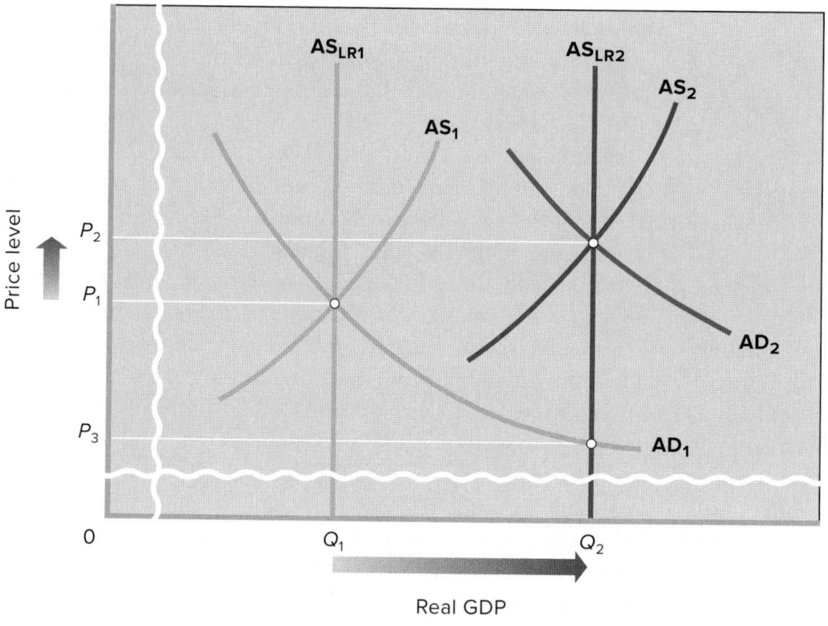

AP FIGURE 32.7 Depicting U.S. growth via the extended AD-AS model. Long-run aggregate supply and short-run aggregate supply have increased over time, as from AS_{LR1} to AS_{LR2} and AS_1 to AS_2. Simultaneously, aggregate demand has shifted rightward, as from AD_1 to AD_2. The actual outcome of these combined shifts has been economic growth, shown as the increase in real output from Q_1 to Q_2, accompanied by mild inflation, shown as the rise in the price level from P_1 to P_2.

economy confronts a new short-run aggregate supply curve AS_2. The changes shown in Figure 32.7 describe the actual U.S. experience: economic growth, accompanied by mild inflation. Real output on average increases at about 3.4 percent annually and inflation averages 2 to 3 percent a year.

Of course, other long-term outcomes besides that depicted are entirely possible. Whether deflation, zero inflation, mild inflation, or rapid inflation accompanies economic growth depends on the extent to which aggregate demand increases relative to long-run aggregate supply. Over long periods, any inflation that accompanies economic growth is exclusively the result of aggregate demand increasing more rapidly than long-run aggregate supply. The expansion of long-run aggregate supply—of potential real GDP—is never the cause of inflation.

AP QUICK REVIEW 32.2

- ✓ In the short run, demand-pull inflation, caused by an increasing aggregate demand, raises both the price level and real output. In the long run, if the economy is operating above full employment, a tightening labor market raises nominal wages, the short-run aggregate supply curve shifts to the left, the price level increases, and the economy settles at full employment.
- ✓ Cost-push inflation results from a reduction in the short-run aggregate supply curve, lowering real output, increasing unemployment, and increasing the price level. Cost-push inflation creates a policy dilemma for the government in that if it engages in an expansionary policy to increase output and reduce unemployment, additional inflation will occur; if it does nothing, the recession will linger until input prices have fallen by enough to return the economy to producing at potential output. If it pursues a contractionary policy to fight inflation, then real output falls and unemployment increases.

AP The Inflation-Unemployment Relationship

LO32.3 Explain the short-run trade-off between inflation and unemployment (the Phillips Curve).

We have just seen that the Fed can determine how much inflation occurs in the economy by how much it causes aggregate demand to shift relative to aggregate supply. Given that low inflation and low unemployment rates are the Fed's major economic goals, its ability to control inflation brings up at least two interesting policy questions: Are low unemployment and low inflation compatible goals or conflicting goals? What explains situations in which high unemployment and high inflation coexist?

The extended AD-AS model supports three significant generalizations relating to these questions:

- Under normal circumstances, there is a short-run trade-off between the rate of inflation and the rate of unemployment.
- Aggregate supply shocks can cause both higher rates of inflation and higher rates of unemployment.
- There is no significant trade-off between inflation and unemployment over long periods of time.

Let's examine each of these generalizations.

The Phillips Curve

We can demonstrate the short-run trade-off between the rate of inflation and the rate of unemployment through the **Phillips Curve,** named after A. W. Phillips, who developed the idea in Great Britain. This curve, generalized in Figure 32.8a, suggests an inverse relationship between the rate of inflation and the rate of unemployment. Lower unemployment rates (measured as leftward movements on the horizontal axis) are associated with higher rates of inflation (measured as upward movements on the vertical axis).

The underlying rationale of the Phillips Curve becomes apparent when we view the short-run aggregate supply curve in Figure 32.9 and perform a simple mental experiment. Suppose that in some short-run period aggregate demand expands from AD_0 to AD_2, either because firms decide to buy more capital goods or the government decides to increase its expenditures. Whatever the cause, in the short run the price level rises from P_0 to P_2 and real output rises from Q_0 to Q_2. As real output rises, the unemployment rate falls.

Now let's compare what would have happened if the increase in aggregate demand had been larger, say, from AD_0 to AD_3. The equilibrium at P_3 and Q_3 indicates that the amount of inflation and the growth of real output would both have been greater (and that the unemployment rate would have been lower). Similarly, suppose aggregate demand during the year had increased only modestly, from AD_0 to AD_1. Compared with our shift from AD_0 to AD_2, the amount of inflation and the growth of real output would have been smaller (and the unemployment rate higher).

The generalization we draw from this mental experiment is this: *Assuming a constant short-run aggregate supply curve,* high rates of inflation are accompanied by low rates of unemployment, and low rates of inflation are accompanied by high rates of unemployment. Other things equal, the expected relationship should look something like Figure 32.8a.

Figure 32.8b reveals that the facts for the 1960s nicely fit the theory. On the basis of that evidence and evidence from other countries, most economists working at the end of the 1960s concluded there was a stable, predictable trade-off between unemployment and inflation. Moreover, U.S. economic

AP FIGURE 32.8 The Phillips Curve: concept and empirical data. (a) The Phillips Curve relates annual rates of inflation and annual rates of unemployment for a series of years. Because this is an inverse relationship, there presumably is a trade-off between unemployment and inflation. (b) Data points for the 1960s seemed to confirm the Phillips Curve concept. (Note: The unemployment rates are annual averages and the inflation rates are on a December-to-December basis.)

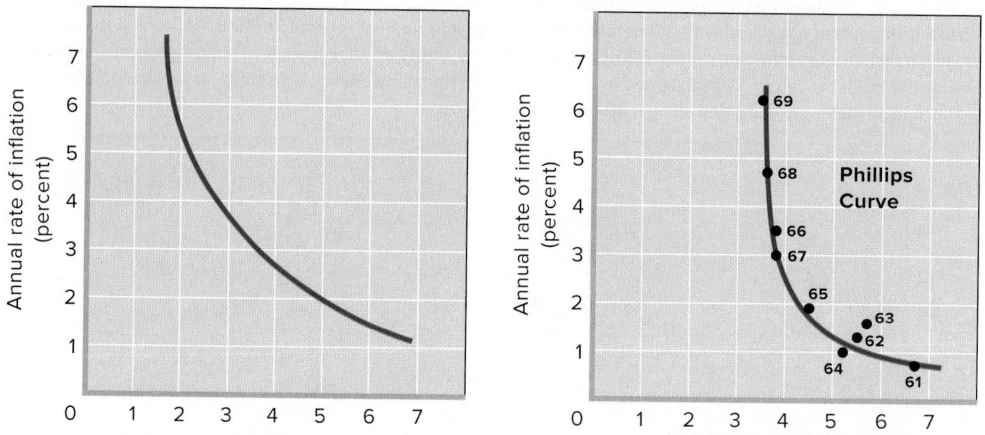

(a)
The concept

(b)
Data for the 1960s

policy was built on that supposed trade-off. According to this thinking, it was impossible to achieve "full employment without inflation": Manipulation of aggregate demand through fiscal and monetary measures would simply move the economy along the Phillips Curve. An expansionary fiscal and monetary policy that boosted aggregate demand and lowered the unemployment rate would simultaneously increase inflation. A restrictive fiscal and monetary policy could be used to reduce the rate of inflation but only at the cost of a higher unemployment rate and more forgone production. Society had to choose between the incompatible goals of price stability and full employment; it had to decide where to locate on its Phillips Curve.

AP FIGURE 32.9 The short-run effect of changes in aggregate demand on real output and the price level. Comparing the effects of various possible increases in aggregate demand leads to the conclusion that the larger the increase in aggregate demand, the higher the rate of inflation and the greater the increase in real output. Because real output and the unemployment rate move in opposite directions, we can generalize that, given short-run aggregate supply, high rates of inflation should be accompanied by low rates of unemployment.

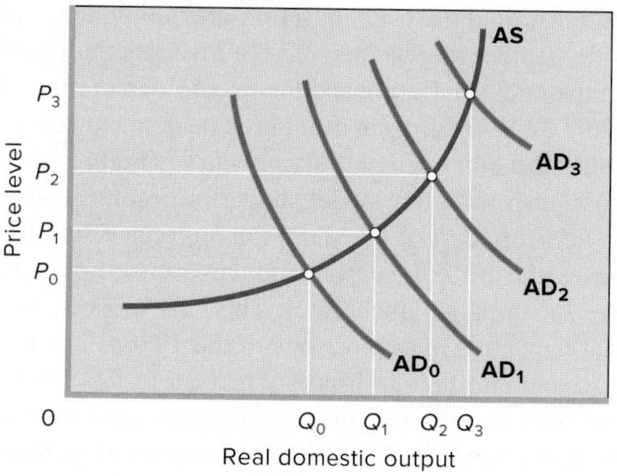

For reasons we will soon see, today's economists reject the idea of a stable, predictable Phillips Curve. Nevertheless, they agree there is a short-run trade-off between unemployment and inflation. *Given short-run aggregate supply,* increases in aggregate demand increase real output and reduce the unemployment rate. As the unemployment rate falls and dips below the natural rate, the excessive spending produces demand-pull inflation. Conversely, when recession sets in and the unemployment rate increases, the weak aggregate demand that caused the recession also leads to lower inflation rates.

Periods of exceptionally low unemployment rates and inflation rates do occur, but only under special sets of economic circumstances. One such period was the late 1990s, when faster productivity growth increased aggregate supply and fully blunted the inflationary impact of rapidly rising aggregate demand (review Figure 26.11).

Aggregate Supply Shocks and the Phillips Curve

The unemployment-inflation experience of the 1970s and early 1980s demolished the idea of an always-stable Phillips Curve. In Figure 32.10, we show the Phillips Curve for the 1960s in blue and then add the data points for 1970 through 2015. Observe that in most of the years of the 1970s and early 1980s, the economy experienced both higher inflation rates

AP **FIGURE 32.10 Inflation rates and unemployment rates, 1960–2015.** A series of aggregate supply shocks in the 1970s resulted in higher rates of inflation *and* higher rates of unemployment. So data points for the 1970s and 1980s tended to be above and to the right of the blue Phillips Curve for the 1960s. In the 1990s, the inflation-unemployment data points slowly moved back toward the 1960s Phillips Curve. Points for the late 1990s and 2000s are similar to those from the 1960s. However, the data point for 2009 (9.3 percent unemployment, −0.4 percent inflation) was located dramatically lower and much farther to the right relative to the data point for 2008 (5.8 percent unemployment, 3.8 percent inflation). That movement reflected negative inflation accompanied by much higher unemployment during 2009. As the economy slowly mended after the Great Recession, the data points for 2011 through 2015 (highlighted in blue) showed inflation and unemployment falling simultaneously—a pattern inconsistent with moving along a single fixed Philips curve.

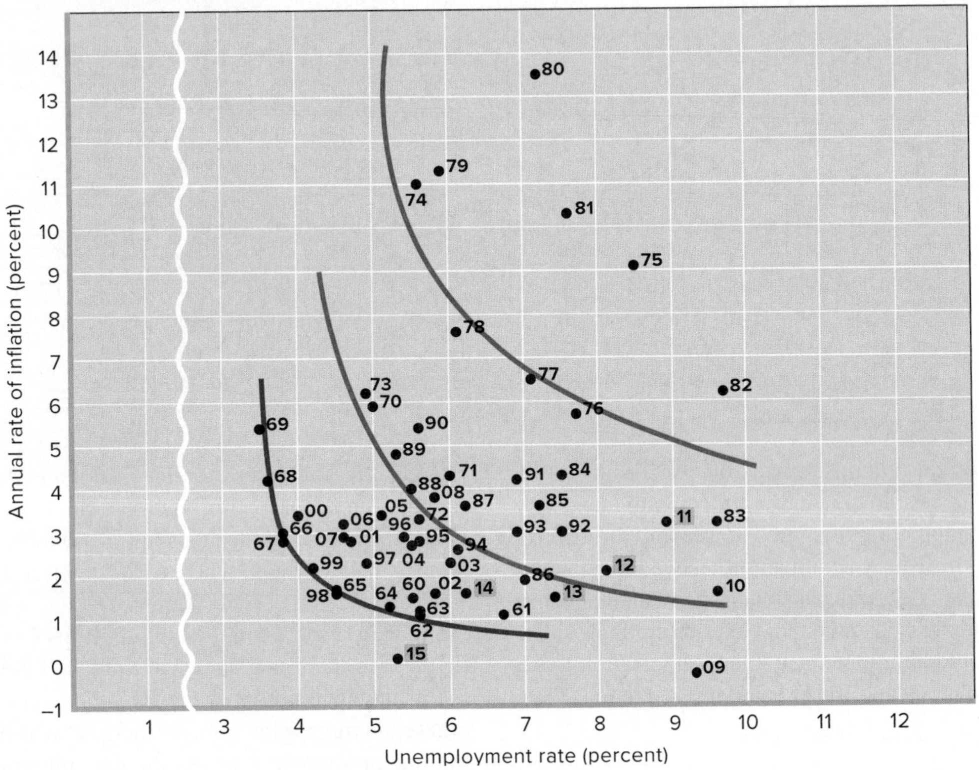

Source: Bureau of Labor Statistics, **www.bls.gov.**

and higher unemployment rates than it did in the 1960s. In fact, inflation and unemployment rose simultaneously in some of those years. This condition is called **stagflation**—a media term that combines the words "stagnation" and "inflation." If there still was any such thing as a Phillips Curve, it had clearly shifted outward, perhaps as shown.

Adverse Aggregate Supply Shocks The data points for the 1970s and early 1980s support our second generalization: Aggregate supply shocks can cause both higher rates of inflation and higher rates of unemployment. A series of adverse **aggregate supply shocks**—sudden, large increases in resource costs that jolt an economy's short-run aggregate supply curve leftward—hit the economy in the 1970s and early 1980s. The most significant of these shocks was a quadrupling of oil prices by the Organization of Petroleum Exporting Countries (OPEC). Consequently, the cost of producing and distributing virtually every product and service rose rapidly. (Other factors working to increase U.S. costs during this period included major agricultural shortfalls, a greatly depreciated dollar, wage hikes previously held down by wage-price controls, and slower rates of productivity growth.)

These shocks shifted the aggregate supply curve to the left and distorted the usual inflation-unemployment relationship. Remember that we derived the inverse relationship between the rate of inflation and the unemployment rate shown in Figure 32.8a by shifting the aggregate demand curve along a stable short-run aggregate supply curve (Figure 32.9). But the cost-push inflation model shown in Figure 32.4 tells us that a *leftward shift* of the short-run aggregate supply curve increases the price level and reduces real output (and increases the unemployment rate). This, say most economists, is what happened in two periods in the 1970s. The U.S. unemployment rate shot up from 4.9 percent in 1973 to 8.5 percent in 1975, contributing to a significant decline in real GDP. In the same period, the U.S. price level rose by 21 percent. The stagflation scenario recurred in 1978, when OPEC increased oil prices by more than 100 percent. The U.S. price level rose by 26 percent over the 1978–1980 period, while unemployment increased from 6.1 to 7.2 percent.

Stagflation's Demise Another look at Figure 32.10 reveals a generally inward movement of the inflation-unemployment points between 1982 and 1989. By 1989, the lingering effects of the earlier period had subsided. One precursor to this favorable trend was the deep recession of 1981–1982, largely caused by a restrictive monetary policy aimed at reducing double-digit inflation. The recession upped the unemployment rate to 9.7 percent in 1982. With so many workers unemployed, those who were working accepted smaller increases in their nominal wages—or, in some cases, wage reductions—in order to preserve their jobs. Firms, in turn, restrained their price increases to try to retain their relative shares of a greatly diminished market.

Other factors were at work. Foreign competition throughout this period held down wage and price hikes in several basic industries such as automobiles and steel. Deregulation of the airline and trucking industries also resulted in wage reductions or so-called wage givebacks. A significant decline in OPEC's monopoly power and a greatly reduced reliance on oil in the production process produced a stunning fall in the price of oil and its derivative products, such as gasoline.

All these factors combined to reduce per-unit production costs and to shift the short-run aggregate supply curve rightward (as from AS_2 to AS_1 in Figure 32.4). Employment and output expanded, and the unemployment rate fell from 9.6 percent in 1983 to 5.3 percent in 1989. Figure 32.10 reveals that the inflation-unemployment points for the late 1990s and 2000s are closer to the points associated with the Phillips Curve of the 1960s than to the points that plot out the data for the late 1970s and early 1980s.

The 2007–2009 recession led to shifts in unemployment and inflation that were inconsistent with a stable Philips curve. In 2008, unemployment was still at a historically moderate 5.8 percent while inflation came in at 3.8 percent. The inflation-unemployment point for 2009, however, moved down and to the right significantly as unemployment jumped to 9.3 percent while the inflation rate fell to a deflationary –0.4 percent. The point for 2010 moved a bit up and to the right as unemployment peaked at 9.6 percent and inflation rose to 1.6 percent. Then the 2011 point moved up and to the left as unemployment began to fall and inflation rose to 3.2 percent. As the economy continued to mend, the points for 2012 through 2015 moved down and to the left as the economy experienced an ongoing pattern of falling inflation coinciding with falling unemployment—a pattern *in*consistent with moving along a single fixed Philips Curve.

The media sometimes express the sum of the unemployment rate and the inflation rate as a rough gauge of the economic discomfort that inflation and unemployment jointly impose on an economy in a particular year. The sum of the two rates is used to compute the *misery index*. For example, a nation with a 5 percent unemployment rate and a 5 percent inflation rate has a misery index number of 10, as does a nation with an 8 percent unemployment rate and a 2 percent inflation rate.

Global Perspective 32.1 shows the misery index for several nations between 2004 and 2014. (It uses average annual inflation rates, not the December-to-December inflation rates used to construct Figure 32.10.) The U.S. misery index number has been neither exceptionally low nor exceptionally high relative to the misery index numbers for the other major economies shown. But bear in mind that economists do not put much stock in the misery index because they do not view the national discomfort associated with a 1 percent change in inflation and a 1 percent change in unemployment as necessarily equivalent. In particular, the misery index can greatly disguise the extent of hardship during a recession. The rise in the unemployment rate in these circumstances causes a huge loss of national output and income (and misery!), even if the higher unemployment rate is partially or fully offset with a decline in the rate of inflation.

GLOBAL PERSPECTIVE 32.1

The Misery Index, Selected Nations, 2004–2014

The U.S. misery index number (the sum of its unemployment rate and inflation rate) has generally been in the midrange of such numbers relative to other major economies in recent years.

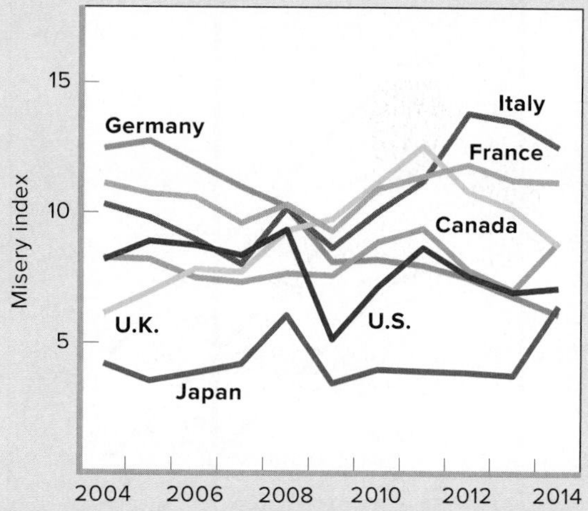

Source: The World Bank, **data.worldbank.org**, and *Global Employment Trends 2014*, International Labour Organization, **ilo.org**. Inflation rates and unemployment rates in this calculation are both on an average-annual basis.

The Long-Run Phillips Curve

LO32.4 Discuss why there is no long-run trade-off between inflation and unemployment.

The overall set of data points in Figure 32.10 supports our third generalization relating to the inflation-unemployment relationship: There is no apparent *long-run* trade-off between inflation and unemployment. Economists point out that when decades (as opposed to a few years) are considered, any rate of inflation is consistent with the natural rate of unemployment prevailing at that time. We know from Chapter 23 that the natural rate of unemployment is the unemployment rate that occurs when cyclical unemployment is zero; it is the full-employment rate of unemployment, or the rate of unemployment when the economy achieves its potential output.

How can there be a short-run inflation-unemployment trade-off but not a long-run trade-off? Figure 32.11 provides the answer.

Short-Run Phillips Curve

Consider Phillips Curve PC_1 in Figure 32.11. Suppose the economy initially is experiencing a 3 percent rate of inflation and a 5 percent natural rate of unemployment. Such short-term curves as PC_1, PC_2, and PC_3 (drawn as straight lines for simplicity) exist because the actual rate of inflation is not always the same as the expected rate.

Establishing an additional point on Phillips Curve PC_1 will clarify this. We begin at a_1, where we assume nominal wages are set on the assumption that the 3 percent rate of inflation will continue. That is, because workers expect output prices to rise by 3 percent per year, they negotiate wage contracts that feature 3 percent per year increases in nominal wages so that these nominal wage increases will exactly offset the expected rise in prices and thereby keep their real wages the same.

But suppose that the rate of inflation rises to 6 percent, perhaps because the Fed has decided to move the AD curve to the right even faster than it had been before. With a nominal wage rate set on the expectation that the 3 percent rate of inflation will continue, the higher product prices raise business profits. Firms respond to the higher profits by hiring more workers and increasing output. In the short run, the economy moves to b_1, which, in contrast to a_1, involves a lower rate of unemployment (4 percent) and a higher rate of inflation (6 percent). The move from a_1 to b_1 is consistent both with an upsloping aggregate supply curve and with the inflation-unemployment trade-off implied by the Phillips Curve analysis. But this short-run Phillips Curve simply is a manifestation of the following principle: *When the actual rate of inflation is higher than expected, profits temporarily rise and the unemployment rate temporarily falls.*

FIGURE 32.11 The long-run vertical Phillips Curve. Increases in aggregate demand beyond those consistent with full-employment output may temporarily boost profits, output, and employment (as from a_1 to b_1). But nominal wages eventually will catch up so as to sustain real wages. When they do, profits will fall, negating the previous short-run stimulus to production and employment (the economy now moves from b_1 to a_2). Consequently, there is no trade-off between the rates of inflation and unemployment in the long run; that is, the long-run Phillips Curve is roughly a vertical line at the economy's natural rate of unemployment.

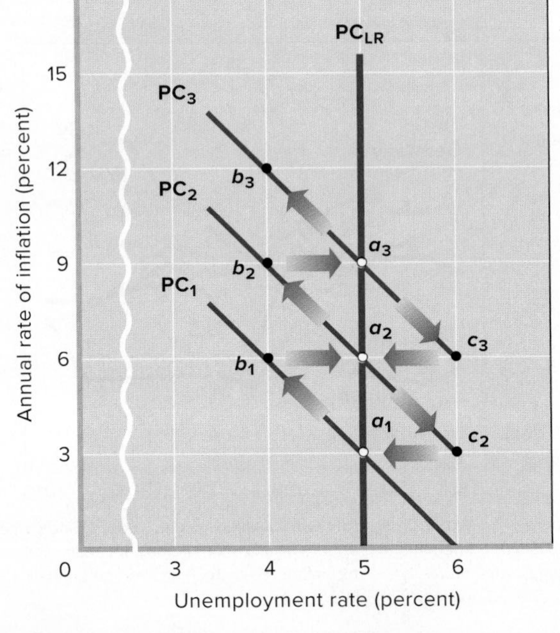

Long-Run Vertical Phillips Curve

But point b_1 is not a stable equilibrium. Workers will recognize that their nominal wages have not increased as fast as inflation and will therefore renegotiate their labor contracts so that they feature faster increases in nominal wages. These faster increases in nominal wages make up for the higher rate of inflation and restore the workers' lost purchasing power. As these new labor contracts kick in, business profits will fall to their prior level. The reduction in profits means that the original motivation to employ more workers and increase output has disappeared.

Unemployment then returns to its natural level at point a_2. Note, however, that the economy now faces a higher actual and expected rate of inflation—6 percent rather than 3 percent. This happens because the new labor contracts feature 6 percent per year increases in wages to make up for the 6 percent per year inflation rate. Because wages are a production cost, this faster increase in wage rates will imply faster future increases in output prices as firms are forced to raise prices more rapidly to make up for the faster future rate of wage growth. Stated a bit differently, the initial increase in inflation will become *persistent* because it leads to renegotiated labor contracts that will perpetuate the higher rate of inflation. In addition, because the new labor contracts are public, it will also be the case that the higher rates of inflation that they will cause will be *expected* by everyone rather than being a surprise.

In view of the higher 6 percent expected rate of inflation, the short-run Phillips Curve shifts upward from PC_1 to PC_2 in Figure 32.11. An "along-the-Phillips-Curve" kind of move from a_1 to b_1 on PC_1 is merely a short-run or transient occurrence. In the long run, after nominal wage contracts catch up with increases in the inflation rate, unemployment returns to its natural rate at a_2, and there is a new short-run Phillips Curve PC_2 at the higher expected rate of inflation.

The scenario repeats if aggregate demand continues to increase. Prices rise momentarily ahead of nominal wages, profits expand, and employment and output increase (as implied by the move from a_2 to b_2). But, in time, nominal wages increase so as to restore real wages. Profits then fall to their original level, pushing employment back to the normal rate at a_3. The economy's "reward" for lowering the unemployment rate below the natural rate is a still higher (9 percent) rate of inflation.

Movements along the short-run Phillips curve (a_1 to b_1 on PC_1) cause the curve to shift to a less favorable position (PC_2, then PC_3, and so on). A stable Phillips Curve with the dependable series of unemployment-rate–inflation-rate trade-offs simply does not exist in the long run. The economy is characterized by a **long-run vertical Phillips Curve.**

The vertical line through a_1, a_2, and a_3 shows the long-run relationship between unemployment and inflation. Any rate of inflation is consistent with the 5 percent natural rate of unemployment. So, in this view, society ought to choose a low rate of inflation rather than a high one.

Disinflation

The distinction between the short-run Phillips Curve and the long-run Phillips Curve also helps explain **disinflation**—reductions in the inflation rate from year to year. Suppose that in Figure 32.11 the economy is at a_3, where the inflation rate is 9 percent. And suppose that a decline in the rate at which aggregate demand shifts to the right faster than aggregate supply (as happened during the 1981–1982 recession) reduces inflation below the 9 percent expected rate, say, to 6 percent. Business profits fall because prices are rising less rapidly than wages. The nominal wage increases, remember, were set on the assumption that the 9 percent rate of inflation would continue. In response to the decline in profits, firms reduce their employment and consequently the unemployment rate rises. The economy temporarily slides downward from point a_3 to c_3 along the short-run Phillips Curve PC_3. *When the actual rate of inflation is lower than the expected rate, profits temporarily fall and the unemployment rate temporarily rises.*

Firms and workers eventually adjust their expectations to the new 6 percent rate of inflation, and thus newly negotiated wage increases decline. Profits are restored, employment rises, and the unemployment rate falls back to its natural rate of 5 percent at a_2. Because the expected rate of inflation is now 6 percent, the short-run Phillips Curve PC_3 shifts leftward to PC_2.

If the rate at which aggregate demand shifts to the right faster than aggregate supply declines even more, the scenario will continue. Inflation declines from 6 percent to, say, 3 percent, moving the economy from a_2 to c_2 along PC_2. The lower-than-expected rate of inflation (lower prices) squeezes profits and reduces employment. But, in the long run, firms respond to the lower profits by reducing their nominal wage increases. Profits are restored and unemployment returns to its natural rate at a_1 as the short-run Phillips Curve moves from PC_2 to PC_1. Once again, the long-run Phillips Curve is vertical at the 5 percent natural rate of unemployment.

AP QUICK REVIEW 32.3

- ✓ As implied by the upsloping short-run aggregate supply (AS) curve, there may be a short-run trade-off between the rate of inflation and the rate of unemployment. This trade-off is reflected in the Phillips Curve (a downward sloping curve in the short run) showing that lower rates of inflation are associated with higher rates of unemployment.
- ✓ In the short run, changes in aggregate demand (AD) are movements along a Phillips curve. AS shocks that produce severe cost-push inflation can cause stagflation—simultaneous increases in the inflation rate and the unemployment rate. With these AS shocks, the Phillips curve will shift. Higher input prices will shift the Phillips curve rightward or upward; lower input prices will shift the Phillips curve leftward or downward.
- ✓ After all nominal wage adjustments play out, the economy should return to its full-employment level of output and its natural rate of unemployment. Thus, the long-run Phillips Curve is vertical at the natural rate of unemployment.

AP Taxation and Aggregate Supply

LO32.5 Explain the relationship among tax rates, tax revenues, and aggregate supply.

A final topic in our discussion of aggregate supply is taxation, a key aspect of **supply-side economics.** "Supply-side economists" or "supply-siders" stress that changes in aggregate supply are an active force in determining the levels of inflation, unemployment, and economic growth. Government policies can either impede or promote rightward shifts of the short-run and long-run aggregate supply curves shown in Figure 32.2. One such policy is taxation.

These economists say that the enlargement of the U.S. tax system has impaired incentives to work, save, and invest. In this view, high tax rates impede productivity growth and hence slow the expansion of long-run aggregate supply. By reducing the after-tax rewards of workers and producers, high tax rates reduce the financial attractiveness of working, saving, and investing.

Supply-siders focus their attention on *marginal tax rates*—the rates on extra dollars of income—because those rates affect the benefits from working, saving, or investing more. In 2016, marginal federal income tax rates varied from 10 to 39.6 percent in the United States.

Taxes and Incentives to Work

Supply-siders believe that how long and how hard people work depends on the amounts of additional after-tax earnings they derive from their efforts. They say that lower marginal tax rates on earned incomes induce more work, and therefore increase aggregate inputs of labor. Lower marginal tax rates increase the after-tax wage rate and make leisure more expensive and work more attractive. The higher opportunity cost of leisure encourages people to substitute work for leisure. This increase in productive effort is achieved in many ways: by increasing the number of hours worked per day or week, by encouraging workers to postpone retirement, by inducing more people to enter the labor force, by motivating people to work harder, and by avoiding long periods of unemployment.

Incentives to Save and Invest

High marginal tax rates also reduce the rewards for saving and investing. For example, suppose that Tony saves $10,000 at 8 percent interest, bringing him $800 of interest per year. If his marginal tax rate is 40 percent, his after-tax interest earnings will be $480, not $800, and his after-tax interest rate will fall to 4.8 percent. While Tony might be willing to save (forgo current consumption) for an 8 percent return on his saving, he might rather consume when the return is only 4.8 percent.

Saving, remember, is the prerequisite of investment. Thus, supply-side economists recommend lower marginal tax rates on interest earned from saving. They also call for lower taxes on income from capital to ensure that there are ready investment outlets for the economy's enhanced pool of saving. A critical determinant of investment spending is the expected *after-tax* return on that spending.

To summarize: Lower marginal tax rates encourage saving and investing. Workers therefore find themselves equipped with more and technologically superior machinery and equipment. Labor productivity rises, and that expands long-run aggregate supply and economic growth, which in turn keeps unemployment rates and inflation low.

The Laffer Curve

In the supply-side view, reductions in marginal tax rates increase the nation's aggregate supply and can leave the nation's tax revenues unchanged or even enlarge them. Thus, supply-side tax cuts need not produce federal budget deficits.

This idea is based on the **Laffer Curve,** named after Arthur Laffer, who popularized it. As Figure 32.12 shows, the Laffer Curve depicts the relationship between tax rates and tax revenues. As tax rates increase from 0 to 100 percent, tax revenues increase from zero to some maximum level (at *m*) and then fall to zero. Tax revenues decline beyond some point because higher tax rates discourage economic activity, thereby shrinking the tax base (domestic output and income). This is easiest to see at the extreme, where the tax rate is 100 percent. Tax revenues here are, in theory, reduced to zero because the 100 percent confiscatory tax rate has halted production. A 100 percent tax rate applied to a tax base of zero yields no revenue.

In the early 1980s, Laffer suggested that the United States was at a point such as *n* on the curve in Figure 32.12. At *n*, tax rates are so high that production is discouraged to the extent that tax revenues are below the maximum at *m*. If the economy is at *n*, then lower tax rates can either increase tax revenues or leave them unchanged. For example, lowering the tax rate from point *n* to point *l* would bolster the economy such that the government would bring in the same total amount of tax revenue as before.

Laffer's reasoning was that lower tax rates stimulate incentives to work, save and invest, innovate, and accept business risks, thus triggering an expansion of real output and income. That enlarged tax base sustains tax revenues even though tax rates are lowered. Indeed, between *n* and *m* lower tax rates result in *increased* tax revenue.

FIGURE 32.12 The Laffer Curve. The Laffer Curve suggests that up to point *m* higher tax rates will result in larger tax revenues. But tax rates higher than *m* will adversely affect incentives to work and produce, reducing the size of the tax base (output and income) to the extent that tax revenues will decline. It follows that if tax rates are above *m*, reductions in tax rates will produce increases in tax revenues.

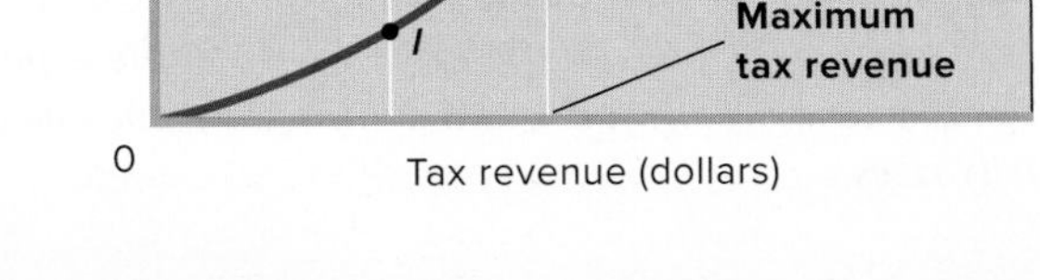

Also, when taxes are lowered, tax avoidance (which is legal) and tax evasion (which is not) decline. High marginal tax rates prompt taxpayers to avoid taxes through various tax shelters, such as buying municipal bonds, on which the interest earned is tax-free. High rates also encourage some taxpayers to conceal income from the Internal Revenue Service. Lower tax rates reduce the inclination to engage in either tax avoidance or tax evasion.

The Laffer curve also implies that for any particular amount of tax revenue that the government can possibly collect, there will be both a high tax rate at which that amount of revenue can be collected as well as a low tax rate at which that amount of revenue can be collected. As an example, compare points *n* an *l* in Figure 32.12. Point *n* has a high tax rate and point *l* has a low tax rate, but they both collect the same amount of tax revenue. So if the government's major goal when setting tax rates is simply to collect a particular total amount of tax revenue, Laffer argued that the government should always opt for the lower tax rate. By doing so, the government would collect the revenue it desired while impinging as little as possible on the private economy.

Criticisms of the Laffer Curve

The Laffer Curve and its supply-side implications have been subject to severe criticism.

Taxes, Incentives, and Time A fundamental criticism relates to the degree to which economic incentives are sensitive to changes in tax rates. Skeptics say ample empirical evidence shows that the impact of a tax cut on incentives is small, of uncertain direction, and relatively slow to emerge. For example, with respect to work incentives, studies indicate that decreases in tax rates lead some people to work more but lead others to work less. Those who work more are enticed by the higher after-tax pay; they substitute work for leisure because the opportunity cost of leisure has increased. But other people work less because the higher after-tax pay enables them to "buy more leisure." With the tax cut, they can earn the same level of after-tax income as before with fewer work hours.

Inflation or Higher Real Interest Rates Most economists think that the demand-side effects of a tax cut are more immediate and certain than longer-term supply-side effects. Thus, tax cuts undertaken when the economy is at or near full employment may produce increases in aggregate demand that overwhelm any increase in aggregate supply. The likely result is inflation or restrictive monetary policy to prevent it. If the latter, real interest rates will rise and investment will decline. This will defeat the purpose of the supply-side tax cuts.

Position on the Curve Skeptics say that the Laffer Curve is merely a logical proposition and assert that there must be some level of tax rates between 0 and 100 percent at which tax revenues will be at their maximum. Economists of all persuasions can agree with this. But the issue of where a particular economy is located on its Laffer Curve is an empirical question. If we assume that we are at point *n* in Figure 32.12, then tax cuts will increase tax revenues. But if the economy is at any point below *m* on the curve, tax-rate reductions will reduce tax revenues.

CONSIDER THIS . . .

Sherwood Forest

Source: © Bettmann/Corbis

The popularization of the idea that tax-rate reductions may increase tax revenues owes much to Arthur Laffer's ability to present his ideas simply. He reportedly took out his pen and drew a curve on a napkin to illustrate his tax ideas to a *Wall Street Journal* editor. The editor retained the napkin and later reproduced the curve in an editorial in *The Wall Street Journal*. The Laffer Curve was born and the idea it portrayed became the centerpiece of economic policy under the Reagan administration (1981–1989), which cut tax rates on personal income by 25 percent over a three-year period.

Laffer illustrated his supply-side views with a story relating to Robin Hood, who, you may recall, stole from the rich to give to the poor. Laffer likened people traveling through Sherwood Forest to taxpayers, whereas Robin Hood and his band of merry men were government. As taxpayers passed through the forest, Robin Hood and his men intercepted them and forced them to hand over their money. Laffer asked audiences, "Do you think that travelers continued to go through Sherwood Forest?"

The answer he sought and got, of course, was "no." Taxpayers will avoid Sherwood Forest to the greatest extent possible. They will lower their taxable income by reducing work hours, retiring earlier, saving less, and engaging in tax avoidance and tax evasion activities. Robin Hood and his men may end up with less revenue than if they collected a relatively small "tax" from each traveler for passage through the forest.

Rebuttal and Evaluation

Supply-side advocates respond to the skeptics by contending that the Reagan tax cuts in the 1980s worked as Laffer predicted. Although the top marginal income tax rates on earned income were cut from 50 to 28 percent in that decade, real GDP and tax revenues were substantially higher at the end of the 1990s than at the beginning.

LAST WORD

Do Tax Increases Reduce Real GDP?*

Determining the Relationship between Changes in Taxes and Permanent Changes in Real GDP Is Fraught with Complexities and Difficulties. University of California-Berkeley Economists Christina Romer and David Romer Have Recently Devised a Novel Way to Approach the Topic. Their Findings Suggest That Tax Increases Reduce Real GDP.†

How do changes in the level of taxation affect the level of economic activity? The simple correlation between taxation and economic activity shows that, on average, when economic activity rises more rapidly, tax revenues also are rising more rapidly. But this correlation almost surely does not reflect a positive effect of tax increases on output. Rather, under our tax system, any positive shock to output raises tax revenues by increasing income.

© Thinkstock/Getty Images RF

In "The Macroeconomic Effects of Tax Changes: Estimates Based on a New Measure of Fiscal Shocks," authors Christina Romer and David Romer observe that this difficulty is just one of many manifestations of a more general problem. Changes in taxes occur for many reasons. And, because the factors that give rise to tax changes often are correlated with other developments in the economy, disentangling the effects of the tax changes from the other effects of these underlying factors is inherently difficult.

To address this problem, Romer and Romer use the narrative record—presidential speeches, executive branch documents, congressional reports, and so on—to identify the size, timing, and principal motivation for all major tax policy actions in the post–World War II United States. This narrative analysis allows them to separate revenue changes resulting from legislation from changes occurring for other reasons. It also allows them to classify legislated changes according to their primary motivation.

Romer and Romer find that despite the complexity of the legislative process, most significant tax changes have been motivated by one of four factors: counteracting other influences in the economy; paying for increases in government spending (or lowering taxes in conjunction with reductions in spending); addressing an inherited budget deficit; and promoting long-run growth. They observe that legislated tax changes taken to counteract other influences on the economy, or to pay for increases in government spending, are very likely to be correlated with other factors affecting the economy. As a result, these observations are likely to lead to unreliable estimates of the effect of tax changes.

Tax changes that are made to promote long-run growth, or to reduce an inherited budget deficit, in contrast, are undertaken for reasons essentially unrelated to other factors influencing output. Thus, examining the behavior of output following these tax changes is likely to provide more reliable estimates of the output effects of tax changes. *The results of this more reliable test indicate that tax changes have very large effects: a tax increase of 1 percent of GDP lowers real GDP by roughly 2 to 3 percent.*

These output effects are highly persistent. The behavior of inflation and unemployment suggests that this persistence reflects long-lasting departures of output from previous levels. Romer and Romer also find that output effects of tax changes are much more closely tied to the actual changes in taxes than news about future changes, and that investment falls sharply in response to tax changes. Indeed, the strong response of investment helps to explain why the output consequences of tax increases are so large.

Romer and Romer find suggestive evidence that tax increases to reduce an inherited budget deficit have much smaller output costs than other tax increases. This is consistent with the idea that deficit-driven tax increases may have important expansionary effects through [improved] expectations and [lower] long-term interest rates, or through [enhanced] confidence.

---

*Abridged from Les Picker, "Tax Increases Reduce GDP," *The NBER Digest*, February/March 2008. The *Digest* provides synopses of research papers in progress by economists affiliated with the National Bureau of Economic Research (NBER).

†Christina Romer and David Romer, "The Macroeconomic Effects of Tax Changes: Estimates Based on a New Measure of Fiscal Shocks," *American Economic Review*, June 2010, pp. 763–801.

But the general view among economists is that the Reagan tax cuts, coming at a time of severe recession, helped boost aggregate demand and return real GDP to its full-employment output and normal growth path. As the economy expanded, so did tax revenues despite the lower tax rates. The rise in tax revenues caused by economic growth swamped the declines in revenues from lower tax rates. In essence, the Laffer Curve shown in Figure 32.12 stretched rightward, increasing net tax revenues. But the tax-rate cuts did not produce extraordinary rightward shifts of the long-run aggregate supply curve. Indeed, saving fell as a percentage of personal income during the period and productivity growth was sluggish. Real GDP sprang back vigorously from recessionary levels, but the economic growth rate soon reverted back to its longer-term average.

Because government expenditures rose more rapidly than tax revenues in the 1980s, large budget deficits occurred. In 1993 the Clinton administration increased the top marginal tax rates from 31 to 39.6 percent to address these deficits. The economy boomed in the last half of the 1990s, and by the end of the decade, tax revenues were so high relative to government expenditures that budget surpluses emerged. In 2001 the Bush administration reduced marginal tax rates over a series of years, partially "to return excess revenues to taxpayers." In 2003 the top marginal tax rate fell to 35 percent. Also, the income tax rates on capital gains and dividends were reduced to 15 percent. Economists generally agree that the Bush tax cuts, along with a highly expansionary monetary policy, helped revive and expand the economy following the recession of 2001. Strong growth of output and income in 2004 and 2005 produced large increases in tax revenues, although large budget deficits remained because spending also increased rapidly. The 2004 deficit was $413 billion and the 2005 deficit was $318 billion. The deficit fell over the next two years, to $162 billion in 2007. But the previously discussed financial crisis plunged the economy into a severe recession beginning in December 2007 and lasting into 2009. That caused income to fall and tax revenues to plummet. Also, the government aggressively pursued expansionary fiscal policy. Budget deficits increased to $459 billion in 2008 and $1.4 trillion in 2009. They decreased in subsequent years, down to around $445 billion in 2015.

Today, there is general agreement that the U.S. economy is operating at a point below *m*—rather than above *m*—on the Laffer Curve in Figure 32.12. In this zone, the overall effect is that personal tax-rate increases raise tax revenues while personal tax-rate decreases reduce tax revenues. But at the same time, economists recognize that, other things being equal, cuts in tax rates reduce tax revenues in percentage terms by less than the tax-rate reductions. Similarly, tax-rate increases do not raise tax revenues by as much in percentage terms as the tax-rate increases. This is true because changes in marginal tax rates alter taxpayer behavior and thus affect taxable income. Although these effects seem to be relatively modest, they need to be considered in designing tax policy—and, in fact, the federal government's Office of Tax Policy created a special division in 2007 devoted to estimating the magnitude of such effects when it comes to proposed changes in U.S. tax laws. Thus, supply-side economics has contributed to how economists and policymakers design and implement fiscal policy.

AP QUICK REVIEW 32.4

- ✓ Supply-side economists focus their attention on government policies that can increase aggregate supply, raising real GDP in the long run, and pressuring downward the price level. Generally, supply-side economists favor lower taxes that will increase incentives to save and to invest, to increase labor effort, and generally to increase real GDP.
- ✓ Put another way, supply-side economists are concerned with the disincentive effect of higher taxes that will reduce economic activity and real GDP.
- ✓ The Laffer Curve relates tax rates to total tax revenues and suggests that, under some circumstances, cuts in tax rates will expand the tax base (output and income) and increase tax revenues.
- ✓ Despite the strength of their commitment to supply-side economics, most economists do recognize that tax policy and other fiscal initiatives do have incentive effects that can affect the level of real GDP.

SUMMARY

LO32.1 Explain the relationship between short-run aggregate supply and long-run aggregate supply.

In macroeconomics, the short run is a period in which nominal wages do not respond to changes in the price level. In contrast, the long run is a period in which nominal wages fully respond to changes in the price level.

The short-run aggregate supply curve is upsloping. Because nominal wages are unresponsive to price-level changes, increases in the price level (prices received by firms) increase profits and real output. Conversely, decreases in the price level reduce profits and real output. However, the long-run aggregate supply curve is vertical. With sufficient time for adjustment, nominal wages rise and fall with the price level, moving the economy along a vertical aggregate supply curve at the economy's full-employment output.

LO32.2 Discuss how to apply the "extended" (short-run/long-run) AD-AS model to inflation, recessions, and economic growth.

In the short run, demand-pull inflation raises the price level and real output. Once nominal wages rise to match the increase in the price level, the temporary increase in real output is reversed.

In the short run, cost-push inflation raises the price level and lowers real output. Unless the government expands aggregate demand, nominal wages will eventually decline under conditions of recession and the short-run aggregate supply curve will shift back to its initial location. Prices and real output will eventually return to their original levels.

If prices and wages are flexible downward, a decline in aggregate demand will lower output and the price level. The decline in the price level will eventually lower nominal wages and shift the short-run aggregate supply curve rightward. Full-employment output will thus be restored.

One-time changes in aggregate demand (AD) and aggregate supply (AS) can only cause limited bouts of inflation. Ongoing mild inflation occurs because the Fed purposely increases AD slightly faster than the expansion of long-run AS (driven by the supply factors of economic growth).

LO32.3 Explain the short-run trade-off between inflation and unemployment (the Phillips Curve).

Assuming a stable, upsloping short-run aggregate supply curve, rightward shifts of the aggregate demand curve of various sizes yield the generalization that high rates of inflation are associated with low rates of unemployment, and vice versa. This inverse relationship is known as the Phillips Curve, and empirical data for the 1960s seemed to be consistent with it.

In the 1970s and early 1980s, the Phillips Curve apparently shifted rightward, reflecting stagflation—simultaneously rising inflation rates and unemployment rates. The higher unemployment rates and inflation rates resulted mainly from huge oil price increases that caused large leftward shifts in the short-run aggregate supply curve (so-called aggregate supply shocks). The Phillips Curve shifted inward toward its original position in the 1980s. By 1989, stagflation had subsided, and the data points for the late 1990s and first half of the first decade of the 2000s were similar to those of the 1960s. The new pattern continued until 2009, when the unemployment rate jumped to 9.3 percent while the inflation rate plummeted to a negative 0.4 percent.

As the economy slowly recovered, unemployment and inflation fell simultaneously between 2011 and 2015—a pattern inconsistent with the economy moving along a single fixed Phillips Curve.

LO32.4 Discuss why there is no long-run trade-off between inflation and unemployment.

Although there is a short-run trade-off between inflation and unemployment, there is no long-run trade-off. Workers will adapt their expectations to new inflation realities, and when they do, the unemployment rate will return to the natural rate. So the long-run Phillips Curve is vertical at the natural rate, meaning that higher rates of inflation do not permanently "buy" the economy less unemployment.

LO32.5 Explain the relationship among tax rates, tax revenues, and aggregate supply.

Supply-side economists focus attention on government policies, such as high taxation, that impede the expansion of aggregate supply. The Laffer Curve relates tax rates to levels of tax revenue and suggests that under some circumstances, cuts in tax rates will expand the tax base (output and income) and increase tax revenues. Most economists, however, believe that the United States is currently operating in the range of the Laffer Curve where tax rates and tax revenues move in the same, not opposite, direction.

Today's economists recognize the importance of considering supply-side effects in designing optimal fiscal policy.

TERMS AND CONCEPTS

short run	stagflation	disinflation
long run	aggregate supply shocks	supply-side economics
Phillips Curve	long-run vertical Phillips Curve	Laffer Curve

The following and additional problems can be found in connect

DISCUSSION QUESTIONS

1. Distinguish between the short run and the long run as they relate to macroeconomics. Why is the distinction important? LO32.1
2. Which of the following statements are true? Which are false? Explain why the false statements are untrue. LO32.1
   a. Short-run aggregate supply curves reflect an inverse relationship between the price level and the level of real output.
   b. The long-run aggregate supply curve assumes that nominal wages are fixed.
   c. In the long run, an increase in the price level will result in an increase in nominal wages.
3. Suppose the government misjudges the natural rate of unemployment to be much lower than it actually is, and thus undertakes expansionary fiscal and monetary policies to try to achieve the lower rate. Use the concept of the short-run Phillips

Curve to explain why these policies might at first succeed. Use the concept of the long-run Phillips Curve to explain the long-run outcome of these policies. LO32.4

4. What do the distinctions between short-run aggregate supply and long-run aggregate supply have in common with the distinction between the short-run Phillips Curve and the long-run Phillips Curve? Explain. LO32.4
5. What is the Laffer Curve, and how does it relate to supply-side economics? Why is determining the economy's location on the curve so important in assessing tax policy? LO32.5
6. Why might one person work more, earn more, and pay more income tax when his or her tax rate is cut, while another person will work less, earn less, and pay less income tax under the same circumstance? LO32.5
7. **LAST WORD** On average, does an increase in taxes raise or lower real GDP? If taxes as a percent of GDP go up 1 percent, by how much does real GDP change? Are the decreases in real GDP caused by tax increases temporary or permanent? Does the intention of a tax increase matter?

AP REVIEW QUESTIONS

1. What will each of the following do to the short-run aggregate supply curve, long-run aggregate supply curve, and/or aggregate demand curve? LO32.1, LO32.2
   - **a.** An increased in government spending.
   - **b.** Expansionary monetary policy over the short run and long run.
   - **c.** Increase in overall productivity.
   - **d.** Decrease in the labor force.
   - **e.** Decrease in personal income tax rates.
   - **f.** Increase in autonomous consumption.
   - **g.** Central Bank's selling of government bonds.
   - **h.** Reduction in this country's average tariff rate.
2. Suppose that AD and AS intersect at an output level that is higher than the full-employment output level. After the economy adjusts back to equilibrium in the long run, the price level and the nominal wage will change in which way? ____________. LO32.2
   - **a.** Nominal wage will be the same and the price level higher.
   - **b.** Nominal wage and the price level will be both unchanged.
   - **c.** Nominal wage will be higher and the price level unchanged.
   - **d.** Nominal wage and the price level will each be higher.
   - **e.** Nominal wage will be higher, but the effect on the price level is indeterminate.
3. Suppose that an economy is in long-run equilibrium. If the price level and real GDP both decline simultaneously and those changes were caused by only one curve shifting, then those changes are best explained as the result of: LO32.2
   - **a.** The AD curve shifting right.
   - **b.** The SAS curve shifting right.
   - **c.** The AD curve shifting left.
   - **d.** The SAS curve shifting left.
   - **e.** The LRAS curve shifting right
4. In the extended analysis of aggregate supply, the long-run aggregate supply curve is: LO32.2
   - **a.** Vertical and the short-run aggregate supply curve is also vertical.
   - **b.** Horizontal and the short-run aggregate supply curve is vertical.
   - **c.** Horizontal and the short-run aggregate supply curve is upward sloping.
   - **d.** Vertical and the short-run aggregate supply curve is upward sloping.
   - **e.** Upward sloping and the short-run aggregate supply curve is vertical.
5. Use graphical analysis to show how each of the following would affect the economy first in the short run and then in the long run. Assume that the United States is initially operating at its full-employment level of output, that prices and wages are eventually flexible both upward and downward, and that there is no counteracting fiscal or monetary policy. LO32.2
   - **a.** Because of a war abroad, the oil supply to the United States is disrupted, sending oil prices rocketing upward.
   - **b.** Construction spending on new homes rises dramatically, greatly increasing total U.S. investment spending.
   - **c.** Economic recession occurs abroad, significantly reducing foreign purchases of U.S. exports.
6. A major adverse (decrease in) aggregate supply shock: LO32.3
   - **a.** Automatically shifts the aggregate demand curve rightward.
   - **b.** Automatically shifts the aggregate demand curve leftward.
   - **c.** Causes the Phillips Curve to shift rightward and upward.
   - **d.** Can be caused by rising productivity.
   - **e.** Can be caused by falling wages.
7. The short-run Phillips Curve suggests that, if government uses an expansionary fiscal policy to stimulate output and employment: LO32.4
   - **a.** Unemployment may actually increase because of the crowding-out effect.
   - **b.** Tax revenues may increase even though tax rates have been reduced.
   - **c.** Inflation will increase in the short run
   - **d.** The natural rate of unemployment may fall.
   - **e.** Both unemployment and inflation may rise.
8. In the extended aggregate demand-aggregate supply model: LO32.4
   - **a.** Long-run equilibrium occurs wherever the aggregate demand curve intersects the short-run aggregate supply curve.
   - **b.** The long-run aggregate supply curve is horizontal.
   - **c.** The price level is the same regardless of the location of the aggregate demand curve.
   - **d.** The price level is the same regardless of the location of the aggregate supply curve.
   - **e.** Long-run equilibrium occurs at the intersection of the aggregate demand curve, the short-run aggregate supply curve, and the long run aggregate supply.

9. Suppose that firms are expecting 6 percent inflation while workers are expecting 9 percent inflation. How much of a pay raise will workers demand if their goal is to maintain the purchasing power of their incomes? LO32.4
   a. 3 percent.
   b. 6 percent.
   c. 9 percent.
   d. 12 percent
   e. 15 percent.
10. Which of the following describes the basis of supply-side economics? LO32.5
    a. High marginal tax rates discourage work, saving, and investment.
    b. High marginal tax rates encourage work, saving, and investment.
    c. Increases in social security taxes and other business taxes shift the aggregate supply curve to the right.
    d. The Federal Reserve should adhere to a monetary rule that limits increases in the money supply to a 5 percent annual rate.
    e. Transfer payments increase incentives to work.
11. Assume that an economy is operating below full employment in the short run. LO32.3, LO32.4
    a. With aggregate supply and demand analysis, show this short-run equilibrium.
    b. Using a graph of the short-run and long-run Phillips curve, label on the short-run Phillips curve as Point A, a possible point of rest for the economy described here.
    c. State a specific fiscal policy action that could help move this economy to full employment?
    d. If the policy described in part C is implemented, show a new possible point of rest on the Phillips Curve and label in point C.
    e. Assume no policy action is taken, describe the mechanism by which this economy could reach full employment.
    f. If the process describe above were to occur, show with your Phillips Curve analysis how the economy reaches full employment.

PROBLEMS

1. Use the figure below to answer the following questions. Assume that the economy initially is operating at price level 120 and real output level $870. This output level is the economy's potential (or full-employment) level of output. Next, suppose that the price level rises from 120 to 130. By how much will real output increase in the short run? In the long run? Instead, now assume that the price level dropped from 120 to 110. Assuming flexible product and resource prices, by how much will real output fall in the short run? In the long run? What is the long-run level of output at each of the three price levels shown? LO32.1

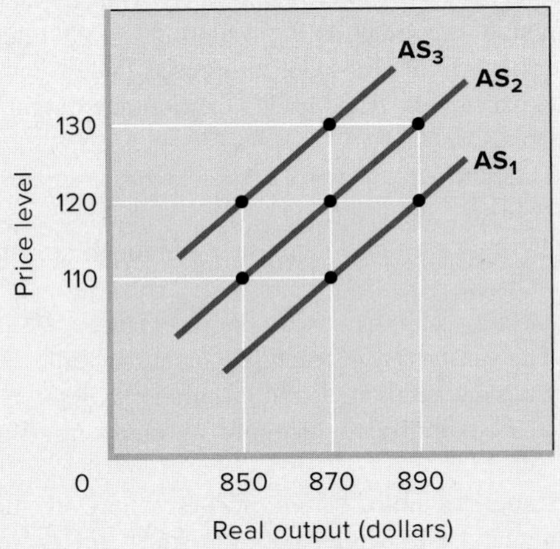

2. **ADVANCED ANALYSIS** Suppose that the equation for a particular short-run AS curve is $P = 20 + 0.5Q$, where P is the price level and Q is real output in dollar terms. What is Q if the price level is 120? Suppose that the Q in your answer is the full-employment level of output. By how much will Q increase *in the short run* if the price level unexpectedly rises from 120 to 132? By how much will Q increase *in the long run* due to the price level increase? LO32.1
3. Suppose that over a 30-year period Buskerville's price level increased from 72 to 138, while its real GDP rose from $1.2 trillion to $2.1 trillion. Did economic growth occur in Buskerville? If so, by what average yearly rate in percentage terms (rounded to one decimal place)? Did Buskerville experience inflation? If so, by what average yearly rate in percentage terms (rounded to one decimal place)? Which shifted rightward faster in Buskerville: its long-run aggregate supply curve (AS_{LR}) or its aggregate demand curve (AD)? LO32.2
4. Suppose that for years East Confetti's short-run Phillips Curve was such that each 1 percentage point increase in its unemployment rate was associated with a 2 percentage point decline in its inflation rate. Then, during several recent years, the short-run pattern changed such that its inflation rate rose by 3 percentage points for every 1 percentage point drop in its unemployment rate. Graphically, did East Confetti's Phillips Curve shift upward or did it shift downward? LO32.3

Chapter 33

Current Issues in Macro Theory and Policy

Learning Objectives

LO33.1 Describe alternative perspectives on the causes of macroeconomic instability, including the views of mainstream economists, monetarists, real-business-cycle advocates, and proponents of coordination failures.

LO33.2 Discuss why new classical economists believe the economy will "self-correct" from aggregate demand and aggregate supply shocks.

LO33.3 Identify and describe the variations of the debate over "rules" versus "discretion" in conducting stabilization policy.

LO33.4 Summarize the fundamental ideas and policy implications of mainstream macroeconomics, monetarism, and rational expectations theory.

AP Chapter Focus

As any academic discipline evolves, it naturally evokes a number of internal disagreements. Economics is no exception. In this chapter we examine a few alternative perspectives on macro theory and policy. A discussion of these alternatives will complete the topics regarding macroeconomic stabilization policies. We focus on the disagreements that various economists have about the answers to three interrelated questions: (1) What causes instability in the economy? (2) Is the economy self-correcting? (3) Should government adhere to *rules* or use *discretion* in setting economic policy?

AP What Causes Macro Instability?

LO33.1 Describe alternative perspectives on the causes of macroeconomic instability, including the views of mainstream economists, monetarists, real-business-cycle advocates, and proponents of coordination failures.

As earlier chapters have indicated, capitalist economies experienced considerable instability during the twentieth century. The United States, for example, experienced the Great Depression, numerous recessions, and periods of inflation. This instability greatly moderated between the early 1980s and 2007, but then the deep recession of 2007–2009 occurred. Economists have different perspectives about why instability like this happens.

Mainstream View

For simplicity, we will use the term "mainstream view" to characterize the prevailing macroeconomic perspective of the majority of economists. According to that view, instability in the economy arises from two sources: (1) price stickiness and (2) unexpected shocks to either aggregate demand or aggregate supply.

As we explained in detail in Chapter 32, in the long run, when both input and output prices are fully flexible and have time to adjust to any changes in aggregate demand or short-run aggregate supply, the economy will always return to producing at potential output. In the shorter run, however, stickiness in either input or output prices will mean that any shock to either aggregate demand or aggregate supply will result in changes in output and employment. Although they are not new to you, let's quickly review shocks to aggregate demand and aggregate supply.

Changes in Aggregate Demand Mainstream macroeconomics focuses on aggregate spending and its components. Recall that the basic equation underlying aggregate expenditures is

$$C_a + I_g + X_n + G = \text{GDP}$$

That is, the aggregate amount of after-tax consumption, gross investment, net exports, and government spending determines the total amount of goods and services produced and sold. In equilibrium, $C_a + I_g + X_n + G$ (aggregate expenditures) is equal to GDP (real output). A decrease in the price level increases equilibrium GDP and thus allows us to trace out a downsloping aggregate demand curve for the economy (see the appendix to Chapter 26). Any change in one of the spending components in the aggregate expenditures equation shifts the aggregate demand curve. This, in turn, changes equilibrium real output, the price level, or both.

Investment spending in particular is subject to wide "booms" and "busts." Significant increases in investment spending are multiplied into even greater increases in aggregate demand and thus can produce demand-pull inflation. In contrast, significant declines in investment spending are multiplied into even greater decreases in aggregate demand and thus can cause recessions.

Adverse Aggregate Supply Shocks In the mainstream view, the second source of macroeconomic instability arises on the supply side. Occasionally, such external events as wars or an artificial supply restriction of a key resource can boost resource prices and significantly raise per-unit production costs. The result is a sizable decline in a nation's aggregate supply, which destabilizes the economy by simultaneously causing cost-push inflation and recession.

Monetarist View

Monetarism (1) focuses on the money supply, (2) holds that markets are highly competitive, and (3) says that a competitive market system gives the economy a high degree of macroeconomic stability. Monetarists argue that the price and wage flexibility provided by competitive markets should cause fluctuations in aggregate demand to alter product and resource prices rather than output and employment. Thus, the market system would provide substantial macroeconomic stability *were it not for government interference in the economy.*

The problem, as monetarists see it, is that government has promoted downward wage inflexibility through the minimum-wage law, pro-union legislation, guaranteed prices for certain farm products, pro-business monopoly legislation, and so forth. The free-market system is capable of providing macroeconomic stability, but, despite good intentions, government interference has undermined that capability. Moreover, monetarists say that government has contributed to the economy's business cycles through its clumsy and mistaken attempts to achieve greater stability through its monetary policies.

Equation of Exchange The fundamental equation of monetarism is the **equation of exchange:**

$$MV = PQ$$

where M is the supply of money; V is the **velocity** of money, that is, the average number of times per year a dollar is spent on final goods and services; P is the price level or, more specifically, the average price at which each unit of physical output is sold; and Q is the physical volume of all goods and services produced.

The left side of the equation of exchange, MV, represents the total amount spent by purchasers of output, while the right side, PQ, represents the total amount received by sellers of that output. The nation's money supply (M) multiplied by the number of times it is spent each year (V) must equal the nation's nominal GDP ($= P \times Q$). The dollar value of total spending has to equal the dollar value of total output.

Stable Velocity Monetarists say that velocity, V, in the equation of exchange is relatively stable. To them, "stable" is not synonymous with "constant," however. Monetarists are aware that velocity has generally trended upward over the last several decades. Shorter pay periods, widespread use of credit cards, and faster means of making payments enable people to hold less money and to turn it over more rapidly than was possible in earlier times. These factors have enabled people to reduce their holdings of cash and checkbook money relative to the size of the nation's nominal GDP.

When monetarists say that velocity is stable, they mean that the factors altering velocity change gradually and predictably and that changes in velocity from one year to the next can be readily anticipated. Moreover, they hold that velocity does not change in response to changes in the money supply itself. Instead, people have a stable desire to hold money relative to holding other financial assets, holding real assets, and buying current output. The factors that determine the amount of money the public wants to hold depend mainly on the level of nominal GDP.

Example: Assume that when the level of nominal GDP is \$400 billion, the public desires \$100 billion of money to purchase that output. That means that V is 4 (= \$400 billion of nominal GDP/\$100 billion of money). If we further assume that the actual supply of money is \$100 billion, the economy is in equilibrium with respect to money; the actual amount of money supplied equals the amount the public wants to hold.

If velocity is stable, the equation of exchange suggests that there is a predictable relationship between the money supply and nominal GDP (= PQ). An increase in the money supply of, say, \$10 billion would upset equilibrium in our example since the public would find itself holding more money or liquidity than it wants. That is, the actual amount of money held (\$110 billion) would exceed the amount of holdings desired (\$100 billion). In that case, the reaction of the public (households and businesses) is to restore its desired balance of money relative to other items, such as stocks and bonds, factories and equipment, houses and automobiles, and clothing and toys. But the spending of money by individual households and businesses would leave more cash in the checkable deposits or billfolds of other households and firms. And they too would try to "spend down" their excess cash balances. But, overall, the \$110 billion supply of money cannot be spent down because a dollar spent is a dollar received.

Instead, the collective attempt to reduce cash balances increases aggregate demand, thereby boosting nominal GDP. Because velocity in our example is 4—that is, the dollar is spent, on average, four times per year—nominal GDP rises from \$400 billion to \$440 billion. At that higher nominal GDP, the money supply of \$110 billion equals the amount of money desired (\$440 billion/4 = \$110 billion), and equilibrium is reestablished.

The \$10 billion increase in the money supply thus eventually increases nominal GDP by \$40 billion. Spending on goods, services, and assets expands until nominal GDP has gone up enough to restore the original 4-to-1 equilibrium relationship between nominal GDP and the money supply.

Note that the relationship GDP/M defines V. A stable relationship between nominal GDP and M means a stable V. And a change in M causes a proportionate change in nominal GDP. Thus, monetarists say that changes in the money supply have a predictable effect on nominal GDP (= $P \times Q$). An increase in M increases P or Q, or some combination of both; a decrease in M reduces P or Q, or some combination of both.

Monetary Causes of Instability Monetarists say that inappropriate monetary policy is the single most important cause of macroeconomic instability. An increase in the money supply directly increases aggregate demand. Under conditions of full employment, that rise in aggregate demand raises the price level. For a time, higher prices cause firms to increase their real output, and the rate of unemployment falls below its natural rate. But once nominal wages rise to reflect the higher prices and thus to restore real wages, real output moves back to its full-employment level and the unemployment rate returns to its natural rate. The inappropriate increase in the money supply leads to inflation, together with instability of real output and employment.

Conversely, a decrease in the money supply reduces aggregate demand. Real output temporarily falls, and the unemployment rate rises above its natural rate. Eventually, nominal wages fall and real output returns to its full-employment level. The inappropriate decline in the money supply leads to deflation, together with instability of real GDP and employment.

The contrast between mainstream macroeconomics and monetarism on the causes of instability thus comes into sharp focus. Mainstream economists view the instability of investment as the main cause of the economy's instability. They see monetary policy as a stabilizing factor. Changes in the money supply raise or lower interest rates as needed, smooth out swings in investment, and thus reduce macroeconomic instability. In contrast, monetarists view changes in the money supply as the main cause of instability in the economy. For example, they say that the Great Depression occurred largely because the Fed allowed the money supply to fall by roughly one-third during that period. According to Milton Friedman, a prominent monetarist,

> And [the money supply] fell not because there were no willing borrowers—not because the horse would not drink. It fell because the Federal Reserve System forced or permitted a sharp reduction in the [money supply], because it failed to exercise the responsibilities assigned to it in the Federal Reserve Act to provide liquidity to the banking system. The Great Contraction is tragic testimony to the power of monetary policy—not, as Keynes and so many of his contemporaries believed, evidence of its impotence.[1]

Real-Business-Cycle View

A third modern view of the cause of macroeconomic instability is that business cycles are caused by real factors that affect aggregate supply rather than by monetary, or spending, factors that cause fluctuations in aggregate demand. In the **real-business-cycle theory,** business fluctuations result from significant changes in technology and resource availability. Those changes affect productivity and thus the long-run growth trend of aggregate supply.

An example focusing on recession will clarify this thinking. Suppose productivity (output per worker) declines sharply because of a large increase in oil prices, which makes it prohibitively expensive to operate certain types of machinery. That decline in productivity implies a reduction in the economy's ability to produce real output. The result would be

[1]Milton Friedman, *The Optimum Quantity of Money and Other Essays* (Chicago: Aldine, 1969), p. 97.

FIGURE 33.1 The real-business-cycle theory. In the real-business-cycle theory, a decline in resource availability shifts the nation's long-run aggregate supply curve to the left from AS_{LR1} to AS_{LR2}. The decline in real output from Q_1 to Q_2, in turn, reduces money demand (less is needed) and money supply (fewer loans are taken out) such that aggregate demand shifts leftward from AD_1 to AD_2. The result is a recession in which the price level remains constant.

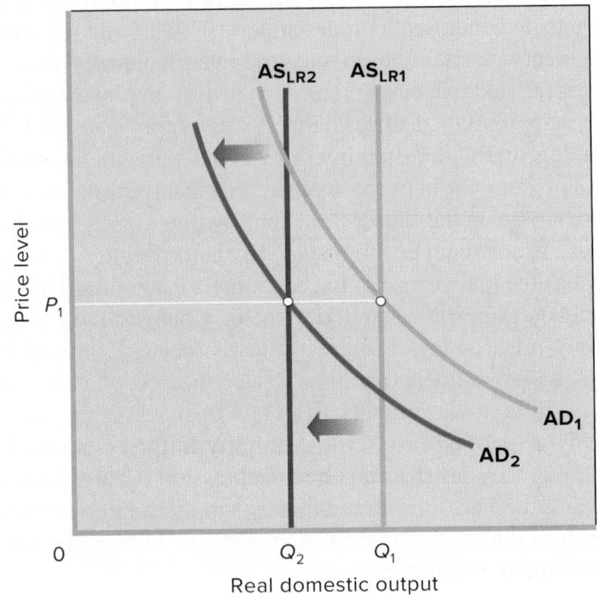

a decrease in the economy's long-run aggregate supply curve, as represented by the leftward shift from AS_{LR1} to AS_{LR2} in Figure 33.1.

As real output falls from Q_1 to Q_2, the public needs less money to buy the reduced volume of goods and services. So the demand for money falls. Moreover, the slowdown in business activity means that businesses need to borrow less from banks, reducing the part of the money supply created by banks through their lending. Thus, the supply of money also falls. In this controversial scenario, changes in the supply of money respond to changes in the demand for money. The decline in the money supply then reduces aggregate demand, as from AD_1 to AD_2 in Figure 33.1. The outcome is a decline in real output from Q_1 to Q_2, with no change in the price level.

Conversely, a large increase in aggregate supply (not shown) caused by, say, major innovations in the production process would shift the long-run aggregate supply curve rightward. Real output would increase, and money demand and money supply would both increase. Aggregate demand would shift rightward by an amount equal to the rightward shift of long-run aggregate supply. Real output would increase, without driving up the price level.

Conclusion: In the real-business-cycle theory, macro instability arises on the aggregate supply side of the economy, not on the aggregate demand side as mainstream economists and monetarists usually claim.

CONSIDER THIS . . .

Too Much Money?

Source: © Baron Wolman/ Getty Images

The severe recession of 2007–2009 fits the mainstream view that recessions are caused by AD shocks rather than the real-business-cycle view that they are caused by AS shocks. Recall that the recession began with a financial crisis that caused significant reductions in investment spending and consumption spending and therefore reduced aggregate demand. As inventories increased, businesses further curtailed their investment spending, and aggregate demand, output, and income dropped even more.

Economists with monetarist leanings, however, cite monetary factors as the main cause of the financial crisis that led to the initial declines in aggregate demand. They argue that the Federal Reserve flooded the economy with too much money and held interest rates too low for too long in promoting recovery from the 2001 recession. In this line of reasoning, the excess money and low interest rates contributed to the bubble in the housing market. When that bubble burst, the resulting loan defaults set in motion the forces that produced the declines in AD and therefore the recession.

All economists agree that the bursting of the housing bubble led to the recession. And too-loose monetary policy may have contributed to the bubble. But economists also cite the role of the very large international flows of foreign savings into the United States during this period. These inflows drove down interest rates and helped to fuel the housing bubble. Other factors such as "pass-the-risk" lending practices, government policies promoting home ownership, and poorly designed and enforced financial regulations certainly came into play. The mainstream view is that causes of the financial crisis and recession are numerous and complex.

Coordination Failures

A fourth and final modern view of macroeconomic instability relates to so-called **coordination failures.** Such failures occur when people fail to reach a mutually beneficial equilibrium because they lack a way to coordinate their actions.

Noneconomic Example Consider first a noneconomic example. Suppose you hear that some people might be getting together at the last minute for an informal party at a nearby beach. But because of a chance of rain, there is some doubt about whether people will actually come out. You make a cell phone call or two to try to get a read on what others are thinking, and then base your decision on that limited information. If you expect others to be there, you will decide to go. If you expect that no one will go, you will decide to stay home. There are several possible equilibrium outcomes, depending on the mix of people's expectations. Let's consider just two. If each person assumes that all the others will go to the party, all will go. The party will occur and presumably everyone will have a good time. But if each person assumes that everyone else will stay home, all will stay home and there will be no party. When the party does not take place, even though all would be better off if it did take place, a coordination failure has occurred.

Macroeconomic Example Now let's apply this example to macroeconomic instability, specifically recession. Suppose that individual firms and households expect other firms and consumers to cut back their investment and consumption spending. As a result, each firm and household will anticipate a reduction of aggregate demand. Firms therefore will reduce their own investment spending since they will anticipate that their future production capacity will be excessive. Households will also reduce their own spending (increase their saving) because they anticipate that they will experience reduced work hours, possible layoffs, and falling incomes in the future.

Aggregate demand will indeed decline and the economy will indeed experience a recession in response to what amounts to a self-fulfilling prophecy. Moreover, the economy will stay at a below-full-employment level of output because, once there, producers and households have no individual incentive to increase spending. If all producers and households would agree to increase their investment and consumption spending simultaneously, then aggregate demand would rise, and real output and real income would increase. Each producer and each consumer would be better off. However, this outcome does not occur because there is no mechanism for firms and households to agree on such a joint spending increase.

In this case, the economy is stuck in an *unemployment equilibrium* because of a coordination failure. With a different set of expectations, a coordination failure might leave the economy in an *inflation equilibrium*. In this view, the economy has a number of such potential equilibrium positions, some good and some bad, depending on people's mix of expectations. Macroeconomic instability, then, reflects the movement of the economy from one such equilibrium position to another as expectations change.

AP QUICK REVIEW 33.1

- ✓ The mainstream view is that macroeconomic instability usually stems from sticky prices, swings in investment spending and, occasionally, from adverse aggregate supply shocks.
- ✓ Monetarists view the economy through the equation of exchange ($MV = PQ$). If velocity V is stable, changes in the money supply M lead directly to changes in nominal GDP ($P \times Q$). For monetarists, changes in M caused by inappropriate monetary policy are the single most important cause of macroeconomic instability. Expansionary shocks are likely to be inflationary, whereas contractionary shocks are likely to increase unemployment.
- ✓ In the real-business-cycle theory, significant changes in "real" factors such as technology, resource availability, and productivity change the economy's long-run aggregate supply, causing macroeconomic instability.
- ✓ Macroeconomic instability can result from coordination failures—less-than-optimal equilibrium positions that occur because businesses and households lack a way to coordinate their actions.

AP Does the Economy "Self-Correct"?

LO33.2 Discuss why new classical economists believe the economy will "self-correct" from aggregate demand and aggregate supply shocks.

Just as there are disputes over the causes of macroeconomic instability, there are disputes over whether or not the economy will correct itself when instability does occur. And economists also disagree on how long it will take for any such self-correction to take place.

New Classical View of Self-Correction

New classical economists tend to be either monetarists or adherents of **rational expectations theory:** the idea that businesses, consumers, and workers expect changes in policies or circumstances to have certain effects on the economy and, in pursuing their own self-interest, take actions to make sure those changes affect them as little as possible. The **new classical economics** holds that when the economy occasionally diverges from its full-employment output, internal mechanisms within the economy will automatically move it back to that output. Policymakers should stand back and let the automatic correction occur, rather than engage in active fiscal and monetary policy. This perspective is often associated with the vertical long-run Phillips Curve, which we discussed in Chapter 32. But we will analyze it here using the extended AD-AS model that was also developed in Chapter 32.

AP FIGURE 33.2 New classical view of self-correction. (a) An unanticipated increase in aggregate demand from AD_1 to AD_2 first moves the economy from *a* to *b*. The economy then self-corrects to *c*. An anticipated increase in aggregate demand moves the economy directly from *a* to *c*. (b) An unanticipated decrease in aggregate demand from AD_1 to AD_3 moves the economy from *a* to *d*. The economy then self-corrects to *e*. An anticipated decrease in aggregate demand moves the economy directly from *a* to *e*. (Mainstream economists, however, say that if the price level remains at P_1, the economy will move from *a* to *f*, and even if the price level falls to P_4, the economy may remain at *d* because of downward wage inflexibility.)

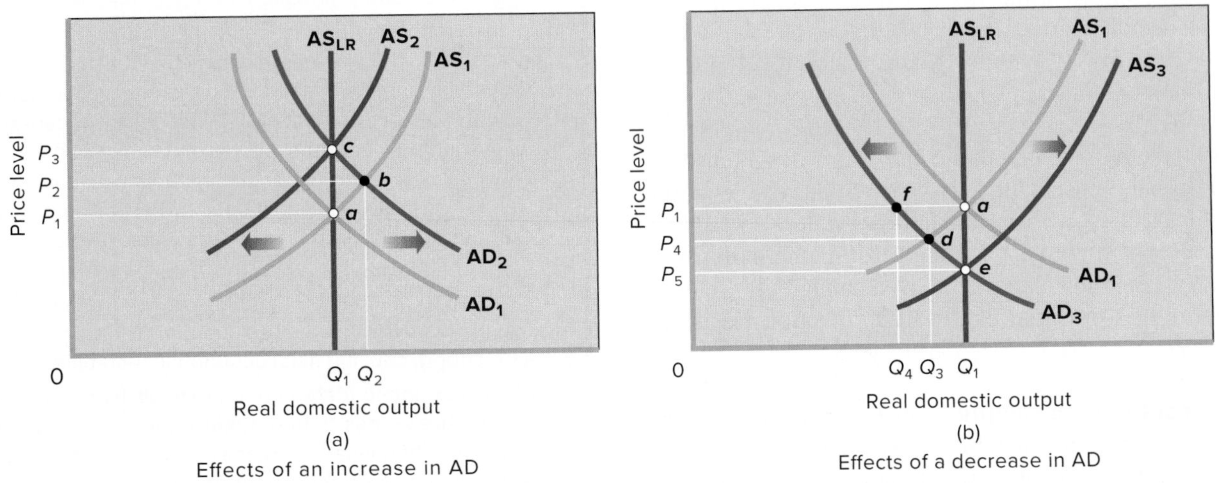

Graphical Analysis Figure 33.2a relates the new classical analysis to the question of self-correction. Specifically, an increase in aggregate demand, say, from AD_1 to AD_2, moves the economy upward along its short-run aggregate supply curve AS_1 from *a* to *b*. The price level rises and real output increases. With the economy producing beyond potential output, high resource demand drives up the prices of labor and other productive inputs. Per-unit production costs increase and the short-run aggregate supply curve shifts leftward, eventually from AS_1 to AS_2. The economy moves from *b* to *c*, and real output returns to its full-employment level, Q_1. This level of output is dictated by the economy's vertical long-run aggregate supply curve, AS_{LR}.

Conversely, a decrease in aggregate demand from AD_1 to AD_3 in Figure 33.2b first moves the economy downward along its short-run aggregate supply curve AS_1 from point *a* to *d*. The price level declines, as does the level of real output. With the economy producing below potential output, low resource demand drives down the prices of labor and other productive inputs. When that happens, per-unit production costs decline and the short-run aggregate supply curve shifts to the right, eventually from AS_1 to AS_3. The economy moves to *e*, where it again achieves its full-employment level, Q_1. As in Figure 33.2a, the economy in Figure 33.2b has automatically self-corrected to its full-employment output and its natural rate of unemployment.

Speed of Adjustment There is some disagreement among new classical economists on how long it will take for self-correction to occur. Monetarists usually hold the *adaptive expectations* view that people form their expectations on the basis of present realities and only gradually change their expectations as experience unfolds. This means that the shifts in the short-run aggregate supply curves shown in Figure 33.2 may not occur for two or three years or even longer. Other new classical economists, however, accept the rational expectations assumption that workers anticipate some future outcomes before they occur. When price-level changes are fully anticipated, adjustments of nominal wages are very quick or even instantaneous. Let's see why.

Although several new theories incorporate rational expectations, our interest here is the new classical version of the rational expectations theory (hereafter, RET). RET is based on two assumptions:

- People behave rationally, gathering and intelligently processing information to form expectations about things that are economically important to them. They adjust those expectations quickly as new developments affecting future economic outcomes occur. Where there is adequate information, people's beliefs about future economic outcomes accurately reflect the likelihood that those outcomes will occur. For example, if it is clear that a certain policy will cause inflation, people will recognize that fact and adjust their economic behavior in anticipation of inflation.
- RET economists assume that all product and resource markets are highly competitive and that prices and wages are flexible both upward and downward. But the RET economists go further, assuming that new information is quickly (in some cases, instantaneously) taken into account in the demand and supply curves of such markets.

The upshot is that equilibrium prices and quantities adjust rapidly to unforeseen events—say, technological change or aggregate supply shocks. They adjust instantaneously to events that have known outcomes—for example, changes in fiscal or monetary policy.

Unanticipated Price-Level Changes The implication of RET is not only that the economy is self-correcting but that self-correction occurs quickly. In this thinking, unanticipated changes in the price level—so-called **price-level surprises**—*do* cause temporary changes in real output. Suppose, for example, that an unanticipated increase in foreign demand for U.S. goods increases U.S. aggregate demand from AD_1 to AD_2 in Figure 33.2a. The immediate result is an unexpected increase in the price level from P_1 to P_2.

But now an interesting question arises. If wages and prices are flexible, as assumed in RET, why doesn't the higher price level immediately cause wages and other input prices to rise, such that there is no increase in real output at all? Why does the economy temporarily move from point *a* to *b* along AS_1? In RET, firms increase output from Q_1 to Q_2 because of misperceptions about rising prices of their own products relative to the prices of other products (and to the prices of labor). They mistakenly think the higher prices of their own products have resulted from increased demand for those products relative to the demands for other products. Expecting higher profits, they increase their own production. But in fact *all* prices, including the price of labor (nominal wages), are rising because of the general increase in aggregate demand. Once firms see that *all* prices and wages are rising, they decrease their production to previous levels.

In terms of Figure 33.2a, the increase in nominal wages shifts the short-run aggregate supply curve leftward, ultimately from AS_1 to AS_2, and the economy moves from *b* to *c*. Thus, the increase in real output caused by the price-level surprise corrects itself.

The same analysis in reverse applies to an unanticipated price-level decrease. In the economy represented by Figure 33.2b, firms misperceive that the prices of their own products are falling due to decreases in the demand for those products relative to other products. They incorrectly anticipate declines in profit and cut production. As a result of their collective actions, real output in the economy falls. Once firms see what is really happening—that *all* prices and wages are dropping—they increase their output to prior levels. The short-run aggregate supply curve in Figure 33.2b shifts rightward from AS_1 to AS_3, and the economy "self-corrects" by moving from *d* to *e*.

Fully Anticipated Price-Level Changes In RET, fully *anticipated* price-level changes do not change real output, even for short periods. In Figure 33.2a, again consider the increase in aggregate demand from AD_1 to AD_2. Businesses immediately recognize that the higher prices being paid for their products are part of the inflation they had anticipated. They understand that the same forces that are causing the inflation result in higher nominal wages, leaving their profits unchanged. The economy therefore moves directly from *a* to *c*. The price level rises as expected, and output remains at its full-employment level Q_1.

Similarly, a fully *anticipated* price-level decrease will leave real output unchanged. Firms conclude that nominal wages are declining by the same percentage amount as the declining price level, leaving profits unchanged. The economy represented by Figure 33.2b therefore moves directly from *a* to *e*. Deflation occurs, but the economy continues to produce its full-employment output Q_1. The anticipated decline in aggregate demand causes no change in real output.

Mainstream View of Self-Correction

Almost all economists acknowledge that the new classical economists have made significant contributions to the theory of aggregate supply. In fact, mainstream economists have incorporated some aspects of RET into their own models. However, most economists strongly disagree with RET on the question of downward price and wage flexibility. While the stock market, foreign exchange market, and certain commodity markets experience day-to-day or minute-to-minute price changes, including price declines, that is not true of many product markets and most labor markets. There is ample evidence, say mainstream economists, that many prices and wages are inflexible downward for long periods. As a result, it may take years for the economy to move from recession back to full-employment output, unless it gets help from fiscal and monetary policy.

Graphical Analysis To understand this mainstream view, again examine Figure 33.2b. Suppose aggregate demand declines from AD_1 to AD_3 because of a significant decline in investment spending. If prices are sticky downward for a while and therefore the price level is temporarily stuck at P_1, the economy will not move from *a* to *d* to *e*, as suggested by RET. Instead, the economy will move from *a* to *f*, as if it were moving along the white horizontal P_1 price line between those two points. Real output will decline from its full-employment level, Q_1, to the recessionary level, Q_4.

But let's assume that large amounts of unsold inventories eventually cause the price level to fall to P_4. Will this lead to the decline in nominal wages needed to shift aggregate supply from AS_1 to AS_3, as suggested by the new classical economists? "Highly unlikely" say mainstream economists. Even more so than prices, nominal wages tend to be inflexible downward. If nominal wages do not decline in response to the decline in the price level, then the short-run aggregate supply curve will not shift rightward. The self-correction mechanism assumed by

RET and new classical economists will break down. Instead, the economy will remain at *d*, experiencing less-than-full-employment output and a high rate of unemployment.

Downward Wage Inflexibility In Chapter 26 we discussed several reasons why firms may not be able to, or may not want to, lower nominal wages. Firms may not be able to cut wages because of wage contracts and the legal minimum wage. And firms may not want to lower wages if they fear potential problems with morale, effort, and efficiency.

While contracts are thought to be the main cause of wage rigidity, so-called efficiency wages and insider-outsider relationships also may play a role. Let's explore both.

Efficiency Wage Theory Recall from Chapter 26 that an **efficiency wage** is a wage that minimizes the firm's labor cost per unit of output. Normally, we would think that the market wage is the efficiency wage since it is the lowest wage at which a firm can obtain a particular type of labor. But where the cost of supervising workers is high or where worker turnover is great, firms may discover that paying a wage that is higher than the market wage will lower their wage cost per unit of output.

Example: Suppose a firm's workers, on average, produce 8 units of output at a $9 market wage but 10 units of output at a $10 above-market wage. The efficiency wage is $10, not the $9 market wage. At the $10 wage, the labor cost per unit of output is only $1 (= $10 wage/10 units of output), compared with $1.12 (= $9 wage/8 units of output) at the $9 wage.

How can a higher wage result in greater efficiency?

- ***Greater work effort*** The above-market wage, in effect, raises the cost to workers of losing their jobs as a result of poor performance. Because workers have a strong incentive to retain their relatively high-paying jobs, they are more likely to provide greater work effort. Looked at differently, workers are more reluctant to shirk (neglect or avoid work) because the higher wage makes job loss more costly to them. Consequently, the above-market wage can be the efficient wage; it can enhance worker productivity so much that the higher wage more than pays for itself.
- ***Lower supervision costs*** With less incentive among workers to shirk, the firm needs fewer supervisory personnel to monitor work performance. This, too, can lower the firm's overall wage cost per unit of output.
- ***Reduced job turnover*** The above-market pay discourages workers from voluntarily leaving their jobs. The lower turnover rate reduces the firm's cost of hiring and training workers. It also gives the firm a more experienced, more productive workforce.

The key implication for macroeconomic instability is that efficiency wages add to the downward inflexibility of wages. Firms that pay efficiency wages will be reluctant to cut wages when aggregate demand declines, since such cuts may encourage shirking, require more supervisory personnel, and increase turnover. In other words, wage cuts that reduce productivity and raise per-unit labor costs are self-defeating.

Insider-Outsider Relationships Other economists theorize that downward wage inflexibility may relate to relationships between "insiders" and "outsiders." Insiders are workers who retain employment even during recession. Outsiders are workers who have been laid off from a firm and unemployed workers who would like to work at that firm.

When recession produces layoffs and widespread unemployment, we might expect outsiders to offer to work for less than the current wage rate, in effect, bidding down wage rates. We also might expect firms to hire such workers to reduce their costs. But, according to the **insider-outsider theory,** outsiders may not be able to underbid existing wages because employers may view the nonwage cost of hiring them to be prohibitive. Employers might fear that insiders would view acceptance of such underbidding as undermining years of effort to increase wages or, worse, as "stealing" jobs. So insiders may refuse to cooperate with new workers who have undercut their pay. Where teamwork is critical for production, such lack of cooperation will reduce overall productivity and thereby lower the firms' profits.

Even if firms are willing to employ outsiders at less than the current wage, those workers might refuse to work for less than the existing wage. To do so might invite harassment from the insiders whose pay they have undercut. Thus, outsiders may remain unemployed, relying on past saving, unemployment compensation, and other social programs to make ends meet.

As in the efficiency wage theory, the insider-outsider theory implies that wages will be inflexible downward when aggregate demand declines. Self-correction may eventually occur but not nearly as rapidly as the new classical economists contend.

AP QUICK REVIEW 33.2

- ✓ New classical economists believe that the economy "self-corrects" when unanticipated events divert it from its full-employment level of real output.
- ✓ In RET, unanticipated price-level changes cause changes in real output in the short run but not in the long run.
- ✓ According to RET, market participants immediately change their actions in response to anticipated price-level changes such that no change in real output occurs.
- ✓ Mainstream economists say that the economy can get mired in recession for several months or more because of downward price and wage inflexibility.
- ✓ Sources of downward wage inflexibility include contracts, efficiency wages, and insider-outsider relationships.
- ✓ Eventually, however, when in recession, wages will be pushed downward, and the economy should return towards full employment.

AP Rules or Discretion?

LO33.3 Identify and describe the variations of the debate over "rules" versus "discretion" in conducting stabilization policy.

These different views on the causes of instability and on the speed of self-correction have led to vigorous debate on macro policy. Should the government adhere to policy rules that prohibit it from causing instability in an economy that is otherwise stable? Or should it use discretionary fiscal and monetary policy, when needed, to stabilize a sometimes-unstable economy?

In Support of Policy Rules

Monetarists and other new classical economists believe policy rules would reduce instability in the economy. They believe that such rules would prevent government from trying to "manage" aggregate demand. That would be a desirable trend because, in their view, such management is misguided and thus is likely to *cause* more instability than it cures.

Monetary Rule Since inappropriate monetary policy is the major source of macroeconomic instability, say monetarists, the enactment of a **monetary rule** would make sense. One such rule would be a requirement that the Fed expand the money supply each year at the same annual rate as the typical growth of the economy's production capacity. That fixed-rate expansion of the money supply would occur whatever the state of the economy. The Fed's sole monetary role would be to use its tools (open-market operations, the discount rate, interest on reserves, and reserve requirements) to ensure that the nation's money supply grew steadily by, say, 3 to 5 percent a year. According to Milton Friedman,

> Such a rule . . . would eliminate . . . the major cause of instability in the economy—the capricious and unpredictable impact of countercyclical monetary policy. As long as the money supply grows at a constant rate each year, be it 3, 4, or 5 percent, any decline into recession will be temporary. The liquidity provided by a constantly growing money supply will cause aggregate demand to expand. Similarly, if the supply of money does not rise at a more than average rate, any inflationary increase in spending will burn itself out for lack of fuel.[2]

Figure 33.3 illustrates the rationale for a monetary rule. Suppose the economy represented there is operating at its full-employment real output, Q_1. Also suppose the nation's long-run aggregate supply curve shifts rightward, as from AS_{LR1} to AS_{LR2}, each year, signifying the average annual increase in potential real output. As you saw in earlier chapters, such annual increases in "potential GDP" result from added resources, improved resources, and improved technology.

[2]As quoted in Lawrence S. Ritter and William L. Silber, *Money*, 5th ed. (New York: Basic Books, 1984), pp. 141–142.

CONSIDER THIS . . .

Source: © Chad Baker/Jason Reed/Ryan McVay/Getty Images RF

On the Road Again

Economist Abba Lerner (1903–1982) likened the economy to an automobile traveling down a road that had traffic barriers on each side. The problem was that the car had no steering wheel. It would hit one barrier, causing the car to veer to the opposite side of the road. There it would hit the other barrier, which in turn would send it careening to the opposite side. To avoid such careening in the form of business cycles, said Lerner, society must equip the economy with a steering wheel. Discretionary fiscal and monetary policy would enable government to steer the economy safely between the problems of recession and demand-pull inflation.

Economist Milton Friedman (1912–2006) modified Lerner's analogy, giving it a different meaning. He said that the economic vehicle does not need a skillful driver who is continuously turning the wheel to adjust to the unexpected irregularities of the route. Instead, the economy needs a way to prohibit the monetary passenger in the back seat from occasionally leaning over and giving the steering wheel a jerk that sends the car off the road. According to Friedman, the car will travel down the road just fine unless the Federal Reserve destabilizes it.

Lerner's analogy implied an internally unstable economy that needs steering through discretionary government stabilization policy. Friedman's modification of the analogy implied a generally stable economy that is destabilized by inappropriate monetary policy by the Federal Reserve. For Lerner, stability required active use of fiscal and monetary policy. For Friedman, macroeconomic stability required a monetary rule forcing the Federal Reserve to increase the money supply at a set, steady annual rate.*

*In his later years, Friedman softened his call for a monetary rule, acknowledging that the Fed had become much more skillful at keeping the rate of inflation in check through prudent monetary policy.

Monetarists argue that a monetary rule would tie increases in the money supply to the typical rightward shift of long-run aggregate supply. In view of the direct link between changes in the money supply and aggregate demand, this would ensure that the AD curve would shift rightward, as from AD_1 to AD_2, each year. As a result, while GDP increases from Q_1 to Q_2, the price level would remain constant at P_1. A monetary rule, then, would promote steady growth of real output along with price stability.

AP **FIGURE 33.3 Rationale for a monetary rule.** A monetary rule that required the Fed to increase the money supply at an annual rate linked to the long-run increase in potential GDP would shift aggregate demand rightward, as from AD_1 to AD_2, at the same pace as the shift in long-run aggregate supply, here, AS_{LR1} to AS_{LR2}. Thus the economy would experience growth without inflation or deflation.

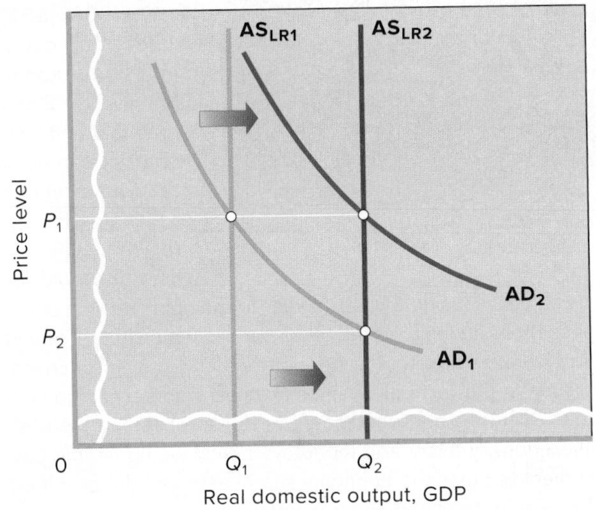

Generally, rational expectations economists also support a monetary rule. They conclude that an expansionary or restrictive monetary policy would alter the rate of inflation but not real output. Suppose, for example, the Fed implements an easy money policy to reduce interest rates, expand investment spending, and boost real GDP. On the basis of past experience and economic knowledge, the public would anticipate that this policy is inflationary and would take protective actions. Workers would press for higher nominal wages; firms would raise their product prices; and lenders would lift their nominal interest rates on loans.

All these responses are designed to prevent inflation from having adverse effects on the real income of workers, businesses, and lenders. But collectively they would immediately raise wage and price levels. So the increase in aggregate demand brought about by the expansionary monetary policy would be completely dissipated in higher prices and wages. Real output and employment would not be increased by the easy money policy.

In this view, the combination of rational expectations and instantaneous market adjustments dooms discretionary monetary policy to ineffectiveness. If discretionary monetary policy produces only inflation (or deflation), say the RET economists, then it makes sense to limit the Fed's discretion and to require that Congress enact a monetary rule consistent with price stability at all times.

In recent decades, the call for a Friedman-type monetary rule has faded. In 2012, the Fed did, however, adopt a flexible version of another type of monetary rule. Under **inflation targeting,** the Fed commits to adjusting monetary policy as necessary to achieve a publicly announced inflation rate. The Fed's choice for its **target rate of inflation** was 2 percent per year, in line with the target rates chosen around the same time by the European Central Bank, the Bank of England, and the Bank of Japan.

Strictly interpreted, inflation targeting would focus the Fed's attention nearly exclusively on controlling inflation and deflation, rather than on counteracting business fluctuations. Proponents of strict inflation targeting generally believe the economy will have fewer, shorter, and less severe business cycles if the Fed adheres to the rule "Set a known inflation goal and achieve it." The Fed, however, decided that its version of inflation targeting would be more flexible, with the Fed reserving the right to use monetary policy as necessary to smooth the business cycle even if doing so might cause inflation to deviate from the target rate of 2 percent.

We discussed another modern monetary rule—the Taylor rule—in Chapter 30. This rule specifies how the Fed should alter the federal funds rate under differing economic circumstances. Another monetary rule, nominal GDP targeting, is discussed in this chapter's Last Word.

Balanced Budget Monetarists and new classical economists question the effectiveness of fiscal policy. At the extreme, a few of them favor a constitutional amendment requiring that the federal government balance its budget annually. Others simply suggest that government be "passive" in its fiscal policy, not intentionally creating budget deficits or surpluses. They believe that deficits and surpluses caused by recession or inflationary expansion will eventually correct themselves as the economy self-corrects to its full-employment output.

Monetarists are particularly strong in their opposition to expansionary fiscal policy. They believe that the deficit spending accompanying such a policy has a strong tendency to "crowd out" private investment. Suppose government runs a budget deficit by printing and selling U.S. securities—that is, by borrowing from the public. By engaging in such borrowing, the government is competing with private businesses for funds. The borrowing increases the demand for money, which then raises the interest rate and crowds out a substantial amount of private investment that would otherwise have been profitable. The net effect of a budget deficit on aggregate demand therefore is unpredictable and, at best, modest.

RET economists reject discretionary fiscal policy for the same reason they reject active monetary policy: They don't think it works. Business and labor will immediately adjust their behavior in anticipation of the price-level effects of a change in fiscal policy. The economy will move directly to the anticipated new price level. Like monetary policy, say the RET theorists, fiscal policy can move the economy along its vertical long-run aggregate supply curve. But because its effects on inflation are fully anticipated, fiscal policy cannot alter real GDP even in the short run. The best course of action for government is to balance its budget.

In Defense of Discretionary Stabilization Policy

Mainstream economists oppose both a strict, Friedman-style monetary rule and a balanced-budget requirement. They believe that monetary policy and fiscal policy are important tools for achieving and maintaining full employment, price stability, and economic growth.

Discretionary Monetary Policy In supporting discretionary monetary policy, mainstream economists argue that the rationale for the Friedman monetary rule is flawed. While there is indeed a close relationship between the money supply and nominal GDP over long periods, in shorter periods this relationship breaks down. The reason is that the velocity of money has proved to be more variable and unpredictable than monetarists contend. Arguing that velocity is variable both cyclically and over time, mainstream economists contend that a constant annual rate of increase in the money supply might not eliminate fluctuations in aggregate demand. In terms of the equation of exchange, a steady rise of *M* does not guarantee a steady expansion of aggregate demand because *V*—the rate at which money is spent—can change.

Look again at Figure 33.3, in which we demonstrated the monetary rule: Expand the money supply annually by a fixed percentage, regardless of the state of the economy. During the period in question, optimistic business expectations might create a boom in investment spending and thus shift the aggregate demand curve to some location to the right of AD_2. (You may want to pencil in a new AD curve, labeling it AD_3.) The price level would then rise above P_1; that is, demand-pull inflation would occur. In this case, the monetary rule will not accomplish its goal of maintaining price stability. Mainstream economists say that the Fed can use a restrictive monetary policy to reduce the excessive investment spending and thereby hold the rightward shift of aggregate demand to AD_2, thus avoiding inflation.

Similarly, suppose instead that investment declines because of pessimistic business expectations. Aggregate demand will then increase by some amount less than the increase from AD_1 to AD_2 in Figure 33.3. Again, the monetary rule fails the stability test: The price level sinks below P_1 (deflation occurs). Or if the price level is inflexible downward at P_1, the economy will not achieve its full-employment output (unemployment rises). An expansionary monetary policy can help avoid each outcome.

Mainstream economists quip that the trouble with the monetary rule is that it tells the policymaker, "Don't do something; just stand there."

Discretionary Fiscal Policy Mainstream economists support the use of fiscal policy to keep recessions from deepening or to keep mild inflation from becoming severe inflation. They recognize the possibility of crowding out but do not think it is a serious problem when business borrowing is depressed, as is usually the case in recession. Because politicians can abuse fiscal policy, most economists feel that it should be held in reserve for situations where monetary policy appears to be ineffective or working too slowly.

As indicated earlier, mainstream economists oppose requirements to balance the budget annually. Tax revenues fall sharply during recessions and rise briskly during periods of demand-pull inflation. Therefore, a law or a constitutional amendment mandating an annually balanced budget would require that the government increase tax rates and reduce government spending during recession and reduce tax rates and increase government spending during economic booms. The first set of actions would worsen recession, and the second set would fuel inflation.

Policy Successes

Finally, mainstream economists point out several specific policy successes in the past four decades:

- A tight money policy dropped inflation from 13.5 percent in 1980 to 3.2 percent in 1983.
- An expansionary fiscal policy reduced the unemployment rate from 9.7 percent in 1982 to 5.5 percent in 1988.
- An easy money policy helped the economy recover from the 1990–1991 recession.
- Judicious tightening of monetary policy in the mid-1990s, and then again in the late 1990s, helped the economy remain on a noninflationary, full-employment growth path.
- In late 2001 and 2002, expansionary fiscal and monetary policy helped the economy recover from a series of economic blows, including the collapse of numerous Internet start-up firms; a severe decline in investment spending; the impacts of the terrorist attacks of September 11, 2001; and a precipitous decline in stock values.
- In 2004 and 2005 the Fed tempered continued expansionary fiscal policy by increasing the federal funds rate in $\frac{1}{4}$ percentage-point increments from 1 percent to 4.25 percent. The economy expanded briskly in those years, while inflation stayed in check. The mild inflation was particularly impressive because the average price of a barrel of crude oil rose from $24 in 2002 to $55 in 2005. The Fed's further increases in interest rates to 5.25 percent in 2006 also kept inflation mild that year and the next despite continued strong growth and oil reaching $99 per barrel in late 2007.
- In 2007 the Fed vigorously responded to a crisis in the mortgage market by ensuring monetary liquidity in the banking system. Besides aggressively lowering the federal funds rate from 5.25 percent in the summer of

2007 to just 2 percent in April 2008, the Fed greatly increased the reserves of the banking system by creating and using its term auction facility. It also undertook other lender-of-last-resort actions to unfreeze credit and prevent a possible collapse of the entire financial system. During the severe recession of 2007–2009, the Fed lowered the federal funds rate further, holding it in the 0 to 0.25 percent range to break the downward slide of the economy and help promote economic recovery.

AP QUICK REVIEW 33.3

- ✓ Mainstream economists disagree with monetarist and rational expectations economists as to whether the Fed should use rules or utilize discretion.
- ✓ Monetarist and rational expectations economists oppose discretion because they believe that discretion adds more instability to the business cycle than it cures. In their view, a monetary rule would require the Fed to expand the money supply each year at the same annual rate as the typical growth of the economy's production capacity.
- ✓ Mainstream economists oppose strict monetary rules and defend both monetary and fiscal policy discretion because they believe that both theory and evidence suggest that discretionary policies help achieve full employment, price stability, and economic growth.

AP Summary of Alternative Views

LO33.4 Summarize the fundamental ideas and policy implications of mainstream macroeconomics, monetarism, and rational expectations theory.

In Table 33.1, we summarize the fundamental ideas and policy implications of three macroeconomic theories: mainstream macroeconomics, monetarism, and rational expectations theory. Note that we have broadly defined new classical economics to include both monetarism and the rational expectations theory since both adhere to the view that the economy tends automatically to achieve equilibrium at its full-employment output.

These different perspectives have obliged mainstream economists to rethink some of their fundamental principles and to revise many of their positions. Although considerable disagreement remains, mainstream macroeconomists agree with monetarists that "money matters" and that excessive growth of the money supply is the major cause of long-lasting, rapid inflation. They also agree with RET proponents and theorists of coordination failures that expectations matter. If government can create expectations of price stability, full employment, and economic growth, households and firms will tend to act in ways to make them happen. In short, thanks to ongoing challenges to conventional wisdom, macroeconomics continues to evolve.

TABLE 33.1 Summary of Alternative Macroeconomic Views

		New Classical Economics	
Issue	**Mainstream Macroeconomics**	**Monetarism**	**Rational Expectations**
View of the private economy	Potentially unstable	Stable in long run at natural rate of unemployment	Stable in long run at natural rate of unemployment
Cause of the observed instability of the private economy	Investment plans unequal to saving plans (changes in AD); AS shocks	Inappropriate monetary policy	Unanticipated AD and AS shocks in the short run
Assumptions about short-run price and wage stickiness	Both prices and wages stuck in the immediate short run; in the short run, wages sticky while prices inflexible downward but flexible upward	Prices flexible upward and downward in the short run; wages sticky in the short run	Prices and wages flexible both upward and downward in the short run
Appropriate macro policies	Active fiscal and monetary policy	Monetary rule	Monetary rule
How changes in the money supply affect the economy	By changing the interest rate, which changes investment and real GDP	By directly changing AD, which changes GDP	No effect on output because price-level changes are anticipated
View of the velocity of money	Unstable	Stable	No consensus
How fiscal policy affects the economy	Changes AD and GDP via the multiplier process	No effect unless money supply changes	No effect because price-level changes are anticipated
View of cost-push inflation	Possible (AS shock)	Impossible in the long run in the absence of excessive money supply growth	Impossible in the long run in the absence of excessive money supply growth

LAST WORD

Market Monetarism

Market Monetarists Call for a New Monetary Rule That Would Institutionalize Fed Policy Responses to Changes in Real Output and Inflation.

In the aftermath of the Great Recession of 2007–2008, a new breed of "market monetarists" suggested that the Fed and other central banks should use prediction markets to adjust monetary policy.

In prediction markets, people can place bets on how likely it is that a particular political or financial outcome will end up happening. There are, for example, many commodities futures markets where people can bet on things like the price of corn next January or the price of oil in five years.

Extensive studies have shown that prediction markets make by far the most accurate predictions about the future—much better than those made by individual experts or even groups of experts attempting to pool their many decades of expertise. The superior prognosticating performance of prediction markets appears to be due to the fact that they incorporate the knowledge and insights of everyone who participates. As a result, even information that is only known to a few nonexperts can affect and improve the prediction.

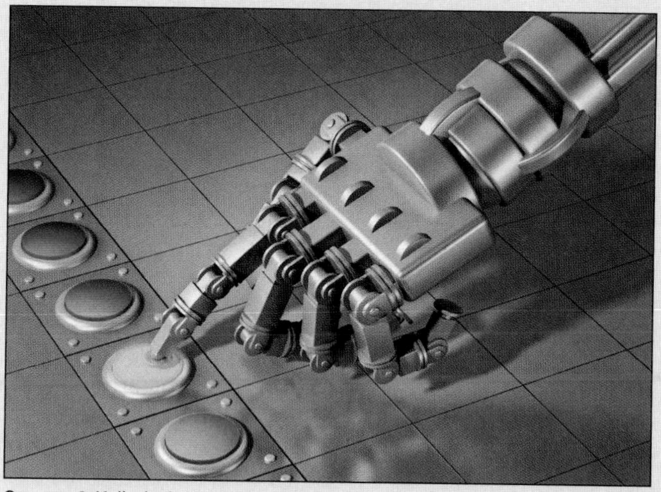

Source: © Kulka/zefa/Corbis

Prediction markets are not perfect. They do make mistakes—for instance predicting the wrong candidate to win the presidential election or predicting that the price of oil will be $46 per barrel in July whereas the actual price ends up being $53 per barrel. But because prediction markets are the best available tool for predicting future outcomes, market monetarists want to piggyback on their predictive accuracy to help the Fed set monetary policy. In particular, they argue that the Fed should set up a prediction market for nominal GDP and then use the predictions generated by that market to adjust monetary policy.

As you know, nominal GDP can grow for two reasons: inflation or increases in real GDP. Market monetarists point out that if you look back over many decades of data, nominal GDP growth in the United States has averaged about 5 percent per year. Of that amount, about 3 percent per year has on average been due to real GDP growth while the remaining 2 percent has been caused by inflation.

What market monetarists want is for the Fed to use a nominal GDP prediction market to guide monetary policy. The Fed's goal would be for the prediction market to always be predicting 5 percent growth in nominal GDP. If the prediction ever deviated from that 5 percent target, the Fed would loosen or tighten monetary policy in whatever way is needed for the prediction to adjust back to 5 percent.

To see how this monetary policy rule would work, suppose that the prediction market for nominal GDP is forecasting only 4 percent nominal GDP growth next year (rather than the desired rate of 5 percent). Because prediction markets make the most accurate forecasts, this 4 percent prediction will be our best available information on what is likely to happen with the economy next year. And since what is likely to happen is less than the target rate of 5 percent, stimulus will be called for. Market monetarists would want the Fed to loosen monetary policy and stimulate the economy until the participants in the nominal GDP prediction market are "voting with their pocketbooks" that nominal GDP will grow by 5 percent next year. When the predicted growth rate reaches 5 percent, the Fed can stop stimulating.

On the flip side, if the prediction market were forecasting 7 percent nominal GDP growth next year rather than the desired 5 percent, market monetarists would want the Fed to tighten monetary policy until the market's prediction fell back down to the 5 percent target rate. That way, contractionary monetary policy would only be applied if and when the prediction market is indicating that the economy is overheating (relative to the 5 percent target growth rate for nominal GDP). Once the prediction market is indicating that the economy is on target again, contractionary actions can end and the Fed can switch to a neutral policy stance (i.e., neither expansionary nor contractionary).

Market monetarism has prompted a vigorous debate. Some opponents argue that "targeting the forecast" would overly constrain the Fed's discretion when reacting to severe crises while others point out that a 5 percent target for nominal GDP growth would prevent real GDP growth from ever exceeding 5 percent per year. So while market monetarism has garnered several prominent proponents, including Nobel Laureate Paul Krugman and former Council of Economic Advisors Chairwoman Christina Romer, the debate over an optimal monetary policy rule will continue.

SUMMARY

LO33.1 Describe alternative perspectives on the causes of macroeconomic instability, including the views of mainstream economists, monetarists, real-business-cycle advocates, and proponents of coordination failures.

The mainstream view is that macro instability is caused by a combination of price stickiness and shocks to aggregate demand or aggregate supply. With prices inflexible in the shorter run, changes in aggregate demand or short-run aggregate supply result in changes in output and employment. In the long run when both input and output prices are fully flexible, the economy will produce at potential output.

Monetarism focuses on the equation of exchange: $MV = PQ$. Because velocity is thought to be stable, changes in M create changes in nominal GDP ($= PQ$). Monetarists believe that the most significant cause of macroeconomic instability has been inappropriate monetary policy. Rapid increases in M cause inflation; insufficient growth of M causes recession. In this view, a major cause of the Great Depression was inappropriate monetary policy, which allowed the money supply to decline by roughly one-third.

Real-business-cycle theory views changes in resource availability and technology (real factors), which alter productivity, as the main causes of macroeconomic instability. In this theory, shifts of the economy's long-run aggregate supply curve change real output. In turn, money demand and money supply change, shifting the aggregate demand curve in the same direction as the initial change in long-run aggregate supply. Real output thus can change without a change in the price level.

A coordination failure is said to occur when people lack a way to coordinate their actions in order to achieve a mutually beneficial equilibrium. Depending on people's expectations, the economy can come to rest at either a good equilibrium (noninflationary full-employment output) or a bad equilibrium (less-than-full-employment output or demand-pull inflation). A bad equilibrium is a result of a coordination failure.

The rational expectations theory rests on two assumptions: (1) With sufficient information, people's beliefs about future economic outcomes accurately reflect the likelihood that those outcomes will occur; and (2) markets are highly competitive, and prices and wages are flexible both upward and downward.

LO33.2 Discuss why new classical economists believe the economy will "self-correct" from aggregate demand and aggregate supply shocks.

New classical economists (monetarists and rational expectations theorists) see the economy as automatically correcting itself when disturbed from its full-employment level of real output. In RET, unanticipated changes in aggregate demand change the price level, and in the short run this leads firms to change output. But once the firms realize that all prices are changing (including nominal wages) as part of general inflation or deflation, they restore their output to the previous level. Anticipated changes in aggregate demand produce only changes in the price level, not changes in real output.

Mainstream economists reject the new classical view that all prices and wages are flexible downward. They contend that nominal wages, in particular, are inflexible downward because of several factors, including labor contracts, efficiency wages, and insider-outsider relationships. This means that declines in aggregate demand lower real output, not only wages and prices.

LO33.3 Identify and describe the variations of the debate over "rules" versus "discretion" in conducting stabilization policy.

Monetarist and rational expectations economists say the Fed should adhere to some form of policy rule, rather than rely exclusively on discretion. The Friedman rule would direct the Fed to increase the money supply at a fixed annual rate equal to the long-run growth of potential GDP. In 2012, the Fed took another path, however, and adopted an inflation target of 2 percent per year, thereby committing itself to adjusting monetary policy to reach that goal except in extreme cases where different rates of inflation might be necessary to smooth the business cycle. Monetarist and rational expectation economists also support maintaining a "neutral" fiscal policy, as opposed to using discretionary fiscal policy to create budget deficits or budget surpluses. A few monetarists and rational expectations economists favor a constitutional amendment requiring that the federal government balance its budget annually.

Mainstream economists oppose strict, Friedman-style monetary rules and a balanced-budget requirement, and defend discretionary monetary and fiscal policies. They say that both theory and evidence suggest that such policies are helpful in achieving full employment, price stability, and economic growth.

LO33.4 Summarize the fundamental ideas and policy implications of mainstream macroeconomics, monetarism, and rational expectations theory.

Macroeconomics continues to evolve because of the debate among the three main schools of economic thought: the mainstream, monetarism, and rational expectations.

Mainstream economics believes the economy to be potentially unstable and prone to business cycles due to sticky prices and wages interacting with economic shocks. The mainstream believes in active monetary and fiscal policy that can change AD through the multiplier process and that changes in the money supply affect the economy by changing the interest rate and investment. The mainstream believes the velocity of money to be unstable and holds that cost-push inflation exists and is caused by AS shocks.

Monetarism believes the economy to be fundamentally stable unless inappropriate monetary policies are applied. It believes wages and prices are fully flexible at all time horizons, allowing the economy to adjust on its own back to equilibrium. It argues that business cycles will only occur if monetary policy is either overly tight or overly loose. To prevent either, monetarists support the application of a *monetary rule* to guide monetary policy. Monetarism views the velocity of money as stable and believes cost-push inflation to be impossible in the long run in the absence of excessive money supply growth. Monetarists believe that fiscal policy cannot affect AD or GDP unless there are accompanying changes in monetary policy. On the other hand, monetary policy can shift AD and thereby affect GDP.

The rational expectations camp believes the economy to be stable in the long run at the natural rate of unemployment due to its assumption that prices are flexible at all time horizons. But over shorter time horizons, recessions and booms can happen due to unexpected AD or AS shocks. Rational expectations proponents support a monetary rule in order to guide expectations, so that monetary policy changes will never be a surprise that could shift the economy away from its equilibrium. They also agree with monetarists in the belief that cost-push inflation should be impossible without excessive money supply growth. Finally, rational expectations economists believe that anticipated fiscal and monetary policy changes will have no effect on GDP because they will lead only to price-level changes. For either to be effective in shifting GDP in the short run, they must come as a surprise.

TERMS AND CONCEPTS

monetarism
equation of exchange
velocity
real-business-cycle theory
coordination failures
rational expectations theory
new classical economics
price-level surprises
efficiency wage
insider-outsider theory
monetary rule
inflation targeting
target rate of inflation

The following and additional problems can be found in connect

DISCUSSION QUESTIONS

1. According to mainstream economists, what is the usual cause of macroeconomic instability? What role does the spending-income multiplier play in creating instability? How might adverse aggregate supply factors cause instability, according to mainstream economists? LO33.1
2. What is an efficiency wage? How might payment of an above-market wage reduce shirking by employees and reduce worker turnover? How might efficiency wages contribute to downward wage inflexibility, at least for a time, when aggregate demand declines? LO33.1
3. How might relationships between so-called insiders and outsiders contribute to downward wage inflexibility? LO33.1
4. Briefly describe the difference between a so-called real business cycle and a more traditional "spending" business cycle. LO33.1
5. Craig and Kris were walking directly toward each other in a congested store aisle. Craig moved to his left to avoid Kris, and at the same time Kris moved to his right to avoid Craig. They bumped into each other. What concept does this example illustrate? How does this idea relate to macroeconomic instability? LO33.1
6. State and explain the basic equation of monetarism. What is the major cause of macroeconomic instability, as viewed by monetarists? LO33.1
7. Use the equation of exchange to explain the rationale for a monetary rule. Why will such a rule run into trouble if *V* unexpectedly falls because of, say, a drop in investment spending by businesses? LO33.1
8. Explain the difference between "active" discretionary fiscal policy advocated by mainstream economists and "passive" fiscal policy advocated by new classical economists. Explain: "The problem with a balanced-budget amendment is that it would, in a sense, require active fiscal policy—but in the wrong direction—as the economy slides into recession." LO33.3
9. You have just been elected president of the United States, and the present chairperson of the Federal Reserve Board has resigned. You need to appoint a new person to this position, as well as a person to chair your Council of Economic Advisers. Using Table 33.1 and your knowledge of macroeconomics, identify the views on macro theory and policy you would want your appointees to hold. Remember, the economic health of the entire nation—and your chances for reelection—may depend on your selection. LO33.4
10. **LAST WORD** Compare and contrast the market monetarist 5 percent target for nominal GDP growth with the older, simpler monetary rule advocated by Milton Friedman.

AP REVIEW QUESTIONS

1. If prices are sticky and gross investment unexpectedly increases, the ________ curve will shift ________. LO33.1
   a. AD; rightward.
   b. AD; leftward.
   c. AS; rightward.
   d. AS; leftward.
   e. Long-run AS; leftward.
2. State the Equation of Exchange. Assume that M is $500 billion and V is 5. What is the level of nominal GDP according to the monetarist equation? If V rises by 10%, then according to the monetarist equation, what will be the new level of nominal GDP? LO33.1
3. According to mainstream macroeconomists, U.S. macro instability has principally resulted over the last century from: LO33.4

a. Investment "booms" and "busts" and, occasionally, adverse aggregate supply shocks.
b. Adherence by the Fed to a monetary rule.
c. Government's attempts to balance its budget.
d. Wide fluctuations in net exports.
e. Wage and price level flexibility.

4. The rational expectations theory assumes that: LO33.4
a. Markets fail to coordinate the actions of households and businesses
b. Firms pay above-market wages to elicit work effort.
c. People behave rationally and that all product and resource prices are flexible both upward and downward.
d. Markets are dominated by monopolistic firms.
e. Fiscal policy changes affect the AS, the price level, and the RDGP.

5. An economy is producing at full employment when AD unexpectedly shifts to the left. A new classical economist would assume that as the economy adjusted back to producing at full employment, the price level and nominal wage would change in which ways? LO33.2
a. The nominal wage would remain constant and the price level will fall.
b. The nominal wage and the price level will both decrease.
c. The nominal wage will fall and the price level will remain constant.
d. Both the nominal wage and the price level will increase.
e. There will be no change in either the nominal wage or in the price level.

6. New classical economists say that an *unanticipated* decrease in aggregate demand first: LO33.4
a. Decreases the price level and real output, and then decreases long-run aggregate supply.
b. Decreases long-run aggregate supply, and then decreases the price level and real output.
c. Decreases short-run aggregate supply, and then decreases long-run aggregate supply.
d. Decreases the price level and real output, and then increases short-run aggregate supply such that the economy returns to the full employment level of output.
e. Increases short-run aggregate supply, and then increases long-run aggregate supply.

7. Place "MON," "RET," or "MAIN" beside the statements that most closely reflect monetarist, rational expectations, or mainstream Keynesian-like views, respectively: LO33.4
a. Anticipated changes in aggregate demand affect only the price level; they have no effect on real output.
b. Downward wage inflexibility means that declines in aggregate demand can cause long-lasting recession.
c. Unanticipated changes in the money supply M increase PQ; at first only Q rises, because nominal wages are fixed, but once workers adapt their expectations to new realities, P rises and Q returns to its former level.
d. Fiscal and monetary policies smooth out the business cycle.
e. The Fed should increase the money supply at a fixed annual rate.

8. Assume that the velocity of money is stable, an increase in the money supply LO33.1
a. Must lead to an increase in the price level.
b. Will increase real GDP.
c. Must increase nominal GDP.
d. Must lead to wage decreases over time.
e. Will increase the long-run aggregate supply in the economy.

9. When the nominal money supply increases and nominal GDP does not changes, what is most likely true? LO33.1
a. The real GDP must have fallen, as the price level increased.
b. The real money supply did not change so the nominal GDP did not change.
c. The increase in the money supply was fully anticipated, so it did not change the price level.
d. The velocity of money fell.
e. The Federal Reserve also reduced the discount rate at the same time.

PROBLEMS

1. Suppose that the money supply and the nominal GDP for a hypothetical economy are \$96 billion and \$336 billion, respectively. What is the velocity of money? How will households and businesses react if the central bank reduces the money supply by \$20 billion? By how much will nominal GDP have to fall to restore equilibrium, according to the monetarist perspective? LO33.1

2. Assume the following information for a hypothetical economy in year 1: money supply = \$400 billion; long-term annual growth of potential GDP = 3 percent; velocity = 4. Assume that the banking system initially has no excess reserves and that the reserve requirement is 10 percent. Also suppose that velocity is constant and that the economy initially is operating at its full-employment real output. LO33.1
a. What is the level of nominal GDP in year 1?
b. Suppose the Fed adheres to a monetary rule through open-market operations. What amount of U.S. securities will it have to sell to, or buy from, banks or the public between years 1 and 2 to meet its monetary rule?

Part ELEVEN AP

International Economics

In the contemporary world, international economic issues are so vital. We will study ***comparative advantage*** and the benefits that can accrue from ***international trade.*** We also will learn how individuals, businesses, and countries with different monetary systems can engage in international economic transactions, both trade and finance, by exchanging money in the ***foreign exchange or international currency market.*** Many of the overall benefits of globalization are shown in this study of international trade and international finance.

Chapter 34

International Trade*

Learning Objectives

LO34.1 List and discuss several key facts about international trade.

LO34.2 Define comparative advantage and demonstrate how specialization and trade add to a nation's output.

LO34.3 Describe how differences between world prices and domestic prices prompt exports and imports.

LO34.4 Analyze the economic effects of tariffs and quotas.

LO34.5 Analyze the validity of the most frequently presented arguments for protectionism.

LO34.6 Identify and explain the objectives of GATT, WTO, EU, eurozone, and NAFTA and discuss offshoring and trade adjustment assistance.

AP Chapter Focus

Backpackers in the wilderness like to think they are "leaving the world behind," but, like Atlas, they carry the world on their shoulders. Much of their equipment is imported—knives from Switzerland, rain gear from South Korea, cameras from Japan, aluminum pots from England, sleeping bags from China, and compasses from Finland. Moreover, they may have driven to the trail-heads in Japanese-made Toyotas or German-made BMWs, sipping coffee from Brazil or snacking on bananas from Honduras.

International trade and the global economy affect all of us daily, whether we are hiking in the wilderness, driving our cars, buying groceries, or working at our jobs. We cannot "leave the world behind." We are enmeshed in a global web of economic relationships, such as trading goods and services, multinational corporations, cooperative ventures among the world's firms, and ties among the world's financial markets.

The focus of this chapter is the trading of goods and services. Then in Chapter 35, we examine the U.S. balance of payments, exchange rates, and U.S. trade deficits.

*Note to Instructors: If you prefer to cover international trade early in your course, you can assign this chapter at the end of either Part 1 or Part 2. This chapter builds on the introductory ideas of opportunity costs, supply and demand analysis, and economic efficiency but does not require an understanding of either market failures or government failures.

Some Key Trade Facts

LO34.1 List and discuss several key facts about international trade.

The following are several important facts relating to international trade.

- U.S. exports and imports have more than doubled as percentages of GDP since 1980.
- A *trade deficit* occurs when imports exceed exports. The United States has a trade deficit in goods. In 2015, U.S. imports of goods exceeded U.S. exports of goods by $529 billion.
- A *trade surplus* occurs when exports exceed imports. The United States has a trade surplus in services (such as air transportation services and financial services). In 2015, U.S. exports of services exceeded U.S. imports of services by $220 billion.
- Principal U.S. exports include chemicals, agricultural products, consumer durables, semiconductors, and aircraft; principal imports include petroleum, automobiles, metals, household appliances, and computers.
- As with other advanced industrial nations, the United States imports many goods that are in some of the same categories as the goods that it exports. Examples: automobiles, computers, chemicals, semiconductors, and telecommunications equipment.
- Canada is the United States' most important trading partner quantitatively. In 2015, about 19 percent of U.S. exported goods were sold to Canadians, who in turn provided 13 percent of imported U.S. goods.
- The United States has a sizable trade deficit with China. In 2015 it was $366 billion.
- Starting in 2012, the shale oil boom in the Plains States greatly reduced U.S. dependence on foreign oil, as can be seen in the statistics that keep track of trade between the United States and the members of OPEC. In 2011, before the boom, the United States imported $191.5 billion of goods (mainly oil) from OPEC while exporting $64.8 billion of goods to those countries. By 2015, U.S. imports had fallen to just $66.2 billion while exports had risen to $72.8 billion. The United States' oil usage had fallen so much that the United States ran its first-ever trade surplus with OPEC in 2015.
- The United States leads the world in the combined volume of exports and imports, as measured in dollars. China, the United States, Germany, Japan, and the Netherlands were the top five exporters by dollar in 2015.

GLOBAL PERSPECTIVE 34.1

Shares of World Exports, Selected Nations

China has the largest share of world exports, followed by Germany and the United States. The eight largest export nations account for about 44.8 percent of world exports.

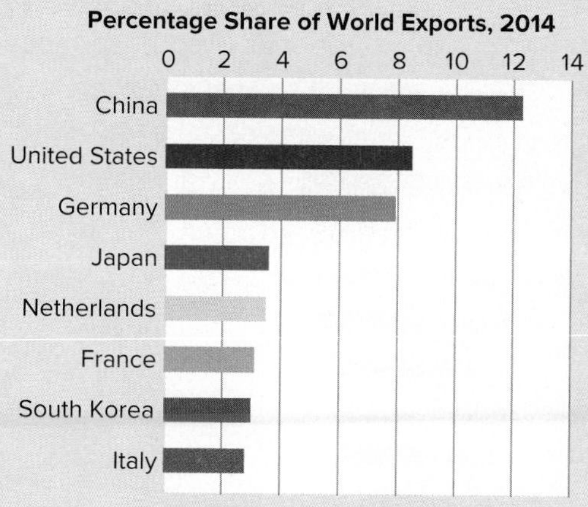

Source: International Trade Statistics, 2015, WTO Publications.

- Currently, the United States provides about 8.5 percent of the world's exports. (See Global Perspective 34.1.)
- Exports of goods and services (on a national income account basis) make up about 13 percent of total U.S. output. That percentage is much lower than the percentage in many other nations, including Belgium, the Netherlands, Germany, Canada, and the United Kingdom. (See Global Perspective 34.2.)
- China has become a major international trader, with an estimated $2.2 trillion of exports in 2015. Other Asian economies—including South Korea, Taiwan, and Singapore—are also active in international trade. Their combined exports exceed those of France, Britain, or Italy.
- International trade links world economies. Through trade, changes in economic conditions in one place on the globe can quickly affect other places.
- International trade is often at the center of debates over economic policy, both within the United States and internationally.

With this information in mind, let's turn to the economics of international trade.

GLOBAL PERSPECTIVE 34.2

Exports of Goods and Services as a Percentage of GDP, Selected Countries

Although the United States is one of the world's largest exporters, as a percentage of GDP, its exports are quite low relative to many other countries.

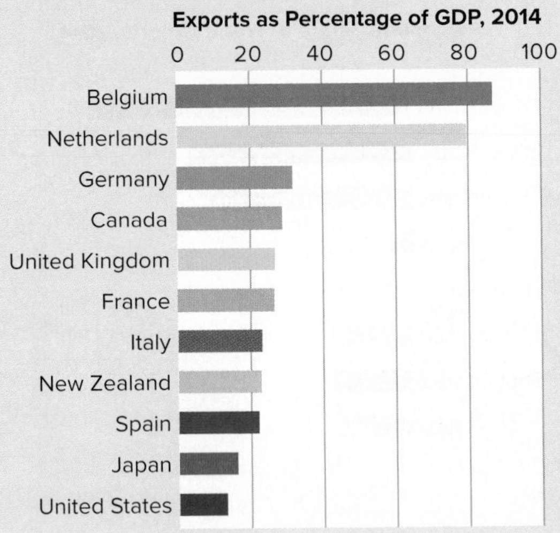

Source: Derived by authors from *IMF International Financial Statistics*, 2015.

The Economic Basis for Trade

LO34.2 Define comparative advantage and demonstrate how specialization and trade add to a nation's output.

Sovereign nations, like individuals and the regions of a nation, can gain by specializing in the products they can produce with the greatest relative efficiency and by trading for the goods they cannot produce as efficiently. The simple answer to the question "Why do nations trade?" is "They trade because it is beneficial." The benefits that emerge relate to three underlying facts:

- The distribution of natural, human, and capital resources among nations is uneven; nations differ in their endowments of economic resources.
- Efficient production of various goods requires different technologies, and not all nations have the same level of technological expertise.
- Products are differentiated as to quality and other attributes, and some people may prefer certain goods imported from abroad rather than similar goods produced domestically.

To recognize the character and interaction of these three facts, think of China, which has abundant and inexpensive labor. As a result, China can produce efficiently (at low cost of other goods forgone) a variety of **labor-intensive goods,** such as textiles, electronics, apparel, toys, and sporting goods.

In contrast, Australia has vast amounts of land and can inexpensively produce such **land-intensive goods** as beef, wool, and meat. Mexico has the soil, tropical climate, rainfall, and ready supply of unskilled labor that allow for the efficient, low-cost production of vegetables. Industrially advanced economies such as the United States and Germany that have relatively large amounts of capital can inexpensively produce goods whose production requires much capital, including such **capital-intensive goods** as airplanes, automobiles, agricultural equipment, machinery, and chemicals.

Also, regardless of their resource intensities, nations can develop individual products that are in demand worldwide because of their special qualities. Examples: fashions from Italy, chocolates from Belgium, software from the United States, and watches from Switzerland.

The distribution of resources, technology, and product distinctiveness among nations is relatively stable in short time periods but certainly can change over time. When that distribution changes, the relative efficiency and success that nations have in producing and selling goods also change. For example, in the past several decades, South Korea has greatly expanded its stock of capital. Although South Korea was primarily an exporter of agricultural products and raw materials a half-century ago, it now exports large quantities of manufactured goods. Similarly, the new technologies that gave us synthetic fibers and synthetic rubber drastically altered the resource mix needed to produce fibers and rubber and changed the relative efficiency of nations in manufacturing them.

As national economies evolve, the size and quality of their labor forces may change, the volume and composition of their capital stocks may shift, new technologies may develop, and even the quality of land and the quantity of natural resources may be altered. As such changes take place, the relative efficiency with which a nation can produce specific goods will also change. As economists would say, comparative advantage can and does sometimes change.

Comparative Advantage

In an open economy (one with an international sector), a country produces more of certain goods (exports) and fewer of other goods (imports) than it would otherwise. Thus, the country shifts the use of labor and other productive resources toward export industries and away from import industries. For example, in the presence of international trade, the United States uses more resources to make commercial aircraft and to grow wheat and fewer resources to make television sets and sew clothes. So we ask: Do such shifts of resources make economic sense? Do they enhance U.S. total output and thus the U.S. standard of living?

CONSIDER THIS . . .

Source: © Digital Vision/Getty Images RF

A CPA and a House Painter

Suppose that Madison, a certified public accountant (CPA), is a swifter painter than Mason, the professional painter she is thinking of hiring. Also assume that Madison can earn $50 per hour as an accountant but would have to pay Mason $15 per hour. And suppose that Madison would need 30 hours to paint her house but Mason would need 40 hours.

Should Madison take time from her accounting to paint her own house, or should she hire the painter? Madison's opportunity cost of painting her house is $1,500 (= 30 hours of sacrificed CPA time × $50 per CPA hour). The cost of hiring Mason is only $600 (= 40 hours of painting × $15 per hour of painting). Although Madison is better at both accounting and painting, she will get her house painted at lower cost by specializing in accounting and using some of her earnings from accounting to hire a house painter.

Similarly, Mason can reduce his cost of obtaining accounting services by specializing in painting and using some of his income to hire Madison to prepare his income tax forms. Suppose Mason would need 10 hours to prepare his tax return, while Madison could handle the task in 2 hours. Mason would sacrifice $150 of income (= 10 hours of painting time × $15 per hour) to do something he could hire Madison to do for $100 (= 2 hours of CPA time × $50 per CPA hour). By specializing in painting and hiring Madison to prepare his tax return, Mason lowers the cost of getting his tax return prepared.

We will see that what is true for our CPA and house painter is also true for nations. Specializing on the basis of comparative advantage enables nations to reduce the cost of obtaining the goods and services they desire.

The answers are affirmative. Specialization and international trade increase the productivity of U.S. resources and allow the United States to obtain greater total output than otherwise would be possible. These benefits are the result of exploiting both *absolute advantages* and *comparative advantages*. A country is said to have an *absolute advantage* over other producers of a product if it is the most efficient producer of that product (by which we mean that it can produce more output of that product from any given amount of resource inputs than can any other producer). A country is said to have a *comparative advantage* over other producers of a product if it can produce the product at a lower opportunity cost (by which we mean that it must forgo less output of alternative products when allocating productive resources to producing the product in question).

In 1776, Adam Smith used the concept of absolute advantage to argue for international specialization and trade. His point was that nations would be better off if each specialized in the production of those products in which it had an absolute advantage and was therefore the most efficient producer:

> It is the maxim of every prudent master of a family, never to attempt to make at home what it will cost him more to make than to buy. The taylor does not attempt to make his own shoes, but buys them of the shoemaker. The shoemaker does not attempt to make his own clothes, but employs a taylor. The farmer attempts to make neither the one nor the other, but employs those different artificers. . . .
>
> What is prudence in the conduct of every private family, can scarce be folly in that of a great kingdom. If a foreign country can supply us with a commodity cheaper than we can make it, better buy it of them with some part of the produce of our own industry, employed in a way in which we have some advantage.[1]

In the early 1800s, David Ricardo extended Smith's idea by demonstrating that it is advantageous for a country to specialize and trade with another country even if it is more productive in all economic activities than that other country. Stated more formally, a nation does not need Smith's absolute advantage—total superiority in the efficiency with which it produces products—to benefit from specialization and trade. It needs only a comparative advantage.

The nearby Consider This box (A CPA and a House Painter) provides a simple, two-person illustration of Ricardo's principle of comparative advantage. Be sure to read it now because it will greatly help you understand the graphical analysis that follows.

AP QUICK REVIEW 34.1

- ✓ International trade enables nations to specialize, increase productivity, and increase the amount of output available for consumption. With trade a country can consume, but not produce, beyond its production possibilities frontier.
- ✓ A country is said to have an *absolute advantage* over the other producers of a product if it can produce the product more efficiently, that is, it can produce more of the product from any given amount of resource inputs than can any other producer. Absolute advantage represents production at lower unit cost.
- ✓ A country is said to have a *comparative advantage* over the other producers of a product if it can produce the product at a lower opportunity cost, that is, it must forgo less of the output of alternative products when allocating resources to producing the product in question. Comparative advantage represents production at lower opportunity cost.

[1]Adam Smith, *The Wealth of Nations* (originally published, 1776; New York: Modern Library, 1937), p. 424.

Two Isolated Nations

Our goal is to place the idea of comparative advantage into the context of trading nations. Our method is to build a simple model that relies on the familiar concepts of production possibilities curves. Suppose the world consists of just two nations, the United States and Mexico. Also for simplicity, suppose that the labor forces in the United States and Mexico are of equal size. Each nation can produce both beef and raw (unprocessed) vegetables but at different levels of economic efficiency. Suppose the U.S. and Mexican domestic production possibilities curves for beef and vegetables are those shown in Figure 34.1a and Figure 34.1b. Note three realities relating to the production possibilities curves in the two graphs:

- ***Constant costs*** The curves derive from the data in Table 34.1 and are drawn as straight lines, in contrast to the bowed-outward production possibilities frontiers we examined in Chapter 1. This means that we have replaced the law of increasing opportunity costs with the assumption of constant costs. This substitution simplifies our discussion but does not impair the validity of our analysis and conclusions. Later we will consider the effects of increasing opportunity costs.
- ***Different costs*** The production possibilities curves of the United States and Mexico reflect different resource mixes and differing levels of technology. Specifically, the differing slopes of the two curves reflect the numbers in the figures and reveal that the opportunity costs of producing beef and vegetables differ between the two nations.
- ***U.S. absolute advantage in both*** A producer (an individual, firm, or country) has an *absolute advantage* over another producer if it can produce more of a product than the other producer using the same amount of resources. Because of our convenient assumption that the U.S. and Mexican labor forces are the same size, the two production possibilities curves show that the United States has an absolute advantage in producing both products. If the United States and Mexico use their entire (equal-size) labor forces to produce either vegetables or beef, the United States can produce more of either than Mexico. The United States, using the same number of workers as Mexico, has greater production possibilities. So output per worker—labor productivity—in the United States exceeds that in Mexico in producing both products.

Opportunity-Cost Ratio in the United States In Figure 34.1a, with full employment, the United States will operate at some point on its production possibilities curve. On that curve, it can increase its output of beef from 0 tons to 30 tons by forgoing 30 tons of vegetables output. So the slope of the production possibilities curve is 1 (= 30 vegetables/30 beef), meaning that 1 ton of vegetables must be sacrificed for each extra ton of beef. In the United States the **opportunity-cost ratio** (domestic exchange ratio) for the two products is 1 ton of vegetables (V) for 1 ton of beef (B), or

United States: $1V \equiv 1B$ (The "≡" sign simply means "equivalent to.")

Within its borders, the United States can "exchange" a ton of vegetables from itself for a ton of beef from itself. Our constant-cost assumption means that this exchange or opportunity-cost relationship prevails for all possible moves from one point to another along the U.S. production possibilities curve.

FIGURE 34.1 Production possibilities for the United States and Mexico. The two production possibilities curves show the combinations of vegetables and beef that the United States and Mexico can produce domestically. The curves for both countries are straight lines because we are assuming constant opportunity costs. (a) As reflected by the slope of *VB* in the left graph, the opportunity-cost ratio in the United States is 1 vegetable ≡ 1 beef. (b) The production possibilities curve *vb* in the right graph has a steeper slope, reflecting the different opportunity-cost ratio in Mexico of 2 vegetables ≡ 1 beef. The difference in the opportunity-cost ratios between the two countries defines their comparative advantages and is the basis for specialization and international trade.

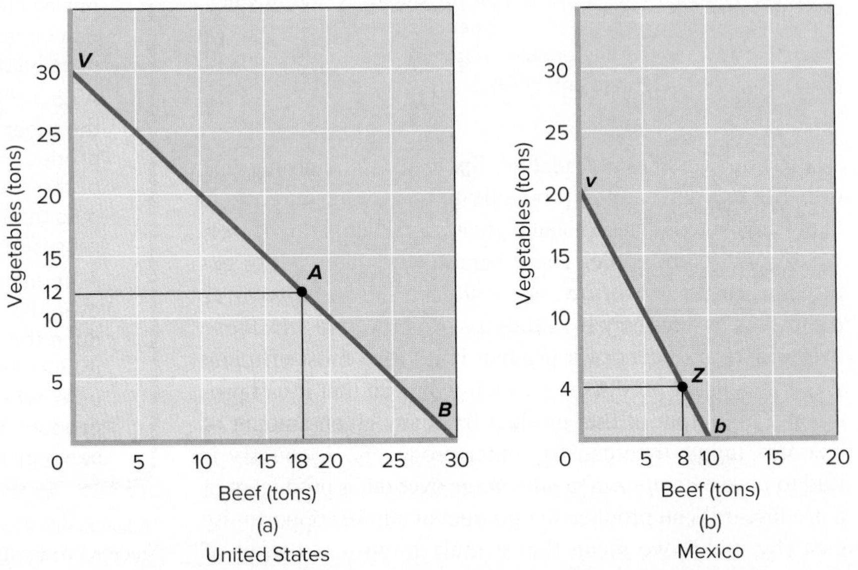

AP TABLE 34.1 International Specialization According to Comparative Advantage and the Gains from Trade

Country	(1) Outputs before Specialization	(2) Outputs after Specialization	(3) Amounts Exported (−) and Imported (+)	(4) Outputs Available after Trade	(5) Gains from Specialization and Trade (4) − (1)
United States	18 beef	30 beef	−10 beef	20 beef	2 beef
	12 vegetables	0 vegetables	+15 vegetables	15 vegetables	3 vegetables
Mexico	8 beef	0 beef	+10 beef	10 beef	2 beef
	4 vegetables	20 vegetables	−15 vegetables	5 vegetables	1 vegetables

Opportunity-Cost Ratio in Mexico Mexico's production possibilities curve in Figure 34.1b represents a different full-employment opportunity-cost ratio. In Mexico, 20 tons of vegetables must be given up to obtain 10 tons of beef. The slope of the production possibilities curve is 2 (= 20 vegetables/10 beef). This means that in Mexico the opportunity-cost ratio for the two goods is 2 tons of vegetables for 1 ton of beef, or

$$\text{Mexico: } 2V \equiv 1B$$

Self-Sufficiency Output Mix If the United States and Mexico are isolated and self-sufficient, then each country must choose some output mix on its production possibilities curve. It will select the mix that provides the greatest total utility or satisfaction. Let's assume that combination point *A* in Figure 34.1a is the optimal mix in the United States. That is, society deems the combination of 18 tons of beef and 12 tons of vegetables preferable to any other combination of the goods available along the production possibilities curve. Suppose Mexico's optimal product mix is 8 tons of beef and 4 tons of vegetables, indicated by point *Z* in Figure 34.1b. These choices by the two countries are reflected in column 1 of Table 34.1.

Specializing Based on Comparative Advantage

A producer (an individual, firm, or nation) has a **comparative advantage** in producing a particular product if it can produce that product at a lower opportunity cost than other producers. Comparative advantage is the key determinant in whether or not nations can gain from specialization and trade. In fact, absolute advantage turns out to be irrelevant.

In our example, for instance, the United States has an absolute advantage over Mexico in producing both vegetables and beef. But it is still the case that the United States can gain from specialization and trade with Mexico. That is because what actually matters is whether the opportunity costs of producing the two products (beef and vegetables) differ in the two countries. If they do, then each nation will enjoy a comparative advantage in one of the products, meaning that it can produce that product at a lower opportunity cost than the other country. As a result, total output can increase if each country specializes in the production of the good in which it has the lower opportunity cost.

This idea is summarized in the **principle of comparative advantage,** which says that total output will be greatest when each good is produced by the nation that has the lowest domestic opportunity cost for producing that good. In our two-nation illustration, the United States has the lower domestic opportunity cost for beef; the United States must forgo only 1 ton of vegetables to produce 1 ton of beef, whereas Mexico must forgo 2 tons of vegetables for 1 ton of beef. The United States has a comparative (cost) advantage in beef and should specialize in beef production. The "world" (that is, the United States and Mexico) in our example would clearly not be economizing in the use of its resources if a high-cost producer (Mexico) produced a specific product (beef) when a low-cost producer (the United States) could have produced it. Having Mexico produce beef would mean that the world economy would have to give up more vegetables than is necessary to obtain a ton of beef.

Mexico has the lower domestic opportunity cost for vegetables. It must sacrifice only $\frac{1}{2}$ ton of beef to produce 1 ton of vegetables, while the United States must forgo 1 ton of beef to produce 1 ton of vegetables. Mexico has a comparative advantage in vegetables and should specialize in vegetable production. Again, the world would not be employing its resources economically if vegetables were produced by a high-cost producer (the United States) rather than by a low-cost producer (Mexico). If the United States produced vegetables, the world would be giving up more beef than necessary to obtain each ton of vegetables. Economizing requires that any particular good be produced by the nation having the lowest domestic opportunity cost or the nation having the comparative advantage for that good. The United States should produce beef, and Mexico should produce vegetables. The situation is summarized in Table 34.2.

A comparison of columns 1 and 2 in Table 34.1 verifies that specialized production enables the world to obtain more

TABLE 34.2 Comparative-Advantage Example: A Summary

Beef	Vegetables
Mexico: Must give up 2 tons of vegetables to get 1 ton of beef.	***Mexico:*** Must give up $\frac{1}{2}$ ton of beef to get 1 ton of vegetables.
United States: Must give up 1 ton of vegetables to get 1 ton of beef.	***United States:*** Must give up 1 ton of beef to get 1 ton of vegetables.
Comparative advantage: United States	***Comparative advantage:*** Mexico

output from its fixed amount of resources. By specializing completely in beef, the United States can produce 30 tons of beef and no vegetables. Mexico, by specializing completely in vegetables, can produce 20 tons of vegetables and no beef. These figures exceed the yields generated without specialization: 26 tons of beef (= 18 in the United States + 8 in Mexico) and 16 tons of vegetables (= 12 in the United States + 4 in Mexico). As a result, the world ends up with 4 more tons of beef (= 30 tons − 26 tons) and 4 more tons of vegetables (= 20 tons − 16 tons) than it would if there were self-sufficiency and unspecialized production.

Terms of Trade

We have just seen that specialization in production will allow for the largest possible amounts of both beef and vegetables to be produced. But with each country specializing in the production of only one item, how will the vegetables that are all produced by Mexico and the beef that is all produced by the United States be divided between consumers in the two countries? The key turns out to be the **terms of trade,** the exchange ratio at which the United States and Mexico trade beef and vegetables.

Crucially, the terms of trade also establish whether each country will find it in its own better interest to bother specializing at all. This is because the terms of trade determine whether each country can "get a better deal" by specializing and trading than it could if it opted instead for self sufficiency. To see how this works, note that because $1B \equiv 1V$ $(= 1V \equiv 1B)$ in the United States, it must get more than 1 ton of vegetables for each 1 ton of beef exported; otherwise, it will not benefit from exporting beef in exchange for Mexican vegetables. The United States must get a better "price" (more vegetables) for its beef through international trade than it can get domestically; otherwise, no gain from trade exists and such trade will not occur.

Similarly, because $1B \equiv 2V$ $(= 2V \equiv 1B)$ in Mexico, Mexico must obtain 1 ton of beef by exporting less than 2 tons of vegetables to get it. Mexico must be able to pay a lower "price" for beef in the world market than it must pay domestically, or else it will not want to trade. The international exchange ratio or terms of trade must therefore lie somewhere between

$$1B \equiv 1V \text{ (United States' cost conditions)}$$

and

$$1B \equiv 2V \text{ (Mexico's cost conditions)}$$

Where between these limits will the world exchange ratio fall? The United States will prefer a rate close to $1B \equiv 2V$, say, $1B \equiv 1\frac{3}{4}V$. The United States wants to obtain as many vegetables as possible for each 1 ton of beef it exports. By contrast, Mexico wants a rate near $1B \equiv 1V$, say, $1B \equiv 1\frac{1}{4}V$. This is true because Mexico wants to export as few vegetables as possible for each 1 ton of beef it receives in exchange.

The actual exchange ratio depends on world supply and demand for the two products. If overall world demand for vegetables is weak relative to its supply and if the demand for beef is strong relative to its supply, the price of vegetables will be lower and the price of beef will be higher. The exchange ratio will settle nearer the $1B \equiv 2V$ figure the United States prefers. If overall world demand for vegetables is great relative to its supply and if the demand for beef is weak relative to its supply, the ratio will settle nearer the $1B \equiv 1V$ level favorable to Mexico. In this manner, the actual exchange ratio that is set by world supply and demand determines how the gains from international specialization and trade are divided between the two nations and, consequently, how the beef that is all produced in the United States and the vegetables that are all produced in Mexico get divided among consumers in the two countries. (We discuss equilibrium world prices later in this chapter.)

Gains from Trade

Suppose the international terms of trade are $1B \equiv 1\frac{1}{2}V$. The possibility of trading on these terms permits each nation to supplant its domestic production possibilities curve with a trading possibilities line (or curve), as shown in **Figure 34.2 (Key Graph).** Just as a production possibilities curve shows the amounts of these products that a full-employment economy can obtain by shifting resources from one to the other, a **trading possibilities line** shows the amounts of the two products that a nation can obtain by specializing in one product and trading for the other. The trading possibilities lines in Figure 34.2 reflect the assumption that both nations specialize on the basis of comparative advantage: The United States specializes completely in beef (at point B in Figure 34.2a), and Mexico specializes completely in vegetables (at point v in Figure 34.2b).

Improved Alternatives With specialization and trade, the United States is no longer constrained by its domestic production possibilities line, which requires it to give up 1 ton of

AP KEY GRAPH

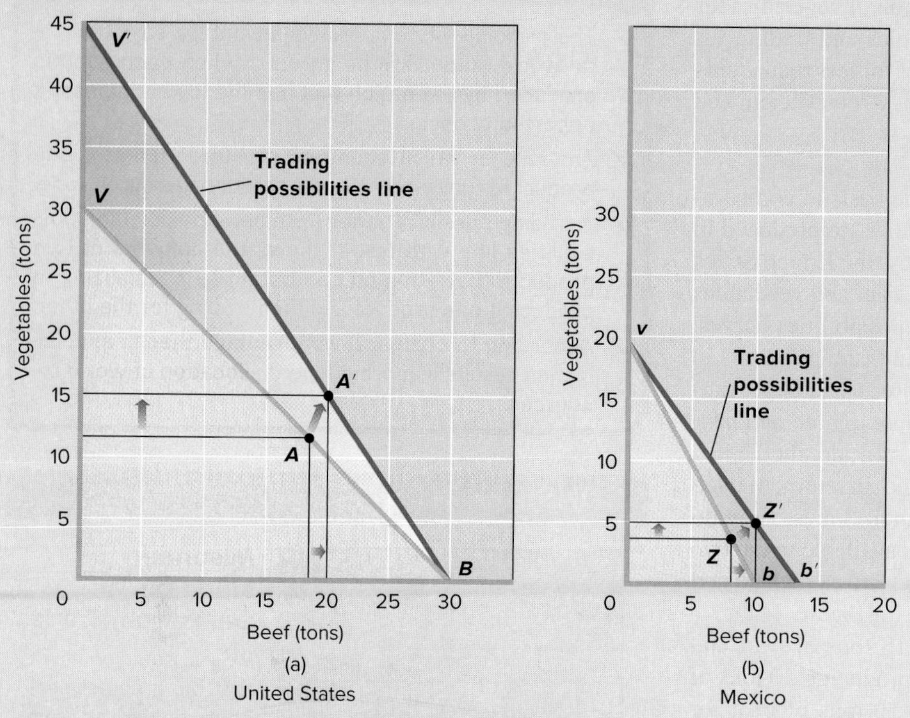

FIGURE 34.2 Trading possibilities lines and the gains from trade. As a result of specialization and trade, both the United States and Mexico can have higher levels of output than the levels attainable on their domestic production possibilities curves. (a) The United States can move from point *A* on its domestic production possibilities curve to, say, *A′* on its trading possibilities line. (b) Mexico can move from *Z* to *Z′*.

QUICK QUIZ FOR FIGURE 34.2

1. The production possibilities curves in graphs (a) and (b) imply:
   - **a.** increasing domestic opportunity costs.
   - **b.** decreasing domestic opportunity costs.
   - **c.** constant domestic opportunity costs.
   - **d.** first decreasing, then increasing domestic opportunity costs.
2. Before specialization, the domestic opportunity cost of producing 1 unit of beef is:
   - **a.** 1 unit of vegetables in both the United States and Mexico.
   - **b.** 1 unit of vegetables in the United States and 2 units of vegetables in Mexico.
   - **c.** 2 units of vegetables in the United States and 1 unit of vegetables in Mexico.
   - **d.** 1 unit of vegetables in the United States and $\frac{1}{2}$ unit of vegetables in Mexico.
3. After specialization and international trade, the world output of beef and vegetables is:
   - **a.** 20 tons of beef and 20 tons of vegetables.
   - **b.** 45 tons of beef and 15 tons of vegetables.
   - **c.** 30 tons of beef and 20 tons of vegetables.
   - **d.** 10 tons of beef and 30 tons of vegetables.
4. After specialization and international trade:
   - **a.** the United States can obtain units of vegetables at less cost than it could before trade.
   - **b.** Mexico can obtain more than 20 tons of vegetables, if it so chooses.
   - **c.** the United States no longer has a comparative advantage in producing beef.
   - **d.** Mexico can benefit by prohibiting vegetables imports from the United States.

Answers: 1. c; 2. b; 3. c; 4. a

beef for every 1 ton of vegetables it wants as it moves up its domestic production possibilities line from, say, point *B*. Instead, the United States, through trade with Mexico, can get $1\frac{1}{2}$ tons of vegetables for every ton of beef that it exports to Mexico, as long as Mexico has vegetables to export. Trading possibilities line BV' thus represents the $1B \equiv 1\frac{1}{2}V$ trading ratio.

Similarly, Mexico, starting at, say, point *v*, no longer has to move down its domestic production possibilities curve, giving up 2 tons of vegetables for each ton of beef it wants. It can now export just $1\frac{1}{2}$ tons of vegetables for each 1 ton of beef that it wants by moving down its trading possibilities line vb'.

Specialization and trade create a new exchange ratio between beef and vegetables, and that ratio is reflected in each nation's trading possibilities line. For both nations, this exchange ratio is superior to the unspecialized exchange ratio embodied in their respective production possibilities curves.

By specializing in beef and trading for Mexico's vegetables, the United States can obtain more than 1 ton of vegetables for 1 ton of beef. By specializing in vegetables and trading for U.S. beef, Mexico can obtain 1 ton of beef for less than 2 tons of vegetables. In both cases, self-sufficiency is inefficient and therefore undesirable.

Greater Output By specializing on the basis of comparative advantage and by trading for goods that are produced in the nation with greater domestic efficiency, the United States and Mexico can achieve combinations of beef and vegetables beyond their own individual production possibilities curves. Specialization according to comparative advantage results in a more efficient allocation of world resources, and larger outputs of both products are therefore available to both nations.

Suppose that at the $1B \equiv 1\frac{1}{2}V$ terms of trade, the United States exports 10 tons of beef to Mexico and, in return, Mexico exports 15 tons of vegetables to the United States. How do the new quantities of beef and vegetables available to the two nations compare with the optimal product mixes that existed before specialization and trade? Point *A* in Figure 34.2a reminds us that the United States chose 18 tons of beef and 12 tons of vegetables originally. But by producing 30 tons of beef and no vegetables and by trading 10 tons of beef for 15 tons of vegetables, the United States can obtain 20 tons of beef and 15 tons of vegetables. This new, superior combination of beef and vegetables is indicated by point *A′* in Figure 34.2a. Compared with the no-trade amounts of 18 tons of beef and 12 tons of vegetables, the United States' **gains from trade** are 2 tons of beef and 3 tons of vegetables.

Similarly, recall that Mexico's optimal product mix was 4 tons of vegetables and 8 tons of beef (point *Z*) before specialization and trade. Now, after specializing in vegetables and trading for beef, Mexico can have 5 tons of vegetables and 10 tons of beef. It accomplishes that by producing 20 tons of vegetables and no beef and exporting 15 tons of its vegetables in exchange for 10 tons of American beef. This new position is indicated by point *Z′* in Figure 34.2b. Mexico's gains from trade are 1 ton of vegetables and 2 tons of beef.

Points *A′* and *Z′* in Figure 34.2 are superior economic positions to points *A* and *Z*. This fact is enormously important! We know that a nation can expand its production possibilities boundary by (1) expanding the quantity and improving the quality of its resources or (2) realizing technological progress. We have now established that international trade can enable a nation to circumvent the output constraint illustrated by its production possibilities curve. An economy can grow by expanding international trade. The outcome of international specialization and trade is equivalent to having more and better resources or discovering and implementing improved production techniques.

Table 34.1 summarizes the transactions and outcomes in our analysis. Please give it one final careful review.

AP QUICK REVIEW 34.2

- ✓ The principle of comparative advantage says that total world output will be greatest when each good is produced by the nation that has the lowest domestic opportunity cost.
- ✓ The rate at which countries can trade units of one product for units of another is called the terms of trade.
- ✓ A trading possibilities line (or a new consumption possibilities line with trade) shows the amounts of two products that a nation can obtain by specializing in producing one product and then trading for the other.
- ✓ According to comparative advantage theory, specialization results in more efficient allocation of world resources.

CONSIDER THIS . . .

Source: © Bloomberg/Getty Images

Misunderstanding the Gains from Trade

It is a common myth that the greatest benefit to be derived from international trade is greater domestic employment in the export sector. This suggests that exports are "good" because they increase domestic employment, whereas imports are "bad" because they deprive people of jobs at home. As we have demonstrated, the true benefit created by international trade is the overall increase in output available through specialization and exchange.

A nation does not need international trade to operate *on* its production possibilities curve. It can fully employ its resources, including labor, with or without international trade. International trade, however, enables a country to reach a point of consumption beyond its domestic production possibilities curve. The gain from trade to a nation is the extra output obtained from abroad—the imports obtained for less sacrifice of other goods than if they were produced at home.

Trade with Increasing Costs

To explain the basic principles underlying international trade, we simplified our analysis in several ways. For example, we limited discussion to two products and two nations. But multiproduct and multinational analysis yield the same conclusions. We also assumed constant opportunity costs (linear production possibilities curves), which is a more substantive simplification. Let's consider the effect of allowing increasing opportunity costs (concave-to-the-origin production possibilities curves) to enter the picture.

Suppose that the United States and Mexico initially are at positions on their concave production possibilities curves where their domestic cost ratios are $1B \equiv 1V$ and $1B \equiv 2V$, as they were in our constant-cost analysis. As before, comparative advantage indicates that the United States should specialize in beef and Mexico in vegetables. But now, as the United States begins to expand beef production, its cost of beef will rise; it will have to sacrifice more than 1 ton of vegetables to get 1 additional ton of beef. Resources are no longer perfectly substitutable between alternative uses, as the constant-cost assumption implied. Resources less and less suitable to beef production must be allocated to the U.S. beef industry in expanding beef output, and that means increasing costs—the sacrifice of larger and larger amounts of vegetables for each additional ton of beef.

Similarly, suppose that Mexico expands vegetable production starting from its $1B \equiv 2V$ cost ratio position. As production increases, it will find that its $1B \equiv 2V$ cost ratio begins to rise. Sacrificing 1 ton of beef will free resources that are capable of producing only something less than 2 tons of vegetables because those transferred resources are less suitable to vegetable production.

As the U.S. cost ratio falls from $1B \equiv 1V$ and the Mexican ratio rises from $1B \equiv 2V$, a point will be reached where the cost ratios are equal in the two nations, perhaps at $1B \equiv 1\frac{3}{4}V$. At this point, the underlying basis for further specialization and trade—differing cost ratios—has disappeared, and further specialization is therefore uneconomical. And, most important, this point of equal cost ratios may be reached while the United States is still producing some vegetables along with its beef and Mexico is producing some beef along with its vegetables. The primary effect of increasing opportunity costs is less-than-complete specialization. For this reason, we often find domestically produced products competing directly against identical or similar imported products within a particular economy.

The Case for Free Trade

The case for free trade reduces to one compelling argument: Through free trade based on the principle of comparative advantage, the world economy can achieve a more efficient allocation of resources and a higher level of material well-being than it can without free trade.

Since the resource mixes and technological knowledge of the world's nations are all somewhat different, each nation can produce particular commodities at different real costs. Each nation should produce goods for which its domestic opportunity costs are lower than the domestic opportunity costs of other nations and exchange those goods for products for which its domestic opportunity costs are high relative to those of other nations. If each nation does this, the world will realize the advantages of geographic and human specialization. The world and each free-trading nation can obtain a larger real income from the fixed supplies of resources available to it.

Government trade barriers lessen or eliminate gains from specialization. If nations cannot trade freely, they must shift resources from efficient (low-cost) to inefficient (high-cost) uses to satisfy their diverse wants. A recent study suggests that the elimination of trade barriers since the Second World War has increased the income of the average U.S. household by at least \$7,000 and perhaps by as much as \$13,000. These income gains are recurring; they happen year after year.[2]

One side benefit of free trade is that it promotes competition and deters monopoly. The increased competition from foreign firms forces domestic firms to find and use the lowest-cost production techniques. It also compels them to be innovative with respect to both product quality and production methods, thereby contributing to economic growth. And free trade gives consumers a wider range of product choices. The reasons to favor free trade are the same as the reasons to endorse competition.

A second side benefit of free trade is that it links national interests and breaks down national animosities. Confronted with political disagreements, trading partners tend to negotiate rather than make war.

AP QUICK REVIEW 34.3

- ✓ International trade enables nations to specialize, increase productivity, and increase consumption.
- ✓ Comparative advantage means total world output will be greatest when each good is produced by the nation that has the lowest domestic opportunity cost.
- ✓ Specialization is usually less than complete among nations because opportunity costs normally rise as any specific nation produces more of a particular good.

AP Supply and Demand Analysis of Exports and Imports

LO34.3 Describe how differences between world prices and domestic prices prompt exports and imports.

Supply and demand analysis reveals how equilibrium prices and quantities of exports and imports are determined. The amount of a good or a service a nation will export or import depends on differences between the equilibrium world price and the equilibrium domestic price. The interaction of *world* supply and demand determines the equilibrium **world price**—the price that equates the quantities supplied and

[2]Scott C. Bradford, Paul L. E. Grieco, and Gary C. Hufbauer, "The Payoff to America from Globalization," *The World Economy,* July 2006, pp. 893–916.

demanded globally. *Domestic* supply and demand determine the equilibrium **domestic price**—the price that would prevail in a closed economy that does not engage in international trade. The domestic price equates quantity supplied and quantity demanded domestically.

In the absence of trade, the domestic prices in a closed economy may or may not equal the world equilibrium prices. When economies are opened for international trade, differences between world and domestic prices encourage exports or imports. To see how, consider the international effects of such price differences in a simple two-nation world, consisting of the United States and Canada, that are both producing aluminum. We assume there are no trade barriers, such as tariffs and quotas, and no international transportation costs.

Supply and Demand in the United States

Figure 34.3a shows the domestic supply curve S_d and the domestic demand curve D_d for aluminum in the United States, which for now is a closed economy. The intersection of S_d and D_d determines the equilibrium domestic price of $1 per pound and the equilibrium domestic quantity of 100 million pounds. Domestic suppliers produce 100 million pounds and sell them all at $1 a pound. So there are no domestic surpluses or shortages of aluminum.

But what if the U.S. economy were opened to trade and the world price of aluminum were above or below this $1 domestic price?

U.S. Export Supply If the aluminum price in the rest of the world (that is, Canada) exceeds $1, U.S. firms will produce more than 100 million pounds and will export the excess domestic output. First, consider a world price of $1.25. We see from the supply curve S_d that U.S. aluminum firms will produce 125 million pounds of aluminum at that price. The demand curve D_d tells us that the United States will purchase only 75 million pounds at $1.25. The outcome is a domestic surplus of 50 million pounds of aluminum. U.S. producers will export those 50 million pounds at the $1.25 world price.

What if the world price were $1.50? The supply curve shows that U.S. firms will produce 150 million pounds of aluminum, while the demand curve tells us that U.S. consumers will buy only 50 million pounds. So U.S. producers will export the domestic surplus of 100 million pounds.

Toward the top of Figure 34.3b we plot the domestic surpluses—the U.S. exports—that occur at world prices above the $1 domestic equilibrium price. When the world and domestic prices are equal (= $1), the quantity of exports supplied is zero (point *a*). There is no surplus of domestic output

FIGURE 34.3 U.S. export supply and import demand. (a) Domestic supply S_d and demand D_d set the domestic equilibrium price of aluminum at $1 per pound. At world prices above $1, there are domestic surpluses of aluminum. At prices below $1, there are domestic shortages. (b) Surpluses are exported (top curve), and shortages are met by importing aluminum (lower curve). The export supply curve shows the direct relationship between world prices and U.S. exports; the import demand curve portrays the inverse relationship between world prices and U.S. imports.

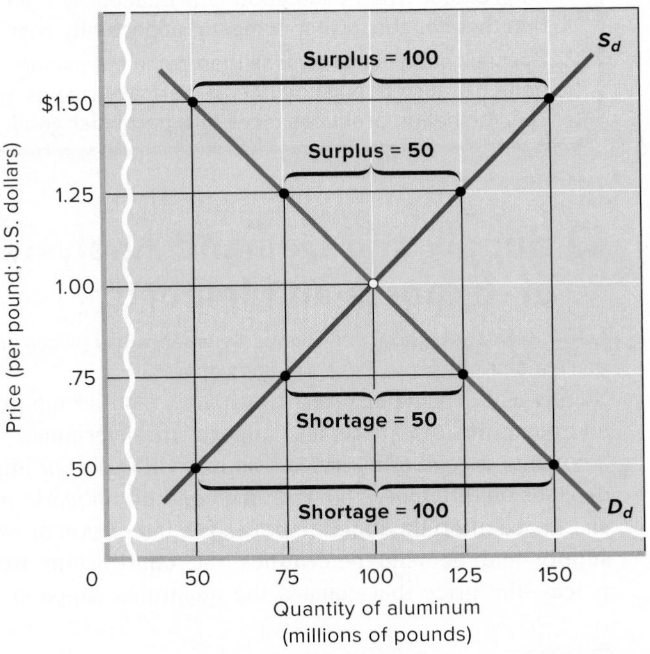

(a)
U.S. domestic aluminum market

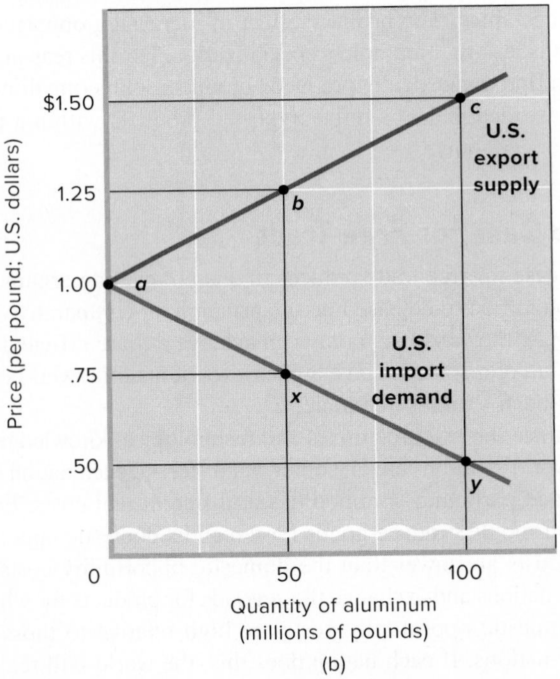

(b)
U.S. export supply and import demand

to export. But when the world price is $1.25, U.S. firms export 50 million pounds of surplus aluminum (point *b*). At a $1.50 world price, the domestic surplus of 100 million pounds is exported (point *c*).

The U.S. **export supply curve,** found by connecting points *a*, *b*, and *c*, shows the amount of aluminum U.S. producers will export at each world price above $1. This curve *slopes upward*, indicating a direct or positive relationship between the world price and the amount of U.S. exports. As world prices increase relative to domestic prices, U.S. exports rise.

U.S. Import Demand If the world price is below the domestic $1 price, the United States will import aluminum. Consider a $0.75 world price. The supply curve in Figure 34.3a reveals that at that price U.S. firms produce only 75 million pounds of aluminum. But the demand curve shows that the United States wants to buy 125 million pounds at that price. The result is a domestic shortage of 50 million pounds. To satisfy that shortage, the United States will import 50 million pounds of aluminum.

At an even lower world price, $0.50, U.S. producers will supply only 50 million pounds. Because U.S. consumers want to buy 150 million pounds at that price, there is a domestic shortage of 100 million pounds. Imports will flow to the United States to make up the difference. That is, at a $0.50 world price U.S. firms will supply 50 million pounds and 100 million pounds will be imported.

In Figure 34.3b, we plot the U.S. **import demand curve** from these data. This *downsloping curve* shows the amounts of aluminum that will be imported at world prices below the $1 U.S. domestic price. The relationship between world prices and imported amounts is inverse or negative. At a world price of $1, domestic output will satisfy U.S. demand; imports will be zero (point *a*). But at $0.75 the United States will import 50 million pounds of aluminum (point *x*); at $0.50, the United States will import 100 million pounds (point *y*). Connecting points *a*, *x*, and *y* yields the *downsloping* U.S. import demand curve. It reveals that as world prices fall relative to U.S. domestic prices, U.S. imports increase.

Supply and Demand in Canada

We repeat our analysis in Figure 34.4, this time from the viewpoint of Canada. (We have converted Canadian dollar prices to U.S. dollar prices via the exchange rate.) Note that the domestic supply curve S_d and the domestic demand curve D_d for aluminum in Canada yield a domestic price of $0.75, which is $0.25 lower than the $1 U.S. domestic price.

The analysis proceeds exactly as above except that the domestic price is now the Canadian price. If the world price is $0.75, Canadians will neither export nor import aluminum

FIGURE 34.4 Canadian export supply and import demand. (a) At world prices above the $0.75 domestic price, production in Canada exceeds domestic consumption. At world prices below $0.75, domestic shortages occur. (b) Surpluses result in exports, and shortages result in imports. The Canadian export supply curve and import demand curve depict the relationships between world prices and exports or imports.

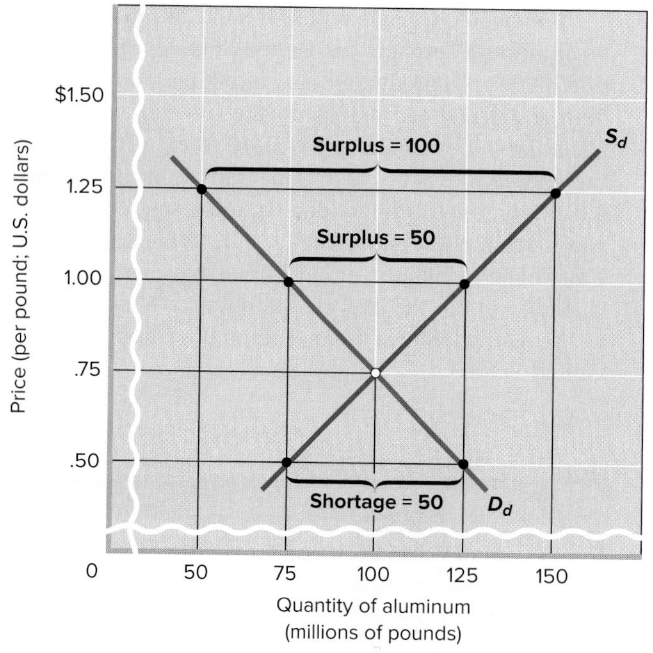

(a)
Canada's domestic aluminum market

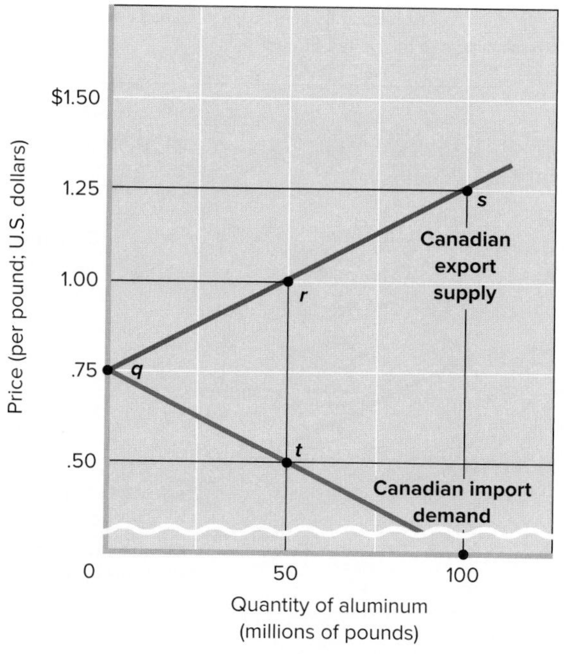

(b)
Canada's export supply and import demand

(giving us point q in Figure 34.4b). At world prices above \$0.75, Canadian firms will produce more aluminum than Canadian consumers will buy. Canadian firms will export the surplus. At a \$1 world price, Figure 34.4b tells us that Canada will have and export a domestic surplus of 50 million pounds (yielding point r). At \$1.25, it will have and will export a domestic surplus of 100 million pounds (point s). Connecting these points yields the upsloping Canadian export supply curve, which reflects the domestic surpluses (and hence the exports) that occur when the world price exceeds the \$0.75 Canadian domestic price.

At world prices below \$0.75, domestic shortages occur in Canada. At a \$0.50 world price, Figure 34.4a shows that Canadian consumers want to buy 125 million pounds of aluminum but Canadian firms will produce only 75 million pounds. The shortage will bring 50 million pounds of imports to Canada (point t in Figure 34.4b). The Canadian import demand curve in that figure shows the Canadian imports that will occur at all world aluminum prices below the \$0.75 Canadian domestic price.

Equilibrium World Price, Exports, and Imports

We now have the tools for determining the **equilibrium world price** of aluminum and the equilibrium world levels of exports and imports when the world is opened to trade. Figure 34.5 combines the U.S. export supply curve and import demand curve in Figure 34.3b and the Canadian export supply curve and import demand curve in Figure 34.4b. The two U.S. curves proceed rightward from the \$1 U.S. domestic price; the two Canadian curves proceed rightward from the \$0.75 Canadian domestic price.

International equilibrium occurs in this two-nation model where one nation's import demand curve intersects another nation's export supply curve. In this case, the U.S. import demand curve intersects Canada's export supply curve at e. There, the world price of aluminum is \$0.88. The Canadian export supply curve indicates that Canada will export 25 million pounds of aluminum at this price. Also at this price the United States will import 25 million pounds from Canada, indicated by the U.S. import demand curve. The \$0.88 world price equates the quantity of imports demanded and the quantity of exports supplied (25 million pounds). Thus, there will be world trade of 25 million pounds of aluminum at \$0.88 per pound.

Note that after trade, the single \$0.88 world price will prevail in both Canada and the United States. Only one price for a standardized commodity can persist in a highly competitive world market. With trade, all consumers can buy a pound of aluminum for \$0.88, and all producers can sell it for that price. This world price means that Canadians will pay more for aluminum with trade (\$0.88) than without it (\$0.75). The increased Canadian output caused by trade raises Canadian per-unit production costs and therefore raises the price of aluminum in Canada. The United States, however, pays less for aluminum with trade (\$0.88) than without it (\$1). The U.S. gain comes from Canada's comparative cost advantage in producing aluminum.

Why would Canada willingly send 25 million pounds of its aluminum output to the United States for U.S. consumption? After all, producing this output uses up scarce Canadian resources and drives up the price of aluminum for Canadians. Canadians are willing to export aluminum to the United States because Canadians gain the means—the U.S. dollars—to import other goods, say, computer software, from the United States. Canadian exports enable Canadians to acquire imports that have greater value to Canadians than the exported aluminum. Canadian exports to the United States finance Canadian imports from the United States.

AP FIGURE 34.5 Equilibrium world price and quantity of exports and imports. In a two-nation world, the equilibrium world price (= \$0.88) is determined by the intersection of one nation's export supply curve and the other nation's import demand curve. This intersection also decides the equilibrium volume of exports and imports. Here, Canada exports 25 million pounds of aluminum to the United States.

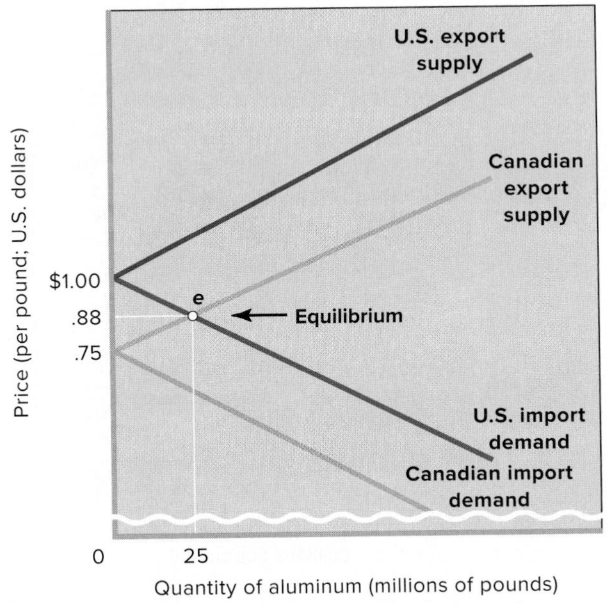

AP QUICK REVIEW 34.4

- ✓ A nation will export a particular product if the world price exceeds the domestic price; it will import the product if the world price is less than the domestic price.

Trade Barriers and Export Subsidies

LO34.4 Analyze the economic effects of tariffs and quotas.

While a nation as a whole gains from trade, trade may harm particular domestic industries and their workers. Those industries might seek to preserve their economic positions by persuading their respective governments to protect them from imports—perhaps through tariffs, import quotas, or other trade barriers.

Indeed, the public may be won over by the apparent plausibility ("Cut imports and prevent domestic unemployment") and the patriotic ring ("Buy American!") of the arguments. The alleged benefits of tariffs are immediate and clear-cut to the public, but the adverse effects cited by economists are obscure and dispersed over the entire economy. When political deal-making is added in—"You back tariffs for the apparel industry in my state, and I'll back tariffs for the auto industry in your state"—the outcome can be a politically robust network of trade barriers. These impediments to free international trade can take several forms.

Tariffs are excise taxes or "duties" on the dollar values or physical quantities of imported goods. They may be imposed to obtain revenue or to protect domestic firms. A **revenue tariff** is usually applied to a product that is not being produced domestically, for example, tin, coffee, or bananas in the case of the United States. Rates on revenue tariffs tend to be modest and are designed to provide the federal government with revenue. A **protective tariff** is implemented to shield domestic producers from foreign competition. These tariffs impede free trade by increasing the prices of imported goods and therefore shifting sales toward domestic producers. Although protective tariffs are usually not high enough to stop the importation of foreign goods, they put foreign producers at a competitive disadvantage. A tariff on imported auto tires, for example, would make domestically produced tires more attractive to consumers.

An **import quota** is a limit on the quantities or total values of specific items that are imported in some period. Once a quota is filled, further imports of that product are choked off. Import quotas are more effective than tariffs in impeding international trade. With a tariff, a product can go on being imported in large quantities. But with an import quota, all imports are prohibited once the quota is filled.

A **nontariff barrier (NTB)** includes onerous licensing requirements, unreasonable standards pertaining to product quality, or simply bureaucratic hurdles and delays in customs procedures. Some nations require that importers of foreign goods obtain licenses and then restrict the number of licenses issued. Although many nations carefully inspect imported agricultural products to prevent the introduction of potentially harmful insects, some countries use lengthy inspections to impede imports. Japan and the European countries frequently require that their domestic importers of foreign goods obtain licenses. By restricting the issuance of licenses, governments can limit imports.

CONSIDER THIS . . .

Buy American?

Source: © Robert W. Ginn/ PhotoEdit

Will "buying American" make Americans better off? No, says Dallas Federal Reserve economist W. Michael Cox:

> A common myth is that it is better for Americans to spend their money at home than abroad. The best way to expose the fallacy of this argument is to take it to its logical extreme. If it is better for me to spend my money here than abroad, then it is even better yet to buy in Texas than in New York, better yet to buy in Dallas than in Houston . . . in my own neighborhood . . . within my own family . . . to consume only what I can produce. Alone and poor.*

Source: W. Michael Cox and Richard Alm, "The Fruits of Free Trade," *2002 Annual Report*, Federal Reserve Bank of Dallas.

A **voluntary export restriction (VER)** is a trade barrier by which foreign firms "voluntarily" limit the amount of their exports to a particular country. VERs have the same effect as import quotas and are agreed to by exporters to avoid more stringent tariffs or quotas. In the late 1990s, for example, Canadian producers of softwood lumber (fir, spruce, cedar, pine) agreed to a VER on exports to the United States under the threat of a permanently higher U.S. tariff.

An **export subsidy** consists of a government payment to a domestic producer of export goods and is designed to aid that producer. By reducing production costs, the subsidies enable the domestic firm to charge a lower price and thus to sell more exports in world markets. Two examples: Some European governments have heavily subsidized Airbus Industries, a European firm that produces commercial aircraft. The subsidies help Airbus compete against the American firm Boeing. The United States and other nations have subsidized domestic farmers to boost the domestic food supply. Such subsidies have artificially lowered export prices on agricultural produce.

Later in this chapter we will discuss some of the specific arguments and appeals that are made to justify protection.

Economic Impact of Tariffs

We will confine our in-depth analysis of the effects of trade barriers to the two most common forms: tariffs and quotas. Once again, we turn to supply and demand analysis for help. Curves D_d and S_d in Figure 34.6 show domestic demand and supply for a product in which a nation, say, the United States, does *not* have a comparative advantage—for example, smartphones. (Disregard curve $S_d + Q$ for now.) Without world trade, the domestic price and output would be P_d and q, respectively.

Assume now that the domestic economy is opened to world trade and that China, which *does* have a comparative advantage in smartphones, begins to sell its smartphones in the United States. We assume that with free trade the domestic price cannot differ from the world price, which here is P_w. At P_w, domestic consumption is d and domestic production is a. The horizontal distance between the domestic supply and demand curves at P_w represents imports of ad. Thus far, our analysis is similar to the analysis of world prices in Figure 34.3.

Direct Effects Suppose now that the United States imposes a tariff on each imported smartphone. The tariff, which raises the price of imported smartphones from P_w to P_t, has four effects:

- ***Decline in consumption*** Consumption of smartphones in the United States declines from d to c as the higher price moves buyers up and to the left along their demand curve. The tariff prompts consumers to buy fewer smartphones and reallocate a portion of their expenditures to less desired substitute products. U.S. consumers are clearly injured by the tariff, since they pay $P_t - P_w$ more for each of the c units they buy at price P_t.
- ***Increased domestic production*** U.S. producers—who are not subject to the tariff—receive the higher price P_t per unit. Because this new price is higher than the pretariff world price P_w, the domestic smartphone industry moves up and to the right along its supply curve S_d, increasing domestic output from a to b. Domestic producers thus enjoy both a higher price and expanded sales; this explains why domestic producers lobby for protective tariffs. But from a social point of view, the increase in domestic production from a to b means that the tariff permits domestic producers of smartphones to bid resources away from other, more efficient, U.S. industries.
- ***Decline in imports*** Chinese producers are hurt. Although the sales price of each smartphone is higher by $P_t - P_w$, that amount accrues to the U.S. government, not to Chinese producers. The after-tariff world price, or the per-unit revenue to Chinese producers, remains at P_w, but the volume of U.S. imports (Chinese exports) falls from ad to bc.
- ***Tariff revenue*** The yellow rectangle represents the amount of revenue the tariff yields. Total revenue from the tariff is determined by multiplying the tariff, $P_t - P_w$ per unit, by the number of smartphones imported, bc. This tariff revenue is a transfer of income from consumers to government and does not represent any net change in the nation's economic well-being. The result is that government gains this portion of what consumers lose by paying more for smartphones.

AP **FIGURE 34.6 The economic effects of a protective tariff or an import quota.** A tariff that increases the price of a good from P_w to P_t will reduce domestic consumption from d to c. Domestic producers will be able to sell more output (b rather than a) at a higher price (P_t rather than P_w). Foreign exporters are injured because they sell less output (bc rather than ad). The yellow area indicates the amount of tariff paid by domestic consumers. An import quota of bc units has the same effect as the tariff, with one exception: The amount represented by the yellow area will go to foreign producers rather than to the domestic government.

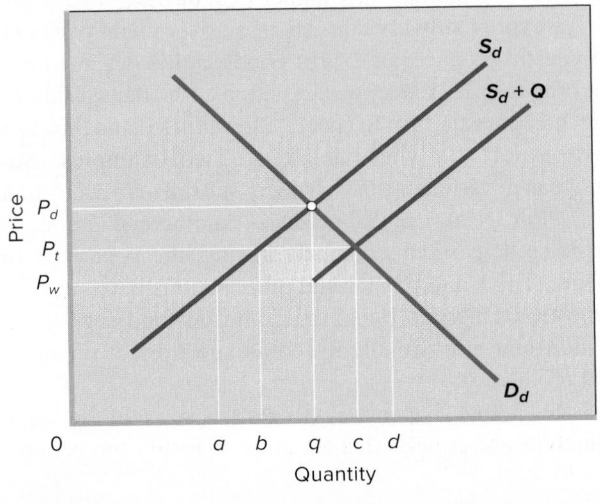

Indirect Effect Tariffs have a subtle effect beyond what our supply and demand diagram can show. Because China sells fewer smartphones in the United States, it earns fewer dollars and so must buy fewer U.S. exports. U.S. export industries must then cut production and release resources. These are highly efficient industries, as we know from their comparative advantage and their ability to sell goods in world markets.

Tariffs directly promote the expansion of inefficient industries that do not have a comparative advantage; they also indirectly cause the contraction of relatively efficient industries that do have a comparative advantage. Put bluntly, tariffs cause resources to be shifted in the wrong direction—and that is not surprising. We know that specialization and world trade lead to more efficient use of world resources and greater world output. But protective tariffs reduce world trade. Therefore, tariffs also reduce efficiency and the world's real output.

Economic Impact of Quotas

We noted earlier that an import quota is a legal limit placed on the amount of some product that can be imported in a given year. Quotas have the same economic impact as a tariff, with one big difference: While tariffs generate revenue for the domestic government, a quota transfers that revenue to foreign producers.

Suppose in Figure 34.6 that, instead of imposing a tariff, the United States prohibits any imports of Chinese smartphones players in excess of *bc* units. In other words, an import quota of *bc* smartphones is imposed on China. We deliberately chose the size of this quota to be the same amount as imports would be under a $P_t - P_w$ tariff so that we can compare "equivalent" situations. As a consequence of the quota, the supply of smartphones is $S_d + Q$ in the United States. This supply consists of the domestic supply plus the fixed amount *bc* (= *Q*) that importers will provide at each domestic price. The supply curve $S_w + Q$ does not extend below price P_w because Chinese producers would not export smartphones to the United States at any price below P_w; instead, they would sell them to other countries at the world market price of P_w.

Most of the economic results are the same as those with a tariff. Prices of smartphones are higher (P_t instead of P_w) because imports have been reduced from *ad* to *bc*. Domestic consumption of smartphones is down from *d* to *c*. U.S. producers enjoy both a higher price (P_t rather than P_w) and increased sales (*b* rather than *a*).

The difference is that the price increase of $P_t - P_w$ paid by U.S. consumers on imports of *bc*—the yellow area—no longer goes to the U.S. Treasury as tariff (tax) revenue but flows to the Chinese firms that have acquired the quota rights to sell smartphones in the United States. For consumers in the United States, a tariff produces a better economic outcome than a quota, other things being the same. A tariff generates government revenue that can be used to cut other taxes or to finance public goods and services that benefit the United States. In contrast, the higher price created by quotas results in additional revenue for foreign producers.

AP QUICK REVIEW 34.5

- ✓ A tariff on a product increases its price, reduces its consumption, increases its domestic production, reduces its imports, and generates tariff revenue for the government.
- ✓ An import quota does the same, except a quota generates excess revenues for foreign producers rather than for the government imposing the quota.

Net Costs of Tariffs and Quotas

Figure 34.6 shows that tariffs and quotas impose costs on domestic consumers but provide gains to domestic producers and, in the case of tariffs, revenue to the federal government. The consumer costs of trade restrictions are calculated by determining the effect the restrictions have on consumer prices. Protection raises the price of a product in three ways: (1) The price of the imported product goes up; (2) the higher price of imports causes some consumers to shift their purchases to higher-priced domestically produced goods; and (3) the prices of domestically produced goods rise because import competition has declined.

Study after study finds that the costs to consumers substantially exceed the gains to producers and government. A sizable net cost or efficiency loss to society arises from trade protection. Furthermore, industries employ large amounts of economic resources to influence Congress to pass and retain protectionist laws. Because these rent-seeking efforts divert resources away from more socially desirable purposes, trade restrictions impose these additional costs on society as well.

Conclusion: The gains that U.S. trade barriers create for protected industries and their workers come at the expense of much greater losses for the entire economy. The result is economic inefficiency, reduced consumption, and lower standards of living.

AP The Case for Protection: A Critical Review

LO34.5 Analyze the validity of the most frequently presented arguments for protectionism.

Despite the logic of specialization and trade, there are still protectionists in some union halls, corporate boardrooms, and congressional conference rooms. What arguments do protectionists make to justify trade barriers? How valid are those arguments?

Military Self-Sufficiency Argument

The argument here is not economic but political-military: Protective tariffs are needed to preserve or strengthen industries that produce the materials essential for national defense. In an uncertain world, the political-military objectives (self-sufficiency) sometimes must take precedence over economic goals (efficiency in the use of world resources).

Unfortunately, it is difficult to measure and compare the benefit of increased national security against the cost of economic inefficiency when protective tariffs are imposed. The economist can only point out that when a nation levies tariffs to increase military self-sufficiency, it incurs economic costs.

All people in the United States would agree that relying on hostile nations for necessary military equipment is not a good idea, yet the self-sufficiency argument is open to serious abuse. Nearly every industry can claim that it makes direct or indirect contributions to national security and hence deserves protection from imports.

Diversification-for-Stability Argument

Highly specialized economies such as Saudi Arabia (based on oil) and Cuba (based on sugar) are dependent on international markets for their income. In these economies, wars, international political developments, recessions abroad, and random fluctuations in world supply and demand for one or two particular goods can cause deep declines in export revenues and therefore in domestic income. Tariff and quota protection are allegedly needed in such nations to enable greater industrial diversification. That way, these economies will not be so dependent on exporting one or two products to obtain the other goods they need. Such goods will be available domestically, thereby providing greater domestic stability.

There is some truth in this diversification-for-stability argument. But the argument has little or no relevance to the United States and other advanced economies. Also, the economic costs of diversification may be great; for example, one-crop economies may be highly inefficient at manufacturing.

Infant Industry Argument

The infant industry argument contends that protective tariffs are needed to allow new domestic industries to establish themselves. Temporarily shielding young domestic firms from the severe competition of more mature and more efficient foreign firms will give infant industries a chance to develop and become efficient producers.

This argument for protection rests on an alleged exception to the case for free trade. The exception is that young industries have not had, and if they face mature foreign competition will never have, the chance to make the long-run adjustments needed for larger scale and greater efficiency in production. In this view, tariff protection for such infant industries will correct a misallocation of world resources perpetuated by historically different levels of economic development between domestic and foreign industries.

There are some logical problems with the infant industry argument. In the developing nations, it is difficult to determine which industries are the infants that are capable of achieving economic maturity and therefore deserving protection. Also, protective tariffs may persist even after industrial maturity has been realized.

Most economists feel that if infant industries are to be subsidized, there are better means than tariffs for doing so. Direct subsidies, for example, have the advantage of making explicit which industries are being aided and to what degree.

Protection-against-Dumping Argument

The protection-against-dumping argument contends that tariffs are needed to protect domestic firms from "dumping" by foreign producers. **Dumping** is the sale of a product in a foreign country at prices either below cost or below the prices commonly charged at home.

Economists cite two plausible reasons for this behavior. First, with regard to below-cost dumping, firms in country A may dump goods at below cost into country B in an attempt to drive their competitors in country B out of business. If the firms in country A succeed in driving their competitors in country B out of business, they will enjoy monopoly power and monopoly prices and profits on the goods they subsequently sell in country B. Their hope is that the longer-term monopoly profits will more than offset the losses from below-cost sales that must take place while they are attempting to drive their competitors in country B out of business.

Second, dumping that involves selling abroad at a price that is below the price commonly charged in the home country (but that is still at or above production costs) may be a form of price discrimination, which is charging different prices to different customers. As an example, a foreign seller that has a monopoly in its home market may find that it can maximize its overall profit by charging a high price in its monopolized domestic market while charging a lower price in the United States, where it must compete with U.S. producers. Curiously, it may pursue this strategy even if it makes no profit at all from its sales in the United States, where it must charge the competitive price. So why bother selling in the United States? Because the increase in overall production that comes about by exporting to the United States may allow the firm to obtain the per-unit cost savings often associated with large-scale production. These cost savings imply even higher profits in the monopolized domestic market.

Because dumping is an "unfair trade practice," most nations prohibit it. For example, where dumping is shown to injure U.S. firms, the federal government imposes tariffs called *antidumping duties* on the goods in question. But relatively few documented cases of dumping occur each year, and specific instances of unfair trade do not justify widespread, permanent tariffs. Moreover, antidumping duties can be abused. Often, what appears to be dumping is simply comparative advantage at work.

Increased Domestic Employment Argument

Arguing for a tariff to "save U.S. jobs" becomes fashionable when the economy encounters a recession (such as the severe recession of 2007–2008 in the United States). In an economy that engages in international trade, exports involve spending on domestic output and imports reflect spending to obtain part of another nation's output. So, in this argument, reducing imports will divert spending on another nation's output to spending on domestic output. Thus, domestic output and employment will rise. But this argument has several shortcomings.

While imports may eliminate some U.S. jobs, they create others. Imports may have eliminated the jobs of some U.S. steel and textile workers in recent years, but other workers have gained jobs unloading ships, flying imported aircraft, and selling imported electronic equipment. Import restrictions alter the composition of employment, but they may have little or no effect on the volume of employment.

The *fallacy of composition*—the false idea that what is true for the part is necessarily true for the whole—is also present in this rationale for tariffs. All nations cannot simultaneously succeed in restricting imports while maintaining their exports; what is true for one nation is not true for all nations. The exports of one nation must be the imports of another nation. To the extent that one country is able to expand its economy through an excess of exports over imports, the resulting excess of imports over exports worsens another economy's unemployment problem. It is no wonder that tariffs and import quotas meant to achieve domestic full employment are called "beggar my neighbor" policies: They achieve short-run domestic goals by making trading partners poorer.

Moreover, nations adversely affected by tariffs and quotas are likely to retaliate, causing a "trade war" (more precisely, a *trade barrier war*) that will choke off trade and make all nations worse off. The **Smoot-Hawley Tariff Act** of 1930 is a classic example. Although that act was meant to reduce imports and stimulate U.S. production, the high tariffs it authorized prompted adversely affected nations to retaliate with tariffs equally high. International trade fell, lowering the output and income of all nations. Economic historians generally agree that the Smoot-Hawley Tariff Act was a contributing cause of the Great Depression.

Finally, forcing an excess of exports over imports cannot succeed in raising domestic employment over the long run. It is through U.S. imports that foreign nations earn dollars for buying U.S. exports. In the long run, a nation must import in order to export. The long-run impact of tariffs is not an increase in domestic employment but, at best, a reallocation of workers away from export industries and to protected domestic industries. This shift implies a less efficient allocation of resources.

Cheap Foreign Labor Argument

The cheap foreign labor argument says that domestic firms and workers must be shielded from the ruinous competition of countries where wages are low. If protection is not provided, cheap imports will flood U.S. markets and the prices of U.S. goods—along with the wages of U.S. workers—will be pulled down. That is, domestic living standards in the United States will be reduced.

This argument can be rebutted at several levels. The logic of the argument suggests that it is not mutually beneficial for rich and poor persons to trade with one another. However, that is not the case. A low-income farmworker may pick lettuce or tomatoes for a rich landowner, and both may benefit from the transaction. And both U.S. consumers and Chinese workers gain when they "trade" a pair of athletic shoes priced at $30 as opposed to U.S. consumers being restricted to buying a similar shoe made in the United States for $60.

Also, recall that gains from trade are based on comparative advantage, not on absolute advantage. Look back at Figure 34.1, where we supposed that the United States and Mexico had labor forces of exactly the same size. Noting the positions of the production possibilities curves, observe that U.S. labor can produce more of either good. Thus, it is more productive. Because of this greater productivity, we can expect wages and living standards to be higher for U.S. labor. Mexico's less productive labor will receive lower wages.

The cheap foreign labor argument suggests that, to maintain its standard of living, the United States should not trade with low-wage Mexico. What if it does not trade with Mexico? Will wages and living standards rise in the United States as a result? No. To obtain vegetables, the United States will have to reallocate a portion of its labor from its relatively more-efficient beef industry to its relatively less-efficient vegetables industry. As a result, the average productivity of U.S. labor will fall, as will real wages and living standards. The labor forces of both countries will have diminished standards of living because without specialization and trade they will have less output available to them. Compare column 4 with column 1 in Table 34.1 or points A' and Z' with A and Z in Figure 34.2 to confirm this point.

Another problem with the cheap foreign labor argument is that its proponents incorrectly focus on labor costs per hour when what really matters is labor costs per unit of output. As an example, suppose that a U.S. factory pays its workers $20 per hour while a factory in a developing country pays its workers $4 per hour. The proponents of the cheap foreign labor argument look at these numbers and conclude—incorrectly—that it is impossible for the U.S. factory to compete with the factory in the developing country. But this conclusion fails to take into account two crucial facts:

- What actually matters is labor costs *per unit of output*, not labor costs *per hour of work*.
- Differences in productivity typically mean that labor costs per unit of output are often nearly identical despite huge differences in hourly labor costs.

To see why these points matter so much, let's take into account how productive the two factories are. Because the U.S. factory uses much more sophisticated technology, better-trained workers, and a lot more capital per worker, one worker in one hour can produce 20 units of output. Since the U.S. workers get paid $20 per hour, this means the U.S. factory's labor cost *per unit of output* is $1. The factory in the developing country is much less productive since it uses less efficient technology and its relatively untrained workers have a lot less machinery and equipment to work with. A worker there produces only 4 units per hour. Given the foreign wage of $4 per hour, this means that the labor cost per unit of output at the factory in the developing country is also $1.

As you can see, the lower wage rate per hour at the factory in the developing country does not translate into lower labor costs per unit—meaning that it won't be able to undersell its U.S. competitor just because its workers get paid lower wages per hour.

Proponents of the cheap foreign labor argument tend to focus exclusively on the large international differences that exist in labor costs per hour. They typically fail to mention that these differences in labor costs per hour are mostly the result of tremendously large differences in productivity and that these large differences in productivity serve to equalize labor costs per unit of output. As a result, firms in developing countries only *sometimes* have an advantage in terms of labor costs per unit of output. Whether they do in any specific situation will vary by industry and firm and will depend on differences in productivity as well as differences in labor costs per hour. For many goods, labor productivity in high-wage countries like the United States is so much higher than labor productivity in low-wage countries that it is actually cheaper *per unit of output* to manufacture those goods in high-wage countries. That is why, for instance, Intel still makes microchips in the United States and why most automobiles are still produced in the United States, Japan, and Europe rather than in low-wage countries.

AP QUICK REVIEW 34.6

✓ Most rationales for trade protections are special-interest requests that, if followed, would create gains for protected industries and their workers at the expense of greater losses for the economy.

AP Multilateral Trade Agreements and Free-Trade Zones

LO34.6 Identify and explain the objectives of GATT, WTO, EU, eurozone, and NAFTA and discuss offshoring and trade adjustment assistance.

Aware of the detrimental effects of trade wars and the general weaknesses of arguments for trade protections, nations have worked to lower tariffs worldwide. Their pursuit of freer trade has been aided by recently emerged special-interest groups that have offset the more-established special-interest groups that have traditionally supported tariffs and quotas. Specifically, lower tariffs are now supported by exporters of goods and services, importers of foreign components used in "domestic" products, and domestic sellers of imported products.

General Agreement on Tariffs and Trade

In 1947, 23 nations, including the United States, signed the **General Agreement on Tariffs and Trade (GATT).** GATT was based on three principles: (1) equal, nondiscriminatory trade treatment for all member nations; (2) the reduction of tariffs by multilateral negotiation; and (3) the elimination of import quotas. Basically, GATT provided a forum for the multilateral negotiation of reduced trade barriers.

Since the Second World War, member nations have completed eight "rounds" of GATT negotiations to reduce trade barriers. The eighth round of negotiations began in Uruguay in 1986. After seven years of complex discussions, in 1993 a new agreement was reached by the 128 nations that were by that time members of GATT. The Uruguay Round agreement took effect on January 1, 1995, and its provisions were phased in through 2005.

Under this agreement, tariffs on thousands of products were eliminated or reduced, with overall tariffs dropping by 33 percent. The agreement also liberalized government rules that in the past impeded the global market for such services as advertising, legal services, tourist services, and financial services. Quotas on imported textiles and apparel were phased out and replaced with tariffs. Other provisions reduced agricultural subsidies paid to farmers and protected intellectual property (patents, trademarks, and copyrights) against piracy.

World Trade Organization

The Uruguay Round agreement established the **World Trade Organization (WTO)** as GATT's successor. Some 161 nations belonged to the WTO in 2015. The WTO oversees trade agreements reached by the member nations, and rules on trade disputes among them. It also provides forums for further rounds of trade negotiations. The ninth and latest round of negotiations—the **Doha Development Agenda**—was launched in Doha, Qatar, in late 2001. (The trade rounds occur over several years in several venues but are named after the city or country of origination.) The negotiations are aimed at further reducing tariffs and quotas, as well as agricultural subsidies that distort trade. You can get an update on the status of the complex negotiations at **www.wto.org.**

GATT and the WTO have been positive forces in the trend toward liberalized world trade. The trade rules agreed upon by the member nations provide a strong and necessary bulwark against the protectionism called for by the special-interest groups in the various nations.

For that reason and others, the WTO is quite controversial. Critics are concerned that rules crafted to expand international trade and investment enable firms to circumvent national laws that protect workers and the environment. Critics ask: What good are minimum-wage laws, worker-safety laws, collective-bargaining rights, and environmental laws if firms can easily shift their production to nations that have weaker laws or if consumers can buy goods produced in those countries?

Proponents of the WTO respond that labor and environmental protections should be pursued directly in nations that have low standards and via international organizations other than the WTO. These issues should not be linked to the process of trade liberalization, which confers widespread economic benefits across nations. Moreover, say proponents of the WTO, many environmental and labor concerns are greatly overblown. Most world trade is among advanced industrial countries, not between them and countries that have lower environmental and labor standards. Moreover, the free flow of goods and resources raises output and income in the developing nations. Historically, such increases in living standards have eventually resulted in stronger, not weaker, protections for the environment and for workers.

The European Union

Countries have also sought to reduce tariffs by creating regional free-trade zones. The most dramatic example is the **European Union (EU).** Initiated in 1958 as the Common Market, in 2003 the EU comprised 15 European nations—Austria, Belgium, Denmark, Finland, France, Germany, Greece, Ireland, Italy, Luxembourg, the Netherlands, Portugal, Spain, Sweden, and the United Kingdom. In 2004, the EU expanded by 10 additional European countries—Cyprus, the Czech Republic, Estonia, Hungary, Latvia, Lithuania, Malta, Poland, Slovakia, and Slovenia. The 2007 addition of Bulgaria and Romania plus the 2013 addition of Croatia expanded the EU to 28 nations.

The EU has abolished tariffs and import quotas on nearly all products traded among the participating nations and established a common system of tariffs applicable to all goods received from nations outside the EU. It has also liberalized the movement of capital and labor within the EU and has created common policies in other economic matters of joint concern, such as agriculture, transportation, and business practices.

EU integration has achieved for Europe what the U.S. constitutional prohibition on tariffs by individual states has achieved for the United States: increased regional specialization, greater productivity, greater output, and faster economic growth. The free flow of goods and services has created large markets for EU industries. The resulting economies of large-scale production have enabled these industries to achieve much lower costs than they could have achieved in their small, single-nation markets.

One of the most significant accomplishments of the EU was the establishment of the so-called **eurozone** or euro area in the early 2000s. As of 2015, 19 members of the EU (Austria, Belgium, Cyprus, Estonia, Finland, France, Germany, Greece, Ireland, Italy, Latvia, Lithuania, Luxembourg, Malta, the Netherlands, Portugal, Slovenia, Slovakia, and Spain) use the euro as a common currency. Notably, the United Kingdom, Denmark, and Sweden have opted not to use the common currency, at least for now. But gone are French francs, German marks, Italian liras, and other national currencies that were once used by eurozone countries.

Economists expect the adoption of the euro to raise the standard of living in the eurozone nations over time. By ending the inconvenience and expense of exchanging currencies, the euro has enhanced the free flow of goods, services, and resources among the eurozone members. Companies that previously sold products in only one or two European nations have found it easier to price and sell their products in all 19 eurozone countries. The euro has also allowed consumers and businesses to comparison shop for outputs and inputs, and this capability has increased competition, reduced prices, and lowered costs.

North American Free Trade Agreement

In 1993 Canada, Mexico, and the United States created a major free-trade zone. The **North American Free Trade Agreement (NAFTA)** established a free-trade area that has about the same combined output as the EU but encompasses a much larger geographic area. NAFTA has eliminated tariffs and other trade barriers among Canada, Mexico, and the United States for most goods and services.

Critics of NAFTA feared that it would cause a massive loss of U.S. jobs as firms moved to Mexico to take advantage of lower wages and weaker regulations on pollution and workplace safety. Also, they were concerned that Japan and South Korea would build plants in Mexico and transport goods tariff-free to the United States, further hurting U.S. firms and workers.

In retrospect, critics were much too pessimistic. Since the passage of NAFTA in 1993, employment in the United States has increased by more than 25 million workers. NAFTA has increased trade among Canada, Mexico, and the United States and has enhanced the standard of living in all three countries.

AP QUICK REVIEW 34.7

- ✓ The General Agreement on Tariffs and Trade (GATT) of 1947 reduced tariffs and quotas and established a process for numerous subsequent rounds of multinational trade negotiations that have liberalized international trade.
- ✓ The World Trade Organization (WTO)—GATT's successor—rules on trade disputes and provides forums for negotiations on further rounds of trade liberalization. The current round of negotiations is called the Doha Development Agenda.
- ✓ The European Union (EU) and the North American Free Trade Agreement (NAFTA) have reduced internal trade barriers among their member nations by establishing multination free-trade zones.

Recognizing Those Hurt by Free Trade

Shifts in patterns of comparative advantage and removal of long-standing trade protection can hurt specific groups of workers. For example, the erosion of the United States' once strong comparative advantage in steel has caused production plant shutdowns and layoffs in the U.S. steel industry. The textile and apparel industries in the United States face similar difficulties. Clearly, not everyone wins from free trade (or freer trade). Some workers lose.

Trade Adjustment Assistance

The **Trade Adjustment Assistance Act** of 2002 introduced some innovative policies to help those hurt by shifts in international trade patterns. The law provides cash assistance (beyond unemployment insurance) for up to 78 weeks for workers displaced by imports or plant relocations abroad. To obtain the assistance, workers must participate in job searches, training programs, or remedial education. Also provided are relocation allowances to help displaced workers move geographically to new jobs within the United States. Refundable tax credits for health insurance serve as payments to help workers maintain their insurance coverage during the retraining and job-search period. Workers who are 50 years of age or older are eligible for "wage insurance," which replaces some of the difference in pay (if any) between their old and new jobs. Many economists support trade adjustment assistance because it not only helps workers hurt by international trade but also helps create the political support necessary to reduce trade barriers and export subsidies.

But not all economists favor trade adjustment assistance. Loss of jobs from imports, sending some work abroad, and plant relocations to other countries are only a small fraction (about 4 percent in recent years) of total job losses in the economy each year. Many workers also lose their jobs because of changing patterns of demand, changing technology, bad management, and other dynamic aspects of a market economy. Some critics ask, "What makes losing one's job to international trade worthy of such special treatment, compared to losing one's job to, say, technological change or domestic competition?" Economists can find no totally satisfying answer.

Offshoring of Jobs

Not only are some U.S. jobs lost because of international trade, but some are lost because of globalization of resource markets. In recent years, U.S. firms have found the outsourcing of work abroad to be increasingly profitable. Economists call this business activity **offshoring**—shifting work previously done by American workers to workers located in other nations. Offshoring is not a new practice but traditionally has involved components for U.S. manufacturing goods. For example, Boeing has long offshored the production of major airplane parts for its "American" aircraft.

Recent advances in computer and communications technology have enabled U.S. firms to offshore service jobs such as data entry, book composition, software coding, call-center operations, medical transcription, and claims processing to countries such as India. Where offshoring occurs, some of the value added in the production process accrues to foreign countries rather than the United States. So part of the income generated from the production of U.S. goods is paid to foreigners, not to American workers.

Offshoring is a wrenching experience for many Americans who lose their jobs, but it is not necessarily bad for the overall economy. Offshoring simply reflects growing specialization and international trade in services, or, more descriptively, "tasks." That growth has been made possible by recent trade agreements and new information and communication technologies. As with trade in goods, trade in services reflects comparative advantage and is beneficial to both trading parties. Moreover, the United States has a sizable trade surplus with other nations in services. The United States gains by specializing in high-valued services such as transportation services, accounting services, legal services, and advertising services, where it still has a comparative advantage. It then "trades" to obtain lower-valued services such as call-center and data-entry work, for which comparative advantage has gone abroad.

Offshoring also increases the demand for complementary jobs in the United States. Jobs that are close substitutes for existing U.S. jobs are lost, but complementary jobs in the United States are expanded. For example, the lower price of writing software code in India may mean a lower cost of software sold in the United States and abroad. That, in turn, may create more jobs for U.S.-based workers such as software designers, marketers, and distributors. Moreover, offshoring may encourage domestic investment and the expansion of firms in the United States by reducing their production costs and keeping them competitive worldwide. In some instances, "offshoring jobs" may equate to "importing competitiveness." Entire firms that might otherwise disappear abroad may remain profitable in the United States only because they can offshore some of their work.

AP QUICK REVIEW 34.8

✓ Increased international trade and offshoring of jobs have harmed some specific U.S. workers and have led to policies such as trade adjustment assistance to try to help them with their transitions to new lines of work.

LAST WORD

Petition of the Candlemakers, 1845

French Economist Frédéric Bastiat (1801–1850) Devastated the Proponents of Protectionism by Satirically Extending Their Reasoning to Its Logical and Absurd Conclusions.

Petition of the Manufacturers of Candles, Waxlights, Lamps, Candlesticks, Street Lamps, Snuffers, Extinguishers, and of the Producers of Oil Tallow, Rosin, Alcohol, and, Generally, of Everything Connected with Lighting.

TO MESSIEURS THE MEMBERS OF THE CHAMBER OF DEPUTIES.

Gentlemen—You are on the right road. You reject abstract theories, and have little consideration for cheapness and plenty. Your chief care is the interest of the producer. You desire to emancipate him from external competition, and reserve the national market for national industry.

We are about to offer you an admirable opportunity of applying your—what shall we call it? your theory? No; nothing is more deceptive than theory; your doctrine? your system? your principle? but you dislike doctrines, you abhor systems, and as for principles, you deny that there are any in social economy: we shall say, then, your practice, your practice without theory and without principle.

We are suffering from the intolerable competition of a foreign rival, placed, it would seem, in a condition so far superior to ours for the production of light, that he absolutely inundates our national market with it at a price fabulously reduced. The moment he shows himself, our trade leaves us—all consumers apply to him; and a branch of native industry, having countless ramifications, is all at once rendered completely stagnant. This rival . . . is no other than the Sun.

What we pray for is, that it may please you to pass a law ordering the shutting up of all windows, skylights, dormer windows, outside and inside shutters, curtains, blinds, bull's-eyes; in a word, of all openings, holes, chinks, clefts, and fissures, by or through which the light of the sun has been in use to enter houses, to the prejudice of the meritorious manufacturers with which we flatter ourselves we have accommodated our country,—a country which, in gratitude, ought not to abandon us now to a strife so unequal.

Source: © J. Luke/PhotoLink/Getty Images RF

If you shut up as much as possible all access to natural light, and create a demand for artificial light, which of our French manufacturers will not be encouraged by it? If more tallow is consumed, then there must be more oxen and sheep; and, consequently, we shall behold the multiplication of artificial meadows, meat, wool, hides, and, above all, manure, which is the basis and foundation of all agricultural wealth.

The same remark applies to navigation. Thousands of vessels will proceed to the whale fishery; and, in a short time, we shall possess a navy capable of maintaining the honor of France, and gratifying the patriotic aspirations of your petitioners, the undersigned candle-makers and others.

Only have the goodness to reflect, Gentlemen, and you will be convinced that there is, perhaps, no Frenchman, from the wealthy coalmaster to the humblest vender of lucifer matches, whose lot will not be ameliorated by the success of this our petition.

Source: Frédéric Bastiat, *Economic Sophisms* (Irvington-on-Hudson, NY: The Foundation for Economic Education, Inc., 1996), abridged, **www.FEE.org**.

SUMMARY

LO34.1 List and discuss several key facts about international trade.

The United States leads the world in the combined volume of exports and imports. Other major trading nations are Germany, Japan, the western European nations, and the Asian economies of China, South Korea, Taiwan, and Singapore. The United States' principal exports include chemicals, agricultural products, consumer durables, semiconductors, and aircraft; principal imports include petroleum, automobiles, metals, household appliances, and computers.

LO34.2 Define comparative advantage and demonstrate how specialization and trade add to a nation's output.

World trade is based on three considerations: the uneven distribution of economic resources among nations, the fact that efficient production of various goods requires particular techniques or combinations of resources, and the differentiated products produced among nations.

Mutually advantageous specialization and trade are possible between any two nations if they have different domestic opportunity-cost ratios for any two products. By specializing on the basis of comparative advantage, nations can obtain larger real incomes with fixed amounts of resources. The terms of trade determine how this increase in world output is shared by the trading nations. Increasing (rather than constant) opportunity costs limit specialization and trade.

LO34.3 Describe how differences between world prices and domestic prices prompt exports and imports.

A nation's export supply curve shows the quantities of a product the nation will export at world prices that exceed the domestic price (the price in a closed, no-international-trade economy). A nation's import demand curve reveals the quantities of a product it will import at world prices below the domestic price.

In a two-nation model, the equilibrium world price and the equilibrium quantities of exports and imports occur where one nation's export supply curve intersects the other nation's import demand curve. A nation will export a particular product if the world price exceeds the domestic price; it will import the product if the world price is less than the domestic price. The country with the lower costs of production will be the exporter and the country with the higher costs of production will be the importer.

LO34.4 Analyze the economic effects of tariffs and quotas.

Trade barriers take the form of protective tariffs, quotas, nontariff barriers, and "voluntary" export restrictions. Export subsidies also distort international trade. Supply and demand analysis demonstrates that protective tariffs and quotas increase the prices and reduce the quantities demanded of the affected goods. Sales by foreign exporters diminish; domestic producers, however, gain higher prices and enlarged sales. Consumer losses from trade restrictions greatly exceed producer and government gains, creating an efficiency loss to society.

LO34.5 Analyze the validity of the most frequently presented arguments for protectionism.

The strongest arguments for protection are the infant industry and military self-sufficiency arguments. Most other arguments for protection are interest-group appeals or reasoning fallacies that emphasize producer interests over consumer interests or stress the immediate effects of trade barriers while ignoring long-run consequences.

The cheap foreign labor argument for protection fails because it focuses on labor costs per hour rather than on what really matters, labor costs per unit of output. Due to higher productivity, firms in high-wage countries like the United States can have lower wage costs per unit of output than competitors in low-wage countries. Whether they do will depend on how their particular wage and productivity levels compare with those of their competitors in low-wage countries.

LO34.6 Identify and explain the objectives of GATT, WTO, EU, eurozone, and NAFTA and discuss offshoring and trade adjustment assistance.

In 1947 the General Agreement on Tariffs and Trade (GATT) was formed to encourage nondiscriminatory treatment for all member nations, to reduce tariffs, and to eliminate import quotas. The Uruguay Round of GATT negotiations (1993) reduced tariffs and quotas, liberalized trade in services, reduced agricultural subsidies, reduced pirating of intellectual property, and phased out quotas on textiles.

GATT's successor, the World Trade Organization (WTO), had 161 member nations in 2015. It implements WTO agreements, rules on trade disputes between members, and provides forums for continued discussions on trade liberalization. The latest round of trade negotiations—the Doha Development Agenda—began in late 2001 and as of 2016 was still in progress.

Free-trade zones liberalize trade within regions. Two examples of free-trade arrangements are the 28-member European Union (EU) and the North American Free Trade Agreement (NAFTA), comprising Canada, Mexico, and the United States. Nineteen EU nations have abandoned their national currencies for a common currency called the euro.

The Trade Adjustment Assistance Act of 2002 recognizes that trade liberalization and increased international trade can create job loss for many workers. The Act therefore provides cash assistance, education and training benefits, health care subsidies, and wage subsidies (for persons aged 50 or older) to qualified workers displaced by imports or relocations of plants from the United States to abroad.

Offshoring is the practice of shifting work previously done by Americans in the United States to workers located in other nations. Although offshoring reduces some U.S. jobs, it lowers production costs, expands sales, and therefore may create other U.S. jobs. Less than 4 percent of all job losses in the United States each year are caused by imports, offshoring, and plant relocation abroad.

TERMS AND CONCEPTS

labor-intensive goods
land-intensive goods
capital-intensive goods
opportunity-cost ratio
comparative advantage
principle of comparative advantage
terms of trade
trading possibilities line
gains from trade
world price
domestic price
export supply curve
import demand curve
equilibrium world price
tariffs
revenue tariff
protective tariff
import quota
nontariff barrier (NTB)
voluntary export restriction (VER)
export subsidy
dumping
Smoot-Hawley Tariff Act
General Agreement on Tariffs and Trade (GATT)
World Trade Organization (WTO)
Doha Development Agenda
European Union (EU)
eurozone
North American Free Trade Agreement (NAFTA)
Trade Adjustment Assistance Act
offshoring

The following and additional problems can be found in connect

DISCUSSION QUESTIONS

1. Quantitatively, how important is international trade to the United States relative to the importance of trade to other nations? What country is the United States' most important trading partner, quantitatively? With what country does the United States have the largest trade deficit? LO34.1
2. Distinguish among land-, labor-, and capital-intensive goods, citing an example of each without resorting to book examples. How do these distinctions relate to international trade? How do distinctive products, unrelated to resource intensity, relate to international trade? LO34.1, LO34.2
3. Explain: "The United States can make certain toys with greater productive efficiency than can China. Yet we import those toys from China." Relate your answer to the ideas of Adam Smith and David Ricardo. LO34.2
4. Suppose Big Country can produce 80 units of X by using all its resources to produce X or 60 units of Y by devoting all its resources to Y. Comparable figures for Small Nation are 60 units of X and 60 units of Y. Assuming constant costs, in which product should each nation specialize? Explain why. What are the limits of the terms of trade between these two countries? How would rising costs (rather than constant costs) affect the extent of specialization and trade between these two countries? LO34.2
5. What is an export supply curve? What is an import demand curve? How do such curves relate to the determination of the equilibrium world price of a tradable good? LO34.3
6. Why is a quota more detrimental to an economy than a tariff that results in the same level of imports as the quota? What is the net outcome of either tariffs or quotas for the world economy? LO34.4
7. "The potentially valid arguments for tariff protection—military self-sufficiency, infant industry protection, and diversification for stability—are also the most easily abused." Why are these arguments susceptible to abuse? LO34.4
8. Evaluate the effectiveness of artificial trade barriers, such as tariffs and import quotas, as a way to achieve and maintain full employment throughout the U.S. economy. How might such policies reduce unemployment in one U.S. industry but increase it in another U.S. industry? LO34.4
9. In 2013, manufacturing workers in the United States earned average compensation of $36.34 per hour. That same year, manufacturing workers in Mexico earned average compensation of $6.82 per hour. How can U.S. manufacturers possibly compete? Why isn't all manufacturing done in Mexico and other low-wage countries? LO34.4
10. How might protective tariffs reduce both the imports and the exports of the nation that levies tariffs? In what way do foreign firms that "dump" their products onto the U.S. market in effect provide bargains to American consumers? How might the import competition lead to quality improvements and cost reductions by American firms? LO34.4
11. Identify and state the significance of each of the following trade-related entities: (*a*) the WTO; (*b*) the EU; (*c*) the eurozone; and (*d*) NAFTA. LO34.6
12. What form does trade adjustment assistance take in the United States? How does such assistance promote political support for free-trade agreements? Do you think workers who lose their jobs because of changes in trade laws deserve special treatment relative to workers who lose their jobs because of other changes in the economy, say, changes in patterns of government spending? LO34.6
13. What is offshoring of white-collar service jobs and how does that practice relate to international trade? Why has offshoring increased over the past few decades? Give an example (other than that in the textbook) of how offshoring can eliminate some American jobs while creating other American jobs. LO34.6
14. **LAST WORD** What was the central point that Bastiat was trying to make in his imaginary petition of the candlemakers?

AP REVIEW QUESTIONS

1. In Country X, a worker can make 5 bicycles per hour. In Country Y, a worker can make 7 bicycles per hour. Which country has an absolute advantage in making bicycles? LO34.2
   a. Country X.
   b. Country Y
2. In Country X, the production of 1 bicycle requires using resources that could otherwise be used to produce 11 lamps. In Country Y, the production of 1 bicycle requires using resources that could otherwise be used to produce 15 lamps. Which country has a comparative advantage in making bicycles? LO34.2
   a. Country X.
   b. Country Y.
3. True or False: If Country X has an absolute advantage over Country Y in producing lamps, it will also have a comparative advantage over Country Y in producing lamps. LO34.2
4. Suppose that the opportunity-cost ratio for sugar and almonds is $4S \equiv 1A$ in Hawaii but $1S \equiv 2A$ in California. Which state has the comparative advantage in producing almonds? LO34.2
   a. Hawaii.
   b. California.
   c. Neither.
   d. Both.
   e. Not enough information to tell.
5. Suppose that the opportunity-cost ratio for fish and lumber is $1F \equiv 1L$ in Canada but $2F \equiv 1L$ in Iceland. Then __________ should specialize in producing fish while __________ should specialize in producing lumber. LO34.2
   a. Canada; Iceland.
   b. Iceland; Canada.
   c. Neither; both.
   d. Canada; neither.
   e. Either; Iceland.
6. Suppose that the opportunity-cost ratio for watches and cheese is $1C \equiv 1W$ in Switzerland but $1C \equiv 4W$ in Japan. LO34.2
   a. Which country has comparative advantage in producing cheese?
   b. Which country has comparative advantage in producing watches?

   At which of the following international exchange ratios (terms of trade) will Switzerland and Japan be willing to specialize and engage in trade with each other?
   *Select **one or more** answers from the choices shown.*
   a. $1C \equiv 3W$.
   b. $1C \equiv \frac{1}{2}W$.
   c. $1C \equiv 5W$.
   d. $\frac{1}{2}C \equiv 1W$.
   e. $2C \equiv 1W$.
7. We see quite a bit of international trade in the real world. And trade is driven by specialization. So why don't we see full specialization—for instance, all cars in the world being made in South Korea, or all the mobile phones in the world being made in China? Choose the best answer from among the following choices. LO34.2
   a. High tariffs.
   b. Extensive import quotas.
   c. Increasing opportunity costs.
   d. Decreasing opportunity costs.
   e. Increasing returns.
8. True or False: International trade based on the principle of comparative advantage creates a less efficient allocation of world economic resources and a reduction in consumption standards in each country. LO34.1
9. Suppose that the current international price of wheat is $6 per bushel and that the United States is currently exporting 30 million bushels per year. If the United States suddenly became a closed economy with respect to wheat, would the domestic price of wheat in the United States end up higher or lower than $6? LO34.3
   a. Higher.
   b. Lower.
   c. The same.
   d. Initially higher, but then fall back to $6.
   e. Initially lower, but then rise back up to $6.
10. Suppose that if Iceland and Japan were both closed economies, the domestic price of fish would be $100 per ton in Iceland and $90 per ton in Japan. If the two countries decided to trade with each other, which of the following could be the equilibrium international price of fish once they begin trading? LO34.3
    a. $75.
    b. $85.
    c. $95.
    d. $105.
    e. $190.
11. There are two countries, Norta and Eartha. Both produce sugar and fish. The table below shows the number of labor hours required to produce a unit of sugar and of fish in each country. LO34.2, LO34.3

	Sugar	Fish (labor hours to produce a unit of each product)
Norta	10	20
Eartha	2	10

    a. Which country has absolute advantage in producing sugar? Explain.
    b. Which country has absolute advantage in producing fish? Explain.
    c. What is the opportunity cost of producing sugar in Norta?
    d. What is the opportunity cost of producing fish in Eartha?
    e. With specialization and trade, which country will produce sugar? Explain.
    f. The international price ratio is such that a unit of fish sells for three times the price of a unit of sugar, say $15 per unit of fish and $5 per unit of sugar. Will these two countries willingly trade and have consumption gains? Explain.
12. Which of the following is true with respect to the classical model of comparative advantage, specialization, and international trade? LO34.2
    a. With trade a country will produce beyond its production possibilities frontier.
    b. With trade a country will reduce its rate of unemployment.
    c. With trade a country will experience a productivity gain with the good it produces and exports, pivoting out the country's production possibilities frontier.
    d. With trade a country can consume beyond its production possibilities frontier.
    e. With trade each product, whether imported or exported, will become cheaper for consumers in the country.

PROBLEMS

1. Assume that the comparative-cost ratios of two products—baby formula and tuna fish—are as follows in the nations of Canswicki and Tunata:

Canswicki: 1 can baby formula ≡ 2 cans tuna fish
Tunata: 1 can baby formula ≡ 4 cans tuna fish

In what product should each nation specialize? Which of the following terms of trade would be acceptable to both nations: (a) 1 can baby formula ≡ $2\frac{1}{2}$ cans tuna fish; (b) 1 can baby formula ≡ 1 can tuna fish; (c) 1 can baby formula ≡ 5 cans tuna fish? **LO34.2**

2. The accompanying hypothetical production possibilities tables are for New Zealand and Spain. Each country can produce apples and plums. Plot the production possibilities data for each of the two countries separately. Referring to your graphs, answer the following: **LO34.2**

New Zealand's Production Possibilities Table (Millions of Bushels)

	Production Alternatives			
Product	**A**	**B**	**C**	**D**
Apples	0	20	40	60
Plums	15	10	5	0

Spain's Production Possibilities Table (Millions of Bushels)

	Production Alternatives			
Product	**R**	**S**	**T**	**U**
Apples	0	20	40	60
Plums	60	40	20	0

a. What is each country's cost ratio of producing plums and apples?
b. Which nation should specialize in which product?
c. Show the trading possibilities lines for each nation if the actual terms of trade are 1 plum for 2 apples. (Plot these lines on your graph.)
d. Suppose the optimum product mixes before specialization and trade were alternative B in New Zealand and alternative S in Spain. What would be the gains from specialization and trade?

3. The following hypothetical production possibilities tables are for China and the United States. Assume that before specialization and trade, the optimal product mix for China is alternative B and for the United States is alternative U. **LO34.2**

a. Are comparative-cost conditions such that the two areas should specialize? If so, what product should each produce?
b. What is the total gain in apparel and chemical output that would result from such specialization?
c. What are the limits of the terms of trade? Suppose that the actual terms of trade are 1 unit of apparel for 1 unit of chemicals and that 4 units of apparel are exchanged for 6 units of chemicals. What are the gains from specialization and trade for each nation?

	China Production Possibilities					
Product	**A**	**B**	**C**	**D**	**E**	**F**
Apparel (in thousands)	30	24	18	12	6	0
Chemicals (in tons)	0	6	12	18	24	30

	U.S. Production Possibilities					
Product	**R**	**S**	**T**	**U**	**V**	**W**
Apparel (in thousands)	10	8	6	4	2	0
Chemicals (in tons)	0	4	8	12	16	20

4. Refer to Figure 3.6. Assume that the graph depicts the U.S. domestic market for corn. How many bushels of corn, if any, will the United States export or import at a world price of \$1, \$2, \$3, \$4, and \$5? Use this information to construct the U.S. export supply curve and import demand curve for corn. Suppose that the only other corn-producing nation is France, where the domestic price is \$4. Which country will export corn; which country will import it? **LO34.3**

35 Chapter

The Balance of Payments, Exchange Rates, and Trade Deficits

Learning Objectives

LO35.1 Explain how currencies of different nations are exchanged when international transactions take place.

LO35.2 Analyze the balance sheet the United States uses to account for the international payments it makes and receives.

LO35.3 Discuss how exchange rates are determined in currency markets that have flexible exchange rates.

LO35.4 Describe the differences between flexible and fixed exchange rates, including how changes in foreign exchange reserves bring about automatic changes in the domestic money supply under a fixed exchange rate.

LO35.5 Explain the current system of managed floating exchange rates.

LO35.6 Identify the causes and consequences of recent U.S. trade deficits.

LO35.7 (Appendix) Explain how exchange rates worked under the gold standard and Bretton Woods.

AP Chapter Focus

If you take a U.S. dollar to the bank and ask to exchange it for U.S. currency, you will get a puzzled look. If you persist, you may get a dollar's worth of change. In other words, one U.S. dollar can buy exactly one U.S. dollar. At the same time, however, for example, on April 5, 2016, 1 U.S. dollar could buy 3,087 Colombian pesos, 1.32 Australian dollars, 0.71 British pound, 1.31 Canadian dollars, 0.88 European euro, 110.48 Japanese yen, or 17.64 Mexican pesos. What explains this seemingly haphazard array of exchange rates?

In Chapter 34 we examined comparative advantage as the underlying economic basis of world trade and discussed the effects of barriers to free trade. Now we introduce the highly important monetary and financial aspects of international trade.

AP International Financial Transactions

LO35.1 Explain how currencies of different nations are exchanged when international transactions take place.

This chapter focuses on international financial transactions, the vast majority of which fall into two broad categories: international trade and international asset transactions. International trade involves either purchasing or selling currently produced goods or services across an international border. Examples include an Egyptian firm exporting cotton to the United States and an American company hiring an Indian call center to answer its phones. International asset transactions involve the transfer of the property rights to either real or financial assets between the citizens of one country and the citizens of another country. International asset transactions include activities like buying foreign stocks or selling your house to a foreigner.

These two categories of international financial transactions reflect the fact that whether they live in different countries or the same country, individuals and firms can only exchange two things with each other: currently produced goods and services or assets. With regard to assets, however, money is by far the most commonly exchanged asset. Only rarely will you encounter a barter situation in which people directly exchange one nonmoney asset for another nonmoney asset—such as trading a car for 500 shares of Microsoft stock or a cow for 30 chickens and a tank of diesel fuel.

As a result, there are two basic types of transactions:

- People trading either goods or services for money.
- People trading assets for money.

In either case, money flows from the buyers of the goods, services, or assets to the sellers of the goods, services, or assets. In the context of international trade, importers are buyers and exporters are sellers. As a result, *imports cause outflows of money while exports cause inflows of money*.

When the buyers and sellers are both from places that use the same currency, there is no confusion about what type of money to use. Americans from California and Wisconsin will use their common currency, the dollar. People from France and Germany will use their common currency, the euro. However, when the buyers and sellers are from places that use different currencies, intermediate asset transactions have to take place: The buyers must convert their own currencies into the currencies that the sellers use and accept.

As an example, consider the case of an English software company that wants to buy a supercomputer made by an American company. The American company sells these high-powered machines for $300,000. To pay for the machine, the English company has to convert some of the money it has (British pounds) into the money that the American company will accept (U.S. dollars). This process is not difficult. As we will soon explain in detail, there are many easy-to-use foreign exchange markets in which those who wish to sell pounds and buy dollars can interact with others who wish to sell dollars and buy pounds. The demand and supply created by these two groups determine the equilibrium exchange rate, which, in turn, determines how many pounds our English company will have to convert to pay for the supercomputer. For instance, if the exchange rate is £1= $2, then the English company will have to convert £150,000 to obtain the $300,000 necessary to purchase the computer.

AP QUICK REVIEW 35.1

- ✓ International financial transactions involve trade either in currently produced goods and services or in preexisting assets.
- ✓ While imports cause outflows of money, exports of goods, services, and assets create inflows of money.
- ✓ If buyers and sellers use different currencies, then foreign exchange transactions take place so that the exporter can be paid in his or her own currency.

AP The Balance of Payments

LO35.2 Analyze the balance sheet the United States uses to account for the international payments it makes and receives.

A nation's **balance of payments** is the sum of all the financial transactions that take place between its residents and the residents of foreign nations. Most of these transactions fall into the two main categories that we have just discussed: international trade and international asset transactions. As a result, nearly all the items included in the balance of payments are things such as exports and imports of goods, exports and imports of services, and international purchases and sales of financial and real assets. But the balance of payments also includes international transactions that fall outside of these main categories—things such as tourist expenditures, interest and dividends received or paid abroad, debt forgiveness, and remittances made by immigrants to their relatives back home.

The Bureau of Economic Analysis at the U.S. Department of Commerce compiles a balance-of-payments statement each year. This statement summarizes all of the millions of payments that individuals and firms in the United States receive from foreigners as well as all of the millions of payments that individuals and firms in the United States make to foreigners. It shows "flows" of inpayments of money *to* the United States and outpayments of money *from* the United States. For convenience, all of these money payments are given in terms of dollars. This is true despite the fact that some of them actually may have been made using foreign currencies—as when, for instance, an American company converts dollars into euros to buy something from an Italian

AP **TABLE 35.1 The U.S. Balance of Payments, 2015 (in Billions)**

CURRENT ACCOUNT		
(1) U.S. goods exports	$+1,513	
(2) U.S. goods imports	−2,273	
(3) *Balance on goods*		$−760
(4) U.S. exports of services	+710	
(5) U.S. imports of services	−491	
(6) *Balance on services*		+219
(7) *Balance on goods and services*		−541
(8) Net investment income	+191*	
(9) Net transfers	−136	
(10) **Balance on current account**		**−486**
CAPITAL AND FINANCIAL ACCOUNT		
Capital account		
(11) *Balance on capital account*		0
Financial account		
(12) Foreign purchases of assets in the United States	+589†	
(13) U.S. purchases of assets abroad	−103†	
(14) *Balance on financial account*		+486
(15) **Balance on capital and financial account**		**+486**
		$ 0

*Includes other, less significant, categories of income.
†Includes one-half of a $275 billion statistical discrepancy that is listed in the capital account.

Source: U.S. Department of Commerce, Bureau of Economic Analysis, **www.bea.gov**. Preliminary 2015 data. The export and import data are on a "balance-of-payment basis" and usually vary from the data on exports and imports reported in the National Income and Product Accounts.

company. When including this outpayment of money from the United States, the accountants who compile the balance-of-payments statement use the number of dollars the American company converted—rather than the number of euros that were actually used to make the purchase.

Table 35.1 is a simplified balance-of-payments statement for the United States in 2015. Because most international financial transactions fall into only two categories—international trade and international asset transactions—the balance-of-payments statement is organized into two broad categories. *The current account* located at the top of the table primarily treats international trade. *The capital and financial account* at the bottom of the table primarily treats international asset transactions.

Current Account

The top portion of Table 35.1 that mainly summarizes U.S. trade in currently produced goods and services is called the **current account.** Items 1 and 2 show U.S. exports and imports of goods (merchandise) in 2015. U.S. exports have a *plus* (+) sign because they are a *credit*; they generate flows of money toward the United States. U.S. imports have a *minus* (−) sign because they are a *debit*; they cause flows of money out of the United States.

Balance on Goods Items 1 and 2 in Table 35.1 reveal that in 2015 U.S. goods exports of $1,513 billion were less than U.S. goods imports of $2,273 billion. A country's *balance of trade on goods* is the difference between its exports and its imports of goods. If exports exceed imports, the result is a surplus on the balance of goods. If imports exceed exports, there is a trade deficit on the balance of goods. We note in item 3 that, in 2015, the United States incurred a trade deficit on goods of $760 billion.

Balance on Services The United States exports not only goods, such as airplanes and computer software, but also services, such as insurance, consulting, travel, and investment advice, to residents of foreign nations. Item 4 in Table 35.1 shows that these service "exports" totaled $710 billion in 2015. Since they generate flows of money toward the United States, they are a credit (thus the + sign). Item 5 indicates that the United States "imports" similar services from foreigners. Those service imports were $491 billion in 2015, and since they generate flows of money out of the United States, they are a debit (thus the − sign). Summed together, items 4 and 5 indicate that the balance on services (item 6) in 2015 was $219 billion. The **balance on goods and services** shown as item 7 is the difference between U.S. exports of goods and services (items 1 and 4) and U.S. imports of goods and services (items

GLOBAL PERSPECTIVE 35.1

U.S. Trade Balances in Goods and Services, Selected Nations, 2015

The United States has large trade deficits in goods and services with several nations, in particular, China, Germany, and Japan.

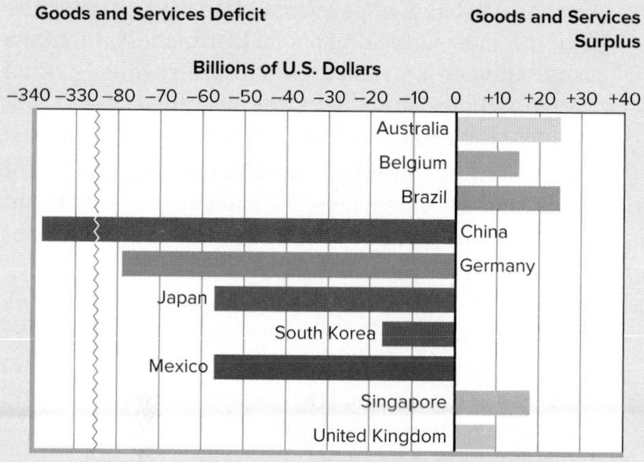

Source: Bureau of Economic Analysis, **www.bea.gov.**

2 and 5). In 2015, U.S. imports of goods and services exceeded U.S. exports of goods and services by $541 billion. So a **trade deficit** of that amount occurred. In contrast, a **trade surplus** occurs when exports of goods and services exceed imports of goods and services. (Global Perspective 35.1 shows U.S. trade deficits and surpluses with selected nations.)

Balance on Current Account Items 8 and 9 are not items relating directly to international trade in goods and services. But they are listed as part of the current account (which is mostly about international trade in goods and services) because they are international financial flows that in some sense compensate for things that can be conceptualized as being *like* international trade in either goods or services. For instance, item 8, *net investment income*, represents the difference between (1) the interest and dividend payments foreigners paid U.S. citizens and companies for the services provided by U.S. capital invested abroad ("exported" capital) and (2) the interest and dividends the U.S. citizens and companies paid for the services provided by foreign capital invested here ("imported" capital). Observe that in 2015 U.S. net investment income was a positive $191 billion.

Item 9 shows net transfers, both public and private, between the United States and the rest of the world. Included here is foreign aid, pensions paid to U.S. citizens living abroad, and remittances by immigrants to relatives abroad. These $136 billion of transfers are net U.S. outpayments (and therefore listed as a negative number in Table 35.1). They are listed as part of the current account because they can be thought of as the financial flows that accompany the exporting of goodwill and the importing of "thank you notes."

By adding all transactions in the current account, we obtain the **balance on current account** shown in item 10. In 2015 the United States had a current account deficit of $486 billion. This means that the U.S. current account transactions created outpayments from the United States greater than inpayments to the United States.

Capital and Financial Account

The bottom portion of the current account statement summarizes U.S. international asset transactions. It is called the **capital and financial account** and consists of two separate accounts: the *capital account* and the *financial account.*

Capital Account The capital account mainly measures debt forgiveness—which is an asset transaction because the person forgiving a debt essentially hands the IOU back to the borrower. It is a "net" account (one that can be either + or −). The $0 billion listed in line 11 tells us that in 2015 foreigners forgave exactly as much debt owed to them by Americans as Americans forgave debt owed to them by foreigners. Any positive (+) entry in line 11 would indicate a credit; positive amounts are an "on-paper" inpayment (asset transfer) by the net amount of debt forgiven.

Financial Account The financial account summarizes international asset transactions having to do with international purchases and sales of real or financial assets. Line 12 lists the amount of foreign purchases of assets in the United States. It has a + sign because any purchase of an American-owned asset by a foreigner generates a flow of money toward the American who sells the asset. Line 13 lists U.S. purchases of assets abroad. These have a − sign because such purchases generate a flow of money from the Americans who buy foreign assets toward the foreigners who sell them those assets.

Items 12 and 13 added together yield a $486 billion balance on the financial account for 2015 (line 14). In 2015 the United States "exported" $589 billion of ownership of its real and financial assets and "imported" $103 billion. Thought of differently, this surplus in the financial account brought in income of $486 billion to the United States. The **balance on capital and financial account** (line 15) is also $486 billion. It is the sum of the $0 billion credit on the capital account and the $486 billion surplus on the financial account. Observe that this $486 billion surplus in the capital and financial account equals the $486 billion deficit in the current account. This is not an accident. The two numbers always equal—or "balance." That's why the statement is called the *balance* of payments. It has to balance. Let's see why.

Why the Balance?

The balance on the current account and the balance on the capital and financial account must always sum to zero because any deficit or surplus in the current account automatically creates an offsetting entry in the capital and financial account. People can only trade one of two things with each other: currently produced goods and services or preexisting assets. Therefore, if trading partners have an imbalance in their trade of currently produced goods and services, the only way to make up for that imbalance is with a net transfer of assets from one party to the other.

To see why this is true, suppose that John (an American) makes shoes and Henri (a Swiss citizen) makes watches and that the pair only trade with each other. Assume that their financial assets consist entirely of money, with each beginning the year with $1,000 in his bank account. Suppose that this year John exports $300 of shoes to Henri and imports $500 of watches from Henri. John therefore ends the year with a $200 goods deficit with Henri.

John and Henri's goods transactions, however, also result in asset exchanges that cause a net transfer of assets from John to Henri equal in size to John's $200 goods deficit with Henri. This is true because Henri pays John $300 for his shoes while John pays Henri $500 for his watches. The *net* result of these opposite-direction asset movements is that $200 of John's initial assets of $1,000 are transferred to Henri. This is unavoidable because the $300 John receives from his exports pays for only the first $300 of his $500 of imports. The only way for John to pay for the remaining $200 of imports is for him to transfer $200 of his initial asset holdings to Henri. Consequently, John's assets decline by $200 from $1,000 to $800, and Henri's assets rise from $1,000 to $1,200.

Consider how the transaction between John and Henri affects the U.S. balance-of-payments statement (Table 35.1), other things equal. John's $200 goods deficit with Henri shows up in the U.S. current account as a −$200 entry in the balance on goods account (line 3) and carries down to a −$200 entry in the balance on current account (line 10).

In the capital and financial account, this $200 is recorded as +$200 in the account labeled foreign purchases of assets in the United States (line 12). This +$200 then carries down to the balance on capital and financial account (line 15). Think of it this way: Henri has in essence used $200 worth of watches to purchase $200 of John's initial $1,000 holding of assets. The +$200 entry in line 12 (foreign purchases of assets in the United States) simply recognizes this fact. This +$200 exactly offsets the −$200 in the current account.

Thus, the balance of payments always balances. Any current account deficit or surplus in the top half of the statement automatically generates an offsetting international asset transfer that shows up in the capital and financial account in the bottom half of the statement. More specifically, current account deficits simultaneously generate transfers of assets to foreigners, while current account surpluses automatically generate transfers of assets from foreigners.

AP QUICK REVIEW 35.2

- ✓ A nation's balance-of-payments statement summarizes all of the international financial transactions that take place between its residents and the residents of all foreign nations. It includes the current account balance and the capital or financial account balance.
- ✓ The current account balance is a nation's exports of goods and services less its imports of goods and services plus its net investment income and net transfers.
- ✓ The capital and financial account balance includes the net amount of the nation's debt forgiveness as well as the nation's sale of real and financial assets to people living abroad less its purchases of real and financial assets from foreigners.
- ✓ The current account balance and the capital and financial account balance always sum to zero because any current account imbalance automatically generates an offsetting international asset transfer.

AP Flexible Exchange Rates

LO35.3 Discuss how exchange rates are determined in currency markets that have flexible exchange rates.

There are two pure types of exchange-rate systems:

- A **flexible- or floating-exchange-rate system** through which demand and supply determine exchange rates and in which no government intervention occurs.
- A **fixed-exchange-rate system** through which governments determine exchange rates and make necessary adjustments in their economies to maintain those rates.

We begin by looking at flexible exchange rates. Let's examine the rate, or price, at which U.S. dollars might be exchanged for British pounds in the market for foreign currency. In **Figure 35.1 (Key Graph)** we show demand D_1 and supply S_1 of pounds. Note that both the demand and supply of pounds are expressed in terms of U.S. dollars. They interact to determine the equilibrium price for pounds—which is expressed in terms of how many dollars are required to purchase one pound.

The *demand-for-pounds curve* D_1 is downsloping because all British goods and services will be cheaper to Americans if pounds become less expensive. That is, at lower dollar prices for pounds, Americans can obtain more pounds and therefore more British goods and services per dollar. To buy those

AP KEY GRAPH

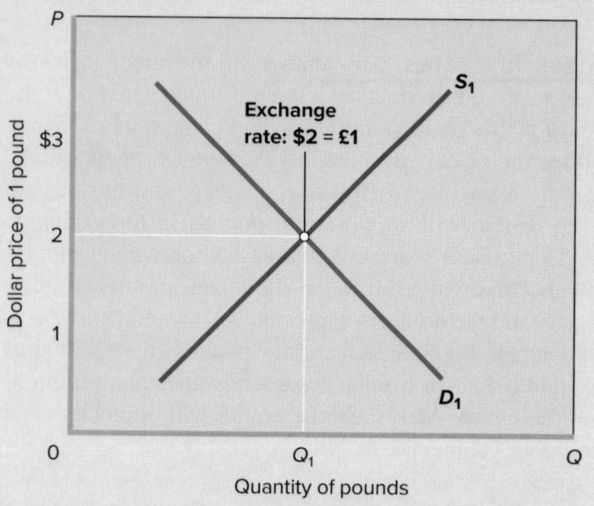

FIGURE 35.1 The market for foreign currency (pounds). The intersection of the demand-for-pounds curve D_1 and the supply-of-pounds curve S_1 determines the equilibrium dollar price of pounds, here, $2. That means that the exchange rate is $2 = £1. Not shown: An increase in demand for pounds or a decrease in supply of pounds will increase the dollar price of pounds and thus cause the pound to appreciate. Also not shown: A decrease in demand for pounds or an increase in the supply of pounds will reduce the dollar price of pounds, meaning that the pound has depreciated.

QUICK QUIZ FOR FIGURE 35.1

1. Which of the following statements is true?
   - **a.** The quantity of pounds demanded falls when the dollar appreciates.
   - **b.** The quantity of pounds supplied declines as the dollar price of the pound rises.
   - **c.** At the equilibrium exchange rate, the pound price of $1 is £$\frac{1}{2}$.
   - **d.** The dollar appreciates if the demand for pounds increases.
2. At the price of $2 for £1 in this figure:
   - **a.** the dollar-pound exchange rate is unstable.
   - **b.** the quantity of pounds supplied equals the quantity demanded.
   - **c.** the dollar price of £1 equals the pound price of $1.
   - **d.** U.S. goods exports to Britain must equal U.S. goods imports from Britain.
3. Other things equal, a leftward shift of the demand curve in this figure:
   - **a.** would depreciate the dollar.
   - **b.** would create a shortage of pounds at the previous price of $2 for £1.
   - **c.** might be caused by a major recession in the United States.
   - **d.** might be caused by a significant rise of real interest rates in Britain.
4. Other things equal, a rightward shift of the supply curve in this figure would:
   - **a.** depreciate the dollar and might be caused by a significant rise of real interest rates in Britain.
   - **b.** depreciate the dollar and might be caused by a significant fall of real interest rates in Britain.
   - **c.** appreciate the dollar and might be caused by a significant rise of real interest rates in the United States.
   - **d.** appreciate the dollar and might be caused by a significant fall of real interest rates in the United States.

Answers: 1. c; 2. b; 3. c; 4. c

cheaper British goods, U.S. consumers will increase the quantity of pounds they demand.

As a concrete example, suppose that you are a U.S. citizen on vacation in London. If it only takes 50 cents to buy 1 pound, you will end up wanting to buy a lot more souvenirs to take home than if it takes $1.50 to buy 1 pound. The lower the dollar price of purchasing a pound, the less expensive British goods and services will appear to you and the more dollars you will want to sell for pounds in order to get "cheap" British products. So the demand curve for pounds slopes downward.

The *supply-of-pounds curve* S_1 is upsloping because the British will purchase more U.S. goods when the dollar price of pounds rises (that is, as the pound price of dollars falls). When the British buy more U.S. goods, they supply a greater quantity of pounds to the foreign exchange market. In other words, they must exchange pounds for dollars to purchase U.S. goods. So, when the dollar price of pounds rises, the quantity of pounds supplied goes up.

As a concrete example, suppose that a Facebook friend from London wants to buy Google stock. Because Google is a U.S. company, he will need dollars to buy Google shares. If he can convert 1 pound into $3, he will want to buy a lot more shares of Google than if each pound only converts into $1.75. The more dollars he can get from selling a pound, the less expensive Google stock will appear to him and the more pounds he will want to sell in order to get "cheap" Google stock. So the supply curve for pounds slopes upward.

The intersection of the supply curve and the demand curve will determine the dollar price of pounds. Here, that price (exchange rate) is $2 for £1. At this exchange rate, the quantities of pounds supplied and demanded are equal; neither a shortage nor a surplus of pounds occurs.

Depreciation and Appreciation

An exchange rate determined by market forces can, and often does, change daily like stock and bond prices. When the dollar price of pounds *rises*, for example, from $2 = £1 to $3 = £1, the dollar has *depreciated* relative to the pound (and the pound has appreciated relative to the dollar). When a currency depreciates, more units of it (dollars) are needed to buy a single unit of some other currency (a pound).

When the dollar price of pounds *falls*, for example, from $2 = £1 to $1 = £1, the dollar has *appreciated* relative to the pound. When a currency appreciates, fewer units of it (dollars) are needed to buy a single unit of some other currency (pounds).

In our U.S.-Britain example, depreciation of the dollar means an appreciation of the pound, and vice versa. When the dollar price of a pound jumps from $2 = £1 to $3 = £1, the pound has appreciated relative to the dollar because it takes fewer pounds to buy $1. At $2 = £1, it took £$\frac{1}{2}$ to buy $1; at $3 = £1, it takes only £$\frac{1}{3}$ to buy $1. Conversely, when the dollar appreciated relative to the pound, the pound depreciated relative to the dollar. More pounds were needed to buy a dollar.

In general, the relevant terminology and relationships between the U.S. dollar and another currency are as follows (where the "≡" sign means "is equivalent to").

- Dollar price of foreign currency increases ≡ dollar depreciates relative to the foreign currency ≡ foreign currency price of dollar decreases ≡ foreign currency appreciates relative to the dollar.
- Dollar price of foreign currency decreases ≡ dollar appreciates relative to the foreign currency ≡ foreign currency price of dollar increases ≡ foreign currency depreciates relative to the dollar.

Determinants of Flexible Exchange Rates

What factors would cause a nation's currency to appreciate or depreciate in the market for foreign exchange? Here are three generalizations:

- If the demand for a nation's currency increases (other things equal), that currency will appreciate; if the demand declines, that currency will depreciate.
- If the supply of a nation's currency increases, that currency will depreciate; if the supply decreases, that currency will appreciate.
- If a nation's currency appreciates, some foreign currency depreciates relative to it.

With these generalizations in mind, let's examine the determinants of exchange rates—the factors that shift the demand or supply curve for a certain currency. As we do so, keep in mind that the other-things-equal assumption is always in force. Also note that we are discussing factors *that change the exchange rate*, not things that change *as a result of* a change in the exchange rate.

Changes in Tastes Any change in consumer tastes or preferences for the products of a foreign country may alter the demand for that nation's currency and change its exchange rate. If technological advances in U.S. wireless phones make them more attractive to British consumers and businesses, then the British will supply more pounds in the exchange market to purchase more U.S. wireless phones. The supply-of-pounds curve will shift to the right, causing the pound to depreciate and the dollar to appreciate.

In contrast, the U.S. demand-for-pounds curve will shift to the right if British woolen apparel becomes more fashionable in the United States. So the pound will appreciate and the dollar will depreciate.

Relative Income Changes A nation's currency is likely to depreciate if its growth of national income is more rapid than that of other countries. Here's why: A country's imports vary directly with its income level. As national income rises in the United States, Americans will buy both more domestic goods and more foreign goods. If the U.S. economy is expanding rapidly and the British economy is stagnant, U.S. imports of British goods, and therefore U.S. demands for pounds, will increase. The dollar price of pounds will rise, so the dollar will depreciate.

Relative Inflation Rate Changes Other things equal, changes in the relative rates of inflation of two nations change their relative price levels and alter the exchange rate between their currencies. The currency of the nation with the higher inflation rate—the more rapidly rising price level—tends to depreciate. Suppose, for example, that inflation is zero percent in Great Britain and 5 percent in the United States so that prices, on average, are rising by 5 percent per year in the United States while, on average, remaining unchanged in Great Britain. U.S. consumers will seek out more of the now relatively lower-priced British goods, increasing the demand for pounds. British consumers will purchase less of the now relatively higher-priced U.S. goods, reducing the supply of pounds. This combination of increased demand for pounds and reduced supply of pounds will cause the pound to appreciate and the dollar to depreciate.

According to the **purchasing-power-parity theory,** exchange rates should eventually adjust such that they equate the purchasing power of various currencies. If a certain market basket of identical products costs $10,000 in the United States and £5,000 in Great Britain, the exchange rate should move to $2 = £1. That way, a dollar spent in the United States will buy exactly as much output as it would if it were first converted to pounds (at the $2 = £1 exchange rate) and used to buy output in Great Britain.

In terms of our example, 5 percent inflation in the United States will increase the price of the market basket from $10,000 to $10,500, while the zero percent inflation in Great Britain will leave the market basket priced at £5,000. For purchasing power parity to hold, the exchange rate would have to move from $2 = £1 to $2.10 = £1. That means the dollar therefore would depreciate and the pound would appreciate. In practice, however, not all exchange rates move precisely to equate the purchasing power of various currencies and thereby achieve "purchasing power parity," even over long periods.

Relative Interest Rates Changes in relative interest rates between two countries may alter their exchange rate. Suppose that real interest rates rise in the United States but stay constant in Great Britain. British citizens will then find the United States a more attractive place in which to loan money directly or loan money indirectly by buying bonds. To make these loans, they will have to supply pounds in the foreign exchange market to obtain dollars. The increase in the supply of pounds results in depreciation of the pound and appreciation of the dollar.

Changes in Relative Expected Returns on Stocks, Real Estate, and Production Facilities International investing extends beyond buying foreign bonds. It includes international investments in stocks and real estate as well as foreign purchases of factories and production facilities. Other things equal, the extent of this foreign investment depends on relative expected returns. To make the investments, investors in one country must sell their currencies to purchase the foreign currencies needed for the foreign investments.

For instance, suppose that investing in England suddenly becomes more popular due to a more positive outlook regarding expected returns on stocks, real estate, and production facilities there. U.S. investors therefore will sell U.S. assets to buy more assets in England. The U.S. assets will be sold for dollars, which will then be brought to the foreign exchange market and exchanged for pounds, which will in turn be used to purchase British assets. The increased demand for pounds in the foreign exchange market will cause the pound to appreciate and therefore the dollar to depreciate relative to the pound.

Speculation Currency speculators are people who buy and sell currencies with an eye toward reselling or repurchasing them at a profit. Suppose speculators expect the U.S. economy to (1) grow more rapidly than the British economy and (2) experience more rapid inflation than Britain. These expectations translate into an anticipation that the pound will appreciate and the dollar will depreciate. Speculators who are holding dollars will therefore try to convert them into pounds. This effort will increase the demand for pounds and cause the dollar price of pounds to rise (that is, cause the dollar to depreciate). A self-fulfilling prophecy occurs: The pound appreciates and the dollar depreciates because speculators act on the belief that these changes will in fact take place. In this way, speculation can cause changes in exchange rates.

Table 35.2 has more illustrations of the determinants of exchange rates; the table is worth careful study.

Disadvantages of Flexible Exchange Rates

Flexible exchange rates may cause several significant problems. These are all related to the fact that flexible exchange rates are often volatile and can change by a large amount in

AP TABLE 35.2 Determinants of Exchange Rates: Factors That Change the Demand for or the Supply of a Particular Currency and Thus Alter the Exchange Rate

Determinant	Examples
Change in tastes	Japanese electronic equipment declines in popularity in the United States (Japanese yen depreciates; U.S. dollar appreciates).
	European tourists reduce visits to the United States (U.S. dollar depreciates; European euro appreciates).
Change in relative incomes	England encounters a recession, reducing its imports, while U.S. real output and real income surge, increasing U.S. imports (British pound appreciates; U.S. dollar depreciates).
Change in relative inflation rates	Switzerland experiences a 3% inflation rate compared to Canada's 10% rate (Swiss franc appreciates; Canadian dollar depreciates).
Change in relative real interest rates	The Federal Reserve drives up interest rates in the United States, while the Bank of England takes no such action (U.S. dollar appreciates; British pound depreciates).
Changes in relative expected returns on stocks, real estate, or production facilities	Corporate tax cuts in the United States raise expected after-tax investment returns in the United States relative to those in Europe (U.S. dollar appreciates; the euro depreciates).
Speculation	Currency traders believe South Korea will have much greater inflation than Taiwan (South Korean won depreciates; Taiwanese dollar appreciates).
	Currency traders think Norway's interest rates will plummet relative to Denmark's rates (Norway's krone depreciates; Denmark's krone appreciates).

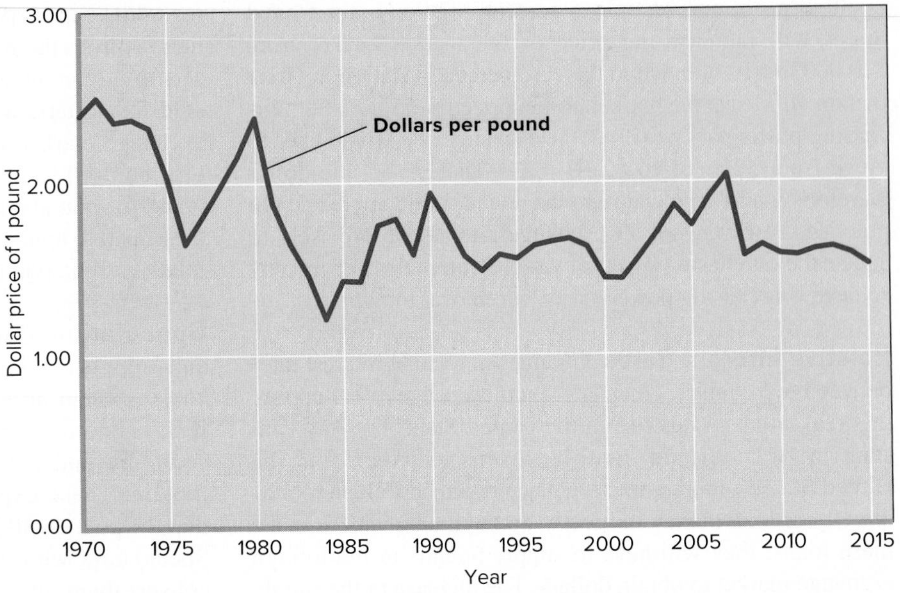

FIGURE 35.2 The dollar-pound exchange rate, 1970–2015. Before January 1971, the dollar-pound exchange rate was fixed at \$2.40 = £1. Since that time, its value has been determined almost entirely by market forces, with only occasional government interventions. Under these mostly flexible conditions, the dollar-pound exchange rate has varied considerably. For instance, in 1981 it took \$2.02 to buy a pound, but by 1985 only \$1.50 was needed to buy a pound. In contrast, between 2001 and 2007 the dollar price of a pound rose from \$1.44 to \$2.00, indicating that the dollar had depreciated relative to the pound. The dollar then sank back to \$1.57 per British pound in 2009 and remained at about that level through 2015.

Source: Economic Report of the President, 2015, Table B-110. Earlier years from prior *Economic Reports.*

just a few weeks or months. In addition, they often take substantial swings that can last several years or more. This can be seen in Figure 35.2, which plots the dollar-pound exchange rate from 1970 through 2016. [You can track other exchange rates, for example, the dollar-euro or dollar-yen rate, by going to the Federal Reserve website, **www.federalreserve.gov,** selecting Economic Research & Data, then Data Releases, and then clicking on "Foreign Exchange Rates (H.10/G.5)" under the heading that reads Exchange Rates and International Data.]

Uncertainty and Diminished Trade The risks and uncertainties associated with flexible exchange rates may discourage the flow of trade. Suppose a U.S. automobile dealer contracts to purchase 10 British cars for £150,000. At the current exchange rate of, say, \$2 for £1, the U.S. importer expects to pay \$300,000 for these automobiles. But if during the 3-month delivery period the rate of exchange shifts to \$3 for £1, the £150,000 payment contracted by the U.S. importer will be \$450,000.

That increase in the dollar price of pounds may thus turn the U.S. importer's anticipated profit into a substantial loss. Aware of the possibility of an adverse change in the exchange rate, the U.S. importer may not be willing to assume the risks involved. The U.S. firm may confine its operations to domestic automobiles, so international trade in this product will not occur.

The same thing can happen with investments. Assume that when the exchange rate is \$3 to £1, a U.S. firm invests \$30,000 (or £10,000) in a British enterprise. It estimates a return of 10 percent; that is, it anticipates annual earnings of \$3,000 or £1,000. Suppose these expectations prove correct in that the British firm earns £1,000 in the first year on the £10,000 investment. But suppose that during the year, the value of the dollar appreciates to \$2 = £1. The absolute return is now only \$2,000 (rather than \$3,000), and the rate of return falls from the anticipated 10 percent to only $6\frac{2}{3}$ percent (= \$2,000/\$30,000). Investment is risky in any case. The added risk of changing exchange rates may persuade the U.S. investor not to venture overseas.

Terms-of-Trade Changes A decline in the international value of its currency will worsen a nation's terms of trade. For example, an increase in the dollar price of a pound will mean that the United States must export more goods and services to finance a specific level of imports from Britain.

Instability Flexible exchange rates may destabilize the domestic economy because wide fluctuations stimulate and then depress industries producing exported goods. If the U.S. economy is operating at full employment and its currency depreciates, the results will be inflationary, for two reasons. (1) Foreign demand for U.S. goods may rise, increasing total spending and pulling up U.S. prices. Also, the prices of all U.S. imports will increase. (2) Conversely, appreciation of the dollar will lower U.S. exports and increase imports, possibly causing unemployment.

Flexible or floating exchange rates also may complicate the use of domestic stabilization policies in seeking full employment and price stability. This is especially true for nations whose exports and imports are large relative to their total domestic output.

AP QUICK REVIEW 35.3

- ✓ Under a flexible exchange rate system, exchange rates are determined by the demand for, and supply of, individual national currencies in the foreign exchange market.
- ✓ Determinants of flexible exchange rates (factors that shift currency supply and demand curves) include (a) changes in tastes; (b) relative national incomes; (c) relative inflation rates; (d) real interest rates; (e) relative expected returns on stocks, real estate, and production facilities; and (f) speculation.
- ✓ The volatility of flexible exchange rates can have some negative consequences, including discouraging international trade, worsening a nation's terms of trade, and destabilizing a nation's domestic economy by depressing export industries.

Fixed Exchange Rates

LO35.4 Describe the differences between flexible and fixed exchange rates, including how changes in foreign exchange reserves bring about automatic changes in the domestic money supply under a fixed exchange rate.

To circumvent the disadvantages of flexible exchange rates, governments have at times fixed or "pegged" their exchange rates. Under a fixed exchange rate, the government stands ready to buy and sell as much currency as is demanded or supplied at the constant (fixed) exchange rate that it announces.

To see how this works, suppose that the U.S. government decides to fix the dollar-pound exchange rate at \$2 = £1. To enforce that peg, the U.S. government must stand ready to exchange both pounds for dollars as well as dollars for pounds at the fixed ratio of \$2 = £1. If Americans want to exchange \$20 billion for pounds, the U.S. government will need to come up with £10 billion pounds (= the required number of pounds at the \$2 = £1 exchange rate). And if Britons wish to exchange £6 billion for dollars, the U.S. government will have to come up with \$12 billion dollars (= required number of dollars at the \$2 = £1 exchange rate).

Foreign Exchange Market Replaced by Government Peg

As long as the U.S. government is able to come up with the necessary amounts of both dollars (to satisfy exchange requests for pounds) and pounds (to satisfy exchange requests for dollars), the fixed exchange rate will preempt the foreign exchange market. All buying and selling of pounds for dollars or dollars for pounds will take place with the U.S. government. The U.S. government will *become* the dollar-pound foreign exchange market.

There will be no other dollar-pound market because, as long as the U.S. government can maintain the peg, there will be no other exchange rate that buyers and sellers would both simultaneously prefer, and thus no possibility of a given buyer and a given seller ever voluntarily agreeing to exchange dollars for pounds at any other exchange rate. To see why, consider an exchange rate like \$3 = £1. U.K. citizens wishing to convert pounds to dollars would prefer \$3 = £1 to the \$2 = £1 exchange rate being offered by the U.S. government because each of their pounds would convert into \$3 rather than \$2. But would U.K. citizens be able to find anyone willing to take the opposite end of the deal and exchange dollars for pounds at a \$3 = £1 exchange rate? The answer is no because anyone wishing to convert dollars to pounds would be able to go to the U.S. government and exchange money at the rate of \$2 = £1, under which they would only have to give up \$2 (rather than \$3) to buy £1. So while U.K. citizens would prefer any exchange rate that gives them more dollars per pound than the \$2 = £1 rate being offered by the U.S. government, they are not going to find anybody willing to exchange money at those rates. So anybody who wants to exchange pounds for dollars will end up dealing with the U.S. government and exchanging money at the \$2 = £1 fixed rate.

You should take a moment to convince yourself that the reverse is also true: While Americans would prefer an exchange rate that requires them to give up less that \$2 for each £1, no U.K. citizen would willingly accept a rate lower than \$2 = £1 because doing so would mean receiving fewer dollars for their pounds than if they exchanged their pounds at the \$2 = £1 exchange rate being offered by the U.S. government. So everyone wishing to exchange dollars for pounds will also end up dealing with the U.S. government and exchanging money at the \$2 = £1 fixed exchange rate.

Please note, however, that if the U.S. government were ever to stop honoring its pledge to exchange dollars for pounds and pounds for dollars at the \$2 = £1 exchange rate, a private market for foreign exchange would instantly pop back into existence to connect the buyers and sellers of dollars and pounds. Because the exchange rate would be determined by supply and demand, it could end up at an equilibrium value that is substantially different from the value of the fixed exchange rate that was just abandoned.

Official Reserves

A government that opts for a fixed exchange rate typically places its central bank in charge of day-to-day operations. It thus becomes the central bank's task to exchange as much local currency for foreign currency and as much foreign currency for local currency as is necessary each day to maintain the peg.

Satisfying requests to exchange foreign currency for local currency is easy, as the central bank has the legal right to print up as much local currency as it wants. But to satisfy requests to exchange local currency for foreign currency, the central bank must maintain a stock (inventory) of foreign currency since it can't legally create additional units of any other country's money.

The stock of the particular foreign currency that is used to maintain the fixed exchange rate will be just one component of the **official reserves** that the central bank will maintain for the government. The official reserves will consist not only of stockpiles of various foreign currencies but also stockpiles of bonds issued by foreign governments, gold reserves, and special reserves held at the International Monetary Fund. The stockpiles of foreign currencies are referred to as **foreign-exchange reserves,** or, less formally, FX reserves.

The Sizes of Currency Purchases and Sales

The amount of foreign and local currency that the central bank will have to buy and sell each day will depend on supply and demand. Consider Figure 35.3, in which we assume that the Fed is fixing the dollar-pound exchange rate at $2 = £1.

Begin by looking at the intersection of demand curve D_1 with supply curve S_1. If this were a free market, the equilibrium exchange rate (determined by where D_1 intersects S_1) would be equal to $2 = £1. But because the Fed is preempting the market by guaranteeing to exchange as many pounds for dollars and as many dollars for pounds as anyone might want to exchange at a price of $2 = £1, there will be no free market for foreign exchange. Instead, the Fed will act as a monopoly currency dealer (middleman) on all currency transactions. It will buy from those who wish to sell and sell to those who wish to buy.

In undertaking those sales, the Fed will find that its reserve of pounds will either remain constant, rise, or fall, depending upon the positions of the demand and supply curves.

FX Reserves Are Constant When Purchases Equal Sales If the demand and supply curves for pounds happen to intersect at the $2 = £1 value of the fixed exchange rate, the Fed's reserve of pounds will remain unchanged in size. This situation is illustrated in Figure 35.3. Demand curve D_1 happens to intersect supply curve S_1 at the fixed exchange rate of $2 = £1. That implies that the quantity supplied of pounds and the quantity demanded of pounds will both equal b at the fixed exchange rate of $2 = £1. So the Fed will be buying and selling an equal number of pounds, which implies that its reserve of pounds will remain constant.

FX Reserves Increase When Sales Exceed Purchases Next, imagine a situation in which the quantity demanded of pounds at the fixed exchange rate exceeds the quantity supplied of pounds at the fixed exchange rate. That happens in Figure 35.3 when the demand curve shifts left to

FIGURE 35.3 Fixed exchange rate with increasing foreign exchange reserves. To maintain a fixed exchange rate of $2 = £1, the central bank will have to buy whatever amount of pounds sellers supply at that price and sell whatever amount of pounds buyers demand at that price. If the demand curve for pounds shifts left to D_0, the quantity of pounds a that the central bank will have to sell to buyers at the fixed exchange rate will be less than the quantity of pounds b that the central bank will have to buy from sellers at that price. The central bank's reserve of pounds will consequently increase by amount ab. Not shown: As the reserve of pounds increases, so will the domestic money supply of dollars.

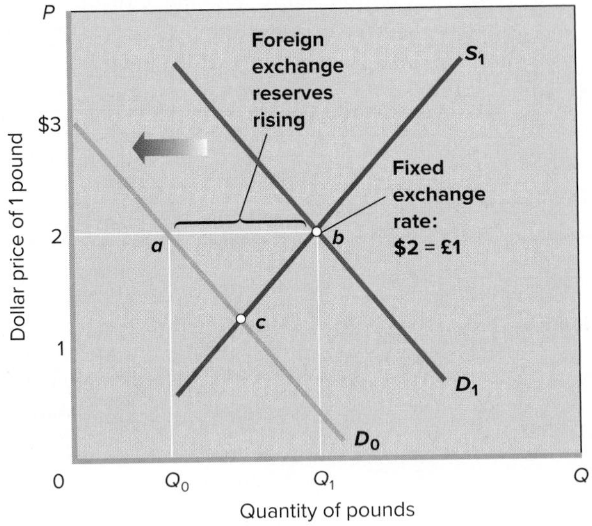

D_0 while the supply curve remains at S_1. In this situation, the Fed will *not* be exchanging equal quantities of pounds for dollars and dollars for pounds. At the fixed $2 = £1 exchange rate, the quantity demanded of pounds along demand curve D_0 will be a while the quantity supplied of pounds along supply curve S_1 will be b. There will be an excess supply of pounds ab that the Fed will end up owning.

That happens because Fed must satisfy both the buyers' desire to purchase a pounds for dollars and the sellers' desire to sell b pounds for dollars. After satisfying both of those desires, the Fed will find that its reserve of pounds has increased by the amount ab since it will have bought more pounds from suppliers than it sold to demanders. *The general rule is that if the quantity supplied of the foreign currency exceeds the quantity demanded at the fixed exchange rate, the central bank will accumulate foreign currency reserves as it accommodates the excess supply.*

Increasing Reserves = Increasing Domestic Money Supply There is a flip side to accumulating foreign currency reserves: The net amount of local currency will also be increasing. This is because when the Fed buys ab more pounds than it sells, it will have to pay for those extra ab pounds by printing up dollars. Those new dollars initially go into the hands of the people who converted pounds into dollars. But as those people spend the newly created dollars for American goods, services, and assets, the general level of prices will tend to rise. Other things equal, rising reserves are inflationary.

Locating Increasing Reserves in the Balance of Payments Increases in foreign exchange reserves appear as a negative (–) item in the U.S. balance of payments statement, specifically as U.S. purchases of foreign assets (line 13 of Table 35.1). Increases in FX reserves are a debit because they represent an outflow of dollars.

Please note that in addition to the possibility of obtaining increased FX reserves as part of a fixed exchange rate regime (as in Figure 35.3), central banks and national governments may also increase FX reserves (whether or not they are pegging the exchange rate) by purchasing foreign currency with either domestic tax revenues or by printing up additional domestic currency. Those increases would also go into line 13 as a negative item.

FX Reserves Decrease When Purchases Exceed Sales Consider Figure 35.4, which reproduces demand curve D_1 and supply curve S_1 from Figure 35.3, but in which we now have a rightward shift of the demand curve from D_1 to D_2. At the fixed exchange rate of \$2 = £1, there will now be more pounds demanded *d* than there will be pounds supplied *b*. As a result of this shortage of pounds, the Fed will find that its reserve of pounds will decrease by *bd* as it sells more pounds for dollars (point *d* along demand curve D_2) than it buys pounds for dollars (point *b* along supply curve S_1). *The general rule is that if the quantity demanded of the foreign currency exceeds the quantity supplied at the fixed exchange rate, the central bank will shed foreign currency reserves as it accommodates the excess demand.*

FIGURE 35.4 Fixed exchange rate with decreasing foreign exchange reserves. To maintain a fixed exchange rate of \$2 = £1, the central bank will have to buy whatever amount of pounds sellers supply at that price and sell whatever amount of pounds buyers demand at that price. If the demand curve for pounds shifts right to D_2, the quantity of pounds *d* that the central bank will have to sell to buyers at the fixed exchange rate will be less than the quantity of pounds *b* that the central bank will have to buy from sellers. The central bank's reserve of pounds will consequently decrease by amount *bd*. Not shown: As the reserve of pounds decreases, so will the domestic money supply of dollars.

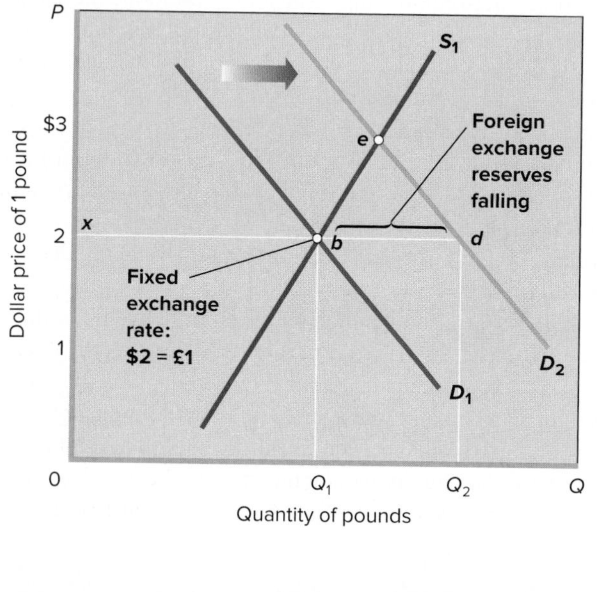

Decreasing Reserves = Decreasing Domestic Money Supply The fall in pound reserves will automatically cause a decrease in the supply of dollars in the U.S. economy because as the Fed sells more pounds than it buys, it will receive more dollars in payment for the *d* pounds that it sells than the number of dollars it has to pay for the *b* pounds that it buys. Because those extra dollars go into the Fed's vaults, they no longer circulate. So in situations such as the one shown in Figure 35.4, there will be fewer dollars flowing around the U.S. economy and thus a tendency for a lower overall price level. Other things equal, decreasing reserves are deflationary.

Locating Decreasing Reserves in the Balance of Payments Decreases in foreign exchange reserves appear as a plus (+) item in the U.S. balance of payments statement, specifically as foreign purchases of U.S. assets (line 12 of Table 35.1). The decreases are a credit because they represent an inflow of dollars.

Please note that in addition to FX reserves declining as part of a fixed exchange rate regime (as in Figure 35.4), central banks and national governments may also decrease FX reserves (whether or not they are fixing an exchange rate) by selling them in exchange for the local currency. Any such decreases would also go into line 12 as a positive item.

Small and Alternating Changes in FX Reserves and the Domestic Money Supply

If the periods of time when the Fed is buying more pounds than it sells (such as *ab* in Figure 35.3) alternate frequently enough with the periods of time when the Fed is selling more pounds than it buys (such as *bd* in Figure 35.4), then the Fed will not have to worry too much about inflation or deflation because any inflationary pressures caused by buying more pounds than it sells will be offset by deflationary pressures caused by selling more pounds than it buys. If the alternation is often enough and the number of dollars is small enough, then the changes in the domestic money supply caused by changes in FX reserves will have very little effect on the domestic price level.

It is also the case that if the periods of surplus and deficit in pound buying and selling alternate frequently enough or only involve modest quantities, the Fed will not have to worry about there being any long-term trend in the size of its pound reserves. The periods of buying more pounds will offset the periods of selling more pounds and the overall quantity of pound reserves will tend to stay about the same on average as time passes.

As a rule of thumb, the changes in both the domestic money supply and the size of the central bank's FX reserves will tend to be small and offsetting if the fixed exchange rate is close in value to the equilibrium exchange rate that would obtain if a free market determined the exchange rate. When the fixed rate is close to the equilibrium rate, any difference between the number of pounds sold and the number of pounds bought will tend to be small and, consequently, there will be little effect on either the domestic money supply or FX reserves.

Large and Continuous Changes in FX Reserves and the Domestic Money Supply

Major economic difficulties can arise if a nation's fixed exchange rate remains either substantially above or substantially below the equilibrium exchange rate for a long period of time.

Large and Continuous Increases in FX Reserves and the Domestic Money Supply First imagine that the disequilibrium situation depicted in Figure 35.3 continued month after month and perhaps even year after year. With the fixed exchange rate substantially above the equilibrium exchange rate determined by where demand curve D_0 intersects supply curve S_1, both FX reserves and the local money supply will increase substantially. The continual increase in the local money supply will impel inflation.

If the anticipated increase in inflation is only modest, the central bank may choose to do nothing in response, and just allow the resulting inflation to occur. But if the injections of new dollars are likely to cause too large an increase in inflation, the central bank will have to either:

- Reset the peg lower (at, say, $1.9 = £1 in Figure 35.3) so that the peg moves closer to the equilibrium exchange rate and thereby reduces the volume of new-dollar creation.
- Abandon the peg altogether so that the equilibrium exchange rate (point *c* in Figure 35.3) would prevail and new-dollar creation would halt.
- Keep the peg the same, but offset the *ab* dollars created in Figure 35.3 with other policy interventions that reduce the domestic money supply. These **sterilization** operations can be accomplished by using either open market operations to sell bonds for dollars or by increasing the banking system's reserve requirements so as to limit the creation of checkable-deposit money. The amount of sterilization will depend upon the central bank's preferences. It can range from just a few dollars all the way up to a complete offset of *ab*. (See the nearby Consider This piece for an example of sterilization in action.)

CONSIDER THIS . . .

Source: © RubberBall Productions/Getty Images RF

China's Inflationary Peg

China's economy boomed in the 1990s and 2000s after it abandoned communism for a market-based economy. China also fixed the value of its currency, the yuan, against the dollar and other foreign currencies to insulate local exporters and investors against exchange rate movements.

The peg that China chose was consistently below the free market equilibrium exchange rate throughout the 2000s so that China's foreign exchange reserves ballooned from just $165 billion in 2000 to a peak of just over $4 trillion in 2014.

China did attempt to gradually reset the peg lower, dropping the fixed exchange rate from about 8.3 yuan = $1 in the early 2000s to about 6.2 yuan = $1 by 2014. But because the yuan price of a dollar remained higher than equilibrium, China aroused accusations in other countries of unfairly subsidizing its export industries by making the yuan artificially cheap.

China also ensured substantial inflationary pressures at home as the number of yuan soared along with the increasing mountain of FX reserves. Inflation spiked as high as 8 percent despite aggressive sterilization efforts and an increase in the reserve ratio for bank lending from 6 percent to 21.5 percent, which left China with the highest reserve ratio by far of any major economy.

Large and Continuous Decreases in FX Reserves and the Domestic Money Supply There is an important difference between having large and continuous increases in FX reserves and the domestic money supply on the one hand (Figure 35.3) and having large and continuous decreases in FX reserves and the domestic money supply on the other hand (Figure 35.4). The difference is caused by the fact that a country's central bank can only legally print the domestic currency. It has no right to print any other country's currency. So if its FX reserves are declining, it cannot simply print up more foreign money to make up for an ongoing decline in its FX reserves.

If the central bank finds itself continually in a situation like Figure 35.4, it has to face the reality that its FX reserves might soon be exhausted. If that were to happen, the country would have to abandon its peg and allow the exchange rate to adjust to its free-market equilibrium value. That might not be a catastrophe, but it would mean that the local economy would have to begin dealing with the volatility and risk associated with a flexible exchange rate. If the central bank wishes to avoid those problems, it will have to figure out a way to either halt, or at least slow, the decline in FX reserves.

One way for the central bank to reduce the rate at which its FX reserves are running out is to reset the peg higher (to, say, \$2.25 = £1 in Figure 35.4). Resetting the peg higher moves the peg closer to the equilibrium exchange rate and thereby reduces the rate at which the central bank's foreign exchange reserves are falling.

Please note, however, that resetting the peg at a higher value will only *slow* the decline in FX reserves if the new value remains below the free-market equilibrium exchange rate. So it is important to consider the policy measures that could be taken to prevent the total exhaustion of the country's FX reserves if the peg cannot be reset all the way up to the free-market equilibrium value.

Trade Policies To maintain a fixed exchange rate, a nation can try to control the flow of trade and finance directly. The United States could try to maintain the \$2 = £1 exchange rate in the face of a shortage of pounds by discouraging imports (thereby reducing the demand for pounds) and encouraging exports (thus increasing the supply of pounds). Imports could be reduced by means of new tariffs or import quotas; special taxes could be levied on the interest and dividends U.S. financial investors receive from foreign investments. Also, the U.S. government could subsidize certain U.S. exports to increase the supply of pounds.

The fundamental problem is that these policies reduce the volume of world trade and change its makeup from what is economically desirable. When nations impose tariffs, quotas, and the like, they lose some of the economic benefits of a free flow of world trade. That loss should not be underestimated: Trade barriers by one nation lead to retaliatory responses from other nations, multiplying the loss.

Exchange Controls and Rationing Another option is to adopt rationing via exchange controls (which are also sometimes referred to as capital controls). Under **exchange controls,** the U.S. government could handle the problem of a pound shortage by requiring that all pounds obtained by U.S. exporters be sold to the federal government. Then the government would allocate or ration this short supply of pounds (represented by *xb* in Figure 35.4) among various U.S. importers, who demand the quantity *xd*. This policy would restrict the value of U.S. imports to the amount of foreign exchange earned by U.S. exports. Assuming balance in the capital and financial account, there would then be no balance-of-payments deficit. U.S. demand for British imports with the value *bd* would simply not be fulfilled.

There are major objections to exchange controls:

- ***Distorted trade*** Like *trade controls* (tariffs, quotas, and export subsidies), exchange controls would distort the pattern of international trade away from the pattern suggested by comparative advantage.
- ***Favoritism*** The process of rationing scarce foreign exchange might lead to government favoritism toward selected importers (big contributors to reelection campaigns, for example).
- ***Restricted choice*** Controls would limit freedom of consumer choice. The U.S. consumers who prefer Volkswagens might have to buy Chevrolets. The business opportunities for some U.S. importers might be impaired if the government were to limit imports.
- ***Black markets*** Enforcement problems are likely under exchange controls. U.S. importers might want foreign exchange badly enough to pay more than the \$2 = £1 official rate, setting the stage for black-market dealings between importers and illegal sellers of foreign exchange.

Domestic Macroeconomic Adjustments A final way to maintain a fixed exchange rate would be to use domestic stabilization policies (monetary policy and fiscal policy) to eliminate the shortage of foreign currency. Tax hikes, reductions in government spending, and a high-interest-rate policy would reduce total spending in the U.S. economy and, consequently, domestic income. Because the volume of imports varies directly with domestic income, demand for British goods, and therefore for pounds, would be restrained.

If these "contractionary" policies served to reduce the domestic price level relative to Britain's, U.S. buyers of consumer and capital goods would divert their demands from British goods to U.S. goods, reducing the demand for pounds. Moreover, the high-interest-rate policy would lift U.S. interest rates relative to those in Britain.

Lower prices on U.S. goods and higher U.S. interest rates would increase British imports of U.S. goods and would increase British financial investment in the United States. Both developments would increase the supply of pounds. The combination of a decrease in the demand for and an increase in the supply of pounds would reduce or eliminate the original U.S. balance-of-payments deficit. In Figure 35.4, the new supply and demand curves would intersect at some new equilibrium point on line *bd*, where the exchange rate remains at \$2 = £1.

Maintaining fixed exchange rates by such means is hardly appealing. The "price" of exchange-rate stability for the United States would be a decline in output, employment, and price levels—in other words, a recession. Eliminating a balance-of-payments deficit and achieving domestic stability are both important national economic goals, but to sacrifice macroeconomic stability simply to defend a currency peg would be to let the tail wag the dog. This chapter's Last Word discusses these concerns in the context of the European monetary union, which can be thought of as a system of permanently fixed exchange rates.

Confusing Payments Terminology

We know that a nation's balance of payments must always balance. It therefore is understandably confusing when economists or the press occasionally refer to a decrease of FX reserves in a country with a fixed exchange rate as a "balance of payments deficit" or an increase of FX reserves as a "balance of payments surplus." This unfortunate terminology often leads to inaccurate interpretations.

When a central bank fixes the exchange rate, all international payments (for trade, services, assets, remittances, etc.) will go through the central bank. If the quantities of foreign currency demanded and supplied aren't equal, the central bank's FX reserves will necessarily rise or fall, as you know from Figures 35.3 and 35.4.

Where FX reserves are rising, the "balance of payments surplus" terminology leads some people to falsely conclude that the United States is in some way "winning" a battle for international payments. After all, it is achieving a larger pile of wealth in the form of increased FX reserves.

What this mistaken interpretation misses is that the increase in FX reserves was not free. Anything gained by one country in terms of higher FX reserves had to be paid for by giving up assets, goods, or services *of an equal value* to another country. What looks like something achieved—a "balance of payments surplus"—results from a failure to account for the items that had to be given up to obtain the increase in FX reserves. This mistake in interpretation is equivalent to a coin dealer exchanging some rare Roman coins for euros but then only counting the increase in the number of euros in his cash box. That would be foolish because he will be failing to account for the fact that he now has fewer rare Roman coins in his possession. Euros were gained, but Roman coins were lost.

So don't be misled by this confusing terminology if you hear or read it. A **balance of payments deficit** is simply a decrease in FX reserves within the overall balance of payments that takes place when a country on a fixed exchange rate is forced to sell FX reserves in order to maintain its currency peg. A **balance of payments surplus** is simply an increase in FX reserves within the overall balance of payments that takes place when a country on a fixed exchange rate is forced to buy FX reserves in order to maintain its currency peg. The balance of payments will always balance. Any increase or decrease in FX reserves in lines 12 or 13 of the Capital and Financial Account in Table 35.1 will be exactly offset by one or more entries of the same total size, but of the opposite sign in lines 1 through 9 of the Current Account. Flows of goods, services, and transfer payments will perfectly offset any increase or decrease in the stock of FX reserves.

AP QUICK REVIEW 35.4

- ✓ To circumvent the disadvantages of flexible exchange rates, at times nations have fixed or "pegged" their exchange rates.
- ✓ Under a system of fixed exchange rates, nations set their exchange rates and then maintain them by buying or selling official reserves of currencies, establishing trade barriers, employing exchange controls, or incurring inflation or recession.
- ✓ Under a fixed exchange rate, any increase (decrease) in foreign exchange reserves will automatically generate an accompanying increase (decrease) in the domestic money supply that can cause inflation (deflation) unless it is offset by other policy actions, such as sterilization.

The Current Exchange Rate System: The Managed Float

LO35.5 Explain the current system of managed floating exchange rates.

Over the past 130 years, the world's nations have used three different exchange-rate systems. From 1879 to 1934, most nations used a gold standard, which implicitly created fixed exchange rates. From 1944 to 1971, most countries participated in the Bretton Woods system, which was a fixed-exchange-rate system indirectly tied to gold. And since 1971, most have used managed floating exchange rates, which mix mostly flexible exchange rates with occasional **currency interventions** during which a government buys or sells foreign exchange in the foreign exchange market in order to alter either supply or demand in a way that will push the exchange rate in the direction the government wants. Naturally, our focus here is on the current exchange-rate system. However, the history of the previous systems and why they broke down is highly fascinating.

The current international exchange-rate system (1971–present) is an "almost" flexible system called **managed floating exchange rates.** Exchange rates among major currencies are free to float to their equilibrium market levels, but nations occasionally use currency interventions in the foreign exchange market to stabilize or alter market exchange rates.

Normally, the major trading nations allow their exchange rates to float up or down to equilibrium levels based on supply and demand in the foreign exchange market. They recognize that changing economic conditions among nations require continuing changes in equilibrium exchange rates. They rely on freely operating foreign exchange markets to accomplish the necessary adjustments. The result has been considerably more volatile exchange rates than those during the Bretton Woods era.

But nations also recognize that certain trends in the movement of equilibrium exchange rates may be at odds with national or international objectives. On occasion, nations therefore intervene in the foreign exchange market by buying or selling large amounts of specific currencies. This way, they can "manage" or stabilize exchange rates by influencing currency demand and supply. In some cases, the interventions are sterilized via open market operations to prevent any change in the domestic money supply.

The current exchange-rate system is thus an "almost" flexible exchange-rate system. The "almost" refers mainly to the occasional currency interventions by governments; it also refers to the fact that the actual system is more complicated than described. While the major currencies such as dollars, euros, pounds, and yen fluctuate in response to changing supply and demand, some developing nations peg their currencies to the dollar and allow their currencies to fluctuate with it against other currencies. Also, some nations peg the value of their currencies to a "basket" or group of other currencies.

How well has the managed float worked? It has both proponents and critics.

In Support of the Managed Float Proponents of the managed-float system argue that it has functioned far better than many experts anticipated. Skeptics had predicted that fluctuating exchange rates would reduce world trade and finance. But in real terms, world trade under the managed float has grown tremendously over the past several decades. Moreover, as supporters are quick to point out, currency crises such as those in Mexico and southeast Asia in the last half of the 1990s were not the result of the floating-exchange-rate system itself. Rather, the abrupt currency devaluations and depreciations resulted from internal problems in those nations, in conjunction with the nations' tendency to peg their currencies to the dollar or to a basket of currencies. In some cases, flexible exchange rates would have made these adjustments far more gradual.

Proponents also point out that the managed float has weathered severe economic turbulence that might have caused a fixed-rate system to break down. Such events as extraordinary oil price increases in 1973–1974 and again in 1981–1983, inflationary recessions in several nations in the mid-1970s, major national recessions in the early 1980s, and large U.S. budget deficits in the 1980s and the first half of the 1990s all caused substantial imbalances in international trade and finance, as did the large U.S. budget deficits and soaring world oil prices that occurred in the middle of the first decade of the 2000s. The U.S. financial crisis and the severe recession of 2007–2009 greatly disrupted world trade. Flexible rates enabled the system to adjust to all these events, whereas the same events would have put unbearable pressures on a fixed-rate system.

Concerns with the Managed Float There is still much sentiment in favor of greater exchange-rate stability. Those favoring more stable exchange rates see problems with the current system. They argue that the excessive volatility of exchange rates under the managed float threatens the prosperity of economies that rely heavily on exports. Several financial crises in individual nations (for example, Mexico, South Korea, Indonesia, Thailand, Russia, and Brazil) were exacerbated by abrupt changes in exchange rates. These crises have led to massive "bailouts" of those economies via loans from the International Monetary Fund (IMF). But the availability of IMF bailouts may spur moral hazard. Nations may undertake risky and inappropriate economic policies because they expect the IMF to bail them out if problems arise. Moreover, some exchange-rate volatility has occurred even when underlying economic and financial conditions were relatively stable, suggesting that speculation plays too large a role in determining exchange rates.

Skeptics say the managed float is basically a "nonsystem" because the guidelines as to what each nation may or may not do with its exchange rates are not specific enough to keep the system working in the long run. Nations inevitably will be tempted to intervene in the foreign exchange market, not merely to smooth out short-term fluctuations in exchange rates but to prop up their currency if it is chronically weak or to manipulate the exchange rate to achieve domestic stabilization goals.

So what are we to conclude? Flexible exchange rates have not worked perfectly, but they have not failed miserably. Thus far they have survived, and no doubt have eased, several major shocks to the international trading system. Meanwhile, the "managed" part of the float has given nations some sense of control over their collective economic destinies. On balance, most economists favor continuation of the present system of "almost" flexible exchange rates.

AP QUICK REVIEW 35.5

- ✓ The managed floating system of exchange rates (1971–present) relies on foreign exchange markets to establish equilibrium exchange rates.
- ✓ Under the system, nations can buy and sell official reserves of foreign currency to stabilize short-term changes in exchange rates or to correct exchange-rate imbalances that are negatively affecting the world economy.
- ✓ Proponents point out that international trade and investment have grown tremendously under the system. Critics say that it is a "nonsystem" and argue that the exchange rate volatility allowed under the managed float discourages international trade and investment. That is, trade and investment would be even larger if exchange rates were more stable.

AP Recent U.S. Trade Deficits

LO35.6 Identify the causes and consequences of recent U.S. trade deficits.

As shown in Figure 35.5a, the United States has experienced large and persistent trade deficits in recent years. These deficits rose rapidly between 2002 and 2006, with the trade deficit on goods and services peaking at $761 billion in 2006.

FIGURE 35.5 U.S. trade deficits, 2002–2015. (a) The United States experienced large deficits in *goods* and in *goods and services* between 2002 and 2012. (b) The U.S. current account, generally reflecting the goods and services deficit, was also in substantial deficit. Although reduced significantly by the recession of 2007–2009, large current account deficits are expected to continue for many years to come.

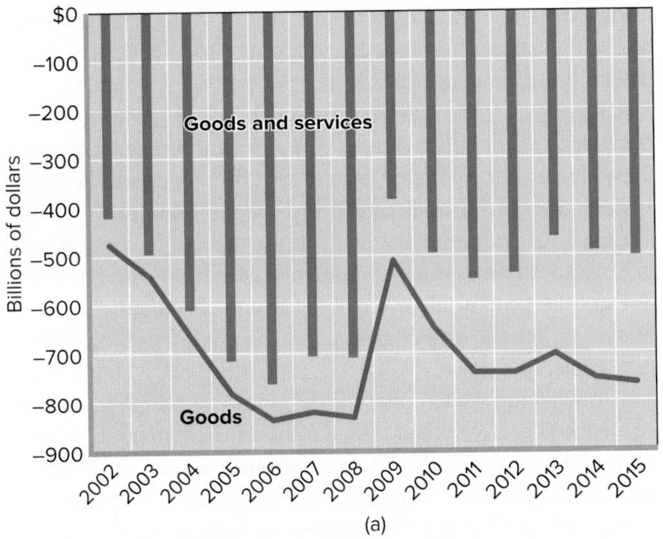

(a)
Balance of trade

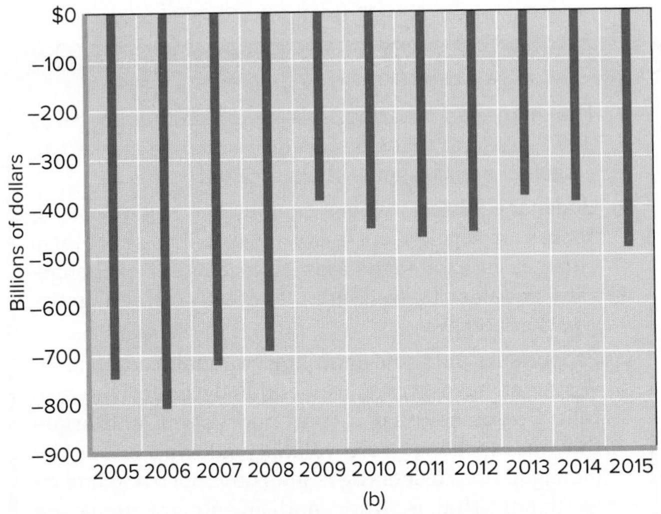

(b)
Balance on current account

Source: Bureau of Economic Analysis, **www.bea.gov.**

The trade deficit on goods and services then declined precipitously to just $383 billion in 2009 as consumers and businesses greatly curtailed their purchases of imports during the recession of 2007–2009. As the economy recovered from the recession, the trade deficit on goods and services began rising again and reached $500 billion in 2015. The current account deficit (Figure 35.5b) reached a record high of $800 billion in 2006, and that amount was 6.0 percent of GDP. The current account deficit declined to $382 billion—2.6 percent of GDP—in the recession year 2009. After the recession, the current account deficit expanded slowly, to $486 billion in 2015. But because GDP had also been growing, the 2015 current account deficit amounted to 2.7 percent of GDP, or about the same percentage as in 2009.

Causes of the Trade Deficits

The large U.S. trade deficits have several causes. First, the U.S. economy expanded more rapidly between 2002 and 2007 than the economies of several U.S. trading partners. The strong U.S. income growth that accompanied that economic growth enabled Americans to greatly increase their purchases of imported products. In contrast, Japan and some European nations suffered recession or experienced relatively slow income growth over that same period. So consumers in those countries increased their purchases of U.S. exports much less rapidly than Americans increased their purchases of foreign imports.

Another factor explaining the large trade deficits is the enormous U.S. trade imbalance with China. In 2015 the United States imported $366 billion more of goods and services from China than it exported to China. Even in the recession year 2009, the trade deficit with China was $220 billion. The 2015 deficit with China was 82 percent larger than the combined deficits with Mexico ($58 billion), Germany ($74 billion), and Japan ($69 billion). The United States is China's largest export market, and although China has greatly increased its imports from the United States, its standard of living has not yet risen sufficiently for its households to afford large quantities of U.S. products. Adding to the problem, China's government has fixed the exchange rate of its currency, the yuan, to a basket of currencies that includes the U.S. dollar. Therefore, China's large trade surpluses with the United States have not caused the yuan to appreciate much against the U.S. dollar. Greater appreciation of the yuan would have made Chinese goods more expensive in the United States and reduced U.S. imports from China. In China a stronger yuan would have reduced the dollar price of U.S. goods and increased Chinese purchases of U.S. exports. That combination—reduced U.S. imports from China and increased U.S. exports to China—would have reduced the large U.S. trade imbalance.

A declining U.S. saving rate (= saving/total income) also contributed to the large U.S. trade deficits. Up until the recession of 2007–2009, the U.S. saving rate declined substantially, while its investment rate (= investment/total income) increased. The gap between U.S. investment and U.S. saving was filled by foreign purchases of U.S. real and financial assets, which created a large surplus on the U.S. capital and financial account. Because foreign savers were willing to finance a large part of U.S. investment, Americans were able to save less and consume more. Part of that added consumption spending was on imported goods.

Finally, many foreigners simply view U.S. assets favorably because of the relatively high risk-adjusted rates of return they provide. The purchase of those assets provides foreign currency to Americans that enables them to finance their strong appetite for imported goods. The capital account surpluses, therefore, may partially cause the high U.S. trade deficits, not just result from those high deficits. The point is that the causes of the high U.S. trade deficits are numerous and not so easy to disentangle.

Implications of U.S. Trade Deficits

The prerecession U.S. trade deficits were the largest ever run by a major industrial nation. Whether the large trade deficits should be of significant concern to the United States and the rest of the world is debatable. Most economists see both benefits and costs to trade deficits.

Increased Current Consumption At the time a trade deficit or a current account deficit is occurring, American consumers benefit. A trade deficit means that the United States is receiving more goods and services as imports from abroad than it is sending out as exports. Taken alone, a trade deficit allows the United States to consume outside its production possibilities curve. It augments the domestic standard of living. But here is a catch: The gain in present consumption may come at the expense of reduced future consumption. When and if the current account deficit declines, Americans may have to consume less than before and perhaps even less than they produce.

Increased U.S. Indebtedness A trade deficit is considered unfavorable because it must be financed by borrowing from the rest of the world, selling off assets, or dipping into official reserves. Recall that current account deficits are financed by surpluses in the capital and financial accounts. Such surpluses require net inpayments of dollars to buy U.S. assets, including debt issued by Americans. Therefore, when U.S. exports are insufficient to finance U.S. imports, the United States increases both its debt to people abroad and the value of foreign claims against assets in the United States. Financing of the U.S. trade deficit has resulted in a larger foreign accumulation of claims against U.S. financial and real assets than the U.S. claim against foreign assets. In 2015, foreigners owned about $7.4 trillion more of U.S. assets (corporations, land, stocks, bonds, loan notes) than U.S. citizens and institutions owned of foreign assets.

If the United States wants to regain ownership of these domestic assets, at some future time it will have to export more than it imports. At that time, domestic consumption will be lower because the United States will need to send more of its output abroad than it receives as imports. Therefore, the current consumption gains delivered by U.S. current account deficits may mean permanent debt, permanent foreign ownership, or large sacrifices of future consumption.

We say "may mean" above because the foreign lending to U.S. firms and foreign investment in the United States increases the U.S. capital stock. U.S. production capacity therefore might increase more rapidly than otherwise because of a large surplus on the capital and financial account. Faster increases in production capacity and real GDP enhance the economy's ability to service foreign debt and buy back real capital, if that is desired.

Trade deficits therefore are a mixed blessing. The long-term impacts of the record-high U.S. trade deficits are largely unknown. That "unknown" worries some economists, who are concerned that foreigners will lose financial confidence in the United States. If that happens, they would restrict their lending to American households and businesses and also reduce their purchases of U.S. assets. Both actions would decrease the demand for U.S. dollars in the foreign exchange market and cause the U.S. dollar to depreciate. A sudden, large depreciation of the U.S. dollar might disrupt world trade and negatively affect economic growth worldwide. Other economists, however, downplay this scenario. Because any decline in the U.S. capital and financial account surplus is automatically met with a decline in the current account deficit, U.S. net exports would rise and the overall impact on the American economy would be slight.

AP QUICK REVIEW 35.6

- ✓ The United States has had large trade deficits and current account deficits in recent decades.
- ✓ Causes include (a) more rapid income growth in the United States than in Japan and some European nations, resulting in expanding U.S. imports relative to exports; (b) the emergence of a large trade deficit with China; (c) continuing large trade deficits with oil-exporting nations; and (d) a large surplus in the capital and financial account, which enabled Americans to reduce their saving and buy more imports.
- ✓ U.S. trade deficits have produced current increases in the living standards of U.S. consumers but the accompanying surpluses on the capital and financial account have increased U.S. debt to the rest of the world and increased foreign ownership of assets in the United States.

LAST WORD

Are Common Currencies Common Sense?

A Shared Currency Precludes Independent Monetary Policies and External Adjustments

When countries use different currencies, international trade is hampered by the deadweight cost of currency-conversion fees, difficulties comparing costs when prices are given in multiple currencies, and exchange-rate risk.

Taken together, these problems suggest a simple solution: Why not use the same currency?

The 19 nations that are members of the eurozone did just that, eliminating their respective local currencies in favor of the euro. When they did, cross-border trade and investment surged, improving the economic prospects of all member nations. Unfortunately, life is full of costs as well as benefits. So while the eurozone countries did dramatically improve international trade and investment among their members, they incurred two major costs.

Source: © Maryna Pleshkun/Shutterstock.com

The Loss of Independent Monetary Policy When a country joins the European Monetary Union, it retains its own central bank, but cedes control over monetary policy to the central authority of the European Central Bank (ECB). To see why this can be problematic, consider a situation in which eurozone member Slovakia is in a recession while the rest of Europe is booming. The ECB has to set a single policy for all members. Because the large majority have booming economies, the ECB will choose to either keep interest rates constant or even raise them—just the opposite of what recessionary Slovakia needs.

The same problem confronts countries such as Zimbabwe, Panama, and El Salvador that have opted to use the U.S. dollar. By switching to U.S. dollars, they have ceded control over monetary policy to the Fed—which will put zero weight on their various local business cycles when setting monetary policy and interest rates for the United States.

The Loss of External Adjustments A country that joins a currency union also loses the ability to maintain competitiveness in international trade by making "external adjustments" to its current account balance. As an example, suppose that Greek goods and services are expensive relative to those produced by other eurozone countries because Greece has restrictive labor laws, low industrial productivity, unnecessarily high tax rates, and a bloated and corrupt public sector. These high costs will tend to cause both a trade deficit and a current account deficit in Greece because Greek consumers will favor less expensive foreign imports while at the same time Greek exporters will be hampered by high production costs.

This situation is not overly problematic if the Greek economy is growing. But if a recession starts, it would be helpful for Greece to figure out a way to boost its competitiveness in international trade and thereby increase the aggregate demand for its goods and services.

If Greece had retained its own currency, the Greek government could simply intervene in the foreign exchange market and devalue the Greek currency. The devaluation would be equivalent to putting all Greek goods and services on sale simultaneously, thereby making them more attractive to foreign consumers. At the same time, the price of foreign goods in Greece would rise, thereby causing local consumers to substitute domestic goods and services for imports. Aggregate demand within Greece would increase. The current account would move toward surplus. The "external adjustment" of devaluation would help Greece with its recession.

But Greece can't devalue; it no longer has its own currency. It can't use the external adjustment of devaluation to help resolve its high costs and lack of competitiveness. Its only way forward will be "internal adjustments" in which changes in the domestic economy lower the Greek cost structure so as to make its products internationally competitive again.

The Greek government could attempt to lower taxes, liberalize labor laws, and reform the bloated and corrupt public sector. But in most countries, those sorts of "structural changes" will be difficult to implement because of strong resistance by special interests or because of prior spending commitments. If they cannot be implemented, a country like Greece will be left with only the most painful type of internal adjustment: a recession-induced deflation in which falling aggregate demand slowly leads to a lower domestic price level. The recession will end, but only after downward price stickiness is overcome and the price level falls by enough to induce consumers both at home and abroad to buy more Greek products.

SUMMARY

LO35.1 Explain how currencies of different nations are exchanged when international transactions take place.

International financial transactions involve trade either in currently produced goods and services or in preexisting assets. Exports of goods, services, and assets create inflows of money, while imports cause outflows of money. If buyers and sellers use different currencies, then foreign exchange transactions take place so that the exporter can be paid in his or her own currency.

LO35.2 Analyze the balance sheet the United States uses to account for the international payments it makes and receives.

The balance of payments records all international trade and financial transactions taking place between a given nation and the rest of the world. The balance on goods and services (the trade balance) compares exports and imports of both goods and services. The current account balance includes not only goods and services transactions but also net investment income and net transfers.

The capital and financial account includes (*a*) the net amount of the nation's debt forgiveness and (*b*) the nation's sale of real and financial assets to people living abroad less its purchases of real and financial assets from foreigners.

The current account and the capital and financial account always sum to zero. A deficit in the current account is always offset by a surplus in the capital and financial account. Conversely, a surplus in the current account is always offset by a deficit in the capital and financial account.

LO35.3 Discuss how exchange rates are determined in currency markets that have flexible exchange rates.

Flexible or floating exchange rates between international currencies are determined by the demand for and supply of those currencies. Under flexible rates, a currency will depreciate or appreciate as a result of changes in tastes, relative income changes, relative changes in inflation rates, relative changes in real interest rates, and speculation. But the fluctuations in the exchange rate that occur under a flexible exchange rate system introduce uncertainty that can reduce the volume of international trade and destabilize the local economy.

LO35.4 Describe the differences between flexible and fixed exchange rates, including how changes in foreign exchange reserves bring about automatic changes in the domestic money supply under a fixed exchange rate.

Some countries have their central banks fix, or peg, their exchange rates to a particular value in order to eliminate the uncertainty about future exchange rates that arises under a floating exchange rate system. Because fixing requires buying and selling foreign currencies, the central bank will maintain reserves (stockpiles) of various foreign currencies. Those foreign exchange (FX) reserves are a subset of a nation's overall collection of official reserves, which can include gold, foreign bonds, and special reserves held with the International Monetary Fund in addition to its holdings of FX reserves.

To maintain a fixed exchange rate, a central bank will simultaneously stand ready to sell as much foreign currency as buyers demand at the fixed exchange rate and buy as much foreign currency as sellers wish to supply at the fixed exchange rate. Those amounts will only be equal if the fixed exchange rate happens to equal the free-market exchange rate that would prevail if the country let the currency float. In other cases, the central bank's stockpile of foreign currency will either be rising or falling.

If FX reserves fall continuously, they may become exhausted. In such situations, the country will have to either abandon the peg, alter the peg, invoke protectionist trade policies, engage in exchange controls, or endure undesirable domestic macroeconomic adjustments.

Countries operating fixed exchange rates must also grapple with the fact that whenever the fixed exchange rate differs from the free-market exchange rate, the domestic money supply will be either rising or falling in tandem with its foreign currency (FX) reserves. That rise or fall in the domestic money supply will cause inflationary or deflationary pressures that policymakers will have to either accept or offset via open-market sterilization operations (bond purchases or sales) or changes in bank reserve ratios.

LO35.5 Explain the current system of managed floating exchange rates.

Since 1971 the world's major nations have used a system of managed floating exchange rates. Market forces generally set rates, although governments intervene with varying frequency to alter their exchange rates.

LO35.6 Identify the causes and consequences of recent U.S. trade deficits.

Between 1997 and 2007, the United States had large and rising trade deficits, which are projected to last well into the future. Causes of the trade deficits include (*a*) more rapid income growth in the United States than in Japan and some European nations, resulting in expanding U.S. imports relative to exports; (*b*) the emergence of a large trade deficit with China; (*c*) continuing large trade deficits with oil-exporting nations; and (*d*) a large surplus in the capital and financial account, which enabled Americans to reduce their saving and buy more imports. The severe recession of 2007–2009 in the United States substantially lowered the U.S. trade deficit by reducing American spending on imports.

U.S. trade deficits have produced current increases in the living standards of U.S. consumers. The accompanying surpluses on the capital and financial account have increased U.S. debt to the rest of the world and increased foreign ownership of assets in the United States. This greater foreign investment in the United States, however, has undoubtedly increased U.S. production possibilities.

TERMS AND CONCEPTS

balance of payments
current account
balance on goods and services
trade deficit
trade surplus
balance on current account
capital and financial account
balance on capital and financial account
flexible- or floating-exchange-rate system
fixed-exchange-rate system
purchasing-power-parity theory
official reserves
foreign exchange reserves
sterilization
exchange controls
balance of payments deficits
balance of payments surplus
currency interventions
managed floating exchange rates

The following and additional problems can be found in connect

DISCUSSION QUESTIONS

1. Do all international financial transactions necessarily involve exchanging one nation's distinct currency for another? Explain. Could a nation that neither imports goods and services nor exports goods and services still engage in international financial transactions? LO35.1
2. Explain: "U.S. exports earn supplies of foreign currencies that Americans can use to finance imports." Indicate whether each of the following creates a demand for or a supply of European euros in foreign exchange markets: LO35.1
   a. A U.S. airline firm purchases several Airbus planes assembled in France.
   b. A German automobile firm decides to build an assembly plant in South Carolina.
   c. A U.S. college student decides to spend a year studying at the Sorbonne in Paris.
   d. An Italian manufacturer ships machinery from one Italian port to another on a Liberian freighter.
   e. The U.S. economy grows faster than the French economy.
   f. A U.S. government bond held by a Spanish citizen matures, and the loan amount is paid back to that person.
   g. It is widely expected that the euro will depreciate in the near future.
3. What do the plus signs and negative signs signify in the U.S. balance-of-payments statement? Which of the following items appear in the current account and which appear in the capital and financial account? U.S. purchases of assets abroad; U.S. services imports; foreign purchases of assets in the United States; U.S. goods exports; U.S. net investment income. Why must the current account and the capital and financial account sum to zero? LO35.2
4. "Exports pay for imports. Yet in 2012 the nations of the world exported about $540 billion more of goods and services to the United States than they imported from the United States." Resolve the apparent inconsistency of these two statements. LO35.2
5. Generally speaking, how is the dollar price of euros determined? Cite a factor that might increase the dollar price of euros. Cite a different factor that might decrease the dollar price of euros. Explain: "A rise in the dollar price of euros necessarily means a fall in the euro price of dollars." Illustrate and elaborate: "The dollar-euro exchange rate provides a direct link between the prices of goods and services produced in the eurozone and in the United States." Explain the purchasing-power-parity theory of exchange rates, using the euro-dollar exchange rate as an illustration. LO35.3
6. Suppose that a Swiss watchmaker imports watch components from Sweden and exports watches to the United States. Also suppose the dollar depreciates, and the Swedish krona appreciates, relative to the Swiss franc. Speculate as to how each would hurt the Swiss watchmaker. LO35.3
7. Explain why the U.S. demand for Mexican pesos is downsloping and the supply of pesos to Americans is upsloping. Assuming a system of flexible exchange rates between Mexico and the United States, indicate whether each of the following would cause the Mexican peso to appreciate or depreciate, other things equal: LO35.3
   a. The United States unilaterally reduces tariffs on Mexican products.
   b. Mexico encounters severe inflation.
   c. Deteriorating political relations reduce American tourism in Mexico.
   d. The U.S. economy moves into a severe recession.
   e. The United States engages in a high-interest-rate monetary policy.
   f. Mexican products become more fashionable to U.S. consumers.
   g. The Mexican government encourages U.S. firms to invest in Mexican oil fields.
   h. The rate of productivity growth in the United States diminishes sharply.
8. Explain why you agree or disagree with the following statements. Assume other things equal. LO35.3
   a. A country that grows faster than its major trading partners can expect the international value of its currency to depreciate.
   b. A nation whose interest rate is rising more rapidly than interest rates in other nations can expect the international value of its currency to appreciate.
   c. A country's currency will appreciate if its inflation rate is less than that of the rest of the world.
9. Would it be accurate to think of a fixed exchange rate as a simultaneous price ceiling and price floor? LO35.2

10. What have been the major causes of the large U.S. trade deficits in recent years? What are the major benefits and costs associated with trade deficits? Explain: "A trade deficit means that a nation is receiving more goods and services from abroad than it is sending abroad." How can that be considered to be "unfavorable"? **LO35.6**

11. **LAST WORD** If a country like Greece that has joined the European Monetary Union can no longer use an independent monetary policy to offset a recession, what sorts of fiscal policy initiatives might it undertake? Give at least two examples.

AP REVIEW QUESTIONS

1. An American company wants to buy a television from a Chinese company. The Chinese company sells its TVs for 1,200 yuan each. The current exchange rate between the U.S. dollar and the Chinese yuan is $1 = 6 yuan. How many dollars will the American company have to convert into yuan to pay for the television? **LO35.1**
   - **a.** $7,200.
   - **b.** $1,200.
   - **c.** $200.
   - **d.** $100.
   - **e.** $60.
2. Assume a system of flexible exchange rates. Suppose that a country has a trade deficit of $50 billion, a balance on the capital (or financial) account of + $110 billion. What should be its balance on its current account over this time period? **LO35.2**
   - **a.** −$10 billion.
   - **b.** −$50 billion.
   - **c.** −$110 billion.
   - **d.** +$50 billion.
   - **e.** +$110 billion.
3. The exchange rate between the U.S. dollar and the British pound starts at $1 = £0.5. It then changes to $1 = £0.75. Given this change, we would say that the U.S. dollar has ____________ while the British pound has ____________. **LO35.3**
   - **a.** Depreciated; appreciated.
   - **b.** Depreciated; depreciated.
   - **c.** Appreciated; depreciated.
   - **d.** Appreciated; appreciated.
   - **e.** Not changed, appreciated.
4. U.S. export transactions create: **LO35.2**
   - **a.** A U.S. demand for foreign monies.
   - **b.** A U.S. demand for U.S. dollars.
   - **c.** A foreign demand for dollars.
   - **d.** A deficit (or negative entry) in the U.S. current account.
   - **e.** A foreign supply of dollars to get more of their local currencies.
5. Suppose that real interest rates fall sharply in the United States, but are unchanged in Great Britain. Other things equal, under a system of freely floating exchange rates, we can expect the demand for pounds in the United States to: **LO35.3**
   - **a.** Decrease, the supply of pounds to increase, and the dollar to appreciate relative to the pound.
   - **b.** Increase, the supply of pounds to increase, and the dollar may either appreciate or depreciate relative to the pound.
   - **c.** Increase, the supply of pounds to decrease, and the dollar to depreciate relative to the pound.
   - **d.** Decrease, the supply of pounds to increase, and the dollar to depreciate relative to the pound.
   - **e.** Remain unchanged, the supply of pounds to decrease and the pound to appreciate.
6. The U.S. demand for euros is: **LO35.3**
   - **a.** Downsloping, because, at lower dollar prices for euros, Americans will want to buy more European goods and services.
   - **b.** Downsloping, because, at higher dollar prices for euros, Americans will want to buy more European goods and services.
   - **c.** Downsloping, because the dollar price of euros and the euro price of dollars are directly related.
   - **d.** Upsloping, because a higher dollar price of euros makes European goods and services more attractive to Americans.
   - **e.** Upsloping, because, at higher dollar prices for euros, Americans will want to buy more European goods and services.
7. Indicate whether each of the following will increase or decrease the demand for dollars or increase or decrease the supply of dollars in foreign exchange markets. Note that in some cases both demand and supply can be affected. **LO35.3**
   - **a.** A desire by American to import more British goods.
   - **b.** An increase in income in the countries with whom the U.S. trades.
   - **c.** A decrease in the real interest rate in the United States.
   - **d.** An increase in the price level within the United States.
   - **e.** An increase in the number of U.S. students studying outside the United States.
   - **f.** A recession in the United States.
8. Draw a properly labeled graph of the market for Euros. Assume that the initial exchange rate is $1.15 per Euro. **LO35.3–35.5**
   - **a.** Assume there is an increase in real interest rates in the Euro zone. Will the demand for and/or supply of Euros change? Explain.
   - **b.** As a result of your answer to part (a), will the value of the Euro to the dollar change? If so, explain the change.
   - **c.** As a result of this change in the exchange rate, will European countries export more goods, the same amount of goods, or fewer goods? Explain.
   - **d.** Assume that the European central bank wishes to reverse the effect on the value of the Euro from the increase in real interest rates in the Euro zone. Will the Central bank buy or sell Euros? Buy or sell dollars? Explain.

9. Draw a properly labeled graph of the market for the dollar with the Yen price per dollar on the vertical axix. Assume that the initial exchange rate is 110 Japanese Yen per dollar. **LO35.3–35.5**
   - **a.** Assume that the Japanese economy expands and incomes increase. What will happened in this market for dollars? Explain.
   - **b.** What will happen to the Yen price per dollar?
   - **c.** As a result of this economic expansion in Japan. What will happen to aggregate demand in the United States?
   - **d.** Given the change in aggregate demand that you identified (part c.) for the U.S. economy, what should happen to real GDP, the price level, and unemployment in the short run in the United States? Explain.

10. Which of the following would represent a debit into the U.S. capital or financial account? **LO35.2**
    - **a.** Japanese investors purchase newly issued U.S. corporate bonds.
    - **b.** A U.S. firm purchases a new textile factory in Costa Rica.
    - **c.** A German firm imports new computers from a firm in the United States.
    - **d.** Korean investors pay dividends to American shareholders in Korean firms.
    - **e.** U.S. residents increase the amount of money they send to family members who live in another country.

PROBLEMS

1. Alpha's balance-of-payments data for 2016 are shown below. All figures are in billions of dollars. What are the (*a*) balance on goods, (*b*) balance on goods and services, (*c*) balance on current account, and (*d*) balance on capital and financial account? **LO35.2**

Goods exports	$+40
Goods imports	−30
Service exports	+15
Service imports	−10
Net investment income	−5
Net transfers	+10
Balance on capital account	0
Foreign purchases of Alpha assets	+20
Alpha purchases of assets abroad	−40

2. China had a $214 billion overall current account surplus in 2012. Assuming that China's net debt forgiveness was zero in 2012 (its capital account balance was zero), by how much did Chinese purchases of financial and real assets abroad exceed foreign purchases of Chinese financial and real assets? **LO35.2**

3. Refer to the following table, in which Q_d is the quantity of loonies demanded, P is the dollar price of loonies, Q_s is the quantity of loonies supplied in year 1, and Q_s' is the quantity of loonies supplied in year 2. All quantities are in billions and the dollar-loonie exchange rate is fully flexible. **LO35.3**

Q_d	P	Q_s	Q_s'
10	125	30	20
15	120	25	15
20	115	20	10
25	110	15	5

   - **a.** What is the equilibrium dollar price of loonies in year 1?
   - **b.** What is the equilibrium dollar price of loonies in year 2?
   - **c.** Did the loonie appreciate or did it depreciate relative to the dollar between years 1 and 2?
   - **d.** Did the dollar appreciate or did it depreciate relative to the loonie between years 1 and 2?
   - **e.** Which one of the following could have caused the change in relative values of the dollar (used in the United States) and the loonie (used in Canadia) between years 1 and 2: (1) More rapid inflation in the United States than in Canadia, (2) an increase in the real interest rate in the United States but not in Canadia, or (3) faster income growth in the United States than in Canadia?

4. Suppose that the current Canadian dollar (CAD) to U.S. dollar exchange rate is $0.85 CAD = $1 US and that the U.S. dollar price of an Apple iPhone is $300. What is the Canadian dollar price of an iPhone? Next, suppose that the CAD to U.S. dollar exchange rate moves to $0.96 CAD = $1 US. What is the new Canadian dollar price of an iPhone? Other things equal, would you expect Canada to import more or fewer iPhones at the new exchange rate? **LO35.3**

5. Return to problem 3 and assume that the exchange rate is fixed at 110. In year 1, what would be the minimum initial size of the U.S. reserve of loonies such that the United States could maintain the peg throughout the year? What about the minimum initial size that would be necessary at the start of year 2? Next, consider only the data for year 1. What peg should the U.S. set if it wants the fixed exchange rate to increase the domestic money supply by $1.2 trillion? **LO35.6**

Previous International Exchange-Rate Systems

LO35.7 Explain how exchange rates worked under the gold standard and Bretton Woods.

This chapter discussed the current system of managed floating exchange rates in some detail. But before this system began in 1971, the world had previously used two other exchange rate systems: the gold standard, which implicitly created fixed exchange rates, and the Bretton Woods system, which was an explicit fixed-rate system indirectly tied to gold. Because the features and problems of these two systems help explain why we have the current system, they are well worth knowing more about.

The Gold Standard: Fixed Exchange Rates

Between 1879 and 1934 the major nations of the world adhered to a fixed-rate system called the **gold standard.** Under this system, each nation must:

- Define its currency in terms of a quantity of gold.
- Maintain a fixed relationship between its stock of gold and its money supply.
- Allow gold to be freely exported and imported.

If each nation defines its currency in terms of gold, the various national currencies will have fixed relationships to one another. For example, if the United States defines \$1 as worth 25 grains of gold, and Britain defines £1 as worth 50 grains of gold, then a British pound is worth 2×25 grains, or \$2. This exchange rate was fixed under the gold standard. The exchange rate did not change in response to changes in currency demand and supply.

Gold Flows If we ignore the costs of packing, insuring, and shipping gold between countries, under the gold standard the rate of exchange would not vary from this \$2 = £1 rate. No one in the United States would pay more than \$2 = £1 because 50 grains of gold could always be bought for \$2 in the United States and sold for £1 in Britain. Nor would the British pay more than £1 for \$2. Why should they when they could buy 50 grains of gold in Britain for £1 and sell it in the United States for \$2?

Under the gold standard, the potential free flow of gold between nations resulted in fixed exchange rates.

Domestic Macroeconomic Adjustments When currency demand or supply changes, the gold standard requires domestic macroeconomic adjustments to maintain the fixed exchange rate. To see why, suppose that U.S. tastes change such that U.S. consumers want to buy more British goods. The resulting increase in the demand for pounds creates a shortage of pounds in the United States (recall Figure 35.4), implying a U.S. balance-of-payments deficit.

What will happen? Remember that the rules of the gold standard prohibit the exchange rate from moving from the fixed \$2 = £1 rate. The rate cannot move to, say, a new equilibrium at \$3 = £1 to correct the imbalance. Instead, gold will flow from the United States to Britain to correct the payments imbalance.

But recall that the gold standard requires that participants maintain a fixed relationship between their domestic money supplies and their quantities of gold. The flow of gold from the United States to Britain will require a reduction of the money supply in the United States. Other things equal, that will reduce total spending in the United States and lower U.S. real domestic output, employment, income, and, perhaps, prices. Also, the decline in the money supply will boost U.S. interest rates.

The opposite will occur in Britain. The inflow of gold will increase the money supply, and this will increase total spending in Britain. Domestic output, employment, income, and, perhaps, prices will rise. The British interest rate will fall.

Declining U.S. incomes and prices will reduce the U.S. demand for British goods and therefore reduce the U.S. demand for pounds. Lower interest rates in Britain will make it less attractive for U.S. investors to make financial investments there, also lessening the demand for pounds. For all these reasons, the demand for pounds in the United States will decline. In Britain, higher incomes, prices, and interest rates will make U.S. imports and U.S. financial investments more attractive. In buying these imports and making these financial investments, British citizens will supply more pounds in the exchange market.

In short, domestic macroeconomic adjustments in the United States and Britain, triggered by the international flow of gold, will produce new demand and supply conditions for pounds such that the \$2 = £1 exchange rate is maintained. After all the adjustments are made, the United States will not have a payments deficit and Britain will not have a payments surplus.

So the gold standard has the advantage of maintaining stable exchange rates and correcting balance-of-payments deficits and surpluses automatically. However, its critical drawback is that nations must accept domestic adjustments in such distasteful forms as unemployment and falling incomes, on the one hand, or inflation, on the other hand. Under the gold standard, a nation's money supply is altered by changes in supply and demand in currency markets, and nations cannot establish their own monetary policy in their own national interest. If the United States, for example, were to experience declining output and income, the loss of gold under the gold standard would reduce the U.S. money supply. That would increase interest rates, retard borrowing and spending, and produce further declines in output and income.

Collapse of the Gold Standard The gold standard collapsed under the weight of the worldwide Depression of the 1930s. As domestic output and employment fell worldwide, the restoration of prosperity became the primary goal of afflicted nations. They responded by enacting protectionist measures to reduce imports. The idea was to get their economies moving again by promoting consumption of domestically produced goods. To make their exports less expensive abroad, many nations redefined their currencies at lower levels in terms of gold. For example, a country that had previously defined the value of its currency at 1 unit = 25 grains of gold might redefine it as 1 unit = 10 grains of gold. Such redefining is an example of **devaluation**—a deliberate action by government to reduce the international value of its currency. A series of such devaluations in the 1930s meant that exchange rates were no longer fixed. That violated a major tenet of the gold standard, and the system broke down.

The Bretton Woods System

The Great Depression and the Second World War left world trade and the world monetary system in shambles. To lay the groundwork for a new international monetary system, in 1944, major nations held an international conference at Bretton Woods, New Hampshire. The conference produced a commitment to a modified fixed-exchange-rate system called an *adjustable-peg system,* or, simply, the **Bretton Woods system.** The new system sought to capture the advantages of the old gold standard (fixed exchange rate) while avoiding its disadvantages (painful domestic macroeconomic adjustments).

Furthermore, the conference created the **International Monetary Fund (IMF)** to make the new exchange-rate system feasible and workable. The new international monetary system managed through the IMF prevailed with modifications until 1971. (The IMF still plays a basic role in international finance; in recent years it has performed a major role in providing loans to developing countries, nations experiencing financial crises, and nations making the transition from communism to capitalism.)

IMF and Pegged Exchange Rates How did the adjustable-peg system of exchange rates work? First, as with the gold standard, each IMF member had to define its currency in terms of gold (or dollars), thus establishing rates of exchange between its currency and the currencies of all other members. In addition, each nation was obligated to keep its exchange rate stable with respect to every other currency. To do so, nations would have to use their official currency reserves to intervene in foreign exchange markets.

Assume again that the U.S. dollar and the British pound were "pegged" to each other at \$2 = £1. And suppose again that the demand for pounds temporarily increases so that a shortage of pounds occurs in the United States (the United States has a balance-of-payments deficit). How can the United States keep its pledge to maintain a \$2 = £1 exchange rate when the new equilibrium rate is, say, \$3 = £1? As we noted previously, the United States can supply additional pounds to the exchange market, increasing the supply of pounds such that the equilibrium exchange rate falls back to \$2 = £1.

Under the Bretton Woods system, there were three main sources of the needed pounds:

- ***Official reserves*** The United States might currently possess pounds in its official reserves as the result of past actions against a payments surplus.
- ***Gold sales*** The U.S. government might sell some of its gold to Britain for pounds. The proceeds would then be offered in the exchange market to augment the supply of pounds.
- ***IMF borrowing*** The needed pounds might be borrowed from the IMF. Nations participating in the Bretton Woods system were required to make contributions to the IMF based on the size of their national income, population, and volume of trade. If necessary, the United States could borrow pounds on a short-term basis from the IMF by supplying its own currency as collateral.

Fundamental Imbalances: Adjusting the Peg The Bretton Woods system recognized that from time to time a nation may be confronted with persistent and sizable balance-of-payments problems that cannot be corrected through the means listed above. In such cases, the nation would eventually run out of official reserves and be unable to maintain its current fixed exchange rate. The Bretton Woods remedy was correction by devaluation, that is, by an "orderly" reduction of the nation's pegged exchange rate. Also, the IMF allowed each member nation to alter the value of its currency by 10 percent, on its own, to correct a so-called fundamental (persistent and continuing) balance-of-payments deficit. Larger exchange-rate changes required the permission of the Fund's board of directors.

By requiring approval of significant rate changes, the Fund guarded against arbitrary and competitive currency devaluations by nations seeking only to boost output in their own countries at the expense of other countries. In our example, devaluation of the dollar would increase U.S. exports and lower U.S. imports, helping to correct the United States' persistent payments deficit.

Demise of the Bretton Woods System Under this adjustable-peg system, nations came to accept gold and the dollar as international reserves. The acceptability of gold as an international medium of exchange derived from its earlier use under the gold standard. Other nations accepted the dollar as international money because the United States had accumulated large quantities of gold, and between 1934 and 1971 it maintained a policy of buying gold from, and selling gold to, foreign governments at a fixed price of $35 per ounce. The dollar was convertible into gold on demand, so the dollar came to be regarded as a substitute for gold, or "as good as gold." The discovery of new gold was limited, but a growing volume of dollars helped facilitate the expanding volume of world trade during this period.

But a major problem arose. The United States had persistent payments deficits throughout the 1950s and 1960s. Those deficits were financed in part by U.S. gold reserves but mostly by payment of U.S. dollars. As the amount of dollars held by foreigners soared and the U.S. gold reserves dwindled, other nations began to question whether the dollar was really "as good as gold." The ability of the United States to continue to convert dollars into gold at $35 per ounce became increasingly doubtful, as did the role of dollars as international monetary reserves. Thus the dilemma was: To maintain the dollar as a reserve medium, the U.S. payments deficit had to be eliminated. But elimination of the payments deficit would remove the source of additional dollar reserves and thus limit the growth of international trade and finance.

The problem culminated in 1971 when the United States ended its 37-year-old policy of exchanging gold for dollars at $35 per ounce. It severed the link between gold and the international value of the dollar, thereby "floating" the dollar and letting market forces determine its value. The floating of the dollar withdrew U.S. support from the Bretton Woods system of fixed exchange rates and effectively ended the system. Nearly all major currencies began to float. This led to the current regime of "managed floating exchange rates" that is described at length in this chapter.

APPENDIX SUMMARY

LO35.7 Explain how exchange rates worked under the gold standard and Bretton Woods.

Before the current system of managed floating exchange rates started in 1971, several different international monetary systems were used.

Between 1879 and 1934, most major trading nations were on the gold standard, in which each nation fixed an exchange rate between its currency and gold. With each nation's currency fixed to gold, the system also implicitly set fixed exchange rates between different national currencies.

Any balance-of-payments imbalance would automatically lead to offsetting international flows of gold. This, in turn, led to automatically occurring domestic macroeconomic adjustments as the country exporting gold automatically encountered a decrease in its money supply while the country importing gold automatically felt an increase in its money supply. When the Great Depression hit, many countries found these automatic adjustments too hard to bear and they abandoned the gold standard.

The Bretton Woods system was implemented after the end of the Second World War and lasted until 1971. Under this system, the United States fixed the value of the U.S. dollar to gold at a rate of $35 per ounce. Other countries then set fixed exchange rates with the dollar so that their currencies were indirectly fixed to gold through the dollar.

The International Monetary Fund was created to administer the Bretton Woods system, which had some flexibility because exchange rates between countries could be adjusted to help offset balance-of-payments imbalances.

As the United States encountered increasingly large balance-of-payments imbalances in the 1960s and early 1970s, its ability to maintain its gold peg of $35 per ounce lost credibility. The United States abandoned the gold standard in 1971, thereby ending the Bretton Woods system. All major currencies then began the current regime of managed floating exchange rates.

APPENDIX TERMS AND CONCEPTS

gold standard

devaluation

Bretton Woods system

International Monetary Fund (IMF)

The following and additional problems can be found in connect

APPENDIX DISCUSSION QUESTIONS

1. Compare and contrast the Bretton Woods system of exchange rates with that of the gold standard. What caused the collapse of the gold standard? What caused the demise of the Bretton Woods system? **LO35.7**

APPENDIX REVIEW QUESTIONS

1. Think back to the gold standard period. If the United States suffered a recession, to what degree could it engage in expansionary monetary policy? **LO35.7**

APPENDIX PROBLEMS

1. Suppose Zeeland pegs its currency, the zee, at 1 zee = 36 grains of gold while Aeeland pegs its currency, the aeellar, at 1 aellar = 10 grains of gold. **LO35.7**
   a. What would the exchange rate be between the zee and the aellar?
   b. How many aellars could you get for 7 zees?
   c. In terms of gold, would you rather have 14.5 zees or 53 aellars?

Selected Economics Statistics for Various Years, 1929–1990

Statistics in rows 1–5 are in billions of dollars in the year specified. Numbers may not add to totals because of rounding.

GDP AND INCOME DATA	1929	1933	1940	1942	1944	1946	1948	1950	1958	1960	1962
1 Gross domestic product	104.6	57.2	102.9	166.0	224.6	227.8	247.8	300.2	482.0	543.3	605.1
1A Personal consumption expenditures	77.4	45.9	71.3	89.0	108.6	144.3	175.0	192.2	296.0	331.6	363.1
1B Gross private domestic investment	17.2	2.3	14.6	11.8	9.2	33.1	50.3	56.5	70.9	86.5	97.0
1C Government purchases	9.6	8.9	15.6	65.5	108.7	43.2	44.0	50.7	114.5	121.0	140.9
1D Net exports of goods and services	0.4	0.1	1.5	−0.3	−2.0	7.2	5.5	0.7	0.5	4.2	4.1
2 Net domestic product	94.2	49.2	92.3	151.1	203.2	202.0	243.4	266.8	419.6	475.4	531.0
3 National income	94.2	49.0	91.5	152.4	201.1	201.5	245.1	267.1	421.7	479.9	535.2
3A Wages and salaries	51.4	29.8	52.8	88.1	124.4	122.6	144.5	158.5	265.1	301.9	332.9
3B Rent	6.1	2.9	3.8	5.5	6.3	6.9	7.5	8.8	14.8	16.5	18
3C Interest	4.6	4	3.3	3.2	2.4	1.9	2.6	3.2	9.6	10.7	14.3
3D Profits	10.8	−0.2	9.9	20.8	25	18.2	31.4	36.1	43.9	54.7	64
3E Proprietor's income	14.0	5.3	12.2	23.3	29.3	35.7	39.3	37.5	50.2	50.6	55.2
3F Taxes on production and imports*	7.3	7.2	9.5	11.5	13.7	16.2	19.8	23.0	38.1	45.5	50.8
4 Personal income	85.3	47.2	79.4	126.7	169.7	182.7	213.7	233.9	379.5	422.5	469.1
5 Disposable income	83.5	46.4	77.7	121.8	152.0	165.5	194.5	215.0	340.9	376.5	417.5
6 Disposable income per capita	685	369	588	903	1,099	1,170	1,326	1,417	1,958	2,083	2,238
7 Personal saving as percent of DI	4.7	−0.8	6.8	26.2	27.9	11.8	8.9	9.3	11.4	10.0	11.1

OTHER STATISTICS	1929	1933	1940	1942	1944	1946	1948	1950	1958	1960	1962
8 Real GDP (billions of 2009 dollars)	1,055.6	777.6	1,265.0	1,770.3	2,237.5	1,959.0	2,018.0	2,181.9	2,832.6	3,105.8	3,379.9
9 Economic growth rate (change in real GDP)	—	−1.3	8.8	18.9	8.0	−11.6	4.1	8.7	−0.7	2.6	6.1
10 Consumer Price Index (1982–1984 = 100)	17.1	13.0	14.0	16.3	17.6	19.5	24.1	24.1	28.9	29.6	30.2
11 Rate of inflation (percent change in CPI)	0.0	−5.1	0.7	10.9	1.7	8.3	8.1	1.3	2.8	1.7	1.0
12 Money supply, *M*1 (billions of $)	26.6	19.9	39.7	55.4	85.3	106.5	112.5	114.1	134.8	140.7	147.8
13 Federal funds interest rate (%)	—	—	—	—	—	—	1.75	2.07	1.57	3.22	2.71
14 Prime interest rate (%)	5.50	1.50	1.50	1.50	1.50	1.50	1.75	2.07	3.83	4.82	4.50
15 Population (millions)	121.8	125.6	132.1	134.9	138.4	141.4	146.6	152.3	174.9	180.7	186.5
16 Civilian labor force (millions)	49.2	51.6	55.6	56.4	54.6	57.5	60.6	62.2	67.6	69.6	70.6
16A Employment (millions)	47.6	38.8	47.5	53.8	54.0	55.3	58.3	58.9	63.0	65.8	66.7
16B Unemployment (millions)	1.6	12.8	8.1	2.7	0.7	2.3	2.3	3.3	4.6	3.9	3.9
17 Unemployment rate (%)	3.2	24.9	14.6	4.7	1.2	3.9	3.8	5.3	6.8	5.5	5.5
18 Productivity growth, business sector (%)	—	—	—	—	—	—	4.4	8.2	2.9	1.8	4.6
19 After-tax manufacturing profit per dollar of sales (cents)	—	—	—	—	—	—	7.0	7.1	4.2	4.4	4.5
20 Price of crude oil (U.S. average, dollars per barrel)	1.27	0.67	1.02	1.19	1.21	1.41	2.60	2.51	3.01	2.88	2.90
21 Federal budget surplus (+) or deficit (−) (billions of dollars)	0.7	−2.6	−2.9	−20.5	−47.6	−15.9	11.8	−3.1	−2.8	0.3	−7.1
22 Public debt (billions of dollars)	16.9	22.5	50.7	79.2	204.1	271.0	252.0	256.9	279.7	290.5	302.9
23 Trade balance on current account (billions of dollars)	—	—	—	—	—	4.9	2.4	−1.8	0.8	2.8	3.4

*Combines items from other smaller accounts.

1964	1966	1968	1970	1972	1974	1976	1978	1980	1982	1984	1986	1988	1990
685.8	815.0	942.5	1,075.9	1,282.4	1,548.8	1,877.6	2,356.6	2,862.5	3,345.0	4,040.7	4,590.1	5,252.6	5,979.6
411.2	480.6	557.4	647.7	769.4	932.0	1,150.2	1,426.2	1,754.6	2,073.9	2,498.2	2,898.4	3,346.9	3,825.6
112.2	144.2	156.9	170.1	228.1	274.5	323.2	478.4	530.1	581.0	820.1	849.1	937.0	993.5
155.5	186.4	226.8	254.2	288.2	343.1	405.8	477.4	590.8	710.0	825.2	974.5	1,078.2	1,238.4
6.9	3.9	1.4	4.0	−3.4	−0.8	−1.6	−25.4	−13.1	−20.0	−102.7	−131.9	−109.4	−77.9
603.4	719.7	829.2	939.1	1,121.5	1,342.6	1,618.4	2,031.5	2,436.5	2,810.7	3,446.4	3,907.9	4,470.2	5,092.8
608.3	719.7	832.1	940.2	1,123.0	1,350.7	1,614.8	2,029.9	2,426.8	2,840.4	3,444.0	3,848.1	4,493.3	5,036.1
376.8	450.3	532.1	625.1	733.6	890.3	1,051.2	1,320.2	1,626.2	1,894.3	2,217.4	2,543.8	2,950	3,342.7
18.8	19.9	20.1	20.7	22.8	23.3	20.6	16.9	19.7	26.1	27.9	21.9	25.1	31.4
17.5	22.5	27.6	40.5	49.3	73.5	89.9	118.8	186.2	277.5	336.1	365.2	394.7	450.1
77.7	96.1	101.7	86.2	117.2	125.7	174.3	238.6	223.6	229.9	337.9	324.4	414.9	417.2
59.1	67.9	73.8	77.8	95.1	112.2	131	166	171.6	171.2	228.2	256.5	325.8	354.4
58.4	63.0	76.8	89.9	105.0	125.7	147.8	169.4	199.5	241.4	296.5	336.3	382.8	440.3
528.4	620.6	730.7	864.6	1,023.6	1,249.3	1,498.1	1,859.5	2,316.8	2,778.8	3,281.3	3,725.1	4,275.3	4,904.5
476.3	554.2	643.8	761.5	899.9	1,098.3	1,325.8	1,630.1	2,018.0	2,424.7	2,903.9	3,287.9	3,770.4	4,311.8
2,482	2,819	3,207	3,713	4,287	5,135	6,079	7,322	8,861	10,442	12,284	13,661	15,386	17,235
11.5	11.1	11.2	12.6	12.1	12.9	11.1	10.2	10.6	11.5	10.7	8.2	7.8	7.8

1964	1966	1968	1970	1972	1974	1976	1978	1980	1982	1984	1986	1988	1990
3,730.5	4,234.9	4,564.7	4,717.7	5,128.8	5,390.2	5,669.3	6,260.4	6,443.4	6,484.3	7,277.2	7,852.1	8,465.4	8,945.4
5.8	6.6	4.9	0.2	5.2	−0.5	5.4	5.6	−0.2	−1.9	7.3	3.5	4.2	1.9
31.0	32.4	34.8	38.8	41.8	49.3	56.9	65.2	82.4	96.5	103.9	109.6	118.3	130.7
1.3	2.9	4.2	5.7	3.2	11.0	5.8	7.6	13.5	6.2	4.3	1.9	4.1	5.4
160.3	172.0	197.4	214.4	249.2	274.2	306.2	357.3	408.5	474.8	551.6	724.7	786.7	824.7
3.50	5.11	5.66	7.18	4.43	10.50	5.05	7.93	13.36	12.26	10.23	6.81	7.57	8.10
4.50	5.63	6.31	7.91	5.25	10.80	6.84	9.06	15.27	14.86	12.04	8.33	9.32	10.01
191.9	196.6	200.7	205.1	209.9	213.9	218.0	222.6	227.2	231.7	235.8	240.1	244.5	249.5
73.1	75.8	78.7	82.8	87.0	91.9	96.2	102.3	106.9	110.2	113.5	117.8	121.7	125.8
69.3	72.9	75.9	78.7	82.2	86.8	88.8	96.0	99.3	99.5	105.0	109.6	115.0	118.8
3.8	2.9	2.8	4.1	4.9	5.2	7.4	6.2	7.6	10.7	8.5	8.2	6.7	7.0
5.2	3.8	3.6	4.9	5.6	5.6	7.7	6.1	7.1	9.7	7.5	7.0	5.5	5.6
3.4	4.1	3.4	2.0	3.2	−1.7	3.2	1.1	−0.2	−0.8	2.7	2.9	1.5	2.1
5.4	5.6	5.2	4.5	4.4	6.4	5.5	5.3	5.6	4.4	4.8	4.6	6.6	4.8
2.88	2.88	2.94	3.18	3.39	6.87	8.19	9.00	21.59	28.52	25.88	12.51	12.58	20.03
−5.9	−3.7	−25.2	−2.8	−23.4	−6.1	−73.7	−59.2	−73.8	−128.0	−185.4	−221.2	−155.2	−221.0
316.1	328.5	368.7	380.9	435.9	483.9	629.0	776.6	909.0	1,137.3	1,564.6	2,120.5	2,601.1	3,206
6.8	3.0	0.6	2.3	−5.8	2.0	4.3	−15.1	2.3	−5.5	−94.3	−147.2	−121.2	−79.0

Selected Economics Statistics for Various Years, 1991–2015

Statistics in rows 1–5 are in billions of dollars in the year specified. Numbers may not add to totals because of rounding.

GDP AND INCOME DATA	1991	1992	1993	1994	1995	1996	1997	1998	1999	2000	2001
1 Gross domestic product	6,174.0	6,539.3	6,878.7	7,308.7	7,664.0	8,100.2	8,608.5	9,089.1	9,665.7	10,289.7	10,625.3
1A Personal consumption expenditures	3,960.2	4,215.7	4,471.0	4,741.0	4,984.2	5,268.1	5,560.7	5,903.0	6,316.9	6,801.6	7,106.9
1B Gross private domestic investment	944.3	1,013.0	1,106.8	1,256.5	1,317.5	1,432.1	1,595.6	1,735.3	1,884.2	2,033.8	1,928.6
1C Government purchases	1,298.2	1,345.4	1,366.1	1,403.7	1,452.2	1,496.4	1,554.2	1,613.5	1,726.0	1,834.4	1,958.8
1D Net exports of goods and services	−28.6	−34.8	−65.2	−92.5	−89.8	−96.4	−102.0	−162.7	−261.4	−380.1	−369.0
2 Net domestic product	5,242.9	5,579.6	5,875.1	6,253.1	6,541.2	6,924.2	7,368.5	7,778.8	8,264.8	8,775.5	9,021.3
3 National income	5,186.1	5,499.8	5,754.8	6,140.1	6,479.4	6,899.5	7,380.3	7,857.3	8,324.3	8,907.0	9,184.7
3A Wages and salaries	3,452	3,671.1	3,820.7	4,010.1	4,202.6	4,422.1	4,714.7	5,077.8	5,410.3	5,856.6	6,046.5
3B Rent	42.0	64.3	93.6	117.5	129.2	147.0	152.0	169.9	183.1	187.7	207.5
3C Interest	408.5	383.7	371.4	365.9	376.5	381.9	414.7	477.8	488.0	565.0	566.4
3D Profits	451.3	475.3	522.0	621.9	703.0	786.1	865.8	804.1	830.2	781.2	754.0
3E Proprietor's income	356.0	402.4	430.5	459.5	484.5	547.4	587.9	644.2	700.4	757.8	836.8
3F Taxes on production and imports*	476.3	503.0	516.6	565.2	583.6	615.0	645.2	683.5	712.3	758.7	773.5
4 Personal income	5,071.1	5,410.8	5,646.8	5,934.7	6,276.5	6,661.9	7,075.0	7,587.7	7,983.8	8,632.8	8,987.1
5 Disposable income	4,484.5	4,800.3	5,000.2	5,244.2	5,532.6	5,829.9	6,148.9	6,561.3	6,876.3	7,400.5	7,752.3
6 Disposable income per capita	17,688	18,684	19,211	19,906	20,753	21,615	22,527	23,759	24,617	26,206	27,179
7 Personal saving as percent of DI	8.2	8.9	7.4	6.3	6.4	5.9	5.7	6.2	4.3	4.0	4.3

OTHER STATISTICS	1991	1992	1993	1994	1995	1996	1997	1998	1999	2000	2001
8 Real GDP (billions of 2009 dollars)	8,938.9	9,256.7	9,510.8	9,894.7	10,163.7	10,549.5	11,022.9	11,513.4	12,071.4	12,565.2	12,684.4
9 Economic growth rate (change in real GDP)	−0.1	3.6	2.7	4.0	2.7	3.8	4.5	4.4	4.8	4.1	1.0
10 Consumer Price Index (1982–1984 = 100)	136.2	140.3	144.5	148.2	152.4	156.9	160.5	163.0	166.6	172.2	177.1
11 Rate of inflation (percent change in CPI)	4.2	3.0	3.0	2.6	2.8	3.0	2.3	1.6	2.2	3.4	2.8
12 Money supply, *M*1 (billions of $)	897.0	1,024.9	1,129.8	1,150.8	1,127.5	1,081.3	1,072.8	1,096.1	1,122.9	1,087.9	1,182.9
13 Federal funds interest rate (%)	5.69	3.52	3.02	4.20	5.84	5.30	5.46	5.35	4.97	6.24	3.89
14 Prime interest rate (%)	8.46	6.25	6.00	7.14	8.83	8.27	8.44	8.35	7.99	9.23	6.92
15 Population (millions)	252.2	255.0	257.8	260.3	262.8	265.2	267.8	270.2	272.7	282.2	285.0
16 Civilian labor force (millions)	126.3	128.1	129.2	131.1	132.3	133.9	136.3	137.7	139.4	142.6	143.7
16A Employment (millions)	117.7	118.5	120.3	123.1	124.9	126.7	129.6	131.5	133.5	136.9	136.9
16B Unemployment (millions)	8.6	9.6	8.9	8.0	7.4	7.2	6.7	6.2	5.9	5.7	6.8
17 Unemployment rate (%)	6.8	7.5	6.9	6.1	5.6	5.4	4.9	4.5	4.2	4.0	4.7
18 Productivity growth, business sector (%)	1.5	4.2	0.5	0.9	0.0	2.9	1.8	3.0	3.5	3.5	3.0
19 After-tax manufacturing profit per dollar of sales (cents)	4.1	3.1	3.7	5.5	6.0	6.5	6.7	6.0	6.4	6.9	5.7
20 Price of crude oil (U.S. average, dollars per barrel)	16.54	15.99	14.25	13.19	14.62	18.46	17.23	10.87	15.56	26.72	21.84
21 Federal budget surplus (+) or deficit (−) (billions of dollars)	−269.2	−290.3	−255.1	−203.2	−164.0	−107.4	−21.9	69.3	125.6	236.2	128.2
22 Public debt (billions of dollars)	3,598.2	4,001.8	4,351.0	4,643.3	4,920.6	5,181.5	5,369.2	5,478.2	5,605.5	5,628.7	5,769.9
23 Trade balance on current account (billions of dollars)	2.9	−51.6	−84.8	−121.6	−113.6	−124.8	−140.7	−215.1	−301.7	−416.3	−396.6

*Combines items from other smaller accounts.

2002	2003	2004	2005	2006	2007	2008	2009	2010	2011	2012	2013	2014	2015**
10,980.2	11,512.2	12,277.0	13,095.4	13,857.9	14,480.3	14,720.3	14,417.9	14,958.3	15,517.9	16,155.3	16,691.5	17,393.1	18,036.6
7,385.3	7,764.4	8,257.8	8,790.3	9,297.5	9,744.4	10,005.5	9,842.9	10,201.9	10,689.3	11,050.6	11,361.2	11,863.4	12,283.7
1,925.0	2,027.9	2,276.7	2,527.1	2,680.6	2,643.7	2,424.8	1,878.1	2,100.8	2,239.9	2,511.7	2,706.3	2,886.5	3,056.6
2,094.9	2,220.8	2,357.4	2,493.7	2,642.2	2,801.9	3,003.2	3,089.1	3,174.0	3,168.7	3,158.6	3,116.1	3,152.1	3,218.3
−425.0	−500.9	−614.8	−715.7	−762.4	−709.8	−713.2	−392.2	−518.5	−580.0	−565.7	−492.0	−508.8	−522.0
9,318.1	9,785.0	10,445.3	11,113.4	11,721.9	12,215.9	12,356.9	12,049.5	12,576.7	13,067.3	13,621.0	14,062.6	14,647.9	15,205.9
9,436.8	9,865.1	10,541.8	11,240.7	12,005.7	12,322.1	12,430.9	12,124.5	12,739.5	13,352.3	14,061.9	14,444.8	15,153.9	15,665.3
6,141.9	6,365.4	6,740.5	7,087.8	7,503.2	7,899.1	8,079.2	7,787.8	7,967.3	8,629.0	8,609.9	8,842.4	9,253.4	9,693.1
217.3	238.0	255.4	238.4	207.5	189.4	262.1	333.7	402.8	485.3	525.3	567.1	606.1	659.6
490.5	466.2	403.5	496.8	580.9	663.4	693.4	563.1	489.4	488.1	527.7	504.6	533.7	524.1
907.2	1,056.4	1,283.3	1,477.7	1,646.5	1,529	1,285.1	1,392.6	1,740.6	1,816.6	1,998.2	2,032.9	2,152.1	2,088.1
871.0	900.1	962.1	979.0	1,053.7	979.2	1,026.5	973.0	1,032.7	1,143.7	1,241.4	1,284.7	1,337.7	1,376.8
808.9	839.0	897.0	961.0	1,013.9	1,062.0	1,084.6	1,074.3	1,106.7	1,149.6	1,159.4	1,213.1	1,270.9	1,323.6
9,149.5	9,487.6	10,049.2	10,610.3	11,389.8	11,995.7	12,430.6	12,082.1	12,435.2	13,254.5	13,915.1	14,073.7	14,809.7	15,458.5
8,099.2	8,486.7	9,003.2	9,401.8	10,037.7	10,507.9	10,995.4	10,937.2	11,243.7	11,801.4	12,403.7	12,395.8	13,022.7	13,519.8
28,127	29,201	30,700	31,763	33,591	34,829	36,104	35,598	36,296	37,804.0	39,441.0	39,129.0	40,794.0	42,026.0
5.0	4.8	4.6	2.6	3.4	3.0	5.0	6.1	5.6	6.0	7.6	5.0	5.6	5.8

2002	2003	2004	2005	2006	2007	2008	2009	2010	2011	2012	2013	2014	2015**
12,909.7	13,270.0	13,774.0	14,235.6	14,615.2	14,876.8	14,833.6	14,417.9	14,779.4	15,020.6	15,354.6	15,612.2	15,982.3	16,397.2
1.8	2.8	3.8	3.4	2.7	1.8	−0.3	−2.8	2.5	1.6	2.2	1.7	2.4	2.6
179.9	184.0	188.9	195.3	201.6	207.3	215.3	214.5	218.1	224.9	229.6	233.0	236.7	237.0
1.6	2.3	2.7	3.4	3.2	2.8	3.8	−0.4	1.6	3.2	2.1	1.5	1.6	0.1
1,220.4	1,306.6	1,375.9	1,374.7	1,366.3	1,374.1	1,604.7	1,695.4	1,836.3	2,160.4	2,440.2	2,660.5	2,927.3	3,087.2
1.67	1.13	1.35	3.21	4.96	5.02	1.93	0.16	0.18	0.10	0.14	0.14	0.07	0.11
4.68	4.12	4.34	6.19	7.96	8.05	5.09	3.25	3.25	3.25	3.25	3.25	3.25	3.25
287.6	290.1	292.8	295.5	298.4	301.2	304.1	306.8	309.3	311.6	313.9	317.1	319.5	321.7
144.9	146.5	147.4	149.3	151.4	153.1	154.3	154.1	153.9	153.6	155.0	155.1	156.1	158.3
136.5	137.7	139.3	141.7	144.4	146.0	145.4	139.9	139.1	139.9	142.5	144.7	147.4	150.1
8.4	8.8	8.1	7.6	7.0	7.1	8.9	14.3	14.8	13.7	12.5	10.4	8.7	8.2
5.8	6.0	5.5	5.1	4.6	4.6	5.8	9.3	9.6	8.9	8.1	6.7	5.6	5.0
4.5	3.9	2.8	1.7	0.9	1.5	0.7	3.1	3.0	0.0	0.7	0.7	0.6	0.8
5.8	7.0	8.0	9.0	9.7	9.3	6.6	8.6	8.1	8.7	8.5	9.3	8.9	7.9
22.51	27.56	36.77	50.28	59.69	66.52	94.04	56.35	74.71	95.73	94.52	95.99	87.39	44.39
−157.8	−377.6	−412.7	−318.3	−248.2	−160.7	−458.6	−1,412.7	−1,294.4	−1,299.6	−1,087.0	−680	−485.0	−439.0
6,198.4	6,760.0	7,354.7	7,905.3	8,451.4	8,950.7	9,986.1	11,875.9	13,528.8	14,764.2	16,050.9	16,738.0	17,824.0	18,151.0
−457.2	−519.1	−628.5	−745.8	−800.6	−710.3	−677.1	−381.9	−442.0	−460.3	−446.5	−366.4	−392.1	−463.0

**Data for 2015 and the years immediately prior are subject to change because of subsequent government data revisions.

Sources: Bureau of Economic Analysis; Bureau of Labor Statistics; Federal Reserve System; *Economic Report of the President, 2016;* and U.S. Energy Information Administration.

GLOSSARY

Note: Terms set in *italic type* are defined separately in this glossary.

45° (degree) line The reference line in a two-dimensional graph that shows equality between the variable measured on the *horizontal axis* and the variable measured on the *vertical axis*. In the *aggregate expenditures model*, the line along which the value of output (measured horizontally) is equal to the value of *aggregate expenditures* (measured vertically).

ability-to-pay principle The idea that those who have greater *income* (or *wealth*) should pay a greater proportion of it as taxes than those who have less income (or wealth).

accounting profit The *total revenue* of a *firm* less its *explicit costs;* the profit (or net income) that appears on accounting statements and that is reported to the government for tax purposes.

acreage allotments A pre-1996 government program that limited the total number of acres to be used in producing (reduced amounts of) various food and fiber products and allocated these acres among individual farmers. These farmers had to limit their plantings to the allotted number of acres to obtain *price supports* for their crops.

actively managed funds *Mutual funds* that have portfolio managers who constantly buy and sell *assets* in an attempt to generate high returns.

actual reserves The funds that a bank has on deposit at the *Federal Reserve Bank* of its district (plus its *vault cash*).

adverse selection problem A problem arising when information known to one party to a contract or agreement is not known to the other party, causing the latter to incur major costs. Example: Individuals who have the poorest health are most likely to buy health insurance.

AFL-CIO An acronym for the American Federation of Labor–Congress of Industrial Organizations; the largest federation of *labor unions* in the United States.

agency shop A place of employment where the employer may hire either *labor union* members or nonmembers but where those employees who do not join the union must either pay union dues or donate an equivalent amount of money to a charity.

aggregate A collection of specific economic units treated as if they were one unit. Examples: the *prices* of all individual *goods* and *services* are combined into the *price level,* and all units of output are aggregated into *gross domestic product*.

aggregate demand A schedule or curve that shows the total quantity of *goods* and *services* that would be demanded (purchased) at various *price levels*.

aggregate demand–aggregate supply (AD-AS) model The macroeconomic model that uses *aggregate demand* and *aggregate supply* to determine and explain the *price level* and the real *domestic output* (*real gross domestic product*).

aggregate expenditures schedule A table of numbers showing the total amount spent on *final goods* and final *services* at different levels of *real gross domestic product* (*real GDP*).

aggregate supply A schedule or curve showing the total quantity of *goods* and *services* that would be supplied (produced) at various *price levels*.

aggregate supply shocks Sudden, large changes in resource costs that shift an economy's aggregate supply curve.

agribusiness The portion of the agricultural and food product industries that is dominated by large corporations.

Agricultural Act of 2014 The agricultural law enacted in the United States in 2014 that eliminated *direct payments* and *countercyclical payments* in favor of two types of *crop insurance—price loss coverage* and *agricultural risk coverage*.

agricultural risk coverage A form of *crop insurance* that pays out if the total revenue generated by all the farmers planting a given crop in a given county falls below a predetermined value.

Alcoa case A 1945 case in which the courts ruled that the possession of monopoly power, no matter how reasonably that power had been used, was a violation of the antitrust laws; temporarily overturned the *rule of reason* applied in the *U.S. Steel case*.

allocative efficiency The apportionment of resources among *firms* and industries to obtain the production of the products most wanted by society (consumers); the output of each product at which its *marginal cost* and *price* or *marginal benefit* are equal, and at which the sum of *consumer surplus* and *producer surplus* is maximized.

anchoring The tendency people have to unconsciously base, or "anchor," the valuation of an item they are currently thinking about on recently considered but logically irrelevant information.

anticipated inflation Increases in the *price level* (*inflation*) that occur at the expected rate.

antitrust laws Legislation (including the *Sherman Act* and *Clayton Act*) that prohibits anticompetitive business activities such as *price fixing,* bid rigging, monopolization, and *tying contracts*.

antitrust policy The use of the *antitrust laws* to promote *competition* and *economic efficiency*.

arbitrage The activity of selling one *asset* and buying an identical or nearly identical asset to benefit from temporary differences in *prices* or *rates of return;* the practice that equalizes prices or returns on similar financial instruments and thus eliminates further opportunities for riskless financial gains.

asset demand for money The amount of *money* people want to hold as a *store of value;* this amount varies inversely with the *interest rate*.

asymmetric information A situation where one party to a market transaction has much more information about a product or service than the other. The result may be an under- or overallocation of resources.

average expected rate of return The *probability-weighted average* of an investment's possible future returns.

average fixed cost (AFC) A *firm*'s total *fixed cost* divided by output (the quantity of product produced).

average product (AP) The total output produced per unit of a *resource* employed (*total product* divided by the quantity of that employed resource).

average propensity to consume (APC) Fraction (or percentage) of *disposable income* that *households* spend on *consumer goods;* consumption divided by *disposable income.*

average propensity to save (APS) Fraction (or percentage) of *disposable income* that *households* save; *saving* divided by *disposable income.*

average revenue Total revenue from the sale of a product divided by the quantity of the product sold (demanded); equal to the *price* at which the product is sold when all units of the product are sold at the same price.

average tax rate Total tax paid divided by total *taxable income* or some other base (such as total income) against which to compare the amount of tax paid. Expressed as a percentage.

average total cost (ATC) A firm's *total cost* divided by output (the quantity of product produced); equal to *average fixed cost* plus *average variable cost.*

average variable cost (AVC) A firm's total *variable cost* divided by output (the quantity of product produced).

backflows The return of workers to the countries from which they originally emigrated.

backward induction A method for solving for the *subgame perfect Nash equilibrium* of a *sequential game* that is presented in *extensive form.*

balance of payments A summary of all the financial transactions that take place between the individuals, *firms,* and governmental units of one nation and those of all other nations during a year.

balance on capital and financial account The sum of the *capital account balance* and the *financial account balance.*

balance on current account The exports of *goods* and *services* of a nation less its imports of goods and services plus its *net investment income* and *net transfers* in a year.

balance on goods and services The exports of *goods* and *services* of a nation less its imports of goods and services in a year.

balance sheet A statement of the *assets, liabilities,* and *net worth* of a *firm* or individual at some given time.

balance-of-payments deficit Misleading term used in the financial press to describe a net decline in a country's *foreign exchange reserves* as it buys and sells foreign exchange in order to maintain a *fixed exchange rate.* The term is misleading because a nation's *balance of payments* statement must always balance (be zero) and can never be in deficit (less than zero).

balance-of-payments surplus Misleading term used in the financial press to describe a net increase in a country's *foreign exchange reserves* as it buys and sells foreign exchange in order to maintain a *fixed exchange rate.* The term is misleading because a nation's *balance of payments* statement must always balance (be zero) and can never be in surplus (greater than zero).

bankrupt A legal situation in which an individual or *firm* finds that it cannot make timely interest payments on money it has borrowed. In such cases, a bankruptcy judge can order the individual or firm to liquidate (turn into cash) its assets in order to pay lenders at least some portion of the amount they are owed.

barrier to entry Anything that artificially prevents the entry of *firms* into an *industry.*

barter The direct exchange of one *good* or *service* for another good or service.

base year The year with which other years are compared when an index is constructed; for example, the base year for a *price index.*

beaten paths Migration routes taken previously by family, relatives, friends, and other migrants.

behavioral economics The branch of economic theory that combines insights from economics, psychology, and biology to make more accurate predictions about human behavior than conventional *neoclassical economics,* which is hampered by its core assumptions that people are fundamentally *rational* and almost entirely self-interested. Behavioral economics can explain *framing effects, anchoring, mental accounting,* the *endowment effect, status quo bias, time inconsistency,* and *loss aversion.*

benefits-received principle The idea that those who receive the benefits of *goods* and *services* provided by government should pay the taxes required to finance them.

beta A relative measure of *nondiversifiable risk* that measures how the nondiversifiable risk of a given *asset* or *portfolio* compares with that of the *market portfolio* (the portfolio that contains every asset available in the financial markets).

bilateral monopoly A market in which there is a single seller (*monopoly*) and a single buyer (*monopsony*).

Board of Governors The seven-member group that supervises and controls the money and banking system of the United States; the Board of Governors of the *Federal Reserve System;* the Federal Reserve Board.

bond A financial device through which a borrower (a *firm* or government) is obligated to pay the principal and interest on a loan at specific dates in the future.

brain drains The exit or *emigration* of highly educated, highly skilled workers from a country.

break-even income The level of *disposable income* at which *households* plan to consume (spend) all their income and to save none of it.

break-even point An output at which a *firm* makes a *normal profit* (*total revenue* = *total cost*) but not an *economic profit.*

Bretton Woods system The international monetary system developed after the Second World War in which *adjustable pegs* were employed, the *International Monetary Fund* help stabilize foreign exchange rates, and gold and the dollar were used as *international monetary reserves.*

British thermal unit (BTU) The amount of energy required to raise the temperature of 1 pound of water by 1 degree Fahrenheit.

budget constraint The limit that the size of a consumer's income (and the *prices* that must be paid for *goods* and *services*) imposes on the ability of that consumer to obtain goods and services.

budget deficit The amount by which expenditures exceed revenues in any year.

budget line A line that shows the different combinations of two products a consumer can purchase with a specific money income, given the products' *prices*.

budget surplus The amount by which the revenues of the federal government exceed its expenditures in any year.

built-in stabilizer A mechanism that increases government's budget deficit (or reduces its surplus) during a recession and increases government's budget surplus (or reduces its deficit) during an expansion without any action by policymakers. The tax system is one such mechanism.

business cycle Recurring increases and decreases in the level of economic activity over periods of years; consists of peak, recession, trough, and expansion phases.

businesses Economic entities (*firms*) that purchase resources and provide *goods* and *services* to the economy.

capital Human-made resources (buildings, machinery, and equipment) used to produce *goods* and *services;* goods that do not directly satisfy human wants; also called capital goods. One of the four *economic resources*.

capital and financial account The section of a nation's *international balance of payments* that records (1) debt forgiveness by and to foreigners and (2) foreign purchases of assets in the United States and U.S. purchases of assets abroad.

capital flight The transfer of savings from *developing countries* to *industrially advanced countries* to avoid government expropriation, taxation, or higher rates of *inflation,* or simply to realize greater returns on *financial investments*.

capital gain The gain realized when *securities* or properties or other assets are sold for a *price* greater than the price paid for them.

capital goods (See *capital.*)

capital-intensive goods Products that require relatively large amounts of *capital* to produce.

capital-saving technology An improvement in *technology* that permits a greater quantity of a product to be produced with a specific amount of *capital* (or permits the same amount of the product to be produced with a smaller amount of capital).

capital-using technology An improvement in *technology* that requires the use of a greater amount of *capital* to produce a specific quantity of a product.

capricious-universe view The view held by some people that fate and outside events, rather than hard work and enterprise, will determine their economic destinies.

cartel A formal agreement among *firms* (or countries) in an *industry* to set the *price* of a product and establish the outputs of the individual firms (or countries) or to divide the market for the product geographically.

cease-and-desist order An order from a court or government agency to a corporation or individual to stop engaging in a specified practice.

Celler-Kefauver Act The federal law of 1950 that amended the *Clayton Act* by prohibiting the acquisition of the assets of one *firm* by another firm when the effect would be less competition.

change in demand A movement of an entire *demand curve* or schedule such that the *quantity demanded* changes at every particular *price;* caused by a change in one or more of the *determinants of demand.*

change in quantity demanded A change in the *quantity demanded* along a fixed *demand curve* (or within a fixed demand schedule) as a result of a change in the *price* of the product.

change in quantity supplied A change in the *quantity supplied* along a fixed *supply curve* (or within a fixed supply schedule) as a result of a change in the product's *price*.

change in supply A movement of an entire *supply curve* or schedule such that the *quantity supplied* changes at every particular *price;* caused by a change in one or more of the *determinants of supply*.

Change to Win A loose federation of American unions that includes the Service Workers and Teamsters unions; the second largest union federation after the *AFL-CIO*.

checkable deposit Any deposit in a *commercial bank* or *thrift institution* against which a check may be written.

circular flow diagram An illustration showing the flow of *resources* from *households* to *firms* and of products from firms to households. These flows are accompanied by reverse flows of money from firms to households and from households to firms.

Clayton Act The federal antitrust law of 1914 that strengthened the *Sherman Act* by making it illegal for *firms* to engage in certain specified practices including *tying contracts, interlocking directorates,* and certain forms of *price discrimination*.

closed shop A place of employment where only workers who are already members of a labor union may be hired.

Coase theorem The idea, first stated by economist Ronald Coase, that some *externalities* can be resolved through private negotiations among the affected parties.

cognitive biases Misperceptions or misunderstandings that cause *systematic errors*. Most result either (1) from *heuristics* that are prone to *systematic errors* or (2) because the brain is attempting to solve a type of problem (such as a calculus problem) for which it was not evolutionarily evolved and for which it has little innate capability.

collateral The pledge of specific assets by a borrower to a lender with the understanding that the lender will get to keep the assets if the borrower fails to repay the loan with cash.

collective bargaining The negotiation of labor contracts between *labor unions* and *firms* or government entities.

collective-action problem The idea that getting a group to pursue a common, collective goal gets harder the larger the group's size. Larger groups are more costly to organize and their members more difficult to motivate because the larger the group, the smaller each member's share of the benefits if the group succeeds.

collusion A situation in which *firms* act together and in agreement (collude) to fix *prices,* divide a market, or otherwise restrict competition.

command system A method of organizing an economy in which property resources are publicly owned and government uses *central economic planning* to direct and coordinate economic activities; *socialism;* communism. Compare with *market system*.

commercial bank A *firm* that engages in the business of banking (accepts deposits, offers checking accounts, and makes loans).

comparative advantage A situation in which a person or country can produce a specific product at a lower opportunity cost than some other person or country; the basis for specialization and trade.

compensating differences Differences in the *wages* received by workers in different jobs to compensate for the nonmonetary differences between the jobs.

compensating wage differential (See *compensating differences.*)

competition The effort and striving between two or more independent rivals to secure the business of one or more third parties by offering the best possible terms.

complementary goods Products and *services* that are used together. When the *price* of one falls, the demand for the other increases (and conversely).

complementary resources Productive inputs that are used jointly with other inputs in the production process; resources for which a decrease in the *price* of one leads to an increase in the demand for the other.

compound interest The accumulation of money that builds over time in an investment or interest-bearing account as new interest is earned on previous interest that is not withdrawn.

conditional cash transfers Anti-poverty programs in which households receive regular cash transfers (grants) as long as they keep their children in school and participate in preventative health-care programs.

conflict diamonds Diamonds that are mined and sold by combatants in war zones in Africa as a way to provide the currency needed to finance their military activities.

conglomerate merger The merger of two *firms* operating in separate industries or separate geographic areas so that neither firm is a supplier, customer, or competitor of the other; any merger that is neither a *horizontal merger* nor a *vertical merger*.

constant returns to scale The situation when a firm's *average total cost* of producing a product remains unchanged in the *long run* as the firm varies the size of its *plant* (and, hence, its output).

constant-cost industry An *industry* in which the entry and exit of *firms* have no effect on the *prices* firms in the industry must pay for resources and thus no effect on production costs.

consumer equilibrium In marginal utility theory, the combination of goods purchased that maximizes *total utility* by applying the *utility-maximizing rule*. In indifference curve analysis, the combination of goods purchased that maximizes *total utility* by enabling the consumer to reach the highest *indifference curve,* given the consumer's *budget line* (or *budget constraint*).

consumer goods Products and *services* that satisfy human wants directly.

Consumer Price Index (CPI) An index that measures the *prices* of a fixed "market basket" of some 300 *goods* and *services* bought by a "typical" consumer.

consumer sovereignty The determination by consumers of the types and quantities of *goods* and *services* that will be produced with the scarce resources of the economy; consumers' direction of production through their *dollar votes*.

consumer surplus The difference between the maximum *price* a consumer is (or consumers are) willing to pay for an additional unit of a product and its market price; the triangular area below the demand curve and above the market price.

consumption of fixed capital An estimate of the amount of *capital* worn out or used up (consumed) in producing the *gross domestic product;* also called depreciation.

consumption schedule A table of numbers showing the amounts *households* plan to spend for *consumer goods* at different levels of *disposable income*.

contractionary fiscal policy A decrease in *government purchases* of *goods* and *services*, an increase in *net taxes,* or some combination of the two, for the purpose of decreasing *aggregate demand* and thus controlling *inflation*.

coordination failure A situation in which people do not reach a mutually beneficial outcome because they lack some way to jointly coordinate their actions; a possible cause of macroeconomic instability.

copayment The percentage of (say, health care) costs that an insured individual pays while the insurer pays the remainder.

core inflation The underlying increases in the *price level* after volatile food and energy *prices* are removed.

corporate income tax A tax levied on the net income (accounting profit) of corporations.

corporation A legal entity ("person") chartered by a state or the federal government that is distinct and separate from the individuals who own it.

corruption The misuse of government power, with which one has been entrusted or assigned, to obtain private gain; includes payments from individuals or companies to secure advantages in obtaining government contracts, avoiding government regulations, or obtaining inside knowledge about forthcoming policy changes.

cost-benefit analysis A comparison of the *marginal costs* of a project or program with the *marginal benefits* to decide whether or not to employ resources in that project or program and to what extent.

cost-of-living adjustment (COLA) An automatic increase in the incomes (*wages*) of workers when *inflation* occurs; often included in *collective bargaining* agreements between *firms* and *unions*. Cost-of-living adjustments are also guaranteed by law for *Social Security* benefits and certain other government *transfer payments*.

cost-push inflation Increases in the *price level* (*inflation*) resulting from an increase in resource costs (for example, raw-material prices) and hence in *per-unit production costs;* inflation caused by reductions in *aggregate supply*.

Council of Economic Advisers (CEA) A group of three persons that advises and assists the president of the United States on economic matters (including the preparation of the annual *Economic Report of the President*).

countercyclical payments (CCPs) Cash *subsidies* paid to farmers when market *prices* for certain crops drop below targeted prices. Payments are based on previous production and are received regardless of the current crop grown.

creative destruction The hypothesis that the creation of new products and production methods destroys the market power of existing monopolies.

credible threat In a *sequential game* with two players, a statement made by Player 1 that truthfully (credibly) threatens a penalizing action against Player 2 if Player 2 does something that Player 1 does not want Player 2 to do. Opposite of *empty threat*.

crop insurance Insurance that farmers can purchase that will pay out if crop selling prices or crop revenues fall below predetermined values.

cross elasticity of demand The ratio of the percentage change in *quantity demanded* of one good to the percentage change in the *price* of some other good. A positive coefficient indicates the two products are *substitute goods;* a negative coefficient indicates they are *complementary goods.*

crowding-out effect A rise in interest rates and a resulting decrease in *planned investment* caused by the federal government's increased borrowing to finance budget deficits and refinance debt.

currency intervention A government's buying and selling of its own currency or foreign currencies to alter international exchange rates.

current account The section in a nation's *international balance of payments* that records its exports and imports of *goods* and *services,* its net *investment income,* and its *net transfers.*

cyclical asymmetry The idea that *monetary policy* may be more successful in slowing expansions and controlling *inflation* than in extracting the economy from severe recession.

cyclical deficit Federal *budget deficit* that is caused by a recession and the consequent decline in tax revenues.

cyclical unemployment A type of *unemployment* caused by insufficient total spending (insufficient *aggregate demand*) and which typically begins in the *recession* phase of the *business cycle.*

cyclically adjusted budget The estimated annual budget deficit or surplus that would occur under existing tax rates and government spending levels if the the economy were to operate at its *full-employment* level of GDP for a year; the *full-employment* budget deficit or surplus.

deadweight loss (See *efficiency loss.*)

debt crisis An economic crisis in which government debt has risen so high that the government is unable to borrow any more money due to people losing faith in the government's ability to repay. Leads to either massive spending cuts or large tax increases, either of which will likely plunge the economy into a *recession.*

decision node In a *strategic game* that is presented in *extensive form,* a point (node) at which a player must make a decision. The decision leads to either another *decision node* or a *terminal node.*

decreasing-cost industry An *industry* in which expansion through the entry of *firms* lowers the *prices* that firms in the industry must pay for resources and therefore decreases their production costs.

deductible The dollar sum of (for example, health care) costs that an insured individual must pay before the insurer begins to pay.

defaults Situations in which borrowers stop making loan payments or do not pay back loans that they took out and are now due.

defensive medicine The recommendation by physicians of more tests and procedures than are warranted medically or economically as a way of protecting themselves against later malpractice suits.

deflation A decline in the general level of *prices* in an economy; a decline in an economy's *price level.*

demand A schedule or curve that shows the various amounts of a product that consumers are willing and able to purchase at each of a series of possible *prices* during a specified period of time.

demand curve A curve that illustrates the *demand* for a product by showing how each possible *price* (on the *vertical axis*) is associated with a specific *quantity demanded* (on the *horizontal axis*).

demand factor (in growth) The requirement that *aggregate demand* increase as fast as *potential output* if *economic growth* is to proceed as quickly as possible.

demand schedule A table of numbers showing the amounts of a *good* or *service* buyers are willing and able to purchase at various *prices* over a specified period of time.

demand shocks Sudden, unexpected changes in demand.

demand-pull inflation Increases in the *price level* (*inflation*) resulting from increases in *aggregate demand.*

demand-side market failures Underallocations of resources that occur when private demand curves understate consumers' full willingness to pay for a *good* or *service.*

demographers Scientists who study the characteristics of human populations.

demographic transition The massive decline in birth rates that occurs once a developing country achieves higher standards of living because the perceived marginal cost of additional children begins to exceed the perceived marginal benefit.

dependent variable A variable that changes as a consequence of a change in some other (independent) variable; the "effect" or outcome.

deregulation The removal of most or even all of the government regulation and laws designed to supervise an industry. Sometimes undertaken to combat *regulatory capture.*

derived demand The demand for a resource that depends on the demand for the products it helps to produce.

determinants of aggregate demand Factors such as consumption spending, *investment,* government spending, and *net exports* that, if they change, shift the aggregate demand curve.

determinants of aggregate supply Factors such as input prices, *productivity,* and the legal-institutional environment that, if they change, shift the aggregate supply curve.

determinants of demand Factors other than *price* that determine the quantities demanded of a *good* or *service.* Also referred to as "demand shifters" because changes in the determinants of demand will cause the *demand curve* to shift either right or left.

determinants of supply Factors other than *price* that determine the quantities supplied of a *good* or *service.* Also referred to as "supply shifters" because changes in the determinants of supply will cause the *supply curve* to shift either right or left.

devaluation A decrease in the governmentally defined value of a currency.

developing countries (DVCs) Many countries of Africa, Asia, and Latin America that are characterized by lack of capital goods, use of nonadvanced technologies, low literacy rates, high unemployment, relatively rapid population growth, and labor forces heavily committed to agriculture.

diagnosis-related group (DRG) system Payments to doctors and hospitals under *Medicare* based on which of hundreds of carefully detailed diagnostic categories best characterize each patient's condition and needs.

dictator game A mutually anonymous behavioral economics game in which one person ("the dictator") unilaterally determines how to split an amount of money with the second player.

differentiated oligopoly An *oligopoly* in which *firms* produce a *differentiated product.*

diffusion The spread of an *innovation* through its widespread imitation.

diminishing marginal utility (See *law of diminishing marginal utility.*)

direct payments Cash subsidies paid to farmers based on past production levels; a permanent transfer payment unaffected by current crop *prices* and current production.

direct relationship The relationship between two variables that change in the same direction, for example, product *price* and quantity supplied; a positive relationship.

discount rate The interest rate that the *Federal Reserve Banks* charge on the loans they make to *commercial banks* and *thrift institutions.*

discouraged workers Employees who have left the *labor force* because they have not been able to find employment.

discrimination The practice of according individuals or groups inferior treatment in hiring, occupational access, education and training, promotion, wage rates, or working conditions even though they have the same abilities, education, skills, and work experience as other workers.

discrimination coefficient A measure of the cost or disutility of prejudice; the monetary amount an employer is willing to pay to hire a preferred worker rather than a nonpreferred worker of the same ability.

diseconomies of scale The situation when a firm's *average total cost* of producing a product increases in the *long run* as the firm increases the size of its *plant* (and, hence, its output).

disinflation A reduction in the rate of *inflation.*

disposable income (DI) *Personal income* less personal taxes; income available for *personal consumption expenditures* and *personal saving.*

diversifiable risk Investment *risk* that investors can reduce via *diversification;* also called idiosyncratic risk.

diversification The strategy of investing in a large number of investments in order to reduce the overall risk to an entire investment *portfolio.*

dividends Payments by a corporation of all or part of its profit to its stockholders (the corporate owners).

division of labor The separation of the work required to produce a product into a number of different tasks that are performed by different workers; *specialization* of workers.

Doha Development Agenda The latest, uncompleted (as of late 2013) sequence of trade negotiations by members of the *World Trade Organization;* named after Doha, Qatar, where the set of negotiations began. Also called the Doha Round.

dollar votes The "votes" that consumers cast for the production of preferred products when they purchase those products rather than the alternatives that were also available.

domestic price The *price* of a *good* or *service* within a country, determined by domestic demand and supply.

dominant strategy In a strategic interaction (*game*) between two or more players, a course of action (strategy) that a player will wish to undertake no matter what the other players choose to do.

dumping The sale of a product in a foreign country at *prices* either below cost or below the prices commonly charged at home.

DuPont cellophane case The antitrust case brought against DuPont in which the U.S. Supreme Court ruled (in 1956) that while DuPont had a monopoly in the narrowly defined market for cellophane, it did not monopolize the more broadly defined market for flexible packaging materials. It was thus not guilty of violating the *Sherman Act.*

durable good A consumer good with an expected life (use) of three or more years.

earmarks Narrow, specially designated spending authorizations placed in broad legislation by senators and representatives for the purpose of providing benefits to *firms* and organizations within their constituencies. Earmarked projects are exempt from competitive bidding and normal evaluation procedures.

earned-income tax credit (EITC) A refundable federal *tax credit* for low-income working people designed to reduce poverty and encourage labor-force participation.

economic cost A payment that must be made to obtain and retain the *services* of a *resource;* the income a *firm* must provide to a resource supplier to attract the resource away from an alternative use; equal to the quantity of other products that cannot be produced when resources are instead used to make a particular product.

economic growth (1) An outward shift in the *production possibilities curve* that results from an increase in resource supplies or quality or an improvement in *technology;* (2) an increase of real output (*gross domestic product*) or real output per capita.

economic immigrants International migrants who have moved from one country to another to obtain economic gains such as better employment opportunities.

economic investment (See *investment.*)

economic perspective A viewpoint that envisions individuals and institutions making rational decisions by comparing the marginal benefits and marginal costs associated with their actions.

economic principle A widely accepted generalization about the economic behavior of individuals or institutions.

economic profit The return flowing to those who provide the economy with the *economic resource* of *entrepreneurial ability;* the *total revenue* of a *firm* less its *economic costs* (which include both *explicit costs* and *implicit costs*); also called "pure profit" and "above-normal profit."

economic rent The *price* paid for the use of land and other natural resources that are in fixed (*perfectly inelastic*) supply.

economic resources The *land, labor, capital,* and *entrepreneurial ability* that are used to produce *goods* and *services;* the *factors of production.*

economic system A particular set of institutional arrangements and a coordinating mechanism for solving the *economizing problem*; a method of organizing an economy, of which the *market system* and the *command system* are the two general types.

economics The social science concerned with how individuals, institutions, and society make optimal (best) choices under conditions of scarcity.

economies of scale The situation when a firm's *average total cost* of producing a product decreases in the *long run* as the firm increases the size of its *plant* (and, hence, its output).

economizing problem The choices necessitated because society's economic wants for *goods* and *services* are unlimited but the resources available to satisfy these wants are limited (scarce).

efficiency factor (in growth) The capacity of an economy to achieve *allocative efficiency* and *productive efficiency* and thereby fulfill the potential for growth that the *supply factors* (*of growth*) make possible; the capacity of an economy to achieve *economic efficiency* and thereby reach the optimal point on its *production possibilities curve*.

efficiency gains from migration The increases in total worldwide output that take place if the additions to output from *immigration* in the destination nation exceed the loss of output from *emigration* from the origin nation.

efficiency loss Reductions in combined consumer and producer surplus caused by an underallocation or overallocation of resources to the production of a *good* or *service*. Also called *deadweight loss*.

efficiency loss of a tax The loss of *net benefits* to society because a tax reduces the production and consumption of a taxed good below the level of *allocative efficiency*. Also called the *deadweight loss* of the tax.

efficiency wage An above-market (above-equilibrium) *wage* that minimizes wage costs per unit of output by encouraging greater effort or reducing turnover.

elastic demand Product or resource demand whose *price elasticity of demand* is greater than 1, so that any given percentage change in *price* leads to a larger percentage change in *quantity demanded*. As a result, quantity demanded is relatively sensitive to (elastic with respect to) price.

elasticity of resource demand A measure of the responsiveness of *firms* to a change in the *price* of a particular *resource* they employ or use; the percentage change in the quantity demanded of the *resource* divided by the percentage change in its *price*.

employer mandate The requirement under the *Patient Protection and Affordable Care Act* (*PPACA*) of 2010 that firms with 50 or more employees pay for insurance policies for their employees or face a fine of $2,000 per employee per year. Firms with fewer than 50 employees are exempt.

empty threat In a *sequential game* with two players, a non-credible (bluffing) statement made by Player 1 that threatens a penalizing action against Player 2 if Player 2 does something that Player 1 does not want Player 2 to do. Opposite of *credible threat*.

endowment effect The tendency people have to place higher valuations on items they possess (are endowed with) than on identical items that they do not possess; perhaps caused by *loss aversion*.

entitlement programs Government programs such as *social insurance, Medicare,* and *Medicaid* that guarantee (entitle) particular levels of transfer payments or noncash benefits to all who fit the programs' criteria.

entrepreneurial ability The human resource that combines the other *economic resources* of *land, labor*, and *capital* to produce new products or make innovations in the production of existing products; provided by *entrepreneurs*.

entrepreneurs Individuals who provide *entrepreneurial ability* to *firms* by setting strategy, advancing innovations, and bearing the financial risk if their firms do poorly.

equality-efficiency trade-off The decrease in *economic efficiency* that may accompany a decrease in *income inequality;* the presumption that some income inequality is required to achieve economic efficiency.

equation of exchange $MV = PQ$, in which M is the supply of *money*, V is the *velocity* of money, P is the *price level,* and Q is the physical volume of *final goods* and final *services* produced.

equilibrium GDP (See *equilibrium real domestic output.*)

equilibrium position In the indifference curve model, the combination of two goods at which a consumer maximizes his or her *utility* (reaches the highest attainable *indifference curve*), given a limited amount to spend (a *budget constraint*).

equilibrium price The *price* in a competitive market at which the *quantity demanded* and the *quantity supplied* are equal, there is neither a shortage nor a surplus, and there is no tendency for price to rise or fall.

equilibrium price level In the *aggregate demand–aggregate supply* (*AD-AS*) *model*, the *price level* at which *aggregate demand* equals *aggregate supply;* the price level at which the aggregate demand curve intersects the aggregate supply curve.

equilibrium quantity (1) The quantity at which the intentions of buyers and sellers in a particular market match at a particular *price* such that the *quantity demanded* and the *quantity supplied* are equal; (2) the profit-maximizing output of a *firm*.

equilibrium real output (See *equilibrium real domestic output.*)

equilibrium world price The *price* of an internationally traded product that equates the quantity of the product demanded by importers with the quantity of the product supplied by exporters; the price determined at the intersection of the export supply curve and the import demand curve.

European Union (EU) An association of 28 European nations (as of mid-2013) that has eliminated tariffs and quotas among them, established common tariffs for imported goods from outside the member nations, eliminated barriers to the free movement of capital, and created other common economic policies.

eurozone The 17 nations (as of 2013) of the 28-member (as of 2013) *European Union* that use the *euro* as their common *currency*. The eurozone countries are Austria, Belgium, Cyprus, Estonia, Finland, France, Germany, Greece, Ireland, Italy, Luxembourg, Malta, the Netherlands, Portugal, Slovakia, Slovenia, and Spain.

excess capacity *Plant* resources that are underused when imperfectly competitive *firms* produce less output than that associated with achieving minimum *average total cost*.

excess reserves The amount by which a *commercial bank*'s or *thrift institution*'s *actual reserves* exceed its *required reserves;* actual reserves minus required reserves.

exchange controls Restrictions that a government may impose over the quantity of foreign currency demand by its citizens and *firms* and over the *rate of exchange* as a way to limit the nation's quantity of *outpayments* relative to its quantity of *inpayments* (in order to eliminate a *payments deficit*).

excise tax A tax levied on the production of a specific product or on the quantity of the product purchased.

excludability The characteristic of a *private good,* for which the seller can keep nonbuyers from obtaining the good.

exclusive unionism The policy, pursued by many *craft unions*, in which a *union* first gets employers to agree to hire only union workers and then excludes many workers from joining the union so as to restrict the supply of labor and drive up wages. Compare with *inclusive unionism.* The policies typically employed by a *craft union.*

exit mechanism The method of resolving workplace dissatisfaction by quitting one's job and searching for another.

expansion The phase of the *business cycle* in which *real GDP, income*, and employment rise.

expansionary fiscal policy An increase in *government purchases* of *goods* and *services*, a decrease in *net taxes,* or some combination of the two for the purpose of increasing *aggregate demand* and expanding real output.

expansionary monetary policy *Federal Reserve System* actions to increase the *money supply,* lower *interest rates,* and expand *real GDP;* an easy money policy.

expectations The anticipations of consumers, *firms*, and others about future economic conditions.

expected rate of return The increase in profit a *firm* anticipates it will obtain by purchasing capital or engaging in research and development (*R&D*); expressed as a percentage of the total cost of the investment (or R&D) activity.

expected-rate-of-return curve As it relates to research and development (*R&D*), a curve showing the anticipated gain in *profit*, as a percentage of R&D expenditure, from an additional dollar spent on R&D.

expenditures approach The method that adds all expenditures made for *final goods* and final *services* to measure the *gross domestic product*.

explicit cost The monetary payment made by a *firm* to an outsider to obtain a *resource*.

export subsidy A government payment to a domestic producer to enable the *firm* to reduce the *price* of a *good* or *service* to foreign buyers.

export supply curve An upward-sloping curve that shows the amount of a product that domestic *firms* will export at each *world price* that is above the *domestic price*.

extensive form A visual representation of a *sequential game* that maps out every possible decision as well as the sequence in which decisions must be made. Also called game-tree format.

external public debt The portion of the public debt owed to foreign citizens, *firms*, and institutions.

externality A cost or benefit from production or consumption that accrues to to someone other than the immediate buyers and sellers of the product being produced or consumed (see *negative externality* and *positive externality*).

extraction cost All costs associated with extracting a natural resource and readying it for sale.

factors of production The four *economic resources: land, labor, capital,* and *entrepreneurial ability.*

fair-return price For *natural monopolies* subject to rate (*price*) regulation, the price that would allow the regulated monopoly to earn a *normal profit;* a price equal to *average total cost.*

fairness A person's opinion as to whether a price, wage, or allocation is considered morally or ethically acceptable.

farm commodities Agricultural products such as grains, milk, cattle, fruits, and vegetables that are usually sold to processors, who use the products as inputs in creating *food products.*

fast-second strategy An approach by a dominant *firm* in which it allows other firms in its *industry* to bear the risk of innovation and then quickly becomes the second firm to offer any successful new product or adopt any improved production process.

federal funds rate The interest rate that U.S. banks and other depository institutions charge one another on overnight loans made out of their *excess reserves.*

Federal Open Market Committee (FOMC) The 12-member group within the *Federal Reserve System* that decides U.S. *monetary policy* and how it is executed through *open-market operations* (in which the Fed buys and sells U.S. government securities to adjust the *money supply*).

Federal Reserve Banks The 12 banks chartered by the U.S. government that collectively act as the *central bank* of the United States. They set monetary policy and regulate the private banking system under the direction of the *Board of Governors* and the *Federal Open Market Committee*. Each of the 12 is a *quasi-public bank* and acts as a *banker's bank* in its designated geographic region.

Federal Reserve Note Paper money issued by the *Federal Reserve Banks.*

Federal Reserve System The U.S. central bank, consisting of the *Board of Governors* of the Federal Reserve and the 12 *Federal Reserve Banks*, which controls the lending activity of the nation's banks and thrifts and thus the *money supply;* commonly referred to as the "Fed."

Federal Trade Commission Act The federal law of 1914 that established the *Federal Trade Commission.*

fee for service In the health care *industry*, payment to physicians for each visit made or procedure performed.

final goods Goods that have been purchased for final use (rather than for resale or further processing or manufacturing.)

financial investment The purchase of a financial asset (such as a *stock, bond,* or *mutual fund*) or real asset (such as a house, land, or factories) or the building of such assets in the expectation of financial gain.

financial services industry The broad category of *firms* that provide financial products and services to help *households* and businesses earn *interest,* receive *dividends,* obtain *capital gains,* insure against losses, and plan for retirement. Includes *commercial banks, thrift institutions,* insurance companies, mutual fund companies, pension funds, investment banks, and *securities* firms.

first-mover advantage In *game theory,* the benefit obtained by the party that moves first in a *sequential game.* A situation that occurs in a *sequential game* if the player who gets to move first has an advantage in terms of final outcomes over the player(s) who move subsequently.

fiscal policy Changes in government spending and tax collections designed to achieve full employment, price stability, and economic growth; also called *discretionary fiscal policy.*

fishery A stock of fish or other marine animal that is composed of a distinct group, for example New England cod, Pacific tuna, or Alaskan crab.

fishery collapse A rapid decline in a *fishery*'s population because its fish are being harvested faster than they can reproduce.

fixed cost Any cost that in total does not change when the *firm* changes its output.

fixed exchange rate A *rate of exchange* that is set in some way and therefore prevented from rising or falling with changes in currency supply and demand.

flexible exchange rate A *rate of exchange* that is determined by the international demand for and supply of a nation's money and that is consequently free to rise or fall because it is not subject to *currency interventions.* Also referred to as a "floating exchange rate."

flexible prices Product *prices* that freely move upward or downward when product demand or supply changes.

follower countries As it relates to *economic growth,* countries that adopt advanced technologies that previously were developed and used by *leader countries.*

food products Processed *farm commodities* sold through grocery stores and restaurants. Examples: bread, meat, fish, chicken, pork, lettuce, peanut butter, and breakfast cereal.

foreign direct investment *Financial investments* made to obtain a lasting ownership interest in *firms* operating outside the economy of the investor; may involve purchasing existing assets or building new production facilities.

foreign purchases effect The inverse relationship between the *net exports* of an economy and its *price level* relative to foreign price levels.

foreign exchange reserves Stockpiles of foreign currencies maintained by a nation's *central bank.* Obtained when the *central bank* sells local currency in exchange for foreign currency in the *foreign exchange market.*

four-firm concentration ratio The percentage of total *industry* sales accounted for by the top four *firms* in an industry.

fractional reserve banking system A system in which *commercial banks* and *thrift institutions* hold less than 100 percent of their checkable-deposit liabilities as reserves of *currency* held in bank vaults or as deposits at the *central bank.*

framing effects In *prospect theory,* changes in people's decision making caused by new information that alters the context, or "frame of reference," that they use to judge whether options are viewed as gains or losses relative to the *status quo.*

free-rider problem The inability of potential providers of an economically desirable *good* or *service* to obtain payment from those who benefit, because of *nonexcludability.*

freedom of choice The freedom of owners of property resources to employ or dispose of them as they see fit, of workers to enter any line of work for which they are qualified, and of consumers to spend their incomes in a manner that they think is appropriate.

freedom of enterprise The freedom of *firms* to obtain economic resources, to use those resources to produce products of the firm's own choosing, and to sell their products in markets of their choice.

Freedom to Farm Act A law passed in 1996 that revamped 60 years of U.S. farm policy by ending *price supports* and *acreage allotments* for wheat, corn, barley, oats, sorghum, rye, cotton, and rice.

frictional unemployment A type of unemployment caused by workers voluntarily changing jobs and by temporary layoffs; unemployed workers between jobs.

full-employment rate of unemployment The *unemployment rate* at which there is no *cyclical unemployment* of the *labor force;* equal to between 5 and 6 percent in the United States because some *frictional* and *structural unemployment* are unavoidable.

future value The amount to which some current amount of *money* will grow if *interest* earned on the amount is left to compound over time. (*See compound interest.*)

gains from trade The extra output that trading partners obtain through specialization of production and exchange of *goods* and *services.*

game An interaction between two or more participants (players) that is strategic so that the choices (strategies) of every participant affect the incentives facing—and thus the choices made by—all of the other participants.

game theory The study of how people behave in strategic situations in which individuals must take into account not only their own possible actions but also the possible reactions of others. Originally developed to analyze the best ways to play games like poker and chess.

GDP gap Actual *gross domestic product* minus *potential output*; may be either a positive amount (a *positive GDP gap*) or a negative amount (a *negative GDP gap*).

General Agreement on Tariffs and Trade (GATT) The international agreement reached in 1947 in which 23 nations agreed to eliminate *import quotas*, negotiate reductions in *tariff* rates, and give each other equal and nondiscriminatory treatment. It now includes most nations and has become the *World Trade Organization.*

Gini ratio A numerical measure of the overall dispersion of income among *households*, families, or individuals; found graphically by dividing the area between the diagonal line and the *Lorenz curve* by the entire area below the diagonal line.

gold standard A historical system of fixed exchange rates in which nations defined their currencies in terms of gold, maintained fixed relationships between their stocks of gold and their money supplies, and allowed gold to be freely exported and imported.

government failure Inefficiencies in resource allocation caused by problems in the operation of the *public sector* (government). Specific examples include the *principal-agent problem*, the *special-interest effect*, the *collective-action problem*, *rent seeking*, and *political corruption.*

government purchases (G) Expenditures by government for *goods* and *services* that government consumes in providing public services as well as expenditures for publicly owned capital that has a long lifetime; the expenditures of all governments in the economy for those *final goods* and final *services*.

gross domestic product (GDP) The total market value of all *final goods* and final *services* produced annually within the boundaries of a nation.

gross output (GO) The dollar value of the economic activity taking place at every stage of production and distribution. By contrast, *gross domestic product* (GDP) only accounts for the value of final output.

gross private domestic investment *(Ig)* Expenditures for newly produced *capital goods* (such as machinery, equipment, tools, and buildings) and for additions to inventories.

growth accounting The bookkeeping of the supply-side elements such as productivity and labor inputs that contribute to changes in *real GDP* over some specific time period.

H1-B provision A provision of the U.S. immigration law that allows the annual entry of 65,000 high-skilled workers in "specialty occupations" such as science, *R&D,* and computer programming to work legally and continuously in the United States for six years.

health maintenance organizations (HMOs) Health care providers that contract with employers, insurance companies, labor unions, or government units to provide health care for their workers or others who are insured.

health savings accounts (HSAs) Tax-free savings accounts into which people with high-deductible health insurance plans can place funds each year. Accumulated funds can be used to pay out-of-pocket medical expenses such as *deductibles* and *copayments*. Unused funds accumulate from year to year and can be used after retirement to supplement *Medicare*.

Herfindahl index A measure of the concentration and competitiveness of an *industry;* calculated as the sum of the squared percentage market shares of the individual *firms* in the industry.

heuristics The brain's low-energy mental shortcuts for making decisions. They are "fast and frugal" and work well in most situations but in other situations result in *systematic errors*.

homogeneous oligopoly An *oligopoly* in which *firms* produce a *standardized product*.

horizontal axis The "left-right" or "west-east" measurement line on a graph or grid.

horizontal merger The merger into a single *firm* of two firms producing the same product and selling it in the same geographic market.

households Economic entities (of one or more persons occupying a housing unit) that provide *resources* to the economy and use the *income* received to purchase *goods* and *services* that satisfy economic wants.

human capital The knowledge and skills that make a person productive.

hyperinflation A very rapid rise in the *price level;* an extremely high rate of *inflation*.

illegal immigrants People who have entered a country unlawfully to reside there; also called unauthorized immigrants.

imitation problem The potential for a *firm*'s rivals to produce a close variation of (imitate) a firm's new product or process, greatly reducing the originator's profit from *R&D* and *innovation*.

immediate market period The length of time during which the producers of a product are unable to change the quantity supplied in response to a change in price and in which there is a *perfectly inelastic supply*.

immediate short-run aggregate supply curve An *aggregate supply* curve for which real *output*, but not the *price level*, changes when the *aggregate demand* curve shifts; a horizontal *aggregate supply* curve that implies an inflexible price level.

imperfect competition All *market structures* except *pure competition;* includes *monopoly, monopolistic competition,* and *oligopoly*.

implicit cost The monetary income a *firm* sacrifices when it uses a *resource* it owns rather than supplying the resource in the market; equal to what the resource could have earned in the best-paying alternative employment; includes a *normal profit*.

import competition The competition that domestic *firms* encounter from the products and *services* of foreign producers.

import demand curve A downsloping curve showing the amount of a product that an economy will import at each *world price* below the *domestic price*.

import quota A limit imposed by a nation on the quantity (or total value) of a good that may be imported during some period of time.

incentive function The inducement that an increase in the price of a commodity gives to sellers to make more of it available (and conversely for a decrease in *price*), and the inducement that an increase in price offers to buyers to purchase smaller quantities (and conversely for a decrease in price).

incentive pay plan A compensation structure that ties worker pay directly to performance. Such plans include piece rates, bonuses, *stock options,* commissions, and *profit-sharing plans*.

inclusive unionism The policy, pursued by *industrial unions,* in which a *union* attempts to include every worker in a given *industry* so as to be able to restrict the entire industry's labor supply and thereby raise wages. Compare with *exclusive unionism*.

income approach The method that adds all the *income* generated by the production of *final goods* and final *services* to measure the *gross domestic product*.

income effect A change in the quantity demanded of a product that results from the change in *real income* (*purchasing power*) caused by a change in the product's *price*.

income elasticity of demand The ratio of the percentage change in the *quantity demanded* of a good to a percentage change in consumer *income;* measures the responsiveness of consumer purchases to income changes.

income inequality The unequal distribution of an economy's total *income* among *households* or families.

income mobility The extent to which *income* receivers move from one part of the income distribution to another over some period of time.

increasing returns An increase in a *firm*'s output by a larger percentage than the percentage increase in its inputs.

increasing-cost industry An *industry* in which expansion through the entry of new *firms* raises the *prices* firms in the industry must pay for *resources* and therefore increases their production costs.

independent unions U.S. unions that are not affiliated with the *AFL-CIO* or *Change to Win.*

independent variable The variable causing a change in some other (dependent) variable.

index funds *Mutual funds* whose *portfolios* exactly match a stock or bond index (a collection of *stocks* or *bonds* meant to capture the overall behavior of a particular category of investments) such as the Standard & Poor's 500 Index or the Russell 3000 Index.

indifference curve A curve showing the different combinations of two products that yield the same satisfaction or *utility* to a consumer.

indifference map A set of *indifference curves,* each representing a different level of *utility,* that together show the preferences of a consumer.

individual transferable quotas (ITQs) Limits (quotas) set by a government or a fisheries commission on the total number or total weight of a species that an individual fisher can harvest during some particular time period; fishers can sell (transfer) the right to use all or part of their respective individual quotas to other fishers.

industrial regulation The older and more traditional type of regulation in which government is concerned with the *prices* charged and the *services* provided to the public in specific *industries.* Differs from *social regulation.*

industrially advanced countries (IACs) High-income countries such as the United States, Canada, Japan, and the nations of western Europe that have highly developed *market economies* based on large stocks of technologically advanced *capital goods* and skilled labor forces.

inelastic demand Product or resource demand for which the *price elasticity of demand* is less than 1, so that any given percentage change in *price* leads to a smaller percentage change in *quantity demanded.* As a result, quantity demanded is relatively insensitive to (inelastic with respect to) price.

inferior good A *good* or *service* whose consumption declines as *income* rises, *prices* held constant.

inflation A rise in the general level of *prices* in an economy; an increase in an economy's *price level.*

inflation targeting The declaration by a *central bank* of a goal for a specific range of *inflation* in a future year, coupled with *monetary policy* designed to achieve the goal.

inflationary expenditure gap In the *aggregate-expenditures model*, the amount by which the *aggregate expenditures schedule* must shift downward to decrease the *nominal GDP* to its full-employment noninflationary level.

inflexible prices Product *prices* that remain in place (at least for a while) even though *supply* or *demand* has changed; stuck prices or sticky prices.

information technology New and more efficient methods of delivering and receiving information through the use of computers, Wi-Fi networks, wireless phones, and the Internet.

infrastructure The interconnected network of large-scale *capital goods* (such as roads, sewers, electrical grids, railways, ports, and the Internet) needed to operate a technologically advanced economy.

injection An addition of spending into the income-expenditure stream: any increment to *consumption, investment, government purchases*, or *net exports.*

innovation The first commercially successful introduction of a new product, use of a new method of production, or creation of a new form of business organization.

insider-outsider theory The hypothesis that nominal wages are inflexible downward because *firms* are aware that workers ("insiders") who retain employment during recession may refuse to work cooperatively with previously unemployed workers ("outsiders") who offer to work for less than the current wage.

insurable risk An eventuality for which both the frequency and magnitude of potential losses can be estimated with considerable accuracy. Insurance companies are willing to sell insurance against such risks.

insurance exchanges Government-regulated markets for health insurance in which individuals seeking to purchase health insurance to comply with the *personal mandate* of the *Patient Protection and Affordable Care Act* (*PPACA*) of 2010 will be able to comparison shop among insurance policies approved by regulators. Each state will have its own exchange.

interest The payment made for the use of (borrowed) *money.*

interest on excess reserves (IOER) *Interest rate* paid by the *Federal Reserve* on bank *excess reserves.*

interest-rate effect The tendency for increases in the *price level* to increase the demand for money, raise interest rates, and, as a result, reduce total spending and real output in the economy (and the reverse for *price-level* decreases).

interest-rate-cost-of-funds curve As it relates to research and development (*R&D*), a curve showing the *interest rate* a *firm* must pay to obtain any particular amount of funds to finance R&D.

interindustry competition The competition for sales between the products of one *industry* and the products of another industry.

interlocking directorate A situation where one or more members of the board of directors of a *corporation* are also on the board of directors of a competing corporation; illegal under the *Clayton Act.*

intermediate goods Products that are purchased for resale or further processing or manufacturing.

International Monetary Fund (IMF) The international association of nations that was formed after the Second World War to make loans of foreign monies to nations with temporary *balance of payments deficits* and, until the early 1970s, manage the international system of pegged exchange rates agreed upon at the Bretton Woods conference. It now mainly makes loans to nations facing possible defaults on private and government loans.

invention The conception of a new product or process combined with the first proof that it will work.

inventories Goods that have been produced but remain unsold.

inverse relationship The relationship between two variables that change in opposite directions, for example, product *price* and quantity demanded; a negative relationship.

inverted-U theory (of R&D) The idea that, other things equal, *R&D* expenditures as a percentage of sales rise with *industry* concentration, reach a peak at a *four-firm concentration ratio* of about 50 percent, and then fall as the ratio further increases.

investment In economics, spending for the production and accumulation of *capital* and additions to *inventories.* (For contrast, see *financial investment.*)

investment demand curve A curve that shows the amounts of *investment* demanded by an economy at a series of *real interest rates.*

investment schedule The tendency of *competition* to cause individuals and *firms* to unintentionally but quite effectively promote the interests of society even when each individual or firm is only attempting to pursue its own interests.

invisible hand The tendency of competition to cause individuals and firms to unintentionally but quite effectively promote the interests of society even when each individual or firm is only attempting to pursue its own interests.

kinked-demand curve A *demand curve* that has a flatter slope above the current *price* than below the current price. Applies to a *noncollusive oligopoly* firm if its rivals will match any price decrease but ignore any price increase.

labor Any mental or physical exertion on the part of a human being that is used in the production of a *good* or *service.* One of the four *economic resources.*

labor force Persons 16 years of age and older who are not in institutions and who are employed or are unemployed and seeking work.

labor productivity Total output divided by the quantity of labor employed to produce it; the *average product* of labor or output per hour of work.

labor-force participation rate The percentage of the working-age population that is actually in the *labor force.*

labor-intensive goods Products requiring relatively large amounts of *labor* to produce.

Laffer Curve A curve relating government tax rates and tax revenues and on which a particular tax rate (between zero and 100 percent) maximizes tax revenues.

laissez-faire capitalism A hypothetical *economic system* in which the government's economic role is limited to protecting private property and establishing a legal environment appropriate to the operation of *markets* in which only mutually agreeable transactions would take place between buyers and sellers; sometimes referred to as "pure *capitalism.*"

land In addition to the part of the earth's surface not covered by water, this term refers to any and all natural resources ("free gifts of nature") that are used to produce *goods* and *services.* Thus, it includes the oceans, sunshine, coal deposits, forests, the electromagnetic spectrum, and *fisheries.* Note that land is one of the four *economic resources.*

land reform Policy changes aimed at creating a more efficient distribution of land ownership in developing countries. Can involve everything from government purchasing large land estates and dividing the land into smaller farms to consolidating tiny plots of land into larger, more efficient private farms.

land-intensive goods Products requiring relatively large amounts of land to produce.

law of demand The principle that, other things equal, an increase in a product's *price* will reduce the quantity of it demanded, and conversely for a decrease in price.

law of diminishing marginal utility The principle that as a consumer increases the consumption of a *good* or *service,* the *marginal utility* obtained from each additional unit of the good or service decreases.

law of diminishing returns The principle that as successive increments of a variable *resource* are added to a fixed resource, the *marginal product* of the variable resource will eventually decrease.

law of increasing opportunity costs The principle that as the production of a good increases, the *opportunity cost* of producing an additional unit rises.

law of supply The principle that, other things equal, an increase in the *price* of a product will increase the quantity of it supplied, and conversely for a price decrease.

leader countries As it relates to *economic growth,* countries that develop and use the most advanced technologies, which then become available to *follower countries.*

leakage (1) A withdrawal of potential spending from the income-expenditures stream via *saving,* tax payments, or *imports;* (2) a withdrawal that reduces the lending potential of the banking system.

learning by doing Achieving greater *productivity* and lower *average total cost* through gains in knowledge and skill that accompany repetition of a task; a source of *economies of scale.*

least-cost combination of resources The quantity of each *resource* that a *firm* must employ in order to produce a particular output at the lowest total cost; the combination at which the ratio of the *marginal product* of a resource to its *marginal resource cost* (to its *price* if the resource is employed in a competitive market) is the same for the last dollar spent on each of the resources employed.

legal cartel theory of regulation The hypothesis that some *industries* seek regulation or want to maintain regulation so that they may form or maintain a legal *cartel.*

legal immigrant A person who lawfully enters a country for the purpose of residing there.

legal tender Any form of *currency* that by law must be accepted by creditors (lenders) for the settlement of a financial debt; a nation's official currency is legal tender within its own borders.

limited liability rule A law that limits the potential losses that an investor in a *corporation* may suffer to the amount that she paid for her shares in the corporation. Encourages *financial investment* by limiting risk.

liquidity The degree to which an asset can be converted quickly into cash with little or no loss of purchasing power. *Money* is said to be perfectly liquid, whereas other assets have lesser degrees of liquidity.

liquidity trap A situation in a severe *recession* in which the *central bank's* injection of additional reserves into the banking system has little or no additional positive impact on lending, borrowing, *investment,* or *aggregate demand.*

loan guarantees A type of investment *subsidy* in which the government agrees to guarantee (pay off) the money borrowed by a private company to fund investment projects if the private company itself fails to repay the loan.

loanable funds theory of interest The concept that the supply of and demand for *loanable funds* determine the equilibrium rate of *interest.*

lockout A negotiating tactic in which a *firm* forbids its unionized workers to return to work until a new *collective bargaining* agreement is signed; a means of imposing costs (lost wages) on union workers.

logrolling The trading of votes by legislators to secure favorable outcomes on decisions concerning the provision of *public goods* and *quasi-public goods.*

long run (1) In *microeconomics,* a period of time long enough to enable producers of a product to change the quantities of all the resources they employ, so that all resources and costs are variable and no resources or costs are fixed. (2) In *macroeconomics,* a period sufficiently long for *nominal wages* and other input *prices* to change in response to a change in a nation's *price level.*

long-run aggregate supply curve The *aggregate supply* curve associated with a time period in which input *prices* (especially *nominal wages*) are fully responsive to changes in the *price level.*

long-run supply curve As it applies to *macroeconomics,* a *supply curve* for which *price,* but not real output, changes when the *demand curves* shifts; a vertical supply curve that implies fully flexible *prices.*

long-run vertical Phillips Curve The *Phillips Curve* after all *nominal wages* have adjusted to changes in the rate of *inflation*; a line emanating straight upward at the economy's *natural rate of unemployment.*

Lorenz curve A curve showing the distribution of income in an economy. The cumulated percentage of families (income receivers) is measured along the horizontal axis and the cumulated percentage of income is measured along the vertical axis.

loss aversion In *prospect theory,* the property of most people's preferences that the pain generated by losses feels substantially more intense than the pleasure generated by gains.

lump-sum tax A tax that collects a constant amount (the tax revenue of government is the same) at all levels of *GDP.*

***M*1** The most narrowly defined *money supply,* equal to *currency* in the hands of the public and the *checkable deposits* of commercial banks and *thrift institutions.*

***M*2** A more broadly defined *money supply,* equal to *M*1 plus *noncheckable savings accounts* (including *money market deposit accounts*), small *time deposits* (deposits of less than $100,000), and individual *money market mutual fund* balances.

macroeconomics The part of *economics* concerned with the performance and behavior of the economy as a whole. Focuses on *economic growth,* the *business cycle, interest rates, inflation,* and the behavior of major economic *aggregates* such as the household, business, and government sectors.

managed floating exchange rate An *exchange rate* that is allowed to change (float) as a result of changes in *currency* supply and demand but at times is altered (managed) by governments via their buying and selling of particular currencies.

marginal analysis The comparison of *marginal* ("extra" or "additional") *benefits* and *marginal costs,* usually for decision making.

marginal cost (MC) The extra (additional) cost of producing 1 more unit of output; equal to the change in *total cost* divided by the change in output (and, in the short run, to the change in total *variable cost* divided by the change in output).

marginal cost-marginal benefit rule As it applies to *cost-benefit analysis,* the tenet that a government project or program should be expanded to the point where the *marginal cost* and *marginal benefit* of additional expenditures are equal.

marginal product (MP) The additional output produced when 1 additional unit of a resource is employed (the quantity of all other resources employed remaining constant); equal to the change in *total product* divided by the change in the quantity of a resource employed.

marginal productivity theory of income distribution The contention that the distribution of *income* is equitable when each unit of each *resource* receives a *money* payment equal to its *marginal revenue product* (its marginal contribution to the revenue of the *firm* using the unit).

marginal propensity to consume (MPC) The fraction of any change in *disposable income* spent for *consumer goods;* equal to the change in consumption divided by the change in disposable income.

marginal propensity to save (MPS) The fraction of any change in *disposable income* that *households* save; equal to the change in *saving* divided by the change in disposable income.

marginal rate of substitution (MRS) The rate at which a consumer is willing to substitute one good for another (from a given combination of goods) and remain equally satisfied (have the same *total utility*); equal to the slope of a consumer's *indifference curve* at each point on the curve.

marginal resource cost (MRC) The amount by which the total cost of employing a *resource* increases when a *firm* employs 1 additional unit of the resource (the quantity of all other resources employed remaining constant); equal to the change in the *total cost* of the resource divided by the change in the quantity of the resource employed.

marginal revenue The change in *total revenue* that results from the sale of 1 additional unit of a *firm*'s product; equal to the change in total revenue divided by the change in the quantity of the product sold.

marginal revenue product (MRP) The change in a firm's *total revenue* when it employs 1 additional unit of a *resource* (the quantity of all other resources employed remaining constant); equal to the change in *total revenue* divided by the change in the quantity of the resource employed.

marginal revenue productivity (See *marginal revenue product.*)

marginal tax rate The *tax* rate paid on an additional dollar of *income.*

marginal utility The extra *utility* a consumer obtains from the consumption of 1 additional unit of a *good* or *service;* equal to the change in *total utility* divided by the change in the quantity consumed.

market Any institution or mechanism that brings together buyers (demanders) and sellers (suppliers) of a particular *good* or *service.*

market failure The inability of a *market* to bring about the allocation of *resources* that best satisfies the wants of society; in particular, the overallocation or underallocation of resources to the production of a particular *good* or *service* because of *externalities* or informational problems or because markets do not provide desired *public goods*.

market portfolio The portfolio consisting of every financial asset (including every *stock* and *bond*) traded in the financial markets. Used to calculate *beta* (a measure of the degree of riskiness) for specific stocks, bonds, and mutual funds.

market structure The characteristics of an *industry* that define the likely behavior and performance of its *firms*. The primary characteristics are the number of firms in the industry, whether they are selling a *differentiated product*, the ease of entry, and how much control firms have over output prices. The most commonly discussed market structures are *pure competition*, *monopolistic competition*, *oligopoly*, pure *monopoly*, and *monopsony*.

market system (1) An *economic system* in which individuals own most *economic resources* and in which *markets* and *prices* serve as the dominant coordinating mechanism used to allocate those resources; *capitalism*. Compare with *command system*. (2) All the product and resource markets of a *market economy* and the relationships among them.

marketing loan program A federal farm subsidy under which certain farmers can receive a loan (on a per-unit-of-output basis) to plant a crop and then, depending on the harvest *price* of the crop, either pay back the loan with interest or keep the loan proceeds while forfeiting their harvested crop to the lender.

median-voter model The theory that under majority rule the median (middle) voter will be in the dominant position to determine the outcome of an election.

Medicaid A federal program that helps finance the medical expenses of individuals covered by the *Supplemental Security Income* (*SSI*) and *Temporary Assistance for Needy Families* (*TANF*) programs.

Medicare A federal program that provides for (1) compulsory hospital insurance for senior citizens, (2) low-cost voluntary insurance to help older Americans pay physicians' fees, and (3) subsidized insurance to buy prescription drugs. Financed by *payroll taxes*.

medium of exchange Any item sellers generally accept and buyers generally use to pay for a *good* or *service; money;* a convenient means of exchanging goods and *services* without engaging in *barter*.

mental accounting The tendency people have to create separate "mental boxes" (or "accounts") in which they deal with particular financial transactions in isolation rather than dealing with them as part of an overall decision-making process that would consider how to best allocate their limited budgets across all possible options by using the *utility-maximizing rule*.

menu costs The reluctance of *firms* to cut *prices* during *recessions* (that they think will be short-lived) because of the costs of altering and communicating their price reductions; named after the cost associated with printing new menus at restaurants.

microcredit Anti-poverty programs that lend small amounts of money to poor entrepreneurs.

microeconomics The part of economics concerned with (1) decision making by individual units such as a *household,* a *firm,* or an *industry* and (2) individual markets, specific *goods* and *services*, and product and resource *prices*.

microfinance The provision of small loans and other financial services to low-income *entrepreneurs* and small-business owners in *developing countries*.

Microsoft case A 2002 antitrust case in which Microsoft was found guilty of violating the *Sherman Act* by engaging in a series of unlawful activities designed to maintain its *monopoly* in operating systems for personal computers; as a remedy the company was prohibited from engaging in a set of specific anticompetitive business practices.

midpoint formula A method for calculating *price elasticity of demand* or *price elasticity of supply* that averages the starting and ending *prices* and quantities when computing percentages.

minimum efficient scale (MES) The lowest level of output at which a *firm* can minimize long-run *average total cost*.

minimum wage The lowest *wage* that employers may legally pay for an hour of work.

modern economic growth The historically recent phenomenon in which nations for the first time have experienced sustained increases in *real GDP per capita*.

monetarism The macroeconomic view that the main cause of changes in aggregate output and the *price level* is fluctuations in the *money supply;* espoused by advocates of a *monetary rule*.

monetary multiplier The multiple of its *excess reserves* by which the banking system can expand *checkable deposits* and thus the *money supply* by making new loans (or buying *securities*); equal to 1 divided by the *reserve requirement*.

monetary policy A central bank's changing of the *money supply* to influence *interest* rates and assist the economy in achieving *price-level stability*, *full employment*, and *economic growth*.

monetary rule (1) A set of guidelines to be followed by a *central bank* that wishes to adjust monetary policy over time to achieve goals such as promoting *economic growth*, encouraging *full employment*, and maintaining a stable *price level*. (2) The guidelines for conducting monetary policy suggested by *monetarism*. As traditionally formulated, the *money supply* should be expanded each year at the same annual rate as the potential rate of growth of *real gross domestic product;* the supply of money should be increased steadily between 3 and 5 percent per year. (Also see *Taylor rule*.)

money Any item that is generally acceptable to sellers in exchange for *goods* and *services*.

money market deposit accounts (MMDAs) Interest-bearing accounts offered by *commercial banks* and *thrift institutions* that invest deposited funds into a variety of short-term *securities*. Depositors may write checks against their balances, but there are minimum-balance requirements as well as limits on the frequency of check writing and withdrawls.

money market mutual funds (MMMFs) *Mutual funds* that invest in short-term *securities*. Depositors can write checks in minimum amounts or more against their accounts.

monopolistic competition A *market structure* in which many *firms* sell a *differentiated product*, entry is relatively easy, each firm has some control over its product *price*, and there is considerable *nonprice competition*.

monopsony A *market structure* in which there is only a single buyer of a good, *service*, or *resource*.

moral hazard problem The possibility that individuals or institutions will change their behavior as the result of a contract or agreement. Example: A bank whose deposits are insured against losses may make riskier loans and investments.

mortgage-backed securities *Bonds* that represent claims to all or part of the monthly mortgage payments from the pools of mortgage loans made by leaders to borrowers to help them purchase residential property.

MR = MC rule The principle that a *firm* will maximize its profit (or minimize its losses) by producing the output at which *marginal revenue* and *marginal cost* are equal, provided product *price* is equal to or greater than *average variable cost*.

MRP = MRC rule The principle that to maximize profit (or minimize losses), a *firm* should employ the quantity of a resource at which its *marginal revenue product* (MRP) is equal to its *marginal resource cost* (MRC), the latter being the wage rate in a purely competitive labor market.

multiple counting Wrongly including the value of *intermediate goods* in the *gross domestic product;* counting the same *good* or *service* more than once.

multiplier The ratio of a change in *equilibrium GDP* to the change in *investment* or in any other component of *aggregate expenditures* or *aggregate demand;* the number by which a change in any such component must be multiplied to find the resulting change in equilibrium GDP.

mutual funds *Portfolios* of *stocks* and *bonds* selected and purchased by mutual fund companies, which finance the purchases by pooling money from thousands of individual investors; includes both *index funds* as well as *actively managed funds*. Fund returns (profits or losses) pass through to each fund's investors.

mutual interdependence A situation in which a change in *price* strategy (or in some other strategy) by one *firm* will affect the sales and profits of another firm (or other firms). Any firm that makes such a change can expect its rivals to react to the change.

myopia Refers to the difficulty human beings have with conceptualizing the more distant future. Leads to decisions that overly favor present and near-term options at the expense of more distant future possibilities.

Nash equilibrium The situation that occurs in some *simultaneous games* wherein every player is playing his or her *dominant strategy* at the same time and thus no player has any reason to change behavior.

national health insurance A program in which a nation's government provides a basic package of health care to all citizens at no direct charge or at a low cost-sharing level. Financing is out of general *tax* revenues.

national income Total *income* earned by *resource* suppliers for their contributions to *gross domestic product* plus *taxes on production and imports;* the sum of wages and salaries, *rent, interest, profit, proprietors' income*, and such taxes.

national income accounting The techniques used to measure the overall production of a country's economy as well as other related variables.

National Labor Relations Act (NLRA) The basic labor-relations law in the United States. Defines the legal rights of unions and management and identifies unfair union and management labor practices; established the *National Labor Relations Board*. Often referred to as the Wagner Act, after the legislation's sponsor, New York Senator Robert F. Wagner.

National Labor Relations Board (NLRB) The board established by the *National Labor Relations Act* of 1935 to investigate unfair labor practices, issue *cease-and-desist orders,* and conduct elections among employees to determine if they wish to be represented by a *labor union*.

natural monopoly An *industry* in which *economies of scale* are so great that a single *firm* can produce the industry's product at a lower average total cost than would be possible if more than one firm produced the product.

natural rate of unemployment (NRU) The *full-employment rate of unemployment;* the *unemployment rate* occurring when there is no cyclical unemployment and the economy is achieving its *potential output*; the unemployment rate at which actual *inflation* equals expected inflation.

near-money Financial *assets* that are not themselves a *medium of exchange* but that have extremely high *liquidity* and thus can be readily converted into *money*. Includes noncheckable *savings accounts*, *time deposits*, and short-term *U.S. government securities* plus savings bonds.

negative self-selection As it relates to international migration, the idea that those who choose to move to another country have poorer *wage* opportunities in the origin country than those with similar skills who choose not to *emigrate*.

negative-sum game In *game theory,* a game in which the gains (+) and losses (−) add up to some amount less than zero; one party's losses exceed the other party's gains. A strategic interaction (*game*) between two or more parties (players) in which the winners' gains are less than the losers' losses so that the gains and losses sum to a negative number.

neoclassical economics The dominant and conventional branch of economic theory that attempts to predict human behavior by building economic models based on simplifying assumptions about people's motives and capabilities. These include that people are fundamentally *rational;* motivated almost entirely by *self-interest;* good at math; and unaffected by *heuristics, time inconsistency,* and *self-control problems*.

net benefits The total benefits of some activity or policy less the total costs of that activity or policy.

net domestic product (NDP) *Gross domestic product* less the part of the year's output that is needed to replace the *capital goods* worn out in producing the output; the nation's total output available for consumption or additions to the *capital stock*.

net exports (X_n) *Exports* minus *imports*.

net private domestic investment *Gross private domestic investment* less *consumption of fixed capital;* the addition to the nation's stock of *capital* during a year.

network effects Increases in the value of a product to each user, including existing users, as the total number of users rises.

new classical economics The theory that, although unanticipated *price-level* changes may create macroeconomic instability in the short run, the economy will return to and stabilize at the full-employment level of domestic output in the long run because *prices* and *wages* adjust automatically to correct movements away from the full-employment output level.

nominal gross domestic product (GDP) *GDP* measured in terms of the *price level* at the time of measurement; *GDP* not adjusted for *inflation*.

nominal income The number of dollars received by an individual or group for its *resources* during some period of time.

nominal interest rate The *interest rate* expressed in terms of annual amounts currently charged for *interest* and not adjusted for *inflation*.

nominal wage The amount of *money* received by a worker per unit of time (hour, day, etc.); money wage.

noncash transfer A *government transfer payment* in the form of *goods* and *services* rather than *money*, for example, food stamps, housing assistance, and job training; also called *in-kind transfers*.

noncompeting groups Collections of workers who do not compete with each other for employment because the skill and training of the workers in one group are substantially different from those of the workers in other groups.

nondiversifiable risk Investment *risk* that investors are unable to reduce via *diversification;* also called systemic risk.

nondurable good A *consumer good* with an expected life (use) of less than three years.

nonexcludability The inability to keep nonpayers (free riders) from obtaining benefits from a certain good; a characteristic of a *public good*.

nonprice competition Competition based on distinguishing one's product by means of *product differentiation* and then *advertising* the distinguished product to consumers.

nonrenewable natural resource Things such as oil, natural gas, and metals, that are either in actual fixed supply or that renew so slowly as to be in virtual fixed supply when viewed from a human time perspective.

nonrivalry The idea that one person's benefit from a certain *good* does not reduce the benefit available to others; a characteristic of a *public good*.

nontariff barriers (NTBs) All barriers other than *protective tariffs* that nations erect to impede international trade, including *import quotas,* licensing requirements, unreasonable product-quality standards, unnecessary bureaucratic detail in customs procedures, and so on.

normal good A *good* or *service* whose consumption increases when *income* increases and falls when income decreases, *price* remaining constant.

normal profit The payment made by a *firm* to obtain and retain *entrepreneurial ability*; the minimum *income* that entrepreneurial ability must receive to induce *entrepreneurs* to provide their entrepreneurial ability to a firm; the level of *accounting profit* at which a firm generates an *economic profit* of zero after paying for entrepreneurial ability.

normative economics The part of economics involving value judgments about what the economy should be like; focused on which economic goals and policies should be implemented; policy economics.

North American Free Trade Agreement (NAFTA) The 1993 treaty that established an international free-trade zone composed of Canada, Mexico, and the United States.

occupational licensing The laws of state or local governments that require that a worker satisfy certain specified requirements and obtain a license from a licensing board before engaging in a particular occupation.

occupational segregation The crowding of women or minorities into less desirable, lower-paying occupations.

official reserves Foreign *currencies* owned by the central bank of a nation.

offshoring The practice of shifting work previously done by domestic workers to workers located abroad.

Okun's law The generalization that any 1-percentage-point rise in the *unemployment rate* above the *full-employment rate of unemployment* is associated with a rise in the *negative GDP gap* by 2 percent of *potential output* (potential *GDP*).

oligopoly A *market structure* in which a few *firms* sell either a *standardized* or *differentiated product,* into which entry is difficult, in which the firm has limited control over product *price* because of *mutual interdependence* (except when there is collusion among firms), and in which there is typically *nonprice competition*.

one-time game A strategic interaction (*game*) between two or more parties (players) that all parties know will take place only once.

open shop A place of employment in which the employer may hire nonunion workers and in which the workers need not become members of a *labor union*.

open-market operations The purchases and sales of U.S. government *securities* that the *Federal Reserve System* undertakes in order to influence *interest rates* and the *money supply;* one method by which the *Federal Reserve* implements *monetary policy*.

opportunity cost The amount of other products that must be forgone or sacrificed to produce a unit of a product.

opportunity-cost ratio An equivalency showing the number of units of two products that can be produced with the same *resources;* the equivalency 1 corn ≡ 3 olives shows that the resources required to produce 3 units of olives must be shifted to corn production to produce 1 unit of corn.

optimal amount of R&D The level of *R&D* at which the *marginal benefit* and *marginal cost* of R&D expenditures are equal.

optimal reduction of an externality The reduction of a *negative externality* such as pollution to the level at which the *marginal benefit* and *marginal cost* of reduction are equal.

other-things-equal assumption The assumption that factors other than those being considered are held constant; *ceteris paribus* assumption.

output effect The possibility that when the *price* of the first of a pair of *substitute resources* falls, the *quantity demanded* of both resources will rise because the reduction in the price of the first resource so greatly reduces production costs that the volume of output created with the two resources increases by so much that the quantity demanded of the second resource increases even after accounting for the *substitution effect*. (See the second definition listed in the entry for *substitution effect*.)

paradox of thrift The seemingly self-contradictory but possibly true statement that increased *saving* may be both good and bad for the economy. It is always good in the long run when matched with increased *investment* spending, but may be bad in the short run if there is a *recession* because it reduces spending on *goods* and *services*. If the increased savings are not translated into increased investment, then the fall in consumption spending will not be made up for by an increase in investment. The overall result will be a decrease in output and employment. If the decline in *GDP* is severe enough, the attempt to save more will actually lead to less overall savings because the higher rate of saving will be applied to a smaller *national income*. Attempts by *households* to save more during a recession may simply worsen the recession and result in less saving.

paradox of voting A situation where paired-choice voting by majority rule fails to provide a consistent ranking of society's preferences for *public goods* or *public services*.

parity concept The idea that year after year the sale of a specific output of a farm product should enable a farmer to purchase a constant amount of nonagricultural *goods* and *services*.

parity ratio The ratio of the *price* received by farmers from the sale of an agricultural commodity to the prices of other goods paid by them; usually expressed as a percentage; used as a rationale for *price supports*.

partnership An unincorporated *firm* owned and operated by two or more persons.

passively managed funds *Mutual funds* whose *portfolios* are not regularly updated by a fund manager attempting to generate high returns. Rather, once an initial portfolio is selected, it is left unchanged so that investors receive whatever return that unchanging portfolio subsequently generates. *Index funds* are a type of passively managed fund.

patent An exclusive right given to inventors to produce and sell a new product or machine for 20 years from the time of patent application.

Patient Protection and Affordable Care Act (PPACA) A major health care law passed by the federal government in 2010. Major provisions include an individual health insurance mandate, a ban on insurers refusing to accept patients with preexisting conditions, and federal (rather than state) regulation of health insurance policies.

payroll tax A *tax* levied on employers of labor equal to a percentage of all or part of the *wages* and salaries paid by them and on employees equal to a percentage of all or part of the wages and salaries received by them.

peak The point in a *business cycle* at which business activity has reached a temporary maximum; the point at which an *expansion* ends and a *recession* begins. At the peak, the economy is near or at *full employment* and the level of real output is at or very close to the economy's capacity.

per se violations Collusive actions, such as attempts by *firms* to fix *prices* or divide a market, that are violations of the *antitrust laws*, even if the actions themselves are unsuccessful.

per-unit production cost The average production cost of a particular level of output; total input cost divided by units of output.

percentage rate of return The percentage gain or loss, relative to the buying *price*, of an *economic investment* or *financial investment* over some period of time.

perfectly elastic demand Product or *resource* demand in which *quantity demanded* can be of any amount at a particular product or resource *price;* graphs as a horizontal *demand curve*.

perfectly inelastic demand Product or *resource* demand in which *price* can be of any amount at a particular quantity of the product or resource that is demanded; when the *quantity demanded* does not respond to a change in price; graphs as a vertical *demand curve*.

personal consumption expenditures (C) The expenditures of *households* for both durable and nondurable *consumer goods*.

personal income (PI) The earned and unearned *income* available to resource suppliers and others before the payment of personal *taxes*.

personal income tax A *tax* levied on the taxable income of individuals, *households*, and unincorporated *firms*.

personal mandate The requirement under the *Patient Protection and Affordable Care Act* (*PPACA*) of 2010 that all U.S. citizens and legal residents purchase health insurance unless they are already covered by employer-sponsored health insurance or government-sponsored health insurance (*Medicaid* or *Medicare*).

Phillips Curve A curve showing the relationship between the *unemployment rate* (on the horizontal axis) and the annual rate of increase in the *price level* (on the vertical axis).

Pigovian tax A *tax* or charge levied on the production of a product that generates *negative externalities*. If set correctly, the tax will precisely offset the overallocation (overproduction) generated by the negative externality.

planned investment The amount that *firms* plan or intend to invest.

political business cycle Fluctuations in the economy caused by the alleged tendency of Congress to destabilize the economy by reducing taxes and increasing government expenditures before elections and to raise taxes and lower expenditures after elections.

political corruption The unlawful misdirection of governmental resources or actions that occurs when government officials abuse their entrusted powers for personal gain. (Also see *corruption*.)

portfolio A specific collection of *stocks, bonds,* or other *financial investments* held by an individual or a *mutual fund*.

positive economics The analysis of facts or data to establish scientific generalizations about economic behavior.

positive-sum game In *game theory*, a game in which the gains (+) and losses (−) add up to more than zero; one party's gains exceed the other party's losses. A strategic interaction (*game*) between two or more parties (players) in which the winners' gains exceed the losers' losses so that the gains and losses sum to something positive.

potential output The real output (*GDP*) an economy can produce when it fully employs its available resources.

poverty rate The percentage of the population with incomes below the official poverty income levels that are established by the federal government.

precommittments Actions taken ahead of time that make it difficult for the future self to avoid doing what the present self desires. See *time inconsistency* and *self-control problems*.

preferred provider organization (PPO) An arrangement in which doctors and hospitals agree to provide health care to insured individuals at rates negotiated with an insurer.

present value Today's value of some amount of *money* that is to be received sometime in the future.

price ceiling A legally established maximum *price* for a *good,* or *service*. Normally set at a price below the *equilibrium price*.

price discrimination The selling of a product to different buyers at different *prices* when the price differences are not justified by differences in cost.

price elasticity of demand The ratio of the percentage change in *quantity demanded* of a product or *resource* to the percentage change in its *price;* a measure of the responsiveness of buyers to a change in the price of a product or resource.

price elasticity of supply The ratio of the percentage change in *quantity supplied* of a product or *resource* to the percentage change in its *price;* a measure of the responsiveness of producers to a change in the price of a product or resource.

price floor A legally established minimum *price* for a *good,* or service. Normally set at a price above the *equilibrium price*.

price index An index number that shows how the weighted-average *price* of a "market basket" of goods changes over time relative to its price in a specific *base year*.

price leadership An informal method that *firms* in an *oligopoly* may employ to set the *price* of their product: One firm (the leader) is the first to announce a change in price, and the other firms (the followers) soon announce identical or similar changes.

price loss coverage A form of *crop insurance* that pays participating farmers if the market price of their output falls below a predetermined value.

price support The term used to refer to *price floors* applied to *farm commodities;* the minimum *price* that the government allows farmers to receive for farm commodities like wheat or corn.

price taker A seller (or buyer) that is unable to affect the *price* at which a product or *resource* sells by changing the amount it sells (or buys).

price war Successive, competitive, and continued decreases in the *prices* charged by *firms* in an oligopolistic *industry*. At each stage of the price war, one *firm* lowers its price below its rivals' price, hoping to increase its sales and revenues at its rivals' expense. The war ends when the price decreases cease.

price-level surprises Unanticipated changes in the *price level*.

prime interest rate The benchmark *interest rate* that banks use as a reference point for a wide range of loans to businesses and individuals.

principal-agent problem (1) At a *firm,* a conflict of interest that occurs when agents (workers or managers) pursue their own objectives to the detriment of the principals' (stockholders') goals. (2) In *public choice theory*, a conflict of interest that arises when elected officials (who are the agents of the people) pursue policies that are in their own interests rather than policies that would be in the better interests of the public (the principals).

principle of comparative advantage The proposition that an individual, region, or nation will benefit if it specializes in producing goods for which its own *opportunity costs* are lower than the opportunity costs of a trading partner, and then exchanging some of the products in which it specializes for other desired products produced by others.

private good A *good,* or *service* that is individually consumed and that can be profitably provided by privately owned *firms* because they can exclude nonpayers from receiving the benefits.

private property The right of private persons and *firms* to obtain, own, control, employ, dispose of, and bequeath *land, capital,* and other property.

probability-weighted average Each of the possible future rates of return from an investment multiplied by its respective probability (expressed as a decimal) of happening.

process innovation The development and use of new or improved production or distribution methods.

producer surplus The difference between the actual *price* a producer receives (or producers receive) and the minimum acceptable price; the triangular area above the *supply curve* and below the market price.

product differentiation A strategy in which one *firm*'s product is distinguished from competing products by means of its design, related *services*, quality, location, or other attributes (except *price*).

product innovation The development and sale of a new or improved product (or service).

product market A market in which products are sold by *firms* and bought by *households*.

production possibilities curve A curve showing the different combinations of two goods or *services* that can be produced in a *full-employment, full-production* economy where the available supplies of *resources* and technology are fixed.

productive efficiency The production of a *good* in the least costly way; occurs when production takes place at the output at which *average total cost* is a minimum and *marginal product* per dollar's worth of input is the same for all inputs.

productivity A measure of average output or real output per unit of input. For example, the productivity of labor is determined by dividing real output by hours of work.

profit-maximizing combination of resources The quantity of each *resource* a *firm* must employ to maximize its *profit* or minimize its loss; the combination of resource inputs at which the *marginal revenue product* of each resource is equal to its *marginal resource cost* (to its *price* if the resource is employed in a competitive market).

progressive tax At the individual level, a *tax* whose *average tax rate* increases as the taxpayer's *income* increases. At the national level, a *tax* for which the *average tax rate* (= tax revenue/*GDP*) rises with *GDP*.

property tax A *tax* on the value of property (*capital, land, stocks* and *bonds,* and other *assets*) owned by *firms* and *households*.

proportional tax At the individual level, a *tax* whose *average tax rate* remains constant as the taxpayer's *income* increases or decreases. At the national level, a *tax* for which the *average tax rate* (= tax revenue/*GDP*) remains constant as *GDP* rises or falls.

prospect theory A *behavioral economics* theory of preferences having three main features: (1) people evaluate options on the basis of whether they generate gains or losses relative to the *status quo;* (2) gains are subject to *diminishing marginal utility*, while losses are subject to diminishing marginal disutility; and (3) people are prone to *loss aversion*.

protective tariff A *tariff* designed to shield domestic producers of a *good* or *service* from the competition of foreign producers.

public assistance programs Government programs that pay benefits to those who are unable to earn *income* (because of permanent disabilities or because they have very low income and dependent children); financed by general *tax* revenues and viewed as public charity (rather than earned rights).

public choice theory The economic analysis of government decision making, politics, and elections.

public debt The total amount owed by the federal government to the owners of government *securities;* equal to the sum of past government *budget deficits* less government *budget surpluses*.

public good A *good* or *service* that is characterized by *nonrivalry* and *nonexcludability*. These characteristics typically imply that no private *firm* can break even when attempting to provide such products. As a result, they are often provided by governments, who pay for them using general *tax* revenues.

public interest theory of regulation The presumption that the purpose of the regulation of an *industry* is to protect the public (consumers) from abuse of the power possessed by *natural monopolies*.

public investments Government expenditures on public capital (such as roads, highways, bridges, mass-transit systems, and electric power facilities) and on *human capital* (such as education, training, and health).

purchasing-power-parity theory The idea that if countries have *flexible exchange rates* (rather than *fixed exchange rates*), the exchange rates between national currencies will adjust to equate the purchasing power of various currencies. In particular, the exchange rate between any two national currencies will adjust to reflect the *price-level* differences between the two countries.

pure competition A *market structure* in which a very large number of *firms* sells a *standardized product,* into which entry is very easy, in which the individual seller has no control over the product *price*, and in which there is no nonprice competition; a market characterized by a very large number of buyers and sellers.

pure monopoly A *market structure* in which one *firm* sells a unique product, into which entry is blocked, in which the single firm has considerable control over product *price*, and in which *nonprice competition* may or may not be found.

pure profit (See *economic profit*.)

pure rate of interest The hypothetical *interest rate* that is completely *risk*-free and not subject to market imperfections; the hypothetical interest rate that would only compensate investors for *time preference*.

purely competitive labor market A *resource market* in which many *firms* compete with one another in hiring a specific kind of *labor*, numerous equally qualified workers supply that labor, and no one controls the market *wage rate*.

quantitative easing (QE) An *open-market operation* in which *bonds* are purchased by a *central bank* in order to increase the quantity of *excess reserves* held by *commercial banks* and thereby (hopefully) stimulate the economy by increasing the amount of lending undertaken by commercial banks; undertaken when interest rates are near zero and, consequently, it is not possible for the central bank to further stimulate the economy with lower interest rates due to the *zero lower bound problem*.

quasi-public good A *good* or *service* to which *excludability* could apply but that has such a large *positive externality* that government sponsors its production to prevent an underallocation of resources.

rational Behaviors and decisions that maximize a person's chances of achieving his or her goals. See *rational behavior*.

rational behavior Human behavior based on comparison of *marginal costs* and *marginal benefits;* behavior designed to maximize *total utility*. See *rational*.

rational expectations theory The hypothesis that *firms* and *households* expect monetary and fiscal policies to have certain effects on the economy and (in pursuit of their own self-interests) take actions that make these policies ineffective.

real GDP (See *real gross domestic product*.)

real GDP per capita *Inflation*-adjusted output per person; *real GDP*/population.

real gross domestic product (GDP) *Gross domestic product* adjusted for *inflation;* gross domestic product in a year divided by the GDP *price index* for that year, the index expressed as a decimal.

real income The amount of *goods* and *services* that can be purchased with *nominal income* during some period of time; nominal income adjusted for *inflation*.

real interest rate The *interest rate* expressed in dollars of constant value (adjusted for *inflation*) and equal to the *nominal interest rate* less the expected rate of inflation.

real wage The amount of *goods* and *services* a worker can purchase with his or her *nominal wage;* the *purchasing power* of the *nominal wage*.

real-balances effect The tendency for increases in the *price level* to lower the real value (or *purchasing power*) of financial *assets* with fixed *money* value and, as a result, to reduce total spending and real output, and conversely for decreases in the *price level*.

real-business-cycle theory A theory that *business cycles* result from changes in *technology* and *resource* availability, which affect *productivity* and thus increase or decrease long-run *aggregate supply*.

recession A period of declining *real GDP*, accompanied by lower *real income* and higher *unemployment*.

recessionary expenditure gap The amount by which the *aggregate expenditures schedule* must shift upward to increase *real GDP* to its full-employment, noninflationary level.

regressive tax At the individual level, a *tax* whose *average tax rate* decreases as the taxpayer's *income* increases. At the national level, a *tax* for which the *average tax rate* (= tax revenue/*GDP*) falls as *GDP* rises.

regulatory agency An agency, commission, or board established by the federal government or a state government to control the *prices* charged and the *services* offered by a *natural monopoly* or *public utility*.

regulatory capture The situation that occurs when a governmental *regulatory agency* ends up being controlled by the industry that it is supposed to be regulating.

remittances Payments by *immigrants* to family members and others located in the immigrants' home countries.

renewable natural resources Things such as forests, water in reservoirs, and wildlife that are capable of growing back or building back up (renewing themselves) if they are harvested at moderate rates.

rent-seeking behavior The actions by persons, *firms*, or unions to gain special benefits from government at the taxpayers' or someone else's expense.

repeated game A strategic interaction (*game*) between two or more parties (players) that all parties know will take place repeatedly.

replacement rate The *total fertility rate* necessary to offset deaths in a country and thereby keep the size of its population constant (without relying on immigration). For most countries, a total fertility rate of about 2.1 births per woman per lifetime.

repo A repurchase agreement (or "repo") is a short-term money loan made by a lender to a borrower that is collateralized with *bonds* pledged by the borrower. The name *repo* refers to how the lender would view the transaction. The same transaction when viewed from the perspective of the borrower would be called a *reverse repo*.

required reserves The funds that each *commercial bank* and *thrift institution* must deposit with its local *Federal Reserve Bank* (or hold as *vault cash*) to meet the legal *reserve requirement;* a fixed percentage of each bank's or thrift's *checkable deposits*.

reserve ratio The fraction of *checkable deposits* that each *commercial bank* or *thrift institution* must hold as reserves at its local *Federal Reserve Bank* or in its own bank vault; also called the *reserve requirement*.

residual claimant In a market system, the economic agent who receives (is claimant to) whatever profit or loss remains (is residual) at a firm after all other *input* providers have been paid. The residual is compensation for providing the economic input of *entrepreneurial ability* and flows to the firm's owners.

resource market A market in which *households* sell and *firms* buy *resources* or the services of resources.

restrictive monetary policy *Federal Reserve System* actions to reduce the *money supply*, increase *interest rates*, and reduce *inflation;* a tight money policy.

revenue tariff A *tariff* designed to produce *income* for the federal government.

reverse repo A reverse repurchase agreement (or "reverse repo") is a short-term money loan that the borrower obtains by pledging *bonds* as collateral. The name *reverse repo* refers to how the borrower would view the transaction. The same transaction when viewed by the lender would be called a *repo*.

right-to-work law A state law (in 23 states) that makes it illegal to require that a worker join a *labor union* in order to retain his or her job; laws that make *union shops* and *agency shops* illegal.

risk The uncertainty as to the future returns of a particular *financial investment* or *economic investment*.

risk premium The *interest rate* above the *risk-free* interest rate that must be paid and received to compensate a lender or investor for *risk*.

risk-free interest rate The *interest rate* earned on short-term U.S. government *bonds*.

rivalry (1) The characteristic of a *private good,* the consumption of which by one party excludes other parties from obtaining the benefit; (2) the attempt by one *firm* to gain strategic advantage over another firm to enhance market share or *profit*.

rule of 70 A method for determining the number of years it will take for some measure to double, given its annual percentage increase. Example: To determine the number of years it will take for the *price level* to double, divide 70 by the annual rate of *inflation*.

rule of reason The rule stated and applied in the *U.S. Steel case* that only combinations and contracts unreasonably restraining trade are subject to actions under the antitrust laws and that size and possession of *monopoly* power are not by themselves illegal. Compare with *per se violation*.

sales tax A *tax* levied on the cost (at retail) of a broad group of products.

saving *Disposable income* not spent for *consumer goods;* equal to *disposable income* minus *personal consumption expenditures;* saving is a flow. Compare with *savings*.

saving schedule A table of numbers that shows the amounts *households* plan to save (plan not to spend for *consumer goods*), at different levels of *disposable income*.

savings account A deposit in a *commercial bank* or *thrift institution* on which *interest* payments are received; generally used for *saving* rather than daily transactions; a component of the *M2 money supply*.

scarcity The limits placed on the amounts and types of *goods* and *services* available for consumption as the result of there being only limited *economic resources* from which to produce output; the fundamental economic constraint that creates *opportunity costs* and that necessitates the use of *marginal analysis* (*cost-benefit analysis*) to make optimal choices.

scientific method The procedure for the systematic pursuit of knowledge involving the observation of facts and the formulation and testing of hypotheses to obtain theories, principles, and laws.

securitization The process of aggregating many individual financial debts, such as mortgages or student loans, into a pool and then issuing new *securities* (typically *bonds*) backed by the pool. The holders of the new securities are entitled to receive the debt payments made on the individual financial debts in the pool.

Security Market Line (SML) A line that shows the *average expected rate of return* of all *financial investments* at each level of *nondiversifiable risk*, the latter measured by *beta*.

self-control problems Refers to the difficulty people have in sticking with earlier plans and avoiding suboptimal decisions when finally confronted with a particular decision-making situation. A manifestation of *time inconsistency* and potentially avoidable by using *precommitments*.

self-interest That which each *firm*, property owner, worker, and consumer believes is best for itself and seeks to obtain.

self-selection As it relates to international migration, the idea that those who choose to move to a new country tend to have greater motivation for economic gain or greater willingness to sacrifice current consumption for future consumption than those with similar skills who choose to remain at home.

sequential game A strategic interaction (*game*) between two or more parties (players) in which each party moves (makes a decision) in a predetermined order (sequence).

service An (intangible) act or use for which a consumer, *firm*, or government is willing to pay.

Sherman Act The federal antitrust law of 1890 that makes *monopoly* and conspiracies to restrain trade criminal offenses.

shocks Sudden, unexpected changes in *demand* (or *aggregate demand*) or supply (or *aggregate supply*).

short run (1) In *microeconomics*, a period of time in which producers are able to change the quantities of some but not all of the *resources* they employ; a period in which some resources (usually *plant*) are fixed and some are variable. (2) In *macroeconomics*, a period in which *nominal wages* and other input *prices* do not change in response to a change in the *price level*.

short-run aggregate supply curve An *aggregate supply* curve relevant to a time period in which input *prices* (particularly *nominal wages*) do not change in response to changes in the *price level*.

short-run supply curve A *supply curve* that shows the quantity of a product a *firm* in a purely competitive *industry* will offer to sell at various *prices* in the *short run;* the portion of the firm's short-run *marginal cost curve* that lies above its *average-variable-cost* curve.

shortage The amount by which the *quantity demanded* of a product exceeds the *quantity supplied* at a particular (below-equilibrium) *price*.

simultaneous consumption The same-time derivation of *utility* from some product by a large number of consumers.

simultaneous game A strategic interaction (*game*) between two or more parties (players) in which every player moves (makes a decision) at the same time.

single-tax movement The political efforts by followers of Henry George (1839–1897) to impose a single *tax* on the value of land and eliminate all other taxes.

skill transferability The ease with which people can shift their work talents from one job, region, or country to another job, region, or country.

slope of a straight line The ratio of the vertical change (the rise or fall) to the horizontal change (the run) between any two points on a straight line. The slope of an upward-sloping line is positive, reflecting a direct relationship between two variables; the slope of a downward-sloping line is negative, reflecting an inverse relationship between two variables.

Smoot-Hawley Tariff Act Legislation passed in 1930 that established very high *tariffs*. Its objective was to reduce *imports* and stimulate the domestic economy, but it resulted only in retaliatory tariffs by other nations.

social insurance programs Programs that replace the earnings lost when people retire or are temporarily unemployed, that are financed by payroll *taxes*, and that are viewed as earned rights (rather than charity).

social regulation Regulation in which government is concerned with the conditions under which *goods* and *services* are produced, their physical characteristics, and the impact of their production on society. Differs from *industrial regulation*.

Social Security The social insurance program in the United States financed by federal *payroll taxes* on employers and employees and designed to replace a portion of the earnings lost when workers become disabled, retire, or die.

socially optimal price The *price* of a product that results in the most efficient allocation of an economy's *resources* and that is equal to the *marginal cost* of the product.

sole proprietorship An unincorporated *firm* owned and operated by one person.

special-interest effect Any political outcome in which a small group ("special interest") gains substantially at the expense of a much larger number of persons who each individually suffers a small loss.

specialization The use of the *resources* of an individual, a *firm*, a region, or a nation to concentrate production on one or a small number of *goods* and *services*.

stagflation *Inflation* accompanied by stagnation in the rate of growth of output and an increase in *unemployment* in the economy; simultaneous increases in the *inflation rate* and the *unemployment rate*.

Standard Oil case A 1911 antitrust case in which Standard Oil was found guilty of violating the *Sherman Act* by illegally monopolizing the petroleum *industry*. As a remedy the company was divided into several competing *firms*.

start-up firm A new *firm* focused on creating and introducing a particular new product or employing a specific new production or distribution method.

start-ups Newly formed firms that are attempting to pioneer a new product or production method.

statistical discrimination The practice of judging an individual on the basis of the average characteristics of the group to which he or she belongs rather than on his or her own personal characteristics.

status quo The existing state of affairs; in *prospect theory*, the current situation from which gains and losses are calculated.

status quo bias The tendency most people have when making choices to select any option that is presented as the default (*status quo*) option. Explainable by *prospect theory* and *loss aversion*.

sterilization *Open market operations* or changes in bank *reserve ratios* undertaken by a *central bank* to offset changes in the domestic *money supply* caused either by the operation of a *fixed exchange rate* or by *currency interventions* made under a *managed floating exchange rate*.

sticky prices (See *inflexible prices*.)

stock (corporate) An ownership share in a corporation.

store of value An *asset* set aside for future use; one of the three functions of *money*.

strategic behavior Self-interested economic actions that take into account the expected reactions of others.

strategic form A matrix representation of a *game* that shows the payouts to every combination of player choices. Can be used for both *simultaneous games* and *sequential games*.

strike The withholding of *labor* services by an organized group of workers (a *labor union*).

structural unemployment *Unemployment* of workers whose skills are not demanded by employers, who lack sufficient skill to obtain employment, or who cannot easily move to locations where jobs are available.

subgame A subset of a larger *game* that begins with a single initial decision node. It includes all subsequent *decision nodes* and/or *terminal nodes*. Most easily seen in *sequential games* presented in *strategic form*.

subgame perfect Nash equilibrium In *sequential games*, a sequence of decisions made by the various players such that no player has an incentive to deviate.

subprime mortgage loans High-*interest-rate* loans to home buyers with above-average credit risk.

substitute goods Products or *services* that can be used in place of each other. When the *price* of one falls, the *demand* for the other product falls; conversely, when the price of one product rises, the demand for the other product rises.

substitute resources Productive inputs that can be used instead of other inputs in the production process; resources for which an increase in the *price* of one leads to an increase in the demand for the other.

substitution effect (1) A change in the quantity demanded of a *consumer good* that results from a change in its relative expensiveness caused by a change in the good's own *price*. (2) The reduction in the *quantity demanded* of the second of a pair of *substitute resources* that occurs when the price of the first resource falls and causes *firms* that employ both resources to switch to using more of the first resource (whose price has fallen) and less of the second resource (whose price has remained the same).

Supplemental Nutrition Assistance Program (SNAP) A government program that provides food money to low-income recipients by depositing electronic money onto *Electronic Benefit Transfer (EBT) cards*. Formerly known as the food-stamp program.

Supplemental Security Income (SSI) A federally financed and administered program that provides a uniform nationwide minimum *income* for the aged, blind, and disabled who do not qualify for benefits under *Social Security* in the United States.

supply A schedule or curve that shows the various amounts of a product that producers are willing and able to make available for sale at each of a series of possible *prices* during a specified period of time.

supply curve A curve that illustrates the *supply* for a product by showing how each possible *price* (on the *vertical axis*) is associated with a specific *quantity supplied* (on the *horizontal axis*).

supply factors (in growth) The four determinants of an economy's physical ability to achieve *economic growth* by increasing *potential output* and shifting out the *production possibilities curve*. The four determinants are improvements in technology plus increases in the quantity and quality of natural resources, human resources, and the stock of capital goods.

supply schedule A table of numbers showing the amounts of a *good* or *service* producers are willing and able to make available for sale at each of a series of possible *prices* during a specified period of time.

supply shocks Sudden, unexpected changes in *aggregate supply*.

supply-side economics A view of *macroeconomics* that emphasizes the role of costs and *aggregate supply* in explaining *inflation, unemployment,* and *economic growth*.

supply-side market failures Overallocations of *resources* that occur when private supply curves understate the full cost of producing a *good* or *service*.

surplus The amount by which the *quantity supplied* of a product exceeds the *quantity demanded* at a specific (above-equilibrium) *price*.

systematic errors Suboptimal choices that (1) are not *rational* because they do not maximize a person's chances of achieving his or her goals and (2) occur routinely, repeatedly, and predictably.

target rate of inflation The publicly announced annual *inflation* rate that a *central bank* attempts to achieve through *monetary policy* actions if it is following an *inflation targeting* monetary policy.

tariff A *tax* imposed by a nation on an imported good.

taste-for-discrimination model A theory that views discrimination as a preference for which an employer is willing to pay.

tax incidence The degree to which a *tax* falls on a particular person or group.

tax subsidy A grant in the form of reduced *taxes* through favorable *tax* treatment. For example, employer-paid health insurance is exempt from federal *income taxes* and *payroll taxes*.

taxes on production and imports A *national income accounting* category that includes such taxes as *sales, excise,* business property taxes, and *tariffs* that *firms* treat as costs of producing a product and pass on (in whole or in part) to buyers by charging a higher *price*.

Taylor rule A *monetary rule* proposed by economist John Taylor that would stipulate exactly how much the *Federal Reserve System* should change *real interest rates* in response to divergences of *real GDP* from potential GDP and divergences of actual rates of *inflation* from a target rate of inflation.

technological advance (1) An improvement in the quality of existing products, the invention of entirely new products, or the creation of new or better ways of producing or distributing products. (2) Any improvement in the methods by which resources are combined such that the same quantity of inputs can be made to yield a combination of outputs that is prefered to any combination of outputs that was previously possible.

Temporary Assistance for Needy Families (TANF) A state-administered and partly federally funded program in the United States that provides financial aid to poor families; the basic welfare program for low-income families in the United States; contains time limits and work requirements.

terminal node In a *sequential game* presented in *extensive form,* a final outcome point (node) showing the payouts to each player if the game ends at that point.

terms of trade The rate at which units of one product can be exchanged for units of another product; the *price* of a *good* or *service;* the amount of one good or service that must be given up to obtain 1 unit of another good or service.

thrift institution A *savings and loan association, mutual savings bank,* or *credit union.*

time deposit An interest-earning deposit in a *commercial bank* or *thrift institution* that the depositor can withdraw without penalty after the end of a specified period.

time inconsistency The human tendency to systematically misjudge at the present time what will actually end up being desired at a future time.

time preference The human tendency for people, because of impatience, to prefer to spend and consume in the present rather than save and wait to spend and consume in the future; this inclination varies in strength among individuals.

time-value of money The idea that a specific amount of *money* is more valuable to a person the sooner it is received because the money can be placed in a financial account or *investment* and earn *compound interest* over time; the *opportunity cost* of receiving a sum of money later rather than earlier.

token money Bills or coins for which the amount printed on the *currency* bears no relationship to the value of the paper or metal embodied within it; for currency still circulating, *money* for which the face value exceeds the commodity value.

total allowable catch (TAC) The overall limit set by a government or a fisheries commission on the total number of fish or tonnage of fish that fishers collectively can harvest during some particular time period. Used to set the fishing limits for *individual transferable quotas* (*ITQs*).

total cost The sum of *fixed cost* and *variable cost.*

total demand for money The sum of the *transactions demand for money* and the *asset demand for money.*

total fertility rate The average number of children per lifetime birthed by a nation's women.

total product (TP) The total output of a particular *good* or *service* produced by a *firm* (or a group of firms or the entire economy).

total revenue (TR) The total number of dollars received by a *firm* (or firms) from the sale of a product; equal to the total expenditures for the product produced by the firm (or firms); equal to the quantity sold (demanded) multiplied by the *price* at which it is sold.

total utility The total amount of satisfaction derived from the consumption of a single product or a combination of products.

total-revenue test A test to determine *elasticity of demand.* Demand is elastic if *total revenue* moves in the opposite direction from a *price* change; it is inelastic when it moves in the same direction as a price change; and it is of unitary elasticity when it does not change when price changes.

Trade Adjustment Assistance Act A U.S. law passed in 2002 that provides cash assistance, education and training benefits, health care subsidies, and *wage* subsidies (for persons age 50 or older) to workers displaced by *imports* or relocations of U.S. *plants* to other countries.

trade deficit The amount by which a nation's *imports* of *goods* (or goods and *services*) exceed its *exports* of goods (or goods and services).

trade surplus The amount by which a nation's *exports* of *goods* (or goods and *services*) exceed its *imports* of goods (or goods and services).

trading possibilities line A line that shows the different combinations of two products that an economy is able to obtain (consume) when it specializes in the production of one product and trades (exports) it to obtain the other product.

tragedy of the commons The tendency for commonly owned *natural resources* to be overused, neglected, or degraded because their common ownership gives nobody an incentive to maintain or improve them.

transactions demand for money The amount of money people want to hold for use as a *medium of exchange* (to make payments); varies directly with *nominal GDP.*

transfer payment A payment of *money* (or *goods* and *services*) by a government to a *household* or *firm* for which the payer receives no *good* or *service* directly in return.

Troubled Asset Relief Program (TARP) A 2008 federal government program that authorized the U.S. Treasury to loan up to $700 billion to critical financial institutions and other U.S. *firms* that were in extreme financial trouble and therefore at high risk of failure.

trough The point in a *business cycle* at which business activity has reached a temporary minimum; the point at which a *recession* ends and an *expansion* (recovery) begins. At the trough, the economy experiences substantial *unemployment* and *real GDP* is less than *potential output.*

tying contract A requirement imposed by a seller that a buyer purchase another (or other) of its products as a condition for buying a desired product; a practice forbidden by the *Clayton Act.*

U.S. government securities U.S. Treasury bills, notes, and *bonds* used to finance *budget deficits;* the components of the *public debt.*

U.S. Steel case The antitrust action brought by the federal government against the U.S. Steel Corporation in which the courts ruled (in 1920) that only unreasonable restraints of trade were illegal and that size and the possession of monopoly power were not by themselves violations of the *antitrust laws.*

ultimatum game A *behavioral economics* game in which a mutually anonymous pair of players interact to determine how an amount of money is to be split. The first player suggests a division. The second player either accepts that proposal (in which case the split is made accordingly) or rejects it (in which case neither player gets anything).

unanticipated inflation An increase of the *price level* (*inflation*) at a rate greater than expected.

unconditional cash transfers Anti-poverty programs that give cash transfers (grants) to poor individuals with no strings attached in the hope that the recipients will improve their economic prospects by spending the money on either education or physical capital.

underemployment A situation in which workers are employed in positions requiring less education and skill than they have.

unemployment The failure to use all available *economic resources* to produce desired *goods* and *services;* the failure of the economy to fully employ its *labor force.*

unemployment compensation (See *unemployment insurance*).

unemployment rate The percentage of the *labor force* unemployed at any time.

unfunded liability A future government spending commitment (liability) for which the government has not legislated an offsetting revenue source.

uninsurable risk An eventuality for which the frequency or magnitude of potential losses is unpredictable or unknowable. Insurance companies are not willing to sell insurance against such risks.

union shop A place of employment where the employer may hire either *labor union* members or nonmembers but where nonmembers must become members within a specified period of time or lose their jobs.

unionization rate The percentage of a particular population of workers that belongs to *labor unions;* alternatively, the percentage of a population of workers that is represented by one union or another in *collective bargaining.*

unit elasticity *Demand* or *supply* for which the *elasticity coefficient* is equal to 1; means that the percentage change in the *quantity demanded* or *quantity supplied* is equal to the percentage change in *price.*

unit of account A standard unit in which *prices* can be stated and the value of *goods* and *services* can be compared; one of the three functions of *money.*

unplanned changes in inventories Changes in *inventories* that *firms* did not anticipate; changes in inventories that occur because of unexpected increases or decreases of aggregate spending (or of *aggregate expenditures*).

user cost The *opportunity cost* of extracting and selling a *nonrenewable natural resource* today rather than waiting to extract and sell the resource in the future; the *present value* of the decline in future revenue that will occur because a nonrenewable natural resource is extracted and sold today rather than being extracted and sold in the future.

usury laws State laws that specify the maximum legal *interest rate* at which loans can be made.

utility The want-satisfying power of a *good* or *service;* the satisfaction or pleasure a consumer obtains from the consumption of a good or service (or from the consumption of a collection of *goods* and *services*).

utility-maximizing rule The principle that to obtain the greatest *total utility,* a consumer should allocate *money income* so that the last dollar spent on each *good* or *service* yields the same *marginal utility* (MU). For two goods X and Y, with prices P_x and P_y, total utility will be maximized by purchasing the amounts of X and Y such that $MU_x/P_x = MU_y/P_y$ for the last dollar spent on each good.

value added The value of a product sold by a *firm* less the value of the products (materials) purchased and used by the firm to produce that product.

variable cost A cost that increases when the *firm* increases its output and decreases when the firm reduces its output.

vault cash The *currency* a bank has on hand in its vault and cash drawers.

velocity The number of times per year that the average dollar in the *money supply* is spent for *final goods* and final *services; nominal gross domestic product* (*GDP*) divided by the *money supply.*

venture capital That part of household *savings* used to finance high-risk business enterprises in exchange for *stock* (and thus a share of any *profit* if the enterprises are successful).

vertical axis The "up-down" or "north-south" measurement line on a graph or grid.

vertical intercept The point at which a line meets the vertical axis of a graph.

vertical merger The merger of one or more *firms* engaged in different stages of the production of a particular *final good.*

very long run In microeconomics, a period of time long enough that *technology* can change and *firms* can introduce new products.

vicious circle of poverty A problem common in some *developing countries* in which their low *per capita incomes* are an obstacle to realizing the levels of *savings* and *investment* needed to achieve rates of growth of output that exceed their rates of population growth.

voice mechanism Communication by workers through their *union* to resolve grievances with an employer.

voluntary export restrictions (VER) Voluntary limitations by countries or *firms* of their exports to a particular foreign nation; undertaken to avoid the enactment of formal trade barriers by the foreign nation.

wage differential The difference between the *wage* received by one worker or group of workers and that received by another worker or group of workers.

wage rate (See *wage.*)

Wall Street Reform and Consumer Protection Act of 2010 The law that gave authority to the *Federal Reserve System* (the Fed) to regulate all large financial institutions, created an oversight council to look for growing risk to the financial system, established a process for the federal government to sell off the assets of large failing financial institutions, provided federal regulatory oversight of asset-backed *securities,* and created a financial consumer protection bureau within the Fed.

wealth effect The tendency for people to increase their consumption spending when the value of their financial and real *assets* rises and to decrease their consumption spending when the value of those assets falls.

welfare cliff A situation in which a welfare recipient's overall income (= welfare benefits plus earned income) would decline if they got a raise or worked more hours. Caused by the abrupt withdrawal of certain welfare benefits at particular income thresholds.

Wheeler-Lea Act The federal law of 1938 that amended the *Federal Trade Commission Act* by prohibiting unfair and deceptive acts or practices of commerce (such as false and misleading advertising and the misrepresentation of products).

will to develop The mental state of wanting *economic growth* strongly enough to change from old to new ways of doing things.

World Bank A bank that lends (and guarantees loans) to *developing countries* to assist them in increasing their *capital stock* and thus in achieving *economic growth.*

world price The international market *price* of a *good* or *service*, determined by world demand and supply.

World Trade Organization (WTO) An organization of 159 nations (as of mid-2013) that oversees the provisions of the current world trade agreement, resolves trade disputes stemming from it, and holds forums for further rounds of trade negotiations.

X-inefficiency The production of output, whatever its level, at a higher average (and total) cost than is necessary for producing that level of output.

zero interest rate policy (ZIRP) A *monetary policy* in which a *central bank* sets *nominal interest rates* at or near zero percent per year in order to stimulate the economy.

zero lower bound problem The constraint placed on the ability of a *central bank* to stimulate the economy through lower interest rates by the fact that *nominal interest rates* cannot be driven lower than zero without causing depositors to withdraw funds from the banking system and thus reduce the ability of banks to stimulate the economy via lending.

zero-sum game In *game theory*, a game in which the gains (+) and losses (−) add up to zero; one party's gain equals the other party's loss. A strategic interaction (*game*) between two or more parties (players) in which the winners' gains exactly offset the losers' losses so that the gains and losses sum to zero.

INDEX

Note: **Bold** type indicates key terms and definitions; page numbers followed by "n" indicates notes; page numbers preceded by "W" indicates Web only chapters.

MICROECONOMICS EXAMINATION

Multiple-Choice Questions

Part A • 70 minutes

Directions: Each of the questions or incomplete statements below is followed by five answers or completions. Select one that is best in each case.

1. Which of the following characteristics best represents a market economy rather than a command economy?
   (A) Exchange of goods and services are controlled by price ceilings and price floors.
   (B) A system of laws establishes rules in the exchange of goods and services.
   (C) Property rights provide incentives for production and exchange.
   (D) Industries are operated and controlled by a central government.
   (E) Central government grants monopoly rights to some firms.

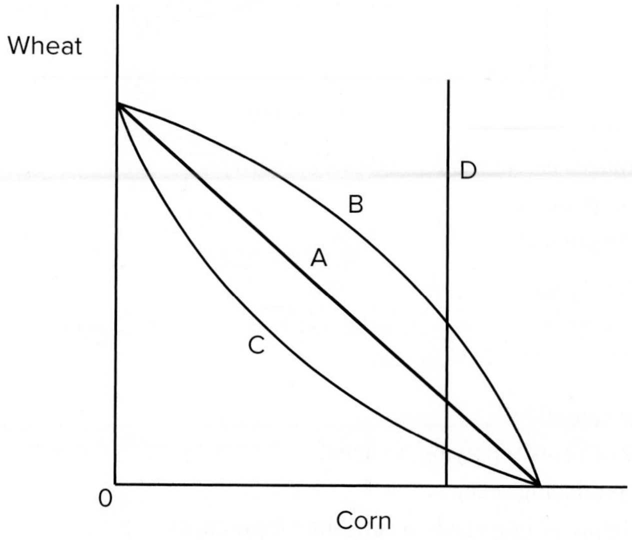

2. The production possibility graph above shows the output combinations of wheat and corn. Which of the lines or curves are consistent with the principle of increasing opportunity cost?
   (A) A only (B) B only (C) C only (D) D only (E) A, B, and C

3. Assume that it takes 10 units of labor to produce a unit of good X and 40 units of labor to produce a unit of good Y. What is the opportunity cost of producing one unit of good X?
   (A) .25 Y (B) 2.5 Y (C) 4 Y (D) 1/.25 X or 4 X (E) 40 labor

4. Price floors are frequently advocated for a good or service to
   (A) correct for a positive externality (spillover benefit)
   (B) alleviate inflationary pressures
   (C) provide for public goods
   (D) create incentives for productive or technical efficiency
   (E) to improve the income level for the producer of a good, like a farmer

Questions 5–6 **refer to the following graph showing the demand for oranges.**

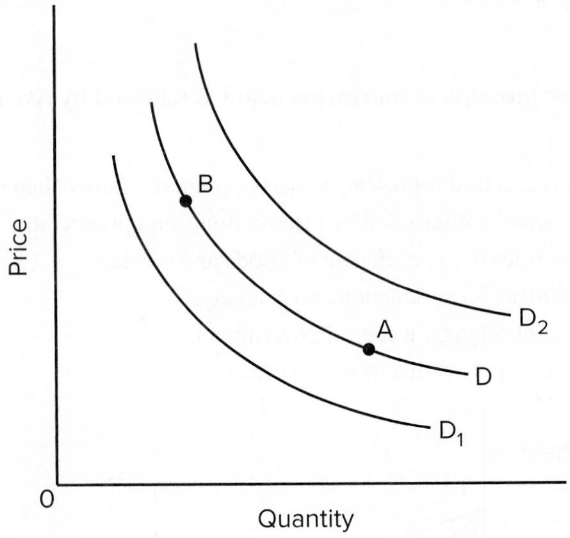

5. An increase in the price of oranges is represented by
(A) movement from point B to point A
(B) movement from point A to point B
(C) shift from D to D_2
(D) shift from D to D_1
(E) shift from D_1 to D_2

6. A shift from D to D_2 could be caused by
(A) a decrease in the number of firms supplying oranges
(B) a decrease in the cost of producing oranges
(C) a drought affecting the supply of grapefruit, a substitute for oranges
(D) a shortage of oranges in the market
(E) a surplus of oranges in the market

7. Assuming that output increases by one, marginal cost can be computed by which of the following methods?
(A) A change in the total variable cost
(B) A change in the total fixed cost
(C) Total cost minus total fixed cost
(D) Total explicit cost minus total implicit cost
(E) Total variable cost minus total fixed cost

8. In the short run, the price of labor divided by the marginal productivity of labor will yield which of the following?
(A) Average total cost
(B) Average variable cost
(C) Marginal cost
(D) The total cost of labor
(E) The profit maximizing output level for the firm

9. If a perfectly competitive firm operates at its profit-maximizing output and earns zero economic profit (or only a normal profit), that firm is operating at a point where

(A) ATC > MR = MC > AVC
(B) ATC < P > MC
(C) P = MC = ATC
(D) P < AR
(E) MR = MC < AVC

10. If a monopolist earning positive economic profit experiences an increase in its fixed cost, which of the following occur to its price, profit, and output?

	Price	Profit	Output
(A)	Increase	Decrease	Decrease
(B)	Increase	Increase	Decrease
(C)	No Change	No Change	No Change
(D)	No Change	Decrease	No Change
(E)	Decrease	Decrease	Decrease

***Questions 11–12* refer to the following market structures.**

I. Perfect competition
II. Monopoly
III. Monopolistic competition
IV. Oligopoly

11. A profit-maximizing firm finds that at its current output the price of the product exceeds the marginal cost of the product. In which of the market structures will a firm increase its output?

(A) I only
(B) II only
(C) II and III only
(D) III and IV only
(E) I, II, III, and IV

12. In which market structure will a firm be most concerned with the issue of interdependence for its output, price, and profits?

(A) I only
(B) II only
(C) III only
(D) IV only
(E) I, II, III, and IV

13. *Weeds,* a local firm, operates in a perfectly competitive market selling flower bouquets. The firm has the following short-run information concerning the selling of bouquets at a current output of 100 bouquets per day.

- Average Revenue = $15.00
- Marginal Cost = $10.00
- Average Total Cost = $10.00
- Average Variable Cost = $5.00

Which of the following actions would be taken by *Weeds* to maximize profits in the short run?

(A) Increase output of the flower bouquets
(B) Increase price of the flower bouquets
(C) Decrease output
(D) Decrease price to equal the average variable cost
(E) Expand the scale of its physical plant size and operation

14. Assuming similar cost functions, which of the following would be the same for perfect competition, monopoly, and for monopolistic-competition models?

(A) Normal (zero) profits would be earned in the long run.
(B) Productive efficiency would be achieved in the long run.
(C) Output would be determined at a point where marginal revenue equals marginal cost.
(D) Allocative efficiency would be achieved in the short run.
(E) Output levels will be the same for all models.

15. The marginal revenue product of labor in a perfectly competitive labor market is downward sloping because

(A) marginal productivity eventually decreases
(B) marginal revenue decreases
(C) the marginal productivity divided by the price of labor decreases
(D) marginal cost of labor increases
(E) firms substitute capital resources for labor resources

For *Questions 16–17,* use the following data about *The Popcorn Store,* operating in a resort town where a teenage laborer can be hired in a perfectly competitive labor market. *The Popcorn Store* currently sells each bag of carmel corn for $2.00 per bag

Quantity of Labor	Marginal Product
1	15
2	30
3	45
4	50
5	40
6	30

16. The law of diminishing returns sets in after the hiring of which laborer?

(A) 1 (B) 2 (C) 3 (D) 4 (E) 5

17. If the prevailing wage rate in the resort town is $70.00 per day, how many laborers will *The Popcorn Store* hire?

(A) 1 (B) 2 (C) 3 (D) 4 (E) 5

18. The free rider problem is associated with the market's inability to produce the social optimum amounts of

(A) inferior goods
(B) goods that are price inelastic
(C) goods that produce negative externalities
(D) public goods
(E) goods for which there are no substitutes

19. The justification for government regulation of business is most convincing if the goal is to

(A) impose minimum wage standards on firms
(B) break up natural monopolies
(C) provide optimal output of the product
(D) insure a fair profit for the business
(E) increase government revenue

Questions 20–21 refer to the following information.

Peter and Sam are gardeners who can produce either fruit or vegetables on the same amount of land. Peter can produce either 100 bushels of vegetables or 200 bushels of fruit whereas Sam can produce either 200 bushels of vegetables or 100 bushels of fruit.

20. Which of the following identifies the absolute advantage and comparative advantage in the production of vegetables and fruit for Peter and Sam?

	Absolute Advantage Fruit	Comparative Advantage Fruit	Absolute Advantage Vegetables	Comparative Advantage Vegetables
(A)	Sam	Peter	Sam	Peter
(B)	Sam	Sam	Peter	Peter
(C)	Peter	Peter	Sam	Peter
(D)	Peter	Peter	Peter	Sam
(E)	Peter	Peter	Sam	Sam

21. Each can increase their consumption of both vegetables and fruit if they adopt which of the following terms of production and trade scenarios?

(A) Peter produces vegetables only and trades 1 bushel of vegetables for 1 bushel of Sam's fruit.
(B) Peter produces fruit only and trades 1 bushel of fruit for 1 bushel of Sam's vegetables.
(C) Peter produces fruit only and trades 1 bushel of fruit for 3 bushels of Sam's vegetables.
(D) Sam produces vegetables only and trades 1 bushel of vegetables for 3 bushels of Peter's fruit.
(E) Sam produces fruit only and trades 1 bushel of fruit for 3 bushels of Peter's vegetables.

22. If tomato juice and orange juice are substitutes, what is the effect if tomato growers experience a drought that destroys a significant amount of the tomato crop?

(A) decrease the quantity demanded of the orange juice
(B) increase the quantity demanded of the tomato juice
(C) increase the quantity demanded of orange juice
(D) decrease the price of tomato juice
(E) have no effect on the quantity demanded of orange juice

23. A surplus of VHS (Video Home System) tapes, *ceteris paribus,* would indicate that which of the following will occur to quantity demanded and quantity supplied in the VHS tape market?

	Quantity demanded	Quantity supplied
(A)	Decrease	Increase
(B)	No change	Increase
(C)	Decrease	No change
(D)	Increase	Increase
(E)	Increase	Decrease

24. Noodles are considered an inferior good and rice a normal good. What is likely to happen to the equilibrium quantities demanded of noodles and rice given an increase in family incomes?

	Noodles	Rice
(A)	Increase	Decrease
(B)	Increase	Increase
(C)	Decrease	Increase
(D)	Decrease	Decrease
(E)	Decrease	No change

25. Good A and Good B have a positive cross elasticity of demand. If the resource cost of making Good A increases, then which of the following will happen in the markets of Good A and B?

	Good A	Good B
(A)	Increase	Decrease
(B)	Increase	Increase
(C)	Decrease	Decrease
(D)	Decrease	Increase
(E)	Decrease	Decrease

26. Kathryn likes drinking milk and eating cookies. With her current consumption, her marginal utility of the last glass of milk is 6 and the marginal utility of her last cookie is 8. Milk costs $1.00 per carton and cookies cost $2.00 per package. This information indicates that Kathryn

(A) has a greater preference for drinking milk than for consuming cookies
(B) is maximizing her total utility of milk, but not of cookies
(C) experiences diminishing marginal utility of milk before that of cookies
(D) can increase her total utilities by purchasing more milk and fewer cookies
(E) possesses a higher total utility for cookies than for milk

Use the following cost graph for a firm to answer questions 27–28

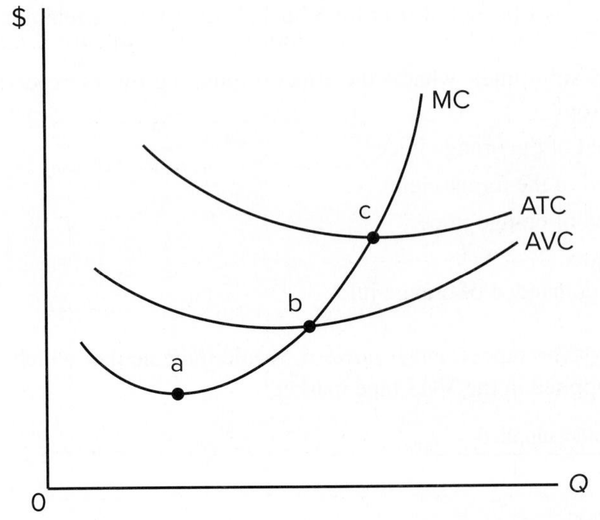

27. For this particular firm, which of the following is true at point b?
(A) Marginal product is at its maximum.
(B) The point of diminishing returns has not yet occurred.
(C) Average fixed costs are increasing.
(D) The shut-down price is below point b.
(E) Marginal cost is equal to marginal productivity.

28. With increasing output, the distance between the ATC curve and the AVC curve changes as a result of
(A) a decrease in average productivity of labor
(B) a decrease in the average fixed cost
(C) specialization and division of labor
(D) economies of scale
(E) increasing marginal returns

29. Diseconomies of scale exist when
(A) marginal utility is zero
(B) a firm produces at a short-run output where MR = MC > ATC
(C) the marginal revenue of labor is zero
(D) long-run average total cost increases as output increases
(E) short-run marginal cost increases as output increases

30. Entry of firms that are earning positive economic profits into a perfectly competitive constant cost industry would have which of the following effects on price and output of an existing individual firm?

	Price	Output
(A)	Decrease	Increase
(B)	Decrease	No change
(C)	Increase	Decrease
(D)	No change	Decrease
(E)	Decrease	Decrease

Questions 31–32 **refer to the following graph that illustrates a single firm that produces a specialized calculator for which there are no substitutes.**

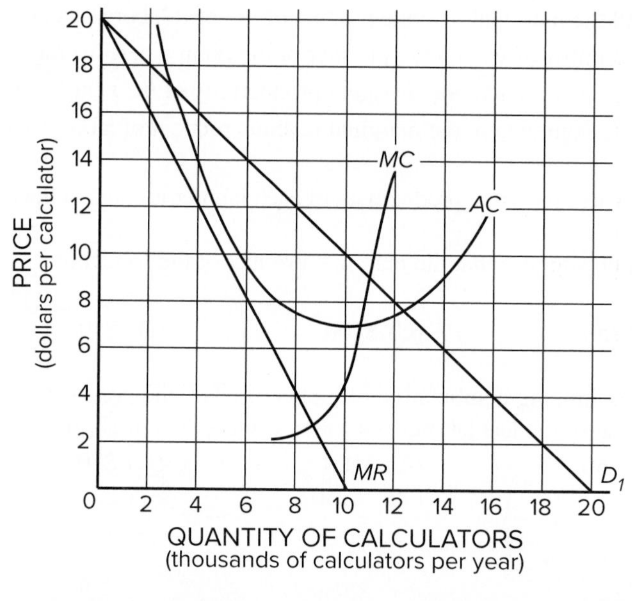

31. What will be the price of the calculator assuming the goal of the firm is to maximize its profits?

(A) Less than $4.00
(B) $7.00
(C) $7.90
(D) $10.00
(E) Greater than $10 but less than $12.00

32. What will be the price of the calculator assuming the goal of the firm is to maximize its total revenue?

(A) $3.00 (B) $7.00 (C) $7.90 (D) $10.00
(E) Greater than $10 but less than $12.00

33. A monopolist and a perfect competitor will both expand their output if which of the following is true?

(A) Price is greater than the average total cost.
(B) Price is greater than the marginal cost.
(C) Marginal revenue is less than the marginal cost.
(D) Marginal revenue is greater than the marginal cost.
(E) Total revenue can increase by lowering the price.

34. A perfectly competitive firm's short run supply curve is described by which of the following?

(A) The segment of the average variable cost curve from its minimum point
(B) The segment of the marginal cost curve lying above its average variable cost
(C) The segment from where marginal cost intersects the average total cost
(D) The segment after the minimum marginal cost
(E) The segment of marginal cost from where marginal revenue equals marginal cost

Questions 35–37 refer to the following information.

Walling Ponies **operates in a perfectly competitive recreational industry offering pony rides to young children. Walling hires teenage workers in a perfectly competitive teenage labor market and rents ponies from a near-by horse farm. She can hire teenage workers to conduct pony rides for children at $100 per day.**

35. How will Walling decide how many laborers to employ?

(A) She will hire workers until the marginal revenue product of the next laborer is equal to $100 per day.
(B) She will hire a sufficient number of workers to produce at the point where average cost equals $100 per day.
(C) She will hire workers at the point where the marginal productivity of the next laborer declines.
(D) She will hire workers at the point where the marginal revenue product of labor is equal to the marginal revenue product of ponies.
(E) She will hire at the point where marginal productivity of each laborer is equal to the average productivity of all workers.

36. At the profit maximizing output, suppose that the marginal product of the last laborer is 4 rides per day. What is the price of each ride?

(A) $400 (B) $250 (C) $100 (D) $50 (E) $25

37. If Walling employs the cost minimizing combination of inputs of labor and ponies, such that the marginal productivity of the last pony is 10 tours and that of the last laborer is 4 tours, what is the rental price of each pony?

(A) $400 (B) $250 (C) $100 (D) $50 (E) $25

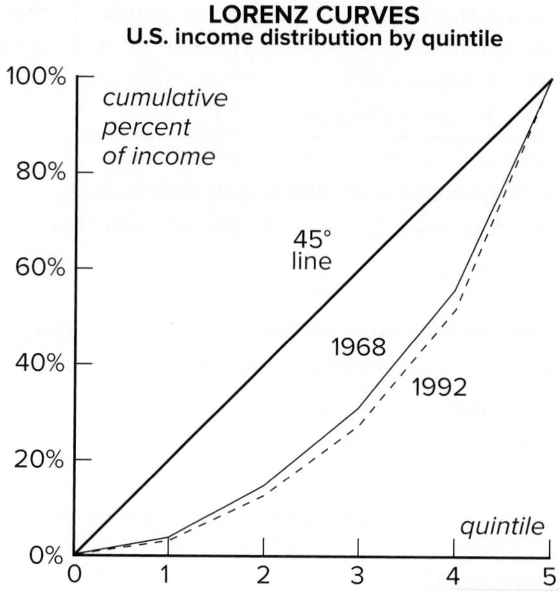

38. From 1968 to 1992, the United States economy most definitely indicates

(A) a decrease in the equality of income among its population
(B) a decrease in real income among U.S. workers
(C) an increase in the national minimum wage laws
(D) an increase in the progressive income tax
(E) a decrease in income of U.S. workers in foreign countries

39. The criteria for efficient allocation of a good or service occurs if the industry operates at a point where

(A) marginal revenue equals marginal cost
(B) marginal private cost equals marginal private benefit
(C) marginal social cost equals marginal social benefit
(D) marginal revenue and marginal cost are below the average total cost
(E) there is no incentive for entry or exiting of firms into the production of the good or service

Questions 40–41 refer to the following production possibility graph of a single country.

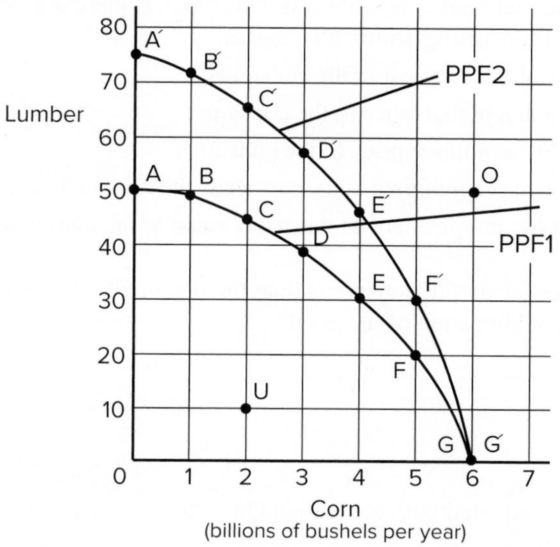

40. The production possibility graph above shows a country's output of corn and lumber, where the production possibility frontier (PPF-1) represents the current output combinations. The movement of the production possibility frontier to production possibility frontier (PPF-2) indicates that

(A) there has been an increase in the demand for lumber
(B) consumers have maintained their current consumption of corn
(C) more resources are devoted to the production of lumber than that of corn
(D) there has been a technological development in the production of lumber but not corn
(E) the cost of producing corn has decreased

41. Each of the points, (A–G), on production possibility frontiers PPF-1 assumes that

(A) resources are variable and can be increased to produce the preferred amount of corn and lumber
(B) the costs of the resources are constant
(C) total output of lumber and corn remain constant
(D) trade that can change the opportunity cost can occur
(E) all resources are being efficiently used in both the production of lumber and corn

Demand and Supply Schedule for Question 42

Price	Quantity Demanded	Quantity Supplied
$5	2,000	0
$10	1,800	300
$15	1,600	600
$20	1,400	900
$25	1,200	1,200
$30	1,000	1,500

42. An effective (binding) price ceiling in the market above would have which of the following effects?

(A) An increase in the demand for the product.
(B) An increase in the supply for the product.
(C) An increase in the marginal utility.
(D) A decrease in the producer surplus.
(E) A decrease in the deadweight loss.

43. A market is currently in an unregulated market equilibrium (Qd = Qs). If there is a negative externality, then which of the following best describes what is occurring within this market?

(A) overproducing the commodity at a lower cost to the consumer
(B) overproducing the commodity at a higher price to the consumer
(C) under producing the commodity at a lower price to the consumer
(D) misallocating resources such that the marginal benefit exceeds the marginal cost
(E) allocating resources such that the marginal social benefit is equal to the marginal social cost

44. In a market where the marginal cost of production is less than the marginal social benefit, which of the following policies would be likely to promote efficient allocation of the good?

(A) A per unit excise tax
(B) A subsidy
(C) A value added tax
(D) A price ceiling
(E) Price regulation where price is equated with the market Qd = Qs

45. A ski resort has decided to increase the price of lift tickets in order to increase the total revenues of the resort. The decision will have the desired affects for the ski resort if the price elasticity of demand is

(A) relatively elastic

(B) relatively unit elastic

(C) relatively inelastic

(D) equal to the price elasticity of supply

(E) greater than the income elasticity of demand

46. The price elasticity of demand for wheat is relatively inelastic. If there is a loss of the wheat crop due to weather and there is a simultaneous research finding that consuming wheat products improves the health of people, then which of the following is likely to occur in the market for wheat and the total revenues of wheat growers?

	Equilibrium Price	Equilibrium Quantity	Total Revenues
(A)	Increase	Increase	Increase
(B)	Increase	Indeterminate	Increase
(C)	Increase	Indeterminate	No change
(D)	Indeterminate	Indeterminate	No change
(E)	Decrease	Decrease	Decrease

47. Government officials desire a policy to discourage the consumption of Good A by imposing an excise tax on the good. The policy will be most effective if which of the following conditions exists for Good A?

I. Price elasticity of demand is relatively inelastic.

II. Price elasticity of demand is relatively elastic.

III. Price elasticity of supply is relatively inelastic.

IV. Price elasticity of supply is relatively elastic.

(A) Condition I only

(B) Conditions I and III only

(C) Conditions I and IV only

(D) Conditions II and III only

(E) Conditions II and IV only

48. In the short run, which of the following conditions must be true if marginal cost equals average total cost?

(A) Marginal cost is greater than average variable cost.

(B) Demand is equal to average total cost.

(C) Diminishing marginal returns will occur after the production of the next unit.

(D) Average fixed cost has reached its lowest level.

(E) Marginal revenue is equal to marginal cost.

49. When average product is equal to marginal product, which of the following is also true for the output level?

(A) Total revenues of the firm will be at their maximum point.

(B) Marginal revenue equals marginal cost.

(C) Normal profits will be earned.

(D) Marginal cost is equal to average variable cost.

(E) Average fixed cost will be at its lowest level.

50. A family experiences a steady increase in income over time and finds that it spends less and less of its income on Good X. Good X must represent which of the following elasticity characteristics?

(A) A price elasticity of demand between 0 and 1
(B) A negative cross price elasticity of demand
(C) A negative income elasticity of demand
(D) A negative elasticity of supply
(E) A unit price elasticity of demand equal to 1

51. The law of diminishing marginal utility explains which of the following?

(A) A downward slope of the marginal product of labor
(B) The downward slope of an individual's demand for a product
(C) The decreasing value of an additional worker in a fixed space
(D) The concave frontier of a production possibility model
(E) An inferior good

52. Assume a firm with fixed input shuts down in the short run and produces no output. Under these conditions what is true about the total cost, total variable cost, and total fixed cost?

	Total Cost	Variable Cost	Fixed Cost
(A)	Positive	0	Positive
(B)	0	0	0
(C)	Positive	Positive	0
(D)	0	0	Positive
(E)	Positive	Positive	Positive

Use the following graphs to answer questions 53–54

Graph 1

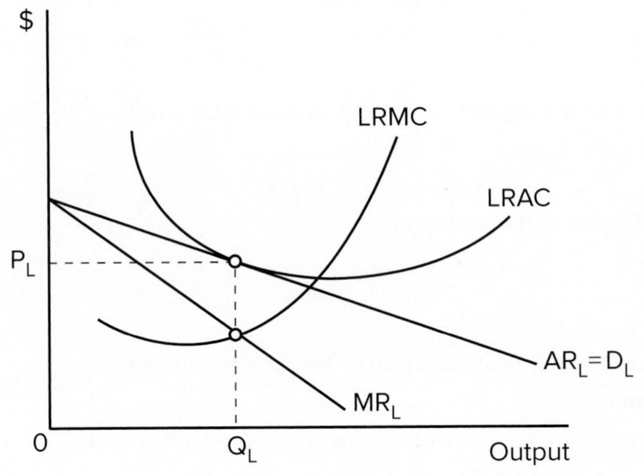

Graph 2

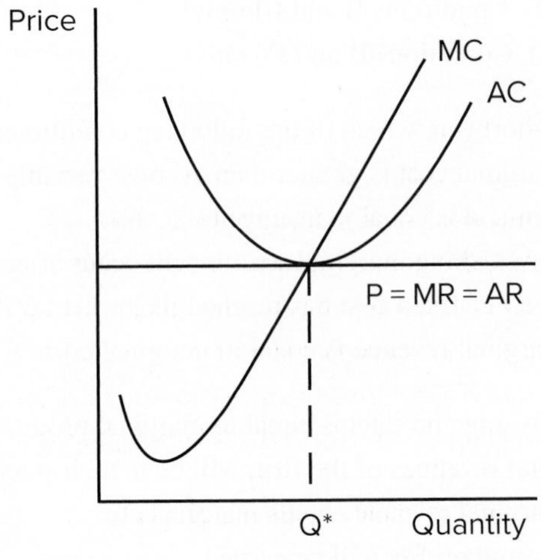

Graph 3

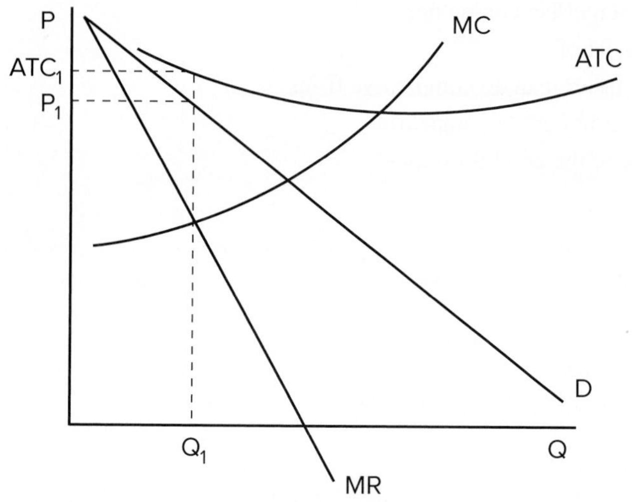

Graph 4

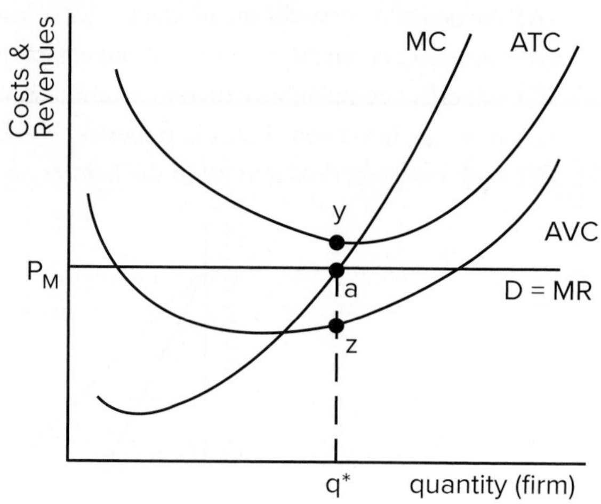

53. Assuming entry and exit in the market, which of the graphical illustrations above would signal firms to exit the market in the long run?

(A) 1 only (B) 2 only (C) 4 only (D) 1 and 3 only (E) 3 and 4 only

54. Assuming the absence of spillover costs or benefits, which of the firms is producing at the socially optimum output in the long run?

(A) 1 only (B) 2 only (C) 1 and 2 only (D) 1, 2, and 4 only (E) 1, 2, 3, and 4

For *Questions 55–56* refer to the payoff matrix below that gives the profits associated with strategic choices of two firms: Chuck's Cab and Vicki's Van, offering transportation services in the same small mid-western city. The first entry in each cell is the profit for Vicki; the second entry is the profit for Chuck.

		Chuck's Cab	
		Morning	Evening
Vicki's Van	Morning	$1,000, $700	$700, $600
	Evening	$750, $950	$900, $800

55. Which of the following is true concerning Chuck's and Vicki's decision to offer their services?

(A) Vicki has a dominant strategy to provide morning service.
(B) Chuck has a dominant strategy to provide evening service.
(C) Chuck has a dominant strategy to provide morning service.
(D) Vicki has a dominant strategy to provide evening service.
(E) Both Chuck and Vicki possess dominant strategies.

56. If Chuck and Vicki choose their own profit strategy without collusion, then which of the following represents the profits for Chuck and Vicki?

	Chuck's Cab	Vicki's Van
(A)	$700	$1,000
(B)	$600	$700
(C)	$950	$750
(D)	$800	$900
(E)	$900	$800

57. A monopolistically competitive firm will face a less elastic demand for labor than a perfect competition firm because

(A) the demand curve for the product is less elastic for an imperfect competitor

(B) imperfect competitors employ more capital goods than labor

(C) imperfect competitors experience diminishing returns faster than do competitive firms

(D) there are fewer substitutes in imperfect competition than in perfect competition

(E) both marginal productivity of the laborer and the price of the good decreases

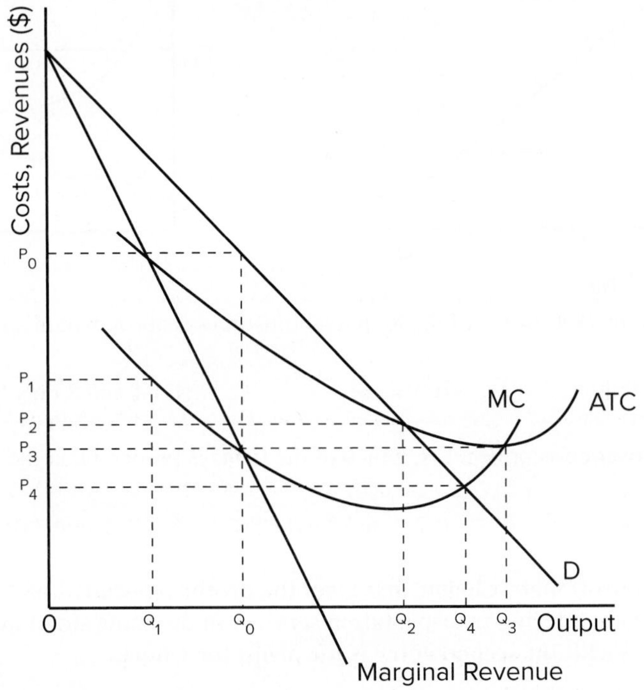

58. According to the graph, the effect of a regulatory policy that would establish a fair return price would mean

(A) the firm would minimize its losses and exit the market

(B) the firm would produce at the lowest average total cost

(C) the firm would produce at the output where price equals average total cost.

(D) the firm would produce at an output level that guarantee economic profit

(E) the firm would produce at an output point where demand equals marginal cost

59. Assume that the demand and supply graph below shows the output of Good X that produces a positive externality. Assuming no government regulation, which of the following is true concerning the output of Good X?

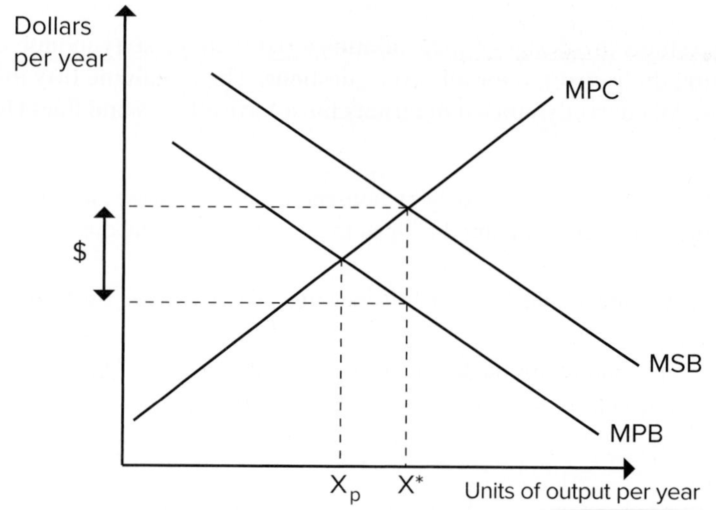

(A) There is sufficient allocation of the good because MPB = MPC at X_p.

(B) There is sufficient allocation of the good because the marginal social benefit (MSB) is greater than the equilibrium price at X_p.

(C) There is sufficient allocation because the marginal social benefit (MSB) will equal the marginal private cost (MPC).

(D) There is an inefficient allocation of resources because the marginal social benefit (MSB) is greater than the marginal private cost (MPC) at X_p.

(E) There is an inefficient allocation because there is a shortage at the market equilibrium, X_p.

60. A monopolist finds that at its current output the price of the product is greater than its marginal revenue, but its marginal cost is equal to marginal revenue. Which of the following is true?

(A) The monopolist is maximizing total revenue.

(B) The monopolist is overproducing the product.

(C) The monopolist is producing at a point of maximum profit.

(D) The monopolist will be guaranteed at most a fair return on its profit.

(E) The monopolist is producing at a point of socially optimum output.

END OF PART A

Free-Response Questions

Part B

Directions: The free-response questions are designed to be administered within a sixty minute time frame. Students should spend ten minutes planning their answers for all three questions. The remaining fifty minutes should be used for answering all three questions. All correctly labeled diagrams must have all axes and lines clearly labeled and must show directional changes.

1. *Stark Tree Farm* grows Douglas fir trees, used primarily by households and businesses for Christmas trees. *Stark* operates in a perfectly competitive market and is currently producing at the profit maximizing output, earning positive economic profits.

(a) Draw correctly labeled side by side graphs for the Christmas tree market and for *Stark Tree Farm* and show each of the following:

(i) The equilibrium price and quantity for the tree industry, labeled as P_{M1} and Q_{M1}.

(ii) The price for Christmas trees from *Stark Tree Farm*, labeled as P_{F1} and quantity produced by *Stark Tree Farm* labeled as Q_{F1}.

(iii) *Stark Tree Farm's* profits

(b) Given your results in Part (a), what long-run adjustment can be expected in the Christmas tree market? Explain

(c) Draw side-by-side graphs showing the Christmas tree industry in long-run equilibrium and the price and output for *Stark Tree Farm*. Use Q_{f2} to show the output.

(d) Given your analysis in part (c), assume now there is an increase in the taste and preferences of consumers to purchase artificial Christmas trees rather than Douglas fir trees. Show on a new graph for the Christmas tree industry the effect on product price and the quantity of Douglas fir Christmas trees in the short run.

(e) Following the change in the equilibrium price identified in part (d), *Stark Tree Farm* continues to produce.

(i) Explain why it would be rational for *Stark Tree Farm* to continue to produce in the short run.

(ii) Will *Stark Tree Farm* continue to operate in the long run? Explain.

2. The City of Cedar provides *Rapid Bus System* (RBS) as the only public form of transportation to citizens of the community. The unregulated *RBS* operates under the conditions of a monopoly that is depicted below.

Rapid Bus System

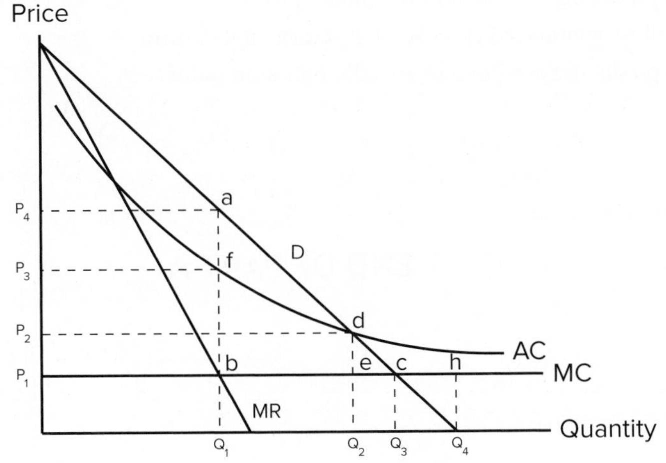

(a) Does the *Rapid Bus System* constitute a natural monopoly? Explain your answer.

(b) Using the graph above do the following:

(i) Identify the price and output for an unregulated profit-maximizing *Rapid Bus System.*

(ii) Identify the price that the city council would set to achieve allocative efficiency.

(iii) Identify the price that the city council would set to achieve a fair return.

(c) Assume that the city council knows that the income elasticity of demand for the bus is −2.0 Explain the effect of an increase in per capita income on ridership (number of riders).

(d) The city council possesses information concerning the price elasticity of demand for the *Rapid Bus System.* It has identified two different routes as with the following elasticities of demand.

- Route 1, Ed =–0.2
- Route 2, Ed = 3.0

(i) Explain how elasticity of demand is calculated.

(ii) If the objective is to increase revenue, should the city council increase, decrease, or make no changes in the bus fares of:

- Route 1
- Route 2

(iii) Explain two conditions needed for the *Rapid Bus System* to price discriminate with these two routes

3. *White Glove Company* is a firm offering moving, transfer, and storage services for households and delivery of furniture for retail businesses. Each job is priced at $200. The company hires equally qualified laborers in a perfectly competitive labor market for $2,000 per month. *White Glove* has the following production function indicating the number of laborers that can be hired and the number of moving jobs each worker can perform in a month.

Number of laborers	Number of Moving Jobs
1	25
2	75
3	135
4	155
5	165
6	160

(a) What are two characteristics of a perfectly competitive labor market, such as the one in which *White Glove Company* operates?

(b) After which laborer do diminishing returns begin or does marginal productivity fall? Explain why this happens.

(c) How will *White Glove Company* determine the number of workers to hire?

(d) How many workers will the firm hire to maximize profits in the short run? Explain how you arrived at your answer.

(e) Assume that *White Glove Company* also rents physical capital (vans and trucks) at the least cost combination of inputs.

(i) How will the *White Glove Company* determine the optimum combination of physical capital (vans and trucks) and labor?

(ii) If the marginal productivity of the last unit of capital is 20 and the firm employs the number of labor indicated in your answer to part (d), what must be the cost per unit of the physical inputs if *White Glove Company* is minimizing the cost of the output produced? Explain your answer.

END OF TEST

MACROECONOMICS EXAMINATION

Multiple-Choice Questions

Part A • 70 minutes

Directions: Each of the questions or incomplete statements below is followed by five answers or completions. Select one that is best in each case

Questions 1–2 **refer to the following graph.**

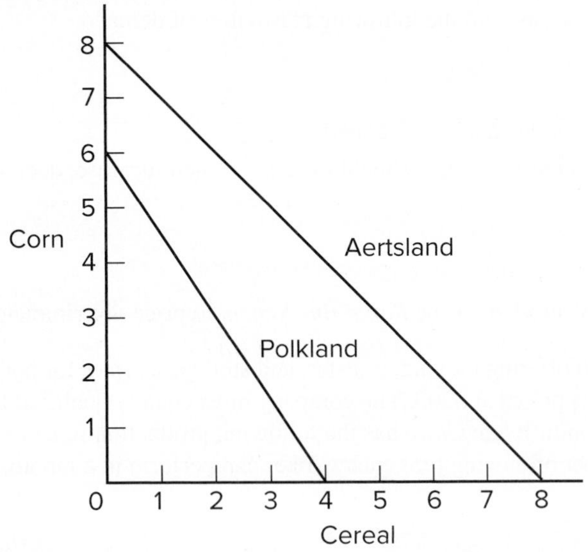

1. Given the graph above, which of the following can be deduced from the production possibilities of cereal and corn by the countries of Polkland and Aertsland?

(A) Trade will not occur between the two countries.
(B) Polkland has an absolute advantage in producing corn.
(C) Polkland must have fewer resources than does Aertsland.
(D) Aertsland has a constant opportunity cost; Polkland has increasing opportunity costs.
(E) Polkland has a comparative advantage in the production of corn.

2. If Aertsland produced 4 units of cereal and 3 units of corn then which of the following is true?

(A) Aertsland is just as efficient as Polkland.
(B) Aertsland has unused resources.
(C) Polkland has an absolute advantage in production of both goods.
(D) Aertsland can improve its output but will encounter an opportunity cost.
(E) Polkland is inefficient in its production possibilities.

3. Compared with the study of microeconomics, the study of macroeconomics is more concerned with which of the following issues?

(A) Policies that correct for negative externalities within the market
(B) The short-run trade-off between the inflation rate and the unemployment rate
(C) The profit-maximizing production level of individual firms
(D) The opportunity cost of producing more of one good and less of another good
(E) The effects of minimum wages on an unskilled labor market

4. The following are expenditures made in the year 2010:

I. A family pays $15,000 for repairs to their house that was built in 1975.
II. A family pays a contractor $150,000 to build a new house.
III. A family pays $1,500 monthly to rent an apartment that was built in 1975.
IV. A contractor purchases the lumber to build a new home.

Which of the above transactions were added to gross domestic product in 2010?
(A) II only
(B) I and II only
(C) II and III only
(D) I, II, and III only
(E) I, II, III, and IV

5. Nominal wages provide information concerning
(A) the current minimum wage that must be paid to employees
(B) the current wage rate in current dollars
(C) the bargaining power of the income earned by workers
(D) the total national income of an economy
(E) the wage differentials that exist among different types of workers

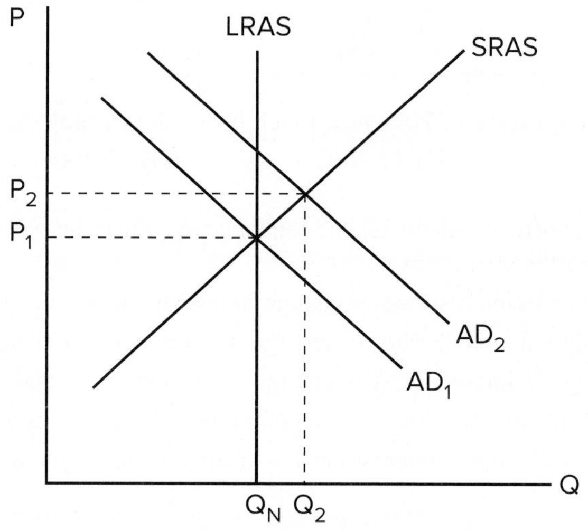

6. Assume the economy depicted in the above graph operates at an equilibrium point where output is Q_N and the price level is P_1. Which of the following conditions would cause the economy to move to output Q_2 and price level P_2?
(A) An appreciation of the country's currency on the foreign exchange market
(B) An increase in technology in the production of consumer goods
(C) An increase in labor productivity due to new technology
(D) An increase in military spending with no change in taxation
(E) A decrease in energy prices

7. Which of the following information would be most useful in understanding the impact of a $100 billion federal income tax decrease on aggregate demand?
(A) The marginal propensity to consume
(B) The reserve requirement
(C) The federal fund rate
(D) The unemployment rate
(E) The current federal deficit

8. An economy experiences a decrease in the unemployment rate as it increases its government spending. This implies that

(A) the aggregate demand curve is downward sloping
(B) the long-run aggregate supply curve has shifted to the right
(C) the economy is operating along the upward sloping aggregate supply curve
(D) the short-run aggregate supply curve has shifted to the right
(E) the economy was previously operating at near capacity

9. A check deposited in Bank B and drawn on Bank A will have which of the following effects?

(A) It will decrease the lending ability of Bank A.
(B) It will decrease the lending ability of the banking system.
(C) It will decrease the total reserves in the banking system.
(D) It will decrease the required reserves in Bank B.
(E) It will decrease the effects of the deposit expansion multiplier.

Wahoo National Bank

Assets		Liabilities	
Reserves	$2,500	Checking deposits	$6,000
Loans Outstanding	$5,500	Net Worth	$3,000
Other Assets	$1,000		
Total	$9,000	Total	$9,000

10. If Wahoo National Bank has a required reserve of 20%, how much in new loans could the bank create?

(A) $0 (B) $1,200 (C) $1,300 (D) $2,500 (E) $2,600

11. Which of the following transmissions correctly identifies the sequence by which the Federal Reserve changes the real gross domestic product using open market operations?

(A) Change in money supply → change in interest rate → change in investment → change in aggregate demand
(B) Change in money supply → change in interest rates → change in net exports → change in capital inflows
(C) Change in federal deficit → change in interest rates → change in aggregate demand
(D) Change in net exports → change in capital inflows → change in interest rates → change in investment
(E) Change in reserve requirements → change in interest rates → change in aggregate demand → change in price levels

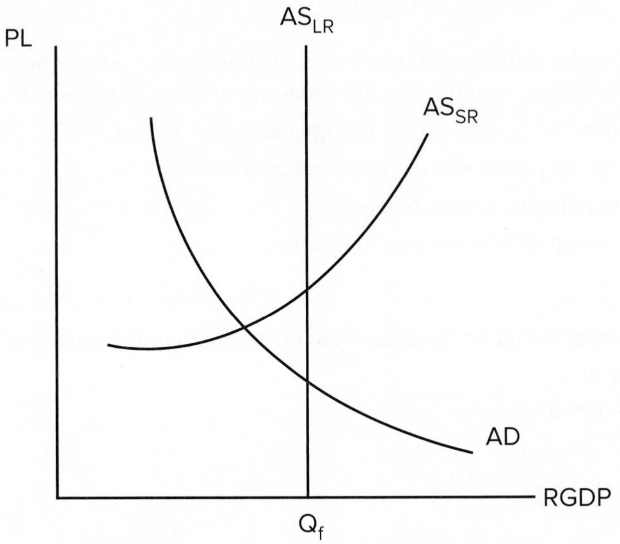

12. The graph above represents

(A) an economy in short run equilibrium with an output more than the full employment level
(B) an economy in short run equilibrium with an output less than the full employment level
(C) an economy in long run equilibrium
(D) an economy in short run equilibrium showing an inflationary gap
(E) an economy suffering stagflation

13. The process by which government spending increases interest rates which, in turn, decreases private investment is referred to as

(A) crowding out
(B) deficit spending
(C) supply shock
(D) stagflation
(E) cost-push inflation

14. The use of taxes rather than government spending is less effective in increasing the level of gross domestic product because

(A) households will retain some of their increased income as savings
(B) households will spend their increased income on investment goods
(C) the timing lag from the changes in disposable income is faster than that of government spending
(D) households are eventually taxed on the increase in their incomes
(E) political decision-makers prefer special interest spending projects

15. According to the short-run Phillips Curve, an economy could achieve lower inflation if it is willing to accept

(A) increasing unemployment
(B) decreasing personal income taxes
(C) increasing government spending
(D) decreasing the international value of the dollar
(E) increasing economic growth

16. Assume that an economy is performing at long-run equilibrium with an upward sloping short-run aggregate supply curve. An increase in government spending would have which of the following effects on real gross domestic product (RGDP) and the price level in the short run?

	Real GDP	Price Levels
(A)	Increase	Increase
(B)	Increase	No change
(C)	No change	No change
(D)	No change	Increase
(E)	Increase	Decrease

17. Which of the following would best demonstrate that economic growth has occurred in an economy?

(A) A decrease in the unemployment rate
(B) Rate of change in the price levels
(C) Growth of aggregate expenditures over time
(D) An increase net exports
(E) An increase in long run aggregate supply over time

18. An increase in the real interest rate would have which of the following effects on investment and long-run economic growth?

	Investment	Economic growth
(A)	Increase	Increase
(B)	Increase	Decrease
(C)	Decrease	Decrease
(D)	Decrease	Increase
(E)	Decrease	No Change

19. The United States has the following international trade transactions:

I. A Chinese firm purchases waste paper from the United States.
II. A U.S. firm buys machine parts from a firm in Mexico.
III. A Chinese company purchases a U.S. treasury bond as an investment.
IV. A U.S. charity group sends money to assist in the restoration of the Great Wall of China.

Which of the following transactions would appear as an increase in the current account of the Balance of Payments for the United States?

(A) I only
(B) II only
(C) II and III only
(D) II and IV only
(E) I, II, and III only

20. Assume an increase in real interest rates in the United States. What are the probable effects on capital flows to the United States, the international value of the dollar, and U.S. net exports?

	Capital flows to the U.S	Value of the Dollar	Net Exports
(A)	Increase	Increase	Decrease
(B)	Increase	Decrease	Increase
(C)	Increase	Decrease	Decrease
(D)	Decrease	Decrease	No change
(E)	Decrease	Increase	No change

21. An increase in global resource allocation can be achieved when

(A) countries first become self-sufficient and then begin trading only their surplus goods
(B) the opportunity costs of producing a good or service are equal between nations
(C) comparative advantages exist between nations and mutual terms of trade can be achieved
(D) absolute advantage in the production of the good or service exists in at least one country
(E) a common medium of exchange exists between or among nations

For *Question 22*, use the following diagrams that show possible changes in the supply and demand for crude oil.

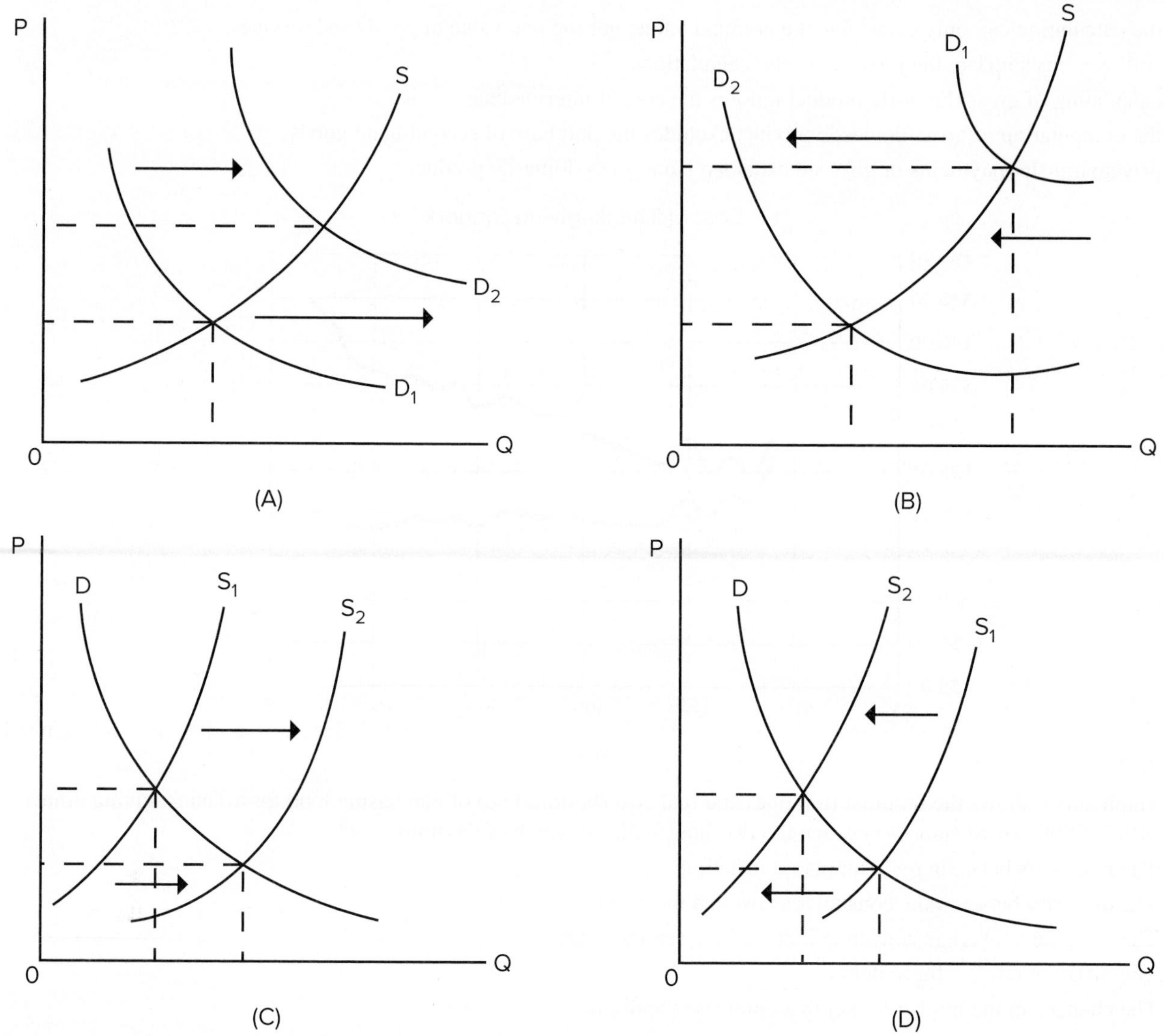

22. Which of the following changes in the short-run market for crude oil would occur if the cost of drilling for oil increased, and a simultaneous oil spill reduced the availability of crude oil?

(A) B only
(B) D only
(C) A and C
(D) B and C
(E) C and D

23. Which of the following is likely during the peak of a business cycle?

(A) A decrease in the price level
(B) A decrease in the unemployment rate
(C) A decrease in gross domestic product
(D) A movement along the production possibility frontier
(E) An increase in the national debt

24. Critics of using gross domestic product as a measure of a country's output suggest that the measure may be misleading because

(A) the calculation can only determine the nominal value, not the real value of goods and services
(B) spillover costs inflate the gross domestic calculations
(C) calculating of gross domestic product ignores the cost of intermediate goods
(D) the computation of gross domestic product excludes the purchase of second-hand goods
(E) private transfer payments or gifts are excluded from gross domestic product

Cost of Thanksgiving Dinners

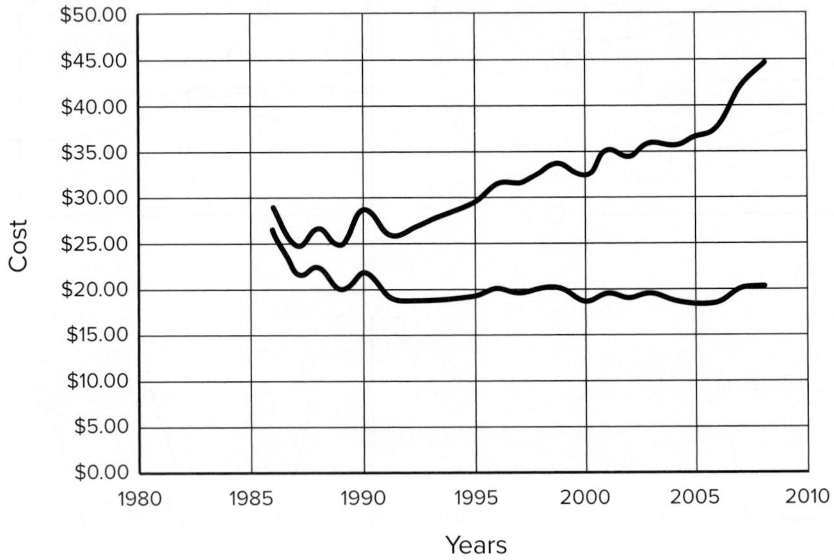

25. The graph above shows the nominal (top line) and real cost (bottom line) of purchasing food for a Thanksgiving dinner from 1987–2009. The distances between the two lines indicate which of the following?

(A) The trade-offs between real output and inflation
(B) The disparity between the consumer's cost and the producer's cost
(C) The increase in average consumer income between the years
(D) The inflation rate for these items
(E) The changes in the market basket that comprise the dinner

26. Which of the following conditions characterize long-run equilibrium in the aggregate demand and aggregate supply model as opposed to short-run equilibrium?

(A) The unemployment rate is zero.
(B) Aggregate demand is equal to short-run aggregate supply.
(C) The economy operates at its natural rate of unemployment.
(D) Leakages and injections are equal in the circular flow model.
(E) The actual inflation rate is less than the expected inflation rate.

27. An increase in the aggregate price level, *ceteris paribus,* increases profitability and provides incentives to produce. This observation explains which of the following?

(A) The slope of the short-run aggregate supply curve
(B) The slope of the long-run aggregate supply curve
(C) The slope of the aggregate demand curve
(D) The self-correction model and the shift of the short-run aggregate supply curve
(E) The shift in the long-run aggregate supply curve

28. An increase in energy costs in a nation results in an increase in the price level and a decrease in real gross domestic product. Which of the following has occurred within the aggregate demand and aggregate supply model?

	Short-run Aggregate Supply	Long-run Aggregate Supply	Aggregate Demand
(A)	Increase	Decrease	Decrease
(B)	Increase	No change	Increase
(C)	Decrease	Decrease	Decrease
(D)	Decrease	No change	No change
(E)	No change	Decrease	No change

29. Which of the following entries constitute a liability for a national commercial bank?

(A) Demand deposits of its customers
(B) Required reserves on hand at the Federal Reserve Banks
(C) Outstanding loans to firms and households
(D) Bonds and securities
(E) Bank property

30. Which of the following policies by the Federal Reserve is aimed at changing federal funds rate?

I. Discount rates
II. Legal reserve requirements
III. Open market operations

(A) I only
(B) II only
(C) III only
(D) I and II only
(E) II and III only

31. The effectiveness of an expansionary monetary policy by the Federal Reserve is limited by

(A) the checks and balances of the executive and the legislative branch
(B) the willingness of banks to lend excess reserves
(C) the current rate of unemployment
(D) the nominal interest rate
(E) the inflation rate

32. Given the flexibility of input prices, the long-run adjustments to real gross domestic product output and the price levels following expansionary fiscal policies will be

	Real GDP	Price Levels
(A)	Increase	Increase
(B)	Increase	Decrease
(C)	No change	Increase
(D)	Decrease	No change
(E)	Decrease	Increase

Questions 33–34 refer to the following diagram.

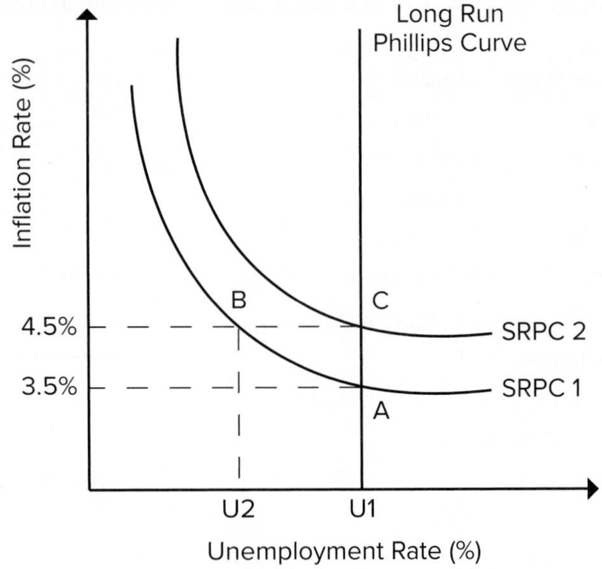

33. From a rational expectations point of view, the movement from point A to point B on the Phillips Curve illustrated above would be caused by an

(A) anticipated increase in inventories
(B) unanticipated supply shock
(C) unanticipated increase in the money supply
(D) anticipated increase in government spending
(E) increase in the international value of the dollar

34. A shift from point B to point C on the Philips Curve illustrated above is equivalent to which of the following in the aggregate demand—aggregate supply model?

(A) An increase in aggregate demand
(B) A decrease in the long-run aggregate supply
(C) An increase in the short-run aggregate supply
(D) A decrease in the aggregate demand
(E) A decrease in the short-run aggregate supply curve

35. What happens to bond prices, interest rates, and investment spending, when the Federal Reserve buys securities and bonds in the open market?

	Bond Prices	Interest	Investment
(A)	Increase	Increase	Increase
(B)	Increase	Decrease	Increase
(C)	Decrease	Increase	Increase
(D)	Decrease	Decrease	Decrease
(E)	Increase	No change	No change

36. A United States Treasury order to sell bonds to pay for federal deficits means which of the following?

(A) The Federal Reserve sells bonds and securities in open market operations.
(B) The supply of loanable funds to the private sector will decrease.
(C) Personal income taxes will increase.
(D) The federal government will decrease its spending.
(E) The effects of crowding out will decrease.

37. Which of the following policies is a likely source of economic growth?
(A) An increase in the real interest rate
(B) An increase in deficit spending
(C) An increase in business inventories
(D) An increase in net exports
(E) An increased in investment in human capital that increases labor productivity

38. Countries tend to trade with each other when each country finds that
(A) one country can produce a greater amount of the good or service compared to another country
(B) price levels of a good or service are similar between countries
(C) a common currency exists to facilitate trade
(D) it can lower the opportunity cost of acquiring a good or service
(E) unemployment is below its potential rate

39. A country that experiences a higher inflation rate, relative to its international trading partners, can expect which of the following short-run effects on net exports and real gross domestic product?

	Net exports	Gross domestic product
(A)	Increase	Increase
(B)	Increase	Decrease
(C)	Decrease	Decrease
(D)	Decrease	Increase
(E)	Decrease	No Change

40. An increase in the long-run aggregate supply of a nation is equivalent to which of the following illustrations?
(A) Movement along a country's production possibility frontier
(B) Movement along the short-run Phillips Curve
(C) Movement along the short-run aggregate supply curve
(D) Outward shift of a country's production possibility frontier
(E) Movement to the peak of the business cycle

41. The simple circular flow model shows that
(A) households are on the buying side of both product and resource markets
(B) businesses are on the selling side of both product and resource markets
(C) households are on the selling side of the resource market and on the buying side of the product market
(D) businesses are on the buying side of the product market and on the selling side of the resource market
(E) businesses are only part of the buying part of the resource market

42. Bagels and cream cheese are complements. Flour is used to produce bagels; milk is used to produce cream cheese. Which of the following factors would cause the price of cream cheese to increase and the equilibrium quantities of bagels to increase?
(A) A decrease in the price of milk
(B) A decrease in the price of flour
(C) An increase in the price of flour and an increase in the price of milk
(D) An increase in the price of flour
(E) A decrease in the price of flour and an increase in the price of milk

43. If the current and expected inflation rate is 2 percent, and your saving strategy is to earn at least 5% on borrowed money, what would be the minimum nominal interest rate that would provide you an incentive to save?
(A) 2% (B) 2.5% (C) 3% (D) 7% (E) 10%

44. Assume you have the following employment data from a local county.

Population (16 years and older)	5,000
Labor Force	3,000
Not working	2,000
Employed full time	2,000
Employed part time	850
Unemployed	150

The unemployment rate in this county is

(A) 5.0% (B) 3.0% (C) 6.6% (D) 31% (E) 25%

45. An increase in the aggregate price level, *ceteris paribus,* causes a decrease in the purchasing power of the real balances of households. This observation helps explains the slope of which curve?

(A) The short-run aggregate supply
(B) The long-run aggregate supply
(C) The aggregate demand curve
(D) The long-run Phillips Curve
(E) The money demanded

46. An increase in labor productivity as a result of new technology will have which of the following effects on inflation and unemployment?

	Inflation	Unemployment
(A)	Increase	Increase
(B)	Increase	Decrease
(C)	Decrease	Decrease
(D)	Decrease	No change
(E)	No change	Increase

47. Federal deficits are generally funded by

(A) the Federal Reserve purchase of bonds and securities in the open market
(B) a decrease in the marginal tax rates
(C) government borrowing in the loanable fund market
(D) cutting of some government programs
(E) investment in research and development

48. Crowding out occurs when

(A) a country has an unfavorable balance of trade on its current account
(B) consumption decreases as a result of an increase in the savings rate
(C) the amount of investment decreases as government borrows to fund deficit spending
(D) government expenditures exceed investment expenditures
(E) capital inflows increase as a result of negative changes in the currency account

49. Incentives that allow households to save and earn tax-free interest income would have which of the following effects on real interest rates and bond prices?

	Real Interest Rates	Bond Prices
(A)	Increase	Increase
(B)	Increase	Decrease
(C)	Decrease	Increase
(D)	Decrease	Decrease
(E)	Decrease	No change

50. The effectiveness of the money multiplier is reduced by which of the following?

(A) Purchases of bonds and securities by the Federal Reserve
(B) The unwillingness of banks to lend money to customers
(C) A decrease in the discount rate and required reserve rates
(D) The international decline of the dollar on the foreign exchange market
(E) An increase in spending and taxation by the federal government

51. An expansionary open market operation in the short-run will lead to

(A) lower interest rates and increases in investment
(B) lower interest rates and increases in government spending
(C) a reduction of required reserves held by banks
(D) an increase in the demand deposit expansion multiplier
(E) higher interest rates and increases in investment

52. An appropriate monetary policy to curtail the effects of accelerating inflation would be to increase

(A) personal income taxes
(B) the international value of the dollar
(C) the sale of Treasury securities and bonds
(D) the money supply
(E) holdings of gold by banks

53. Assume an economy is operating at full employment with price stability, and the government now finds it must I increase military spending by 20 billion dollars. With a marginal propensity to consume of .80, how can the government increase its spending while maintaining price stability within the economy?

(A) Increase taxes by $16 billion
(B) Increase taxes by $20 billion
(C) Increase taxes by $25 billion
(D) Increase taxes by $100 billion
(E) Increase taxes by $80 billion

54. Assume the economy has been operating at full employment for two successive years, with an increasing nominal gross domestic product. Which of the following must be considered to assess whether there has been economic growth in this economy?

(A) Capital consumption allowance
(B) The number of labor hours in a work week
(C) The unemployment rate
(D) The amount of public (government) spending
(E) Price level change

55. Assume that a country, which had a balanced current account, increases its imports sharply. What is theeffect on its current account balance and the international value of its currency?

	Current Account Balance	International Value of Currency
(A)	Deficit	Decreases
(B)	Deficit	Increases
(C)	No change	Decreases
(D)	Surplus	Increases
(E)	Surplus	Decreases

56. Which of the following events would cause the United States dollar to appreciate relative to its trading partners?
(A) Overseas tourism by Americans increases
(B) Prices in the United States fall relative to its trading partners
(C) Increased capital outflow from the United States to its trading partners
(D) U.S. firms import foreign technology products
(E) Increase in the unemployment rate of trading partners

57. Long-run equilibrium within the aggregate demand and aggregate supply models means
(A) the economy is operating at full employment
(B) the federal government has a balanced budget
(C) the expected inflation rate is zero
(D) the business cycle has reached its peak
(E) the current account and the capital (financial) account are both in balance

58. The Federal Reserve increases or decreases the money supply by
(A) ordering the U.S. Treasury to issue or retire bonds
(B) printing more or less money
(C) selling or buying securities and bonds on the open market
(D) changing the marginal tax rates
(E) increasing or decreasing its gold deposits

59. Which of the following policies would be advocated by government decision-makers in an economy with falling price levels and increasing unemployment?
(A) Increase in government spending with an increase in the money supply
(B) Increase in government spending with an increase in personal income taxes
(C) Decrease in government spending and an increase in personal income taxes
(D) Decrease in government spending and a decrease in the money supply
(E) Increase in the tax rate of corporate profits and a decrease in personal income tax rates

60. As a result of recessionary fears, consumers decrease their spending and increase their savings rates. Which of the following will occur in the In the loanable funds market and in the money market.

	Loanable Funds	Money Market
(A)	Increase in the supply	Increase in the supply
(B)	Increase in the supply	Decrease in the demand
(C)	Decrease in the demand	Decrease in the demand
(D)	Decrease in the demand	Increase in the supply
(E)	Increase in the demand	Increase in the demand

END OF PART A

Free Response Questions

Part B

Directions: The free response questions are designed to be administered within a sixty minute time frame. Students should spend ten minutes planning their answer for all three questions. The remaining fifty minutes should be used to answer all three questions. All correctly labeled diagrams must have all axes and lines clearly labeled and must show directional changes.

1. Assume that the United States economy is in a recession.

(a) Using a correctly labeled aggregate demand and aggregate supply graph, show the current equilibrium real gross domestic product, price level, and the full employment gross domestic product.

(b) Assume that the recession shown in part (a), falls below the fully employed economy by 500 billion dollars. Using marginal propensity to consume of 0.8, calculate the following:

(i) The minimum amount of government spending required to restore the economy to full employment (with no change in taxes)

(ii) The minimum amount of a tax change required to restore the economy to a full employment (with no change in government spending)

(c) Assume that the current nominal interest rate is 8%, and that the rate of investment will increase by $25 billion for every one percent decrease in the interest rate. Assume that the marginal propensity to consume continues to be 0.8.

(i) By how much will the interest rate be required to change to increase aggregate demand by $500?

(ii) How can the change in the interest rate using open market operations (indicated in part c(i)) be done?

(iii) What will happen to bond prices in the short run? Explain.

(d) Explain the mechanism by which the change in the interest rate may restore a fully employed economy.

(e) Assume that interest rates remain constant elsewhere in the world. Given the change in the United States interest rate (identified in c(i)),

(i) Use a correctly labeled graph of the dollar market to show what will happen to the international value of the dollar in relation to foreign currencies?

(ii) Explain the effect of the interest rate change on the international value of the dollar

2. Suppose that an economy is currently in long-run equilibrium.

(a) Draw a correctly labeled aggregate demand and aggregate supply graph, showing

(i) the current output (Y_f), and

(ii) current price levels (PL_1)

(b) Assume that the central government enacts a health care program that ensures government payment for essential medical care for all citizens. On your graph in part (a), show the impact of the government policy on the price levels and real gross domestic product.

(i) Explain the impact on the unemployment rate in the short run.

(c) Draw a correctly labeled short-run and long-run Phillips Curve.

(i) Identify as point X the long-run equilibrium associated with your graph

(ii) Show the impact of your analysis in part (b) on the Phillips Curve and label the new short-run equilibrium as point Y.

(iii) Have real wages increased, decreased, or remained the same at point Y in comparison to point X? Explain.

(d) Assume that all input prices are flexible and the markets adjust to equilibrium.

(i) With these flexible input prices, explain the long-run impact of the government policy, part (b) on the price level, real gross domestic product, and unemployment.

(ii) Show the long-run effects that you explained in part d(i) on both the short-run Phillips Curve of part (c) and the long-run Phillips curve. Label the new equilibrium point as point Z.

3. Supply and demand analysis is common to both the study of microeconomics and macroeconomics. Draw two columns I and II to do the following.

(i) In column (I) draw a correctly labeled short-run supply and demand graph for the gasoline market; in column (II) a correctly labeled aggregate demand and short-run and long-run aggregate supply curves for an economy. For each graph identify the equilibrium quantities.

(ii) Is the equilibrium identified in both graphs efficient? Explain.

(iii) Provide one reason for why the demand and aggregate demand curves drawn in column I and II are downward sloping.

(iv) Suppose that there is a change in technology that provides new sources of oil, a major factor of production. Explain how this event would impact supply and demand for the gasoline market and for the aggregate economy.

END OF TEST